SOURCEBOOK ON GERMAN LAW

Second Edition

Cavendish
Publishing
Limited

London • Sydney • Portland, Oregon

SOURCEBOOK ON GERMAN LAW

Second Edition

Raymond Youngs,
LLB (Lond), LLM (Lond) (Brigid M Cotter prizes),
Solicitor, Senior Lecturer in Law,
Southampton Institute of Higher Education,
Associate Lecturer, University of Surrey,
Senior Research Fellow, Institute of Global Law,
University College, London

Cavendish
Publishing
Limited

London • Sydney • Portland, Oregon

Second edition first published in Great Britain 2002 by
Cavendish Publishing Limited, The Glass House,
Wharton Street, London WC1X 9PX, United Kingdom
Telephone: + 44 (0)20 7278 8000   Facsimile: + 44 (0)20 7278 8080
Email: info@cavendishpublishing.com
Website: www.cavendishpublishing.com

Published in the United States by Cavendish Publishing
c/o International Specialized Book Services,
5804 NE Hassalo Street, Portland,
Oregon 97213-3644, USA

Published in Australia by Cavendish Publishing (Australia) Pty Ltd
3/303 Barrenjoey Road, Newport, NSW 2106, Australia

© Youngs, R	2002
First edition	1994
Reprinted	1998
Second edition	2002

British Library Cataloguing in Publication Data
Youngs, Raymond
Sourcebook on German law – 2nd ed
I Law – Germany
349.4'3

Library of Congress Cataloguing in Publication Data
Data available

ISBN 1-85941-678-0

1 3 5 7 9 10 8 6 4 2

Printed and bound in Great Britain

PREFACE TO THE SECOND EDITION

Over seven years have now passed since the first edition of this book and many changes have taken place in the Basic Law, the Civil Code and Criminal Code. These have, where relevant, been incorporated into this edition. I would also have liked to replace the cases with more modern ones, but this proved too ambitious for the time available, so I have had to content myself with including a few new ones at the expense of the old. The new ones are not all modern, but some reflect such topical subjects as mass slaughter of animals, the use of drugs, the legacy of East Germany, and computers and the internet. Also, instead of serving up the standard diet of cases from the Federal Constitutional Court and the Bundesgerichtshof, I have included two cases from the Federal Administrative Court and one from an Oberlandesgericht. The cases which appear for the first time in this edition are referred to as: the cattle slaughter case; the cannabis application rejection case; the right to give the opposite view cases; the land purchase mistake case; the computer non-disclosure case; the shooting at the disco case; the internet auction case; the kite case; and the referendum mistake case.

The European Union also has a higher profile; one of the new cases is partly based on EU law, and some of the amendments to the Civil Code are in pursuance of EU Directives. Perhaps all the amendments to the Civil Code look on to a day when parts of private law will be codified at a European level and the most modern parts of the national codes will exert the most influence on the ultimate wording of such a document.

Material on German law has become more freely available and some book sources are mentioned in a further reading list at the end of the book. Articles on German law can be identified through the database Legaltrac, so I have only made a passing reference to some articles where I have attempted to explore a theme more deeply. Websites are an increasingly useful source, and a substantial number of translations of German cases now appear on the website of the Institute of Global Law, University College, London: www.ucl.ac.uk/laws/global_law. Other sources worth mentioning (some in English and some in German) include in particular: www.jura.uni-sb.de; www.kanzlei.de; www.iecl.iuscomp.org/gla; http://dejure.org.

Raymond Youngs
Southampton Institute
May 2002

PREFACE TO THE FIRST EDITION

'Positive law lives in the general consciousness of a people and hence we have to call it people's law.'
von Savigny

My initial idea in writing this book was to produce a selection of original German legal material together with some commentary on it, one particular source of inspiration being the *Sourcebook on French Law* by Rudden. There were a number of reasons why this was not achievable, the most important of which were:

1 I thought it was desirable to include material which gave an introduction to five basic areas of law: the constitution, human rights, contract, tort and crime.

2 In view of the fact that the French language is much more widely known than German, a full translation of the material seemed necessary.

3 German case decisions are usually much longer than French ones.

4 In view of the pressure on space created by these factors, extracts from academic writings could not realistically be included, and commentary had to be brief and selective.

Like any book containing cases and materials, coverage of the law has to be patchy and incomplete, even in areas included in some detail. The purpose of the book, however, is to facilitate study of some specific areas in greater depth than a textbook would permit, perhaps with the aid of other sources, either German or, where available, English (such as the incomparably wider and deeper treatment of tort in the German *Law of Torts: A Comparative Introduction* by Markesinis (3rd edn, Oxford: Clarendon); inevitably, there is some duplication of tort cases between that book and this one).

I have also had in mind the needs of students who are intending to study German law in Germany under programmes such ERASMUS and SOCRATES, and who ought to be familiar with the language as well as the content of German law before they start.

Some cases represent significant legal developments and others are just illustrations. Apart from their substantive law content, some present images of post-war Germany: the aftermath of the Third Reich (the film director case; the publication of a letter case); features of post-war West Germany such as the economic miracle (the investment aid act case) and student unrest (the newspaper delivery obstruction case); the pathway to reunification (the all Germany election case) and its consequences (the shootings at the Berlin wall case; the East German politicians trial publicity cases); and Germany's place in the new world order (the Bosnia flight exclusion zone case). Some cases present interesting comparisons in different kinds of legal reasoning: contrast the moral argument in the base motive case with the historical and sociological content of the housework day case; the analysis of old case law in the rough ill-treatment case with the analysis of statutory purpose in the arrested admiral case; the bold academic theorising in the Hamburg parking case and the conceptual arguments in the neglected assistance case with the application of the provisions of the Code in the cases concerning declarations of will. Cases like the film director case, and the shootings at the Berlin wall case are jurisprudential studies in themselves.

I owe a great debt to a number of people without whom this book would not have been possible, in particular: my brother-in-law and sister-in-law Wolf and Geraldine Paul, who (respectively) helped me with some difficult pieces of German and some particularly intractable software problems; and typed some parts of the manuscript; my wife Daphne, and my children David, Geoffrey, Rosemary and Emma who put up with a lot while the book was being written and still (in the case of the first three) gave some help with the typing; my parents-in-law, Mr and Mrs Barber, who prepared the index; Jürgen Meinz of the Beamtenfachhochschule at Hof who gave some helpful advice about contents; Cavendish who went to great pains introducing order into an initially chaotic manuscript in a short space of time; Professor Cooper, my Head of Division, who provided support and assistance while the book was being written; Sara Navas, who typed a large part of the manuscript. The responsibility for any errors remains solely mine.

I would also like to thank JCB Mohr (Paul Siebeck) (in respect of the decisions of the Bundesverfassungsgericht) Verlag CH Beck (in respect of the cases contained in the Neue Juristische Wochenschrift) and Carl Heymanns Verlag KG (in respect of of the decisions of the Bundesgerichtshof) for their kind permission for the reproduction of cases in this book.

Raymond Youngs
Southampton Institute
1994

CONTENTS

Preface to the Second Edition   *v*
Preface to the First Edition   *vii*
Table of Abbreviations   *xv*
Table of Cases   *xxvii*
Table of Statutes   *xxxix*

1   INTRODUCTION   **1**
GENERAL APPROACH   1
   Selectivity   1
   Translation   2
   Particular words and expressions   2
SOURCES OF GERMAN LAW   4
   Generally   4
   Hierarchy   4
   Judicial decisions and academic writings   5
   European Union law   5

2   THE CONSTITUTION   **7**
NATURE   7
   Generally   7
THE GERMAN STATE   9
   The Basic Law   9
   Preamble   9
POLITICAL PARTIES   11
FLAG   11
INTERNATIONAL RELATIONS   13
   European Union   13
   International relations generally   17
THE BOSNIA FLIGHT EXCLUSION ZONE CASE   19
THE STATES   43
EXTERNAL RELATIONS   49
CITIZENS' RIGHTS   49
OFFICIALS AND AUTHORITIES   51
COERCION BY THE FEDERATION   53
THE LEGISLATURE   53
   Federal Parliament   53
THE ALL GERMANY ELECTION CASE   53
   Other legislative bodies   83
THE EXECUTIVE   83
   The President   83
   Federal Government   83
LEGISLATION   83
   The Federation and the States   83
   Altering the Constitution   83

Regulations   85
Special cases   85
Coming into force   87
ADMINISTRATION   87
THE JUDICIARY   87
    The Courts   87
    Federal Constitutional Court   89
    Federal Courts   93
    Judges   93
    Constitutional issues   95
    Special courts   97
    Criminal law and the right to be heard   97
    Freedom   99
FINANCE   99
DEFENCE   99
TRANSITIONAL AND FINAL PROVISIONS   101

3 HUMAN RIGHTS   **105**
INTRODUCTION   105
    Nature of Basic Rights   105
    Who can claim Basic Rights?   106
    Against whom can Basic Rights be claimed?   106
    Limitations on the Basic Rights   107
THE PRINCIPLE OF PROPORTIONALITY   108
    Status in English law   108
    Status in German law   108
THE ARRESTED ADMIRAL CASE   111
THE BASIC RIGHTS THEMSELVES   129
THE CATTLE SLAUGHTER CASE   128
THE HOUSEWORK DAY CASE   141
THE CANNABIS APPLICATION REJECTION CASE   159
THE RIGHT TO GIVE THE OPPOSITE VIEW CASES   173
THE INVESTMENT AID ACT CASE   193

4 RIGHTS AND OBLIGATIONS   **229**
THE CIVIL CODE   229
PERSONS   229
    Natural persons   231
LEGAL TRANSACTIONS   239
    Legal transactions, declarations of will and contracts   239

DECLARATIONS OF WILL   241
  The concept   241
THE UNINTENDED DECLARATION OF WILL CASE   243
THE LAND PURCHASE MISTAKE CASE   261
THE COMPUTER NON-DISCLOSURE CASE   283
  Requirements as to form   297
  How a declaration of will becomes effective   299
THE MISDIRECTED WITHDRAWAL DECLARATION CASE   301
  Interpretation of a declaration of will   313
  Illegality   313
  Impropriety   315
INVALIDITY OF A LEGAL TRANSACTION   315
AVOIDANCE GENERALLY   315
PERIODS AND DATES; AND LIMITATION   317
EXERCISE OF RIGHTS   317
SPECIAL DEFENCES   319
THE SHOOTING AT THE DISCO CASE   321

5   CONTRACT   331
OFFER AND ACCEPTANCE   331
  Offer   333
THE INTERNET AUCTION CASE   333
  Acceptance   359
NEED FOR AGREEMENT   361
AUCTIONS   363
INTERPRETATION OF CONTRACTS   363
CONDITIONS   363
AGENCY   367
CONSENT   367
PERFORMANCE   369
  Generally   369
  Payments   371
  Compensation   373
FRUSTRATION   375
FAULT   377
THE FALL IN THE SUPERMARKET CASE   377
THE TERMINATION OF NEGOTIATIONS CASE   393
IMPOSSIBILITY   397
THE ALLERGY TO HAIR TONIC CASE   399
DELAY   411
CONTENT OF A CONTRACT   415
  Generally   415
  Determinations   423

MUTUAL CONTRACTS 425
   Generally 425
PROMISE IN FAVOUR OF A THIRD PARTY 429
REMAINDER OF THE SECOND BOOK 431

6   **TORT** **433**
NATURE 433
TWO GENERAL PRINCIPLES OF LIABILITY 435
   General 435
   Statutory 437
THE FOWL PEST CASE 439
THE PUBLICATION OF A LETTER CASE 469
THE NEWSPAPER DELIVERY OBSTRUCTION CASE 481
HARM TO FINANCIAL STATUS 503
HARM CONTRARY TO MORALITY 503
THE FILM DIRECTOR CASE 505
LIMITATION OF LIABILITY 559
PLURALITY OF DEFENDANTS 561
VICARIOUS LIABILITY 563
   Employers 563
THE FALLEN TELEGRAPH POLE CASE 565
   Supervisors 573
STRICT LIABILITY AND ANIMALS 575
   Animals 575
   Other cases 575
LIABILITY FOR BUILDINGS 577
LIABILITY OF OFFICIALS 579
THE AIR TRAFFIC CONTROLLERS' STRIKE CASE 579
THE KITE CASE 605
LIABILITY AS BETWEEN DEFENDANTS 609
COMPENSATION 609
   Personal injury 609
   Other cases 613
LIMITATION 615

7   **CRIMINAL LAW** **617**
HISTORY AND EFFECTIVE SCOPE 617
   Non-retroactivity 619
   Temporal scope 619
THE SHOOTINGS AT THE BERLIN WALL CASE 621
   Spatial scope 683
   Time and place of act 683
   Young people 685

Contents

DEFINITIONS — 685

PRINCIPLES — 687

    Omissions, acting for another, intention and negligence — 687

    Mistakes — 687

THE REFERENDUM MISTAKE CASE — 689

    Punishment linked to consequence — 697

    Criminal incapacity — 699

ATTEMPT — 699

PERPETRATORS AND PARTICIPANTS — 701

    Perpetrators — 701

    Participants — 701

SELF-DEFENCE AND EMERGENCIES — 703

    Self-defence — 703

    Emergency — 705

ASSESSMENT OF PUNISHMENT — 707

    One crime or offence — 707

    Several crimes or offences — 711

CRIMES OF INSULT — 715

THE INSULT OF SOLDIERS CASE — 715

CRIMES AGAINST LIFE — 731

THE BASE MOTIVE CASE — 733

BODILY INJURY — 739

THE ROUGH ILL-TREATMENT CASE — 741

Bibliography — 751

Index — 753

TABLE OF ABBREVIATIONS

AcP	Archiv für die civilistische Praxis Archive for Civil Practice
AGBG	Gesetz zur Regelung des Rechts der Allgemeinem Geschaftsbedingungen General Conditions of Business/Contract Act
AK-GG	Kommentar zum GG, Reihe Alternativ-kommentar Commentary on the BL, alternative commentary series
AMG	Arzneimittelgesetz Medicines Act
AO	Abgabenordnung Internal Revenue Code
AP	Arbeitsrechtliche Praxis Labour Law Practice
ArbRecht	Arbeitsrecht Employment law
AT	Allgemeiner Teil General Part
AVV, AVwV	Allgemeine Verwaltungsvorschrift General Administrative Order
AZO	Arbeitszeitordnung Working Hours Order
BAG	Bundesarbeitsgericht Federal Labour Court
BAnz	Bundesanzeiger Federal Advertiser
BayObLG	Bayerisches Oberstes Landgericht Bavarian Upper State Court
BB	Betriebs-Berater Business Adviser

BDiszG	Bundesdisziplinargesetz Federal Disciplinary Act
BFSG	Gesetz über die Bundesanstalt für Flugsicherung Federal Institute for Flight Safety Act
BG	Bürgerliches Gesetzbuch Civil Code
BGBl	Bundesgesetzblatt Federal Law Gazette
BGH	Bundesgerichtshof Federal Supreme Court
BGH LM	see LM
BGHR	BGH-Rechtsprechung Strafsachen Federal Supreme Court case law – criminal cases
BGHSt	Entscheidungen des Bundesgerichtshofs in Strafsachen Decisions of the Federal Supreme Court in criminal cases
BGHZ	Entscheidungen des Bundesgerichtshofs in Zivilsachen Decisions of the Federal Supreme Court in civil cases
BStBl	Bundessteuerblatt Federal Tax Gazette
BTDrucks	Bundestag-Drucksachen Federal Parliament – Printed Material
BtMG	Betaubungsmittelgesetz Narcotics Act
BVerfG	Bundesverfassungsgericht Federal Constitutional Court

BVerfGE	Entscheidungen des Bundesverfassungsgerichts Federal Constitutional Court Decisions
BVerfGG	Gesetz über das Bundesverfassungsgericht Federal Constitutional Court Act
BVerwG	Bundesverwaltungsgericht Federal Administrative Court
BVerwGE	Entscheidungen des Bundesverwaltungsgerichts Federal Administrative Court Decisions
BWahlG	Bundeswahlgesetz Federal Elections Act
CoR	Computerreport Computer Report
DB	Der Betrieb Business (a legal journal)
DDR	Deutsche Demokratische Republik German Democratic Republic
DJT	Deutsche Juristentag German Lawyers Conference
DR	Deutsches Recht (Zeitschrift) German Law (Journal)
DRiZ	Deutsche Richterzeitung German Judicial Journal
DVBl	Deutsches Verwaltungsblatt German Administrative Gazette
EGBGB	Einführungsgesetz zum Bürgerliches Gesetzbuch Introductory Act to the Civil Code

EGStGB	Einführungsgesetz zum Strafgesetzbuch Introductory Act to the Criminal Code
Erste IHDV	Erste Verordnung zur Durchführung des Gesetzes über die Investitionshilfe der gewerblichen Wirtschaft First Regulation for Administration of the Investment Aid for Industry Act
EStG	Einkommensteuergesetz Income Tax Act
EuGH	Europäischer Gerichtshof European Court of Justice
EuGRZ	Europäische Grundrechte Zeitschrift European Human Rights Journal
FS	Festschrift Celebratory or commemorative Publication
GA	Goltdammers Archiv Goltdammer's Archives
GBl	Gesetzblatt Statutes Gazette
GewO	Gewerbe Ordnung Business Order
GG	Grundgesetz Basic Law
GmbH	Gesellschaft mit beschränkter Haftung Private limited company
GSSt	Großer Senat Strafsachen Decisions of the Great Senate in criminal cases

GVBl	Gesetz- und Verordnungsblatt Statutes and Regulations Gazette
GVG	Gerichtsverfassungsgesetz Organisation of the Courts Act
HATG	Hausarbeitstaggesetz Housework Day Act
HbgPresseG	Hamburg Pressegesetz Hamburg Press Act
HEZ	Höchstrichterliche Entscheidungen, Sammlung von Entscheidungen der Oberlandesgerichte und der obersten Gerichte in Zivilsachen Highest judicial decisions, collection of decisions of the upper State courts and of the highest courts in civil cases
HGB	Handelsgesetzbuch Commercial Code
HRR	Höchstrichterliche Rechtsprechung Case Law of Highest Courts
IHG	Gesetz über Investitionshilfe für gewerblichen Wirtschaft Investment Aid for Industry Act
IPbürgR	Internationale Pakt über bürgerliche und politische Rechte International Convention on Civil and Political Rights
JR	Juristische Rundschau Legal Review
JuS	Juristische Schulung Legal Training
JW	Juristische Wochenschrift Legal Weekly Journal

JZ	Juristenzeitung Jurists Gazette
KG	Kammergericht Supreme Court
KK	Karlsruher Kommentar (zur Strafprozeßordnung) Karlsruhe Commentary (on the Criminal Procedure Code)
KRG	Kontrollratgesetz (Allied) Control Council Act
KritV	Kritische Vierteljahresschrift für Gesetzgebung und Rechtswissenschaft Critical Quarterly Journal for legislation and jurisprudence
KunstUrhG	Kunst Urheber Gesetz Artistic Copyright Act
LebMG	Lebensmittelgesetz Food Act
LG	Landgericht State Court
LitUrhG	Gesetz betreffend das Urheberrecht an Werken der Literatur und der Tonkunst Literary Copyright Act (Act concerning copyright in works of literature and music)
LK	Leipziger Kommentar Leipzig Commentary
LM	Lindenmaier-Möhring, Nachschlagewerk des Bundesgerichtshofs Lindenmaier-Möhring, Reference book of the Federal Supreme Court
LuftVG	Luftverkehrgesetz Air Traffic Act

LuftVO	Luftverkehrordnung Air Traffic Order
LZ	Leipziger Zeitschrift für Deutsches Recht Leipzig Journal for German Law
MDR	Monatsschrift für deutsches Recht Monthly Journal of German Law
MMR	Multimedia und Recht Multimedia and the law
MRK	Menschenrechtskonvention Convention on Human Rights
NJ	Neue Justiz New Justice
NJW	Neue Juristische Wochenschrift New Legal Weekly Journal
NRW	Nordrhein Westfalen North Rhine Westphalia
NStZ	Neue Zeitschrift für Strafrecht New Journal of Criminal Law
NVwZ	Neue Zeitschrift für Verwaltungsrecht New Journal for Administrative Law
NZWehrr	Neue Zeitschrift für Wehrrecht New Journal for Defence Law
OG	Oberstes Gericht der DDR Supreme Court (of the DDR)
OHGSt	Entscheidungen des Obersten Gerichtshofes für die Britische Zone in Strafsachen Decisions of the Supreme Court for the British Zone in criminal matters
OLG	Oberlandesgericht Upper State Court

OVG	Oberverwaltungsgericht Upper Administrative Court
PartG	Parteiengesetz Parties Act
PDS	Partei des Demokratischen Sozialismus Party of Democratic Socialism
RFH	Reichfinanzhof Reich Revenue Court
RG	Reichsgericht Reich High Court
RGBl	Reichsgesetzblatt Reich Laws Gazette
RGRK	BGB, Kommentar, herausgegeben von Reichsgerichtsräten und Bundesrichtern Commentary on the BGB by Reich Justices and Federal Judges
RGSt	Entscheidungen des Reichsgerichts in Strafsachen Decisions of the Reich High Court in criminal cases
RGZ	Entscheidungen des Reichsgerichts in Zivilsachen Decisions of the Reich High Court in civil cases
RHG, RHaftPflG	Reichshaftspflichtgesetz Reich Liability Act
SED	Sozialistische Einheitspartei Deutschlands Socialist Unity Party of Germany (East German Communists)
SJZ	Süddeutsche Juristenzeitung South German Legal Gazette
StGB	Strafgesetzbuch Criminal Code

StGH	Staatsgerichtshof Constitutional Court (of an individual State)
StPO	Strafprozeßordnung Criminal Procedure Code
StR	Strafrecht Criminal Law
StrÄndG	Strafrechtsänderungsgesetz Criminal Law Amendment Act
StrRG	Strafregistergesetz Criminal Register Act
StV	Strafverteidiger (Zeitschrift) Defence Lawyer (Journal)
StVG	Straßenverkehrgesetz Road Traffic Act
UWG	Gesetz gegen den unlauteren Wettbewerb Unfair Competition Act
UZwG	Gesetz über den unmittelbaren Zwang bei Ausübung öffentlicher Gewalt durch Vollzugsbeamte des Bundes Application of Force Act (Act concerning direct force exercised by public authority by an executive official of the Federation)
UZwGBw	Gesetz über die Anwendung unmittelbaren Zwanges und die Ausübung besonderer Befugnisse durch Soldaten der Bundeswehr und zivile Wachpersonen Application of Military Force Act (Act concerning the application of direct force and the exercise of special powers by soldiers of the Federal Army and civilian guards)

VDB	Vergleichende Darstellung des Deutschen und ausländischen Strafrechts, 1906 f Besonderer Teil Comparative presentation of German and foreign criminal law, 1906 f Special Part
VersR	Versicherungsrecht (Zeitschrift) Insurance Law (Journal)
VG/VGH	Verwaltungsgericht/ Verwaltungsgerichtshof Administrative Court
VerwRspr	Verwaltungsrechtsprechung Administrative law case law
VkBl	Amtsblatt des Bundesministers für Verkehr Official Journal of the Federal Minister for Transport
VVDStRL	Veröffentlichungen der Vereinigungen Deutscher Staatsrechtlehrer Publications of the Associations of German Teachers of Public Law
VwGO	Verwaltungsgerichtsordnung Administrative Courts Order
WPflG	Wehrpflichtgesetz Military Service Act
WM	Wertpapiermitteilungen Security News
WStG	Wehrstrafgesetz Military Crimes Act
(Z)	Zivilsache(n) Civil case(s)
ZaöRV	Zeitschrift für ausländisches öffentliches Recht und Völkerrecht Journal of Foreign Public and International Law

ZBR	Zeitschrift für Beamtenrecht Journal for the Law relating to Officials
ZHR	Zeitschrift für das gesamte Handelsrecht und Wirtschaftsrecht Journal of Commercial Law and Business Law
ZLR	Zeitschrift für Luftrecht Journal of Air Law
ZPO	Zivilprozeßordnung Civil Procedure Code
ZR	Zivilrecht Civil Law
ZRP	Zeitschrift für Rechtspolitik (Beilage zur NJW) Journal of Legal Politics (supplement to NJW)
ZStW	Zeitschrift für die gesamte Strafrechtswissenschaft Journal of Criminal Jurisprudence

TABLE OF CASES

GERMAN
AcP
AcP 1965, 311 — 451
AcP 1967, 290 — 449

BAG
BAG 1, 51 = AP no 1 — 155
BAG 13, 1 = AP no 19 (Grand Senate 16 3 1962) — 145, 149, 151
BAG 26 10 1978 — 155

BAnz (FA)
BAnz no 45 of 6.3.1958 = BGB1 III 7831–1–1 — 455

BayObLG
BayObLG Cr 1958, 34 — 721
BayObLG NstZ 1983, 126 — 719
BayObLG NstZ 1983, 265 — 719
[1974] 2 CMLR 540 Solange I = BVerfGE 37, 271 — 15
[1987] 3 CMLR 225 Solange II = BVerfGE 52, 178 — 15, 97

BB
BB 1959, 1186 = VersR 1960, 342 — 405
BB 1964, 319 — 453
BB 1965, 439 — 455
BB 1979, 477 = AP no 27 — 145, 155
Baden-Württemberg StGH, VerwRspr 4, 1 — 213

BGB1
BGB1 1954 II 14 — 667
BGB1 1973 II 421 — 631
BGB1 1973 II 1534 — 649
BGB1 III 7831 — 455

BGHSt
BGHSt 2, 38 — 721
BGHSt 2, 194 — 689
BGHSt 2, 196 — 691
BGHSt 2, 201 — 697
BGHSt 2, 203 — 695
BGHSt 2, 209 — 697
BGHSt 2, 234 — 627, 647
BGHSt 3, 132 base motive case — 733
BGHSt 4, 1 — 689
BGHSt 6, 186 — 725
BGHSt 11, 207 — 719, 721
BGHSt 18, 87 — 675
BGHSt 21, 371 — 719, 725
BGHSt 23, 46 — 489, 493
BGHSt 25, 277 rough ill-treatment case — 741
BGHSt 26, 99 — 657
BGHSt 30, 1 — 631, 633
BGHSt 32, 293 — 631, 633

BGHSt 32, 310   719, 725
BGHSt 33, 97   629
BGHSt 35, 379   657, 673
BGHSt 36, 83 insult of soldiers case   715
BGHSt 37, 320   631
BGHSt 38, 1   631
BGHSt 38, 18   631
BGHSt 38, 88   631
BGHSt 39, 1 shootings at the Berlin wall case   109, 621

BGHZ
BGHZ 6, 330   383, 385
BGHZ 7, 338   605
BGHZ 9, 373 = NJW 53, 1297   567
BGHZ 11, 192   589
BGHZ 13, 334 publication of a letter case   469
BGHZ 15, 224   443
BGHZ 16, 54   265, 279
BGHZ 16, 111   595
BGHZ 21, 102   251, 255
BGHZ 22, 383   589
BGHZ 23, 36   595
BGHZ 24, 21   461
BGHZ 25, 250   443
BGHZ 29, 65   489, 597
BGHZ 33, 247   447
BGHZ 34, 32   261
BGHZ 34, 375   603
BGHZ 36, 252   489, 597
BGHZ 38, 200   597
BGHZ 40, 91   443, 453
BGHZ 40, 99   445
BGHZ 40, 101   443
BGHZ 40, 104   445
BGHZ 42, 176   583
BGHZ 45, 296   489, 493, 597, 599
BGHZ 47, 207 = NJW 1967, 1022   291
BGHZ 48, 118   451, 453
BGHZ 48, 310   465
BGHZ 49, 350   387, 447
BGHZ 51, 91 fowl pest case   387, 389, 439
BGHZ 56, 40   593
BGHZ 56, 296   387
BGHZ 59, 30 newspaper delivery obstruction case   481, 597
BGHZ 59, 172   405
BGHZ 60, 221 = NJW 1973, 752   395
BGHZ 61, 118   409
BGHZ 61, 227   387, 389
BGHZ 63, 35   593
BGHZ 64, 46 allergy to hair tonic case   399
BGHZ 65, 196   593
BGHZ 66, 51 fall in the supermarket case   377
BGHZ 69, 297   315

BGHZ 69, 128 air traffic controllers strike case 579
BGHZ 70, 337 = NJW 1978, 1374 291
BGHZ 71, 262 259
BGHZ 72, 382 = NJW 1979, 718 291

BVerfGE
BVerfGE [1994] NJ 46 107
BVerfGE 2 BvE 1/90 57
BVerfGE 2 BvQ 17/93 [1993] EuGRZ 326 19
BVerfGE 1, 14 215
BVerfGE 1, 144 221
BVerfGE 1, 264 201
BVerfGE 1, 208 61, 69
BVerfGE 2, 1 Socialist Reich Party 515
BVerfGE 2, 266 211, 217
BVerfGE 2, 307 215
BVerfGE 3, 19 211, 221
BVerfGE 3, 34 199
BVerfGE 3, 58 211
BVerfGE 3, 225 149, 647, 665
BVerfGE 3, 288 211
BVerfGE 3, 359 199
BVerfGE 3, 383 199
BVerfGE 3, 407 203
BVerfGE 4, 7 investment aid act case 193
BVerfGE 4, 31 = NJW 1954, 1601 81
BVerfGE 5, 9 149, 151
BVerfGE 5, 85 Communist Party 515, 521
BVerfGE 6, 32 515, 543
BVerfGE 6, 55 515
BVerfGE 6, 84 = NJW 1957, 377 61, 69, 515
BVerfGE 6, 132 647
BVerfGE 7, 198 film director case 505
BVerfGE 7, 377 Chemists 185
BVerfGE 8, 1 599
BVerfGE 8, 85 = NJW 1964, 1715 179
BVerfGE 10, 59 91, 149
BVerfGE 12, 113 493
BVerfGE 14, 121 = NJW 1962, 1493 63
BVerfGE 15, 337 149
BVerfGE 18, 85, 92 91
BVerfGE 19, 342 arrested admiral case 111
BVerfGE 20, 162 493
BVerfGE 21, 329 149
BVerfGE 22, 349 157
BVerfGE 24, 278 493, 719
BVerfGE 25, 236 157
BVerfGE 25, 256 Blinkfüer 495
BVerfGE 25, 269 665
BVerfGE 30, 173 Mephisto case 129, 173
BVerfGE 31, 1 149
BVerfGE 32, 98 = NJW 1972, 327 165
BVerfGE 36, 1 655

BVerfGE 37, 217   149, 151
BVerfGE 37, 271 Solange I = [1974] 2 CMLR 540   15
BVerfGE 42, 163   719
BVerfGE 43, 213   149
BVerfGE 44, 125 = NJW 1977, 1054   59
BVerfGE 51, 222 = NJW 1979, 2463   59, 61
BVerfGE 51, 252   61
BVerfGE 52, 178 Solange II = [1987] 3 CMLR 225   15, 97
BVerfGE 52, 223 = NJW 1980, 575   165
BVerfGE 52, 369 housework day case   143
BVerfGE 53, 135   109
BVerfGE 55, 159   109
BVerfGE 58, 300 Gravel   191
BVerfGE 69, 315 Brokdorf   183
BVerfGE 73, 1 = NJW 1986, 2492   59
BVerfGE 73, 40 = NJW 1986, 2487   59
BVerfGE 73, 206 Mutlangen   183
BVerfGE 74, 264 Boxberg   191
BVerfGE 78, 350 = NJW 1989, 285   59
BVerfGE 90, 145 = NJW 1994, 1577   165, 167, 169
BVerfGE 96, 375 [399] = NJW 1998, 519   135
BVerfGE 97, 125 = NJW 1998, 1381   177, 179
BVerfGE 101, 1 [37] = NJW 1999, 3523   129
BVerfGE 101, 361 = NJW 2000, 1021   179

BVerwG
BVerfG 3 C 20/00, 21.12.2000   159
BVerfG 1 BvQ 35/01, 24.8.2001   175
BVerfG 1 BvQ 36/01, 30.8.2001   179

DB
DB 1971, 2302   257
DB 1973, 1129 (BAG)   251
DB 1975, 2075   257
DB 1976, 1018 (BAG) = NJW 1976, 1284   309
DB 2000, 666 Wilkens   347, 349, 355, 357

DRiZ
DRiZ 1941, 637 = HRR 1941, 225   443
DRiZ 1968, 266   453

DVBl
DVBl 1974, 820 = ZBR 1974, 369 = NJW 1975, 1905   595

HRR
HRR 1931 no 376   743
HRR 1935 no 1276   745
HRR 1941, 225 = GJJ 1941, 637   443

JR
JR 1968, 287   455

JuS

JuS 1968, 347	451
JuS 1978, 674	721

JZ

JZ 1960, 470	729
JZ 1962, 553	387
JZ 1965, 475	387
JZ 1968, 494	455
JZ 1968, 497	449
JZ 1968, 714	449
JZ 1971, 73	599
JZ 1984, 948	633
JZ 1992, 665	633
JZ 1992, 990	667

LM

LM 254 E no 2	389
LM 276 Fa no 1	395
LM 459 BGB no 4	265

MDR

MDR 1953, 401	725
MDR 1954, 515	383
MDR 1966, 491	463
MDR 1974, 921	597

NJW

NJW 1953, 58	249
NJW 1953, 1297	567
NJW 1954, 913 (BGH) fallen telegraph pole case	565
NJW 1954, 1601 = BVerfGE 4, 31	81
NJW 1956, 1193	389
NJW 1957, 377 = FCCD 6, 84	61, 69, 515
NJW 1957, 746 (BGH) = LM	395
NJW 1957, 1688 (BAG)	515
NJW 1959, 670	597
NJW 1959, 1676	387
NJW 1960, 77	387
NJW 1960, 720 = WM 1960, 582	383
NJW 1961, 868	409
NJW 1962, 31	379, 463
NJW 1962, 1493 = BVerfGE 14, 121	63
NJW 1964, 33 = WM 1963, 1327	387, 389
NJW 1964, 34	465
NJW 1964, 272	637
NJW 1964, 811	291
NJW 1965, 965 (BGH)	309
NJW 1965, 1757 = WM 1965, 871	387
NJW 1967, 2199	395
NJW 1968, 247	465
NJW 1968, 1279	459, 603

NJW 1968, 1323	447
NJW 1968, 1593	449
NJW 1968, 1597	451
NJW 1968, 1598	449
NJW 1968, 1929	447
NJW 1968, 2102	249
NJW 1968, 2240 (BGH)	465
NJW 1969, 41 = WM 1968, 1354	389
NJW 1969, 1207	597
NJW 1970, 38 = WM 1969, 1358	389
NJW 1970, 653	291
NJW 1970, 1840	395
NJW 1971, 886	597
NJW 1971, 1422	251
NJW 1971, 1795 = WM 1971 749	291
NJW 1972, 2217 = WM 1972, 1124	405
NJW 1973, 752 = BGHZ 60, 221	395
NJW 1974, 1503 = Betr 1974, 1427	295
NJW 1974, 1641	409
NJW 1974, 1762 (BGHZ))	719
NJW 1975, 43	395
NJW 1975, 1774 termination of negotiations case	393
NJW 1975, 1905	595
NJW 1976, 103 (BGH)	593
NJW 1976, 1284 L	309
NJW 1977, 22	637, 649
NJW 1977, 626 (BGHZ)	719
NJW 1977, 1054 = BVerfGE 44, 125	59
NJW 1979, 1101	629
NJW 1979, 2032 misdirected withdrawal declaration case	301
NJW 1979, 2463 = BVerfGE 51, 222	59, 61
NJW 1981, 1522	719
NJW 1981, 2050 = LM 276 Fc BGB no 12 = WM 1981, 689	291
NJW 1981, 2117 (BGHZ)	719
NJW 1986, 1262	719
NJW 1986, 2492 = BVerfGE 73, 1	59
NJW 1986 2487 = BVerfGE 74, 40	59
NJW 1989, 285 = BVerfGE 78, 350	59
NJW 1997, 165	339, 341
NJW 2000, 94	347
NJW 2000, 167	339
NJW 2000, 3216	161
NJW 2002, 363	333
NJW 53, 1297 = BGHZ 9, 373	567

NStZ

NStZ BUSC 1983, 126	719
NStZ BUSC 1983, 265	719
NStZ 1987, 224	675
NStZ 1987, 554	725
NStZ 1997, 498	167

OHGSt

OHGSt 2, 231	665
OHG JR 1978, 422	719

OLG

OLG of Cologne, NJW 1950, 702	307
OLG of Düsseldorf, NJW 1979, 59	633
OLG of Düsseldorf (C), NJW 1981, 1522	719
OLG of Düsseldorf, NJW 1983, 1277	633
OLGof Düsseldorf (C), NJW 1986, 1262	719
OLG of Hamburg, 7 U 75/01, 15.8.2001	177
OLG of Hamburg 7 U 77/01	181
OLG of Hamburg NZWehrr 77/70	725

RFH

RFH 27, 321	213

RG

RG GRUR 1940, 375	295
RG Recht 1912 no 1273	279
RG Recht 1912 no 2797	279
RG WarnRspr 1911 no 192	279
RG WarnRspr 1911 no 368	279
RG WarnRspr 1912 no 205	279
RG case law 1, 292	719

RG

RG DR 1940, 26	745
RG DR 1941, 492	745
RG DR 1943, 993	607
RG DR 1944, 330	745
RG LZ 1915, 60	719
RG JW 1912, 461 = SeuffArch 67 no 198	267
RG JW 1917, 236	275
RG JW 1925, 2752	273, 275
RG JW 1931, 865	607
RG JW 1932, 31	719
RG JW 1938, 1879	745
RG JW 1938, 2808	745

RGSt

RGSt 19, 136	743
RGSt 31, 185	721
RGSt 32, 113	743
RGSt 33, 46	719, 721
RGSt 62, 160	745

RGZ

RGZ 21, 308	279
RGZ 41, 43	475
RGZ 50, 191	309
RGZ 51, 1	279
RGZ 57, 358	273

RGZ 59, 240	279
RGZ 61, 84	279
RGZ 61, 171	265
RGZ 64, 266	279
RGZ 69, 242	477
RGZ 69, 401	475
RGZ 72, 175	475
RGZ 78, 239	381
RGZ 79, 397	475, 477
RGZ 82, 333	475
RGZ 85, 343	475
RGZ 87, 1	451
RGZ 94, 1	475
RGZ 96, 148	591
RGZ 99, 148	363
RGZ 99, 214	279
RGZ 100, 205	273, 275
RGZ 104, 257	589
RGZ 107, 277	475
RGZ 111, 233	291
RGZ 113, 414	475
RGZ 115, 416	475
RGZ 116, 287	565
RGZ 123, 312	475
RGZ 127, 31	567
RGZ 135, 339	265
RGZ 138, 254	265
RGZ 138, 354	265
RGZ 142, 116	497
RGZ 151, 50	477
RGZ 154, 117	595
RGZ 155, 257	531
RGZ 157, 228	569
RGZ 158, 83	595
RGZ 161, 193	277
RGZ 162, 7	475
RGZ 170, 155	459
RGZ 170, 246	445
RGZ 170, 380	307

SJZ
SJZ 1946, 105	647
SJZ 1947, 642	475

VersR
VersR 1956, 410	449
VersR 1956, 765	405
VersR 1960, 217	585
VersR 1960, 342 = BB 1959, 1186	405
VersR 1961, 231	459
VersR 1963, 339	603
VersR 1966, 875	603

VersR 1967, 69, 352   489
VersR 1967, 69, 851   489
VersR 1967, 685   459
VersR 1973, 443   603

VG
VG Frankfurt aM Decision of 1.3.2001 – 1 G 429/01 (V)   131

VkBl
VkBl 1954, 26   585

WM
WM 1960, 582 = NJW 1960, 720   383
WM 1963, 1327 = NJW 1964, 33   387, 389
WM 1965, 871 = NJW 1965, 1757   387
WM 1968, 300 = LM   387
WM 1968, 1354 = NJW 1969, 41   389, 447
WM 1969, 1358 = NJW 1970, 38   389
WM 1972, 1124 = NJW 1972, 2217   405
WM 1975, 157   291
WM 1976, 448   251
WM 1977, 394   291
WM 1998, 1949   357

ZBR
ZBR 1974, 369   595

ZHR
ZHR 1965, 269   445
ZHR 1967, 173   451
ZHR 1967, 176   455
ZHR 1967, 179   449
ZHR 1967, 180   453

ZR
BGH, judgment of 20.5.1952 – I StR 490/51   695
BGH, judgment of 10.7.1952 – IV StR 73/52   697
BGH, judgment of 31.3.1953 – I ZR 584/52   725
BGH, judgment of 14.1.1954 – III ZR 221/52 (Frankfurt/M)   565
BGH, judgment of 5.11.1955 – VI ZR 199/54 = VersR 1956, 765   405
BGH, judgment of 25.4.1956 – VI ZR 34/35 = NJW 1956, 1193   389
BGH, judgment of 15.5.1959 – VI ZR 109/58 = NJW 1959, 1676   387
BGH, judgment of 20.10.1959 – VI ZR 152/58
   = VersR 1960, 342 = BB 1959, 1186   405
BGH, judgment of 30.1.1961 – III ZR 225/59 = NLW 1961, 868   409
BGH, judgment of 26.9.1961 – VI ZR 92/61   383
BGH, judgment of 8.5.1965 – VI ZR 58/65 = LM   389
BGH, judgment of 9.10.1968 – VIII ZR 173/66 = WM 1968, 1354   447
BGH, judgment of 14.1.1969 – VI ZR 196/67 = VersR 69, 352   489
BGH, judgment of 20.6.1969 – VI ZR 234/67 = VersR 69, 851   489
BGH, judgment of 30.9.1969 – VI ZR 254/67 = WM 1972/1124
   = NJW 1972, 2217   389

BGH, judgment of 11.7.1972 – VI ZR 194/70 = VersR 1956, 765 405
BGH, judgment of 12.6.1975 – X ZR 25/73 (Hamm) 393
BGH, judgment of 27.7.1978 – V ZR 180/77 (Frankfurt) 321
BGH, judgment of 13.7.1983 – VIII ZR 142/82 (Düsseldorf) 283
BGH, judgment of 24.1.1984 – V ZR 866/83 725
Civil Senate, judgment of 23.10.1952, VEW (defendant) v E
(claimant) – III ZR 364/51 605
Civil Senate, judgment of 25.5.1954 Dr M (plaintiff) v
D W Publishers Ltd (defendant) – I ZR 211/53 469
Civil Senate, judgment of 14.12.1960, P (defendant) v D (claimant)
– V ZR 40/60 261
Civil Senate, judgment of 13.7.1963 = BGHZ 40, 91 453
Civil Senate, judgment of 26.11.1968, V Ltd (defendant) v
B (plaintiff), VI ZR 212/66 439
Civil Senate, judgment of 30.5.1972, A (defendant) v FS (plaintiff)
– VI ZR 6/71 481
Civil Senate, judgment of 19.2.1975, FL (plaintiff) v
Fa O (defendant) – VIII ZR 144/73 399
Civil Senate, judgment of 28.1.1976, D (defendant) v
L (plaintiff) – VIII ZR 246/74 377
Civil Senate, judgment of 16.6.1977, FRG (defendant) v
Fa N (plaintiff) – III ZR 179/75 579
Criminal Senate, judgment of 23.12.1952, against Z and
B – II StR 612/52 689
Criminal Senate (3rd), judgment of 23.1.1974, v W – III ZR 324/73 741
Criminal Senate (1st), judgment of 9.1.1989, v P – I ZR 641/88 715
Criminal Senate, judgment of 3.11.1992, v W and H – V ZR 370/92 621
Vacational Criminal Senate (1st), judgment of 25.7.1952, v
Sch – I ZR 272/52 733
BAG, judgment of 10.5.1957 = NJW 1957, 1688 515
BGH, judgment of 26.9.1961 – VI ZR 92/61 = NLW 1962, 31 = LM 379
BGH, judgment of 11.5.1979 – V ZR 177/77 (Düsseldorf) 301
Great Senate for criminal cases, judgment of 18.3.1952 – GSSt 2/51 689, 691
Senate judgment of 1.4.1953 – VI ZR 77/52 465
Senate judgment of 21.4.1956 – VI ZR 36/55 = VersR 1956, 410 449
Senate judgment of 15.1.1958 – 1 BvR 400/51 505
Senate, judgment of 5.1.1960 – VII ZR 1/59 = NJW 1960, 720
= WM 1960, 582 383
Senate, judgment of 3.1.1961 – VI ZR 67/60 = VersR 1961, 231 459
Senate, judgment of 26.9.1961 – VI ZR 922/61 463
Senate, judgment of 16.10.1963 – VIII ZR 28/62
= WM 1963, 1327 = NJW 1964, 33 387, 389
Senate, judgment of 23.6.1965 – VIII ZR 201/63
= WM 1965, 871 = NJW 1965, 1757 387
Senate judgment 18.1.1966 – VI ZR 184/64 = MDR 1966, 491 463
Senate, judgment of 21.3.1967 – VI ZR 164/65 455
Senate, judgment of 4.4.1967 – VI ZR 98/65 = VersR 1967, 685 459
Senate, judgment of 17.10.1967 – VI ZR 70/66 = NJW 1968 247 465
Senate, judgment of 10.1.1968 – VIII ZR 104/65
= WM 1968, 300 = LM 387

Senate, judgment of 12.3.1968 – VI ZR 178/66 = NJW 1968, 1279   459
Senate, judgment of 30.4.1968 – VI ZR 29/67 = NJW 1968 1323   447
Senate, judgment of 18.6.1968 – VI ZR 120/67 = NJW 1968 1929   447
Senate, judgment of 9.10.1968 – VIII ZR 173/66 = WM 1968, 1354
    = NJW 19679, 41   389

EUROPEAN COURT OF JUSTICE
Harz v Deutsche Tradex GmbH (case 79/83) [1986] 2 CMLR 430   107
Internationale Handelsgesellschaft GmbH v EV St (Case 11/70)
    [1972] CMLR 55   108
Rewe-Zentral AG v Bundesmonopolverwaltung für Branntwein
    (Cassis de Dijon) (Case 120/78) [1979] 3 CMLR 494   109
Von Colson v Land Nordrhein Westfalen (Case 14/83)
    [1986] 2 CMLR 430   107

UNITED KINGDOM
Bebee v Sales (1916) 32 TLR 413   573
Buron v Denman (1848) 2 Exch 167   629
Byrne v Boadle (1863) 2 H & C 722   435

Carlill v Carbolic Smoke Ball Co [1893] 1 QB 256   241
Council for Civil Service Unions v Minister for the Civil Service
    [1984] 3 All ER 935 HL   108

Derbyshire County Council v Times Newspapers
    [1992] 3 All ER 65   715

Fairline Shipping Corporation v Adamson [1974] 2 All ER 967   241
Felthouse v Bindley (1862) 11 CB (NS) 869   241

Gorris v Scott (1874) LR 9 Exch 125   437

Jones v Padavatton [1969] 2 All ER 616   241
Jones v Vernon's Pool Ltd [1938] 2 All ER 626   241

Limpus v London General Omnibus Co (1862) 1 H & C 526   563

Moorcock, The (1889) 14 PD 64   371
Musgrave v Pulido (1897) 5 App Cas 102   629

Pharmaceutical Society v Boots Cash Chemist (Southern) Ltd
    [1952] 2 All ER 456; [1953] 1 All ER 482   333

R v Desmond, Barrett and Others, The Times, 28 April 1868   637
R v Secretary of State for Employment ex p Equal Opportunities
    Commission and Another, The Times, 4 March 1994   141
R v Secretary of State for the Home Department ex p Brind
    [1991] 1 All ER 720 HL   108
Rose v Plenty [1976] 1 All ER 97   563

Saunders v Anglia Building Society [1970] 3 All ER 961   259

Ward v Tesco Stores Ltd [1976] 2 All ER 219   435

USA
Tennessee v Garner, 1985 US Supreme Court 471 US 1   655

TABLE OF STATUTES

GERMANY

Administrative Courts
  Order (VwGO)—
    42 . . . . 131, 133
    123 . . . . 131, 133
    137 163
(Allied) Control Council Act
  (KRG)—
    II 217
    no 10 . . . . 541, 545
Animals Protection Act—
    1 129
Application of Force
  Act (UZwG)—
    11 . . . . 645, 657
Application of Military
  Force Act (UZwGBw)—
    15 657
    16 . . . . 645, 657
Air Traffic Act (LuftVG)—
    1 583
    29 . . . . 585, 593
    31 585
Air Traffic Order (LuftVO)—
    26 . . . . 585, 587, 593, 595

Basic Law (GG) 1, 4, 7, 9, 13, 15,
          27, 43, 55, 75, 83–89, 117,
          123, 129, 157, 177, 205, 207,
          491, 645, 659
    X 203
    1–19 7
    1 . . . . 83, 85, 107, 129, 131, 135,
          137, 139, 197, 207, 469,
          475, 519, 531
    2 . . . . 111, 115, 117, 121, 127,
          139, 165, 193, 197, 205, 207,
          221, 469, 475, 541, 583
    3 . . . . 141, 143, 145, 147, 149,
          151, 155, 197, 201, 211, 221
    4 . . . . 157, 159, 163, 165
    5 . . . 173, 175, 177, 179, 181, 183, 227,
          481, 491, 505, 507, 511, 513,
          519, 523, 525, 527, 531, 559, 719
    6 . . . . 105, 181

    7 181
    8 . . . . 183, 227, 481, 491
    9 . . . . 183, 197, 221, 227
    10 . . . . 185, 227
    11 . . . . 185, 227
    12 . . . . 107, 185, 207
    12 a 93, 185, 187
    13 . . . . 189, 227
    14 . . . . 7, 191, 193, 197, 207,
          209, 223, 227
    15 . . . . 197, 207, 223
    16 223
    16 a 223, 227
    17 . . . . 223, 227
    17 a 227
    18 227
    19 . . . . 108, 173, 201, 207, 227
    20 . . . . 9, 11, 15, 83, 85,
          91, 197, 207, 497
    21 . . . . 11, 55, 57, 59
    22 11
    23 . . . . 13, 15, 97, 101
    24 . . . . 15, 17, 25, 27
    25 . . . . 15, 41, 97, 105, 629
    26 . . . . 41, 93
    27 41
    28 . . . . 43, 91
    29 . . . . 43, 45, 47
    30 47
    31 . . . . 4, 47
    32 49
    33 49
    34 . . . . 51, 579, 583, 587, 589, 591
    35 . . . . 51, 185
    36 51
    37 53
    38 . . . . 53, 55, 57, 59, 101
    39–49 83
    50 101
    50–53 83
    53 a 83
    54–61 83
    59 25
    62–69 83
    70–78 . . . . 47, 83
    70 197

72 89
74 . . . . 193, 201, 203
74 a. 95
79 . . . . 13, 15, 83, 85, 101
80 . . . . 85, 215, 217
80 a. 85, 187
81 85
82 87
83–91 87
84 203
87 a. 25, 27, 185, 727
91 185
91 a. 87
91 b. 87
92 87
93 89
94 91
95 . . . . 93, 95
96 93
97 93
98 95
99 95
100 97
101 97
102 97
103 . . . . . . 97, 619, 621, 627, 659, 663,
               665, 667, 669, 671
104 . . . . 99, 107, 117, 139
104 a–115. 99
105 203
110 . . . . 197, 223
115 . . . . 197, 205
115 a–115 l 99
115 a. 187
116–142 101
116 101
119 101
123 101
140 101
143 101
144 101
145 101
146 . . . . 69, 103

Civil Code – Introductory Act
(EGBGB)—
6 645
Civil Code (BGB) . . . 1, 7, 229, 261, 331,
               369, 433, 437, 469, 511, 575
1 . . . . 161, 231, 235, 263
2 . . . . 231, 645
3–6 231
7–11 233
12 233
13 233
14 233
15–20 233
21–29 233
28 . . . . 395, 475
30 . . . . 569, 573
31 . . . . 569, 573
89 . . . . 569, 573
90–103 233
104 235
105 235
106 235
107–113 235
107 235
108 . . . . 235, 267
109 237
110 237
111 . . . . 237, 367
112 . . . . 237, 265, 269
113 239
114–115 239
116 . . . . 243, 253, 255, 279, 351
117 243
118 . . . . 243, 253, 281
119 . . . . 243, 247, 249, 251,
               253, 257, 259, 261, 263,
               265, 267, 269, 271, 273,
               275, 277, 279, 281, 333, 355
120 . . . . 249, 279, 281
121 . . . . 243, 249, 273, 279, 355
122 . . . . 247, 249, 253, 281, 453
123 . . . . 261, 273, 275, 281,
               283, 291, 295, 317
124 295

125 297
126 . . . . 297, 299
126 a. 297, 299
126 b. 297
127 297
127 a. 299
128 . . . . 299, 361
129 299
130 . . . . 299, 301
131 . . . . 235, 311
132 311
133 . . . . 313, 349, 363, 387
134 . . . . 313, 333, 357
135 313
136 313
137 313
138 . . . . 315, 371
139 315
140 315
141 . . . . 315, 355
142 . . . . 253, 279, 295, 315, 355
143 . . . . . . 243, 257, 279, 295, 315, 355
144 317
145 . . . . 9, 333, 339, 343, 353
146 . . . . 7, 359
147 359
148 359
149 359
150 . . . . 251, 359
151 . . . . 325, 333, 335, 337, 361
152 361
153 361
154 361
155 361
156 . . . . 333, 347, 349, 363
157 . . . . 253, 313, 363, 371, 387
158 . . . . 363, 365
159 363
160 . . . . 363, 365
161 365
162 365
163 365
164–181 367
164 . . . . 333, 337
166 343
167 . . . . 343, 353

181 353
182 . . . . 235, 367
183 . . . . 235, 367
184 . . . . 235, 367
185 367
186–193 317
194–225 317
195 . . . . 383, 391
210 295
211 295
226 317
227 . . . . 319, 321, 323, 325, 435
228 . . . . 319, 435
229 319
230 319
231 319
241 . . . . 369, 399, 419, 427
242. . . . . 251, 299, 363,
                                   369, 371, 453
243 371
244 371
245 371
246 371
247 371
248 373
249 . . . . 373, 439, 605
250 373
251 373
252 . . . . 373, 605
253 . . . . 375, 611
254 . . . . 375, 389, 501, 611
255 375
256–274 375
273 425
275 . . . . 357, 371, 375, 411,
                         419, 427, 429, 453
276 . . . . 329, 377, 381, 393,
                         395, 397, 455, 463, 603
277 397
278 . . . . 375, 383, 397, 441, 459
279 397
280 . . . . 377, 397, 399, 411
281 . . . . 397, 411, 421
282 . . . . 379, 383, 397, 399, 409
283 . . . . 357, 377, 397, 411
284 . . . . 377, 411, 421

285 . . . . 377, 411
286 . . . . 397, 411
287 413
288 413
289–291 413
292 413
293–304 413
305 . . . . 333, 415, 417, 419
306 . . . . 417, 419
307 . . . . 417, 419
308 419
309 419
310 419
311 . . . . 377, 419, 421
312 421
313 421
314 421
315 . . . . 333, 351, 423
316 423
317 423
318 423
319 423
320 425
321 425
323 . . . . 421, 425, 429
324 427
325 427
326 . . . . 377, 427
327 429
328 . . . . 377, 387, 429
329 431
330–332 431
333 431
334 431
335 431
346–348 399
349 307
373 451
426 499
433 . . . . 385, 399
441 . . . . 427, 429
446 265
459 . . . . 261, 265, 267, 269,
                              271, 273, 445
477 . . . . 265, 269, 271

536 465
618 443
760 609
762 . . . . 333, 357
766 255
771 245
823–826 561
823 . . . . 295, 321, 329, 433, 435,
                    437, 439, 449, 457, 459,
            461, 469, 473, 481, 487, 489,
            529, 565, 567, 569, 571, 573,
                    579, 595, 597, 603, 715
824 . . . . 473, 503, 597
825 503
826 . . . . 433, 475, 487, 503,
                    505, 511, 513, 517, 531,
                              591, 597, 605
827 . . . . 377, 559, 561
828 . . . . 377, 561
829 . . . . 561, 609
830 . . . . 481, 497, 499, 501, 561
831 . . . . 383, 449, 455, 465,
                              563, 565, 567, 609
832 . . . . 233, 465, 573, 609
833 . . . . 465, 575, 605, 609
834 . . . . 465, 575, 609
835 . . . . 575, 609
836 . . . . . . 465, 565, 571, 573, 577, 609
837 . . . . 577, 609
838 . . . . 577, 609
839 . . . . 565, 567, 579, 583,
                              587, 591, 593, 595, 601
840 . . . . 499, 609
841 609
842 609
843 . . . . 609, 611
844 . . . . 443, 611
845 . . . . 443, 611
846 611
847 . . . . 329, 375, 611
848 613
849 613
850 613
851 613
852 . . . . 383, 615

853 615
872 577
904 329
1356 155

Civil Procedure Code (ZPO)—
112 117
187 307
286 . . . . 277, 279, 465
302 247
561 599
563 309
599 247

Commercial Code (HGB)—
1 255
124 201
161 201
350 255

Control Council Act—
II 217
no 10 . . . . 541, 545

Criminal Law
  Amendment Act
  (StrÄndG) 635

Criminal Code –
  Introductory Act
  (EGStGB)—
315 . . . . 627, 631, 633, 657

Criminal Code
  (StGB) 1, 7, 437, 617
1 619
2 . . . . 619, 621, 627, 631, 633,
                    645, 657, 667, 671, 673,
                    675, 681
3 . . . . 631, 633, 683
4 683
5 . . . . 631, 683
6 . . . . 631, 681, 683
7 . . . . 621, 631, 633, 683
8 683
9 683
10 685
11 . . . . 677, 685, 713, 731
12 685
13 687
14 . . . . 687, 701

15 687
16 687
17 . . . . 627, 681, 687, 689
18 697
19 699
20 699
21 699
22 699
23 . . . . 699, 703
24 701
25 . . . . 561, 673, 675, 701
26 . . . . 561, 701
27 561
28 701
29 . . . . 701, 703
30 703
31 703
32 . . . . 319, 325, 703
33 703
34 . . . . 319, 323, 705
35 705
41 711
43 a 713
44 711
46 707
46 a 707
47 709
48 709
49 . . . . 687, 699, 701, 703,
                          705, 707, 709
50 709
51 711
52 . . . . 545, 553, 711, 713
53 . . . . 325, 713
54 713
55 713
59 . . . . 689, 695
80 683
81–83 683
94–100 a 683
130 . . . . 715, 727, 729
185 . . . . 715, 721, 723, 725
186 . . . . 473, 715, 731
187 . . . . 473, 637, 715, 727, 731
188 731

189 . . . . 721, 731
190 731
192 731
193 . . . . 725, 731
194 . . . . 723, 725, 731
195–198 731
199 731
200 731
211 . . . . 113, 731, 733, 735
212 . . . . 113, 627, 671, 673, 735
213 . . . . . . 625, 627, 629, 635, 671, 735
216 737
217 737
218–219 b 737
220 737
220 a. 113, 683, 737
221 737
222 737
223 . . . . 739, 743, 747
223 a. 745
223 b 741, 743, 745, 747
224 . . . . 739, 747
225 . . . . 739, 741, 747
226 . . . . 737, 747, 747, 749
227 747
228 749
229 749
230 749
231 749
234 a. 631, 683
240 . . . . 437, 487
241 a. 631, 683
Criminal Procedure
  Code (StPO) 115
  11 a. 711
  94 711
  112 . . . . 111, 113, 115, 121,
                             123, 125, 127
  116 . . . . . . 111, 113, 115, 121, 125, 127
  120 121
  121 121
  376 693

Declaration of the Rights of
  Men and Citizens 1789 521
Disappearance Act (VerschG)—
  9 231

First Regulation for Administration
  of the Investment Aid for
  Industry Act (Erste IHDV)—
  2 213
  14 . . . . 215, 217
  23 . . . . 215, 217
  24 . . . . 215, 217
Federal Constitutional
  Court Act (BVerfGG)—
  23 201
  26 529
  32 . . . . 29, 175, 177, 181
  34 157
  34 a. 81
  35 81
  64 31
  90 . . . . 199, 505, 513, 519
  95 . . . . 115, 157
Federal Elections
  Act (BWahlG) 63, 65, 71, 73, 81
  6 . . . . 55, 57, 59, 71
  18 65
  21 63
  34 71
  53 . . . . 55, 57, 67, 69, 71
Federal Institute for
  Flight Safety Act (BFSG) 585
  1 . . . . 585, 593, 595
  2 . . . . 585, 593
  3 585
Food Act (LebMG)—
  3 459
  4 459
Free Time Order 151

General Administrative
  Order (AVV) —
  1 .... 585, 593
  3 .... 585, 595
  6 .... 585, 593, 595
  10 .... 585, 593
  13 595
  19 595
  23 595
General Conditions of
  Business/Contract
  Act (AGBG)........... 333, 345, 347,
                            371, 415
  .... 333, 345, 347, 415
  1 .... 333, 341, 345, 347
  2 .... 333, 341, 345, 353
  4 347
  6 357
  9 347
  10 .... 333, 347
  24 347

Housework Day Act, North
  Rhine Westphalia
  (HATG NRW) 143, 145, 147
  1.................... 143, 145, 149,
                       151, 155, 157
  2 .... 145, 153

Implementation Provisions to the
Animal Diseases Act—
  87 455
Income Tax Act (EStG)—
  7–7e 215
Internal Revenue Code (AO)—
  264 197
Investment Aid for Industry
  Act (FLG I, 7)
  (IHG) 193, 195, 197, 199,
             201, 203, 205, 207, 209, 211,
             215, 219, 221, 223, 585
  1 193
  2 213

3 213
6 .... 215, 217
7 .... 215, 217
10 .... 215, 217
20 217
21 217
29 .... 203, 219
38 .... 215, 217
Investment Aid for Industry
  (Amendment No 1) Act
  (FLG I, 585) (IHG)......... 193, 195
  3 219
Investment Aid for Industry
  (Amendment No 2) Act
  (FLG I, 107) (IHG)......... 193, 195

Literary Copyright Act
  (LitUrhG)—
  1 475

Medicines Act (AMG) 437, 459
  3 459
  6 459
  19 467
Military Crimes Act (WStG) 675
  1 675
  5 .... 621, 627, 675, 677
Military Service Act (WPflG) —
  4 723

Narcotics Act (BtMG)........... 167
  3 .... 159, 161, 165, 173
  5 .... 159, 161, 163
  29 167
  29ff.......................... 167

Organisation of the Courts
  Act (GVG)—
  121 689

Parties Act (PartG)—
  2 65

Press Act (HbgPresseG)—
11 . . . . 469, 473, 479
Product Liability
Act 399, 575
Protection of
Mothers Act 151

Reich Constitution 1919—
118 523
Reich Liability Act (RHG)—
1 607
Road Traffic Act
(StVG) 575

Signature Act 297
Soldiers Act—
1 723
11 37
State Liability Act 579

Telegraph Lines Act 569
12 569
Transport of Persons
Act 415

Unfair Competition Act (UWG)—
3 295
13 295
13 a 281
Unification Treaty 617, 629, 633
3 101
5 69
18 629
19 . . . . 101, 629
41 101
App I, Ch III 631

Weimar Constitution 101
118 519
131 567
Working Hours Order (AZO) 151
16–19 151

**GERMAN DEMOCRATIC
REPUBLIC**
Border Act 621, 637, 651, 661
17 633
18 633
26 . . . . 625, 627, 663
27 . . . . 625, 627, 633, 635, 637,
639, 641, 643, 645, 657,
659, 661, 663

Constitution 75
3 69
8 653
30 . . . . 659, 663
48 661
49 661
51 649
85–94 669
89 659
90 661
91 669
95 669
96 661
Criminal Code – German
Democratic Republic
(StGB-DDR)
1 635
5 631
22 673
112 . . . . 627, 671
113 . . . . 627, 671
213 . . . . . . 627, 633, 635, 637, 657, 663
258 . . . . 627, 675

4th Penal Law Amendment
Act 18 12 1987
(LG GDR I 301) 659

Directive of 15 2 1982
(LG GDR I, 187) 653
Directive of 28 6 1979
(LG GDR I, 151)
17 653

Passport Act
 (LG GDR I 148) 651, 653
Passport and Visa
 Order 28 6 1979 653

Regulation of 20 11 1988
 (LG GDR I, 271) 653

Statute of Approval to the
 Electoral Treaty 75
Statute on the Electoral
 Law Treaty 67, 71
Statute Regarding Election to
 the Peoples Chamber—
 1, 60 79
 81 65
Statute Regarding Elections to
 the State Parliament—
 1, 960 79
Statute Regarding Parties and Other
 Political Alliances—
 5 65

FRANCE
Civil Code. 331
 1110 259
 1382 . . . . 433, 435
 1383 . . . . 433, 435

Declaration of Human Rights—
 Art 9. 119
 11 119

INTERNATIONAL LEGISLATION
Amsterdam Treaty 133
 Protocol 2 . . . . 131, 133

Directive 93/13 419
Directive 97/7—
 9 369

Directive 99/44 427
Directive 2000/35—
 3 371

European Convention on
 Human Rights. . . . 105, 223, 645, 659
 5 119
 6 . . . . 117, 119
 7 667
 10 715
 64 667

EC Treaty 133
 5 107
 177 97
 239 133
 249 137
 311 133
EEC Treaty (Treaty of Rome)—
 Art 119. 141
European Union Charter of
 Fundamental Rights 129
 1 . . . . 131, 135

International Convention on Civil
 and Political Rights. . . . 649, 651, 655
 3 655
 6 . . . . 651, 655, 657, 659, 663
 12 . . . . 649, 651, 653, 657, 663

Maastricht Treaty (TEU) 15

NATO Treaty. 39
 11 35

Regulation 1254/1999—
 Art 38. 139
Regulation 2777/2000 . . . . 131, 133,
                                   137, 139

Statute of International Military
  Tribunal of Nuremberg—
  8 669
  15 667

United Nations Charter—
  Ch VII 35
United Nations Drugs
  Convention—
  3 171
United Nations General Declaration
  of Human Rights. 119

UNITED KINGDOM
Animals Act 1971 575

Contracts (Rights of Third
  Parties) Act 1999 429

Employment Protection
  (Consolidation) Act 1978 141

Law Reform (Contributory
  Negligence) Act 1945 375

CHAPTER ONE

INTRODUCTION

GENERAL APPROACH

Selectivity

This book has been necessarily selective in the areas of law covered and the source materials chosen in respect of those areas. The purpose of the book is to introduce the reader to German legal material over a wide area, and this does not permit comprehensive treatment of the categories involved.

As to the areas covered, some themes are developed fairly fully (although even here the material may not represent the full picture) particularly if there is a relevant case included, whilst others are only touched on, or omitted. The wide subject area and the length of some of the source material has necessitated this rather arbitrary treatment. For instance, in the chapter on criminal law only a selection of crimes is included, and in the chapter on contract, there is nothing about special types of contract like contracts of sale or for services.

I have limited these source materials to extracts from the Basic Law and the Civil and Criminal Codes (with amendments), and the judgments in cases heard by the Federal Constitutional Court and the Federal Supreme Court. There would have been a strong case for including extracts from academic writings, in view of their importance in German law, but space does not permit it, and they are in any case referred to extensively in the judgments. I have included the whole of each of the court judgments. The reason for this was that each judgment tells a story, and it is easier to understand the arguments against a complete picture. Sometimes the case will deal with several separate issues which arguably should be physically separated, so that they appear in the parts of the book where those issues are dealt with, but I have refrained from splitting any judgments, as this makes it harder to associate and therefore understand the separate sections.

The cases have been selected partly for their significance in relation to German law, partly because of the contrast they provide to English law, and partly for their political or topical interest.

Translation

The translations are of a fairly basic, inelegant nature, because I have tried to keep as close as possible to the structure of the original material. This original material should, where possible, be used rather than the translation, as no translation can do full justice to the original. To mention just two examples, the use of the subjunctive in German for reported speech ensures that it is apparent how much of a court judgment is merely presenting the arguments of the parties. There are also certain words and expressions, some of which are listed below, which cause particular difficulties when attempting to convey their meaning in English. The literal nature of the translation is intended to assist students, who may only have a smattering of German, to identify words and phrases in the original text.

Professor Markesinis in his article 'Judge, Jurist and the Study and Use of Foreign Law'[1] draws attention to the need to interpret foreign legal material and then appropriately adapt it to make its 'immigration' possible into a different legal system, and he gives illustrations of how this can be achieved. In many cases the English translations in this book are a starting point for such an exercise; the original texts will facilitate taking it further.

Particular words and expressions

There are some particular German words and expressions which deserve comment, as they have no simple English equivalent.

Berufung and Revision. These could both be translated as appeal, but this would overlook the fact that a Berufung is a full appeal at a lower level, but a Revision is an appeal to a higher court on the law only. I have therefore translated Revision as 'appeal in law'.

Gesetz. See below, under Sources of German Law. Since, however, as appears from that section, on a narrow theoretical view, most German law originates from Gesetz in the wide sense, it is sometimes appropriate to translate it as the word 'law'. I have not found it possible to be consistent here, and I accept that it may be better to opt for the conventional approach and translate Gesetz as 'law' in most cases.

Gesellschaft. This does not only mean 'company' in the sense of a limited company; a German partnership is a Gesellschaft.

Gläubiger and Schuldner. The temptation is to translate these terms as debtor and creditor respectively, but they have a wider meaning in

---

1 (1993) 109 LQR 622 (Markesinis), p 624.

German law: they are used for obligations to pay money; but also for other obligations as well. I have therefore translated them respectively as obligee and obligor.

Land and Länder. I have translated these words as State and States respectively, as they are not immediately comprehensible to the English reader, especially the plural Länder. However, I have also had to use the word State when referring to the functions of Government in general, whether of the Federation or of the individual States.

Recht. This can be used in the objective sense, to mean law; or it can be used subjectively, to mean a right.

Rechtsgut. This means the subject matter of a legal right, but I have usually translated it as 'legal interest'.

Rechtsstaat. This signifies a State which is governed by the rule of law, and also implies such principles as proportionality and legal certainty. Because of the difficulty of incorporating this into the translation each time (especially when it appears in adjectival form: rechtstaatliche) I have simply rendered it as a constitutional State (or, in adjectival form, constitutional).

Rechtsprechung. This has usually been translated as 'case law', but the implication is not thereby intended that it is case law in the English sense. The status of the judicial decision as a possible source of law is, however, considered below.

Verbrechen and Vergehen. I have translated these respectively as 'crimes' and 'offences' since this seems to be the simplest way of conveying the difference in the seriousness; but I have also had to find an English expression to cover both. For this I have used criminal act, or criminal offence. I have used delict where the German word was **Delikt**, but it needs to be borne in mind that Delikt can also mean a tort.

Verkehr. This is a difficult word, as besides other meanings, it can refer to traffic, business, and the affairs of life in general. I have sometimes translated it as 'business' for simplicity when it may in fact carry the wider meaning.

Verkehrsicherheit. This is one of those words which, although it is not immediately apparent, has a specialised legal meaning. It refers to protection from risks in the affairs of life.

SOURCES OF GERMAN LAW

Generally

There are two accepted sources of German law: statute law (Gesetz) and customary law (Gewohnheitsrecht). The second is however now far less important than it was: it is unwritten law based on a long standing practice which has been appropriately recognised. It may be that two further sources have developed: judicial decisions and European Community law.

Gesetz has a wide meaning and a narrow one. In its narrow meaning, it would only cover statutes passed by the German Federal Parliament, ie, the Codes (which are statutory provisions relating to a large area of law, arranged in a logical manner) and other legislation. In its wide meaning, which is the one used in the previous paragraph, it includes any law enacted by a competent authority, and would also cover the Constitution and the legislation passed by the Parliaments of the States.

Hierarchy

Within Gesetz, in its wide meaning, there is a hierarchy of norms, ie, the various types of Gesetz rank differently in priority, and, in the event of an inconsistency, a type with a higher priority will prevail over a type with a lower priority. The inconsistent lower priority norm will be invalid.

The form of Gesetz which ranks highest is the Constitution (the Basic Law). Next comes Gesetz in the narrow sense (but excluding, or course, any of constitutional rank). After this, we have regulations (Rechtsverordnungen). These are norms made by the Executive (which includes the Government, its ministers and administrative authorities) under the authority of a Gesetz or (occasionally) the Basic Law. Finally, there are bye-laws (Satzungen) which are made by public institutions at a lower level than the State within the area of their competence. They may cover matters like parking and refuse disposal.

There is then the relationship between Federal law and State law. Article 31 of the Basic Law provides that Federal law prevails over State law, but for reasons explained in Chapter Two the article is rarely applied.

Judicial decisions and academic writings

The judge's function is normally merely to interpret the law. However, rules sometimes have to be extended to cover situations not mentioned in them, gaps may need to be filled, and more detailed content given to general rules. Judicial decisions can therefore be, in practice, a source of German law although judges in later cases are not usually bound to follow such decisions as in the English system. The courts have developed concepts like collapse of the foundation of a transaction, positive breach of contract, and the established and exercised pursuit of a business, and they have given content to concepts such as good faith and good morals. The courts are also prepared in some cases to extend statutory provisions by analogy (although this cannot be done in criminal law to the disadvantage of a defendant). However, as will be observed from the cases, German courts quote from academic writings as well as from decisions in past cases. The prevailing judicial opinion and the prevailing academic doctrine may diverge. All these considerations may make for uncertainty in the application of the detail of the law.

European Union law

See Chapter Two, p 12 and onwards.

THE CONSTITUTION

NATURE

Generally

The Basic Law was only intended to be a temporary Constitution, applying to the western zone of Germany until unification was achieved. Article 146 now provides that it is to remain in effect until it is replaced by a democratically approved one. Various amendments have been made to the Basic Law in the course of its comparatively short history.

The first 19 articles of the Basic Law relate to human rights and are therefore dealt with in Chapter Three.

There is an important principle known as the unity of the Constitution: different interests need to be reconciled under it. The provisions of the Basic Law are interpreted, if possible, so as not to conflict with its other provisions, but sometimes the requirements of one article have to be balanced against the requirements of another.

The Basic Law, largely because of its nature but also partly because of the speed with which it was drafted, cannot be interpreted in such a precise manner as the Civil Code or Criminal Code. The Basic Law needs not only to be interpreted, but also constitutional norms may need to be 'concretised' for individual cases. This is because constitutional norms are often very generally worded, and may represent a compromise position between two extreme points of view. A constitutional law concept may also have a different meaning to the same concept in another branch of law, eg, the constitutional law concept of property in Art 14 of the GG is different from the civil law concept.

The Federal Constitutional Court shows restraint in interpreting the Basic Law, in particular in relation to political issues. Its decisions reveal that certain matters are left to the legislator and (independently) to the executive. The judiciary also have a protected core area of power. 'This task of and authority for "creative discovery of law" has never, in principle, been denied to the judge – at any rate under the authority of the Basic Law' (BVerfGE 34, 269, 287: Soraya).

THE GERMAN STATE

Das Grundgesetz

Der Parlamentarische Rat hat am 23. Mai 1949 in Bonn am Rhein in öffentlicher Sitzung festgestellt, daß das am 8. Mai des Jahres 1949 vom Parlamentarischen Rat beschlossene Grundgesetz für die Bundesrepublik Deutschland in der Woche vom 16.–22. Mai 1949 durch die Volksvertretungen von mehr als Zweidritteln der beteiligten deutschen Länder angenommen worden ist.

Auf Grund dieser Feststellung hat der Parlamentische Rat, vertreten durch seine Präsidenten, das Grundgesetz ausgefertigt und verkündet.

Das Grundgesetz wird hiermit gemäß Artikel 145 Absatz 3 im Bundesgesetzblatt veröffentlicht:

Präambel

Im Bewußtsein seiner Verantwortung vor Gott und den Menschen, von dem Willen beseelt, als gleichberechtigtes Glied in einem vereinten Europa dem Frieden der Welt zu dienen, hat sich das Deutsche Volk kraft seiner verfassungsgebenden Gewalt dieses Grundgesetz gegeben.

Die Deutschen in den Ländern Baden-Württemberg, Bayern, Berlin, Brandenburg, Bremen, Hamburg, Hessen, Mecklenburg-Vorpommern, Niedersachsen, Nordrhein-Westfalen, Rheinland-Pfalz, Saarland, Sachsen, Sachsen-Anhalt, Schleswig-Holstein, und Thüringen haben in freier Selbstbestimmung die Einheit und Freiheit Deutschlands vollendet. Damit gilt dieses Grundgesetz für das gesamte Deutsche Volk.

II Der Bund und die Länder

Art 20 [Bundesstaatliche Verfassung; Widerstandsrecht] (1) Die Bundesrepublik Deutschland ist ein demokratischer und sozialer Bundesstaat.

(2) Alle Staatsgewalt geht vom Volke aus. Sie wird vom Volke in Wahlen und Abstimmungen und durch besondere Organe der Gesetzgebung, der vollziehenden Gewalt und der Rechtsprechung ausgeübt.

(3) Die Gesetzgebung ist an die verfassungsmäßige Ordnung, die vollziehende Gewalt und die Rechtsprechung sind an Gesetz und Recht gebunden.

(4) Gegen jeden, der es unternimmt, diese Ordnung zu beseitigen, haben alle Deutschen das Recht zum Widerstand, wenn andere Abhilfe nicht möglich ist.

THE GERMAN STATE

The Basic Law

The Parliamentary Council on the 23 May 1949 at Bonn on the Rhine in open session has established that the Basic Law for the Federal Republic of Germany adopted by the Parliamentary Council on the 8 May of the year 1949 was accepted in the week 16–22 May 1949 by the diets of more than two thirds of the participating German States.

On the basis of this finding, the Parliamentary Council, represented by its presidents, has signed and promulgated the Basic Law.

The Basic Law is hereby published, in accordance with Art 145 para 3, in the *Federal Law Gazette*:

Preamble

In the consciousness of their responsibility before God and man, inspired by the desire to assist world peace as an equal member in a united Europe, the German people, by virtue of their power to form a Constitution, have made for themselves this Basic Law.

The German people in the States of Baden-Württemberg, Bavaria, Berlin, Brandenburg, Bremen, Hamburg, Hesse, Mecklenberg-Vorpommern, Niedersachsen, Nordrhein-Westfalen, Rheinland-Pfalz, Saarland, Sachsen, Sachsen-Anhalt, Schleswig-Holstein, and Thüringen have in free self-determination secured the unity and liberty of Germany. This Basic Law therefore applies for the whole German people.

§ I relates to the Basic Rights and is covered in Chapter Three.

II The Federation and the States

Art 20 [Federal Constitution; right of resistance] (1) The Federal Republic of Germany is a democratic and social Federal State.

(2) All State power proceeds from the people. It is exercised by the people in elections and referenda and by special organs of the legislature, the executive and the judiciary.

(3) The legislature is bound to the constitutional order and the executive and judiciary are bound to statute and law.

(4) All Germans have the right of resistance against those who attempt to set aside this order if other redress is not possible.

The democratic, social and Federal aspects of the German State are legal principles. Democracy, however, relates to the State and its power and not to society (BVerfGE 57, 295). Federalism means that the Federation and the States each exercise their own sovereign authority. (Contrast English local authorities where the authority is delegated or derived.)

Paragraph 4 of this article was raised unsuccessfully as a defence by the defendant in the newspaper delivery obstruction case: see Chapter Six, p 481.

POLITICAL PARTIES

Article 21 [Parteien] (1) Die Parteien wirken bei der politischen Willensbildung des Volkes mit. Ihre Gründung ist frei. Ihre innere Ordnung muß demokratischen Grundsätzen entsprechen. Sie müssen über die Herkunft und Verwendung ihrer Mittel sowie über ihr Vermögen öffentlich Rechenschaft geben.

(2) Parteien, die nach ihren Zielen oder nach dem Verhalten ihrer Anhänger darauf ausgehen, die freiheitliche demokratische Grundordnung zu beeinträchtigen oder zu beseitigen oder den Bestand der Bundesrepublik Deutschland zu gefährden, sind verfassungswidrig. Über die Frage der Verfassungswidrigkeit entscheidet das Bundesverfassungsgericht.

(3) Das Näherer regeln Bundesgesetze.

FLAG

Art. 22 [Bundesflagge] Die Bundesflagge ist schwarz-rot-gold.

POLITICAL PARTIES

Article 21 [Parties] (1) Parties contribute towards the formation of the political will of the people. They may be freely established. Their internal order must correspond to democratic principles. They must render public account regarding the origin and use of their means as well as their property.

(2) Parties which, according to their goals or according to the conduct of their adherents, aim at prejudicing or setting aside the free democratic basic order or endangering the stability of the Federal Republic of Germany are unconstitutional. The Federal Constitutional Court decides on the question of unconstitutionality.

(3) The details are to be regulated by Federal statutes.

The Socialist Reich Party (BVerfGE 2, 1) and the Communist Party of Germany (BVerfGE 5, 85) have been banned under this article as a result of proceedings before the Federal Constitutional Court. The decisions are lengthy; the judgment about the Communist Party in 1956 runs to over 300 pages! It decided that its failure to recognise a free democratic order was not in itself sufficient to make a party unconstitutional; the party had to take an active and aggressive anti-establishment stance. It did not matter whether the unconstitutional intentions were for immediate implementation. The right of resistance under Art 20(4) of the GG was only for use in the last resort, and then only for the maintenance or restoration of the existing legal order. The party was to be dissolved and its property expropriated by the Federal Republic. The court decided that the ban did not however necessarily legally prevent a communist party taking part in elections for the whole of Germany in the event of reunification.

FLAG

Article 22 [Federal flag] The Federal flag is black, red and gold.

INTERNATIONAL RELATIONS

European Union

Art. 23 [Verwirklichung der Europäischen Union; Beteiligung des Bundesrates, der Bundesregierung] (1) Zur Verwirklichung eines vereinten Europas wirkt die Bundesrepublik Deutschland bei der Entwicklung der Europäischen Union mit, die demokratischen, rechtsstaatlichen, sozialen und föderativen Grundsätzen und dem Grundsatz der Subsidiarität verpflichtet ist und einen diesem Grundgesetz im wesentlichen vergleichbaren Grundrechtsschutz gewährleistet. Der Bund kann hierzu durch Gesetz mit Zustimmung des Bundesrates Hoheitsrechte übertragen. Für die Begründung der Europäischen Union sowie für Änderungen ihrer vertraglichen Grundlagen und vergleichbare Regelungen, durch die dieses Grundgesetz seinem Inhalt nach geändert oder ergänzt wird oder solche Änderungen oder Ergänzungen ermöglicht werden, gilt Artikel 79 Abs. 2 und 3.

(2) In Angelegenheiten der Europäischen Union wirken der Bundestag und durch den Bundesrat die Länder mit. Die Bundesregierung hat den Bundestag und den Bundesrat umfassend und zum frühestmöglichen Zeitpunkt zu unterrichten.

(3) Die Bundesregierung gibt dem Bundestag Gelegenheit zur Stellungnahme vor ihrer Mitwirkung an Rechtsetzungsakten der Europäischen Union. Die Bundesregierung berücksichtigt die Stellungnahmen des Bundestages bei den Verhandlungen. Das Nähere regelt ein Gesetz.

(4) Der Bundesrat ist an der Willensbildung des Bundes zu beteiligen, soweit er an einer entsprechenden innerstaatlichen Maßnahme mitzuwirken hätte oder soweit die Länder innerstaatlich zuständig wären.

(5) Soweit in einem Bereich ausschließlicher Zuständigkeiten des Bundes Interessen der Länder berührt sind oder soweit im übrigen der Bund das Recht zur Gesetzgebung hat, berücksichtigt die Bundesregierung die Stellungnahme des Bundesrates. Wenn im Schwerpunkt Gesetzgebungsbefugnisse der Länder, die Einrichtung ihrer Behörden oder ihre Verwaltungsverfahren betroffen sind, ist bei der Willensbildung des Bundes insoweit die Auffassung des Bundesrates maßgeblich zu berücksichtigen; dabei ist die gesamtstaatliche Verantwortung des Bundes zu wahren. In Angelegenheiten, die zu Ausgabenerhöhungen oder Einnahmeminderungen für den Bund führen können, ist die Zustimmung der Bundesregierung erforderlich.

INTERNATIONAL RELATIONS

European Union

Article 23 [Realisation of the European Union; participation of the Federal Council and the Federal Government] (1) The Federal Republic of Germany is to contribute towards the realisation of a united Europe in the development of the European Union which is committed to democratic, constitutional, social and Federal principles and the principle of subsidiarity and guarantees a protection of Basic Rights which is substantially comparable to this Basic Law. The Federation can transfer sovereign rights to it by statute with the consent of the Federal Council. Article 79 paras 2 and 3 apply for the founding of the European Union as well as for alterations of its treaty principles and comparable rules insofar as this Basic Law is thereby altered or added to in respect of its content or such alterations or additions are made possible.

(2) In affairs of the European Union the Federal Parliament and the States, operating through the Federal Council, are to collaborate. The Federal Government must keep the Federal Parliament and the Federal Council comprehensively informed at the earliest possible point in time.

(3) The Federal Government is to give the Federal Parliament the opportunity to comment before the Federal Government's participation in acts by the European Union establishing law. The Federal Government is to have regard to the expressed opinion of the Federal Parliament in the negotiations. The details are to be regulated by statute.

(4) The Federal Council is to participate in the formation of the will of the Federation insofar as it would have to participate in a corresponding internal measure or insofar as the States would be internally competent.

(5) Insofar as in a particular area of exclusive competence of the Federation interests of the States are affected or insofar as in other respects the Federation has the right to legislate, the Federal Government is to have regard to the expressed opinion of the Federal Council. If the legislative powers of the States, the organisation of their authorities or their administrative procedures are affected in a crucial respect, the view of the Federal Council is, to this extent, to be taken into account as the determining factor in the formation of the will of the Federation; at the same time the responsibility of the Federation for all the States is to be preserved. In matters which can lead to increases in expenditure or reduction in income for the Federation, the consent of the Federal Government is necessary.

(6) Wenn im Schwerpunkt ausschließliche Gesetzgebungsbefugnisse der Länder betroffen sind, soll die Wahrnehmung der Rechte, die der Bundesrepublik Deutschland als Mitgliedstaat der Europäischen Union zustehen, vom Bund auf einen vom Bundesrat benannten Vertreter der Länder übertragen werden. Die Wahrnehmung der Rechte erfolgt unter Beteiligung und in Abstimmung mit der Bundesregierung; dabei ist die gesamtstaatliche Verantwortung des Bundes zu wahren.

(7) Das Nähere zu den Absätzen 4 bis 6 regelt ein Gesetz, das der Zustimmung des Bundesrates bedarf.

(6) If exclusive legislative powers of the States are affected in a crucial respect, the protection of the rights which belong to the Federal Republic of Germany as a Member State of the European Union will be transferred from the Federation to a States' representative named by the Federal Council. The protection of the rights is to ensue with participation by, and in agreement with, the Federal Government; at the same time the responsibility of the Federation for all the States is to be preserved.

(7) Details in respect of paras 4–6 will be regulated by a statute which requires the consent of the Federal Council.

The old Art 23 provided that the Basic Law was to apply, for the time being, to the States of West Germany, and in other parts of Germany it was to become effective on their accession. This article was no longer needed after unification. This new Art 23 was introduced in 1992 to take account of certain constitutional problems which had been encountered in connection with European Community law. West Germany's accession to the European Communities was originally based on Art 24, below, and the relationship between European Community law and German law was based on Art 25. This article created a problem, as it only established the precedence of international law over ordinary law, and did not say anything as to its relationship with constitutional law. In the Internationale Handelsgesellschaft or Solange I case (BVerfGE 37, 271; [1974] 2 CMLR 540) in 1974, the Federal Constitutional Court said that the German courts should still be able to test European Community law against German constitutional rights insofar as it may be deficient (solange is the German for insofar). In the Wünsche Handelsgesellschaft or Solange II case (BVerfGE 52, 178; [1987] 3 CMLR 225), in 1986, however, the Federal Constitutional Court stated that fundamental rights were now sufficiently protected by the European Court of Justice, and had priority without needing to be reviewed in the light of the German Constitution. The basis of the decisions was the transfer of powers to the European Community under Art 24, confirmed by the Accession Act. What had taken place in between 1974 and 1986 in the European Community to justify this change of view? The other problem was that certain European Community matters were within the competence of the States rather than the Federation and this issue was a basic unchangeable constitutional principle under Arts 20 and 79 of the Basic Law.

In a judgment of 12 October 1993 [1994] 1 CMLR 57, the Federal Constitutional Court decided that the law ratifying the Treaty on European Union (Maastricht) was compatible with the Basic Law.

The cattle slaughter case gives an example of the relationship between European Community law and national law: see Chapter Three, p 129.

International relations generally

Art. 24 [Kollektives Sicherheitssystem] (1) Der Bund kann durch Gesetz Hoheitsrechte auf zwischenstaatliche Einrichtungen übertragen.

(1a) Soweit die Länder für die Ausübung der staatlichen Befugnisse und die Erfüllung der staatlichen Aufgaben zuständig sind, können sie mit Zustimmung der Bundesregierung Hoheitsrechte auf grenznachbarschaftliche Einrichtungen übertragen.

(2) Der Bund kann sich zur Wahrung des Friedens einem System gegenseitiger kollektiver Sicherheit einordnen; er wird hierbei in die Beschränkungen seiner Hoheitsrechte einwilligen, die eine friedliche und dauerhafte Ordnung in Europa and zwischen den Völkern der Welt herbeiführen und sichern.

(3) Zur Regelung zwischenstaatlicher Streitigkeiten wird der Bund Vereinbarungen über eine allgemeine, umfassende, obligatorische, internationale Schiedsgerichtsbarkeit beitreten.

International relations generally

Article 24 [Collective security system] (1) The Federation can, by statute, transfer sovereign rights to international organisations.

(1a) Insofar as the States are competent for the exercise of government powers and the fulfilment of government responsibilities, they can transfer sovereign rights to institutions on their borders with the consent of the Federal Government.

(2) The Federation can arrange a system of mutual collective security, for the preservation of peace; by this means it will acquiesce in the limitations on its sovereign rights which produce and secure a peaceful and lasting order in Europe and between the peoples of the world.

(3) For the settlement of international disputes, the Federation will enter into agreements regarding a general, comprehensive, obligatory, international arbitration system.

THE BOSNIA FLIGHT EXCLUSION ZONE CASE

BVerfGE Band 88 II S. 173

Nr. 17

Urteil des Zweiten Senats vom 8. April 1993 aufgrund der mündlichen Verhandlung vom 7. April 1993

– 2 BvE 5/93 und 2 BvQ 11/93 –

In dem Verfahren

1 über den Antrag festzustellen, daß die Entscheidungen

(a) der Bundesregierung vom 2. April 1993, die Soldaten der deutschen Bundeswehr auch bei der durch VN-Sicherheitsrats-Resolution 816 nun angelegten militärischen Durchsetzung der Überflugverbote über Bosnien in den AWACS-Frühwarn- und Einsatzführungssystemen dritter Staaten weiter Dienst tun zu lassen bzw. sie von dort nicht zurückzurufen sowie

(b) des Bundesministers der Verteidigung, die betreffenden Soldaten eben diesen Dienst in den AWACS-Maschinen auch in der jetzigen Phase möglicher militärischer Verwicklung weiter ausüben zu lassen, gegen Art. 20 Abs. 3 sowie gegen Art. 87 a Abs. 2, 79 Abs. 1 und 2 GG verstoßen, *hier*: Antrag auf Erlaß einer einstweiligen Anordnung,

Antragsteller: 1) Fraktion der F.D.P. im Deutschen Bundestag, vertreten durch den Vorsitzenden, Bundeshaus, Bonn, 2) Frau Ina Albowitz und weitere 54 Abgeordnete der F.D.P.-Bundestagsfraktion, Bundeshaus, Bonn,- Bevollmächtigter zu 1) und 2): Prof. Dr. Edzard Schmidt-Jortzig, Graf-Spee-Straße 18 a, Kiel -, Bevollmächtigter zu 1): Rechtsanwalt Prof. Dr. Rüdiger Zuck, Robert-Koch-Straße 2, Stuttgart -,

Antragsgegner: 1) die Bundesregierung, vertreten durch den Bundeskanzler, Adenauerallee 139/141, Bonn, 2) der Bundesminister der Verteidigung, Hardthöhe, Bonn, – Bevollmächtigter zu 1) und 2): Prof. Dr. Dieter Blumenwitz, Tannenstraße 2, Baldham – 2 BvE 5/93 –;

THE BOSNIA FLIGHT EXCLUSION ZONE CASE

The interest of this case for the English law student lies not only in the unfamiliar concept of testing a Government decision as to the deployment of forces against the provisions of the Constitution; there is also a parallel to be drawn between the balancing exercise carried out on the issue of whether a temporary order should be issued, and the principles established as to whether a temporary injunction should be issued in English law. In the decision of the BVerfG 2 BvQ 17/93 of 23 June 1993; [1993] EuGRZ 326 similar issues were considered in relation to the sending of troops to Somalia, and it was decided the no *further* troops should be sent without the consent of the Federal Parliament.

BVerfGE Volume 88 II p 173

No 17

Judgment of the Second Senate of 8 April 1993 on the basis of the oral hearing of 7 April 1993

– 2 BvE 5/93 and 2 BvQ 11/93 –

In the proceedings

1 to make a finding on the application that the decisions

(a) of the Federal Government of 2 April 1993 to make the soldiers of the German army carry out further service in the military implementation, planned under UN Security Council Resolution 816, of the flight ban over Bosnia, in the AWACS Early Warning and Quick Response Systems of third States (or not to recall them from there), as well as;

(b) of the Federal Minister for Defence to make the soldiers concerned continue to carry out this service in the AWACS aircraft in the present phase of possible military development violated Art 20 para 3 as well as Art 87 a para 2 and 79 para 1 and 2 of the GG: application for issue of a provisional order:

applicants: 1) parliamentary party of the FDP (Free Democratic Party) in the German Parliament, represented by the Chairman, Parliament House, Bonn 2) Mrs Ina Albowitz and 54 other MPs of the FDP parliamentary party, Parliament House, Bonn (here follow details of legal representation),

respondents: 1) the Federal Government, represented by the Federal Chancellor, Adenauerallee 139/141, Bonn, 2) the Federal Defence minister, Hardthöhe, Bonn (here follow details of legal representation) – 2 BvE 5/93 –;

2 über den Antrag, im Wege der einstweiligen Anordnung

(a) die Durchführung des Beschlusses des Bundeskabinetts vom 2. April 1993, mit dem der Verbleib der Soldaten der Bundeswehr in den zur Überwachung des Luftraums über Bosnien-Herzegowina eingesetzten AWACS-Flugzeugen angeordnet wird, einstweilen bis zur Entscheidung über den alsbald anzustrengenden Organstreit auszusetzen und

(b) die Antragsgegnerin anzuweisen, die Soldaten der Bundeswehr aus den zur Überwachung des Luftraums über Bosnien-Herzegowina eingesetzten AWACS-Flugzeugen einstweilen bis zur Entscheidung über den alsbald anzustrengenden Organstreit abzuziehen, Antragstellerin: Fraktion der SPD im Deutschen Bundestag, vertreten durch den Vorsitzenden, Bundeshaus, Bonn, - Bevollmächtigter: Prof. Dr. Michael Bothe, Theodor-Heuss-Straße 6, Bensheim, Antragsgegnerin: die Bundesregierung, vertreten durch den Bundeskanzler, Adenauerallee 139/141, Bonn, – Bevollmächtiger: Prof. Dr. Dieter Blumenwitz, Tannenstraße 2, Baldham – 2 BvQ 11/93 –.

Entscheidungsformel:

Die Anträge werden abgelehnt.

Gründe:

A

Die zur gemeinsamen Entscheidung verbundenen Verfahren betreffen den Beschluß der Bundesregierung über die Beteiligung deutscher Soldaten an der Durchsetzung des von den Vereinten Nationen verhängten Flugverbotes im Luftraum über Bosnien-Herzegowina.

I

1 Der Sicherheitsrat der Vereinten Nationen verhängte mit der Resolution 781 vom 9. Oktober 1992 ein Flugverbot für Militärflugzeuge im Luftraum über Bosnien-Herzegowina und ersuchte die Schutztruppe der Vereinten Nationen (UNPROFOR), es zu überwachen. Die Mitglieder der Nordatlantikpakt-Organisation (NATO) übernahmen diese Aufgabe und setzten dazu AWACS (Airborne Warning and Control System – luftgestütztes Frühwarn- und Kontrollsystem) – Fernaufklärer ein, in denen Soldaten verschiedener NATO-Mitgliedsländer als integrierte Einheit tätig sind. Mit diesen Flugzeugen werden Flugbewegungen aus großer Höhe erfaßt; sie können zugleich als Feuerleitstand für den Einsatz von Jagdflugzeugen gegen gegnerische Flugzeuge dienen. Etwa ein Drittel des militärischen Personals des AWACS-Verbandes sind Soldaten der Bundeswehr in verschiedenen Funktionen.

2 regarding the application for a provisional order

(a) to suspend the execution of the decision of the Federal Cabinet of 2 April 1993 by which the soldiers of the Federal Army are ordered to stay in the AWACS aircraft which are used for the surveillance of the airspace over Bosnia-Herzegovina for the time being until the decision in the public institutions action which is to be brought immediately and

(b) to instruct the respondent to remove the soldiers of the Federal Army from the AWACS aircraft used for surveillance of the airspace over Bosnia-Herzegovina for the time being until the decision in the public institutions action which is to be brought immediately,

applicant: parliamentary party of the SPD (Socialist Party of Germany) in the German Parliament, represented by the Chairman, Parliament House, Bonn (here follow details of legal representation),

respondent: the Federal Government, represented by the Federal Chancellor, Adenauerallee 139/141, Bonn (here follow details of legal representation) – 2 BvQ 11/93.

Decision:

The applications are rejected.

Reasons:

A

The proceedings, combined for the purpose of a joint decision, concern the decision of the Federal Government regarding the participation of German soldiers in the carrying out of the ban on flights in the airspace over Bosnia-Herzegovina imposed by the United Nations.

I

1 The Security Council of the United Nations by its resolution 781 of 9 October 1992 imposed a ban on flights for military aircraft in the airspace over Bosnia-Herzegovina and requested the protection force of the United Nations (UNPROFOR) to supervise it. The members of the North Atlantic Treaty Organisation (NATO) took over this task and also deployed for that purpose Airborne Warning and Control System (AWACS) distance reconnaissance planes in which soldiers of different NATO Member States operated as an integrated unit. With these aircraft, flight movements are detected from a great height; they can at the same time serve as a command post for directing fire for the deployment of fighter aircraft against hostile aircraft. About a third of the military personnel of the AWACS unit are soldiers of the Federal Army in various functions.

Am 31. März 1993 verabschiedete der Sicherheitsrat der Vereinten Nationen die Resolution 816, deren hier maßgebliche Bestimmungen in Nrn. 1 und 4 lauten:

Der Sicherheitsrat ... in Ausführung des Kapitels VII der Charta der Vereinten Nationen ...

1. beschließt, das durch die Resolution 781 (1992) erlassene Verbot auf alle Flüge mit Starrflügel- oder Drehflügelluftfahrzeugen im Luftraum der Republik Bosnien und Herzegowina auszudehnen, wobei dieses Verbot nicht für von UNPROFOR nach Absatz 2 genehmigte Flüge gilt;

2 ...

3 ...

4 ermächtigt die Mitgliedstaaten, sieben Tage nach der Verabschiedung dieser Resolution im Auftrag des Sicherheitsrats sowie unter der Voraussetzung, daß sie eng mit dem Generalsekretär und UNPROFOR zusammenarbeiten, einzeln oder durch regionale Organisationen oder Abmachungen im Falle weiterer Verstöße alle notwendigen Maßnahmen im Luftraum der Republik Bosnien und Herzegowina zu ergreifen, um die Einhaltung des in Absatz 1 genannten Flugverbotes unter angemessener Berücksichtigung der jeweiligen Umstände sowie der Art der Flüge sicherzustellen; ...

Am 2. April 1993 traf die Bundesregierung gegen die Stimmen der F.D.P.- Minister folgende Entscheidung:

4 Sie [die Bundesregierung] ist einverstanden, daß der NATO-AWACS-Verband nummehr in Übereinstimmung mit Sicherheitsratsresolution 816 vom 31.03.1993 auch unter deutscher Beteiligung daran mitwirkt, dieses Flugverbot durchzusetzen.

Der NATO-Rat erklärte mit Beschluß vom 2. April 1993 seine Bereitschaft, die Umsetzung der vom Sicherheitsrat beschlossenen Resolution 816 zu unterstützen. Er bestätigte darüber hinaus seine Zustimmung zu den einzelnen Durchsetzungsphasen, den Einsatzrichtlinien sowie den sonstigen Planungen.

2 Die Verfassungsmäßigkeit des Beschlusses der Bundesregierung ist zwischen den Mitgliedern, die den Unionsparteien angehören, und denen, die F.D.P.-Mitglieder sind, sowie zwischen den Koalitionsparteien umstritten. Man kam überein, daß die Bundesregierung mit der Mehrheit ihrer Mitglieder den Beschluß fassen könne, die F.D.P.-Fraktion hiergegen aber einen Antrag beim Bundesverfassungsgericht stellen werde mit dem Ziel, die Verfassungswidrigkeit dieses Beschlusses feststellen zu lassen; mit diesem Antrag sollte ein Antrag auf Erlaß einer einstweiligen Anordnung verbunden werden, um den Vollzug der Regierungsentscheidung zu hindern. Solche Anträge haben die Antragsteller im Verfahren 2 BvE 5/93 gestellt.

On 31 March 1993 the Security Council of the United Nations passed Resolution 816, the significant provisions of which in nos 1 and 4 read:

The Security Council ... in execution of Chapter VII of the Charter of the United Nations ...

1 resolves to extend the ban imposed by Resolution 781 (1992) to all flights with fixed wing and swing wing aircraft in the airspace of the Republic of Bosnia and Herzegovina, without this ban applying to flights approved by UNPROFOR in accordance with para 2;

2 ...

3 ...

4 empowers the Member States, seven days after the passing of this resolution on behalf of the Security Council as well as on condition that they cooperate closely with the General Secretary and UNPROFOR individually or by regional organisations or arrangements in case of further violations to take all necessary measures in the air space of the Republic of Bosnia and Herzegovina in order to ensure the observation of the flying ban mentioned in para 1, subject to appropriate consideration of the actual circumstances as well as the type of flights ...

On 2 April 1993 the Federal Government made the following decision against the votes of the FDP Ministers:

4 It (the Federal Government) has agreed that the NATO-AWACS unit will co-operate from now on in conformity with Security Council resolution 816 of 31 March 1993 with German participation as well to give effect to this flying ban.

The NATO Council declared by its resolution of 2 April 1993 its preparedness to support the transposition of Security Council resolution 816 into action. Besides this it confirmed its agreement to the individual implementation phases, the deployment guidelines and the other plans as well.

2 The constitutionality of the decision of the Federal Government is disputed between the members who belong to the Union parties and those who are members of the FDP, as well as between the Coalition parties. Agreement was reached that the Federal Government could make the decision with the majority of its members, but the FDP parliamentary party would make an application to the Federal Constitutional Court with the objective of establishing the unconstitutionality of this decision; an application for the issue of a temporary order was to be joined with this application, in order to prevent the carrying out of the Government's decision. The applicants have made such applications in the proceedings 2 BvE 5/93.

3 Die Bundestagsfraktion der SPD hält den Beschluß der Bundesregierung ebenfalls für verfassungswidrig und beantragt den Erlaß einer einstweiligen Anordnung.

II

1 Die Antragsteller vertreten die Auffassung, die Entscheidung der Bundesregierung verletze die Rechte des Bundestages; die Fraktionen seien befugt, diese Rechte im Wege der Prozeßstandschaft geltend zu machen. Die Abgeordneten der F.D.P.-Fraktion seien darüberhinaus in eigenen parlamentarischen Mitwirkungsrechten verletzt.

Der Kampfeinsatz von Bundeswehrsoldaten außerhalb des NATO-Bündnisgebietes ohne Eintritt des Bündnisfalles sei weder durch Art. 87 a Abs. 2 GG noch durch Art. 24 Abs. 2 GG gedeckt. Hierfür hätte es einer Änderung des Grundgesetzes bedurft. Art. 87 a Abs. 2 GG statuiere im Erfordernis eines 'ausdrücklichen' Zulassens des Streitkräfteeinsatzes einen spezifischen Übergehungsschutz zugunsten des verfassungsändernden Gesetzgebers. Die SPD-Fraktion macht darüber hinaus geltend, daß die Bundesregierung durch den angegriffenen Beschluß an einem inhaltlichen Wandel der NATO- und WEU-Verträge mitwirke und dadurch Rechte des Bundestages aus Art. 59 Abs. 2 GG verletze. Außerdem fehle die gesetzliche Grundlage, um deutsche Soldaten dem Kommando des NATO-Oberbefehlshabers Europa zu unterstellen.

2 Der Erlaß der einstweiligen Anordnung sei zur Abwehr schwerer Nachteile zum gemeinen Wohl dringend geboten. Leben und Gesundheit deutscher Soldaten würden gefährdet, ohne daß dies parlamentarisch entschieden und verantwortet worden sei. Die militärische Durchsetzung des Flugverbotes stelle eine bewaffnete kriegerische Konfrontation dar. Dies könne den Soldaten der Bundeswehr und ihren Angehörigen nur auf der Grundlage einer gesicherten Rechtslage zugemutet werden.

Sollte die einstweilige Anordnung nicht ergehen und kämen deshalb Soldaten zu Schaden, werde die angegriffene Maßnahme später jedoch im Hauptsacheverfahren für verfassungswidrig erklärt, so wäre dies für 'die soziologische Verfassung des deutschen Staates, das Integrationsgefühl der Bürger und die Rechtfertigungsnachfrage der Betroffenen geradezu verheerend'.

Die SPD-Fraktion macht geltend, die Bundesrepublik schaffe durch die Beteiligung an der Militäraktion einen für sie völkerrechtlich verbindlichen Vertrauenstatbestand und enge faktisch den Spielraum des verfassungsändernden Gesetzgebers ein. Allein deshalb sei die Beteiligung des Parlamentes nach Art. 59 Abs. 2 GG erforderlich. Der Entscheidung der Bundesregierung liege eine neue Verfassungsauslegung zugrunde; sollte diese keinen Bestand haben, so beeinträchtige der neuerliche Wechsel das Vertrauen der Soldaten und der Verbündeten in die Verläßlichkeit und Berechenbarkeit der Bundesrepublik.

3 The parliamentary party of the SDP also considers the decision of the Federal Government to be unconstitutional and applies for issue of a temporary order.

II

1 The applicants argue that the decision of the Federal Government violates the rights of the Federal Parliament; the parliamentary parties are authorised to claim these rights by virtue of an authority to institute proceedings.[1] The MPs of the FDP parliamentary party are also adversely affected in respect of their own parliamentary rights of participation.

The deployment of soldiers of the Federal Army in action outside the area of the NATO alliance, without a case for alliance action arising, is covered neither by Art 87 a para 2 of the GG nor by Art 24 para 2 of the GG. It would have required a change of the Basic Law for this. Article 87 a para 2 of the GG[2] lays down in its requirement of an 'express' permitting of deployment of troops a specific protection for the possibility of the legislator changing the Constitution. The SDP parliamentary party claims in addition to this that the Federal Government is, by the decision which is under challenge, taking part in a change in the content of the NATO and WEU treaties and thereby infringing the rights of the Federal Parliament under Art 59 para 2 of the GG. Besides this, the statutory basis is lacking for putting German soldiers under the command of the NATO Supreme Commander for Europe.

2 The issue of the temporary order was urgently needed for the prevention of serious disadvantages for the common good. The life and health of German soldiers were endangered without this being decided and defended in Parliament. The military implementation of the flight ban represented an armed warlike confrontation. This could only be required of the soldiers of the Federal Army and their relatives on the basis of a secure legal position. If the temporary order was not issued and soldiers therefore came to harm, and the measure which is under challenge was nevertheless declared later in the main proceedings to be unconstitutional, this would be 'simply devastating for the sociological Constitution of the German State, the feeling of integration of the citizens and the demand for justification by those affected'.

The SDP parliamentary party claims that the Federal Government, by participation in military action, created a situation of trust which was binding on it in international law and effectively narrowed the scope of the legislator for changing the Constitution. On that account alone the participation of Parliament in accordance with Art 59 para 2 of the GG was necessary. The decision of the Federal Government was based on a new interpretation of the Constitution; if this were to have no continuing existence, the further change would impair the confidence of the soldiers and the allies in the dependability and predictability of the Federal Republic.

---

1   This term means authority to start proceedings in one's own name in respect of a right belonging to another.

2   Article 87 a(2) provides: Except for defence, the armed forces may only be deployed insofar as this Basic Law expressly permits it.

Das AWACS-System bleibe auch ohne deutsche Beteiligung funktionsfähig. Der wesentliche Schaden einer einstweiligen Anordnung könne nur auf politischem Gebiet liegen; sie beende jedoch den politischen Begründungsnotstand für die deutsche Zurückhaltung bei der Beteiligung an internationalen militärischen Maßnahmen zur Friedenssicherung überzeugend und belege die Kraft des deutschen Rechtsstaates.

Die verfassungsrechtlichen Beschränkungen des Einsatzes der Bundeswehr seien im Ausland bekannt. Es werde nicht erwartet, daß die Bundesrepublik sich über ihre Verfassung hinwegsetze. Umgekehrt könnte eine Änderung der Praxis ohne Änderung der Verfassung oder ohne eine verfassungsgerichtliche Klarstellung den Eindruck erwecken, die bisher vorgebrachten Bedenken seien nicht gewichtig, ja sogar nur vorgeschoben gewesen. Da zur Beteiligung an den militärischen Maßnahmen aufgrund der Sicherheitsratsresolution weder aufgrund der VN-Charta noch des NATO-Vertrages eine Verpflichtung bestehe, könne der Bundesrepublik nicht die Nichterfüllung ihrer völkerrechtlichen Verpflichtungen vorgehalten werden.

III

Die Antragsgegner halten die Anträge für unzulässig, jedenfalls für unbegründet.

1 Den Fraktionen fehle die Antragsbefugnis, weil zwischen ihnen und der Bundesregierung nicht das erforderliche verfassungsrechtliche Rechtsverhältnis bestehe. Art. 87 a Abs. 2 GG sei nicht dazu bestimmt, Rechte des Bundestages zur Gesetzgebung zu gewährleisten.

2 (a) Die Zulässigkeit von Kampfeinsätzen von Soldaten der Bundeswehr im Rahmen der NATO zur Durchsetzung von Zwangsmaßnahmen, die vom VN-Sicherheitsrat verhängt worden sind, ergebe sich aus Art. 24 Abs. 2 GG. Art. 87 a Abs. 2 GG stehe dem nicht entgegen. Dieser Einsatz der Streitkräfte verlange keine Mitwirkung des Parlaments.

(b) Der Verbleib der deutschen Soldaten an Bord der AWACS-Flugzeuge führe zu keiner in die Zukunft wirkenden allgemeinen völkerrechtlichen Bindung der Bundesrepublik. Die Bundesregierung könne völkerrechtlich ihre Haltung in den NATO-Gremien und gegenüber den Vereinten Nationen ändern und die deutschen Soldaten aus dem AWACS-Verband zurückziehen. Der verfassungsändernde Gesetzgeber werde deshalb nicht vor vollendete Tatsachen gestellt.

Die Gefahren für die deutschen Soldaten in den AWACS-Flugzeugen seien nicht größer als bei den seit Monaten laufenden Überwachungsflügen und geringer als bei den humanitären Hilfsflügen. Die behaupteten konkreten Gefährdungen seien wegen der Einsatzbedingungen nicht gegeben.

The AWACS system would remain capable of operating even without German participation. The appreciable harm of a temporary order could only lie in the political sphere; it would however convincingly bring to an end the emergency as to political reasoning for German restraint in participation in international military measures for the securing of peace and prove the power of the German Constitutional State.

The constitutional law limitations on the deployment of the Federal Army were known in other countries. It would not be expected that the Federal Republic would disregard its Constitution. On the other hand, a change in practice without a change of the Constitution or without a constitutional court elucidation could give rise to the impression that the doubts which had been expressed so far had not been important - had even in fact only been pleaded as excuses. As no obligation existed to participate in military measures on the basis of the Security Council resolution either on the basis of the UN Charter or the NATO treaty, the Federal Republic could not be charged with the non-fulfilment of its international law obligations.

III

The respondents consider the applications to be inadmissible, or at any rate unfounded.

1 The parliamentary parties lack the authority to make application because the necessary constitutional law relationship does not exist between them and the Federal Government. Article 87 a para 2 of the GG is not intended to guarantee the rights of the Federal Parliament to legislate.

2 (a) The permissibility of the deployment of soldiers of the Federal Army in action within the framework of NATO for the implementation of coercive measures which have been imposed by the UN Security Council follows from Art 24 para 2 of the GG. Article 87 a para 2 of the GG is not opposed to it. This deployment of troops does not require the participation of Parliament.

(b) The presence of German soldiers on board the AWACS aircraft would not lead to any general international law commitment of the Federal Republic which would take effect into the future. The Federal Government could change its attitude in international law in the NATO committees and as against the United Nations and withdraw the German soldiers from the AWACS unit. The legislator changing the Constitution would not therefore be presented with completed facts.

The dangers for German soldiers in the AWACS aircraft would not be greater than with the surveillance flights which had been taking place for a matter of months and would be less than with the humanitarian aid flights. The real dangers which had been asserted would, because of the conditions of deployment, not be present.

Erginge die einstweilige Anordnung, bliebe der Organstreit in der Hauptsache aber erfolglos, so ergäben sich schwerwiegende Nachteile für die Bundesrepublik. Ohne deutsche Beteiligung sei die Einsatzfähigkeit des AWACS-Verbandes in Frage gestellt, jedenfalls aber nachhaltig eingeschränkt. Das von den Vereinten Nationen verhängte Flugverbot sei zeitlich und räumlich nur noch lückenhaft durchzusetzen.

Bündnispolitisch würde der Erlaß einer einstweiligen Anordnung zu einem Vertrauensverlust bei den NATO-Partnern führen, der letztlich die Verteidigungsfähigkeit Deutschlands mindere. Das Zurückziehen deutscher Kräfte aus einem integrierten Verband komme einer Aukündigung der Bündnissolidarität gleich. Die Bundesrepublik habe die Solidarität ihrer Partner immer wieder eingefordert. Bei einem Abzug des deutschen Personals aus dem AWACS-Verband würde gerade in dem Augenblick das die NATO-Allianz ausmachende Prinzip der Gegenseitigkeit unterlaufen, in dem die Partnerstaaten Solidarität erwarteten. Zugleich werde die Entwicklung von Strategie und Organisation der NATO, die sich in Richtung auf multinationale Verbände bewege, empfindlich gestört.

IV

In der mündlichen Verhandlung haben sich Mitglieder des Bundestages und der Bundesregierung sowie Generale der Bundeswehr geäußert. Der Generalsekretär der NATO hat zu bündnispolitischen Fragen Stellung genommen.

B

Eine einstweilige Anordnung kann nicht ergehen.

1 Nach § 32 Abs. 1 BVerfGG kann das Bundesverfassungsgericht im Streitfall einen Zustand durch einstweilige Anordnung vorläufig regeln, wenn dies zur Abwehr schwerer Nachteile, zur Verhinderung drohender Gewalt oder aus einem anderen wichtigen Grund zum gemeinen Wohl dringend geboten ist. Bei der Prüfung dieser Voraussetzungen ist ein besonders strenger Maßstab anzulegen, wenn eine Maßnahme mit völkerrechtlichen oder außenpolitischen Auswirkungen betroffen ist (vgl. auch BVerfGE 83, 162 [171f.]).

Dabei müssen die Gründe, welche für die Verfassungswidrigkeit der angegriffenen Maßnahme sprechen, außer Betracht bleiben, es sei denn, die in der Hauptsache begehrte Feststellung erwiese sich von vornherein als unzulässig oder offensichtlich unbegründet. Das Bundesverfassungsgericht wägt die Nachteile, die einträten, wenn die einstweilige Anordnung nicht erginge, die Maßnahme aber später für verfassungswidrig erklärt würde, gegen diejenigen ab, die entstünden, wenn die Maßnahme nicht in Kraft träte, sie sich aber im Hauptsacheverfahren als verfassungsgemäß erwiese (vgl. BVerfGE 86, 390 [395]; st. Rspr.).

If the temporary order was issued, but the public institutions action were unsuccessful in the main issue, serious disadvantages would result for the Federal Republic. Without German participation, the deployment capability of the AWACS unit would be put in question and at any rate effectively limited. The flight ban imposed by the United Nations could only be implemented with gaps in time and in space.

The issue of a temporary order would lead, in the politics of the alliance, to a loss of confidence on the part of the NATO partners, which in the end would reduce Germany's defence capability. The withdrawal of German forces from an integrated unit would be equivalent to giving notice of withdrawal from alliance solidarity. The Federal Republic had repeatedly demanded the solidarity of its colleagues. By withdrawal of German personnel from the AWACS unit, the principle of mutuality which made up the NATO alliance would be undermined just at the moment in which the partner States expected solidarity. At the same time the development of the strategy and organisation in NATO, which was moving in the direction of multi-national alliances, would be severely disturbed.

IV

In the oral hearing the members of the Federal Parliament and the Federal Government as well as the Generals of the Federal Army expressed their opinions. The General Secretary of NATO expressed his view on questions concerning the politics of the alliance.

B

A temporary order cannot be issued.

1 In accordance with § 32 para 1 of the BVerfGG the Federal Constitutional Court can provisionally regulate a situation by a temporary order in a disputed case if this is urgently necessary for the averting of serious disadvantages, for the prevention of threatened force, or for some other important reason for the common good. In the examination of these prerequisites an especially stringent standard is to be applied if a measure is concerned with the effects of international law or foreign politics (compare also BVerfGE 83, 162 [171 and onwards]).

At the same time the reasons which argue for the unconstitutionality of the measures challenged must be left out of consideration unless the finding sought in the main proceedings shows itself from the start to be inadmissible or obviously unfounded. The Federal Constitutional Court weighs the disadvantages which would arise if the temporary order were not issued, but the measure was later declared to be unconstitutional against those which would arise if the measure did not come into force, but it showed itself in the main proceedings to be in accordance with the Constitution (compare BVerfGE 86, 390 [395]; consistent case law).

2 Der Antrag der Antragsteller im Verfahren 2 BvE 5/93 und der angekündigte Antrag der Antragstellerin im Verfahren 2 BvQ 11/93 gegen die Bundesregierung sind weder von vornherein unzulässig noch offensichtlich unbegründet. Diese Anträge sind insbesondere nicht deshalb unzulässig, weil es etwa an einer Maßnahme im Sinne des § 64 Abs. 1 BVerfGG fehlte. Der Beschluß der Bundesregierung vom 2. April 1993 stellt eine solche Maßnahme dar. Er entscheidet mit rechtserheblicher Wirkung über die Teilnahme deutscher Soldaten an der Überwachung und Durchsetzung des Flugverbots über Bosnien-Herzegowina durch den NATO-AWACS-Verband nach Maßgabe der Resolutionen 781, 786 und 816 des Sicherheitsrates der Vereinten Nationen. Seine Umsetzung bedarf, wie sich auch aus der mündlichen Vehandlung ergeben hat, selbst dann keiner erneuten Beschlußfassung durch die Bundesregierung, wenn das Bundesverfassungsgericht die Anträge auf Erlaß einer einstweiligen Anordnung als unzulässig verwerfen oder mit der Begründung zurückweisen würde, der Organstreit sei unzulässig. Dies hat Bundesminister Bohl in der mündlichen Verhandlung ausdrücklich bestätigt. Dem Beschluß liegt danach auch kein mündlicher oder stillschweigender Vorbehalt dieses Inhalts zugrunde. Die Möglichkeit, daß der Beschluß bei veränderter politischer Lage aufgehoben oder geändert werden könnte, bedeutet nicht, daß ihm Rechtserheblichkeit nicht zukäme.

Einer weiteren Prüfung der Zulässigkeit der Organstreitverfahren bedarf es nicht, weil die Anträge auf Erlaß einer einstweiligen Anordnung aufgrund der gebotenen Folgenabwägung keinen Erfolg haben.

3 (a) Ergeht die einstweilige Anordnung, erweist sich aber der Einsatz deutscher Soldaten später verfassungsrechtlich als zulässig, drohen der Bundesrepublik Deutschland schwere Nachteile.

2 The application of the applicants in the proceedings 2 BvE 5/93 and the application announced by the applicant in the proceedings 2 BvQ 11/93 against the Federal Government are neither inadmissible from the start nor obviously unfounded. These applications are in particular not inadmissible just because there was no measure in the sense of § 64 para 1 of the BVerfGG. The decision of the Federal Government of 2 April 1993 represents such a measure. It decides, with significant effects in law, about the participation of German soldiers in the surveillance and implementation of the flight ban over Bosnia-Herzegovina by the NATO-AWACS unit according to the requirements of Resolutions 781, 786 and 816 of the Security Council of the United Nations. Its transposition into action did not, as also followed from the oral hearing, even require a renewed decision by the Federal Government if the Federal Constitutional Court rejected the applications for issue of a temporary order as inadmissible or refused them on the ground that the public institutions action was inadmissible. This was expressly confirmed by Federal Minister Bohl in the oral hearing. According to this, no oral or tacit reservation to this effect was at the basis of this decision. The possibility that the decision could be changed or changed in an altered political climate does not mean that it did not possess legal significance.

A further examination of the admissibility of the public institutions action is not needed, because the applications for issue of a temporary order are unsuccessful on the basis of the necessary weighing of the consequences.

3 (a) If the temporary order is issued, but the deployment of German soldiers later shows itself to be permissible in constitutional law, serious disadvantages threaten the Federal Republic of Germany.

Die Bundesrepublik Deutschland unterhält und betreibt von Anfang an zusammen mit elf anderen, der NATO angehörenden Nationen den NATO-Frühwarnverband (AWACS-Verband) als voll integrierten Verband des Bündnisses. Sein allgemeiner Auftrag besteht darin, im Rahmen der integrierten NATO-Luftverteidigung Frühwarnung zu betreiben und die Luftlageerstellung zu unterstützen. Der deutsche Anteil am militärischen Personal beträgt über 30%; die Flugsicherung wird ausschließlich von Deutschen gewährleistet. Die mündliche Verhandlung hat ergeben, daß dem Einsatz gerade dieses Verbandes für die Durchsetzung des Flugverbots eine Schlüsselrolle zukommt. Wenn die gefestigte, auf eingehender Schulung beruhende Zusammenarbeit bei den Einsätzen des AWACS-Verbandes aufgrund vorangegangener Resolutionen des VN-Sicherheitsrates gerade in dem Zeitpunkt abgebrochen würde, in dem nach Auffassung der Bündnispartner ein besonders gewichtiger Einsatz ansteht, so müßte dies nach Einschätzung der Bundesregierung, aber auch des Generalsekretärs der NATO, von den Bündnispartnern – ungeachtet etwaiger Möglichkeiten, das Auscheiden deutscher Soldaten auszugleichen – als eine empfindliche Störung der von der Völkerrechtsgemeinschaft autorisierten und von der NATO unterstützten Maßnahme empfunden werden.

Die mündliche Verhandlung hat zudem ergeben, daß bei einem Abzug der deutschen Soldaten aus dem AWACS-Verband dessen Einsatzfähigkeit erheblich beeinträchtigt, die Durchsetzung des Flugverbots mithin gefährdet wäre. Die auf Zusammenarbeit der jeweils 17-18 Besatzungsmitglieder unterschiedlicher Nationen beruhende Einsatzfähigkeit des Verbandes würde nach Auskunft des Kommandeurs der Einheit, Brigadegeneral Ehmann, bei Herausnahme der deutschen Besatzungen selbst unter Ausschöpfung aller Möglichkeiten nach 14 Tagen – gemessen am Einsatzauftrag – entscheidend geschwächt. Die mit der Resolution 816 des Sicherheitsrats beabsichtigte politische Signalwirkung würde so verfehlt. Das Bundesverfassungsgericht hat keine Anhaltspunkte, die zu der Annahme zwingen, daß diese Einschätzungen fehlerhaft sein könnten.

The Federal Republic of Germany, together with eleven other nations belonging to NATO, has maintained and managed the NATO Early Warning Unit (AWACS Unit) from the start as a fully integrated unit of the alliance. Its general commission consists in managing the early warning within the framework of the integrated NATO air defence and supporting the generation of the reporting of the situation in the air. The German share of military personnel consists of over 30%; flight safety is guaranteed exclusively by Germans. The oral hearing showed that the deployment of this particular unit has a key role for the implementation of the flight ban. If the established co-operation, based on thorough training, in the deployment of the AWACS unit on the basis of the preceding resolutions of the UN Security Council was discontinued just at that point in time in which, according to the opinion of the alliance partners, an especially important deployment was under consideration, this would, according to the evaluation of the Federal Government and also of the General Secretary of NATO, necessarily have been perceived by the alliance partners – notwithstanding various possibilities of making up for the withdrawal of German soldiers – as a severe disturbance to a measure authorised by the international law community and supported by NATO.

The oral hearing showed in addition that on a withdrawal of German soldiers from the AWACS unit its deployment capability would be substantially impaired and therefore the implementation of the flight ban endangered. The deployment capability of the unit which was based on the co-operation of the 17–18 crew members (at any given time) from different nations would, according to information from the commander of the unit, Brigadier General Ehmann, be decidedly weakened by the removal of the German crews, even on exhausting all the possibilities, after 14 days – running from the order as to deployment. The political signal intended by Resolution 816 of the Security Council would thus be unsuccessful. The Federal Constitutional Court has no compelling reasons to suppose that these evaluations could be incorrect.

Führt das Verfahren in der Hauptsache zu einer abschließenden Klärung dahin, daß die Verfassung die Beteiligung deutscher Streitkräfte an der Maßnahme nicht erlaubt, so muß das Bündnis das Ausscheiden deutscher Soldaten hinnehmen, selbst wenn dadurch die Einsatzfähigkeit des integrierten NATO-Verbandes empfindlich geschwächt würde und nur noch eine lückenhafte Durchsetzung des Flugverbotes möglich wäre. Es handelte sich dann um die Klärung der verfassungsrechtlichen Grundlage eines Mitgliedstaates für den Einsatz seiner Streitkräfte, wie sie auch nach Art. 11 des NATO-Vertrages jedem Bündnispartner vorbehalten ist. Solange indes die Verfassungsrechtsfrage noch offen ist, läge ein schwerer Nachteil vor, wenn die Bundesregierung entgegen ihrer Rechtsauffassung und politischen Einschätzung die deutschen Soldaten aus dem Verband abziehen müßte, sich später aber erwiese, daß die Verfassung die Mitwirkung deutscher Streitkräfte zuläßt. Dadurch würde das Vertrauen, das sich die Bundesrepublik Deutschland innerhalb des Bündnisses durch ihre bisherige stetige Mitwirkung in dem AWACS-Verband erworben hat, aufs Spiel gesetzt.

Die Haltung der Bundesregierung zum AWACS-Einsatz beruht maßgeblich auf der Tatsache, daß der Sicherheitsrat in seiner Resolution 816 diese Maßnahme im Rahmen des Friedensauftrages nach Kapitel VII VN-Charta autorisiert hat und erwartet, daß die in ihr angesprochenen Mitgliedstaaten einzeln oder durch regionale Organisationen sich daran beteiligen. Diese Erwartung wurde in der mündlichen Verhandlung sowohl vom Bundesminister des Auswärtigen wie vom Bundesminister der Verteidigung bestätigt; ihre Grundlage ist die Mitgliedschaft der Bundesrepublik Deutschland in den Vereinten Nationen und in der NATO. Unbeschadet der in der Vergangenheit und gegenwärtig geäußerten verfassungsrechtlichen Vorbehalte hat die Bundesrepublik Deutschland gerade in jüngster Zeit in einer Reihe von internationalen Dokumenten ihre Bereitschaft bekundet, im Rahmen der verschiedenen Bündnissysteme friedenserhaltende und friedensherstellende Operationen unter der Autorität des VN-Sicherheitsrats zu unterstützen (vgl. etwa das neue Strategische Konzept des Bündnisses, veröffentlicht auf der Tagung der Staats- und Regierungschefs des Nordatlantikrates am 7. und 8. November 1991 in Rom, Bulletin des Presse- und Informationsamtes der Bundesregierung Nr. 128 vom 13. November 1991, S. 1039 [1045 unter Nr. 42]; die sogenannte Petersberg-Erklärung der Westeuropäischen Union vom 19. Juni 1992, Bulletin Nr. 68 vom 23. Juni 1992, S. 649, unter I.2., II. 4.; Kommuniqué der Ministertagung des Nordatlantikrates vom 17. Dezember 1992 in Brüssel, Bulletin Nr. 141 vom 29. Dezember 1992, S. 1305 [1309 unter Nr. 6–8]).

If the proceedings in the main issue lead to a definite clarification to the effect that the Constitution does not permit the participation of German forces in the measures, the Alliance will have to accept the withdrawal of German soldiers, even if the deployment capability of the integrated NATO unit would thereby be severely weakened and only a defective implementation of the flight ban would be possible. It would then be a matter of clarification of the basis in the constitutional law of a Member State for the deployment of its forces, as is, according to Art 11 of the NATO Treaty, reserved to every alliance partner. As long, however, as the constitutional law position is still open, there would be a serious disadvantage if the Federal Government had, contrary to its view of the law and political assessment of the position, to withdraw the German soldiers from the unit but it later turned out that the Constitution permits the participation of German forces. The trust which the Federal Republic of Germany has earned within the Alliance by its constant participation up until now in the AWACS unit would thereby be put at stake.

The stance of the Federal Government on AWACS deployment is determined by the fact that the Security Council, in its Resolution 816, authorised this measure in the framework of a peace mission in accordance with Chapter VII of the UN Charter and expects the Member States addressed in it to participate in it individually or by regional organisations. This expectation was confirmed in the oral hearing by the Federal Minister for Foreign Affairs as well as by the Federal Defence Minister. Its basis is the Federal Republic of Germany's membership of the United Nations and NATO. Without prejudice to constitutional law reservations expressed in the past and currently, the Federal Republic of Germany has in recent times declared in a series of international documents its preparedness, within the framework of the different alliance systems, to support operations to keep peace and establish peace under the authority of the UN Security Council (compare the new Strategic Concept of the Alliance, published at the Conference of Heads of States and Governments of the North Atlantic Council on 7 and 8 November 1991 in Rome, Bulletin of the Press and Information Office of the Federal Government no 128 of 13 November 1991, p 1039 [1045 under no 42]; the so-called Petersberg Declaration of the West European Union of 19 June 1992, Bulletin no 68 of 23 June 1992, p 649, under I.2, II.4; Communiqué of the Council of Ministers of the North Atlantic Council of 17 December 1992 in Brussels, Bulletin no 141 of 29 December 1992, p 1305 [1309 under nos 6–8]).

Erginge die einstweilige Anordnung, müßte die Bundesrepublik Deutschland, indem sie ihre Mitwirkung an dem integrierten multinationalen Verband im Rahmen einer völkerrechtlich vereinbarten Friedenssicherungsaufgabe im Augenblick der Aktion abbricht, die durch ihr bisheriges Verhalten begründete Erwartung enttäuschen. Angesichts der Unaufschiebbarkeit der Maßnahme könnte sie den ihr obliegenden Beitrag zur Friedenssicherung gerade jetzt nicht leisten, wo er gefordet ist. Ein Vertrauensverlust bei den Bündnispartnern und allen europäischen Nachbarn wäre unvermeidlich, der dadurch entstehende Schaden nicht wiedergutzumachen.

(b) Demgenüber wiegen die Nachteile weniger schwer, die entstehen, wenn die einstweilige Anordnung nicht erlassen wird, die Mitwirkung deutscher Soldaten sich später aber als unzulässig erweist.

Durch eine Mitwirkung deutscher Soldaten in dem AWACS-Verband – sie allein ist Gegenstand dieses Urteils – wird kein völkerrechtlich erheblicher Vertrauenstatbestand begründet. Eine solche Mitwirkung kann auf der Grundlage des anhängigen Verfahrens und des vorliegenden Urteils nur als vorläufige, in ihre Fortsetzung vom Ausgang der Hauptsacheverfahren abhängige Zusammenarbeit gedeutet werden, zumal wenn die Bundesregierung dies den beteiligten auswärtigen Staaten notifizieren wird.

Ein wesentlicher Schaden erwächst dem Gemeinwohl auch nicht aus der Situation der zum Einsatz kommenden deutschen Soldaten. Nach der in der mündlichen Verhandlung vorgetragenen Einschätzung des Generalinspekteurs der Bundeswehr, General Naumann, und des Kommandeurs des AWACS-Verbandes, Brigadegeneral Ehmann, besteht für die Soldaten bei der gegebenen Einsatzplanung keine erhebliche militärische Gefährdungslage; deren Eintreten sei zudem militärpolitisch wenig wahrscheinlich.

Der Soldat trägt auch kein rechtliches Risiko, wenn sich später die Verfassungswidrigkeit des Einsatzes ergeben sollte. Die Tätigkeit des Verbandes hält sich im Rahmen des Beschlusses des Sicherheitsrates 816 vom 31. März 1993 und steht im Einklang mit der Zielsetzung der Charta der Vereinten Nationen, den Weltfrieden und die internationale Sicherheit zu gewährleisten, unabhängig von der abschließenden Klärung der Frage, ob die Bundesregierung seinen Einsatz anordnen durfte. Die Verantwortung für die verfassungsrechtliche Zulässigkeit dieser Anordnung tragen nicht die an dem Einsatz beteiligten Soldaten sondern die Bundesregierung. Das Gesetz stellt die Soldaten von dieser Verantwortlichkeit frei (§ 11 Soldatengesetz).

If the temporary order was issued, the Federal Republic of Germany would have to disappoint the expectation based on its conduct heretofore since it would be discontinuing, in the moment of action, its participation in the integrated multi-national unit within the framework of an exercise to secure peace, agreed under international law. In the face of the urgency of the measures, it would not be able to provide the contribution to the securing of peace incumbent on it just at the time it is required. A loss of trust with the alliance partners and all the European neighbours would be unavoidable and the harm arising therefrom could not be made good.

(b) Over against this, the disadvantages which arise if the temporary order is not issued but the participation of German soldiers proves later to be impermissible are less serious.

No situation of trust which is significant in international law will be established by participation of German soldiers in the AWACS unit – and this participation alone is the subject of the judgment. Such a participation can, on the basis of the pending proceedings and the judgment under consideration, only be interpreted as provisional co-operation, dependant for its continuation on the outcome of the main proceedings, especially if the Federal Government notifies this to the participating foreign States.

Neither would substantial harm to the common good arise from the situation of the German soldiers being deployed. According to the assessment of the Inspector General of the Federal Army, General Naumann and of the Commander of the AWACS unit, Brigadier General Ehmann, expressed in the oral proceedings, no situation of substantial military danger exists for the soldiers in the given deployment plan; the occurrence of such a situation was moreover not very likely from the point of view of military policy.

The soldier also carries no legal risk if the unconstitutionality of the deployment should manifest itself later. The activity of the unit is kept within the framework of Resolution 816 of the Security Council of 31 March 1993 and is in harmony with the objective set by the Charter of the United Nations, to guarantee world peace and international security, independently of the final resolution of the question of whether the Federal Republic is permitted to order its deployment. The responsibility for the permissibility of this order in constitutional law is not borne by the soldiers who participate in the deployment, but by the Federal Republic. Statute frees the soldiers from this responsibility (§ 11 of the Soldiers Act).

Allerdings kann in einer Lage, in der Soldaten der Bundeswehr erstmalig zu einem Kampfeinsatz geschickt werden und dieser nicht der unmittelbaren Verteidigung gegen Angriffe auf die Bundesrepublik oder einen ihrer Bündnispartner dient, ein Nachteil für das gemeine Wohl daraus erwachsen, daß bei späterer Festellung der Verfassungswidrigkeit des Einsatzes das Vertrauen der Soldaten darauf enttäuscht wird, daß eine so weittragende Entscheidung auf einer gesicherten verfassungsrechtlichen Grundlage beruht. Dieser Nachteil tritt hier jedoch an Bedeutung zurück; die Bundeswehrführung wird darauf verweisen können, daß ihre Befehle auf einer verantwortlichen Beurteilung der komplexen Rechtslage durch die dafür zuständige, demokratisch legitimierte Bundesregierung beruhten.

Auch für die innerstaatliche Ordnung entsteht kein nicht wiedergutzumachender Nachteil. Vollendete Tatsachen werden nicht geschaffen. Erkennbar ist für die Bürger in Deutschland, daß über die Zweifel an der verfassungrechtlichen Zulässigkeit einer Mitwirkung deutscher Soldaten bei der Durchsetzung der Sicherheitsratsresolution 816 vom 31. März 1993 derzeit noch nicht entschieden ist, die in der Hauptsache zu treffende Entscheidung aber sofort befolgt werden wird. Deshalb kann weder für das Rechtsbewußtsein in Deutschland noch für das Vertrauen in die verfassungsrechtliche Gebundenheit der Bundesrepublik Deutschland ein Schaden entstehen. Eine wie immer geartete Präjudizierung künftiger Entscheidungen von Verfassungsorganen tritt nicht ein. Entgegen der seitens der Antragsteller geäußerten Auffassung konnte daher bei der Entscheidung über die Hauptsache das Argument nicht gehört werden, der Einsatz des AWACS-Verbandes unter Beteilung deutscher Soldaten habe als Element der Staatspraxis Gewicht für die Auslegung des NATO-Vertrages.

Die Überzeugungskraft der Argumente, mit denen die Antragsteller ihre abweichende Gewichtung der bei Nichterlaß einer einstweiligen Anordnung befürchteten Nachteile begründen, leidet im übrigen daran, daß mit den Anträgen nur der Abzug des fliegenden Personals des AWACS-Verbandes begehrt wird, obwohl die vorgetragenen Bedenken – abgesehen von der Frage nach einer potentiellen Gefährdung – in gleicher Weise für das Bodenpersonal gelten, dessen Einsatz sie bis zur Entscheidung in der Hauptsache hinzunehmen bereit sind.

C

Das Urteil ist im Ergebnis mit 5:3 Stimmen ergangen.

(gez.)	Mahrenholz	Böckenförde	Klein
	Graßhof	Kruis	Kirchhof
	Winter		Sommer

Certainly, in a situation in which soldiers of the Federal Army are sent for the first time for deployment in conflict, this does not serve the purpose of direct defence against attacks on the Federal Republic or one of its Alliance partners, a disadvantage for the general good can arise from the fact that on it being later established that the deployment is contrary to the Constitution, the confidence of the soldiers that such a far-reaching decision is based on a secured constitutional law foundation will be disappointed. The disadvantage, however, recedes in importance; the Federal Army command will be able to refer to the fact that its commands are based on a responsible assessment of the complex legal situation by the Federal Government which is competent for this purpose and democratically legitimated.

For the internal order also, no disadvantage arises which cannot be made good. No *faits accomplis* are produced. Citizens of Germany can recognise that no decision is yet being made regarding the doubts about the permissibility in constitutional law of the participation of German soldiers in the implementation of the Security Council Resolution 816 of 31 March 1993, but the decision to be taken in the main proceedings will be immediately obeyed. Therefore, no harm can arise either for the legal consciousness in Germany, or for confidence in the Federal Republic of Germany being bound by constitutional law. The usual kind of prejudice to future decisions of constitutional organs does not arise. Contrary to the opinion expressed on the part of the applicants, no argument could be heard at the decision about the main issue, as to the effect that the deployment of the AWACS unit, with the participation of German soldiers would have, as an element of State practice, weight for the interpretation of the NATO Treaty.

The persuasive power of the arguments on which the applicants base their divergent weighting of the disadvantages feared if a temporary order were not to be issued suffers additionally from the fact that the applications only seek the withdrawal of the flight personnel of the AWACS unit, although the doubts expressed – apart from the question of potential danger – are valid in the same way for the ground personnel, whose deployment they are ready to accept until the decision in the main issue.

C

The judgment is issued in its outcome by a majority of five votes to three.

(Signatures)

Art. 25 [Völkerrecht Bestandteil des Bundesrechtes] Die allgemeinen Regeln des Völkerrechtes sind Bestandteil des Bundesrechtes. Sie gehen den Gesetzen vor und erzeugen Rechte und Pflichten unmittelbar für die Bewohner des Bundesgebietes.

Art. 26 [Verbot des Angriffskrieges] (1) Handlungen, die geeignet sind und in der Absicht vorgenommen werden, das friedliche Zusammenleben der Völker zu stören, insbesondere die Führung eines Angriffskrieges vorzubereiten, sind verfassungswidrig. Sie sind unter Strafe zu stellen.

(2) Zur Kriegsführung bestimmte Waffen dürfen nur mit Genehmigung der Bundesregierung hergestellt, befördert und in Verkehr gebracht werden. Das Nähere regelt ein Bundesgesetz.

Art. 27 ...

Article 25 [International law element of Federal law] The general rules of international law are an element of Federal law. They take precedence over statutes and produce rights and duties directly for the inhabitants of the territory of the Federation.

Article 26 [Prohibition of war of aggression] (1) Actions which are appropriate for and are undertaken with the intention of disturbing the peaceful co-existence of peoples, and especially to prepare for the conduct of a war of aggression are unconstitutional. They are to be punishable.

(2) Weapons designed for the conduct of war may only be produced, transported and brought into circulation with the consent of the Federal Government. Details will be regulated by a Federal Statute.

(Article 27 relates to the merchant fleet.)

THE STATES

Art. 28 [Verfassung der Länder] (1) Die verfassungsmäßige Ordnung in den Ländern muß den Grundsätzen des republikanischen, demokratischen und sozialen Rechtsstaates im Sinne dieses Grundgesetzes entsprechen. In den Ländern, Kreisen und Gemeinden muß das Volk eine Vertretung haben, die aus allgemeinen, unmittelbaren, freien, gleichen und geheimen Wahlen hervorgegangen ist. Bei Wahlen in Kreisen und Gemeinden sind auch Personen, die die Staatsangehörigkeit eines Mitgliedstaates der Europäischen Gemeinschaft besitzen, nach Maßgabe von Recht der Europäischen Gemeinschaft wahlberechtigt und wählbar. In Gemeinden kann an die Stelle einer gewählten Körperschaft die Gemeindeversammlung treten.

(2) Den Gemeinden muß das Recht gewährleistet sein, alle Angelegenheiten der örtlichen Gemeinschaft im Rahmen der Gesetze in eigener Verantwortung zu regeln. Auch die Gemeindeverbände haben im Rahmen ihres gesetzlichen Aufgabenbereiches nach Maßgabe der Gesetze das Recht der Selbstverwaltung. Die Gewährleistung der Selbstverwaltung umfaßt auch die Grundlagen der finanziellen Eigenverantwortung; zu diesen Grundlagen gehört eine den Gemeinden mit Hebesatzrecht zustehende wirtschaftskraftbezogene Steuerquelle.

(3) Der Bund gewährleistet, daß die verfassungsmäßige Ordnung der Länder den Grundrechten und den Bestimmungen der Absätze 1 und 2 entspricht.

Art. 29 [Neugliederung des Bundesgebietes] (1) Das Bundesgebiet kann neu gegliedert werden, um zu gewährleisten, daß die Länder nach Größe und Leistungsfähigkeit die ihnen obliegenden Aufgaben wirksam erfüllen können. Dabei sind die landsmannschaftliche Verbundenheit, die geschichtlichen und kulturellen Zusammenhänge, die wirtschaftliche Zweckmäßigkeit sowie die Erfordernisse der Raumordnung und der Landesplanung zu berücksichtigen.

(2) Maßnahmen zur Neugliederung des Bundesgebietes ergehen durch Bundesgesetz, das der Bestätigung durch Volksentscheid bedarf. Die betroffenen Länder sind zu hören.

THE STATES

Article 28 [Constitution of the States] (1) The constitutional order in the States must correspond with the principles of the republican, democratic and social constitutional State in the sense of this Basic Law. In the States, districts and communities the people must have a representation which results from general, direct, free, equal and secret elections. In elections in the districts and communities, persons who possess the nationality of a Member State of the European Community are entitled to vote and are electable in accordance with the law of the European Community. In communities, a community meeting can take the place of an elected body.

(2) The communities must be guaranteed the right to regulate all the affairs of the local community on their own responsibility within the framework of statute law. Associations of communities also have the right to self-government within the framework of the area of their statutory duties in accordance with statute law. The guarantee of self-government also includes the fundamentals of financial responsibility; these fundamentals include a tax source belonging to the communes with the right to fix the rate of assessment and related to economic power.

(3) The Federation will guarantee that the constitutional order of the States corresponds to the Basic Rights and the provisions of paras 1 and 2.

This gives an institutional guarantee of communal self-administration: BVerfGE 1, 167. But this does not relate to the particular local government structure; since the Basic Law came into force, substantial reforms have been made.

Article 29 [Reorganisation of the Federal territory] (1) The territory of the Federation can be reorganised in order to guarantee that the States in accordance with their size and efficiency can effectively fulfil the duties incumbent upon them. In this connection the regional affiliations, the historical and cultural connections and the economic suitability as well as the requirements of environmental planning and land planning are to be considered.

(2) Measures for reorganisation of the territory of the Federation are to be made by Federal statute which needs confirmation by referendum. The affected States must be heard.

(3) Der Volksentscheid findet in den Ländern statt, aus deren Gebieten oder Gebietsteilen ein neues oder neu umgrenztes Land gebildet werden soll (betroffene Länder). Abzustimmen ist über die Frage, ob die betroffenen Länder wie bisher bestehenbleiben sollen oder ob das neue oder neu umgrenzte Land gebildet werden soll. Der Volksentscheid für die Bildung eines neuen oder neu umgrenzten Landes kommt zustande, wenn in dessen künftigem Gebiet und insgesamt in den Gebieten oder Gebietsteilen eines betroffenen Landes, deren Landeszugehörigkeit im gleichen Sinne geändert werden soll, jeweils eine Mehrheit der Änderung zustimmt. Er kommt nicht zustande, wenn im Gebiet eines der betroffenen Länder eine Mehrheit die Änderung ablehnt; die Ablehnung ist jedoch unbeachtlich, wenn in einem Gebietsteil, dessen Zugehörigkeit zu dem betroffenen Land geändert werden soll, eine Mehrheit von zwei Dritteln der Änderung zustimmt, es sei denn, daß im Gesamtgebiet des betroffenen Landes eine Mehrheit von zwei Dritteln die Änderung ablehnt.

(4) Wird in einem zusammenhängenden, abgegrenzten Siedlungs- und Wirtschaftsraum, dessen Teile in mehreren Ländern liegen und der mindestens eine Million Einwohner hat, von einem Zehntel der in ihm zum Bundestag Wahlberechtigten durch Volksbegehren gefordert, daß für diesen Raum eine einheitliche Landeszugehörigkeit herbeigeführt werde, so ist durch Bundesgesetz innerhalb von zwei Jahren entweder zu bestimmen, ob die Landeszugehörigkeit gemäß Absatz 2 geändert wird, oder daß in den betroffenen Ländern eine Volksbefragung stattfindet.

(5) Die Volksbefragung ist darauf gerichtet festzustellen, ob eine in dem Gesetz vorzuschlagende Änderung der Landeszugehörigkeit Zustimmung findet. Das Gesetz kann verschiedene, jedoch nicht mehr als zwei Vorschläge der Volksbefragung vorlegen. Stimmt eine Mehrheit einer vorgeschlagenen Änderung der Landeszugehörigkeit zu, so ist durch Bundesgesetz innerhalb von zwei Jahren zu bestimmen, ob die Landeszugehörigkeit gemäß Absatz 2 geändert wird. Findet ein der Volksbefragung vorgelegter Vorschlag eine den Maßgaben des Absatzes 3 Satz 3 und 4 entsprechende Zustimmung, so ist innerhalb von zwei Jahren nach der Durchführung der Volksbefragung ein Bundesgesetz zur Bildung des vorgeschlagenen Landes zu erlassen, das der Bestätigung durch Volksentscheid nicht mehr bedarf.

(6) Mehrheit im Volksentscheid und in der Volksbefragung ist die Mehrheit der abgegebenen Stimmen, wenn sie mindestens ein Viertel der zum Bundestag Wahlberechtigten umfaßt. Im übrigen wird das Nähere über Volksentscheid, Volksbegehren und Volksbefragung durch ein Bundesgesetz geregelt; dieses kann auch vorsehen, daß Volksbegehren innerhalb eines Zeitraumes von fünf Jahren nicht wiederholt werden können.

(3) The referendum will take place in the States from whose territories, or parts of whose territories, a new State or a State with new borders is to be formed ('affected States'). Votes are to be cast on the question of whether the affected States should remain as they have been or whether the new State or the State with new borders shall be formed. The referendum for the formation of a new State or a State with new borders succeeds if there is a majority in its future area and, collectively, in those territories or parts of territories of an affected State whose State membership is to be changed in the same way. It does not succeed if, in the territory of one of the affected States, a majority rejects the change; the rejection is however not to be taken into account if in a part of a territory whose membership of the affected State is to be changed a majority of two-thirds approves the change; unless a majority of two-thirds in the entire territory of the affected State rejects the change.

(4) If in a coherent and defined residential and economic area, parts of which are in several States and which has at least a million inhabitants, a tenth of the persons entitled to vote for the Federal Parliament in it demand by petition that unified adherence to a State is brought about for this area, then either it must be determined by a Federal statute within two years whether the adherence will be changed in accordance with para 2 or a plebiscite will take place in the States affected.

(5) The plebiscite is directed towards establishing whether a change in adherence to be proposed in the statute will find agreement. The statute can put forward different but no more than two proposals in the plebiscite. If a majority agrees with a proposed change of adherence, then it must be determined within two years by a Federal statute whether the adherence will be changed in accordance with para 2. If a proposal put forward in the plebiscite finds agreement corresponding to the provisions of para 3 sentences 3 and 4, then within two years of the implementation of the plebiscite, a Federal statute for the formation of the proposed State is to be issued which no longer needs confirmation by referendum.

(6) A majority in a referendum and in a plebiscite is a majority of votes given, if it includes the votes of at least a quarter of those entitled to vote for the Federal Parliament. Apart from this, details about referenda, petitions and plebiscites are to be regulated by a Federal statute; this can also provide that petitions can not be repeated within a period of five years.

(7) Sonstige Änderungen des Gebietsbestandes der Länder können durch Staatsverträge der beteiligten Länder oder durch Bundesgesetz mit Zustimmung des Bundesrates erfolgen, wenn das Gebiet, dessen Landeszugehörigkeit geändert werden soll, nicht mehr als 50,000 Einwohner hat. Das Nähere regelt ein Bundesgesetz, das der Zustimmung des Bundesrates and der Mehrheit der Mitglieder des Bundestages bedarf. Es muß die Anhörung der betroffenen Gemeinden und Kreise vorsehen.

(8) Die Länder können eine Neugliederung für das jeweils von ihnen umfaßte Gebiet oder für Teilgebiete abweichend von den Vorschriften der Absätze 2 bis 7 durch Staatsvertrag regeln. Die betroffenen Gemeinden und Kreise sind zu hören. Der Staatsvertrag bedarf der Bestätigung durch Volksentscheid in jedem beteiligten Land. Betrifft der Staatsvertrag Teilgebiete der Länder, kann die Bestätigung auf Volksentscheide in diesen Teilgebieten beschränkt werden; Satz 5 zweiter Halbsatz findet keine Anwendung. Bei einem Volksentscheid entscheidet die Mehrheit der abgegebenen Stimmen, wenn sie mindestens ein Viertel der zum Bundestag Wahlberechtigten umfaßt; des Nähere regelt ein Bundesgesetz. Der Staatsvertrag bedarf der Zustimmung des Bundestages.

Art. 30 [Funktionen der Länder] Die Ausübung der staatlichen Befugnisse und die Erfüllung der staatlichen Aufgaben ist Sache der Länder, soweit dieses Grundgesetz keine andere Regelung trifft oder zuläßt.

Art. 31 [Vorrang des Bundesrechts] Bundesrecht bricht Landesrecht.

(7) Other changes in the territorial extent of the States can result from State treaties of the affected States or by Federal statute approved by the Federal Council if the territory, whose State membership is to be changed, has no more than 50,000 inhabitants. Details are to be regulated by a Federal statute which needs to be approved by the Federal Council and by a majority of members of the Federal Parliament. It must provide for the affected districts and communities to be heard.

(8) The States can regulate a reorganisation by a treaty in a manner which deviates from the provisions of paras 2–7 for the territory included in them or for parts of it. The communes and districts affected are to be heard. The treaty needs confirmation by a referendum in each participating State. If the treaty concerns parts of the States, the confirmation can be limited to referenda in these parts; the second half sentence of sentence 5 has no application. In a referendum, a decision is made by a majority of votes given, if they include at least a quarter of the persons entitled to vote for the Federal Parliament; details will be regulated by a Federal statute. The treaty needs the consent of the Federal Parliament.

Article 30 [Functions of the States] The exercise of public powers and the fulfilment of public duties is a matter for the States, insofar as no other rule is made or permitted by this Basic Law.

Article 31 [Priority of Federal law] Federal law has priority over State law.

This article gives a misleading picture of the relationship between Federal law and State law. In fact, the legislative competences of the Federation and the States are clearly laid down in Arts 70–78 of the Basic Law and each type of legislation has priority in its own proper sphere. Cases where this article could be applied will therefore be very rare.

EXTERNAL RELATIONS

Art. 32 [Auswärtige Beziehungen] (1) Die Pflege der Beziehungen zu auswärtigen Staaten ist Sache des Bundes.

(2) Vor dem Abschlusse eines Vertrages, der die besonderen Verhältnisse eines Landes berührt, ist das Land rechtzeitig zu hören.

(3) Soweit die Länder für die Gesetzgebung zuständig sind, können sie mit Zustimmung der Bundesregierung mit auswärtigen Staaten Verträge abschließen.

CITIZENS' RIGHTS

Art. 33 [Staatsbürgerliche Rechte] (1) Jeder Deutsche hat in jedem Lande die gleichen staatsbürgerlichen Rechte und Pflichten.

(2) Jeder Deutsche hat nach seiner Eignung, Befähigung und fachlichen Leistung gleichen Zugang zu jedem öffentlichen Amte.

(3) Der Genuß bürgerlicher und staatsbürgerlicher Rechte, die Zulassung zu öffentlichen Ämtern sowie die im öffentlichen Dienste erworbenen Rechte sind unabhängig von dem religiösen Bekenntnis. Niemandem darf aus seiner Zugehörigkeit oder Nichtzugehörigkeit zu einem Bekenntnisse oder einer Weltanschauung ein Nachteil erwachsen.

(4) Die Ausübung hoheitsrechtlicher Befugnisse ist als ständige Aufgabe in der Regel Angehörigen des öffentlichen Dienstes zu übertragen, die in einem öffentlich-rechtlichen Dienst- und Treueverhältnis stehen.

(5) Das Recht des öffentlichen Dienstes ist unter Berücksichtigung der hergebrachten Grundsätze des Berufsbeamtentums zu regeln.

EXTERNAL RELATIONS

Article 32 [External relations] (1) Control of relations with foreign States is a matter for the Federation.

(2) Before the conclusion of a treaty affecting the special circumstances of a State, that State has to be heard in good time.

(3) Insofar as the States are competent to legislate, they can conclude treaties with foreign States with the consent of the Federal Government.

CITIZENS' RIGHTS

Article 33 [Rights of national citizens] (1) Every German has the same civic rights and duties in each State.

(2) Every German is to have, according to his aptitude, qualifications and vocational achievement, equal access to every public office.

(3) The enjoyment of civil and civic rights, access to public office, and any rights acquired while holding public office are independent of religious persuasion. No disadvantage may result to anyone from his adherence or non-adherence to a creed or ideology.

(4) The exercise of sovereign legal powers as a permanent task is as a rule to be assigned to members of the public service who are in a public law relationship of service and loyalty.

(5) The law of the public service is to be regulated with regard to the traditional principles of the professional civil service.

OFFICIALS AND AUTHORITIES

Art. 34 [Haftung bei Amtspflichtverletzung] Verletzt jemand in Ausübung eines ihm anvertrauten öffentlichen Amtes die ihm einem Dritten gegenüber obliegende Amtspflicht, so trifft die Verantwortlichkeit grundsätzlich den Staat oder die Körperschaft, in deren Dienst er steht. Bei Vorsatz oder grober Fahrlässigkeit bleibt der Rückgriff vorbehalten. Für den Anspruch auf Schadensersatz und für den Rückgriff darf der ordentliche Rechtsweg nicht ausgeschlossen werden.

Art. 35 [Rechts- und Amtshilfe] (1) Alle Behörden des Bundes und der Länder leisten sich gegenseitig Rechts- und Amtshilfe.

(2) Zur Aufrechterhaltung oder Wiederherstellung der öffentlichen Sicherheit oder Ordnung kann ein Land in Fällen von besonderer Bedeutung Kräfte und Einrichtungen des Bundesgrenzschutzes zur Unterstützung seiner Polizei anfordern, wenn die Polizei ohne diese Unterstützung eine Aufgabe nicht oder nur unter erheblichen Schwierigkeiten erfüllen könnte. Zur Hilfe bei einer Naturkatastrophe oder bei einem besonders schweren Unglücksfall kann ein Land Polizeikräfte anderer Länder, Kräfte und Einrichtungen anderer Verwaltungen sowie des Bundesgrenzschutzes und der Streitkräfte anfordern.

(3) Gefährdet die Naturkatastrophe oder der Unglücksfall das Gebiet mehr als eines Landes, so kann die Bundesregierung, soweit es zur wirksamen Bekämpfung erforderlich ist, den Landesregierungen die Weisung erteilen, Polizeikräfte anderen Ländern zur Verfügung zu stellen, sowie Einheiten des Bundesgrenzschutzes und der Streitkräfte zur Unterstützung der Polizeikräfte einsetzen. Maßnahmen der Bundesregierung nach Satz 1 sind jederzeit auf Verlangen des Bundesrates, im übrigen unverzüglich nach Beseitigung der Gefahr aufzuheben.

Art. 36 [Beamte der Bundesbehörden] (1) Bei den obersten Bundesbehörden sind Beamte aus allen Ländern in angemessenem Verhältnis zu verwenden. Die bei den übrigen Bundesbehörden beschäftigten Personen sollen in der Regel aus dem Lande genommen werden, in dem sie tätig sind.

(2) Die Wehrgesetze haben auch die Gliederung des Bundes in Länder und ihre besonderen landsmannschaftlichen Verhältnisse zu berücksichtigen.

OFFICIALS AND AUTHORITIES

Article 34 [Liability for breach of official duty] If someone, in the exercise of a public office entrusted to him, breaches the official duty incumbent upon him as against a third party, responsibility falls in principle on the State or the body in whose service he is. A right of recourse is reserved in cases of intention or gross negligence. Ordinary legal proceedings may not be excluded in respect of the claim for compensation for harm and the right of recourse.

In connection with this article, see the air traffic controllers' strike case in Chapter Six, p 579.

Article 35 [Legal and official assistance] (1) All authorities of the Federation and the States are to give each other legal and official assistance.

(2) For the maintenance or restoration of public security or order a State can demand, in cases of special importance, personnel and equipment of the Federal Border Protection Force for the support of its police force, if the police, without this support, could not carry out a task or could only do so with substantial difficulty. A State can, in the case of a natural disaster or an especially severe accident, demand the assistance of police forces of other States, of personnel and equipment of other administrations as well as of the Federal Border Protection Force, and of the armed forces.

(3) If the natural disaster or accident endangers the territory of more than one State, the Federal Government can, insofar as it is necessary for effectively combating the problem, order the State governments to put police forces at the disposal of other States, and to use units of the Federal Border Protection Force and of the armed forces to support the police. Measures of the Federal Government in accordance with sentence 1 are to be revoked at any time upon demand of the Federal Council, or in other cases immediately after the danger has been removed.

Article 36 [Officials of Federal authorities] (1) In the highest Federal authorities, officials from all the States are to be employed in appropriate proportions. Persons employed in the other Federal authorities are as a rule to be taken from the State in which they are active.

(2) Defence statutes must also take into consideration the division of the Federation into States and the special regional relationships of their inhabitants.

COERCION BY THE FEDERATION

Art. 37 [Bundeszwang] (1) Wenn ein Land die ihm nach dem Grundgesetze oder einem anderen Bundesgesetze obliegenden Bundespflichten nicht erfüllt, kann die Bundesregierung mit Zustimmung des Bundesrates die notwendigen Maßnahmen treffen, um das Land im Wege des Bundeszwanges zur Erfüllung seiner Pflichten anzuhalten.

(2) Zur Durchführung des Bundeszwanges hat die Bundesregierung oder ihr Beauftragter das Weisungsrecht gegenüber allen Ländern und ihren Behörden.

THE LEGISLATURE

Federal Parliament

III Der Bundestag

Art. 38 [Wahl] (1) Die Abgeordneten des Deutschen Bundestages werden in allgemeiner, unmittelbarer, freier, gleicher und geheimer Wahl gewählt. Sie sind Vertreter des ganzen Volkes, an Aufträge und Weisungen nicht gebunden und nur ihrem Gewissen unterworfen.

(2) Wahlberechtigt ist, wer das achtzehnte Lebensjahr vollendet hat; wählbar ist, wer das Alter erreicht hat, mit dem die Volljährigkeit eintritt.

(3) Das Nähere bestimmt ein Bundesgesetz.

COERCION BY THE FEDERATION

Article 37 [Federal coercion] (1) If a State does not fulfil the Federal obligations incumbent upon it according to the Basic Law or another Federal statute, the Federal Government can, with the agreement of the Federal Council, take the necessary measures by way of Federal coercion in order to induce the State to fulfil its duties.

(2) For the carrying out of Federal coercion, the Federal Government, or its agent, has the right to give instructions as against all States and their authorities.

THE LEGISLATURE

Federal Parliament

III The Federal Parliament
Article 38 [Election] (1) The members of the German Federal Parliament are to be elected in general, direct, free, equal and secret elections. They are representatives of the whole people, not bound by mandates and instructions and only subject to their consciences.

(2) Any person who has completed his 18th year is entitled to vote; any person who has reached the age of majority is electable.

(3) A Federal statute will provide for the details.

THE ALL GERMANY ELECTION CASE

This case requires some understanding of the German electoral system. Voters in Germany have two votes in the Federal Parliament elections. They cast the first for their preferred candidate, and the second for their preferred party. Some seats in Parliament are allocated to candidates chosen by the first vote; the remainder are chosen from the party lists of candidates (which are prepared for the individual States and are therefore called State lists) in such proportions that each party's total representation in Parliament is proportionate to the percentage of the second votes cast for that party. But if that percentage is less than 5%, no candidates will be taken from that party's State list.

The Federal Constitutional Court had already held this 5% barrier clause in the relevant electoral statute (which prevents small parties being represented in the Federal Parliament) to be valid in constitutional law in BVerfGE 6, 84. It became apparent, however, prior to the first elections for the whole of Germany after unification, that this clause would have a particularly adverse effect on the East German parties. This case therefore decided the clause to be invalid, ie, in the context of that election. This was because it infringed the constitutional law norms of formal electoral equality and equality of chances for the parties.

THE ALL GERMANY ELECTION CASE

BVerfG NJW 1990 Band 47 S. 3001

1 Wahlrecht für die gesamtdeutsche Wahl am 2.12.1990

GG Art. 21 I, 38 I; BWahlG §§ 6 VI 1, 53 II

1 Aus den Grundsätzen der formalen Wahlrechtsgleichheit und der Chancengleichheit der Parteien folgt, daß dem Gesetzgeber bei der Ordnung des Wahlrechts zu politischen Körperschaften nur ein eng bemessener Spielraum für Differenzierungen verbleibt. Sie bedürfen zu ihrer Rechtfertigung stets eines zwingenden Grundes.

2 (a) Die Vereinbarkeit einer Sperrklausel mit dem Grundsatz der Gleichheit der Wahl kann nicht ein für allemal abstrakt beurteilt werden. Bei ihrem Erlaß sind die Verhältnisse des Landes, für das sie gelten soll, zu berücksichtigen.

(b) Findet der Wahlgesetzgeber besondere Umstände vor, die ein Quorum von 5 v. H. unzulässig werden lassen, so muß er ihnen Rechnung tragen. Dabei steht es ihm grundsätzlich frei, auf eine Sperrklausel zu verzichten, deren Höhe herabzusetzen oder andere geeignete Maßnahmen zu ergreifen. Hält er es für ratsam, an seiner Sperrklausel von 5 v. H. festzuhalten, aber ihre Auswirkungen zu mildern, so muß das Mittel, zu dem er sich entschließt, um die gebotene Milderung zu bewirken, seinerseits mit der Verfassung vereinbar sein, insbesondere den Grundsätzen der Wahlrechtsgleichheit und der Chancengleichheit der Parteien genügen.

3 Ein Wahlgesetz, das es Parteien ermöglicht, ihre Landeslisten zu verbinden, um als bloße Zählgemeinschaft die 5 v. H.-Klausel zu überwinden (Listenverbindung), gewichtet – anders als eine Regelung, die es Parteien erlaubt, eine gemeinsame Liste aufzustellen (Listenvereinigung)-, den Erfolg von Wählerstimmen ohne zwingenden Grund ungleich und verstößt daher gegen den Grundsatz der Wahl- und Chancengleichheit.

4 (a) Die erste gesamtdeutsche Wahl des Deutschen Bundestages findet unter besonderen Umständen statt, die eine unveränderte Aufrechterhaltung der herkömmlichen, wahlgebietsbezogenen Sperrklausel von 5 v. H. nicht erlauben.

(b) Unter den besonderen Bedingungen dieser Wahl ist eine Sperrklausel verfassungsrechtlich unbedenklich, die nicht auf das gesamte Wahlgebiet bezogen ist, sondern Parteien am Verhältnisausgleich teilnehmen läßt, wenn sie entweder im bisherigen Gebiet der Bundesrepublik Deutschland einschließlich Berlin (West) oder im Gebiet der Deutschen Demokratischen Republik einschließlich Berlin (Ost) 5 v. H. der für ihre Landeslisten abgegebenen Stimmen erreichen.

THE ALL GERMANY ELECTION CASE

BVerfG NJW 1990 Volume 47 p 3001

1 Electoral law for the election for the whole of German on the 2 December 1990

GG Art 21 I, 38 I; BWahlG §§ 6 VI 1, 53 II

1 It follows from the principles of formal electoral law equality and equality of chance for the parties that only a narrow measure of latitude remains for the legislator for discriminating in the regulation of election law for political bodies. Such discriminations always need a pressing ground for their justification.

2 (a) The reconcilability of a barrier clause with the principle of equality in the election cannot be assessed once and for all in abstract terms. The circumstances of the State for which it is to apply have to be considered when it is enacted.

(b) If the electoral legislator meets with special circumstances which cause a quorum of 5% to become impermissible, he must take them into account. At the same time he is, in principle, free to relinquish a barrier clause, to reduce its limit, or to use other appropriate measures. If he regards it as advisable to adhere to his barrier clause of 5%, but to mitigate its effects, the means upon which he determines in order to effect the required mitigation must be reconcilable with the Constitution and especially satisfy the principles of election law equality and equality of chances of the parties.

3 An election statute which makes it possible for parties to combine their State lists, as a mere partnership made for counting purposes, in order to overcome the 5% clause (combination of lists) – in contrast to a regime which allows the parties to make up a common list (fusion of lists) – weights the result of electors' votes unequally without any compelling ground and therefore offends against the principle of election equality and equality of chances.

4 (a) The first election for the whole of Germany, for the German Federal Parliament, takes place under special circumstances which do not permit an unchanged preservation of the traditional barrier clause of 5% based on the electoral area.

(b) Under the special conditions of this election a barrier clause is unobjectionable in constitutional law if it is not based on the whole electoral area but allows parties to participate in the proportional settlement if they reach 5% of the votes cast for their State lists, either in the former territory of the Federal Republic of Germany inclusive of Berlin (West), or in the territory of the German Democratic Republic inclusive of Berlin (East).

(c) Die unterschiedlichen Startbedingungen der im Gebiet der Deutschen Demokratischen Republik zur Wahl antretenden Parteien und politischen Vereinigungen können allein durch die Regionalisierung der Sperrklausel nicht hinreichend ausgeglichen werden. Als Ausgleich bietet sich die Zulassung von Listenvereinigungen für Parteien und politische Vereinigungen an, soweit sie im Gebiet der Deutschen Demokratischen Republik ihren Sitz haben.

BVerfG, Urt. v. 29.9.1990 – 2 BvE 1/90 u. a.

Zum Sachverhalt: Die Ast. (die Bundespartei 'Die Republikaner', die Partei 'die Grünen' und die Linke Liste/PDS) wollen als politische Parteien an der ersten gesamtdeutschen Wahl am 2. 12. 1990 teilnehmen. Sie beantragten im Organstreitverfahren festzustellen: Der Deutsche Bundestag hat dadurch gegen die Rechte der Ast. aus Art. 38 I GG i. V. mit Art. 21 GG verstoßen, daß er in Art. 1 des Gesetzes zu dem Vertrag vom 3.8.1990 zur Vorbereitung und Durchführung der ersten gesamtdeutschen Wahl des Bundestages zwischen der Bundesrepublik Deutschland und der Deutschen Demokratischen Republik sowie zu dem Änderungsvertrag vom 20.8.1990 diesem Vertrag sowie dem Änderungsvertrag zugestimmt hat und in Art. 2 Nr. 2 des oben genannten Gesetzes mit einer Neufassung des § 53 II BWahlG unter Aufrechterhaltung der Sperrklausel des § 6 IV BWahlG i.d.F. der Bekanntmachung vom 1.9.1975 (BGBl I, 2325) vorgesehen hat, daß Landeslisten verschiedener Parteien, die in keinem Land – ausgenommen Berlin – nebeneinander Listenwahlvorschläge einreichen, durch Erklärung gegenüber dem Bundeswahlleiter verbunden werden können.

Zwei Ast. beantragten außerdem festzustellen: Der Bundesrat hat die Ast. dadurch in ihren Rechten aus Art. 38 I GG i.V. mit Art. 21 GG verletzt, daß er Art. 1 und Art. 2 Nr. 2 des Gesetzes zu dem Vertrag vom 3.8.1990 zur Vorbereitung und Durchführung der ersten gesamtdeutschen Wahl des Bundestages zwischen der Bundesrepublik Deutschland und der Deutschen Demokratischen Republik sowie dem Änderungsvertrag vom 20.8.1990 zugestimmt hat.

Die mit den Organstreitverfahren zur gemeinsamen Entscheidung verbundenen Verfassungsbeschwerden richteten sich gleichfalls gegen das Gesetz zum Wahlrechtsvertrag. Die Bf., Mitglieder der Partei 'die Grünen', sind zur Wahl zum 12. Deutschen Bundestag wahlberechtigt und bewerben sich um Bundestagssitze, die Bf. zu 1 als Wahlkreiskandidatin, der Bf. zu 2 hat auf Platz 5 einer Landesliste seiner Partei einen Listenplatz erhalten. Das *BVerfG* hat entschieden:

I In den Verfassungsbeschwerde-Verfahren:

1 § 53 II BWahlG i.d.F. des Gesetzes vom 29.8.1990 zu dem Vertrag vom 3.8.1990 zur Vorbereitung und Durchführung der ersten gesamtdeutschen Wahl des Deutschen Bundestages zwischen der Bundesrepublik Deutschland und der Deutschen Demokratischen Republik sowie dem Änderungsvertrag vom 20.8.1990 (BGBl II, 813) verletzt die Bf. in ihrem Recht auf Gleichheit der Wahl nach Art. 38 I GG und ist nichtig.

(c) The differing starting conditions of the parties and political alliances entering the election in the area of the German Democratic Republic cannot be sufficiently compensated for by regionalisation of the barrier clause alone. The permitting of fusions of lists for parties and political alliances, insofar as they have their domicile in the territory of the German Democratic Republic, presents itself as providing a compensatory effect.

BVerFG judgment of 29 September 1990 – 2 BvE 1/90.

On the facts of the case: The applicants (the Federal party 'the Republicans', 'the Greens' party and the Left List/PDS) want to participate as political parties in the first election for the whole of Germany on 2 December 1990. They proposed to establish in the public institutions action: The German Federal Parliament has violated the rights of the applicants under Art 38 I of the GG in combination with Art 21 of the GG by virtue of the fact that, in Art 1 of the Statute to the Treaty of 3 August 1990 between the Federal Republic of Germany and the German Democratic Republic on the preparation and implementation of the first election for the whole of Germany for the Federal Parliament as well as to the Treaty of 20 August 1990 amending this Treaty, the Federal Parliament agreed to this Treaty as well as to the Amendment Treaty; and Art 2 no 2 of the above mentioned Statute with a new formulation of § 53 II of the BWahlG preserving the barrier clause of § 6 IV of the BWahlG in the formulation published on 1 September 1975 (BGBl I, 2325) has provided that the State lists of various parties which do not submit election list proposals at the same time in any State – with the exception of Berlin – can be joined by a declaration made to the Federal Election Director.

Two applicants proposed additionally to establish: The Federal Council infringed the rights of the applicants under Art 38 I of the GG in combination with Art 21 of the GG by virtue of the fact that it agreed to Art 1 and Art 2 no 2 of the Statute to the Treaty of 3 September 1990 between the Federal Republic of Germany and the German Democratic Republic on the preparation and implementation of the first election for the whole of Germany for the Federal Parliament as well as to the Amendment Treaty of 20 September 1990.

The constitutional complaints, which are combined with the public institutions action for the purpose of a joint decision, are likewise directed against the Statute on the Election Law Treaty. The complainants, members of 'the Greens' party, are entitled to vote at the election for the 12th German Federal Parliament and are competing for Federal Parliament seats, the first complainant as constituency candidate; the second complainant has received a list place in the fifth place on a State list of his party. The Federal Constitutional Court has decided:

I In the constitutional complaint proceedings:

1 § 53 II of the BWahlG in the formulation of the Statute of the 29 August 1990 to the Treaty of the 3 August 1990 between the Federal Republic of Germany and the German Democratic Republic on the preparation and implementation of the first election for the whole of Germany for the Federal Parliament as well as the Amendment Treaty of 20 August 1990 (BGBl II, 813) infringes the right of the complainants to equality in the election under Art 38 I of the GG and is void.

2. § 6 VI 1 Alt. 1 BWahlG i.V. mit Art. 1 des zu 1 genannten Gesetzes vom 29.8.1990 verletzt die Bf. in ihrem Recht auf Gleichheit der Wahl nach Art. 38 I 1 GG, soweit er für die erste gesamtdeutsche Wahl des Deutschen Bundestages die Sperrklausel auf das gesamte Wahlgebiet bezieht; insoweit ist die Bestimmung mit dem Grundgesetz unvereinbar.

II In den Organstreitverfahren:

Der Deutsche Bundestag hat durch Beschluß des zu I 1 genannten Gesetzes vom 29.8.1990 die Ast., der Bundesrat hat durch die von ihm erklärte Zustimmung zu diesem Gesetz die Ast. der Verfahren zu 1 und 3 in dem aus Nummer I des Tenors ersichtlichen Umfang in ihrem Recht auf Chancengleichheit nach Art. 21 I und Art. 38 I GG verletzt.

Aus den Gründen: C. Anträge und Verfassungsbeschwerden sind begründet.

I Der für die Wahl zum Deutschen Bundestag in Art. 38 I 1 GG gewährleistete Grundsatz der gleichen Wahl ist nach der ständigen Rechtsprechung des *BVerfG* wegen des Zusammenhangs mit dem egalitären demokratischen Prinzip im Sinne einer strengen und formalen Gleichheit zu verstehen (vgl. insb. *BVerfGE* 51, 222 [234] = NJW 1979, 2463 m. w. Nachw.; *BVerfGE* 78, 350 [357f.] = NJW 1989, 285). Die durch das Grundgesetz errichtete demokratische Ordnung gewichtet also im Bereich der Wahlen die Stimmen aller Staatsbürger unbeschadet der zwischen ihnen bestehenden Unterschiede gleich. Daher ist eine Differenzierung des Zählwertes und grundsätzlich auch – bei der Verhältniswahl – des Erfolgswertes der Wählerstimmen ausgeschlossen.

Da es vor allem die Parteien sind, die die Bürger für die Wahlen zu politischen Handlungseinheiten organisatorisch zusammenschließen, ergibt sich aus dem formalisierten Gleichheitssatz im Bereich der Wahlen, daß auch der Grundsatz gleicher Wettbewerbschancen der politischen Parteien und Wählervereinigungen in demselben formalen Sinne zu verstehen ist. Das Recht der Parteien auf Chancengleichheit bei Wahlen folgt aus ihrem in Art. 21 I, 38 I 1 GG umschriebenen verfassungsrechtlichen Status und aus der Bedeutung, die der darin verbürgten Freiheit der Parteigründung und dem Mehrparteienprinzip für die freiheitliche Demokratie zukommt (vgl. *BVerfGE* 73, 1 [28f.] = NJW 1986, 2492; *BVerfGE* 73, 40 [88f.] = NJW 1986, 2487; st. Rspr.). Es beherrscht den Wahlvorgang wie die Wahlvorbereitung. Die Demokratie kann nicht funktionieren, wenn nicht die Parteien grundsätzlich unter gleichen rechtlichen Bedingungen in den Wahlkampf eintreten (vgl. *BVerfGE* 44, 125 [146] = NJW 1977, 1054). Regelt der Gesetzgeber den Bereich der politischen Willensbildung bei Wahlen in einer Weise, die die Chancengleichheit der politischen Parteien und Wählervereinigungen verändern kann, sind seinem Gestaltungsspielraum besonders enge Grenzen gesetzt; ihm ist grundsätzlich jede unterschiedliche Behandlung der Parteien und Wählergruppen verfassungskräftig versagt (vgl. *BVerfGE* 51, 222 [235] = NJW 1979, 2463 m. w. Nachw.).

2 § 6 VI 1 alternative 1 of the BWahlG in combination with Art 1 of the statute mentioned at 1 of 29 August 1990 infringes the complainants' right to equality in the election under Art 38 I 1 of the GG insofar as it applies the barrier clause to the whole electoral area for the first election for the whole of Germany for the German Federal Parliament; to this extent the provision is irreconcilable with the Basic Law.

II In the public institutions action: The German Federal Republic has infringed the right to equality of chances, under Art 21 I and Art 38 I of the GG, of the applicants by passing the statute of 29 August 1990 mentioned at I 1 and the Federal Council by declaring its agreement to this statute has infringed the right to equality of chances, under those articles, of the first and third applicants in the action to the extent evident from Number 1 of the judgment.

Reasons: C. The applications and constitutional complaints are well founded.

I The principle of election equality, guaranteed for the election to the German Federal Parliament in Art 38 I 1 of the GG, is in accordance with the consistent case law of the *BVerfG* to be understood in the sense of a strict and formal equality because of the connection with the egalitarian democratic principle (compare especially *BVerfGE* 51, 222 [234] = NJW 1979, 2463 with further references; *BVerfGE* 78, 350 [357 and onwards] = NJW 1989, 285). The democratic order set up by the Basic Law thus, in the realm of elections, evaluates the votes of all the citizens of the State equally without regard to the differences existing between them. Therefore differentiation of the computed value and in principle also – for an election by proportional representation – the effective value of the electors' votes is excluded.

As it is above all the parties which unite the citizens organisationally for the elections into political operational units, it follows from the formalised equality requirement in the realm of elections that the principle of equal chances of competition for the political parties and electoral alliances is also to be understood in the same formal sense. The right of the parties to equality of chances in the elections follows from their constitutional law status described in Arts. 21 I and 38 I 1 of the GG and from the importance which belongs to the freedom of party formation guaranteed in it and the multi-party principle for free democracy (compare *BVerfGE* 73, 1 [28 and onwards] = NJW 1986, 2492; BVerfGE 73, 40 [88 and onwards] = NJW 1986, 2487; consistent case law). It controls the election procedure in the same way as preparation for the election. Democracy cannot function if the parties do not enter the election contest in principle under the same legal conditions (compare *BVerfGE* 44, 125 [146] = NJW, 1977, 1054). When the legislator regulates the area of formation of political will in elections in a manner which can change the equality of chances of the political parties and electoral alliances, especially narrow boundaries are set for its creative latitude; in principle, any different treatment of parties or electoral groupings is, by virtue of the Constitution, denied to him (compare *BVerfGE* 51, 222 [235] = NJW 1979, 2463 with further references).

Aus den Grundsätzen der formalen Wahlrechtsgleichheit und der Chancengleichheit der Parteien folgt mithin, daß dem Gesetzgeber bei der Ordnung des Wahlrechts zu politischen Körperschaften nur ein eng bemessener Spielraum für Differenzierungen verbleibt. Diese bedürfen hier stets zu ihrer Rechtfertigung eines zwingenden Grundes. Als ein Grund von hinreichend zwingendem Charakter, der Differenzierungen bei der Wahlrechtsgleichheit im System der Verhältniswahl rechtfertigt, ist in der Rechtsprechung des *BVerfG* wiederholt die Sicherung der Funktionsfähigkeit der zu wählenden Volksvertretung angesehen worden (vgl. etwa *BVerfGE* 1, 208 [247f.]; 4, 31 [40] = NJW 1954, 1601; *BVerfGE* 6, 84 [92, 93f.] = NJW 1957, 377; *BVerfGE* 51, 222 [236] = NJW 1979, 2463). Das dem Verhältniswahlsystem eigene Prinzip, den politischen Willen der Wählerschaft in der zu wählenden Körperschaft möglichst wirklichkeitsnah abzubilden, kann eine Aufspaltung der Volksvertretung in viele kleine Gruppen zur Folge haben, die die Bildung einer stabilen Mehrheit erschweren oder verhindern würde. Soweit es zur Sicherung der Handlungs- und Entscheidungsfähigkeit des Parlaments geboten ist, darf der Gesetzgeber deshalb bei der Verhältniswahl den Erfolgswert der Stimmen unterschiedlich gewichten.

Um dieses Zieles willen ist es dem Gesetzgeber grundsätzlich gestattet, die Funktionsfähigkeit der zu wählenden Volksvertretung durch eine Sperrklausel zu sichern. Dabei ist ein Quorum von 5 v. H. in aller Regel verfassungsrechtlich nicht zu beanstanden. Indessen hat das *BVerfG* schon früh betont, daß die Vereinbarkeit einer Sperrklausel mit dem Grundsatz der Gleichheit der Wahl nicht ein für allemal abstrakt beurteilt werden kann. Eine Wahlrechtsbestimmung könne in dem einen Staat zu einem bestimmten Zeitpunkt gerechtfertigt sein und in einem anderen Staat oder zu einem anderen Zeitpunkt nicht; bei ihrem Erlaß seien die Verhältnisse des Landes, für das sie gelten solle, zu berücksichtigen (vgl. *BVerfGE* 1, 208 [259]; s. auch *BVerfGE* 51, 252 [236f.]). Daran wird festgehalten: Eine gegenüber der herkömmlichen abweichende Beurteilung der Sperrklausel kann sich danach – sei es auch nur vorübergehend – als notwendig erweisen, wenn sich innerhalb des Staates die Verhältnisse wesentlich ändern, etwa durch eine kurzfristig vor der Wahl eintretende erhebliche Erweiterung des räumlichen Geltungsbereichs des Wahlgesetzes um ein Gebiet von anderer Parteienstruktur.

It therefore follows from the principles of formal electoral law equality and equality of chances of the parties that only a narrow measure of latitude for differentiations remains for the legislator in the regulation of electoral law for political bodies. Such differentiations always need a pressing reason for their justification here. The securing of the functional capability of the representatives of the people who are to be elected has repeatedly been regarded in the case law of the *BVerfG* as a reason of sufficiently pressing character which justifies differentiations in electoral law equality in the system of proportional representation (compare *BVerfGE* 1, 208 [247 and onwards]; 4, 31 [40] = NJW 1954, 1601; *BVerfGE* 6, 84 [92, 93 and onwards] = NJW 1957, 377; *BVerfGE* 51, 222 [236] = NJW 1979, 2463). The principle peculiar to the proportional representation system, to portray the political will of the electorate as nearly as possible to reality in the body which is to be elected, can have as a result the splitting up of the elected representatives of the people into many small groups, which would impede or prevent the formation of a stable majority. Insofar as it is required for the securing of the capability of parliament to operate and decide, the legislator may for that reason weight the effective value of the votes differently in a proportional representation election.

For the sake of this objective, the legislator is permitted, in principle, to secure the functional capability of the representatives of the people who are to be elected by a barrier clause. In this connection, a quorum of 5% is as a rule not to be objected to in constitutional law. However, the *BVerfG* emphasised early on that the reconcilability of a barrier clause with the principle of equality in elections cannot be abstractly assessed once and for all. A provision of electoral law could be justified in one State at a certain point in time and not in another State at another point in time; the circumstances of the State to which it is to apply are to be considered at the time it is made (compare *BVerfGE* 1, 208 [259]; see also *BVerfGE* 51, 252 [236 and onwards]). In that connection it is emphasised that an assessment of the barrier clause which diverges from the traditional one can afterwards prove to be necessary – even if only temporarily – if circumstances within a State change substantially, perhaps by a substantial widening of the spatial area of validity of the electoral statute, occurring shortly before the election, by an area with another party structure.

Findet der Wahlgesetzgeber in diesem Sinne besondere Umstände vor, so muß er ihnen Rechnung tragen. Dabei steht es ihm grundsätzlich frei, auf eine Sperrklausel zu verzichten, deren Höhe herabzusetzen oder andere geeignete Maßnahmen zu ergreifen. Hält er es für ratsam, an einer Sperrklausel von 5 v. H. festzuhalten, aber ihre Auswirkungen zu mildern, so muß das Mittel, zu dem er sich entschließt, um die gebotene Milderung zu bewirken, seinerseits mit der Verfassung vereinbar sein, insbesondere also den Grundsätzen der Wahlrechtsgleichheit und der Chancengleichheit der Parteien genügen. Eine die Wirkung der Sperrklausel mildernde Vorschrift läßt sich mithin nicht allein damit rechtfertigen, daß sie im Vergleich zu deren uneingeschränkter Geltung eine 'Vergünstigung' darstellt. Vielmehr kann verfassungsrechtlich nur eine Regelung Bestand haben, die sich gegenüber dem Wahlwettbewerb der Parteien neutral verhält (vgl. *BVerfGE* 14, 121 [134] = NJW 1962, 1493). Diese Neutralität kann auch fordern, daß der Gesetzgeber bei Sperrklauseln rechtlich veranlaßte Verzerrungen des Wahlwettbewerbs nicht unbeachtet lassen darf, die sich als besondere Umstände in dem erwähnten Sinne darstellen.

II Die erste gesamtdeutsche Wahl des Deutschen Bundestages, auf die sich die beanstandeten gesetzgeberischen Maßnahmen beziehen, findet unter besonderen, so nicht wiederkehrenden Umständen statt, denen der Wahlgesetzgeber bei einer Sperrklausel Rechnung tragen muß. Sie unterscheidet sich von anderen Wahlen dadurch, daß die politischen Parteien und Vereinigungen sich kurzfristig auf ein erweitertes Wahlgebiet einstellen müssen, ein Teil der an der Wahl teilnehmenden Parteien und Vereinigungen sich außerdem erst seit wenigen Monaten organisieren und politisch betätigen konnte.

1 Die Erstreckung des Bundeswahlgesetzes auf das Gebiet der Länder der Deutschen Demokratischen Republik hat zur Folge, daß diese Länder Teile des Wahlgebiets im Sinne der Regelungen des Bundeswahlgesetzes werden (§ 21 BWahlG). Sodann findet die erste gesamtdeutsche Wahl bereits ein Jahr nach der friedlichen Revolution in der Deutschen Demokratischen Republik statt. Zwischen der Herstellung eines gesamtdeutschen Wahlgebiets, das zwei vierzig Jahre getrennte Gebiete vereinigt, und dem Tag der ersten gesamtdeutschen Wahl werden gerade drei Monate liegen. Diese Entwicklung läßt einer Reihe von Parteien keine ausreichende Möglichkeit, ihren Wirkungsbereich auf das jeweils neu hinzugekommene Wahlgebiet auszuweiten und sich dort mit Aussicht auf Erfolg darzustellen und um Wählerstimmen zu werben. Insbesondere haben die Parteien bis zur Bundestagswahl nur begrenzt Gelegenheit, sich in den neu hinzugekommenen Wahlgebieten an Kommunal- oder Landtagswahlen zu beteiligen und dadurch dem Wähler Programm und Kandidaten bekannt zu machen.

If the electoral legislator finds special circumstances in this sense, he must take them into account. In this connection he is free in principle to forego a barrier clause, to reduce its limit or to take other appropriate measures. If he regards it as advisable to adhere to a barrier clause of 5% but to mitigate its effects, the means upon which he determines to effect the required mitigation must, for his part, be reconcilable with the Constitution and especially satisfy the principles of electoral law equality and equality of chances of the parties. A provision mitigating the effect of the barrier clause cannot therefore be justified only on the grounds that, in comparison to the unrestricted effect of such a clause, it represents a 'concession'. Rather can a requirement only survive in constitutional law if it operates neutrally in respect of the election contest of the parties (compare *BVerfGE* 14, 121 [134] = NJW 1962, 1493). This neutrality can also require that the legislator may not, in connection with barrier clauses, ignore distortions of the election contest which are caused by law and which present themselves as special circumstances in the sense mentioned.

II The first election for the whole of Germany for the German Federal Parliament, to which the legislative measures objected to refer, takes place under special circumstances which will not therefore recur and of which the electoral legislator must take account in connection with a barrier clause. It differs from other elections by virtue of the fact that the political parties and alliances must, in a short period, adapt themselves to a widened electoral area and additionally part of the parties and alliances participating in the election could only organise themselves and become politically active during the last few months.

1 The extension of the Federal Elections Act to the territory of the States of the German Democratic Republic has as a consequence that these States become parts of the electoral area in the sense of the requirements of the Federal Elections Act (§ 21 of the BWahlG). The first election for the whole of Germany takes place only a year after the peaceful revolution in the German Democratic Republic. Between the restoration of an electoral area of the whole of Germany, which unites two territories separated for 40 years and the day of the first election for the whole of Germany there will be just three months. This development leaves a number of parties no sufficient possibility to widen their effective area to the electoral area newly added at that time and to present themselves there with the prospect of success and to solicit the votes of electors. In particular the parties have only limited opportunity, until the Federal Parliament election, to participate in the municipal or State Parliament elections and thereby to make known to the voter their programme and candidates in the newly added electoral areas.

(a) Bei dieser Ausgangslage belastet eine auf das gesamte Wahlgebiet bezogene 5 v. H.-Sperrklausel die zum Teil bis heute nur auf dem Gebiet der Deutschen Demokratischen Republik tätigen Parteien gegenwärtig ungleich stärker als die bisher nur in der Bundesrepublik Deutschland tätigen Parteien. Nach den Feststellungen des Bundestagsausschusses Deutsche Einheit (BT-Dr 11/7652 – neu, S. 5) führt die Beibehaltung dieser Sperrklausel für die in ihrem Wirkungsbereich bisher auf das Gebiet der Deutschen Demokratischen Republik beschränkten Parteien und politischen Vereinigungen dazu, daß sie – bezogen auf ihren bisherigen Tätigkeitsbereich – 23,75 v. H. der Zweitstimmen erzielen müssen, um die 5 v. H.- Hürde zu überspringen und damit im Bundestag vertreten zu sein. Dementsprechend müssen die Parteien in der Bundesrepublik Deutschland – bezogen auf ihren bisherigen Wirkungsraum – etwas über 6 v. H. der Zweitstimmen erreichen.

Ein weiterer besonderer, vom Wahlgesetzgeber zu berücksichtigender Umstand ergibt sich daraus, daß Parteien und politische Vereinigungen außerhalb der Nationalen Front sich erst seit dem Umbruch in der Deutschen Demokratischen Republik organisieren und betätigen konnten. Im Vergleich zu den langjährig tätigen Parteien sind deshalb ihre organisatorischen, personellen und finanziellen Handlungsgrundlagen weniger weit ausgebildet; auch für die Entwicklung ihrer Programmatik und ihrer Zusammenarbeit mit anderen politischen Gruppen steht ihnen nur eine kurze Zeit zur Verfügung.

(b) Diese Unterschiede sind nicht von den politischen Parteien und Vereinigungen zu verantworten oder ihnen aus sonstigen Gründen zuzurechnen. Sie haben ihre Ursache vielmehr in der Veränderung des geltenden Rechts. Bis zur Erstreckung des Bundeswahlgesetzes waren in der Bundesrepublik Deutschland nur politische Parteien mit Sitz oder Geschäftsleitung im bisherigen Geltungsbereich des Gesetzes zu Wahlvorschlägen befugt (§ 18 BWahlG, § 2 III Nr. 2 PartG). Bei den Wahlen zur Volkskammer der Deutschen Demokratischen Republik am 18.3.1990 stand ein Wahlvorschlagsrecht nur Parteien und politischen Vereinigungen mit Sitz im Staatsgebiet der Deutschen Demokratischen Republik zu (§ 8 I des Gesetzes über die Wahl zur Volkskammer der Deutschen Demokratischen Republik vom 18.3.1990 vom 20.2.1990 [GB1 I, 60]; § 5 II des Gesetzes über Parteien und andere politische Vereinigungen vom 21.2.1990 [GBl I, 66]). Der Wahlvertrag vom 29.8.1990 ersetzt das bisher in der Deutschen Demokratischen Republik geltende Wahlrecht und modifiziert das Bundeswahlgesetz mit Wirkung für die Bundesrepublik Deutschland durch die Erweiterung des Wahlgebiets und die Beteiligung von Parteien und politischen Vereinigungen mit unterschiedlichen organisatorischen Ausgangsbedingungen, also in zwei für die Chancengleichheit der Parteien wesentlichen Punkten.

(a) From this starting point, a 5% barrier clause applied to the whole electoral area burdens the parties which until now were to some extent active only on the territory of the German Democratic Republic much more heavily at present than the parties only active until now in the Federal Republic of Germany. According to the findings of the Federal Parliament Committee on German Unity (BTDrucks – 11/7652 – new, p 5), the retention of the barrier clause leads, in relation to the parties and political alliances limited until now in their effective area to the territory of the German Democratic Republic, to their having to – based on the area of their activity until now – aim for 23.75% of the second votes in order to overcome the 5% hurdle and thereby be represented in the Federal Parliament. In comparison, the parties in the Federal Republic of Germany – based on their effective area until now – must reach something over 6% of the second votes.

A further special circumstance which must be considered by the electoral legislator arises from the fact that parties and political alliances, apart from the National Front, could only organise themselves and become active since the revolutionary change in the German Democratic Republic. In comparison to the parties which had been active over a long period, their organisational, personnel and financial fundamentals of operation are therefore not so fully developed; and only a short time is available to them for the development of their programme and their collaboration with other political groups.

(b) These differences are not the responsibility of the political parties and alliances or to be attributed to them on other grounds. They are caused by the change in the applicable law. Until the extension of the Federal Elections Act, only political parties with a domicile or business management within the area of applicability of the Act were authorised to make election proposals in the Federal Republic of Germany (§ 18 of the BWahlG; § 2 III no 2 of the PartG). In the elections to the Peoples Chamber of the German Democratic Republic on 18.3.1990 the right to make an election proposal only belonged to parties and political alliances with a domicile in the State territory of the German Democratic Republic (§ 81 of the Statute regarding the Election to the Peoples Chamber of the German Democratic Republic of the 18.3.1990 of 20.2.1990 [GBl I, 60]; § 5 II of the Statute regarding Parties and Other Political Alliances of 21.2.1990 [GBl I, 66]). The Election Treaty of 29.8.1990 replaces the electoral law applying until now in the German Democratic Republic and modifies the Federal Elections Act with effect for the Federal Republic of Germany by the widening of the electoral area, and the participation of parties and political alliances with differing organisational starting conditions, and therefore in two points of significance for the equality of chances of the parties.

Auch die Unterschiedlichkeit der organisatorischen Ausgangsbedingungen beruht auf Rechtsgründen. Nach der früher in der Deutschen Demokratischen Republik geltenden Verordnung über die Gründung und Tätigkeit von Vereinigungen vom 6.11.1975 (GBl I, 723) bedurften Vereinigungen zur Ausübung ihrer Tätigkeit der staatlichen Anerkennung (§ 2 I); diese wurde nur gewährt, wenn die Vereinigungen in ihrem Charakter und ihrer Zielstellung den Grundsätzen der sozialistischen Gesellschaftsordnung entsprachen (§ 1 II). Politische Parteien durften nur innerhalb der Nationalen Front der Deutschen Demokratischen Republik bestehen (Art. 3 II der Verfassung der Deutschen Demokratischen Republik vom 6.4.1968 i.d.F. vom 7.10.1974 [GBl I, 425]). Diese Gründungs- und Betätigkeitsverbote sind erst seit kurzem entfallen.

Diese durch die Rechtsordnung hergestellten Unterschiede sind nicht Verschiedenheiten, die der Wahlgesetzgeber auf Grund seiner Neutralitätspflicht hinzunehmen hätte, sondern Ungleichheiten, die er bei einer Sperrklauselregelung nicht unbeachtet lassen darf.

2 Entgegen der von dem Neuen Forum in der mündlichen Verhandlung vertretenen Auffassung liegt kein besonderer, vom Wahlrechtsgesetzgeber zu berücksichtigender Umstand in den Aufgaben, die in Art. 5 des Einigungsvertrages angesprochen sind. Danach wird den gesetzgebenden Körperschaften 'empfohlen', sich mit den im Zusammenhang mit der deutschen Einigung aufgeworfenen Fragen zur Änderung oder Ergänzung des Grundgesetzes zu befassen, insbesondere auch mit der Frage der Anwendung des Art. 146 GG und in deren Rahmen einer Volksabstimmung. Damit wird der 12. Deutsche Bundestag nicht selbst zu einer verfassungsgebenden oder verfassungsentwerfenden Versammlung im Sinne einer Betätigung der verfassungsgebenden Gewalt. Es kann deshalb dahinstehen, ob solche Aufgaben die Anwendung einer Sperrklausel ausschlössen.

III 1 Mit der Feststellung, daß bei der ersten gesamtdeutschen Bundestagswahl besondere Umstände vorliegen, die ein Festhalten an einer auf das gesamte Wahlgebiet bezogenen 5 v. H.-Sperrklausel verbieten, hat es jedoch nicht sein Bewenden. Der Gesetzgeber hat nämlich die Wirkung der Sperrklausel durch § 53 II BWahlG abgeschwächt. Damit wollte er ermöglichen, 'daß Parteien, die in einem der beiden deutschen Staaten gebildet worden sind und sich noch nicht durch Zusammenschluß mit einer Partei im anderen Staat die organisatorische Basis für die gesamtdeutsche Wahl geschaffen haben, Listenverbindungen eingehen und damit das Gesamtgewicht der für sie abgegebenen Zweitstimmen in der Wahl zur Wirkung bringen' (BTDrucks 11/7624 S. 21; vgl. auch den Bericht über die Beratungen des Ausschusses Deutsche Einheit betreffend den Entwurf des Gesetzes zum Wahlrechtsvertrag mit dem Hinweis, daß sich eine große Mehrheit im Ausschuß den Überlegungen von Bundesinnenminister *Dr. Schäuble* angeschlossen habe, nach denen es ein Anliegen gewesen sei, 'dem Umstand gerecht zu werden, daß es nach 40 Jahren Teilung Gruppierungen und Parteien gebe, die bisher nur in einem oder anderen Teil Deutschlands politisch tätig sein konnten', BTDrucks 11/7652 – neu, S. 7).

The difference in the organisational starting conditions is also based on legal grounds. According to the Regulation regarding the Founding and Activity of Societies of 6 November 1975 (GBl I, 723) formerly applying in the German Democratic Republic, alliances needed State recognition for the exercise of their activity (§ 2 I); this would only be granted if the societies corresponded to the principles of the socialist order of society in their character and their objectives (§ 1 II). Political parties could only exist within the National Front of the German Democratic Republic (Art 3 II of the Constitution of the German Democratic Republic of 6 April 1968 in the version of 7 October 1974 [GBl I, 425]. These prohibitions on founding and activity have only recently been lifted.

These differences, established by the legal order, are not differences which the electoral legislator had to accept on the basis of his duty of neutrality, but inequalities which he could not leave out of consideration in a barrier clause regime.

2 Contrary to the view advocated by the New Forum in the oral hearing, there is no special circumstance which is to be considered by the electoral legislator in the duties which are addressed in Art 5 of the Unification Treaty. According to this the legislative bodies are 'recommended' to consider the questions posed in connection with German Unification on alterations or additions to the Basic Law and especially with the question of the application of Art 146 of the GG and of a referendum within that framework. The 12th Federal German Parliament itself does not thereby become a constitution-creating or constitution-designing assembly in the sense of an activity of constitution-creating power. It can therefore remain undecided whether such duties would exclude the application of a barrier clause.

III 1 The matter does not however rest with the finding that special circumstances were present at the first Federal Parliament election for the whole of Germany which forbid adherence to a 5% barrier clause applied to the whole electoral area. The legislator has in fact weakened the effect of the barrier clause by § 53 II of the BWahlG. He intended thereby to enable 'parties, which had been formed in one of the two German States and had not yet created for themselves the organisational basis for the election for the whole of Germany by merger with a party in the other State, to enter into combinations of lists and thereby to bring into effect the total amount of the second votes given for them in the election' (BTDrucks 11/7624, p 21; compare also the Report on the Deliberations of the Committee on German Unity regarding the proposal for the Statute to the Electoral Law Treaty with the reference to the fact that a large majority in the Committee had agreed with the opinions of the Federal Minister of the Interior *Dr Schäuble* according to which there had been a wish 'to take into account the circumstance that after 40 years of division there were groupings and parties who, until now, could only be politically active in one or the other part of Germany' BTDrucks 11/7652 – new, p 7).

Dementsprechend ist die in Rede stehende Regelung daraufhin zu prüfen, ob sie die besondere Erschwernis, die für politische Parteien und Vereinigungen angesichts der Erweiterung des Wahlgebiets und der damit verbundenen verschärften Sperrwirkung einer wahlgebietsbezogenen Sperrklausel von 5 v. H. entstanden ist, in verfassungsrechtlich nicht zu beanstandender Weise ausräumt.

2 Diese Frage ist zu verneinen.

(a) Das Eingehen einer Listenverbindung ist durch die Konkurrenzklausel des § 53 II BWahlG eingeschränkt. Sie bewirkt, daß nur solchen Parteien die Verbindung ihrer Listen ermöglicht wird, die in keinem Land – ausgenommen Berlin – nebeneinander Listenwahlvorschläge einreichen. Damit hat sie eine - gegenläufige - Differenzierung des Erfolgswertes derjenigen Wählerstimmen zur Folge, die einer Liste mit weniger als 5 v. H. der Stimmen gelten. Deshalb muß sie sich an den Anforderungen der formalen Gleichheit messen lassen. Diesen ist – ungeachtet noch zu erörternder grundsätzlicher Bedenken gegen Listenverbindungen verschiedener Parteien überhaupt – schon deshalb nicht genügt, weil sie nicht alle Parteien in gleicher Weise begünstigt, auf die der Grundgedanke des § 53 II BWahlG zutrifft (vgl. *BVerfGE* 6, 84 [97, 98] = NJW 1957, 377).

Eine Chance, trotz Nichterreichens des Quorums am Verhältnisausgleich teilzunehmen, erhalten von vornherein nur einzelne der kleineren Parteien. Abstrakt steht die Listenverbindungsmöglichkeit zwar allen Parteien und politischen Vereinigungen offen. Das Wahlrecht hat sich aber nicht an abstrakt konstruierten Fällen, sondern an der politischen Wirklichkeit zu orientieren (*BVerfGE* 1, 208 [259]). Nimmt man sie in den Blick, so reduziert sich die Zahl möglicher Listenverbindungen drastisch. Der weit überwiegende Teil der Parteien, auf die der Grundgedanke des § 53 II BWahlG zutrifft, wird keinen Partner für eine Listenverbindung finden, ohne daß dies im Programm oder in anderen von der Partei beeinflußbaren Umständen begründet ist. Denn anders als bei einer uneingeschränkten Listenverbindungsmöglichkeit können unter der Geltung der Konkurrenzklausel praktisch immer nur zwei Parteien eine Listenverbindung eingehen, wenn sie den damit bezweckten Erfolg – die Überwindung der Sperrklausel - erreichen wollen. Das gilt jedenfalls dann, wenn die Parteien – wie es die Regel ist – zumindest im Gebiet der Deutschen Demokratischen Republik oder im Gebiet der Bundesrepublik Deutschland in allen Ländern Listenwahlvorschläge einreichen.

Accordingly, the regime under discussion is to be examined to see whether it removes, in a way that cannot be faulted in constitutional law, the special difficulty which has arisen for political parties and alliances in the face of the widening of the electoral area and, connected with that, the increased exclusionary effect of a barrier clause of 5% related to the electoral area.

2 This question is to be answered in the negative.

(a) Entering into a combination of lists is limited by the competition clause of § 53 II of the BWahlG. Its effect is that only those parties are enabled to combine their lists which do not submit electoral list proposals at the same time in any State – except Berlin. It thereby has as a consequence a – contrary – differentiation of the effective value of those election votes which relate to a list with less than 5% of the votes. It must therefore be measured against the requirements of formal equality. These are – leaving out of account fundamental doubts yet to be discussed about combination of lists of different parties – not satisfied simply because it does not favour in the same manner all parties to which the basic concept of § 53 II of the BWahlG applies (compare *BVerfGE* 6, 84 [97, 98] = NJW 1957, 377).

Only some of the smaller parties receive, from the start, a chance to participate in the proportional adjustment in spite of non-attainment of the quorum. In the abstract, the possibility of combination of lists is available to all parties and political alliances. But electoral law must orientate itself not to abstractly invented cases, but to political reality (*BVerfGE* 1, 208 [259]). If one takes this into account, the number of possible combinations of lists is reduced drastically. By far the greater part of the parties to whom the basic concept of § 53 II of the BWahlG applies will find no partner for a list combination, without this being based on the programme or on other circumstances which can be influenced by the party. This is because, in contrast to the position under an unlimited possibility for combination of lists, in practice under the regime of the competition clause only two parties can ever enter into a combination of lists if they want to attain the result intended thereby – the overcoming of the barrier clause. That applies in any case if the parties – as is the rule – submit electoral list proposals at least in the territory of the German Democratic Republic of Germany or in the territory of the Federal Republic of Germany in all States.

Können danach nicht beliebig viele Listen miteinander verbunden werden, so sind erfolgversprechend nur Verbindungen solcher Parteien, bei denen (wie es dem Bild des Huckepacknehmens entspricht) mindestens ein Partner in seinem Bezugsgebiet (Deutsche Demokratische Republik oder Bundesrepublik Deutschland) über ein hinreichendes Wählerpotential verfügt und deswegen in der Lage ist, die Schwäche des Partners auszugleichen. Wegen der unterschiedlichen Größe der beiden zu einem Wahlgebiet zusammengefügten Teile Deutschlands kommen dabei als Listenverbindungspartner für kleinere Parteien praktisch nur Parteien in Betracht, die in der Bundesrepublik mit einem nennenswerten Stimmenanteil rechnen können. Von diesen wenigen Parteien hatten im Zeitpunkt der Verabschiedung des Gesetzes zum Wahlvertrag bereits drei ihre Fusion mit Schwesterparteien im anderen Gebiet vollzogen oder angekündigt. Damit scheiden sie unter der Geltung der Konkurrenzklausel als Partner aus, weil sie in jedem Bundesland Listenwahlvorschläge einreichen werden.

Mithin hat von vornherein nur ein sehr kleiner Teil der Parteien, auf die der Grundgedanke des § 53 II BWahlG zutrifft, überhaupt eine reale Chance, einen Partner zu finden, der zur Überwindung der 5 v. H. Klausel verhelfen könnte. Das verletzt die Chancengleichheit der Parteien.

(b) Unabhängig hiervon führt jede Listenverbindung – ob mit oder ohne Konkurrenzklausel – zu einem Verstoß gegen die Chancengleichheit, weil sie den Erfolg von Wählerstimmen ungleich gewichtet, ohne daß dafür ein zwingender, sachlicher Grund angeführt werden kann. Dies ergibt sich aus folgenden Erwägungen:

(aa) Es entspricht dem System der Verhältniswahl, wie es im Bundeswahlgesetz ausgeformt ist, daß die Wahl nach von den Parteien aufgestellten Landeslisten erfolgt (vgl. § 6 I i.V. mit § 34 II Nr. 2 BWahlG). Auf eine solche Landesliste abgegebene Stimmen bleiben gem. § 6 VI BWahlG – abgesehen von den dort weiter vorgesehenen, hier aber nicht zu erörternden Sonderregelungen – bei der Verteilung der Sitze unberücksichtigt, wenn die jeweilige Partei nicht mindestens 5 v. H. der im Wahlgebiet abgegebenen gültigen Stimmen erhalten hat. Die darin liegende unterschiedliche Gewichtung des Erfolgswertes von Wahlstimmen trifft alle Parteien gleichermaßen, sofern sie die mit dieser Sperrklausel aufgestellte Hürde – die Vereinigung von mindestens 5 v. H. der im Wahlgebiet abgegebenen Stimmen auf sich - nicht überwinden können.

If, according to this, one cannot combine as many lists as are desired with each other, the only combinations promising success are of those parties in which (corresponding to the piggy back picture) at least one partner has in its reference area (German Democratic Republic or Federal Republic of Germany) a sufficient potential of voters at its disposal and for this reason is in a position to make up for the weakness of the partner. Because of the different size of the two parts of Germany which are joined to form one electoral area, the only partners which come practically into consideration are those which can reckon on a significant share of votes in the Federal Republic. Of these few parties, at the point in time of the passing of the Statute on the Electoral Treaty three had already completed or announced their fusion with sister parties in the other territory. They are thereby excluded as partners under the effect of the competition clause as they will submit electoral list proposals in every State in the Federation.

Therefore from the start only a very small part of the parties to which the basic concept of § 53 II of the BWahlG applies has any real chance of finding a partner which could help to overcome the 5% clause. That violates the equality of chances of the parties.

(b) Independently of this, every combination of lists – whether with or without a competition clause – leads to a violation of the equality of chances because it evaluates the results of the elector's votes unequally, without it being possible to adduce a pressing material reason for this. This arises from the following considerations:

(aa) It conforms to the system of proportional representation as provided for in the Federal Elections Act that the election takes place in accordance with the State lists established by the parties (compare § 6 I in combination with § 34 II no 2 of the BWahlG). On such a State list votes cast remain, in accordance with § 6 VI of the BWahlG – apart from the special rules further provided for there, but not to be discussed here – out of consideration on the distribution of seats if the party under consideration did not receive at least 5% of the votes validly cast in the electoral area. The differing weighting of the effective value of the election votes present in this affects all parties in the same way insofar as they cannot overcome the hurdle set up by this barrier clause – the appropriating of at least 5% of the votes cast in the electoral area.

Diese gleichmäßige Wirkung der Sperrklausel wird für diejenigen Parteien wieder durchbrochen, die gegenüber dem Bundeswahlleiter eine Verbindung ihrer Listenwahlvorschläge erklären. Diese Erklärung bewirkt, daß für die Überwindung der Sperrklausel der Prozentsatz maßgeblich ist, der sich aus der Summe der auf die verbundenen Landeslisten abgegebenen Stimmen errechnet. Auf diese Weise können bei der Sitzverteilung Parteien berücksichtigt werden, die je für sich im Wahlgebiet die 5 v. H. -Grenze verfehlt hätten und damit ohne Mandat geblieben wären. Überwindet gar eine der die Listenverbindung eingehenden Parteien bereits aus eigener Kraft die Sperrklausel, so braucht die zweite an der Listenverbindung beteiligte Partei dazu nichts mehr beizutragen. Listenverbindungen haben daher nicht nur zur Folge, sondern auch zum Ziel, daß sie die Wirkung von Sperrklauseln unterschiedlich gestalten, je nachdem, ob durch eine Erklärung gegenüber dem Bundeswahlleiter Listen verbunden worden sind oder nicht.

Dem unterschiedlichen Erfolgswert der auf eine verbundene Landesliste abgegebenen Wählerstimmen gegenüber den Wählerstimmen, die auf eine nicht verbundene Landeslist entfallen sind, entspricht auch ein unterschiedlicher Erfolgswert der jeweils einzelnen Wahlstimme: Jeder Wähler, der seine Stimme für eine der verbundenen Listen abgibt, kann dadurch dazu beitragen, daß auch die auf die andere Liste entfallenden Stimmen im Verhältnisausgleich Berücksichtigung finden. Er verhilft also einer Liste zum Erfolg, für die er seine Stimme nicht abgegeben hat. Eine derart unterschiedliche Gewichtung der Wählerstimmen widerspricht dem Grundsatz der formalen Wahlrechtsgleichheit in so grundlegender Weise, daß schon von daher kein rechtfertigender Grund für die damit einhergehende Chancenungleichheit der Parteien in Betracht kommt.

(bb) Demgegenüber haftet einer Listen*vereinigung*, wie sie das Wahlrecht der Deutschen Demokratischen Republik kennt (vgl. unten IV 2), ein solcher Verstoß gegen die Wahlgleichheit nicht an. Während die Listenverbindung zur Überwindung der Sperrklausel eine bloße Zählgemeinschaft bildet, setzt die Listenvereinigung eine verfestigte Form des Zusammenwirkens voraus. Bei einer solchen Vereinigung stellen mehrere Parteien oder politische Vereinigungen eine gemeinsame Liste auf, die die Bewerber verschiedener Parteien in eine feste Rangfolge bringt und sich den Wählern stellt. Damit wird die gleichmäßige Wirkung der Sperrklausel also gerade nicht aufgehoben; auch auf eine Listenvereinigung müssen so viele Stimmen entfallen, wie zur Überwindung der Sperrklausel erforderlich sind. Die Zulassung von Listenvereinigungen macht daher den Erfolgswert von abgegebenen Wählerstimmen nicht über dasjenige Maß hinaus ungleich, welches vom Zweck einer Sperrklausel gedeckt ist. Die Zulassung einer Listenvereinigung enthält daher lediglich eine Ausnahme von dem Grundsatz des Bundeswahlgesetzes, daß nur einzelne Parteien oder politische Vereinigungen einen Listenwahlvorschlag machen können. Die Listenverbindung beachtet zwar diese gesetzliche Vorgabe, durchbricht demgegenüber aber den in der Wahlrechtsgleichheit angelegten Verfassungssatz, daß das Hindernis einer Sperrklausel für alle Listenwahlvorschläge in gleicher Weise gelten soll.

This uniform effect of the barrier clause is broken again for those parties which make a declaration to the Federal Election Manager of a combination of their electoral list proposals. This declaration causes the percentage which is conclusive for the overcoming of the barrier clause to be the one which is calculated from the sum of the votes cast on the combined State lists. In this way, parties can be considered in the distribution of seats which would each for themselves have failed to attain the 5% limit in the electoral area and thereby would have remained without a mandate. If one of the parties taking part in a combination of lists overcomes the barrier clause by its own power, the second party participating in the combination of lists does not need to contribute anything more to it. Combinations of lists have developed for that reason not only as a consequence but also as an objective that they shape the effect of barrier clauses differently according to whether lists have been combined by a declaration to the Federal Elections Manager or not.

The differing effective value of electors' votes cast falling to a combined State list as against electors' votes cast falling to a non-combined State list is also reflected in a differing effective value of the single election vote: every voter who casts his vote for one of the combined lists can thereby contribute to the votes falling to the other list also being considered in the proportional adjustment. He thus assists the success of a list for which he has not cast his vote. A differing weighting of this kind of electors' votes contradicts the principle of formal electoral law equality in so fundamental a manner that for that very reason no justifying ground falls to be considered for the accompanying inequality of the parties' chances.

(bb) Over against this, such a violation of electoral equality does not attach to a *fusion* of lists as the electoral law of the German Democratic Republic recognises it (compare below, IV 2). Whilst a combination of lists forms a mere numerical partnership for the overcoming of the barrier clause, the fusion of lists presupposes a solid form of co-operation. In such a fusion, several parties or political alliances establish a common list which brings the candidates of the different parties into a firm order of rank which is presented to the voters. The uniform effect of the barrier clause is thus not removed; such number of votes must be cast for a fusion of lists as are necessary for overcoming the barrier clause. The permitting of fusions of lists therefore does not make the effective value of the votes cast unequal beyond the extent which is covered by the purpose of a barrier clause. The permitting of a fusion of lists therefore merely comprises an exception from the principle of the Federal Elections Act that only single parties or political alliances can make an electoral list proposal. The combination of lists certainly has regard to this legal handicap, but on the other hand violates the constitutional principle applied in electoral law equality that the obstacle of a barrier clause is to apply in the same way for all electoral list proposals.

IV Aus dem bisher Gesagten folgt nicht, daß der Gesetzgeber von Verfassungs wegen gehalten ist, bei der ersten gesamtdeutschen Wahl von einer Sperrklauselregelung überhaupt abzusehen.

1 (a) Allerdings kommt eine allgemeine Absenkung der Sperrklausel bei Aufrechterhaltung ihrer Bezogenheit auf das gesamte Wahlgebiet nicht in Betracht. Es darf nämlich auch hier nicht unberücksichtigt bleiben, daß sich die Parteien, die ihren Betätigungsraum bislang allein in der Deutschen Demokratischen Republik hatten, durch die Erweiterung des Wahlgebiets im Verhältnis zu den Parteien der Bundesrepublik Deutschland ungleichen Ausgangsbedingungen ausgesetzt sehen. Sie müssen sich, um ihre Chancen auf einen bestimmten Stimmenanteil zu wahren, gewissermaßen aus dem Stand heraus um ein neues Wählerpotential bemühen, das um mehr als das Dreieinhalbfache die Zahl der Wahlberechtigten in der Deutschen Demokratischen Republik, also in ihrem bisherigen Wahlgebiet, übersteigt; demgegenüber macht das vergleichbare Handicap für Parteien der Bundesrepublik Deutschland wegen der viel höheren Zahl der in ihrem bisherigen Wahlgebiet ansässigen Wahlberechtigten nicht einmal ein Drittel aus. Diese ungleichen Ausgangsbedingungen sind – wie bereits dargelegt – die notwendige Folge aus der Zusammenführung der beiden bisher selbständigen Wahlgebiete zu einem einheitlichen Wahlgebiet und damit erst durch eine rechtliche Regelung, nämlich das Zustimmungsgesetz zum Wahlvertrag, geschaffen worden.

Daraus folgt, daß der Gesetzgeber von Verfassungs wegen gehindert ist, eine von ihm für notwendig erachtete Sperrklausel in der Weise festzulegen, daß sie gerade an die in Rede stehende ungleiche Ausgangslage anknüpft, sie also zum Ausgangspunkt für eine Regelung nimmt, die darauf abzielt, im Interesse eines funktionsfähigen Parlaments den Erfolgswert der Wählerstimmen unterschiedlich zu gewichten. In diesem Falle wird - wegen der beschriebenen ungleichen Ausgangslage – eine Ungleichheit, die durch die Funktion einer Sperrklausel nicht zu rechtfertigen ist, rechtlich verfestigt: Die Parteien in der Deutschen Demokratischen Republik müßten nämlich zur Überwindung der Sperrklausel stets einen weitaus größeren Anteil an Wählern in ihrem bisherigen Wahlgebiet gewinnen, also hier einen entsprechend größeren Erfolg bei der Wahl haben, als es für die Parteien in der Bundesrepublik, bezogen auf deren bisheriges Wahlgebiet, erforderlich ist. So hätte beispielsweise eine Minderung der wahlgebietsbezogenen Sperrklausel auf etwa 1,2 v. H. zwar die Wirkung, daß die Parteien der Deutschen Demokratischen Republik nicht mehr als 5 v. H. der Wählerstimmen, bezogen auf die frühere Deutsche Demokratische Republik gewinnen müßten, um dieses Hindernis zu überwinden. Sie würden also im Ergebnis nicht härter getroffen als dies bei einer auf das bisherige Wahlgebiet bezogenen 5 v. H.-Klausel der Fall wäre. Den Parteien der Bundesrepublik genügte dagegen schon ein Anteil von etwa 1,6 v. H. der Stimmen, bezogen auf ihr bisheriges Wahlgebiet, um an der Sitzverteilung teilzunehmen. Diese Ungleichheit besteht in ihrer Relation auch bei einer Senkung der Sperrklausel unter 1,2 v. H. fort; sie haftet jeder wahlgebietsweiten einheitlichen Sperrklausel an.

IV It does not follow from what has been said so far that the legislator is constrained by virtue of the Constitution to abandon a barrier clause regime altogether in the first election for the whole of Germany.

1 (a) Certainly a general lowering of the barrier clause accompanied by maintenance of its applicability to the whole electoral area does not come into consideration. It is not of course to be left out of consideration here that the parties which had their area of activity until now in the German Democratic Republic alone see themselves as exposed to unequal starting conditions in comparison with the parties of the Federal Republic of Germany by the widening of the electoral area. They must, in order to preserve their chances of a certain share of the votes, strive to a certain degree from their existing position for a new vote's potential which exceeds by more than three and a half times the number of persons entitled to vote in the German Democratic Republic, ie, in their electoral area up till now; on the other hand the comparable handicap for parties of the Federal Republic of Germany does not even constitute a third because of the much higher number of persons entitled to vote who are resident in their electoral area heretofore. These unequal starting conditions are, as already explained, the necessary consequence of the bringing together of the two hitherto independent electoral areas into a single electoral area, and have been created by a legal regime, namely the Statute of Approval to the Electoral Treaty.

It follows from this that the legislator by virtue of the Constitution is prevented from laying down the barrier clause regarded by him as necessary in such a way that it connects directly to the unequal initial situation under discussion and therefore takes it as a starting point for a regime which aims to weight the effective value of electors' votes differently in the interests of creating a parliament capable of functioning. In this case an inequality which cannot be justified by the function of a barrier clause – because of the unequal initial situation described – is legally established. The parties in the German Democratic Republic would always have to win a far greater fraction of the voters in what had been their election area until now to overcome the barrier clause and therefore have a correspondingly greater success in the election than is necessary for the parties in the Federal Republic in reference to what had until now been their electoral area. So, for example, a reduction of a barrier clause related to the electoral area to perhaps 1.2% would have had the effect that the parties of the German Democratic Republic would have had to win no more than 5% of the electors' votes in respect of the former German Democratic Republic in order to overcome this obstacle. They would therefore, in the result, not be worse affected than would be the case under a 5% clause relating to what had until now been the electoral area. On the other hand a share of about 1.6% of the votes in relation to their electoral area so far would suffice for the parties of the Federal Republic in order to participate in the distribution of seats. This inequality of relationship persists even for a reduction of the barrier clause below 1.2%; it attaches to any uniform barrier clause applying to the whole electoral area.

Damit verletzt eine solche Sperrklausel, wie immer ihre Höhe festgestzt sein mag, die Chancengleichheit zu Lasten der Parteien der Deutschen Demokratischen Republik. Sie verhielte sich gegenüber den politischen Parteien – angesichts der auf Rechtsgegebenheiten beruhenden unterschiedlichen Ausgangslage – nicht mehr neutral, sondern bedeutete eine Intervention zugunsten der Parteien der Bundesrepublik Deutschland.

(b) Verfassungsrechtlich unbedenklich ist hingegen eine regionalisierte Sperrklausel, die einerseits auf das bisherige Gebiet der Bundesrepublik Deutschland einschließlich Berlins (West), andererseits auf das Gebiet der Deutschen Demokratischen Republik einschließlich Berlins (Ost) bezogen und für beide Bezugsgebiete in gleicher Höhe festgesetzt wird. Die Ungleichheit, daß nach der Herstellung der staatlichen Einheit Parteien der Deutschen Demokratischen Republik sich sofort auf einem Wahlgebiet der Auseinandersetzung und Konkurrenz zu stellen haben, das – gemessen an der Bevölkerung – um mehr als 300 v. H. größer ist als ihr bisheriges, während die Vergrößerung bei den Parteien der Bundesrepublik Deutschland nur etwa 27 v. H. ausmacht, würde mit der regionalisierten Sperrklausel nicht Ausgangspunkt für eine den Erfolgswert der Wählerstimmen unterschiedlich gewichtende Regelung sein; sie würde auf diese Weise nicht auf die rechtliche Ebene gehoben und damit rechtlich sanktioniert. Statt dessen würden den Parteien hier wie dort – bezogen auf ihren ungleichen Start – im wesentlichen nicht ungleiche, sondern gerade gleiche Chancen eingeräumt und dementsprechend auch die gleiche Unterstützung durch die Wähler abverlangt. Dagegen läßt sich nicht einwenden, daß eine in diesem Sinne regionale Sperrklausel bei der im Wahlrecht gebotenen formalen Betrachtungsweise dazu führe, daß im Gebiet der Deutschen Demokratischen Republik abgegebene Stimmen im Rahmen des Verhältnisausgleichs größeres Gewicht erhielten. Auch eine strikte und formale Gleichheit, wie sie dem demokratischen Prinzip entspricht, läßt sich bei der hier gegebenen ungleichen Ausgangslage nur durch die Anknüpfung der formalen Gleichheit an das jeweilige Bezugsgebiet herstellen. Der Umstand, daß – wegen der Abhängigkeit des Erfolgswerts der Wahlstimme von einem bestimmten Stimmenanteil – in dem einen Bezugsgebiet für diesen Stimmenanteil mehr Stimmen aufgebracht werden müssen als in dem anderen, führt daher nicht zu einem Gleichheitsverstoß, wenn – wie hier – diese Bezugsgebiete ihrerseits nach Gleichheitsgesichtspunkten gebildet werden.

Such a barrier clause therefore violates the equality of chances of the parties to the disadvantage of the parties of the German Democratic Republic, however its limit may be established. It would no longer be neutral as against the political parties – in the face of the differing initial situation based on legal realities – but would signify an intervention in favour of the parties of the Federal Republic of Germany.

(b) On the other hand, it would be constitutionally unobjectionable to have a regionalised barrier clause, which on the one hand related to the area of the Federal Republic of Germany up to now, inclusive of Berlin (West) and on the other hand to the area of the German Democratic Republic inclusive of Berlin (East) and which is established at the same level for both reference areas. The inequality arising from the fact that, after the restoration of State unity, parties of the German Democratic Republic have to take their stand immediately in argument and competition in an electoral area which – measured by its population – is more than 300% larger than its area so far, whilst the enlargement for the parties of the Federal Republic of Germany only amounts to about 27% this would not, with the regionalised barrier clause, count as a starting point for a regime evaluating the effective value of the electors' votes differently; it would in this way not be raised to the legal plane and therefore be legally permitted. Instead of this the parties here as well as there would – in relation to their unequal start – be granted chances which were in substance not unequal but exactly equal and accordingly the same support by the electors would also be requested. No objection could be raised against this to the effect that a barrier clause which was regional in this sense would in the formal method of consideration required by electoral law, lead to votes cast in the German Democratic Republic receiving greater weight in the framework of the proportional adjustment. A strict and formal equality corresponding with the democratic principle can only be restored in the face of the unequal starting point existing here by attaching formal equality to the actual reference area. The fact that - because of the dependence of the effective value of the vote on a determined share of the votes – in the one reference area more votes must be cast to attain this share of the votes than in the other does not lead to an infringement of equality if – as here – the reference areas are for their part formed according to the standpoint of equality.

2 Die bloße Regionalisierung einer Sperrklausel – ungeachtet ihrer Höhe – genügt allerdings hier den Anforderungen der Chancengleichheit noch nicht. Sie allein vermag die unterschiedlichen Startbedingungen bei dieser ersten gesamtdeutschen Wahl nicht hinreichend auszugleichen. Sie bestehen für die im Gebiet der Deutschen Demokratischen Republik zur Wahl antretenden Parteien und politischen Vereinigungen wie gezeigt darin, daß einige von ihnen im Wahlkampf – in mehr oder weniger starkem Maße – auf eine Ausstattung zurückzugreifen in der Lage sind, die ihnen in der Zeit der Parteidiktatur der SED aufzubauen möglich war, während andere, von dieser Diktatur verfolgt und unterdrückt, erst nach deren Sturz beginnen konnten, sich zu organisieren. Dieser auch in der mündlichen Verhandlung geltend gemachte Nachteil besteht für die letztgenannten Gruppierungen auch gegenüber allen im bisherigen Gebiet der Bundesrepublik Deutschland zur Wahl antretenden Parteien und politischen Vereinigungen. Er bedarf des Ausgleichs. Dafür bietet sich der in der Deutschen Demokratischen Republik in dem Gesetz über die Wahlen zur Volkskammer der Deutschen Demokratischen Republik am 18.3.1990 vom 20.2.1990 (GBl I, 60) und in dem Gesetz über die Wahlen zu den Landtagen in der Deutschen Demokratischen Republik vom 22.7.1990 (GBl I, 960) beschrittene Weg einer Listenvereinigung an. Macht der Gesetzgeber von dieser Möglichkeit für die Wahl zum 12. Deutschen Bundestag Gebrauch und gestattet er dementsprechend im Gebiet der Deutschen Demokratischen Republik Listenvereinigungen unter den für die Wahlen zu den Landtagen bestehenden gesetzlichen Voraussetzungen für Parteien und politische Vereinigungen, soweit sie oder ihre Landesverbände in dem Gebiet der Deutschen Demokratischen Republik ihren Sitz haben, so wird der Diskriminierung Rechnung getragen, denen nicht wenige jetzt in der Deutschen Demokratischen Republik sich betätigende Parteien und politische Vereinigungen in der Zeit der SED-Herrschaft ausgesetzt waren. Ihnen bleibt so auch erspart, sich im Blick auf die bevorstehende Bundestagswahl binnen kürzeste Frist um andere Organisationsformen bemühen zu müssen, die das Wahlrecht voraussetzt oder nahelegt. Solche, aus politischen Organisationen im Gebiet der Deutschen Demokratischen Republik gebildete Listenvereinigungen können im gesamten Wahlgebiet kandidieren.

2 The simple regionalisation of a barrier clause – without regard to its level – certainly does not yet satisfy the requirements of equality of chances. On its own it cannot sufficiently make up for the different starting conditions for this first election for the whole of Germany. They exist, for the parties and political alliances entering the election in the area of the German Democratic Republic, as has been shown by the fact that some of them are – to a greater or lesser degree – in a position in the election campaign to rely on resources which could build them up in the time of the party dictatorship of the SED whilst others, which were suppressed and persecuted by this dictatorship, were only able to begin to get organised for the first time after its overthrow. This disadvantage, which was also argued in the oral hearing, exists for the last mentioned groupings as against all parties and political alliances entering the election from the territory of the Federal Republic of Germany. It needs to be compensated for. For this purpose, the beaten path of a fusion of lists offers itself in the German Democratic Republic as in the Statute of 20.2.1990 (GBl I, 60) regarding the elections to the Peoples Chamber of the German Democratic Republic on 18.3.1990 and in the Statute of 22.7.1990 (GBl I, 960) regarding the elections to the State Parliaments in the German Democratic Republic. If the legislator makes use of this possibility for the election for the 12th Federal German Parliament and if he accordingly allows fusions of lists in the territory of the German Democratic Republic under the statutory conditions existing for parties and political alliances in respect of elections to the State Parliaments insofar as they or their State associations have their domicile in the territory of the German Democratic Republic, allowance will be made for the discrimination to which not a few of the parties and political alliances which are now active in the German Democratic Republic were exposed during the period of the SED dominance. They will therefore also be saved having to strive to adopt within the shortest period of time, with a view to the imminent Federal Parliament elections, other forms of organisation which electoral law presupposes or suggests. Such fusions of lists, formed from political organisations in the territory of the German Democratic Republic, can field candidates in the whole electoral area.

3 Das die Sperrklausel rechtfertigende Ziel bleibt auch bei einer so gearteten Regionalisierung, verbunden mit der Möglichkeit der Bildung von Listenvereinigungen durch im bisherigen Gebiet der Deutschen Demokratischen Republik tätige Parteien und politische Vereinigungen, gewahrt. Zwar werden auf diese Weise kleine Parteien nicht in gleichem Umfang von der Vertretung im Parlament ferngehalten wie bei einer einheitlichen, auf das Wahlgebiet bezogenen oder auch bei einer regionalisierten Sperrklausel ohne die Möglichkeit der Bildung von Listenvereinigungen. Indessen geht von einer solchen Regelung für die Wahl zum 12. Deutschen Bundestag – und nur sie ist Gegenstand der Beurteilung – durchaus noch eine wirksame Sperrwirkung aus. Der Gesetzgeber wäre auch in der Lage, die regionalisierte Sperrklausel im Blick auf die besondere Bedeutung der ersten gesamtdeutschen freien Wahl unterhalb von 5 v. H. anzusetzen; das ist ebenso eine Frage seiner Gestaltungsfreiheit wie die Entscheidung über das 'Ob' einer Sperrklausel (vgl. *BVerf GE* 4, 31 [40] = NJW 1954, 1601). Verwehrt wäre ihm allerdings - aus Gründen der Wahlrechtsgleichheit-, die regionalisierte Sperrklausel für die beiden Bezugsgebiete unterschiedlich festzulegen.

D Die Auslagenerstattung zugunsten der Bf. im Verfassungsbeschwerde-Verfahren ergibt sich aus § 34 a II BVerfGG.

Die Ast. in den Organstreitverfahren haben durch die Vorbereitung und Durchführung der Verfahren zur Klärung von Fragen grundsätzlicher Bedeutung beigetragen, die im Hinblick auf die erste gesamtdeutsche Wahl von besonderer verfassungrechtlicher Tragweite sind. Daher erschien es dem *Senat* billig, ausnahmsweise die Erstattung der Auslagen gem. § 34 a III BVerfGG anzuordnen.

E Aus dem Urteil ergibt sich, daß der Gesetzgeber neue wahlrechtliche Regelungen zu treffen hat. Dabei ist allerdings äußerst kurzfristiges Handeln geboten, denn der Gesetzgeber hat dafür zu sorgen, daß zwischen dem Zeitpunkt der Verkündung einer Neuregelung and den – gegebenenfalls zu ändernden – Terminen des Bundeswahlgesetzes den Parteien und politischen Vereinigungen der notwendige Zeitraum verbleibt, um sich auf die neue Gesetzeslage einzustellen.

Bundestag, Bundesrat und Bundesregierung haben in der mündlichen Verhandlung erklärt, sie seien bei Ergehen einer die Verfassungswidrigkeit der streitbefangenen Vorschriften feststellenden Entscheidung des *Senats* willens und in der Lage, rechtzeitig im Blick auf den vom Bundespräsidenten als Wahltag bestimmten 2.12.1990 die erforderlichen Änderungen des Bundeswahlgesetzes vorzunehmen. Davon geht der *Senat* aus. Er sieht deshalb im gegenwärtigen Zeitpunkt davon ab, durch Erlaß einer Anordnung nach § 35 BVerfGG selbst die rechtliche Grundlage für die Durchführung der Wahlen bereitzustellen.

F Diese Entscheidung ist einstimmig ergangen.

3 The objective which justifies the barrier clause remains protected even with a regionalisation formulated in this manner, combined with the possibility of forming fusions of lists by parties and political alliances active in what was until now the territory of the German Democratic Republic. In this way, small parties will certainly not be held back from representation in Parliament to the same extent as with a uniform barrier clause relating to the electoral area or even with a regionalised barrier clause, without the possibility of formation of fusion of lists. However, an effective barrier effect still arises from such a regime for the election for the 12th Federal Parliament – and only that is the subject of the judgment. The legislator would also be in a position to set the regionalised barrier clause at under 5% having regard to the special significance of the first free elections for the whole of Germany; that is just as much a question of his freedom in drafting as the decision about whether to have a barrier clause (compare *BVerfGE* 4, 31 [40] = NJW 1954, 1601). He would certainly be prevented - on the grounds of electoral law equality – from fixing the regionalised barrier clause at different levels for the two reference areas.

D The reimbursement of expenses in favour of the complainants in the constitutional complaint proceedings results from § 34 a II of the BVerfGG.

The applicants in the public institutions action have contributed, by the preparation and carrying through of proceedings, to the elucidation of questions of fundamental importance which are of special constitutional law importance with regard to the first election for the whole of Germany. It therefore seems fair to the *Senate* to order, by way of exception, the reimbursement of expenses in accordance with § 34 a III of the BVerfGG.

E It follows from the judgment that the legislator has to make new electoral law regulations. Very rapid action is of course required here, because the legislator has to take care that between the point in time of the announcement of a new regime and the deadlines of the Federal Elections Act – to be altered if necessary – the necessary time remains for the parties and political alliances to adapt to the new statutory position.

The Federal Parliament, the Federal Council and the Federal Government have explained in the oral hearing that they are, on issue of a decision by the *Senate* establishing the unconstitutionality of the provisions which are the subject of the dispute willing and in a position to undertake the necessary alterations to the Federal Elections Act in time, having regard to the election day of 2 December 1990 determined by the Federal President. The *Senate* is proceeding on this basis. At the present point in time it therefore refrains from providing the legal basis itself for the carrying through of the elections by issue of an order in accordance with § 35 of the BVerfGG.

F This decision is issued unanimously.

Other legislative bodies

IV Der Bundesrat

IVa Gemeinsamer Ausschuß

THE EXECUTIVE

The President

V Der Bundespräsident

Federal Government

VI Die Bundesregierung

LEGISLATION

The Federation and the States

VII Die Gesetzgebung des Bundes

Altering the Constitution

Art. 79 [Änderungen des Grundgesetzes] (1) Das Grundgesetz kann nur durch ein Gesetz geändert werden, das den Wortlaut des Grundgesetzes ausdrücklich ändert oder ergänzt. Bei völkerrechtlichen Verträgen, die eine Friedensregelung, die Vorbereitung einer Friedensregelung oder den Abbau einer besatzungsrechtlichen Ordnung zum Gegenstand haben oder der Verteidigung der Bundesrepublik zu dienen bestimmt sind, genügt zur Klarstellung, daß die Bestimmungen des Grundgesetzes dem Abschluß und dem Inkraftsetzen der Verträge nicht entgegenstehen, eine Ergänzung des Wortlautes des Grundgesetzes, die sich auf diese Klarstellung beschränkt.

(2) Ein solches Gesetz bedarf der Zustimmung von zwei Dritteln der Mitglieder des Bundestages und zwei Dritteln der Stimmen des Bundesrates.

(3) Eine Änderung dieses Grundgesetzes, durch welche die Gliederung des Bundes in Länder, die grundsätzliche Mitwirkung der Länder bei der Gesetzgebung oder die in den Artikeln 1 und 20 niedergelegten Grundsätze berührt werden, ist unzulässig.

(Articles 39–48 contain further provisions about the Federal Parliament. Article 49 is revoked.)

Other legislative bodies

IV Federal Council: Arts 50–53

IVa Common Committee: Art 53 a

THE EXECUTIVE

The President

V Federal President: Arts 54–61

Federal Government

VI Federal Government: Arts 62–69

LEGISLATION

The Federation and the States

VII Legislative Powers of the Federation

Articles 70–78 set out the legislative powers of the Federation and the States and certain procedural matters. It is a basic principle of legislative competence that it belongs to the States unless the Basic Law expressly says otherwise. In reality, however few legislative powers are left to the complete control of the States (in particular police law, construction control law, and education law).

Altering the Constitution

Article 79 [Changes in the Basic Law] (1) The Basic Law can only be changed by a statute which expressly alters or adds to the wording of the Basic Law. For international treaties which have as their objective a peaceful settlement, preparation for a peaceful settlement or the dismantling of an occupation regime or are intended to assist the defence of the Federal Republic, an addition to the wording of the Basic Law which is limited to an explanation that the provisions of the Basic Law are not opposed to the conclusion and coming into force of the treaties will suffice as such an explanation.

(2) Such a statute needs agreement of two thirds of the members of the Federal Parliament and two thirds of the votes of the Federal Council.

(3) A change of this Basic Law which affects the division of the Federation into States, the co-operation in principle of the States in legislation or the principles laid down in Arts 1 and 20 is not permitted.

Regulations

Art. 80 [Erlass von Rechtsverordnungen] (1) Durch Gesetz können die Bundesregierung, ein Bundesminister oder die Landesregierungen ermächtigt werden, Rechtsverordnungen zu erlassen. Dabei müssen Inhalt, Zweck und Ausmaß der erteilten Ermächtigung im Gesetze bestimmt werden. Die Rechtsgrundlage ist in der Verordnung anzugeben. Ist durch Gesetz vorgesehen, daß eine Ermächtigung weiter übertragen werden kann, so bedarf es zur Übertragung der Ermächtigung einer Rechtsverordnung.

(2) ...

(3) Der Bundesrat kann der Bundesregierung Vorlagen für den Erlaß von Rechtsverordnungen zuleiten, die seiner Zustimmung bedürfen.

(4) Soweit durch Bundesgesetz oder auf Grund von Bundesgesetzen Landesregierungen ermächtigt werden, Rechtsverordnungen zu erlassen, sind die Länder zu einer Regelung auch durch Gesetz befugt.

Special cases

...

Article 79(3) is a very important paragraph which ensures that no fundamental changes can take place in the Basic Law. Note that the only specific articles which are referred to are Arts 1 and 20, not Arts 1–20.

Regulations

Article 80 [Issue of regulations] (1) The Federal Government, a Federal Minister or the State governments can be authorised by statute to issue regulations. In this connection the content, purpose and extent of the authorisation granted must be determined in the statute. The legal basis must be stated in the regulation. If it is provided by statute that an authorisation can be further transferred, a regulation is needed for the transfer of the authorisation.

(Paragraph (2) states the cases in which the agreement of the Federal Council is needed for regulations.)

(3) The Federal Council can bring proposals for the making of regulations which need its agreement before the Federal Government.

(4) Insofar as State governments are empowered by a Federal statute or on the basis of Federal statutes to make regulations, the States are also authorised to regulate by statute.

The requirements of this article were considered in the investment aid act case: see Chapter Three, p 193. The purpose of the article was to restrict the use of regulations so as to avoid the abuse of this power which had occurred under the Weimar Republic and the Third Reich.

Special cases

(Articles 80 a and 81 contain special provisions regarding the declaration of a state of tension and passing of certain legislative proposals when a legislative emergency is declared.)

Coming into force

Art. 82 [Verkündung und Inkrafttreten der Gesetze] (1) Die nach den Vorschriften dieses Grundgesetzes zustande gekommenen Gesetze werden vom Bundespräsidenten nach Gegenzeichnung ausgefertigt und im Bundesgesetzblatte verkündet. Rechtsverordnungen werden von der Stelle, die sie erläßt, ausgefertigt und vorbehaltlich anderweitiger gesetzlicher Regelung im Bundesgesetzblatte verkündet.

(2) Jedes Gesetz und jede Rechtsverordnung soll den Tag des Inkrafttretens bestimmen. Fehlt eine solche Bestimmung, so treten sie mit dem vierzehnten Tage nach Ablauf des Tages in Kraft, an dem das Bundesgesezblatt ausgegeben worden ist.

ADMINISTRATION

VIII Die Ausführung der Bundesgesetze und die Bundesverwaltung

VIII a Gemeinschaftsaufgaben

THE JUDICIARY

The Courts

IX Die Rechtsprechung

Art. 92 [Gerichtsorganisation] Die rechsprechende Gewalt ist den Richtern anvertraut; sie wird durch das Bundesverfassungsgericht, durch die in diesem Grundgesetze vorgesehenen Bundesgerichte und durch die Gerichte der Länder ausgeübt.

Coming into force

Article 82 [Publication and coming into force of statutes] (1) Statutes which have come into existence in accordance with the provisions of this Basic Law will be, after counter-signature, signed by the Federal President and published in the *Federal Law Gazette*. Regulations will be signed by the authority which issues them and, subject to any other regulation by statute, published in the *Federal Law Gazette*.

(2) Every statute and every regulation shall determine the day when it is to come into force. In the absence of such a determination, they come into force on the 14th day after the end of the day in which the *Federal Law Gazette* has been issued.

ADMINISTRATION

VIII The implementation of the Federal statutes and the Federal administration (Arts 83–91)

VIII a Cooperative tasks (Arts 91 a and 91 b)

THE JUDICIARY

The Courts

IX The administration of justice

Article 92 [Organisation of the courts] The judicial power is entrusted to the judges; it is to be exercised by the Federal Constitutional Court, by the Federal courts provided for in this Basic Law and by the courts of the States.

Federal Constitutional Court

Art. 93 [Bundesverfassungsgericht, Zuständigkeit] (1) Das Bundesverfassungsgericht entscheidet:

1 über die Auslegung dieses Grundgesetzes aus Anlaß von Streitigkeiten über den Umfang der Rechte und Pflichten eines obersten Bundesorgans oder anderer Beteiligter, die durch dieses Grundgesetz oder in der Geschäftsordnung eines obersten Bundesorgans mit eigenen Rechten ausgestattet sind;

2 bei Meinungsverschiedenheiten oder Zweifeln über die förmliche und sachliche Vereinbarkeit von Bundesrecht oder Landesrecht mit diesem Grundgesetze oder die Vereinbarkeit von Landesrecht mit sonstigem Bundesrechte auf Antrag der Bundesregierung, einer Landesregierung oder eines Drittels der Mitglieder des Bundestages;

2 a bei Meinungsverschiedenheiten, ob ein Gesetz den Voraussetzungen des Artikels 72 Abs. 2 entspricht, auf Antrag des Bundesrates, einer Landesregierung oder der Volksvertretung eines Landes;

3 bei Meinungsverschiedenheiten über Rechte und Pflichten des Bundes und der Länder, insbesondere bei der Ausführung von Bundesrecht durch die Länder und bei der Ausübung der Bundesaufsicht;

Federal Constitutional Court

The Constitution, said Chief Justice Hughes, is what the judges say it is. The Federal Constitutional Court has had a very important role in developing the Basic Law by its decisions. It is made up of two senates of eight judges, one of which considers legal issues, including the Basic Rights, and the other deals with disputes between the organs of government.

Although many of this court's decisions are of a political nature, either in the narrow or the broad sense of the word, and the judges are chosen by the legislature, their independence is regarded as very important. In a speech at Wetzlar in 1993, to commemorate the first sitting there of the Reichskammergericht 300 years before, Professor Dr Roman Herzog, President of the Federal Constitutional Court, commented on this issue. He said that the non-partisan nature and independence of the court in their present form were a result of the achievements of the 18th and (largely) the 19th centuries. There were always critics of the procedure for choosing judges, and there was room for improvement in it. Nevertheless, he had never known of a judge having been chosen for the court on the 'ticket' of one of the large parties and who therefore advocated their policies in the court's deliberations. However, he acknowledged that each judge brought with him his basic ideological principles and these of course also approximated to a greater or lesser degree to those of a particular party. See 'Cold neutrality? A comparison of the standards of the House of Lords with those of the German Federal Constitutional Court' (2000) 20 OJLS 391.

Article 93 [Federal Constitutional Court: competence] The Federal Constitutional Court decides:

1 on the interpretation of this Basic Law on the occasion of disputes about the scope of the rights and duties of an upper Federal organ or other parties involved provided by their own rights by this Basic Law or in the standing orders of an upper Federal organ;

2 on differences of opinion or doubts about the formal and substantive compatibility of Federal law or State law with this Basic Law or the compatibility of State law with other Federal law, on a proposal from the Federal Government, a State government or a third of the members of the Federal Parliament;

2 a on differences of opinion as to whether a statute corresponds to the prerequisites of Art 72 para 2, on the application of the Federal Council, a State government or the legislature of a State;

3 on differences of opinion about rights and duties of the Federation and the States, in particular on the execution of Federal law by the States and on the exercise of Federal supervision;

4 in anderen öffentlich-rechtlichen Streitigkeiten zwischen dem Bunde und den Ländern, zwischen verschiedenen Ländern oder innerhalb eines Landes, soweit nicht ein anderer Rechtsweg gegeben ist;

4 a über Verfassungsbeschwerden, die von jedermann mit der Behauptung erhoben werden können, durch die öffentliche Gewalt in einem seiner Grundrechte oder in einem seiner in Artikel 20 Abs. 4, 33, 38, 101, 103 und 104 enthaltenen Rechte verletzt zu sein;

4 b über Verfassungsbeschwerden von Gemeinden und Gemeindeverbänden wegen Verletzung des Rechts auf Selbstverwaltung nach Artikel 28 durch ein Gesetz, bei Landesgesetzen jedoch nur, soweit nicht Beschwerde beim Landesverfassungsgericht erhoben werden kann;

5 in den übrigen in diesem Grundgesetze vorgesehenen Fällen.

(2) Das Bundesverfassungsgericht wird ferner in den ihm sonst durch Bundesgesetz zugewiesenen Fällen tätig.

Art. 94 [Bundesverfassungsgericht, Zusammensetzung] (1) Das Bundesverfassungsgericht besteht aus Bundesrichtern und anderen Mitgliedern. Die Mitglieder des Bundesverfassungsgerichtes werden je zur Hälfte vom Bundestage und vom Bundesrate gewählt. Sie dürfen weder dem Bundestage, dem Bundesrate, der Bundesregierung noch entsprechenden Organen eines Landes angehören.

(2) Ein Bundesgesetz regelt seine Verfassung und das Verfahren und bestimmt, in welchen Fällen seine Entscheidungen Gesetzeskraft haben. Es kann für Verfassungsbeschwerden die vorherige Erschöpfung des Rechtsweges zur Voraussetzung machen und ein besonderes Annahmeverfahren vorsehen.

4 in other public law disputes between the Federation and the States, between the different States or within a State, insofar as another legal remedy is not provided;

4 a on constitutional complaints which can be commenced by anyone who asserts that one of his Basic Rights or one of his rights contained in Art 20 paras 4, 33, 38, 101, 103 and 104 has been violated by the exercise of public authority;

4 b on constitutional complaints by communities and associations of communities because of violation by a statute of the right of self-government in accordance with Art 28; but in the case of State statutes, only insofar as a complaint cannot be made to the State Constitutional Court;

5 in the other cases provided for in this Basic Law.

(2) The Federal Constitutional Court will also act in the other cases assigned to it by Federal statute.

Paragraph 4a of this article, which in theory, relates to any action by the executive, the judiciary or the legislature, must obviously be subject to limitations, or it would be used too extensively. The complainant must normally exhaust all other remedies available to him before resorting to the constitutional complaint (see Art 94 II, below) although this may be relaxed in cases of great importance or urgency. The complainant must also have *locus standi* in the sense that he must be personally affected. Further, in the case of an administrative act, it must be addressed to him; in the case of a legislative act, it must normally have been applied to his disadvantage by a court or administrative authority (but see, eg, BVerfGE 10, 59, 66); and in the case of a judicial act it must be a sufficiently substantial infringement (see, eg, BVerfGE 18, 85, 92 and onwards).

Article 94 [Federal Constitutional Court: composition] (1) The Federal Constitutional Court will consist of Federal judges and other members. The members of the Federal Constitutional Court will be chosen as to one half by the Federal Parliament and as to the other half by the Federal Council. They may not belong to the Federal Parliament, the Federal Council or the Federal Government nor to corresponding bodies of a State.

(2) A Federal statute will regulate its constitution and procedure and will determine in which cases its decisions are to have the authority of law. It can make the prior exhaustion of legal remedies a pre-condition for constitutional complaints and provide for a special procedure as to admissibility.

Federal Courts

Art. 95 [Oberste Bundesgerichtshöfe] (1) Für die Gebiete der ordentlichen, der Verwaltungs-, der Finanz-, der Arbeits- und der Sozialgerichtsbarkeit errichtet der Bund als oberste Gerichtshöfe den Bundesgerichtshof, das Bundesverwaltungsgericht, den Bundesfinanzhof, das Bundesarbeitsgericht und das Bundessozialgericht.

(2) Über die Berufung der Richter dieser Gerichte entscheidet der für das jeweilige Sachgebiet zuständige Bundesminister gemeinsam mit einem Richterwahlausschuß, der aus den für das jeweilige Sachgebiet zuständigen Ministern der Länder und einer gleichen Anzahl von Mitgliedern besteht, die vom Bundestage gewählt werden.

(3) Zur Wahrung der Einheitlichkeit der Rechtsprechung ist ein Gemeinsamer Senat der in Absatz 1 genannten Gerichte zu bilden. Das Nähere regelt ein Bundesgesetz.

Art. 96 [Bundesgerichte] (1) Der Bund kann für Angelegenheiten des gewerblichen Rechtsschutzes ein Bundesgericht errichten.

(2) Der Bund kann Wehrstrafgerichte für die Streitkräfte als Bundesgerichte errichten. Sie können die Strafgerichtsbarkeit nur im Verteidigungsfalle sowie über Angehörige der Streitkräfte ausüben, die in das Ausland entsandt oder an Bord von Kriegsschiffen eingeschifft sind. Das Nähere regelt ein Bundesgesetz. Diese Gerichte gehören zum Geschäftsbereich des Bundesjustizministers. Ihre hauptamtlichen Richter müssen die Befähigung zum Richteramt haben.

(3) Oberster Gerichtshof für die in Absatz 1 und 2 genannten Gerichte ist der Bundesgerichtshof.

(4) Der Bund kann für Personen, die zu ihm in einem öffentlich-rechtlichen Dienstverhältnis stehen, Bundesgerichte zur Entscheidung in Disziplinarverfahren und Beschwerdeverfahren errichten.

(5) Für Strafverfahren auf den Gebieten des Artikels 26 Abs. 1 und des Staatsschutzes kann ein Bundesgesetz mit Zustimmung des Bundesrates vorsehen, daß Gerichte der Länder Gerichtsbarkeit des Bundes ausüben.

Judges

Art. 97 [Unabhängigkeit der Richter] (1) Die Richter sind unabhängig und nur dem Gesetze unterworfen.

Federal Courts

Article 95 [Upper Federal Courts] (1) For the areas of ordinary, administrative, revenue, employment and social jurisdiction, the Federation will set up as upper courts the Federal Supreme Court, the Federal Administrative Court, the Federal Revenue Court, the Federal Labour Court and the Federal Social Court.

(2) Decisions on the appointment of the judges for these courts will be made by the competent Federal Minister for the actual subject area together with a Judicial Appointments Committee which will consist of the ministers of the States who are competent for the actual subject area and an equal number of members who will be selected by the Federal Parliament.

(3) For the preservation of unity in case law, a common senate is to be formed of the courts mentioned in para 1. Details will be regulated by a Federal statute.

Article 96 [Federal Courts] (1) The Federation can establish a Federal Court for protection of industrial property rights.

(2) The Federation can establish as Federal courts military criminal courts for the armed forces. They can exercise criminal jurisdiction only in a state of defence[3] or in respect of members of the armed forces which are sent to foreign countries or are on board warships. Details will be regulated by a Federal statute. These courts belong to the area of responsibility of the Federal Justice Minister. Their full time judges must have qualification for judicial office.

(3) The highest court for the courts mentioned in paras 1 and 2 is the Federal Supreme Court.

(4) The Federation can establish Federal courts for decisions in disciplinary proceedings and complaint proceedings for persons who are in a public law service relationship to it.

(5) For criminal proceedings in the areas of Art 26 para 1 and State protection a Federal statute can provide, with the agreement of the Federal Council, that courts of the States exercise the jurisdiction of the Federation.

Judges

Article 97 [Independence of the judges] (1) The judges are independent and subject only to law.

---

3   See footnote 1 to Art 12 a, Chapter Three, p 187.

(2) Die hauptamtlich und planmäßig endgültig angestellten Richter können wider ihren Willen nur kraft richterlicher Entscheidung und nur aus Gründen und unter den Formen, welche die Gesetze bestimmen, vor Ablauf ihrer Amtszeit entlassen oder dauernd oder zeitweise ihres Amtes enthoben oder an eine andere Stelle oder in den Ruhestand versetzt werden. Die Gesetzgebung kann Altersgrenzen festsetzen, bei deren Erreichung auf Lebenszeit angestellte Richter in den Ruhestand treten. Bei Veränderung der Einrichtung der Gerichte oder ihrer Bezirke können Richter an ein anderes Gericht versetzt oder aus dem Amte entfernt werden, jedoch nur unter Belassung des vollen Gehaltes.

Art. 98 [Rechtsstellung der Richter] (1) Die Rechtstellung der Bundesrichter ist durch besonderes Bundegesetz zu regeln.

(2) Wenn ein Bundesrichter im Amte oder außerhalb des Amtes gegen die Grundsätze des Grundgesetzes oder gegen die verfassungsmäßige Ordnung eines Landes verstößt, so kann das Bundesverfassungsgericht mit Zweidrittelmehrheit auf Antrag des Bundestages anordnen, das der Richter in ein anderes Amt oder in den Ruhestand zu versetzen ist. Im Falle eines vorsätzlichen Verstoßes kann auf Entlassung erkannt werden.

(3) Die Rechtsstellung der Richter in den Ländern ist durch besondere Landesgesetze zu regeln. Der Bund kann Rahmenvorschriften erlassen, soweit Artikel 74 a Abs. 4 nichts anderes bestimmt.

(4) Die Länder können bestimmen, daß über die Anstellung der Richter in den Ländern der Landesjustizminister gemeinsam mit einem Richterwahlausschuß entscheidet.

(5) Die Länder können für Landesrichter eine Absatz 2 entsprechende Regelung treffen. Geltendes Landesverfassungsrecht bleibt unberührt. Die Entscheidung über eine Richteranklage steht dem Bundesverfassungsgericht zu.

Constitutional issues

Art. 99 [Verfassungsstreit innerhalb eines Landes] Dem Bundesverfassungsgerichte kann durch Landesgesetz die Entscheidung von Verfassungsstreitigkeiten innerhalb eines Landes, den in Artikel 95 Abs. 1 genannten obersten Gerichtshöfen für den letzten Rechtszug die Entscheidung in solchen Sachen zugewiesen werden, bei denen es sich um die Anwendung von Landesrecht handelt.

(2) The full time judges who are systematically and permanently employed can only be dismissed or permanently or temporarily relieved of their office or removed to another post or retired early against their will before the expiry of their period of office by virtue of a judicial decision and only for reasons and with the formalities determined by statute law. Legislation can set age limits on which judges who are employed for life will retire. On a change of the arrangement of the courts or their areas, judges can be transferred to another court or be removed from office but only on the basis that they continue to receive full salary.

Article 98 [Legal position of judges] (1) The legal position of Federal judges is to be regulated by a special Federal statute.

(2) If a Federal judge in office or out of office violates the principles of the Basic Law or the constitutional order of a State, the Federal constitutional Court can, on a proposal from the Federal Parliament, by a two thirds majority, order the judge to be transferred to another office or compulsorily retired. In the case of an intentional violation, dismissal can be ordered.

(3) The legal position of judges in the States is to be regulated by special State statutes. The Federation can issue framework provisions insofar as Art 74 a para 4 does not provide otherwise.

(4) The States can decide that the State Justice Minister will make decisions about the appointment of judges in the States together with a Judicial Appointments Committee.

(5) The States can make a provision corresponding to para 2 for State judges. Applicable State constitutional law remains unaffected. The decision on the impeachment of a judge is for the Federal Constitutional Court.

Constitutional issues

Article 99 [Constitutional conflict within a State] The resolution of constitutional disputes within a State can be referred by a State statute to the Federal Constitutional Court and the resolution of those matters which concern the application of State law can be referred in the last resort to the upper courts mentioned in Art 95 para 1.

Art. 100 [Verfassungswidrigkeit von Gesetzen] (1) Hält ein Gericht ein Gesetz, auf dessen Gültigkeit es bei der Entscheidung ankommt, für verfassungswidrig, so ist das Verfahren auszusetzen und, wenn es sich um die Verletzung der Verfassung eines Landes handelt, die Entscheidung des für Verfassungsstreitigkeiten zuständigen Gerichtes des Landes, wenn es sich um die Verletzung dieses Grundgesetzes handelt, die Entscheidung des Bundesverfassungsgerichtes einzuholen. Dies gilt auch, wenn es sich um die Verletzung dieses Grundgesetzes durch Landesrecht oder um die Unvereinbarkeit eines Landesgesetzes mit einem Bundesgesetze handelt.

(2) Ist in einem Rechtsstreite zweifelhaft, ob eine Regel des Völkerrechtes Bestandteil des Bundesrechtes ist und ob sie unmittelbar Rechte und Pflichten für den Einzelnen erzeugt (Artikel 25), so hat das Gericht die Entscheidung des Bundesverfassungsgerichtes einzuholen.

(3) Will das Verfassungsgericht eines Landes bei der Auslegung des Grundgesetzes von einer Entscheidung des Bundesverfassungsgerichtes oder des Verfassungsgerichtes eines anderen Landes abweichen, so hat das Verfassungsgericht die Entscheidung des Bundesverfassungsgerichtes einzuholen.

Special courts

Art. 101 [Ausnahmegerichte] (1) Ausnahmegerichte sind unzulässig. Niemand darf seinem gesetzlichen Richter entzogen werden.

(2) Gerichte für besondere Sachgebiete können nur durch Gesetz errichtet werden.

Criminal law and the right to be heard

Art. 102 [Abschaffung der Todesstrafe] Die Todesstrafe ist abgeschafft.

Art. 103 [Grundrechte des Angeklagten] (1) Vor Gericht hat jedermann Anspruch auf rechtliches Gehör.

(2) Eine Tat kann nur bestraft werden, wenn die Strafbarkeit gesetzlich bestimmt war, bevor die Tat begangen wurde.

(3) Niemand darf wegen derselben Tat auf Grund der allegemeinen Strafgesetze mehrmals bestraft werden.

Article 100 [Unconstitutionality of statutes] (1) If a court holds a statute, the validity of which is at issue in a decision, to be unconstitutional, proceedings must be suspended, and if it concerns the violation of the Constitution of a State, the decision of the court of the State which is competent for constitutional disputes must be sought, and if it concerns the violation of this Basic Law, the decision of the Federal Constitutional Court is to be sought. This also applies if it concerns the violation of this Basic Law by State law or the irreconcilability of a State statute with a Federal statute.

(2) If in a legal dispute it is in doubt whether a rule of international law is a constituent part of Federal law and whether it creates direct rights and duties for the individual (Art 25), the court must seek the decision of the Federal Constitutional Court.

(3) If the constitutional court of a State wants to deviate in the interpretation of the Basic Law from a decision of the Federal Constitutional Court or the constitutional court of another State, the constitutional court must seek the decision of the Federal Constitutional Court.

Special courts

Article 101 [Extraordinary courts] (1) Extraordinary courts are not permitted. No-one may be deprived of his access to a statutory judge.

(2) Courts for special subject areas can only be set up by statute.

The Wünsche Handelsgesellschaft or Solange II case (BVerfGE 52, 178; [1987] 3 CMLR 225) decided that the European Court of Justice was a statutory court for the purpose of para 1 sentence 2 of this article, and access could therefore be claimed to it within the appropriate limits. What would be the implications in German law, therefore, of a refusal to make a reference to the European Court of Justice under Art 234 of the European Community Treaty?

Criminal law and the right to be heard

Article 102 [Abolition of the death penalty] The death penalty is abolished.

Article 103 [Basic rights of a defendant] (1) Everyone has a claim to a legal hearing before a court.

(2) An act can only be punished if its criminality was determined by statute before the act was committed.

(3) No-one may be punished several times because of the same act on the basis of general criminal statutes.

The effect of para 2 was an issue in the shootings at the Berlin wall case: see Chapter Seven, p 621 and onwards.

Freedom

Art. 104 [Rechtsgarantien bei Freiheitsentziehung] (1) Die Freiheit der Person kann nur auf Grund eines förmlichen Gesetzes und nur unter Beachtung der darin vorgeschriebenen Formen beschränkt werden. Festgehaltene Personen dürfen weder seelisch noch körperlich mißhandelt werden.

(2) Über die Zulässigkeit und Fortdauer einer Freiheitsentziehung hat nur der Richter zu entscheiden. Bei jeder nicht auf richterlicher Anordnung beruhenden Freiheitsentziehung ist unverzüglich eine richterliche Entscheidung herbeizuführen. Die Polizei darf aus eigener Machtvollkommenheit niemanden länger als bis zum Ende des Tages nach dem Ergreifen in eigenem Gewahrsam halten. Das Nähere ist gesetzlich zu regeln.

(3) Jeder wegen des Verdachtes einer strafbaren Handlung vorläufig Festgenommene ist spätestens am Tage nach der Festnahme dem Richter vorzuführen, der ihm die Gründe der Festnahme mitzuteilen, ihn zu vernehmen und ihm Gelegenheit zu Einwendungen zu geben hat. Der Richter hat unverzüglich entweder einen mit Gründen versehenen schriftlichen Haftbefehl zu erlassen oder die Freilassung anzuordnen.

(4) Von jeder richterlichen Entscheidung über die Anordnung oder Fortdauer einer Freiheitsentziehung ist unverzüglich ein Angehöriger des Festgehaltenen oder eine Person seines Vertrauens zu benachrichtigen.

FINANCE

X Das Finanzwesen

DEFENCE

X a Verteidigungsfall

Freedom

Article 104 [Legal guarantees on deprivation of freedom] (1) Freedom of the person can only be restricted on the basis of a formal statute and only having regard to the formalities prescribed therein. Detained persons may not be ill-treated either mentally or bodily.

(2) Only a judge must decide on the permissibility and continuation of a deprivation of freedom. A judicial decision must be made without delay in respect of any deprivation of freedom which is not based on a judicial order. The police are not, on the basis of their own authority, permitted to detain anyone in their own custody for a longer period than to the end of the day after the apprehension. Details are to be regulated by statute.

(3) Every person who has been provisionally arrested on suspicion of a criminal act is to be brought, at the latest on the day after the arrest, before a judge who must communicate to him the reasons for the arrest, interrogate him and give him the opportunity to make objections. The judge must immediately either order the issue of a written arrest warrant, including reasons, or order his release.

(4) Every judicial decision about an order for, or the continuation of, a deprivation of freedom is to be notified without delay to a relative of the arrested person or a person whom he trusts.

FINANCE

X Finance
(Arts 104 a–115)

DEFENCE

X a Defence
(Arts 115 a–115 l)

TRANSITIONAL AND FINAL PROVISIONS

XI Übergangs- und Schlußbestimmungen

Art. 143 [Abweichungen von Bestimmungen des Grundgesetz als Übergangsrecht] (1) Recht in dem in Artikel 3 des Einigungsvertrags genannten Gebiet kann längstens bis zum 31. Dezember 1992 von Bestimmungen dieses Grundgesetzes abweichen, soweit und solange infolge der unterschiedlichen Verhältnisse die völlige Anpassung an die grundgesetzliche Ordnung noch nicht erreicht werden kann. Abweichungen dürfen nicht gegen Artikel 19 Abs. 2 verstoßen und müssen mit den in Artikel 79 Abs. 3 genannten Grundsätzen vereinbar sein.

(2) Abweichungen von den Abschnitten II, VIII, VIII a, IX, X und XI sind längstens bis zum 31. Dezember 1995 zulässig.

(3) Unabhängig von Absatz 1 und 2 haben Artikel 41 des Einigungsvertrags und Regelungen zu seiner Durchführung auch insoweit Bestand, als sie vorsehen, daß Eingriffe in das Eigentum auf dem in Artikel 3 dieses Vertrags genannten Gebiet nicht mehr rückgängig gemacht werden.

Art. 144 [Ratifizierung des Grundgesetzes] (1) Dieses Grundgesetz bedarf der Annahme durch die Volksvertretungen in zwei Dritteln der deutschen Länder, in denen es zunächst gelten soll.

(2) Soweit die Anwendung dieses Grundgesetzes in einem der in Artikel 23 aufgeführten Länder oder in einem Teile eines dieser Länder Beschränkungen unterliegt, hat das Land oder der Teil des Landes das Recht, gemäß Artikel 38 Vertreter in den Bundestag und gemäß Artikel 50 Vertreter in den Bundesrat zu entsenden.

Art. 145 [Verkündung des Grundgesetzes] (1) Der Parlamentarische Rat stellt in öffentlicher Sitzung unter Mitwirkung der Abgeordneten Groß-Berlins die Annahme dieses Grundgesetzes fest, fertigt es aus und verkündet es.

(2) Dieses Grundgesetz tritt mit Ablauf des Tages der Verkündung in Kraft.

(3) Es ist im Bundesgesetzblatte zu veröffentlichen.

TRANSITIONAL AND FINAL PROVISIONS

XI Transitional and final provisions

(Articles 116–142)

This section of the Basic Law contains a number of miscellaneous provisions, in particular on German nationality (Art 116) fugitives and exiles (Art 119) the continuing validity of old law (Art 123 and onwards) and the continuing validity of certain articles of the Weimar Constitution relating to religious matters (Art 140).

Article 143 [Deviations from the provisions of the Basic Law as transitional law] (1) Law in the territory mentioned in Art 3 of the Unification Treaty can deviate from provisions of this Basic Law until 31 December 1992 at the latest, insofar as complete adjustment to the Basic Law order cannot yet be reached as a consequence of the differing circumstances. Deviations are not permitted to violate Art 19 para 2 and must be reconcilable with the principles mentioned in Art 79 para 3.

(2) Deviations from Sections II, VIII, VIII a, IX, X and XI are permissible until 31 December 1995 at the latest.

(3) Independently of paragraphs 1 and 2, Art 41 of the Unification Treaty and the rules for its implementation are to remain in effect insofar as they provide that interferences with property in the territory mentioned in Art 3 of this Treaty are no longer to be revoked.

Article 144 [Ratification of the Basic Law] (1) This Basic Law needs to be accepted by representative assemblies in two thirds of the German States in which it is, for the time being, to be effective.

(2) Insofar as the application of this Basic Law is subject to limitations in one of the States listed in Art 23[4] or in a part of one of these States, the State or the part of the State has the right to send representatives in accordance with Art 38 to the Federal Parliament and in accordance with Art 50 to the Federal Council.

Article 145 [Publication of the Basic Law] (1) The Parliamentary Council in open session with the cooperation of the deputies from Great Berlin will confirm the acceptance of this Basic Law, sign it and publish it.

(2) This Basic Law comes into effect at the end of the day of publication.

(3) It is to be published in the *Federal Law Gazette*.

---

4   The reference here is to the old form of Art 23: see the comment immediately following the new form of this article at p 15.

Art. 146 [Geltungsdauer des Grundgestezes] Dieses Grundgesetz, das nach Vollendung der Einheit und Freiheit Deutschlands für das gesamte deutsche Volk gilt, verliert seine Gültigkeit an dem Tage, an dem eine Verfassung in Kraft tritt, die von dem deutschen Volke in freier Entscheidung beschlossen worden ist.

Article 146 [Period of validity of the Basic Law] This Basic Law, which applies after the completion of the unity and freedom of Germany for all the German people, will lose its validity on the day in which a Constitution comes into effect which has been determined by a free decision of the German people.

CHAPTER THREE

HUMAN RIGHTS

INTRODUCTION

This is a difficult subject conceptually for the English law student. The Basic Rights are what we would call human rights, and the English approach to human rights is that people have the right to do what the law does not prevent them from doing. In England, a law which deprived a person of what legal theorists would regard as human right would be construed as far as possible in that person's favour. But the limitations here are significant: there is no authoritative definition of a human right; and rules of construction cannot achieve much in the face of clear wording. Even the European Convention of Human Rights is only an aid to construction in English law. (The Convention has been incorporated into German law, but only as ordinary statute law. It does not therefore have the status of constitutional law, nor even, possibly, of public international law under Art 25 of the Basic Law.)

Because the Basic Rights are part of the Constitution, the Federal Constitutional Court can declare legislation invalid if it contravenes these rights. The executive and the judiciary are also bound by them.

Nature of Basic Rights

The Basic Rights are rights of persons that the State shall refrain from doing in certain things. The Basic Rights may also have positive aspects, ie, the person benefiting may have the right to claim action by the State in his favour. This may be implied; or it may be express: see Art 6 IV.

Sometimes two or more Basic Rights appear to apply to a situation. It will then sometimes be a question of deciding which is the more or the most specialised – although this is often a difficult question to answer! But sometimes the situation will be due to a potential conflict, and it is then a question of deciding which shall prevail: see, for instance, the film director case (Chapter Six, p 505).

Who can claim Basic Rights?

(a) Nationality

There are certain rights such as freedom of assembly (Art 8), freedom of association (Art 9), freedom of movement (Art 11) and freedom of vocation (Art 12) which are for Germans alone. But most of the Basic Rights can be claimed by anyone.

(b) Age

Minors are just as entitled to Basic Rights as adults; but there are obvious practical problems. A child must be represented by its parents in court proceedings, including those in which Basic Rights become relevant. And parents have a right to bring up their children, which is protected by Art 6 II. Conflicts between the child and its parents may need to be resolved by the Guardianship Court.

(c) Corporate bodies

Private bodies (if German) can rely on appropriate Basic Rights, eg, Arts. 3 and 14: see Art 19 III and in particular the investment aid act case at p 193; but public bodies cannot use Basic Rights unless this is specifically provided for. There are however Basic Rights in relation to court proceedings which may benefit corporate bodies generally. See on this issue BVerfGE 68, 193 (guilds).

Against whom can Basic Rights be claimed?

(a) Direct effect

The Basic Rights bind all State authorities, including those of the individual States. (The States will also be bound by their own Basic Rights: these must be consistent with the Federal Basic Rights, ie, they can be wider but must not be narrower. In practice they are not usually very important.) The rights can therefore be claimed against anyone in authority.

(b) Secondary effect

There is however argument as to the extent to which the Basic Rights may have a secondary effect in the realm of private law. It is claimed that they are, in principle, operative against the State, but they are also values which penetrate private law, especially its vaguer concepts like good morals and good faith. There are practical difficulties about the application of this, however. And there is also the question of what happens when the State is acting like a private organisation: is this another case of secondary effect of the Basic Rights?

An alternative view is that the Basic Rights only bind those in authority, but this includes the judges, even when they are deciding private law issues. There is an interesting parallel here with the principle of indirect effect of European Community Directives: see *Von Colson v Land Nordrhein Westfalen* (Case 14/83) [1986] 2 CMLR 430; and *Harz v Deutsche Tradex GmbH* (Case 79/83) [1986] 2 CMLR 430. These cases were based on the requirement of Art 5 of the European Community Treaty that Member States should take all appropriate measures to ensure fulfilment of their Community obligations. The European Court of Justice said this included an obligation on the national courts to interpret the provisions of national law in such a way as to ensure that the provisions of a Directive, which has not been implemented but should have been, are achieved.

The film director case (Chapter Six, p 505) provides a good example of this principle. The Federal Constitutional Court decisions BGH NJW 1994, 1278, BGH NJW 1994, 1341 and BGH NJW 1995, 592 shows how contract law may also be affected.

Limitations on the Basic Rights

(a) Generally

The starting point is an assumption that the individual is free to do what is not expressly forbidden.

Occasionally there will be a limitation on this in the Basic Rights themselves.

In other cases it is left to the legislator to make limitations. Frequently, the relevant article will say this is only to be done on the basis of a statute. This does not exclude the possibility of an exception being made by regulations or bye-laws, provided they are made on the basis of a statute. (In the case, however, of Art 104 (right to personal freedom) (see Chapter Two, p 99) limitations can only be made by a formal statute.)

(b) Basic Rights without the 'statutory reservation'

If the Basic Right does not even provide for a limitation, can the power to make a statute-based one be assumed? Sometimes the absence is obviously intended, as with Art 1: right to human dignity. But in other cases, the opposite would seem to be appropriate, eg, Art 12 I: choice of a vocation. Can the reservation be implied?

The Federal Constitutional Court says that such Basic Rights can only be limited in individual relationships by conflicting Basic Rights of third parties and other legal values invested with constitutional status, eg, State security (having regard to the unity of the Constitution and the total order of values protected by it). To this extent, there can be an unwritten 'statutory reservation'.

(c) Basic Rights with the 'statutory reservation'

Even here the legislator's powers are not unlimited. Statutes must be valid, and must comply with Art 19. Article 19 I imposes procedural requirements, and Art 19 II contains a substantive requirement. This is after the Basic Right has been invaded, a central core must be left. There is much academic argument about what this can be: see the allusion to this concept in the East German politicians trial publicity cases, p 153. Whatever the concept may mean, however, its importance is dwarfed by the principle of proportionality.

THE PRINCIPLE OF PROPORTIONALITY

Status in English law

The concept of proportionality has become known to English lawyers through the medium of European Community law. European Community law took it, of course, from German law: see the European Court of Justice decision in *Internationale Handelsgesellschaft GmbH v EV St* (Case 11/70) [1972] CMLR 255. The interesting issue in English law is whether there is any prospect of it being extended to areas of English law in which European Community law plays no part. The suggestion was received with some sympathy in *Council of Civil Service Unions v Minister for the Civil Service* [1984] 3 All ER 935; but not in *R v Secretary of State for the Home Department ex p Brind* [1991] 1 All ER 720.

Status in German law

The principle of proportionality is not expressly set out in the Basic Law, but it governs the amount of the core which must be left in a Basic Right. The Federal Constitutional Court regards it as inherent in the Constitutional State principle and the nature of the Basic Rights themselves. It is applied to laws themselves, but may also be applied to the way in which those laws are implemented.

It is made of three parts:

(a) Appropriateness

The law must be appropriate for attaining its objective. The Federal Constitutional Court decided that it was inappropriate for the legislator to require a falconer to have technical knowledge about weapons, when he used none (BVerfGE 55, 159).

(b) Necessity

The law must be necessary for attaining its objective, and not go too far: see the arrested admiral case, below.

(c) Balancing

The purpose and method of the law should be weighed against each other: they should not be out of proportion to each other. This requirement is the one which is most commonly breached. The legislator might make serious interferences with liberty for a comparatively trivial purpose. Would a significant reduction in the interference possibly only result in an insignificant effect on the desired consequences? In a case about a ban on the bringing into circulation of food which might be confused with chocolate, the Federal Constitutional Court said a strict labelling requirement would have sufficed (BVerfGE 53, 135). The similarity with European Court of Justice cases such as *Rewe-Zentral AG v Bundesmonopolverwaltung für Branntwein (Cassis de Dijon)* (Case 120/78) [1979] 3 CMLR 494 is striking.

Notice how the principle of proportionality is applied in deciding how the law of the German Democratic Republic should be interpreted in the shootings at the Berlin Wall case: Chapter Seven, p 621 and onwards.

THE ARRESTED ADMIRAL CASE

BVerfGE Band 19 S. 342

39 Nach dem verfassungsrechtlichen Grundsatz der Verhältnismäßigkeit ist auch bei einem auf § 112 Abs. 4 StPO gestützten Haftbefehl eine Haftverschonung in entsprechender Anwendung des § 116 StPO möglich.

> Beschluß des Ersten Senats vom 15. Dezember 1965
>
> – 1 BvR 513/65 –
>
> in dem Verfahren über die Verfassungsbeschwerde des Admirals a.D. ... – Bevollmächtigte: Rechtsanwälte ... – gegen 1. den Haftbefehl des Landgerichts Hamburg vom 9. August 1965 - (37) 135/65 (141 Js 170/61 StA Hamburg) – 2 den Beschluß des Hanseatischen Oberlandesgerichts Hamburg vom 23. August 1965 – 2 b Ws 70/65.

Entscheidungsformel:

Der Beschluß des Hanseatischen Oberlandesgerichts Hamburg vom 23. August 1965 – 2b Ws 70/65 – verletzt das Recht des Beschwerdeführers aus Artikel 2 Absatz 2 des Grundgesetzes. Er wird deshalb aufgehoben. Die Sache wird an das Hanseatische Oberlandesgericht zurückverwiesen.

Gründe:

I

1 Das Gesetz zur Änderung der Strafprozeßordnung und des Gerichtsverfassungsgesetzes vom 19. Dezember 1964 (BGBl. I S. 1067), das am 1. April 1965 in Kraft getreten ist (sogenannte Kleine Strafprozeßnovelle), hat u. a. das Recht der Untersuchungshaft neu geregelt; dabei verfolgt es im ganzen die Tendenz, Anordnung und Dauer der Haft zu beschränken. Die bisherigen Haftvoraussetzungen sind 'objektiviert' worden, d. h., es müssen 'bestimmte Tatsachen' festgestellt werden, aus denen sich die genau umschriebenen Tatbestände der Flucht- oder Verdunkelungsgefahr ergeben. Andererseits hat die Novelle bei Sittlichkeitsverbrechen den Haftgrund der Wiederholungsgefahr neu eingeführt und schließlich in § 112 Abs. 4 StPO folgendes bestimmt:

THE ARRESTED ADMIRAL CASE

This case is chiefly of importance for its application of the principle of proportionality to the rules about arrest. It also however contains interesting comment about the origin of this principle, and the relevance of the general principles of human rights to the issue in question. Compare the approach to statutory interpretation at the end of the case with the English approach.

BVerfGE Volume 19 p 342

39 According to the constitutional law principle of proportionality an exemption from arrest by corresponding application of § 116 of the StPO is possible also for a warrant based on § 112 para 4 of the StPO.

Decision of the First Senate on 15 December 1965

– 1 BvR 513/65 –

in the proceedings concerning the constitutional complaint of Admiral aD ... authorised representatives: lawyers ... against 1 the warrant of the State Court of Hamburg of 9 August 1965 – (37) 135/65 (141 Js 170/61 StA Hamburg) – 2 the decision of the Hanseatic Upper State Court of Hamburg of 23 August 1965 – 2 b Ws 70/65.

Decision:

The decision of the Hanseatic Upper State Court of Hamburg of 23 August 1965 – 2 b Ws 70/65 – violates the right of the complainant under Art 2 para 2 of the Basic Law. It is therefore quashed. The matter is referred back to the Hanseatic Upper State Court.

Reasons:

I

1 The Criminal Procedure Code and Court Constitution Statute (Amendment) Act of 19 December 1964 (BGBl I, 1067) which came into force on 1 April 1965 (the so-called Short Criminal Procedure Amendment) amongst other things made new rules as to the right to arrest for investigation; there follows from this a general tendency to limit the ordering and length of arrests. The prerequisites for arrest applying until now have been 'objectivised', ie, 'certain facts' must be established from which the precisely described essential elements of danger of flight and of suppression of evidence arise. On the other hand the Amendment has newly introduced danger of repetition as a ground of arrest for sexual crimes and finally in § 112 para 4 of the StPO provided as follows:

Gegen den Beschuldigten, der eines Verbrechens wider das Leben nach den §§ 211, 212 oder § 220 a Abs. 1 Nr. 1 des Strafgesetzbuches dringend verdächtig ist, darf die Untersuchungshaft auch angeordnet werden, wenn ein Haftgrund nach Absatz 2 und 3 nicht besteht.

Die Fälle der sogenannten Haftverschonung sind in § 116 StPO gegenüber der früheren Regelung erweitert worden. Nicht nur bei Fluchtgefahr, sondern auch bei Verdunkelungsgefahr und Wiederholungsgefahr ist die Aussetzung des Vollzuges des Haftbefehls möglich, wenn mit weniger einschneidenden Maßnahmen der Zweck der Untersuchungshaft erreicht werden kann. § 112 Abs. 4 StPO ist in § 116 StPO nicht erwähnt.

2 Die Frage, ob auch dann, wenn der Haftbefehl allein auf § 112 Abs. 4 StPO gestützt ist, eine Aussetzung des Vollzuges nach § 116 StPO verfügt werden kann, ist im Schrifttum und insbesondere auch in der Rechtsprechung der Oberlandesgerichte streitig. Einige wollen unter Berufung auf den Wortlaut des § 116 StPO diese Möglichkeit ausschließen, andere halten es trotz des Wortlauts mit verschiedener Begründung für geboten, auch bei einer Verhaftung nach § 112 Abs. 4 StPO zur Haftverschonung zu gelangen. Eine dritte Gruppe hält es für möglich, auch bei Verbrechen gegen das Leben den Vollzug des Haftbefehls gemäß § 116 StPO auszusetzen, wenn er allein oder zusätzlich auf § 112 Abs. 2 oder 3 StPO gestützt wird. Einen Überblick über die Auffassungen in Literatur und Rechtsprechung gibt Kleinknecht, MDR 1965, 785; vgl. auch OLG Köln, Beschluß vom 24. September 1965 – HEs 73/65 – und OLG Stuttgart, Beschluß vom 27. Oktober 1965 – 3 HEs 48/65.

II

1 Der Beschwerdeführer, ein Admiral a.D., der im 76. Lebensjahr steht, ist wegen Mordes angeklagt. Es wird ihm zur Last gelegt, er habe 1944 als Marineattaché der Deutschen Botschaft in Tokio den Befehl gegeben, Untersuchungsgefangene, die auf Blockadebrechern nach Deutschland verschifft wurden, im Fall der Selbstversenkung mit dem Schiff untergehen zu lassen. Auf Grund eines gemäß § 112 Abs. 4 StPO erlassenen Haftbefehls des Landgerichts Hamburg vom 9. August 1965 wurde der Beschwerdeführer am 11. August 1965 verhaftet. Die Beschwerde gegen den Haftbefehl hat das Hanseatische Oberlandesgericht Hamburg durch Beschluß vom 23. August 1965 verworfen: Angesichts der Schwere des Deliktes, dessen der Beschwerdeführer verdächtig sei, komme es nicht darauf an, ob auch Haftgründe im Sinne des § 112 Abs. 2 StPO beständen. Eine Haftentlassung nach § 116 StPO müsse außer Betracht bleiben, da die Aussetzung eines nach § 112 Abs. 4 StPO erlassenen Haftbefels gesetzlich ausgeschlossen sei.

Arrest for investigation can also be ordered against an accused who is under strong suspicion of a crime against life under §§ 211, 212 or § 220 a para 1 no 1 of Criminal Code, if a ground for arrest under paras 2 and 3 does not exist.

The cases of so-called arrest exemption are widened by § 116 of the StPO in comparison to the earlier regime. Suspension of execution of the warrant is possible not only where there is danger of flight but also where there is danger of suppression of evidence and danger of repetition, if the purpose of the arrest for investigation can be reached with less radical measures. § 112 para 4 of the StPO is not mentioned in § 116 of the StPO.

2 The question whether, if the warrant is based on § 112 para 4 of the StPO alone, a suspension of execution can be ordered under § 116 of the StPO is disputed in academic writings and especially in the case law of the Upper State Court. Some would exclude this possibility by appealing to the wording of § 116 of the StPO; others consider it, for varying reasons and, in spite of the wording, to be necessary even with an arrest under § 112 para 4 of the StPO to resort to the arrest exemption. A third group consider it to be possible to suspend the execution of the warrant according to § 116 of the StPO even with a crime against life, if it is solely or additionally supported by § 112 para 2 or 3 of the StPO. An overview of the opinions in academic literature and case law is given by Kleinknecht, MDR 1965, 785; compare also OLG of Cologne, decision of 24 September 1965 – HEs 73/65 – and OLG of Stuttgart, decision of 27 October 1965 – 3 HEs 48/65.

II

1 The complainant, Admiral aD, who is 76 years old, is accused of murder. The accusation is that as naval attaché of the German Embassy in Tokyo in 1944 he gave a command that prisoners awaiting trial who were shipped to Germany on blockade runners were to be left to go down with the ship if it was scuttled. The complainant was arrested on 11 August 1965 on the basis of a warrant issued by the State Court of Hamburg on 9 August 1965 in accordance with § 112 para 4 of the StPO. The complaint against the warrant has been rejected by the Hanseatic Upper State Court of Hamburg by a decision of 23 August 1965: in the light of the severity of the delict of which the claimant is suspected, it does not depend on whether grounds for arrest exist in the sense of § 112 para 4 of the StPO. A release from custody in accordance with § 116 of the StPO must be left out of consideration, as suspension of a warrant issued under § 112 para 4 of the StPO is excluded by statute.

Gegen den Beschluß des Oberlandesgerichts hat der Beschwerdeführer Verfassungsbeschwerde erhoben. Er rügt, durch falsche Auslegung der Strafprozeßordnung werde er in seinem Grundrecht aus Art 2 Abs. 2 GG verletzt. Andere Gerichte hielten die Haftverschonung bei einem auf § 112 Abs. 4 StPO gestützten Haftbefehl für zulässig. Hätte das Oberlandesgericht eine solche Auslegung, die allein verfassungsmäßig sei, gewählt, dann hätte der Vollzug des Haftbefehls ausgesetzt werden müssen. Der Beschwerdeführer wisse seit fünf Jahren von den Ermittlungen gegen sich; er habe sich zur Durchführung des Verfahrens jederzeit zur Verfügung gestellt. Er sei allseits hochgeachtet und würde sich jederzeit nach bestimmten Weisungen richten, die das Gericht zur Abwendung der Haft treffen würde. Der Beschwerdeführer beantragt:

1 den Beschluß des Hanseatischen Oberlandesgerichts vom 23. August 1965 insoweit aufzuheben, als durch ihm die Aussetzung des Vollzuges des Haftbefehls vom 9. August 1965 wegen gesetzlicher Unzulässigkeit der Aussetzung gemäß § 116 StPO abgelehnt worden ist,

2 die Sache zur Entscheidung über die Aussetzung des Vollzuges des Haftbefehls an ein zuständiges Gericht zurückzuverweisen (§ 95 Abs. 2 BVerfGG).

II

2 Der Bundesminister der Justiz hält die Verfassungsbeschwerde für unbegründet. Die Neuordnung des Haftrechts verfolge das Ziel, dem Grundsatz der Verhältnismäßigkeit entsprechend die Anordnung und Dauer der Untersuchungshaft zu beschränken. Demnach seien im allgemeinen die Schwere des Deliktes und die Höhe der zu erwartenden Strafe kein Grund mehr, unter erleichterten Voraussetzungen einen Haftbefehl zu erlassen. Der besondere Haftgrund des § 112 Abs. 4 StPO sei keine modifizierte Aufrechterhaltung des alten § 112 Abs. 2 Nr. 1 StPO, der bei Verbrechen den Fluchtverdacht gesetzlich vermutete, sondern komme auch dann in Betracht, wenn Fluchtverdacht oder Verdunkelungsgefahr gerade nicht vorlägen. Der hohe Respekt vor dem Rechtgut des menschlichen Lebens, das das höchste Schutzgut unserer Gesellschaftsordnung sei, habe den Gesetzgeber veranlaßt, diesen Haftgrund einzuführen, der besonders dann herangezogen werden könne, wenn kein 'klassischer' Haftgrund vorliege. Deshalb lasse sich in diesen Fällen der Zweck der Untersuchungshaft nicht durch Haftverschonung unter Auflagen erreichen. Dem Grundsatz der Verhältnismäßigkeit trage das Gesetz insofern Rechnung, als es in leichteren Fällen von Verbrechen gegen das Leben dem Richter gestatte, vom Erlaß eines Haftbefehls nach § 112 Abs. 4 StPO abzusehen; statt dessen könne er Haftbefehl nach § 112 Abs. 2 oder 3 StPO erlassen, falls die gesetzliche Voraussetzungen hierfür vorlägen, dann aber auch den Vollzug des Haftbefehls gemäß § 116 StPO aussetzen.

The complainant has raised a constitutional complaint against the decision of the Upper State Court. He claims that his basic right under Art 2 para 2 of the GG has been violated by incorrect interpretation of the Criminal Procedure Code. Other courts have held the arrest exemption to be permissible on a warrant supported by § 112 para 4 of the StPO. Had the Upper State Court chosen such an interpretation, which is the only constitutional one, the execution of the warrant would then have had to be suspended. The complainant knew for the last five years about the investigations against him; he had made himself available at all times for the carrying through of the proceedings. He was highly respected everywhere and would conduct himself at all times according to specified instructions which the court would make on setting aside the arrest. The complainant applies for the following:

1 the quashing of the decision of the Hanseatic Upper State Court of 23 August 1965 insofar as that suspension of the execution of the warrant of 9 August 1965 was refused by it because of the legal impermissibility of the suspension according to § 116 of the StPO,

2 The reference back to a competent court of the issue for decision about the suspension of the execution of the warrant (§ 95 para 2 of the BVerfGG).

II

2 The Federal Minister of Justice considers the constitutional complaint to be unfounded. The new regime for the law of arrest pursues the goal, in accordance with the principle of proportionality, of limiting the ordering and length of arrest for investigation. According to this, the seriousness of the delict and the severity of the penalty to be expected are in general no longer a basis for issuing a warrant on the basis of less severe prerequisites. The special ground for arrest in § 112 para 4 of the StPO is not a modified continuation of the old § 112 para 2 no 1 of the StPO, which created a legal presumption of suspicion of flight on commission of a crime; but falls to be considered even when suspicion of flight or the danger of suppression of evidence are not present. The high respect for the legally protected right of human life, which is the highest protected value of our social order, has caused the legislator to introduce this ground of arrest which could in particular be brought forward if no 'classical' ground of arrest was present. Therefore, the purpose of arrest for investigation cannot be attained in these cases by arrest exemption subject to conditions. Statute therefore takes the principle of proportionality into account to the extent that it allows the judge in less serious cases of crimes against life to refrain from issue of a warrant in accordance with § 112 para 4 of the StPO. Instead of this he could issue a warrant under § 112 para 2 or 3 of the StPO if the statutory prerequisites for this were present, but then suspend the execution of the warrant in accordance with § 116 of the StPO.

Die Verfassungsbeschwerde sei schon deshalb unbegründet, weil kein spezifisches Verfassungsrecht verletzt sei. Die verschiedenen Auslegungen, die auch für Mord- und Totschlagsverdächtige eine Haftverschonung zuließen, seien allenfalls vertretbar, aber nicht zwingend von der Verfassung geboten. Weder das Übermaßverbot noch der Verhältnismäßigkeitsgrundsatz forderten, den der schlimmsten Verbrechen Verdächtigen auf freiem Fuß zu lassen.

Verfassungsrecht sei auch nicht dadurch verletzt worden, daß das Gericht im konkreten Fall sein Ermessen anders hätte gebrauchen müssen. Denn die Annahme des besonderen Haftgrundes des Absatzes 4 des § 112 StPO sei auch bei dem Alter des Beschwerdeführers und unter dem Gesichtspunkt, daß die vorgeworfene Tat über 20 Jahre zurückliege, nicht unvertretbar, mithin nicht willkürlich.

III

Die Verfassungsbeschwerde ist begründet.

1 In dem Rechtsinstitut der Untersuchungshaft wird das Spannungsverhältnis zwischen dem in Art 2 Abs. 2 und Art 104 GG gewährleisteten Recht des Einzelnen auf persönliche Freiheit und den unabweisbaren Bedürfnissen einer wirksamen Strafverfolgung deutlich sichtbar. Die rasche und gerechte Ahndung schwerer Straftaten würde in vielen Fällen nicht möglich sein, wenn es den Strafverfolgungsbehörden ausnahmslos verwehrt wäre, den mutmaßlichen Täter schon vor der Verurteilung festzunehmen und bis zum Urteil in Haft zu halten. Andererseits ist die volle Entziehung der persönlichen Freiheit durch Einschließung in eine Haftanstalt ein Übel, das im Rechtsstaat grundsätzlich nur dem zugefügt werden darf, der wegen einer gesetzlich mit Strafe bedrohten Handlung rechtskräftig verurteilt worden ist. Diese Maßnahme schon gegen einen einer Straftat lediglich Verdächtigen zu ergreifen kann nur in streng begrenzten Ausnahmefällen zulässig sein. Dies ergibt sich auch aus der grundsätzlichen Unschuldsvermutung, die es ausschließt, auch bei noch so dringendem Tatverdacht gegen den Beschuldigten im Vorgriff auf die Strafe Maßregeln zu verhängen, die in ihrer Wirkung der Freiheitsstrafe gleichkommen. Diese Unschuldsvermutung ist zwar im Grundgesetz nicht ausdrücklich statuiert, entspricht aber allgemeiner rechtsstaatlicher Überzeugung und ist durch Art 6 Abs. 2 der Europäischen Menschenrechtskonvention auch in das positive Recht der Bundesrepublik eingeführt worden.

The constitutional complaint is unfounded because no specific constitutional right has been harmed. The different interpretations which permit an arrest exemption even for those suspected of murder and manslaughter are justifiable if need be, but are not obligatory under the Constitution. Neither the prohibition on excessive action nor the proportionality principle required a person who is suspected of the worst crimes to be set free.

Constitutional law has also not been violated simply because the court in a particular case should have exercised its discretion in another way. This is because acceptance of the special ground of arrest in para 4 of § 112 of the ZPO is not unjustifiable and not therefore arbitrary even taking into account the age of the complainant and from the point of view that the reprehensible act took place over 20 years ago.

III

The constitutional complaint is justified.

1 In the legal institution of arrest for investigation, the relationship of tension between the right of the individual to personal freedom guaranteed in Art 2 para 2 and Art 104 of GG and the irrefutable needs of effective criminal prosecution are clearly visible. The speedy and just punishment of serious criminal acts would not in many cases be possible if it was without exception forbidden to the criminal authorities to apprehend the suspected perpetrator before conviction and keep him under arrest until the court's decision. On the other hand, the total deprivation of personal freedom by confinement in a remand institution is an evil which, in a constitutional State, ought, in principle, only be inflicted on a person who, because of an action lawfully threatened with punishment, has been convicted in a legally valid manner. To take this measure against a person merely suspected of a criminal act can only be permissible in strictly circumscribed cases. This also follows from the principle of the presumption of innocence, which excludes, even in the case of the strongest suspicion against the accused, the imposition of measures in anticipation of punishment which are in effect equal to a prison sentence. This presumption of innocence is certainly not expressly laid down in the Basic Law, but it corresponds to the general conviction in constitutional States and has also been introduced into the positive law of the Federal Republic by Art 6 para 2 of the European Convention of Human Rights.

Eine vertretbare Lösung dieses Konflikts zweier für den Rechtsstaat gleich wichtiger Prinzipien läßt sich nur erreichen, wenn den vom Standpunkt der Strafverfolgung aus erforderlich und zweckmäßig erscheinenden Freiheitsbeschränkungen ständig der Freiheitsanspruch des noch nicht verurteilten Beschuldigten als Korrektiv entgegengehalten wird. Dies bedeutet: Die Untersuchungshaft muß in Anordnung und Vollzug von dem Grundsatz der Verhältnismäßigkeit beherrscht werden; der Eingriff in die Freiheit ist nur hinzunehmen, wenn und soweit einerseits wegen dringenden auf konkrete Anhaltspunkte gestützten Tatverdachts begründete Zweifel an der Unschuld des Verdächtigen bestehen, andererseits der legitime Anspruch der staatlichen Gemeinschaft auf vollständige Aufklärung der Tat und rasche Bestrafung des Täters nicht anders gesichert werden kann als dadurch, daß der Verdächtige vorläufig in Haft genommen wird. Die Verfolgung anderer Zwecke durch die Untersuchungshaft ist jedenfalls grundsätzlich ausgeschlossen; namentlich darf sie nicht nach Art einer Strafe einen Rechtsgüterschutz vorwegnehmen, dem das materielle Strafrecht dienen soll.

2 Die neuere Rechtsentwicklung trägt diesen Grundsätzen Rechnung. Die Allgemeine Erklärung der Menschenrechte der Vereinten Nationen vom 10. Dezember 1948 betont im Anschluß an die französische Erklärung der Menschenrechte von 1789 die Unschuldsvermutung nachdrücklich (Art 11 Abs. 1 in Verbindung mit Art 9). Die Europäische Menschenrechtskonvention wiederholt diesen Grundsatz (Art 6 Abs. 2) und umschreibt in Artikel 5 genau die Voraussetzungen, unter denen im Rechtsstaat die Beschränkung der persönlichen Freiheit allein zulässig ist. Das Ministerkomitee des Europarats hat dazu neuerdings eine Empfehlung an die Mitgliedstaaten beschlossen (Mitteilungen des Europarats, veröffentlicht in der Beilage zum Bundesanzeiger Nr. 102 vom 3. Juni 1965, S. 38), die u. a. folgende Richtlinien enthält:

> Die Untersuchungshaft darf niemals zwingend sein. Die Justizbehörde wird eine diesbezügliche Entscheidung unter Berücksichtigung aller Umstände des jeweiligen Falles treffen.
> Die Untersuchungshaft muß als eine Ausnahmemaßnahme betrachtet werden.
> Die Untersuchungshaft darf nur in solchen Fällen angeordnet und beibehalten werden, wo sie unbedingt notwendig erscheint. Sie darf auf keinen Fall als Strafmaßnahme Anwendung finden.
> Andere Maßnahmen, welche die Untersuchungshaft ersetzen könnten, sind ebenfalls anzuführen.

A justifiable solution to this conflict of two principles which are equally important for the constitutional State can only be reached if the limitations on freedom, which appear to be necessary and appropriate from the standpoint of criminal prosecution are continually, as a corrective, set against the claim to freedom of the accused who has not yet been convicted. This means: arrest for investigation must, as to its ordering and execution, be governed by the principle of proportionality. The invasion of freedom is only to be accepted if and insofar as, on the one hand, because of strong suspicion with a solid basis, justified doubt exists as to the innocence of the suspected person; and, on the other hand, the legitimate claim of the State community to complete explanation of the deed and rapid punishment of the perpetrator cannot be otherwise secured than by the provisional taking of the suspected person into custody. The pursuit of other purposes by arrest for investigation is in every case excluded on principle; in particular it may not anticipate by way of punishment the protection of legal rights which substantive criminal law should provide for.

2 The more recent development in the law takes account of these principles. The General Declaration of Human Rights by the United Nations on 10 December 1948 expressly emphasises the presumption of innocence following the French Declaration of Human Rights of 1789 (Art 11 para 1 in combination with Art 9). The European Convention on Human Rights repeats this principle (Art 6 para 2) and in Art 5 describes precisely the only prerequisites under which, in a constitutional State, the limitation of personal freedom is permissible. The Committee of Ministers of the European Council has in addition recently determined on a recommendation to the Member States (Communications of the European Council, published in the Appendix to the *Federal Advertiser* no 102 of 3 June 1965, p 38) which contains, *inter alia*, the following guidelines:

> Arrest for investigation may never be obligatory. The Justice authority will make a decision with reference to this on consideration of all the circumstances of the actual case.

> Arrest for investigation must be regarded as an exceptional measure.

> Arrest for investigation may only be ordered and continued in those cases where it appears to be absolutely necessary. It may not be applied in any case as a penal measure.

> Other measures, which could replace arrest for investigation, are to be conducted likewise.

In der Bundesrepublik Deutschland hat der Grundsatz der Verhältnismäßigkeit verfassungsrechtlichen Rang. Er ergibt sich aus dem Rechtsstaatsprinzip, im Grunde bereits aus dem Wesen der Grundrechte selbst, die als Ausdruck des allgemeinen Freiheitsanspruchs des Bürgers gegenüber dem Staat von der öffentlichen Gewalt jeweils nur so weit beschränkt werden dürfen, als es zum Schutz öffentlicher Interessen unerläßlich ist. Für das Grundrecht der persönlichen Freiheit folgt dies auch aus der besonderen Bedeutung, die gerade diesem Grundrecht als der Basis der allgemeinen Rechtsstellung und Entfaltungsmöglichkeit des Bürgers zukommt und die das Grundgesetz dadurch anerkennt, daß es in Art 2 Abs. 2 die Freiheit der Person als 'unverletzlich' bezeichnet.

Die Strafprozeßnovelle vom 19. Dezember 1964, deren Ziel eine verfassungskonforme Ausgestaltung des Strafverfahrens war, will dem Grundsatz der Verhältnismäßigkeit im Untersuchungshaftrecht allgemein Geltung verschaffen. Er wird, was die Voraussetzungen der Haftanordnung anlangt, in § 112 Abs. 1 Satz 2 StPO generell ausgesprochen und für Vollzug und Dauer der Haft in §§ 116, 120, 121 StPO wiederholt. Er kommt vor allem auch darin zum Ausdruck, daß – trotz genauer Umschreibung der Voraussetzungen für den Erlaß eines Haftbefehls – dieser niemals obligatorisch ist, sondern stets im pflichtmäßigen Ermessen des Richters steht; das folgt aus dem Wort 'darf' in § 112 Abs. 1 und 4 StPO.

3 Bei der ihm hiernach obliegenden Abwägung hat der Richter stets im Auge zu behalten, daß es der vornehmliche Zweck und der eigentliche Rechtfertigungsgrund der Untersuchungshaft ist, die Durchführung eines geordneten Strafverfahrens zu gewährleisten und die spätere Strafvollstreckung sicherzustellen; ist sie zu einem dieser Zwecke nicht mehr nötig, so ist es unverhältnismäßig und daher grundsätzlich unzulässig, sie anzuordnen, aufrechtzuerhalten oder zu vollziehen. Die Haftgründe der Fluchtgefahr und der Verdunkelungsgefahr (§ 112 Abs. 2 StPO) dienen ersichtlich diesem Zweck. Der Haftgrund der Wiederholungsgefahr in § 112 Abs. 3 StPO geht zwar darüber hinaus, indem er den Schutz der Allgemeinheit vor weiteren Straftaten, also einen präventiv-polizeilichen Gesichtspunkt, für die Verhängung der Untersuchungshaft genügen läßt. Er kann jedoch damit gerechtfertigt werden, daß es hier um die Bewahrung eines besonders schutzbedürftigen Kreises der Bevölkerung vor mit hoher Wahrscheinlichkeit drohenden schweren Straftaten geht; auch erscheint es zweckmäßiger, diesen Schutz den bereits mit der Aufklärung der begangenen Straftat befaßten Strafverfolgungsbehörden und damit dem Richter anzuvertrauen als der Polizei.

In the Federal Republic of Germany, the principle of proportionality has constitutional law status. It arises out of the principle of the constitutional State, in principle even from the nature of the Basic Rights themselves, which as an expression of the citizen's general claim to freedom as against the State, may be limited at any time by public authority only so far as this is imperative for the protection of public interests. For the basic right of personal freedom, this also follows from the special meaning which is appropriate to this Basic Right as the basis of the citizen's general legal position and opportunity for development and which the Basic Law acknowledges by, in Art 2 para 2, describing the freedom of the person as 'inviolable'.

The Criminal Procedure Amendment of 19 December 1964, the goal of which was an organisation of criminal proceedings which would conform to the Constitution intended to give the principle of proportionality general validity in the law relating to arrest for investigation. So far as concerns the prerequisites for an order for arrest, it is stated generally in § 112 para 1 sentence 2 of the StPO and is repeated for the execution and length of the arrest in §§ 116, 120 and 121 of the StPO. It is expressed pre-eminently in the fact that – despite exact description of the prerequisites for the issue of a warrant – this is never obligatory, but is always at the discretion of the judge which is to be exercised in accordance with his duty. This follows from the word 'may' in § 112 paras 1 and 4 of the StPO.

3 In the assessment, which is accordingly incumbent upon him, the judge must always keep in mind that the chief purpose and real ground of justification for arrest for investigation is to guarantee the carrying through of orderly criminal proceedings and to ensure the later execution of punishment. If it is no longer necessary for one of these purposes, it is disproportionate and therefore impermissible in principle to order, maintain or execute it. Danger of flight and danger of suppression of evidence (§ 112 para 2 of the StPO) obviously serve this purpose as grounds for arrest. Danger of repetition in § 112 para 3 of the StPO as a ground for arrest certainly exceeds this, in that it lets the protection of the general public from further criminal acts, ie, a preventative policing consideration, suffice for the imposition of arrest for investigation. It can, however, be justified on the grounds that the particular case concerns preservation of a section of the population particularly needing protection from serious criminal acts which are threatened with high probability; it also seems more appropriate to entrust this protection to the crime investigation authorities already concerned with the clearing up of the criminal act which has been committed – and therefore to the judge rather than to the police.

Der neu eingeführte § 112 Abs. 4 StPO müßte dagegen rechtsstaatliche Bedenken erwecken, wenn er dahin auszulegen wäre, daß bei dringendem Verdacht eines der hier bezeichneten Verbrechen gegen das Leben die Untersuchungshaft ohne weiteres, d. h. ohne Prüfung weiterer Voraussetzungen, verhängt werden dürfte. Eine solche Auslegung wäre mit dem Grundgesetz nicht vereinbar. Es kann schon zweifelhaft sein, ob sie dem Wortlaut der Bestimmung entspricht; denn dieser legt es nahe, der Vorschrift nur subsidiäre Geltung beizumessen, sie also nur anzuwenden, wenn zuvor das Vorliegen eines Haftgrundes nach Absatz 2 geprüft und verneint worden ist. Aber auch wenn man dieser Auslegung nicht folgt, fordert der Grundsatz der Verhältnismäßigkeit, daß der Richter auch bei Anwendung des § 112 Abs. 4 StPO den Zweck der Untersuchungshaft nie aus dem Auge verliert. Weder die Schwere der Verbrechen wider das Leben noch die Schwere der (noch nicht festgestellten) Schuld rechtfertigen für sich allein die Verhaftung des Beschuldigten; noch weniger ist die Rücksicht auf eine mehr oder minder deutlich feststellbare 'Erregung der Bevölkerung' ausreichend, die es unerträglich finde, wenn ein 'Mörder' frei umhergehe. Es müssen vielmehr auch hier stets Umstände vorliegen, die die Gefahr begründen, daß ohne Festnahme des Beschuldigten die alsbaldige Aufklärung und Ahndung der Tat gefährdet sein könnte. Der zwar nicht mit 'bestimmten Tatsachen' belegbare, aber nach den Umständen des Falles doch nicht auszuschließende Flucht- oder Verdunkelungsverdacht kann u. U. bereits ausreichen. Ebenso könnte die ernstliche Befürchtung, daß der Beschuldigte weitere Verbrechen ähnlicher Art begeht, für den Erlaß eines Haftbefehls genügen. § 112 Abs. 4 StPO ist in engem Zusammenhang mit Absatz 2 zu sehen; er läßt sich dann damit rechtfertigen, daß mit Rücksicht auf die Schwere der hier bezeichneten Straftaten die strengen Voraussetzungen der Haftgründe des Absatzes 2 gelockert werden sollen, um die Gefahr auszuschließen, daß gerade besonders gefährliche Täter sich der Bestrafung entziehen.

The newly introduced § 112 para 4 of the StPO would on the other hand have had to give rise to constitutional misgivings if it were to be interpreted to the effect that arrest for investigation might on its own, ie, without proof of further prerequisites, be imposed where there was strong suspicion of one of the crimes against life described here. Such an interpretation would not be reconcilable with the Basic Law. It can be doubted whether it corresponds with the wording of the provision; because this suggests attaching only subsidiary validity to the provision, thus only applying it if the presence of a ground of arrest under para 2 has been previously considered and denied. But even if one does not follow this interpretation, the principle of proportionality requires that the judge doesn't ever lose sight of the purpose of arrest for investigation even when applying § 112 para 4 of the StPO. Neither the seriousness of the crime against life nor the seriousness of the (not yet established) guilt justify on their own the arrest of the accused; even less sufficient is consideration of a more or less clearly ascertainable 'excitement of the population' which would find it unacceptable that a 'murderer' should be moving around freely. There must always be circumstances present, even here, which substantiate the danger that the immediate clearing up and punishment of the deed could be endangered unless the accused is arrested. Suspicion of flight or suppression of evidence not verifiable by 'definite facts', but not in the circumstances of the case to be excluded, can in certain circumstances, suffice. Likewise the serious fear that the accused will commit further offences of a similar kind could suffice for the issue of a warrant. § 112 para 4 of the StPO is to be seen in close relationship with para 2; it then permits justification of the relaxation of the strict prerequisites for the grounds of arrest in para 2, in consideration of the seriousness of the criminal acts here described in order to exclude the danger that especially dangerous perpetrators will escape punishment.

4 Eine besondere Ausprägung des Grundsatzes der Verhältnismäßgkeit stellt § 116 StPO dar. Er legt dem Richter die Pflicht auf, bei jeder Verhaftung wegen Flucht-, Verdunkelungs- und Wiederholungsgefahr zu prüfen, ob der Zweck der Untersuchungshaft nicht auch durch weniger einschneidende Freiheitsbeschränkungen erreicht werden kann. Ist das der Fall, so ist der Vollzug des Haftbefehls auszusetzen. Die vorstehenden Darlegungen über die allgemeine Bedeutung des Verhältnismäßigkeitsgrundsatzes im Haftrecht führen zu dem Ergebnis, daß eine Haftverschonung auch möglich sein muß, wenn der Haftbefehl auf § 112 Abs. 4 StPO gestützt wird. Weder Wortlaut noch Sinn des § 112 StPO verbieten es, auch bei Verbrechen gegen das Leben den Haftbefehl auf Absatz 2, gegebenenfalls auf Absatz 3 zu stützen. Es wäre ein ungereimtes Ergebnis und würde dem Prinzip der Verhältnismäßigkeit klar widersprechen, wenn zwar bei Flucht- oder Verdunkelungsgefahr im Sinne des § 112 Abs. 2 StPO ohne Rücksicht auf die Schwere der Straftat der Beschuldigte stets nach § 116 StPO von der Haft verschont werden könnte, andererseits aber bei geringerer Gefahr von Flucht oder Verdunkelung der Beschuldigte von jeder für den Zweck des Strafverfahrens ausreichenden milderen Maßnahme schlechthin ausgeschlossen wäre. Wenn eine Aufhebung des Haftbefehls die Durchführung des Strafverfahrens gefährden könnte, eine Aussetzung des Haftbefehls mit bestimmten Auflagen aber ausreicht, dann darf der Richter nicht gezwungen sein, die Haft fortdauern zu lassen. Die Minderung des Schutzes des Beschuldigten, die in der Einführung des Haftgrundes des § 112 Abs. 4 StPO und damit in der Erleichterung des Erlasses eines Haftbefehls liegt, muß durch die Zulassung einer Haftverschonung einigermaßen ausgeglichen und darf nicht durch ihre Versagung in der Wirkung noch gesteigert werden.

Der Einwand, der Richter könne, wenn er eine Haftverschonung für angebracht halte, von dem Erlaß eines Haftbefehls nach § 112 Abs. 4 StPO überhaupt absehen oder ihn aufheben, wäre unberechtigt. Damit würde der Ermessensbereich des Richters in einer dem Verhältnismäßigkeitsgrundsatz widersprechenden Weise verengt. Er hätte nur die Wahl zwischen unbeschränkter Freilassung und voller Freiheitsentziehung. Es kann aber sehr wohl Fälle geben, in denen es angemessen und für die Zwecke des Strafverfahrens ausreichend ist, den Beschuldigten in einer 'kontrollierten Freiheit' zu belassen, indem gegen ihn Maßnahmen der in § 116 StPO bezeichneten Art verhängt werden.

4 § 116 of the StPO represents a particular expression of the principle of proportionality. It places on the judge the duty to examine, on every arrest made because of the danger of flight, suppression of evidence or repetition, whether the purpose of the arrest for investigation cannot also be reached by less radical limitations on freedom. If that is the case, the execution of the warrant is to be suspended. The above explanations about the general meaning of the principle of proportionality in the law of arrest lead to the conclusion that an arrest exemption must also be possible if the warrant is supported by § 112 para 4 of the StPO. Neither the wording nor the sense of § 112 of the StPO forbid a warrant, even in connection with crimes against life, to be based on para 2 or on para 3 if need be. It would be an inconsistent result and would clearly contradict the principle of proportionality if, where there was danger of flight or suppression of evidence in the sense of § 112 para 2 of the StPO there could always be exemption from arrest under § 116 of the StPO, without consideration of the seriousness of the criminal act of the accused, but on the other hand where there was less danger of flight or suppression of evidence, the accused would be entirely excluded from every less severe measure which would suffice for the purpose of the criminal proceedings. If an annulment of the warrant could endanger the carrying through of the criminal proceedings but a suspension of the warrant with certain conditions would suffice, then the judge cannot be compelled to let the arrest continue. The reduction in the accused's protection which lies in the introduction of the ground of arrest in § 112 para 4 of the StPO and because of that in the facilitating of the issue of a warrant must be compensated for to some extent by the authorisation of an arrest exemption and it may not be increased by its denial in practice.

The objection that the judge could, if he considered an arrest exemption to be appropriate, refrain altogether from issuing a warrant in accordance with § 112 para 4 of the StPO or revoke it, would be unwarranted. That would result in the judge's area of discretion being narrowed in a manner which would contradict the principle of proportionality. He would only have the choice between unrestricted release and total deprivation of freedom. There can very well be cases, however, in which it is appropriate and sufficient for the purposes of the criminal proceedings, to leave the accused in a 'controlled freedom' in which measures of the kind described in § 116 of the StPO are imposed against him.

5 Angesichts der Bedeutung des Grundrechts der persönlichen Freiheit einerseits, der Anforderungen einer wirkungsvollen, aber in rechtsstaatlichen Formen verlaufenden Strafverfolgung andererseits und des Grundsatzes der Verhältnismäßigkeit des Eingriffs in Verbindung mit der Unschuldsvermutung zugunsten des Beschuldigten muß auch bei einer Verhaftung auf Grund des § 12 Abs. 4 StPO eine Haftverschonung möglich sein. Demgegenüber können Bedenken aus dem Wortlaut des § 116 StPO zurücktreten. Diese Bestimmung regelt die Voraussetzungen einer Aussetzung des Vollzuges einer Haftbefehls nicht erschöpfend, wie die von den Gerichten seit jeher geübte Praxis beweist, den Vollzug eines Haftbefehls auch bei Haftunfähigkeit des Beschuldigten auszusetzen. Überdies erscheint es nach der Entstehungsgeschichte des Gesetzes vom 19. Dezember 1964 nicht ausgeschlossen, daß diese Auslegung dem wahren Willen des Gesetzgebers entspricht und nur versehentlich im Wortlaut nicht zum Ausdruck gekommen ist: Die Haftgründe des § 112 Abs. 3 – Wiederholungsgefahr bei Sittlichkeitsverbrechen – und Abs. 4 – schwere Verbrechen gegen das Leben – waren in den ursprünglichen Entwürfen der Fraktionen und der Bundesregierung nicht vorgesehen (BT-Drucks. IV/63 und IV/178). Erst der Rechtsausschuß des Bundestages nahm einen Vorschlag an, der inhaltlich dem heutigen § 112 Abs. 4 StPO entsprach, sich aber allgemein auf besonders schwere Fälle bezog (Protokoll Nr. 37). Der Bundestag stimmte in der zweiten Beratung dem § 112 StPO in der vom Rechtsausschuß vorgeschlagenen Form zu und beschloß, § 116 StPO dahin zu ergänzen, daß auch der Vollzug eines nach § 112 Abs. 3 oder Abs. 4 StPO erlassenen Haftbefehls unter gewissen Bedingungen ausgesetzt werden könne. Unwidersprochen wurde die Auffassung vertreten, daß es auch bei Wiederholungsgefahr und bei Vorliegen besonders schwerer Verbrechen Fälle gebe, in denen bei Erfüllung von Auflagen der Vollzug des Haftbefehls unterbleiben könne. Vor der dritten Beratung im Bundestag beschloß dann der Rechtsausschuß die Streichung des Absatzes 4 in § 112 StPO und brachte die Verbrechen wider das Leben bei der Haftvoraussetzung der Wiederholungsgefahr in Absatz 3 unter. Folgerichtig strich er in § 116 StPO die Bezugnahme auf § 112 Abs. 4 StPO (BT - Drucks. IV/2378). In der dritten Beratung nahm der Bundestag einen Änderungsantrag an, in dem der § 112 Abs. 4 StPO in der heute geltenden Fassung wiederhergestellt wurde, ohne jedoch erneut in § 116 StPO eine Haftverschonung für die Fälle des § 112 Abs. 4 StPO einzuführen.

Bei einer somit auch im Fall des § 112 Abs. 4 StPO möglichen Haftverschonung wird der Richter die jeweils erforderlichen Maßnahmen in entsprechender Anwendung des § 116 Abs. 1 bis 3 StPO zu treffen haben.

6 Der angefochtene Beschluß läßt den Grundsatz der Verhältnismäßigkeit außer acht. Dies geschieht bereits durch die Bestätigung des Haftbefehls, in der die vorstehend dargelegte Rechtsauffassung nicht berücksichtigt wird, vor allem aber dadurch, daß die Möglichkeit einer Aussetzung des Haftbefehls schlechthin verneint wird. Der Beschluß verletzt also das Grundrecht des Beschwerdeführers aus Art 2 Abs. 2 GG und ist deshalb aufzuheben.

5 In the light of the meaning of the basic right of personal freedom on the one hand, of the requirements of effective prosecution of crimes which nevertheless proceeds in a form consistent with the rule of law on the other hand, and the principle of the proportionality of the intrusion combined with the presumption of innocence in favour of the accused, an arrest exemption must be possible even for an arrest on the basis of § 112 para 4 of the StPO. Over against this, doubts based on the wording of § 116 of the StPO can recede. This provision does not regulate the prerequisites of a suspension of the execution of a warrant exhaustively, as is demonstrated by the long-standing practice of the courts, in also suspending the execution of a warrant because of the unsuitability of the accused for arrest. It appears, moreover, from the history of the origin of the statute of 19 December 1964, not to be impossible that this interpretation corresponds to the true intention of the legislator and it is only through an oversight that it has not been expressed in the wording: the grounds of arrest of § 112 para 3 – danger of repetition with sexual crimes – and para 4 – serious crimes against life were not provided for in the original proposals of the parliamentary parties and of the Federal Government (BTDrucks IV/63 and IV/178). The Legal Committee of the Federal Parliament first accepted a proposal which corresponded in content to the present day § 112 para 4 of the StPO, but referred in general to especially serious cases (Report no 37). The Federal Parliament agreed on the second reading to § 112 of the StPO in the form proposed by the Legal Committee and decided to amend § 116 of the StPO to the effect that the execution of a warrant issued under § 112 para 3 or para 4 of the StPO could also be suspended under certain circumstances. The view was taken, without being challenged, that there were also cases, where there was danger of repetition or especially serious crimes were present, in which, on the fulfilment of conditions, there should be no execution of the warrant. Before the third reading in the Federal Parliament, the Legal Committee decided on the deletion of para 4 of § 112 of the StPO and put crimes against life under the danger of repetition precondition for arrest in para 3. Consequently, it deleted the reference in § 116 of the StPO to § 112 para 4 of the StPO (BTDrucks IV/2378). In the third reading the Federal Parliament accepted a proposal for an amendment in which § 112 para 4 of the StPO was restored in the current version without however again introducing in § 116 of the StPO an arrest exemption for the cases in § 112 para 4 of the StPO.

On an arrest exemption, which is therefore also possible in the case of § 112 para 4 of the StPO, the judge will have to take the measures necessary at any time by corresponding application of § 116 paras 1–3 of the StPO.

6 The contested decision leaves the principle of proportionality out of consideration. This occurred through the confirmation of the warrant, in which the view of the law explained above was not considered but especially through the fact that the possibility of a suspension of the warrant was simply denied. The decision thus violates the basic right of the complainant under Art 2 para 2 of the GG and is therefore to be quashed.

THE BASIC RIGHTS THEMSELVES

Grundgesetz

I Die Grundrechte

Art. 1 [Schutz der Menschenwürde] (1) Die Würde des Menschen ist unantastbar. Sie zu achten und zu schützen ist Verpflichtung aller staatlichen Gewalt.

(2) Das deutsche Volk bekennt sich darum zu unverletzlichen und unveräußerlichen Menschenrechten als Grundlage jeder menschlichen Gemeinschaft, des Friedens und der Gerechtigkeit in der Welt.

(3) Die nachfolgenden Grundrechte binden Gesetzgebung, vollziehende Gewalt und Rechtsprechung als unmittelbar geltendes Recht.

THE CATTLE SLAUGHTER CASE

THE BASIC RIGHTS THEMSELVES

Basic Law

I The Basic Rights

Article 1 [Protection of Human Dignity] (1) The dignity of the human being is inviolable. It is the duty of all State authority to have regard to it and to protect it.

(2) Therefore the German people acknowledge inviolable and inalienable human rights as the foundation of every human community, peace and justice in the world.

(3) The following basic rights bind the legislature, the executive and the judiciary as directly valid law.

This right has its negative aspects, eg, that prisoners who are serving a life sentence, but who are not a danger to the public, have a right to hope for an early release. It also has positive aspects, eg, a duty to provide social services at an appropriate level for such people as the sick. It does not end with death: see the Mephisto case (BVerfGE 30, 173).

THE CATTLE SLAUGHTER CASE

The chief interest in this case is the unsuccessful attempt to extend human dignity to cover the treatment of animals. One particular feature which will be of interest to English readers is the application of the Charter of Fundamental Rights for the European Union.

In 1998 there had been an unsuccessful attempt to include a provision in the Basic Law stating that 'Animals are to be regarded as fellow creatures. They are protected within the framework of statutes from avoidable suffering and harm'. There is a coalition paper by the current governing parties which says that the Federal government will develop a new initiative for the inclusion of animal protection in the Basic law. § 1 of the Animals Protection Act states that the Act is based on 'the responsibility of human beings for animals, to protect their lives and well being as fellow creatures'. This 'principle of ethically-based animal protection' is subject to the limitations of the principle of proportionality (BVerfGE 101, 1 [37] = NJW 1999, 3523).

VG Frankfurt a.M. NJW 2001, 1295

23 Massentötung von Rindern

GG Art. 1 I; Verordnung (EG) Nr. 2777/2000

1 Die Zulässigkeit einer auf vorbeugende Unterlassung gerichteten einstweiligen Anordnung nach § 123 VwGO setzt in analoger Anwendung von § 42 II VwGO das Vorliegen einer Antragsbefugnis voraus.

2 Das Protokoll Nr. 5 zum Amsterdamer Vertrag über den Tierschutz und das Wohlergehen der Tiere enthält nur eine Zielbestimmung für staatliches Handeln und vermittelt keine subjektiven Rechte.

3 Die Garantie der Menschenwürde in Art 1 der Charta der grundrechte der Europäischen Union und in Art 1 I GG schützt allein die Würde des Menschen, nicht der Tiere. Ein Recht auf ethischen Tierschutz kann aus der Garantie der Menschenwürde nicht hergeleitet werden.

Die Menschenwürde vermittelt daher kein subjektives Recht für ein Rechtsschutzersuchen, mit dem sich ein Bürger dagegen wendet, dass Rinder allein aus Gründen der Stützung des Rindfleischmarkts getötet werden.

5 Das Gericht hat keine erheblichen Zweifel an der Gültigkeit der Verordnung (EG) Nr. 2777/2000, die die nationale Marktordnungsbehörde verpflichtet, angebotene Rinder aufzukaufen, zu töten und unschädlich beseitigen zu lassen.

VG Frankfurt a.M., Beschl. v. 1.3.2001 – 1 G 429/01 (V)

Zum Sachverhalt: Die Ast. wenden sich dagegen, dass die Ag., gestützt auf die Verordnung (EG) Nr. 2777/2000 der Kommission vom 18. 12. 2000 (ABIEG) Nr. L 321/47) über außerordentliche Stützungsmaßnahmen für den Rindfleischmarkt Maßnahmen zum Ankauf von Rindern ergreift, um diese zu töten und anschließend unschädlich beseitigen zulassen. Die Ast. betreiben einen kontrollierten ökologischen Bauernhof, auf dem sie nur Getreide, Gemüse und Obst anbauen. Nutztiere halten sie nicht, weil sie Tiere nicht töten können und wollen. Sie wollen verhindern, dass in der Bundesrepublik Deutschland 400 000 Rinder aus deutschen Zuchtbetrieben aus Gründen der Marktstützung angekauft, getötet, zu Tiermehl verarbeitet und verbrannt werden. Sie vertreten die Auffassung, der Schutz der Menschenwürde in Art. 1 GG setze auch der Behandlung von Tieren Grenzen.

Das *VG* hat den Antrag abgelehnt.

VG Frankfurt aM 2001, 1295

23 Mass cull of cattle

GG Art 1 I; EC Regulation 2777/2000

1 The permissibility of an interim prohibitory injunction under § 123 of the VwGO assumes the existence of authority to make an application by analogy with § 42 II of the VwGO.

2 Protocol No 5 to the Amsterdam Treaty about the protection and the welfare of animals only contains an objective for State action and does not convey any subjective rights.

3 The guarantee of human dignity in Art 1 of the Charter of Fundamental Rights for the European Union and in Art 1 I of the GG only protects the dignity of human beings, not animals. No right to ethical protection of animals can be derived from the guarantee of human dignity.

4 Human dignity does not therefore convey any subjective right for a request for legal protection by which a citizen could object to cattle being killed solely on the ground of support of the cattle meat market.

5 The court has no substantial doubt about the validity of EC Regulation 2777/2000, which obliges the national market order authority to buy up cattle offered, to kill them and to have them safely disposed of.

VG Frankfurt aM, Decision of 1.3.2001 – 1 G 429/01 (V)

Facts: The applicant objects to the fact that the respondent on the basis of EC Regulation 2777/2000 by the Commission dated 18.12.2000 (OJ no L 321/47) about exceptional support measures for the cattle meat market is taking measures to buy cattle in order to kill them and immediately afterwards to have them safely disposed of. The applicants carry on a controlled ecological farm where they only grow cereals, vegetables and fruit. They keep no economically useful animals, because they cannot and will not kill animals. They want to prevent 400,000 head of cattle from German breeding businesses in the German Federal Republic being purchased, slaughtered, processed into animal feed and burnt on the grounds of market support. They hold the view that the protection of human dignity in Art 1 of the GG also sets limits to the treatment of animals.

The administrative court rejected the application.

Aus den Gründen:

II Der Antrag der Ast. ist bereits unzulässig. Den Ast. fehlt die erforderliche Antragsbefugnis.

Die Ast. wollen in der Sache erreichen, dass die Ag. nicht zur Koordinierung der Schlachtung von rund 400 000 Rindern in Anwendung der Verordnung (EG) Nr. 2777/2000 tätig wird. Dieses Begehren der Ast. ist rechtlich als vorbeugende Unterlassungs- bzw. Feststellungsklage einzuordnen. Die Zulässigkeit einer solchen Klage in der Hauptsache setzt in analoger Anwendung von § 42 II VwGO voraus, dass der jeweilige Kläger zur Klage befugt ist (vgl. hierzu *BVerwG*, NVwZ 1991, 470; *Kopp* VwGO, 11. Aufl., § 42 Rdnr. 62 m. w. Nachw.). Zweck der Klagebefugnis ist es, die Popularklage auszuschließen, die dem auf Individualrechtsschutz ausgerichteten Rechtsschutzsystem der VwGO fremd ist. Diese subjektiv rechtliche Begrenzung gilt entsprechend § 42 II VwGO auch für das einstweilige Anordnungsverfahren nach § 123 VwGO (vgl. VGH *Kassel*, NVwZ 1986, 766).

An solchen subjektiven Rechten, auf die sich die Ast. berufen könnten, fehlt es hier. Die Ast., die selbst keine Nutztiere halten, sind von den Maßnahmen der Ag. auf Grund der Verordnung (EG) Nr. 2777/2000 unmittelbar nicht betroffen.

Ein subjektives Recht können die Ast. auch nicht aus dem Protokoll über den Tierschutz und das Wohlergehen der Tiere herleiten, das dem Vertrag von Amsterdam zur Änderung des Vertrages über die Europäische Union und der Verträge zur Gründung der europäischen Gemeinschaften beigefügt ist (ABlEG Nr. C 340/110 v. 10.11.1997). Nach dem zitierten Protokoll tragen die Gemeinschaft und die Mitglieder bei der Festlegung und Durchführung der Politik der Gemeinschaft in den Bereichen Landwirtschaft, Verkehr, Binnenmarkt, und Forschung den Erfordernissen des Wohlergehens der Tiere in vollem Umfang Rechnung; sie berücksichtigen hierbei die Rechts- und Verwaltungsvorschriften und die Gepflogenheiten der Mitgliedstaaten insbesondere in Bezug auf religiöse Riten, kulturelle Traditionen und das regionale Erbe. Die Protokolle, die dem EG-Vertrag im gegenseitigen Einvernehmen der Mitgliedstaaten beigefügt wurden, sind gem. Art. 311 EGV integraler Bestandteil des EG-Vertrages und haben damit den gleichen Rang wie der EG-Vertrag selbst (vgl. *Geiger*, EGV, 2. Aufl. [1995], Art. 239 Rdnr. 2; *Bleckmann/Pieper*, in: *Dauses*, Hdb. des EU-WirtschaftsR, B I-3).

Das Protokoll über den Tierschutz und das Wohlergehen der Tiere enthält jedoch lediglich eine Zielbestimmung für die Durchführung und Festlegung der Politik der Gemeinschaft, jedoch keine Regelung, die inhaltlich unbedingt und hinreichend genau ist, um im Einzelfall angewendet zu werden.

Grounds:

II The application of the applicants is impermissible. The applicants lack the necessary authority to make the application.

The applicants want to ensure in this matter that the respondent does not act to co-ordinate the slaughter of about 400,000 head of cattle in application of EC Regulation 2777/2000. This wish of the applicants is to be classified legally as a claim for a preventative injunction or declaration. The permissibility of such a claim in the main issue assumes, applying § 42 II VwGO by analogy, that the claimant in question is authorised to make the claim (see, on this *BVerwG*, NVwZ 1991, 470; *Kopp* VwGO, 11th edn, § 42 marginal no 62 with other references). The purpose of the concept of authority to make the claim is to exclude the popular claim, which is foreign to the legal protection system of the VwGO, which is directed to individual legal protection. This subjective law limitation applies according to § 42 II of the VwGO for the interim order proceedings under § 123 of the VwGO as well (see VGH *Kassel*, NVwZ 1986, 766).

Such subjective rights to which the applicants could refer are lacking here. The applicants who have no economically useful animals themselves are not directly affected by the measures of the respondent on the basis of EC Regulation 2777/2000.

Nor can the applicants derive a subjective right from the Protocol about the protection and wellbeing of animals which is appended to the Treaty of Amsterdam on the Amendment of the Treaty concerning the European Union and the Treaties on the founding of the European Communities (OJ no C 340/110 of 10.11.1997). Under the Protocol quoted, the Community and the members take fully into account in the establishment and implementation of Community policy in the areas of agriculture, transport, the internal market and research the requirements of the wellbeing of animals. They consider in this connection the legal and administrative provisions and the customs of the Member States in particular in relation to religious rites, cultural traditions and regional heritage. The Protocols which were appended to the EC Treaty by mutual agreement of the Member States are an integral component of the EC Treaty according to Art 311 of the Treaty and therefore have the same ranking as the Treaty itself (see *Geiger*, *EC Treaty*, 2nd edn [1995], Art 239 marginal no 2; *Bleckmann/Pieper*, in: Dauses, *Handbook of European Business Law*, B I-3).

But the Protocol about the protection and wellbeing of animals merely contains a goal for the execution and establishment of the policy of the Community and not a regime which is unconditional and sufficiently precise in content to be applied in the individual case.

Entgegen der Ansicht der Ast. ergibt sich ein solches Recht nicht aus der Garantie der Menschenwürde, die jetzt in Art. 1 der Grundrechtecharta der Europäischen Union Anerkennung gefunden hat.

Das Grundrecht der Würde des Menschen ist in der Rechtsprechung des *EuGH* – soweit ersichtlich – bisher nicht ausdrücklich erwähnt; es ist jedoch davon auszugehen, dass es im Hinblick auf die generelle Anerkennung der Grundrechte durch den *EuGH* auch Bestandteil der europäischen Grundrechte ist. Denn der *EuGH* hat wiederholt entschieden, dass die Grundrechte zu den allgemeinen Rechtsgrundsätzen gehören, die er zu wahren hat, und dass er bei der Gewährleistung dieser Rechte von ihnen auszugehen hat (vgl. hierzu *EuGH*, Slg. 1969, 419 [425] st. Rspr.; vgl. auch *Rengeling*, Grundrechtsschutz in der europ. Gemeinschaft, S. 133 m. w. Nachw.). Der Schutzbereich des europäischen Grundrechts der Menschenwürde geht jedoch nicht über den Schutzbereich der Menschenwürde aus Art. 1 I GG hinaus.

Entgegen der Ansicht der Ast. ergibt sich ein subjektives Recht bereits nicht aus der grundgesetzlich geschützten Garantie der Menschenwürde (Art 1 I GG).

Art. 1 I 1 GG erklärt die Würde des Menschen für unantastbar. Sie zu achten und zu schützen wird zur vornehmsten Pflicht aller staatlichen Gewalt erhoben (Art. 1 I 2 GG). Mit der Menschenwürde als oberstem Wert des Grundgesetzes und tragendem Konstitutionsprinzip ist der soziale Wert und Achtungsanspruch des Menschen verbunden, der es verbietet, ihn zum bloßen Objekt des Staates zu machen oder ihn einer Handlung auszusetzen, die seine Subjektqualität prinzipiell in Frage stellt (vgl. *BVerfGE* 96, 375 [399] = NJW 1998, 519 = LM H. 6/1998 § 249 [A] BGB Nr. 114a). Unter Rückgriff auf die Menschenwürde wird teilweise vertreten, dass die Menschenwürde jedenfalls mittelbar auch den Schutz der Tiere umfasse und so der Idee des ethischen Tierschutzes Verfassungsrang zukomme (vgl. *v. Münch/Kunig*, GG I, 4. Aufl. [1992], Art. 1 Rdnr. 16; *Erbel*, DVBl 1986, 1235 [1251]; *Starck*, in: *v. Mangoldt/Klein/Starck*, GG, 3. Aufl. [1985], Art. 5 Rdnr. 269). Diese Auffassung stützt sich darauf, dass es mit der Würde des Menschen nicht vereinbar ist, mit Tieren unangemessen umzugehen. Der unangemessene Umgang mit Tieren führe mittelbar auch zu einem die Würde des Mitmenschen beeinträchtigenden Verhalten.

Contrary to the view of the applicants, such a right does not arise from the guarantee of human dignity which has now found recognition in Art 1 of the Charter of Fundamental Rights of the European Union.

The basic right of human dignity has not – so far as is evident – been expressly mentioned so far in the case law of the ECJ, but in view of the ECJ's general acceptance of basic rights, it must be assumed that it is also a component of European fundamental rights. This is because the ECJ has repeatedly decided that the basic rights belong to the general principles of law which it has to maintain, and that in the guaranteeing of these rights it has to proceed on the basis of them (see on this EuGH, Slg. 1969, 419 [425], consistent case law; see also *Rengeling*, Protection of Fundamental Rights in the European Community, p 133 with further references). The protected area of the European basic right of human dignity does not however go beyond the protected area of human dignity under Art 1 I of the GG.

Contrary to the view of the applicants, no subjective right arises from the guarantee of human dignity protected by the Basic Law (Art 1 I of the GG).

Art 1 I 1 of the GG declares human dignity to be inviolable. Having regard to it and protecting it are elevated to the primary duty of all State power (Art 1 I 2 of the GG). The social value of human beings and their claim to regard, which prevents them being made mere objects of the State or exposing them to action which in principle puts their subjective quality in question (see *BVerfGE* 96, 375 [399] = NJW 1998, 519 = LM H. 6/1998 § 249 [A] BGB Nr. 114 a) is connected with human dignity as the chief value of the Basic Law and a leading constitutional principle. It is partly claimed, having recourse to the concept of human dignity, that human dignity in any case indirectly includes the protection of animals and therefore the idea of ethical protection of animals acquires constitutional rank (see *v München/Kunig*, GG I, 4th edn, 1992 [Art 1] marginal no 16; *Erbel*, DVBl 1986, 1235 [1251]; *Starck*, in: *v. Mangoldt/Klein/Starck*, GG, 3rd edn [1985], Art 5 marginal no 269). This view is based on the idea that it is irreconcilable with human dignity to handle animals improperly. Improper treatment of animals would lead indirectly to behaviour which would impair the dignity of fellow human beings.

Dieser Auffassung vermag sich die erkennende *Kammer* nicht anzuschließen. Art. 1 I GG schützt die Würde des Menschen, nicht der Tiere (*Dreier*, in: *ders.* [Hrsg.], GG I, 1996 Art. 1 Rdnr. 63). Tierschutz hat - anders formuliert - mit Menschenwürde nichts zu tun (vgl. *Jarass/Pieroth*, GG, 4. Aufl. [1997], Art. 1 Anm. 11; *Höfling*, in: *Sachs*, GG, 2. Aufl. [1989], Art. 1 Rdnr. 30). Gegen die Auffassung, die dem ethischen Tierschutz Verfassungsrang zubilligen will, spricht insbesondere die anthropozentrische Ausrichtung des Grundgesetzes, die ausschließlich den Schutz des Menschen und nicht der anderen Lebewesen zum Ziel hat. Die Interessen eines Tieres selbst können deshalb nicht als Bestandteil der Menschenwürdegarantie betrachtet werden. Zudem droht bei einer Ausweitung der Menschenwürdegarantie auch auf den Tierschutz eine Überstrapazierung des Art. 1 I GG, der die Würde des Menschen vor Verletzungen schützen soll und nicht im Sinne seiner 'Besserung' zum Vehikel höchst ehrenhafter, aber partikulärer moralischer Standards werden soll. Auch angesichts einer kulturell gefestigten und auf absehbare Zeit wohl nicht grundlegend veränderten Praxis systematischer Aufzucht von Tieren zum Zwecke ihres späteren Verzehrs – Musterfall der Behandlung als bloßes Objekt – kann vom Tier als integralem Bestandteil der Menschenwürde keine Rede sein (so ausdrücklich: *Dreier*, Art. 1 Rdnr. 64).

Ungeachtet der Frage der Zulässigkeit des Antrags ist der Antrag auf Gewährung auf vorläufigen vorbeugenden Rechtsschutz aber auch deshalb ohne Erfolg, weil die Maßgaben des *EuGH* für die Gewährung vorläufigen Rechtsschutzes durch nationale Verwaltungsgerichte gegenüber Maßnahmen nationaler Behörden in Anwendung von primärem oder sekundärem Gemeinschaftsrecht nicht vorliegen. Vorliegend wollen die Ast. im Ergebnis im einstweiligen Rechtsschutzverfahren erreichen, dass die nationale Marktordnungsbehörde keinerlei Maßnahmen zur Umsetzung der Verordnung (EG) Nr. 2777/2000 ergreift. Da somit nach dem Willen der Ast. in der Bundesrepublik Deutschland vorläufig eine Verordnung der EG, die nach Art. 249 EGV in allen ihren Teilen verbindlich und unmittelbar in jedem Mitgliedstaat gilt, außer Anwendung bleiben soll, kann der begehrte einstweilige Rechtsschutz im Übrigen nur unter den Voraussetzungen gewährt werden, die der *EuGH* für die Gewährung vorläufigen Rechtsschutzes durch nationale Verwaltungsgerichte gegenüber sekundärem Gemeinschaftsrecht entwickelt hat (vgl. *EuGH*, Slg. 1995, I-3761 = NJW 1996, 1333 – Atlanta I). Voraussetzung für die Gewährung vorläufigen Rechtsschutzes ist danach:

1 dass das nationale Gericht erhebliche Zweifel an der Gültigkeit der Gemeinschaftsordnung hat,

2 die Frage dieser Gültigkeit dem *EuGH* vorlegt,

3 die Eilentscheidung dringlicher ist und

This chamber cannot follow this view. Article 1 I of the GG protects the dignity of humans, not animals (*Dreier*, in: the same (ed), GG I, 1996 Art 1 marginal no 63). Protection of animals has – to put it differently – nothing to do with human dignity (see *Jarass/Pieroth*, GG, 4th edn [1997], Art 1 marginal no 11; *Höfling*, in: *Sachs*, GG, 2nd edn [1989], Art 1 marginal no 30). In particular, the human centred approach of the Basic Law, which has as its exclusive object the protection of the human being and not of other forms of life, argues against the view that would give ethical animal protection constitutional rank. The interests of an animal itself can therefore not be regarded as a component of the human dignity guarantee. Besides this, widening the guarantee of human dignity to include protection of animals would threaten to overstretch Art 1 I of the GG, which is to protect human dignity from violations and not, in the sense of 'bettering' it, to become the vehicle of highly honourable but particular moral standards. In the face of a culturally established practice not fundamentally altered throughout many generations of systematic breeding of animals for the purpose of their subsequent consumption – a classic example of treatment as a mere object – there can be no question of animals being an integral part of human dignity (thus, expressly: *Dreier*, Art 1 marginal no 64).

Apart from the question of the admissibility of the application, the application for the granting of provisional preventative legal protection is however also unsuccessful, as the conditions of the ECJ for the granting of provisional legal protection by national administrative courts against measures of national authorities in application of primary or secondary Community law are not present. In this case the complainants want to achieve by proceedings for temporary legal protection the result that the national market order authority takes no measures for the implementation of EC Regulation 2777/2000. As the complainants therefore want an EC Regulation (which according to Art 249 of the EC Treaty is binding in all its parts and applies directly in every Member State) to remain temporarily inapplicable in the Federal Republic of Germany, the desired temporary legal protection can anyway only be granted under the prerequisites which the ECJ has developed for the granting of provisional legal protection by national administrative courts against secondary Community law (see *EuGH* Slg. 1995, I-3761 = NJW 1996, 1333 – Altanta I). The prerequisites for the granting of temporary legal protection are accordingly:

1   that the national court has substantial doubt about the validity of the EC order,

2   it lays the question of this validity before the ECJ,

3   rapid decision is very urgent and

4 den Ast. ein schwerer, nicht wieder gutzumachender Schaden droht und

5 wenn das Gericht die Interessen der Gemeinschaft angemessen berücksichtigt.

Diese Voraussetzungen liegen hier nicht vor. Das Gericht hat schon keine erheblichen Zweifel an der Gültigkeit der streitbefangenen Gemeinschaftsverordnung. Die Verordnung findet entgegen der Auffassung der Ast. ihre Rechtsgrundlage in Art 38 II i.V. mit Art 38 I der Verordnung (EG) Nr. 1254/99 des Rates vom 17.5.1999 (ABIEG Nr. L. 160/21 v. 26.6.1999). Nach Art. 38 I können die notwendigen Maßnahmen ergriffen werden, wenn auf dem Gemeinschaftsmarkt ein erheblicher Preisanstieg oder erheblicher Preisrückgang festgestellt und damit zu rechnen ist, dass diese Lage anhält und dadurch Marktstörungen auftreten oder aufzutreten drohen.

Vorliegend sind – wie sich aus der ersten Begründungserwägung zur Verordnung (EG) Nr. 2777/2000 der Kommission ergibt, die Erzeugerpreise im Hinblick auf den Zusammenbruch des Rindfleischmarkts erheblich zurückgegangen, ohne dass ein Ende dieser Marktstörung absehbar ist, so dass die Kommission außerordentliche Stützungsmaßnahmen für erforderlich gehalten hat. Sonstige Bedenken gegen die Gültigkeit der einschlägigen Verordnung sind weder ersichtlich noch dargetan. Insbesondere verstößt die Verordnung nicht gegen primäres Gemeinschaftsrecht oder allgemeine Rechtsgrundsätze, wozu auch die Menschenwürde gehört.

(Mitgeteilt von Vors. Richter am VG W. Schäfer, Frankfurt a. M.)

Art. 2 [Allgemeines Persönlichkeitsrecht] (1) Jeder hat das Recht auf die freie Entfaltung seiner Persönlichkeit, soweit er nicht die Rechte anderer verletzt und nicht gegen die verfassungsmäßige Ordnung oder das Sittengesetz verstößt.

(2) Jeder hat das Recht auf Leben und körperliche Unversehrtheit. Die Freiheit der Person ist unverletzlich. In diese Rechte darf nur auf Grund eines Gesetzes eingegriffen werden.

4   the complainant is threatened by severe damage which cannot be made good and

5   if the court takes the interests of the Community into account appropriately.

These prerequisites are not present here. The court has no substantial doubt about the validity of the disputed Community Regulation. Contrary to the view of the complainants, the Regulation finds its legal basis in Art 38 II in combination with Art 38 I of EC Regulation 1254/199 of the Council of 17.5.1999 (OJ no L 160/21 of 26.6.1999). According to Art 38 I, the necessary measures can be taken if a substantial rise or fall in price on the community market is established, and it is to be expected that this situation will remain and market disturbances will thereby arise or threaten to arise.

As emerges from the first reason for EC Regulation 2777/2000 by the Commission, the producers' prices here have substantially decreased, having regard to the collapse of the beef market, and no end to this market disturbance is foreseeable, so that the Commission has considered exceptional support measures to be necessary. No other doubts about the validity of the relevant Regulation are either evident or stated. In particular the Regulation does not violate primary EC law or general legal principles (which include human dignity).

(Submitted by the presiding judge at the Administrative Court, W Schäfer, Frankfurt aM.)

Article 2 [General right to personality] (1) Everyone has the right to the free development of his personality, insofar as he does not injure the rights of others or violate the constitutional order or the moral law.

(2) Everyone has the right to life and physical integrity. The freedom of the individual is inviolable. These rights may only be restricted on the basis of a statute.

This article, together with Art 1, gives a general right to privacy and non-interference in personal affairs. It covers things like the extent to which a person can be required to give information and belong to associations of a public nature. The investment aid act case (in relation to corporate bodies) (see p 193), the publication of a letter case (see Chapter Six, p 469) the film director case (see Chapter Six, p 505) and the insult of soldiers case (see Chapter Seven, p 715) give examples of the extent and limitations of the right.

Article 2 I gives the right not, eg, to be spied on and may for instance be relevant to the degree of publicity which can be given in the search for a criminal.

Article 2 II applies only to natural persons. It will be subject to limitations: killing may sometimes be considered necessary, eg, to save the life of another. But Nazi-style euthanasia would be unconstitutional. And the right to life could also be endangered by compulsion to carry out tasks which involve great risk.

See also Art 104 in Chapter Two, p 97 in relation to personal freedom.

Art. 3 [Gleichheit vor dem Gesetz] (1) Alle Menschen sind vor dem Gesetz gleich.

(2) Männer und Frauen sind gleichberechtigt. Der Staat fördert die tatsächliche Durchsetzung der Gleichberechtigung von Frauen und Männern und wirkt auf die Beseitigung bestehender Nachteile hin.

(3) Niemand darf wegen seines Geschlechtes, seiner Abstammung, seiner Rasse, seiner Sprache, seiner Heimat und Herkunft, seines Glaubens, seiner religiösen oder politischen Anschauungen benachteiligt oder bevorzugt werden. Niemand darf wegen seiner Behinderung benachteiligt werden.

Article 3 [Equality before the law] (1) All human beings are equal before the law.

(2) Men and women have equal rights. The State promotes the actual implementation of equality of rights of women and men and works towards the elimination of existing disadvantages.

(3) No-one may be disadvantaged or advantaged on account of his sex, parentage, race, language, homeland and origin, belief, or religious or political views. No one may be disadvantaged because of his disability.

The general requirement of equality in para 1 means that essentially similar cases should be treated similarly, and essentially different cases should be treated in a way that corresponds to their difference. The Federal Constitutional Court has approved different retirement ages for doctors and midwives, because their professional profiles were different. The paragraph prevents the application of arbitrary rules. The legislator's task is not, however, made impossibly difficult, because he only has to find a solution which does not clearly contravene this paragraph, and he may be able to avoid a breach by including a special clause to cover exceptional cases.

Paragraphs 2 and 3 have their limitations, eg, certain types of employment and political extremists respectively.

THE HOUSEWORK DAY CASE

There is a familiarity now for the English law student in the idea of assessing national legislation for its compatibility with a superior norm which requires equality between the sexes: see *R v Secretary of State for Employment ex p Equal Opportunities Commission and Another, The Times*, 4 March 1994, relating to a successful challenge of certain provisions of the Employment Protection (Consolidation) Act 1978, on the basis that they were incompatible with Art 119 of the Treaty of Rome. It is however noteworthy that the successful challenge there was by the Equal Opportunities Commission; the challenge by an individual, Mrs Day, was unsuccessful. In the housework day case a successful challenge was mounted by an individual.

THE HOUSEWORK DAY CASE

BVerfGE Band 52 S. 369

16 Mit Art. 3 Abs. 2 GG ist es unvereinbar, wenn alleinstehenden Frauen mit eigenem Hausstand, nicht aber Männern in gleicher Lage ein Anspruch auf Hausarbeitstag gewährt wird.

Beschluß des Ersten Senats vom 13. November 1979

– 1 BvR 631/78 –

in dem Verfahren über die Verfassungsbeschwerde des Herrn M ... a) gegen das Urteil des Arbeitsgerichts Köln vom 17. Februar 1978 – 12 Ca 7967/77 –, b) mittelbar gegen § 1 des Gesetzes des Landes Nordrhein-Westfalen über Freizeitgewährung für Frauen mit eigenem Hausstand vom 27. Juli 1948 (GVBl. 1949 S. 6).

Entscheidungsformel:

1 § 1 des Gesetzes des Landes Nordrhein-Westfalen über Freizeitgewährung für Frauen mit eigenem Hausstand vom 27. Juli 1948 (*Gesetz- und Verordnungsbl.* 1949 S. 6) ist mit Artikel 3 Absatz 2 des Grundgesetzes unvereinbar, soweit der Hausarbeitstag weiblichen, aber nicht männlichen alleinstehenden Arbeitnehmern mit eigenem Hausstand gewährt wird.

2 Das Urteil des Arbeitsgerichts Köln vom 17. Februar 1978 – 12 Ca 7967/77 – verletzt das Grundrecht des Beschwerdeführers aus Artikel 3 Abs. 2 des Grundgesetzes und wird aufgehoben. Die Sache wird an das Arbeitsgericht zurückverwiesen.

3 Das Land Nordrhein-Westfalen hat dem Beschwerdeführer die notwendigen Auslagen zu erstatten.

Gründe:

A

Die Verfassungsbeschwerde betrifft die Verfassungsmäßigkeit des § 1 des Gesetzes des Landes Nordrhein-Westfalen über Freizeitgewährung für Frauen mit eigenem Hausstand vom 27. Juli 1948 (HATG NRW), soweit es einen Hausarbeitstag weiblichen, aber nicht männlichen alleinstehenden Arbeitnehmern mit eigenem Hausstand gewährt.

THE HOUSEWORK DAY CASE

BVerfGE Volume 52 p 369

16 It is incompatible with Art 3 para 2 of the GG for a claim to a housework day to be granted to single women with their own households but not to men in the same position.

Decision of the First Senate of 13 November 1979

– 1 BvR 631/78 –

in the proceedings about the constitutional complaint of Mr. M ... a) against the judgment of the Labour Court of Cologne of 17 January 1978 – 12 Ca 7967/77 –, b) indirectly against § 1 of the Statute of the State of North Rhine Westphalia concerning the granting of free time for women with their own households of 27 July 1948 (GVB1 1949, 6)

Decision:

1 § 1 of the Statute of the State of North Rhine Westphalia concerning the granting of free time for women with their own households of 27 July 1948 (*Statutes and Regulations Gazette* 1949, p 6) is incompatible with Art 3 para 2 of the Basic Law insofar as the housework day is granted to female, but not to male, single employees with their own households.

2 The judgment of the Labour Court of Cologne of 17 February 1978 – 12 Ca 7967/77 – violates the basic right of the complainant arising from Art 3 para 2 of the Basic Law and is quashed. The matter is referred back to the Labour Court.

3 The State of North Rhine Westphalia must reimburse the complainant for the necessary expenses.

Reasons:

A

The constitutional complaint concerns the constitutionality of § 1 of the Statute of the State of North Rhine Westphalia concerning the granting of free time for women with their own households of 27 July 1948 (Housework Day Act, North Rhine Westphalia – HATG NRW), insofar as it grants a housework day to female, but not male, single employees with their own households.

I

1 Die Gewährung des Hausarbeitstages geht zurück auf § 2 Abs. 1 Buchst. b der Anordnung des Reichsarbeitsministers über Arbeitszeitverkürzung für Frauen, Schwerbeschädigte und minderleistungsfähige Personen (Freizeitanordnung) vom 22. Oktober 1943 (Reichsarbeitsblatt I S. 508). Bedingt durch die Kriegsverhältnisse mußten in immer stärkerem Maße Frauen als Arbeitskräfte herangezogen werden. Der Doppelbelastung mit Berufs- und Hausarbeit wurde durch die Gewährung eines unbezahlten Hausarbeitstages Rechnung getragen.

Nach dem Zweiten Weltkrieg wurde das Hausarbeitstagsrecht durch Gesetze der Länder Bremen (Gesetz über den Hausarbeitstag vom 29. Juni 1948 – GBl. S. 95), Hamburg (Gesetz über den Hausarbeitstag vom 17. Februar 1949 – GVBl. S. 15), Niedersachsen (Gesetz betr. hauswirtschaftliche Freizeit für Frauen – Hausarbeitstag – vom 9. Mai 1949 - GVBl. S. 104) und Nordrhein-Westfalen erweitert. Diese Gesetze stimmen darin überein, daß sie weiblichen Arbeitnehmern mit eigenem Hausstand den Anspruch auf einen freien und – insoweit abweichend von der Freizeitanordnung – bezahlten Hausarbeitstag gewähren. In den Ländern ohne eigene Hausarbeitstagsgesetze gilt die Freizeitanordnung weiter. In den Ländern mit Hausarbeitstagsgesetzen gilt sie insoweit, als nicht ihre Bestimmungen weitergehenden Gesetzen widersprechen.

2 Die Vorschrift des § 1 HATG NRW lautet:

In Betrieben und Verwaltungen aller Art haben Frauen mit eigenem Hausstand, die im Durchschnitt wöchentlich mindestens 40 Stunden arbeiten, Anspruch auf einen arbeitsfreien Wochentag (Hausarbeitstag) in jedem Monat.

Nach der gefestigten Rechtsprechung des Bundesarbeitsgerichts können nicht nur verheiratete, sondern auch alleinstehende Arbeitnehmerinnen, die einen eigenen Hausstand führen, einen Hausarbeitstag beanspruchen. Ein eigener Hausstand im Sinne des § 1 HATG NRW liegt bei einer alleinstehenden Frau vor, wenn sie mindestens einen Raum ganz oder überwiegend mit Einrichtungsgegenständen ausgestattet hat und darin ohne ausreichende Hilfe die anfallenden, mit einem Haushalt üblicherweise verbundenen Arbeiten im wesentlichen selbst verrichtet. Das Bundesarbeitsgericht hält die Vorschrift in dieser Auslegung mit Art. 3 Abs. 2 GG für vereinbar. Sie knüpfe an die typische Arbeitsteilung der Geschlechter an und sei als Arbeitschutzrecht für erwerbstätige Frauen anzusehen (BAG – Gr. Sen – Beschluß vom 16. März 1962, BAG 13, 1 = AP Nr. 19 zu § 1 HausarbTagsG NRW; seither ständige Rechtsprechung vgl. zuletzt BAG-Urteil vom 26. Oktober 1978, BB 1979, S. 477 = [demnächst] AP Nr. 27 zu § 1 HausarbTagsG NRW).

I

1 The granting of the housework day goes back to § 2 para 1 letter b of the Order of the Labour Minister of the Reich regarding the shortening of working time for women, the seriously disabled and less capable persons (Free Time Order) of 22 October 1943 (*Reich Labour Gazette I*, p 508). Due to the limitations of war conditions, women had to be called in as a work force in ever increasing numbers. The double burden of vocational work and housework was taken into account by the granting of an unpaid housework day.

After the Second World War, the right to a housework day was extended by statutes of the States of Bremen (Housework Day Act of 29 June 1948 – GB1, 95), Hamburg (Housework Day Act of 17 February 1949 – GVB1, 15), Lower Saxony (Housekeeping Free Time for Women (Housework Day) Act of 9 May (1949 – GVB1, 104) and North Rhine Westphalia. These statutes agree with one another in that they grant female employees with their own households a claim to a free and – in this respect deviating from the Free Time Order – paid housework day. In the States without their own housework day statutes, the Free Time Order remains valid. In the States with housework day statutes, it is valid insofar as the provisions of statutes going beyond it do not contradict it.

2 The provisions of § 1 of the HATG NRW state:

In businesses and administrations of every kind, women with their own households, who work on average at least 40 hours a week, have a claim to a work free week day (housework day), in each month.

According to the confirmed case law of the Federal Labour Court, not only married but also single female employees who conduct their own households can claim a housework day. One's own household, in the sense of § 1 HATG NRW, exists for a single woman if she has fitted out at least one room entirely or predominantly with furnishing facilities, and in the main carries out there herself, without sufficient help, the work arising which is connected in practice with a household. The Federal Labour Court regards this interpretation of the provisions as being compatible with Art 3 para 2 of the GG. It links with the typical division of work between the sexes and is to be regarded as a work protection right for working women (BAG Grand Senate – decision of 16 March 1962, BAG 13, 1 = AP no 19 at § 1 Housework Day Act NRW; since then consistent case law, compare finally BAG judgment of 26 October 1978, BB 1979, 477 = [to be published soon] AP no 27 on § 1 Housework Day Act NRW).

II

1 Der Beschwerdeführer ist Krankenpfleger im Dienst des Landes Nordrhein-Westfalen. Er ist ledig und wohnt allein in einer Wohnung von ca. 80 qm. Er arbeitet 40 Stunden an sechs Tagen in der Woche. Sein Arbeitgeber lehnte seinen Antrag vom 1. Oktober 1977 ab, ihm von Oktober 1977 an einen Hausarbeitstag zu gewähren. Im arbeitsgerichtlichen Verfahren beantragte er zuletzt, das Land Nordrhein-Wesfalen zu verurteilen ihm für einen arbeitsfreien Hausarbeitstag im Monat Oktober 1977 eine Abgeltung von 120 DM brutto zu zahlen.

2 Das Arbeitsgericht hat die Klage abgewiesen. Es führt aus:

Der von dem Beschwerdeführer geltend gemachte Anspruch finde weder in dem Hausarbeitstagsgesetz des Landes Nordrhein-Westfalen noch in Art. 3 Abs. 2 GG eine Rechtsgrundlage. Im Hausarbeitstagsgesetz seien als Anspruchsberechtigte nur Frauen genannt. Wenn das Gesetz wegen Verstoßes gegen Art. 3 GG unwirksam wäre, weil es Frauen unzulässig begünstige, habe das nicht die von dem Beschwerdeführer erhoffte Rechtsfolge daß Männer die gleichen Rechte erhielten. Es sei Sinn des Gleichberechtigungssatzes, die Frauen, die bisher rechtlich benachteiligt gewesen seien, auf den Status der Männer anzuheben. Aus Art. 3 GG könne nicht abgeleitet werden, daß den Männern – wenn der Gesetzgeber in seinem Bestreben, die Frauen den Männern gleichzustellen, über das Ziel 'hinausgeschossen' sei und die Frauen 'überprivilegiert' habe – die den Frauen gewährten Rechte auch eingeräumt werden müßten.

3 Mit der gegen das Urteil des Arbeitsgerichts gerichteten Verfassungsbeschwerde rügt der Beschwerdeführer, daß das Hausarbeitstagsgesetz des Landes Nordrhein-Westfalen gegen Art. 3 Abs. 2 und 3 GG verstoße. Er trägt vor: Die Nichtgewährung des Hausarbeitstages an männliche Arbeitnehmer könne mit dem Hinweis auf die traditionelle Arbeitsteilung der Geschlechter nicht gerechtfertigt werden. Zwar werde eine Arbeitsteilung, nach der die Frau den Haushalt führe und der Mann im Berufsleben stehe, noch häufig praktiziert. Als gesellschaftliches Prinzip sei dieser Grundsatz jedoch längst überwunden. Es gelte heute gesellschaftlich keineswegs mehr als anrüchig, wenn eine Frau am Berufsleben teilnehme. Auch sei es nicht mehr typisch, daß die alleinstehende Frau ihren Haushalt selbst führe, während bei dem Mann das Gegenteil der Fall sei. Es sei ausschließlich eine Frage der finanziellen Situation oder der persönlichen Neigung, ob eine alleinstehende Person, gleichgültig ob Mann oder Frau, sich selbst versorge oder gegen Bezahlung durch Dritte versorgen lasse. Entscheide sie sich für die Selbstversorgung, sei die Situation für Mann und Frau gleich. Im übrigen komme dem Gleichberechtigungsgrundsatz eine gewisse korrigierende Funktion hinsichtlich dessen zu, was bisher als typische Rollenverteilung angesehen worden sei.

II

1 The complainant is a male nurse in service in the State of North Rhine Westphalia. He is single and lives alone in an apartment of about 80 sq.m He works 40 hours on six days in the week. His employer refused his request of 1 October 1977 to grant him a housework day from October 1977 onwards. In the Labour Court proceedings, he finally applied for the State of North Rhine Westphalia to be adjudged liable to pay him compensation of 120 DM gross for a work free housework day in the month of October 1977.

2 The Labour Court rejected the claim. It explains:

The claim raised by the complainant finds no legal basis in either the Housework Day Act of the State of North Rhein Westphalia nor in Art 3 para 2 of the GG. In the Housework Day Act, only women are mentioned as persons entitled to claim. If the statute were ineffective because of violation of Art 3 of the GG, because it benefited women in an impermissible way, that would not have the legal consequences hoped for by the complainant, that men should receive the same rights. The point of the equal rights requirement was to raise women, who until now had been legally disadvantaged, to the status of men. It could not be deduced from Art 3 of the GG that men – if the legislator in his endeavour to put women on an equal footing to men had 'overshot' the objective, and 'overprivileged' women – had also to be given the rights granted to women.

3 By the constitutional complaint against the judgment of the Labour Court, the complainant objects that the Housework Day Act of the State of North Rhine Westphalia violates Art 3 para 2 and 3 of the GG. He states: the failure to grant a housework day to male employees could not be justified by reference to the traditional division of work between the sexes. Certainly, a division of work by which the woman carries out the housework and the man is working is still commonly practised. As a social principle, however, this rule had long since been overtaken. Today it was regarded socially as being no longer in any way improper if a woman was working. It was also no longer typical for the single woman herself to run her household, whilst with a man the opposite was the case. It was exclusively a question of the financial situation or of personal inclination whether a single person, regardless of whether he or she was a man or a woman, looked after himself or herself or arranged for himself or herself to be looked after by a third party for payment. If she decided in favour of looking after herself, the situation for men and women would be equal. Besides this, a certain correcting function was appropriate for the equal rights principle in relation to what had until now been regarded as a typical division of roles.

III

Die Bundesregierung, der Ministerpräsident des Landes Nordrhein-Westfalen und das Bundesarbeitsgericht haben auf die bisherige Rechtsprechung des Bundesarbeitsgerichts hingewiesen und im übrigen von Stellungnahmen abgesehen.

B

Die zulässige Verfassungsbeschwerde ist begründet. § 1 HATG NRW ist mit Art. 3 Abs. 2 GG unvereinbar, soweit die Vorschrift nur für alleinstehende Frauen mit eigenem Hausstand die Gewährung eines Hausarbeitstages vorsieht.

I

Gegenstand der verfassungsrechtlichen Prüfung ist § 1 HATG NRW in der Auslegung, die das Bundesarbeitsgericht der Vorschrift mit dem Beschluß seines Großen Senats vom. 16. März 1962 (BAG 13, 1 = AP Nr. 19 zu S. 1 HausarbTagsG NRW) gegeben hat und seither seiner Rechtsprechung zugrunde legt Danach haben im Bereich des Landes Nordrhein-Westfalen alle arbeitenden Frauen ohne Rücksicht auf ihren Familienstand einen Anspruch auf den Hausarbeitstag, wenn sie in einem bestimmten zeitlichen Umfang arbeiten und einen eigenen Hausstand haben und selbst führen; für männliche Arbeitnehmer die sich in der gleichen Lage befinden, sieht § 1 HATG NRW dagegen nach dem insoweit eindeutigen Wortlaut einen Anspruch auf den Hausarbeitstag nicht vor. Von dieser Rechtslage geht auch das Arbeitsgericht in dem mit der Verfassungsbeschwerde angefochtenen Urteil aus.

Prüfungsmaßstab ist Art. 3 Abs. 2 GG. Das dort ausgesprochene Gebot der Gleichberechtigung von Männern und Frauen konkretisiert den allgemeinen Gleichheitssatz und verbietet, daß der Geschlechtsunterschied einen beachtlichen Grund für Differenzierungen im Recht abgeben kann. Das schließt allerdings nach der ständigen Rechtsprechung des Bundesverfassungsgerichts Regelungen nicht aus, die im Hinblick auf die objektiven biologischen und funktionalen (arbeitsteiligen) Unterschiede nach der Natur des jeweiligen Lebensverhältnisses zwischen Männern und Frauen differenzieren (vgl. BVerfGE 3, 225 [242]; 5, 9 [12]; 10, 59 [74]; 15, 337 [343]; 21, 329 [343f.]; 31, 1 [4f.]; 37, 217 [249f.]; 43, 213 [225]). Auf solche Merkmale läßt sich die Unterscheidung, die die Regelung des § 1 HATG NRW trifft - jedenfalls bei Alleinstehenden -, nicht zurückzuführen.

II

Die Regelung des § 1 HATG NRW knüpft bei der Bestimmung, welchen Personen der Hausarbeitstag zu gewähren ist, allein an den Geschlechtsunterschied an und nimmt damit ein verfassungsrechtlich unzulässige Differenzierung vor.

III

The Federal Government, the Prime Minister of the State of North Rhine Westphalia and the Federal Labour Court have referred to the past case law of the Federal Labour Court and apart from this have refrained from taking a position.

B

The constitutional complaint is permissible and well founded. § 1 of the HATG NRW is irreconcilable with Art 3 para 2 of the GG insofar as its provisions only provide for the granting of a housework day for single women with their own households.

I

The object of the constitutional law examination is § 1 of the HATG NRW, in the interpretation which the Federal Labour Court has given to this provision by the decision of its Grand Senate of 16 March 1962 (BGBl 13, 1 = AP no 19 on § 1 Housework Day Act NRW) and which has since laid the basis of its case law. According to this, all working women in the area of the State of North Rhine Westphalia have, without regard to their family status, a claim to a housework day if they work for a certain time period and have their own household and run it themselves; for male employees who find themselves in the same situation, § 1 of the HATG NRW does not on the other hand provide a claim to a housework day according to its wording which is in this respect unambiguous. The Labour Court also proceeded from this legal position in the judgment which is challenged by the constitutional complaint.

The standard for the examination is Art 3 para 2 of the GG. The requirement expressed there for the granting of equal rights to men and women concretises the general requirement of equality and prevents a difference in sex from being allowed to give a relevant reason for differentiating in law. That certainly does not, according to the consistent case law of the Federal Constitutional Court, exclude rules which, having regard to the objective biological and functional (based in the division of labour) distinctions, differentiate according to the nature of prevailing relationships of life between men and women (compare BVerfGE 3, 225 [242]; 5, 9 [12]; 10, 59 [74]; 15, 337 [343]; 21, 329 [343 and onwards]; 31, 1 [4 and onwards]; 37, 217 [249 and onwards]; 43, 213 [225]). The differentiation which the requirements of § 1 HATG NRW makes – at any rate with single persons – cannot be put down to such characteristics.

II

The requirements of § 1 of the HATG NRW are linked, by the provision as to the persons to whom the housework day is to be granted, only to a difference on account of sex and because of that make a differentiation impermissible in constitutional law.

1 Mit der Gewährung eines Hausarbeitstages soll der Arbeitnehmerin Gelegenheit gegeben werden, Arbeiten zu erledigen, die sich nur schwer im täglichen Nebeneinander von Beruf und Haushalt bewältigen lassen, insbesondere umfangreiche Wasch- und Putzarbeiten (vgl. Binder-Wehberg, Ungleichbehandlung von Mann und Frau, 1970, S. 128 unter Hinweis auf den erwähnten Beschluß des Großen Senats des Bundesarbeitsgerichts vom 16. März 1962). Diese Zielsetzung wird bereits in den der Freizeitordnung vorangegangenen Erlassen des Reichsarbeitsministers zur Zulassung von Arbeitszeitverkürzungen durch das Gewerbeaufsichtsamt erkennbar (zit. bei Bulla, Mutterschutzgesetz und Frauenarbeitsrecht, 1954, 2. Buch, Teil B, Rdnr. 3, S. 541). In einem Erlaß vom 12. Dezember 1939 heißt es: 'Verkürzte Arbeitszeiten an einzelnen Werktagen können ferner angeordnet werden, um verheirateten Frauen, insbesondere Frauen mit Kindern, die Vesorgung ihres Haushalts zu erleichtern.' In einem nachfolgenden Erlaß vom 31. Juli 1940 ist unter anderem bestimmt:

> Den Frauen ist zur Erledigung ihrer häuslichen Aufgaben nach Möglichkeit eine verkürzte Arbeitszeit an etwa zwei Tagen in der Woche einzuräumen. Falls ihnen diese Arbeitszeitverkürzungen aus betrieblichen Gründen nicht gewährt werden können, soll ihnen innerhalb von zwei Wochen ein voller Arbeitstag (Waschtag) freigegeben werden.

2 Eine Doppelbelastung durch Berufstätigkeit und Haushaltsführung kann auch bei Männern in Betracht kommen. Dies gilt insbesondere für Alleinstehende, die sich in einer eigenen Wohnung selbst versorgen, da bei ihnen Berufstätigkeit und Haushaltsführung zwangsläufig in einer Person zusammentreffen. Soweit ein alleinstehender Arbeitnehmer die Doppelbelastung durch Beruf und Haushalt trägt, ist es nicht gerechtfertigt, ihn bei der Gewährung des Hausarbeitstages anders als eine alleinstehende Arbeitnehmerin zu behandeln. Objektive biologische oder funktionale (arbeitsteilige) Unterschiede prägen das hier zu ordnende Lebensverhältnis nicht so entscheidend, daß die vergleichbaren Elemente daneben vollkommen zurücktreten müßten und die verschiedene rechtliche Regelung mit den Begriffen 'Benachteiligen' und 'Bevorzugen' nicht mehr sinnvoll zu erfassen wäre (vgl. BVerfGE 37, 217 [249] m.w.N.).

(a) Es gehört nicht zu den geschlechtsbedingten Eigenheiten von Frauen, Hausarbeit zu verrichten. Wenn in diesem Bereich gleichwohl in erster Linie die Tätigkeit von Frauen erwartet wird, beruht dies allein auf der herkömmlichen Vorstellung, daß es der Frau zufällt, den Haushalt ganz oder mindestens überwiegend zu besorgen.

1 With the granting of a housework day, the female worker is to be given the opportunity to carry out work which could only, with difficulty, be dealt with in the daily juxtaposition of vocation and household, especially extensive washing and cleaning work (compare Binder-Wehberg, Unequal Treatment of Men and Women, 1970, p 128 with reference to the said decision of the Grant Senate of the Federal Labour Court of 16 March 1962). This objective is already recognisable in the decrees of the Reich Labour Minister preceding the Free Time Order for the authorisation of reductions in working time by the Factory Inspectorate (quoted in Bulla, Protection of Mothers Act and Women's Labour Law, 1954, 2nd Book, Part B, marginal no 3, p 541). In a decree of 12 December 1939 it states: 'Shortened working periods on individual working days can be further ordered to facilitate for married women, especially women with children, the care of their households.' In a subsequent decree of 31 July 1940 it is provided, amongst other things:

> A shortened work period on approximately two days in the week is to be granted if possible to women for the carrying out of their household tasks. In case these shortenings of work periods cannot be granted to them for business reasons, a full working day (wash day) is to be released for them every two weeks.

2 A double burden through vocational activity and running of a household can also come under consideration for men. This is especially true for single persons who look after themselves in their own dwellings, as for them vocational activity and running of a household unavoidably coincide in one person. Insofar as a single employee bears the double burden of vocation and household, it is not justified to treat him differently from a single female employee as to the granting of a housework day. Objective biological or functional (based on the division of labour) distinctions do not shape the relationship of life to be arranged here so decisively that the comparable elements in relation to it must completely recede and the different legal regime could no longer be sensibly understood by the concepts 'disadvantaging' and 'preferring' (compare BVerfGE 37, 217 [249] with further references).

(a) Carrying out housework does not belong to the characteristics of women which are dependent on sex. If the activity of women is nevertheless primarily expected in this area, this is only based on the traditional idea that it falls to the woman to attend to the housekeeping entirely or at least predominantly.

Die bisherige Regelung kann auch nicht mit einer geringeren Leistungsfähigkeit der Frau gerechtfertigt werden. Dabei kann dahinstehen, ob Frauen allgemein gegen körperliche Anstrengungen weniger widerstandsfähig und gesundheitlichen Schädigungen stärker ausgesetzt sind als Männer. Jedenfalls ist es nicht Sinn des Hausarbeitstages, eine etwaige schwächere Konstitution der Frau auszugleichen. Dem wird für den Bereich des Arbeitslebens durch die besonderen Arbeitsschutzvorschriften der §§ 16 bis 19 der Arbeitszeitordnung Rechnung getragen (vgl. Binder-Wehberg, a.a.O., S. 130ff.; Denecke-Neumann, AZO, 9. Aufl., 1976, 16 Rdnr. 1; Dürig in: Maunz-Dürig-Herzog-Scholz GG, Art. 3 Abs. 2 Rdnr. 43). Solche Arbeitsschutzbestimmungen, die auf die besondere Schutzwürdigkeit der Frau abstellen - vor allem Mutterschutzgesetze -, sind mit Art. 3 Abs. 2 GG vereinbar, weil dadurch nur Lebensumstände berücksichtigt werden, die ausschließlich die Frauen betreffen (vgl. BVerfGE 5, 9 [12]; Dürig, a.a.O., Art. 3 Abs. 2 Rdnr. 13).

Auch durch die Entstehungsgeschichte wird bestätigt, daß die Vorschrift des § 1 HATG NRW nicht an biologische Eigenschaften der Frau, insbesondere nicht an eine geringere körperliche Leistungsfähigkeit anknüpft. Durch die Gewährung des Hausarbeitstages soll der mit Beruf und Haushalt doppelt belasteten Arbeitnehmerin Gelegenheit und Zeit gegeben werden größere Haushaltsarbeiten zu erledigen, die mehr Zeit als den nach Arbeitsende jeweils verbleibenden Teil des Tages in Anspruch nehmen. Die Regelung beruht nicht auf der Abwägung der unterschiedlichen Leistungsfähigkeit von Männern und Frauen im Arbeitsleben, wie sie den Vorschriften der Arbeitszeitordnung nach ihrem Gesamtzusammenhang ersichtlich zugrunde liegt, sondern ausschließlich auf einer Bewertung der Doppelbelastung durch Beruf und Haushalt. Von dieser Doppelbelastung kann ein männlicher Arbeitnehmer, der daneben einen Haushalt führt, in gleicher Weise betroffen sein. Der Umfang der zu erledigenden Hausarbeit ist nicht geringer, wenn der Haushalt von einem Mann statt von einer Frau geführt wird. Bei dieser Sachlage kann die Gewährung des bezahlten Hausarbeitstages nur an Frauen mit den biologischen Unterschieden der Geschlechter nicht begründet werden.

Auch der Gedanke des Mutterschutzes der berufstätigen Frau hat in der Regelung des § 1 HATG NRW keinen Niederschlag gefunden (a.A.: BAG 13, 1). Die Vorschrift gewährt den Hausarbeitstag vorbehaltlich der übrigen Voraussetzungen allen Frauen ohne Rücksicht auf das Lebensalter, eine bestehende Schwangerschaft oder vorhandene Kinder, knüpft also in keiner Weise an Merkmale der Mutterschaft an. Im übrigen hatte der Gesetzgeber schon lange vor der ersten Regelung des Hausarbeitstages die Materie des Mutterschutzes besonders gesetzlich geregelt. Zum Zeitpunkt des Erlasses der Freizeitordnung galt das Gesetz zum Schutze der erwerbstätigen Mutter (Mutterschutzgesetz) vom 17 Mai 1942 (RGBl I S. 321), das später durch das Gesetz vom 24. Januar 1952 (BGBl I S. 69) abgelöst wurde (vgl. jetzt: Mutterschutzgesetz in der Fassung der Bekanntmachung vom 18. April 1968, zuletzt geändert durch Art. 2 des Gesetzes vom 27 Juni 1979 [BGBl I S. 823]).

The existing regime also cannot be justified by a smaller capacity for work on the part of the woman. At the same time it can be left undecided whether women in general are less resistant to bodily exertions and are more at the mercy of harm to their health than men. In any case, it is not the point of the housework day to compensate for a possibly weaker constitution of the woman. Account is taken of this in the sphere of working life by the special work protection provisions of §§ 16–19 of the Working Hours Order (compare Binder-Wehberg, *loc cit*, p 130 and onwards; Denecke-Neuman, AZO, 9th edn, 1976, 16 marginal no 1; Dürig in: Maunz-Dürig-Herzog-Scholz, GG, Art 3 para 2 marginal no 43). Such work protection provisions, which take into account the special need for protection of women – pre-eminently the Protection of Mothers Act – are compatible with Art 3 para 2 of the GG, because only those circumstances of life are taken into consideration by them which exclusively affect women (compare BVerfGE 5, 9 [12]; Dürig, *loc cit*, Art 3 para 2 marginal no 13).

It is also confirmed by the history of its origin that the provisions of § 1 of the HATG NRW do not relate to biological characteristics of women, and particularly not to a smaller physical capacity for work. By the granting of the housework day, the female worker, doubly burdened by vocation and housekeeping is given time and opportunity to carry out greater tasks of housework which claim more time than the part of any day which remains at the end of work. The regime is not based on a weighing up of the different capacity for work of men and women in working life, as obviously lies at the root of the provisions of the Working Hours Order according to their total context, but exclusively on an evaluation of the double burden of vocation and housework. A male worker who also runs a household can be affected in the same way by this double burden. The content of the housework to be carried out is not smaller if the household is run by a man instead of a woman. In view of this state of affairs, the granting of the paid housework day to women only cannot be justified by the biological differences of the sexes.

The concept of maternity protection for the working woman has also found no expression in the regime of § 1 of the HATG NRW (another view: BAG 13, 1). The provisions grant the housework day, subject to the other prerequisites, to all women without regard to their age, the existence of a pregnancy or the presence of children and thus do not relate in any way to the characteristics of motherhood. The legislator had incidentally regulated the substance of maternity protection separately by statute long before the first regulating of the housework day. At the point in time at which the Free Time Order was issued, the Statute for the protection of the working mother (Protection of Mothers Act) of 17 May 1942 (RGBl I, 321) was effective, and this was later superseded by the Statute of 24 January 1952 (BGBl I, 69) (compare now: Protection of Mothers Act in the form published on 18 April 1968, finally amended by Art 2 of the Statute of 27 June 1979 [BGBl I, 823]).

(b) Die Vorschrift des § 1 HATG NRW kann auch nicht durch funktionale (arbeitsteilige) Unterschiede der Geschlechter gerechtfertigt werden. Allerdings entspricht es einer hergebrachten Vorstellung, daß die Haushaltsführung als eine der Frau zufallende Aufgabe bei der Aufteilung der soziologischen Funktionen zwischen den Geschlechtern empfunden wird. Von dieser Rollenverteilung gehen auch diejenigen Stimmen in der Literatur aus, die allgemein die Berechtigung der gegenwärtigen Hausarbeitstagsregelung bei Mehrpersonenhaushalten für verfassungsrechtlich unbedenklich halten (vgl. Bulla, a.a.O., Rdnr. 35, S. 559f.; Dürig, a.a.O., Art 3 Abs. 2 Rdnr. 43; Nikisch, Arbeitsrecht, 2. Aufl., 1955, 1. Bd., § 40 II 3, S. 466; Friedrich Klein, Rechtsgutachten zur Auslegung des § 1 des nordrhein-westfälischen Gesetzes über Freizeitgewährung für Frauen mit eigenem Hausstand ..., erstattet gegenüber dem Bundesarbeitsgericht in dem erwähnten Verfahren des Großen Senats, S. 43f.; Scheffler, Ehe und Familie, in: Bettermann-Nipperdey-Scheuner, Die Grundrechte, 4. Bd., 1. Halbbd., S. 245 [309]; differenzierend Binder-Wehberg, a.a.O., S. 130f.). Ob aufgrund des neuen Familienrechts (§ 1356 BGB) sich bei Eheleuten die Aufteilung der beiderseitigen Aufgaben in Beruf, Haushalt und Familie grundlegend geändert hat (verneinend Urteil des Bundesarbeitsgerichts vom 26. Oktober 1978, BB 1979, 477 = [demnächst] AP Nr. 27 zu § 1 HausarbTagsG NRW) und ob daraus Folgerungen bei der verfassungsrechtlichen Beurteilung des Rechts des Hausarbeitstages zu ziehen sind, kann in diesem Verfahren dahingestellt bleiben. Jedenfalls verletzt die einseitige Hausarbeitstagsregelung zugunsten der alleinstehenden Frauen den Grundsatz der Gleichberechtigung nach Art. 3 Abs. 2 GG. Diese Frauen unterscheiden sich in keinem wesentlichen Punkt von Männern in gleicher Lage. Dabei ist es auch unerheblich, ob es für die alleinstehende berufstätige Frau der typischen Gestaltung der sozialen Verhältnisse entspricht, daß sie im Gegensatz zum Mann den Haushalt selbständig führt (so Hueck-Nipperdey, Lehrbuch des Arbeitsrechts, 7. Aufl., 1963, 1. Bd., § 69 II 3 Fußn. 13, S. 719, die mit dieser Erwägung einen Verfassungsverstoß verneinen; ebenso BAG 1, 51 = AP Nr. 1 zu Art. 3 GG). Selbst wenn dies auch heute noch zutreffend sein sollte, rechtfertigt es nicht die Benachteiligung der Männer, die ihren eigenen Haushalt tatsächlich selbst führen. Es verstößt gegen den Gleichberechtigungsgrundsatz, wenn den privaten Interessen der weiblichen Arbeitnehmer an einer bestimmten außerbetrieblichen Tätigkeit durch eine Ungleichbehandlung Rechnung getragen wird (Binder-Wehberg, a.a.O., S. 131). Im übrigen stellt auch das Bundesarbeitsgericht in seiner Rechtsprechung nicht darauf ab, ob – alleinstehende – Frauen typischerweise ihren Haushalt selbst führen, sondern auf die im Einzelfall zu treffende Feststellung, ob die alleinstehende Frau 'ohne ausreichende Hilfe die anfallenden mit einem Haushalt üblicherweise verbundenen Arbeiten im wesentlichen selbst verrichtet' (BAG, AP Nr. 26 zu § 1 HausarbTagsG NRW). Entsprechende Feststellungen können in gleicher Weise auch bei Männern mit eigenem Hausstand getroffen werden.

(b) The provisions of § 1 of the HATG NRW can also not be justified by functional (based on the division of labour) distinctions between the sexes. Certainly it corresponds to a traditional idea that the running of the household is felt to be a task falling to the woman in the division of sociological functions between the sexes. This division of roles is also used as a starting point for those voices in academic writings who in general consider the entitlement under the present housework day regime for households consisting of more than one person to be unobjectionable in constitutional law (compare Bulla *loc cit,* marginal no 35, p 559 and onwards; Dürig, *loc cit*, Art 3 para 2 marginal no 43; Nikisch, Labour Law, 2nd edn, 1955 Vol I § 40 II 3, p 466; Friedrich Klein, Legal opinion on the interpretation of § 1 of the Statute of North Rhine Westphalia concerning the granting of free time for women with their own households ... reported to the Federal Labour Court in the said proceedings of the Grand Senate, p 43 and onwards; Scheffler, Marriage and Family in: Bettermann-Nipperdey-Scheuner, *The Basic Rights*, Vol 4 Subvolume 1 p 245 [309]; differentiating Binder-Wehberg, *loc cit*, p 130 and onwards). Whether on the basis of the new family law (§ 1356 of the BGB) the allocation of mutual duties in relation to vocation, housekeeping and the family have fundamentally changed between married persons (denied by the judgment of the Federal Labour Court of 26 October 1978, BB 1979, 477 = [to be published soon] AP no 27 on § 1 of the Housework Day Act NRW), and whether inferences are to be drawn from that in a constitutional law assessment of the law about housework days, can remain undecided in these proceedings. In any case, the one-sided housework day regime in favour of single women violates the principle of equal rights according to Art 3 para 2 of the GG. These women are different in no significant respect from men in the same situation. In this connection it is also unimportant whether for the single working woman it corresponds to the typical formation of social relationships that she, in contrast to a man, runs the household independently (as in Hueck-Nipperdey, Textbook of Labour Law, 7th edn, 1963, Vol 1 69 II 3 footnote 13, p 719, which for this reason denies violation of the Constitution; as also in BAG 1, 51 = AP no 1 on Art 3 of the GG). Even if this should be pertinent today, it does not justify the disadvantaging of men who actually run their own households themselves. It violates the equal rights principle if through unequal treatment account is taken of the private interests of women workers in a certain private activity (Binder-Wehberg, *loc cit*, p 131). Also, the Federal Labour Court, incidentally, in its case law, does not take into account whether single women typically run their households themselves, but takes into account the assessment to be made in the individual case of whether the single woman 'substantially carries out herself without sufficient help the work arising which is in practice connected with a household'. (BAG, AP no 26 on § 1 of the Housework Day Act NRW). Corresponding assessments can also be made in the same manner for men with their own households.

III

Das Bundesverfassungsgericht kann die Vorschrift des § 1 HATG NRW nicht für nichtig erklären, sondern muß sich darauf beschränken, ihre Verfassungswidrigkeit festzustellen, da dem Gesetzgeber verschiedene Wege offenstehen, die von der Verfassung geforderte Gleichheit herzustellen (vgl. BVerfGE 25, 236 [252]).

Das Urteil des Arbeitsgerichts Köln ist aufzuheben, da es auf der für verfassungswidrig erklärten Vorschrift des § 1 HATG NRW beruht (§ 95 Abs. 2 BVerfGG). Die Sache ist an das Arbeitsgericht zurückzuverweisen. Wenn dieses sein Verfahren aussetzt, wird dem Beschwerdeführer die Chance offengehalten, an einer etwaigen Erweiterung des Rechts auf einen Hausarbeitstag durch den Gesetzgeber teilzunehmen (vgl. BVerfGE 22, 349 [363]).

Die Entscheidung über die Erstattung der notwendigen Auslagen beruht auf § 34 Abs. 4 BVerfGG.

(gez.) Dr. Benda   Dr. Böhmer   Dr. Simon

Dr. Faller   Dr. Hesse   Dr. Katzenstein

  Dr. Niemeyer   Dr. Heußner

Art. 4 [Glaubens-, Gewissens- und Bekenntnisfreiheit. Kriegsdienstverweigerung] (1) Die Freiheit des Glaubens, des Gewissens und die Freiheit des religiösen und weltanschaulichen Bekenntnisses sind unverletzlich.

(2) Die ungestörte Religionsausübung wird gewährleistet.

(3) Niemand darf gegen sein Gewissen zum Kriegsdienst mit der Waffe gezwungen werden. Das Nähere regelt ein Bundesgesetz.

III

The constitutional court cannot declare the provisions of the § 1 of the HATG NRW to be invalid but must confine itself to establishing that they are contrary to the Constitution, as various ways are available to the legislator for restoring the equality required by the Constitution (compare BVerfGE 25, 236 [252]).

The judgment of the Labour Court of Cologne is to be quashed, as it is based on the provisions of § 1 of the HATG NRW declared to be contrary to the Constitution (§ 95 para 2 of the BVerfGG). The matter is to be referred back to the Labour Court. If this Court suspends its proceedings, the chance would be kept open for the complainant to participate in a possible widening of the right to a housework day by the legislator (compare BVerfGE 22, 349 [363]).

The decision about the reimbursement of the necessary expenses is based on § 34 para 4 of the BVerfGG.

(Signatures of judges)

Article 4 [Freedom of belief, conscience and creed; refusal of military service] (1) Freedom of belief and of conscience, and freedom of religious and ideological creed are inviolable.

(2) The undisturbed practice of religion is guaranteed.

(3) No-one may be forced into armed military service against his conscience. Details are to be regulated by a Federal Statute.

THE CANNABIS APPLICATION REJECTION CASE

BVerwG NJW 2001, 1365

16 Religionsfreiheit und Anbau von Cannabis

GG Art. 4; BtMG §§ 3,5 I Nrn. 5 u. 6.

Eine Ausnahmegenehmigung vom Verbot des Cannabisanbaus nach § 3 BtMG kann nicht mit der Begründung beansprucht werden, der Genuss von Marihuana sei Teil der Religionsausübung.

BVerwG, Urt. v. 21.12.2000 – 3 C 20/00 (Berlin)

Zum Sachverhalt:

Der Kl. ist Sänger und Liedkomponist. Mit Schreiben vom 30.8.1993 beantragte er beim Bundesgesundheitsamt die Erteilung einer Erlaubnis zum Anbau von indischem Hanf in kleinen Mengen (fünf bis zehn Pflanzen pro Jahr). Dazu trug er vor, er bekenne sich zum Glauben der Rastas. Für die schwerpunktmäßig in Jamaica ansässigen Rastas sei das einheimische Marihuana – Cannabis sativa – das 'heilige Kraut', von dem an mehreren Stellen der Bibel gesprochen werde. Marihuana gelte unter der Mehrzahl der Rastas als Nahrung für das Gehirn und als Heilmittel. Es werde bei rituellen Versammlungen geraucht. In Ausübung seines Grundrechts der Religionsfreiheit wolle er Marihuanapflanzen zum Eigenverbrauch in geringem Umfang anbauen, ernten und später bei Rastazeremonien konsumieren. Er werde dafür sorgen, dass die Marihuanapflanzen nur auf seinem eigenen Grundstück angebaut und von ihm allein geerntet würden, so dass ein Missbrauch durch unbefugte Personen ausgeschlossen sei.

Mit Bescheid vom 7.12.1993 lehnte das Bundesgesundheitsamt den Antrag mit der Begründung ab, eine Erlaubnis für das nach dem Betäubungsmittelgesetz nicht verkehrsfähige Betäubungsmittel Cannabis könne nur ausnahmsweise zu wissenschaftlichen oder anderen im öffentlichen Interesse liegenden Zwecken erteilt werden; eine solche Zweckbestimmung könne dem Antrag nicht entnommen werden. Den Widerspruch des Kl. wies das Bundesgesundheitsamt mit Bescheid vom 17.5.1994 zurück. Die Klage auf Erteilung der beantragten Erlaubnis hat das *VG* abgewiesen. Die Berufung des Kl. hat das OVG zurückgewiesen.

Die Revision des Kl. blieb ohne Erfolg.

THE CANNABIS APPLICATION REJECTION CASE

BVerwG NJW 2001, 1365

This case is in form an unsuccessful challenge to a refusal by the administrative authorities to grant permission to grow cannabis. Its constitutional interest lies in the rejection of religious freedom under Art 4 of the Basic Law as a ground for challenging the decision. I have not been able to trace any reference in the Bible to a 'sacred herb'.

BVerwG NJW 2001, 1365

16 Religious freedom and the cultivation of cannabis

GG Art 4; BtMG §§ 3, 5 I nos 5 and 6.

An approval of an exception to the prohibition on the cultivation of cannabis under § 3 of the BtMG cannot be claimed on the basis that the consumption of marijuana is part of a religious exercise.

BVerwG, judgment of 21.12.2000 – 3 C 20/00 (Berlin)

Facts:

The claimant is a singer and composer of songs. By a letter of the 30.8.1993 he applied to the Federal Health Office for granting of a permission to grow small amounts of indian hemp (five to 10 plants a year). In this connection, he stated that he professed the Rastafarian religion. For Rastafarians, who were principally resident in Jamaica, the indigenous plant marijuana – Cannabis sativa – was the 'sacred herb' which was mentioned in several places in the Bible. The majority of Rastafarians regarded Marihuana as food for the brain and a medicine. It was smoked at ritual gatherings. In the exercise of his basic right of religious freedom, he wanted to grow the plants in small quantities for his own use, to harvest them, and later consume them at Rastafarian ceremonies. He would make sure that the marijuana plants were only grown on his land and were only harvested by him, so that misuse by unauthorised persons was excluded.

The Federal Health Office rejected his application by a decision of 7.12.1993 on the grounds that a permission for cannabis, which was a prohibited narcotic according to the BtMG, could only be given exceptionally for scientific or other purposes in the public interest. Such a purpose could not be deduced from the application. The Federal Health Office rejected the applicant's objection by its decision of the 17.5.1994. The claim for the giving of the permission he requested was rejected by the *VG*. The claimant's appeal was dismissed by the OVG.

The claimant's appeal in law was unsuccessful.

Aus den Gründen:

II Die Revision ist unbegründet. Die Entscheidung des BerGer., dass dem Kl. die begehrte Erlaubnis zum Anbau von Cannabis in geringen Mengen nicht erteilt werden darf, verletzt kein Bundesrecht.

1 Grundlage des Begehrens ist § 3 BtMG i. d. F. der Bekanntmachung vom 1.3.1994 (BGBl I, 358). Danach bedarf einer Erlaubnis des Bundesinstituts für Arzneimittel und Medizinprodukte, wer Betäubungsmittel anbauen will (§ 3 I Nr. 1). Für die Anlage 1 des Gesetzes aufgeführten Betäubungsmittel kann die Erlaubnis nur ausnahmsweise zu wissenschaftlichen oder anderen im öffentlichen Interesse liegenden Zwecken erteilt werden (Abs. 2). Cannabis gehört – abgesehen von hier nicht interessierenden Ausnahmen – zu den in dieser Anlage genannten nichtverkehrsfähigen Betäubungsmitteln. Sein Anbau ist mithin erlaubnispflichtig, aber nur unter den genannten Voraussetzungen erlaubnisfähig. Diese Voraussetzungen liegen hier nicht vor.

Dass der Kl. die Erlaubnis nicht zu wissenschaftlichen Zwecken begehrt, liegt auf der Hand. Der Anbau soll auch keinen anderen im öffentlichen Interesse liegenden Zwecken dienen. Ein öffentliches Interesse ist gegeben, wenn das Vorhaben zumindest auch einem gegenwärtigen Anliegen der Allgemeinheit entspricht (vgl. *Weber*, BtMG, § 3 Rdnr. 82; vgl. auch *Eberth/Müller*, BetäubungsmittelR, § 3 BtMG Rdnr. 27). So hat das *BVerfG* aus der Angabe des Gesetzeszwecks in § 5 I Nr. 6 BtMG, die notwendige medizinische Versorgung der Bevölkerung sicherzustellen, entnommen, dass therapeutische Zwecke ein öffentliches Interesse an der Verwendung von Betäubungsmitteln begründen können (vgl. NJW 2000, 3126). Unter Umständen kommen auch gewichtige wirtschaftliche Belange einer Region als Grund für die Bejahung eines öffentlichen Interesses in Betracht (vgl. *Körner*, BtMG, 4. Aufl. [1994], § 3 Rdnr. 15).

Ein Anliegen der Allgemeinheit verbindet sich mit dem vom Kl. erstrebten Cannabisanbau jedoch nicht. Die Bevölkerung hat keinerlei Vorteil von einer solchen Freigabe. Irgendeinen Gewinn kann sie davon nicht erwarten. Auch nach dem eigenen Vorbringen des Kl. geht es ihm nur darum, seine eigenen Bedürfnisse zu befriedigen. Dass er diese mit seiner Religionszugehörigkeit begründet, ändert daran nichts. Er weist sogar selbst darauf hin, dass es in Deutschland nur sehr wenige Rastifaris gebe, so dass die Gefahr einer Ausweitung des Cannabiskonsums nicht gegeben sei. Es geht also nicht um ein Anliegen, das von einer Vielzahl von Menschen geteilt wird und damit der Allgemeinheit zugerechnet werden könnte. Die Voraussetzungen einer Erlaubniserteilung nach § 3 II BtMG liegen daher nicht vor.

Grounds:

II The appeal in law is unfounded. The appeal court's decision that the claimant ought not to be given the desired permission for the cultivation of cannabis in small amounts does not violate Federal law.

The basis of the request is § 3 of the BtMG in the version promulgated on 1.3.1994 (BGBl I, 358). According to this, a person who wants to cultivate narcotics needs a permission from the Federal Institute for Medicines and Medicinal Products (§ 3 I no 1). For the narcotics listed in Appendix 1 of the Act, the permission can only exceptionally be given for scientific or other purposes in the public interest (para 2). Cannabis belongs – apart from exceptions of no interest to us here – to the narcotics mentioned in this Appendix which are prohibited. Its cultivation therefore needs permission, but permission can only be given under the prerequisites mentioned. These prerequisites are not present here.

It is obvious that the claimant does not seek the permission for scientific purposes. The cultivation is also not to serve any other purposes in the public interest. A public interest is present when the proposal corresponds at least to a present matter of concern of the general public (see *Weber*, BtMG, § 3 marginal no 82; see also *Eberth/Müller*, BetäubungsmittelR, BtMG § 3 marginal no 27). Thus the *BVerfG* deduced from the giving of the purpose of the Act in § 5 I no 6 BtMG, of securing the necessary medical care of the population, that therapeutic purposes can form the basis of a public interest in the use of narcotics (see NJW 2000, 3126). In certain circumstances, important business interests of a region also come into consideration as a ground for finding a public interest (see *Körner*, BtMG, 4th edn [1994], § 3 marginal no 15).

However, the cultivation of cannabis sought by the claimant is not associated with any matter of concern to the general public. The population gets no advantage of any kind from such a release. It cannot expect any gain from it. Even according to the claimant's own case, it is only a question of satisfying his own needs. The fact that he bases this on his religion changes nothing. He even points out himself that there were only very few Rastafarians in Germany, which meant that there was no danger of the spread of the consumption of cannabis. It is therefore not a question of a matter of concern which is shared by numbers of people and could thereby be attributed to the general public. The prerequisites for the giving of permission under § 3 II of the Narcotics Act are therefore not present.

2 Darüber hinaus steht der Erlaubniserteilung auch § 5 I Nr. 6 BtMG entgegen. Danach ist die Erlaubnis zu versagen, wenn die Art und der Zweck des beantragten Verkehrs nicht mit dem Zweck des Gesetzes, den Missbrauch von Betäubungsmitteln sowie das Entstehen oder Erhalten einer Betäubungsmittelabhängigkeit soweit wie möglich auszuschließen, vereinbar ist. Die Erteilung der begehrten Erlaubnis könnte Signalwirkung entfalten. Selbst wenn man davon absieht, dass der Kl. ausweislich der vom Bekl. im Revisionsverfahren vorgelegten Internetseiten ein engagierter Verfechter der generellen Freigabe des Cannabiskonsums ist, liegt die Gefahr nahe, dass die Erteilung der Erlaubnis unter Bezugnahme auf religiöse Bedürfnisse in der Öffentlichkeit als Hinweis auf einen einfachen Weg zum legalen Cannabisgenuss verstanden werden könnte. Diese Gefahr liegt besonders nahe, weil der Kl., wie er in der mündlichen Verhandlung vor dem erkennenden *Senat* erklärt hat, in seinen Konzerten öffentlich auf die Bedeutung des Cannabisgenusses für sein Leben und seine Musik hinweist. Das erklärte Ziel des Gesetzes, den Missbrauch von Betäubungsmitteln sowie das Entstehen oder Erhalten einer Betäubungsmittelabhängigkeit soweit wie möglich auszuschließen, wäre damit nicht vereinbar.

2 Zu Unrecht rügt der Kl., die vorgenommene Auslegung des Betäubungsmittelgesetzes verletze sein Grundrecht auf ungestörte Religionsausübung nach Art 4 II GG und sei daher verfassungswidrig.

3.1 Das BerGer. ist davon ausgegangen, dass die Versagung der beantragten Erlaubnis den Schutzbereich des Art. 4 GG berühre. Es hat festgestellt, Rastafari sei eine Religion, die in den 30er Jahren auf Jamaika entstanden sei. Dagegen ist nichts zu errinern (vgl. auch Brockhaus-Enzyklopädie, Stichwort 'Rastafari'). Das BerGer. hat weiter festgestellt, dass der Kl. dieser Religion anhängt und dass zu ihren wesentlichen rituellen Vollzügen das gemeinsame Rauchen von Marihuana gehört. Auf welchen Erkenntnisgrundlagen diese Feststellungen im Einzelnen beruhen, ist weder dem angefochtenen Urteil noch den Akten nachvollziehbar zu entnehmen. Möglicherweise ist der *Senat* daran gleichwohl gem. § 137 II VwGO gebunden, zumal hiergegen von keiner Seite Rügen erhoben worden sind. Dem braucht hier jedoch nicht weiter nachgegangen zu werden, da zu Gunsten des Kl. unterstellt werden kann, dass die tatsächlichen Feststellungen des BerGer. Bestand haben und die Versagung der begehrten Erlaubnis in das Grundrecht des Kl. auf freie Religionsausübung eingreift. Dies führt gleichwohl nicht zum Erfolg der Klage.

2 Besides this the giving of permission is contrary to § 5 I no 6 of the Narcotics Act. According to this, permission is to be refused if the kind and purpose of the dealings which are the subject of the application are not reconcilable with the purpose of the Act, which is to exclude as far as possible the misuse of narcotics and the formation or continuation of narcotic dependence. The giving of the desired permission could have a knock-on effect. Even ignoring the fact that the claimant, according to the internet pages produced by the defendant in the appeal in law proceedings, is a committed advocate for the general lifting of restrictions on the consumption of cannabis, the danger arises that the giving of permission with reference to religious needs could be understood by the public as an indication of a simple way to legal cannabis consumption. This danger is especially present because the claimant, as he stated in the oral hearing before this Senate, refers publicly in his concerts to the significance of the consumption of cannabis for his life and music. The declared goal of the Act, which was to exclude as far as possible the misuse of narcotics and the formation or the continuation of narcotic dependence, would not be reconcilable with this.

3 The claimant was not correct in objecting that the interpretation which had been made of the Narcotics Act violated his basic right to the undisturbed exercise of religion under Art 4 II of the GG and was therefore unconstitutional.

3.1 The appeal court proceeded on the basis that the denial of the permission applied for affected the area protected by Art 4 of the GG. It has established that Rastafarianism was a religion which emerged in the 1930s in Jamaica. Nothing can be brought forward to contradict this (see also the Brockhaus Encyclopaedia under the heading 'Rastafarianism'). The appeal court has further established that the claimant was an adherent of this religion and that the communal smoking of marijuana was part of its fundamental ritual performances. The detailed evidential basis for these findings cannot be comprehensibly deduced either from the disputed judgment or from the documents. Possibly the Senate is however bound by the findings in accordance with § 137 II of the VwGO, especially as no objections have been raised to them on either side. But it is not necessary to go into this further here, as it could be assumed in the claimant's favour that the factual findings of the appeal court are valid, and the refusal of the desired permission violates the basic right of the claimant to free exercise of his religion. But this does not lead to the success of his claim.

Ohne Bedeutung ist in diesem Zusammenhang, dass das Anliegen des Kl. im Rahmen des Glaubensvollzuges allein den *Genuss* von Cannabis betrifft, während das Erlaubnisbegehren sich auf den *Anbau* von Cannabis richtet. Hierzu trägt der Kl. vor, der eigene Anbau solle ihn von dem kriminell besetzten Drogenmarkt unabhängig machen. In der Tat setzt der Genuss in jedem Fall irgendeine Form der Beschaffung voraus. Nach § 3 I Nr. 1 BtMG ist aber zu jeder Form der Beschaffung, etwa zur Einfuhr oder zum Erwerb von Cannabis, eine Erlaubnis notwendig, deren Erteilung jeweils von denselben Voraussetzungen abhängt. Wenn der Genuss von Cannabis zum Schutzbereich der Glaubensfreiheit gehört, kann für die Beschaffung nichts anderes gelten. Unter diesen Umständen erscheint der eigene Anbau jedenfalls nicht sozialschädlicher als andere Formen des Erwerbs.

3.2 Das BerGer. hat die Notwendigkeit einer verfassungskonformen Auslegung des Erlaubnistatbestands, insbesondere des Merkmals der 'im öffentlichen Interesse liegenden Zwecke', verneint, weil das Grundrecht auf Religionsfreiheit gegenüber dem gleichfalls Verfassungsrang genießenden Schutzgut der Volksgesundheit zurücktreten müsse. Es hat dazu auf die Gefahren des Cannabiskonsums für die Allgemeinheit abgestellt. Dies ist aus Rechtsgründen nicht zu beanstanden.

3.2.1 Keine Probleme wirft der Ausgangspunkt des BerGer. auf, dass das Grundrecht auf Religionsfreiheit durch die verfassungsrechtliche Gewährleistung anderer Schutzgüter beschränkt werden kann. Gerät Art. 4 GG in Kollision mit einer anderen Verfassungsnorm, so ist einer Abwägung erforderlich (vgl. u. a. *BVerfGE* 32, 98 [108] = NJW 1972, 327; *BVerfGE* 52, 223 [246f.] = NJW 1980, 575; *Jarass/Pieroth*, GG, 5. Aufl., Art 4 Rdnr. 19). Außer Zweifel steht auch dass der Schutz der Volksgesundheit verfassungsrechtlichen Rang genießt (vgl. *BVerfGE* 90, 145 [174f.] = NJW 1994, 1577). In Art 2 II GG wird jedermann das Recht auf Leben und körperliche Unversehrtheit gewährleistet. Betäubungsmittelmissbrauch und Drogenabhängigkeit stellen eine schwere Gefahr für die Volksgesundheit dar. Ihre Abwehr kann folglich auch Eingriffe in andere Grundrechte rechtfertigen.

Die hiernach gebotene Abwägung ergibt, dass es verfassungsrechtlich nicht geboten ist, für den Anbau von Cannabis zum Zwecke der Religionsausübung im Gesetz die Erteilung einer Ausnahmeerlaubnis vorzusehen.

The fact that the claimant's request within the framework of a religious exercise only concerns the *consumption* of cannabis, whilst his desire for a permit is directed to the *cultivation* of cannabis, is without significance in this connection. The claimant says on this subject that cultivating the plant himself will make him independent of the criminal drug market. In fact consumption in every case assumes some form of production. But according to § 3 I no 1 of the BtMG, a permit is necessary for every form of obtaining cannabis, for instance for import or purchase, and the giving of this permit depends in each case on the same prerequisites. If the consumption of cannabis belongs to the protected area of freedom of belief, nothing different can apply to the obtaining of it. Under these circumstances, growing the plant oneself does not in any case appear to be more socially harmful than other forms of acquisition.

3.2 The appeal court denied the need for an interpretation of the requirements for the permit which conforms to the constitution, in particular in respect of the characteristic of 'purposes in the public interest', because the basic right to freedom of religion had to give place to the protected interest of public health, which likewise enjoyed constitutional rank. It has on this issue taken into account the dangers of cannabis consumption for the general public. This is not open to objection on legal grounds.

3.2.1 The starting point of the appeal court, that the basic right to religious freedom can be limited by the constitutional law guarantee of other protected interests, raises no problems. If Art 4 of the GG comes into collision with another constitutional norm, then balancing is necessary (see, amongst others, *BVerfGE* 32, 98 [108] = NJW 1972, 327; *BVerfGE* 52, 223 [246f.] = NJW 1980, 575; *Jarass/Pieroth*, GG, 5th edn, Art 4 marginal no 19). It is also beyond doubt that the protection of public health enjoys constitutional law rank (see *BVerfGE* 90, 145 [174f.] = NJW 1994, 1577). In Art 2 II of the GG everyone is guaranteed the right to life and corporeal integrity. Misuse of narcotics and drug dependency represent a serious danger for public health. Their defence can consequently even justify invasions of other basic rights.

The result of the balancing which is accordingly required is that it is not required in constitutional law to provide in the statute for the giving of a permit by way of exception for the cultivation of cannabis for the purposes of the exercise of religion.

3.2.2 Dabei ist zunächst das – geringe – Maß der Belastung zu berücksichtigen, das sich aus dem Fehlen einer Erlaubnismöglichkeit ergibt. Zwar erfüllt der unerlaubte Anbau von Cannabis auch in geringen Mengen zum Eigenverbrauch, wie er Gegenstand des Erlaubnisantrags ist, den Straftatbestand des § 29 I Nr. 3 BtMG. In seinem Beschluss vom 9.3.1994 (*BVerfGE* 90, 145 = NJW 1994, 1577) hat das *BVerfG* die Strafandrohung in den genannten Fällen aber nur deshalb als mit dem Verhältnismäßigkeitsgrundsatz vereinbar angesehen, weil der Gesetzgeber den Strafverfolgungsbehörden eine ganze Reihe von Möglichkeiten an die Hand gegeben hat, dem geringeren Unwertgehalt dieser Taten durch ein Absehen von der Strafverfolgung Rechnung zu tragen. Das *BVerfG* hat sogar die Behörden aufgefordert, für die Wahrnehmung dieser Möglichkeiten einheitliche Maßstäbe zu schaffen. Die Versagung der Erlaubnismöglichkeit ist mithin nicht gleichbedeutend mit der Gefahr der Bestrafung bei einer Verletzung des Anbauverbots.

Dementsprechend geht das Anliegen des Kl. erklärtermaßen dahin, seinen Cannabisgenuss offiziell zu legalisieren. Hierzu erstrebt er die Erlaubnis. Die Erteilung der Erlaubnis würde zwar die Strafbarkeit von vornherein ausschließen, weil die Strafnormen der §§ 29ff. BtMG sämtlich auf unerlaubtes Verhalten abstellen. Daraus ist im Gegenschluss aber nicht zu folgern, dass der Kl. ohne die Erlaubnis einer Strafverfolgung ausgesetzt wäre. Er hat im Berufungsverfahren ausdrücklich vorgetragen, dass ihm wegen der geringen Menge des anzubauenden Cannabis keine Strafverfolgung drohe. Wo insoweit im Einzelnen die Grenzen liegen (vgl. auch *BVerfG*, NStZ 1997, 498), bedarf hier keiner Klärung. Entscheidend ist, dass die strafrechtlichen Normen hinreichenden Spielraum gewähren, um – sogar ohne Rückgriff auf das Grundrecht der Religionsfreiheit – dem jeweiligen Unwertgehalt des Verstoßes gegen das Betäubungsmittelgesetz Rechnung zu tragen bis hin zum völligen Absehen von Strafe.

3.2.2 In this connection, first of all the – small – degree of disadvantage has to be considered which will follow from the absence of any possibility of a permit. It is true that the cultivation of cannabis without permission, even in small amounts for personal use, as is the subject of the application for the permit here, fulfils the definition of the crime under § 29 I no 3 of the BtMG. In its decision of the 9.3.1994 (*BVerfGE* 90, 145 = NJW 1994, 1577) the *BVerfG* however saw the threat of a penalty in the cases mentioned as only reconcilable with the principle of proportionality because the legislator had put into the hands of the criminal prosecution authorities a whole string of possibilities of taking into account the smaller degree of reprehensibility of these acts by refraining from prosecution. The *BVerfG* even invited the authorities to create unified standards for the implementation of these possibilities. The refusal of the possibility of a permit is therefore not synonymous with the risk of punishment on the violation of a ban on cultivation.

Accordingly the claimant's request is stated to be directed towards legalising his consumption of cannabis officially. He seeks the permit for this purpose. The giving of the permit would admittedly exclude criminality from the outset because all the criminal norms of §§ 29ff of the BtMG are geared to unlawful behaviour. It is not however to be concluded by way of contrast from this that the claimant would be exposed to a criminal prosecution without the permit. He has expressly stated in the original appeal proceedings that because of the small amount of cannabis to be cultivated he was not threatened with criminal prosecution. Where the boundaries lie in detail in this respect (see also *BVerfG*, NStZ 1997, 498) needs no clarification here. The decisive factor is that the criminal law norms grant sufficient leeway in order – even without resorting to the basic right of religious freedom – to take account of the particular degree of reprehensibility of the violation of Narcotics Act right up to completely refraining from punishment.

Allerdings würde eine Erlaubnis Personen in der Situation des Kl. ein höheres Maß an Rechtssicherheit im Hinblick auf eine etwaige Strafbarkeit ihres Verhalten gewähren. Außerdem würde es sie von dem Stigma befreien, überhaupt etwas Gesetzwidriges zu tun. Bei der Frage, ob diesen Anliegen durch eine normative Ausnahmeregelung Rechnung getragen werden muss, ist aber zu berücksichtigen, dass der Cannabisgenuss im Rahmen der Religionsausübung jedenfalls in Deutschland offenkundig ein Phänomen ist, das nur ganz wenige Personen betrifft. So hat etwa das *BVerfG* zur unterschiedlichen Behandlung von Cannabis und Alkohol durch den Gesetzgeber darauf hingewiesen, dass alkoholhaltige Substanzen in Form von Wein auch im religiösen Kult verwandt werden (*BVerfGE* 90, 145 [197] = NJW 1994, 1577). Die Verwendung von Cannabis im Rahmen kultischer Handlungen kam dagegen nicht in den Blick. Eine derart seltene Erscheinung wäre vom Gesetz nur dann im Rahmen des Erlaubnisverfahrens zu regeln, wenn anderenfalls die freie Religionsausübung in gravierender Weise eingeschränkt wäre. Das ist aber nicht der Fall.

3.2.3 Überdies ist in die Abwägung einzustellen, dass das generelle Verbot des Verkehrs mit Cannabis dem Schutz der Gesundheit Einzelner und der Bevölkerung insgesamt zu dienen bestimmt und geeignet ist. Das *BVerfG* hat in seinem bereits zitierten Beschluss vom 9.3.1994 (*BVerfGE* 90, 145 [181] = NJW 1994, 1577) festgestellt, dass sich die von Cannabisprodukten ausgehenden Gesundheitsgefahren aus heutiger Sicht zwar als geringer darstellen, als der Gesetzgeber bei Erlass des Gesetzes angenommen hat, dass aber dennoch auch nach dem jetzigen Erkenntnisstand nicht unbeträchtliche Gefahren und Risiken verbleiben, so dass die Gesamtkonzeption des Gesetzes in Bezug auf Cannabisprodukte weiterhin vor der Verfassung Bestand hat. Hingewiesen wird dazu unter anderem auf die kaum bestrittene Möglichkeit einer psychischen Abhängigkeit. Auch werden Äußerungen der Wissenschaft angeführt, dass der Dauerkonsum von Cannabisprodukten zu Verhaltensstörungen, Lethargie, Gleichgültigkeit, Angstgefühlen, Realitätsverlust und Depressionen führen könne und dies gerade die Persönlichkeitsentwicklung von Jugendlichen nachhaltig zu stören vermöge. Der vorliegende Rechtsstreit hat keine Erkenntnisse erbracht, die dieser Einschätzung des *BVerfG* zuwider liefen. Nach der Stellungnahme des Oberbundesanwalts beim *BVerwG*, die im Einvernehmen mit den Bundesministerien für Gesundheit, des Innern und der Justiz abgegeben worden ist, haben auch die nach Ergehen der Entscheidung des *BVerfG* durchgeführten Forschungen den Beweis einer generellen Unbedenklichkeit des Genusses von Cannabisprodukten nicht erbracht.

Admittedly a permit would grant to persons in the claimant's situation a higher degree of legal certainty in respect of possible criminality of their behaviour. Besides this, it would free them from the stigma of having done anything unlawful at all. But in relation to the question of whether account must be taken of this request by a normative exception regime, it must be borne in mind that the consumption of cannabis within the framework of the exercise of religion is, at any rate in Germany, manifestly a phenomenon which concerns only quite a small number of people. Thus, for instance, the *BVerfG* has, in relation to the differing treatment of cannabis and alcohol by the legislator, referred to the fact that substances containing alcohol in the form of wine are also used in religious worship (*BVerfGE* 90, 145 [197] = NJW 1994, 1577). The use of cannabis within the framework of religious activities did not on the other hand come into consideration. A phenomenon of such a rare kind would only have to be regulated by the statute within the framework of the permit procedure if otherwise the free exercise of religion would be limited in a serious way. That, however, is not the case.

3.2.3 Besides, there must be included in the balancing exercise the fact that the general prohibition on dealings with cannabis is intended and appropriate to serve the protection of the health of individuals and the population as a whole. The *BVerfG* established in its decision of the 9.3.1994 which has already been quoted (*BVerfGE* 90, 145 [181] = NJW 1994, 1577) that the dangers to health which arise from cannabis products admittedly appear to be smaller from today's standpoint than the legislator assumed on the passing of the statute; but that not inconsiderable dangers and risks remain even according to the present state of knowledge, so that the concept of the statute as a whole with reference to cannabis products still endures in the eyes of the Constitution. Reference is made on this subject, amongst other things, to the scarcely disputed possibility of a psychological dependency. Scientific statements are also quoted to the effect that consumption of cannabis produces over a long period can lead to behavioural disturbances, lethargy, indifference, feelings of anxiety, loss of reality and depression, and this can disrupt the development of the personality of young people in a lasting way. The present case has not produced any findings which run counter to this assessment of the *BVerfG*. According to the opinion of the Chief Federal Attorney of the Federal Administrative Court which has been submitted in agreement with the Federal Ministries for Health, the Interior and Justice, the researches carried out after the making of the decision of the *BVerfG* have also produced no proof of general harmlessness of the consumption of cannabis products.

Ferner ist zu beachten, dass sich die nationale gesetzliche Regelung, die auf eine möglichst weit gehende Einschränkung des Verkehrs mit Cannabisprodukten zielt, in ein System internationaler Abkommen einfügt. So haben die Vereinten Nationen in Art. 3 I des Suchtstoffübereinkommens 1988 (BGBl II 1993, 1137) das vorsätzliche Anbauen der Cannabispflanze zum Zwecke der Gewinnung von Suchtstoffen als strafwürdige Handlung deklariert und die Vertragsparteien zu entsprechenden Regelungen verpflichtet. Die Einschätzung des Bundesgesetzgebers, das generelle Verbot des Verkehrs mit Cannabisprodukten sei erforderlich, um Gesundheit und Wohl der Menschen vor ernstlichen Gefahren zu bewahren, deckt sich folglich mit der Ansicht eines großen Teils der Völkergemeinschaft und mit einer von der Bundesrepublik völkerrechtlich übernommenen Verpflichtung.

Zu Unrecht meint der Kl. in die gebotene Abwägung dürften die allgemeinen Gefahren des Marihuanagebrauchs nicht eingestellt werden, weil sie bei dem zur Genehmigung gestellten Anbau geringer Mengen von Cannabis zum gelegentlichen Eigengebrauch aus religiösen Gründen nicht einträten. Dabei übersieht er, dass die Frage, ob der Gesetzgeber aus verfassungsrechtlichen Gründen im Hinblick auf das Grundrecht der Religionsfreiheit gehalten ist, eine Ausnahmeerlaubnis für Fälle der in Rede stehenden Art vorzusehen, die normative Ebene betrifft. Auf dieser Ebene sind generalisierende, vom konkreten Einzelfall abstrahierende Erwägungen nicht nur zulässig, sondern sogar geboten.

In diesem Rahmen gewinnt insbesondere die oben bereits angesprochene Gefahr der Signalwirkung einer Erlaubniserteilung Gewicht. Gerade labile Jugendliche könnten dadurch verführt werden, die mit dem Gebrauch von Cannabisprodukten verbundenen Risiken zu unterschätzen und sich selbst zu schädigen. Darüber hinaus würde die Möglichkeit einer Erlaubniserteilung aus religiösen Gründen der Gefahr des Missbrauchs Tür und Tor öffnen. Der Hinweis, dass im Rahmen oder auch unter dem Deckmantel des Rastafari-Kults erlaubterweise Marihuana genossen werden könne, ließe sich leicht zu einer breiten Bresche in das Verbot des Cannabis-Gebrauchs ausweiten. Die Tatsache, dass der Kl. selbst im Internet seinen Prozess mit dem allgemeinen Feldzug gegen das Cannabis-Verbot verbindet, ist hierfür ein deutlicher Beleg.

Demgegenüber bietet der Verweis, auf die differenzierten Sanktionsmöglichkeiten des Strafrechts eine Basis, den berechtigten Anliegen des Kl. ebenso wie den Schutzbedürfnissen der Allgemeinheit voll gerecht zu werden.

It further has to be borne in mind that the national statutory regime, which aims for a limitation which is as extensive as possible of trade in cannabis products, fits into a system of international agreements. Thus the United Nations in Art 3 I of the Drugs Convention 1988 (BGBl II 1993, 1137) have declared the international cultivation of the cannabis plant for the purpose of production of drugs to be criminal activity and obliged the treaty partners to create corresponding regimes. The assessment of the Federal legislator that the general prohibition on dealings with cannabis was necessary in order to preserve the health and wellbeing of human beings from serious dangers consequently coincides with the view of a great part of the international community and with a duty undertaken by the Federal Republic in public international law.

The claimant is wrong in thinking that the general dangers of the use of marijuana ought not to be included in the required balancing exercise because they would not occur on the cultivation of small amounts of cannabis for occasional personal use on religious grounds, as put forward for the permit. In this connection, he overlooks the fact that the question of whether the legislator is required on constitutional law grounds, having regard to the basic right of religious freedom, to provide an exceptional permission for cases of the kind in question concerns the normative plane. On this plane, generalised considerations, abstracted from the actual individual case, are not only permissible, but even required.

Within this framework, the danger already addressed above of the knock-on effect of the granting of a permit gains particular weight. Weak young people could thereby be misled to underestimate the risks associated with the use of cannabis products, and harm themselves. In addition to this, the possibility of granting a permit on religious grounds would open the door to the danger of misuse. The indication that within the framework or even under the guise of the Rastafarian cult marijuana could be consumed with permission could easily be broadened into a wide breach in the prohibition of the use of cannabis. The fact that the claimant himself on the internet links his proceedings with the general campaign against the ban on cannabis is clear evidence of this.

Over against this, the reference to the differentiated possibilities of sanctions in criminal law offers a basis for doing full justice to the legitimate request of the claimant as well as the general public's needs for protection.

3.2.4 Aus alldem ergibt sich, dass § 3 II BtMG mit der Verfassung vereinbar ist, soweit er für den Betäubungsmittelverkehr aus religiösen Gründen keine Erlaubnismöglichkeit vorsieht. Zu einer Reduktion der gesetzlichen Regelung im Wege der verfassungskonformen Auslegung besteht kein Anlass.

Art. 5 [Recht der freien Meinungsäußerung] (1) Jeder hat das Recht, seine Meinung in Wort, Schrift und Bild frei zu äußern und zu verbreiten und sich aus allgemein zugänglichen Quellen ungehindert zu unterrichten. Die Pressefreiheit und die Freiheit der Berichterstattung durch Rundfunk und Film werden gewährleistet. Eine Zensur findet nicht statt.

(2) Diese Rechte finden ihre Schranken in den Vorschriften der allgemeinen Gesetze, den gesetzlichen Bestimmungen zum Schutze der Jugend und in dem Recht der persönlichen Ehre.

(3) Kunst und Wissenschaft, Forschung und Lehre sind frei. Die Freiheit der Lehre entbindet nicht von der Treue zur Verfassung.

THE RIGHT TO GIVE THE OPPOSITE VIEW CASES

BVerfG NJW 2002, 356

4 Recht auf Gegendarstellung – Gysi I

GG Art 5 I, II; HbgPresseG § 11

1 Das Gegendarstellungsrecht lässt Raum für eine Auslegung, nach der in Fällen offensichtlicher Unwahrheit der Gegendarstellung ein berechtigtes Interesse an ihrem Abdruck verneint wird.

3.2.4 From all this, it follows that § 3 II of the BtMG is reconcilable with the Constitution, insofar as it provides no possibility for a permit for trading in narcotics on religious grounds. There is no ground for reducing the statutory regime by way of interpretation so as to conform to the Constitution.

Article 5 [Right to free expression of opinion] (1) Everyone has the right to express and disseminate his opinion freely by word, writing and picture and to inform himself from generally accessible sources without restraint. Freedom of the press and of reporting by radio and film are guaranteed. Censorship is not to take place.

(2) These rights are limited by the provisions of general statutes, statutory rules for the protection of the young and the right to personal honour.

(3) Art, science, research and teaching are free. Freedom of teaching does not exonerate from loyalty to the Constitution.

This article was applied in the newspaper delivery obstruction case (see Chapter Six, p 481), in which it was held that it did not justify coercion. It was also considered in the insult of soldiers case: see Chapter Seven, p 715.

Examples of the application of the exception about personal honour are to be found in the film director case (Chapter Six, p 505 and onwards) and in the Mephisto case (BVerfGE 30, 173). The exception for 'general' statutes (or laws) refers to statutes which apply to an large indefinite number of persons and circumstances. (Note the provision in Art 19 I which forbids generally any restriction on basic rights by statutes about individual cases.) See the film director case (Chapter Six, p 505 and onwards) for a definition of a general statute. An example of an application of this exception is the right of journalists to refuse to disclose their sources, on the ground that this would impair their chances of operating effectively.

THE RIGHT TO GIVE THE OPPOSITE VIEW CASES

Gregor Gysi took over from Egon Krenz as the leader of the east German Communist Party (the SED) after it had changed its name to the Democratic Socialist Party (PDS). The central issue in this case is the interesting concept of the right to present the opposite point of view (as opposed to a mere right to demand a correction) in certain cases where a person has been made the subject of a publication.

BVerfG NJW 2002, 356

4 Right to presentation of the opposite view – Gysi I

GG, Art 5 I, II; HbgPresseG § 11

1 The right to presentation of the opposite view leaves room for an interpretation according to which, in cases of obvious untruthfulness of the presentation, a justified interest in its printing is denied.

2 Die Deutung der in einem Presseartikel verwendeten Formulierung 'Gregor Gysi, ein registrierter Stasi-Spitzel' als Tatsachenbehauptung und nicht als wertende Meinungsäußerung begegnet in verfassungrechtlicher Hinsicht keinen durchgreifenden Bedenken. (Leitsätze der Redaktion.)

BVerfG (1. Kammer des Ersten Senats), Beschl. v. 24.8.2001 – 1 BvQ 35/01

Zum Sachverhalt:

Der abgelehnte Antrag auf Erlass einer einstweiligen Anordnung betraf die Verpflichtung zum Abdruck einer Gegendarstellung. Anlass der Gegendarstellung bildete die in dem Artikel 'Ist Gregor Gysi ein Prophet oder der Wolf im Schafspelz' ('Die Welt' vom 23.6.2001, S. 3) verwendete Formulierung 'Gregor Gysi, ein registrierter Stasi-Spitzel'.

Aus den Gründen:

Nach § 32 I BVerGG kann das *BVerfG* im Streitfall einen Zustand durch einstweilige Anordnung vorläufig regeln, wenn dies zur Abwehr schwerer Nachteile, zur Verhinderung drohender Gewalt oder aus einem anderen wichtigen Grund zum gemeinen Wohl dringend geboten ist. Bei der Prüfung, ob die Voraussetzungen des § 32 I BVerfGG vorliegen, sind die Erfolgsaussichten der von der Ast. angekündigten Verfassungsbeschwerde insoweit relevant, als dem Eilrechtsschutzbegehren nach § 32 I BVerfGG nicht entsprochen werden kann, wenn die angekündigte Verfassungsbeschwerde unzulässig oder offensichtlich unbegründet ist. Maßgebend für die Beurteilung ist der Verfahrensstand im Zeitpunkt der Entscheidung.

Die Voraussetzungen für den Erlass der begehrten einstweiligen Anordnung liegen nicht vor. Denn die angekündigte Verfassungsbeschwerde ist bei derzeitigem Verfahrensstand nach Aktenlage offensichtlich unbegründet.

Es sind keine Anhaltspunkte dafür ersichtlich, dass die Ast. durch die in der Antragsschrift bezeichneten Entscheidungen des *LG Hamburg* oder durch das noch ausstehende Berufungsurteil des *OLG Hamburg* im einstweiligen Verfügungsverfahren (7 U 75/01) in ihrem Grundrecht auf Pressefreiheit (Art. 5 I 2 GG) verletzt worden ist bzw. verletzt werden könnte.

2 The interpretation of the expression used in a press article 'Gregor Gysi, a registered Stasi informer' as an assertion of fact and not as an evaluating expression of opinion does not meet with any effectual objections in a constitutional law respect. (Editorial summaries.)

BVerfG (first chamber of the first Senate), decision of 24.8.2001 – 1 BvQ 35/01

Facts:

The rejected application for issue of an interim injunction concerned the duty to print a presentation of the opposite point of view. The cause for such a presentation was the expression 'Gregor Gysi, a registered Stasi informer' in the article 'Is Gregor Gysi a prophet or a wolf in sheep's clothing?' (*Die Welt*, 23.6.2001, p 3).

Grounds:

According to § 32 I of the BVerfGG, the Federal Constitutional Court can, in the case in question, provisionally regulate a situation by an interim injunction, if this is urgently required for the common good for the avoidance of grave disadvantages, for the prevention of threatened force, or on some other important ground. In examining whether the prerequisites of § 32 I of the BVerfGG are present, the prospects of success of the constitutional complaint notified by the applicant are relevant to the extent that the request for rapid protection of rights under § 32 I of the BVerfGG cannot be complied with if the constitutional complaint notified is impermissible or obviously unfounded. The decisive factor for the assessment is the stage of the proceedings at the point in time of the decision.

The prerequisites for the issue of the interim injunction requested are not present. This is because the constitutional complaint notified is obviously unfounded at the present stage of the proceedings according to the state of the documents.

There are no obvious indications for saying that the applicant has been harmed or could by harmed by the decisions by the Hamburg State Court described in the application or by the still outstanding appeal judgment of the Hamburg Upper State Court in the interim injunction proceedings (7 U 75/01) in its basic right to freedom of the press (Art 5 I 2 of the GG).

Die Grundlage dieser Einschätzung bildet der Beschluss der *OLG* vom 15.8.2001 (7 U 75/01), mit dem der Antrag der Ast. zurückgewiesen worden ist, die Zwangsvollstreckung aus den bezeichneten Entscheidungen des *LG* einstweilen einzustellen. Seinen Beschluss begründet das *OLG* damit, dass die Berufing der Ast. keine hinreichende Aussicht auf Erfolg biete. Damit können die in den Gründen dieses Beschlusses weiter enthaltenen Ausführungen des *OLG* jedenfalls im Verfahren nach § 32 I BVerfGG als Grundlage für die Einschätzung der Erfolgsaussichten der von der Ast. angekündigten Verfassungsbeschwerde gegen die im einstweiligen Verfügungsverfahren ergangenen und noch zu ergehenden Entscheidungen des *LG* und des *OLG* herangezogen werden.

Der Ast. ist zustimmen, dass die zivilgerichtlichen Entscheidungen den Schutzbereich ihres Grundrechts aus Art. 5 I 2 GG betreffen. Das Grundrecht auf Pressefreiheit wird aber nach derzeitigem Sachstand nicht verletzt.

Die gesetzliche Grundlage, auf die sich die angegriffenen Entscheidungen stützen (§ 11 HbgPresseG), steht mit dem Grundgesetz in Einklang (vgl. *BVerfGE* 97, 125 [145ff.] = NJW 1998, 1381). § 11 HbgPresseG ist ein allgemeines Gesetz i.S. des Art. 5 II GG. Die mit ihm getroffenen Regelungen beschränken die Pressefreiheit nicht unverhältnismäßig (vgl. *BVerfGE* 97, 125 [146] = NJW 1998, 1381).

Es ist nicht davon auszugehen, dass die Zivilgerichte im Ausgangsverfahren bei der Auslegung und Anwendung von § 11 HbgPresseG die Bedeutung und Tragweite der Pressefreiheit nicht hinreichend beachtet haben beziehungsweise ihr nicht hinreichend Rechnung tragen werden.

So begegnet die Deutung der in dem Artikel verwendeten Formulierung 'Gregor Gysi, ein registrierter Stasi-Spitzel' als Tatsachenbehauptung und nicht als wertende Meinungsäußerung in verfassungrechtliche Hinsicht keinen durchgreifenden Bedenken. Auch besteht kein Anlass zu der Annahme, dass mögliche andere Deutungen der Formulierung, die zu einem für die Ast. günstigeren Ergebnis des einstweiligen Verfügungsverfahrens führen könnten, nicht in Betracht gezogen bzw. nicht mit einer nachvollziehbaren Begründung ausgeschlossen worden sind.

The basis of this assessment is formed by the decision of the Upper State Court of the 15.8.2001 (7 U 75/01) (by which the applicant's application has been rejected temporarily) to suspend the execution of the decisions of the State Court which have been described. The Upper State Court gives as its reason for its decision the fact that the applicant's appeal offers no sufficient prospect of success. The observations of the Upper State Court further contained in the reasons for this decision can in any case be referred to in the proceedings under § 32 I of the BVerfGG as the basis for the assessment of the prospects of success of the constitutional complaint notified by the applicant against the decisions of the State Court and the Upper State Court issued and still to be issued in the interim injunction proceedings.

It is necessary to agree with the applicant that the civil court decisions concern the protected area of its basic right under Art 5 I 2 of the GG. However, the basic right to freedom of the press is not violated according to the current state of the case.

The statutory basis on which the decisions under challenge are founded (§ 11 of the HbgPresseG) is in harmony with the Basic Law (see *BVerfGE* 97, 125 [145ff] = NJW 1998, 1381). § 11 of the HbgPresseG is a general statute in the sense of Art 5 II of the GG. The rules made by it do not limit press freedom disproportionately (see *BVerfGE* 97, 125 [146] = NJW 1998, 1381).

It must not be assumed that the civil courts in the initial proceedings in the interpretation and application of § 11 of the HbgPresseG have not paid sufficient regard to the importance and scope of press freedom (or will not take it sufficiently into account).

Thus the meaning of the expression 'Gregor Gysi, a registered Stasi informer' used in the article as an assertion of facts and not as an evaluating statement of opinion meets with no effectual objections in a constitutional law respect. There is also no cause for assuming that possible other meanings of the expression, which could lead to an outcome of the proceedings for an interim injunction which was more favourable for the applicant, have not been taken into consideration (or have not been excluded with comprehensible reasoning).

Das presserechtliche Gegendarstellungsrecht setzt weder den Nachweis der Unwahrheit der Erstmitteilung noch den der Wahrheit der Gegendarstellung voraus. Die Wahrheitsunabhängigkeit der Gegendarstellung ist Folge des aus der staatlichen Schutzpflicht für das Persönlichkeitsrecht folgenden Gebots der Sicherstellung gleicher publizistischer Wirkung. Das Gegendarstellungsrecht lässt Raum für eine Auslegung, nach der in Fällen offensichtlicher Unwahrheit der Gegendarstellung ein berechtigtes Interesse an ihrem Abdruck verneint wird (vgl. *BVerfGE* 97, 125 [147f.] = NJW 1998, 1381). Unter Zugrundelegung des durch das *BVerfG* anzuwendenden Prüfungsmaßstabs (vgl. *BVerfGE* 18, 85 [92f.] = NJW 1964, 1715; *BVerfGE* 101, 361 [388] = NJW 2000, 1021; st. Rspr.) ist aus verfassungsrechtlicher Sicht nicht zu beanstanden, dass die Zivilgerichte die von *Gysi* beanspruchte Gegendarstellung im Ausgangsverfahren nicht als offensichtlich unwahr bzw. irreführend gewürdigt haben.

BVerfG NJW 2002, 357

5 Recht auf Gegendarstellung – Gysi II

GG Art 5 I, II; HbgPresseG § 11

Zum Umfang des Rechts auf Gegendarstellung bei einer aus Tatsachenbehauptung und Meinungsäußerung bestehenden redaktionellen Anmerkung. (Leitsatz der Redaktion)

BVerfG (1. Kammer des Ersten Senats), Beschl. v. 30.8.2001 – 1 BvQ 36/01

Zum Sachverhalt:

Der Antrag auf Erlass einer einstweiligen Anordnung betraf die Verpflichtung zum Abdruck einer Gegendarstellung. Die Ast. hat in einer redaktionellen Anmerkung (*'Die Welt'* vom 25.7.2001) zu einer den Gegner des Ausgangsverfahrens – Herrn *Gregor Gysi* – betreffenden Gegendarstellung die Bundesbeauftragte für die Unterlagen des Staatssicherheitsdienstes der ehemaligen DDR, *Marianne Birthler*, mit dem Satz zitiert: 'Da Herr *Dr. Gysi* sich konspirativ mit der Stasi getroffen hat, da er Aufträge entgegengenommen und umgesetzt hat, da er Informationen geliefert hat, können wir davon sprechen, dass er über Jahre hinaus wie ein IM gearbeitet hat.' Die Ast. ist auf Antrag von Herrn *Gysi* im Wege der einstweiligen Verfügung zum Abdruck einer (erneuten) Gegendarstellung verurteilt worden. Der Antrag auf Erlass einer einstweiligen Anordnung wurde abgelehnt.

The right to presentation of the opposite point of view under press law does not assume either the proof of the untruth of the first communication nor of the truth of the presentation of the opposite view. The fact that the presentation of the opposite view is independent of the truth is a consequence of the requirement that, following from the duty of the State to protect the right of personality, equal media effect should be guaranteed. The right to present the opposite view leaves room for an interpretation according to which, in cases of obvious untruthfulness of that presentation, a justified interest in printing it is denied (see *BVerfGE* 97, 125 [147f] = NJW 1998, 1381). On the basis of the examination standard to be applied by the *BVerfG* (see *BVerfGE* 18, 85 [92f] = NJW 1964, 1715; *BVerfGE* 101, 361 [388] = NJW 2000, 1021; consistent case law) it is not to be objected to from a constitutional law point of view that the civil courts have assessed the presentation of the opposite view claimed by *Gysi* in the original proceedings as not obviously untrue or misleading.

BVerfG NJW 2002, 357

5 Right to presentation of the opposite view – Gysi II

GG, Art 5 I, II; HbgPresseG § 11

On the scope of the right to presentation of the opposite view on a editorial comment consisting of an assertion of facts and statement of opinion. (Editorial summary.)

BVerfG (first chamber of the first Senate), decision of 30.8.2001 – 1 BvQ 36/01

Facts:

The application for issue of an interim injunction concerned the duty to print a presentation of the opposite view. The applicant has in an editorial comment (*'Die Welt'* of the 25.7.2001) on a presentation of the opposite view concerning the opponent in the original proceedings – Mr *Gregor Gysi* – quoted the Federal official responsible for the documents of the state security service of the former DDR, Marianne Birthler, with the sentence: 'As Dr Gysi has met conspiratorially with the Stasi, as he has accepted and implemented instructions, as he has delivered information, we can say that he has worked for years as an IM (informeller Mitarbeiter: informal co-worker).' The applicant has been ordered by interim injunction on the application of Mr Gysi to print a (fresh) presentation of the opposite view. The application for issue of an interim order was refused.

Aus den Gründen:

Die Voraussetzungen für den Erlass der begehrten einstweiligen Anordnung (§ 32 I BVerfGG) liegen nicht vor, da die angekündigte Verfassungsbeschwerde bei dem derzeitigen Verfahrensstand nach Aktenlage offensichtlich unbegründet ist. Es sind keine Anhaltspunkte dafür ersichtlich, dass die Ast. durch die in der Antragsschrift bezeichneten Entscheidungen des *LG Hamburg* oder durch das noch ausstehende Berufungsurteil des *OLG Hamburg* im einstweiligen Verfügungsverfahren (7 U 77/01) in ihrem Grundrecht auf Pressefreiheit (Art. 5 I 2 GG) verletzt worden ist bzw. verletzt werden könnte. Als dem Gegendarstellungsanspruch zugängliche Tatsachenbehauptung wurde lediglich der erste Teil des wiedergegebenen Zitats gewertet, während der letzte Halbsatz als nicht gegendarstellungsfähige Meinungsäußerung angesehen wurde. Dies ist aus verfassungsrechtlicher Sicht nicht zu beanstanden. Dementsprechend wurde Herrn *Gysi* auch nur hinsichtlich der tatsächlichen Elemente des von der Ast. widergegebenen Zitats die Möglichkeit einer Erwiderung eingeräumt. Die Zivilgerichte haben auch nicht verkannt, dass der Gegendarstellungsanspruch weder den Nachweis der Unwahrheit der Erstmitteilung noch den der Wahrheit der Gegendarstellung voraussetzt. Schließlich ist auch nicht zu beanstanden, dass die Zivilgerichte davon ausgegangen sind, die Ast. habe nicht glaubhaft gemacht, die von Herrn *Gysi* beanspruchte Gegendarstellung im Ausgangsverfahren sei offensichtlich unwahr bzw. irreführend.

Art. 6 [Ehe, Familie, nichteheliche Kinder] (1) Ehe und Familie stehen unter dem besonderen Schutze der staatlichen Ordnung.

(2) Pflege und Erziehung der Kinder sind das natürliche Recht der Eltern und die zuvörderst ihnen obliegende Pflicht. Uber ihre Betätigung wacht die staatliche Gemeinschaft.

(3) Gegen den Willen der Erziehungsberechtigten dürfen Kinder nur auf Grund eines Gesetzes von der Familie getrennt werden, wenn die Erziehungsberechtigten versagen oder wenn die Kinder aus anderen Gründen zu verwahrlosen drohen.

(4) Jede Mutter hat Anspruch auf den Schutz und die Fürsorge der Gemeinschaft.

(5) Den unehelichen Kindern sind durch die Gesetzgebung die gleichen Bedingungen für ihre leibliche und seelische Entwicklung und ihre Stellung in der Gesellschaft zu schaffen wie den ehelichen Kindern.

Art. 7 [Schulwesen] (1) Das gesamte Schulwesen steht unter der Aufsicht des Staates.

(2) Die Erziehungsberechtigten haben das Recht, über die Teilnahme des Kindes am Religionsunterricht zu bestimmen.

Reasons:

The prerequisites for the issue of the desired interim order (§ 32 I of the BVerfGG) are not present, as the constitutional complaint notified is obviously unfounded at the current stage of the proceedings according to the state of the documents. There are no evident indications for saying that the applicant has been harmed or could be harmed in its basic right to press freedom (Art 5 I 2 of the GG) by the decisions of the Hamburg State Court described in the application or by the appeal judgment of the Hamburg Upper State Court, which is still outstanding, in the interim injunction proceedings (7 U 77/01). Only the first part of the quotation which was reproduced was assessed as an assertion of facts available for the claim to a presentation of the opposite view, while the last half sentence was regarded as an expression of opinion not capable of generating a presentation of the opposite view. This is not open to objection from a constitutional law viewpoint. Accordingly Mr *Gysi* was granted the possibility of a reply only in respect of the factual elements of the quotation repeated by the applicant. The civil courts have also not failed to recognise that the claim to presentation of the opposite view assumes neither the proof of the untruthfulness of the first communication nor of the truth of the presentation of the opposite view. Finally it is also not open to objection that the civil courts assumed that the applicant had not made it credible that the presentation of the opposite view claimed by Mr *Gysi* in the original proceedings was obviously untrue or misleading.

Article 6 [Marriage, family and illegitimate children] (1) Marriage and the family are under the special protection of the public order.

(2) Care and upbringing of children are the natural rights of parents and the foremost duty incumbent upon them. The public community has to watch over their activity.

(3) Children may only be separated from the family, against the will of those authorised to bring them up, on the basis of a statute, if such persons fail or if the children are threatened with neglect for other reasons.

(4) Every mother has a claim to protection and care from the community.

(5) Illegitimate children are to be provided for by legislation with the same conditions for their physical and spiritual development and their place in society as legitimate children.

Article 7 [Educational system] (1) The whole education system is under the supervision of the State.

(2) Those authorised to bring up a child have the right to determine its participation in religious instruction.

(3) Der Religionsunterricht ist in den öffentlichen Schulen mit Ausnahme der bekenntnisfreien Schulen ordentliches Lehrfach. Unbeschadet des staatlichen Aufsichtsrechtes wird der Religionsunterricht in Übereinstimmung mit den Grundsätzen der Religionsgemeinschaften erteilt. Kein Lehrer darf gegen seinen Willen verpflichtet werden, Religionsunterricht zu erteilen.

(4) Das Recht zur Errichtung von privaten Schulen wird gewährleistet. Private Schulen als Ersatz für öffentliche Schulen bedürfen der Genehmigung des Staates und unterstehen den Landesgesetzen. Die Genehmigung ist zu erteilen, wenn die privaten Schulen in ihren Lehrzielen und Einrichtungen sowie in der wissenschaftlichen Ausbildung ihrer Lehrkräfte nicht hinter den öffentlichen Schulen zurückstehen und eine Sonderung der Schüler nach den Besitzverhältnissen der Eltern nicht gefördert wird. Die Genehmigung ist zu versagen, wenn die wirtschaftliche und rechtliche Stellung der Lehrkräfte nicht genügend gesichert ist.

(5) Eine private Volksschule ist nur zuzulassen, wenn die Unterrichtsverwaltung ein besonderes pädagogisches Interesse anerkennt oder, auf Antrag von Erziehungsberechtigten, wenn sie als Gemeinschaftsschule, als Bekenntnis- oder Weltanschauungsschule errichtet werden soll und eine öffentliche Volksschule dieser Art in der Gemeinde nicht besteht.

(6) Vorschulen bleiben aufgehoben.

Art. 8 [Versammlungsfreiheit] (1) Alle Deutschen haben das Recht, sich ohne Anmeldung oder Erlaubnis friedlich und ohne Waffen zu versammeln.

(2) Für Versammlungen unter freiem Himmel kann dieses Recht durch Gesetz oder auf Grund eines Gesetzes beschränkt werden.

Art. 9 [Vereinigungsfreiheit] (1) Alle Deutschen haben das Recht, Vereine und Gesellschaften zu bilden.

(2) Vereinigungen, deren Zwecke oder deren Tätigkeit den Strafgesetzen zuwiderlaufen oder die sich gegen die verfassungsmäßige Ordnung oder gegen den Gedanken der Völkerverständigung richten, sind verboten.

(3) Religious instruction is to be a regular subject in public schools, with the exception of secular schools. Without prejudice to the State's right of supervision, religious instruction is to be given in accordance with principles of religious communities. No teacher may be obliged to give religious instruction against his will.

(4) The right to set up private schools is guaranteed. Private schools as substitutes for public schools need the approval of the State and are governed by statutes of the State. Such approval is to be given if private schools are not inferior to public schools in their teaching aims and arrangements as well as in the scholarly development of the teachers, and separation of the pupils according to the means of their parents is not promoted. Approval is to be refused if the economic and legal standing of the teachers is not adequately secured.

(5) A private primary school is only to be permitted if the education authority has a particular pedagogic interest in it, or if, on a proposal from those authorised to bring children up, it is to be set up as a community school or a denominational or ideological school and a public primary school of this type does not exist in the district.

(6) Preparatory schools remain abolished.

Article 8 [Freedom of assembly] (1) All Germans have the right to assemble peacefully and without weapons, without announcement or permission.

(2) This right can be limited by statute or on the basis of a statute in respect of meetings in the open air.

This right was considered in the newspaper delivery obstruction case (see Chapter Six, p 481 and onwards), in particular as to its relationship with Art 5, and the issue of what is a peaceful demonstration. For more recent views on this issue, however, see, eg, BVerfGE 69, 315 (Brokdorf) and 73, 206 (Mutlangen).

Article 9 [Freedom of association] (1) All Germans have the right to form associations and societies.

(2) Associations whose purposes or activities are contrary to the criminal laws or which are directed against the constitutional order or the conceptions of understanding between peoples are forbidden.

(3) Das Recht, zur Wahrung und Förderung der Arbeits- und Wirtschaftsbedingungen Vereinigungen zu bilden, ist für jedermann und für alle Berufe gewährleistet. Abreden, die dieses Recht einschränken oder zu behindern suchen, sind nichtig, hierauf gerichtete Maßnahmen sind rechtswidrig. Maßnahmen nach den Artikeln 12 a, 35 Abs. 2 und 3, Artikel 87 a Abs. 4 und Artikel 91 dürfen sich nicht gegen Arbeitskämpfe richten, die zur Wahrung und Förderung der Arbeits- und Wirtschaftsbedingungen von Vereinigungen im Sinne des Satzes 1 geführt werden.

Art. 10 [Brief-, Post- und Fernmeldegeheimnis] (1) Das Briefgeheimnis sowie das Post- und Fernmeldegeheimnis sind unverletzlich.

(2) Beschränkungen dürfen nur auf Grund eines Gesetzes angeordnet werden. Dient die Beschränkung dem Schutze der freiheitlichen demokratischen Grundordnung oder des Bestandes oder der Sicherung des Bundes oder eines Landes, so kann das Gesetz bestimmen, daß sie dem Betroffenen nicht mitgeteilt wird und daß an die Stelle des Rechtsweges die Nachprüfung durch von der Volksvertretung bestellte Organe und Hilfsorgane tritt.

Art. 11 [Freizügigkeit] (1) Alle Deutschen genießen Freizügigkeit im ganzen Bundesgebiet.

(2) Dieses Recht darf nur durch Gesetz oder auf Grund eines Gesetzes und nur für die Fälle eingeschränkt werden, in denen eine ausreichende Lebensgrundlage nicht vorhanden ist und der Allgemeinheit daraus besondere Lasten entstehen würden oder in denen es zur Abwehr einer drohenden Gefahr für den Bestand oder die freiheitliche demokratische Grundordnung des Bundes oder eines Landes, zur Bekämpfung von Seuchengefahr, Naturkatastrophen oder besonders schweren Unglücksfällen, zum Schutze der Jugend vor Verwahrlosung oder um strafbaren Handlungen vorzubeugen, erforderlich ist.

Art. 12 [Berufsfreiheit] (1) Alle Deutschen haben das Recht, Beruf, Arbeitsplatz und Ausbildungsstätte frei zu wählen. Die Berufsausübung kann durch Gesetz oder auf Grund eines Gesetzes geregelt werden.

(2) Niemand darf zu einer bestimmten Arbeit gezwungen werden, außer im Rahmen einer herkömmlichen allgemeinen, für alle gleichen öffentlichen Dienstleistungspflicht.

(3) Zwangsarbeit ist nur bei einer gerichtlich angeordneten Freiheitsentziehung zulässig.

(3) The right to form associations for the preservation and advancement of conditions of labour and business is guaranteed for everyone and for all vocations. Agreements which limit this right or seek to impede it are invalid; measures with this object in view are contrary to law. Measures under Arts 12 a, 35 para 2 and 3, Art 87 a para 4 and Art 91 may not be directed against labour disputes which are conducted for the preservation and advancement of conditions of labour and business by associations in the sense of sentence 1.

Paragraph 3 includes the right not only to join such associations, but to engage in their activities; and also the right not to join them (as to which see the investment aid act case, p 193). Members of such associations can however be expelled for a satisfactory reason.

Article 10 [Privacy of letters and postal and telephone services] (1) The privacy of letters as well as of the postal and telephone services are inviolable.

(2) Limitations may only be made on the basis of a statute. If the limitation serves the protection of the free and democratic basic order or the stability or security of the Federation or of a State, the statute can provide that the limitation shall not be communicated to the person affected and that verification by organs (constituted by popular representation) and auxiliary organs replaces legal proceedings.

Article 11 [Freedom of movement] (1) All Germans enjoy freedom of movement in the whole of the Federal territory.

(2) This right may only be limited by statute, or on the basis of a statute and then only for cases in which a sufficient basis in life is not present and special burdens would arise out of it for the general public; or in which it is necessary, in order to prevent a danger which threatens the stability or the free democratic basic order of the Federation or of a State, for combating the danger of disease, natural catastrophes or especially serious accidents, for protection of the young from neglect, or to prevent criminal acts.

Article 12 [Freedom of vocation] (1) All Germans have the right to choose a vocation, place of work and place of education freely. The exercise of a vocation can be regulated by statute or on the basis of a statute.

(2) No-one may be forced to carry out a particular type of work, except within the framework of a traditional, general, public duty of service which is the same for everyone.

(3) Forced labour is only permissible on a withdrawal of freedom which is judicially determined.

In the chemist's case (BVerfGE 7, 377), the Federal Constitutional Court took the view that vocational activity included both choice and exercise of that activity. Statutory limitations might apply to either; and such limitations insofar as they applied to admission might be justifiable, eg, examinations, but not limitation on numbers of licences for economic reasons.

Art. 12 a [Dienstverpflichtungen] (1) Männer können vom vollendeten achtzehnten Lebensjahr an zum Dienst in den Streitkräften, im Bundesgrenzschutz oder in einem Zivilschutzverband verpflichtet werden.

(2) Wer aus Gewissensgründen den Kriegsdienst mit der Waffe verweigert, kann zu einem Ersatzdienst verpflichtet werden. Die Dauer des Ersatzdienstes darf die Dauer des Wehrdienstes nicht übersteigen. Das Nähere regelt ein Gesetz, das die Freiheit der Gewissensentscheidung nicht beeinträchtigen darf und auch eine Möglichkeit des Ersatzdienstes vorsehen muß, die in keinem Zusammenhang mit den Verbänden der Streitkräfte und des Bundesgrenzschutzes steht.

(3) Wehrpflichtige, die nicht zu einem Dienst nach Absatz 1 oder 2 herangezogen sind, können im Verteidigungsfalle durch Gesetz oder auf Grund eines Gesetzes zu zivilen Dienstleistungen für Zwecke der Verteidigung einschließlich des Schutzes der Zivilbevölkerung in Arbeitsverhältnisse verpflichtet werden; Verpflichtungen in offentlich-rechtliche Dienstverhältnisse sind nur zur Wahrnehmung polizeilicher Aufgaben oder solcher hoheitlichen Aufgaben der öffentlichen Verwaltung, die nur in einem öffentlich-rechtlichen Dienstverhältnis erfüllt werden können, zulässig. Arbeitsverhältnisse nach Satz 1 können bei den Streitkräften, im Bereich ihrer Versorgung sowie bei der öffentlichen Verwaltung begründet werden; Verpflichtungen in Arbeitsverhältnisse im Bereiche der Versorgung der Zivilbevölkerung sind nur zulässig, um ihren lebensnotwendigen Bedarf zu decken oder ihren Schutz sicherzustellen.

(4) Kann im Verteidigungsfalle der Bedarf an zivilen Dienstleistungen im zivilen Sanitäts- und Heilwesen sowie in der ortsfesten militärischen Lazarettorganisation nicht auf freiwilliger Grundlage gedeckt werden, so können Frauen vom vollendeten achtzehnten bis zum vollendeten fünfundfünfzigsten Lebensjahr durch Gesetz oder auf Grund eines Gesetzes zu derartigen Dienstleistungen herangezogen werden. Sie dürfen auf keinen Fall zum Dienst mit der Waffe verpflichtet werden.

(5) Für die Zeit vor dem Verteidigungsfalle können Verpflichtungen nach Absatz 3 nur nach Maßgabe des Artikels 80 a Abs. 1 begründet werden. Zur Vorbereitung auf Dienstleistungen nach Absatz 3, für die besondere Kenntnisse oder Fertigkeiten erforderlich sind, kann durch Gesetz oder auf Grund eines Gesetzes die Teilnahme an Ausbildungsveranstaltungen zur Pflicht gemacht werden. Satz 1 findet insoweit keine Anwendung.

(6) Kann im Verteidigungsfalle der Bedarf an Arbeitskräften für die in Absatz 3 Satz 2 genannten Bereiche auf freiwilliger Grundlage nicht gedeckt werden, so kann zur Sicherung dieses Bedarfs die Freiheit der Deutschen, die Ausübung eines Berufs oder den Arbeitsplatz aufzugeben, durch Gesetz oder auf Grund eines Gesetzes eingeschränkt werden. Vor Eintritt des Verteidigungsfalles gilt Absatz 5 Satz 1 entsprechend.

Article 12 a [Conscription] (1) Men can be required, from the completion of their 18th year, to serve in the military forces, in the Federal Border Protection Force or in a civil defence corps.

(2) A person who refuses to do armed military service for reasons of conscience can be required to do substituted service. The length of substituted service may not exceed the length of military service. Details are to be regulated by a statute which may not restrict freedom of decision on grounds of conscience and must also provide for the possibility of substituted service which has no connection with the units of the military forces or the Federal Border Protection Force.

(3) Conscripted persons who are not called to service in accordance with paras 1 or 2 can, if a state of defence[1] exists, be required to do civilian service in employment relationships for the purposes of defence (inclusive of protection of the civilian population) by a statute or on the basis of a statute; duties in public law service relationships are however only permissible here for the maintenance of police duties or such sovereign duties of the public administration as can only be fulfilled in a public law service relationship. Employment relationships, in accordance with sentence 1, can be established with the military forces in the area of providing for them, as well as with the public administration; duties in employment relationships in the area of providing for the civilian population are only permissible to cover their vitally necessary needs or to ensure their protection.

(4) If, when there is a state of defence, the need for civilian services in the public health and medical services as well as in the stationary military hospital organisation cannot be covered on a voluntary basis, women from the completion of their 18th year until the completion of their 55th year can be called to those kinds of services by a statute or on the basis of a statute. They may not in any case be obliged to carry out service with weapons.

(5) For the period before the state of defence, the duties in accordance with para 3 can only be established in accordance with the requirements of Art 80 a para 1. For preparation for the services in accordance with para 3 for which special knowledge or skills are necessary, participation in training arrangements can be required, by a statute or on the basis of a statute. Sentence 1 has to that extent no application.

(6) If, when there is a state of defence, the need for labour for the areas named in para 3 sentence 2 cannot be covered on a voluntary basis, the freedom of Germans to give up the exercise of a vocation or a place of work can be limited by a statute or on the basis of a statute to provide for this need. Before a state of defence arises, para 5 sentence 1 has corresponding effect.

---

1 This is a state of affairs in which Federal territory is the subject of armed attack or immediately threatened by such an attack. The Federal Parliament with the consent of the Federal Council decides whether this is the case by virtue of Art 115 a of the GG.

Art. 13 [Unverletzlichkeit der Wohnung] (1) Die Wohnung ist unverletzlich.

(2) Durchsuchungen dürfen nur durch den Richter, bei Gefahr im Verzuge auch durch die in den Gesetzen vorgesehenen anderen Organe angeordnet und nur in der dort vorgeschriebenen Form durchgeführt werden.

(3) Begründen bestimmte Tatsachen den Verdacht, daß jemand eine durch Gesetz einzeln bestimmte besonders schwere Straftat begangen hat, so dürfen zur Verfolgung der Tat auf Grund richterlicher Anordnung technische Mittel zur akustischen Überwachung von Wohnungen, in denen der Beschuldigte sich vermutlich aufhält, eingesetzt werden, wenn die Erforschung des Sachverhalts auf andere Weise unverhältnismäßig erschwert oder aussichtslos wäre. Die Maßnahme ist zu befristen. Die Anordnung erfolgt durch einen mit drei Richtern besetzten Spruchkörper. Bei Gefahr im Verzuge kann sie auch durch einen einzelnen Richter getroffen werden.

(4) Zur Abwehr dringender Gefahren für die öffentliche Sicherheit, insbesondere einer gemeinen Gefahr oder einer Lebensgefahr, dürfen technische Mittel zur Überwachung von Wohnungen nur auf Grund richterlicher Anordnung eingesetzt werden. Bei Gefahr im Verzüge kann die Maßnahme auch durch eine andere gesetzlich bestimmte Stelle angeordnet werden; eine richerliche Entscheidung ist unverzüglich nachzuholen.

(5) Sind technische Mittel ausschließlich zum Schutze der bei einem Einsatz in Wohnungen tätigen Personen vorgesehen, kann die Maßnahme durch eine gesetzlich bestimmte Stelle angeordnet werden. Eine anderweitige Verwertung der hierbei erlangten Erkenntnisse ist nur zum Zwecke der Strafverfolgung oder der Gefahrenabwehr und nur zulässig, wenn zuvor die Rechtmäßigkeit der Maßnahme richterlich festgestellt ist; bei Gefahr im Verzuge ist die richterliche Entscheidung unverzüglich nachzuholen.

(6) Die Bundesregierung unterrichtet den Bundestag jährlich über den nach Absatz 3 sowie über den im Zuständigkeitsbereich des Bundes nach Absatz 4 und, soweit richterlich überprüfungsbedürftig, nach Absatz 5 erfolgten Einsatz technische Mittel. Ein vom Bundestag gewähltes Gremium übt auf der Grundlage dieses Berichts die parlamentarische Kontrolle aus. Die Länder gewährleisten eine gleichwertige parlamentarische Kontrolle.

Article 13 [Inviolability of the home] (1) The home is inviolable.

(2) Searches may only be ordered by a judge (or where there is danger in delay, by the other organs provided for in statutes) and only executed in the form provided for by statute.

(3) If there are definite facts on which to base the suspicion that someone has committed a serious crime which has been individually determined by statute, technical means for the acoustic surveillance of dwellings in which the accused is probably residing may be employed by judicial order for prosecution in respect of the act, if the investigation of the case in another way would be disproportionately difficult or without prospect of success. The measure must be time limited. The order is to be made by a court consisting of three judges. If danger would arise from delay it can also be made by a single judge.

(4) To avert urgent dangers for public safety, in particular a general danger or a danger to life, technical means for surveillance of dwellings may only be employed on the basis of a judicial order. If danger would arise from delay the measure can also be ordered by another authority determined by statute; a judicial decision must be obtained without delay.

(5) If technical means are planned exclusively for the protection of the persons deployed in dwellings, the measure can be ordered by an authority determined by statute. Other use of the information obtained by this means is only permissible for the purpose of criminal prosecution or to avert danger and if the legality of the measure is judicially established beforehand; if danger would arise from delay the judicial decision must be obtained without delay.

(6) The Federal Government will inform the Federal Parliament annually about the employment of technical means taking place under para 3, under para 4 within the area of competence of the Federation and under para 5 insofar as judicial examination is needed. A panel elected by the Federal Parliament will exercise parliamentary control on the basis of this report. The States guarantee parliamentary control of an equal standard.

(7) Eingriffe und Beschränkungen dürfen im übrigen nur zur Abwehr einer gemeinen Gefahr oder einer Lebensgefahr für einzelne Personen, auf Grund eines Gesetzes auch zur Verhütung dringender Gefahren für die öffentliche Sicherheit und Ordnung, insbesondere zur Behebung der Raumnot, zur Bekämpfung von Seuchengefahr oder zum Schutze gefährdeter Jugendlicher vorgenommen werden.

Art. 14 [Eigentum, Erbrecht und Enteignung] (1) Das Eigentum und das Erbrecht werden gewährleistet. Inhalt und Schranken werden durch die Gesetze bestimmt.

(2) Eigentum verpflichtet. Sein Gebrauch soll zugleich dem Wohle der Allgemeinheit dienen.

(3) Eine Enteignung ist nur zum Wohle der Allgemeinheit zulässig. Sie darf nur durch Gesetz oder auf Grund eines Gesetzes erfolgen, das Art und Ausmaß der Entschädigung regelt. Die Entschädigung ist unter gerechter Abwägung der Interessen der Allgemeinheit und der Beteiligten zu bestimmen. Wegen der Höhe der Entschädigung steht im Streitfalle der Rechtsweg vor den ordentlichen Gerichten offen.

(7) Interferences and limitations may in other respects only be made for guarding against a common danger or danger to the lives of individual persons, or, on the basis of a statute, for prevention of pressing dangers for public safety and order, especially to eliminate shortage of space, to combat danger of disease or to protect endangered young persons.

Article 14 [Property, right of inheritance and expropriation] (1) Property and inheritance are guaranteed. Content and limitations are to be determined by statutes.

(2) Property imposes duties. Its use is at the same time to serve the good of the general public.

(3) An expropriation is only permissible for the good of the general public. It can only take place by a statute or on the basis of a statute which regulates the type and measure of the compensation. Compensation is to be determined by a just balancing of the interests of the general public and of the persons involved. In case of dispute, legal proceedings are available before the ordinary courts in respect of the level of compensation.

Property in the constitutional sense has a different meaning to property in the civil law sense, and means every right which has a value.

Paragraph 2 requires the legislator to carry out a balancing act between the needs of private property and the requirements of the social order.

Expropriation under para 3 means any sufficiently serious interference with property. This might be carried out by statute, or, more commonly, on the basis of statutory authority. The gravel extraction case (BVerfGE 58, 300) fell to be considered under the former category. A statute revoked licences for the extraction of gravel. This was however held to be a determination of the contents and limits of a right rather than an expropriation, because extraction could continue for a further 17 years.

Special considerations arise when the expropriation is for the benefit of a private body; see, eg, BVerfGE 74, 264.

THE INVESTMENT AID ACT CASE

BVerfGE Band 4 S. 7

2

1 Art. 74 Nr. 11 GG begründet die Zuständigkeit des Bundes auch für Gesetze, die ordnend und lenkend in das Wirtschaftsleben eingreifen.

2 Wirtschaftslenkende Gesetze verstoßen nicht schon deshalb gegen den Gleichheitssatz, weil sie die Wettbewerbslage verändern. Sie können auch im Interesse einzelner Gruppen erlassen werden, jedoch nur, wenn dies durch das öffentliche Wohl geboten ist und schutzwürdige Interessen anderer nicht willkürlich vernachlässigt werden.

3 Ein gesetzlicher Eingriff in die Freiheit der Disposition über Betriebsmittel ist mit Art. 2 Abs. 1 GG vereinbar, sofern ein angemessener Spielraum zur Entfaltung der Unternehmerinitiative verbleibt.

4 Art. 14 GG schützt nicht das Vermögen als solches.

5 Die Liquidität des Betriebes ist kein der Eigentumsgarantie unterliegendes Recht.

6 Ein bestimmtes Wirtschaftssystem ist durch das Grundgesetz nicht gewährleistet.

7 Offene Handelsgesellschaften und Kommanditgesellschaften können unter ihrer Firma Verfassungsbeschwerde erheben.

8 Verfassungsbeschwerden können auch telegrafisch eingelegt werden.

Urteil des Ersten Senats vom 20. Juli 1954

– 1 BvR 459, 484, 548, 555, 623, 651, 748, 783, 801/52, 5, 9/53, 96, 114/54 –

in dem Verfahren über die Verfassungsbeschwerden verschiedener Firmen gegen das Bundesgesetz über die Investitionshilfe der gewerblichen Wirtschaft vom 7. Januar 1952 (BGBl. I S. 7) - IHG -, abgeändert durch Gesetze vom 22. August 1952 (BGBl. I S. 585) – 1. Änd. IHG – und vom 30. März 1953 (BGBl. I S. 107) – 2.ÄndIHG –.

THE INVESTMENT AID ACT CASE

This is one of those constitutional law cases where the economic policies of the legislator are subjected to review. This is carried out with understandable restraint, but one of the interesting features of the case is its wide-ranging assessment of the legislation involved against a number of basic rights and constitutional principles.

BVerfGE Volume 4 p 7

2

1 Article 74 no 11 of the GG is the basis for the competence of the Federation for statutes which intervene in the business world in a regulating and directing fashion.

2 Statutes which direct business do not contravene the requirement of equality simply because they change the conditions of competition. They can also be issued in the interests of single groups but only, however, if this is required for the public good and the interests of others which are worthy of protection are not arbitrarily neglected.

3 A statutory invasion of the freedom of disposition of working capital is reconcilable with Art 2 para 1 of the GG, insofar as appropriate latitude remains for the development of entrepreneurial initiative.

4 Article 14 of the GG does not protect property as such.

5 The liquidity of a business is not a right which is subject to the property guarantee.

6 The Basic Law does not guarantee a particular economic system.

7 General partnerships and limited partnerships can make constitutional complaints under their firm names.

8 Constitutional complaints can also be lodged telegraphically.

Judgment of the First Senate on 20 July 1954

– 1 BvR 459, 484, 548, 555, 623, 651, 748, 783, 801/52, 5, 9/53, 96, 114/54 –

in the proceedings concerning the constitutional complaints of various firms against the Federal Investment Aid for Industry Act of 7 January 1952 (BGBl I, 7) - IHG -, amended by statutes of 22 August 1952 (BGBl I, 585) – Investment Aid for Industry (Amendment no 1) Act – and of 30 March 1953 (BGBl I, 107) – Investment Aid for Industry (Amendment no 2) Act.

Entscheidungsformel:

Die Verfassungsbeschwerden werden zurückgewiesen.

Gründe:

A

Der wirtschaftliche Aufschwung, der in der Bundesrepublik nach der Währungsreform einsetzte, wirkte sich nicht sofort in allen Wirtschaftszweigen gleichmäßig aus. Während Teile der gewerblichen Wirtschaft mit Hilfe steuerlicher Vergünstigungen oder durch Freigabe der Preise in erheblichem Umfange Investitionen vornehmen konnten, fehlten dem Kohlenbergbau und der eisenschaffenden Industrie, die beide noch an Höchstpreise gebunden waren, die notwendigen Investitionsmittel. Darin lag die Gefahr eines Sinkens der Produktion. Überlegungen, wie den sog. Engpaßindustrien geholfen werden könne, beschäftigten auch den Gemeinschaftsausschuß der gewerblichen Wirtschaft, in dem die Spitzenverbände der gewerblichen Wirtschaft vertreten sind. Er beschloß am 27. April 1951, die gewerbliche Wirtschaft solle einen Betrag von 1 Milliarde DM als Investitionshilfe freiwillig zur Verfügung stellen. Dieser Plan ließ sich jedoch nicht verwirklichen. Nach eingehenden Verhandlungen kam es daher schließlich zu einer gesetzlichen Regelung durch das Gesetz über die Investitionshilfe der gewerblichen Wirtschaft vom 7. Januar 1952 (BGB1 I S. 7) - IHG, abgeändert durch Gesetze vom 22. August 1952 (BGB1 I S. 585) und vom 30. März 1953 (BGB1 I S. 107).

Nach diesem Gesetz hat die gewerbliche Wirtschaft zur Deckung des vordringlichen Investitionsbedarfs des Kohlenbergbaues, der eisenschaffenden Industrie und der Energiewirtschaft einen einmaligen Beitrag in Höhe von 1 Milliarde DM aufzubringen. Bemessungsgrundlage ist ein Betrag, der für jeden Betrieb aus Gewinn und Umsatz der Jahre 1950 und 1951 errechnet wird. Der Aufbringungssatz beträgt 3,5 v. H. der Bemessungsgrundlage.

Bei der Aufbringung wirken die Finanzbehörden der Länder, vor allem die Finanzämter mit. Der Aufbringungsschuldner hat gegenüber dem zuständigen Finanzamt Erklärungen über die Berechnungsgrundlage und den Aufbringungsbetrag abzugeben. Kommt er dieser Verpflichtung nicht oder nicht ordnungsgemäß nach, so kann das Finanzamt von sich aus den Aufbringungsbetrag festsetzen. Hiergegen steht dem Aufbringungsschuldner die Berufung an das Finanzgericht offen.

Decision:

The constitutional complaints are rejected.

Reasons:

A

The economic uplift which began in the Federal Republic after the currency reform did not take immediate effect in all branches of industry equally. Whilst parts of industry could carry out investment on a considerable scale with the help of tax concessions or through the decontrol of prices, the coal mining and iron producing industries, which were both still tied to maximum prices, lacked the necessary means of investment. There was a danger of a fall in production as a result of this. The Joint Committee of Industry in which the chief associations of industry are represented deliberated on how the so-called bottleneck industries could be helped. It decided on 27 April 1951 that industry should voluntarily make available a sum of one thousand million DM as investment aid. This plan was not, however, put into effect. After detailed negotiations there was, in the end, statutory regulation by the Investment Aid for Industry Act of 7 January 1952 (BGBl I, 7) – IHG, amended by statutes of 22 August 1952 (BGBl I, 585) and of 30 March 1953 (BGBl I, 107).

According to this statute, industry had to raise a single sum of one thousand million DM to cover the urgent investment needs of the coal mining industry, the iron production industry and the energy industry. The basis of assessment is a sum which is calculated for every business on the basis of profit and turnover for the years 1950 and 1951. The levy requirement amounts to 3.5% of the basis of assessment.

The tax authorities of the States, especially the tax offices, are to be involved in the levy. The party liable for the levy must submit declarations about the basis of calculation and the sum due under the levy to the competent tax office. If it does not carry out this duty, or does not carry it out properly, the tax office can assess the sum due under the levy itself. In this case the party liable for the levy may appeal to the Revenue Court.

Das Aufkommen aus der Investitionshilfe bildet ein mit eigener Rechtspersönlichkeit ausgestattetes Sondervermögen, dessen Vorstand die Industriekreditbank (das 'Kreditinstitut') ist. Aus dem Sondervermögen werden den begünstigten Betrieben Darlehen zu Investitionszwecken gewährt; als Ausgleich müssen die Betriebe dem Sondervermögen Aktien oder Schuldverschreibungen im Nennbetrag des Darlehens zur Zeichnung anbieten. Diese Wertpapiere können von den Aufbringungsschuldnern mittels einer Erwerbsberechtigung übernommen werden, die sie durch Zahlung ihres Aufbringungsbetrages erlangen. Die Aufbringungsbeträge sind bis zur Zuteilung der Wertpapiere mit 4%, nach Ablauf von 18 Monaten mit 5% verzinslich. Machen die Aufbringungsschuldner von ihrem mit der Erwerbsberechtigung verbundenen Wahlrecht nicht fristgemäß Gebrauch, so werden ihnen die zum Ausgleich gedachten Wertpapiere durch das Kreditinstitut zugeteilt.

Über die Verwendung der Investitionshilfemittel sowie über die Bedingungen, unter denen sie den Begünstigten zu gewähren sind, beschließt ein Kuratorium aus neunzehn Mitgliedern, dessen Beschlüsse hinsichtlich der Auswahl der Begünstigten und der Höhe der bewilligten Mittel der Bestätigung des Bundesministers der Wirtschaft bedürfen. Durch den bestätigten Beschluß wird das begünstigte Unternehmen verpflichtet, über die bewilligten Investitionsmittel hinaus für das begünstigte Vorhaben eigene Mittel in Höhe der dann entfallenden Aufbringungspflicht zu verwenden.

B

Die Beschwerdeführer unterliegen der Aufbringungspflicht nach dem Investitionshilfegesetz. Die Beschwerdeführer zu 8, 47, 76, 77 und 78 haben Aufbringungsbescheide der zuständigen Finanzämter erhalten, gegen die sie Rechtsmittel eingelegt haben. In den Berufungsverfahren der Beschwerdeführer zu 8 und zu 76 haben die Finanzgerichte Münster und Kiel das Verfahren gemäß § 264 Abs. 1 AO bis zur Entscheidung des Bundesverfassungsgerichts über die Verfassungsbeschwerden ausgesetzt.

Die Beschwerdeführer zu 1–76 haben mit z. T. voneinander abweichenden Anträgen Verfassungsbeschwerde gegen das Investitionshilfegesetz, teilweise auch gegen die dazu ergangenen Durchführungsverordnungen, die Beschwerdeführer zu 77 und 78 gegen die ihnen gegenüber ergangenen Aufbringungsbescheide erhoben. Das Ziel aller Beschwerdeführer ist die Nichtigerklärung des Investitionshilfegesetzes oder einzelner seiner Vorschriften wegen Verletzung der Art. 1, 2, 3, 9, 14, 15, 20, 70, 110 und 115 GG, sowie ungeschriebener Verfassungsgrundsätze.

The revenue from the investment aid forms a special fund endowed with its own legal personality whose board is the Industry Credit Bank (the 'Credit Institute'). The assisted businesses are granted loans from the special fund for investment purposes; in return the businesses must offer to the special fund shares or debentures for subscription in the nominal amount of the loan. These securities can be taken over by the party liable to the levy by means of a commercial authorisation, which they obtain by payment of the amount of their levy. The amounts levied bear interest at 4% until allotment of the securities and at 5% after the lapse of 18 months. If the parties liable to the levy do not make use in time of their voting right connected with the commercial authorisation the securities intended as recompense will be allocated to them by the Credit Institute.

A committee with 19 members decides about the use of the investment aid, as well as the conditions under which it is to be granted to those assisted. The committee's decisions in relation to the selection of those to be assisted and the level of aid to be allowed need the confirmation of the Federal Minister for the Economy. As a result of the confirmed decision, the assisted undertaking will be obliged to use its own resources, to the amount of the levy obligation (which then ceases to apply) for the assisted purpose, over and above the investment aid allowed.

B

The complainants are subject to the duty to pay the levy in accordance with the Investment Aid Act. The 8th, 46th, 76th, 77th and 78th complainants have received levy decisions from the competent tax offices, against which they have lodged legal proceedings. In the appeal proceedings of the 8th and 76th complainants, the Finance Courts of Münster and Kiel have suspended the proceedings in accordance with § 264 para 1 of the Internal Revenue Code until the decision of the constitutional court about the constitutional complaint.

The 1st–76th complainants have raised complaints against the Investment Aid Act by applications which partially differ from one another. The complaints are also partly raised against the implementing Regulations issued for the purpose of the Act and the 77th and 78th complainants have raised complaints against the levy decisions which have been issued against them. The objective of all the complainants is a declaration that the Investment Aid Act or individual provisions of it are invalid on the grounds of the violation of Arts 1, 2, 3, 9, 14, 15, 20, 70, 110 and 115 of the GG as well as unwritten constitutional principles.

Die Verfassungsbeschwerden sind dem Bundestag, dem Bundesrat und der Bundesregierung zur Stellungnahme zugeleitet worden. Der Bundestag und der Bundesrat haben sich zur Sache nicht geäußert. Die Bundesregierung hält die Einwände der Beschwerdeführer gegen die Verfassungsmäßigkeit des Investitionshilfegesetzes für unbegründet.

In der mündlichen Verhandlung, in der die Verfassungsbeschwerden zur gemeinsamen Verhandlung und Entscheidung verbunden wurden, waren die Beschwerdeführer zu 1–51 und 73–78 und die Bundesregierung vertreten.

C

1 Das Investitionshilfegesetz kann unmittelbar mit der Verfassungsbeschwerde angegriffen werden, weil es in die Rechtsstellung der Betroffenen eingreift, ohne daß es eines Vollzugsaktes bedarf (BVerfGE 3, 34 [36]). Der Zulässigkeit der Verfassungsbeschwerden gegen das Gesetz steht nicht entgegen, daß gegen die Beschwerdeführer zu 8, 47 und 76 Aufbringungsbescheide ergangen sind. In diesem Falle haben sie die Möglichkeit, sowohl das Gesetz unmittelbar als auch den Vollzugsakt mit der Verfassungsbeschwerde anzugreifen.

2 Auch die gegen den Aufbringungsbescheid gerichteten Verfassungsbeschwerden der Beschwerdeführer zu 77 und 78 sind demgemäß zulässig, obwohl sie die Jahresfrist zur Einlegung der Verfassungsbeschwerde unmittelbar gegen das Investitionshilfegesetz versäumt haben.

Der Rechtsweg gegen die Aufbringungsbescheide ist allerdings nicht erschöpft, aber den Beschwerdeführern erwüchse ein schwerer und unabwendbarer Nachteil, wenn sie zunächst auf den Rechtsweg verwiesen würden; in den bereits anhängigen Verfahren über die Verfassungsmäßigkeit des Investitionshilfegesetzes würde mit Wirkung für und gegen alle entschieden werden, ohne daß sie Gelegenheit gehabt hätten, ihre Argumente vorzutragen. Im Hinblick auf die grundsätzlichen verfassungsrechtlichen Fragen, die das Investitionshilfegesetz aufwirft, sind die Verfassungsbeschwerden auch von allgemeiner Bedeutung. Die Voraussetzungen des § 90 Abs. 2 Satz 2 BVerfGG liegen daher vor.

3 Sämtliche Beschwerdeführer sind antragsberechtigt.

(a) Soweit sie juristische Personen sind, können sie jedenfalls die von ihnen behauptete Verletzung des Gleichheitssatzes mit der Verfassungsbeschwerde geltend machen, weil dieser seinem Wesen nach auf juristische Personen anwendbar ist (vgl. BVerfGE 3, 383; auch BVerfGE 3, 359 [363]).

The constitutional complaints have been brought before the Federal Parliament, the Federal Council and the Federal Government for comment. The Federal Parliament and the Federal Council have made no comment in the matter. The Federal Government consider the objections of the complainants against the constitutionality of the Investment Aid Act to be unfounded.

In the oral hearing in which the constitutional complaints were joined for a joint hearing and decision, the 1st–51st and 73rd–78th complainants and the Federal Government were represented.

C

1 The Investment Aid Act can be challenged directly by constitutional complaint, because it interferes with the legal standing of those affected, without needing an executive act (BVerfGE 3, 34 [36]). It does not militate against the admissibility of the constitutional complaints against the statute that levy decisions have been issued against the 8th, 47th and 76th complainants. In this case they have the possibility of challenging the statute directly as well as the executive act by means of a constitutional complaint.

2 The constitutional complaints of the 77th and 78th complainants directed against the levy decision are also accordingly admissible although they were made directly against the Investment Aid Act outside the one year period for lodging a constitutional complaint.

Ordinary legal remedies against the levy decisions have certainly not been exhausted, but a severe and unavoidable disadvantage would accrue to the complainants if they were referred in the first instance to ordinary legal proceedings; in the proceedings already pending about the constitutionality of the Investment Aid Act a decision would be made with effect for and against all parties without them having had the opportunity to bring forward their arguments. With regard to the basic constitutional law questions which the Investment Aid Act poses, the constitutional complaints are also of general importance. The prerequisites of § 90, para 2 sentence 2 of the BVerfGG are therefore present.

3 All the complainants are entitled to make an application.

(a) Insofar as they are legal persons they can raise the violation claimed by them of the equality requirement by means of constitutional complaint, because it is by its nature applicable to legal persons (compare BVerfGE 3, 383; also BVerfGE 3, 359 [363]).

(b) Soweit Offene Handelsgesellschaften und Kommanditgesellschaften Verfassungsbeschwerden eingelegt haben, sind diese
ebenfalls zulässig. Diese Gesellschaften können unter ihrer Firma Rechte
erwerben, Verbindlichkeiten eingehen und vor Gericht als Partei
auftreten (§§ 124 Abs. 1, 161 Abs. 2 HGB). Dann handeln die unter einer
gemeinschaftlichen Firma zusammengeschlossenen Gesellschafter. Ein
solches Handeln kommt auch bei der Verteidigung von Grundrechten in
Frage, wenn sich der staatliche Eingriff auf das gesamthänderisch
gebundene Gesellschaftsvermögen oder das von der Gesellschaft
betriebene Handelsgewerbe bezieht. Ein solcher Eingriff in das
Gesellschaftsvermögen erfolgt durch das Investitionshilfegesetz, denn
für den Aufbringungsbetrag haftet bei Offenen Handelsgesellschaften
und Kommanditgesellschaften neben dem Vermögen der Gesellschafter
auch das der Gesellschaft.

Welche Grundrechtsverletzungen diese Gesellschaften rügen
können, ist aus dem Grundgedanken des Art. 19 Abs. 3 GG zu
beantworten. Jedenfalls steht ihnen das Grundrecht aus Art. 3 Abs. 1
GG, auf das sie sich berufen, in dem oben bezeichneten Rahmen zu.

4 Der Beschwerdeführer zu 76 hat die Verfassungsbeschwerde
telegrafisch eingelegt. Damit ist die Schriftform des § 23 Abs. 1 BVerfGG
gewahrt.

D

Die Angriffe der Beschwerdeführer richten sich zunächst gegen das
Gesetz im ganzen.

1 Ein Teil von ihnen macht geltend, der Bund sei zum Erlaß des
Gesetzes nicht zuständig gewesen. Das Bundesverfassungsgericht hat
diese Frage von Amts wegen geprüft (BVerfGE 1, 264 [271]).

Die Bundesregierung leitet das Gesetzgebungsrecht des Bundes
zutreffend aus Art. 74 Nr. 11 GG her. Wortlaut und
Entstehungsgeschichte dieser Bestimmung bieten keinen Anhalt, die
Gesetzgebungsbefugnis des Bundes auf Gesetze zu beschränken, die
lediglich organisatorischen Inhalt haben oder nur die
Rechtsbeziehungen der in Art. 74 Nr. 11 GG einzeln aufgeführten
Wirtschaftszweige regeln. Nach Art. 74 Nr. 11 GG können auch
Bundesgesetze erlassen werden, die ordnend und lenkend in das
Wirtschaftsleben eingreifen. Das Investitionshilfgesetz ist ein solches
Gesetz; es bezweckt, Kapital zu Investitionszwecken aus einem
bestimmten Bereich der Wirtschaft in einen anderen zu leiten.

(b) Insofar as general partnerships and limited partnerships have lodged constitutional complaints, they are likewise admissible. These partnerships can acquire rights under their firm names, enter into obligations and appear in court as a party (§§ 124 paras 1, 161 para 2 of the HGB). Partners who are bound together are then trading under a corporate name. Such trading also comes into consideration where the basic rights are being defended if the government intervention relates to the partnership's resources committed to corporate use or the business carried on by the partnership. Such an intervention in the partnership's resources results from the Investment Aid Act, because with general partnerships and limited partnerships the resources of the partnership as well as those of the members are liable for the sum levied.

Which basic right violations may be objected to by these partnerships is to be answered in accordance with the basic ideas of Art 19 para 3 of the GG. In any case, they are entitled, within the framework described above, to the basic right from Art 3 para 1 of the GG to which they refer.

4 The 76th complainant lodged the constitutional complaint telegraphically. In this respect the correct form of writing under § 23 para 1 of the BVerfGG has been adhered to.

D

The challenges of the complainants are directed at first against the statute as a whole.

1 Part of them assert that the Federation was not competent for the issue of the statute. The Federal Constitutional Court examined this question by virtue of its official position (BVerfGE 1, 264 [271]).

The Federal Government correctly deduces the Federation's right to legislate from Art 74 no 11^2 of the GG. The wording and origins of this provision offer no support for limiting the legislative authority of the Federation to statutes which merely have an organisational content or only regulate the legal relationships of the branches of industry set out individually in Art 74 no 11 of the GG. In accordance with Art 74 no 11 of the GG Federal statutes can also be issued which intervene in the business world in a regulating and directing fashion. The Investment Aid Act is such a statute; it aims to transfer capital from one specified sphere of industry to another for investment purposes.

---

2 Article 74 of the GG lists the concurrent legislative powers of the Federation and the States, ie, the States only have power insofar as the Federation has not already made use of these powers. No 11 is 'Industrial law (mining, industry, the energy industry, trade, business, commerce, banking and the stock market, private law insurance)'.

Es bleibt aber zu prüfen, ob das gewählte Mittel, die Auferlegung einer Geldleistung, der Investitionshilfe den Charakter einer Steuer im Sinne des Abschnitts X des Grundgesetzes verleiht. Dann würde die Gesetzgebungszuständigkeit des Bundes ausschließlich nach Art. 105 GG zu beurteilen sein, der insoweit Art. 74 Nr. 11 GG vorgeht (vgl. Gutachten des Bundesverfassungsgerichts vom 16. Juni 1954 – 1 P BvV 2/52, BVerfGE 3, 407).

Die Investitionshilfe weist allerdings einige einer Steuer verwandte Züge auf. Ihr wahrer Rechtscharakter kann aber nur aus der Gesamtheit der wirtschaftlichen Vorgänge entnommen werden, die das Investitionshilfegesetz bewirkt. Es bezweckt die Umlenkung von Investitionsmitteln, um einen Investitionsbedarf zu befriedigen, der vom Gesetzgeber für vordringlich erachtet wurde. Dieser erwartete, daß durch die aufgebrachten Mittel Investitionsvorhaben in mehrfacher Höhe der Investitionshilfe ausgelöst werden würden. Deshalb haben die begünstigten Betriebe auch eigene Mittel einzusetzen (§ 29 Abs. 5 Satz 2 IHG). Soweit das Investitionhilfegesetz lenkend in den Wirtschaftsablauf eingreift, knüpft es an den marktwirtschaftlichen Vorgang der Zeichnung von Wertpapieren an. Obwohl die Aufbringungsschuldner zunächst die öffentlich-rechtliche Pflicht haben, den auf sie entfallenden Betrag zu zahlen, münden ihre Leistungen doch schließlich in privatrechtliche Beziehungen in Form aktienrechtlicher Beteiligungen oder verbriefter Gläubiger-Schuldnerbeziehungen ein; letztlich stehen dabei Leistungen der Aufbringungsschuldner und Gegenleistungen der begünstigten Unternehmen einander gegenüber. Die Aufbringungsbeträge gelangen nur als durchlaufende Mittel in das Sondervermögen Investitionshilfe, das nicht staatliche Einkünfte verwaltet, sondern der staatlichen Kreditlenkung dient, indem es die Herstellung der Rechtsbeziehungen zwischen den Aufbringungsschuldnern und den begünstigten Unternehmen vermittelt. Dies alles zeigt, daß die Investitionshilfe sich ihrem Wesen nach von einer Steuer unterscheidet.

Die Investitionshilfe wird auch nicht etwa dadurch zu einer Steuer, daß Finanzbehörden bei ihrer Aufbringung mitwirken. Diese können auch zu anderen als finanzhoheitlichen Zwecken tätig werden. Dem Gesetzgeber konnte es sachgerecht erscheinen, die Finanzbehörden einzuschalten, weil sich die Mitwirkung der Industrie- und Handelskammern im Aufbringungsverfahren als undurchführbar erwies. Daß damit durch ein Bundesgesetz bestimmte, fachlich geeignete Landesbehörden zur Durchführung des Gesetzes herangezogen werden, ist angesichts der Zustimmung des Bundesrats verfassungsrechtlich unbedenklich (Art. 84 Abs. 1 GG).

But it remains to be examined whether the chosen means, the imposition of a money payment, confer on the investment aid the character of a tax in the sense of section X of the Basic Law. Then the legislative competence of the Federation would fall to be determined exclusively according to Art 105 of the GG which to that extent takes precedence over Art 74 no 11 of the GG (compare the opinion of the Federal Constitutional Court of 16 June 1954 – 1 P BvV 2/52, BVerfGE 3, 407).

The investment aid certainly exhibits some of the features analogous to a tax. Its true legal character can however only be inferred from the totality of the business transactions which the Investment Aid Act produces. It aims at the diversion of investment resources to satisfy an investment need which is regarded by the legislator as pressing. The legislator expects that by the resources raised, investment plans of several times the level of the investment aid will be released. Therefore, the assisted businesses must also put in their own resources (§ 29 para 5 sentence 2 of the IHG). Insofar as the Investment Aid Act intervenes in the course of business affairs in a directing manner, it links it with the market economy event of the drawing of securities. Although the parties liable for the levy have a public law duty at first to pay the amount which falls on them, their obligations finally turn into private law relationships in the form of legal participation by virtue of a shareholding or documented creditor-debtor relationships; ultimately the obligations of the parties liable for the levy and the counter obligations of the assisted undertakings correspond to each other. The amounts levied only reach the special fund for investment aid as a continuous resource and the fund does not manage government income, but serves the government directing of credit in that it facilitates the production of legal relationships between the parties liable for the levy and the assisted undertakings. This all shows that investment aid is by its very nature different from a tax.

The investment aid also does not turn into a tax just because tax authorities are involved in its levy. These authorities can also be active for other purposes than public financial ones. It could appear proper to the legislator to call in the tax authorities because the involvement of chambers of commerce in levy proceedings showed itself as being impracticable. It is constitutionally completely unobjectionable in view of the agreement of the Federal Council that a Federal statute should enlist designated, appropriate specialist State authorities for the implementation of the statute (Art 84 para 1 of the GG).

Bedenken gegen die Gesetzgebungszuständigkeit des Bundes würden sich auch dann nicht ergeben, wenn man die Investitionshilfe als Zwangsanleihe ansehen wollte. Nach herrschender Meinung werden Zwangsanleihen wegen der Rückzahlung und Verzinsung des Anleihebetrages nicht zu den Steuern gerechnet. Entgegen der Auffassung einiger Beschwerdeführer ist die Auferlegung von Zwangsanleihen auch nicht durch Art. 115 GG verboten. Diese Vorschrift bezieht sich überhaupt nur auf Anleihen, die – anders als die Investitionshilfe – eine Verschuldung des Bundes zur Folge haben.

2 Zum Erlaß des Investitionshilfegesetzes bedurfte es auch nicht, wie einige Beschwerdeführer behaupten, wegen besonderer Intensität des Eingriffs einer ausdrücklichen verfassungsrechtlichen Ermächtigung. Die Grenzen für die Ausnutzung einer durch das Grundgesetz gewährten Gesetzgebungskompetenz werden ausschließlich durch die Grundrechte und sonstigen Verfassungsgrundsätze bestimmt.

3 Die Beschwerdeführer meinen, das Investitionshilfegesetz verstoße gegen das Grundrecht auf freie Entfaltung der Persönlichkeit, weil es sie in ihrer freien Unternehmerinitiative beschränke.

Art. 2 Abs. 1 GG ist nicht verletzt. Dabei ist gleichgültig, von welcher grundsätzlichen Auffassung über die Bedeutung dieser Verfassungsbestimmung man ausgeht.

Sieht man in Art. 2 Abs. 1 GG nur den Schutz eines Mindestmaßes menschlicher Handlungsfreiheit, ohne das der Mensch seine Wesensanlage als geistig-sittliche Person überhaupt nicht entfalten kann, so ragt das Investitionshilfegesetz in diesen Bereich nicht hinein, denn die eigenverantwortliche freie Unternehmerpersönlichkeit wird durch das Investitionshilfegesetz nicht berührt.

Doubts about the legislative competence of the Federation would not arise here if one wished to regard the investment aid as a forced loan. According to the prevailing opinion, forced loans are not reckoned as taxes because of the payment back and the payment of interest on the sum lent. Contrary to the view of some of the complainants, the imposition of forced loans is not forbidden by Art 115 of the GG. In any case this provision only refers to loans which – in contrast to investment aid – have an indebtedness to the Federation as their consequence.

2 An express constitutional law authorisation on account of the special intensity of the interference was not necessary for the enactment of the Investment Aid Act, as some complainants claim. The boundaries for use of a legislative competence granted by the Basic Law are exclusively determined by the Basic Rights and other constitutional principles.

3 The complainants consider that the Investment Aid Act contravenes the Basic Right to free development of the personality, because it is limited it in its free entrepreneurial initiative.

Article 2 para 1 of the Basic Law is not infringed. In this connection it makes no difference from which fundamental view about the meaning of this constitutional rule one proceeds.

If one sees in Art 2 para 1 of the GG only the protection of an indispensable minimum of human freedom of action without which the human being cannot develop his essential characteristics as a spiritual and moral person, the Investment Aid Act does not intrude into this realm, because the free and autonomous entrepreneurial personality is not affected by the Investment Aid Act.

Erblickt man weitergehend in diesem Grundrecht eine umfassende Gewährleistung der Handlungsfreiheit, so besteht diese von vornherein nur, soweit sie nicht die Rechte anderer verletzt und nicht gegen die verfassungsmäßige Ordnung oder das Sittengesetz verstößt. Das Menschenbild des Grundgesetzes ist nicht das eines isolierten souveränen Individuums; das Grundgesetz hat vielmehr die Spannung Individuum – Gemeinschaft im Sinne der Gemeinschaftsbezogenheit und Gemeinschaftsgebundenheit der Person entschieden, ohne dabei deren Eigenwert anzutasten. Das ergibt sich insbesondere aus einer Gesamtsicht der Art. 1, 2, 12, 14, 15, 19 und 20 GG. Dies heißt aber: der Einzelne muß sich diejenigen Schranken seiner Handlungsfreiheit gefallen lassen, die der Gesetzgeber zur Pflege und Förderung des sozialen Zusammenlebens in den Grenzen des bei dem gegebenen Sachverhalt allgemein Zumutbaren zieht, vorausgesetzt, daß dabei die Eigenständigkeit der Person gewahrt bleibt. In diesem Rahmen hält sich das Investitionshilfegesetz. Kein Aufbringungsschuldner ist an der so verstandenen Entfaltung seiner Persönlichkeit gehindert, wenn das Gesetz zeitweilig seine Dispositionsbefugnis über Betriebsmittel beschränkt und durch hoheitlichen Zwang Rechtsbeziehungen zwischen ihm und den begünstigten Unternehmen herbeiführt. Trotz dieser Beschränkung bleibt noch den Betroffenen weiter Spielraum, um sich als verantwortliche Unternehmer wirtschaftlich frei zu entfalten.

Verfassungsrechtlich unbedenklich ist das Investitionshilfegesetz erst recht, wenn man in Art. 2 Abs. 1 GG zwar eine umfassende Gewährleistung der Handlungsfreiheit erblickt, dann aber zur verfassungsmäßigen Ordnung, die die Handlungsfreiheit einschränkt, alle formell und materiell verfassungsmäßigen Rechtsnormen rechnet. Vom Standpunkt dieser Auffassung genügt der in diesem Urteil geführte Nachweis, daß das Investitionshilfegesetz mit den sonstigen Bestimmungen des Grundgesetzes im Einklang steht.

Da Art. 2 Abs. 1 GG keinesfalls verletzt ist, kann dahingestellt bleiben, ob und inwieweit auch juristische Personen, Offene Handelsgesellschaften und Kommanditgesellschaften sich auf diese Bestimmung berufen können.

4 Die Beschwerdeführer machen weiter geltend, das Investitionshilfegesetz verletze die verfassungsmäßige Eigentumsgarantie. Einige qualifizieren die Investitionshilfe als verfassungsrechtlich unzulässige Enteignung, weil sie nicht im öffentlichen Interesse liege und keine oder nur unzulängliche Entschädigung gewähre; andere verneinen den Enteignungscharakter der Investitionshilfe, erblicken aber in ihr einen im Grundgesetz nicht vorgesehenen und daher unzulässigen Eingriff in das Eigentum.

If one sees in this Basic Right, in a far reaching way, a comprehensive guarantee of freedom of action, this can from the outset only exist insofar as it does not violate the rights of others and does not offend against the constitutional order or the moral law. The picture of the human being in the Basic Law is not that of an isolated sovereign individual; the Basic Law has resolved the tension of the individual with society much more in the sense of relations to society and ties of a person to society, without at the same time infringing his own worth. That follows in particular from looking at Arts 1, 2, 12, 14, 15, 19 and 20 of the GG together. But this means: the individual must put up with those limitations on his freedom of action which the legislator draws for the care and advancement of communal social life within the boundaries of what is generally reasonable in the given circumstances, provided that the independence of the person is preserved at the same time. The Investment Aid Act keeps within this framework. No party liable for the levy is constrained in the development of its personality understood in this sense, even if the Act temporarily limits its authority to dispose of business resources and brings legal relationships into existence between it and the assisted undertakings by sovereign compulsion. In spite of this limitation, the affected party still has further scope to develop freely in the economic sphere as a responsible undertaking.

The Investment Aid Act is definitely unobjectionable from a constitutional law point of view if one sees a comprehensive guarantee of freedom of action in Art 2 para 1 of the GG, but then attributes all formal and material constitutional legal norms to the constitutional order which limits the freedom of action. From the standpoint of this view, the proof furnished in this judgment that the Investment Aid Act is in harmony with the other provisions of the Basic Law suffices.

As Art 2 para 1 of the GG is not in any way violated, it can be left open whether and to what extent legal persons, general partnerships and limited partnerships, can also refer to this provision.

4 The complainants further claim that the Investment Aid Act violates the constitutional property guarantee. Some designate the investment aid as a constitutionally impermissible expropriation because it is not in the public interest and it grants no or insufficient compensation; others deny the expropriation character of the investment aid, but see in it an invasion of property which is not provided for in the Basic Law and therefore not permitted.

Auf das Grundrecht aus Art. 14 GG können sich seinem Wesen nach auch juristische Personen berufen. Ein gleiches gilt für Handelsgesellschaften, soweit die Eingriffe sich auf gesamthänderisch gebundenes Eigentum beziehen.

Die Rügen sind jedoch unbegründet, denn das Investitionshilfegesetz ordnet keinen Eingriff in das verfassungsrechtlich geschützte Eigentum der Beschwerdeführer an. Wenngleich der Umfang der durch Art. 14 GG geschützten Objekte in Schrifttum und Rechtsprechung umstritten ist, besteht doch Einmütigkeit darüber, daß Art. 14 GG nicht das Vermögen gegen Eingriffe durch Auferlegung von Geldleistungspflichten schützt. Solche Geldleistungspflichten, wie sie das Investitionshilfegesetz vorsieht, berühren nicht die Eigentumsgarantie des Grundgesetzes.

Daran kann auch die Überlegung nichts ändern, daß durch die Erfüllung einer Zahlungspflicht die Liquidität des Bestriebsvermögens vermindert wird. Das gehört zum Wesen jeder Geldleistungspflicht. Die Liquidität eines Betriebes ist zwar eine 'wirtschaftliche Position', aber kein selbständiges Recht; die Frage der Eigentumsgarantie kann daher überhaupt nicht aufgeworfen werden.

5 Die Beschwerdeführer wenden ferner ein, die Aufteilung der Wirtschaft in gebende und nehmende Betriebe verstoße gegen den Gleichheitssatz, den Grundsatz der wirtschaftspolitischen Neutralität des Grundgesetzes und die bisherige Wirtschafts- und Sozialordnung; die Investitionshilfe sei kein marktkonformes Mittel.

Das Grundgesetz garantiert weder die wirtschaftspolitische Neutralität der Regierungs- und Gesetzgebungsgewalt noch eine nur mit marktkonformen Mitteln zu steuernde 'soziale Marktwirtschaft'.

Die 'wirtschaftspolitische Neutralität' des Grundgesetzes besteht lediglich darin, daß sich der Verfassungsgeber nicht ausdrücklich für ein bestimmtes Wirtschaftssystem entschieden hat. Dies ermöglicht dem Gesetzgeber die ihm jeweils sachgemäß erscheinende Wirtschaftspolitik zu verfolgen, sofern er dabei das Grundgesetz beachtet.

Die gegenwärtige Wirtschafts- und Sozialordnung ist zwar eine nach dem Grundgesetz mögliche Ordnung, keineswegs aber die allein mögliche. Sie beruht auf einer vom Willen des Gesetzgebers getragenen wirtschafts- und sozialpolitischen Entscheidung, die durch eine andere Entscheidung ersetzt oder durchbrochen werden kann. Daher ist es verfassungsrechtlich ohne Bedeutung, ob das Investitionshilfegesetz im Einklang mit der bisherigen Wirtschafts- und Sozialordnung steht und ob das zur Wirtschaftslenkung verwandte Mittel 'marktkonform' ist.

The basic right in Art 14 can also, by its nature, be referred to by legal persons. The same applies for trading organisations insofar as the invasions relate to property committed to corporate use.

The criticisms are however unfounded because the Investment Aid Act does not order any invasion of the property of the complainants as protected by constitutional law. Although the extent of the objects protected by Art 14 of the GG is disputed in academic literature and case law there is unanimity over the fact that Art 14 of the GG does not protect property against invasions by the imposition of duties to pay money. Such impositions, as provided for by the Investment Aid Act, do not affect the property guarantee of the Basic Law.

The consideration that through the fulfilment of a duty of payment the liquidity of the resources of a business may be reduced can change nothing in this respect. That is inherent in the nature of every duty to pay money. The liquidity of a business is certainly an 'economic position', but not an independent right; the question of the property guarantee therefore certainly cannot be raised.

5 The complainants object further that the division of the economy into donating and receiving businesses contravenes the equality requirement, the principle of the political-economic neutrality of the Basic Law and the present economic and social order; the investment aid is not a measure in conformity with market.

The Basic Law guarantees neither political-economic neutrality of the executive and legislative powers nor a 'social market economy' to be controlled only by measures in conformity with the market.

The 'political-economic neutrality' of the Basic Law consists only in the fact that the draftsman of the constitution did not decide expressly in favour of a particular economic system. This enables the legislator to follow the economic policy which seems to him at any time to be proper, as long as he observes the Basic Law at the same time.

The present economic and social order is certainly a possible order under the Basic Law, but definitely not the only possible one. It is based on an economic and socio-political decision produced by the will of the legislator. This decision can be replaced or annulled by another decision. Therefore it is of no importance from a constitutional law point of view whether the Investment Aid Act is in harmony with the present economic and social order and whether the method used for economic direction is in 'conformity with the market'.

Der Gleichheitssatz ist nicht verletzt. Er darf nicht dazu benutzt werden, den weiten Ermessensspielraum einzuengen, den das Grundgesetz dem Gesetzgeber einräumt. Nur die Überschreitung oder der Mißbrauch des gesetzgeberischen Ermessens verstoßen gegen den Gleichheitssatz (vgl. BVerfGE 2, 266 [280]; 3, 19 [24f.]; 3, 58 [135f.]; 3, 288 [337]).

Das Bundesverfassungsgericht ist nicht befugt, Gesetze daraufhin zu prüfen, ob sie im ganzen oder in einzelnen Bestimmungen zweckmäßig sind. Das gilt auch für Gesetze, die konkrete Maßnahmen verwirklichen wollen und gegenstandslos werden, nachdem diese durchgeführt sind. Auch sie sind vom Bundesverfassungsgericht im Hinblick auf Art. 3 Abs. 1 GG nur daraufhin zu prüfen, ob der Gesetzgeber die äußersten Grenzen seines Ermessens innegehalten und dieses nicht mißbraucht hat. Allerdings kann bei Gesetzen der eben erwähnten Art leichter als bei anderen Gesetzen erkennbar sein, ob die gesetzliche Regelung der Eigenart des Sachverhalts noch entspricht, durch sie gerechtfertigt wird und am Gedanken der Gerechtigkeit orientiert ist. Insofern mag dem Gleichheitssatz hier eine erhöhte praktische Bedeutung zukommen. Die Prüfungsbefugnis des Bundesverfassungsgerichts wird dadurch jedoch nicht erweitert, der Prüfungsmaßstab des Art. 3 Abs. 1 GG bleibt stets derselbe. Prüft man das Investitionshilfegesetz an diesem Maßstab, dann ergibt sich, daß der Gesetzgeber die äußersten Grenzen des ihm eingeräumten Ermessens nicht überschritten hat. Dabei ist zu berücksichtigen, daß jede Wirtschaftslenkungsmaßnahme, indem sie gestaltend in den Ablauf des sozialen Lebens eingreift, das freie Spiel der Kräfte mehr oder weniger korrigiert. Das schließt grundsätzlich auch die Möglichkeit ein, Gesetze im Interesse einzelner Gruppen zu erlassen. Allerdings müssen solche Gesetze durch das öffentliche Interesse geboten sein und dürfen nicht willkürlich die schutzwürdigen Interessen anderer vernachlässigen.

Dem trägt das Investitionshilfegesetz Rechnung. Die Aufbringungsschuldner erhalten in Höhe ihres Aufbringungsbetrages Wertpapiere, die Zinsen, ggf. Dividende abwerfen und von denen nach der Sachlage angenommen werden kann, daß sie einen der allgemeinen wirtschaftlichen Entwicklung entsprechenden Realwert behalten. Bis zum Erwerb der Wertpapiere wird der Aufbringungsbetrag steuerfrei verzinst. Die wirtschaftlichen Interessen der Aufbringungsschuldner werden also nicht willkürlich benachteiligt, selbst wenn der eigene Investitionsbedarf zurückgestellt werden muß.

E

1 Die Angriffe der Beschwerdeführer gegen einzelne Vorschriften des Investitionshilfegesetzes werden vornehmlich mit angeblichen Verletzungen des Gleichheitssatzes begründet. Der Gesetzgeber hat jedoch auch insoweit die seinem Ermessen gezogenen Schranken nicht überschritten.

The requirement of equality is not violated. It may not be used to narrow the broad discretionary powers which the Basic Law grants to the legislator. Only the exceeding or misuse of the legislative discretion offend the requirement of equality (compare BVerfGE 2, 266 [280]; 3, 19 [24 and onwards]; 3, 58 [135 and onwards]; 3, 288 [337]).

The Federal Constitutional Court is not authorised to examine statutes as to whether they are expedient as a whole or in individual provisions. That is also true for statutes which are intended to put concrete measures into effect and become purposeless after these have been carried through. They are also only to be examined by the Federal Constitutional Court, in the light of Art 3 para 1 of the GG, as to whether the legislator has kept within the outermost limits of his discretion and has not misused this. Certainly it can be more easily discernible with statutes of the kind just mentioned, than with other statutes, whether the statutory regulation corresponds to the characteristics of the subject matter, is justified by it and is adapted to the concept of justice. To this extent the requirement of equality may here be given an increased practical importance. The Federal Constitutional Court's authority to examine is not however widened by this; the examination yardstick of Art 3 para 1 of the GG remains continually the same. If one tests the Investment Aid Act against this yardstick, then it is revealed that the legislator has not exceeded the outermost limits of the discretion granted to him. At the same time it is to be taken into account that every measure directing the economy, in that it intervenes formatively in the course of social life, corrects the free play of forces to a greater or lesser extent. That also includes, as a matter of principle, the possibility of issuing statutes in the interests of individual groups. Such statutes must of course be required by the public interest and may not arbitrarily neglect the interests of others which are worthy of protection.

The Investment Aid Act takes this into account. The parties liable for the levy receive securities to the amounts of the sums levied which yield interest, or dividends if applicable, and from which it can, according to the circumstances, be accepted that they have a real value corresponding to general business development. Until acquisition of the securities, the sum levied bears tax free interest. The business interests of the parties liable for the levy are thus not arbitrarily disadvantaged, even when their own investment needs have to be shelved.

E

1 The contentions of the complainants against the individual provisions of the Investment Aid Act are chiefly founded on alleged violations of the requirement of equality. The legislator has however in this respect also not exceeded the limits drawn for his discretion.

(a) Das gilt zunächst für die Beschränkung der Aufbringungspflicht auf die Betriebe der gewerblichen Wirtschaft (§ 2 IHG). Diese ist von jeher als besonderes Objekt öffentlicher Lasten anerkannt (Gewerbesteuer, Industriebelastung, Osthilfe). In der Rechtsprechung sind sogar Sondersteuern für einzelne Berufsstände und Gewerbezweige als mit dem Gleichheitssatz vereinbar angesehen worden (vgl. RFH 27, 321 [322]; Württ.-Bad. StGH, VerwRspr. 4, 1 [10f.]), wenn sie mit der Eigenart des Sachverhalts begründet werden können. Das gilt auch für das Investitionshilfegesetz. Im Hinblick auf die besondere Verbundenheit der begünstigten Industrie mit der übrigen gewerblichen Wirtschaft hält sich die Entscheidung des Gesetzgebers, nur diese zur Investitionshilfe heranzuziehen, im Rahmen des ihm zustehenden Ermessens.

(b) Das gleiche gilt für die in § 3 IHG angeordneten Freistellungen von der Aufbringungspflicht. Sie entsprechen größtenteils dem Gewerbesteuerrecht, an das das Investitionshilfegesetz auch bei der Abgrenzung des Kreises der Aufbringungspflichtigen anknüpft. Die in öffentlicher Hand befindlichen Unternehmen sind freigestellt, weil sie in erster Linie der Erfüllung eines öffentlichen Zweckes und nicht der Erzielung von Gewinnen dienen und ihre Heranziehung zur Investitionshilfe sich möglicherweise – entgegen der Absicht des Gesetzgebers – als Belastung des Steuerzahlers ausgewirkt hätte. Auch die nicht in öffentlicher Hand befindlichen öffentlichen Verkehrsbetriebe dienen in besonderem Maße öffentlichen Zwecken, was in dem ihnen auferlegten Kontrahierungszwang verbunden mit der sozialen Staffelung ihrer Tarife zum Ausdruck kommt. Die Sonderbehandlung der land- und forstwirtschaftlichen Genossenschaften stimmt mit dem Gewerbesteuerrecht überein und entspricht ihrer besonderen Struktur. Sie leisten grundsätzlich Gemeinschaftshilfe für ihre Mitglieder. Erstreckt sich aber ihr Geschäftsbetrieb auch auf Nichtmitglieder, ohne daß ihnen dies durch Gesetz oder behördliche Anordnung vorgeschrieben wäre, so sind sie voll aufbringungspflichtig (§ 2 der Ersten Verordnung zur Durchführung des Gesetzes über die Investitionshilfe der gewerblichen Wirtschaft [Erste IHDV] vom 5. April 1952 [BGBl. I S. 232]).

(a) That applies first to the limitation of the levy duty to businesses in industry (§ 2 of the IHG). This has always been recognised as the special object of public burdens (trade tax, industry charge, eastern aid). In case law, even special taxes for individual vocations and branches of trade have been seen as reconcilable with the requirement of equality (compare RFH 27, 321 [322]; Baden-Württemberg StGH, VerwRspr 4, 1 [10 and onwards]) if they can be based on the characteristics of the subject matter. That applies also to the Investment Aid Act. In view of the special closeness of the assisted industry to the remainder of industry, the decision of the legislator to enlist only this for investment aid keeps within the framework of the discretion which belongs to him.

(b) The same applies to the exemptions from the duty to pay the levy provided for in § 3 of the IHG. They correspond for the greater part to the trade tax law, with which the Investment Aid Act links in respect of the delimiting of the circle of those under a duty to pay the levy. Those undertakings which are in the public sector are exempted principally because they serve the fulfilment of a public purpose and not the realisation of profit and bringing them in for investment aid might possibly have had the effect, contrary to the intention of the legislator, of burdening the taxpayer. The public transport services which are not in public ownership also serve public purposes to a special extent, which is expressed in the obligation to contract which is placed upon them, together with the social gradation of their tariffs. The special treatment of the agriculture and forestry co-operatives agrees with the trade tax law and corresponds to their special structure. In principle they provide communal aid for their members. But if their business also extends to non-members without this being stipulated for them by statute or official order, they are fully liable for the levy (§ 2 of the First Regulation for Administration of the Investment Aid for Industry Act [Erste IHDV] of 5 April 1952 [BGBl I, 232]).

(c) Zu Unrecht wenden sich die Beschwerdeführer auch gegen die Bemessungsgrundlage. Daß sie an das Wirtschaftsergebnis der Jahre 1950 und 1951 anknüpft, macht das Investitionshilfegesetz nicht zu einem rückwirkenden. Diese Anknüpfung an in der Vergangenheit liegende Tatbestände folgt aus der Natur der Investitionshilfe als einer Sofortmaßnahme. Ob Gewinn und Umsatz in der gewählten Verknüpfung die bestmögliche Bemessungsgrundlage darstellen, hat das Bundesverfassungsgericht nicht nachzuprüfen. Jedenfalls ist sie nicht schlechthin ungeeignet und daher mit dem Gleichheitssatz vereinbar. Das gilt auch für die Regelung, daß die gemäß §§ 7 bis 7 e EStG vorgenommenen Investitionen bei Berechnung der Bemessungsgrundlage dem Gewinn zugeschlagen werden. Da diese Investitionen geeignet waren, die wirtschaftliche Kraft der betreffenden Unternehmen zu stärken, war der Gesetzgeber nicht verpflichtet, die bereits bei der Einkommensteuer begünstigten Vorgänge abermals durch Nichtberücksichtigung der dafür gemachten Aufwendungen bei der Investitionshilfe zu begünstigen.

(d) Die Beschwerdeführer wenden sich auch gegen die Sonderregelung in §§ 14, 23, 24 der Ersten IHDV, in der sie eine unzulässige Begünstigung der Rundfunkgesellschaften, des Großhandels und der Organgesellschaften erblicken. Einige verneinen auch die Gültigkeit der in §§ 10, 38 IHG erteilten Ermächtigung zur Änderung der Bemessungsgrundlage und des Aufbringungssatzes im Wege einer Durchführungsverordnung. Dies ist als Vorfrage zu prüfen.

Art. 80 Abs. 1 Satz 2 GG schließt Ermächtigungen aus, die so unbestimmt sind, daß nicht vorausgesehen werden kann, in welchen Fällen und mit welcher Tendenz von ihnen Gebrauch gemacht wird und welchen Inhalt die auf Grund solcher Ermächtigungen erlassenen Verordnungen haben können (BVerfGE 1, 14 [60]). Ermächtigungsinhalt, -zweck und -ausmaß müssen sich, wenn sie nicht ausdrücklich im Gesetz bestimmt sind, jedenfalls mit Deutlichkeit aus ihm ergeben (vgl. BVerfGE 2, 307 [334f.]).

Der Inhalt der Ermächtigung ist in §§ 10, 38 IHG ausdrücklich bestimmt: die Bundesregierung wird ermächtigt, die Bemessungsgrundlage oder den Aufbringungssatz abweichend von der allgemeinen Regelung der §§ 6, 7 festzustellen. Auch der Zweck der Ermächtigung kommt deutlich im Gesetz zum Ausdruck: es soll in den Fällen, in denen die allgemeine Bemessungsgrundlage oder der allgemeine Aufbringungssatz nicht anwendbar sind oder zu einer übermäßigen und unangemessenen Belastung führen würden, eine Regelung getroffen werden, die die betreffenden Wirtschaftszweige unter Berücksichtigung ihrer besonderen Eigenart etwa ebenso belastet wie die übrigen.

(c) The complainants also argue, unjustifiably, against the basis of assessment. The fact that it links to business outcomes in the years 1950 and 1951 does not make the Investment Aid Act a retrospective one. This link to a state of affairs existing in the past follows from the nature of the investment aid as an immediate measure. Whether profit and turnover in the combination chosen represent the best possible basis of assessment is not for the Federal Constitutional Court to examine. In any case, it is not completely unsuitable, and is therefore reconcilable with the equality requirement. That also applies to the rule that the investments taken on in accordance with §§ 7–7e of the EStG will be added to the profit when calculating the basis of assessment. As these investments were appropriate for strengthening the economic power of the undertaking concerned, the legislator was not obliged, as to events which had already been treated favourably in connection with income tax, to treat them favourably again by ignoring expenditure on them in connection with investment aid.

(d) The complainants also object to the special rule in §§ 14, 23 and 24 of the Erste IHDV in which they see an impermissible advantage to broadcasting companies, wholesale trade and subsidiary companies. Some also deny the validity of the authorisation conferred by §§ 10 and 38 of the IHG to change the basis of assessment and the levy requirement by administrative regulation. This is to be examined as a preliminary question.

Article 80 para 1 sentence 2 of the GG excludes authorisations which are so uncertain that it cannot be foreseen in which cases and for what use will be made of them and what content regulations issued on the basis of such authorisations can have (BVerfGE 1, 14 [60]). The content, purpose and extent of the authorisation must, if they are not expressly determined in the statute at all events be evident from it (compare BVerfGE 2, 307 [334 and onwards]).

The content of the authorisation is determined expressly in §§ 10 and 38 of the IHG: the Federal Government is authorised to determine the basis of assessment or the levy requirement in a way which diverges from the general regime of §§ 6 and 7. The purpose of the authorisation is also clearly expressed in the statute: in cases in which the general basis of assessment or the general levy requirement is not applicable or would lead to an excessive and inappropriate burden, a rule is to be made which imposes burdens on the branches of industry in question to the same extent broadly as the others, taking into consideration their special character.

Zweifelhaft kann sein, ob das Ausmaß der Ermächtigung im Gesetz bestimmt ist. Das Ausmaß kann jedoch hier mit hinreichender Deutlichkeit aus ihrem begrenzten Zweck erschlossen werden: soweit die Ermächtigung dazu dienen soll, eine übermäßige und unangemessene Belastung zu beseitigen, liegt darin zugleich eine Bestimmung ihres Ausmaßes. Eine nach §§ 10, 38 IHG ergehende Rechtsverordnung darf die Lage der Aufbringungsschuldner im Vergleich zur Regelung in §§ 6, 7 IHG keinesfalls verschlechtern; sie darf sie aber auch nur insoweit verbessern, als dies erforderlich ist, um das Übermaß und die Unangemessenheit der Belastung zu beseitigen. Aus § 10 IHG geht hervor, daß Entsprechendes auch für die Fälle gelten soll, in denen der allgemeine Aufbringungssatz überhaupt nicht anwendbar ist. Auch hier soll im Ergebnis eine Belastung erreicht werden, die der der übrigen Wirtschaftszweige entspricht. Nur bei dieser Auslegung kann die Ermächtigung noch mit Art. 80 Abs. 1 Satz 2 GG vereinbart werden (vgl. BVerfGE 2, 266 [282]).

So gesehen dient § 10 IHG geradezu der Verwirklichung des Gleichheitssatzes.

Auch die §§ 14, 23, 24 der Ersten IHDV verstoßen nicht gegen den Gleichheitssatz, da sie von sachlichen Erwägungen getragen sind. Bei den Rundfunkgesellschaften konnte die normale Bemessungsgrundlage nicht gewählt werden, da sie unterschiedlich organisiert sind und steuerlich verschieden behandelt werden. Für die Abweichung beim Großhandel war seine besonders hohe Umsatz-Intensität maßgebend. Die Behandlung der Organgesellschaften folgt den Grundsätzen des Gewerbesteuerrechts. Die Umsatzsteuerpflicht der sog. Innenumsätze zwischen beherrschtem und beherrschendem Unternehmen beruht auf Besatzungsrecht (Art. II KRG Nr. 15), das vom früheren deutschen Recht abweicht. Wenn der Bundesgesetzgeber diese Regelung nicht übernahm, handelte er nicht willkürlich.

(e) Die Beschwerdeführer beanstanden weiter, daß die aufbringungspflichtige Wirtschaft in manchen Fällen gezwungen sei, Bankkredite zu hohen Zinsen aufzunehmen oder Teile ihres Umlaufvermögens zu veräußern. Sie erblicken auch hierin eine Verletzung des Gleichheitssatzes, weil ein Gleiches den begünstigten Industriezweigen nicht zugemutet werde.

Die Notwendigkeit der von den Beschwerdeführern erwähnten Maßnahmen kann sich in der Tat daraus ergeben, daß ihnen Stundung und Erlaß nicht gewährt werden, wenn sie sich die Mittel zur Aufbringung der Investitionshilfe durch Aufnahme eines Bankkredits im Rahmen ihres üblichen Kreditvolumens oder durch Veräußerung von Gegenständen des Umlaufvermögens beschaffen können (§§ 20, 21 IHG in Verbindung mit Abschnitt 3 der Vorläufigen Verwaltungsrichtlinien über Stundung und Erlaß bei der Investitionshilfe vom 15. Juli 1952 [BAnz. Nr. 136 vom 17. Juli 1952; BStBI I S. 559] und Abschnitt 1 und 4 der Endgültigen Verwaltungsrichtlinien über Stundung und Erlaß bei der Investitionshilfe vom 11. August 1953 [BAnz. Nr. 155 vom 14. August 1953; BStBI I S. 341]).

It can be doubted whether the extent of the authorisation is determined in the statute. The extent can however be inferred here with sufficient clarity from its limited purpose: in as much as the authorisation is intended to enable the setting aside of an excessive and inappropriate burden, a determination of its extent is at the same time contained in this. A legal Regulation based on §§ 10 and 38 of the IHG may not in any case make the position of the party liable for the levy worse than it would be in comparison with the regime under §§ 6 and 7 of the IHG; it may however improve it only insofar as this is necessary to set aside the excessiveness and inappropriateness of the burden. It follows from § 10 of the IHG that corresponding considerations are to apply for the cases in which the general levy requirement is certainly not applicable. Here too a burden is to be imposed which in its outcome corresponds to that for the remaining branches of industry. The authorisation can only be made compatible with Art 80 para 1 sentence 2 of the GG by means of this interpretation (compare BVerfGE 2, 266 [282]).

Looked at in this way, § 10 of the IHG plainly serves the realisation of the requirement of equality.

§§ 14, 23 and 24 of the Erste IHDV also do not offend against the requirement of equality, as they are supported by practical considerations. With broadcasting companies, the normal basis of assessment could not be chosen, because they are differently organised and differently treated for tax purposes. The especially high intensity of turnover was decisive for the difference for the wholesale trade. The treatment of subsidiary companies follows the principles of trade tax law. The liability to sales tax of the so-called internal turnover as between controlled and controlling undertakings is based on occupation law (Art II KRG no 15) which deviates from earlier German law. When the Federal legislator did not adopt this regime he was not acting arbitrarily.

(e) The complainants object further that the sector of industry liable to the levy has been compelled in many cases to take out bank loans at high interest or to dispose of parts of its working capital. They see in this too a violation of the equality requirement because the same is not expected of the assisted branches of industry.

The need for the measures mentioned by the complainants can actually arise from the fact that they are not allowed deferment of payment and remission if they can get themselves the means of paying investment aid by the taking out of a bank loan within the framework of their usual volume of credit or by the disposal of assets from their working capital (ss 20 and 21 of the IHG in conjunction with § 3 of the Provisional Administrative Guidelines regarding Deferment of Payment and Remission in respect of Investment Aid of 15 July 1952 ([BAnz no 136 of 17 July 1952; BStBI I, 559] and §§ 1 and 4 of the Final Administrative Guidelines regarding Deferment of Payment and Remission in connection with Investment Aid of 11 August 1953 [BAnz no 155 of 14 August 1953; BStBI I, 341]).

Das verstößt jedoch nicht gegen den Gleichheitssatz. Die Aufnahme von Krediten ist in der gewerblichen Wirtschaft nichts Ungewöhnliches, und es wird den Aufbringungsschuldnern nicht zugemutet, über ihr übliches Kreditvolumen hinauszugehen. Bei der Veräußerung von Gegenständen des Umlaufvermögens soll die Substanz des Betriebes unberührt bleiben, und die Aufbringungsschuldner sind nicht gezwungen, Gegenstände unter den Wiederbeschaffungspreisen zu veräußern.

Gemäß § 29 Abs. 5 Satz 2 IHG müssen auch die begünstigten Unternehmen über die bewilligten Investitionsmittel hinaus eigene Mittel in Höhe der dann entfallenden Aufbringungspflicht für das begünstigte Vorhaben aufwenden. Das bedeutet, daß auch sie gegebenenfalls Kredite aufnehmen und Gegenstände ihres Umlaufvermögens veräußern müssen, um in den Genuß der Investitionshilfemittel zu kommen.

(f) Unbegründet ist auch die Rüge der Beschwerdeführer, die Menschenwürde, der Gleichheitssatz und das Rechtsstaatsprinzip seien verletzt, weil das Investitionshilfegesetz die Aufbringungsschuldner zwinge, Betriebe zu unterstützen, mit denen sie im Wettbewerb stehen. Sie rügen also eine durch das Investitionshilfegesetz zu ihren Ungunsten verursachte Verschiebung der Wettbewerbslage.

Jede Wirtschaftslenkungsmaßnahme stellt aber einen Eingriff in das freie Spiel der Wirtschaft und die sich daraus ergebende Wettbewerbslage dar. Sind Wirtschaftslenkungsmaßnahmen verfassungsrechtlich zulässig, so können sie nicht schon dadurch unzulässig werden, daß sie die Wettbewerbslage verändern. Ihre Unzulässigkeit könnte sich nur aus besonderen Umständen ergeben, die den Schluß auf ein willkürliches Handeln des Gesetzgebers rechtfertigen würden.

Solche besonderen Umstände liegen beim Investitionshilfegesetz nicht vor. Eine unmittelbare Unterstützung von Wettbewerbern durch die Aufbringungsschuldner ist nach der Struktur des Gesetzes ausgeschlossen. Allenfalls könnte in Ausnahmefällen eine mittelbare Unterstützung in Betracht kommen, indem Investitionshilfemittel an Betriebe zugeteilt werden, die mit einzelnen Betriebsabteilungen im Wettbewerb zu aufbringungspflichtigen Betrieben stehen. Der Gesetzgeber ist jedoch auch insoweit bemüht gewesen, jede mögliche über den Rahmen der Aufbringungspflicht hinausgehende Belastung der Aufbringungsschuldner auszuschließen. Er hat deshalb sogar die Vorschriften des § 29 Abs. 6 IHG – mit Wirkung auf bereits abgeschlossene Verträge (Art. 3 des 1. ÄndIHG) – geändert, als sich herausstellte, daß das Gesetz in seiner ursprünglichen Fassung dem Kuratorium nur unzulängliche Einflußmöglichkeiten auf die Verwendung der Investitionshilfemittel bei den begünstigten Unternehmen gab.

That does not however offend against the requirement of equality. The taking out of loans is nothing unusual in industry and it is not expected of parties liable for the levy to go above their usual volume of credit. The substance of the business should remain untouched by the disposal of assets from the working capital and the party liable for the levy is not compelled to dispose of assets at below the replacement prices.

According to § 29 para 5 sentence 2 of the IHG the benefited undertakings must use their own resources, to the amount of the allocated levy obligation, for the benefited purpose, over and above the investment resources allotted. This means that they must also, if necessary, take out loans and dispose of assets from their working capital in order to enjoy the investment aid funds.

(f) The criticism of the complainants that human dignity, the requirement of equality and the constitutional state principle are violated because the Investment Aid Act compels the parties who are liable for the levy to support businesses with which they are in competition is also unfounded. They are criticising in effect a shifting in the competition situation caused by the Investment Aid Act to their disadvantage.

However, every measure directing the economy represents an inroad into the free play of the economy and the competition situation resulting from it. If measures directing the economy are permissible in constitutional law, they cannot be impermissible simply because they change the competition situation. Their impermissibility could only result from special circumstances which would justify the conclusion that there had been arbitrary action on the part of the legislator.

Such special circumstances are not present with the Investment Aid Act. Direct support of competitors by the parties liable for the levy is excluded by the structure of the statute. At most, in exceptional cases, indirect support could fall to be considered in that investment aid funds are allocated to businesses which have separate business divisions which are in competition with businesses liable for the levy. The legislator has however also been in this respect at pains to exclude every possible burden on the parties liable for the levy which goes beyond the framework of the levy duty. He has for this reason even changed the rules of § 29 para 6 of the IHG – applying to contracts which have already been concluded (Art 3 of the Investment Aid for Industry (Amendment no 1) Act) – as it appeared that the Act in its original form gave to the Committee insufficient possibilities of influencing the expenditure of the investment aid funds by the benefited undertakings.

(g) Wenn die Beschwerdeführer schließlich meinen, der Gesetzgeber habe den Gleichheitssatz verletzt, weil er die Vorschläge des Gemeinschaftsausschusses der gewerblichen Wirtschaft ohne hinreichende sachliche Nachprüfung übernommen und keine fundierten Ermessenserwägungen angestellt habe, so kommt diesem Gesichtspunkt keine selbständige Bedeutung zu.

Ob ein Gesetz den Gleichheitssatz verletzt, richtet sich nicht danach, wie es zustandegekommen ist, sondern ausschließlich nach seinem sachlichen Inhalt. Da gegen den Inhalt des Investitionshilfegesetzes keine durchgreifenden im Verfahren der Verfassungsbeschwerde prüfbaren verfassungsrechtlichen Bedenken bestehen, können aus der Art seiner parlamentarischen Behandlung, insbesondere aus dem Aufgreifen des Vorschlages des Gemeinschaftsausschusses der gewerblichen Wirtschaft durch die Bundesregierung, keine Einwände aus dem Gesichtspunkt des Art. 3 GG hergeleitet werden.

(h) Die Rüge, Investitionshilfemittel seien zum Teil auch nichtbedürftigen Betrieben zugutegekommen, richtet sich nicht gegen das Investitionshilfegesetz, sondern gegen seine Durchführung. Die Möglichkeit, daß beim Vollzug des Gesetzes einzelne unsachgemäße Maßnahmen getroffen werden, läßt aber die Verfassungsmäßigkeit des Gesetzes unberührt (BVerfGE 1, 144 [149]; 3, 19 [33]).

2 Die Beschwerdeführer rügen weiter, ihnen werde, soweit Aktien zwangsweise zugeteilt würden, eine Zwangsmitgliedschaft als Aktionär der Gesellschaft auferlegt. Das verstoße gegen das Grundrecht einer aus Art. 2 und 9 GG abzuleitenden 'negativen Vereinsfreiheit'.

Bisher steht noch nicht fest, ob überhaupt Aktien zwangsweise zugeteilt werden. Die Zuteilung bedurfte jedenfalls eines besonderen Vollzugsaktes. Die Beschwerdeführer sind also nicht im üblichen Sinne aktuell und unmittelbar betroffen. Dennoch soll die Rüge geprüft werden, weil immerhin der Entschluß der Beschwerdeführer, ein Übernahmeangebot des Kreditinstituts anzunehmen, von der Zulässigkeit der Aktienzuweisung abhängen könnte.

Auch wenn man mit der herrschenden Meinung annimmt, daß Art. 2 Abs. 1 oder Art. 9 Abs. 1 GG einen verfassungsrechtlichen Schutz vor Zwangsinkorporierungen in *bestimmte* Vereine oder Gesellschaften gewähren, würde dieses Grundrecht der 'negativen Vereinsfreiheit' durch die Zwangszuteilung von Aktien nicht verletzt werden. Die Aufbringungsschuldner würden zwar durch die Zuteilung von Aktien formell Mitglieder der betreffenden Aktiengesellschaft. Im Wirtschaftsleben wird die Aktie jedoch überwiegend als bloßes Vermögensrecht angesehen. Das ist um so mehr gerechtfertigt, als sich aus dem Erwerb voll eingezahlter Aktien bestehender Aktiengesellschaften für den Aktionär mitgliedschaftliche Pflichten in aller Regel nicht ergeben.

(g) Finally, if the complainants consider that the legislator has violated the requirement of equality because he has taken over the proposals of the Joint Committee of Industry without sufficient verification and arranged no satisfactorily based exercise of discretion, this point of view has no independent significance.

Whether a law violates the requirement of equality does not depend upon how it came into existence, but exclusively according to its factual content. As there are no doubts in constitutional law which are effectual and examinable in the constitutional complaints procedure in respect of the content of the Investment Aid Act, no objections from the point of view of Art 3 of the GG can be derived from the manner of its treatment in Parliament, or in particular from the taking up by the Federal Government of the proposal of the Joint Committee of Industry.

(h) The criticism that investment aid funds have partly also benefited businesses which are not in need is not directed against the Investment Aid Act but against its administration. The possibility that in the execution of the Act individual inappropriate measures will be taken does not affect the constitutionality of the statute (BVerfGE 1, 144 [149]; 3, 19 [33]).

2 The complainants further object that insofar as shares were compulsorily allocated to them, forced membership of a company as a shareholder has been imposed upon them. That offends against the basic right of a 'negative freedom of association', to be deduced from Arts 2 and 9 of the GG.

Up to now it has not been established whether shares have been compulsorily allocated. The allocation would need a special executive act. The complainants are also not, in the usual sense, currently and directly affected. The criticism should however be examined because, after all, the decision of the complainants to accept an offer for the take-up of shares from the Credit Institute could depend on the permissibility of the share allocation.

Even if one accepts, in accordance with the prevailing opinion, that Art 2 para 1 or Art 9 para 1 of the GG grant a constitutional law protection against compulsory incorporation into *particular* associations or companies, this basic right of 'negative freedom of association' would not be violated by compulsory allocation of shares. The parties liable for the levy certainly became formal members of the company concerned by the allocation of shares. However, in business life, the share is predominantly regarded as a mere right of property. That is all the more justified as no member's duties for the shareholder generally arise from the acquisition of fully paid-up shares in existing companies.

3 Gegen die Einschaltung des 'Sondervermögens Investitionshilfe' wird geltend gemacht, das Investitionshilfegesetz schaffe so eine verfassungswidrige berufsständische Ordnung, bewirke eine unzulässige Sozialisierung von Geldmitteln und verletze die aus Art. 110 GG herzuleitende Etatisierungspflicht.

Daß die Einschaltung des Sondervermögens eine berufsständische Ordnung begründe, kann ernstlich nicht geltend gemacht werden. Ebensowenig ist einzusehen, wie dadurch eine Sozialisierungsmaßnahme bewirkt worden sein soll. Das Sondervermögen verwandelt die Einzahlungen der Aufbringungsschuldner nicht in Gemeineigentum, sondern es ist lediglich Durchgangsstelle.

Die Rüge, Art. 110 GG sei durch das Investitionshilfegesetz verletzt worden, ist im Verfahren der Verfassungsbeschwerde an sich nicht zu prüfen. Eine Prüfung von Amts wegen würde im übrigen ergeben, daß die Investitionshilfemittel, da sie keine Bundeseinnahmen sind (vgl. oben D 1), nicht in den Bundeshaushalt aufgenommen werden müssen.

Da die Prüfung keine Verfassungswidrigkeiten ergeben hat, sind die Verfassungsbeschwerden als unbegründet zurückzuweisen.

Art. 15 [Sozialisierung] Grund und Boden, Naturschätze und Produktionsmittel können zum Zwecke der Vergesellschaftung durch ein Gesetz, das Art und Ausmaß der Entschädigung regelt, in Gemeineigentum oder in andere Formen der Gemeinwirtschaft überführt werden. Für die Entschädigung gilt Art. 14 Abs. 3 Satz 3 und 4 entsprechend.

Art. 16 [Ausbürgerung, Auslieferung] (1) Die deutsche Staatsangehörigkeit darf nicht entzogen werden. Der Verlust der Staatsangehörigkeit darf nur auf Grund eines Gesetzes und gegen den Willen des Betroffenen nur dann eintreten, wenn der Betroffene dadurch nicht staatenlos wird.

(2) Kein Deutscher darf an das Ausland ausgeliefert werden. Durch Gesetz kann eine abweichende Regelung für Auslieferungen an einen Mitgliedstaat der Europäischen Union oder an einen internationalen Gerichtshof getroffen werden, soweit rechtsstaatliche Grundsätze gewährt sind.

Art. 16a [Asylrecht, sichere Drittstaaten, sicherer Herkunftsstaat] (1) Politisch Verfolgte genießen Asylrecht.

3 Against the bringing in of 'special fund investment aid' it is claimed that the Investment Aid Act creates a business regime contrary to the Constitution, it produces a impermissible socialisation of money resources and violates the duty to estimate State expenditure which is to be deduced from Art 110 of the GG.

It cannot seriously be claimed that the introduction of the special fund is the basis of a business regime. It is just as hard to see how a socialisation measure could have been produced thereby. The special fund does not change the payments of the parties liable for the levy into public property, but it is merely a transitional stage.

The criticism that Art 110 of the GG has been violated by the Investment Aid Act is not in itself to be examined in the procedure for the constitutional complaint. Besides this, an official examination would demonstrate that the investment aid fund, as it is not Federal revenue (see D.1, above), does not have to be taken into the Federal budget.

As the examination has revealed nothing contrary to the Constitution, the constitutional complaints are to be rejected as unfounded.

Article 15 [Socialisation] Land, natural resources and means of production can be transferred, for the purposes of nationalisation, to common ownership or to other forms of cooperative economy by a statute which regulates the type and measure of compensation. Article 14 para 3 sentences 3 and 4 have corresponding effect as to such compensation.

Article 16 [Loss of citizenship, extradition] (1) German citizenship cannot be withdrawn. The loss of citizenship may only take place on the basis of a statute and can only occur against the will of the person affected if he does not become Stateless as a result.

(2) No German may be handed over to another country. A differing regime can be made by statute for handing over to a Member State of the European Union or to an international court, insofar as constitutional principles are guaranteed.

Article 16a [Right of asylum, safe third States, safe State of origin] (1) Persons persecuted for political reasons enjoy the right of asylum.

(2) Auf Absatz 1 kann sich nicht berufen, wer aus einem Mitgliedstaat der Europäischen Gemeinschaften oder aus einem anderen Drittstaat einreist, in dem die Anwendung des Abkommens über die Rechtsstellung der Flüchtlinge und der Konvention zum Schutze der Menschenrechte und Grundfreiheiten sichergestellt ist. Die Staaten außerhalb der Europäischen Gemeinschaften, auf die die Voraussetzungen des Satzes 1 zutreffen, werden durch Gesetz, das der Zustimmung des Bundesrates bedarf, bestimmt. In den Fällen des Satzes 1 können aufenthaltsbeendende Maßnahmen unabhängig von einem hiergegen eingelegten Rechtsbehelf vollzogen werden.

(3) Durch Gesetz, das der Zustimmung des Bundesrates bedarf, können Staaten bestimmt werden, bei denen auf Grund der Rechtslage, der Rechtsanwendung und der allgemeinen politischen Verhältnisse gewährleistet erscheint, daß dort weder politische Verfolgung noch unmenschliche oder erniedrigende Bestrafung oder Behandlung stattfindet. Es wird vermutet, daß ein Ausländer aus einem solchen Staat nicht verfolgt wird, solange er nicht Tatsachen vorträgt, die die Annahme begründen, daß er entgegen dieser Vermutung politisch verfolgt wird.

(4) Die Vollziehung aufenthaltsbeendender Maßnahmen wird in den Fällen des Absatzes 3 und in anderen Fällen, die offensichtlich unbegründet sind oder als offensichtlich unbegründet gelten, durch das Gericht nur ausgesetzt, wenn ernstliche Zweifel an der Rechtmäßigkeit der Maßnahme bestehen; der Prüfungsumfang kann eingeschränkt werden und verspätetes Vorbringen unberücksichtigt bleiben. Das Nähere ist durch Gesetz zu bestimmen.

(5) Die Absätze 1 bis 4 stehen völkerrechtlichen Verträgen von Mitgliedstaaten der Europäischen Gemeinschaften untereinander und mit dritten Staaten nicht entgegen, die unter Beachtung der Verpflichtungen aus dem Abkommen über die Rechtstellung der Flüchtlinge und der Konvention zum Schutze der Menschenrechte und Grundfreiheiten, deren Anwendung in den Vertragsstaaten sichergestellt sein muß, Zuständigkeitsregelungen für die Prüfung von Asylbegehren einschließlich der gegenseitigen Anerkennung von Asylentscheidungen treffen.

Art. 17 [Petitionsrecht] Jederman hat das Recht, sich einzeln oder in Gemeinschaft mit anderen schriftlich mit Bitten oder Beschwerden an die zuständigen Stellen und an die Volksvertretung zu wenden.

(2) A person cannot rely on para 1 if he enters from a Member State of the European Communities or from another third State in which the application of the Agreement on the Legal Status of Fugitives and the Convention on the Protection of Human Rights and Basic Freedoms is secured. The States outside the European Communities to which the requirements of sentence 1 apply will be determined by statute which will require the consent of the Federal Council. In cases to which sentence 1 applies, measures bringing residence to an end can be implemented, independently of legal proceedings lodged against this.

(3) States can be determined by statute, which needs the approval of the Federal Council, in which, on the basis of the state of the law, the application of the law and the general political circumstances, it appears to be guaranteed that neither political persecution nor inhuman nor degrading punishment or treatment take place there. It is assumed that a foreigner from such a State is not persecuted as long as he does not put forward facts which form the basis for supposing that, contrary to this assumption, he is politically persecuted.

(4) The implementation of measures bringing residence to an end will only be halted by the court in the cases mentioned in para 3 and in other cases which are obviously unfounded, or are to be considered as unfounded if serious doubts exist as to the legality of the measure; the scope of the examination can be limited, and belated allegations are to remain out of consideration. Details are to be determined by statute.

(5) Paragraphs 1–4 are not opposed to international law treaties of Member States of the European Communities between themselves and with third States, which (taking into consideration the obligations arising from the Agreement on the Legal Status of Fugitives and the Convention on the Protection of Human Rights and Basic Freedoms, the application of which must be secured in the treaty States) make rules as to competence for examination of those seeking asylum, including the mutual recognition of asylum decisions.

Paragraph 1 of Art 16 a used to be the last sentence of para 2 of Art 16. Because of the controversy which surrounded this issue following reunification, it has been transferred to a separate article and made subject to qualifications.

Article 17 [Right of petition] Everyone has the right singly or in common with others to apply or complain in writing to the competent authorities or to representative bodies.

Art. 17 a [Einschränkung von Grundrechten bei Soldaten] (1) Gesetze über Wehrdienst und Ersatzdienst können bestimmen, daß für die Angehörigen der Streitkräfte und des Ersatzdienstes während der Zeit des Wehr- oder Ersatzdienstes das Grundrecht, seine Meinung in Wort, Schrift und Bild frei zu äußern und zu verbreiten (Artikel 5 Abs. 1 Satz 1 erster Halbsatz), das Grundrecht der Versammlungsfreiheit (Artikel 8) und das Petitionsrecht (Artikel 17), soweit es das Recht gewährt, Bitten oder Beschwerden in Gemeinschaft mit anderen vorzubringen, eingeschränkt werden.

(2) Gesetze, die der Verteidigung einschließlich des Schutzes der Zivilbevölkerung dienen, können bestimmen, daß die Grundrechte der Freizügigkeit (Artikel 11) und der Unverletzlichkeit der Wohnung (Artikel 13) eingeschränkt werden.

Art. 18 [Verwirkung von Grundrechten] Wer die Freiheit der Meinungsäußerung, insbesondere die Pressefreiheit (Artikel 5 Absatz 1), die Lehrfreiheit (Artikel 5 Absatz 3), die Versammlungsfreiheit (Artikel 8), die Vereinigungsfreiheit (Artikel 9), das Brief-, Post- und Fernmeldegeheimnis (Artikel 10), das Eigentum (Artikel 14) oder das Asylrecht (Artikel 16 a) zum Kampfe gegen die freiheitliche demokratische Grundordnung mißbraucht, verwirkt diese Grundrechte. Die Verwirkung und ihr Ausmaß werden durch das Bundesverfassungsgericht ausgesprochen.

Art. 19 [Einschränkung von Grundrechten] (1) Soweit nach diesem Grundgesetz ein Grundrecht durch Gesetz oder auf Grund eines Gesetzes eingeschränkt werden kann, muß das Gesetz allgemein und nicht nur für den Einzelfall gelten. Außerdem muß das Gesetz das Grundrecht unter Angabe des Artikels nennen.

(2) In keinem Falle darf ein Grundrecht in seinem Wesensgehalt angetastet werden.

(3) Die Grundrechte gelten auch für inländische juristische Personen, soweit sie ihrem Wesen nach auf diese anwendbar sind.

(4) Wird jemand durch die öffentliche Gewalt in seinen Rechten verletzt, so steht ihm der Rechtsweg offen. Soweit eine andere Zuständigkeit nicht begründet ist, ist der ordentliche Rechtsweg gegeben. Artikel 10 Absatz 2 Satz 2 bleibt unberührt.

Article 17 a [Limitation of Basic Rights for soldiers] (1) Statutes about military service and substituted service can provide that the basic right to express and disseminate one's opinion freely in word, writing and picture (Art 5 para 1 sentence 1, first half sentence), the basic right of freedom of assembly (Art 8) and the right of petition (Art 17), insofar as it grants the right to make requests or complaints jointly with others, is limited for members of the military services and substituted services during the period of such military service or substituted service.

(2) Statutes which concern defence, inclusive of protection of the civil population, can provide that the basic rights of free movement (Art 11) and the inviolability of the home (Art 13) are limited.

Article 18 [Forfeiture of Basic Rights] A person who misuses the freedom of expression of opinion, especially press freedom (Art 5 para 1), the freedom to teach (Art 5 para 3), the freedom of assembly (Art 8), the freedom of association (Art 9), the privacy of letters and postal and telephone services (Art 10), property (Art 14) or the right of asylum (Art 16 a) to contest the free democratic basic order forfeits these basic rights. The forfeiture and its extent will be declared by the Federal Constitutional Court.

Article 19 [Limitation of Basic Rights] (1) Insofar as a basic right can, according to this Basic Law, be limited by a statute or on the basis of a statute, the statute must be a general one and not only applicable to an individual case. Besides this the statute must identify the basic right by reference to the article.

(2) A basic right may not in any case be violated in its essential content.

(3) The basic rights are applicable to domestic legal persons insofar as these rights are applicable to such by their nature.

(4) If a person's rights are infringed by the exercise of public authority, legal proceedings are available to him. Insofar as another competent authority has not been established, ordinary legal proceedings are available. Article 10 para 2 sentence 2 remains unaffected.

CHAPTER FOUR

RIGHTS AND OBLIGATIONS

THE CIVIL CODE

The Civil Code (BGB) came into effect in Germany on 1 January 1900 after a preparatory period of nearly 26 years.

It was not replaced during the national socialist period, although there were proposals for this. Instead, it was interpreted in such a way as to conform to the prevailing ideology, and this applied in particular to the 'general clauses', eg, the requirements of good faith and good morals.

Specifically national socialist laws were repealed by the Control Council Acts when Germany was occupied.

When Germany was divided, the BGB still applied in the East as well as the West, but it was handled in a different way. It was subsequently progressively amended in the DDR in view of its inconsistency with the State's ideology. The contract ceased to be an instrument of private autonomy and became instead a tool in a State-planned economy.

As a result of unification, the BGB and subsidiary statutory provisions now apply again fully in the new States in the East, subject to a few exceptions. There are however transitional provisions to avoid hardship.

PERSONS

The two kinds of persons recognised in German law as capable of having rights and duties are the natural person (a human being) and the legal person. Legal competence (Rechtsfähigkeit) which is referred to in the first article of the Civil Code set out below means the capacity to have rights and duties.

Natural persons

(1) Birth

Bürgerliches Gesetzbuch

Erstes Buch. Allgemeiner Teil

Erster Abschnitt. Personen

Erster Titel. Natürliche Personen

§ 1 [Beginn der Rechtsfähigkeit] Die Rechtsfähigkeit des Menschen beginnt mit der Vollendung der Geburt.

(2) Death

(3) Capacity and competence

§ 2 [Eintritt der Volljährigkeit] Die Volljährigkeit tritt mit der Vollendung des achtzehnten Lebensjahres ein.

§§ 3–6 (aufgehoben)

Natural persons

(1) Birth

First Book. General Part

First Section. Persons

First Title. Natural Persons

§ 1 [Commencement of legal capacity] The legal capacity of a human being begins with the completion of birth.

Nevertheless a natural person can acquire rights before birth.

(2) Death

Legal capacity ends with death, but there are provisions for this to be presumed by means of a judicial declaration of death in the case of a person who has disappeared (§ 9 of the VerschG = Disappearance Act).

(3) Capacity and competence

Legal capacity is to be distinguished from competence to act, which is a human being's capacity for behaviour which has legal consequences. This includes transaction competence and tortious competence. These are respectively the capacity to enter into legal transactions and the capacity to commit torts.

§ 2 [Attainment of majority] Majority commences on the completion of the 18th year of life.

§§ 3–6 (repealed)

(4) Right to a name

§ 12 [Namensrecht] Wird das Recht zum Gebrauch eines Namens dem Berechtigten von einem anderen bestritten oder wird das Interesse des Berechtigten dadurch verletzt, daß ein anderer unbefugt den gleichen Namen gebraucht, so kann der Berechtigte von dem anderen Beseitigung der Beeinträchtigung verlangen. Sind weiterer Beeinträchtigungen zu besorgen, so kann er auf Unterlassung klagen.

§ 13 [Verbraucher] Verbraucher ist jede natürliche Person, die ein Rechtsgeschäft zu einem Zwecke abschließt, der weder ihrer gewerblichen noch ihrer selbständigen beruflichen Tätigkeit zugerechnet werden kann.

§ 14 [Unternehmer] (1) Unternehmer ist eine natürliche oder juristische Person oder eine rechtsfähige Personengesellschaft, die bei Abschluss eines Rechtsgeschäfts in Ausübung ihrer gewerblichen oder selbständigen beruflichen Tätigkeit handelt.

(2) Eine rechtsfähige Personengesellschaft ist eine Personengesellschaft, die mit der Fähigkeit ausgestattet ist, Rechte zu erwerben und Verbindlichkeiten einzugehen.

§§ 15–20 (aufgehoben)

(5) Legal persons

(6) Property

§§ 7–11 relate to domicile.

(4) Right to a name

This really only relates to the names of citizens, but it has been extended to cover other names. It might therefore be a personal name, or it might be the name of business (the 'Firma') which can be transferred with the business. The right can be infringed by refusal to acknowledge the name; or by unauthorised use of it if some deception as to identity is involved.

It is one aspect of the right to personality: see the publication of a letter case in Chapter Six, p 469. It is also an 'other right' under § 823 para 1 of the BGB: see Chapter Six, p 435.

To what extent is the right to use of a name protected in English law in (a) the business sphere and (b) the personal sphere?

§ 12 [Right to a name] If the right to the use of a name by the person entitled to it is disputed by another, or if the interest of the person entitled to it is harmed by the unauthorised use by another of the same name, the person entitled can require from that other removal of the infringement. If further infringements fail to be dealt with, he can sue for cessation.

§ 13 [Consumer] A consumer is any natural person who concludes a legal transaction for a purpose which cannot be attributed to his commercial or independent vocational activity.

§ 14 [Undertaking] (1) An undertaking is a natural or legal person or a legally competent association of persons which in concluding a legal transaction acts in the exercise of its commercial or independent vocational activity.

(2) A legally competent association of persons is an association of persons which is provided with the capacity to acquire rights and enter into obligations.

§§ 15–20 (repealed)

(5) Legal persons

§§ 21–89 of the BGB relate to legal persons: associations (Vereine), institutions (Stiftungen) and legal persons in public law.

(6) Property

§§ 90–103 of the BGB relate to things (Sachen) and animals. These articles define and categorise physical property, and its products, benefits and burdens.

(7) *Legal competence*

Dritter Abschnitt. Rechtsgeschäfte

Erster Titel. Geschäftsfähigkeit

§ 104 [Geschäftsunfähigkeit] Geschäftsunfähig ist:

1 wer nicht das siebente Lebensjahr vollendet hat;

2 wer sich in einem die freie Willensbestimmung ausschließenden Zustande krankhafter Störung der Geistestätigkeit befindet, sofern nicht der Zustand seiner Natur nach ein vorübergehender ist.

§ 105 [Nichtigkeit der Willenserklärung] (1) Die Willenserklärung eines Geschäftsunfähigen ist nichtig.

(2) Nichtig ist auch eine Willenserklärung, die im Zustande der Bewußtlosigkeit oder vorübergehender Störung der Geistestätigkeit abgegeben wird.

§ 106 [Beschränkte Geschäftsfähigkeit Minderjähriger] Ein Minderjähriger, der das siebente Lebensjahr vollendet hat, ist nach Maßgabe der §§ 107 bis 113 in der Geschäftsfähigkeit beschränkt.

§ 107 [Einwilligung des gesetzlichen Vertreters] Der Minderjährige bedarf zu einer Willenserklärung, durch die er nicht lediglich einen rechtlichen Vorteil erlangt, der Einwilligung seines gesetzlichen Vertreters.

§ 108 [Vertragsschluß ohne Einwilligung] (1) Schließt der Minderjährige einen Vertrag ohne die erforderliche Einwilligung des gesetzlichen Vertreters, so hängt die Wirksamkeit des Vertrags von der Genehmigung des Vertreters ab.

(7) Legal competence

Legal competence (Geschäftsfähigkeit), which is considered in the following Title, must be distinguished from legal capacity (Rechtsfähigkeit) which we encountered in § 1 of the BGB. Legal competence means the ability to give and accept (see § 131 of the BGB, below) declarations of will.

Besides legal competence and incompetence, German law recognises partial competence. This applies in the case of minors between the ages of 7 and 18, and there are provisions for such minors to be protected by a legal representative. The major issue in relation to minors is whether the transaction includes a legal disadvantage. If so, the consent of the minor's legal representative is needed. Whether there is such a disadvantage is a complicated value judgment, for which a number of rules have been devised.

If the consent of the legal representative is needed for a transaction by a minor (§ 107 of the BGB) this should be given beforehand: see §§ 182 and 183 of the BGB. However, in the case of transactions of a contractual nature, approval can instead be given subsequently: see § 184 of the BGB.

Third section. Legal transactions

First Title. Legal competence

§ 104 [Legal incompetence] The following are not legally competent:

1 a person who has not completed his 7th year;

2 a person who suffers from a condition of disturbance of mental activity through disease, which prevents the free power of decision (insofar as this condition is not by its nature a transitory one).

§ 105 [Invalidity of declaration of will] (1) A declaration of will which is made by a person who is legally incompetent is void.

(2) A declaration of will is also void if it is made in a condition of unconsciousness or transitory disturbance of mental activity.

§ 106 [Limited legal competence of a minor] A minor who has completed his 7th year is limited in his legal competence in accordance with §§ 107–113.

§ 107 [Consent of the legal representative] The minor needs the consent of his legal representative for a declaration of will by which he does not merely obtain a legal advantage.

§ 108 [Conclusion of a contract without consent] (1) If a minor concludes a contract without the necessary consent of his legal representative, the effectiveness of the contract depends on the ratification of the representative.

(2) Fordert der andere Teil den Vertreter zur Erklärung über die Genehmigung auf, so kann die Erklärung nur ihm gegenüber erfolgen; eine vor der Aufforderung dem Minderjährigen gegenüber erklärte Genehmigung oder Verweigerung der Genehmigung wird unwirksam. Die Genehmigung kann nur bis zum Ablaufe von zwei Wochen nach dem Empfange der Aufforderung erklärt werden; wird sie nicht erklärt, so gilt sie als verweigert.

(3) Ist der Minderjährige unbeschränkt geschäftsfähig geworden, so tritt seine Genehmigung an die Stelle der Genehmigung des Vertreters.

§ 109 [Widerrufsrecht des anderen Teils] (1) Bis zur Genehmigung des Vertrags ist der andere Teil zum Widerrufe berechtigt. Der Widerruf kann auch dem Minderjährigen gegenüber erklärt werden.

(2) Hat der andere Teil die Minderjährigkeit gekannt, so kann er nur widerrufen, wenn der Minderjährige der Wahrheit zuwider die Einwilligung des Vertreters behauptet hat; er kann auch in diesem Falle nicht widerrufen, wenn ihm das Fehlen der Einwilligung bei dem Abschlusse des Vertrags bekannt war.

§ 110 [Bewirkung der Leistung mit eigenen Mitteln] Ein von dem Minderjährigen ohne Zustimmung des gesetzlichen Vertreters geschlossener Vertrag gilt als von Anfang an wirksam, wenn der Minderjährige die vertragsmäßige Leistung mit Mitteln bewirkt, die ihm zu diesem Zwecke oder zu freier Verfügung von dem Vertreter oder mit dessen Zustimmung von einem Dritten überlassen worden sind.

§ 111 [Einseitige Rechtsgeschäfte] Ein einseitiges Rechtsgeschäft, das der Minderjährige ohne die erforderliche Einwilligung des gesetzlichen Vertreters vornimmt, ist unwirksam. Nimmt der Minderjährige mit dieser Einwilligung ein solches Rechtsgeschäft einem anderen gegenüber vor, so ist das Rechtsgeschäft unwirksam, wenn der Minderjährige die Einwilligung nicht in schriftlicher Form vorlegt und der andere das Rechtsgeschäft aus diesem Grunde unverzüglich zurückweist. Die Zurückweisung ist ausgeschlossen, wenn der Vertreter den anderen von der Einwilligung in Kenntnis gesetzt hatte.

§ 112 [Selbständiger Betrieb eines Erwerbsgeschäfts] (1) Ermächtigt der gesetzliche Vertreter mit Genehmigung des Vormundschaftsgerichts den Minderjährigen zum selbständigen Betrieb eines Erwerbsgeschäfts, so ist der Minderjährige für solche Rechtsgeschäfte unbeschränkt geschäftsfähig, welche der Geschäftsbetrieb mit sich bringt. Ausgenomen sind Rechtsgeschäfte, zu denen der Vertreter der Genehmigung des Vormundschaftsgerichts bedarf.

(2) Die Ermächtigung kann von dem Vertreter nur mit Genehmigung des Vormundschaftsgerichts zurückgenommen werden.

(2) If the other party asks the representative for a statement about ratification, the statement can only be effective against him. A statement of ratification or refusal of ratification to the minor before the request is ineffective. The ratification can only be given during the period of two weeks from receipt of the request; if it is not given, it is to be considered as refused.

(3) If the minor has attained unlimited legal competence, his ratification takes the place of the ratification of the representative.

§ 109 [Right of revocation by the other party] (1) Until ratification of the contract, the other party has the right of revocation. The revocation can also be made as against the minor.

(2) If the other party knew about the minority, he can only revoke if the minor falsely asserted that the representative had given his consent. Even in this case he cannot revoke if the absence of consent was known to him at the conclusion of the contract.

§ 110 [Effecting performance with own means] A contract concluded by the minor, without the agreement of the legal representative, counts as effective from its commencement if the minor effects contractual performance with means which are made available to him by the representative (or by a third person with the representative's agreement) for this purpose or for use as the minor wishes.

§ 111 [One-sided legal transactions] A one-sided legal transaction, which the minor undertakes without the necessary consent of the legal representative, is ineffective. If the minor undertakes such a legal transaction with this consent as against another person, this transaction is ineffective if the minor does not produce the consent in a written form and the other person rejects the legal transaction on this ground without delay. Rejection is excluded if the representative had apprised the other person of the consent.

§ 112 [Independent operation of a commercial business] (1) If the legal representative (with the approval of the Guardianship Court) authorises the minor to operate a commercial business independently, the minor has unlimited competence for such legal transactions as the operation of the business brings with it. Legal transactions for which the representative needs the approval of the Guardianship Court are excepted.

(2) The authorisation can only be revoked by the representative with the approval of the Guardianship Court.

§ 113 [Dienst- oder Arbeitsverhältnis] (1) Ermächtigt der gesetzliche Vertreter den Minderjährigen, in Dienst oder in Arbeit zu treten, so ist der Minderjährige für solche Rechtsgeschäfte unbeschränkt geschäftsfähig, welche die Eingehung oder Aufhebung eines Dienst- oder Arbeitsverhältnisses der gestatteten Art oder die Erfüllung der sich aus einem solchen Verhältnis ergebenden Verpflichtungen betreffen. Ausgenomen sind Verträge, zu denen der Vertreter der Genehmigung des Vormundschaftsgerichts bedarf.

(2) Die Ermächtigung kann von dem Vertreter zurückgenommen oder eingeschränkt werden.

(3) Ist der gesetzliche Vertreter ein Vormund, so kann die Ermächtigung, wenn sie von ihm verweigert wird, auf Antrag des Minderjährigen durch das Vormundschaftsgericht ersetzt werden. Das Vormundschaftsgericht hat die Ermächtigung zu ersetzen, wenn sie im Interesse des Mündels liegt.

(4) Die für einen einzelnen Fall erteilte Ermächtigung gilt im Zweifel als allgemeine Ermächtigung zur Eingehung von Verhältnissen derselben Art.

§§ 114 und 115 (aufgehoben)

LEGAL TRANSACTIONS

§ 113 [Service or work relationship] (1) If the legal representative authorises the minor to enter service or work, the minor has unlimited competence for such legal transactions as concern the commencement or termination of a service or work relationship of the permitted kind or the fulfilment of the obligations arising from such a relationship. Contracts for which the representative needed the approval of the Guardianship Court are excepted.

(2) The authorisation can be revoked or restricted by the representative.

(3) If the legal representative is a guardian, and the authorisation is refused by him, it can be substituted by the Guardianship Court on the application of the minor. The Guardianship Court has the authority to substitute if it is in the interest of the minor.

(4) An authorisation which is given for a single case takes effect in case of doubt as a general authorisation for entering into relationships of the same kind.

§§ 114 and 115 (repealed)

LEGAL TRANSACTIONS

Legal transactions, declarations of will and contracts

There are three important basic concepts in this area of German civil law: the legal transaction, the declaration of will and the contract. The contract is the most significant form of legal transaction; a declaration (or declarations) of will is (or are) (a) necessary component part(s) of a legal transaction, although there may be some other necessary components as well.

There are certain factual requirements which must be present for a legal transaction to exist: for instance, if the legal transaction is a contract, an offer must be accepted before the contract can come into existence. (Both the offer and the acceptance are declarations or will.) There are further requirements which must be satisfied for a legal transaction to be effective, eg, contravention of good morals makes a legal transaction void.

Legal transactions may be one-sided or many-sided. The former category includes a will, and termination of a contract if one party has power to take this step. The latter category includes a contract, a marriage and a disposal of property.

DECLARATIONS OF WILL

DECLARATIONS OF WILL

The concept

It is necessary to distinguish between the declaration of will, which is intended to be legally binding, and the non-binding declaration which is made by 'grace and favour' (Gefälligskeitzusage). The distinction is a matter of interpretation, and a variety of factors have to be taken into consideration, including the surrounding circumstances.

Compare this with the English law concept of intention to create legal relations in cases such as *Carlill v Carbolic Smoke Ball Co* [1893] 1 QB 256; *Jones v Vernon's Pools Ltd* [1938] 2 All ER 626; and *Jones v Padavatton* [1969] 2 All ER 616.

A declaration of will might be deduced from a person's conduct, eg, when someone avails themselves of a service for which payment is due. But conduct would be insufficient if statute or a legal transaction required the declaration to take some particular form. There are also circumstances where conduct gives rise to a presumption of a declaration of will. Silence cannot normally amount to a declaration of will, but:

(a) statute will sometimes confer on it the status of a declaration of will;

(b) under customary law silence in the context of a businessman's confirmatory letter will sometimes amount to consent; and

(c) silence may be regarded sometimes as consent under case law.

Compare the position here with English cases such as *Felthouse v Bindley* (1862) 11 CB (NS) 869; and *Fairline Shipping Corporation v Adamson* [1974] 2 All ER 967.

Declarations of will can be divided into those which do not need to be received (eg, wills) and those which do (eg, offers to enter into contracts). The former are effective when given the latter are only effective when given and received.

Zweiter Titel. Willensklärung

§ 116 [Geheimer Vorbehalt] Eine Willenserklärung ist nicht deshalb nichtig, weil sich der Erklärende insgeheim vorbehält, das Erklärte nicht zu wollen. Die Erklärung ist nichtig, wenn sie einem anderen gegenüber abzugeben ist und dieser den Vorbehalt kennt.

§ 117 [Scheingeschäft] (1) Wird eine Willenserklärung, die einem anderen gegenüber abzugeben ist, mit dessen Einverständnisse nur zum Schein abgegeben, so ist sie nichtig.

(2) Wird durch ein Scheingeschäft ein anderes Rechtsgeschäft verdeckt, so finden die für das verdeckte Rechtsgeschäft geltenden Vorschriften Anwendung.

§ 118 [Mangel der Ernstlichkeit] Eine nicht ernstlich gemeinte Willenserklärung, die in der Erwartung abgegeben wird, der Mangel der Ernstlichkeit werde nicht verkannt werden, ist nichtig.

THE UNINTENDED DECLARATION OF WILL CASE

BGHZ Band 91 S. 325

39 Trotz fehlenden Erklärungsbewußtseins (Rechtsbindungswillens, Geschäftswillens) liegt eine Willenserklärung vor wenn der Erklärende bei Anwendung der im Verkehr erforderlichen Sorfalt hätte erkennen und vermeiden können daß seine Äußerung nach Treu und Glauben und der Verkehrsitte als Willenserklärung aufgefaßt werden durfte, und wenn der Empfänger sie auch tatsächlich so verstanden hat. Sie kann gemäß §§ 119, 121, 143 BGB angefochten werden.

BGB §§ 116ff., 119

IX. Zivilsenat. Urt. v 7. Juni 1984 i.S. Kreis- und Stadtsparkasse D. (Bekl.) w. Sch. GmbH (Kl.) IX ZR 66/83.

I Landgericht München II

II Oberlandesgericht München

Second Title. Declaration of Will

§ 116 [Secret reservation] A declaration of will is not invalid because the maker of it secretly makes a reservation of not intending what is declared. The declaration of will is invalid if it is to be made as against another and if that other person knows the reservation.

See the internet auction case, Chapter Five, p 333.

§ 117 [Sham transaction] (1) If a declaration of will which is to be made as against another is, with his agreement, only given as a sham it is invalid.

(2) If another legal transaction is concealed by a sham transaction, the rules effective for the legal transaction which has been concealed are to be applied.

§ 118 [Lack of sincerity] A declaration of will which is not seriously intended, which is made in the expectation that the lack of sincerity will not fail to be recognised, is invalid.

THE UNINTENDED DECLARATION OF WILL CASE

This case shows that despite the use of the expression declaration of will, the intention of the declarant is not always the determining factor. The issue may be how the recipient could reasonably have understood it, and how he in fact understood it. If this results in a contract coming into existence, the issue then becomes whether the declarant can avoid it.

BGHZ Volume 91 p 325

39 In spite of the absence of the conscious making of a declaration (intention to be bound, business intention), a declaration of will is present if the declarer, by using the care necessary in the affairs of life, could have perceived that his statement might, according to good faith and business custom, be regarded as a declaration of will, and if the recipient did in fact also understand it. It can be avoided in accordance with §§ 119, 121, 143 of the BGB.

BGB §§ 116 and onwards, 119

IXth Civil Senate. Judgment of 7 June 1984 in the matter of the District and City Saving Bank D (defendant) v Sch GmbH (plaintiff). IX CiL 66/83.

I State Court of Munich II

II Upper State Court of Munich

Die Klägerin, die Hallen aus Stahl herstellte, hatte von ihrer Kundin, der Firma SVG-GmbH (im folgenden: SVG) verlangt, Bankbürgschaften zur Sicherung aus Lieferungen herrührender Verbindlichkeiten beizubringen. Das sagte der Geschäftsführer der SVG auch zu. Er nahm einen von der Klägerin am 4. September 1981 ausgestellten, auf die SVG gezogenen Wechsel über 259 046,83 DM für diese Firma an. Am 8. September 1981 richtete die beklagte Sparkasse folgendes Schreiben an die Klägerin:

> Unsere Bürgschaft in Höhe von 50 000 DM 1 zugunsten Firma SVG-GmbH
> Sehr geehrte Damen,
> sehr geehrte Herren,
> zugunsten der Firma SVG-GmbH haben wir gegenüber Ihrer Firma die selbstschuldnerische Bürgschaft in Höhe von 150 000 DM übernommen.
> Wir wären ihnen für eine kurze Mitteilung sehr verbunden wie hoch sich die Verpflichtungen der Firma SVG-GmbH bei Ihnen derzeit belaufen.
> ...

Die Klägerin antwortete unter dem 17. September 1981:

> Wir danken für Ihr Schreiben vom 8.9.1981 und haben gerne zur Kenntnis genommen, daß Sie gegenüber der Firma SVG-GmbH... die selbstschuldnerische Bürgschaft gegenüber unserer Firma in Höhe von 150 000 DM übernommen haben.
> Unsere Forderungen an die oben genannte Firma betragen mit heutigem Stand öS 1 652 717,83, welches einem Gegenwert von 236 102,54 DM entspricht.
> ...

Am 24. September 1981 schrieb die Beklagte an die Klägerin:

> Zu Ihrem Schreiben vom 17.9.1981 teilen wir Ihnen mit, daß wir an Sie gegenüber der oben bezeichneten Firma (SVG-Gesellschaft mit beschränkter Haftung) keine selbstschuldnerische Bürgschaft in Höhe von 150 000 DM übernommen haben. Die in Ihrem Schreiben angeführten Ausführungen treffen daher nicht zu.
> ...

Nachdem die Klägerin am 28. September 1981 auf den Widerspruch zu dem Schreiben vom 8. September 1981 hingewiesen hatte, entgegenete die Beklagte unter dem 6. Oktober 1981:

> ...

The plaintiff which made steel structures had asked its customer SVG Ltd ('SVG') to produce bank securities to guarantee obligations arising from supplies. That was agreed to by the director of SVG. He accepted a bill of exchange for 259,046.83 DM drawn by the plaintiff on SVG on 4 September 1981 for this firm. On 8 September 1981, the defendant's savings bank sent the following letter to the plaintiff:

> Our security in the sum of 150,000 DM in favour of SVG Ltd
> Dear Mesdames,
> Dear Sirs,
> For the benefit of SVG Ltd we have taken over as against your company the directly enforceable[1] security in the sum of 150,000 DM.
> We should be obliged to you for a brief communication as to the extent of the obligation of SVG Ltd to you at this moment.
> ...

The plaintiff answered on 17 September 1981:

> We thank you for your letter of the 8 September 1981 and are pleased to learn that you have, in respect of SVG Ltd ... taken over the directly enforceable security as against our company in the sum of 150,000 DM.
> Our claims on the above named company amount to 1,652,717.83 Austrian schillings as at today's date which corresponds to an equivalent of 236,102.54 DM.

On 24 September 1981 the defendant wrote to the plaintiff:

> In reply to your letter of the 17 September 1981 we inform you that we have not taken over any directly enforceable security in your favour in the sum of 150,000 DM as against the above named company (SVG Ltd). The statements made in your letter are therefore not correct.
> ...

After the plaintiff referred on the 28 September 1981 to the contradiction to the letter of the 8 September 1981, the defendant replied on the 6 October 1981:

---

1 This is a security under which the person granting it cannot raise the objection under § 771 of the BGB that there has not yet been an unsuccessful execution against the principal debtor.

Bei dem Schreiben vom 8. September 1981 ging unsere Zweigstelle davon aus, daß gegenüber der Firma Sch. Hallen Bau GmbH eine Bürgschaft besteht. Diese Annahme beruhte auf einem Irrtum. Im Dezember 1980 war auch die Übernahme eine Bürgschaft gegenüber der Firma Sch. im Gespräch. Diese Bürschaft kam jedoch nie zustande ...

Mit Schreiben vom 17. November 1981 focht die Beklagte 'eine etwa erteilte Bürgschaftserklärung nochmals wegen Irrtums vorsorglich an'.

Am 8. Dezember 1981 ging der Wechsel über 259 046,83 DM mangels Zahlung der Bezogenen zu Protest.

Das Landgericht erkannte die Klägerin am 12. August 1982 durch Vorbehaltsurteil 150 000 DM nebst Prozeßzinsen zu. Es erklärte dieses Urteil am 11. November 1982 für vorbehaltslos. Das Oberlandesgericht wies die zu gemeinsamer Verhandlung und Entscheidung verbundenen Berufungen zurück. Die Revision der Beklagten hatte keinen Erfolg.

Aus den Gründen:

...

I Auf Grund der dem Tatrichter vorbehaltenen Würdigung unstreitiger Umstände steht fest: Die Klägerin durfte das Schreiben vom 8. September 1981 dahin auffassen, daß die Beklagte mit ihm eine selbstschuldnerische Bürgschaft bis 150 000 DM für die aus Lieferungen von Stahlhallen herrührenden Verbindlichkeiten der SVG, zu denen auch die Schuld aus dem von dieser Gesellschaft akzeptierten und nicht eingelösten Wechsel vom 4. September 1981 gehört, gegenüber der Klägerin eingehen wollte. Die Klägerin hat das Schreiben auch so verstanden und das in ihm erkannte Vertragsangebot angenommen. Insoweit erhebt die Revision keine Beanstandungen.

1 Wie sie jedoch zutreffend ausführt, ist nach der Unterstellung des Tatrichters für die Revisionsinstanz davon auszugehen, daß die Vertreter der Beklagten mit ihrem Schreiben vom 8. September 1981 nur eine tatsächliche Mitteilung machen wollten, also bei der Unterzeichnung und Absendung nicht den Willen, ja nicht einmal des Bewußtsein hatten, eine verbindliche rechtsgeschäftliche Erklärung abzugeben. Dann aber, so macht die Revision geltend, fehle es am Tatbestand einer Willenserklärung. Ihrer Beseitigung durch Anfechtung nach § 119 Abs. 1 BGB bedürfe es mithin nicht. Allenfalls ein nicht dargelegter Vertrauensschaden sei analog § 122 BGB zu ersetzen, wenn die Beklagte die mögliche Deutung ihres Verhaltens als Willenserklärung bei Anwendung pflichtgemäßer Sorgfalt hätte erkennen können.

In the letter of 8 September 1981 our branch office proceeded on the basis that a security existed as against Sch Hallen Bau Ltd. This supposition was based on an error. In December 1980, the taking over of a security in respect of the company Sch was under consideration. This security however never came into existence ...

By a letter of 17 November 1981 the defendant avoided 'again, as a precaution, on the grounds of mistake, a security declaration which had possibly been made'.

On 8 December 1981 the bill for 259,046.83 DM together with procedural interest went to protest for want of payment by the drawee.

The State Court awarded the plaintiff 150,000 DM together with procedural interest on 12 August 1982 by a reservation judgment.[2] It declared this judgment to be unconditional on 11 November 1982. The Upper State Court rejected the appeals which were combined for joint proceedings and decision. The appeal in law of the defendant was unsuccessful.

Reasons:

...

I On the basis of the assessment, reserved to the judge of fact, of the undisputed circumstances, it is established: The plaintiff was entitled to interpret the letter of 8 September 1981 to the effect that the defendant wanted to enter into a directly enforceable security as against the plaintiff to the sum of 150,000 DM for the liabilities of SVG arising out of the deliveries of steel structures. The obligation arising from the bill of exchange of 4 September 1981 accepted by this company and not honoured also belongs to these liabilities. The plaintiff also interpreted the letter in this way and accepted the contractual offer recognised in it. In this respect the appeal raises no objections.

1 According to the assumption of the judge of fact for the court for the appeal in law, one should, as it pertinently states, proceed on the basis that the representatives of the defendant by their letter of 8 September 1981 only wanted to make a factual communication and therefore by signing and sending the letter did not have the intention, or even the consciousness, of making a binding legally effective declaration. But then, as the appeal in law asserts, the essential elements of a declaration of will were lacking. Its nullification by avoidance in accordance with § 119 para 1 of the BGB was not therefore needed. In any event, harm arising from breach of trust,[3] which has not been demonstrated, would be established by analogy[4] with § 122 if the defendant could have recognised the possible interpretation of its conduct as a declaration of will by the use of such care as it had a duty to show.

---

2 This is a judgment which contains a reservation in respect of objections by the defendant: see §§ 302 and 599 of the ZPO.

3 See further as to this concept the termination of negotiations case in Chapter Five, p 393.

4 Argument by analogy is permitted in civil law, but not in criminal law in a manner which would be to the disadvantage of the defendant.

Der Angriff ist unbegründet.

(a) Die Ansicht, daß das Erklärungsbewußtsein ein konstitutives Erfordernis der Willenserklärung sei, sein Fehlen also ohne Anfechtung Nichtigkeit zur Folge habe und allenfalls analog § 122 BGB oder aus *culpa in contrahendo* eine Haftung des Erklärenden auf Ersatz des Vertrauensschadens in Betracht komme, vertreten insbesondere Enneccerus/Nipperdey, Allgemeiner Teil des bürgerlichen Rechts 15. Aufl. 1 Band 2. Halbband S. 901ff.; Lehmann/Hübner, Allgemeiner Teil des BGB, 15. Aufl., § 34 III 1 b = S. 260; H. Lange BGB Allg. Teil 12. Aufl., S. 229; Fabricius JuS 1966, 1, 8; Wieacker JZ 1967, 385, 389; Thiele JZ 1969, 405, 407; Canaris, *Die Vertrauenshaftung im deutschen Privatrecht*, 1971, S. 427ff., 548ff.; derselbe NJW 1974, 521, 527, 528; Frotz, *Verkehrsschutz im Vertretungsrecht*, 1972, S. 469ff.; Staudinger/Dilcher, BGB, 12. Aufl. vor § 116 Rdnr. 18/27, 80/83 (vgl. auch Schmidt-Salzer JR 1969, 279, 282, 284, 288). Der Auffassung, daß die ohne jenes Bewußtsein abgegebene Erklärung, die ihr Empfänger als rechtsgeschäftliche verstehen durfte, zunächst wirksam sei, aber wie ein Erklärungsirrtum gemäß §§ 119 Abs. 1. 120, 121 BGB angefochten werden könne, sind vor allem Larenz, *Methode der Auslegung des Rechtsgeschäfts* S. 82ff.; derselbe BGB Allg. Teil 6. Aufl., S. 343ff.; Flume, Allg. Teil 3. Aufl. Bd. 2 S. 449f., allerdings nicht für die konkludente Handlung; Lange/Köhler, BGB Allg. Teil 17. Aufl., S. 240ff.; Gudian AcP 169, 232ff.; Kellmann JuS 1971, 609, 612f.; von Craushaar AcP 174, 2, 6ff.; Brox, *Die Einschränkung der Irrtumsanfechtung* [1960] S. 50ff.; derselbe in Erman, BGB, 7. Aufl. vor § 116 Rdnr. 3; MünchKomm/Kramer vor § 116 Rdnr. 13 und § 119 Rdnr. 78ff.; Soergel/Hefermehl, BGB, 11. Aufl. vor § 116 Rdnr. 12 bis 15; Bydlinski eingehend in JZ 1975, 1.

The argument is unjustified.

(a) The view that consciousness of making a declaration is a fundamental requirement of a declaration of will, and therefore its absence would result in nullity without the need for avoidance and in any event by analogy with § 122 of the BGB or through *culpa in contrahendo*[5] liability of the declarer for compensation for the damage due to breach of trust would fall to be considered, is defended especially by Enneccerus/Nipperdey, General Part of the Civil Code, 15th edn, Vol 1 Part 2, p 901 and onwards; Lehmann/Hübner, General Part of the BGB, 15th edn, § 34 III 1 b = p 260; H Lange, General Part of the BGB, 12th edn, p 229; Fabricius JuS 1966, 1, 8,; Wieacker JZ 1967, 385, 389; Thiele JZ 1969, 405, 407; Canaris, *Liability for Breach of Trust in German Private Law,* 1971, p 427 and onwards, 548 and onwards; the same, NJW 1974, 521, 527, 528; Frotz, *Protection of Business in Agency Law,* 1972, p 469 and onwards; Staudinger/Dilcher, BGB 12th edn, preceding § 166 marginal no 18/27, 80/83 (compare also Schmidt-Salzer JR 1969, 279, 282, 284, 288). The view that a declaration, which was given without that consciousness which its recipient might understand as legally effective, is initially effective but could be challenged as a mistaken declaration in accordance with §§ 119 para 1, 120 and 121 of the BGB is held primarily by Larenz, *Methods of Interpretation of the Legal Transaction,* p 82 and onwards; the same, General Part of the BGB, 6th edn, p 343 and onwards; Flume, General Part, 3rd edn, Vol 2 p 449 and onwards, but at all events not for decisive action;[6] Lange/Köhler, General Part of the BGB, 17th edn, p 240 and onwards; Gudian AcP 169, 232 and onwards; Kellmann JuS 1971, 609, 612 and onwards; von Craushaar AcP 174, 2, 6 and onwards; Brox, *Restriction on Avoidance for Mistake* [1960] p 50 and onwards; the same in Erman, BGB, 7th edn, preceding § 116 marginal no 3; Münich Commentary/Kramer preceding § 116 marginal no 13 and § 119 marginal no 78 and onwards; Soergel/Hefermehl, BGB, 11th edn, preceding § 116 marginal nos 12–15; Bydlinski in detail in JuS 1975, 1.

---

5 *Culpa in contrahendo* (obligation in connection with conclusion of a contract) is a concept which has been developed from customary law independently of the Civil Code. It gives rise to a duty to compensate when there has been a violation of a precontractual duty.

6 Decisive action here means action with a clear purpose but without an express declaration, eg, offer by conduct to enter into a contract.

Der Bundesgerichtshof hat die Frage bisher nicht abschließend entschieden. Er hat sie in den Urteilen vom 20 Oktober 1952 – IV ZR 44/52 = NJW 1953, 58 und vom 11. Juli 1968 – II ZR 157/65 = NJW 1968, 2102 ausdrücklich offengelassen. Aus der Entscheidung vom 10. Mai 1968 – V ZR 221/64 = JR 1968, 420, 421 kann nicht eindeutig entnommen werden, daß der Bundesgerichtshof das Erklärungsbewußtsein für konstitutiv halte. Dort ist ausgeführt, daß der Glaube an einen Rechtsübergang kraft Gesetzes den rechtsgeschäftlichen Willen *und* seine Erklärung nicht ersetzen könne. Dagegen nehmen das eine Gefälligkeitshandlung betreffende Urteil BGHZ 21, 102, 106ff. und die Entscheidungen des Bundesarbeitsgerichts in NJW 1971, 1422, 1423 und in DB 1973, 1129, 1130 an, daß es nicht auf den verborgen gebliebenen inneren Willen des Erklärenden, sondern darauf ankomme, wie der Erklärungsgegner nach Treu und Glauben und unter Berücksichtigung aller Begleitumstände die Äußerung verstehen durfte. Im Urteil vom 14 März 1963 – VII ZR 257/61 (= LM BGB § 150 Nr. 6) sieht der Bundesgerichtshof anscheinend das Erklärungsbewußtsein als Voraussetzung einer Willenserklärung an, legt aber auch dar, daß derjenige, der durch schlüssiges Verhalten den Eindruck erweckt, er habe einen Geschäftswillen gehabt und geäußert, ohne ihn tatsächlich zu haben, sich nach § 242 BGB so behandeln lassen müsse, wie wenn er einen Geschäftswillen gehabt hätte. Nach dem Urteil des Bundesgerichtshofs vom 23. Februar 1976 – II ZR 177/74 (WM 1976, 448) ist die Unterzeichnung einer Handelsregisteranmeldung durch einen Gesellschafter für die übrigen Gesellschafter regelmäßig dahin zu verstehen, daß er auch im Innenverhältnis billige, was er dort erklärt habe. Dabei sei die Frage, ob ein Rechtsbindungswille vorhanden ist, nicht nach dem verborgen gebliebenen inneren Willen des erklärenden Gesellschafters, sondern danach zu beurteilen, ob sein Verhalten aus der Sicht der Mitgesellschafter nach Treu und Glauben mit Rücksicht auf die Verkehrssitte als Ausdruck eines bestimmten Willens erscheint. In diesem Urteil wird auch eine Anfechtung nach § 119 Abs. 1 BGB für möglich erachtet. Die dort entwickelten Grundsätze wurden allerdings bisher auf Erklärungen, die nicht die gesellschaftsrechtlichen Verhältnisse nach außen und innen zu verändern geeignet sind, soweit ersichtlich, nicht übertragen.

The Federal Supreme Court has not decided the matter definitively so far. It has expressly left it open in the judgments of 20 October 1952 – IV ZR 44/52 = NJW, 1953, 58 and of 11 July 1968 – II ZR 157/65 = NJW, 1868, 2102. It cannot be clearly inferred from the decision of 10 May 1968 – V ZR 221/64 = JR 1968, 420, 421 that the Federal Supreme Court considers consciousness of making a declaration as fundamental. There it is stated that belief in a legal transition taking effect by virtue of the law could not replace the intention to create legal relations *and* its declaration. On the other hand, the judgment regarding a 'grace and favour' transaction, BGHZ 21, 102, 106, and onwards, and the decisions of the Federal Labour Court in NJW 1971, 1422, 1423, and in DB 1973, 1129, 1130 accept that it does not depend on the inner intention of the declarer which remained hidden, but on how the other party might understand the statement according to good faith and following consideration of all surrounding circumstances. In the judgment of 14 March 1963 – VII ZR 257/61 (= LM BGB § 150 no 6) the Federal Supreme Court apparently regards the consciousness of making a declaration as a pre-requisite of a declaration of will but states also that a person who through decisive action, creates the impression that he has had and expressed an intention to create legal relations, without really having it, must let himself be treated according to § 242 of the BGB as if he had an intention to create legal relations. According to the judgment of the Federal Supreme Court of 23 February 1976 – II ZR 177/74 (WM 1976, 448) the signing of a trade register notification by a company member for the other company members is normally to be understood as approving also in the inner relationship what he has there declared. In this connection, the question of whether an intention to be legally bound is present is not to be judged according to the inner intention of the company member making the declaration, which remained hidden, but according to whether his conduct appears, in the eyes of the fellow company members as the expression of a fixed intention, in accordance with good faith and having regard to business custom. In this judgment, an avoidance in accordance with § 119 para 1 of the BGB is also regarded as possible. The principles developed there, though, have certainly not so far been carried over to declarations which were not appropriate to change relationships in company law externally and internally, as far as can be seen.

(b) Der erkennende Senat ist von den Erwägungen des II. Zivilsenats ausgehend der Auffassung, daß es zur Wirksamkeit der Bürgschaftsverpflichtung nicht darauf ankommt ob die Vertreter der Beklagten bei der Unterzeichnung und Absendung ihres Schreibens vom 8. September 1981 den Willen oder auch nur das Bewußtsein hatten eine rechtsgeschäftliche Erklärung abzugeben. Dafür sind in Anlehnung an Bydlinski (aaO) und Kramer (MünchKomm § 119 Rdn. 81ff.) folgende Gründe maßgebend: In den §§ 116ff. BGB ist der Begriff der Willenserklärung nicht definiert. Insbesondere aus dem Wortlaut des § 119 BGB kann nichts gegen die hier vertretene Ansicht hergeleitet werden. 'Eine Erklärung dieses Inhalts' hat nicht nur nicht abgeben wollen, wer sich einen anderen rechtsgeschäftlichen Inhalt vorgestellt hatte, sondern auch derjenige, der keine rechtsgeschäftliche Erklärung hatte abgeben wollen. Aus § 118 BGB ist nicht zu schließen daß fehlendes Erklärungsbewußtsein (oder fehlender Geschäftswille) ohne Anfechtung immer zur Nichtigkeit führe. Will der Erklärende, wie in § 118 BGB vorausgesetzt, bewußt keine Bindung in der Erwartung, daß dies auch erkannt werde, so entspricht die Nichtigkeit seinem Willen; ihm braucht die Wahl, das Erklärte gegen *und für* sich gelten zu lassen oder nach § 119 BGB anzufechten, nicht eröffnet zu werden. Damit nicht zu vergleichen ist eine Erklärung ohne das Bewußtsein, daß sie als rechtsgeschäftliche verstanden wird. Sie steht der irrtümlichen, als rechtserheblich gewollten Erklärung sehr viel näher. Wer erklärt zu kaufen, sich aber Verkauf vorstellt, befindet sich in einer ganz ähnlichen Lage wie derjenige, der das für Kauf übliche Zeichen gibt, aber nicht an Kauf denkt. In beiden Fällen erscheint es angemessen, dem Erklärenden die Wahl zu lassen, ob er nach § 119 Abs. 1 BGB anfechten will und dann das Vertrauensinteresse nach § 122 BGB ersetzen muß oder ob er bei seine Erklärung stehen bleiben will und dann eine etwaige Gegenleistung erhält, die ihn günstiger stellen könnte als seine einseitige Verpflichtung zum Ersatz des Vertrauensschadens.

Mit dieser Wahlmöglichkeit ist auch das Bedenken ausgeräumt, daß ohne Erklärungsbewußtsein keine Privatautonome Gestaltung in Selbstbestimmung vorliege, die durch Selbstverantwortung allein nicht ersetzt werden könne. Das Recht der Willenserklärung baut nicht nur auf der Selbstbestimmung des Rechtsträgers auf; es schützt in §§ 119, 157 BGB das Vertrauen des Erklärungsempfängers und die Verkehrssicherheit, indem es den Erklärenden auch an nicht vorgestellte und, was dem gleichzuachten ist, an nicht bewußt in Geltung gesetzte Rechtsfolgen bindet. Die Befugnis des Erklärenden, der in beiden Fällen die tatsächlich in seiner Erklärung zum Ausdruck gebrachten Rechtsfolgen nicht gewollt hat, diese durch Anfechtung rückwirkend (§ 142 Abs. 1 BGB) zu vernichten oder gelten zu lassen, trägt dem Gedanken der Selbstbestimmung ausreichend Rechnung (so auch Soergel/Hefermehl aaO).

(b) The deciding Senate, proceeding from the deliberations of the second Civil Senate, is of the view that, for the purpose of the effectiveness of the security obligation, it is not a question of whether the representatives of the defendant had, when signing and sending their letter of 8 September 1981, the intention or even only the consciousness of giving a legally effective declaration. The following grounds, following Bydlinski (*loc cit*) and Kramer (Münich Commentary § 119 marginal no 81 and onwards) are authoritative in this respect: In § 116 and onwards of the BGB the concept of the declaration of will is not defined. In particular nothing can be drawn from the text of § 119 of the BGB against the view which is advocated here. Not only did the person who had imagined another legally effective content not want to give 'a declaration of this content', but also the person who did not want to give any legally effective declaration at all. It is not to be concluded from § 118 of the BGB that the absence of consciousness of making a declaration (or the lack of any business intention) would always lead to invalidity without avoidance. If the declarant, as assumed in § 118 of the BGB, consciously intended the declaration not to be binding, in the expectation that this would also be recognised, the invalidity corresponds to his intention. The choice of allowing what is declared to be valid against him *and in his favour* or avoiding it under § 119 of the BGB does not need to be available to him. A declaration without the consciousness that it will be understood as legally effective is not comparable with that. It is very much nearer to the declaration which is mistaken but which is intended to be legally effective. A person who declares that he will buy, but imagines that he is selling, finds himself in quite a similar position to a person who gives the usual indications for a purchase but does not think of purchase. In both cases it seems appropriate to leave the declarant the choice of whether he wants to avoid, in accordance with § 119 para 1 of the BGB, and have to compensate the interest of anyone trusting on the validity of the declaration in accordance with § 122 of the BGB or if he wants to stand by his declaration, and receive a possible consideration in return, which could put him in a better position than his one-sided duty to compensate for the damage caused by the trust put in the declaration.

This possibility of choice also dispels the counter argument that without consciousness of making a declaration no personal autonomous self-determined structuring can be present and that this cannot be replaced by personal responsibility alone. The law, as to declarations of will, does not only build on the right of self-determination of the possessor of rights; it protects in §§ 119 and 157 of the BGB the trust of the recipient of the declaration and protection from risks in the affairs of life in that it also binds the declarant to legal consequences which were not imagined and (which has to be considered as equivalent) not consciously made effective. The power of the declarant, who in both cases did not desire the legal consequences which were actually expressed in his declaration, to annul these consequences retrospectively by avoidance (§ 142 para 1 of the BGB) or to allow them to remain valid takes sufficient account of the concept of self-determination (as also in Soergel/Hefermehl *loc cit*).

Eine Willenserklärung liegt bei fehlendem Erklärungsbewußtsein allerdings nur dann vor, wenn sie als solche dem Erklärenden zugerechnet werden kann. Das setzt voraus, daß dieser bei Anwendung der im Verkehr erforderlichen Sorgfalt hätte erkennen und vermeiden können, daß seine Erklärung oder sein Verhalten vom Empfänger nach Treu und Glauben und mit Rücksicht auf die Verkehrssitte als Willenerklärung aufgefaßt werden durfte (so neben Bydlinski und Kramer insbesondere Larenz, Gudian und Brox jeweils aaO; vgl. auch BGHZ 21, 102, 106; Palandt/Heinrichs, BGB, 43. Aufl. vor § 116 Anm. 4 b).

2 Die Revision rügt von diesem Rechtsstandpunkt aus weiter, das Berufungsgericht habe keine Feststellungen getroffen, aus denen sich ergebe, daß die Vertreter der Beklagten die Deutung ihres Verhaltens als Willenserklärung bei pflichtgemäßer Sorgfalt hätten erkennen können. Diese Rüge greift nicht durch. Angesichts des Wortlauts des von den Vertretern der Beklagten verfaßten Schreibens vom 8. September 1981, mit dem sie erstmals Verbindung zur Klägerin aufnahmen, bedurfte es keine Begründung durch den Tatrichter, daß sich den Repräsentanten der Beklagten die Erkenntnis hätte aufdrängen müssen, der Empfänger werde ihr Schreiben als verbindliches Angebot auf Abschluß eines Bürgschaftsvertrags verstehen; denn in der den Formerfordernissen des § 766 BGB genügenden Erklärung sind Gläubiger und Schuldner bezeichnet, die Verbindlichkeiten, die verbürgt werden sollen, ausreichend bestimmt und der Verbürgungswille objectiv zum Ausdruck gebracht. Jedenfalls eine Sparkasse oder Bank die eine solche Erklärung einem Gläubiger ihres Kunden zugehen läßt, muß bei Anwendung der im Kreditgewerbe erforderlichen Sorgfalt damit rechnen, daß der Empfänger die Erklärung entsprechend ihrem Inhalt als Bürgschaftsverpflichtung auffassen werde. Dem steht nicht entgegen, daß die Beklagte, wie die Revision in diesem Zusammenhang geltend macht, bei Bürgschaftsübernahme entsprechend der Verkehrsitte einen Vordruck verwende. Denn auch den vertretungsberechtigten Leitern einer Zweigstelle der Beklagten Sparkasse muß bekannt sein, daß Willenserklärungen bindend nicht nur in Formularen abgegeben werden können, zumal ein Kaufmann (§ 1 Abs. 2 Nr. 4 HGB) eine Bürgschaft auch formfrei übernehmen kann (§ 350 HGB).

II Die Entscheidung des Berufungsgerichts, daß die Beklagte ihre Erklärung vom 8. September 1981 nicht wirksam angefochten habe, läßt entgegen den Angriffen der Revision keinen Rechtsfehler erkennen.

A declaration of will is of course only present in cases of absence of consciousness of making the declaration if it can be attributed, as such, to the declarant. That assumes that this person, by application of the care necessary in the affairs of life, could have recognised that his declaration or his behaviour might have been understood as a declaration of will, according to good faith and having regard to business custom, and avoided this consequence (as in Bydlinski and Kramer, especially Larenz, Gudian and Brox, each *loc cit*; compare also BGHZ 21, 102, 106; Palandt/Heinrichs BGB, 43rd edn, preceding § 116 note 4 b).

2 The appeal in law further argues from this legal standpoint that the appeal court made no findings from which it would follow that the representatives of the defendant could, by exercising the care they were under a duty to show, have recognised the interpretation of their behaviour as a declaration of will. This criticism is not justified. In the light of the wording of the letter of 8 September 1981 composed by the representatives of the defendant, by which it made contact with the plaintiff for the first time, no grounds were needed from the judge of fact for saying the representatives of the defendant would have been compelled to recognise that the recipient would understand their letter as a binding offer for the conclusion of a contract for the granting of security. This is because in the declaration, which satisfies the formal requirements of § 766 of the BGB, the creditor and debtor are described, the obligations which are to be guaranteed are sufficiently determined and the intention to guarantee expressed objectively. In any case a savings bank or bank which allows such a declaration to reach a creditor of its customer must, by applying the care necessary in credit business, take into account that the recipient will understand the declaration, according to its content, as a security obligation. The fact that the defendant, as is claimed by the appeal in this connection, uses, in accordance with business custom, a form on the take up of a security, does not militate against this. It must be known, even to the managers of a branch of the defendant savings bank who have authority to represent it, that declarations of will can be given in a binding manner otherwise than by forms, and in particular a businessman (§ 1 para 2 no 4 of the HGB) can also take over a security without a form (§ 350 of the HGB).

II The decision of the appeal court, that the defendant has not effectively avoided its declaration of 8 September 1981, reveals, contrary to the arguments in the appeal in law, no mistake in law.

1 Das Schreiben der Beklagten vom 24. September 1981 erfüllt nicht die Voraussetzungen einer Anfechtungserklärung im Sinne des § 143 Abs. 1 BGB. Anfechtungserklärung ist jede Willenserklärung, die unzweideutig erkennen läßt, daß das Rechtsgeschäft rückwirkend beseitigt werden soll. Es bedarf dabei nicht des ausdrücklichen Gebrauchs des Wortes 'anfechten'. Es kann je nach den Umständen durchaus genügen, wenn eine nach dem objectiven Erklärungswert der Willensäußerung übernommene Verpflichtung bestritten oder nicht anerkannt oder wenn ihr widersprochen wird. In jedem Fall ist aber erforderlich, daß sich *unzweideutig* der Wille ergibt, das Geschäft gerade *wegen des Willensmangels* nicht bestehenlassen zu wollen (BGH Urteile vom 28. September 1954 - I ZR 180/52 = LM BGB § 119 Nr. 5; vom 7. Oktober 1971 – VII ZR 177/69 = DB 1971, 2302; vom 26. Juni 1975 – II ZR 35/74 = DB 1975, 2075 jeweils mit Nachweisen).

Davon ausgehend hebt das Berufungsgericht zutreffend hervor, daß das Schreiben vom 24. September 1981 diesen Anforderungen nicht genügt, weil es keinerlei Hinweis auf einen Willensmangel enthalte. Unter Willensmangel versteht der Tatrichter zu Recht auch das Fehlen des Erklärungsbewußtseins. Die Revision meint dagegen, in dem Sonderfall, daß eine ohne Erklärungsbewußtsein vorgenommene Handlung angefochten werden solle, sei das Schreiben vom 24. September 1981 als Anfechtungserklärung ausreichend. Dem ist jedoch nicht so. Auch wenn der aus einer Äußerung in Anspruch Genommene ohne Erklärungsbewußtsein gehandelt hat, muß in der Anfechtung ein wie auch immer umschriebener Willensmangel wie in den anderen Fällen der Anfechtung wegen Irrtums erkennbar werden; denn der redlicher Erklärungsempfänger hat eine schutzwürdiges Interesse daran, unverzüglich zu erfahren, ob der Gegner seine Erklärung wegen eines Willensmangels rückwirkend beseitigen will (vgl. dazu Bylinski JZ 1975, 1, 5). Daß das Schreiben der Beklagten vom 24. September 1981 mehr als die bloße Verneinung der Übernahme der Bürgschaft zum Ausdruck gebracht habe, macht auch die Revision nicht geltend.

2 Das Berufungsgericht nimmt an, daß die Beklagte mit ihrem Schreiben vom 6. Oktober 1981 verspätet, nämlich nicht ohne schuldhaftes Zögern angefochten habe (§ 121 Abs. 1 BGB). Dies sei erst 15 Tage nach Kenntnis des Anfechtungsgrundes geschehen. Zwar sei in aller Regel dem Irrenden eine angemessene Überlegungsfrist zuzugestehen. Sie diene der vernünftigen Überlegung der Frage, ob der Irrende wirklich anfechten oder es bei der trotz Irrtums abgegebenen Erklärung bewenden lassen wolle. Da aber die Beklagte auf keinen Fall an der Bürgschaftsverpflichtung habe festhalten wollen, habe sie auch keine längere Frist zur Überlegung dafür gebraucht, ob sie anfechten wolle oder nicht. Mithin habe die Beklagte gezögert. Dieses Zögern sei zumindest fahrlässig gewesen. Die Beklagte habe ein nicht Verschulden nicht dargelegt und nicht bewiesen. Ihr Antwortschreiben vom 24. September 1981 zeige, daß ihre Überlegungen bis zu diesem Zeitpunkt abgeschlossen gewesen seien.

1 The letter of the defendant of 24 September 1981 does not fulfil the requirements of an avoidance declaration in the sense of § 143 para 1 of the BGB. An avoidance declaration is any declaration of will which unambiguously makes known that the legal transaction is to be set aside retrospectively. The express use of the word 'avoid' is not necessary here. It can, according to the circumstances, be completely sufficient, if an obligation which has, according to the objective value of the expression of will, been taken up is disputed, or not acknowledged, or if it is contradicted. But in each case it is necessary that the intention is unambiguously revealed that the transaction is not intended to remain in existence because of the lack of intention (BGH judgments of 28 September 1954 – I ZR 180/52 = LM BGB § 119 no 5; of 7 October 1971 – VII ZR 177/69 = DB 1971, 2302; of 26 June 1975 – II ZR 35/74 = DB 1975, 2075 each with references).

Proceeding from here, the appeal court pertinently emphasises that the letter of 24 September 1981 does not satisfy these requirements because it contains no kind of reference to a lack of intention. The judge of fact correctly understood lack of intention as including the absence of the consciousness of making a declaration. The appeal in law, on the other hand, takes the view that, in the special case of avoiding a transaction undertaken without the consciousness of making a declaration, the letter of 24 September 1981 would be sufficient as a declaration of avoidance. That is, however, not so. Even when the person who is the subject of a claim based on a statement has acted without the consciousness of making a declaration, a lack of intention, described as usual, must, as in other cases of avoidance for mistake, be recognisable in the avoidance; because the honest recipient of the declaration of will has an interest deserving protection in knowing, without delay, whether the opposite party wants to set aside his declaration retrospectively because of a lack of intention (compare to this Bydlinski JZ 1975 1, 5). The appeal in law does not assert that the letter of the defendant of 24 September 1981 did more than express a bare denial of the take up of the security.

2 The appeal court accepts that the defendant, by its letter of 6 October 1981, belatedly, that is to say not without culpable delay, effected avoidance (§ 121 para 1 of the BGB). This first occurred 15 days after knowledge of the ground for avoidance. Certainly as a rule an appropriate period for consideration is to be granted to the mistaken party. It assists intelligent consideration of the question of whether the mistaken party really wants to avoid or to be content with the declaration which has been given in spite of the error. But as the defendant did not wish, under any circumstances, to adhere to the security obligation, it did not need a longer period for consideration of whether it wanted to avoid or not. Therefore, the defendant delayed. This delay was at least negligent. The defendant has neither explained nor proved a defence. Its answering letter of 24 September 1981 shows that its considerations up to this point in time had been concluded.

Demgegenüber wendet die Revision ein, der Beklagten sei eine längere Überlegungsfrist als vom Berufungsgericht zugestanden einzuräumen, weil sie sich nicht bewußt gewesen sei, gegenüber der Klägerin eine Bürgschaftsverpflichtung abgegeben zu haben. Es sei deshalb für sie erforderlich gewesen die tatsächliche und rechtliche Lage eingehend zu prüfen. Danach sei die Anfechtung im Schreiben vom 6. Oktober 1981 noch rechtzeitig.

Die Rüge ist unbegründet. Die Beklagte hat in der Berufungsbegründung selbst vorgetragen, den Anfechtungsgrund durch das am 21. September 1981 eingegangene Schreiben der Klägerin vom 17. September 1981 erkannt zu haben. Dementsprechend geht auch die Revision davon aus, daß die Beklagte durch dieses Schreiben Kenntnis vom Anfechtungsgrund erlangt, nämlich erfahren hat, daß entgegen ihrer Vorstellung die Klägerin das Schreiben vom 8. September 1981 als Bürgschaftserklärung aufgefaßt hatte und so auch verstehen durfte. Dann ist kein Grund ersichtlich, weshalb die Beklagte, die ihre Überlegungen spätestens bei der Abfassung der Antwort vom 24. September 1981 abgeschlossen hatte, mit der Absendung der Anfechtungserklärung bis 6. Oktober 1981 zugewartet hat. Unter diesen Umständen kann der Vorwurf des Tatrichters, die Beklagte habe fahrlässig gezögert, nicht beanstandet werden. Er hat die Anforderungen an eine unverzügliche Anfechtung nicht überspannt.

(1) Mistake

§ 119 [Anfechtbarkeit wegen Irrtums] (1) Wer bei der Abgabe einer Willenserklärung über deren Inhalt im Irrtume war oder eine Erklärung dieses Inhalts überhaupt nicht abgeben wollte, kann die Erklärung anfechten, wenn anzunehmen ist, daß er sie bei Kenntnis der Sachlage und bei verständiger Würdigung des Falles nicht abgegeben haben würde.

(2) Als Irrtum über den Inhalt der Erklärung gilt auch der Irrtum über solche Eigenschaften der Person oder der Sache, die im Verkehr als wesentlich angesehen werden.

Over against this, the appeal in law raises the objection that the defendant should have been granted a longer time for consideration than was allowed by the appeal court, because it had not been conscious of having entered into a security obligation in favour of the plaintiff. It was therefore necessary for it to examine thoroughly the factual and legal situation. Therefore, the avoidance in the letter of 6 October 1981 is in time.

The criticism is unfounded. The defendant has itself stated in the grounds of appeal that it recognised the ground for avoidance from the plaintiff's letter of 17 September 1981, which arrived on 21 September 1981. Accordingly, the appeal proceeds on the basis that the defendant, through this letter, obtained knowledge of the ground for avoidance, that is to say learnt that, contrary to its impression, the plaintiff had understood the letter of 8 September 1981 as a declaration of security and it was permissible to understand it in this way. There is then no apparent ground on account of which the defendant, which had concluded its considerations at the latest on composition of the answer of 24 September 1981, waited till the 6 October 1981 for the dispatching of the declaration of avoidance. Under these circumstances the accusation of the judge of fact that the defendant negligently delayed cannot be objected to. He did not extend the requirements of a prompt avoidance too far.

(1) Mistake

§ 119 [Voidability as a result of mistake] (1) A person who was, on the making of a declaration of will, mistaken about the contents or who did not want to give a declaration with these contents at all can avoid the declaration if it is to be supposed that he would not have made it, if he had known the circumstances and had had a rational appreciation of the case.

See the internet auction case, Chapter Five, p 333.

(2) A mistake about such characteristics of the person or thing as are seen as material in the affairs of life also counts as a mistake about the contents of a declaration.

The mistakes referred to in § 119 II are those relating to the essential characteristics of the person or thing involved. A comparison can be drawn here with the requirements of Art 1110 of the French Civil Code. This may not be the case where the mistake is about the value, and it could not cover an external issue.

People who sign documents not knowing their contents are generally bound by them; but avoidance under § 119 I is possible if the document is not of a kind that could have been expected in the circumstances, eg, BGHZ 71, 262. Compare this with the English approach to *non est factum* in cases such as *Saunders v Anglia Building Society* [1970] 3 All ER 961.

THE LAND PURCHASE MISTAKE CASE
BGHZ 34, 32

BGHZ Band 34 S. 32

1 Der Käufer kann den Kaufvertrag vor dem Gefahrübergang auch dann wegen Irrtums nach § 119 Abs. 2 BGB anfechten, wenn er ausnahmsweise vor diesem Zeitpunkt zur Geltendmachung der Rechte nach §§ 459ff BGB befugt ist.

2 Es ist eine Frage der Willensauslegung, ob im einzelnen Fall in der Anfechtung wegen arglistiger Täuschung zugleich eine solche wegen Irrtums über eine verkehrswesentliche Eigenschaft im Sinne des § 119 Abs. 2 BGB zu erblicken ist.

3 Das Eigentum an einer Sache ist keine verkehrswesentliche Eigenschaft.

BGB §§ 119 Abs. 2, 123, 459ff

V. Zivilsenat. Urt. vom 14. Dezember 1960 i.S. P. (Bekl.) w. D. (Kl.) V ZR 40/60.

I Landgericht Paderborn

II Oberlandesgericht Hamm

Der Kläger verkaufte in notarieller Urkunde vom 27. November 1957 ein Grundstück in V. an die Beklagte. Im Zeitpunkt des Kaufabschlusses stand des Grundstück noch im Miteigentum je zur Hälfte des Klägers und seiner Ehefrau. Diese hat am 13. Dezember 1957 ihren Miteigentumsanteil an den Kläger aufgelassen. Dessen Eintragung im Grundbuch ist am 7. Januar 1958 erfolgt.

Die Beklagte hat u. a.:

1 mit Schreiben vom 13. Dezember 1957 Wandlung verlangt mit der Begründung, das verkaufte Grundstück liege im Bereich einer bereits geplanten Umgehungsstraße;

2 mit Schreiben vom 23. Dezember 1957 aus diesem Grunde ferner den Kaufvertrag wegen arglistiger Täuschung angefochten und zugleich mit Rücksicht darauf, daß der Kläger nur Miteigentümer des Grundstücks war, alle mit der Veräußerung zusammenhängenden Willenserklärungen widerrufen.

Die auf Zahlung eines Teils des Kaufpreises gerichtete Klage hatte in den Vorinstanzen Erfolg.

Die Revision der Beklagten führte zur Aufhebung des Berufungsurteils und zur Zurückweisung.

THE LAND PURCHASE MISTAKE CASE

This case concerns the availability of the grounds of mistake and deceit for avoiding a contract. It related to a sale of land, however, so further remedies came into consideration from the part of the Civil Code which deals with property sales.

BGHZ Volume 34 p 32

1 The purchaser can avoid a purchase contract for mistake in accordance with § 119 para 2 of the BGB before the passing of risk even if exceptionally he is authorised before this time to claim rights under §§ 459ff of the BGB.

2 It is a question of interpretation of intention whether in an individual case there can be seen in an avoidance for deceit at the same time an avoidance for mistake about a characteristic of importance in the affairs of life in the sense of § 119 para 2 of the BGB.

3 Ownership of an item of property is not a characteristic of importance in the affairs of life.

BGB §§ 119 para 2, 123, 459ff and onwards

Vth Civil Senate judgment of 14. December 1960 in the case of P (defendant) v D (claimant) – V ZR 40/60.

I State Court of Paderborn

II Upper State Court of Hamm

The claimant sold a piece of land in V to the defendant by a notarial deed of the 27 November 1957. At the point in time of the conclusion of the purchase the piece of land was still in the joint ownership (one half each) of the claimant and his wife. The latter transferred her share in the joint ownership to the claimant on the 13 December 1957. The entry of this in the Land Register occurred on the 7 January 1958.

The defendant has (amongst other things):

1 demanded cancellation of the sale contract by a letter of the 13 December 1957, on the basis that the piece of land sold lies in the path of a by-pass which had already been planned;

2 also avoided the purchase contract for fraudulent deception by a letter of the 23 December 1957 on this ground and, at the same time, having regard to the fact that the claimant was only the co-owner of the piece of land, revoked all declarations of intention connected with the disposal.

The claim for payment of part of the purchase price was successful at the previous instances.

The appeal in law by the defendant led to quashing of the judgment of the appeal court and reference back.

Aus den Gründen:

1 Die Revision wendet sich in erster Linie gegen die Ausführungen des Berufungsgerichts über die geplante Umgehungsstraße, durch die nach der Auskunft der Amtsverwaltung V. vom 20. Januar 1959 das ganze Grundstück in Anspruch genommen wird.

(a) Gegenüber der Auffassung des Berufungsgerichts, der von der Beklagten hinsichtlich der geplanten Umgehungsstraße geltend gemachte Wandlungsanspruch sei nicht begründet, weil nach § 1 des Kaufvertrags Gewährleistungsansprüche ausgeschlossen seien und der Kläger den Mangel nicht arglistig verschwiegen habe, macht die Revision dem Berufungsgericht zum Vorwurf, es habe sich dabei nicht mit dem Wortlaut des Vertrags auseinandergesetzt, nach dem der Verzicht der Beklagten auf Gewährleistungsansprüche sich nur auf 'Güte, Grenzen und Beschaffenheit' erstreckt habe; hierunter falle aber nicht der durch die Umgehungsstraße bedingte Mangel. Damit kann die Revision keinen Erfolg haben. Das Berufungsgericht hat den Wortlaut der vereinbarten Klausel über den Gewährleistungsausschluß im Tatbestand seines Urteils aufgeführt und die Klausel dahin ausgelegt, daß damit alle Gewährleistungsansprüche, also auch der hinsichtlich der Umgehungsstraße ausgeschlossen sein sollten. Mit dem Wortlaut der Klausel ist dies nicht unvereinbar.

(b) Soweit das Berufungsgericht die auf die geplante Umgehungsstraße gestützte Anfechtung des Kaufvertrags wegen arglistiger Täuschung nicht für begründet hält, greift die Revision nicht die Verneinung einer arglistigen Täuschung durch den Kläger, sondern lediglich die Ablehnung der Umdeutung der erklärten Anfechtung wegen arglistiger Täuschung in eine solche wegen Irrtums über eine verkehrswesentliche Eigenschaft im Sinne des § 119 Abs. 2 BGB an.

Reasons:

1 The appeal in law is first directed against the findings of the appeal court about the planned by-pass, by which the whole piece of land is claimed, according to information of the 20 January 1959 from the administrative authority (*Amtsverwaltung* at V).

(a) Contrary to the view of the appeal court (that the claim raised by the defendant to cancellation of the sale contract in respect of the planned by-pass was not well founded, because claims to guarantees were excluded according to § 1 of the purchase contract and the claimant was not deceitfully silent about the defect) the appeal in law accuses the appeal court of not having looked critically at the wording of the contract, according to which the defendant's renunciation of guarantee claims only extended to 'quality, boundaries and composition'; but the defect relating to the by-pass did not come under this. The appeal in law cannot be successful here. The appeal court quoted the wording of the agreed clause about the exclusion of a guarantee in the text of its judgment and interpreted the clause to the effect that all guarantee claims (and thus also those in relation to the by-pass) should thereby be excluded. This is not irreconcilable with the wording of the clause.

(b) Insofar as the appeal court holds the avoidance of the purchase contract for fraudulent deception on the basis of the planned by-pass not to be well founded, the appeal in law does not challenge the denial of fraudulent deception by the claimant, but merely the refusal of conversion of the avoidance declared for fraudulent deception into an avoidance for mistake about a characteristic of significance in the affairs of life in the sense of § 119 para 2 of the BGB.

Vor der Entscheidung hierüber ist die Prüfung der Frage angebracht, ob diese Irrtumsanfechtung nicht wegen des von der Beklagten geltend gemachten Wandlungsanspruchs unbeachtlich wäre. Auszugehen ist dabei von der vom Bundesgerichtshof bestätigten und auch im Schrifttum weitgehend gebilligten Rechtsprechung des Reichgerichts, nach der die Vorschriften der §§ 459ff. BGB als Sondervorschriften die Anwendung des § 119 Abs. 2 BGB ausschließen (RGZ 61, 171, 175; 135, 339, 340; 138, 354, 356; BGHZ 16, 54, 57; LM § 459 BGB Nr. 4; BGB-RGRK, 11. Aufl., § 459 Anm. 36; Staudinger, BGB, 11. Aufl., § 459 Vorbem. 16; Palandt, BGB, 19. Aufl., § 459 Vorbem. 2 d; Erman, BGB, 2. Aufl., § 459 Anm. 5 a; Enneccerus/Lehmann, Schuldrecht 15. Bearb. § 112 III 2 S. 456). Begründet wird diese Auffassung damit, der mit den Vorschriften über die Wandlung erstrebte, insbesondere in den kurzen Verjährungsfristen des § 477 BGB zum Ausdruck kommende Zweck, im Interesse der im Verkehr erforderlichen Sicherheit eine glatte Abwicklung der Kaufgeschäfte in verhältnismäßig kurzer Zeit zu ermöglichen, würde nicht erreicht werden, wenn wegen eines Mangels des Kaufgegenstandes im Sinne der §§ 459ff BGB, der zugleich eine verkehrswesentliche Eigenschaft im Sinne des § 119 Abs. 2 BGB darstellt, die Anfechtung nach dieser Vorschrift gegeben wäre. Die aufgeführte Rechtsprechung gilt allerdings nur, wenn und soweit nach den Sonderbestimmungen der §§ 459ff BGB die Gewährschaftshaftung wegen Sachmangels dem Käufer Schutz gewährt (RGZ 138, 354, 356), wenn also die Gewährleistungsansprüche bereits entstanden sind. Dies ist aber nach § 459 BGB erst mit dem Gefahrübergang auf den Käufer und damit nach § 446 BGB erst dann der Fall, wenn die Übergabe der verkauften Sache, bei Grundstücken die Eintragung des Käufers als Eigentümer im Grundbuch, wenn diese der Übergabe vorausgeht, erfolgt ist. Es wird deshalb mit Recht die Ansicht vertreten, daß gegen die Anwendbarkeit des § 119 Abs. 2 BGB in der Zeit vor dem Gefahrübergang kein Hindernis besteht.

Before a decision on this issue, it is appropriate to examine the question of whether this avoidance for mistake would not be irrelevant because of the claim for cancellation raised by the defendant. In this connection, one must proceed on the basis of the case law of the Reich High Court confirmed by the Federal Supreme Court and also extensively approved in the academic literature according to which the provisions of §§ 459ff of the BGB as special provisions exclude the application of § 119 para 2 of the BGB (RGZ 61, 171, 175; 135, 339, 340; 138, 354, 356; BGHZ 16, 54, 57; LM § 459 BGB no 4; BGB-RGRK, 11th edn, § 459 note 36; Staudinger, BGB, 11th edn, § 459 introductory note 16; Palandt, BGB, 19th edn, § 459 introductory note 2 d; Erman, BGB, 2nd edn, § 459 note 5 a; Enneccerus/Lehmann, Schuldrecht, 15th Revision, § 112 III 2, p 456). This view is based on the fact that the purpose sought by the provisions about cancellation, expressed in particular in the short limitation periods of § 477 of the BGB, of enabling smooth execution of purchase transactions in a relatively short time in the interest of the certainty necessary in the affairs of life, would not be attained if because of a defect in the subject matter of the purchase in the sense of §§ 459ff and onwards of the BGB which at the same time represented a characteristic which is of significance in the affairs of life in the sense of § 119 para 2 of the BGB, the avoidance would be given in accordance with this provision. The case law quoted admittedly only applies if and insofar as, according to the special provisions of §§ 459ff of the BGB, the guarantee liability because of a defect in the thing affords protection for the purchaser (RGZ 138, 354, 356), ie, if the claims to guarantee have already arisen. But according to §§ 459 and onwards of the BGB this is only the case with the transfer of risk to the purchaser and therefore according to § 446 of the BGB when the handing over of the object sold occurs and with pieces of land, the entry of the purchaser as owner in the Land Register if this precedes the handing over. The view is therefore correctly taken that no obstacle exists to the applicability of § 119 para 2 of the BGB in the period before the passing of risk.

Da die in dem Kaufvertrag zwischen den Parteien für den 15. Januar 1958 vereinbarte Übergabe des verkauften Grundstücks an die Beklagte noch nicht erfolgt und diese auch noch nicht als Eigentümerin im Grundbuch eingetragen ist, würde somit der Zulässigkeit einer von der Beklagten wegen der geplanten Umgehungsstraße erklärten Anfechtung wegen Irrtums nach § 119 Abs. 2 BGB nichts im Wege stehen. Die Frage des Ausschlusses dieser Anfechtung stellt sich hier aber deshalb, weil nach der in der Rechtsprechung und im Schriftum vertretenen Auffassung, welcher der Senat beitritt, der Käufer ausnahmsweise auch schon vor dem Gefahrübergang berechtigt ist, die Gewährleistungsansprüche geltend zu machen, nämlich dann, wenn der Mangel der Sache unbehebbar oder die zugesicherte Eigenschaft der Sache nicht mehr zu verschaffen ist oder wenn der Verkäufer die Behebung bzw. Verschaffung endgültig abgelehnt hat (RG JW 1912, 461 = SeuffArch 67 Nr. 198; RG Nachschlagewerk § 459 BGB Nr. 151; OLG Hamburg HEZ 1, 271; BGB RGRK aaO § 459 Anm. 12; Staudinger aaO § 459 Anm. 6; Palandt aaO § 459 Anm. 1; Erman aaO § 459 Anm. 4; Enneccerus/Lehmann aaO § 108 II 1 a S. 434). Diese Rechtsprechung stellt mit Recht darauf ab, daß es in den aufgeführten Ausnahmefällen mit Treu und Glauben nicht zu vereinbaren wäre, wenn dem Käufer zugemutet würde, die verkaufte Sache nur deshalb anzunehmen, um die im Gesetz für die Gewährleistungsansprüche aufgestellte Voraussetzung des Gefahrübergangs zu schaffen, und sie nach dann erklärter Wandlung sofort wieder an den Verkäufer zurückzugeben. Ein Ausnahmefall in dem aufgeführten Sinn liegt hier vor, da der Kläger die Durchführung der geplanten Umgehungsstraße nicht verhindern und damit den hierdurch bedingten Mangel des verkauften Grundstücks nicht beheben kann. Es kommt deshalb auf die Frage an, ob in den Fällen, in denen ausnahmsweise die Gewährleistungsansprüche schon vor dem Gefahrübergang geltend gemacht werden können, im gleichen Umfang nicht auch die Anfechtung wegen Irrtums über eine verkehrswesentliche Eigenschaft der verkauften Sache nach § 119 Abs. 2 BGB als ausgeschlossen anzusehen ist.

As the handing over (agreed in the purchase contract between the parties for the 15 January 1958) to the defendant of the piece of land which has been sold has not yet ensued and she has also not yet been registered as owner in the Land Register, nothing would therefore stand in the way of the permissibility of an avoidance for mistake in accordance with § 119 para 2 of the BGB by the defendant because of the planned by-pass. The question of exclusion of this avoidance presents itself here however because according to the view taken in the case law and in the literature, to which the Senate accedes, the purchaser is exceptionally entitled even before the passing of the risk to raise guarantee claims, namely when the defect in the thing is not removable, or when the promised characteristic of the thing can no longer be provided, or if the seller has finally refused the removal or the provision (RG JW 1912, 461 = SeuffArch 67 no 198; RG Reference Work § 459 BGB no 151; OLG Hamburg HEZ 1, 271; BGB RGRK, *loc cit*, § 459 no 12; Staudinger, *loc cit*, § 459 note 6; Palandt, *loc cit*, § 459 note 1; Erman, *loc cit*, § 459 note 4; Enneccerus/Lehmann, *loc cit*, § 108 II 1 a, p 434). This case law correctly takes into account that it would not be reconcilable with good faith in the exceptional cases quoted, if it would be expected of the purchaser only to accept the thing sold in order to create the prerequisite of passing of the risk put forward in the law for guarantee claims and to give it back again immediately to the seller after the then declared cancellation. An exceptional case in the sense quoted is present here as the claimant cannot prevent the implementation of the planned by-pass and therefore cannot remove the defect relating to this in the piece of land sold. It is therefore a question of whether in the cases in which exceptionally the guarantee claims can be raised before the passing of the risk, avoidance for mistake about a characteristic of the thing sold which is of significance in the affairs of life in accordance with § 119 para 2 of the BGB is not also to be regarded as excluded to the same extent.

Diese Frage ist, soweit ersichtlich, in der Rechtsprechung bisher noch nicht erörtert worden. Im Schriftum wird zu ihr nur vereinzelt Stellung genommen. Von Erman (aaO § 459 Anm. 5) wird, allerdings ohne nähere Begründung, die Ansicht vertreten, dem Käufer ständen die Rechte auf Grund der allgemeinen Vorschriften, und damit auch das Recht der Anfechtung wegen Irrtums nach § 119 Abs. 2 BGB, vor dem Gefahrübergang auch dann zu, wenn er ausnahmsweise vor diesem Zeitpunkt zur Geltendmachung der Rechte nach Maßgabe der §§ 459ff BGB befugt sei. Nach Staudinger (aaO § 459 Vorbem. 9) müssen, wenn ausnahmsweise die Sachmängelrechte schon vor dem Gefahrübergang geltend gemacht werden können, z. B. bei Unbehebbarkeit des Mangels, mit dieser ihrer Entstehung für andere Rechtsbehelfe die Grundsätze für die Zeit nach dem Entstehen der Mängelgewährrechte, also die Grundsätze für die Zeit nach dem Gefahrübergang gelten, weil die Beschränkungen der anderen Rechtsbehelfe sich ja gerade aus den bestehenden Gewährleistungsrechten ergäben; hieraus wird gefolgert, daß, wenn die Gewährleistungsansprüche schon vor dem Gefahrübergang geltend gemacht werden können, auch schon vor diesem das Anfechtungsrecht nach § 119 Abs. 2 BGB ausgeschlossen ist (Staudinger aaO § 459 Vorbem. 16 a). Bei Enneccerus/Lehmann (aaO § 112 III 2 S. 457) wird zu der hier zu entscheidenden Frage dahin Stellung genommen, daß bei unbehebbaren Mängeln die Gewährleistungsansprüche zwar bereits vor dem Gefahrübergang entstanden seien, die Gründe, aus denen die Absicht der Verdrängung der Irrtumsanfechtung gefolgert werde, jedoch voraussetzen dürften, daß die Gewährleistungsansprüche als verjährbare entstanden seien. Aus dieser Formulierung könnte zwar, wenn man sie für sich allein betrachtet, entnommen werden, daß eine Irrtumsanfechtung ausgeschlossen ist, weil nach § 477 BGB der Lauf der Verjährungsfristen erst vom Zeitpunkt der Ablieferung (bei beweglichen Sachen) und der Übergabe (bei Grundstücken) beginnt. Unter Berücksichtungung der ihr unmittelbar vorausgehenden Darlegungen wird die Formulierung aber mit Staudinger (aaO § 459 Vorbem. 16 a) dahin verstanden werden müssen, daß die Irrtumsanfechtung schon vor dem Gefahrübergang zwar nicht ausgeschlossen ist, weil vor diesem schon die Gewährleistungsansprüche entstanden sind, daß aber in diesem Falle auch der Lauf der Verjährungsfristen des § 477 BGB entsprechend früher beginnt. Von Flume (Eigenschaftsirrtum und Kauf 1948 S. 37ff., 134ff.) wird schließlich die Ansicht vertreten, daß die Rechte des Käufers in den §§ 459ff. BGB ausschließlich geregelt seien und deshalb eine Irrtumsanfechtung nach § 119 Abs. 2 BGB auf jeden Fall und damit auch schon vor dem Gefahrübergang ausgeschlossen sei.

So far as is evident, this question has not yet been discussed in the case law. It is only occasionally commented on in the academic literature. The view is taken by Erman (*loc cit*, § 459 note 5), admittedly without a precise basis, that the purchaser would also be entitled to the rights on the basis of the general provisions and therefore also the right to avoidance for mistake under § 119 para 2 of the BGB before the passing of the risk if exceptionally he was authorised before this point in time to claim the rights under § 459ff and onwards of the BGB. According to Staudinger (*loc cit*, § 459 introductory note 9) if exceptionally the rights in respect of defects in the thing can be claimed before the passing of the risk (eg, if the defect is not removable) with their coming into existence for other legal remedies the principles for the period after the coming into existence of the defects guarantee rights (ie, the principles for the period after the passing of the risk) must apply, because the limitations of the other legal remedies would arise precisely from the existing guarantee rights; from this it is concluded that if the guarantee claims can be claimed before the passing of the risk, the right of avoidance under § 119 para 2 of the BGB is also excluded before this (Staudinger, *loc cit*, § 459 introductory note 16 a). In Enneccerus/Lehmann (*loc cit*, § 112 III 2, p 457) the position is taken in relation to the question to be decided here that, with defects that cannot be removed, the guarantee claims had certainly arisen before the passing of the risk, but the grounds on which the intention to displace avoidance for mistake is deduced might presuppose that the guarantee claims have arisen as time limited. From this formulation it could certainly be deduced, if one considered it on its own, that avoidance for mistake is excluded because according to § 477 of the BGB the running of the limitation periods starts from the point in time of the delivery (for moveable things) and handing over (for pieces of land). Having regard to the explanations immediately preceding it, the formulation in Staudinger (*loc cit*, § 459 introductory note 16 a) must however be understood to the effect that avoidance for mistake is certainly not excluded before the passing of the risk because the guarantee claims have arisen before this, but that in this case the running of the limitation periods in § 477 of the BGB also begins correspondingly sooner. Finally, the view is taken by Flume (*Mistake as to Characteristic and Purchase*, 1948, pp 37ff and onwards and 134ff and onwards) that the rights of the purchaser were exclusively regulated in §§ 459ff and onwards of the BGB and therefore an avoidance for mistake under § 119 para 2 of the BGB was excluded in every case and therefore also before the passing of the risk.

Aus dieser letzteren Ansicht kann für die hier zu entscheidende Frage deshalb nichts entnommen werden, weil sie auf der Ablehnung der vom Bundesgerichtshof bestätigten Rechtsprechung des Reichgerichts beruht, daß die Bestimmungen der §§ 459ff. BGB das Anfechtungsrecht nach § 119 Abs. 2 BGB erst vom Zeitpunkt des Gefahrübergangs ab und damit erst nach der Entstehung der Gewährleistungsansprüche ausschließen, und deshalb bei ihr das Problem, ob dieser Ausschluß auch dann gilt, wenn der Käufer die Gewährleistungsansprüche ausnahmsweise schon vor dem Gefahrübergang geltend machen kann, überhaupt nicht auftaucht.

Bei der Würdigung der übrigen Ansichten kommt der Senat mit Erman zum Ergebnis, daß dem Käufer die Rechte auf Grund der allgemeinen Vorschriften, und damit auch das Recht der Anfechtung wegen Irrtums nach § 119 Abs. 2 BGB, vor dem Gefahrübergang auch dann zustehen, wenn er ausnahmsweise vor diesem Zeitpunkt zur Geltendmachung der Rechte nach Maßgabe der §§ 459ff. BGB befugt ist. Dis Ansichten von Staudinger und Enneccerus/Lehmann, daß mit der Vorverlegung des für die Geltendmachung der Gewährleistungsansprüche maßgebenden Zeitpunkts auch der Zeitpunkt, von dem ab das Anfechtungsrecht nach § 119 Abs. 2 BGB ausgeschlossen ist, vorzuverlegen sei, und die weitere Ansicht von Enneccerus/Lehmann, daß dann auch die Verjährungsfristen des § 477 BGB entsprechend früher zu laufen beginnen müßten, sind zwar an sich folgerichtig. Hierbei ist jedoch übersehen, daß die dem Käufer eingeräumte Befugnis, die Gewährleistungsansprüche ausnahmsweise schon vor dem Gefahrübergang geltend zu machen, eine Vergünstigung für den Käufer darstellt, die aus dem Grundsatz von Treu und Glauben hergeleitet wird. Dieser Grundsatz erfordert es aber nicht, die aufgeführten weiteren Folgerungen zu ziehen. Denn wenn der Käufer mit der ihm eingeräumten Befugnis zur früheren Geltendmachung der Gewährleistungsansprüche entsprechend früher auch das Anfechtungsrecht nach § 119 Abs. 2 BGB verlieren würde, dann könnte von einer solchen Vergünstigung nicht mehr gesprochen werden. Hinzu kommt, daß der Käufer im Einzelfall auf die frühere Geltendmachung der Gewährleistungsansprüche etwa deshalb keinen Wert legt, weil er ein Interesse daran hat, daß ihm zunächst einmal die Kaufsache übergeben wird, damit er ihren Zustand feststellen und sich schlüssig werden kann, ob er einen Gewährleistungsanspruch überhaupt und, bejahendenfalls, welchen er geltend machen soll.

From this latter view nothing can therefore be deduced for the question which is to be decided here, because it is based on the rejection in the case law of the Reich High Court confirmed by the Federal Supreme Court of the idea that the provisions of §§ 459ff and onwards of the BGB exclude the right of avoidance under § 119 para 2 of the BGB only from the point in time of the passing of the risk onwards and therefore only after the coming into existence of the guarantee claims; and therefore in relation to it the problem does not arise at all of whether this exclusion also applies if the purchaser can exceptionally raise the guarantee claims before the passing of the risk.

In assessing the remaining views, the Senate comes with Ermann to the conclusion that the rights on the basis of the general provisions, and therefore also the right to avoidance for mistake under § 119 para 2 of the BGB before the passing of the risk, still belong to the purchaser even if exceptionally he is authorised before this point in time to enforce the rights under §§ 459 of the BGB. The views of Staudinger and Enneccerus/Lehmann, that with the bringing forward of the point in time which is decisive for the enforcement of the guarantee claims, the point in time is also to be brought forward from which the right of avoidance under § 119 para 2 of the BGB is excluded, and the further view of Enneccerus/Lehmann that then the limitation periods of § 477 of the BGB must also begin to run correspondingly earlier, are certainly in themselves consistent. This however overlooks the fact that the authority granted to the purchaser exceptionally to enforce the guarantee claims before the passing of the risk represents a benefitting of the purchaser which is derived from the principle of good faith. But this principle does not require the drawing of the further conclusions which are set out. This is because if the purchaser, with the authority granted to him for the earlier enforcement of guarantee claims, would at a correspondingly earlier point in time lose the right of avoidance under § 119 para 2 BGB as well, then there could no longer be any talk of such a benefitting. In addition to this, the purchaser in the individual case will perhaps place no value on the earlier enforcement of the guarantee claims, because he has an interest in the thing purchased being first of all handed over to him so that he can establish what its condition is and can make up his mind about whether he is to enforce a guarantee claim at all, and, if so, which.

Gerade in einem solchen Fall wäre es aber nicht gerechtfertigt, dem Kläger das Anfechtungsrecht nach § 119 Abs. 2 BGB schon von dem Zeitpunkt ab zu versagen, in dem er die Befugnis zur Geltendmachung der Gewährleistungsansprüche hat. Dafür, daß dem Käufer das Anfechtungsrecht vor dem Gefahrübergang nicht zu versagen ist, spricht ferner eine Erwägung praktischer Art. Es kommt nämlich in diesem Falle auf die insbesondere dann, wenn die Unbehebbarkeit des Mangels nicht ohne weiteres feststeht, zweifelhafte Frage nicht mehr an, von welchem Zeitpunkt vor dem Gefahrübergang ab das Anfechtungsrecht auszuschließen wäre. Schließlich wird dadurch, daß das Anfechtungsrecht des Käufers vor dem Gefahrübergang durch die vorher mögliche Geltendmachung der Gewährleistungsansprüche nicht ausgeschlossen ist, ein schutzwürdiges Interesse des Verkäufers, insbesondere sein Interesse an einer glatten Abwicklung des Kaufgeschäfts in verhältnismäßig kurzer Zeit nicht berührt. Denn wenn der Käufer von seinem Anfechtungsrecht bis zum Gefahrübergang keinen Gebrauch gemacht hat, hat er es nach der vom Bundesgerichtshof gebilligten Rechtsprechung des Reichsgerichts, daß die Vorschriften der §§ 459ff. BGB Sondervorschriften seien, für die Zukunft verloren.

Da somit die von der Beklagten wegen der geplanten Umgehungsstraße erklärte Anfechtung wegen Irrtums über eine verkehrswesentliche Eigenschaft im Sinne des § 119 Abs. 2 BGB nicht schon dadurch ausgeschlossen wäre, daß die Beklagte wegen dieses Mangels den Wandlungsanspruch geltend machen konnte und auch geltend gemacht hat, bedarf es noch der Stellungnahme zu der Meinung der Revision, die wegen der geplanten Umgehungsstraße erklärte Anfechtung wegen arglistige Täuschung sei in eine solche wegen Irrtums nach § 119 Abs. 2 BGB umzudeuten.

Das Berufungsgericht hat eine Umdeutung in diesem Sinne unter Bezugnahme auf RG JW 1925, 2752 abgelehnt. Bei der von der Revision erbetenen Nachprüfung dieser Auffassung des Berufungsgerichts ist davon auszugehen, daß beim Vorliegen der Anfechtungsgründe sowohl des § 119 als auch des § 123 BGB die auf die letztere Vorschrift gestützte Anfechtung zugleich die Behauptung eines Irrtums über diejenige Tatsache enthält, über die der Anfechtende getäuscht sein will, und deshalb eine Anfechtung wegen arglistiger Täuschung auch eine solche wegen Irrtums enthalten kann (LM § 119 BGB Nr. 5; RGZ 57, 358, 362; 100, 205, 207/208; BGB-RGRK aaO § 121 Anm. 2; Palandt, aaO § 123 Anm. 1 b).

But it is in just such a case that it would not be justified to deny to the purchaser the right of avoidance under § 119 para 2 of the BGB from the point in time at which he has the authority for the enforcement of guarantee claims onwards. Further, a consideration of a practical kind speaks in favour of not denying to the purchaser the right of avoidance before the passing of the risk. In this case it is no longer an issue of the doubtful (especially if the non-removability of the defect is not easily established) question of the point in time before the passing of the risk from which the right of avoidance would be excluded. In the end it is by that fact that the right of avoidance of the purchaser before the passing of the risk is not excluded by the enforcement of the guarantee claims which is possible in advance, that an interest of the seller which is worthy of protection, in particular his interest in a smooth completion of the purchase transaction in a comparatively short period, is not affected. This is because if the purchaser has made no use of his right of avoidance until the passing of the risk, he has, according to the case law of the Reich High Court approved by the Federal Supreme Court to the effect that the provisions of §§ 459ff and onwards of the BGB are special provisions, lost it for the future.

As therefore the avoidance declared by the defendant because of a mistake about a characteristic significant in the affairs of life in the sense of § 119 para 2 of the BGB, ie, because of the planned by-pass, would not be excluded just because the defendant could raise (and also has raised) the claim to cancellation because of this defect, a decision is still needed on the view expressed in the appeal in law that the avoidance declared because of the planned by-pass for fraudulent deception could be converted into such a declaration for mistake under § 119 para 2 of the BGB.

The appeal court has refused a conversion in this sense with reference to RG JW 1925, 2752. In the re-examination of this view of the appeal court requested by the appeal in law, one must proceed on the basis that where grounds of avoidance are present under § 119 as well as § 123 of the BGB, the avoidance based on the latter provision contains at the same time the assertion of a mistake about that fact as to which the person making the avoidance claims to be deceived and therefore an avoidance for fraudulent deception can also contain an avoidance for mistake (LM § 119 BGB no 5; RGZ 57, 358, 362; 100, 205, 207/208; BGB-RGRK, *loc cit*, § 121 note 2; Palandt, *loc cit*, § 123 note 1 b).

Das Reichsgericht hat jedoch in mehreren Urteilen die Auffassung vertreten, daß die Partei, die ihre Anfechtung bisher nur auf arglistige Täuschung gestützt hat, in jedem Fall im Prozeß zum Ausdruck bringen muß, daß sie sich auch auf Irrtum berufen will (außer JW 1925, 2752 noch WarnRspr 1916 Nr. 7; 1917 Nr. 236 und SeuffArch 83 Nr. 1; ebenso BGB-RGRK aaO). Zur Begründung dieser Auffassung hat das Reichsgericht ausgeführt, daß derjenige, der einen Vertrag wegen arglistiger Täuschung anfechte, damit noch nicht die Unwirksamkeit des Vertrags durch eine in ihren Voraussetzungen und rechtlichen Folgen verschiedene Anfechtung wegen Irrtums herbeiführen wolle und daß es auch gegen den Beibringungsgrundsatz verstoßen würde, wenn eine lediglich auf arglistige Täuschung gestützte Anfechtung auch als solche wegen Irrtums berücksichtigt würde, ohne daß der Anfechtende sich darauf berufen habe. Wie von der Revision mit Recht hervorgehoben wird, hat das Reichsgericht demgegenüber in einem weiteren Urteil (RGZ 100, 205, 207/208) geprüft, ob die vorliegende Anfechtung wegen arglistiger Täuschung auch eine solche wegen Irrtums in sich schließen und zum Ausdruck bringen sollte, und damit im Gegensatz zu seinen anderen Entscheidungen nicht, wenigstens nicht in erste Linie, auf die ausdrückliche Berufung des Anfechtenden auf Irrtum im Prozeß, sondern auf den aus der Anfechtungserklärung zu ermittelnden Willen des Anfechtenden abgestellt. Der Senat folgt dieser Auffassung. Das Erfordernis der Berufung des Anfechtenden auf Irrtum im Prozeß wäre zwar geeignet, eindeutig klare Verhältnisse zu schaffen. Es ist jedoch kein Grund ersichtlich. eine Irrtumsanfechtung auch dann unberücksichtigt zu lassen, wenn der Anfechtende sich auf diese zwar nicht ausdrücklich berufen hat, aus der Anfechtungserklärung sich jedoch ergibt, daß er auch wegen Irrtums anfechten wollte. Es ist deshalb eine Frage der Willensauslegung, ob im einzelnen Falle in der Anfechtung wegen arglistiger Täuschung zugleich eine solche wegen Irrtums über eine verkehrswesentliche Eigenschaft im Sinne des § 119 Abs. 2 BGB zu erblicken ist (ebenso Staudinger aaO § 123 Anm. 28). Dabei kann allerdings der (auch vom Reichsgericht in RGZ 100, 205 mitberücksichtigte) Umstand, daß der Anfechtende sich im Prozeß nicht auf Irrtumsanfechtung berufen hat, einen Anhaltspunkt dafür abgeben, daß er sich hierauf auch nicht berufen wollte.

The Reich High Court has however in several judgments taken the view that the party which has based its avoidance so far only on fraudulent deception must in each case state in the proceedings that it will refer to mistake (besides JW 1925, 2752, WarnRspr 1916 no 7; 1917 no 236 and SeuffArch 83 no 1; likewise BGB-RGRK, *loc cit*). As a basis for this view, the Reich High Court has stated that the person who avoids a contract for fraudulent deception would not thereby wish to bring about the ineffectiveness of the contract by avoidance for mistake, which is different in its prerequisites and legal consequences, and that it would also violate the principle that proceedings are under the control of the parties if an avoidance based merely on fraudulent deception was also considered as an avoidance for mistake, without the person making the avoidance having referred to it. As the appeal in law correctly emphasises, the Reich High Court has on the other hand in a further judgment (RGZ 100, 205, 207/208) examined whether the present avoidance for fraudulent deception should also contain in itself and express an avoidance for mistake and thereby, in contrast to its other decisions, did not take into account (or at least not primarily) the express reference of the person making the avoidance to mistake in the proceedings, but the intention of the person making the avoidance to be ascertained from the avoidance declaration. The Senate follows this view. The requirement of reference by the person making the avoidance to mistake in the proceedings would certainly be appropriate to create clear relationships in an unambiguous manner. No ground is however evident for leaving avoidance for mistake out of account if the person making the avoidance has admittedly not referred expressly to this, but it follows from the avoidance declaration that he also wanted to avoid for mistake. It is therefore a question of interpretation of the intention whether in the individual case an avoidance for mistake for a characteristic of significance in the affairs of life in the sense of § 119 para 2 of the BGB is at the same time to be seen in the avoidance for fraudulent deception (likewise Staudinger, *loc cit*, § 123 note 28). In this connection, the fact (also taken into account by the Reich High Court in RGZ 100, 205) that the person making the avoidance did not refer in the proceedings to avoidance for mistake can certainly provide a ground for concluding that he also did not want to refer to it.

Bei diesem Ergebnis kommt es somit darauf an, ob aus der von der Beklagten wegen der geplanten Umgehungsstraße erklärten Anfechtung wegen arglistiger Täuschung zu entnehmen ist, daß sie insoweit auch Irrtumsanfechtung geltend machen wollte. Dies zu bejahen, bestehen nach der Auffassung des Senats keine Bedenken, weil die Beklagte, wie sich aus ihren zahlreichen Angriffen gegen den Bestand des Kaufvertrags ergibt, von diesem auf jede nur mögliche Weise, auch durch Irrtumsanfechtung wegen der geplanten Umgehungsstraße, wenn die anderen Angriffe ohne Erfolg bleiben sollten, loskommen wollte. Hinzu kommt, daß sie sich, wie noch erörtert wird, wegen des Umstandes, daß der Kläger im Zeitpunkt des Abschlusses des Kaufvertrags nur Miteigentümer des Grundstücks war, außer auf Anfechtung wegen arglistiger Täuschung auch ausdrücklich auf Anfechtung wegen Irrtums berufen hat.

Die jetzt noch zu entscheidende Frage, ob die geplante Umgehungsstraße eine verkehrswesentliche Eigenschaft im Sinne des § 119 Abs. 2 BGB darstellt, ist vom Berufungsgericht, von seinem Standpunkt aus verständlich, nicht behandelt worden. Ihre Beantwortung hängt, wie von der Revision mit Recht hervorgehoben wird, davon ab, inwieweit im Zeitpunkt des Abschlusses des Kaufvertrags der Plan der Umgehungsstraße bereits gediehen war, ob also die Auskunft der Amtsverwaltung V. vom 20. Januar 1959 dahin, daß durch die Umgehungsstraße das ganze Grundstück in Anspruch genommen werde und das darauf stehende Gebäude deshalb abgerissen werden müsse, auch schon für den Zeitpunkt des Abschlusses des Kaufvertrags gilt (vgl. hierzu RGZ 161, 193, 194/195; Staudinger aaO § 119 Anm. 2).

2 Eine arglistige Täuschung der Beklagten durch den Kläger mit Rücksicht darauf, daß im Zeitpunkt des Abschlusses des Kaufvertrags die eine Miteigentumshälfte des Grundstücks noch im Eigentum der Ehefrau des Klägers stand, hat das Berufungsgericht mit der Begründung verneint, nach dem Ergebnis der Beweisaufnahme habe der Kläger bei Abschluß des Kaufvertrags mit Einwilligung seine Ehefrau gehandelt und diese sei nur versehentlich nicht im Kaufvertrag mit aufgeführt worden.

Auch hiergegen wendet sich die Revision nicht. Sie rügt aber Verletzung des § 286 ZPO, weil die Beklagte insoweit die Anfechtung des Kaufvertrags auch auf Irrtum gestützt habe und das Berufungsgericht hierauf nicht eingegangen sei.

Die Rüge ist nicht begründet.

With this outcome it is therefore a question of whether it can be deduced from the avoidance declared by the defendant for fraudulent deception because of the planned by-pass that she also, in this respect, intended to claim avoidance for mistake. There are no difficulties about confirming this, according to the view of the Senate, because the defendant (as follows from her numerous challenges to the continued existence of the purchase contract) wanted to escape from it in any possible way, and therefore also by avoidance for mistake because of the planned by-pass, if the other challenges should be unsuccessful. In addition to this, there is the fact that she, as will be discussed, has referred expressly to avoidance for mistake besides avoidance for fraudulent deception, because of the fact that the claimant at the point in time of the conclusion of the purchase contract was only a co-owner of the piece of land.

The question which has now still to be decided, as to whether the planned by-pass represents a characteristic of significance in the affairs of life in the sense of § 119 para 2 of the BGB, has not been dealt with by the appeal court, understandably from its point of view. The answer to it depends, as is correctly emphasised by the appeal in law, on the stage the plan for the by-pass had reached at the point in time of the conclusion of the purchase contract, ie, whether the information of the administrative authority (*Amtsverwaltung*) at V of the 20 January 1959 to the effect that the whole piece of land will be claimed by the by-pass and the building standing on it must therefore be demolished, also applies at the point in time of the conclusion of the purchase contract (see on this RGZ 161, 193, 194/195; Staudinger, *loc cit*, § 119 note 2).

2 Fraudulent deception of the defendant by the claimant (having regard to the fact that at the point in time of the conclusion of the purchase contract one half share in the co-ownership of the piece of land was owned by the wife of the claimant) was denied by the appeal court on the basis that according to the outcome of the taking of evidence, the claimant acted on the concluding of the purchase contract with the agreement of his wife and she had only been omitted from the purchase contract inadvertently.

The appeal in law does not object to this. It complains however of a violation of § 286 of the ZPO, because the defendant has in this respect based the avoidance of the purchase contract on mistake also and the appeal court has not paid attention to this.

The complaint is not well founded.

Das Übergehen der Berufung der Beklagten auf Irrtum stellt allerdings einen Verstoß gegen § 286 ZPO dar. Hierauf beruht jedoch das Berufungsurteil nicht, weil entgegen der Meinung der Revision die Voraussetzungen des § 119 Abs. 2 BGB nicht gegeben sind. Als verkehrswesentliche Eigenschaften einer Sache im Sinne dieser Vorschrift kommen zwar nicht nur ihre natürliche Beschaffenheit, sondern auch die vorhandenen tatsächlichen und rechtlichen Verhältnisse in Betracht, die infolge ihrer Beschaffenheit und Dauer auf die Brauchbarkeit und den Wert von Einfluß sind (RGZ 21, 308, 311; 52, 1, 2; 59, 240, 243; 61, 84, 86; 64, 266, 269; 99, 214; BGB RGRK aaO § 119 Anm.17; Siebert/Hefermehl, BGB, 9. Aufl., § 119 Anm. 20; Enneccerus/Nipperdey, Allgemeiner Teil des Bürgerlichen Rechts, 15. Aufl., § 168 II 1 a S. 1044; vgl. auch BGHZ 16, 54, 57); so wurden bei Grundstücken als verkehrswesentliche Eigenschaften anerkannt: die Grenzen (RG Recht 1912 Nr. 2797), der Umfang und die Lage (RG WarnRspr 1911 Nr. 368; 1912 Nr. 205), die Bebaubarkeit und die gewerbliche Verwendbarkeit (RG WarnRspr 1911 Nr. 172) und die mit dem Eigentum verbundenen Berechtigungen (RG Recht 1912 Nr. 1273). Aus dieser Begriffsbestimmung in Verbindung mit den aufgeführten Beispeilen ergibt sich aber, daß sich verkehrswesentliche Eigenschaften einer Sache nur aus solchen tatsächlichen und rechtlichen Verhältnissen ergeben können, welche die Beziehung der Sache zum Umwelt betreffen (vgl. Erman aaO § 119 Anm. 10), also durch Umstände bedingt sind, die außerhalb der Sache selbst liegen. Dies trifft für das Eigentum der Sache nicht zu. Es ist nicht ersichtlich, inwiefern dieses auf die Brauchbarkeit und den Wert der Sache Einfluß haben kann. Das Eigentum an einer Sache ist deshalb keine verkehrswesentliche Eigenschaft im Sinne des § 119 Abs. 2 BGB für den Fall, daß der Irrtum auf Seiten des Verkäufers liegt.

§ 120 [Anfechtbarkeit wegen falscher Übermittlung] Eine Willensklärung, welche durch die zur Übermittlung verwendete Person oder Einrichtung unrichtig übermittelt worden ist, kann unter der gleichen Voraussetzung angefochten werden wie nach § 119 eine irrtümlich abgegebene Willenserklärung.

§ 121 [Anfechtungsfrist] (1) Die Anfechtung muss in den Fällen der § 119, 120 ohne schuldhaftes Zögern (unverzüglich) erfolgen, nachdem der Anfechtungsberechtigte von dem Anfechtungsgrund Kenntnis erlangt hat. Die einem Abwesenden gegenüber erfolgte Anfechtung gilt als rechtzeitig erfolgt, wenn die Anfechtungserklärung unverzüglich abgesendet worden ist.

(2) Die Anfechtung ist ausgeschlossen, wenn seit der Abgabe der Willenserklärung zehn Jahre verstrichen sind.

The ignoring by the defendant's appeal of mistake admittedly represents a violation of § 286 of the ZPO. But the judgment in the appeal is not based on this, because contrary to the opinion of the appeal in law, the prerequisites of § 119 para 2 of the BGB are not present. It is true that it is not only the natural qualities of a thing but also its existing factual and legal relationships which, in consequence of its qualities and prospective life, are of influence on its usefulness and value which come to be considered as the characteristics of it which are of significance in the affairs of life in the sense of this provision (RGZ 21, 308, 311; 52, 1, 2; 59, 240, 243; 61, 84, 86; 64, 266, 269; 99, 214; BGB RGRK, *loc cit*, § 119 note 17; Siebert/Hefermehl, BGB, 9th edn, § 119 note 20; Enneccerus/Nipperdey, General Part of Civil Law, 15th edn, § 168 II 1 a p 1044; see also BGHZ 16, 54, 57). Thus, in relation to pieces of land, the following have been acknowledged as characteristics which are of significance in the affairs of life: boundaries (RG Recht 1912 no 2797), area and location (RG WarnRspr 1911 no 368; 1912 no 205) suitability for building and commercial utility (RG WarnRspr 1911 no 172) and the entitlements associated with ownership (RG Recht 1912 no 1273). It follows however from this definition, in combination with the examples listed, that characteristics of a thing which are of significance in the affairs of life can only arise from those factual and legal relationships which concern the relationship of the thing to the surrounding world (see Erman, *loc cit*, § 119 note 10), ie, which are caused by circumstances which are outside the thing itself. This does not apply to the ownership of the thing. It is not evident in what respect this can have an influence on the usefulness and value of the thing. The ownership of the thing is therefore not a characteristic which is of significance in the affairs of life in the sense of § 119 para 2 of the BGB for the case where the mistake is on the side of the seller.

§ 120 [Voidability as a result of incorrect communication] A declaration of will which has been incorrectly communicated by the person or institution used for the communication can be avoided under the same prerequisite as a mistakenly made declaration according to § 119.

§ 121 [Period for avoidance] (1) The avoidance must, in the cases of §§ 119 and 120, follow without reprehensible delay (promptly) after the person entitled to avoid has obtained knowledge of the ground for avoidance. Avoidance, as against an absent person, counts as having been punctually effected if the avoidance declaration has been despatched promptly.

(2) Avoidance is excluded if 10 years have elapsed since the making of the declaration of will.

As to the operation of this article, see the unintended declaration of will case, p 243 and the internet auction case, Chapter Five, p 333. For further provisions about the exercise of the right of avoidance, see §§ 142 and 143, p 315.

(2) Duty to compensate

§ 122 [Schadensersatzpflicht des Anfechtenden] (1) Ist eine Willenserklärung nach § 118 nichtig oder auf Grund der §§ 119, 120 angefochten, so hat der Erklärende, wenn die Erklärung einem anderen gegenüber abzugeben war, diesem, andernfalls jedem Dritten den Schaden zu ersetzen, den der andere oder der Dritte dadurch erleidet, daß er auf die Gültigkeit der Erklärung vertraut, jedoch nicht über den Betrag des Interesses hinaus, welches der andere oder der Dritte an der Gültigkeit der Erklärung hat.

(2) Die Schadensersatzpflicht tritt nicht ein, wenn der Beschädigte den Grund der Nichtigkeit oder der Anfechtbarkeit kannte oder infolge von Fahrlässigkeit nicht kannte (kennen mußte).

(3) Deception and threats

§ 123 [Anfechtbarkeit wegen Täuschung oder Drohung] (1) Wer zur Abgabe einer Willenserklärung durch arglistige Täuschung oder widerrechtlich durch Drohung bestimmt worden ist, kann die Erklärung anfechten.

(2) Hat ein Dritter die Täuschung verübt, so ist eine Erklärung, die einem anderen gegenüber abzugeben war, nur dann anfechtbar, wenn dieser die Täuschung kannte oder kennen mußte. Soweit ein anderer als derjenige, welchem gegenüber die Erklärung abzugeben war, aus der Erklärung unmittelbar ein Recht erworben hat, ist die Erklärung ihm gegenüber anfechtbar, wenn er die Täuschung kannte oder kennen mußte.

(2) Duty to compensate

§ 122 [Duty of the person avoiding to compensate for damage] (1) If a declaration of will is invalid according to § 118 or avoided on the ground of §§ 119 or 120, the declarer must, if the declaration was to be made as against another, compensate this other person, or otherwise each third person, for the damage which this other person or the third person suffers as a result of trusting in the validity of the declaration, but not, however, over and above the amount of the interest which the other person or the third person has in the validity of the declaration.

(2) The duty to compensate for damage does not arise if the injured party knew the ground of invalidity or of voidability or did not know it as a result of negligence (ought to have known it).

Note the consideration of § 122 in the fowl pest case: see Chapter Six, p 439.

(3) Deception and threats

§ 123 [Voidability on account of deception or threat] (1) Whoever has been caused to make a declaration of will by fraudulent deception or by threat, in a manner contrary to law, can avoid the declaration.

(2) If a third person has practised the deceit, a declaration which was to be made as against another person is only avoidable if this person knew the deceit or ought to have known of it. Insofar as another person than the one as against whom the declaration was to be made has obtained a right immediately from the declaration, the declaration is avoidable as against him if he knew the deception or ought to have known it.

If there is a duty to state the truth, failure to do so can amount to deceit. Statements of opinion are not covered. The concept is similar to fraudulent misrepresentation in English law. See the land purchase mistake case, p 261, as to the relationship between fraud and mistake. As to negligent and innocent misrepresentation, see § 13 a of the Unfair Competition Act, and the concept of mistake.

Note how much wider the concept of threat is than the English concept of duress, eg, it need not even come from the other party to the contract. The requirement of unlawfulness can be satisfied in a variety of ways and it need not be criminal unlawfulness. Threat of an irrelevant prosecution would suffice.

THE COMPUTER NON-DISCLOSURE CASE

BGH NJW 1933, 2493

3 BGB § 123 (Aufklärung über Senkung des Herstellerlistenpreises während Vertragsverhandlungen)

Zur Frage, ob der Verkäufer (Händler), der bei den Vertrags-verhandlungen auf der Grundlage seines Listenpreises einen Nachlaß von 30% gewährt hat, verpflichtet ist, dem Käufer eine nach Abschluß der Vertragsverhandlungen, aber vor Unterzeichnung des Vertrages erfolgte erhebliche Senkung des Herstellerlistenpreises mitzuteilen.

BGH, Urt. v. 13.7.1983 – VIII ZR 142/82 (Düsseldorf)

Zum Sachverhalt:

Die Parteien streiten über die Rückabwicklung eines Kaufvertrages über einen Computer. Der Kl. der seit 1968 in seinem Steuerberaterbüro einen K-Computer A für Buchhaltungs aufzeichnungen und steuerliche Berechnungen verwendete, verhandelte Anfang 1975 mit der Bekl. zu 1 (im folgenden: die Bekl.) über den Erwerb eines K-Computers B, dessen Listenpreis damals 163065 DM ohne Magnetbandstation, Bänder und sonstiges Zubehör betrug. Nachdem der Kl. zum Ausdruck gebracht hatte, daß er für die Anlage einschließlich Bandstation und Zubehör nur ca. 120 000 DM investieren könne, bot ihm die Bekl. am 7.3.1975 ein Modell des Typs C einschließlich Bandstation unter Anrechnung des zurückgenommenen Gerätes zum Preis von 1 707 780 DM zuzüglich Mehrwertsteuer an. Nachdem der Kl. die Modellbezeichnung beanstandet hatte, kam es am 11.3.1975 zu erneuten Gesprächen, in denen die Bekl. erklärte, sie habe die Modellbezeichnung C nur gewählt, damit der reduzierte Preis für das Modell B gegenüber Konkurrenzunternehmen nicht offengelegt werde. Der für die Bekl. auftretende Verkaufsleiter M überließ dem Kl. eine Notiz, die den Listenpreis der Bekl. für das Modell B einschließlich Bandstation mit 179 600 DM (163 065 DM + 16 535 DM) und den des Kontenzuführgerätes mit 8450 DM wiedergibt. Der Kl. unterzeichnete daraufhin am 11.3.1975 einen 'Auftrag' über das Modell B einschließlich Bandstation und Kontenzuführgerät zum Preise von 121 230 DM unter Vorbehalt des Rücktritts bis zum 25.3.1975. In diesem Auftrag, der zu seiner Wirksamkeit der Auftragsbestätigung der Bekl. bedurfte, war auf das Angebot vom 7.3.1975 Bezug genommen.

THE COMPUTER NON-DISCLOSURE CASE

In this case, liability for fraudulent deceit because of a failure to disclose was considered. This does not pose the same problems as in English law, where the emphasis is on misrepresentation. However, in respect of the failure in question (non-disclosure of a fall in the manufacturer's list price after negotiations had begun), there was no duty to disclose.

BGH NJW 1933, 2493

3 BGB § 123 (Explanation about lowering of the manufacturer's list price during contractual negotiations)

On the question of whether the seller (dealer) who, in contractual negotiations on the basis of his list price, has granted a discount of 30% is under a duty to inform the buyer about a substantial lowering of the manufacturer's list price occurring after the conclusion of the contractual negotiations but before the signing of the contract.

BGH, judgment of 13.7.1983 – VIII ZR 142/82 (Düsseldorf)

Facts:

The parties are in dispute about the cancellation of a purchase contract about a computer. The claimant had used a K computer A in his tax advice office for book-keeping records and tax calculations since 1968. He negotiated at the beginning of 1975 with the first defendant ('the defendant') about the acquisition of a K computer B, the list price of which amounted to 163,065 DM, without tapedeck, tapes and other accessories. After the claimant had said that he could only invest about 120,000 DM for the equipment inclusive of tapedeck and accessories, the defendant offered him on the 7.3.1975 a type C model, inclusive of tapedeck, taking into account the apparatus which was traded in, at the price of 1,707,780 DM (this figure must be a misprint) plus VAT. After the claimant had queried the description of model, renewed talks took place on the 11.3.1975 in which the defendant stated that it had only chosen model description C in order that the reduced price for model B would not be revealed to competing undertakings. The sales manager M representing the defendant let the claimant have a note which quotes the defendants' list price for model B inclusive of tapedeck as 179,600 DM (163,065 DM + 16,535 DM) and that of the account feed apparatus as 8,450 DM. The claimant thereupon signed an 'order' on the 11.3.1975 for model B inclusive of tapedeck and account feed apparatus at the price of 121,230 DM, with a proviso for withdrawal up to the 25.3.1975. In this order, which needed the confirmation of the defendant to be effective, reference was made to the offer of the 7.3.1975.

Nachdem der Kl. anschließend noch einmal Gespräche mit Konkurrenzunternehmen geführt hatte, unterzeichnete er am 21.3.1975 einen von der Bekl. am 17.3.1975 vorbereiteten schriftlichen 'Auftrag', der ohne Bezugnahme auf das Angebot vom 7.3.1975 mit dem Auftrag vom 11.3.1975 identisch war. Diesmal behielt er sich keinen Rücktritt vor. Die Bekl. bestätigte diesen Auftrag am 24.3.1975. Im September 1975 wurde der Computer an den Kl. geliefert und von diesem in Betrieb genommen. Der Kl. veräußerte die Computeranlage nach seinem Vorbringen an die Firma U weiter und schloß mit ihr einen Leasingvertrag über 60 Monate. Den mit der Bekl. vereinbarten Kaufpreis zahlte die Leasingfirma an die Bekl. Mit Rundschreiben vom 10.3.1975, das der Bekl. am 14.3.1975 zugegangen war, hatte die Firma K ihren Hardware-Listenpreis für das vom Kl. bestellte Modell ohne Zubehör von 155 300 DM auf 86 900 DM herabgesetzt. Die Bekl. änderte ihren Listenpreis daraufhin auf 91245 DM, nach ihrer Behauptung jedoch erst zum 1.9.1975. Die Senkung des Listenpreises durch die Firma K teilte sie dem Kl. nicht mit. Da die Computeranlage die Erwartungen des Kl. nicht voll erfüllte, versuchte er, sie im Jahre 1976 als gebrauchte Anlage zu veräußern. Dabei will er am 29.10.1976 erfahren haben, daß seine Anlage im März 1975 nur einen Marktpreis von ca. 120 000 DM bis 130 000 DM gehabt habe. Mit Schreiben vom 9.11.1976 erklärte er daraufhin die Anfechtung des Kaufvertrages vom 21./24.3.1975 gegenüber der Bekl. mit der Begründung, die Bekl. habe ihm die Anlage unter Vortäuschung eines ungewöhnlich hohen Nachlasses vom Listenpreis verkauft, während der ausgehandelte Kaufpreis in Wirklichkeit dem zur Zeit des Vertragsschlusses gültigen Listenpreis entsprochen habe. Der Nachlaß vom Listenpreis sei für seine Kaufentscheidung maßgebend gewesen, weil er davon ausgegangen sei, daß er die Anlage ohne nennenswerte Verluste wieder veräußern könne, falls sie seinen Erwartungen nicht entspreche. Mit der Klage hat der Kl. die Bekl. als Gesamtschuldner auf Rückzahlung des Kaufpreises und auf Ersatz gezahlter Leasingvergütung Zug um Zug gegen die Rückübereignung der Computeranlage in Anspruch genommen und den zu erstattenden Betrag unter Anrechnung einer Nutzungsentschädigung auf 109 767,90 DM errechnet.

Das LG hat der Klage stattgegeben, das BerGer. hat sie abgewiesen. Die Revision des Kl. hatte keinen Erfolg.

After the claimant had conversations once again with competing undertakings, he signed on 21.3.1975 a written 'order' prepared by the defendant on the 17.3.1975 which without the reference to the offer of the 7.3.1975, was identical with the order of the 11.3.1975. This time he reserved no right of withdrawal for himself. The defendant confirmed this order on the 24.3.1975. In September 1975 the computer was delivered to the claimant and put into use by him. The claimant transferred the computer system according to his evidence, to the U firm and concluded with it a leasing contract for 60 months. The leasing firm paid to the defendant the purchase price agreed with him. By a circular of 14.3.1975 which reached the defendant on the 17.3.1975, the K firm had reduced their hardware list price for the model ordered by the claimant, without accessories, from 155,300 DM to 86,900 DM. The defendant thereupon changed its list price to 91,245 DM, but only (according to their assertion) from the 1.9.1975. It did not communicate to the claimant the lowering of the list price by the K firm. As the computer equipment did not fully fulfil the expectations of the claimant, he sought to dispose of it as a used system equipment in 1976. He claims to have discovered on the 29.10.1976 that his system had only had a market price of about 20,000 DM to 130,000 DM in March 1975. By a letter of the 9.11.1976 he thereupon declared his avoidance of the purchase contract of the 21/24.3.1975 as against the defendant on the basis that the defendant had sold him the system under the pretence of an unusually high discount on the listed price, whilst the negotiated purchase price in reality corresponded to the current listed price at the time of the conclusion of the contract. The discount on the list price was decisive for his decision to purchase, because he had proceeded on the basis that he could dispose of the system again without significant loss, if it did not correspond to his expectations. By the action, the claimant claimed against the defendants as joint debtors for the repayment of the purchase price and for compensation for the leasing reimbursement which had been paid, simultaneously with the transfer back of the computer system and calculated the sum to be reimbursed, taking into account compensation for use, at 109,767.90 DM.

The State Court allowed the claim but the appeal court rejected it. The appeal in law of the claimant was unsuccessful.

Aus den Gründen:

I Nach Ansicht des BerGer. steht dem Kl. die geltend gemachte Forderung weder als Bereicherungs- noch als Schadenersatzanspruch aus Verschulden bei Vertragsschluß zu.

1 Es läßt dahingestellt, ob der Kl. zur Geltendmachung der eingeklagten Ansprüche aktiv legitimiert ist und ob seine Anfechtung rechtzeitig erfolgt ist. Ein Bereicherungsanspruch des Kl. auf Rückzahlung des Kaufpreises scheidet nach Auffassung des BerGer. deshalb aus, weil der Kl. den Kaufvertrag mangels eines Anfechtungsgrundes nicht wirksam angefochten habe. Eine arglistige Täuschung durch die Bekl., die den Kl. zur Anfechtung berechtigt hätte, liege nicht vor. Weder habe die Bekl. dem Kl. falsche Tatsachen vorgespiegelt, weil die letzte vor Vertragsschluß liegende Erklärung der Bekl., der Listenpreis des Computers mit Zubehör betrage etwa 180 000 DM, zu diesem Zeitpunkt den Tatsachen entsprochen habe, noch habe die Bekl. den Kl. durch das Verschweigen der Listenpreissenkung getäuscht und ihn dadurch in unredlicher Weise zum Kaufentschluß veranlaßt. Denn eine arglistige Täuschung durch Verschweigen setze voraus, daß hinsichtlich der verschwiegenen Umstände eine Offenbarungspflicht bestehe. Die für das Bestehen einer solchen Verpflichtung erforderlichen Voraussetzungen seien im vorliegenden Fall nicht erfüllt. Zwischen den Parteien habe kein besonderes Treueverhältnis bestanden, das der Bekl. eine besondere Rücksichtnahme auf die Interessen des Kl. geboten habe. Die Bekl. sei nicht verpflichtet gewesen, den Kl. über die Senkung des Listenpreises ihres Lieferanten aufzuklären, weil dies in den Bereich ihrer Preiskalkulation gehört habe.

2 Mangels einer Offenbarungspflicht der Bekl. scheide auch ein Schadensersatzanspruch des Kl. wegen Verschuldens der Bekl. bei Vertragsschluß aus.

Reasons:

I According to the view of the appeal court, the claimant is not entitled to a claim based on fault on conclusion of the contract either on the basis of enrichment or on the basis of compensation for harm.

1 It leaves undecided whether the claimant is effectively authorised for the making of the claims which he has brought and whether his avoidance took place in time. A claim for unjust enrichment by the claimant for repayment of the purchase price has to be ruled out, according to the view of the appeal court, because the claimant has not effectively avoided the purchase contract in view of the lack of a ground for avoidance. There is no deceit by the defendant which would have justified the claimant in avoiding the contract. Neither has the defendant led the claimant into believing false facts, because the last declaration by the defendant before the conclusion of the contract, that the list price of the computer with the accessories amounted to about 180,000 DM corresponded with the facts at this point in time, nor had the defendant deceived the claimant by remaining silent about the reduction in the list price and thereby caused him in a dishonest fashion to decide to buy. This is because deceit by silence assumes that a duty to reveal exists in relation to the facts as to which silence was kept. The necessary prerequisites for the existence of such a duty were not fulfilled in the present case. No special relationship of fidelity existed between the parties which required the defendant to show a special consideration for the interests of the claimant. The defendant was not obliged to inform the claimant about the lowering of the list price of their supplier, because this belonged to the area of its price calculations.

2 In view of the absence of a duty to reveal by the defendant, a claim by the claimant to compensation for fault by the defendant on conclusion of a contract was ruled out as well.

II Dagegen wendet sich die Revision ohne Erfolg.

1 Soweit das BerGer. zu dem Ergebnis gelangt ist, die Bekl. habe den Kl. am 11.3.1975 nicht durch Vorspiegelung falscher Tatsachen getäuscht, ist dies aus Rechtsgründen nicht zu beanstanden. Das BerGer. leitet seine Überzeugung aus dem Umstand ab, daß die in der am 11.3.1975 übergebenen Aktennotiz des Verkaufsleiters M zu erblickende Erklärung, der Listenpreis der Bekl. für das gewünschte Modell B betrage nebst Zubehör 179 600 DM, den Tatsachen entsprochen habe. Diese Feststellung deckt sich mit dem unstreitigen Sachverhalt. Wenn demgegenüber die Revision geltend macht, es sei nach der Lebenserfahrung und den Umständen des Falles davon auszugehen, daß die Bekl. bzw, deren Verkaufsleiter zum damaligen Zeitpunkt von einer Senkung der Listenpreise des Herstellers gewußt habe, und daraus folgert, der Kl. sei durch die Angabe des Listenpreises der Bekl. über den Marktwert der Anlage getäuscht worden, kann dem nicht gefolgt werden. Mangels entsprechender Feststellungen des BerGer. über den Stand der Kenntnis der Bekl. von der Preisentwicklung bei der Herstellerfirma und angesichts des Umstandes, daß das die Mitteilung über die Listenpreissenkung enthaltende Schreiben der Herstellerfirma vom 10.3.1975 der Bekl. unstreitig erst am 14.3.1975 zugegangen ist, reichen die Lebenserfahrung und die von der Revision herausgestellte wirtschaftliche Verflechtung der Herstellerfirma mit der Bekl. nicht aus, um mit hinreichender Sicherheit den Schluß ziehen zu können, die Bekl. habe schon am 11.3.1975 gewußt, daß und gegebenenfalls in welchem Umfange die Herstellerfirma ihre Listenpreise gesenkt habe. Dies hat der Kl. in der Vorinstanz auch selbst nicht behauptet.

2 Die Ausführungen des BerGer., mit denen es eine arglistige Täuschung seitens der Bekl. durch Verschweigen wesentlicher Umstände verneint, lassen gleichfalls keine Rechtsfehler erkennen. Entgegen der Auffassung der Revision kann nach Lage des Falles eine arglistige Täuschung nicht darin erblickt werden, daß die Bekl. dem Kl. die Senkung des Herstellerlistenpreises nicht vor dem endgültigen Vertragsschluß vom 21./24.3.1975 mitgeteilt, sondern ihn im dem Glauben gelassen hat, er erwerbe eine Anlage, deren Marktgeltung erheblich höher sei als der vereinbarte Kaufpreis.

II The appeal in law was unsuccessfully directed against this.

1 Insofar as the appeal court reached the conclusion that the defendant did not deceive the claimant on the 11.3.1975 by leading him into believing false facts, this is not to be objected to on legal grounds. The appeal court derives its conviction from the fact that in the statement which was to be seen in the memo of the sales manager M handed over on the 11.3.1975 that the list price of the defendant for the desired model B with accessories was 179,600 DM, corresponded with the facts. This finding coincides with the undisputed facts of the case. When in contrast the appeal in law claims that from experience of life and from the circumstances of the case one has to proceed on the basis that the defendant or its sales manager knew of a lowering of the list prices of the manufacturer at that point in time and deduces from this that the claimant was deceived by the giving of the list price of the defendant about the market value of the system, it cannot be followed. In the absence of corresponding findings by the appeal court about the state of knowledge of the defendant about the price developments with the manufacturing firm and in the face of the fact that the letter by the manufacturing firm of the 10.3.1975 containing the communication about the lowering of the list price indisputably only reached the defendant on the 14.3.1975, experience of life and the business involvement of the manufacturing firm with the defendant set out in the appeal in law do not suffice to enable the conclusion to be drawn with sufficient certainty that the defendant knew on the 11.3.1975 that the manufacturing firm had lowered its list prices and, if appropriate, to what extent. This was not even alleged by the claimant himself in the court of first instance.

2 The findings of the appeal court, in which it denies deceit on the part of the defendant through the withholding of important facts, likewise reveal no mistakes of law. Contrary to the view of the appeal in law, deceit cannot, according to the facts of the case, be seen in the fact that the defendant did not inform the claimant of the lowering of the manufacturer's list price before the final conclusion of the contract of the 21./24.3.1975, but left him in the belief that he was acquiring a system the market value of which was substantially higher than the agreed purchase price.

(a) Das bewußte Verschweigen von Tatsachen durch wissentliches Dulden eines Irrtums des Vertragspartners stellt nur dann eine arglistige Täuschung dar, wenn gegenüber dem Vertragspartner eine Rechtspflicht zur Offenbarung bestand. Eine allgemeine Rechtspflicht, den Vertragspartner über alle Umstände aufzuklären, die auf seine Entschließung Einfluß haben könnten, gibt es nicht. Eine Aufklärungspflicht läßt sich immer nur aus besonderen Gründen anhand der Umstände des Einzelfalles bejahen (*Krüger=Nieland*, in RGRK, 12. Aufl., § 123 Rdnr. 16; *Kramer*, in: MünchKomm, § 123 Rdnrn. 15, 16; *Soergel-Hefermehl*, BGB, 11. Aufl., § 123 Rdnr. 6). Eine derartige Pflicht hat die Rechtsprechung aus den konkreten, zwischen den Partnern bestehenden Vertragsbeziehungen dann abgeleitet, wenn das Verschweigen von Tatsachen gegen den Grundsatz von Treu und Glauben verstoßen würde und der Erklärungsgegner die Mitteilung der verschwiegenen Tatsache nach der Verkehrsauffassung erwarten durfte (*Senat* NJW 1981, 2050 = LM § 276 Fc BGB Nr. 12 = WM 1981, 689; WM 1977, 394 [396]; 1975, 157 [158], *BGHZ* 72, 382 [388] = NJW 1979, 718; *BGHZ* 70, 337 [342] = NJW 1978, 1374; *BGHZ* 47, 207 [211] = NJW 1967, 1022; *RGZ* 111, 233 [235]). Bei einem Kaufvertrag besteht wegen der widerstreitenden Interessen grundsätzlich keine Rechtspflicht des Verkäufers, den Käufer von sich aus über alle Umstände aufzuklären, die für dessen Vertragsentschluß von Bedeutung sein könnten (*Senat* NJW 1971, 1795 [1799] = WM 1971, 749; NJW 1970, 653 [655]; *Kramer*, in MünchKomm, § 123 Rdnr. 17). Doch hängt der Umfang der rechtlich gebotenen Aufklärung des Vertragspartners nicht nur von der Art des angestrebten Vertrages ab. Ohne Rücksicht darauf können sich während der Vertragsverhandlungen Umstände ergeben, die nach den Grundsätzen von Treu und Glauben eine Rechtspflicht auch des Verkäufers zur Aufklärung des Vertragspartners begründen können (vgl. *Senat*, NJW 1964, 811). Eine derartige Situation kann dann vorliegen, wenn sich die Vertragsverhandlungen über einen längeren Zeitraum hinwegziehen, ein gewisses Vertrauensverhältnis zwischen den Vertragspartnern entstanden ist und seitens des Verkäufers im Rahmen dieser Verhandlungen Angaben gemacht werden, die für die Kaufentscheidung erkennbar von wesentlicher Bedeutung sind, deren tatsächliche Grundlagen aber noch vor Vertragsschluß entfallen und die sich damit als unrichtig herausstellen.

(a) Deliberate silence about facts by knowingly tolerating a mistake of the other contracting party only represents deceit if a legal duty to disclose existed as against the other contracting party. There is no general legal duty to explain to the other contracting party all the circumstances which could have an influence on his decision. A duty to explain can only be found for special reasons on the basis of the circumstances of the individual case (*Krüger = Nieland*, in RGRK, 12th edn, § 123 marginal no 16; *Kramer*, in: MünchKomm, § 123 marginal nos 15, 16; *Soergel-Hefermehl*, BGB, 11th edn, § 123 marginal no 6). The case law has derived such a duty from the actual contractual relationships existing between the parties when silence about facts would violate the principle of good faith and the recipient of the declaration might according to the view in affairs of life have expected communication of the fact as to which silence was maintained (*Senate* NJW 1981, 2050 = LM § 276 Fc BGB no 12 = WM 1981, 689; WM 1977, 394 [396]; 1975, 157 [158], *BGHZ 72*, 382 [388] = NJW 1979, 718; *BGHZ 70*, 337 [342] = NJW 1978, 1374; *BGHZ 47*, 207 [211] = NJW 1967, 1022; *RGZ 111*, 233 [235]). In a purchase contract, because of the conflicting interests, there is in principle no legal duty by the seller to explain to the purchaser of his own accord about all the circumstances which could be of importance for his contractual decision (*Senate* NJW 1971, 1795 [1799] = WM 1971, 749; NJW 1970, 653 [655]; *Kramer*, in MünchKomm, § 123 marginal no 17). But the scope of the explanation of the other contracting party required by law does not only depend on the type of contract intended. Without regard to this, circumstances can arise during the contractual negotiations which according to the principles of good faith can found a legal duty by the seller to provide information to the other contracting party (see *Senate*, NJW 1964, 811). Such a situation can be present if the contractual negotiations stretch over a lengthy period of time, a certain relationship of trust has arisen between the contracting parties and information is given by the seller within the framework of these negotiations which is obviously of substantial importance for the decision to purchase, but the factual basis for it has disappeared before the conclusion of the contract and it therefore turns out to be incorrect.

(b) Das BerGer. hat eine Offenbarungspflicht der Bekl. unter Anwendung der vorerwähnten Grundsätze rechtsfehlerfrei verneint. Die Senkung des Herstellerpreises hatte allerdings zur Folge, daß der zwischen den Parteien vereinbarte Kaufpreis für die Computeranlage fast genau dem Preis entsprach, den die Bekl. bei einer Änderung ihrer eigenen Preisliste auf der Grundlage des neuen Herstellerpreises gefordert hätte, so daß die vom Kl. nach seiner Behauptung gehegte Erwartung, er erhalte eine Anlage, deren Marktwert erheblich über dem vereinbarten Kaufpreis liege, tatsächlich fehlgeschlagen ist. Eine entsprechende Aufklärungspflicht der Bekl. hätte jedoch nur bestanden, wenn diese Erwartung für den Kaufentschluß des Kl. nicht nur mitentscheidend, sondern ihre motivierende Kraft für die Bekl. erkennbar gewesen wäre. Hierzu hat das BerGer. unter im Rahmen tatrichterlichen Ermessens liegender Würdigung des Ergebnisses der in erster Instanz durchgeführten Beweisaufnahme festgestellt, für die Bekl. sei als entscheidungserhebliche Vorstellung des Kl. allein erkennbar gewesen, daß dieser für den ausgewählten Computer nur rd. 120 000 DM investieren könne oder wolle. Angesichts des Umstandes, daß der vereinbarte Preis jedenfalls dem Marktwert des Computers entsprach und der Herstellerlistenpreis nach den nicht angegriffenen Feststellungen des BerGer. nicht Gegenstand der Vertragsverhandlungen war, bestand für die Bekl. daher keine aus dem Grundsatz von Treu und Glauben ableitbare Verpflichtung, dem Kl. ihre Kalkulation zu offenbaren und ihn über die Marktverhältnisse, insbesondere darüber aufzuklären, daß der Hersteller seine Listenpreise gesenkt hatte und es ihr so wirtschaftlich leichter fiel, den ihrerseits angebotenen Preis zu halten. Das gilt um so mehr, als der Kl. bei den Vertragsverhandlungen mit dem Ziel, die Bekl. zu einem Entgegenkommen bei der Preisgestaltung zu bewegen, ein Konkurrenzangebot der Firma N zu 110 000 DM für eine offensichtlich gleichwertige Anlage ins Spiel gebracht und so zu erkennen gegeben hatte, daß er über das Preisniveau der für seine Zwecke infrage kommenden Computeranlagen informiert war. Angesichts dieser Sachlage ist es auch ohne Belang, ob – was das BerGer. als möglich unterstellt hat – die Verhandlungsführer der Bekl. gegenüber dem Kl. erklärt haben, der Preis von ca. 120 000 DM bedeute einen Preisnachlaß von etwa 30%, die Bekl. müsse bei dieser Preisgestaltung auf einen Gewinn verzichten und versuchen, bei ihrem Lieferanten selbst einen Preisnachlaß zu erhalten. Wie zu entscheiden gewesen wäre, wenn der von der Bekl. geforderte Preis von 121 230 DM nicht dem Marktwert der Computeranlage im März 1975 entsprochen hätte, sondern deutlich höher gelegen hätte, kann hier offenbleiben.

(b) The appeal court denied a duty on the part of the defendant to disclose information, by applying the previously mentioned principles in a manner which was free from legal errors. The lowering of the manufacturer's price admittedly had as a consequence that the purchase price agreed between the parties for the computer system almost exactly corresponded to the price which the defendant would have demanded on an alteration of its own price list on the basis of the new manufacturer's price, so that the expectation which the claimant claimed to have had that he was receiving a system the market value of which was substantially above the agreed purchase price, has in fact not been attained. A corresponding duty on the part of the defendant to give information would however only have existed if this expectation was not only one of the decisive factors in the claimant's decision to purchase, but would have been the motivating factor in a manner which was obvious to the defendant. On this point, the appeal court established by an assessment of the outcome of the taking of evidence carried out by the court of first instance which was within the framework of the discretion of the judge of fact, that the only idea obvious to the defendant which the claimant had which was important for his decision was that he wanted to or could invest only about 120,000 DM for the chosen computer. In view of the fact that the agreed price in any case corresponded to the market value of the computer and that, according to the findings of the appeal court which had not been challenged, the manufacturer's list price was not the subject of the contractual negotiations, there was therefore no duty for the defendant which could be derived from the principle of good faith to reveal its calculations to the claimant and to inform him about market conditions; and in particular that the manufacturer had lowered his list price and it was therefore easier for it from a business point of view to keep to the price which it had offered. That is all the more so as the claimant had brought into the contractual negotiations a competing offer from the firm N at 110,000 DM for a system which obviously had the same value and with the objective of inducing the defendant to make a concession about the price structure and had thus given it to be understood that he was informed about the price level of the computer systems which came into consideration for his purposes. In the light of this state of affairs, it is also unimportant whether – as the appeal court assumed to be possible – the negotiators for the defendant stated to the claimant that the price of about 120,000 DM meant a discount of about 30% and the defendant would have to give up making a profit at this level of pricing and attempt to obtain a discount from its suppliers. What decision would have had to be made if the price of 121,230 DM demanded by the defendant had not corresponded to the market value of the computer system in March 1975 but had been clearly higher, can remain open here.

3 Da die Bekl. keine ihr obliegende Offenbarungspflicht verletzt hat, läßt sich der Klageanspruch auch nicht auf § 826 BGB oder auf ein Verschulden der Bekl. bei Vertragsschluß stützen.

III Ohne Erfolg macht die Revision schließlich geltend, daß dem Kl. ein Anspruch auf Freistellung vom Vertrag gem. § 823 II BGB i.V. mit § 3 UWG zustehe. Die Revision übersieht, daß die bei einem schuldhaften Verstoß gegen § 3 UWG eingreifende Sonderregulation des § 13 II UWG die Anwendung des § 823 II BGB ausschließt (*BGH*, NJW 1974, 1503 = Betr 1974, 1427 [1429]; *RG*, GRUR 1940, 375 [378]; *Baumbach-Hefermehl*, WettbewerbsR, 13. Aufl., § 3 UWG Rdnr. 403). Anspruchsberechtigt i.S. des § 13 II UWG ist indessen nur ein geschädigter Mitbewerber. Auf die in diesem Zusammenhang von der Revision aufgeworfene Frage, ob § 3 UWG für den Verbraucher ein Schutzgesetz i.S. des § 823 II BGB ist (verneinend: *BGH*, NJW 1974, 1503; bejahend: *Baumbach-Hefermehl*, § 3 UWG Rdnr. 403), braucht deshalb nicht eingegangen zu werden.

(4) *Avoidance for deception or threats*

§ 124 [Anfechtungsfrist] (1) Die Anfechtung einer nach § 123 anfechtbaren Willenserklärung kann nur binnen Jahresfrist erfolgen.

(2) Die Frist beginnt im Falle der arglistigen Täuschung mit dem Zeitpunkt, in welchem der Anfechtungsberechtigte die Täuschung entdeckt, im Falle der Drohung mit dem Zeitpunkt, in welchem die Zwangslage aufhört. Auf den Lauf der Frist finden die für die Verjährung geltenden Vorschriften der §§ 206, 210 und 211 entsprechende Anwendung.

(3) Die Anfechtung ist ausgeschlossen, wenn seit der Abgabe der Willenserklärung zehn Jahre verstrichen sind.

3 As the defendant has not breached any duty of disclosure incumbent upon it, the claim can also not be based on § 826 of the BGB or on fault of the defendant in relation to the conclusion of the contract.

III The appeal in law finally claims unsuccessfully that the claimant had a claim to be released from the contract in accordance with § 823 II of the BGB in combination with § 3 of the UWG. The appeal in law overlooks the fact that the special regime of § 13 II of the UWG which applies on a culpable violation of § 3 of the UWG excludes the application of § 823 II of the BGB (*BGH*, NJW 1974, 1503 = Betr 1974, 1427 [1429]; *RG* GRUR 1940, 375 [378]; *Baumbach-Hefermehl*, WettbewerbsR, 13th edn, UWG, § 3 marginal no 403). However, the only person entitled to claim in the sense of § 13 II of the UWG is a competitor who has been harmed. It is not therefore necessary to go into the question raised in this connection by the appeal in law of whether § 3 of the UWG is a protective statute for the consumer of the sense of § 823 II of the BGB (denied in *BGH*, NJW 1974, 1503; affirmed in *Baumbach-Hefermehl*, UWG, § 3 marginal no 403).

(4) Avoidance for deception or threats

§ 124 [Period for avoidance] (1) The avoidance of a declaration of will avoidable according to § 123 can only occur within the period of a year.

(2) The period begins in the case of fraudulent deception with the point in time at which the person entitled to avoid discovers the deception and in the case of threat with the point in time at which the state of compulsion ceases. The rules of §§ 206, 210 and 211 applying to limitation of actions have corresponding application to the running of the period for avoidance.

(3) Avoidance is excluded if since the making of the declaration of will 10 years have elapsed.

For further provisions about the exercise of the right of avoidance, see §§ 142 and 143, p 315.

Requirements as to form

§ 125 [Nichtigkeit wegen Formmangels] Ein Rechtsgeschäft, welches der durch Gesetz vorgeschrieben Form ermangelt, ist nichtig. Der Mangel der durch Rechtsgeschäft bestimmten Form hat im Zweifel gleichfalls Nichtigkeit zur Folge.

§ 126 [Schriftform] (1) Ist durch Gesetz schriftliche Form vorgeschrieben, so muß die Urkunde von dem Aussteller eigenhändig durch Namensunterschrift oder mittels notariell beglaubigten Handzeichens unterzeichnet werden.

(2) Bei einem Vertrag muss die Unterzeichnung der Parteien auf derselben Urkunde erfolgen. Werden über den Vertrag mehrere gleichlautende Urkunden aufgenommen, so genügt es, wenn jede Partei die für die andere Partei bestimmte Urkunde unterzeichnet.

(3) Die schriftliche Form kann durch die elektronische Form ersetzt werden, wenn sich nicht aus dem Gesetz ein anderes ergibt.

(4) Die schriftliche Form wird durch die notarielle Beurkundung ersetzt.

§ 126 a [Elektronisch Form] (1) Soll die gesetzlich vorgeschriebene schriftliche Form durch die elektronische Form ersetzt werden, so muss der Aussteller der Erklärung dieser seinen Namen hinzufügen und das elektronische Dokument mit einer qualifizierten elektronischen Signatur nach dem Signaturgesetz versehen.

(2) Bei einem Vertrag müssen die Parteien jeweils ein gleichlautendes Dokument in der in Absatz 1 bezeichneten Weise elektronisch signieren.

§ 126 b [Textform] Ist durch Gesetz Textform vorgeschrieben, so muss die Erklärung in einer Urkunde oder auf andere zur dauerhaften Wiedergabe in Schriftzeichen geeignete Weise abgegeben, die Person des Erklärenden genannt und der Abschluss der Erklärung durch Nachbildung der Namensunterschrift oder anders erkennbar gemacht werden.

§ 127 [Vereinbarte Form] (1) Die Vorschriften des § 126, des § 126 a oder des § 126 b gelten im Zweifel auch für die durch Rechtsgeschäft bestimmte Form.

(2) Zur Wahrung der durch Rechtsgeschäft bestimmten schriftlichen Form genügt, soweit nicht ein anderer Wille anzunehmen ist, die telekommunikative Übermittlung und bei einem Vertrag der Briefwechsel. Wird eine solche Form gewählt, so kann nachträglich eine dem § 126 entsprechende Beurkundung verlangt werden.

Requirements as to form

§ 125 [Invalidity due to lack of form] A legal transaction which lacks the form prescribed by statute, is invalid. The lack of form required by a legal transaction has likewise the consequence of invalidity in case of doubt.

§ 126 [Written form] (1) If written form is prescribed by statute, the document must be signed by the author with his own hand or signed by means of a notarially attested mark.

(2) With a contract, the signature of the parties must be made on the same document. If several identical documents are drawn up in respect of the contract, it suffices if each party signs the document intended for the other party.

(3) Written form can be replaced by electronic form, unless a different consequence is to be deduced from statute.

(4) Notarial authentication can take the place of written form.

§ 126 a [Electronic form] (1) If the statutorily prescribed written form is to be replaced by the electronic form, the person making the declaration must add his name to this and provide the electronic document with a qualified electronic signature in accordance with the Signature Act.

(2) For a contract, the parties must each sign electronically an identical document in the manner described in para 1.

§ 126 b [Text form] If text form is prescribed by statute, the declaration must be given in a document or in another manner appropriate for permanent reproduction in letters, the declarant must be named and the conclusion of the declaration be made recognisable by a copy of the signature of the name or otherwise.

§ 127 [Agreed form] (1) The provisions of § 126, § 126 a or § 126 b apply in case of doubt for the form determined by a legal transaction also.

(2) Telecommunication suffices for the observation of the written form provided for by a legal transaction, insofar as no different intention is to be assumed; and exchange of letters for a contract. If such a form is chosen, a document corresponding to § 126 can be required afterwards.

(3) Zur Wahrung der durch Rechtsgeschäft bestimmten elektronischen Form genügt, soweit nicht ein anderer Wille anzunehmen ist, auch eine andere als die in § 126 a bestimmte elektronische Signatur und bei einem Vertrag der Austausch von Angebots- und Annahmeerklärung, die jeweils mit einer elektronischen Signatur versehen sind. Wird eine solche Form gewählt, so kann nachträglich eine dem § 126 a entsprechende elektronische Signierung oder, wenn diese einer der Parteien nicht möglich ist, eine dem § 126 entsprechende Beurkundung verlangt werden.

§ 127 a [Ersatz für notarielle Beurkundung] Die notarielle Beurkundung wird bei einem gerichtlichen Vergleich durch die Aufnahme der Erklärungen in ein nach der Vorschriften der Zivilprozeßordnung erichtetes Protokoll ersetzt.

§ 128 [Notarielle Beurkundung] Ist durch Gesetz notarielle Beurkundung eines Vertrags vorgeschrieben, so genügt es, wenn zunächst der Antrag und sodann die Annahme des Antrags von einem Notar beurkundet wird.

§ 129 [Öffentliche Beglaubigung] (1) Ist durch Gesetz für eine Erklärung öffentliche Beglaubigung vorgeschrieben, so muß die Erklärung schriftlich abgefaßt und die Unterschrift des Erklärenden von einem Notar beglaubigt werden. Wird die Erklärung von dem Aussteller mittels Handzeichens unterzeichnet, so ist die im § 126 Abs. 1 vorgeschriebene Beglaubigung des Handzeichens erforderlich und genügend.

(2) Die öffentliche Beglaubigung wird durch die notarielle Beurkundung der Erklärung ersetzt.

How a declaration of will becomes effective

§ 130 [Wirksamwerden der Willensklärung gegenüber Abwesenden] (1) Eine Willenserklärung, die einem anderen gegenüber abzugeben ist, wird, wenn sie in dessen Abwesenheit abgegeben wird, in dem Zeitpunkte wirksam, in welchem sie ihm zugeht. Sie wird nicht wirksam, wenn dem anderen vorher oder gleichzeitig ein Widerruf zugeht.

(2) Auf die Wirksamkeit der Willenserklärung ist es ohne Einfluß, wenn der Erklärende nach der Abgabe stirbt oder geschäftsunfähig wird.

(3) Diese Vorschriften finden auch dann Anwendung, wenn die Willenserklärung einer Behörde gegenüber abzugeben ist.

(3) A different electronic signature than that provided for in §126 a suffices for the observation of the electronic form provided for by a legal transaction, insofar as no different intention is to be assumed; and the exchange of offer and acceptance declarations which are each provided with an electronic signature for a contract. If such a form is chosen, an electronic signature corresponding to § 126 a or, if this is not possible for one of the parties, a document corresponding to § 126 can be required afterwards.

The statutory requirements as to form may be relaxed on the basis of § 242 (good faith) in cases of intolerable hardship – and even then not in the case of certain family and inheritance matters. Contractual requirements as to form may be relaxed more easily.

§ 127 a [Replacement for notarial authentication] Notarial authentication is replaced, on a judicial compromise, by the taking of depositions in a record drawn up in accordance with the rules as to civil procedure.

§ 128 [Notarial authentication] If notarial authentication of a contract is prescribed by statute, it suffices if first the offer and then the acceptance of the offer is authenticated by a notary.

§ 129 [Public attestation] (1) If public attestation is prescribed by statute for a declaration, the declaration must be drawn up in writing and the signature of the declarant attested by a notary. If the declaration is signed by the author by means of a mark, the attestation of the mark prescribed in § 126 para 1 is necessary and sufficient.

(2) Notarial authentication of the declaration can take the place of public attestation.

How a declaration of will becomes effective

§ 130 [How the declaration of will becomes effective as against absent persons] (1) A declaration of will which is to be made as against another becomes, if it is made in his absence, effective at the point in time at which it reaches him. It does not become effective if a revocation reaches the other previously or at the same time.

(2) It has no impact on the effectiveness of a declaration of will if the declarant dies or becomes incompetent after he makes it.

(3) These rules also apply if the declaration is to be made as against an authority.

THE MISDIRECTED WITHDRAWAL
DECLARATION CASE

NJW 1979 Heft 40 S. 2032

2 BGB § 130 (Voraussetzungen für das Wirksamwerden empfangsbedürftiger Willenserklärungen)

Für das Wirksamwerden einer empfangsbedürftigen Willenserklärung ist - außer dem Zugehen an den Erklärungsgegner – erforderlich, aber auch ausreichend, daß sie mit Willen des Erklärenden in den Verkehr gelangt ist und der Erklärende damit rechnen konnte und gerechnet hat, daß sie (sei es auch auf Umwegen) den richtigen Empfänger erreichen werde.

BGH, Urt. v. 11.5.1979 – V ZR 177/77 (Düsseldorf)

THE MISDIRECTED WITHDRAWAL
DECLARATION CASE

As we have seen, it is only some declarations of will which need to reach another person in order to become effective. This case concerns what has to happen to such declarations.

NJW 1979 Volume 40 p 2032

2 § 130 of the BGB (Prerequisites for declarations of will which need to be received becoming effective)

For a declaration of will which needs to be received to become effective it is, unless it reaches the opposite party, necessary and also sufficient that it has come into circulation in accordance with the intention of the declarant and the declarant could count upon it and has counted upon it reaching the right recipient, even if by indirect means.

BGH judgment of 11.5.1979 – V CiL 177/77 (Düsseldorf)

Zum Sachverhalt:

Die Kl. Eheleute erwarben aufgrund notariellen Vertrages vom 4.9.1975 ein Grundstück, das mit einem Bauerngehöft bestanden ist. Zum Ausgleich für Leistungen des Bekl. beim Ausbau der Gebäude schlossen die Parteien gleichzeitig einen notariellen Versorgungsvertrag, durch den sich die Kl. gegenüber dem Bekl. neben persönlichen Dienstleistungen zur Bestellung eines unentgeltlichen Wohnrechts an einer Wohnung verpflichteten. Wegen ersatzweise zu erbringender Geldleistungen unterwarfen sie sich der sofortigen Zwangvollstreckung. Im Zusammenhang mit der Begründung des Wohnrechts wurde in dem Versorgungsvertrag niedergelegt, daß eine Baugenehmigung, die dem Bekl. im Jahre 1970 für den Anbau erteilt worden war, auf die Kl. 'umgeschrieben' werden sollte. Abschließend wurde ihnen ein Rücktrittsrecht mit folgendem Wortlaut eingeräumt: 'Für den Fall, daß die erwähnte Baugenehmigung nicht bis zum 23.9.1975 auf die ... (Kl.) umgeschrieben sein sollte, sind die ... (Kl.) berechtigt, von dem heutigen Vertrag zurückzutreten. Der Rücktritt ist spätestens am 30.9.1975 schriftlich zu erklären. Das Rücktrittsrecht entfällt, wenn die Rücktrittsvoraussetzungen wegfallen, ehe der Rücktritt ausgeübt ist.' Unter dem 24.9.1975 erklärten die Kl. in einem an den beurkundenden Notar gerichteten Schreiben unter Hinweis auf das Fehlen der Baugenehmigung den Rücktritt vom Versorgungsvertrag. Der Notar leitete das Schreiben an den Bekl. weiter; bei ihm ging es am 30.9.1975 ein. Ein weiteres Schreiben, in dem sie ihre Rücktrittser-klärung wiederholten, richteten die Kl. am 30.9.1975 unmittelbar an den Bekl.; es erreichte ihn ebenfalls noch an diesem Tage. Auf eine Bauvoranfrage stellte der Oberkreisdirektor am 30.9.1975 dem Bekl. durch einen Vorbescheid 'vorbehaltlich der Zustimmung des Landeskonservators' die Genehmigung des geplanten Bauvorhabens in Aussicht. Mit Schreiben vom 3.10.1975 widersprach der Bekl. den Rücktrittserklärungen. Mit der Klage verfolgen die Kl. den Antrag, die – vom Bekl. inzwischen eingeleitete – Zwangsvollstreckung für unzulässig zu erklären.

LG und OLG haben der Vollstreckungsabwehrklage stattgegeben. Die Revision des Bekl. führte zur Aufhebung und Zurückverweisung.

Facts:

The plaintiffs (a married couple) acquired, on the basis of a notarial contract of the 4.9.1975 a piece of land which is the site of a farmstead. As compensation for the services of the defendant for the extension of the buildings, the parties concluded at the same time a notarial service contract by which the plaintiffs committed themselves to reserve to the defendant a free right of residence in a dwelling, in addition to personal services. Because of money payments to be made by way of compensation, they submitted to immediate execution proceedings. In connection with the establishment of the right of residence, it was laid down in the service contract that a permission to build which had been given to the defendant in the year 1970 for the building on should be 'transferred' to the plaintiffs. Finally, a right of withdrawal was granted to them in the following words: 'In case the said permission to build should not be transferred to ... (plaintiffs) until the 23.9.1975 the ... (plaintiffs) are entitled to withdraw from this contract. The withdrawal must be declared in writing on the 30.9.1975 at the latest. The right of withdrawal lapses if the withdrawal prerequisites cease to apply before withdrawal has taken place.' On the 24.9.1975 the plaintiffs declared their withdrawal from the service contract in a document, referring to absence of permission to build, directed to the authenticating notary. The notary forwarded the document on to the defendant; it was received on the 30.9.1975. A further document, in which they repeated their withdrawal declaration was sent by the plaintiffs directly to the defendant on the 30.9.1975; it reached him on this same day. In reply to a preliminary request for building, the district chief executive on the 30.9.1975 promised the defendant permission for the planned building proposal by a preliminary decision 'subject to the consent of the State curator'. By a letter of the 3.10.1975 the defendant refuted the withdrawal declarations. The plaintiffs are pursuing, in the action, an application for a declaration that the execution, initiated by the defendant in the meantime, is not permissible.

The State Court and the Upper State Court have granted the request for rejection of the execution. The appeal in law of the defendant led to quashing and reference back.

Aus den Gründen:

I Das BerGer. hat die Auffassung vertreten, daß die Kl. durch ihr Schreiben vom 24.9.1975 wirksam von dem Versorgungsvertrag zurückgetreten seien:

Daß die Rücktrittserklärung nicht an den Bekl., sondern an den beurkundenden Notar gerichtet gewesen sei, schade nicht, weil der Notar das Schreiben an den Bekl. weitergeleitet habe und es dort noch innerhalb der bis zum 30.9.1975 vereinbarten Frist eingegangen sei. Im Zeitpunkt des Zugehens beim Bekl. hätten die Rücktrittsvoraussetzungen noch vorgelegen; denn der positive Vorbescheid des Oberkreisdirektors sei dem Bekl. erst gegen 12 Uhr ausgehändigt worden, der Eilbrief des Notars hingegen habe dem für den Wohnort des Bekl. zuständigen Postamt schon um 8 Uhr vorgelegen und müsse daher spätestens um 10 Uhr in den Briefkasten des Bekl. eingeworfen worden sein. Unter diesen Umständen komme es nicht mehr auf den Zeitpunkt an, in dem das zweite, unmittelbar an den Bekl. gerichtete Rücktrittsschreiben vom 30.9.1975 bei diesem eingegangen sei.

II Diese Ausführungen halten der – von Amts wegen anzustellenden – rechtlichen Nachprüfung nicht stand.

Reasons:

I The appeal court defended the view that the plaintiffs by their letter of the 24.9.1975 effectively withdrew from the service contract:

The fact that the withdrawal declaration was not directed to the defendant but to the authenticating notary does not matter because the notary forwarded the letter to the defendant and it arrived there within the agreed period which ended on the 30.9.1975. At the point in time it reached the defendant the prerequisites for withdrawal would have been present; because the positive preliminary decision of the district chief executive was first delivered to the defendant at around 12 o'clock, and the express letter from the notary had already come to the appropriate post office for the defendant's place of residence by 8 o'clock and must hence have been put into the letter box of the defendant by 10 o'clock at the latest. Under these circumstances it is no longer a matter of the point in time at which the second withdrawal document of the 30.9.1975, which was sent to the defendant directly, reached him.

II These statements do not stand up to the legal re-examination which there is an official duty to conduct.

1 Wie auch das BerGer. nicht verkennt, bedurfte der Rücktritt von dem Versorgungsvertrag einer Erklärung gegenüber dem anderen Teile (§ 349 BGB), mithin gegenüber dem Bekl. Das BerGer stellt hierzu fest, die Kl. seien offenbar irrtümlich davon ausgegangen, daß der Notar als Beurkundungsperson der richtige Adressat für die Rücktrittserklärung sei; sie hätten ihm nicht nur ankündigen wollen, wie sie sich gegenüber dem Bekl. zu verhalten gedächten, sondern hätten durch die an ihn gerichtete Rücktrittserklärung die Rücktrittsfolgen gegenüber dem Bekl. auslösen wollen. Die Übersendung an den falschen Empfänger sei, so meint das BerGer., dadurch 'korrigiert' worden, daß der Notar das Rücktrittsschreiben dem Bekl. übersandt habe; der Inhalt des Schreibens und die Begleitumstände gäben mithin keinen Anlaß, in Zweifel zu ziehen, daß die Kl. 'gegenüber dem Bekl. von ihrem Rücktrittsrecht Gebrauch machen' wollten. Diese Ausführungen verkennen die Voraussetzungen für das Wirksamwerden empfangsbedürftiger Willenserklärungen. Zwar brauchen auch solche Erklärungen nicht unmittelbar an den Erklärungsgegner abgesandt zu werden; sie können ihm auch über Dritte zugeleitet werden, doch darf dies nicht mehr oder weniger zufällig, sondern muß zielgerichtet geschehen. Es gibt im bürgerlichen Recht keinen dem § 187 ZPO für die Heilung von Zustellungsmängeln entsprechenden Grundsatz, wie ihn das BerGer. seiner Beurteilung anscheinend zugrunde gelegt hat. Erforderlich, aber auch ausreichend ist – neben dem Zugehen – vielmehr, daß die Willenserklärung mit Willen des Erklärenden in den Verkehr gelangt und der Erklärende damit rechnen konnte und gerechnet hat, sie werde (auf welchem Wege auch immer) den Erklärungsgegner erreichen (*Flume*, Allg. Teil des Bürgerlichen Rechts, 2. Band: Das Rechtsgeschäft, 2. Aufl., § 14 Anm. 2; *Soergel-Hefermehl*, BGB, 11. Aufl., § 130 Rdnr. 6; *Förschler* in: MünchKomm, § 130 Rdnr. 10; vgl. auch RGZ 170, 380 [382]; *OLG Köln*, NJW 1950, 702). Feststellungen in dieser Richtung hat das BerGer. – aus seiner Sicht folgerichtig – nicht getroffen. Das angefochtene Urteil kann daher mit der gegebenen Begründung nicht aufrechterhalten werden.

1 As the appeal court did not fail to recognise, withdrawal from the services contract required a declaration against the other party (§ 349 of the BGB), ie, the defendant. The appeal court also established on this issue that the plaintiffs assumed, clearly mistakenly, that the notary as the authenticator was the correct addressee for the withdrawal declaration. They would not only have wanted to give him notice of how they intended to act as against the defendant, but they would also have wanted, by the withdrawal declaration directed to him, to trigger the consequences of withdrawal as against the defendant. The appeal court considered the dispatch to the wrong recipient was corrected by the fact that the notary had sent the withdrawal document to the defendant. The content of the document and the surrounding circumstances therefore gave no cause to doubt that the plaintiffs wanted 'to make use of their right of withdrawal as against the defendant'. These statements misjudge the prerequisites for declarations of will which need to be received becoming effective. Such declarations certainly do not need to be sent directly to the opposite party; they can be sent to him through a third party. This may however not happen more or less accidentally, but must occur with that purpose in view. There is no principle in civil law corresponding to § 187 of the ZPO for the curing of defects in service, which the appeal court has apparently taken as a basis for its decision. Rather is it necessary (but also sufficient) that, in addition to actual arrival, the declaration has come into circulation in accordance with the intention of the declarant, and the declarant could count upon it, and has counted upon it reaching (by whatever means) the party against whom the declaration was made (*Flume*, General Part of the Civil Code, Vol 2: *The Legal Transaction*, 2nd edn, § 14 note 2; *Soergel-Hefermehl*, BGB, 11th edn, § 130 marginal no 6; *Förschler* in: Münich Commentary, § 130 marginal no 10; compare also RGZ 170, 380 [382]; OLG Cologne, NJW 1950, 702). The appeal court has not logically, from its point of view, made findings in this respect. The judgment challenged can therefore not be sustained by the reasoning given.

2 Das Berufungsurteil stellt sich auch nicht aus anderen Gründen im Ergebnis als richtig dar (§ 563 ZPO). Zwar ist zwischen den Parteien unstreitig, daß das an den Bekl. gerichtete Rücktrittsschreiben der Kl. vom 30.9.1975 ebenfalls an diesem Tage – und damit innerhalb der vertraglich vorgesehenen Frist – beim Bekl. eingegangen ist. Der genaue Zeitpunkt des Zugehens und damit die Reihenfolge der Aushändigung des Vorbescheides und des Eingangs der Rücktrittserklärung – ist im Berufungsurteil offen geblieben. Obwohl die Darlegungs- und Beweislast für den rechtserhaltenden Umstand (Replik), daß im Zeitpunkt des Zugangs der Rücktrittserklärung das Rücktrittsrecht bereits erloschen war, beim Bekl. liegt, läßt sich der Rechtsstreit im gegenwärtigen Stadium nicht nach der Verteilung der Darlegungs- und Beweislast entscheiden. Nachdem der Prozeß bisher aus der unzutreffenden Sicht geführt worden ist, daß das Rücktrittsschreiben vom 24.9.1975 durch Weiterleitung seitens des Notars an den Bekl. ohne weiteres wirksam werden konnte, ist den Parteien vielmehr Gelegenheit zu geben, zum genauen Zeitpunkt des Zugehens des zweiten Schreibens beim Bekl. näheres vorzutragen.

3 Sollte die erneute Verhandlung bezüglich des ersten Rücktrittsschreibens ergeben, daß die Kl. damit gerechnet haben, der Notar werde das Schreiben – wie geschehen – an den Bekl. weiterleiten, so hinge die Wirksamkeit jener Rücktrittserklärung von im Berufungsurteil und von der Revision angesprochenen weiteren Fragen ab. Für ihre Beurteilung wären folgende Erwägungen maßgebend:

(a) Im Anschluß an die ständige Rechtsprechung und herrschende Meinung (RGZ 50, 191 [194]; BGH, NJW 1965, 965 [966]; BAG, Betr 1976, 1018 = NJW 1976, 1284 L; Förschler, in: MünchKomm, § 130 Rdnr. 16 m. w. Nachw.) ist mit dem BerGer. davon auszugehen, daß eine schriftliche Willenserklärung zugegangen ist, sobald sie in verkehrsüblicher Art in die tatsächliche Verfügungsgewalt des Addresaten gelangt und ihm in dieser Weise die Möglichkeit der Kenntnisnahme verschafft ist. Briefsendungen sind danach im allgemeinen bereits dann als zugegangen anzusehen, wenn sie in den Briefkasten des Empfängers eingeworfen werden. Für Eilbriefe gilt entgegen der Meinung der Revision nichts anderes.

(b) Nicht zu beanstanden ist der vom BerGer. angewendete Erfahrungssatz, daß Eilbotensendungen gem. § 33 PostO im Wege bevorzugter Zustellung vor der allgemeinen Post zugestellt werden.

(c) Die Erhebung von den Kl. angebotener Beweise dafür, 'daß der Einwurf in den Briefkasten *nach* der Mittagsstunde wahrscheinlich ist', erübrigt sich, da der Bekl. mit der Darlegung einer bloßen Wahrscheinlichkeit seiner Darlegungs- und Beweislast für die zur Beendigung des Rücktrittsrechts führenden Umstände nicht genügt.

The appeal judgment does not appear in its outcome to be correct on other grounds as well (§ 563 of the ZPO). It is certainly not disputed between the parties that the plaintiff's withdrawal document of the 30.9.1975 directed to the defendant also reached the defendant on this day, and therefore within the period provided for by the contract. The exact point in time of the receipt, and therefore the sequence of the delivery of the preliminary decision and the arrival of the withdrawal declaration, is left open in the appeal judgment. Although the burden of explanation and proof for the facts supporting the right (reply[7]), ie, that at the point in time of the arrival of the withdrawal declaration the right of withdrawal had already lapsed, lies with the defendant, the legal dispute at the present stage is not to be decided according to the allocation of the burden of explanation and proof. Since the proceedings have until now been conducted from the incorrect point of view that the withdrawal document of the 24.9.1975 could become effective simply by forwarding it, by the notary, to the defendant, it is much more appropriate to give the parties the opportunity to present further details about the exact point in time of the receipt of the second document by the defendant.

3 If the renewed hearing should reveal that in relation to the first withdrawal document the plaintiffs counted on it that the notary would forward the document to the defendant, as in fact happened, the effectiveness of that withdrawal document would depend on further questions addressed in the original appeal judgment and in the appeal in law. For assessing it, the following considerations would be decisive:

(a) Following the consistent case law and the prevailing opinion (RGZ 50, 191 [194]; BGH, NJW 1965, 965 [966]; BAG, DB 1976, 1018 = NJW 1976, 1284 L; Förschler, in Münich Commentary, § 130 marginal no 16 with further references) one should proceed, as did the appeal court, on the basis that a written declaration has arrived as soon as it has reached the actual power of control of the addressee in the usual business manner and in this way he is provided with the possibility of becoming aware of its contents. According to this, letters are in general to be regarded as having been received if they are put into the letter box of the recipient. There is no different rule for express letters, contrary to the view expressed in the appeal in law.

(b) There can be no objection to the empirical principle applied by the appeal court that express dispatches in accordance with § 33 of the Postal Regulations are delivered before the ordinary post, by way of preferential delivery.

(c) The investigation of the evidence offered by the plaintiffs for the fact 'that the insertion in the letter box probably occurred *after* midday' is unnecessary, as the defendant, by submission of a mere probability, does not satisfy his burden of explanation and proof for the circumstances leading to the termination of the right of withdrawal.

---

7 This means reply in the English sense of the plaintiff's response to new matters raised in a defendant's defence.

(d) Entgegen der Ansicht der Revision ist aus Rechtsgründen nicht die Vertragsauslegung geboten, daß – unabhängig von der genauen zeitlichen Reihenfolge des Zugangs – das Rücktrittsrecht schon dann entfallen sollte, wenn die Rücktrittserklärung und die behördliche Klärung der Zulässigkeit des Bauvorhabens auf denselben Tag fielen. Die gegenteilige Auslegung des BerGer. ist frei von Rechtsfehlern.

(e) Es verstößt nicht gegen Treu und Glauben, daß die Kl. den Versorgungsvertrag hinfällig machten, obwohl fristgemäß feststand, daß der Ausbau des Gebäudes baubehördlich genehmigt werde. Da der Vertrag für die Ausübung des Rücktrittsrechts nur den Zeitraum vom 23. bis zum 30.9.1975 vorsah, handelten die Kl. nicht treuwidrig, indem sie am letzten Tage der Frist den Rücktritt erklärten. Dieser Gefahr hätte der Bekl. nach der vertraglichen Risikoverteilung (nur) dadurch entgehen können, daß er den positiven Vorbescheid bereits bis zum 23.9.1975 herbeiführte.

§ 131 [Wirksamwerden gegenüber nicht voll Geschäftsfähigen] (1) Wird die Willenserklärung einem Geschäftsunfähigen gegenüber abgegeben, so wird sie nicht wirksam, bevor sie dem gesetzlichen Vertreter zugeht.

(2) Das gleiche gilt, wenn die Willenserklärung einer in der Geschäftsfähigkeit beschränkten Person gegenüber abgegeben wird. Bringt die Erklärung jedoch der in der Geschäftsfähigkeit beschränkten Person lediglich einem rechtlichen Vorteil, oder hat der gesetzliche Vertreter seine Einwilligung erteilt, so wird die Erklärung in dem Zeitpunkte wirksam, in welchem sie ihr zugeht.

§ 132 [Ersatz des Zugehens durch Zustellung] (1) Eine Willenserklärung gilt auch dann als zugegangen, wenn sie durch Vermittlung eines Gerichtsvollziehers zugestellt worden ist. Die Zustellung erfolgt nach den Vorschriften der Zivilprozeßordnung.

(2) Befindet sich der Erklärende über die Person desjenigen, welchem gegenüber die Erklärung abzugeben ist, in einer nicht auf Fahrlässigkeit beruhenden Unkenntnis oder ist der Aufenthalt dieser Person unbekannt, so kann die Zustellung nach den für die öffentliche Zustellung einer Ladung geltenden Vorschriften der Zivilprozeßordnung erfolgen ...

(d) Contrary to the view expressed in the appeal in law, it is not necessary on legal grounds to interpret the contract so that – independently of the exact time sequence of the receipt – the right of withdrawal should lapse if the declaration of withdrawal and the official clarification of the permissibility of the building proposal occurred on the same day. The appeal court's interpretation to the contrary is free from legal errors.

(e) It is not a breach of good faith that the plaintiffs invalidated the service contract even though it was established in time that the extension of the building was authorised by the building authority. As the contract only allowed the period from 23 to 30.9.1975 for the exercise of the right of withdrawal, the plaintiffs did not act contrary to good faith by declaring withdrawal on the last day of the period. The defendant could (only) have escaped this danger, in accordance with the contractual apportionment of risks, by causing the positive preliminary decision to be made by the 23.9.1975 at the latest.

§ 131 [Effectiveness against a person not fully competent] (1) If the declaration of will is made against an incompetent person, it is not effective before it reaches the legal representative.

(2) The same applies if the declaration of will is made against a person of limited competence. If however the declaration only gives the person of limited competence a legal advantage or if the legal representative has given his consent, the declaration will be effective at the point in time at which it reaches that person.

§ 132 [Replacement of receipt by service] (1) A declaration of will counts as having been received if it has been served by the agency of a bailiff. The service takes place according to the rules of civil procedure.

(2) If the declarant is in a state of ignorance (which is not due to negligence) as to the person as against whom the declaration is to be made, or if the residence of this person is unknown, the service can take place according to the rules of civil process applying to the service of a summons by publication ...

The remainder of this paragraph relates to the court which is to have competence to give approval in such cases.

Interpretation of a declaration of will

§ 133 [Auslegung einer Willenserklärung] Bei der Auslegung einer Willenserklärung ist der wirkliche Wille zu erforschen und nicht an dem buchstäblichen Sinne des Ausdrucks zu haften.

Illegality

(1) Generally

§ 134 [Gesetzliches Verbot] Ein Rechtsgeschäft, das gegen ein gesetzliches Verbot verstößt, ist nichtig, wenn sich nicht aus dem Gesetz ein anderes ergibt.

(2) As to alienation

§ 135 [Gesetzliches Veräußerungsverbot] (1) Verstößt die Verfügung über einen Gegenstand gegen ein gesetzliches Veräußerungsverbot, das nur den Schutz bestimmter Personen bezweckt, so ist sie nur diesen Personen gegenüber unwirksam. Der rechtsgeschäftlichen Verfügung steht eine Verfügung gleich, die im Wege der Zwangsvollstreckung oder der Arrestvollziehung erfolgt.

(2) Die Vorschriften zugunsten derjenigen welche Rechte von einem Nichtberechtigten herleiten, finden entsprechende Anwendung.

§ 136 [Behördliches Veräußerungsverbot] Ein Veräußersungsverbot, das von einem Gericht oder von einer anderen Behörden innerhalb ihrer Zuständigkeit erlassen wird, steht einem gesetzlichen Veräußerungsverbote der im § 135 bezeichneten Art gleich.

§ 137 [Rechtsgeschäftliches Veräußerungsverbot] Die Befugnis zur Verfügung über ein veräußerliches Recht kann nicht durch Rechtsgeschäft ausgeschlossen oder beschränkt werden. Die Wirksamkeit einer Verpflichtung, über ein solches Recht nicht zu verfügen, wird durch diese Vorschrift nicht berührt.

Interpretation of a declaration of will

§ 133 [Interpretation of a declaration of will] In the interpretation of a declaration of will, the real intention is to be ascertained, and the literal sense of what is expressed is not to be followed.

§§ 133 and 157 (see Chapter Five, p 363) do not contain comprehensive rules for interpretation of (respectively) declarations of will and contracts. The remaining rules are contained in case law and doctrine, and in particular require consideration of prior negotiations, purpose and context. A different interpretation may be reached, depending on whether one looks at the declaration from the point of view of the maker of it, or from that of anyone to whom it is addressed, or simply objectively. There are therefore different rules, eg, for declarations, which need to be received, and for wills.

Illegality

(1) Generally

§ 134 [Statutory prohibition] A legal transaction which is contrary to a statutory prohibition is invalid unless a different consequence is to be deduced from the statute.

See the internet auction case, Chapter Five, p 333.

(2) As to alienation

§ 135 [Statutory prohibition on alienation] (1) If the disposal of an item contravenes a statutory prohibition on alienation which only has in view the protection of certain persons, it is only ineffective as against those persons. The disposal by legal transaction is equivalent to a disposal which occurs by way of legal execution or the carrying out of an attachment.

(2) The rules for the benefit of those who derive rights from a person who is not entitled have corresponding application.

§ 136 [Alienation prohibition by an authority] A prohibition on alienation which is issued by a court or by another authority within its competence is equivalent to a statutory prohibition on alienation of the kind described in § 135.

§ 137 [Alienation prohibited by a legal transaction] The authority to dispose of an alienable right cannot be excluded or limited by a legal transaction. The effectiveness of an obligation not to dispose of such a right is not affected by this rule.

Impropriety

§ 138 [Sittenwidriges Rechtsgeschäft; Wucher] (1) Ein Rechtsgeschäft, das gegen die guten Sitten verstößt, ist nichtig.

(2) Nichtig ist insbesondere ein Rechtsgeschäft, durch das jemand unter Ausbeutung der Zwangslage, der Unerfahrenheit, des Mangels an Urteilsvermögen oder der erheblichen Willensschwäche eines anderen sich oder einem Dritten für eine Leistung Vermögensvorteile versprechen oder gewähren läßt die in einem auffälligen Mißverhältnis zu der Leistung stehen.

INVALIDITY OF A LEGAL TRANSACTION

§ 139 [Teilnichtigkeit] Ist ein Teil eines Rechtsgeschäfts nichtig, so ist das ganze Rechtsgeschäft nichtig, wenn nicht anzunehmen ist, daß es auch ohne den nichtigen Teil vorgenommen sein würde.

§ 140 [Umdeutung] Entspricht ein nichtiges Rechtsgeschäft den Erfordernissen eines anderen Rechtsgeschäfts, so gilt das letztere, wenn anzunehmen ist, daß dessen Geltung bei Kenntnis der Nichtigkeit gewollt sein würde.

§ 141 [Bestätigung des nichtigen Rechtsgeschäfts] (1) Wird ein nichtiges Rechtsgeschäft von demjenigen, welcher es vorgenommen hat, bestätigt, so ist die Bestätigung als erneute Vornahme zu beurteilen.

(2) Wird ein nichtiger Vertrag von den Parteien bestätigt, so sind diese im Zweifel verpflichtet, einander zu gewähren, was sie haben würden, wenn der Vertrag von Anfang an gültig gewesen wäre.

AVOIDANCE GENERALLY

§ 142 [Wirkung der Anfechtung] (1) Wird ein anfechtbares Rechtsgeschäft angefochten, so ist es als von Anfang an nichtig anzusehen.

(2) Wer die Anfechtbarkeit kannte oder kenne mußte, wird, wenn die Anfechtung erfolgt, so behandelt, wie wenn er die Nichtigkeit des Rechtsgeschäfts gekannt hätte oder hätte kennen müssen.

§ 143 [Anfechtungserklärung] (1) Die Anfechtung erfolgt durch Erklärung gegenüber dem Anfechtungsgegner.

Impropriety

§ 138 [Immoral legal transaction; taking unfair advantage] (1) A legal transaction which contravenes good morals is void.

(2) In particular, a legal transaction is void by which someone through exploitation of the predicament, inexperience, lack of judgment, or significant weakness of the will of another causes to be promised or granted to himself or a third person in return for a performance economic advantages which are conspicuously disproportionate to the performance.

Good morals means the feeling of propriety of all fair and right thinking persons; see BGHZ 69, 297. Regard must be had to the legal order and in particular the Basic Law. Transactions contravening this concept can take many forms, but the English law categories of unreasonable restraint of trade and sexual immorality would be included. See the Prostitutionsgesetz of the 20.12.01 (BGBl I, 3983).

INVALIDITY OF A LEGAL TRANSACTION

§ 139 [Partial invalidity] If part of a legal transaction is invalid, the whole transaction is invalid if it cannot be assumed that it would have been entered into even without the invalid part.

Compare this to the English rules on whether a transaction is divisible.

§ 140 [Conversion] If an invalid legal transaction corresponds to the requirements of another legal transaction, the latter is valid if it can be assumed that validity of this transaction would have been desired on knowledge of the invalidity.

§ 141 [Confirmation of an invalid legal transaction] (1) If an invalid legal transaction is confirmed by the person who entered into it, the confirmation is to be regarded as a renewal of the entry into it.

(2) If an invalid contract is confirmed by the parties, these are obliged, in case of doubt, to grant to each other what they would have if the contract had been valid from the start.

AVOIDANCE GENERALLY

§ 142 [Effect of voidability] (1) If a voidable legal transaction is avoided, it is to be regarded as void from the start.

(2) Any person who knew of the voidability or ought to have known of it, will, if avoidance follows, be treated as if he had known of the invalidity of the legal transaction or ought to have known of it.

§ 143 [Declaration of avoidance] (1) Avoidance occurs by a declaration made as against the opposing party.

(2) Anfechtungsgegner ist bei einem Vertrage der andere Teil, im Falle des § 123 Abs. 2 Satz 2 derjenige, welcher aus dem Vertrag unmittelbar ein Recht erworben hat.

(3) Bei einem einseitigen Rechtsgeschäft, das einem anderen gegenüber vorzunehmen war, ist der andere der Anfechtungsgegner. Das gleiche gilt bei einem Rechtsgeschäfte, das einem anderen oder einer Behörde gegenüber vorzunehmen war, auch dann, wenn das Rechtsgeschäft der Behörde gegenüber vorgenommen worden ist.

(4) Bei einem einseitigen Rechtsgeschäft anderer Art ist Anfechtungsgegner jeder, der auf Grund des Rechtsgeschäfts unmittelbar einen rechtlichen Vorteil erlangt hat. Die Anfechtung kann jedoch, wenn die Willenserklärung einer Behörde gegenüber abzugeben war durch Erklärung gegenüber der Behörde erfolgen; die Behörde soll die Anfechtung demjenigen mitteilen, welcher durch das Rechtsgeschäft unmittelbar betroffen worden ist.

§ 144 [Bestätigung des anfechtbaren Rechtsgeschäfts] (1) Die Anfechtung ist ausgeschlossen, wenn das anfechtbare Rechtsgeschäft von dem Anfechtungsberechtigten bestätigt wird.

(2) Die Bestätigung bedarf nicht der für das Rechtsgeschäft bestimmten Form.

PERIODS AND DATES; AND LIMITATION

EXERCISE OF RIGHTS

Sechster Abschnitt. Ausübung der Rechte. Selbtsverteidigung. Selbsthilfe

§ 226 [Schikaneverbot] Die Ausübung eines Rechtes ist unzulässig, wenn sie nur den Zweck haben kann, einem anderen Schaden zuzufügen.

(2) The opposing party is, in the case of a contract, the other party, and in the case of § 123 para 2 sentence 2 the person who has obtained a right directly from the contract.

See the internet auction case, Chapter Five, p 333.

(3) In the case of a one-sided legal transaction which was to be entered into as against another person, that other is the opposing party. The same applies in the case of a legal transaction which was to be entered into as against either another person or an authority, even if the transaction has been entered into as against the authority.

(4) In the case of a one-sided legal transaction of the other kind, the opposing party is each person who has received a legal advantage directly on the basis of the legal transaction. The avoidance can, however, if the declaration of will was to be given as against an authority, take place by declaration as against the authority; the authority shall communicate the avoidance to the person who has been directly affected by the legal transaction.

§ 144 [Confirmation of an avoidable legal transaction] (1) Avoidance is excluded if the avoidable legal transaction is confirmed by the person entitled to avoid it.

(2) The confirmation does not need to be in the required form for the legal transaction.

PERIODS AND DATES; AND LIMITATION

These are dealt with in (respectively) the Fourth and Fifth Sections of the BGB (§§ 186–193 and 194–225).

EXERCISE OF RIGHTS

Sixth Title. Exercise of Rights. Self-defence. Self-help

§ 226 [Prohibition of vexatiousness] The exercise of a right is not permitted if it can only have the purpose of causing harm to another.

This could apply to a person who erects a building with the sole purpose of obstructing another person's view.

SPECIAL DEFENCES

§ 227 [Notwehr] (1) Eine durch Notwehr gebotene Handlung ist nicht widerrechtlich.

(2) Notwehr ist diejenige Verteidigung, welche erforderlich ist, um einen gegenwärtigen rechtswidrigen Angriff von sich oder einem anderen abzuwenden.

§ 228 [Notstand] Wer eine fremde Sache beschädigt oder zerstört, um eine durch sie drohende Gefahr von sich oder einem anderen abzuwenden, handelt nicht widerrechtlich, wenn die Beschädigung oder die Zerstörung zur Abwendung der Gefahr erforderlich ist and der Schaden nicht außer Verhältnis zu der Gefahr steht. Hat der Handelnde die Gefahr verschuldet, so ist er zum Schadenersatze verpflichtet.

§ 229 [Selbsthilfe] Wer zum Zwecke der Selbsthilfe eine Sache wegnimmt, zerstört oder beschädigt oder wer zum Zwecke der Selbsthilfe einen Verpflichteten, welcher der Flucht verdächtigt ist, festnimmt oder den Widerstand des Verpflichteten gegen eine Handlung, die dieser zu dulden verpflichtet ist, beseitigt, handelt nicht widerrechtlich, wenn obrigkeitliche Hilfe nicht rechtzeitig zu erlangen ist und ohne sofortiges Eingreifen die Gefahr besteht, daß die Verwirklichung des Anspruchs vereitelt oder wesentlich erschwert werde.

§ 230 [Grenzen der Selbsthilfe] (1) Die Selbsthilfe darf nicht weiter gehen, als zur Abwendung der Gefahr erforderlich ist.

(2) Im Falle der Wegnahme von Sachen ist, sofern nicht Zwangsvollstreckung erwirkt wird, der dingliche Arrest zu beantragen.

(3) Im Falle der Festnahme des Verpflichteten ist, sofern er nicht wieder in Freiheit gesetzt wird, der persönliche Sicherheitsarrest bei dem Amtsgerichte zu beantragen, in dessen Bezirke die Festnahme erfolgt ist; der Verpflichtete ist unverzüglich dem Gerichte vorzuführen.

(4) Wird der Arrestantrag verzögert oder abgelehnt, so hat die Rückgabe der weggenommenen Sachen und die Freilassung des Festgenommenen unverzüglich zu erfolgen.

§ 231 [Irrtümliche Selbsthilfe] Wer eine der im § 229 bezeichneten Handlungen in der irrigen Annahme vornimmt, daß die für den Ausschluß der Widerrechtlichkeit erforderlichen Voraussetzungen vorhanden seien, ist dem anderen Teile zum Schadenersatze verpflichtet, auch wenn der Irrtum nicht auf Fahrlässigkeit beruht.

SPECIAL DEFENCES

§ 227 [Self-defence] (1) An action required by self-defence is not unlawful.

(2) Self-defence is that defence which is necessary in order to divert a present unlawful attack from oneself or from another.

Compare this to § 32 of the StGB. See the shooting at the disco case, p 321.

§ 228 [Emergency] A person who harms or destroys an object belonging to another in order to divert from himself or another a danger which threatens as a result of it does not act unlawfully if the harm or the destruction is necessary for the diversion of the danger and the harm is not out of proportion to the danger. If the person so acting is to blame for the danger, he is obliged to compensate for the harm.

Compare this to § 34 of the StGB.

§ 229 [Self-help] A person who, for the purpose of self-help, takes away, destroys or harms an object or who, for the purpose of self-help, apprehends a person under an obligation who is suspected of flight, or puts an end to the resistance of such a person against an action which he is obliged to permit, does not act unlawfully if official help is not obtainable in time and the danger exists that without immediate intervention the realisation of the claim will be frustrated or substantially impeded.

§ 230 [Limits of self-help] (1) Self-help may not go further than is necessary for the prevention of the danger.

(2) In the case of the removal of objects, insofar as legal execution is not effected, judicial arrest is to be applied for.

(3) In the case of the apprehension of a person under an obligation, insofar as he is not set at liberty again, personal arrest for security purposes is to be applied for in the county court in whose area the apprehension took place; the person under the obligation is to be brought before the court without delay.

(4) If the application for arrest is delayed or refused, the return of the objects taken away and the release of the persons arrested must ensue without delay.

§ 231 [Mistaken self-help] A person who carries out one of the actions described in § 229 on the mistaken supposition that the prerequisites necessary for the exclusion of unlawfulness are present is obliged to compensate the other party for harm, even if the mistake was not based on negligence.

THE SHOOTING AT THE DISCO CASE

8 BGB §§ 823, 227 (Ersatzpflicht des Schädigers wegen dessen Verhalten vor Eintritt der Notwehrlage)

Zur Pflicht eines Gastwirts, unter besonderen Umständen auf die Herbeiführung einer Notwehrsituation gegenüber unbefugten Eindringlingen deshalb zu verzichten, weil die zu gewärtigende Notwendigkeit des Schußwaffengebrauchs andere Gäste erheblich gefährden müßte.

BGH, Urt. v. 27.6.1978 – VI ZR 180/77 (Frankfurt)

Zum Sachverhalt:

Der Bekl. war Mitinhaber einer Discothek, in der es am späten Abend des 27.7.1971 zu einer Schlägerei zwischen Mitgliedern einer Rockerbande und dem von dieser angegriffenen Bekl. kam. Dabei machte dieser von einer mitgeführten Schußwaffe Gebrauch, mit der er, nachdem er einen erfolglosen Warnschuß abgegeben hatte, den Bandenführer durch zwei gezielte Schüsse tödlich verletzte. Eine der beiden Kugeln durchschlug dessen Bauchdecke, prallte nach Wiederaustritt aus dem Körper auf den Boden, verirrte sich von da als Querschläger auf die nahe Tanzfläche und drang dort dem gerade tanzenden, an dem Raufhandel nicht beteiligten, seinerzeit noch nicht ganz 17-jährigen Kl. in den Bauch. Diese Verwundung machte die operative Entferning der Milz erforderlich.

Der Kl. nimmt den Bekl. wegen fahrlässig verursachter Körperverletzung auf Schadensersatz in Anspruch. Das LG hat nur einen Teil des bezifferten Klageanspruchs zugesprochen und die Ersatzpflicht hinsichtlich späterer materieller Schäden festgestellt, den Schmerzensgeldanspruch jedoch abgewiesen. Die Berufung des Kl. führte auch zu einer Verurteilung zur Zahlung von Schmerzensgeld dem Grunde nach; die Anschlußberufung des Bekl. blieb erfolglos. Die – zugelassene – Revision des Bekl. hatte keinen Erfolg.

Aus den Gründen:

... II 1 Das BerGer. hält den Bekl. für verpflichtet, dem Kl. aus unerlaubter Handlung (§ 823 BGB) Schadensersatz zu leisten. Es führt hierzu aus:

THE SHOOTING AT THE DISCO CASE

This was a claim in tort for negligently inflicted injury, but the facts are bizarre. The problem was that the defendant acted in self-defence in shooting an intruder, but the court wanted to find him liable to the claimant, who was accidentally injured by the bullet. It did so by looking at the defendant's actions as a whole, including his rashness in allowing the confrontation to take place.

8 BGB §§ 823, 227 (Duty of wrongdoer to compensate because of his conduct before the commencement of a self-defence situation)

On the duty of a landlord to refrain in special circumstances from bringing about a self-defence situation in relation to unauthorised intruders because the necessity which was to be expected of the use of firearms would necessarily seriously endanger other guests.

BGH, judgment of 27.6.1978 – VI ZR 180/77 (Frankfurt)

Facts:

The defendant was the co-proprietor of a discotheque in which, late in the evening of the 27.7.1971 a brawl arose between the members of a group of rockers and the defendant, who was attacked by them. In the course of this, he made use of a gun which he had brought with him, by which, after he had fired a warning shot which brought no result, he fatally injured the leader of the group with two aimed shots. One of the two bullets penetrated his abdominal wall, rebounded from the floor after exit from his body, and ricocheted from there to the nearby dance floor and penetrated the abdomen of the claimant who was not quite 17 at the time and was dancing there. He had not been taking part in the brawl. This injury necessitated the removal of his spleen by an operation.

The claimant claims compensation from the defendant for negligently causing physical injury. The State Court granted part only of the sum claimed and established a duty to compensate in relation to later material harm. However, it rejected the claim for damages for pain and suffering. The claimant's appeal led to a judgment in principle for the payment of damages for pain and suffering. The cross appeal of the defendant was unsuccessful. The appeal in law of the defendant was permitted, but was unsuccessful.

Reasons:

... II 1 The appeal court considers that the defendant is under a duty to compensate the claimant in tort (§ 823 of the BGB). On this issue it explains:

Daß der Bekl. den Schuß auf den Anführer der Rocker in einer Notwehrlage abgefeuert habe, mache die dadurch ungewollt eingetretene Körperverletzung des Kl. nicht rechtmäßig, weil der Rechtfertigungsgrund des § 227 BGB nur gegenüber dem Angreifer zum Tragen komme, nicht jedoch gegenüber einem Dritten, der unbeabsichtigt durch die Notwehrhandlung verletzt werde. Es könne demnach nur darum gehen, ob die Körperverletzung des Kl. durch den Bekl. aufgrund besonderer Umstände entschuldigt, nicht dagegen, ob sie gerechtfertigt gewesen sei. Im vorliegenden Fall müsse fahrlässiges Handeln des Bekl. bejaht werden. Wer aber wie im Streitfall innerhalb eines Lokals mit vielen Gästen im Zuge einer Auseinandersetzung auf jemanden schieße, müsse regelmässig damit rechnen, daß Dritte durch den Schuß zu Schaden kommen könnten. Das gelte hier um so mehr, als der Bekl. kurz vor der Schußabgabe seine Brille verloren habe und deshalb nur schlecht habe sehen können. Die mögliche Verletzung eines Dritten, wie sie auch dann eingetreten sei, sei durchaus vorauszusehen gewesen. Eine dem strafrechtlichen entschuldigenden Notstand des § 34 StGB entsprechende Regelung gebe es für das Zivilrecht nicht, wenngleich im Bereich des zivilrechtlichen Haftungsrecht dem rechtwidrig handelnden Schädiger wohl kaum ein Schuldvorwurf zu machen sein werde, wenn er schuldlos in eine Lage gerate, die zum Schutze seiner Gesundheit oder sogar seines Lebens eine Abwehrmaßnahme herausfordere, die auch am Angriff nicht beteiligte Dritte nicht nur gefährde, sondern sogar verletze. Im Streitfall könne daher das Verschulden des Bekl. nicht darin gesehen werden, daß er während des gegen ihn gerichteten Angriffs der Rocker zur Schußwaffe gegriffen habe; wohl aber müsse ihm angelastet werden, daß er trotz der von ihm erkannten Gefahr und der in Kauf genommenen Wahrscheinlichkeit, zur Selbstverteidigung von der Waffe Gebrauch machen zu müssen, nicht davon abgesehen habe, noch vor Eintreffen der Polizei in sein Lokal zu gehen und auf diese Weise den Rockern den angedrohten Angriff auf seine Person erst zu ermöglichen.

2 Diesen Ausführungen kann nur im Ergebnis beigepflichtet werden. Es kommt im Streitfall nicht darauf an, zu der Auffassung des BerGer. Stellung zu nehmen, der Gebrauch der Schußwaffe gegen die angreifenden Rocker sei zwar aus der gegebenen Notwehrlage heraus gerechtfertigt gewesen, er müsse aber insoweit als rechtswidrig beurteilt werden, als es dadurch nicht nur zu einer – letztlich tödlichen – Verletzung des Anführers der Rocker, sondern auch zu einer – unstreitig ungewollten – Beeinträchtigung der körperlichen Unversehrtheit des Klägers gekommen sei.

The firing by the defendant of a shot at the leader of the rockers in a self-defence situation would not make the claimant's physical injury (which arose unintentionally from it) lawful. This is because the ground of justification in § 227 of the BGB would only be effective against the attacker and not against a third party who was unintentionally injured by the act of self-defence. It could accordingly only be a question of whether the physical injury of the claimant by the defendant was excused on the basis of special circumstances, and not of whether it was justified. In the present case, the defendant's behaviour has to be described as negligent. A person who (as in the case in question) shoots at someone inside a bar with many guests present in the course of a confrontation must as a rule take into account the fact that third parties could come to harm as a result of the shot. That is all the more applicable here as the defendant had lost his glasses shortly before the firing of the shot and therefore could not see properly. Possible injury to a third party (of the kind which actually occurred) was definitely foreseeable. There was no provision for the civil law corresponding to the emergency of § 34 of the StGB which is an excuse in criminal law. It was however true that in the realm of civil liability law, an accusation of blame was certainly scarcely to be made against the defendant who acts in a manner contrary to law when, without any fault on his part, he got into a situation which for the protection of his health or even his life required defensive action, which not only endangered but harmed third parties who did not take part in the attack. In this case, the fault of the defendant could therefore not be seen in the fact that he had resorted to using a gun during the attack by the rockers against him. He had however to be blamed for the fact that, in spite of the danger recognised by him and the probability, which he accepted, that he would have to make use of a weapon in self-defence, he had not refrained from going into his bar before the arrival of the police, thus enabling the rockers to make the threatened attack on his person.

2 It is only possible to agree with the outcome of these observations. It is not necessary in the present case to express an opinion on the view of the appeal court that the use of a gun against the attacking rockers was justified by the given self-defence situation but that it had to be judged to be illegal insofar as not only an injury (which was ultimately fatal) of the leader of the rockers but also an invasion of the physical integrity of the claimant (it being undisputed that this was unintentional) had thereby resulted.

Selbst wenn man – entgegen der wohl herrschenden Meinung (z.B. *Baldus*, in: LK, 9. Aufl., § 53 StGB Rdnrn. 27, 23, wo auch auf die Gegenmeinung hingewiesen wird; *Samson*, in SKStGB, 2. Aufl., § 32 Rdnr. 18: ausf. und m. w. Nachw. versehen *Schönke-Shröder*, StGB, 19. Aufl. Rdnr. 32; *Larenz*, BGB AT, 4. Aufl., § 151c; *Erman-Hefermehl*, BGB, 6. Aufl., § 227 Rdnr. 15) – eine solche 'Spaltung' der Rechtswidrigkeit verneinen wollte anderte dies an dem Ergebnis nichts. Denn im Streitfall folgt die Verpflichtung des Bekl., dem Kl. Schadensersatz zu leisten, aus der Wertung von dessen gesamtem Verhalten vor Eintritt der Notwehrlage. Die ihm zuzurechnende rechtswidrige und für die Verletzung des Kl. auch adäquatkausale Handlung liegt nämlich bereits darin, daß er noch vor dem Eintreffen der Polizei seine Diskothek entsprechend der tatrichterlichen Feststellung in bewußter Erkenntnis des Umstandes aufsuchte, daß sein Erscheinen die Auseinandersetzung mit der Rockerbande geradezu heraufbeschwören werde, und daß es dabei für ihn zu einer nur mit der mitgenommenen Waffe abzuwehrenden Notwehrlage kommen könne.

(a) Entgegen der Auffassung der Revision sprechen rechtsgrundsätzliche Erwägungen nicht dagegen, im Streitfall eine Pflicht des Bekl. zu bejahen, die Diskothek nicht vor dem Erscheinen der von ihm bereits herbeigerufenen Polizei zu betreten. Es geht hierbei nicht um die Frage der Zumutung eines Zurückweichens vor einem gegenwärtigen rechtswidrigen Angriff (vgl. *Johannsen*, in: RGRK, 12. Aufl., § 227 Rdnr. 8; *Larenz*, § 15 I b; *Staudinger-Coing*, BGB, 11. Aufl., § 227 Rdnr. 7); ein solcher lag in der Zeit bis zum Eintreffen des Bekl. in seinem Lokal nicht vor. Vielmehr war dieser aus seiner Verpflichtung gegenüber seinen in der Diskothek anwesenden Gästen, die mit seinem Streit mit den Rockern nichts zu tun hatten, gehalten, einen tätlichen Zusammenstoß mit diesen zu vermeiden, wenn er – wie im Berufungsurteil von der Revision unangefochten festgestellt – damit rechnete, daß es im Verlaufe einer solchen Auseinandersetzung auch zu einer für ihn lebensbedrohenden und dann den Gebrauch der bewußt mitgeführten Pistole notwendig machenden Lage kommen könne. Auch der Kl., zudem einer der mit dem Bekl. in vertraglichen Beziehungen stehenden Gäste, hatte daher Anspruch auf Vermeidung einer Situation, in der der Bekl. – wenn auch gegenüber den ihn angreifenden Rockern gerechtfertigt – zur Verteidigung seines Lebens zur Waffe greifen mußte.

Even if one wanted to deny such a 'splitting' of the illegality – and this is contrary to the prevailing opinion: eg, *Baldus*, in: LK, 9th edn, StGB, § 53 marginal nos 27 and 23, where the contrary opinion is also referred to; *Samson*, in SKStGB, 2nd edn, § 32 marginal no 18; (detailed and provided with further references) *Schönke-Schröder*, StGB, 19th edn, marginal no 32, *Larenz*, BGB AT, 4th edn, § 151c; *Erman-Hefermehl*, BGB, 6th edn, § 227 marginal no 15 – this would not make any change in the outcome. This is because in the present case the duty of the defendant to compensate the claimant follows from the assessment of his behaviour as a whole before the self-defence situation arose. The unlawful action to be attributed to him, and which was an adequate cause of the injury to the claimant, lies in the fact that before the arrival of the police he, according to the findings of the judge of fact, visited his discotheque in the conscious knowledge of the fact that his appearance would provoke the confrontation with the group of rockers and that the result for him could be a self-defence situation which could only be averted with the weapon which he took with him.

(a) Contrary to the view of the appeal in law, considerations of legal principle do not militate against finding in the present case a duty on the part of the defendant not to enter the discotheque before the appearance of the police who had already been summoned by him. It is not a question here of the imposition of a requirement to draw back in the face of a present unlawful attack (see *Johannsen*, in: RGRK, 12th edn, § 227 marginal no 8; *Larenz*, § 15 I b; *Staudinger-Coing*, BGB, 11th edn, § 227 marginal no 7): such a situation did not exist in the period up to the arrival of the defendant in his club. Instead he was required by his duty to his guests present in the discotheque, who had nothing to do with his dispute with the rockers, to avoid a physical clash with them, if he – as the appeal court judgment establishes (and this is not challenged by the appeal in law) – reckoned that in the course of such a confrontation a situation could arise which threatened his life and which could then make necessary the use of the pistol which he had deliberately brought with him. The claimant, one of the guests, moreover, who was in a contractual relationship with the defendant, had a claim therefore for the avoidance of a situation in which the defendant would have to resort for defending his life to a weapon – even if this was justified as against the rockers who were attacking him.

Dem kann der Bekl. nicht mit dem Hinweis begegnen, er habe die allein von den Rockern herbeigeführte Lage nicht provoziert. Darauf hat es jedenfalls dann nicht anzukommen, wenn es um die Pflichtem geht, die diesen als Inhaber der Diskothek gegenüber seinen Gästen trafen. Deren Interesse an der Vermeidung von Gefahren, die von einem Raufhandel zwischen Wirt und Rockern auszugehen pflegen, hatten sich seine Eigeninteressen unterzuordnen, falls es sich nicht um die Sorge für seine eigene Sicherheit und Unversehrtheit handelte. Man muß dem Bekl. aus der Gesamtsituation freilich zugestehen, daß es ihm als Mitinhaber der Diskothek nötig erscheinen durfte, sich in dieser aufzuhalten, wenn die Anwesenheit der Rocker eine allgemeine Gefahrenlage nicht nur für die Ausstattung des Lokals, sondern möglicherweise auch für die körperliche Unversehrtheit von Angestellten und Gästen begründete; dann aber war von ihm zu verlangen, daß er sich dabei nicht den Rockern zeigte, sondern sich, jedenfalls zunächst, in einem Nebenraum aufhielt. Daß dem Hindernisse entgegengestanden hätten, ist nicht ersichtlich.

(b) Bei richtiger Beurteilung der Umstände muß auch das Betreten des Lokals durch den Bekl. als adäquat ursächlich für die Verletzung des Kl. gewertet werden. Das Verhalten der Rockerbande war deutlich dahin gerichtet, gegen den Bekl. als einen der Mitinhaber der Diskothek tätlich vorzugehen, wie sie diesem schon angedroht hatten. Es war daher damit zu rechnen, daß sie mit ihrem Vorhaben begannen, sobald er auftauchte; daß sie schon vorher gegen andere Personen gewalttätig geworden waren, ist nicht festgestellt und wird von der Revision auch nicht geltend gemacht. Daraus aber ergab sich dann als naheliegende Folge, daß der Gebrauch einer Schußwaffe die Gefahr der – wenn auch ungewollten – Verletzung eines der anwesenden Gäste mit sich brachte, weil die Möglichkeit nahelag, daß ein im Zuge der tätlichen Auseinandersetzung abgegebener Schuß wie im Streitfall nicht nur den Angreifer traf.

This cannot be met by the defendant by reference to the fact that he had not provoked the situation, which had been caused by the rockers alone. It does not in any case depend on that, if it is a question of the duties which applied to him as proprietor of the discotheque as a against his guests. His personal interests had to be subordinated to their interest in the avoidance of dangers which usually proceed from a brawl between a landlord and rockers, if it was not a question of concern for his own safety and freedom from bodily harm. It has to be admitted in favour of the defendant on the basis of the whole situation that it might appear necessary to him as co-proprietor of the discotheque to be present in it when the presence of the rockers created a general situation of danger not only for the furnishings of the club, but also possibly for the freedom of the employees and the guests from bodily injury. But then it was to be expected of him not to show himself to the rockers but to remain in a neighbouring room, at any rate at first. It was not obvious that there would have been obstacles to this.

(b) On a correct assessment of the circumstances, the entering of the club by the defendant must be rated as adequately causal for the claimant's injury. The conduct of the group of rockers was clearly directed towards taking physical action against the defendant as one of the co-proprietors of the discotheque, as they had already threatened him. It was therefore to be expected that they would begin with their plan as soon as he appeared. It has not been established that they had previously been violent against other persons and this is not claimed by the appeal in law either. But the natural consequence arising from this was that the use of a firearm carried with it the danger of an injury – even though unintended – to one of the guests present, because the possibility arose that a shot fired in the course of the physical confrontation would not only hit the attacker, as in the case in question.

(c) Letzlich kann auch kein Zweifel darüber bestehen, daß der Bekl. in der Lage war bei Beachtung der ihm obliegenden Sorgfalt den schließlich eingetretenen und den Kl. schädigenden Erfolg vorauszusehen, so daß er i.S. von § 276 BGB für dessen Verletzung verantwortlich ist und aus § 823 BGB Schadensersatz zu leisten hat. Das hat das BerGer. – wenn auch in seinen Überlegungen von einen anderen Ausgangspunkt ableitend – zutreffend ausgeführt. Zu dieser Bejahung fahrlässigen und demnach schuldhaften Verhaltens führen bereits die Überlegungen, wie sie vorstehend zur Frage der Kausalität angestellt wurden. Die Möglichkeit der Verletzung eines der anwesenden Gäste lag entgegen der Meinung der Revision nicht fern, falls es zu dem vom Bekl. selbst als wahrscheinlich angenommenen Schußwechsel mit den Rockern kam. Im Verlaufe einer tätlichen Auseinandersetzung, insbesondere auch aus einer Notwehrlage heraus abgegebene Pistolenschüsse sind in der Regel nicht sicher gezielt und stellen schon deshalb in einem voll besetzten Lokal eine erhebliche Gefährdung für alle Gäste dar.

3 Hat somit der Bekl. wegen unerlaubter Handlung für den dem Kl. entstandenen Schaden einzustehen und auch für immaterielle Einbußen (§ 847 BGB) eine Entschädigung zu leisten, so kommt es nicht mehr darauf an, ob dem Kl., wie das LG gemeint hat, auch aus einer analogen Anwendung von § 904 BGB ein Anspruch zustehen könnte.

(c) Finally there can be doubt about the fact that the defendant was in a position, when observing the degree of care incumbent upon him, to foresee the consequence which finally occurred and caused harm to the claimant, so that he is responsible in the sense of § 276 of the BGB for his injury and has to provide compensation under § 823 of the BGB. The appeal court has explained that correctly – even though setting out from a different starting point in its considerations. The considerations as employed above on the question of causality lead to this finding of negligent and accordingly culpable behaviour. The possibility of injury of one of the guests present was, contrary to the opinion of the appeal in law, not out of the question if it came to an exchange of shots with the rockers, which was accepted by the defendant himself as probable. Pistol shots fired in the course of a physical confrontation, especially arising out of a self-defence situation, are as a rule not safely aimed, and therefore on that account alone represent a substantial risk for all guests in a fully occupied club.

3 If the defendant has therefore to assume liability in tort for the harm which has occurred to the claimant and also to provide compensation for non-material losses (§ 847 of the BGB), it does not matter any longer whether the claimant, as the State Court thought, could also be entitled to a claim from an application of § 904 of the BGB by analogy.

CHAPTER FIVE

CONTRACT

OFFER AND ACCEPTANCE

Logically, simple agreements will almost always be reached by someone putting a proposition to another person, which that person then accepts. In German law, therefore, as well as in English law, a contract comes into existence by offer and acceptance. In contrast to the position in the French Civil Code, the concepts of offer and acceptance are actually dealt with in the German Civil Code. They are however both species of the declaration of will referred to in Chapter Four, and contract is a species of the legal transaction also referred to in the same chapter.

Offer

(1) Definition

Bürgerliches Gesetzbuch

Erstes Buch. Allgemeiner Teil

Dritter Abschnitt. Rechtsgeschäfte

Dritter Titel. Vertrag

§ 145 [Bindung an den Antrag] Wer einem anderen die Schließung eines Vertrags anträgt, ist an den Antrag gebunden, es sei denn, daß er die Gebundenheit ausgeschlossen hat.

THE INTERNET AUCTION CASE

OLG Hamm NJW 2001, 1142

13 Vertragsschluss bei Internetauktion

BGB §§ 145ff., 151, 156, 315, 119ff., 134, 762; AGBG §§ 1,2,10 Nr. 5,9 II Nr. 1; GewO § 34b

Im Rahmen einer Internetauktion kann ein wirksamer Vertragsschluss darin liegen, dass der Anbietende unter Verzicht auf die Annahmeerklärung bedingungsgemäß sein Warenangebot freisahaltet und bei Ablauf der vorgegebenen Bietzeit ein wirksames Gebot vorliegt. Die Regeln der *invitatio ad offerendum* finden insoweit keine Anwendung. Auch ist der im letzten Gebot liegende Erwerbspreis, auch wenn er auffällig hinter dem Marktpreis zurückbleibt, verbindlich, solange es der die Ware Anbietende in der Hand hatte, durch Setzen eines Mindestgebots auf den Erwerbspreis Einfluss zu nehmen. (Leitsatz der Redaktion.)

OLG Hamm, Urt. v. 14.12.2000 – 2 U 58/00 (nicht rechtskräftig).

Offer

(1) Definition

First book; General Part

Third section. Legal transactions

Third title. Contract

§ 145 [Binding effect of offer] A person who offers the conclusion of a contract to another person is bound by the offer unless he has excluded this binding effect.

Despite the wording of § 145, an offer can be made to a group of persons, even if they are not defined. However, the offer must be either certain or capable or being rendered certain, as in English law. The *essentialia negotii* (essential contractual issues) must be covered by it. The offer must also be intended to be binding. Mere provision of information would be an *invitatio ad offerendum* (invitation to treat). In a self-service store, the offer would appear to be the selection of goods by the customer, as in English law (see *Pharmaceutical Society v Boots Cash Chemist (Southern) Ltd* [1952] 2 All ER 456; [1953] 1 All ER 482) but see the discussion on this point in the fall in the supermarket case, p 377.

THE INTERNET AUCTION CASE

This seemed an appropriate case with which to replace the cases in the first edition about factual contracts, as it relates to a new method of creating a contract. The AGBG (General Conditions of Business/Contract Act) has now been incorporated into the Civil Code: see §§ 305 *et seq*, p 415. An appeal in law against the court's decision in this case was unsuccessful: BGH NJW 2002, 363.

OLG Hamm NJW 2001, 1142

13 Conclusion of contract by internet auction

BGB §§ 145ff and onwards, 151, 156, 315, 119ff and onwards, 134, 762; AGBG §§ 1,2,10 No 5, 9 II no 1; GewO § 34b

Within the framework of an internet auction a contract can be effectively concluded by the offeror releasing his offer of goods in accordance with conditions, renouncing his right to a declaration of acceptance and, on expiry of the offer period set, an effective bid being present. The rules about the *invitatio ad offerendum* (invitation to treat) have no application in this respect. The purchase price in this last bid is also binding, even if it is conspicuously below the market price, so long as the offeror of the goods had power to influence the purchase price by the setting of a minimum bid. (Editorial summary.)

OLG Hamm, judgment of 14.12.2000 – 2 U 58/00 (not legally binding).

Zum Sachverhalt:

Die ricardo.de AG in Hamburg verkauft über das Internet eigene Gegenstände gegen Höchstgebot, vermittelt auf diesem Wege Vertragsabschlüsse mit anderen Anbietern und gibt unter der Bezeichnung 'ricardo private auktionen' auch Dritten die Möglichkeit, eigene Verkaufsveranstaltungen durchzuführen. Vor der Teilnahme müssen sich die Teilnehmer bei 'ricando.de' anmelden und dabei die Anerkennung der AGB durch Doppelklick erklären. Bereits auf der Homepage von 'ricardo.de' wird auf die AGB für 'ricardo.de' Verkaufsveranstaltungen (AGB) hingewiesen. Die Teilnehmer können durch zweimaliges Anklicken den Text der AGB in druckgerechter Form abrufen. Die AGB lauten unter anderem wie folgt:

§ 3 *Beschreibung des Kaufgegenstands, Verkaufsangebot bei privaten Auktionen.* (1) ricardo.de ermöglicht es Teilnehmern, im Eigentum des jeweiligen Teilnehmers stehende Gegenstände, die im Rahmen von *private auktionen* verkauft werden sollen, auf Angebotsseiten öffentlich zu präsentieren.

(5) Der anbietende Teilnehmer wird im Rahmen der Freischaltung der Angebotsseite aufgefordert, die in Abs. 4 und § 5 IV genannten Zusicherungen und Erklärungen gegenüber ricardo.de abzugeben. ricardo.de handelt dabei als Empfangsvertreter aller anderen Teilnehmer, § 164 III BGB. Die Freischaltung erfolgt erst, wenn der anbietende Teilnehmer die geforderten Zusicherungen und Erklärungen abgegeben hat.

§ 4 *Vertragsangebot.* (1) Für die von ricardo.de im Rahmen von *ricardo auktionen* und die von anbietenden Teilnehmern im Rahmen von *private auktionen* angebotenen Gegenstände können alle Teilnehmer mit Ausnahme des in Abs. 2 genannten Personenkreises während des jeweils für den angebotenen Gegenstand angegebenen Angebotszeitraums (§ 6) verbindliche Kaufangebote über die ricardo.de-Website abgeben.

(3) Die Angebote sind verbindlich und unwiderruflich. Sie erlöschen ohne weiteres mit Ablauf des übernächsten Werktags nach dem Ende des jeweiligen Angebotszeitraums, wenn sie nicht bis dahin von ricardo.de oder dem anbietenden Teilnehmer angenommen worden sind, § 151 S. 2 BGB.

Facts:

Ricardo.de AG in Hamburg sells its own assets over the internet to the highest bidder, and in this way arranges the conclusion of contracts with other offerors. It also gives to third parties under the name 'ricardo private auctions' the possibility of carrying out their own sale events. Before participating, the participants must register with 'ricardo.de' and at the same time declare their acceptance of the general conditions of contract by a double click. Reference is made on the home page of ricardo.de itself to the general conditions of contract for 'ricardo.de' sale events (general conditions). The participants can call up the text of the general conditions in printer friendly form by double clicking. The general conditions state, amongst other things, as follows:

§ 3 *Description of the object in the sale, sale offer in private auctions.* (1) ricardo.de enables participants to present publicly on offer pages objects in the ownership of the participant in question which are to be sold by *private auction.*

(5) The participant making the offer is invited within the framework of the release of the offer page to give the assurances and declarations mentioned in para 4 and § 5 IV to ricardo.de. ricardo.de acts in this connection as the receiving agent of all other participants: § 164 III of the BGB. Release occurs when the participant making the offer has given the assurances and declarations asked for.

§ 4 *Contractual offer.* (1) For the objects offered by ricardo.de in the framework of *ricardo auctions* and by participants making offers within the framework of *private auctions*, all participants, with the exception of the group of persons mentioned in para 2, can submit binding offers to buy through the ricardo.de website during the offer period (§ 6) given in each case for the object offered.

(3) The offers are binding and irrevocable. They lapse automatically with the expiry of the next working day but one after the end of the offer period in question, if they have not been accepted until then by ricardo.de or the participant making the offer: § 151 sentence 2 of the BGB.

(5) Um eine ordnungsgemäße Durchführung von *ricardo auktionen* und *private auktionen* sicherzustellen ist ricardo.de berechtigt, Angebote ohne Angabe von Gründen, insbesondere jedoch Angebote von Teilnehmern, die:

(a) von ricardo.de gem. § 1 III von der Teilnahme an Verkaufsveranstaltungen ausgeschlossen werden könnten oder;

(b) gem. Abs, 2 kein Kaufangebot abgeben dürfen,

zurückzuweisen; insofern stehen die Kaufangebote unter der auflösenden Bedingung, dass sie von ricardo.de nicht innerhalb von einer Woche nach Ende des jeweiligen Angebotszeitraums zurückgewiesen werden.

(7) Bei Angeboten, die im Rahmen von *private auktionen* abgegeben werden, handelt ricardo.de als Empfangsvertreter der anbietenden Teilnehmer, § 164 III BGB.

§ 5 *Annahme eines Vertragsangebots.* (1) Der Vertrag über einen angebotenen Gegenstand kommt ohne Erklärung gegenüber dem Teilnehmer, der das Vertragsangebot abgegeben hat (nachfolgend auch 'Antragender' genannt), bereits durch Annahme des Vertragsangebots zu Stande. Der Antragende verzichtet auf eine Annahmeerklärung, § 151 S. 1 BGB. Über die Annahme seines Vertragsantrags wird der Antragende alsbald, spätestens jedoch bis 24 Uhr des zweiten Werktags nach Ende des Angebotszeitraums (§ 6) von ricardo.de per E-mail unter der von ihm angegebenen E-Mail-Adresse unterrichtet.

(4) Bei *private auktionen* erklärt der anbietende Teilnehmer bereits mit der Freischaltung seiner Angebotsseite gem. § 3 V die Annahme des höchstens unter Berücksichtigung von § 4 IV und V wirksam abgegebenen Kaufangebots. Der anbietende Teilnehmer wird von ricardo.de vom Zustandekommen des Kaufvertrags alsbald, spätestens jedoch bis 24 Uhr des zweiten Werktags nach Ende des Angebotszeitraums (§ 6) per E-mail unter der von dem anbietenden Teilnehmer angegebenen E-mail Adresse unterrichtet.

§ 6 *Angebotszeitraum.* (1) Angebote zum Vertragsschluss können nur während eines für den jeweiligen Gegenstand von ricardo.de festgelegten Zeitraums abgegeben werden ('Angebotszeitraum'). Bei *private auktionen* wird ricardo.de die Wünsche des anbietenden Teilnehmers nach Möglichkeit berücksichtigen.

(3) ricardo.de ist berechtigt, den Angebotszeitraum nach eignenem Ermessen zu verkürzen oder zu verlängern oder Veranstaltungen ohne Abschluss eines Vertrags abzubrechen.

(5) In order to ensure an orderly implementation of *ricardo auctions* and *private auctions*, ricardo.de is entitled to reject offers without the giving of reasons, in particular offers of participants which:

(a) could be excluded by ricardo.de in accordance with § 1 III from participation in sale events; or

(b) in accordance with para 2 are not allowed to give any offer to purchase,

in this respect offers to purchase are subject to the resolutive condition that they are not rejected by ricardo.de within a week after the end of the offer period in question.

(7) In the case of offers which are given within the framework of *private auctions*, ricardo.de acts as the receiving agent of the offering participant, § 164 III of the BGB.

§ 5 *Acceptance of a contractual offer.* (1) The contract about an object offered comes into existence without a declaration to the participant who has given the contractual offer (hereafter called the 'offeror'), by acceptance of the contractual offer. The offeror gives up his right to a declaration of acceptance: § 151 sentence 1 of the BGB. The offeror will be informed by ricardo.de by email at the email address given by him about the acceptance of his contractual offer as soon as possible but at the latest before midnight of the second working day after the end of the offer period (§ 6).

(4) In the case of *private auctions* the offering participant declares by the release of his offer page in accordance with § 3 V the acceptance of the highest offer to buy which has been effectively given, taking into consideration § 4 IV and V. The offering participant will be informed by ricardo.de by email at the email address given by the offering participant of the coming into existence of the purchase contract as soon as possible but at the latest before midnight of the second working day after the end of the offer period (§ 6).

§ 6 *Offer period.* (1) Offers for conclusion of a contract can only be submitted during a period fixed by ricardo-de for the object in question ('offer period'). In *private auctions* ricardo.de will consider the wishes of the offering participant if possible.

(3) ricardo.de is entitled to shorten or lengthen the offer period or to break off events without the conclusion of a contract according to its own discretion.

Der Bekl. ist BWL-Student, der im Rahmen seines Ende 1997 angemeldeten Gewerbes nach seinen Angaben ca. 20 bis 50 Neufahrzeuge als EU-Reimporte auf Kundenbestellung auf 'konventionellem Wege' verkauft hat. 1999 führte er unter 'ricardo private auktionen' eine eigene Verkaufsveranstaltung durch und bot unter dem Namen A-Automobile einen Neuwagen mit der Beschreibung: 'Passat Variant TDI 110' ... bei einem Startpreis von 10 DM ohne Angabe eines Mindestpreises vom 22.7.1999, 21.33 Uhr, bis zum 27.7.1999, 21.35 Uhr an. Ein Neufahrzeug mit diesen Ausstattungs- merkmalen hatte im Autohandel einen Listenpreis von ca. 57 000 DM. Innerhalb der Bieterzeit gab der Kl. als 963ster und letzter Bieter online ein Gebot über 26 350 DM ab. Am 27.7.1999 um 21.54 Uhr erhielt er von 'ricardo.de' per E-Mail die Nachricht, dass er 'bei ricardo private (...) für 26 350 DM den Zuschlag bei der Auktion von A-Automobile mit dem Titel VW Passat Variant TDI 110 PS – Neuwagen (Auktions-Nr.: 174 124) erhalten' habe. Neben der Beglückwünschung zum erhaltenen Zuschlag wies 'ricardo.de' den Kl. unter Angabe der E-Mail-Adresse und Telefon- /Fax-Nummer des Bekl. darauf hin, 'sich mit A-Automobile in Verbindung (zu setzen), um Versand und Bezahlung schnell und einfach zu regeln'. Daraufhin nahm der Kl. am 28. und 29.7.1999 jeweils telefonisch Kontakt mit dem Bekl. auf. Im Rahmen dieser Telefonate lehnte der Bekl. die Lieferung des von ihm angebotenen Fahrzeugs zu dem vom Kl. gebotenen Kaufpreis i.H. von 26 350 DM ab.

Die auf Lieferung eines Pkw VW Passat Variant TDI, 110 PS, mit den weiteren vorbeschriebenen Ausstattungsmerkmalen gerichtete Klage, Zug um Zug gegen Zahlung von 26 350 DM, hat das LG abgewiesen ... Die Berufung des Kl. hatte Erfolg.

Aus den Gründen:

I Die Parteien haben einen Kaufvertrag über einen Pkw des beschriebenen Typs zu einem Kaufpreis von 26 350 DM durch *Angebot und Annahme* – via Internet – geschlossen. Zutreffend hat das LG insoweit ausgeführt, dass Rechtsgeschäfte im Internet den allgemeinen Regeln des bürgerlichen Rechts folgen (*Palandt/Heinrichs*, BGB, 59. Aufl., § 145 Rdnrn. 6ff.), so dass es für den wirksamen Abschluss des Kaufvertrags eines Angebots und einer entsprechenden Annahme bedurfte, §§ 145ff. BGB. Diese Erklärungen konnten rechtswirksam auch online per Mausklick abgeben werden (*Ernst*, NJW-CoR 1997, 165).

The defendant is a business student who, within the framework of his business, registered at the end of 1997, sold, according to his statement, about 20 to 50 new vehicles as EU reimports on customer order in conventional ways. In 1999 he carried out his own sale event under the title 'ricardo private auctions' and offered under the name A-car a new car with the description Passat Variant TDI 110 (*here followed details of the car*) at a starting price of 10 DM without the setting of a reserve price from 22.7.1999, 21.33 hours to 27.7.1999, 21.35 hours. A new vehicle with these features had a list price in the car trade of about 57,000 DM. Within the period for bidding, the claimant as the 963rd and last bidder on line submitted a bid for 26,350 DM. On 27.7.1999 at 21.54 hours he received from 'ricardo.de' by email the news that he had 'obtained at ricardo private (...) for 26,350 DM the acceptance of the bid at the auction of A-car with the title VW Passat Variant TDI 110 PS – new car (Auction no 174,124)'. Besides the congratulations on the acceptance received, 'ricardo.de' indicated to the claimant, giving the email address and telephone/fax number of the defendant, that he should (get) in contact with A-car in order to arrange dispatch and payment quickly and simply. The claimant then made contact by telephone on the 28. and 29.7.1999 with the defendant. Within the framework of these telephone calls the defendant declined to deliver the vehicle offered by him at the purchase price for which the claimant had made a bid, the sum of 26,350 DM.

The claim, which was for delivery of a VW Passat Variant TDI car, 110 PS, with the further features described above, in return for simultaneous payment of 26,350 DM, was rejected by the State Court (references omitted). The claimant's appeal was successful.

Reasons:

I The parties have concluded a purchase contract for a car of the type described at a purchase price of 26,350 DM by offer and acceptance – via the internet. The State Court also correctly stated in this respect that legal transactions on the internet follow the general rules of civil law (*Palandt/Heinrichs*, BGB, 59th edn, § 145 marginal nos 6ff), so that for the effective conclusion of a sale contract an offer and a corresponding acceptance is needed: §§ 145ff and onwards of the BGB. These declarations could be submitted in a legally effective way online by a click of the mouse (*Ernst*, NJW-CoR 1997, 165).

1 Entgegen den Ausführungen des LG neigt der *Senat* dazu, in der Freischaltung der Angebotsseite durch den Bekl. für die hier streitige Auktion nicht lediglich eine 'invitatio ad offerendum', sondern bereits ein rechtsverbindliches Angebot auf Abschluss eines entsprechenden Kaufvertrags zu sehen.

(a) Wie vom LG zutreffend ausgeführt sind bei der rechtlichen Bewertung der Parteierklärungen (auch) die AGB von 'ricardo.de' zu berücksichtigen.

(1) Diese wurden von den Parteien *gegenüber 'ricardo.de'* wirksam i.S. des § 2 AGBG einbezogen, da die Teilnehmer beriets auf der Startseite sowie nochmals bei der Anmeldung bei 'ricardo.de' auf die AGB hingewiesen werden und die Bestimmungen sowohl online eingesehen als auch in druckgerechter Form von den Teilnehmern abgerufen werden können. Damit ist den Anforderungen des § 2 AGBG Genüge getan, wie die *Kammer* zutreffend ausgeführt hat (so auch *Ulrici*, JuS 2000, 947 [948]; *Ernst* NJW-CoR 1997, 165 [167]). Da die Anerkennung der AGB für alle Teilnehmer zwingende Voraussetzung für die Teilnahme an Veranstaltungen von ricado.de ist, durfte und musste jeder Teilnehmer von einer entsprechenden Anerkennung der Bedingungen durch alle anderen Teilnehmer ausgehen. So haben die Parteien auch übereinstimmend jeweils gegenüber ricardo.de erklärt, dass sie im Verhältnis Antragender/Annehmender zu den Bedingungen von ricardo.de kontrahieren wollen. Soweit diese Bedingungen Regelungen hinsichtlich des Vertragsschlusses unter den Teilnehmern enthielten, musste und durfte daher jeder Teilnehmer aus der maßgeblichen Sicht des objektiven Empfängerhorizonts davon ausgehen, dass den abgegebenen Erklärungen der in den AGB beigemessene Erklärungswert zukommt.

(2) Auf eine wirksame Einbeziehung der Bestimmungen nach § 2 AGBG *im Verhältnis der Parteien zueinander* kommt es dabei nicht an. Denn bei den Vertragsbestimmungen handelt es sich, bezogen auf die Parteien, *nicht* um AGB i.S. der §§ 1ff. AGBG, da keiner von beiden Vertragsparteien Verwender der AGB ist; diese sind vielmehr von einem Dritten, nämlich dem Unternehmen ricardo.de, das die Plattform für die Auktion anbietet, zur Voraussetzung der Teilnahme an dem System gemacht worden. Darauf, dass Vertragsbedingungen 'gestellt' sein müssen, um als AGB i.S. der §§ 1ff. AGBG zu gelten, kann angesichts der eindeutigen gesetzlichen Regelung – entgegen der von *Wiebe* (MMR 2000, 323 [325]) vertretenen Auffassung – insbesondere auch nicht unter Hinweis auf ein 'berechtigtes Interesse aller Beteiligten an einer einheitlichen Marktordnung' im Verhältnis 'Verkäufer/Käufer' verzichtet werden.

1 Contrary to the statements of the State Court, the *Senate* inclines to the view that in the release of the offer page by the defendant for the auction which is in dispute here, there is not merely an *'invitatio ad offerendum* (invitation to treat)' but a legally binding offer to conclude a corresponding purchase contract.

(a) As the State Court correctly stated, in the legal assessment of the declarations of the parties, the general conditions of 'ricardo.de' are (also) to be considered.

(1) These were effectively included by the parties in the sense of § 2 of the AGBG as against *ricardo.de*, as the participants were referred to the general conditions of contract on the home page as well as on registering with 'ricardo.de' and the provisions can be looked at online as well as retrieved in printer friendly form by the participants. The requirements of § 2 of the AGBG are complied with, as the *chamber* has correctly stated (thus also in *Ulrici*, JuS 2000, 947 [948]; *Ernst* NJW-CoR 1997, 165 [167]). As the recognition of the general conditions is an imperative prerequisite for all participants for participation in events by ricardo.de, every participant might and had to proceed on the basis of a corresponding recognition of the conditions by all other participants. The parties have thus also declared concurrently in each case as against ricardo.de that they would contract on the conditions of ricardo.de in the relationship of offeror/acceptor. Insofar as these conditions contained rules in relation to the conclusion of the contract between the participants, every participant (from the objective viewpoint of the recipient, which was crucial here) therefore had to and might proceed on the basis that the declarations acquired the value as declarations which were attached to them in the general conditions.

(2) It does not depend here on an effective inclusion of the provisions in accordance with § 2 of the AGBG *in the relationship of the parties with each other*. This is because with the contractual provisions, in relation to the parties, it is *not* a question of the general conditions in the sense of §§ 1ff and onwards of the AGBG, as neither of the two contractual parties is a user of the general conditions. Instead, these have been made a prerequisite of participation in the system by a third party, namely the undertaking ricardo.de, which offers the platform for the auction. The idea that the contractual conditions must be 'placed' in order to apply as general conditions in the sense of §§ 1ff of the AGBG can in the light of the unambiguous statutory regime be abandoned – contrary to the view propounded by *Wiebe* (MMR 2000, 323 [325]) – and in particular not even with reference to a 'justified interest of all participants in a unified market order' in the relationship of 'seller/buyer'.

Ebenso wenig kommt es bei der Auslegung des Erklärungsverhaltens der Parteien auf die Frage der Wirksamkeit der Klauseln *im Verhältnis zu ricardo.de* an, da beide Parteien die Regelungen unabhängig von ihrer rechtlichen Qualifizierung anerkannt haben und damit als Erklärungsempfänger die daraufhin abgegebenen Erklärungen im Sinne dieser Bestimmungen verstehen mussten.

(3) Damit bilden die AGB von ricardo.de die Auslegungsgrundlage, wie die Parteien als Erklärungsempfänger bzw. ricardo.de gem. § 166 I BGB als nach § 3 V und § 4 VII der AGB jeweils i.S. von § 167 I Alt. 1 BGB bevollmächtigter Empfangsvertreter die jeweilig abgegebenen Erklärungen der Parteien nach dem objektiven Empfängerhorizont verstehen durften. Zwar regelt § 3 I AGB, dass ricardo.de den Teilnehmern ermöglicht, Gegenstände, die im Rahmen von 'private auktionen' verkauft werden sollen, auf Angebotsseiten öffentlich zu präsentieren, was für eine bloße 'invitatio ad offerendum' spricht. Im Übrigen regeln die §§ 3 IV, 4 I, 4 IV, 4 VII, 5 I der AGB, dass das Kaufangebot von den Bietern abgegeben wird und der Verkäufer nach § 5 IV AGB durch das Freischalten der Angebotsseite antizipiert die Annahme des letzten innerhalb der Bietzeit wirksam abgegebenen Gebots erklärt. Dabei handelt es sich aber rechtlich um 'Falschbezeichnungen' (*'falsa demonstratio'*). Denn die Freischaltung der Angebotsseite erfüllt unabhängig von ihrer Bezeichnung in den AGB alle Voraussetzungen eines Angebots i.S. des § 145 BGB.

So ist unter einem Angebot i.S. des § 145 BGB jede mit Rechtsbindungswillen abgegebene einseitige empfangsbedürftige Willenserklärung zu verstehen, die auf Abschluss eines Vertrags gerichtet ist, dessen Gegenstand und Inhalt in der Erklärung hinreichend bestimmt oder bestimmbar ist, wobei eine ausreichende Bestimmbarkeit auch dann vorliegt, wenn der Anbietende die Festlegung einzelner Vertragspunkte dem Angebotsempfänger überlässt (*Palandt/Heinrichs*, § 145 Rdnrn. 1f. m. w. Nachw.). Kennzeichend für das Angebot ist dabei, dass dieses der Annahme in der Regel zeitlich vorangeht (*Palandt/Heinrichs*, Vorb. § 145 Rdnr. 4).

Nor does it depend on the question of the effectiveness of the clauses *in the relationship to ricardo.de* when interpreting the declarations, as both parties have recognised the rules independently of their legal qualification and must therefore as recipients of these declarations have understood the declarations submitted on this basis in the sense of these provisions.

(3) The general conditions of ricardo.de therefore form the basis of interpretation as to how the parties as recipients of declarations or ricardo.de in accordance with § 166 I of the BGB as the authorised agents for receipt under § 3 V and § 4 VII of the general conditions in each case in the sense of § 167 I alternative 1 of the BGB might, in accordance with the objective recipient's viewpoint, understand the declarations in question submitted by the parties. It is true that § 3 I of the general conditions provides that ricardo.de enables the participants to present publicly on offer pages objects which are to be sold within the framework of 'private auctions', which argues in favour of a mere *'invitatio ad offerendum* (invitation to treat)'. Besides this, §§ 3 IV, 4 I, 4 IV, 4 VII and 5 I of the general conditions provide that the offer to purchase is submitted by the bidders and the seller, according to § 5 IV of the general conditions, by the release of the offer page declares in anticipation the acceptance of the last bid effectively submitted within the bidding period. But this is legally a question of 'false descriptions' (*'falsa demonstratio'*). This is because the release of the offer page fulfils all the prerequisites of an offer in the sense of § 145 of the BGB, independently of its description in the general conditions.

Thus an offer in the sense of § 145 of the BGB is to be understood as including every unilateral declaration of will submitted with the intention that it will be binding in law and needing to be received, which is directed to the conclusion of a contract and subject matter and content of which is sufficiently determined in the declaration or is determinable. In this connection, sufficient determinability is present if the offeror leaves the fixing of individual contractual points to the recipient of the offer (*Palandt/Heinrichs*, § 145 marginal nos 1f with further references). It is at the same time characteristic of the offer that this as a rule precedes the acceptance in time (*Palandt/Heinrichs*, preamble to § 145 marginal no 4).

Aus § 5 IV der AGB ergibt sich sinngemäß, dass die Freischaltung der Angebotsseite die rechtlich verbindliche Erklärung auf Abschluss eines Kaufvertrags über den angebotenen Gegenstand enthält. Die allgemeine Erwägung, die im Zweifel für die Annahme einer unverbindlichen *'invitatio ad offerendum'* spricht, dass nämlich der in seinen Kapazitäten eingeschränkte Warenanbieter keine rechtsverbindlicher Erklärung abgeben wolle, um nicht gegenüber allen potenziellen Auktionsteilnehmern rechtlich verpflichtet zu sein, greift nicht ein, da das Angebot insoweit beschränkt ist, als es gem. § 5 der AGB nur durch das am Ende der Bietzeit abgegebene höchste Gebot angenommen werden konnte. Diese Erklärung ist auch hinsichtlich der wesentlichen Vertragsbestandteile hinreichend bestimmt bzw. bestimmbar. Denn neben der bestimmten Angabe des Kaufgegenstands sind durch die AGB von ricardo.de sowohl der Vertragspartner als auch der Kaufpreis hinreichend bestimmbar. So ergibt sich aus dem durch die AGB von ricardo.de festgelegten Auktionsablauf der Vertragspartner als der letzte Bieter innerhalb der vorgesehenen Bietzeit. Ebenso ist die Erklärung des Bekl. hinsichtlich des Kaufpreises im Hinblick auf die Regelung in den AGB, dass der Kaufpreis im Rahmen des Auktionsverfahrens durch das gegenseitige Überbieten durch die Bieter bis zum Ablauf des festgelegten Auktionszeitraums bestimmt wird, hinreichend bestimmbar.

Die Bezeichnung als vorweggenommene bindende Annahmeerklärung ist somit lediglich eine 'Falschbenennung' einer tatsächlich auf Abschluss eines Vertrags gerichteten Erklärung, die alle Voraussetzungen eines Angebots erfüllt. Das auf dieses Angebot erfolgte höchste Gebot des Kl. stellt danach dessen Annahme dar.

(4) Auch unter dem Gesichtspunkt der 'AGB-Kontrolle' bestehen keine Bedenken hinsichtlich der Wirksamkeit der auf § 5 IV AGB beruhenden Erklärung.

(a) Das folgt schon daraus, dass die Regelungen *im Verhältnis der Parteien zueinander*, wie ausgeführt, *nicht* der Kontrolle nach dem AGB-Gesetz unterliegen, da keine der Parteien Verwender i.S. des § 1 AGBG ist, das heißt die Bestimmungen von keiner der Parteien der anderen i.S. des § 1 AGBG 'gestellt' wurden. Auch aus der zeitlichen Reihenfolge der Anmeldungen der Teilnehmer bei 'ricardo.de' per Login mit Benutzername und Passwort unter Anerkennung der Bedingungen kann auf ein 'Stellen' i.S. des § 2 AGBG nicht geschlossen werden, da die Anmeldungsreihenfolge rein zufällig ist.

From § 5 IV of the general conditions it follows logically that the release of the offer page contains the legally binding declaration for conclusion of a purchase contract regarding the object offered. The general consideration which in case of doubt argues for the assumption of a non-binding *'invitatio ad offerendum* (invitation to treat)', ie, that the offeror of goods who is limited in his capacity did not intend to give any legally binding declaration, so as not to be under a legal obligation as against all potential participants in the auction, does not apply, as the offer is limited insofar as, according to § 5 of the general conditions, it could only be accepted by the highest offer submitted by the end of the bidding period. This declaration is also sufficiently determined or determinable with regard to the fundamental components of the contract. This is because, besides the definite particulars of the subject matter of the purchase, the contractual partner as well as the purchase price are sufficiently determinable through the general conditions of ricardo.de. Thus the contractual partner emerges, from the course of events in the auction laid down by the general conditions of ricardo.de, as the last bidder within the bidding time provided for. Likewise the declaration of the defendant in respect of the purchase price, having regard to the regime in the general conditions that the purchase price is determined in the framework of the auction proceedings by the mutual outbidding by the bidders until expiry of the period fixed for the auction, is sufficiently determinable.

The description as an anticipated binding declaration of acceptance is therefore merely a 'false description' of a declaration which is actually directed to conclusion of a contract, which fulfils all the prerequisites for an offer. The highest bid of the claimant following on this offer accordingly represents his acceptance.

(4) Nor are there any objections from the point of view of 'general conditions control' in relation to the effectiveness of the declaration based on § 5 IV of the general conditions.

(a) That follows simply from the fact that the rules *in the relationship of the parties to each other*, as explained, are *not* subject to control under the General Conditions of Business/Contract Act, as neither of the parties is a consumer in the sense of § 1 of the AGBG, that is to say that the provisions were not 'put' by either of the parties to the other in the sense of § 1 of the AGBG. Nor is it possible to infer a 'placing' in the sense of § 2 of the AGBG from the sequence in time of the registrations of the participants at 'ricardo.de' by login with user name and password in acceptance of the conditions as the sequence of registrations is purely accidental.

(b) Selbst wenn man aber – entgegen der Ansicht des *Senats* – auch zwischen den Parteien von einer Anwendbarkeit des AGB-Gesetzes ausginge, neigt der *Senat* dazu, nach der Interessenlage (allein) den anbietenden Teilnehmer (Bekl.) als Verwender i.S. des § 1 AGBG anzusehen (so wohl auch *Wilmer*, NJW-CoR 2000, 94 [99]). Denn der Verkäufer bedient sich des von 'ricardo.de' bereitgestellten Verkaufsportals, um unter Anerkennung und Geltung der dortigen AGB seine Ware an potenzielle Bieter zu verkaufen. Insoweit macht er sich deren AGB, zumindest soweit sie Modalitäten des Kaufvertragsabschlusses vorsehen, zu eigen. Unabhängig vom Zeitpunkt des Login fungiert er dabei als Initiator des Verkaufs, da es nur durch seine Teilnahme am System überhaupt zum Abschluss eines Kaufvertrags – mit welchem Käufer auch immer – über den von ihm angebotenen Gegenstand kommen kann. Als Verwender unterfiele der Bekl. im Verhältnis zum Bieter (Kl.) aber nicht dem Schutzzweck des AGB-Gesetzes.

(c) Selbst wenn man aber – entgegen der Ansicht des *Senats* – den Käufer als Verwender ansähe, so verstieße die Bestimmung des § 5 IV AGB weder gegen § 10 Nr. 5 AGBG noch gegen § 9 II Nr. 1 AGBG. § 10 Nr. 5 AGBG wäre wegen § 24 Nr. 1 AGBG schon nicht anwendbar, weil der Bekl., der nach seinen Angaben seit Anmeldung des Gewerbes Ende 1997 nebenberuflich ca. 20 bis 50 EU-Reimporte auf Kundenbestellung durchführte, als 'Unternehmer' i.S. des § 24 Nr. 1 AGBG anzusehen ist.

Ohnedies läge auch kein Verstoß gegen § 10 Nr. 5 AGBG vor, da die Klausel keine Erklärungsfiktion aufstellt, sondern i.V. mit § 4 V AGB nur die *Verpflichtung* beinhaltet, mit der Freischaltung der Angebotsseite die rechtsverbindliche Erklärung auf Abschluss eines Kaufvertrags abzugeben (vgl. auch *Wiebe*, MMR 2000, 284). Ebenso wenig läge ein Verstoß gegen § 9 II Nr. 1 AGBG – wegen Abweichung vom Leitbild des § 156 BGB – vor. Eine *unangemessene Benachteiligung* des Vertragspartners des Verwenders könnte nämlich nicht angenommen werden (so auch *Wiebe*, MMR 2000, 284 [286]; *Ulrici*, JuS 2000, 947 [949]; *Wilkens*, DB 2000, 666 [668]).

(b) Even if one were, however, to proceed on the basis – contrary to the view of the *Senate* – of applicability of the AGBG between the parties, also the *Senate* tends to regard (only) the offering participant (the defendant) as consumer in the sense of § 1 of the AGBG, according to the state of the parties' interests (thus also *Wilmer*, NJW-CoR 2000, 94 [99]). This is because the seller makes use of the sale portal provided by 'ricardo.de' in order to sell his goods to potential bidders subject to the acceptance and validity of the general conditions there. In this respect he adopts its general conditions, at least insofar as they provide modalities for conclusion of purchase contracts. Independently of the point in time of the login, he acts in this connection as initiator of the sale, as only by his participation in the system can it come to a conclusion of a purchase contract – with whatever purchaser – about the object offered by him. As consumer, the defendant would not however come within the protective purpose of the AGBG in the relationship to the bidder (the claimant).

(c) However, even if one were – contrary to the view of the *Senate* – to see the purchaser as a consumer, the provisions of § 5 IV of the general conditions would not violate § 10 no 5 of the AGBG nor § 9 II no 1 of that Act. § 10 no 5 of that Act would not be applicable because of § 24 no 1 of that Act, as the defendant who, according to his own statement, since registration of the business at the end of 1997, carried out as a sideline about 20–50 EU reimports on customer orders, is to be seen as an 'undertaking' in the sense of § 24 no 1 of the AGBG.

In any case, no violation of § 10 no 5 of the AGBG would be present as the clause does not put forward any declaration fiction but in combination with § 4 V of the general conditions only contains the *duty* to submit the legally binding declaration to conclude a purchase contract with the release of the offer page (see also *Wiebe*, MMR 2000, 284). Nor was there any violation of § 9 II no 1 of the AGBG – because of deviation from the model of § 156 of the BGB. An *unreasonable disadvantage* to the contractual partner of the consumer could not be assumed (thus also *Wiebe*, MMR 2000, 284 [286]; *Ulrici*, JuS 2000, 947 [949]; *Wilkens*, DB 2000, 666 [668]).

So spräche zwar die vom *LG* zutreffend angeführte Unausgereiftheit des Verfahrens, wonach ein 'Ausbieten' auf Grund des begrenzten Zeitraums und der kleinen Bietschritte unter Umständen nicht möglich sei und die Bieter in Kenntnis des festgelegten Zeitraums unter Umständen bis zum Ende zögerten, um erst in der Schlussphase zu bieten, für eine Unangemessenheit. Denn in derartigen Fällen besteht wegen des Fehlens eines Auktionators i.S. des § 156 BGB grundsätzlich nicht die Möglichkeit, die Auktion situationsbedingt zu verlängern, um auf diese Weise für den anbietenden Teil einen günstigen Vertragsabschluss zu erreichen. § 6 III AGB sieht zwar eine solche Verlängerungsmöglichkeit für 'ricardo.de' vor, von dieser ist aber vorliegend kein Gebrauch gemacht worden.

Gegen die Annahme einer unangemessenen Benachteiligung spräche aber entscheidend, dass der anbietende Teilnehmer den Verlauf der Auktion durch die Angabe eines Mindest- und Startpreises, der Größe der Bietschritte sowie des Bietzeitraums nachhaltig beeinflussen und sein Risiko damit in Grenzen halten kann.

Im Übrigen ist allgemein bekannt, dass es sich bei Auktionen um risikoreiche Transaktionsformen handelt. So geht der anbietende Teilnehmer dieses Risiko bewusst ein, um gleichsam die Chance wahrzunehmen, durch die Preisbestimmung mittels des gegenseitigen Überbietens der Bieter einen guten Preis zu erlangen, der möglicherweise sogar über dem Marktpreis liegt. Dass sich diese Chance unter Umständen nicht realisiert, liegt in der Natur der Auktion. Im Übrigen bietet erst die Verfahrensgestaltung ohne Auktionator die Möglichkeit, den Angebotszeitraum auf mehrere Wochen auszudehnen, was die einzelne Warenpräsentation für einen wesentlich größeren Personenkreis zugänglich macht und somit in der Regel die Erzielung eines angemessenen Preises sicherstellt (*Wilkens*, DB 2000, 666 [668]).

(d) Soweit der Bekl. geltend macht, dass sich Bedenken hinsichtlich der Ernsthaftigkeit und Verbindlichkeit der Angebote wegen des Zulassungsverfahrens nach § 1 AGB und der Rücknahmemöglichkeit der Anmeldung nach § 4 III AGB ergäben, kann dies allenfalls die Wirksamkeit *dieser Regelungen* berühren, nicht jedoch die des § 5 IV der AGB. Gleiches gilt hinsichtlich der Bedenken bezüglich § 4 V AGB.

(b) Im Übrigen hat das *LG* zu Recht angenommen, dass bei der Auslegung einer Erklärung neben dem Wortlaut auch außerhalb des Erklärungsakts liegende Begleitumstände aus der Sicht des objektiven Empfängerhorizonts miteinzubeziehen sind (*Palandt/Heinrichs*, § 133 Rdnr. 15 m. w. Nachw.).

The incomplete nature of the procedure which was correctly mentioned by the State Court – and according to which an 'offer for sale' would perhaps not be possible on the basis of the limited period of time and the small steps in the bidding, and the bidder in the knowledge of the fixed period of time perhaps would have hesitated until the end in order to bid for the first time in the final phase – would admittedly have argued in favour of unreasonableness. This is because in cases of this kind, due to the absence of an auctioneer in the sense of § 156 of the BGB, the possibility in principle does not exist of lengthening the auction on the basis of the situation, in order by this means to reach a favourable conclusion of a contract for the offering party. § 6 III of the general conditions admittedly provides for the possibility of such a lengthening for 'ricardo.de', but no use has been made of this here.

But the crucial argument against assumption of an unreasonable disadvantage is the fact that the offering participant can influence the course of the auction on a permanent basis by giving a minimum price and a starting price, the size of the steps in the bidding and the bidding period, and thereby keep his risk within limits.

Besides this, it is generally known that auctions are forms of transaction full of risks. The offering participant therefore goes into this risk consciously, in order, so to speak, to exploit the chance, through price determination by means of mutual outbidding by the bidders, of obtaining a good price, which might possibly even be over the market price. The fact that this chance might possibly not be realised lies in the nature of an auction. In addition to this, the formulation of the proceedings without an auctioneer offers the possibility of extending the offer period to several weeks which makes the individual presentation of goods accessible for a substantially greater circle of persons and therefore as a rule guarantees the obtaining of a reasonable price (*Wilkens*, DB 2000, 666 [668]).

(d) Insofar as the defendant claims that doubts arose in relation to the seriousness and binding nature of the offers because of the admission procedure under § 1 of the general conditions and the possibility of withdrawal of the registration under § 4 III of the general conditions, this can at the most affect the effectiveness of *these rules*, but not however those of § 5 IV of the general conditions. The same applies in relation to the doubts about § 4 V of the general conditions.

(b) Besides this the State Court has correctly assumed that in the interpretation of a declaration, besides the wording, accompanying circumstances from the objective viewpoint of a recipient but outside the actual act of declaration are to be included (*Palandt/Heinrichs*, § 133 marginal no 15 with further references).

(1) Der *Senat* kann allerdings der *Kammer*, die ausgeführt hat, dass diese Begleitumstände *gegen* die Annahme einer auf Abschluss eines Kaufvertrags unter dem Einstandspreis gerichteten Erklärung sprächen, *nicht* folgen. Die *Kammer* hat gemeint, der Kl. habe nicht davon ausgehen dürfen, dass der Bekl. die Auktion als Werbeveranstaltung habe nutzen wollen und Vermögenseinbußen durch einen Verkauf des Pkw *unter dem Einkaufspreis* einkalkuliert habe. Dem ist aber entgegenzuhalten, dass der Bekl. als Verkaufsplattform gerade eine Internet*auktion* benutzt hat und den Pkw nicht zu einem Festpreis, sondern mit einem Startpreis von lediglich 10 DM anbot, was ihm die potenzielle Möglichkeit verschaffte, einen größeren Bieterkreis zu erreichen. Die vom Bekl. gewählte Verkaufsform spricht daher *für* eine auf Abschluss eines Kaufvertrags über den Pkw zu jedem Kaufpreis oberhalb des Startpreises gerichtete Willenserklärung (so auch *Ulrici*, JuS 2000, 947 [949]).

Entgegen den Ausführungen des *LG* ist also aus der Sicht eines objektiven Erklärungsempfängers, der Kenntnis von der Möglichkeit der Festsetzung eines (weit höheren) Mindestgebots hat, auf den Willen des Erklärenden zu schließen, mit jedem Gebot über dem festgelegten Startpreis einverstanden zu sein, selbst wenn dieses noch so niedrig liegt (so auch *Ulrici*, JuS 2000, 947 [950]). Der geheim gehaltene Wille, den Pkw erst ab Erreichen des Einkaufspreises verkaufen zu wollen, ist nach § 116 BGB unbeachtlich.

Das Risiko, den Pkw möglicherweise lediglich für wenige hundert DM 'zum Schleuderpreis' verkaufen zu müssen, kann der Verkäufer durch die Angabe eines entsprechend hohen Mindestgebots gerade vermeiden. Macht er dies nicht, so ist bei verständiger Würdigung anzunehmen, dass er aus Marketing- oder sonstigen Gründen bei der Versteigerung auch hohe Verluste in Kauf zu nehmen bereit ist.

Auch der Umstand, dass der Anbieter nach Freischaltung der Angebotsseite keinerlei Korrekturmöglichkeit mehr hat, vermag keine andere Bewertung zu rechtfertigen, da dem Erklärenden dieser Umstand bei Bestätigung seiner Angaben gegenüber 'ricardo.de' erkennbar war. Nimmt er die der Freischaltung zeitlich vorgelagerten Korrekturmöglichkeiten *nicht* wahr, so geschieht dies auf sein Risiko.

(2) Eine Beschränkung der Erklärung des Bekl. auf Gebote im Rahmen der Billigkeit folgt auch nicht dem Rechtsgedanken des § 315 BGB, da die Parteien ausdrücklich eine andere Regelung hinsichtlich der Leistungsbestimmung – nämlich durch Bieterwettstreit – getroffen haben und somit ein Zweifelsfall i.S. des § 315 BGB *nicht* vorliegt. Die Leistungsbestimmung wurde angesichts der Festlegung von Startpreis und Bieterschritten auch nicht in das Belieben des Kl. gestellt.

(1) The *Senate* can admittedly *not* follow the *chamber*, which stated that these accompanying circumstances argued *against* the assumption of a declaration directed towards the conclusion of a purchase contract below the cost price. The chamber thought that the claimant was not allowed to proceed on the basis that the defendant wanted to use the auction as a business event and had included in his calculations losses by a sale of the car *below the wholesale price*. It must however be set against this that the defendant has used an internet *auction* as a sale platform and offered the car not at a fixed price but with a starting price of merely 10 DM, which provided him with the potential possibility of reaching a greater circle of bidders. The form of sale chosen by the defendant therefore argues *in favour of* a declaration of will directed to conclusion of a purchase contract regarding the car at any purchase price over the starting price (thus also *Ulrici*, JuS 2000, 947 [949]).

Contrary to the observations of the State Court from the point of view of an objective recipient of a declaration who knew of the possibility of the setting of a (much higher) minimum bid, it is necessary to infer the will of the declarant to be in agreement with every bid over the fixed starting price, even if this was as low as it could be (thus also *Ulrici*, JuS 2000, 947 [950]). The secretly held intention of wanting to sell the car only after reaching the wholesale price is of no importance according to § 116 of the BGB.

The risk of possibly having to sell the car for merely a few hundred DM 'at a knockdown price' can be avoided by the seller giving an appropriately high reserve price. If he does not do this, then it is to be assumed on a sensible assessment that he is ready on marketing or other grounds to accept high losses in the auction.

Even the fact that after release of the offer page the offeror has no longer any opportunity to make corrections cannot justify any other evaluation, as this fact could be recognised by the declarant on confirmation of his instructions to 'ricardo.de'. If he does *not* take advantage of the opportunties for correction at a point in time before the release, this takes place at his own risk.

(2) Limitation of the defendant's declaration to bids within the framework of fairness also does not follow the legal concept in § 315 of the BGB, as the parties have expressly made another regime in relation to the performance provision – namely by competition in bidding – and therefore a case of doubt in the sense of § 315 of the BGB is *not* present. The performance provision was also not put in the claimant's complete discretion, in view of the fixing of the starting price and the steps for bidders.

Es entspricht vielmehr dem *Prinzip der Privatautonomie*, dass denjenigen, der sich in Anbetracht der mit Auktionen verbundenen Chancen und Risiken für diese Verkaufsform entscheidet, auch die Pflicht trifft, die Folgen bei Realisierung der Risiken zu tragen. So darf der privatautonom erklärte Wille nicht – wie vom *LG* im Ergebnis vorgenommen – durch den 'vernünftigen' Willen ersetzt werden ('Es gibt ihn doch, den gerechten Preis', *Wiebe*, MMR 2000, 284), denn die Privatautonomie gestattet – in den hier nicht tangierten Grenzen der §§ 134, 138 BGB – auch (ganz) unvernünftiges Verhalten.

2 Selbst wenn man aber entgegen der Ansicht des *Senats* in der Freischaltung der Angebotsseite kein Angebot i.S. des § 145 BGB sähe, so stellte es in jedem Fall eine antizipierte Annahmeerklärung hinsichtlich des in diesem Fall durch den letzten Bieter – hier des Kl. – im Angebotszeitraum wirksam abgegebenen Angebots dar. Das *LG* hat zutreffend ausgeführt, dass keine grundsätzlichen Bedenken bezüglich der Zulässigkeit einer derartigen antizipierten Annahme bestehen. Dies folgt aus dem Grundsatz der Privatautonomie und der damit verbundenen Freiheit, Risiken einzugehen.

3 Die Erklärungen sind den Parteien jeweils dergestalt *zugegangen*, dass 'ricardo.de' von den Parteien durch wirksame Anerkennung der AGB als Empfangsvertreter bezüglich der Erklärungen in §§ 3 V, 4 VII AGB bevollmächtigt würde. Wie das *LG* zutreffend ausgeführt hat, haben die Parteien im Verhältnis zu 'ricardo.de' die AGB i.S. des § 2 AGBG wirksam in den Vertrag einbezogen (s. o.), so dass eine Bevollmächtigung i.S. des § 167 I 1 BGB *gegenüber dem Vertreter* erfolgt ist.

Die Bestellung von 'ricardo.de' zum Empfangsvertreter beider Parteien verstößt auch nicht gegen § 181 BGB. Unabhängig von der Frage, ob die Vorschrift nach ihrem Schutzzweck auf den Empfangsvertreter überhaupt anwendbar ist, ist die Doppelvertretung in jedem Fall als gestattet i.S. des § 181 BGB anzusehen, da sie jeweils in Kenntnis der Bestellung durch die andere Partei erfolgte.

It corresponds instead with the *principle of private autonomy* that the person who, in view of the chance and risks associated with auctions, decides in favour of this form of sale also has the duty of bearing the consequences on realisation of the risks. Thus, the declared will, based on private autonomy, cannot – as was undertaken by the State Court in the end result – be replaced by the 'sensible' will ('All the same, there is a fair price', *Wiebe*, MMR 2000, 284), because private autonomy also allows (completely) stupid behaviour – within the limits of §§ 134 and 138 of the BGB, which were not reached here.

2 Even if, contrary to the view of the *Senate*, one were to see in the release of the offer page no offer in the sense of § 145 of the BGB, then it represented in each case an anticipated declaration of acceptance in relation to the offer effectively submitted in this case by the last bidder – here the claimant – in the offer period. The State Court has correctly observed that no objections in principle exist in relation to the permissibility of an anticipated acceptance of this kind. This follows from the principle of private autonomy and the freedom associated with this to incur risks.

3 The declarations *reached* the parties in each case in such a way that 'ricardo.de' was authorised by the parties, by effective recognition of the general conditions, as the receiving agent in relation to the declarations in §§ 3 V and 4 VII of the general conditions. As the State Court has correctly observed, the parties in the relationship to 'ricardo.de' have effectively included into the contract the AGBG (see above), so that an authorisation in the sense of § 167 I 1 of the BGB *as against the agent* has occurred.

The appointment of 'ricardo.de' as the receiving agent of both parties does not violate § 181 of the BGB. Independently of the question of whether the provision, according to its protective purpose, is applicable to the receiving agent at all, double representation is in each case to be regarded as permitted in the sense of § 181 of the BGB, as it occurred in each case in the knowledge of the appointment by the other party.

II 1 Die Willenserklärung des Bekl. ist nicht durch Anfechtung nach §§ 119, 142 I BGB untergegangen.

(a) Insoweit fehlt es bereits an einem Anfechtungsgrund. Ein vom Bekl. geltend gemachter Erklärungsirrtum i.S. des § 119 I Alt. 2 BGB durch versehentliche Eingabe eines Startpreises von 10 DM an Stelle von 10 000 DM lag nicht vor. Es fehlte insoweit an einer entsprechenden Fehlvorstellung. So hat der Bekl. im Rahmen der persönlichen Anhörung gem. § 141 ZPO eingeräumt, dass es ihm infolge Zeitdrucks bei Einrichtung der Angebotsseite 'egal' gewesen sei, was er inhaltlich eingegeben und dass er sich auf die Kontrollfrage 'Alles recht so?' durch 'ricardo.de' vor der Freischaltung seine Eingaben und die rechtlichen Hinweise zwecks Zeitersparnis nicht durchgelesen habe. An einem zur Anfechtung berechtigenden Irrtum fehlt es aber, wenn der Erklärende die Erklärung in dem Bewusstsein abgibt, ihren Inhalt nicht genau zu kennen (*Palandt/Heinrichs*, § 119 Rdnr. 9 m. w. Nachw.).

(b) Im Übrigen fehlt es auch an der Ursächlichkeit des Irrtums für die Abgabe der Willenserklärung, da der erzielte Kaufpreis von 26 350 DM über dem angeblich gewollten Startpreis von 10 000 DM liegt. Die Erwägung, dass bei einem höheren Startpreis innerhalb der Bietzeit ein höheres letztes Gebot möglich gewesen wäre (so *Ulrici* JuS 2000, 947 [951]), ist spekulativ und kann nicht zur Bejahung der Ursächlichkeit herangezogen werden. Dies gilt insbesondere auch vor dem Hintergrund, dass es bei einem höheren Startpreis unter Umständen keine so rege Bieterbeteiligung gegeben hätte. Zweifel gehen hier zu Lasten des Bekl.

(c) Im Übrigen fehlt es an der *Unverzüglichkeit* der Anfechtungserklärung i.S. des § 121 BGB. Dabei mag dahinstehen, ob man – entgegen dem Wortlaut des § 121 BGB – für den Fristbeginn *hier* nicht auf den Auktionsbeginn abstellen kann (s. *Ulrici*, JuS 2000, 947 [951]), sondern auf den Zeitpunkt der Kenntniserlangen von der Person des Käufers abstellen muss, da dem Bekl. erst ab diesem Zeitpunkt die Abgabe der Anfechtungserklärung gegenüber dem Anfechtungsgegner i.S. des § 143 I, II BGB möglich war (so auch *Wilkens*, DB 2000, 666 [668]). Die Anfechtungserklärung ist, wie vom Bekl. auch schriftsätzlich vorgetragen, erst in dem Anwaltsschreiben vom 6.8.1999 und nicht bereits in den Ende Juli geführten Telefonaten zwischen den Parteien abgegeben worden. Denn der bezüglich der Telefonate erfolgte Vortrag, der Bekl. habe mitgeteilt, er habe sich 'verklickt' und wolle deswegen den Vertrag nicht gegen sich gelten lassen, steht im Widerspruch zu seinem Vorbringen, man habe seinerzeit einen Aufhebungsvertrag geschlossen. Eine am 6.8.1999 abgegebene Anfechtungserklärung erfolgte nicht mehr unverzüglich i.S. des § 121 BGB.

II 1 The declaration of will by the defendant was not destroyed by avoidance under §§ 119 and 142 I of the BGB.

(a) In this respect there is not even a ground of avoidance. A declaration mistake in the sense of § 119 I alternative 2 of the BGB, as claimed by the defendant, by inadvertent input of a starting price of 10 DM, in place of 10,000 DM was not present. In this respect an appropriate defective concept is lacking. The defendant has admitted within the framework of the personal hearing in accordance with § 141 of the ZPO that, in consequence of the pressure of time in the setting up of the offer page, it was 'all the same' to him what he submitted as contents and that, on the confirmation question 'Everything OK?' by 'ricardo.de' before the release, he had not read through his submissions and the legal advice, in order to save time. But there is no mistake giving a right to avoidance, if the declarant is submitting the declaration in the consciousness of not knowing its content exactly (*Palandt/Heinrichs*, § 119 marginal no 9 with further references).

(b) Apart from this, causality of the mistake for the submission of the declaration of will is also lacking, as the purchase price of 26,350 DM achieved is above the starting price of 10,000 DM which was alleged to be desired. The argument that, if there had been a higher starting price, a higher final offer would have been possible within the offer period (as in *Ulrici* JuS 2000, 947 [951]) is speculative and cannot be utilised to affirm causality. This applies in particular against the background that had there been a higher starting price there would possibly not have been such vigorous bidder participation. Doubts on this subject go to the disadvantage of the defendant.

(c) Besides this, there was a failure to make the avoidance declaration *without delay* in the sense of § 121 of the BGB. In this connection it may be left undecided whether – contrary to the wording of § 121 of the BGB – the beginning of the period *here* can be taken not as the beginning of the auction (see *Ulrici* JuS 2000, 947 [951]) but must be taken as the point in time when the identity of the purchaser is known, since it was only from this point in time that the giving of the avoidance declaration to the person who should receive it in the sense of § 143 I and II of the BGB was possible for the defendant (thus also *Wilkens*, DB 2000, 666 [668]). The declaration of avoidance is, as stated by the defendant in their written case, only given in the lawyer's letter of the 6.8.1999 and not in the telephone conversations between the parties at the end of July. This is because the argument made in relation to the telephone conversations that the defendant had said he had 'clicked by mistake' and therefore did not want the contract to be valid against him is in contradiction to his statement that a cancellation contract had been concluded at that time. An avoidance declaration given on the 6.8.1999 did not occur without delay in the sense of § 121 of the BGB.

2 Der Vertrag ist auch nicht wegen Verstoßes gegen ein gesetztliches Verbot nichtig, § 134 BGB. In Betracht käme ein Verstoß gegen § 34 b I GewO und § 34 b VO Nr. 5 b GewO. Diese Vorschriften richten sich aber nur an den Auktionsveranstalter, weshalb sie schon aus diesem Grunde nicht zur Nichtigkeit des Vertrags zwischen den Parteien führen können.

III Der Anspruch des Kl. auf Lieferung und Übereignung eines Pkw des im Tenor beschriebenen Typs ist auch nicht nach § 275 BGB wegen nachträglichen Unvermögens untergegangen ... Insoweit kann dahinstehen, ob die Parteien eine Stück- oder Gattungsschuld vereinbart haben. Denn abgesehen von fehlenden Beweisangeboten durch den Bekl. ist eine Bewieserhebung über die Frage, ob dem Bekl. die Lieferung des speziellen oder eines entsprechenden Neufahrzeugs – wie dieser behauptet – wegen Weiterverkaufs des ursprünglich vorhandenen Fahrzeugs und einer inzwischen eingetretenen Produktionsänderung nicht mehr möglich ist, nicht erforderlich, da feststeht, dass der Bekl. auf Grund des Weiterverkaufs ein mögliches Unvermögen zu vertreten hätte. Sollte sich in der Zwangsvollstreckung ergeben, dass dem Bekl. die Erfüllung des Klageanspruchs tatsächlich unmöglich ist, so hat der Kl. die Möglichkeit des Vorgehens nach § 283 BGB (*Palandt/Heinrichs*, § 275 Rdnr. 25 m. w. Nachw. aus der Rspr.; *OLG Hamm*, WM 1998, 1949 [1950] m. w. Nachw.).

V Die Verbindlichkeit ist auch klagbar. Bei der Internetauktion handelt es sich nicht um ein Glückspiel i.S. des § 762 BGB (so auch *Wiebe*, MMR 2000, 284 [285]; *Wilkens*, DB 2000, 666 [668]). Bei einem Glücksspiel hängen Gewinn und Verlust (hauptsächlich) vom Zufall, nicht aber von der Einwirkung der Parteien ab. Bei der vorliegenden Auktion war aber nur die Höhe des zu erzielenden Preises ungewiss, und auch hier hatte der Anbieter Möglichkeiten der Einwirkung durch Festlegung eines Mindest- sowie Startpreises, der Bietschritte und des Bietzeitraums.

Daran ändert sich auch nichts dadurch, dass 'ricardo.de' nach § 6 III AGB berechtigt war, den Angebotszeitraum nach eigenem Ermessen zu verkürzen oder zu verlängern oder Veranstaltungen ohne Abschluss eines Vertrags abzubrechen. Denn den Begriff des Spiels i.S. des § 762 BGB zeichnet insbesondere aus, dass sich der Zweck in der Unterhaltung und/oder Gewinnerzielung erschöpft, das heißt ein ernster sittlicher oder wirtschaftlicher Geschäftszweck fehlt (*Palandt/Sprau*, § 762 Rdnr. 2). Vorliegend verfolgten beide Parteien dagegen den wirtschaftlichen Zweck, das Fahrzeug zu einem – aus ihrer jeweiligen Sicht – günstigen Kaufpreis zu verkaufen bzw. zu erwerben. Dass eine solche Auktion spekulativen Charakter hat, macht sie noch nicht zum Spiel i.S. von § 762 BGB (*Wiebe*, MMR 2000, 284 [285]).

2 The contract is also not void because of violation of a statutory prohibition: § 134 of the BGB. A violation of § 34 b I of the GewO and § 34 b VO no 5 b of the GewO would have come into consideration. But these provisions are only directed against the organiser of the auction, for which reason they cannot lead simply on this ground to nullity of the contract between the parties.

III The claimant's claim to delivery and transfer of a car of the type described in the judgment also did not lapse under § 275 of the BGB because of subsequent impossibility ... In this respect it can be left undecided whether the parties have agreed an obligation relating to a class or relating to a specific object. This is because apart from the absence of offers of proof by the defendant, it is not necessary to obtain evidence on the question of whether the delivery of the special or a corresponding new car for the defendant – as he asserts – is no longer possible because of the selling on of the original vehicle available and a change in production which has taken place in the meantime, as it is certain that the defendant would have to be responsible for any possible impossibility on the ground of selling on. If it should emerge in the execution proceedings that the fulfilment of the claim is actually impossible for the defendant, the claimant has the possibility of proceeding under § 283 of the BGB (*Palandt/Heinrichs*, § 275 marginal no 25 with further references from the case law; *OLG Hamm*, WM 1998, 1949 [1950] with further references).

V The obligation is also enforceable. An internet auction is not a game of chance in the sense of § 762 of the BGB (thus also *Wiebe*, MMR 2000, 284 [285]; *Wilkens*, DB 2000, 666 [668]). In a game of chance, gain and loss depend (chiefly) on accident but not on the influence of the parties. But in the auction in this case only the amount of the price to be obtained was uncertain and even here the offeror had opportunities for influence by fixing a reserve price as well as a start price, the bidding steps and the bidding period.

Nothing here is changed by the fact that 'ricardo.de' was entitled under § 6 III of the general conditions to shorten or lengthen the offer period according to its own discretion, or to break off arrangements without conclusion of a contract. This is because the concept of the game in the sense of § 762 of the BGB is distinguished in particular by the fact that the purpose does not go beyond the entertainment and/or obtaining of gain, that is to say a serious moral or economic business purpose is lacking (*Palandt/Sprau*, § 762 marginal no 2). Both parties here were on the other hand pursuing the business purpose of selling or acquiring the vehicle at what was in their respective opinions a favourable purchase price. The fact that such an auction has a speculative character does not make it into a game in the sense of § 762 of the BGB (*Wiebe*, MMR 2000, 284 [285]).

(2) *Lapse of offer*

§ 146 [Erlöschen des Antrags] Der Antrag erlischt, wenn er dem Antragenden gegenüber abgelehnt oder wenn er nicht diesem gegenüber nach den §§ 147 bis 149 rechtzeitig angenommen wird.

Acceptance

(1) *Time for acceptance*

§ 147 [Annahmefrist] (1) Der einem Anwesenden gemachte Antrag kann nur sofort angenommen werden. Dies gilt auch von einem mittels Fernsprechers oder einer sonstigen technischen Einrichtung von Person zu Person gemachten Antrage.

(2) Der einem Abwesenden gemachte Antrag kann nur bis zu dem Zeitpunkt angenommen werden, in welchem der Antragende den Eingang der Antwort unter regelmäßigen Umständen erwarten darf.

§ 148 [Bestimmung einer Annahmefrist] Hat der Antragende für die Annahme des Antrags eine Frist bestimmt, so kann die Annahme nur innerhalb der Frist erfolgen.

§ 149 [Verspätet zugegangene Annahmeerklärung] Ist eine dem Antragenden verspätet zugegangene Annahmeerklärung dergestalt abgesendet worden, daß sie bei regelmäßiger Beförderung ihm rechtzeitig zugegangen sein würde, und mußte der Antragende dies erkennen, so hat er die Verspätung dem Annehmenden unverzüglich nach dem Empfange der Erklärung anzuzeigen, sofern es nicht schon vorher geschehen ist. Verzögert er die Absendung der Anzeige, so gilt die Annahme als nicht verspätet.

(2) *Acceptance as a new offer*

§ 150 [Verspätete und abändernde Annahme] (1) Die verspätete Annahme eines Antrags gilt als neuer Antrag.

(2) Eine Annahme unter Erweiterungen, Einschränkungen oder sonstigen Änderungen gilt als Ablehnung verbunden mit einem neuen Antrage.

(2) Lapse of offer

§ 146 [Lapsing of the offer] The offer lapses if it is refused as against the offeror, or if it is not accepted in time as against him in accordance with §§ 147–149.

Despite the more precise rules on this subject in comparison with English law, they may be avoided in practice by the use of words indicating an intention not to be bound like 'freibleibend' (subject to alteration) or 'ohne Obligo' (without recourse).

Acceptance

(1) Time for acceptance

§147 [Period for acceptance] (1) An offer made to a person who is present can only be accepted immediately. This also applies to an offer made by one person to another by telephone, or some other technical apparatus.

(2) An offer made to an absent person can only be accepted up to the point in time at which the offeror might expect the arrival of the answer in usual circumstances.

§ 148 [Fixing of a period for acceptance] If the offeror has fixed a period for the acceptance of the offer, acceptance can only take place within this period.

§ 149 [Declaration of acceptance arriving belatedly] If a declaration of acceptance which reaches the offeror late has been sent in such a way that it would have reached him punctually on regular dispatch, and if the offeror must have realised this, he should notify the delay to the acceptor immediately after the receipt of the declaration, insofar as this has not already happened. If he delays the dispatch of the notification, the acceptance is not to be regarded as belated.

(2) Acceptance as a new offer

§ 150 [Delayed or conditional acceptance] (1) Delayed acceptance of an offer counts as a new offer.

(2) An acceptance with additions, limitations or other alterations counts as refusal combined with a new offer.

(3) Method of acceptance

§ 151 [Annahme ohne Erklärung gegenüber dem Antragenden] Der Vertrag kommt durch die Annahme des Antrags zustande, ohne daß die Annahme dem Antragenden gegenüber erklärt zu werden braucht, wenn eine solche Erklärung nach der Verkehrsitte nicht zu erwarten ist oder der Antragende auf sie verzichtet hat. Der Zeitpunkt, in welchem der Antrag erlischt, bestimmt sich nach dem aus dem Antrag oder den Umständen zu entnehmenden Willen des Antragenden.

§ 152 [Annahme bei notarieller Beurkundung] Wird ein Vertrag notariell beurkundet, ohne daß beide Teile gleichzeitig anwesend sind, so kommt der Vertrag mit der nach § 128 erfolgten Beurkundung der Annahme zustande, wenn nicht ein anderes bestimmt ist. Die Vorschrift des § 151 Satz 2 findet Anwendung.

(4) Death or incompetence of offeror

§ 153 [Tod oder Geschäftsunfähigkeit des Antragenden] Das Zustandekommen des Vertrags wird nicht dadurch gehindert, daß der Antragende vor der Annahme stirbt oder geschäftsunfähig wird, es sei denn, daß ein anderer Wille des Antragenden anzunehmen ist.

NEED FOR AGREEMENT

§ 154 [Offener Einigungsmangel; fehlende Beurkundung] (1) Solange nicht die Parteien sich über alle Punkte eines Vertrags geeinigt haben, über die nach der Erklärung auch nur einer Partei eine Vereinbarung getroffen werden soll, ist im Zweifel der Vertrag nicht geschlossen. Die Verständigung über einzelne Punkte ist auch dann nicht bindend, wenn eine Aufzeichnung stattgefunden hat.

(2) Ist eine Beurkundung des beabsichtigten Vertrags verabredet worden, so ist im Zweifel der Vertrag nicht geschlossen, bis die Beurkundung erfolgt ist.

§ 155 [Versteckter Einigungsmangel] Haben sich die Parteien bei einem Vertrage, den sie als geschlossen ansehen, über einen Punkt, über den eine Vereinbarung getroffen werden sollte, in Wirklichkeit nicht geeinigt, so gilt das Vereinbarte, sofern anzunehmen ist, daß der Vertrag auch ohne eine Bestimmung über diesen Punkt geschlossen sein würde.

(3) Method of acceptance

In English law it is not always necessary for acceptance to reach the offeror. *Carlill v Carbolic Smoke Ball Co* **[1893] 2 QB 256 is a classic example. German law also provides for this in certain circumstances.**

§ 151 [Acceptance without a declaration as against the offeror] A contract comes into existence by acceptance of an offer without the acceptance needing to be declared as against the offeror, if such a declaration is not to be expected according to business custom or the offeror has renounced his right to it. The point in time at which the offer lapses is to be determined according to the intention of the offeror to be gleaned from the offer or the circumstances.

See the internet auction case, p 333.

§ 152 [Acceptance with notarial authentication] If a contract is notarially authenticated without both parties being present at the same time, the contract comes into existence when the authentication of the acceptance takes place according to § 128, insofar as no other provision is made. The provisions of § 151 sentence 2 are to be applied.

(4) Death or incompetence of an offeror

§ 153 [Death or legal incompetence of offeror] The formation of the contract is not prevented by the offeror dying or becoming incompetent before acceptance, unless a contrary intention of the offeror is to be assumed.

NEED FOR AGREEMENT

§ 154 [Patent lack of agreement; authentication lacking] (1) As long as the parties have not agreed about all points of a contract as to which, according to the declaration of even only one party, agreement should be made, the contract has, in case of doubt, not been concluded. Agreement about individual points is still not binding if a record has been made.

(2) If authentication of the intended contract has been agreed, the contract has, in case of doubt, not been concluded until the authentication has taken place.

§ 155 [Concealed lack of agreement] If the parties to a contract, which they regard as concluded, have in reality not agreed about a point about which an agreement should be made, what has been agreed is valid insofar as it is to be assumed that the contract would have been concluded even without a determination about this point.

AUCTIONS

§ 156 [Vertragsschluß bei Versteigerung] Bei einer Versteigerung kommt der Vertrag erst durch den Zuschlag zustande. Ein Gebot erlischt, wenn ein Übergebot abgegeben oder die Versteigerung ohne Erteilung des Zuschlags geschlossen wird.

INTERPRETATION OF CONTRACTS

§ 157 [Auslegung von Verträgen] Verträge sind so auszulegen, wie Treu und Glauben mit Rücksicht auf die Verkehrssitte es erfordern.

CONDITIONS

Vierter Titel. Bedingung. Zeitbestimmung

§ 158 [Aufschiebende und auflösende Bedingung] (1) Wird ein Rechtsgeschäft unter einer aufschiebenden Bedingung vorgenommen, so tritt die von der Bedingung abhängig gemachte Wirkung mit dem Eintritte der Bedingung ein.

(2) Wird ein Rechtsgeschäft unter einer auflösenden Bedingung vorgenommen, so endigt mit dem Eintritte der Bedingung die Wirkung des Rechtsgeschäfts; mit diesem Zeitpunkte tritt der frühere Rechtszustand wieder ein.

§ 159 [Rückbeziehung] Sollen nach dem Inhalte des Rechtsgeschäfts die an den Eintritt der Bedingung geknüpften Folgen auf einen früheren Zeitpunkt zurückbezogen werden, so sind im Falle des Eintritts der Bedingung die Beteiligten verpflichtet, einander zu gewähren, was sie haben würden, wenn die Folgen in dem früheren Zeitpunkt eingetreten wären.

§ 160 [Haftung während der Schwebezeit] (1) Wer unter einer aufschiebenden Bedingung berechtigt ist, kann im Falle des Eintritts der Bedingung Schadensersatz von dem anderen Teile verlangen, wenn dieser während der Schwebezeit das von der Bedingung abhängige Recht durch sein Verschulden vereitelt oder beeinträchtigt.

AUCTIONS

§ 156 [Conclusion of a contract at an auction] At an auction a contract comes into existence by knocking down (to a bidder). A bid lapses if a higher bid is made or the auction is closed without the item being knocked down.

See the internet auction case, p 333.

INTERPRETATION OF CONTRACTS

§ 157 [Interpretation of contracts] Contracts are to be interpreted as required by good faith, with regard to business custom.

See § 133 (Chapter Four, p 313) and § 242 (p 369) and the comments on these. Further interpretation rules will apply to contracts, eg, if the intention of parties does not correspond with what they actually stated, the contract must nevertheless be interpreted in the light of their actual intention. In RGZ 99, 148, agreement was reached on the sale of a certain type of fish. The fact that it was misdescribed in the contract did not matter. Special rules apply where a particular form is prescribed for a contract.

CONDITIONS

Fourth Title. Conditions. Determination of time

§ 158 [Conditions precedent and subsequent] (1) If a legal transaction is entered into subject to a condition precedent, the effect made dependent on the condition occurs when the condition takes effect.

(2) If a legal transaction is entered into subject to a condition subsequent, the effect of the transaction ends with the fulfilment of the condition; at this point in time the former legal situation becomes effective again.

§ 159 [Retrospective effect] If, according to the content of a legal transaction, the consequences connected with the fulfilment of a condition are related back to an earlier point in time, the parties are obliged, in the case of fulfilment of the condition to grant to each other what they would have if the consequences had arisen at the earlier point in time.

§ 160 [Liability during the period of suspense] (1) A person who has a right under a condition precedent can in case of fulfilment of the condition claim compensation from the other party if during the period of suspense this person has through his own fault frustrated or infringed the right dependent on the condition.

(2) Den gleichen Anspruch hat unter denselben Voraussetzungen bei einem unter einer auflösenden Bedingung vorgenommenen Rechtsgeschäfte derjenige, zu dessen Gunsten der frühere Rechtszustand wieder eintritt.

§ 161 [Zwischenverfügungen] (1) Hat jemand unter einer aufschiebenden Bedingung über einen Gegenstand verfügt, so ist jede weitere Verfügung, die er während der Schwebezeit über den Gegenstand trifft, im Falle des Eintritts der Bedingung insoweit unwirksam, als sie die von der Bedingung abhängige Wirkung vereiteln oder beeinträchtigen würde. Einer solchen Verfügung steht eine Verfügung gleich, die während der Schwebezeit im Wege der Zwangsvollstreckung oder der Arrestvollziehung oder durch den Konkursverwalter erfolgt.

(2) Dasselbe gilt bei einer auflösenden Bedingung von den Verfügungen desjenigen, dessen Recht mit dem Eintritte der Bedingung endigt.

(3) Die Vorschriften zugunsten derjenigen, welche Rechte von einem Nichtberechtigten herleiten, finden entsprechende Anwendung.

§ 162 [Unzulässige Einwirkung auf die Bedingung] (1) Wird der Eintritt der Bedingung von der Partei, zu deren Nachteil er gereichen würde, wider Treu und Glauben verhindert, so gilt die Bedingung als eingetreten.

(2) Wird der Eintritt der Bedingung von der Partei, zu deren Vorteil er gereicht, wider Treu und Glauben herbeigeführt, so gilt der Eintritt als nicht erfolgt.

§ 163 [Zeitbestimmung] Ist für die Wirkung eines Rechtsgeschäfts bei dessen Vornahme ein Anfangs- oder ein Endtermin bestimmt worden, so finden im ersteren Falle die für die aufschiebende, im letzteren Falle die für die auflösende Bedingung geltenden Vorschriften der §§ 158, 160, 161 entsprechende Anwendung.

(2) In the case of a legal transaction entered into subject to a condition subsequent, the person for whose benefit the former legal situation takes effect again has the same claim under the same conditions.

§ 161 [Disposals in the interim period] (1) If someone disposes of an object subject to a condition precedent, every further disposal which he makes during the period of suspense in relation to the object is, in case of fulfilment of the condition, ineffective so far as the effect dependent on the condition would frustrate or infringe it. Such a disposal is equivalent to a disposal which takes place during the period of suspense by way of a legal execution or the carrying out of an arrest or through the receiver in bankruptcy.

(2) The same applies in the case of a condition subsequent in relation to the disposals of a person whose right ends with the fulfilment of the condition.

(3) The rules for the benefit of those who derive rights from a person who is not entitled have corresponding application.

§ 162 [Impermissible influence upon the condition] (1) If the fulfilment of the condition is prevented in a manner contrary to good faith by the party who would be disadvantaged by it, the condition counts as fulfilled.

(2) If the fulfilment of the condition is brought about in a manner contrary to good faith by the party who would be advantaged by it, the fulfilment is not to count as having taken place.

§ 163 [Time determination] If, when a legal transaction is entered into, a commencement or termination date has been fixed for the operation of the transaction, the rules of §§ 158, 160 and 161 for, in the former case, conditions precedent and for, in the latter case, conditions subsequent, have corresponding application.

AGENCY

CONSENT

Sechster Titel. Einwilligung. Genehmigung

§ 182 [Zustimmung] (1) Hängt die Wirksamkeit eines Vertrags oder eines einseitigen Rechtsgeschäfts, das einem anderen gegenüber vorzunehmen ist, von der Zustimmung eines Dritten ab, so kann die Erteilung sowie die Verweigerung der Zustimmung wohl dem einen als dem anderen Teile gegenüber erklärt werden.

(2) Die Zustimmung bedarf nicht der für das Rechtsgeschäft bestimmten Form.

(3) Wird ein einseitiges Rechtsgeschäft, dessen Wirksamkeit von der Zustimmung eines Dritten abhängt, mit Einwilligung des Dritten vorgenommen, so finden die Vorschriften des § 111 Satz 2, 3 entsprechende Anwendung.

§ 183 [Wideruflichkeit der Einwilligung] Die vorherige Zustimmung (Einwilligung) ist bis zur Vornahme des Rechtsgeschäfts widerruflich, soweit nicht aus dem ihrer Erteilung zugrunde liegenden Rechtsverhältnisse sich ein anderes ergibt. Der Widerruf kann sowohl dem einen als dem anderen Teile gegenüber erklärt werden.

§ 184 [Rückwirkung der Genehmigung] (1) Die nachträgliche Zustimmung (Genehmigung) wirkt auf den Zeitpunkt der Vornahme des Rechtsgeschäfts zurück, soweit nicht ein anderes bestimmt ist.

(2) Durch die Rückwirkung werden Verfügungen nicht unwirksam, die vor der Genehmigung über den Gegenstand des Rechtsgeschäfts von dem Genehmigenden getroffen worden oder im Wege der Zwangsvollstreckung oder der Arrestvollziehung oder durch den Konkursverwalter erfolgt sind.

§ 185 [Verfügung eines Nichtberechtigten] (1) Eine Verfügung, die ein Nichtberechtigter über einen Gegenstand trifft, ist wirksam, wenn sie mit Einwilligung des Berechtigten erfolgt.

(2) Die Verfügung wird wirksam, wenn der Berechtigte sie genehmigt oder wenn der Verfügende den Gegenstand erwirbt oder wenn er von dem Berechtigten beerbt wird und dieser für die Nachlaßverbindlichkeiten unbeschränkt haftet. In den beiden letzteren Fällen wird, wenn über den Gegenstand mehrere miteinander nicht in Einklang stehende Verfügungen getroffen worden sind, nur die frühere Verfügung wirksam.

AGENCY

The rules on this subject are contained in the Fifth Title of the Civil Code (§§ 164–181).

CONSENT

Sixth title. Assent. Approval

§ 182 [Consent] (1) If the effectiveness of a contract, or a one-sided legal transaction which is to take place as against another, depends on the consent of a third party, the giving or refusal of the consent can be declared to one party or the other.

(2) The consent does not need the form prescribed for the legal transaction.

(3) If a one-sided legal transaction which depends for its effectiveness on the consent of a third party takes place with the assent of the third party the rules in § 111 sentences 2 and 3 have corresponding application.

§ 183 [Revocability of assent] Prior consent (assent) is revocable until the transaction takes place insofar as the legal relationship which underlies the giving of it does not give rise to a different conclusion. The revocation can be declared to the one party or the other.

§ 184 [Retroactivity of approval] (1) Subsequent consent (approval) takes effect retrospectively at the point in time of the taking place of the legal transaction, insofar as no other provision is made.

(2) Disposals do not become ineffective due to retroactivity, if they were made before the approval in respect of the object of the legal transaction by the person giving the approval or took place by way of a legal execution or the carrying out of an arrest or through the receiver in bankruptcy.

§ 185 [Disposal by a person not entitled] (1) A disposal which is made in respect of an object by a person not entitled to make it is effective if it takes place with the assent of the person who is entitled.

(2) The disposal becomes effective if the person entitled to make it approves it or if the person making the disposal acquires the object or if his heir is the person entitled and that person is liable to an unlimited extent for the obligations in respect of the estate. In the two latter cases, only the earlier disposal is effective if several disposals have been made in respect of the object which are not in accord with one another.

PERFORMANCE

Zweites Buch. Recht der Schuldverhältnisse

Erster Abschnitt. Inhalt der Schuldverhältnisse

Erster Titel. Verpflichtung zur Leistung

§ 241 [Pflichten aus dem Schuldverhältnis] (1) Kraft des Schuldverhältnisses ist der Gläubiger berechtigt, von dem Schuldner eine Leistung zu fordern. Die Leistung kann auch in einem Unterlassen bestehen.

(2) Das Schuldverhältnis kann nach seinem Inhalt jeden Teil zur Rücksicht auf die Rechte, Rechtsgüter und Interessen des anderen Teils verpflichten.

§ 241a [Unbestellte Leistungen] (1) Durch die Lieferungen unbestellter Sachen oder durch die Erbringung unbestellter sonstiger Leistungen durch einen Unternehmer an einen Verbraucher wird ein Anspruch gegen diesen nicht begründet.

(2) Gesetzliche Ansprüche sind nicht ausgeschlossen, wenn die Leistung nicht für den Empfänger bestimmt war oder in der irrigen Vorstellung einer Bestellung erfolgte und der Empfänger dies erkannt hat oder bei Anwendung der im Verkehr erforderlichen Sorgfalt hätte erkennen können.

(3) Eine unbestellte Leistung liegt nicht vor, wenn dem Verbraucher statt der bestellten eine nach Qualität und Preis gleichwertige Leistung angeboten und er darauf hingewiesen wird, dass er zur Annahme nicht verpflichtet ist und die Kosten der Rücksendung nicht zu tragen hat.

§ 242 [Leistung nach Treu und Glauben] Der Schuldner ist verpflichtet, die Leistung so zu bewirken, wie Treu und Glauben mit Rücksicht auf die Verkehrssitte es erfordern.

PERFORMANCE

Generally

The second book of the Civil Code contains the law relating to obligation relationships, general and special. The special ones include particular obligations by virtue of a contract or other act of a party, such as sale, exchange, loan, etc and obligations arising by virtue of statutory provisions such as unjust enrichment and tort. For reasons of space, the only special relationship considered in this book is tort (see Chapter Six). The following provisions of the Civil Code relate to general obligation relationships.

BGB

Second Book. Law of Obligation Relationships

First section. Content of Obligation Relationships

First Title. Obligation to perform

§ 241 [Duties from the obligation relationship] (1) By virtue of the obligation relationship, the obligee is entitled to demand performance from the obligor. Performance can also consist of an omission.

(2) The obligation relationship can, according to its content, oblige each party to have consideration for the rights, legal entitlements and interests of the other party.

Apart from the duty to perform (or to compensate for non-performance), there will be secondary duties as to how performance must take place, and other matters connected with performance such as the provision of information. See on this last issue, the allergy to hair tonic case, p 399.

§ 241a [Unsolicited services] (1) The delivery of unsolicited goods or the carrying out of other unsolicited services by an undertaking in favour of consumer does not found a claim against the latter.

(2) Statutory claims are not excluded if the service was not intended for the recipient or occurred under the mistaken impression that an order had been given and the recipient knew this or could have known it by applying the care necessary in the affairs of life.

(3) An unsolicited service is not present if the consumer is offered, instead of what was ordered, a performance of equal value according to quality and price and it is pointed out to him that he is not obliged to accept it and he does not have to bear the costs of sending it back.

This provision serves to transpose Art 9 of EC Directive 97/7.

§ 242 [Performance in accordance with good faith] The obligor is obliged to effect performance as required by good faith with regard to business custom.

§ 243 [Gattungsschuld] (1) Wer eine nur der Gattung nach bestimmte Sache schuldet, hat eine Sache von mittlerer Art und Güte zu leisten.

(2) Hat der Schuldner das zur Leistung einer solchen Sache seinerseits Erforderliche getan, so beschränkt sich das Schuldverhältnis auf diese Sache.

Payments

§ 246 [Gesetzlicher Zinssatz] Ist eine Schuld nach Gesetz oder Rechtsgeschäft zu verzinsen, so sind vier vom Hundert für das Jahr zu entrichten, sofern nicht ein anderes bestimmt ist.

§ 247 [Basiszinssatz] (1) Der Basiszinssatz beträgt 3,62 Prozent. Er verändert sich zum 1. Januar und 1. Juli eines jeden Jahres um die Prozentpunkte, um welche die Bezugsgröße seit der letzten Veränderung des Basiszinssatzes gestiegen oder gefallen ist. Bezugsgröße ist der Zinssatz für die jüngste Hauptrefinanzierungsoperation der Europäischen Zentralbank vor dem ersten Kalendertag des betreffenden Halbjahrs.

(2) Die Deutsche Bundesbank gibt den geltenden Basiszinssatz unverzüglich nach den in Absatz 1 Satz 2 genannten Zeitpunkten im Bundesanzeiger bekannt.

This has been an extremely fruitful category of the Civil Code, and should be read with §§ 138 and 157. It has resulted in clauses being implied into contracts in a manner which can be compared to the principle in *The Moorcock* (1889) 14 PD 64. It has however also been used in some cases to justify alteration of contracts, as with some loan agreements in the inflation period after the First World War, when some borrowers were required to pay back as capital more than the mere amount of Marks they had borrowed. This in turn has led to the development of the concept of collapse of the foundation of the transaction, which sometimes operates similarly to the English doctrine of frustration (although in this connection, see also § 275), but which is applied where possible so as to preserve the contract. It has given rise to certain rules about contractual terms which have been further developed by the legislature in the AGBG (the General Conditions of Business/Contract Act 1976). (These are now included in the Civil Code itself, §§ 305 and onwards: see p 415.) This contains provisions as to when general conditions of business which a party seeks to introduce will become part of a contract, and controls their content by means of prohibitions on certain general and individual clauses. A party may also sometimes be denied the right to rely on a transaction being void if such reliance would be contrary to § 242. Besides this there are indications of it being used as a general equitable principle. See for instance, the fowl pest case, Chapter Six, p 439.

§ 243 [Obligation relating to a class] (1) A person who is only obliged to provide a thing determined according to its class has to provide a thing of average type and quality.

(2) If the obligor has, on his side, done what is necessary for the provision of such a thing, the obligation relationship is restricted to this thing.

Payments

(§§ 244 and 245 of the BGB relate to currency and coinage for money payments.)

§ 246 [Statutory rate of interest] If a debt is subject to interest in accordance with statute or a legal transaction, 4% per year is to be paid insofar as no other rate has been determined.

§ 247 [Basic rate of interest] (1) The basic rate of interest is 3.62%. It changes on the 1 January and the 1 July of every year by the percentage points by which the base factor has risen or fallen since the last change in the basic rate of interest. The base factor is the interest for the most recent major refinancing operation of the European Central Bank before the first calendar day of the half year concerned.

(2) The Deutsche Bundesbank will make known the applicable basic rate of interest without delay, in respect of the points in time mentioned in para 1 sentence 2, in the Bundesanzeiger (*Federal Gazette*).

This provision serves to transpose Art 3 of EC Directive 2000/35.

§ 248 [Zinseszinsen] (1) Eine im voraus getroffene Vereinbarung, daß fällige Zinsen wieder Zinsen tragen sollen, ist nichtig.

(2) Sparkassen, Kreditanstalten und Inhaber von Bankgeschäften können im voraus vereinbaren, daß nicht erhobene Zinsen von Einlagen als neue verzinsliche Einlagen gelten sollen.

Compensation

(1) General rules

§ 249 [Art und Umfang des Schadensersatzes] Wer zum Schadensersatze verpflichtet ist, hat den Zustand herzustellen, der bestehen würde, wenn der zum Ersatze verpflichtende Umstand nicht eingetreten wäre. Ist wegen Verletzung einer Person oder wegen Beschädigung einer Sache Schadensersatz zu leisten, so kann der Gläubiger statt der Herstellung den dazu erforderlichen Geldbetrag verlangen.

§ 250 [Schadensersatz in Geld nach Fristsetzung] Der Gläubiger kann dem Ersatzpflichtigen zur Herstellung eine angemessene Frist mit der Erklärung bestimmen, daß er die Herstellung nach dem Ablaufe der Frist ablehne. Nach dem Ablaufe der Frist kann der Gläubiger den Ersatz in Geld verlangen, wenn nicht die Herstellung rechtzeitig erfolgt; der Anspruch auf die Herstellung ist ausgeschlossen.

§ 251 [Schadensersatz in Geld ohne Fristsetzung] (1) Soweit die Herstellung nicht möglich oder zur Entschädigung des Gläubigers nicht genügend ist, hat der Ersatzpflichtige den Gläubiger in Geld zu entschädigen.

(2) Der Ersatzpflichtige kann den Gläubiger in Geld entschädigen, wenn die Herstellung nur mit unverhältnismäßigen Aufwendungen möglich ist. Die aus der Heilbehandlung eines verletzten Tieres entstandenen Aufwendungen sind nicht bereits dann unverhältnismäßig, wenn sie dessen Wert erheblich übersteigen.

(2) Special rules

§ 252 [Entgangener Gewinn] Der zu ersetzende Schaden umfaßt auch den entgangenen Gewinn. Als entgangen gilt der Gewinn, welcher nach dem gewöhnlichen Laufe der Dinge oder nach den besonderen Umständen, insbesondere nach den getroffenen Anstalten und Vorkehrungen, mit Wahrscheinlichkeit erwartet werden konnte.

§ 248 [Compound interest] (1) An agreement made in advance that interest which is due is to bear interest is void.

(2) Savings banks, credit institutions and proprietors of bank businesses can agree in advance that interest not collected from an investment shall count as a new interest-bearing investment ...

Here follow special provisions in relation to credit institutions.

Compensation

(1) General rules

§ 249 [Nature and extent of compensation for harm] A person who is obliged to make compensation for harm has to restore the conditions which would have existed if the circumstance giving rise to the obligation to make compensation had not occurred. If compensation for harm is to be made because of injury to a person or because of damage to an object, the obligee can, instead of restoration, demand the sum of money necessary for it.

§ 249 was considered in the fowl pest and air traffic controllers strike cases: see Chapter Six, pp 439 and 579 respectively.

§ 250 [Monetary compensation for harm after the setting of a period] The obligee can set for the person obliged to make compensation an appropriate period for restoration by a declaration that he will refuse restoration after the expiry of the period. After the expiry of the period the obligee can demand the compensation in money if restoration does not ensue; the claim to restoration is excluded.

§ 251 [Monetary compensation for harm without the setting of a period] (1) Insofar as restoration is not possible or is not sufficient for indemnifying the obligee, the person obliged to make compensation must indemnify the obligee in money.

(2) The person obliged to make compensation can indemnify the obligee in money if restoration is possible only with disproportionate expenditure. Expenses which have arisen from the remedial treatment of an injured animal are not disproportionate simply because they significantly exceed its value.

(2) Special rules

§ 252 [Lost profit] The harm to be compensated for also includes lost profit. Profit counts as lost if, according to the ordinary course of things or according to the special circumstances, in particular, according to arrangements and provisions which have been made, it could be expected with probability.

This category of compensation was considered in the air traffic controllers strike case: see Chapter Six, p 579.

§ 253 [Immaterieller Schaden] Wegen eines Schadens, der nicht Vermögensschaden ist, kann Entschädigung in Geld nur in den durch das Gesetz bestimmten Fällen gefordert werden.

§ 254 [Mitverschulden] (1) Hat bei der Entstehung des Schadens ein Verschulden des Beschädigten mitgewirkt, so hängt die Verpflichtung zum Ersatze sowie der Umfang des zu leistenden Ersatzes von den Umständen, insbesondere davon ab, inwieweit der Schaden vorwiegend von dem einen oder dem anderen Teile verursacht worden ist.

(2) Dies gilt auch dann, wenn sich das Verschulden des Beschädigten darauf beschränkt, daß er unterlassen hat, den Schuldner auf die Gefahr eines ungewöhnlich hohen Schadens aufmerksam zu machen, die der Schuldner weder kannte noch kennen mußte, oder daß er unterlassen hat, den Schaden abzuwenden oder zu mindern. Die Vorschrift des § 78 findet entsprechende Anwendung.

§ 255 [Abtretung der Ersatzansprüche] Wer für den Verlust einer Sache oder eines Rechtes Schadensersatz zu leisten hat, ist zum Ersatze nur gegen Abtretung der Ansprüche verpflichtet, die dem Ersatzberechtigten auf Grund des Eigentums an der Sache oder auf Grund des Rechtes gegen Dritte zustehen.

FRUSTRATION

§ 275 [Ausschluss der Leistungspflicht] (1) Der Anspruch auf Leistung ist ausgeschlossen, soweit diese für den Schuldner oder für jedermann unmöglich ist.

(2) Der Schuldner kann die Leistung verweigern, soweit diese einen Aufwand erfordert, der unter Beachtung des Inhalts des Schuldverhältnisses und der Gebote von Treu und Glauben in einem groben Missverhältnis zu dem Leistungsinteresse des Gläubigers steht. Bei der Bestimmung der dem Schuldner zuzumutenden Anstrengungen ist auch zu berücksichtigen, ob der Schuldner das Leistungshindernis zu vertreten hat.

§ 253 [Immaterial harm] For harm which is not financial harm, compensation in money can only be demanded in the cases determined by statute.

The restrictive effect of this provision combined with § 847 has been ignored by the courts in relation to the right of personality. However, it prevented the girl in the fall in the supermarket case (see p 377) from recovering damages for pain and suffering.

§ 254 [Contributory fault] (1) If a fault on the part of the person harmed contributed to the origin of the harm, the obligation to make compensation as well as the extent of the compensation to be made depends on the circumstances and especially on to what extent the harm was predominantly caused by one party or the other.

(2) This also applies if the fault of the person harmed is limited to the fact that he omitted to draw the obligor's attention to the danger of an unusually high level of harm which the obligor neither knew nor ought to have known or that he omitted to prevent or lessen the harm. The provisions of § 278 apply correspondingly.

The scope of § 254 is wider than that of the Law Reform (Contributory Negligence) Act 1945. It applies to liability in tort and contract, and it covers failure to warn and to mitigate damage as well as contribution to the source of the damage. It was raised as a defence in the newspaper delivery obstruction case (see Chapter Six, p 481) but, not perhaps surprisingly, was unsuccessful.

§ 255 [Transfer of claims for compensation] A person who has to provide compensation for harm for the loss of an object or a right is only obliged to make compensation on transfer of the claims to which the person entitled to compensation has a right on the basis of ownership of the object or on the basis of the right against third parties.

(There follows in §§ 256–274 further detailed rules about performance.)

FRUSTRATION

§ 275 [Exclusion of duty to perform] (1) The claim to performance is excluded insofar as this is impossible for the obligor or for anyone.

(2) The obligor can refuse the performance insofar as this requires an expenditure which, having regard to the content of the obligation relationship and the requirements of good faith, is in gross disproportion to the interest of the obligee in performance. In determining the efforts to be expected of the obligor, it also has to be considered whether the obligor is responsible for the hindrance to performance.

(3) Der Schuldner kann die Leistung ferner verweigern, wenn er die Leistung persönlich zu erbringen hat und sie ihm unter Abwägung des seiner Leistung entgegenstehenden Hindernisses mit dem Leistungsinteresse des Gläubigers nicht zugemutet werden kann.

(4) Die Rechte des Gläubigers bestimmen sich nach den §§ 280, 283 bis 285, 311 und 326.

FAULT

§ 276 [Verantwortlichkeit des Schuldners] (1) Der Schuldner hat Vorsatz und Fahrlässigkeit zu vertreten, wenn eine strengere oder mildere Haftung weder bestimmt noch aus dem sonstigen Inhalt des Schuldverhältnisses, insbesondere aus der Übernahme einer Garantie oder eines Beschaffungsrisikos, zu entnehmen ist. Die Vorschriften der §§ 827 und 828 finden entsprechende Anwendung.

(2) Fahrlässig handelt, wer die im Verkehr erforderliche Sorgfalt außer Acht lässt.

(3) Die Haftung wegen Vorsatzes kann dem Schuldner nicht im Voraus erlassen werden.

THE FALL IN THE SUPERMARKET CASE

BGHZ Band 66 S. 51

7 Begleitet ein Kind seine Mutter zum Einkauf in einen Selbstbedienungsladen, so können ihm, wenn es dort zu Fall kommt, unter dem Gesichtspunkt eines Vertrages mit Schutzwirkung zugunsten Dritter Schadensersatzansprüche aus Verschulden bei Vertragsschluß zustehen.

BGB §§ 276, 328

VIII Zivilsenat. Urt. v. 28. Januar 1976 i.S. Fa.D.-GmbH (Bekl.) w. L. (Kl.). VIII ZR 246/74.

(3) The obligor can further refuse performance if he has to carry out the performance personally and it cannot be expected of him on balancing the hindrance to his performance with the interest of the obligee in performance.

(4) The rights of the obligee are determined in accordance with §§ 280, 283–285, 311a and 326.

This provision also serves to transpose EC Directive 99/44. See also the internet auction case, p 333.

FAULT

§ 276 [Responsibility of the obligor] (1) The obligor is responsible for intention and negligence if a stricter or more lenient liability is neither determined nor is to be deduced from the other content of the obligation relationship, in particular from the adoption of a guarantee or of a risk of production. The provisions of §§ 827 and 828 apply correspondingly.

(2) A person acts negligently if he does not have regard to the care necessary in the affairs of life.

(3) The obligor cannot be released from liability for intentional acts in advance.

THE FALL IN THE SUPERMARKET CASE

This case involves the extension of contractual protection to cover liability which was not the subject of the contract in favour of someone who was not a party to it. It therefore seems an unusual case to the English law student, but there is a familiarity about the concept of potential dual liability in tort and contract and the comparison of these liabilities to see which is more favourable to the plaintiff.

BGHZ Volume 66 p 51

7 If a child accompanies its mother on a purchase in a self-service store, it can be entitled, if it falls down, to claims for compensation for harm based on fault on making of the contract from the standpoint of a contract with protective effects in favour of a third party.

BGB §§ 276 and 328

VIIIth Civil Senate. Judgment of 28 January 1976 in the case of the Company D Ltd (defendant) v L (plaintiff) – VIII ZR 246/74.

I Landgericht Trier

II Oberlandesgericht Koblenz

Am 2. November 1963 begab sich die damals 14 Jahre alte Klägerin mit ihre Mutter in die Filiale der Beklagten in Sch., einen kleineren Selbstbedienungsladen. Während die Mutter nach Aussuchen der Waren noch an der Kasse stand, ging die Klägerin um die Kasse herum zur Packablage, um ihrer Mutter beim Einpacken behilflich zu sein. Dabei fiel sie zu Boden und zog sich einen schmerzhaften Gelenkbluterguß am rechten Knie zu, der eine längere ärztliche Behandlung erforderlich machte.

Mit der Behauptung, sie sei auf einem Gemüseblatt ausgerutscht, hat die Klägerin die Beklagte aus Verletzung der Verkehrssicherungspflicht in Anspruch genommen und mit ihrer am 5. März 1970 erhobenen Klage u. a. Ersatz des durch den Unfall in Höhe von 701,51 DM entstandenen und des künftig noch entstehenden Vermögensschadens verlangt. Die Beklagte hat bestritten, daß die Klägerin auf einem Gemüseblatt ausgerutscht sei, hilfsweise ihr Verschulden an dem Unfall in Abrede gestellt und sich überdies auf Verjährung berufen.

Das Landgericht hat die Klage wegen Verjährung abgewiesen. Das Berufungsgericht hat ihr – und zwar unter Berücksichtigung eines Mitverschuldens der Klägerin zu 1/4 – in Höhe von 497,11 DM stattgegeben und außerdem die Verpflichtung der Beklagten zum Ersatz von 3/4 des der Klägerin künftig noch erwachsenden Schadens festgestellt. Die zugelassene Revision der Beklagten hatte keinen Erfolg.

Aus den Gründen:

I Das Berufungsgericht sieht als erwiesen an, daß die Klägerin in der Nähe der Packablage auf einem am Boden liegenden Gemüseblatt ausgerutscht ist und sich dabei Verletzungen zugezogen hat, die die geltendgemachten Aufwendungen erforderlich gemacht haben und einen Zukunftsschaden nicht ausschließen. Diese Feststellungen lassen einen Rechtsfehler nicht erkennen.

II Nach Ansicht des Berufungsgerichts hat die Beklagte den ihr obliegenden Nachweis daß sie hinsichtlich der Vekehrssicherheit in ihrem Ladenlokal alle ihr zuzumutende Sorgfalt beachtet habe und der Unfall nur darauf zurückzuführen sei, daß ein anderer Kunde kurz zuvor ein Gemüseblatt habe zu Boden fallen lassen, nicht geführt. Auch diese Ausführungen sind aus Rechtsgründen nicht zu beanstanden. Sie entsprechen hinsichtlich der Verkehrssicherungspflicht eines Warenhausinhabers und der insoweit aus § 282 BGB hergeleiteten Umkehr der Beweislast bei Schadensersatzansprüchen aus Verschulden bei Vertragsschluß, auf die das Berufungsgericht seine Entscheidung stützt, der ständigen Rechtsprechung des Bundesgerichtshofs (BGH Urteil vom 26. September 1961 – VI ZR 92/61 = NJW 1962, 31 = LM BGB § 276 (Fa) Nr. 13; vgl. auch RGZ 78, 239).

I State Court of Trier

II Upper State Court of Koblenz

On 2 November 1963, the plaintiff, at that time was 14 years old, went with her mother into the defendant's branch in Sch, a small self-service store. Whilst the mother was, after selecting goods, still standing at the checkout, the plaintiff went round the check-out to the packing area, in order to help her mother with the packing. In doing this, she fell to the floor, and sustained a painful bruise on the joint of the right knee, which necessitated long medical treatment.

The plaintiff claimed against the defendant for breach of the duty to protect against ordinary risks, by asserting that she slipped on a vegetable leaf, and by her action commenced on 5 March 1970 demanded amongst other things compensation in the sum of 701.51 DM for the financial loss which had arisen as a result of the accident and for financial loss arising in the future. The defendant disputed that the plaintiff slipped on a vegetable leaf, subsidiarily denied its fault in relation to the accident and besides this relied on limitation.

The State Court rejected the claim for limitation reasons. The appeal court granted it – in view of contributory fault on the part of the plaintiff amounting to 1/4 – in the sum of 497.11 DM and in addition found that the defendant was liable to compensate the plaintiff for 3/4 of the harm arising to her in the future. The admissible appeal in law of the defendant was unsuccessful.

Reasons:

I The appeal court regards as proved that the plaintiff slipped on a vegetable leaf lying on the ground in the neighbourhood of the packing area and in doing so received injuries which necessitated the expenses claimed and not exclude the possibility of future harm. These findings do not reveal an error of law.

II According to the view of the appeal court, the defendant has not furnished the proof incumbent upon it that it had observed all the care expected of it to protect against ordinary risks in its shop, and the accident was only to be attributed to the fact that another customer had let a vegetable leaf fall to the ground shortly before. These statements cannot be objected to on legal grounds. They correspond, with regard to the duty of the proprietor of a department store to protect against ordinary risks and the reversal, derived in this respect from § 282 of the BGB, of the burden of proof in claims for compensation for damage for fault on the making of a contract, on which the appeal court based its decision, with the consistent case law of the Federal Supreme Court (BGH judgment of 26 September 1961 – VI ZR 92/61 = NJW 1962, 31 = LM BGB § 276 (Fa) no 13; compare also RGZ 78, 239).

III Die Beklagte hafte daher – so führt das Berufungsgericht weiter aus – unter Berücksichtigung des Mitverschuldens der Klägerin auf 3/4 des eingetretenen und künftig noch zu erwartenden Schadens – und zwar nicht nur aus unerlaubter Handlung sondern auch wegen Verschuldens bei Vertragsschluß, weil sie die mit Eröffnung des Selbstbedienungsladens der Klägerin selbst gegenüber übernommene vertragliche Schutz- und Fürsorgepflicht verletzt habe. Überdies ergebe sich auch unter dem Gesichtspunkt eines Vertrages mit Schutzwirkung zugunsten Dritter ein Schadensersatzanspruch der Klägerin weil deren Mutter während des Unfalls in Vertragsverhandlungen mit der Beklagten gestanden habe und die Klägerin als Hilfsperson in den Schutzbereich dieses vertragsähnlichen Schuldverhältnisses einbezogen gewesen sei. Für Ansprüche aus Verschulden bei Vertragsschluß gelte aber die dreißigjährige Verjährungsfrist, so daß die Verjährung insoweit durch die Klageerhebung rechtzeitig unterbrochen sei.

III The defendant is therefore liable, so the appeal court further states, taking into account the contributory fault of the plaintiff, to 3/4 of the damage which has occurred and which is to be expected in the future, and not only on the basis of tort, but also because of fault in the making of a contract because it breached the contractual duties of protection and care assumed as against the plaintiff herself with the opening of the self-service shop. Moreover, a claim by the plaintiff to compensation for harm also followed from the point of view of a contract with protective effect in favour of a third party because the plaintiff's mother was in contractual negotiations with the defendant at the time of the accident and the plaintiff as an assistant had been drawn into the area of protection of this quasi-contractual obligation relationship. However, for claims for fault on the making of a contract the 30 year limitation period applied, so that the limitation period in this respect had been interrupted by the commencement of an action within the time limit.

IV Diese Ausführungen halten – jedenfalls im Ergebnis – einer rechtlichen Nachprüfung stand.

Allerdings bestehen gegen die Haupterwägung des Berufungsgerichts Bedenken, die Beklagte hafte, auch ohne daß es der Heranziehung des Gesichtspunktes eines Vertrages mit Schutzwirkung zugunsten Dritter bedürfe, der Klägerin unmittelbar aus Verschulden bei Vertragsschluß (*culpa in contrahendo*). Die Haftung aus *culpa in contrahendo*, die den Geschädigten in Fällen wie dem vorliegenden gegenüber der allgemeinen deliktischen Haftung aus Verletzung der Verkehrssicherungspflicht – etwa in Hinblick auf die verschärfte Gehilfenhaftung (§ 278 BGB gegenüber § 831 BGB), die längere Verjährungsfrist (§ 195 BGB gegenüber § 852 BGB) und die Umkehr der Beweislast (§ 282 BGB) – wesentlich günstiger stellt, beruht auf einem in Ergänzung des geschriebenen Rechtes geschaffenen gesetzlichen Schuldverhältnis, das aus der Aufnahme von Vertragsverhandlungen entspringt und vom tatsächlichen Zustandekommen eines Vertrages und seiner Wirksamkeit weitgehend unabhängig ist (BGHZ 6, 330, 333; ständige Rechtsprechung; vgl. Larenz Schuldrecht, 11. Aufl. Bd. I S. 94, 96f. mit weiteren Nachweisen). Die aus diesem Schuldverhältnis hergeleitete Haftung für die Verletzung von Schutz- und Obhutspflichten findet bei Fällen der vorliegenden Art ihre Rechtfertigung darin, daß der Geschädigte sich zum Zwecke der Vertragsverhandlungen in den Einflußbereich des anderen Teiles begeben hat und damit redlicherweise auf eine gesteigerte Sorgfalt seines Verhandlungspartners vertrauen kann (vgl. dazu auch Senatsurteil vom 5. Januar 1960 - VIII ZR 1/59 = NJW 1960, 720 = WM 1960, 582; Larenz aaO sowie MDR 1954, 515; Nirk in Festschrift für Möhring 1965, S. 385ff., 392). Das bestätigt gerade der vorliegende Fall, in dem die Mutter der Klägerin zum Zwecke des Kaufabschlusses die Verkaufsräume der Beklagten aufsuchen und sich damit einer Gefährdung, wie sie erfahrungsgemäß der verstärkte Publikumsverkehr vor allem in der Kassenzone eines Selbstbedienungsladens mit sich bringt, aussetzen mußte. Voraussetzung für eine Haftung aus *culpa in contrahendo* ist bei derartigen Kaufverträgen aber stets, daß der Geschädigte sich mit dem Ziel des Vertragsabschlusses oder doch der Anbahnung 'geschäftlicher Kontakte' (so Larenz, Schuldrecht aaO S. 94ff. und MDR 1954, 515) – also als zumindest *möglicher* Kunde, wenn auch vielleicht noch ohne feste Kaufabsicht – in die Verkaufsräume begeben hat (vgl. BGH Urteil vom 26. September 1961 – VI ZR 92/61 aaO; Nirk aaO S. 392).

IV These statements stand up to legal examination at any rate in the outcome.

Certainly doubts exist about the major strand of reasoning of the appeal court that the defendant is liable, even without needing to refer to the point of view of a contract with protective effect in favour of a third party, to the plaintiff directly for fault during the making of a contract (*culpa in contrahendo*).[1] The liability from *culpa in contrahendo* puts the person harmed in a substantially more favourable position in cases like the present one, as against general delictual liability for breach of the duty to protect against ordinary risks – having regard to the higher degree of liability for assistants (§ 278 of the BGB as against § 831 of the BGB), the longer limitation period (§ 195 of the BGB as against § 852 of the BGB) and the reversal of the burden of proof (§ 282 of the BGB). It is based on a legal obligation relationship created to complete the written law which originates from the taking up of contractual negotiations and which is largely independent of the actual coming into existence of a contract and its effectiveness (BGHZ 6, 330, 333; consistent case law; compare Larenz, The Law of Obligations, 11th edn, Vol I p 94, 96 and onwards, with further references). The liability derived from this obligation relationship for the breach of duties of protection and care finds its justification in cases of the present kind in the fact that the person who has suffered harm entered the sphere of influence of the other party for the purpose of contractual negotiations and can therefore honestly trust in the increased care of his partner in the negotiations (on this compare also the Senate's judgment of 5 January 1960 – VIII ZR 1/59 = NJW 1960, 720 = WM 1960, 582; Larenz, *loc cit* as well as MDR 1954, 515; Nirk in Commemorative Publication for Möhring 1965, p 385 and onwards, 392). That confirms exactly the present case in which the mother of the plaintiff went to visit the sale premises of the defendant for the purpose of the conclusion of purchases and thereby exposed herself to a danger of the kind that, according to experience, the increased movements of the public bring above all in the checkout zone of a self-service store. A prerequisite for liability in *culpa in contrahendo* is however always that with purchase contracts of this kind the person who has suffered harm entered the sale premises with the objective of the conclusion of a contract or the opening up of 'business contacts' (thus Larenz, The Law of Obligations, *loc cit*, p 94 and onwards and MDR 1954, 515) – therefore at least as a *possible* customer, even if perhaps without a firm intention of purchase (compare BGH judgment of 26 September 1961 – VI ZR 92/61, *loc cit*, Nirk, *loc cit*, p 392).

---

1   *Culpa in contrahendo* is explained in note 5 in Chapter Four, p 249.

Dabei mag dahinstehen, ob es angesichts der Besonderheiten des Kaufes in einem Selbstbedienungsladen bereits ausreicht, wenn der Kunde beim Betreten der Verkaufsräume zunächst lediglich die Absicht hat, sich einen Überblick über das Warenangebot zu verschaffen und sich dadurch möglicherweise zum Kauf anregen zu lassen, oder wenn er vorerst nur einen vorbereitenden Preisvergleich mit Konkurrenzunternehmen vornehmen will. Jedenfalls fehlt es für eine über die deliktische Haftung hinausgehende vertragliche Haftung aus *culpa in contrahendo* dann an einer hinreichenden Rechtfertigung, wenn die den Selbstbedienungsladen betretende Person von vornherein gar keine Kaufabsicht hatte – etwa weil sie, abgesehen von dem vom Berufungsgericht erwähnten Fall des Ladendiebes, die Geschäftsräume ausschließlich als Schutz vor Witterungseinflüssen aufsuchen oder als Durchgang zu einer anderen Straße oder überhaupt nur als Treffpunkt mit anderen Personen benutzen wollte. Die Abgrenzung mag im Einzelfall vor allem deswegen schwierig sein, weil sie auf eine innere und somit nur schwer beweisbare Willensrichtung abstellt. Im vorliegenden Fall ist jedoch unstreitig, daß die Klägerin von vornherein nicht die Absicht hatte, selbst einen Kaufvertrag mit der Beklagten abzuschließen, vielmehr lediglich ihre Mutter begleitete und diese bei ihrem Kauf unterstützen wollte. Eine unmittelbare Anwendung der Haftung aus Verschulden der Beklagten bei Vertragsschluß der Klägerin gegenüber scheidet mithin aus.

V Gleichwohl erweist sich das Berufungsurteil im Ergebnis als richtig, weil die Hilfserwägung des Berufungsgerichts die Entscheidung trägt.

1 Wäre die Mutter der Klägerin auf dieselbe Weise wie ihre Tochter zu Schaden gekommen, so bestünden gegen die Haftung der Beklagten aus *culpa in contrahendo* – davon geht ersichtlich auch die Revision aus – keine Bedenken. Dabei bedarf es keiner Stellungnahme zu der im Schrifttum umstrittenen Frage, ob in einem Selbstbedienungsladen der Kaufvertrag dadurch zustandekommt, daß der Käufer das ihm mit der Aufstellung der Waren gemachte Angebot durch Vorweisen der ausgesuchten Ware an der Kasse – sich bis zu diesem Zeitpunkt eine endgültige Entscheidung vorbehaltend – annimmt, oder ob in dem Aufstellen der Ware lediglich die Aufforderung zur Abgabe eines Angebotes liegt, das der Kunde seinerseits mit dem Vorweisen gegenüber der Kassiererin abgibt und das letztere durch Registrieren für den Selbstbedienungsladen annimmt (vgl. zum Meinungsstand Mezger in BGB-RGRK, 12. Aufl. vor § 433 Rdn. 55 mit weiteren Nachweisen). Jedenfalls läßt der Zusammenhang der Urteilsgründe, wenn es auch an einer ausdrücklichen Feststellung des Berufungsgerichts in dieser Richtung fehlt, erkennen, daß in Unfallzeitpunkt zwischen der Beklagten und der Mutter der Klägerin, die die zum Kauf vorgesehen Waren bereits endgültig ausgewählt hatte, bereits ein die Haftung aus *culpa in contrahendo* rechtfertigendes gesetzliches Schuldverhältnis (BGHZ 6, 330, 333) bestand.

In this connection it may be left undecided whether, in the light of the peculiarities of purchase in a self-service store, it suffices if the customer, on entry of the sale premises, at first merely has the intention to get a general view of the goods on offer and thereby possibly to let himself be induced to make a purchase; or if he wants first of all only to undertake a preparatory price comparison with rival undertakings. At any rate there would be no sufficient justification for a contractual liability based on *culpa in contrahendo* going beyond delictual liability, if the person entering the self-service store had from the start no intention to purchase at all – perhaps because – apart from the case of the shoplifter mentioned by the appeal court, he wanted to go to the business premises exclusively as protection from the effect of the weather or to use them as a passage to another street or only as a meeting point with other persons. The demarcation line may be difficult to draw in the individual case, primarily because it is geared to an inner intention which can therefore only be proved with difficulty. In the present case, it is however undisputed that the plaintiff did not, from the start, have the intention of concluding a purchase contract with the defendant herself, but rather merely accompanied her mother and wanted to support her in her purchases. A direct application of liability as against the plaintiff through fault of the defendant on making of the contract is therefore excluded.

V Nevertheless the appeal judgment shows itself to be correct in its outcome because the supplementary line of reasoning of the appeal court supports the decision.

1 If the mother of the plaintiff had come to harm in the same manner as her daughter, no doubt would have existed about the liability of the defendant under *culpa in contrahendo*. The appeal in law obviously proceeds on this basis. In this connection, no opinion needs to be expressed on the question, which is disputed in the literature, of whether in a self-service store the purchase contract comes into existence by virtue of the fact that the purchaser accepts the offer made to him by the display of the goods by production of the selected item at the checkout, reserving a final decision until this point in time – or whether in the display of the goods there is merely an invitation for the submission of an offer, which the customer for his part submits by the production of the item to the check-out assistant and the latter accepts on behalf of the self-service store by ringing it up (compare on the state of opinion Mezger in BGB RGRK, 12th edn, before § 433 marginal no 55 with further references). In any case the context of the reasons for the judgment reveal, even if there is no express finding of the appeal court in this direction, that at the point in time of the accident there already existed between the defendant and the mother of the plaintiff, who had already finally chosen the goods provided for purchase, a legal obligation relationship justifying liability under *culpa in contrahendo* (BGHZ 6, 330, 333).

2 Auf dieses gesetzliche Schuldverhältnis kann sich auch die Klägerin zur Rechtfertigung ihrer vertraglichen Schadensersatzansprüche berufen. Es entspricht seit langem gefestigter Rechtsprechung insbesondere des erkennenden Senats, daß unter besonderen Voraussetzungen auch außenstehende, am Vertragsschluß selbst nicht beteiligte Dritte in den Schutzbereich eines Vertrages einbezogen sind mit der Folge, daß ihnen zwar kein Anspruch auf Erfüllung der primären Vertragspflicht, wohl aber auf den durch den Vertrag gebotenen Schutz und die Fürsorge zusteht, und daß sie aus der Verletzung dieser vertraglichen Nebenpflichten Schadensersatzansprüche in eigenem Namen geltendmachen können (Senatsurteile vom 16. Oktober 1963 – VIII ZR 28/62 = WM 1963, 1327 = NJW 1964, 33, vom 23. Juni 1965 – VIII ZR 201/63 = WM 1965, 871 = NJW 1965, 1757, vom 10 Januar 1968 – VIII ZR 104/65 = WM 1968, 300 = LM BGB § 328 Nr. 33; BGHZ 49, 350; 56, 269; 61, 227). Die rechtsdogmatische Frage, ob sich ein derartiger 'Vertrag mit Schutzwirkung zugunsten Dritter' (s. Larenz, *Schuldrecht* aaO S. 183f. und NJW 1960, 77f.) – wovon bisher die Rechtsprechung ausgegangen ist – aus der ergänzenden Auslegung eines insoweit lückenhaften Vertrages herleitet (§§ 133, 157 BGB), oder ob sich unmittelbare vertragsähnliche Ansprüche, wie im Schrifttum im zunehmendem Maße angenommen wird, aus vom hypothetischen Parteiwillen losgelösten Gründen – etwa aus Gewohnheitsrecht oder aufgrund richterlicher Rechtsfortbildung – ergeben, bedarf hier keiner Vertiefung und Entscheidung (vgl. zur letztgenannter Ansicht etwa Palandt/Heinrichs, BGB, 35. Aufl., § 328 Anm. 2 b; Larenz, Schuldrecht aaO S. 185f.; Gernhuber, Festschrift für Nikisch 1958 S. 249ff. und JZ 1962, 553; Esser, Schuldrecht, 4. Aufl., Teil I S. 399; Canaris, JZ 1965, 475). Nach beiden Auffassungen kommt es jedenfalls entscheidend darauf an, daß der Vertrag nach seinem Sinn und Zweck und unter Berücksichtigung von Treu und Glauben eine Einbeziehung des Dritten in seinen Schutzbereich erfordert und die eine Vertragspartei – für den Vertragsgegner erkennbar – redlicherweise damit rechnen kann, daß die ihr geschuldete Obhut und Fürsorge in gleichem Maße auch dem Dritten entgegengebracht wird (vgl. BGHZ 51, 91, 96; 56, 269; BGH Urteil vom 15. Mai 1959 – VI ZR 109/58 = NJW 1959 1676). Kaufverträge generell von dieser rechtlich möglichen Vertragsgestaltung auszunehmen besteht – das zeigen insbesondere Käufe in Ladenlokalen bei denen sich der Käufer u. U. mit dem Dritten in den Einflußbereich des Verkäufers begeben muß – kein rechtfertigender Anlaß. Das nimmt auch der VI. Zivilsenat in der o. g. Entscheidung BGHZ 51, 91 (96) nicht an.

2 The plaintiff also can refer to this legal obligation relationship for the justification of her contractual claims for compensation. It corresponds to long established case law, especially that of the deciding Senate, that in special conditions even third party outsiders who did not themselves take part in the making of the contract are included in the area of protection of a contract with the consequence that a claim belongs to them, not for fulfilment of the primary contractual duty, but for the protection and care required by the contract, and that they can claim compensation for harm in their own name for breach of these contractual subsidiary duties (Senate's judgments of 16 October 1963 – VIII ZR 28/62 = WM 1963, 1327 = NJW 1964, 33, of 23 June 1965 – VIII ZR 201/63 = WM 1965, 871 = NJW 1965, 1757, of 10 January 1968 – VIII ZR 104/65 = WM 1968, 300 = LM BGB § 328 no 33; BGHZ 49, 350; 56, 269; 61, 227). The question of legal theory as to whether 'a contract with protective effect in favour of a third party' of this kind (see Larenz, *The Law of Obligations, loc cit,* p 183 and onwards and NJW 1960, 77 and onwards) – from which the case law has proceeded until now – derives from the complementary interpretation of a contract which is in this respect incomplete (§§ 133 and 157 of the BGB), or whether direct quasi-contractual claims, as is accepted to an increasing extent in the literature, result from reasons detached from the hypothetical intention of the party – perhaps from customary law or on the basis of judicial development of the law – does not need deeper consideration or decision here (compare, as to the last mentioned view, Palandt/Heinrichs, BGB, 35th edn, § 328 note 2 b; Larenz, The Law of Obligations, *loc cit,* p 185 and onwards; Gernhuber, Commemorative Publication for Nikisch 1958, p 249 and onwards, and JZ 1962, 553; Esser, The Law of Obligations, 4th edn, Part I, p 399; Canaris, JZ 1965, 475). According to both views, the decisive question is that the contract according to its sense and purpose, and having regard to good faith, requires an inclusion of the third party into its area of protection and the one party to the contract can honestly reckon – and this was capable of being recognised by the other contractual partner – on the protection and care owed to her being offered to the same extent to the third party also (compare BGHZ 51, 91, 96; 56, 269; BGH judgment of the 15 May 1959 – VI ZR 109/58 = NJW 1959, 1676). There is no cause which would justify the exempting of purchase contracts generally from this legally possible construction – and this is shown especially by purchases in shops for which the purchaser must, in certain circumstances, enter the area of influence of the seller with the third party. That is also not accepted by the VIth Civil Senate in the above mentioned decision BGHZ 51, 91 (96).

3 Allerdings erfordert die Einbeziehung Dritter in den Schutzbereich eines Vertrages – soll die vom Gesetzgeber getroffene unterschiedliche Ausgestaltung von Vertrags- und deliktischer Haftung nicht aufgegeben oder verwischt werden – eine Beschränkung auf eng begrenzte Fälle (BGH Urteil vom 25. April 1956 – VI ZR 34/35 = NJW 1956, 1193 mit Anmerkung von Larenz; Senatsurteil vom 9. Oktober 1968 – VIII ZR 173/66 = WM 1968, 1354 = NJW 1969, 41; BGH Urteil vom 30. September 1969 – VI ZR 254/67 = WM 1969, 1358 = NJW 1970, 38; BGHZ 51, 91, 96 and 61, 227, 234). Ob insoweit der bloße Umstand, daß der Kunde sich bei der Anbahnung und Abwicklung des Kaufvertrages in einem Selbstbedienungsladen eines Dritten bedient, für die Annahme einer Schutzwirkung ausreichen würde, kann dahingestellt bleiben; denn im vorliegenden Fall kommt hinzu, daß die Mutter der Klägerin im Innenverhältnis 'für Wohl und Wehe' ihrer Tochter verantwortlich war (BGHZ 51, 91, 96) und damit – auch für die Beklagte erkennbar – allein schon aus diesem Grunde redlicherweise davon ausgehen durfte, daß die sie begleitende Tochter denselben Schutz genießen würde wie sie selbst. In einem derartigen engen familienrechtlichen Band hat die Rechtsprechung von jeher eine Rechtfertigung für die Erstreckung der vertraglichen Schutzwirkung gesehen (BGH Urteil vom 8. Mai 1965 VI ZR 58/55 = LM BGB § 254 [E] Nr. 2; Senatsurteil vom 16. Oktober 1963 – VIII ZR 28/62 = WM 1963, 1327 = NJW 1964, 33; BGHZ 61, 227, 234).

3 The inclusion of the third party in the protected area of a contract needs of course – if the different shaping of contractual and delictual liability by the legislator is not to be given up or obliterated – to be restricted to narrowly defined cases (BGH judgment of 25 April 1956 – VI ZR 34/35 = NJW 1956, 1193 with comment by Larenz; judgment of the Senate of 9 October 1968 – VIII ZR 173/66 = WM 1968, 1354 = NJW 1969, 41; BGH judgment of 30 September 1969 - VI ZR 254/67 = WM 1969, 1358 = NJW 1970, 38; BGHZ 51, 91, 96 and 61, 227, 234). Whether in this respect the mere circumstance that the customer makes use of a third party in the preparation for and carrying out of the purchase contract in a self-service shop would suffice for the acceptance of a protective effect can remain undecided; because in the present case there is the additional factor that the mother of the plaintiff was responsible in the internal relationship 'for weal and woe' of her daughter (BGHZ 51, 91, 96) and thereby – and this was also recognisable by the defendant – on this ground alone might honestly proceed on the basis that the daughter accompanying her would enjoy the same protection as herself. In a close family law bond of this kind, case law has always seen a justification for the extension of the contractual protective effect (BGH judgment of 8 May 1965 VI ZR 58/55 = LM BGB § 254 [E] no 2; judgment of the Senate of 16 October 1963 – VIII ZR 28/62 = WM 1963, 1327 = NJW 1964, 33; BGHZ 61, 227, 234).

4 Daß im vorliegenden Fall der Kaufvertrag im Zeitpunkt des Unfalls noch nicht abgeschlossen war, ist im Ergebnis ohne entscheidende rechtliche Bedeutung. Gerade wenn man die Schutz- und Fürsorgepflicht als maßgeblichen Inhalt des durch die Anbahnung von Vertragsverhandlungen begründeten gesetzlichen Schuldverhältnisses ansieht und berücksichtigt, daß der Vertragspartner diese Obhutspflicht gleichermaßen vor wie nach Vertragsabschluß schuldet, ist die Einbeziehung dritter, in gleicher Hinsicht schutzwürdiger Personen in dieses gesetzliche Schuldverhältnis nur folgerichtig (vgl. Larenz, *Schuldrecht* aaO S. 188). Es würde im übrigen auch an jedem vernünftigen rechtfertigenden Grund dafür fehlen, die vertragliche Haftung vom reinen Zufall abhängig zu machen, ob die Vertragsverhandlungen im Zeitpunkt der Schädigung schon zum endgültigen Vertragsabschluß geführt hatten; das zeigt eindringlich der vorliegende Fall, in dem die 'Kaufverhandlungen' im wesentlichen abgeschlossen waren und der Vertragsabschluß im Unfallzeitpunkt – möglicherweise bedingt durch eine von der Mutter der Klägerin nicht zu verantwortende Verzögerung bei der Abfertigung an der Kasse – jedenfalls unmittelbar bevorstand. Die Meinung der Revision, eine Kumulation von Haftung aus '*culpa in contrahendo*' und 'Einbeziehung eines Dritten in die Schutzwirkung eines Vertrages' führe zu eine nicht mehr überschaubaren Ausweitung des Risikos für den Verkäufer, wendet sich im Grunde gegen die Berechtigung beider Rechtsinstitute überhaupt. Der insoweit in der Tat nicht von der Hand zu weisenden Gefahr einer Ausuferung hat die Rechtsprechung jedoch, wie bereits ausgeführt wurde, von jeher dadurch Rechnung getragen, daß sie an die Einbeziehung Dritter in den Schutzbereich eines Vertrages strenge Anforderungen gestellt hat. Im Rahmen lediglich *vor*vertraglicher Rechtsbeziehungen mag hierbei möglicherweise besondere Zurückhaltung geboten sein. Aber auch bei noch so enger Grenzziehung bestehen jedenfalls dann gegen die Erstreckung der Schutzwirkung keine Bedenken, wenn – wie hier – der Schädiger sich dem Ansinnen der die Vertragsverhandlungen führenden Mutter, ihrem später zu Schaden gekommenen Kind von vorneherein ausdrücklich den gleichen Schutz wie ihr selbst einzuräumen, redlicherweise nicht hätte widersetzen können. Sowiet schließlich die Revision meint, die lange Verjährungsfrist – verbunden zudem mit einer Umkehr der Beweislast – verschlechtere in derartigen Fällen die Beweissituation für den als Schädiger in Anspruch Genommenen in unerträglicher Weise, bietet sich als Korrektiv die Verwirkung an, für deren Vorliegen es hier allerdings an jedem Anhalt fehlt.

VI Da somit der Klägerin unmittelbare und im Hinblick auf § 195 BGB nicht verjährte Schadensersatzansprüche gegen die Beklagte zustehen, ist die angefochtene Entscheidung im Ergebnis rechtlich nicht zu beanstanden.

4 The fact that in the present case the purchase contract had not yet been concluded at the point in time of the accident is in the result without decisive legal significance. If one regards the duty of protection and care as the controlling content of the legal obligation relationship based on the opening of contractual negotiations, and considers that the other contracting party owes this duty of care in the same way before as well as after the conclusion of the contract, the inclusion of third persons who are in a similar respect worthy of protection in this legal obligation relationship is only logical (compare Larenz, *The Law of Obligations, loc cit,* p 188). There would incidentally be no sensible justifying reason for making the contractual liability dependent on the pure accident of whether the contractual negotiations had, at the point in time of the harm, already led to the final conclusion of the contract; that is shown forcibly by the present case in which the 'purchase negotiations' were substantially concluded and the conclusion of the contract was in any case immediately imminent – subject perhaps to a delay in being dealt with at the checkout, for which the mother of the plaintiff would not be responsible – at the point in time of the accident. The opinion of the appeal in law that a cumulation of liability from *culpa in contrahendo* and 'inclusion of a third party in the protective effect of a contract' would lead to a widening of risk for the seller which would no longer be easily comprehensible really opposes in principle the legitimacy of both legal concepts. The danger, in reality, in this respect, which is not to be rejected out of hand, of an opening of the floodgates has however, as already explained, always been taken into account by the case law by virtue of the fact that it has placed strict requirements on the inclusion of a third person in the protective area of a contract. Within the framework of merely *pre*-contractual legal relations, special caution may possibly be required in this connection. But even with however narrow a drawing of the boundary, there are in any case no doubts about the extension of the protective effect if, as here, the person causing the harm could not honestly have opposed the request of the mother conducting the contractual negotiations of granting explicitly as a matter of course for the child who later came to be harmed the same protection as for herself. Finally, insofar as the appeal in law expresses the view that the long period of limitation, in association moreover with a reversal of the burden of proof, worsens the evidential situation in cases of this kind for the person causing the harm against whom a claim has been made in an intolerable manner, forfeiture (any basis for the presence of which is certainly lacking here) presents itself as a corrective.[2]

VI As therefore the plaintiff is entitled to direct claims to compensation for harm against the defendant which are not, having regard to § 195 of the BGB, time expired, the contested decision is not to be objected to in its outcome on legal grounds.

---

2   Forfeiture here is the loss of a right to claim because of delay, and it follows from the principle of good faith. There is an interesting comparison to be made with the equitable principle of laches.

THE TERMINATION OF NEGOTIATIONS CASE

BGH NJW 1975 Heft 39 S. 1774

3 BGB § 276 (Ersatz des Vertrauensschadens bei grundlosem Abbruch der Vertragsverhandlungen)

Zum Ersatz des Vertrauensschadens beim Abbruch von Vertragsverhandlungen.

BGH, Urt. v. 12.6.1975 – X ZR 25/73 (Hamm)

Die Klägerin macht Ansprüche gegen die Beklagte geltend, weil es nicht zu dem Abschluß eines Lizenzvertrages gekommen sei, der der Klägerin von dem Vorstandsmitglied der Beklagten, K., zugesichert worden sei.

Das LG hat die Klage abgewiesen. Das OLG hat den Klageanspruch im wesentlichen dem Grunde nach für gerechtfertigt erklärt.

Die Revision der Beklagten hatte keinen Erfolg.

Aus den Gründen:

I 2.a) Das Berufungsgericht spricht der Klägerin dem Grunde nach einen Anspruch auf Ersatz des Vertrauensschadens wegen Verschuldens bei Vertragsschluß zu. Die Beklagte habe durch die Art ihrer Verhandlungen mit K. die berechtigte Erwartung begründet, daß es zum Abschluß eines Lizenzvertrags mit der Klägerin kommen würde. Es hält das Vertrauen der Klägerin hierauf für schutzwürdig. Grundlage für die Erwartung der Klägerin, die Beklagte werde mit ihr einen Lizenzvertrag schließen, bilde nicht allein das Schreiben v. 15.8.1968, mit dem K. in die Lage versetzt werden sollte, die erforderlichen Schritte bei den iranischen Behörden zu ergreifen. Auf Grund der weiteren Verhandlungen, insbesondere der sich daran anschließenden Korrespondenz, in der es um Preis- und Kalkulationsfragen, die Ausstattung und die Baupläne des zu errichtenden Fabrikgebäudes ging, sei diese Erwartung aufrechterhalten und noch verstärkt worden. Wenn sich die Gründung der Gesellschaft und die Errichtung der Fabrikanlagen auch – möglicherweise länger, als ursprünglich erwartet – hingezogen habe, so sei doch ersichtlich gewesen, daß Schritte in dieser Richtung unternommen wurden und daß mit der Entstehung von Kosten zu rechnen war. Wenn die Beklagte sich nunmehr zurückzog, so habe sie das nicht tun können, ohne der Klägerin die im Vertrauen auf die Zusage gemachten Aufwendungen zu ersetzen. Im Zusammenhang mit der Prüfung der Frage, ob der Klägerin der Anspruch auf Ersatz des Vertrauensschadens zustehe, obwohl K. die Verhandlungen geführt habe und die Klägerin erst im November 1969 gegründet worden sei, hat das Berufungsgericht weiter folgendes ausgeführt: ...

THE TERMINATION OF NEGOTIATIONS CASE

This case is another instance of the permitting of a pre-contractual claim. In English law, there can be no liability until a contract is formed, and this has sometimes given rise to unsatisfactory consequences, eg, in a period of rapidly rising house prices there was an attempt to introduce a bill providing for compensation for prospective purchasers who had been the victims of 'gazumping'.

BGH NJW 1975 Volume 39 p 1774

3 BGB § 276 (Compensation for damage due to violation of trust on groundless termination of contractual negotiations)

On compensation for damage for violation of trust on termination of contractual negotiations.

BGH, judgment of 12.6.1975 – X ZR 25/73 (Hamm)

The plaintiff is making claims against the defendant because a licence contract, which had been granted to the plaintiff by a member of the board of the defendant had not been concluded.

The State Court dismissed the action. The Upper State Court declared the claim to be substantially justified in principle.

The appeal in law of the defendant was unsuccessful.

Reasons:

I 2.a) The appeal court awards to the plaintiff in principle a claim to compensation for violation of trust because of fault on the making of a contract. The defendant, by the manner of its negotiations with K established the justified expectation that a licence contract with the plaintiff would be concluded. It considers the plaintiff's trust in this to be worthy of protection. The basis for the expectation of the plaintiff that the defendant would conclude a licence contract with it is not only formed by the letter of the 15.8.1968 by which K was to be put in a position to take the necessary steps with the Iranian authorities. On the basis of further negotiations, in particular the following correspondence which concerned questions of price and calculation, the fittings and the building plans of the factory building to be erected, this expectation was maintained and further strengthened. If the founding of the company, and the erection of the factory buildings also, became protracted – possibly for longer than originally expected – it was however obvious that steps in this direction had been undertaken, and the incurring of expenses had to be reckoned with. If the defendant now withdrew, it could not do this without compensating the plaintiff for expenditure incurred in reliance on the undertaking. In connection with the examination of the question of whether the plaintiff was entitled to a claim to compensation for harm caused by violation of trust although K had conducted the negotiations and the plaintiff had only been formed in November 1969, the appeal court further stated as follows: ...

(b) Die Revision hat demgegenüber in der mündlichen Verhandlung gerügt, das Berufungsgericht habe zu geringe Anforderungen an das Maß des bei den Vertragsverhandlungen erwarteten Vertrauens gestellt, das eine Haftung auf Ersatz des Vertrauensschadens auslöse, wenn die Vertragsverhandlungen abgebrochen werden.

3 Grundlage der Haftung für Verschulden bei Vertragsverhandlungen ist enttäuschtes Vertrauen (BGHZ 60, 221, 226 = NJW 1973, 752 m. w. Nachw.). Unter diesem Gesichtspunkt verpflichtet auch der grundlose Abbruch der Vertragsverhandlungen zum Ersatz des Vertrauensschadens, wenn derjenige, der die Verhandlungen abbricht, zuvor durch sein Verhalten das Vertrauen geweckt oder genährt hatte, der Vertrag werde mit Sicherheit zustande kommen (BGH, NJW 1957, 746 = LM § 276 [Fa] BGB Nr. 1; BGH, LM § 276 [Fa] BGB Nr. 11, 23 = NJW 1967, 2199; LM § 276 [Fa] BGB Nr. 28, 34 = NJW 1970, 1840; NJW 1975, 43, 44, jeweils m. w. Nachw.). Diese Verpflichtung besteht als Folge der Haftung für Auswirkungen eines Vertrauenstatbestandes gegenüber demjenigen, bei dem Vertrauen auf das Zustandekommen des in Aussicht genommenen Vertrages hervorgerufen worden ist (BGH, LM § 276 [Fa] BGB Nr. 34 unter III 2 a = NJW 1970, 1840). Soweit der in Aussicht genommene Vertrag mit einer noch zu gründenden Gesellschaft geschlossen werden sollte, hängt es von den Umständen des Einzelfalles ab, ob eine demnächst gegründete Gesellschaft nach dem Gang der Verhandlungen darauf vertrauen durfte, daß der in Aussicht genommene Vertrag mit ihr zustande kommen werde. Bei einer derartigen Sachlage kann zwar der andere Teil ein Interesse daran haben, sich seine Entschließungsfreiheit voll zu bewahren, bis er genauere Kenntnis über Art und Zusammensetzung der zu gründenden Gesellschaft erlangt hat. Der andere Teil kann aber auch, wenn es sich um eine von seinem Verhandlungspartner zu gründende Gesellschaft handelt, diesem einen gewissen Gestaltungsspielraum zugestehen und insoweit, wenn er sich auf das Zustandekommen des Vertrages verlassen darf, seine eigene Entschließungsfreiheit einschränken. Das hat das Berufungsgericht angenommen. Es hat den vorgetragenen Sachverhalt dahin gewürdigt, daß die Beklagte keine besonderen Ansprüche an die zu gründende Gesellschaft gestellt habe, daß die Klägerin den nach den Umständen an sie zu stellenden Erwartungen genüge und deshalb darauf vertrauen durfte, daß die Beklagte sie als Vertragspartnerin akzeptiere und den Lizenzvertrag mit ihr abschließe. Diese tatrichterliche Würdigung wird von der Revision nicht mit Verfahrensrügen angegriffen. Sie ist möglich und deshalb für das Revisionsgericht bindend. Sie rechtfertigt die daraus abgeleitete Folgerung, daß der Klägerin wegen des ihr gegenüber begründeten Vertrauenstatbestandes Ansprüche aus Verschulden bei den Vertragsverhandlungen zustehen ...

(b) The appeal in law has on the other hand raised the objection in the oral hearing that the appeal court has placed requirements which are too small on the extent of the trust expected in the contractual negotiations which would produce liability to compensate for harm caused by violation of trust if the contractual negotiations were broken off.

3 The basis of liability for fault in contractual negotiations is disappointed trust (BGHZ 60, 221, 226 = NJW 1973, 752 with further references). From this point of view, the groundless breaking off of contractual negotiations gives rise to an obligation to compensate for harm caused by violation of trust if the person who breaks off the negotiations had previously, by his conduct, awakened or supported the confidence that the contract would certainly come into existence (BGH, NJW 1957, 746 = LM § 276 [Fa] BGB no 1; BGH, LM § 276 [Fa] BGB no 11, 23 = NJW 1967, 2199; LM § 276 [Fa] BGB no 28, 34 = NJW 1970, 1840; NJW 1975, 43, 44, each with further references). This duty exists as a consequence of the liability for the effects of a situation of trust as against the person in whom confidence in the coming into existence of the proposed contract has been induced (BGB, LM § 276 [Fa] BGB no 34 under III 2 a = NJW 1970, 1840). Insofar as the proposed contract was to be concluded with a company yet to be formed, it depends on the circumstances of the individual case whether a company which was formed soon after the course of the negotiations could trust that the proposed contract would come into existence with it. In a state of affairs of this kind the other party can have an interest in fully preserving his freedom of decision until he has obtained more exact knowledge about the type and composition of the company to be formed. But the other party can also, if it is a matter of a company to be formed by his negotiating partner, grant to him a certain formative scope, and, to this extent, if he may rely on the coming into existence of the contract, limit his own freedom of decision. This was accepted by the appeal court. It assessed the stated circumstances to the effect that the defendant had placed no special claims on the company to be formed, and that the plaintiff was satisfied with the expectations to be placed on it in accordance with the circumstances, and could therefore trust that the defendant would accept it as contractual partner and conclude the licence contract with it. This assessment of the judge of fact was not attacked by the appeal in law with procedural objections. It is possible and therefore binding on the court for the appeal in law. It justifies the inference derived from it that the plaintiff, because of the confidence situation established in its favour, is entitled to claims based on fault in the contractual negotiations.

§ 277 [Sorgfalt in eigenen Angelegenheiten; grobe Fahrlässigkeit] Wer nur für diejenige Sorgfalt einzustehen hat, welche er in eigenen Angelegenheiten anzuwenden pflegt, ist von der Haftung wegen grober Fahrlässigkeit nicht befreit.

§ 278 [Verantwortlichkeit des Schuldners für Dritte] Der Schuldner hat ein Verschulden seines gesetzlichen Vertreters und der Personen, deren er sich zur Erfüllung seiner Verbindlichkeit bedient, in gleichem Umfang zu vertreten wie eigenes Verschulden. Die Vorschrift des § 276 Abs. 3 findet keine Anwendung.

IMPOSSIBILITY

§ 279 [weggefallen]

§ 280 [Schadensersatz wegen Pflichtverletzung] (1) Verletzt der Schuldner eine Pflicht aus dem Schuldverhältnis, so kann der Gläubiger Ersatz des hierdurch entstehenden Schadens verlangen. Dies gilt nicht, wenn der Schuldner die Pflichtverletzung nicht zu vertreten hat.

(2) Schadensersatz wegen Verzögerung der Leistung kann der Gläubiger nur unter der zusätzlichen Voraussetzung des § 286 verlangen.

(3) Schadensersatz statt der Leistung kann der Gläubiger nur unter den zusätzlichen Voraussetzungen des § 281, des § 282 oder des § 283 verlangen.

§ 281 [Schadensersatz statt der Leistung wegen nicht oder nicht wie geschuldet erbrachter Leistung] (1) Soweit der Schuldner die fällige Leistung nicht oder nicht wie geschuldet erbringt, kann der Gläubiger unter den Voraussetzungen des § 280 Abs. 1 Schadensersatz statt der Leistung verlangen, wenn er dem Schuldner erfolglos eine angemessene Frist zur Leistung oder Nacherfüllung bestimmt hat. Hat der Schuldner eine Teilleistung bewirkt, so kann der Gläubiger Schadensersatz statt der ganzen Leistung nur verlangen, wenn er an der Teilleistung kein Interesse hat. Hat der Schuldner die Leistung nicht wie geschuldet bewirkt, so kann der Gläubiger Schadensersatz statt der ganzen Leistung nicht verlangen, wenn die Pflichtverletzung unerheblich ist.

(2) Die Fristsetzung ist entbehrlich, wenn der Schuldner die Leistung ernsthaft und endgültig verweigert oder wenn besondere Umstände vorliegen, die unter Abwägung der beiderseitigen Interessen die sofortige Geltendmachung des Schadensersatzanspruchs rechtfertigen.

§ 277 [Care in own affairs; gross negligence] A person who only has to answer for that care which he is accustomed to apply in his own affairs is not freed from liability for gross negligence.

§ 278 [Responsibility of obligor for third parties] The obligor has to answer for a fault on the part of his legal representative and of persons whom he uses for the fulfilment of his obligations to the same extent as for his own fault. The provisions of § 276 para 3 do not apply.

This instance of strict liability can, in some cases, make up for the possibility of an employer escaping vicarious liability in tort. This could occur in the *culpa in contrahendo* situation arising in cases like the fall in the supermarket case: see p 377. See also consideration of § 278 in the fowl pest case, Chapter Six, p 439.

IMPOSSIBILITY

§ 279 [repealed]

§ 280 [Compensation for violation of duty] (1) If the obligor violates a duty from the obligation relationship, the obligee can demand compensation for the harm arising from this. This does not apply if the obligor is not responsible for the violation of duty.

(2) The obligee can only demand compensation for delay in performance under the additional prerequisite of § 286.

(3) The obligee can only demand compensation instead of performance under the additional prerequisites of § 281, § 282 or § 283.

§ 281 [Compensation instead of performance for performance not carried out or not carried out as owed] (1) Insofar as the obligor does not carry out the performance due, or does not carry it out as owed, the obligee can demand compensation instead of performance under the prerequisites of § 280 para 1 if he has fixed for the obligor an appropriate period for performance or later fulfilment without success. If the obligor effects a partial performance, the obligee can only demand compensation instead of the whole performance if he has no interest in the partial performance. If the obligor has not effected performance as owed, the obligee cannot demand compensation instead of the whole performance if the violation of duty is insignificant.

(2) The setting of the period can be dispensed with if the obligor refuses performance seriously and finally or if special circumstances are present which, on balancing the interests on both sides, justify the immediate making of a compensation claim.

(3) Kommt nach der Art der Pflichtverletzung eine Fristsetzung nicht in Betracht, so tritt an deren Stelle eine Abmahnung.

(4) Der Anspruch auf die Leistung ist ausgeschlossen, sobald der Gläubiger statt der Leistung Schadensersatz verlangt hat.

(5) Verlangt der Gläubiger Schadensersatz statt der ganzen Leistung, so ist der Schuldner zur Rückforderung des Geleisteten nach den §§ 346 bis 348 berechtigt.

§ 282 [Schadensersatz statt der Leistung wegen Verletzung einer Pflicht nach § 241 Abs. 2] Verletzt der Schuldner eine Pflicht nach § 241 Abs. 2, kann der Gläubiger unter den Voraussetzungen des § 280 Abs. 1 Schadensersatz statt der Leistung verlangen, wenn ihm die Leistung durch den Schuldner nicht mehr zuzumuten ist.

THE ALLERGY TO HAIR TONIC CASE

BGHZ Band 64 S. 46

6 Zur Frage, welche Hinweispflicht den Verkäufer eines kosmetischen Präparates (Haartonicum) trifft, wenn das von ihm hergestellte und vertriebene Mittel allergische Reaktionen auslösen kann.

BGB §§ 282, 433

VIII Zivilsenat. Urt. v 19. Februar 1975 i.S. F.L. (Kl.) w. Fa O. (Bekl.). VIII ZR 144/73.

I Landgericht Zweibrücken

(3) If the setting of a period does not come into consideration because of the type of violation of duty, a warning will take its place.

(4) The claim to performance is excluded as soon as the obligee has demanded compensation instead of performance.

(5) If the obligee demands compensation instead of the whole performance, the obligor is entitled to demand back what has been performed in accordance with §§ 346–348.

§ 282 [Compensation instead of performance because of violation of a duty under § 241 para 2] If the obligor violates a duty under § 241 para 2, the obligee can demand compensation instead of performance under the prerequisites of § 280 para 1, if performance by the obligor can no longer be expected from the obligee's point of view.

THE ALLERGY TO HAIR TONIC CASE

This case concerns a manufacturer's duty of explanation about the risks in respect of his product, and also involves consideration of the burden of proof. On the issue of product liability generally, see the Product Liability Act 1989.

BGHZ Volume 64 p 46

6 On the question of what duty to give instructions applies to the seller of a cosmetic preparation (hair tonic) if the product produced and sold by him can cause allergic reactions.

BGB §§ 282 and 433

VIIIth Civil Senate. Judgment of 19 February 1975 in the case of FL (plaintiff) v Fa O (defendant) – VIII ZR 144/73.

I State Court of Zweibrücken

II Oberlandesgericht Zweibrücken

Der Kläger benutzte seit Juni 1959 in seinem Friseurgeschäft ein von der Beklagten hergestelltes und von ihr in Großpackungen bezogenes Haartonicum. Ende August 1960 traten bei ihm an den Händen Hautausschläge auf, deren Herkunft zunächst nicht geklärt werden konnte und die in der Folgezeit trotz zunächst ambulanter und dann wiederholter stationärer Behandlungen nicht nachhaltig beseitigt werden konnten. Im März 1961 ermittelte die Universitätshautklinik in M. als Ursache für die Hauterkrankung eine Überempfindlichkeit gegen dieses Tonicum, von dem der Kläger bis August 1960 insgesamt etwa 150 Packungen verbraucht und das er auch in der Folgezeit bei seinen jeweils kürzeren Versuchen, seine Tätigkeit wieder aufzunehmen, benutzt hatte. Während die Beklagte den für den Einzelkunden bestimmten Packungen Prospekte mit dem Hinweis beigefügt hatte, daß das Tonicum bei besonderer Empfindlichkeit in einzelnen Fällen Hautreaktionen (Allergien) hervorrufen könne und dann zu einem Absetzen geraten werde, enthielten die den Friseurpackungen beigefügten Prospekte – jedenfalls damals – diesen Hinweis nicht. Obwohl der Kläger sofort nach Feststellung der Ursache für seine Erkrankung das Tonicum nicht mehr verwendete, trat der Hautausschlag immer wieder auf. Das veranlaßte ihn, im Juli 1962 seinen Friseurberuf aufzugeben.

Mit der Begründung, die Beklagte habe dafür einzustehen, daß sich bei ihm zunächst eine monovalente Überempfindlichkeit gegen das streitige Tonicum und seit 1961 eine polyvalente Überempfindlichkeit auch gegen andere im Friseurgewerbe verwendete Mittel gebildet habe, hat der Kläger die Beklagte auf Schadensersatz wegen Verdienstausfalls in Anspruch genommen.

Hätte die Beklagte – so behauptet er – ihn auf die mit der Verwendung des Tonicums verbundenen Gefahren hingewiesen, so hätte er nicht nur beim ersten Auftreten von Hautreizungen dieses Mittel nicht mehr verwendet, sondern sich auch von Anfang an durch Hautschutzsalben und Desinfektionen wirksam gegen Allergien geschützt, gegebenenfalls von der Verwendung des Mittels überhaupt abgesehen. Die Beklagte bezweifelt, daß der Kläger überhaupt einen solchen Hinweis beachtet hätte; jedenfalls sei der unterbliebene Hinweis, zu dem sie ohnehin nicht verpflichtet gewesen sei, deswegen für den jetzt geltend gemachten Schaden nicht ursächlich, weil sich nicht feststellen lasse, daß beim ersten Auftreten von Hautreizungen eine polyvalente Überempfindlichkeit noch habe verhindert werden können.

Landgericht und Berufungsgericht haben die Klage abgewiesen. Die Revision des Klägers hatte Erfolg.

II Upper State Court of Zweibrücken

The plaintiff, in his hairdresser's business used, from June 1959 onwards, a hair tonic which was produced by the defendant and put by it into large packages. At the end of August 1960 a skin rash appeared on the plaintiff's hands, the origin of which could not at first be established. Despite initial out-patient treatment, and later repeated in-patient treatment in the period which followed, the rash could not be permanently removed. In March 1961 the University Skin Clinic in M established that the cause of the skin disease was over-sensitivity to this hair tonic, of which the plaintiff had used up to about 150 bottles altogether, until August 1960, and, in his on each occasion shorter attempts to resume his occupation in the ensuing period, had used more. Whilst the defendant had attached to packets, bound for individual customers, leaflets warning that the tonic could bring about allergic reactions in individual cases of special sensitivity, and then cessation of application was advised, the leaflets attached to packets for hairdressers did not – at any rate at that time – contain this indication. Although the plaintiff stopped using the tonic as soon as the cause of his illness was established, the rash kept on reappearing. That caused him to give up his occupation as a hairdresser in July 1962.

The plaintiff has made a claim against the defendant for compensation for harm due to loss of income, on the basis that the defendant has to be responsible for the fact that first a single substance hypersensitivity in respect of the tonic which is the subject of the dispute and since 1961 a multiple hypersensitivity as well in respect of other products used in the hairdresser's trade has developed.

The plaintiff maintains that if the defendant had drawn his attention to the dangers associated with the use of the tonic, he would, on the first appearance of skin irritations, not only no longer have used this product, but would have protected himself effectively from the start against allergies by protective skin ointments and antiseptics, and if necessary refrained altogether from the use of the product. The defendant doubts that the plaintiff would really have paid attention to such a warning; in any case the absence of a warning (which it was not obliged to give anyway) was not the cause of the harm now claimed for because it could not be established that on the first appearance of the skin irritations a multiple hypersensitivity could still have been prevented.

The State Court and the appeal court dismissed the action. The plaintiff's appeal in law was successful.

Aus den Gründen:

1 Das Berufungsgericht legt der Beklagten nicht zur Last, daß sie das Haartonicum trotz der ihr bekannten Nebenwirkungen überhaupt in Verkehr gebracht und an den Kläger verkauft habe; angesichts des im wesentlichen negativen Ergebnisses der sorgfältig durchgeführten Versuchsreihen habe sie annehmen dürfen, daß von dem Präparat lediglich eine nur geringfügige Gefährdung für speziell allergisch veranlagte Personen ausgehen könne und es damit insgesamt ungefährlich sei.

Diese Ausführungen lassen einen Rechtsfehler nicht erkennen. Ob und in welchem Umfang bei einem kosmetischen Präparat schädliche Nebenwirkungen hingenommen werden können und der Hersteller bzw. Händler sich auf die Beifügung eines warnenden Hinweises beschränken darf, richtet sich nach der gegebenen Interessenlage im Einzelfall (vgl. dazu Schmidt-Salzer, *Produkthaftung* 1973. S. 68ff.) und unterliegt damit in erster Linie tatrichterliche Würdigung. Im vorliegenden Fall hatte die Beklagte in mehreren unterschiedlich ausgestalteten Versuchsreihen das Tonicum und den in ihm enthaltenen Wirkstoff klinisch und in Friseurbetrieben eingehend und sorgfältig auf seine Wirksamkeit und etwaige Nebenwirkungen untersuchen lassen. Zwar ist die Feststellung des Berufungsgerichts, bei den im Krankenhaus L. durchgeführten Testreihen habe sich lediglich bei zwei – ohnehin als Patienten einer Hautklinik besonders empfindlich – Personen eine allergische Reaktion gezeigt, ersichtlich aktenwidrig; tatsächlich handelte es sich bei einer der insgesamt 166 behandelten Personen, bei der sich eine ausgesprochene und heftige Unverträglichkeit gezeigt hatte, um einen hautgesunden und nicht an allergischen Krankheiten leidenden Arzt. Gleichwohl waren die Fälle der Unverträglichkeit – gemessen an der Zahl der behandelten Personen – zahlenmäßig derart gering, daß das Berufungsgericht das Inverkehrbringen des Tonicums unter Abwägung der für und gegen seine Verwendung sprechenden Umstände als vertretbar ansehen konnte; dies um so mehr, als das Tonicum – wie zwischen den Parteien unstreitig ist – als Mittel zur Bekämpfung von Seborrhoe und ähnlichen Erkrankungen durchaus geeignet war und die Kassenärztliche Bundesvereinigung ihre Mitglieder zur Verordnung dieses Mittels auch für Patienten der sozialen Krankenversicherung autorisiert hatte.

Reasons:

1 The appeal court does not charge the defendant with having brought the hair tonic into circulation and having sold it to the plaintiff in spite of the side effects known to it; in the light of the substantially negative results of the series of tests which had been carefully carried out, it had been able to accept that only a mere trifling danger for specially allergically disposed persons could arise from the preparation and it was therefore on the whole not dangerous.

No error of law can be detected in the statements. Whether and to what extent harmful side effects can be accepted with a cosmetic preparation and the manufacturer or the dealer may limit himself to the addition of a warning is to be determined according to the given situation as to the interests in the individual case (compare to this Schmidt-Salzer, *Product Liability*, 1973, p 68 and onwards) and is therefore primarily subject to assessment by the judge of fact. In the present case the defendant had had the tonic, and the hormone contained in it, exhaustively and carefully investigated clinically and in hairdresser's businesses in differently framed series of tests for its effectiveness and possible side effects. Certainly the findings of the appeal court, that in the series of tests carried out in the hospital at L, an allergic reaction only showed itself with two persons, who were, moreover, as patients of a skin clinic, especially sensitive, is obviously contrary to the documents. Actually, it was a question of one out of a total of 166 persons treated in whom a pronounced and violent intolerance had shown itself – a doctor with healthy skin and not suffering from allergic diseases. Nevertheless, the cases of intolerance - measured against the number of persons treated – were numerically so small that the appeal court could regard the bringing of the tonic into circulation as defendable, on weighing the circumstances for and against its use; and all the more so because the tonic – as is not disputed between the parties – was entirely suitable as a means to combat seborrhoea and similar diseases and the Federal Association of General Practitioners had authorised their members to prescribe this product for patients on social health insurance as well.

2 Allerdings durfte die Beklagte angesichts der bei der Erprobung aufgetretenen Unverträglichkeiten das Tonicum nicht ohne Hinweis auf mögliche Nebenwirkungen auf den Markt bringen.

(a) Daß den Hersteller und Händler eines Erzeugnisses, von dem spezifische Gefahren ausgehen können, eine derartige Verpflichtung zur Aufklärung und Warnung trifft, ist in der Rechtsprechung seit langem anerkannt und folgt – neben der allgemein deliktsrechtlichen Verpflichtung zur Gefahrenabwehr – für den vorliegenden Fall aus einer dahingehenden kaufvertragsrechtlichen Nebenpflicht (BGH Urteile vom 5. November 1955 - VI ZR 199/54 = VersR 1956, 765, vom 20. Oktober 1959 – VI ZR 152/58 = VersR 1960, 342 = BB 1959, 1186 sowie vom 11. Juli 1972 – VI ZR 194/70 = WM 1972, 1124 = NJW 1972, 2217, insoweit in BGHZ 59, 172 nicht abgedruckt; Schmidt-Salzer aaO). Der Umstand, daß die Nebenwirkungen nur in seltenen Fällen auftraten, befreite die Beklagte von dieser Verpflichtung nicht, zumal auch der von ihr mit der Prüfung des Tonicums beauftragte Chefarzt der dermatologischen Abteilung des Städtischen Krankenhauses L. sie ausdrücklich auf die Notwendigkeit einer derartigen Warnung hingewiesen hatte.

2 Certainly the defendant ought not to have brought the tonic on to the market without warning about the possible side effects in the light of the intolerances which had arisen on testing.

(a) It has been recognised for a long time in case law that such an obligation to provide explanation and warning applies to the manufacturer of and dealer in a product from which specific dangers can arise and this follows – beside the general obligation in the law of tort to prevent dangers – for the present case from a comprehensive collateral duty from the law of sales contracts (BGH judgments of 5 November 1955 – VI ZR 199/54 = VersR 1956, 765, of 20 October 1959 – VI ZR 152/58 = VersR 1960, 342 = BB 1959, 1186 as well as of 11 July 1972 – VI ZR 194/70 = WM 1972, 1124 = NJW 1972, 2217, insofar as not printed in BGHZ 59, 172; Schmidt-Salzer, *loc cit*). The fact that the side effects only arose in rare cases did not free the defendant from this obligation, especially as the senior consultant of the dermatological department of the City Hospital at L commissioned by it with the examination of the tonic had expressly drawn its attention to the necessity of a warning of this kind.

(b) Welchen Inhalt eine derartige Aufklärung im konkreten Fall haben muß, richtet sich nach dem Zweck der Aufklärungspflicht. Sie soll dem Betroffenen Klarheit über die ihm unter Umständen drohende Gefahr verschaffen und ihn in die Lage versetzen, rechtzeitig von der Verwendung des Mittels überhaupt Abstand zu nehmen oder der Gefahr durch wirksame Gegenmittel soweit wie möglich entgegenzuwirken. Im vorliegenden Fall erachtet es das Berufungsgericht als ausreichend wenn die Käufer darauf hingewiesen worden wären, es könne bei besonders empfindlichen und dazu veranlagten Personen eine allergische Hautreaktion auftreten. Damit hat das Berufungsgericht das Ausmaß der dem einzelnen unter Umständen drohenden Gefahr und infolgedessen den Umfang der Aufklärungspflicht verkannt. Ein derartiger Hinweis hätte die Käufer, sofern sie sich nicht bereits als zur Allergie neigend kannten und deswegen besonders vorsichtig waren, lediglich veranlaßt, beim ersten Auftreten von Reizerscheinungen das Tonicum abzusetzen und künftig zu meiden. Damit aber hätte ein Schaden nicht in allen Fällen mehr verhindert werden können. Wie im Gutachten der Universitäts-Hautklinik M. vom 4. Mai 1961 ausgeführt ist, entspricht es der Erfahrung, daß die durch die Verwendung eines derartigen Tonicums ausgelösten allergischen Reaktionen nicht nur zu einer dauerden monovalenten Überempfindlichkeit gerade gegenüber diesem Mittel, sondern sehr bald auch zu einer polyvalenten Überempfindlichkeit gegenüber anderen Präparaten führen können; das ziehen beide Parteien auch nicht ernsthaft in Zweifel. Gerade in Fällen, in denen zur Allergie neigende Personen dieses Mittel – wie der Kläger als Friseur – in größerem Umfang verwenden, besteht daher die naheliegende Gefahr, daß die zunächst nur monovalente Überempfindlichkeit eine völlige oder doch teilweise Berufsunfähigkeit zur Folge hat und damit zu schweren beruflichen und wirtschaftlichen Schäden führt. Es kommt hinzu, daß die Entwicklung zu einer irreparablen Überempfindlichkeit bereits weitgehend abgeschlossen sein kann, bevor der Betroffene die ersten allergischen Reaktionen verspürt, von dieser Möglichkeit geht gerade auch die Beklagte, wie ihr Prozeßvortrag zur Kausalität im vorliegenden Fall zeigt, aus.

(b) The content, which an explanation of this kind must have in the actual case, depends upon the purpose of the duty of explanation. It must provide the person affected with clarity regarding the danger which threatens him in certain circumstances, and put him in a situation promptly to give up the use of the product altogether or to counteract the danger by effective antidotes as far as possible. In the present case the appeal court considers it to be sufficient if the purchasers had been referred to the fact that an allergic skin reaction could occur with persons who are especially sensitive and with a predisposition to it. In this respect the appeal court has failed to recognise the extent of the danger threatening the individual in certain cases and, because of that, the scope of the duty of explanation. An indication of this kind would merely have caused the purchasers, insofar as they did not already know that they had a tendency to allergy and therefore were especially careful, to discontinue use of the tonic on the first occurrence of symptoms of irritation and to avoid it in future. But, by this means, harm could not have been prevented in all cases. As is explained in the opinion of 4 May 1961 of the University Skin Clinic at M, it corresponds with experience that the allergic reactions caused by the use of a tonic of this kind can lead not only to a lasting single substance hypersensitivity merely in respect of this product, but very soon to a multiple hypersensitivity to other preparations as well; and this is not seriously called in question by the parties. In precisely those cases in which persons with a tendency to allergy use this product to a substantial extent – like the plaintiff as a hairdresser – the obvious danger exists that the hypersensitivity, which is at first related to a single substance, will have a complete or partial occupational incapacity as its consequence and therefore lead to severe occupational and economic harm. Added to this is the fact that development to an irreparable hypersensitivity can already be largely established before the person affected becomes aware of the first allergic reactions. The defendant has also proceeded on the basis of this possibility, as its submissions at the trial in the present case on causality show.

(c) Bei dieser Sachlage wäre der bloße Hinweis auf mögliche allergische Hautreaktionen mit dem Rat, dann das Tonicum abzusetzen, jedenfalls gegenüber den Käufern, die das Mittel für den Verbrauch in ihrem Gewerbebetrieb bezogen, nicht ausreichend gewesen. Die Ansicht, Friseuren gegenüber sei ein warnender Hinweis überhaupt entbehrlich, weil diese nach Berufsausbildung und -erfahrung ohnehin mit Nebenwirkungen bei jedem Haartonicum rechnen müßten, hat die Beklagte mit Rücksicht auf die gegenteilige Auskunft der Handwerkskammer D. nicht mehr aufrechterhalten. Vielmehr hätte die Beklagte - ohne daß es hier eines weiteren Eingehens auf die Fassung des warnenden Hinweises im einzelnen bedarf - jedenfalls Friseure in den für sie bestimmten Packungen auf die nicht auszuschließende Gefahr einer sich unbemerkt vollziehenden Entwicklung zu einer irreparablen polyvalenten Überempfindlichkeit hinweisen müssen. Insoweit hat die Beklagte auch schuldhaft gehandelt. Da sie das Haartonicum selbst entwickelt, hergestellt und vertrieben hat, wäre es ihre Sache gewesen, im einzelnen darzulegen und zu beweisen, daß sie auch bei der gebotenen Sorgfalt mit einer derart weitgehenden, in ihrem Gefahrenbereich wurzelnden Gefahr nicht rechnen mußte (vgl. § 282 BGB). Diesen Nachweis hat sie nicht erbracht.

(d) Allerdings wäre die Verletzung der Hinweispflicht für den eingetretenen Schaden nur dann ursächlich, wenn pflichtgemäßes Handeln den Schaden mit Sicherheit verhindert hätte; eine bloße Möglichkeit oder eine gewisse Wahrscheinlichkeit genügen nicht (BGH Urteil vom 30. Januar 1961 – III ZR 225/59 = NJW 1961, 868, 870). Das Berufungsgericht sieht insoweit – wenn auch auf der Grundlage der von ihm als ausreichend erachteten, weniger weitgehenden Aufklärungspflicht – weder als erwiesen noch überhaupt als hinreichend wahrscheinlich an, daß der Kläger bei Kenntnis der möglichen Nebenwirkungen von der Verwendung des Haartonicums überhaupt abgesehen oder jedenfalls von vornherein geeignete Schutzmaßnahmen (Verwendung von Schutzsalben, regelmäßige Desinfektion der Hände) getroffen hätte. Damit hat das Berufungsgericht die Bewieslast verkannt. Verletzt jemand eine vertragliche Aufklärungspflicht, so trifft ihn – abweichend von dem Grundsatz, daß der Geschädigte im Regelfall den Ursachenzusammenhang zwischen Vertragsverletzung und eingetretenem Schaden zu beweisen hat – das Risiko der Unaufklärbarkeit des Ursachenzusammenhangs jedenfalls insoweit, als in Frage steht, wie der andere Teil gehandelt hätte, wenn er pflichtgemäß ins Bild gesetzt worden wäre (BGHZ 61, 118, 122). Diese Rechtsprechung trägt mit der Umkehr der Beweislast dem Umstand Rechnung, daß der Zweck derartiger Aufklärungspflichten auch darin besteht, Klarheit darüber zu schaffen, ob der Vertragsgegner, wenn ihm das jeweilige Risiko in seiner ganzen Tragweite bewußt gemacht wird, trotzdem an der ins Auge gefaßten Maßnahme – hier Verwendung des Tonicums – festhalten oder von ihr Abstand nehmen will; er soll daher, wenn diese Frage nur hypothetisch zu entscheiden ist, von der ihn typischerweise treffenden Beweisnot entlastet werden (vgl. auch Hofmann NJW 1974, 1641). Die Beklagte hätte also nachweisen müssen, daß der Kläger auch in Kenntnis des vollen Umfangs der Gefahr einen Hinweis mit dem oben dargelegten Inhalt unbeachtet gelassen hätte, wobei ihr gegebenenfalls der Beweis des ersten Anscheins zustatten kam.

(c) In these circumstances the mere reference to the possible allergic skin reactions with the advice to discontinue the use of the tonic would have been insufficient, in any case as against purchasers who obtained the product for use in their businesses. The view that a warning to hairdressers was really unnecessary because they, in accordance with their vocational training and experience, had to take account of the side effects of each hair tonic was no longer maintained by the defendant having regard to the contrary information of the trade association at D. The defendant – without there being any need here for a further investigation in detail of the form of the wording of the warning – should in any case have drawn the attention of hairdressers, in the packets intended for them, to the danger, which could not be excluded, of an unnoticed development into an irreversible multiple hypersensitivity. In this respect the defendant has acted culpably. As it developed, manufactured and distributed the hair tonic itself, it would have been for it to explain in detail and to demonstrate that it did not have to take into account, even with the necessary care, such an extensive danger rooted in its sphere of risk (compare § 282 of the BGB). It has not produced this proof.

(d) Certainly breach of the duty to warn would only have been the cause of the harm which has arisen if action in accordance with the duty would, with certainty, have prevented the harm; a mere possibility or a certain probability do not suffice (BGH judgment of 30 January 1961 – III ZR 225/59 = NLW 1961, 868, 870). The appeal court – even though on the basis of a duty to explain which was less extensive but regarded by it as sufficient – in this respect regards it neither as proved nor really as sufficiently probable that the plaintiff, on knowing the possible side effects, would have refrained at all from use of the hair tonic or in any case taken from the start appropriate protective measures (use of protective ointments, regular disinfection of the hands). The appeal court thereby failed to recognise the burden of proof. If someone breaches a contractual duty of explanation, he – as an exception to the principle that the person harmed has as a rule to prove the causal connection between breach of the contract and harm which has arisen – bears the risk of inexplicability of the casual connection in any case insofar as it is in question how the other party would have acted if he, in accordance with the duty, had been put into the picture (BGHZ 61, 118, 122). This case law, by reversal of the burden of proof, takes account of the fact that the purpose of this kind of duty of explanation is also to produce clarity on the question of whether the other party to the contract, if the actual risk is made known to him in its complete scope, will nevertheless adhere to the steps contemplated – here, use of the tonic – or to refrain from them; he is therefore to be, if this question is only to be decided hypothetically, freed from the necessity of proof which typically falls upon him (compare also Hofmann NJW 1974, 1641). The defendant therefore would have had to prove that the plaintiff even in the knowledge of the full extent of the danger would have paid no attention to a warning with the content explained above (in connection with which proof based on first appearance would possibly be of advantage to it).

(e) Das hat das Berufungsgericht verkannt. Da die insoweit beweispflichtige Beklagte keinen Beweis angetreten hat und überdies den ihr obliegenden, ein hypothetisches Verhalten des Klägers betreffenden Nachweis, daß dieser im Jahre 1960 – also vor nahezu 15 Jahren – bei ausreichendem Hinweis gleichwohl das Haartonicum zunächst weiter verwendet hätte, heute auch nicht mehr führen könnte, ist sie beweisfällig geblieben. Der Schadensersatzanspruch des Klägers ist mithin dem Grunde nach gerechtfertigt.

DELAY

§ 283 [Schadensersatz statt der Leistung bei Ausschluss der Leistungspflicht] Braucht der Schuldner nach § 275 Abs. 1 bis 3 nicht zu leisten, kann der Gläubiger unter den Voraussetzungen des § 280 Abs. 1 Schadensersatz statt der Leistung verlangen. § 281 Abs. 1 Satz 2 und 3 und Abs. 5 findet entsprechende Anwendung.

§ 284 [Ersatz vergeblicher Aufwendungen] Anstelle des Schadensersatzes statt der Leistung kann der Gläubiger Ersatz der Aufwendungen verlangen, die er im Vertrauen auf den Erhalt der Leistung gemacht hat und billigerweise machen durfte, es sei denn, deren Zweck wäre auch ohne die Pflichtverletzung des Schuldners nicht erreicht worden.

§ 285 [Herausgabe des Ersatzes] (1) Erlangt der Schuldner infolge des Umstands, auf Grund dessen er die Leistung nach § 275 Abs. 1 bis 3 nicht zu erbringen braucht, für den geschuldeten Gegenstand einen Ersatz oder einen Ersatzanspruch, so kann der Gläubiger Herausgabe des als Ersatz Empfangenen oder Abtretung des Ersatzanspruchs verlangen.

(2) Kann der Gläubiger statt der Leistung Schadensersatz verlangen, so mindert sich dieser, wenn er von dem in Absatz 1 bestimmten Recht Gebrauch macht, um den Wert des erlangten Ersatzes oder Ersatzanspruchs.

§ 286 [Verzug des Schuldners] (1) Leistet der Schuldner auf eine Mahnung des Gläubigers nicht, die nach dem Eintritt der Fälligkeit erfolgt, so kommt er durch die Mahnung in Verzug. Der Mahnung stehen die Erhebung der Klage auf die Leistung sowie die Zustellung eines Mahnbescheids im Mahnverfahren gleich.

(2) Der Mahnung bedarf es nicht, wenn:

1 für die Leistung eine Zeit nach dem Kalender bestimmt ist,

2 der Leistung ein Ereignis vorauszugehen hat und eine angemessene Zeit für die Leistung in der Weise bestimmt ist, dass sie sich von dem Ereignis an nach dem Kalender berechnen lässt,

(e) The appeal court failed to recognise this. As the defendant, who was in this respect under a duty of proof, undertook no proof and moreover even today could not bring the proof incumbent upon it relating to hypothetical conduct of the plaintiff that he, in 1960 – therefore nearly 15 years ago, following sufficient warning would nevertheless have continued to use the hair tonic for the time being, it remained under an unfulfilled obligation of proof. The claim for compensation for harm by the plaintiff is therefore justified in principle.

DELAY

§ 283 [Compensation instead of performance on exclusion of the duty of performance] If the obligor does not need to perform in accordance with § 275 paras 1–3, the obligee can demand compensation instead of performance under the prerequisites of § 280 para 1. § 281 para 1 sentences 2 and 3 and para 5 have corresponding application.

See the internet auction case, p 333.

§ 284 [Compensation for abortive expenditure] In place of compensation instead of performance the obligee can demand compensation for expenditure which he has made (and could justifiably make) in reliance on receiving the performance unless its purpose would not have been attained even without the obligor's violation of duty.

§ 285 [Handing over of compensation] If the obligor obtains as a result of the circumstance on the basis of which he does not need to carry out the performance in accordance with § 275 paras 1–3 compensation or a claim to compensation for the object which is the subject of the obligation, the obligee can demand the handing over of what has been received as compensation, or the transfer of the claim to compensation.

(2) If the obligor can demand compensation instead of performance, then this reduces, if he makes use of the right provided for in para 1, by the value of the compensation obtained or the claim to compensation.

§ 286 [Delay of the obligor] (1) If the obligor does not effect performance after a warning by the obligee which is made after performance becomes due, the warning results in him being in delay. The warning is equivalent to the institution of proceedings for performance as well as the delivery of a warning order in warning proceedings.

(2) The warning is not needed, if:

1 a time is fixed for the performance according to the calendar;

2 an event must precede the performance and an appropriate time is fixed for the performance in such a way that it can be reckoned from the event onwards according to the calendar;

3 der Schuldner die Leistung ernsthaft und endgültig verweigert,

4 aus besonderen Gründen unter Abwägung der beiderseitigen Interessen der sofortige Eintritt des Verzugs gerechtfertigt ist.

(3) Der Schuldner einer Entgeltforderung kommt spätestens in Verzug, wenn er nicht innerhalb von 30 Tagen nach Fälligkeit und Zugang einer Rechnung oder gleichwertigen Zahlungsaufstellung leistet; dies gilt gegenüber einem Schuldner, der Verbraucher ist, nur, wenn auf diese Folgen in der Rechnung oder Zahlungsaufstellung besonders hingewiesen worden ist. Wenn der Zeitpunkt des Zugangs der Rechnung oder Zahlungsaufstellung unsicher ist, kommt der Schuldner, der nicht Verbraucher ist, spätestens 30 Tage nach Fälligkeit und Empfang der Gegenleistung in Verzug.

(4) Der Schuldner kommt nicht in Verzug, solange die Leistung infolge eines Umstands unterbleibt, den er nicht zu vertreten hat.

§ 287 [Verantwortlichkeit während des Verzugs] Der Schuldner hat während des Verzugs jede Fahrlässigkeit zu vertreten. Er haftet wegen der Leistung auch für Zufall, es sei denn, dass der Schaden auch bei rechtzeitiger Leistung eingetreten sein würde.

§ 288 [Verzugszinsen] (1) Eine Geldschuld ist während des Verzugs zu verzinsen. Der Verzugszinsatz beträgt für das Jahr fünf Prozentpunkte über dem Basiszinsatz.

(2) Bei Rechtsgeschäften, an denen ein Verbraucher nicht beteilgt ist, beträgt der Zinssatz für Entgeltforderungen acht Prozentpunkte über dem Basiszinsatz.

(3) Der Gläubiger kann aus einem anderen Rechtsgrund höhere Zinsen verlangen.

(4) Die Geltendmachung eines weiteren Schadens ist nicht ausgeschlossen.

§ 292 [Haftung bei Herausgabepflicht] (1) Hat der Schuldner einen bestimmten Gegenstand herauszugeben, so bestimmt sich von dem Eintritte der Rechtshängigkeit an der Anspruch des Gläubigers auf Schadensersatz wegen Verschlechterung, Unterganges oder einer aus einem anderen Grunde eintretenden Unmöglichkeit der Herausgabe nach den Vorschriften, welche für das Verhältnis zwischen dem Eigentümer und dem Besitzer von dem Eintritte der Rechtshängigkeit des Eigentumsanspruchs an gelten, soweit nicht aus dem Schuldverhältnis oder dem Verzuge des Schuldners sich zugunsten des Gläubigers ein anderes ergibt.

(2) Das gleiche gilt von dem Anspruche des Gläubigers auf Herausgabe oder Vergütung von Nutzungen und von dem Anspruche des Schuldners auf Ersatz von Verwendungen.

3 the obligor refuses performance seriously and finally;

4 the immediate commencement of delay is justified on special grounds, on balancing the interests of both parties.

(3) The obligor in respect of a demand for payment is in delay at the latest when he does not effect performance within 30 days after it becomes due and an account or an equivalent payment statement is received; this applies as against an obligor who is a consumer only if his attention has particularly been drawn to these consequences in the account or payment statement. If the time of the arrival of the account or payment statement is uncertain, the obligor who is not a consumer is in delay at the latest 30 days after performance has become due and counter-performance has been received.

(4) The obligor is not in delay as long as performance does not occur as a result of a circumstance for which he is not responsible.

This provision also partly serves to transpose EC Directive 2000/35.

§ 287 [Responsibility during delay] The obligor is responsible for all negligence during the delay. He is liable because of the performance for chance events also, unless the harm would have occurred even on punctual performance.

§ 288 [Interest for delay] (1) Interest is due on a money debt during a period of delay. The rate of interest for delay for the year amounts to five percentage points above the basic interest rate.

(2) In the case of legal transactions in which a consumer is not involved, the rate of interest for demands for payment amounts to eight percentage points above the basic interest rate.

(3) The obligee can demand higher interest on another legal ground.

(4) A claim for further loss is not excluded.

This provision also partly serves to transpose EC Directive 2000/35.

(§§ 289–291 contain further provision as to the payment of interest.)

§ 292 [Liability under duty to deliver] (1) If the obligor has to deliver a certain object, the claim of the obligee to compensation for harm for deterioration, destruction or an impossibility of delivery arising from some other reason is determined from the moment that the matter becomes sub judice onwards according to the provisions which apply to the relationship between the owner and the possessor from the moment the claim to ownership becomes sub judice onwards, insofar as some other provision does not arise in favour of the obligee from the obligation relationship or the delay of the obligor.

(2) The same applies to the claim of the obligee to delivery or compensation for benefits produced and to the claim of the obligor to compensation for expenses.

(§§ 293–304 relate to delay by the obligee.)

CONTENT OF A CONTRACT

Generally

Zweiter Abschnitt. Gestaltung rechtsgeschäftlicher Schuldverhältnisse durch Allgemeine Geschäftsbedingungen

§ 305 [Einbeziehung Allgemeiner Geschäftsbedingungen in den Vertrag] (1) Allgemeine Geschäftsbedingungen sind alle für eine Vielzahl von Verträgen vorformulierten Vertragsbedingungen, die eine Vertragspartei (Verwender) der anderen Vertragspartei bei Abschluss eines Vertrags stellt. Gleichgültig ist, ob die Bestimmungen einen äußerlich gesonderten Bestandteil des Vertrags bilden oder in die Vertragsurkunde selbst aufgenommen werden, welchen Umfang sie haben, in welcher Schriftart sie verfasst sind und welche Form der Vertrag hat. Allgemeine Geschäftsbedingungen liegen nicht vor, soweit die Vertragsbedingungen zwischen den Vertragsparteien im Einzelnen ausgehandelt sind.

(2) Allgemeine Geschäftsbedingungen werden nur dann Bestandteil eines Vertrags, wenn der Verwender bei Vertragsschluss:

1 die anderer Vertragspartei ausdrücklich oder, wenn ein ausdrücklicher Hinweis wegen der Art des Vertragsschlusses nur unter unverhältnismäßigen Schwierigkeiten möglich ist, durch deutlich sichtbaren Aushang am Orte des Vertragsschlusses auf sie hinweist und

2 der anderen Vertragspartei die Möglichkeit verschafft, in zumutbarer Weise, die auch eine für den Verwender erkennbare körperliche Behinderung der anderen Vertragspartei angemessen berücksichtigt, von ihrem Inhalt Kenntnis zu nehmen,

und wenn die andere Vertragspartei mit ihrer Geltung einverstanden ist.

(3) Die Vertragsparteien können für eine bestimmte Art von Rechtsgeschäften die Geltung bestimmter Allgemeiner Geschäftsbedingungen unter Beachtung der in Absatz 2 bezeichneten Erfordernisse im Voraus vereinbaren.

§ 305a [Einbeziehung in besonderen Fällen] Auch ohne Einhaltung der in § 305 Abs. 2 Nr. 1 und 2 bezeichneten Erfordernisse werden einbezogen, wenn die andere Vertragspartei mit ihrer Geltung einverstanden ist,

1 die mit Genehmigung der zuständigen Verkehrsbehörde oder auf Grund von internationalen Übereinkommen erlassenen Tarife und Ausführungsbestimmungen der Eisenbahnen und die nach Maßgabe des Personenbeförderungsgesetzes genehmigten Beförderungs-bedingungen der Straßenbahnen, Obusse und Kraftfahrzeuge im Linienverkehr in den Beförderungsvertrag,

CONTENT OF A CONTRACT

Generally

Second section. Formulation of obligation relationships in legal transactions by general conditions of contract

§ 305 [Incorporation of general conditions of contract into the contract] (1) General conditions of contract are all contractual conditions predetermined for many contracts which one contracting party (the user) puts to the other party at the conclusion of a contract. It does not matter whether the provisions form an outwardly separated component of the contract or are incorporated into the contract document itself, what scope they have, in what kind of written form they are composed and what form the contract has. General conditions of contract are not present insofar as the contractual conditions are negotiated individually between the parties.

(2) General conditions of contract are only a component of a contract if the user on conclusion of the contract:

1 refers the other party to them expressly or, if an express reference is only possible with disproportionate difficulties because of the way the contract is concluded by a clearly visible notice at the place of conclusion of the contract and

2 provides the other party with the opportunity of becoming acquainted with their content in a reasonable manner which also takes appropriate account of any physical disability of the other party which the user can recognise,

and if the other party is in agreement with their applicability.

(3) The parties can agree in advance the applicability of certain general conditions of contract, having regard to the requirements described in para 2, for a particular type of legal transaction.

Similar provisions to §§ 305 *et seq* were contained in the General Conditions of Contract Act. See the internet auction case, p 333.

§ 305a [Incorporation in special cases] Even without the observation of the requirements described in § 305 para 2 nos 1 and 2, if the other contracting party is in agreement with their applicability,

1 the tariffs and implementation provisions of the railways issued with the approval of the competent transport authority or on the basis of international treaties and the transport conditions of trams, buses and motor vehicles in regular services approved in accordance with the Transport of Persons Act are included into the transportation contract.

2 die im Amtsblatt der Regulierungsbehörde für Telekommunikation und Post veröffentlichten und in den Geschäftsstellen des Verwenders bereitgehaltenen Allgemeinen Geschäftsbedingungen:

(a) in Beförderungsverträge, die außerhalb von Geschäftsräumen durch den Einwurf von Postsendungen in Briefkästen abgeschlossen werden,

(b) in Verträge über Telekommunikations-, Informations- und andere Dienstleistungen, die unmittelbar durch Einsatz von Fernkommunikationsmitteln und während der Erbringung einer Telekommunikationsdienstleistung in einem Mal erbracht werden, wenn die Allgemeinen Geschäftsbedingungen der anderen Vertragspartei nur unter unverhältnismäßigen Schwierigkeiten vor dem Vertragsschluss zugänglich gemacht werden können.

§ 305b [Vorrang der Individualabrede] Individuelle Vertragsabreden haben Vorrang vor Allgemeinen Geschäftsbedingungen.

§ 305c [Überraschende und mehrdeutige Klauseln] (1) Bestimmungen in Allgemeinen Geschäftsbedingungen, die nach den Umständen, insbesondere nach dem äußeren Erscheinungsbild des Vertrags, so ungewöhnlich sind, dass der Vertragspartner des Verwenders mit ihnen nicht zu rechnen braucht, werden nicht Vertragsbestandteil.

(2) Zweifel bei der Auslegung Allgemeiner Geschäftsbedingungen gehen zu Lasten des Verwenders.

§ 306 [Rechtsfolgen bei Nichteinbeziehung und Unwirksamkeit] (1) Sind Allgemeine Geschäftsbedingungen ganz oder teilweise nicht Vertragsbestandteil geworden oder unwirksam, so bleibt der Vertrag im Übrigen wirksam.

(2) Soweit die Bestimmungen nicht Vertragsbestandteil geworden oder unwirksam sind, richtet sich der Inhalt des Vertrags nach den gesetzlichen Vorschriften.

(3) Der Vertrag ist unwirksam, wenn das Festhalten an ihm auch unter Berücksichtigung der nach Absatz 2 vorgesehenen Änderung eine unzumutbare Härte für eine Vertragspartei darstellen würde.

§ 306a [Umgehungsverbot] Die Vorschriften dieses Abschnitts finden auch Anwendung, wenn sie durch anderweitige Gestaltungen umgangen werden.

§ 307 [Inhaltskontrolle] (1) Bestimmungen in Allgemeinen Geschäftsbedingungen sind unwirksam, wenn sie den Vertragspartner des Verwenders entgegen den Geboten von Treu and Glauben unangemessen benachteiligen. Eine unangemessene Benachteiligung kann sich auch daraus ergeben, dass die Bestimmung nicht klar und verständlich ist.

(2) Eine unangemessene Benachteiligung ist im Zweifel anzunehmen, wenn eine Bestimmung

2 the general conditions of contract published in the official gazette of the regulatory authority for telecommunications and post and kept available in the places of business of the user:

(a) are included into transportation contracts which are concluded outside business premises by the insertion of postal packages into letterboxes;

(b) are included into contracts about telecommunication, information and other services which are directly produced by use of methods of communication from a distance and during the production of a telecommunication service are produced at once if the general conditions of contract can only be made accessible to the other party before the conclusion of the contract with disproportionate difficulties.

§ 305b [Priority of the individual arrangement] Individual contractual arrangements have priority over general conditions of contract.

§ 305c [Surprising and ambiguous clauses] (1) Provisions in general conditions of contract which in the circumstances, in particular according to the outward appearance of the contract, are so unusual that the contracting partner of the user does not need to take them into account are not a component of the contract.

(2) Doubts in the interpretation of general conditions of contract are resolved to the disadvantage of the user.

§ 306 [Legal consequences of non-inclusion and ineffectiveness] (1) If general conditions of contract have wholly or partly not become a component of the contract or are ineffective, the contract remains effective in other respects.

(2) Insofar as the provisions have not become a component of the contract or are ineffective, the content of the contract will be controlled by the statutory provisions.

(3) The contract is ineffective if adhering to it, even taking into consideration the amendment provided for under para 2, would represent an unreasonable hardship for a contracting party.

§ 306a [Prohibition of evasion] The provisions of this section will also apply if they are evaded by the use of other forms.

§ 307 [Control of content] (1) Provisions in general conditions of contract are ineffective if they unreasonably disadvantage the contracting partner of the user contrary to the requirements of good faith. An unreasonable disadvantage can arise from the fact that the provision is not clear and comprehensible.

(2) An unreasonable disadvantage is to be assumed in case of doubt if a provision

1 mit wesentlichen Grundgedanken der gesetzlichen Regelung, von der abgewichen wird, nicht zu vereinbaren ist oder

2 wesentliche Rechte oder Pflichten, die sich aus der Natur des Vertrags ergeben, so einschränkt, dass die Erreichung des Vertragszwecks gefährdet ist.

(3) Die Absätze 1 und 2 sowie die §§ 308 und 309 gelten nur für Bestimmungen in Allgemeinen Geschäftsbedingungen, durch die von Rechtsvorschriften abweichende oder diese ergänzende Regelungen vereinbart werden. Andere Bestimmungen können nach Absatz 1 Satz 2 in Verbindung mit Absatz 1 Satz 1 unwirksam sein.

§ 308 ...

§ 309 ...

§ 310 ...

Zweites Buch. Recht der Schuldverhältnisse

Dritter Abschnitt. Schuldverhältnisse aus Verträgen

Erster Titel. Begründung, Inhalt und Beendigung

Erster Untertitel. Begründung

§ 311 [Rechtsgeschäftliche und rechtsgeschäftsähnliche Schuldverhältnisse] (1) Zur Begründung eines Schuldverhältnisses durch Rechtsgeschäft sowie zur Änderung des Inhalts eines Schuldverhältnisses ist ein Vertrag zwischen den Beteilgten erforderlich, soweit nicht das Gesetz ein anderes vorschreibt.

(2) Ein Schuldverhältnis mit Pflichten nach § 241 Abs. 2 entsteht auch durch

1 die Aufnahme von Vertragsverhandlungen,

2 die Anbahnung eines Vertrags, bei welcher der eine Teil im Hinblick auf eine etwaige rechtsgeschäftliche Beziehung dem anderen Teil die Möglichkeit zur Einwirkung auf seine Rechte, Rechtsgüter und Interessen gewährt oder ihm diese anvertraut, oder

3 ähnliche geschäftliche Kontakte.

(3) Ein Schuldverhältnis mit Pflichten nach § 241 Abs. 2 kann auch zu Personen entstehen, die nicht selbst Vertragspartei werden sollen. Ein solches Schuldverhältnis entsteht insbesondere, wenn der Dritte in besonderem Maße Vertrauen für sich in Anspruch nimmt und dadurch die Vertragsverhandlungen oder den Vertragsschluss erheblich beeinflusst.

§ 311a [Leistungshindernis bei Vertragsschluss] (1) Der Wirksamkeit eines Vertrags steht es nicht entgegen, dass der Schuldner nach § 275 Abs. 1 bis 3 nicht zu leisten braucht und das Leistungshindernis schon bei Vertragsschluss vorliegt.

1 is not reconcilable with essential basic concepts of the statutory regime from which there is a deviation or

2 limits essential rights or duties which arise from the nature of the contract in such a way that the attainment of the purpose of the contract is endangered.

(3) Paragraphs 1 and 2 as well as §§ 308 and 309 only apply to provisions in general conditions of contract by which rules deviating from provisions of law or supplementing them are agreed. Other provisions can be ineffective in accordance with para 1 sentence 2 in combination with paragraph 1 sentence 1.

§§ 308 and 309 set out clauses which are prohibited and § 310 defines the area of application of this part of the Civil Code.

§§ 305–310 also serve to transpose EC Directive 93/13.

Second Book. Law of obligation relationships

Third section. Obligation relationships arising from contracts

First title. Establishment, content and termination

First Subtitle. Establishment

§ 311 [Obligation relationships arising from legal transactions and similar obligation relationships] (1) For the establishment of an obligation relationship by a legal transaction as well as the amendment of the content of an obligation relationship, a contract between the participants is necessary insofar as statute does not prescribe otherwise.

(2) An obligation relationship with duties in accordance with § 241 para 2 also arises through

1 the opening up of contractual negotiations,

2 the initiation of a contract in which one party, having regard to a possible relationship in the nature of a legal transaction, grants to the other party the possibility of exerting an effect on his rights, legal entitlements and interests, or entrusts these to him, or

3 similar business contacts.

(3) An obligation relationship with duties in accordance with § 241 para 2 can also arise in favour of persons who were not themselves to be contracting parties. Such an obligation relationship arises in particular when the third party claims reliance for himself to a special extent and thereby substantially influences the contractual negotiations or the conclusion of the contract.

§ 311a [Hindrance to performance on conclusion of contract] (1) It is not inconsistent with the effectiveness of a contract that the obligor does not need to perform under § 275 paras 1–3 and the hindrance to performance is already present on conclusion of the contract.

(2) Der Gläubiger kann nach seiner Wahl Schadensersatz statt der Leistung oder Ersatz seiner Aufwendungen in dem in § 284 bestimmten Umfang verlangen. Dies gilt nicht, wenn der Schuldner das Leistungshindernis bei Vertragsschluss nicht kannte und seine Unkenntnis auch nicht zu vertreten hat. § 281 Abs. 1 Satz 2 und 3 und Abs. 5 findet entsprechende Anwendung.

§ 313 [Störung der Geschäftsgrundlage] (1) Haben sich Umstände, die zur Grundlage des Vertrags geworden sind, nach Vertragsschluss scherwiegend verändert und hätten die Parteien den Vertrag nicht oder mit anderem Inhalt geschlossen, wenn sie diese Veränderung vorausgesehen hätten, so kann Anpassung des Vertrags verlangt werden, soweit einem Teil unter Berücksichtigung aller Umstände des Einzelfalls, insbesondere der vertraglichen oder gesetzlichen Risikoverteilung, das Festhalten am unveränderten Vertrag nicht zugemutet werden kann.

(2) Einer Veränderung der Umstände steht es gleich, wenn wesentliche Vorstellungen, die zur Grundlage des Vertrags geworden sind, sich als falsch herausstellen.

(3) Ist eine Anpassung des Vertrags nicht möglich oder einem Teil nicht zumutbar, so kann der benachteiligte Teil vom Vertrag zurücktreten. An die Stelle des Rücktrittsrechts tritt für Dauerschuldverhältnisse das Recht zur Kündigung.

§ 314 [Kündigung von Dauerschuldverhältnissen aus wichtigem Grund] (1) Dauerschuldverhältnisse kann jeder Vertragsteil aus wichtigem Grund ohne Einhaltung einer Kündigungsfrist kündigen. Ein wichtiger Grund liegt vor, wenn dem kündigenden Teil unter Berücksichtigung aller Umstande des Einzelfalls und unter Abwägung der beiderseitigen Interessen die Fortsetzung des Vertragsverhältnisses bis zur vereinbarten Beendigung oder bis zum Ablauf einer Kündigungsfrist nicht zugemutet werden kann.

(2) Besteht der wichtige Grund in der Verletzung einer Pflicht aus dem Vertrag, ist die Kündigung erst nach erfolglosem Ablauf einer zur Abhilfe bestimmten Frist oder nach erfolgloser Abmahnung zulässig. § 323 Abs. 2 findet entsprechende Anwendung.

(3) Der Berechtigte kann nur innerhalb einer angemessenen Frist kündigen, nachdem er vom Kündigungsgrund Kenntnis erlangt hat.

(4) Die Berechtigung, Schadensersatz zu verlangen, wird durch die Kündigung nicht ausgeschlossen.

(2) The obligee can demand compensation for harm instead of performance or compensation for his expenses in the scope determined by § 284, according to his choice. This does not apply if the obligor did not know of the hindrance to performance on the conclusion of the contract and is also not answerable for his lack of knowledge. § 281 para 1 sentences 2 and 3 and para 5 have corresponding application.

§§ 311 b, 311 c, 312 and 312 a–312 f relate to special forms of contract.

§ 313 [Disturbance of the basis of a transaction] (1) If circumstances which have become the basis of a contract have seriously altered after the conclusion of a contract and if the parties would not have concluded the contract or would have concluded it with a different content if they had foreseen this change, then adaptation of the contract can be demanded, insofar as adhering to the unaltered contract cannot be expected of one party taking into consideration all the circumstances of the individual case, in particular the contractual or statutory division of risks.

(2) If essential ideas which have become the basis of the contract turn out to be false, that is to be equated to an alteration of the circumstances.

(3) If an adaptation of the contract is not possible or not reasonable towards one party, the disadvantaged party can withdraw from the contract. For long term obligation relationships the right to terminate takes the place of the right of withdrawal.

§ 314 [Notice in respect of long term relationships on important grounds] (1) Long term relationships can be terminated by any contracting party on an important ground without the observation of a period of notice. An important ground is present if the continuation of the contractual relationship to the agreed termination or to the expiry of a notice period cannot be expected of the party giving notice, taking into consideration all the circumstances of the individual case and balancing the interests of both sides.

(2) If the important ground consists in the violation of a duty under the contract, termination is only permissible after the expiry without result of a period determined for remedy or after a warning without result. § 323 para 2 has corresponding application.

(3) The person so entitled can only terminate within a reasonable period after he has obtained knowledge of the ground for termination.

(4) The entitlement to demand compensation for harm is not excluded by the termination.

Determinations

§ 315 [Bestimmung der Leistung durch eine Partei] (1) Soll die Leistung durch einen der Vertragschließenden bestimmt werden, so ist im Zweifel anzunehmen, daß die Bestimmung nach billigem Ermessen zu treffen ist.

(2) Die Bestimmung erfolgt durch Erklärung gegenüber dem anderen Teile.

(3) Soll die Bestimmung nach billigem Ermessen erfolgen, so ist die getroffene Bestimmung für den anderen Teil nur verbindlich, wenn sie die Billigkeit entspricht. Entspricht sie nicht der Billigkeit, so wird die Bestimmung durch Urteil getroffen; das gleiche gilt, wenn die Bestimmung verzögert wird.

§ 316 [Bestimmung der Gegenleistung] Ist der Umfang der für eine Leistung versprochenen Gegenleistung nicht bestimmt, so steht die Bestimmung im Zweifel demjenigen Teile zu, welcher die Gegenleistung zu fordern hat.

§ 317 [Bestimmung der Leistung durch einen Dritten] (1) Ist die Bestimmung der Leistung einem Dritten überlassen, so ist im Zweifel anzunehmen, daß sie nach billigem Ermessen zu treffen ist.

(2) Soll die Bestimmung durch mehrere Dritte erfolgen, so ist im Zweifel Übereinstimmung aller erforderlich; soll eine Summe bestimmt werden, so ist, wenn verschiedene Summen bestimmt werden, im Zweifel die Durchschnittsumme maßgebend.

§ 318 [Anfechtung der Bestimmung] (1) Die einem Dritten überlassene Bestimmung der Leistung erfolgt durch Erklärung gegenüber einem der Vertragschließenden.

(2) Die Anfechtung der getroffenen Bestimmung wegen Irrtums, Drohung oder arglistiger Täuschung steht nur den Vertragschließenden zu; Anfechtungsgegner ist der andere Teil. Die Anfechtung muß unverzüglich erfolgen, nachdem der Anfechtungsberechtigte von dem Anfechtungsgrunde Kenntnis erlangt hat. Sie ist ausgeschlossen, wenn dreißig Jahre verstrichen sind, nachdem die Bestimmung getroffen worden ist.

§ 319 [Unwirksamkeit der Bestimmung; Ersetzung] (1) Soll der Dritte die Leistung nach billigem Ermessen bestimmen, so ist die getroffene Bestimmung für die Vertragschließenden nicht verbindlich, wenn sie offenbar unbillig ist. Die Bestimmung erfolgt in diesem Falle durch Urteil; das gleiche gilt, wenn der Dritte die Bestimmung nicht treffen kann oder will oder wenn er sie verzögert.

Determinations

§ 315 [Determination of performance by a party] (1) If performance is to be determined by one of the persons making the contract, in case of doubt it is to be accepted that the determination is to be made in accordance with fair judgment.

(2) The determination is to be made by declaration as against the other party.

(3) If the determination is to be made in accordance with fair judgment, the determination in question is only binding on the other party if it is reasonable. If it is not reasonable, the determination is to be made by court judgment; the same applies if the determination is delayed.

See the internet auction case, p 333.

§ 316 [Determination of performance in return] If the scope of the performance promised in return for another performance is not determined, in case of doubt the determination is for the party who can demand the performance first mentioned.

§ 317 [Determination of performance by a third party] (1) If the determination of the performance is left to a third party, in case of doubt it is to be accepted that it is to be made in accordance with fair judgment.

(2) If the determination is to be made by several third parties, in case of doubt the agreement of all is necessary; if a sum is to be determined, and different sums are determined, in case of doubt the average sum is the authoritative one.

§ 318 [Challenge of the determination] (1) A determination of performance left to a third party is to take place by declaration as against one of the contracting parties.

(2) Challenge of the determination in question because of mistake, threat or fraudulent deception is only for the contracting parties; the respondent to the challenge is the other party. The challenge must follow without delay after the person entitled to challenge has obtained knowledge of the ground for challenge. It is excluded when 30 years have elapsed after the determination has been made.

§ 319 [Ineffectiveness of the determination; replacement] (1) If the third party has to determine performance in accordance with fair judgment, the determination in question is not binding on the contracting parties if it is obviously unfair. The determination is to take place in this case by court judgment; the same applies if the third party cannot or will not make the determination or if it delays in making it.

(2) Soll der Dritte die Bestimmung nach freiem Belieben treffen, so ist der Vertrag unwirksam, wenn der Dritte die Bestimmung nicht treffen kann oder will oder wenn er sie verzögert.

MUTUAL CONTRACTS

Generally

Zweiter Titel. Gegenseitiger Vertrag

§ 320 [Einrede des nichterfüllten Vertrags] (1) Wer aus einem gegenseitigen Vertrage verpflichtet ist, kann die ihm obliegende Leistung bis zur Bewirkung der Gegenleistung verweigern, es sei denn, daß er vorzuleisten verpflichtet ist. Hat die Leistung an mehrere zu erfolgen, so kann dem einzelnen der ihm gebührende Teil bis zur Bewirkung der ganzen Gegenleistung verweigert werden. Die Vorschrift des § 273 Abs. 3 findet keine Anwendung.

(2) Ist von der einen Seite teilweise geleistet worden, so kann die Gegenleistung insoweit nicht verweigert werden, als die Verweigerung nach den Umständen, insbesondere wegen verhältnismäßiger Geringfügigkeit des rückständigen Teiles, gegen Treu und Glauben verstoßen würde.

§ 321 [Unsicherheitseinrede] (1) Wer aus einem gegenseitigen Vertrag vorzuleisten verpflichtet ist, kann die ihm obliegende Leistung verweigern, wenn nach Abschluss des Vertrags erkennbar wird, dass sein Anspruch auf die Gegenleistung durch mangelnde Leistungsfähigkeit des anderen Teils gefährdet wird. Das Leistungsverweigerungsrecht entfällt, wenn die Gegenleistung bewirkt oder Sicherheit für sie geleistet wird.

(2) Der Vorleistungspflichtige kann eine angemessene Frist bestimmen, in welcher der andere Teil Zug um Zug gegen die Leistung nach seiner Wahl die Gegenleistung zu bewirken oder Sicherheit zu leisten hat. Nach erfolglosem Ablauf der Frist kann der Vorleistungspflichtige vom Vertrag zurücktreten. § 323 findet entsprechende Anwendung.

§ 322 (weggefallen)

§ 323 [Rücktritt wegen nicht oder nicht vertragsgemäß erbrachter Leistung] (1) Erbringt bei einem gegenseitigen Vertrag der Schuldner eine fällige Leistung nicht oder nicht vertragsgemäß, so kann der Gläubiger, wenn er dem Schuldner erfolglos eine angemessene Frist zur Leistung oder Nacherfüllung bestimmt hat, vom Vertrag zurücktreten.

(2) Die Fristsetzung ist entbehrlich, wenn

(2) If the third party is to make the determination as he pleases, the contract is ineffective if the third party cannot or will not make the determination or if he delays in making it.

MUTUAL CONTRACTS

Generally

Second title. Mutual contract

§ 320 [Objection of the unfulfilled contract] (1) A person who is under an obligation from a mutual contract can refuse the performance which is incumbent upon him until the effecting of performance in return, unless he is obliged to effect performance beforehand. If performance has to take place towards several persons, the individual can be refused the part which is due to him until the effecting of the whole performance in return. The provisions of § 273 para 3 have no application.

(2) If performance by one side has partly taken place, performance in return cannot be refused insofar as the refusal would, according to the circumstances, and especially because of the proportionate insignificance of the outstanding part, violate good faith.

§ 321 [Objection of uncertainty] (1) A person who is obliged to effect performance beforehand under a mutual contract can refuse the performance which is incumbent upon him if, after conclusion of the contract, it is evident that his claim to performance in return is endangered by lack of ability to perform on the part of the other party. The right to refuse performance lapses when the performance in return is effected or security is provided for it.

(2) The person obliged to effect performance beforehand can determine an appropriate period in which the other party has, simultaneously with this performance, to effect performance in return or to provide security, according to his choice. After the period has expired without result, the person obliged to effect performance beforehand can withdraw from the contract. § 323 has corresponding application.

§ 322 (repealed)

§ 323 [Withdrawal because of no performance or performance not in accordance with the contract] (1) If an obligor in a mutual contract does not effect performance which is due or does not effect it in accordance with the contract, the obligee can withdraw from the contract, if he has determined for the obligor an appropriate period for performance or subsequent fulfilment without result.

(2) The setting of a period can be dispensed with, if

1 der Schuldner die Leistung ernsthaft und endgültig verweigert,

2 der Schuldner die Leistung zu einem im Vertrag bestimmten Termin oder innerhalb einer bestimmten Frist nicht bewirkt und der Gläubiger im Vertrag den Fortbestand seines Leistungsinteresses an die Rechtzeitigkeit der Leistung gebunden hat oder

3 besondere Umstände vorliegen, die unter Abwägung der beiderseitigen Interessen den sofortigen Rücktritt rechtfertigen.

(3) Kommt nach der Art der Pflichtverletzung eine Fristsetzung nicht in Betracht, so tritt an deren Stelle eine Abmahnung.

(4) Der Gläubiger kann bereits vor dem Eintritt der Fälligkeit der Leistung zurücktreten, wenn offensichtlich ist, dass die Voraussetzungen des Rücktritts eintreten werden.

(5) Hat der Schuldner eine Teilleistung bewirkt, so kann der Gläubiger vom ganzen Vertrag nur zurücktreten, wenn er an der Teilleistung kein Interesse hat. Hat der Schuldner die Leistung nicht vertragsgemäß bewirkt, so kann der Gläubiger vom Vertrag nicht zurücktreten, wenn die Pflichtverletzung unerheblich ist.

(6) Der Rücktritt ist ausgeschlossen, wenn der Gläubiger für den Umstand, der ihn zum Rücktritt berechtigen würde, allein oder weit überwiegend verantwortlich ist oder wenn der vom Schuldner nicht zu vertretende Umstand zu einer Zeit eintritt, zu welcher der Gläubiger im Verzug der Annahme ist.

§ 324 [Rücktritt wegen Verletzung einer Pflicht nach § 241 Abs. 2] Verletzt der Schuldner bei einem gegenseitigen Vertrag eine Pflicht nach § 241 Abs. 2, so kann der Gläubiger zurücktreten, wenn ihm ein Festhalten am Vertrag nicht mehr zuzumuten ist.

§ 325 [Schadensersatz und Rücktritt] Das Recht, bei einem gegenseitigen Vertrag Schadensersatz zu verlangen, wird durch den Rücktritt nicht ausgeschlossen.

§ 326 [Befreiung von der Gegenleistung und Rücktritt beim Ausschluss der Leistungspflicht] (1) Braucht der Schuldner nach § 275 Abs. 1 bis 3 nicht zu leisten, entfällt der Anspruch auf die Gegenleistung; bei einer Teilleistung findet § 441 Abs. 3 entsprechende Anwendung. Satz 1 gilt nicht, wenn der Schuldner im Falle der nicht vertragsgemäßen Leistung die Nacherfüllung nach § 275 Abs. 1 bis 3 zu erbringen braucht.

1 the obligor refuses performance seriously and finally,

2 the obligor does not effect performance at a date determined in the contract or within a determined period and in the contract the obligee has linked the continued existence of his interest in performance to the punctuality of performance or

3 special circumstances are present which justify immediate withdrawal on balancing the interests of both parties.

(3) If because of the type of violation of duty the setting of a period does not come into consideration, a warning will take its place.

(4) The obligee can withdraw even before performance becomes due if it is obvious that the prerequisites for withdrawal will occur.

(5) If the obligor has effected partial performance, the obligee can only withdraw from the whole contract if he has no interest in partial performance. If the obligor has not effected performance in accordance with the contract, the obligee cannot withdraw from the contract if the violation of duty is insignificant.

(6) Withdrawal is excluded if the obligee is responsible alone or overwhelmingly for the circumstance which would justify him withdrawing or if the circumstance for which the obligor is not answerable occurs at a time at which the obligee is in delay in acceptance.

This provision also serves to transpose EC Directive 99/44.

§ 324 [Withdrawal because of violation of a duty under § 241 para 2] If the obligor violates a duty under § 241 para 2 in a mutual contract, the obligee can withdraw if adhering to the contract can no longer be expected of him.

§ 325 [Compensation and withdrawal] The right to demand compensation in respect of a mutual contract is not excluded by withdrawal.

§ 326 [Release from performance in return and withdrawal on exclusion of the duty of performance] (1) If the obligor does not need to perform under § 275 paras 1–3, the claim to performance in return lapses; on a partial performance § 441 para 3 has corresponding application. Sentence 1 does not apply, if the obligor in the case of performance which is not in accordance with the contract needs to effect subsequent fulfilment under § 275 paras 1–3.

(2) Ist der Gläubiger für den Umstand, auf Grund dessen der Schuldner nach § 275 Abs. 1 bis 3 nicht zu leisten braucht, allein oder weit überwiegend verantwortlich oder tritt dieser vom Schuldner nicht zu vertretende Umstand zu einer Zeit ein, zu welcher der Gläubiger im Verzug der Annahme ist, so behält der Schuldner den Anspruch auf die Gegenleistung. Er muss sich jedoch dasjenige anrechnen lassen, was er infolge der Befreiung von der Leistung erspart oder durch anderweitige Verwendung seiner Arbeitskraft erwirbt oder zu erwerben böswillig unterlässt.

(3) Verlangt der Gläubiger nach § 285 Herausgabe des für den geschuldeten Gegenstand erlangten Ersatzes oder Abtretung des Ersatzanspruchs, so bleibt er zur Gegenleistung verpflichtet. Diese mindert sich jedoch nach Maßgabe des § 441 Abs. 3 insoweit, als der Wert des Ersatzes oder des Ersatzanspruchs hinter dem Wert der geschuldeten Leistung zurückbleibt.

(4) Soweit die nach dieser Vorschrift nicht gechuldete Gegenleistung bewirkt ist, kann das Geleistete nach den §§ 346 bis 348 zurückgefordert werden.

(5) Braucht der Schuldner nach § 275 Abs. 1 bis 3 nicht zu leisten, kann der Gläubiger zurücktreten; auf den Rücktritt findet § 323 mit der Maßgabe entsprechende Anwendung, dass die Fristsetzung entbehrlich ist.

§ 327 (weggefallen)

PROMISE IN FAVOUR OF A THIRD PARTY

Dritter Titel. Versprechen der Leistung an einen Dritten

§ 328 [Vertrag zugunsten Dritter] (1) Durch Vertrag kann eine Leistung an einen Dritten mit der Wirkung bedungen werden, daß der Dritte unmittelbar das Recht erwirbt, die Leistung zu fordern.

(2) In Ermangelung einer besonderen Bestimmung ist aus den Umständen, insbesondere aus dem Zwecke des Vertrags, zu entnehmen, ob der Dritte das Recht erwerben, ob das Recht des Dritten sofort oder nur unter gewissen Voraussetzungen entstehen und ob den Vertragschließenden die Befugnis vorbehalten sein soll, das Recht des Dritten ohne dessen Zustimmung aufzuheben oder zu ändern.

(2) If the obligee is responsible alone or overwhelmingly for the circumstance on the basis of which the obligor does not need to perform under § 275 paras 1–3 or if this circumstance for which the obligor is not answerable occurs at a time at which the obligee is in delay in acceptance, the obligor retains the claim to performance in return. He must however allow to be reckoned against him what he has saved as a result of the release from performance or acquires by other use of his power to work or wilfully neglects to acquire.

(3) If the obligee demands in accordance with § 285 restitution of the compensation acquired for the object owed or transfer of the claim to compensation, he remains obliged to effect performance in return. This however reduces in accordance with § 441 para 3 insofar as the value of the compensation or of the claim to compensation remains less than the value of the performance owed.

(4) Insofar as the performance in return which is not owed according to this provision is effected, what is performed can be demanded back in accordance with §§ 346–348.

(5) If the obligor does not need to perform in accordance with §§ 275 paras 1–3, the obligee can withdraw; on the withdrawal § 323 has corresponding application with the proviso that the setting of a period can be dispensed with.

This provision also serves to transpose EC Directive 99/44.

§ 327 (repealed)

PROMISE IN FAVOUR OF A THIRD PARTY

Third title. Promise of performance to a third party

§ 328 [Contract in favour of a third party] (1) Performance towards a third party can be stipulated for by contract with the effect that the third party acquires the right directly to demand performance.

(2) In the absence of a special provision, it is to be inferred from the circumstances, especially the purpose of the contract, whether the third party should acquire the right, whether the right of the third party should arise immediately or only under certain circumstances and whether the authority should be reserved to the contracting parties to remove or change the right of the third party without his consent.

See the fall in the supermarket case, p 377. See also now (as to English law) the Contracts (Rights of Third Parties) Act 1999.

§ 329 [Auslegungsregel bei Erfüllungsübernahme] Verpflichtet sich in einem Vertrage der eine Teil zur Befriedigung eines Gläubigers des anderen Teiles, ohne die Schuld zu übernehmen, so ist im Zweifel nicht anzunehmen, daß der Gläubiger unmittelbar das Recht erwerben soll, die Befriedigung von ihm zu fordern.

§ 333 [Zurückweisung des Rechts durch den Dritten] Weist der Dritte das aus dem Vertrag erworbene Recht dem Versprechenden gegenüber zurück, so gilt das Recht als nicht erworben.

§ 334 [Einwendungen des Schuldners gegenüber dem Dritten] Einwendungen aus dem Vertrage stehen dem Versprechenden auch gegenüber dem Dritten zu.

§ 335 [Forderungsrecht des Versprechensempfängers] Der Versprechensempfänger kann, sofern nicht ein anderer Wille der Vertragschließenden anzunehmen ist, die Leistung an den Dritten auch dann fordern, wenn diesem das Recht auf die Leistung zusteht.

REMAINDER OF THE SECOND BOOK

Vierter Titel. Draufgabe. Vertragsstrafe

Fünfter Titel. Rücktritt; Widerrufs- und Rückgaberecht bei Verbraucherverträgen

Vierter Abschnitt. Erlöschen der Schuldverhältnisse

Erster Title. Erfüllung

Zweiter Titel. Hinterlegung

Dritter Title. Aufrechnung

Vierter Title. Erlaß

Fünfter Abschnitt. Übertragung der Forderung

Sechster Abschnitt. Schuldübernahme

Siebenter Abschnitt. Mehrheit von Schuldnern und Gläubigern

Achter Abschnitt. Einzelne Schuldverhältnisse

§ 329 [Rule of interpretation on taking over of fulfilment] If one party commits himself in a contract to satisfy an obligee of the other party, without taking over the obligation, it is not to be assumed, in case of doubt, that the obligee is to acquire the right directly to demand satisfaction from him.

(§§ 330–332 relate to life insurance and annuities and the effect of death.)

§ 333 [Rejection of the right by the third party] If the third party rejects, as against the promisor, the right acquired from the contract, the right does not take effect as acquired.

§ 334 [Objections of the obligor as against the third party] Objections arising from the contract belong to the promisor as against the third party as well.

§ 335 [Right of demand of recipient of the promise] The recipient of the promise can, insofar as a different intention of the contracting parties is not be assumed, also demand performance towards the third party if the right to performance belongs to that person.

REMAINDER OF THE SECOND BOOK

Fourth title. Deposit. Contractual penalty

Fifth title. Withdrawal; right of revocation and return for consumer contracts

Fourth section. Extinguishment of obligation relationships

First title. Fulfilment

Second title. Deposition

Third title. Settling of accounts

Fourth Title. Release

Fifth section. Transfer of the demand

Sixth section. Taking over of the obligation

Seventh section. Plurality of obligors and obligees

Eighth section. Individual obligation relationships

(This section consists of 27 titles, the last of which is tort: see Chapter Six.)

TORT

NATURE

The English law of tort consists of a large number of individual torts of varying importance, each with their own principles of liability. The French law of tort has been very largely based on Art 1382 of the Civil Code, supplemented by Art 1383. The German law of tort is somewhere in between these two positions. There is no general principle of liability; see the fallen telegraph pole case, p 565. There are three general bases of liability: §§ 823 paras 1 and 2, and § 826. There are also a number of specific articles in the Civil Code which create liability in narrowly defined areas. As with both other legal systems, there are also specific statutory provisions, sometimes creating strict liability.

TWO GENERAL PRINCIPLES OF LIABILITY

Bürgerliches Gesetzbuch

Fünfundzwanzigster Titel. Unerlaubte Handlungen

§ 823 [Schadensersatzpflicht] (1) Wer vorsätzlich oder fahrlässig das Leben, den Körper, die Gesundheit, die Freiheit, das Eigentum oder ein sonstiges Recht eines anderen widerrechtlich verletzt, ist dem anderen zum Ersatze des daraus entstehenden Schadens verpflichtet.

TWO GENERAL PRINCIPLES OF LIABILITY

Twenty-fifth Title. Tort

§ 823 I creates a very broad category of liability, rather like Arts 1382 and 1383 of the French Civil Code, only a little more specific. § 823 II creates a general category of statutory liability.

General

§ 823 [Duty to compensate for harm] (1) A person who intentionally or negligently injures the life, body, health, freedom, property or other right of another unlawfully is obliged to compensate the other for the harm arising from this.

(1) Scope

This paragraph covers omissions as well as intentional and negligent acts. The issues, familiar in English law, of causation and duty may have to be considered. The requirement of unlawfulness may be satisfied by direct injury to one of the legal interests listed here; or by there being a duty (Verkehrsicherungsflicht) which has been breached. There may however be a justification; see, for example, §§ 227 and 228 of the BGB and the shooting at the disco case (see Chapter Four, p 321).

(2) Burden of proof

This generally falls on the plaintiff, but there is a German equivalent of the doctrine of *res ipsa loquitur* as it operates in such cases as *Byrne v Boadle* (1863) 2 H & C 722; and *Ward v Tesco Stores Ltd* [1976] 2 All ER 219. There are good illustrations of the application of this in the fowl pest case below, and in the fallen telegraph pole case which appears later at p 565.

(3) Catalogue of rights

One of the issues here is whether a right described in § 823 I has been infringed. The following cases provide illustrations of such rights. In the newspaper delivery obstruction case the carrying on of a business was classified as an 'other right', and the same view was taken in the air traffic controllers' strike case: see p 579; but note the discussion as to whether this was only available when other rights were not. Rights such as a right to personal honour and to privacy and the right of a parent to care for a child are also classified as 'other rights'.

Statutory

(2) Die gleiche Verpflichtung trifft denjenigen, welcher gegen ein den Schutz eines anderen bezweckendes Gesetz verstößt. Ist nach dem Inhalte des Gesetzes ein Verstoß gegen dieses auch ohne Verchulden möglich, so tritt die Ersatzpflicht nur im Falle des Verschuldens ein.

Statutory

(2) The same obligation applies to a person who offends against a statutory provision which has in view the protection of another. If, according to the content of the statutory provision, a violation of it is also possible without fault, the duty to compensate only arises in case of fault.

The purpose of the statutory provision here may affect the persons who can claim, and the harm for which they can claim.

There are a number of provisions of the criminal law which will give rise to liability under this paragraph, and it is under this paragraph that defamation claims will often be made, because defamation is primarily a crime in German law, and only becomes a tort by virtue of the fact that there has been an infringement of a statutory provision: see the 14th section of the Criminal Code in Chapter Seven, p 715. However, there is a particular form of defamation for which specific provision is made in the Civil Code, as set out below.

Three other examples of liability arising under § 823 II are the fowl pest case (see p 439) where it was stated that it would create liability in combination with the Medicines Act; and the newspaper delivery obstruction case (p 481) where the creation of liability in combination with § 240 of the StGB was considered and the computer non-disclosure case, Chapter Four, p 283 where the possibility of liability arising in combination with the Unfair Competition Act was discussed.

The statutory provision must protect the interests of an individual and not merely the public; and the harm done to the plaintiff must be within the ambit of the provision. Compare the approach here to that of the case of *Gorris v Scott* (1874) JR 9 Exch 125.

THE FOWL PEST CASE

BGHZ Band 51 S. 91

16 (a) Wird bei bestimmungsgemäßer Verwendung eines Industrieerzeugnisses eine Person oder eine Sache dadurch geschädigt, daß das Produkt fehlerhaft hergestellt war, so muß der Hersteller beweisen, daß ihn hinsichtlich des Fehlers kein Verschulden trifft.

(b) Erbringt der Hersteller diesen Beweis nicht, so haftet er nach Deliktsgrundsätzen. Ein Zwischenerwerber kann den bei einem Dritten eingetretenen Schaden nicht nach Vertragsrecht liquidieren.

BGB §§ 823, 249

VI. Zivilsenat. Urt. v. 26. November 1968 i.S. V. GmbH (Bekl.) w. B. (Kl.). VI ZR 212/66.

I Landgericht Mönchengladbach

II Oberlandesgericht Düsseldorf

Die Klägerin, die eine Hühnerfarm betreibt, ließ am 19. November 1963 ihre Hühner durch den Tierarzt Dr. H. gegen Hühnerpest impfen. Einige Tage danach brach jedoch die Hühnerpest aus. Mehr als 4000 Hühner verendeten, über 100 mußten notgeschlachtet werden.

Die Klägerin nimmt die Beklagte, ein Impfstoffwerk, auf Ersatz ihrer Schäden in Anspruch. Der Tierarzt hatte für die Impfung den von der Beklagten hergestellten Impfstoff XY verwendet. Diesen hatte er Anfang November 1963 in 500 ccm-Flaschen von der Beklagten bezogen. Die Flaschen stammten aus der Charge ALD 210, die die Beklagte am 18. Oktober 1963 im Staatlichen Paul-Ehrlich-Institut in Frankfurt a. M. hatte prüfen lassen; dabei war die Charge freigegeben worden. Anschließend hatte die Beklagte sie in ihrem Betrieb auf handelsübliche Gefäße abgefüllt. Bei Behältnissen unter 500 ccm geschieht dies unter luftdichtem Abschluß bei Unterdruck; bei größeren Flaschen ließ es die Beklagte im offenen Eingußverfahren durchführen, jedoch im abgeschlossenen Raum bei ultravioletter Bestrahlung.

THE FOWL PEST CASE

This is case on the border land of tort and contract. It concerns a defective vaccine, and the person whose chickens were killed by it had no contract with the manufacturer. There is a discussion of possible contractual remedies, but the conclusion is that liability only arises in tort, although the burden of proof is shifted to the manufacturer, so it was for him to disprove fault, not for the plaintiff to prove it.

BGHZ Volume 51 p 91

16 (a) If a person or thing is harmed by the agreed use of an industrial product due to the fact that the product was defectively manufactured, the manufacturer must prove that no blame rests with him in relation to the fault.

(b) If the manufacturer does not supply this proof, he is liable according to tortious principles. An intermediate transferee cannot claim for harm to a third party according to contract law.

BGB §§ 823, 249

VIth Civil Senate. Judgment of 26 November 1968 in the matter of V Ltd (defendant) v B (plaintiff) – VI ZR 212/66.

I State Court of Mönchengladbach

II Upper State Court of Düsseldorf

The plaintiff, who runs a chicken farm, had her chickens vaccinated on 19 November 1963 by the veterinary surgeon Dr H against fowl pest. However, some days afterwards fowl pest broke out. More than 4,000 chickens died and more than 100 had to be slaughtered.

The plaintiff claims against the defendant vaccine manufacturers for compensation for the harm. The veterinary surgeon had used the vaccine XY manufactured by the defendant. He had obtained this at the beginning of November 1963 from the defendant in 500 cc bottles. The bottles came from the batch ALD 210, which the defendant had caused to be examined on 18 October 1963 in the State run Paul Ehrlich Institute in Frankfurt am Main; the batch had been passed as a result. Afterwards, the defendant filled containers of the normal kind in commercial use. For containers under 500 cc this occurs in an airtight compartment in a partial vacuum; with larger bottles the defendant arranged for this to be carried out through an open infusion process, but in a closed room irradiated with ultra-violet rays.

Als Dr. H. wenige Tage darauf am 22. November 1963 bei dem Landwirt R. die Hühner impfte, brach auch dort die Hühnerpest aus. Dasselbe trat Ende November 1963 bei drei Geflügelzüchtern in Württemberg ein, die ihre Hühner ebenfalls mit dem Impfstoff der Beklagten aus der Charge ALD 210 hatten impfen lassen. Als daraufhin das Tierärztliche Unterschungsamt Stuttgart mehrere Flaschen dieser Charge von der Bundesforschungsanstalt für Viruskrankheiten der Tiere in Tübingen untersuchen ließ, wurden in einigen Flaschen bakterielle Verunreinigungen und noch aktive ND (Newcastle Disease)- Viren festgestellt, die nicht ausreichend immunisiert worden waren. Auch das Paul-Ehrlich-Institut stellte fest, daß einige der ihm zur Überprüfung eingesandten Flaschen unsteril waren und in ihnen ND-Virus nachgewiesen werden konnte. Die Beklagte hat bestritten, daß der Ausbruch der Hühnerpest auf die Verwendung ihres Impfstoffes zurückzuführen sei. Jedenfalls könne die fehlende Sterilität der Flaschen nicht die Ursache gewesen sein. Hierzu hat sie sich auf das von ihr überreichte Gutachten von Prof. Dr. E. bei der Bundesforschungsanstalt für Viruserkrankungen berufen. Sie hat für die Arbeiter und die Leiterin ihrer Virus-Abteilung den Entlastungsbeweis angetreten.

Landgericht und Oberlandesgericht haben den Klageanspruch dem Grunde nach für gerechtfertigt erklärt. Die Revision der Beklagten hatte keinen Erfolg.

Aus den Gründen:

Das Berufungsgericht geht davon aus, daß der in den an Dr. H. gelieferten Flaschen enthaltene Impfstoff durch Bakterien verunreinigt gewesen sei, und hält für erwiesen, daß der Ausbruch der Hühnerpest hierauf zurückzuführen sei. Selbst der von der Beklagten zugezogene Gutachter Prof. Dr. E. vermöge nicht auszuschließen, daß es zu der Verunreinigung durch eine Fahrlässigkeit der beim Abfüllen von der Beklagten beschäftigten Personen gekommen sei. Für deren Verschulden müsse sie gemäß § 278 BGB im Verhältnis zu dem Käufer des Impfstoffes, dem Tierarzt, einstehen. Dieser aber sei berechtigt gewesen, den bei der Klägerin eingetretenen Schaden ersetzt zu verlangen. Da er seinen Ersatzanspruch an die Klägerin abgetreten habe, sei der Klageanspruch dem Grunde nach gerechtfertigt.

I Die Grundsätze über die *Drittschadensliquidation* können im vorliegenden Falle nicht angewendet werden.

When Dr H vaccinated chickens a few days afterwards on 22 November 1963, at farmer R's, premises fowl pest broke out there as well. The same occurred at the end of November 1963 at three poultry breeders in Württemberg, who had also had their chickens vaccinated with the defendant's vaccine from the batch ALD 210. When the Veterinary Investigation Office at Stuttgart thereupon had several bottles of this batch investigated by the Federal Research Institute for Viral Diseases of Animals in Tübingen, in some bottles bacterial contamination and still active and ND (Newcastle Disease) viruses were identified, which had not been rendered sufficiently immune. The Paul Ehrlich Institute also established that some of the bottles, sent to it for examination, were non-sterile and ND-virus could be traced in them. The defendant has disputed that the outbreak of fowl pest can be traced back to the application of their vaccine. In any case, the lack of sterility of the bottle could not have been the cause. In this connection it referred to the opinion supplied by it of Professor Dr E of the Federal Research Institute for Viral Diseases. It has offered exculpatory proof in respect of its vicarious liability for the employees and manageress of its virus department.

The State Court and the Upper State Court have stated the claim to be justified in principle. The appeal in law of the defendant was unsuccessful.

Reasons:

The appeal court proceeded on the basis that the vaccine contained in the bottles delivered to Dr H was contaminated by bacteria and considered it to be proved that the outbreak of fowl pest was to be traced back to this. Even the assessor, Professor Dr E, brought in by the defendant, cannot exclude the possibility that the contamination occurred through negligence of the persons employed by the defendant in the filling process. It must be liable for their fault, in accordance with § 278 of the BGB, in the relationship with the purchaser of the vaccine, the veterinary surgeon. He, however, was entitled to ask for compensation for the harm which occurred to the plaintiff. As he has made his claim to compensation to the plaintiff, the claim in the action is justified in principle.

I The principles as to *claims for harm to a third party* cannot be applied in the present case.

1 Grundsätzlich kann auf Grund eines Vertrages nur der den Ersatz eines Schadens verlangen, bei dem der Schaden tatsächlich eingetreten ist und dem er rechtlich zur Last fällt. Tritt der Schaden bei einem Dritten ein, so haftet ihm der Schädiger - von besonderen Ausnahmen abgesehen (vgl. § 618 Abs. 3 mit §§ 844, 845 BGB) – nur nach Deliktsrecht. Diese Unterscheidung zwischen begünstigter Vertragshaftung und begrenzter Deliktshaftung gehört zum System des geltenden Haftungsrechts und ist nicht nur ein theoretisches Dogma. Nur in besonderen Fällen hat die Rechtsprechung Ausnahmen zugelassen, nämlich dann, wenn das Durch den Vertrag geschützte Interesse infolge besonderer Rechtsbeziehungen zwischen dem aus dem Vertrag berechtigten Gläubiger und dem Träger des Interesses dergestalt auf den Dritten 'verlagert' ist, daß der Schaden rechtlich ihn und nicht den Gläubiger trifft. Daraus darf der Schädiger keinen Vorteil zum Nachteil des Dritten ziehen: er muß dem Gläubiger den Drittschaden ersetzen. Das gilt – von den seltenen Fällen einer 'Gefahrentlastung' abgesehen (BGHZ 40, 91, 100) – dann, wenn der Gläubiger für Rechnung des Dritten kontrahiert hatte (BGHZ 25, 250, 258) oder wenn die Sache, deren Obhut der Schuldner versprochen hatte, nicht dem Gläubiger, sondern dem Dritten gehörte (BGHZ 15, 224).

(a) Ein solcher Ausnahmefall liegt hier nicht vor. Eine 'Interessenverknüpfung' kraft mittelbarer Stellvertretung kommt nicht in Betracht. Dr. H. hatte den Impfstoff nicht im Auftrage und nicht für Rechnung der Klägerin gekauft. Als er ihn bei der Beklagten bestellte und bezog, wußte er noch nicht, bei welchem Landwirt er ihn anwenden werde. In aller Regel wird ein Tierarzt – wie durchweg ein Werkunternehmer sein Material – seine Medikamente selbst dann nicht im Auftrag und für Rechnung eines Patienten oder Auftraggebers kaufen, wenn er sie zur Ausführung eines ihm schon erteilten Behandlungsauftrages benötigt. Der dem Urteil des Reichsgerichts DR 1941, 637 = HRR 1941, 225 zugrunde liegende Sachverhalt lag entscheidend anders.

Hier geht es auch nicht um einen der Fälle, in denen die dem Schuldner in Obhut gegebene Sache nicht dem Vertragsgegner, sondern einem Dritten gehört. Zwar mag Dr. H. eine 'Obhutspflicht' bezüglich der Hühner der Klägerin obgelegen haben. Drittschadensliquidation setzt aber voraus, daß die Obhutspflicht zwischen Gläubiger und Schuldner bestanden hat (BGHZ 40, 101). Das war hier nicht der Fall.

1 In principle, on the basis of a contract, compensation can only be demanded for harm by the person to whom the harm has actually occurred and who is legally burdened by it. If the harm occurs to a third party, the person causing the harm is only liable to him, apart from special exceptions (compare § 618 para 3 with §§ 844 and 845 of the BGB), under the law of tort. This difference between favourable contractual liability and limited tortious liability is part of the system of the effective law of liability and is not only a theoretical doctrine. Case law has only permitted exceptions in special cases, namely when the interest protected by the contract is, in consequence of special legal relationships between the obligee under the contract and the holder of the interest, 'shifted' to a third party in such a manner that the harm legally affects him and not the obligee. The person causing the harm cannot take any advantage from this to the disadvantage of the third party: he must compensate the obligee for the harm to the third party. That applies, apart from the rare cases of 'relief from risks' (BGHZ 40, 91, 100), if the obligee had contracted for the account of a third party (BGHZ 25, 250, 258) or the thing which the obligor promised to protect does not belong to the obligee but to the third party (BGHZ 15, 224).

(a) Such an exceptional case is not present here. A 'connection of interests' by virtue of indirect representation does not come into consideration. Dr H had not bought the vaccine by order of, or on account of, the plaintiff. When he ordered and received it from the defendant, he did not yet know for which farmer he would use it. As a rule a veterinary surgeon – as with an undertaker of work in respect of his material – will buy his medicines himself and not by order of and on account of a patient or customer if he needs them for the carrying out of an order for treatment which has already been given to him. The circumstances which formed the basis of the judgment of the Reich High Court (DRiZ 1941, 637 = HRR 1941, 225) were decidedly different.

It is also here not a question of one of the cases in which the thing which is given to the obligor to protect does not belong to the other contracting party but to a third party. Certainly a 'duty to protect' in relation to the plaintiff's chickens may have fallen on Dr H But claiming for harm to a third party presupposes that the duty to protect existed between obligee and obligor (BGHZ 40, 101). That was not the case here.

(b) Von diesen Grundsätzen geht an sich auch das Berufungsgericht aus. Es ist sich auch dessen bewußt, daß grundsätzlich der Hersteller und Lieferant einer Ware, die sein Käufer an einen Dritten weiterverkauft hat, nicht schon auf Grund des Kaufvertrages für Schäden einzustehen braucht, die einem Dritten entstanden sind (BGHZ 40, 104, 105). Dennoch glaubt es, im vorliegenden Fall die Liquidierung des Drittschadens zulassen zu können. Hier habe die einwandfreie Beschaffenheit des Impfstoffes entscheidend im Interesse der Klägerin, an deren Hühnern er angewendet wurde, gelegen. Der Tierarzt habe die Beschaffenheit des Impfstoffes nicht überprüfen können, sondern sich auf sorgfältige Herstellung durch die Beklagte verlassen müssen. Diese habe daher davon ausgehen müssen, daß ihre Pflicht zu einwandfreier Lieferung nicht nur gegenüber dem Tierarzt, sondern gegenüber den jeweiligen Hühnerhaltern bestanden habe.

(c) Diese Erwägungen reichen nicht aus, um einen Fall zulässiger Drittschadensliquidation anzunehmen. Der Bundesgerichtshof hat bereits in seinem Urteil BGHZ 40, 99ff. betont, daß dem durch Mängel der Kaufsache geschädigten Dritten nicht schon durch eine auf Treu und Glauben gestützte Auslegung des Kaufvertrages ein aus diesem Vertrag abgeleiteter Ersatzanspruch gewährt werden kann. Er ist in dieser Entscheidung von dem Urteil des Reichsgerichts RGZ 170, 246 abgerückt. Auch das Berufungsgericht hat keine konkreten Anhaltspunkte dafür festgestellt, weshalb die Beklagte bereit und willens gewesen sein sollte, ihrem Vertragsgegner, dem Tierarzt, weitergehende Schadensersatzansprüche einzuräumen, als sie nach dem gesetzlichen Kaufrecht mußte. Zudem setzt Drittschadensliquidation voraus, daß nur ein Schaden entstanden ist, der sich, wäre nicht 'zufällig' ein Dritter Träger des geschützten Rechtsgutes, bei dem Gläubiger ausgewirkt hätte. Von einer solchen 'Verlagerung' des Schadens kann hier nicht gesprochen werden. Dieser ist hier sowohl tatsächlich wie rechtlich bei der Klägerin eingetreten, während er bei einer echten Schadensverlagerung tatsächlich, wenn auch nicht rechtlich, beim Gläubiger eintritt. Er konnte nicht ebensogut beim Tierarzt wie bei den Hühnerhaltern eintreten, sondern nur bei diesen und nicht, worauf es entscheidend ankommt, statt beim Tierarzt bei ihnen.

Die bisher von der Rechtsprechung zugelassenen Fälle einer Drittschadensliquidation lassen sich auch nicht um einen Fall der hier vorliegenden Art erweitern. Andernfalls müßte auch der Hersteller und Lieferant von Lebens- und Genußmitteln, von Wasch- und Arzneimitteln usw. den beim Endverbraucher entstehenden Schaden nicht bloß aus Delikt, sondern aus Kaufrecht ersetzen. Denn auch er weiß, so wie sein Käufer, der Groß- oder Zwischen- und Einzelhändler, daß sich etwaige Schäden nicht beim Händler, sondern erst beim Endabnehmer zeigen werden. Daraus allein läßt sich aber noch nicht eine vertragliche Haftung des Herstellers gegenüber dem Endabnehmer ableiten. Die Frage, wie dessen Interessen gewahrt werden können, ist somit nicht mittels Drittschadensliquidation zu lösen (so auch Soergel/Ballerstedt, BGB, 10. Aufl. Bem. 43 vor § 459; Esser, *Schuldrecht* Bd. I, 3. Aufl., S. 297; von Caemmerer, ZHR 1965, 269, 277).

(b) The appeal court also proceeded from these principles. It was also aware of the fact that in principle the manufacturer and supplier of a commodity which its purchaser has sold on to a third party does not need, simply on the basis of the purchase contract, to be responsible for harm which arises to a third party (BGHZ 40, 104, 105). It believed however that it was able to permit the claim for harm to a third party in the present case. Here, the faultless condition of the vaccine would have been decidedly in the interests of the plaintiff, on whose chickens it was used. The veterinary surgeon would not have been able to examine the condition of the vaccine but would have had to rely on careful manufacture by the defendant. The defendant would therefore have had to proceed on the basis that its duty to make a faultless supply existed not only as against the veterinary surgeon but also as against the actual keepers of chickens.

(c) These considerations do not suffice to accept a case of permissible claim for harm to a third party. The Federal Supreme Court has already emphasised in its judgment BGHZ 40, 99 and onwards that a third party harmed due to defects in the thing sold cannot be granted, by an interpretation of the purchase contract supported by the principle of good faith, a claim to compensation derived from this contract. It has in this decision, moved away from the judgment of the Reich High Court RGZ 170, 246. The appeal court also did not establish a concrete basis for why the defendant should have been ready and willing to grant to the other contracting party, the veterinary surgeon, more extensive claims for compensation for damage than it had to according to the statutory rights on purchase. Moreover, claiming of harm to a third party presupposes that only one harm has arisen which would have taken effect against the obligee, had there not been 'coincidentally' a third party who was the holder of the protected subject matter of a right. One cannot speak here of such a 'shifting' of the harm. This has occurred here actually as well as legally to the plaintiff, whilst for a true shifting of harm it occurs actually, if not also legally, to the obligee. It could not occur just as much to the veterinary surgeon as to the keepers of chickens but only to these latter and not, which is the decisive question, to them instead of to the veterinary surgeon.

The cases of claims for harm to a third party permitted so far by case law do not allow themselves to be widened to a case of the kind present here. Otherwise the manufacturer and supplier of food and luxuries, of detergents and medicines etc. would have to compensate for the damage arising to the final consumer not merely in tort but in the law of purchase. For he also knows, as well as his purchaser, the wholesaler, middleman and retailer that possible harm shows itself for the first time, not to the dealer, but to the final recipient. But contractual liability of the manufacturer to the final recipient cannot be derived from this alone. The question of how the interests of this person can be preserved is therefore not to be resolved by means of a claim for harm to a third party (as also in Soergel/Ballerstedt, BGB, 10th edn, note 43 before § 459: Esser; *Law of Obligations Vol I*, 3rd edn, p 297; von Caemmerer, ZHR 1965, 269, 277).

2 Das Berufungsgericht hat seine Ansicht auch damit begründet, hier ergebe sich aus Sinn und Zweck des Vertrages eine Fürsorgepflicht des Herstellers zugunsten des Dritten. Dies könnte dahin verstanden werden, als wolle das Berufungsgericht der Klägerin einen Ersatzanspruch aus einem *Vertrag mit Schutzwirkung zugunsten Dritter* zubilligen. Auch dem könnte nicht gefolgt werden.

(a) Der Bundesgerichtshof hat zwar unter diesem rechtlichen Gesichtspunkt unter bestimmten Umständen auch einem am Vertrag nicht beteiligten Dritten Ersatzansprüche zugebilligt (BGHZ 33, 247, 249 und 49, 350, 351 mit Nachweisen). Diese Grundsätze können hier jedoch nicht herangezogen werden.

Keineswegs kann schon jeder, der infolge einer Sorgfaltsverletzung des Schuldners Schaden erlitten hat, einen eigenen Ersatzanspruch aus dem Vertrag zwischen Gläubiger und Schuldner ableiten (Senatsurteil vom 30. April 1968 - VI ZR 29/67 -, NJW 1968, 1323). Der Senat hat in seinem Urteil vom 18. Juni 1968 (VI ZR 120/67, NJW 1968, 1929) erneut darauf hingewiesen, daß das Gesetz zwischen unmittelbar und mittelbar Geschädigten unterscheidet und daß die Haftung aus einem Vertrag grundsätzlich an das Band geknüpft ist, das den Schuldner mit seinem Partner verbindet (vgl. auch BGH Urt. v. 9. Oktober 1968 -VIII ZR 173/66 -, WM 1968, 1354). Andernfalls besteht die Gefahr, daß der Schuldner das Risiko, das er bei Abschluß eines Vertrages eingeht, nicht mehr einkalkulieren kann. Daher wäre es nicht mehr mit den Grundsätzen von Treu und Glauben, aus denen der Vertrag mit Schutzwirkung zugunsten Dritter gerade entwickelt worden ist, zu vereinbaren, wenn der Schuldner für so weitgehende Folgen seiner Vertragsverletzung haften müßte. Das kann nur dann angenommen werden, wenn der Gläubiger sozusagen für das Wohl und Wehe des Dritten mitverantwortlich ist, weil dessen Schädigung auch ihn trifft, indem er ihm gegenüber zu Schutz und Fürsorge verpflichtet ist. Dieses Innenverhältnis zwischen dem Gläubiger und einem Dritten, durchweg gekennzeichnet durch einen personenrechtlichen Einschlag, führt zur Schutzwirkung zugunsten des Dritten, nicht das Verhältnis zwischen dem Gläubiger und seinem Vertragspartner. Ein solches Verhältnis liegt bei einem Kauf- oder einem Werkvertrag in aller Regel nicht vor (vgl. Larenz, *Schuldrecht*, 9. Aufl., II § 37 IV).

(b) Auch im vorliegenden Fall fehlt es an solchen engen Beziehungen zwischen dem Gläubiger (Tierarzt) und seinen Auftraggebern. (Wird ausgeführt.)

2 The appeal court has also based its view on the idea that here, from the sense and purpose of the contract, a duty of care by the manufacturer arises in favour of the third party. This could be understood as meaning that the appeal court wanted to grant to the plaintiff a claim to compensation from a *contract with protective effect in favour of a third party*. This can also not be followed.

(a) The Federal Supreme Court has certainly, from this legal point of view, in certain circumstances granted claims to compensation to a third party not participating in the contract (BGHZ 33, 247, 249 and 49, 350, 351 with references). These principles cannot, however, be brought into play here.

In no way is it possible for anyone who has suffered harm in consequence of a lack of care by the obligor to derive his own claim to compensation from the contract between the obligee and the obligor (judgment of the Senate of 30 April 1968 - VI ZR 29/67 -, NJW 1968, 1323). The Senate in its judgment of 18 June 1968 (VI ZR 120/67, NJW 1968, 1929) referred again to the fact that statute differentiates between those who are directly and indirectly harmed and that liability under a contract is in principle connected to the bond which binds the obligor to his partner (compare also BGH judgment of 9 October 1968 - VIII ZR 173/66 -, WM 1968, 1354). Otherwise the danger exists that the obligor will not be able any longer to calculate the risk which he incurs on conclusion of a contract. It would therefore no longer be compatible with the principles of good faith, from which the contract with protective effect in favour of a third party has been developed if the obligor had to be liable for such extensive consequences of his violation of the contract. That can only be accepted if the obligee, so to speak, shares responsibility for the weal and woe of the third party, because harm to this party affects him as well in that he is under a duty of protection and care to him. This inner relationship between the obligee and a third party, usually characterised by the imprint of the personal rights, leads to protective effect in favour of the third party, not the relationship between the obligee and his contractual partner. Such a relationship is not present in a purchase or work contract as a rule (compare Larenz, *Law of Obligations*, 9th edn, II § 37 IV).

(b) In the present case there are also no such close relationships between the obligee (veterinary surgeon) and his customers. (This is amplified.)

II Wird somit das angefochtene Urteil von der ihm gegebenen Begründung nicht getragen, so war zu prüfen, ob es sich mit anderer Begründung aufrechterhalten läßt. Die Klägerin hat ihre Klage nicht nur auf Ansprüche gestützt, die sie aus dem von Dr. H. mit der Beklagten geschlossenen Kaufvertrag ableiten wollte, sondern sich auch auf die §§ 823ff. BGB berufen. Außerdem hat sie die in letzter Zeit, vor allem auf dem Deutschen Juristentag 1968 (vgl. JZ 1968, 714), eingehend erörterte Frage der unmittelbaren Haftung des Warenherstellers gegenüber dem Endverbraucher (*Produzentenhaftung*) ins Feld geführt (vgl. Karlsruher Forum 1963, Beiheft zum VersR: *Haftung des Warenherstellers*; Simitis, *Grundfragen der Produzentenhaftung*, 1965, und sein Gutachten zum Deutschen Juristentag 1968; vgl. auch die Nachweise bei Weitnauer, NJW 1968, 1593).

1 Auch die Befürworter einer weitergehenden Haftung des Produzenten gehen durchweg davon aus, daß sie sich weder mittels Drittschadensliquidation noch mittels eines Vertrages mit Schutzwirkung zugunsten Dritter begründen lasse. Sie wollen dem Verbraucher einen eigenen, nicht vom Vertrag Käufer-Hersteller abhängigen Ersatzanspruch gewähren, der sich als 'action directe' unmittelbar gegen den Hersteller richten soll – so wie der vom Gesetz gewährte Ersatzanspruch aus §§ 823ff. BGB. Indes sehen sie diesen Deliktsanspruch nicht mehr als ausreichend und sachgerecht an, weil er in der Regel reine Vermögensschäden nicht deckt, und vor allem, weil er dem Produzenten, insbesondere bei bloßen 'Fabrikationsfehlern', die Möglichkeit offenläßt, sich zu entlasten (§ 831 BGB).

Der hier zu entscheidende Fall gibt keinen Anlaß zur Prüfung der Frage, ob an der Rechtsprechung festzuhalten ist, daß sich der Produzent bei Fabrikationsfehlern auf § 831 BGB berufen kann (dagegen – im Anschluß an Simitis, *Grundfragen* S. 72, und Gutachten S. 51 – der Deutsche Juristentag 1968; siehe aber auch Rehbinder, ZHR 1967, 179/180; Weitnauer, AcP 1967, 290; NJW 1968, 1598; Canaris, JZ 1968, 497) und daß bei solchen Fehlern nicht *prima facie* von einem Verschulden des Herstellers ausgegangen werden könne (Senatsurteil vom 21. April 1956 - VI ZR 36/55 -, VersR 1956, 410). Denn hier steht nicht fest, daß der Impfstoff deshalb reaktivierte Viren enthielt, weil eine Hilfskraft der Beklagten einen Fehler begangen hat. Vielmehr kann das auch auf Ursachen beruhen, die im Herstellungs-, insbesondere im Abfüllverfahren der Beklagten liegen. Der vorliegende Fall nötigt auch nicht dazu, zur Problematik der Produzentenhaftung in vollem Umfang Stellung zu nehmen. Hier kommt es nur auf das Folgende an.

II If, therefore, the judgment which is challenged is not supported by the reasoning given for it, it has to be examined whether it can be supported with other reasoning. The plaintiff has supported her action not only by claims which she sought to derive from the purchase contract concluded by Dr H with the defendant, but she has also referred to §§ 823 and onwards of the BGB. Besides this she has brought in the question exhaustively discussed in recent times, principally in the German Lawyers Conference 1968 (compare JZ 1968, 714), of the direct liability of the manufacturer of goods to the final consumer (*manufacturers' liability*) (compare Karlsruhe Forum 1963, Supplement to VersR: *Liability of the Manufacturer of Goods*; Simitis, *Basic Questions of the Liability of Manufacturers*, 1965 and his opinion at the German Lawyers Conference, 1968; compare also the references in Weitnauer, NJW 1968, 1593).

1 Even the supporters of an extensive liability for manufacturers usually proceed on the basis that it is established neither by means of a claim for harm to a third party nor by means of a contract with protective effect in favour of a third party. They want to grant to the consumer his own claim to compensation, not dependent on the contract between the purchaser and the manufacturer, which is to be brought as a 'direct action' directly against the manufacturer, like the claim to compensation granted by statute in §§ 823 and onwards of the BGB. However, they regard this claim in tort as no longer being sufficient and proper because, as a rule, it does not cover pure economic harm and principally because it leaves open to the manufacturer, especially in relation to mere 'manufacturing errors' the possibility of exculpating itself (§ 831 of the BGB).

The cause to be decided here gives no occasion for examining the question of whether the case law that the manufacturer can refer to in § 831 of the BGB in relation to manufacturing errors is to be adhered to (for a contrary view, following Simitis, *Basic Questions*, p 72 and *Opinion*, p 51, the German Lawyers Conference; but see also Rehbinder ZHR 1967, 179/180; Weitnauer AcP 1967, 290; NJW 1968, 1598; Canaris JZ 1968, 497) and that one could, not in the case of such errors, proceed *prima facie* from fault on the part of the manufacturer (judgment of the Senate of 21 April 1956 - VI ZR 36/55 -, VersR 1956, 410). For it has not been established here that the vaccine contained reactivated viruses because an assistant of the defendant made a mistake. Rather could it be founded on causes which are present in the manufacturing process, in particular the infusion process, of the defendant. The present case does not require the taking of a view on the problem of product liability in its full extent. Here, the question is only as follows.

(a) Der Klageanspruch würde ohne weiteres zuzusprechen sein, wenn der von Diederichsen (*Die Haftung des Warenherstellers*, 1967) vertretenen Ansicht gefolgt werden könnte, daß der Hersteller für jede Art von Fehlern des Produkts ohne Rücksicht auf Verschulden, also wie bei einer Gefährdungs- oder gar Erfolgshaftung ('strict liability'), einstehen müsse. Diederichsen glaubt, dies aus 'rechtssoziologischen und rechtstheoretischen Überlegungen' dem geltenden Recht entnehmen zu können. Es kann jedoch schon zweifelhaft sein, ob sein Standpunkt rechtspolitisch zu befürworten wäre. Jedenfalls läßt sich eine Haftung ohne Verschulden mit den Grundsätzen des geltenden Haftungsrechts nicht vereinbaren. Die in einzelnen Gesetzen angeordnete Gefährdungshaftung – meist zudem bis zu unterschiedlichen Höchstgrenzen – auch auf die Produzentenhaftung auszudehnen, ist dem Richter verwehrt. Vielmehr muß der Gesetzgeber entscheiden, ob und inwieweit dem Hersteller eine stärker objektivierte Haftung aufzuerlegen ist (vgl. *die Begründung des Referentenentwurfs eines Gesetzes über Änderung und Ergänzung schadensersatzrechtlicher Vorschriften*, 1967, S. 102).

(b) Ebensowenig ist es – von besonders gelagerten Fällen abgesehen (vgl. Lukes, JuS 1968, 347) – rechtlich möglich, dem Endabnehmer dadurch einen direkten Ersatzanspruch zu gewähren, daß ein zwischen ihm und dem Produzenten unmittelbar, wenn auch stillschweigend, abgeschlossener Garantievertrag angenommen wird (so Müller, AcP 1965, 311). Darin, daß der Produzent seine Ware unter Benennung seiner Urheberschaft, nämlich mit seinem Etikett, in Originalverpackungen, unter seinem Warenzeichen oder der von ihm geprägten Bezeichnung (Markenwaren) usw. vertreiben läßt, liegt im allgemeinen noch keine Willenserklärung in dem Sinne, daß er dem Verbraucher für sorgfältige Herstellung einstehen wolle (vgl. RGZ 87, 1; Schlegelberger/Hefermehl, HGB, 4. Aufl. Bem. 51 vor § 373; Simitis, Gutachten zum DJT 1968 S. 24 mit weiteren Nachweisen). In aller Regel läßt sich sogar in der Werbung für Markenwaren, die den Endabnehmer in besonders eindringlicher Weise anspricht, noch keine Zusage finden, für etwaige Mängel der Ware haften zu wollen (BGHZ 48, 118, 122/123). Das kann auch dann nicht angenommen werden, wenn es um die, zudem erheblich weitergehende Frage geht, ob der Hersteller auch einem Endabnehmer seines Produkts direkt haften wolle (vgl. Rehbinder, ZHR 1967, 173; Weitnauer, NJW 1968, 1597).

(a) The claim would only succeed, without more, if the view advocated by Diederichsen (*The Liability of Manufacturers of Goods*, 1967) could be followed, that the manufacturer must be responsible for every kind of defect of the product without regard to fault and therefore as with risk liability or even result liability ('strict liability'). Diederichsen believes this can be concluded from present law out of socio-legal and legal theory considerations. It can however be doubted whether his point of view is to be advocated on grounds of legal politics. In any case, liability without fault is not reconcilable with the principles of current liability law. The judge is prevented from extending the risk liability prescribed in individual statutory provisions – most, moreover, to different limits – to manufacturers liability as well. Rather must the legislator decide whether and how far a stronger objective liability is to be imposed on the manufacturer (compare the *Reasoning of the Experts' Draft of a Statute regarding the Alteration and Supplementing of Legal Provisions for Compensation for Damage*, 1967, p 102).

(b) It is not possible either from a legal point of view, apart from exceptional cases (compare Lukes JuS 1968, 347), to grant the ultimate purchaser a direct claim to compensation by accepting a directly, even though tacitly, concluded guarantee contract between him and the manufacturer (as in Miller AcP 1965, 311). In general, no declaration of will to the effect that the manufacturer will be responsible for careful production is contained in the fact that he permits his goods to be sold under the designation of his authorship, that is with his label in original packaging, under his trade mark or a mark imprinted by him (proprietary goods) etc (compare RGZ 87, 1; Schlegelberger/Hefermehl HGB, 4th edn, note 51 before § 373; Simitis, opinion on DJT 1968, p 24 with further references). As a rule, even in the advertising of proprietary goods, which is addressed to the ultimate purchaser in an especially forcible way, no promise to be liable for possible defects in the goods is found (BGHZ 48, 118, 122/123). That cannot be accepted either where the considerably more extensive question of whether a manufacturer is willing to be liable to an ultimate purchaser of his product is concerned (compare Rehbinder ZHR 1967, 173; Weitnauer NJW, 1968, 1597).

(c) Außer Frage steht auch, daß dem Endabnehmer ein Ersatzanspruch nicht schon aus Verletzung der aus 'sozialem Kontakt' angeblich folgenden Schutzpflichten gewährt werden kann (vgl. Lorenz in der *Festschrift für Nattorp*, 1961, S. 83; Soergel/Schmidt aaO Bem. 5 vor § 275). Zwischen Hersteller und Abnehmer bestehen keine geschäftlichen Beziehungen; sie sollen auch nicht angebahnt und demnächst abgeschlossen werden. Die soziologisch gewiß vorhandenen Beziehungen haben rechtlich nicht das Gewicht, daß aus ihnen Haftungsansprüche kraft rechtlicher Sonderbeziehungen folgten. Das gilt auch für den Versuch von Weimar, die Haftung des Produzenten aus der Generalklausel des § 242 BGB abzuleiten (Untersuchungen zum Problem der Produktenhaftung, *Basler Studien zur Rechtswissenschaft* Heft 79 S. 69ff., und DRiZ 1968, 266).

2 Besondere Überlegung verdient der Gedanke, eine auf dem Gesetz beruhende, aus dem Vertrauensgedanken entwickelte quasikontraktliche Sonderrechtsbeziehung zwischen Hersteller und Verbraucher anzuerkennen. In der Tat dürften die Beziehungen, die zwischen dem Käufer eines schadenstiftenden Produktes und dessen Hersteller vor Eintritt des Schadens bestanden haben, von engerer Art sein als die, die den Hersteller mit 'jedermann' dann – und erst dann – in Verbindung bringen, wenn dieser durch sein Produkt zu Schaden kommt. Diesen 'Jedermann' auf deliktische Ansprüche zu verweisen, ist gerecht. Hinsichtlich der Ersatzansprüche eines Käufers dagegen könnte erwogen werden, sie auch dann aus Vertragsrecht abzuleiten, wenn er die Ware nicht beim Hersteller direkt, sondern über einen Händler gekauft hat.

(a) Von derartigen Sonderrechtsbeziehungen zwischen Hersteller und Abnehmer der Ware ausgehend hatte zunächst Lorenz (auf dem Karlsruher Forum 1963) die Ansicht vertreten, der Hersteller müsse für das Vertrauen, das er mit einem Produkt, verstärkt durch die Werbung, beim Verbraucher erweckt habe, entsprechend § 122 BGB einstehen. Diesen Gedanken hat der VIII. Zivilsenat des Bundesgerichtshofs am Schluß seines Urteils vom 13. Juli 1963 (BGHZ 40, 91, 108) erwähnt. Er hat damit aber keine Stellung nehmen wollen. In seinem Urteil BGHZ 48, 118 hat er es abgelehnt, der Werbung haftungsbegründende Kraft zuzulegen. Daß sie im Ringen um den 'König Kunde' immer umfangreicher und, betriebswirtschaftlich gesehen, immer bedeutungsvoller geworden ist, besagt noch nicht, daß ihr rechtlich die Bedeutung einer Haftungszusage zukäme. So versteht sie ein verständiger Verbraucher auch nicht. Lorenz hat denn auch seinen Gedanken – den vor allem Markert (BB 1964, 319ff.) und Rehbinder (ZHR 1967, 180ff.) aufgenommen hatten – nicht weiterverfolgt (s. Kieler Tagung für Rechtsvergleichung 1965, Heft 28 der Schriftenreihe für Rechtsvergleichung S. 51/52).

(c) It is also beyond doubt that the ultimate purchaser cannot be granted a claim to compensation arising from violation of the duties of protection allegedly following from 'social contact' (compare Lorenz in the *Commemorative Publication for Nattorp*, 1961, p 83; Soergel/Schmidt, *loc cit*, note 5 before § 275). Between manufacturer and purchaser there are no business relationships; neither are they about to be opened and soon concluded. The sociological relationships which are certainly present do not have such legal weight that liability claims by virtue of special relationships in law should follow from them. That also applies to the attempt of Weimar to derive liability of manufacturers from the general clause in § 242 of the BGB (Investigations of the Problem of liability of manufacturers, *Basle Studies in Jurisprudence*, Vol 79 p 69 and onwards and DRiZ 1968, 266).

2 The idea of recognising a special quasi-contractual legal relationship between manufacturer and consumer, based on statute and developed from the concept of trust, deserves special consideration. In fact the relationships, which have existed between the purchaser of a product causing harm and its manufacturer before the harm occurred, ought to be of a closer kind than those which bring the manufacturer into a relation with 'everyone' when, and only when, this person comes to harm through his product. To refer this 'everyone' to tortious claims is correct. In relation to a purchaser's claims to compensation, it could be borne in mind on the other hand that they could also be derived from contract law if he has not bought the product from a manufacturer direct, but had bought it via a dealer.

(a) Proceeding from those kinds of special relationships in law between manufacturer and purchaser of the product, Lorenz (at the Karlsruhe Forum in 1963) first defended the view that the manufacturer must be responsible in accordance with § 122 of the BGB for the trust which he has induced in the consumer by the product and which has been strengthened by the advertising. This concept was mentioned by the VIIIth Civil Senate of the Federal Supreme Court at the end of its judgment of 13 July 1963 (BGHZ 40, 91, 108). But it did not intend thereby to take up a definite stance. In its judgment BGHZ 48, 118 declined to attribute to advertising the power of founding liability. The fact that in struggling for the 'King Customer' advertising has become continually more comprehensive and, looked at from a business point of view, continually more important, does not signify that the meaning of an acceptance of liability should legally belong to it. An intelligent consumer does not understand it in this way either. Lorenz also did not further pursue his concept – which had been taken up principally by Markert (BB 1964, 319 and onwards) and Rehbinder (ZHR 1967, 180 and onwards) (see Kiel Conference for Comparative Law, 1965, Volume 28 of the series of writings on Comparative Law, pp 51/52).

(b) Auf dem Grundgedanken von Lorenz bauen die Lösungsversuche auf, die Haftung des Herstellers aus einem Einstehen für in Anspruch genommenes und vom Verbraucher gewährtes Vertrauen, entsprechend den für *culpa in contrahendo* entwickelten Rechtssätzen, abzuleiten (vgl. Rehbinder, BB 1965, 439 und ZHR 1967, 176; Steffen, JR 1968, 287, und vor allem Canaris, JZ 1968, 494).

Es ist indes zweifelhaft, ob diese Überlegungen tragfähig sein könnten, im Wege einer Fortbildung des Rechts dem Verbraucher einen Ersatzanspruch zu gewähren, der, so wie der deliktische Anspruch, nicht ohne weiteres abbedungen werden könnte, andererseits nicht vom Entlastungsbeweis des § 831 BGB bedroht wäre. Der Senat hat sich schon in seinem Urteil vom. 21. März 1967 (VI ZR 164/65, LM BGB § 276 [Ha] Nr. 4) gegen die Versuche gewandt, die Haftung eines außerhalb des Vertrages stehenden Dritten aus in Anspruch genommenem Vertrauen zu begründen, und betont, daß damit die durch den Vertrag gezogene Abgrenzung zwischen schuldrechtlichem und deliktischem Haftungsbereich in folgenschwerer Weise durchbrochen würde. Ob die dort gegen eine Haftungsausdehnung bei positiver Vertragsverletzung ausgesprochenen Bedenken auch gegen die Einbeziehung des Produzenten in eine vertragsähnliche Haftung sprechen, braucht im vorliegenden Fall nicht abschließend entschieden zu werden. Auch braucht der Frage nicht nachgegangen zu werden, wie einem durch das Produkt Geschädigten ein solcher quasikontraktlicher Anspruch zugesprochen werden soll, wenn er das Produkt nicht gekauft hatte, sondern bei dessen Benutzung durch ihn selbst oder durch andere zu Schaden gekommen war. Im vorliegend zu entscheidenden Fall handelt es sich nicht um hintereinander geschaltete, rechtlich selbständige Kaufverträge in einer 'Absatzkette', bei der der Verkäufer in der Tat oft der bloße 'Verteiler' des Herstellers geworden ist, ein 'Durchgriff' daher naheliegt. Hier stand vielmehr zwischen der Klägerin und der Beklagten ein Tierarzt, der allein zu entscheiden hatte, welchen Impfstoff er benutzte. Ihm und nicht einer etwaigen Werbung der Beklagten hatte die Klägerin ihr Vertrauen gewährt. Sie wäre nicht imstande gewesen, selbst den Impfstoff bei der Beklagten unmittelbar oder im Handel zu kaufen: die Beklagte durfte ihn nur an den Tierarzt abgeben und nur dieser durfte ihn anwenden (§ 87 der Ausführungsvorschriften zum Viehseuchengesetz idF v. 1. März 1958, BAnz Nr. 45 v. 6. März 1958 = BGB1 III 7831-1-1). Schon deshalb scheidet hier der Gedanke aus, zwischen den Parteien hätten vertragsähnliche Beziehungen bestanden. Die Klägerin war nicht 'Verbraucherin' des Impfstoffes, auch nicht dessen 'Benutzerin', sondern, rechtlich gesehen, 'nur' die Geschädigte. Als solche ist sie aber auf deliktische Ersatzansprüche beschränkt.

(b) On Lorenz's basic concept are built the attempted explanations which derive liability of the manufacturer from his being responsible for the trust which has been claimed from and granted by the consumer corresponding to the legal rules developed for *culpa in contrahendo* (compare Rehbinder, BB 1965, 439 and ZHR 1967, 176; Steffen, JR 1968, 287, and principally Canaris, JZ, 1968, 494).

It is nevertheless doubtful whether these considerations could be capable of granting the consumer a claim to compensation by way of further development of the law, which claim, like the tortious claim, could not be automatically excluded, but on the other hand would not be threatened by the exculpatory proof of § 831 of the BGB. The Senate has already, in its judgment of 21 March 1967 (VI ZR 164/65, LM BGB § 276 [Ha] no 4) turned against attempts to base liability of a third party standing outside the contract on trust which has been claimed and emphasises that the demarcation drawn by the contract between the areas of liability under the law of obligations and under the law of tort would be broken down in a manner which would have grave consequences. Whether the doubts expressed there about an extension of liability in respect of positive breach of contract also militate against the inclusion of the manufacturer in a liability similar to that in contract does not need to be finally decided in the present case. Nor is it necessary to investigate the question of how a person suffering harm from the product is to be granted such a quasi-contractual claim if he had not bought the product, but had come to harm through the use of it by himself or by others. In the case to be decided here, it is not a question of purchase contracts connected one after the other but legally independent, in a 'sale chain' in which the seller has in fact often become the mere 'distributor' of the manufacturer, where therefore a 'robust approach' suggests itself. Here, between the plaintiff and the defendant there was a veterinary surgeon who alone had to decide which vaccine he would use. The plaintiff had put her trust in him and not in some possible advertisement of the defendant. She would not have been in a position to buy the vaccine from the defendant herself directly or on the market; the defendant could only give it to the veterinary surgeon and he was the only person who could use it (§ 87 of the Implementation Provisions to the Animal Diseases Act in the version of 1 March 1958, BAnz no 45 of 6 March 1958 = BGBl III 7831-1-1). Simply for this reason the idea is ruled out here that relationships similar to a contract had existed between the parties. The plaintiff was not a 'consumer' of the vaccine and not its 'user' either but, looked at from a legal point of view 'only' the person suffering harm. As such, she is limited to claims for compensation in tort.

III Nach dem vom Berufungsgericht festgestellten Sachverhalt sind die Voraussetzungen des § 823 BGB erfüllt. Der von der Beklagten gelieferte Impfstoff war fehlerhaft und die Ursache für die Erkrankung der Hühner. Auch wenn hier, wie oben ausgeführt, die Regeln des Vertragsrechts nicht anwendbar sind, so muß dennoch davon ausgegangen werden, daß der Beklagten ein eigenes Verschulden zur Last fällt. Wird jemand bei bestimmungsgemäßer Verwendung eines Industrieerzeugnisses dadurch an einem der in § 823 Abs. 1 BGB geschützten Rechtsgüter geschädigt, daß dieses Produkt fehlerhaft hergestellt war, so ist es Sache des Herstellers, die Vorgängen aufzuklären, die den Fehler verursacht haben, und dabei darzutun, daß ihn hieran kein Verschulden trifft.

1 Nicht in Frage steht, daß auch bei der 'Produzentenhaftung' der Geschädigte nachzuweisen hat, daß der Schaden durch einen Fehler des Produktes verursacht ist. Die Klägerin hatte daher zu beweisen, daß die Geflügelpest bei ihren Hühnern ausgebrochen ist, weil der Impfstoff von der Beklagten stammte und bei seiner Auslieferung aktive Viren enthielt.

Diesen Beweis hat das Berufungsgericht als erbracht angesehen. (Wird ausgeführt.)

2 Das Berufungsgericht geht bei Prüfung der Frage, worauf es zurückzuführen ist, daß der Impfstoff unabgetötete Viren enthielt, von der Tatsache aus, daß sowohl das Paul-Ehrlich-Institut wie die Bundesforschungsanstalt in den von ihnen untersuchten Flaschen Bakterien festgestellt haben. Es legt seiner Würdigung im wesentlichen zugrunde, was Prof. Dr. E. in seinem Gutachten ausgeführt hatte. Dieser hatte erklärt, mit hoher Wahrscheinlichkeit sei anzunehmen, daß die Bakterien beim Abfüllvorgang, nämlich bei dem im Betriebe der Beklagten von Hand ausgeführten Umschütten des Impstoffes aus den großen Behältern, in die Flaschen geraten seien. Schon mehrfach sei beobachtet worden, daß Viren, die – wie hier – durch Zusatz von Formaldehyd abgetötet worden seien, unter bestimmten Umständen wieder aktiv geworden seien. Es sei daher möglich, daß es hier die Bakterien gewesen seien, die eine Reaktivierung der Viren ausgelöst hätten. Auf Grund dieser Ausführungen des Sachverständigen glaubt das Berufungsgericht feststellen zu können, daß die bakterielle Verunreinigung der Flaschen die Ursache der Reaktivierung gewesen sei. Dazu weist es darauf hin, daß durch den Teil der Charge, der nicht bakteriell verunreinigt gewesen sei, keine Schäden entstanden seien, während dies bei den Flaschen der Fall gewesen sei, die von Dr. H. und im Kreise Heilbronn benutzt und in denen anschließend die Bakterien festgestellt wurden. Auch Dr. E. halte es für möglich, daß die Verunreinigung des Impfstoffs 'durch menschliches Versagen' einer der Personen verursacht worden sei, die die Beklagte beim Abfüllen des Impfstoffes beschäftigt habe.

III According to the facts of the case as established by the appeal court, the prerequisites of § 823 of the BGB are fulfilled. The vaccine delivered by the defendant was defective and was the reason for the chickens becoming ill. Even if, as explained above, the rules of contract law are not applicable here, one must nevertheless proceed on the basis that the defendant bears the responsibility of a fault of its own. If someone, by the use as agreed of an industrial product, is harmed in one of the legal interests protected in § 823 para 1 of the BGB, because this product was defectively manufactured, it is for the manufacturer to clarify the events which caused the mistake and thereby to demonstrate that there was no fault on his part in this respect.

1 There is no doubt that even for 'manufacturer's liability' the person suffering harm has to prove that the harm is caused by a defect in the product. The plaintiff had therefore to prove that the fowl pest broke out amongst her chickens because the vaccine came from the defendant and contained active viruses on its delivery.

This proof has been regarded by the appeal court as furnished. (This is explained.)

2 In examination of the question of what caused the vaccine to contain viruses which had not been destroyed, the appeal court proceeded from the fact that the Paul Ehrlich Institute as well as the Federal Research Institute identified bacteria in the bottles investigated by them. What Professor Dr E had stated in his opinion forms substantially the basis of its assessment. He had explained that it was to be accepted as a high probability that the bacteria had entered the bottles in the decanting process, that is, in the pouring of the vaccine from the large containers which was carried out in the defendant's business by hand. It has been observed on several occasions that viruses which have been, as here, destroyed by the addition of formaldehyde, have become active again under certain circumstances. It is therefore possible that it was the bacteria here which had caused a reactivation of viruses. On the basis of these statements by the expert, the appeal court believed it could establish that the bacterial contamination of the bottles was the cause of the reactivation. In addition it indicates that no harm arose from the part of the batch which had not been contaminated by bacteria, whilst this had been the case with the bottles which had been used by Dr H and in the Helbronn area and in which bacteria had subsequently been identified. Dr E also regards it as possible that the contamination of the vaccine was caused 'by human failure' on the part of one of the persons whom the defendant had employed in the decanting of the vaccine.

3 Die Revision greift diese Würdigung des Berufungsgerichts an. Ihre Rügen haben keinen Erfolg.

Richtig ist zwar, daß das Berufungsgericht kein Verschulden der Beklagten selbst als bewiesen angesehen hat. Vielmehr hat es lediglich angenommen, daß wahrscheinlich eine Hilfsperson den Schaden verschuldet habe. Eine Haftung der Beklagten gemäß § 278 BGB läßt sich indessen, wie oben dargetan, nicht aus der Anwendung des Vertragsrechts ableiten. Das nötigt aber nicht dazu, den Rechtsstreit an den Tatrichter zurückzuverweisen. Denn es war auch dann Sache der Beklagten, sich zu entlasten, wenn die Klägerin sich nur auf § 823 BGB stützen kann.

(aa) Dies ergibt sich schon daraus, daß der Ersatzanspruch der Klägerin auch aus § 823 Abs. 2 BGB folgt. Denn die Beklagte hat durch die Auslieferung der gefährlichen Flaschen mit Impfstoff gegen ein Schutzgesetz verstoßen. Dieser Impfstoff, ein Arzneimittel im Sinne des Arzneimittelgesetzes vom 16. Mai 1961 (§ 3 Abs. 3 AMG), war geeignet, bei den Hühnern schädliche, ja tödliche Wirkungen hervorzurufen. § 6 AMG verbietet es, derartigen Impfstoff in den Verkehr zu bringen. Diese Vorschrift stellt – nicht anders als der für gesundheitsschädliche Lebensmittel geltende § 3 LebMG (vgl. RGZ 170, 155, 156 zu § 4 LebMG) – ein Gesetz zum Schutz der gefährdeten Menschen oder Tiere dar. Ist aber ein Verstoß gegen ein Schutzgesetz bewiesen, so spricht eine Vermutung dafür, daß dies schuldhaft geschehen ist. Der das Schutzgesetz Übertretende muß daher Umstände dartun und beweisen, die geeignet sind, die Annahme seines Verschuldens auszuräumen (Senatsurteil vom 12. März 1968 - VI ZR 178/66 -, NJW 1968, 1279). Diesen Beweis hat ein Betriebsinhaber nicht geführt, wenn eine mögliche Ursache ungeklärt geblieben ist, die in der Sphäre seiner Verantwortlichkeit liegt und ein schadensursächliches Verschulden enthalten würde (Senatsurteile vom 3. Januar 1961 - VI ZR 67/60 -, VersR 1961, 231, und vom 4. April 1967 - VI ZR 98/65 -, VersR 1967, 685).

(bb) Diese Beweislastregelung würde aber auch dann gelten, wenn die Klägerin ihren Ersatzanspruch allein auf Absatz 1 des § 823 BGB stützen könnte. Auch dann war es Sache der Beklagten, sich zu entlasten.

3 The appeal in law disputes this assessment of the appeal court. Its arguments are however unsuccessful.

It is certainly true that the appeal court did not regard any fault of the defendant itself as proved. Rather it merely accepted that an assistant was probably to blame for the damage. Liability of the defendant in accordance with § 278 of the BGB cannot however be derived from the application of contract law, as demonstrated above. That does not however require the action to be referred back to the judge of fact. It was also for the defendant to exculpate itself if the plaintiff could only rely on § 823 of the BGB.

(aa) This results from the fact that the claim to compensation by the plaintiff also follows from § 823 para 2 of the BGB. This is because the defendant has violated a protective statute by the delivery of dangerous bottles of vaccine. This vaccine, a medicine in the sense of the Medicines Act of 16 May 1961 (§ 3 para 3 of the AMG), was apt to bring about harmful, in fact fatal, effects in the chicken. § 6 of the AMG forbids the bringing of that kind of vaccine into circulation. This provision represents – no differently than § 3 of the Food Act which is effective for food which is harmful to health (compare RGZ 170, 155, 156 on § 4 of the LebMG) – a statute for the protection of endangered animals or humans. If, however, a violation of a protective statute is proved, there is a presumption that this has occurred culpably. The infringer of the protective statute must therefore demonstrate and prove circumstances which are apt to displace the presumption of his fault (judgment of the Senate of 12 March 1968 - VI ZR 178/66 -, NJW 1968, 1279). This proof has not been shown by a proprietor of a business if a possible cause which lies in the sphere of his responsibility and which would contain fault which would cause harm has remained unsolved (judgments of the Senate of 3 January 1961 – VI ZR 67/60 – VersR 1961, 231, and of 4 April 1967 - VI ZR 98/65 -, VersR 1967, 685).

(bb) This rule as to the burden of proof would however also apply if the plaintiff could only base her claim to compensation on para 1 of § 823 of the BGB. Then also it would be for the defendant to exculpate itself.

Zwar hat in aller Regel der Geschädigte, der sich auf § 823 Abs. 1 BGB stützt, nicht nur die Kausalität zwischen seinem Schaden und dem Verhalten des Schädigers darzutun und notfalls zu beweisen, sondern auch dessen Verschulden (BGHZ 24, 21, 29). Jedoch hängt die Möglichkeit dieses Nachweises der subjektiven Voraussetzungen erheblich davon ab, inwieweit der Geschädigte den objektiven Geschehensablauf in seinen Einzelheiten aufklären kann. Das aber ist vor allem dann mit besonderen Schwierigkeiten verknüpft, wenn es um Vorgänge geht, die sich bei der Herstellung des Produkts im Betriebe abgespielt haben. Die Rechtsprechung ist daher seit langem dem Geschädigten dadurch zu Hilfe gekommen, daß sie sich mit dem Nachweis einer Kausalkette begnügt hat, die nach der Lebenserfahrung zunächst für ein 'Organisationsverschulden' des Herstellers spricht. Hierbei kann jedoch für Schadensersatzansprüche aus 'Produzentenhaftung' nicht stehengeblieben werden. Allzuoft wird der Betreibsinhaber die Möglichkeit dartun, daß der Fehler des Produkts auch auf eine Weise verursacht worden sein kann, die den Schluß auf sein Verschulden nicht zuläßt - ein Nachweis, der zumeist wiederum auf Vorgängen im Betriebe des Schädigers beruht, daher vom Geschädigten schwer zu widerlegen ist. Infolgedessen kann der Hersteller dann, wenn es um Schäden geht, die aus dem Gefahrenbereich seines Betriebes erwachsen sind, noch nicht dadurch als entlastet angesehen werden, daß er Möglichkeiten aufzeigt, nach denen der Fehler des Produkts auch ohne ein in seinem Organisationsbereich liegendes Verschulden entstanden sein kann. Dies gebieten in den Fällen der Produzentenhaftung die schutzbedürftigen Interessen des Geschädigten - gleich ob Endabnehmer, Benutzer oder Dritter; andererseits erlauben es die schutzwürdigen Interessen des Produzenten, von ihm den Nachweis seiner Schuldlosigkeit zu verlangen.

Certainly the person suffering harm who relies on § 823 para 1 of the BGB has as a rule not only to demonstrate and, if necessary, prove the causality between the harm he has suffered and the conduct of the person causing it, but also the fault of that person (BGHZ 24, 21, 29). However, the possibility of this proof of subjective prerequisites is considerably dependent on how far the person suffering damage can explain the objective sequence of events in its particulars. But that is above all attended with special difficulties when it concerns events which have occurred in the manufacture of products in business. Case law has therefore over a long period of time come to the aid of the person suffering damage by satisfying itself with proof of a chain of causation which at first sight, according to experience of life, argues for a 'fault in the organisation' of the manufacturer. Things cannot however remain here for claims for compensation for harm arising from 'manufacturer's liability'. All too often the proprietor of a business will demonstrate the possibility that the defect in the product can also be caused in a way which does not permit the conclusion that he is at fault; a proof which generally again rests on events in the business of the person causing the harm and therefore is difficult to refute by the person suffering the harm. In consequence the manufacturer cannot, when it is a question of harm which has arisen from the risk area of his business, be regarded as exculpated because he shows possibilities according to which the defect in the product could also have arisen without a fault existing within the scope of his organisation. The interests of the person harmed which need protection, regardless of whether he is an ultimate purchaser, user or third party, demand this in cases of manufacturer's liability; on the other hand, the interests of the manufacturer which need protection permit the requiring from him of proof of absence of fault on his part.

Diese Beweisregel greift freilich erst ein, wenn der Geschädigte nachgewiesen hat, daß sein Schaden im Organisations- und Gefahrenbereich des Herstellers, und zwar durch einen objektiven Mangel oder Zustand der Verkehrswidrigkeit ausgelöst worden ist. Dieser Beweis wird vom Geschädigten sogar dann verlangt, wenn er den Schädiger wegen Verletzung vertraglicher oder vorvertraglicher Schutz- und Nebenpflichten in Anspruch nimmt (Senatsurteile vom 26. September 1961 - VI ZR 92/61 -, LM BGB § 276 [Fa] Nr. 13 = NJW 1962, 31, und vom 18. Januar 1966 - VI ZR 184/64 -, MDR 1966, 491). Nichts anderes gilt, wenn er den Produzenten wegen Verletzung der Verkehrssicherungspflicht in Anspruch nimmt. Hat er aber diesen Beweis geführt, so ist der Produzent 'näher daran', den Sachverhalt aufzuklären und die Folgen der Beweislosigkeit zu tragen. Er überblickt die Produktionssphäre, bestimmt und organisiert den Herstellungsprozeß und die Auslieferungskontrolle der fertigen Produkte. Oft machen die Größe des Betriebes, seine komplizierte, verschachtelte, auf Arbeitsteilung beruhende Organisation, verwickelte technische, chemische oder biologische Vorgänge und dergleichen es dem Geschädigten praktisch unmöglich, die Ursache des schadenstiftenden Fehlers aufzuklären. Er vermag daher dem Richter den Sachverhalt nicht in solcher Weise darzulegen, daß dieser zuverlässig beurteilen kann, ob der Betriebsleitung ein Versäumnis vorzuwerfen ist oder ob es sich um einen von einem Arbeiter verschuldeten Fabrikationsfehler, um einen der immer wieder einmal vorkommenden 'Ausreißer' oder gar um einen 'Entwicklungsfehler' gehandelt hat, der nach dem damaligen Stand der Technik und Wissenschaft unvorhersehbar war. Liegt so aber die Ursache der Unaufklärbarkeit im Bereich des Produzenten, so gehört sie auch zu seiner Risikosphäre. Dann ist es sachgerecht und zumutbar, daß ihn das Risiko der Nichterweislichkeit seiner Schuldlosigkeit trifft.

This rule of proof, of course, only applies if the person suffering harm has proved that his harm has been caused in the area of the organisation and the area of the risk of the manufacturer and by an objective fault or a condition which is contrary to good business. This proof is even required of the person suffering harm when he claims against the person causing the harm for breach of contractual or pre-contractual protective or subsidiary duties (judgments of the Senate of 26 September 1961 - VI ZR 92/61 -, LM BGB § 276 [Fa] no 13 = NJW 1962, 31, and of 18 January 1966 - VI ZR 184/64 -, MDR 1966, 491). The position is no different if he claims against the manufacturer for breach of the business duty of care. But if he has adduced this proof, the manufacturer is 'closer to it' for clarifying the facts of the case or bearing the consequences of absence of proof. He surveys the sphere of production, determines and organises the process of manufacture and the supervision of delivery of the finished products. Often the size of the business, its complicated, segmented organisation based on division of work, intricate technical, chemical or biological processes and the like make it practically impossible for the person suffering harm to elucidate the cause of the defect which brought about the damage. He may therefore not be able to explain the facts of the case to the judge in such a manner that he can reliably assess whether the management of the business is to be accused of neglect or whether it was a matter of a flaw in manufacture which was the fault of a worker, one of the continually recurring 'runaways' or even a 'development defect' which according to the state of technology and science at that time was unforeseeable. If however the cause of the inexplicability lies in the sphere of the manufacturer, it also belongs to his area of risk. Then it is proper and reasonable that he bears the risk of not being able to prove his freedom from blame.

Von solcher Beweisregel ist die Rechtsprechung schon immer bei vertraglichen oder quasivertraglichen Sonderrechtsbeziehungen zwischen Geschädigtem (Gläubiger) und Schädiger (Schuldner) ausgegangen (BGHZ 48, 310, 312; BGH LM BGB § 536 Nr. 6 a = NJW 1964, 34; BGH NJW 1968, 2240). Es ist kein durchgreifender Grund ersichtlich, warum diese Beweisregel nicht dann für nach Deliktsrecht zu entscheidende Haftungsfälle ebenso gelten soll, wenn die ihr zugrunde liegenden Erwägungen auch hier zutreffen. Schon § 831 BGB erlegt dem Geschäftsherrn in bestimmten Beziehungen einen Entlastungsbeweis auf – ähnliches gilt in den Haftungsfällen der §§ 832, 833, 834 BGB. Vor allem gilt dies in den Fällen der §§ 836ff. BGB. Hier verlangt das Gesetz zwar von dem durch den Einsturz eines Gebäudes Geschädigten den Beweis, daß sein Schaden 'die Folge fehlerhafter Errichtung oder mangelhafter Unterhaltung' des Gebäudes war, erlegt aber dem Besitzer usw. den Beweis dafür auf, daß er alles getan hat, um die Gefahren, die von seinem Gebäude ausgehen konnten, abzuwenden. Die in diesen Vorschriften angeordnete Umkehr der Behauptungs- und Beweislast geht nicht immer davon aus, das Verschulden des Schädigers sei zu vermuten. Vielmehr beruht sie überwiegend auf dem Gedanken, daß der Schädiger eher als der Geschädigte in der Lage ist, die für den Vorwurf der Fahrlässigkeit maßgebenden Vorgänge aufzuklären, daß es daher gerecht sei, ihn das Risiko einer Unaufklärbarkeit tragen zu lassen. Der Senat hat schon in seinem Urteil vom 1. April 1953 (VI ZR 77/52, LM ZPO § 286 [C] Nr. 12) darauf hingewiesen, vom Kläger könne nicht der für ihn gewöhnlich fast unmögliche Nachweis verlangt werden, daß die schadenstiftende Sache durch ein Verschulden des Geschäftsinhabers oder seiner Angestellten in den Betrieb gekommen sei. Vor allem hat der Senat bereits in seinem Urteil vom 17. Oktober 1967 (VI ZR 70/66, NJW 1968, 247) ausgesprochen, es sei Sache des Produzenten, sich zu entlasten, wenn der Geschädigte keine Angaben darüber machen könne, in welchen Einzelpunkten schuldhafte Pflichtverletzungen der Unternehmensleitung vorgelegen hätten. Die moderne Entwicklung der Warenproduktion, an der oft nachträglich nur schwer zu ermittelnde Personen oder Maschinen beteiligt sind und die auf nur noch vom Fachmann zu durchschauenden und zu kontrollierenden Fertigungsprozessen beruht verlangt eine Fortbildung des Beweisrechts in der Richtung, wie sie das Gesetz in § 836 BGB vorgezeichnet hat (vgl. Simitis, Gutachten zum DJT 1968 S. 92ff.; Stoll in Festschrift für von Hippel, 1967, S. 557).

Dabei wird es allerdings – so wie bei der für positive Vertragsverletzungen anerkannten Umkehrung der Beweislast - stets auf die in der jeweiligen Fallgruppe gegebene Interessenlage ankommen. Die Frage, ob auch dem Inhaber eines kleineren Betriebes, dessen Herstellungsverfahren überschaubar und durchsichtig ist (Familien- und Einmannbetriebe, landwirtschaftliche Erzeuger und dergleichen), die Übernahme des Beweisrisikos zugemutet werden kann, bedarf hier keiner Prüfung. In den Fällen der hier vorliegenden Art ist es jedenfalls Sache des Herstellers, sich zu entlasten.

Case law has always been based on such a rule of proof in contractual or quasi-contractual special legal relationships between the person suffering harm (the obligee) and the person causing harm (obligor) (BGHZ 48, 310, 312; BGH LM BGB § 536 no 6a = NJW 1964, 34; BGH NJW 1968, 2240). There is no evident decisive reason as to why this rule of proof should not be just as valid for liability cases to be decided according to the law of tort if the considerations which form a basis for it are appropriate here also. § 831 of the BGB already imposes on the employer in certain respects a burden of exculpatory proof – similar rules apply in the cases of liability under §§ 832, 833 and 834 of the BGB. This applies above all in the cases of §§ 836 and onwards of the BGB. Here statute demands from a person, suffering harm due to the collapse of a building proof, that the harm was 'the consequence of defective erection or deficient maintenance' of the building, but imposes on the possessor, etc. the burden of proof that he has done everything to avert the dangers which could emanate from the building. The reversal of the burden of assertion and proof required by these provisions does not always proceed on the basis that fault by the person causing the harm is to be presumed. Rather is it based predominantly on the consideration that the person causing the harm rather than the person suffering it is in a position to explain the determining events in respect of the accusation of negligence and that it is therefore right to leave him to bear the risk of anything being inexplicable. The Senate has already in its judgment of 1 April 1953 (VI ZR 77/52, LM ZPO § 286 [C] no 12) referred to the fact that the plaintiff could not be asked for the proof, which would usually be almost impossible for him, that the thing causing the harm came into circulation through a fault on the part of the proprietor of the business, or his employees. The Senate has above all in its judgment of 17 October 1967 (VI ZR 70/66, NJW 1968, 247) already stated that it was for the manufacturer to exculpate himself if the person suffering harm cannot make any statements as to the individual points in which culpable breaches of duty on the part of the management of the undertaking had been present. The modern development of production of goods in which persons or machines have participated, who or which can often only be ascertained afterwards with difficulty, and which are based on manufacturing processes which can only be understood and controlled by an expert demand a further development of the law of proof in the direction which the statutory provision in § 836 of the BGB has indicated (compare Simitis, Opinion at the DJT 1968, p 92 and onwards; Stoll in the Commemorative Publication for von Hippel, 1967, p 557).

At the same time it will certainly, as with the reversal of the burden of proof recognised for positive breaches of contract, always depend on the position as to the interests in the respective groups of cases. The question of whether the taking over of the risk of proof can also be expected of the proprietor of a small business whose manufacturing procedure is comprehensible and transparent (family and one man businesses, agricultural producers and the like) does not need to be examined here. In the cases of the sort present here, it is, in each case, for the manufacturer to exculpate himself.

4 Diesen Entlastungsbeweis hat die Beklagte nicht erbracht.

(a) Nach dem von ihr selbst vorgelegten Gutachen von Prof. Dr. E. ist es möglich, daß Unachtsamkeit einer beim Abfüllen tätigen Hilfskraft zur Verunreinigung der Flaschen geführt hat. Er hält das Verfahren, Gefäße über 500 ccm, also auch die an Dr. H. gelieferten Flaschen, mittels Umschüttens von Hand abzufüllen und sie nicht, wie dies bei den kleineren Gefäßen geschieht, mittels einer Apparatur zu füllen, für eine 'ältere Methode', die zwar noch 'tragbar', aber verbesserungsbedürftig sei. Für dieses Von-Hand-Abfüllen müsse zumindest eine entsprechend höhere 'Arbeitskapelle' mit UV-Ausleuchtung konstruiert werden. Außerdem müsse die 'bescheidene apparative Ausstattung' des Betriebes erweitert werden, indem Trockensterilisatoren angeschafft würden, damit die zu füllenden größeren Gefäße besser, vor allem ohne längere Unterbrechung sterilisiert werden könnten. Prof. Dr. E. hat ferner darauf hingewiesen, daß mangels Temperatur- und Druckschreiber nicht kontrolliert werden konnte, ob die beim Autoklavieren erforderliche hohe Temperatur auch wirklich erreicht wurde. Er hat daher die Verwendung von Farbumschlag-Röhrchen empfohlen. Außerdem hat er geraten, den Abfüllraum von Zeit zu Zeit durch Aufstellen von Agar-oder Blutplatten auf seinen Keimgehalt zu prüfen.

Der Gutachter meint nun zwar trotz dieser Verbesserungsvorschläge, die Herstellungsmethoden der Beklagten seien 'nicht unzulänglich' und 'erfüllten die Normalanforderungen'. Auch die Abfüllmethode verbürge ein ausreichendes Maß an Sicherheit, wenn sie auch verbesserungsbedürftig sei. Abschließend meint er, die Beklagte habe keine der notwendigen Sicherungsmaßnahmen fahrlässig außer acht gelassen. Die bakterielle Verunreinigung könne zwar durch mangelnde Beachtung der gebotenen Vorsichtsmaßnahmen verursacht, könne aber trotz Beachtung dieser Maßnahmen eingetreten sein.

(b) Dieser Auffassung des Sachverständigen über das Maß der erforderlichen Sorgfalt kann nicht gefolgt werden. Auch er geht davon aus, daß bei der Herstellung von Impfstoffen, bei denen lebende Viren abgeschwächt werden müssen, 'ein höchstmögliches Maß an Sicherheit' verlangt werden muß. Eben deshalb unterliegen Impfstoffwerke strenger staatlicher Überwachung (§ 19 AMG mit den nach Abs. 5 noch maßgebenden landesrechtlichen Vorschriften). Die von Prof. Dr. E. angeführten Mängel in der Ausstattung des Betriebes der Beklagten, vor allem hinsichtlich des Abfüllens von Hand, stehen einer Feststellung entgegen, daß der Leitung der Beklagten keine fahrlässigen Versäumnisse zur Last fielen. Die von ihm empfohlenen Änderungen lagen keineswegs fern und stellten an die Beklagte weder technisch noch finanziell unzumutbare Anforderungen. Es ist nicht auszuschließen, daß diese zusätzlichen Sicherungsmaßnahmen die Abfüllung gefährlichen Impfstoffes verhütet hätten.

4 This exculpatory proof has not been produced by the defendant.

(a) According to the opinion of Professor Dr E which it produced it is possible that lack of attention by one assistant engaged in the decanting led to the contamination of the bottles. He considers the procedure of filling vessels of over 500 cc (therefore including the bottles delivered to Dr H) by means of decanting by hand and not, as occurs with the smaller vessels, filling them by means of machinery to be an 'older method', which is certainly still 'acceptable', but needs improvement. At least a correspondingly superior 'work station' with ultraviolet illumination must be constructed for this decanting by hand. Moreover the 'modest apparatus fittings' of the business must be extended by obtaining dry sterilisers, so that the larger vessels to be filled could be better sterilised, above all without long interruption. Professor Dr E has further indicated that in default of temperature and pressure gauges being able to be controlled, no control could be exercised over whether the necessary high temperature was really reached in the autoclave process. He therefore recommended the use of colour change test tubes. Additionally, he advised testing the decanting room from time to time by the positioning of agar dishes and blood dishes for its germ content.

The assessor considers that in spite of these proposals for improvement, the manufacturing methods of the defendant were 'not inadequate' and 'fulfilled the normal requirements'. Also the decanting method guarantees a sufficient measure of safety even if it needs improvement. Finally, he thinks that the defendant did not leave any of the necessary safety measures negligently out of consideration. The bacterial contamination could certainly be caused by lack of attention to the necessary precautionary measures, but could have occurred despite consideration of these measures.

(b) This opinion of the expert about the measure of necessary care cannot be followed. Even he proceeds on the basis that in the manufacture of vaccines in which living viruses must be rendered ineffective 'a level of safety which is a high as possible' must be demanded. It is just for this reason that vaccine factories are subject to strong Government surveillance (§ 19 of the AMG with the State law rules which are authoritative according to para 5). The defects cited by Professor Dr E in the equipment of the business of the defendant and above all in relation to the decanting by hand militate against a finding that the management of the defendant was not responsible for any neglect. The changes recommended by him were not in any way taken too far and did not place on the defendant demands which were either technically or financially unreasonable. It cannot be excluded that these additional safety measures would have prevented the decanting of dangerous vaccine.

THE PUBLICATION OF A LETTER CASE

BGHZ Band 13 S. 334

43 Briefe oder sonstige private Aufzeichnungen dürfen in der Regel nicht ohne Zustimmung des noch lebenden Verfassers und nur in der vom Verfasser gebilligten Weise veröffentlicht werden. Das folgt aus dem in Artt 1, 2 GrundG verankerten Schutz der Persönlichkeit und gilt daher auch dann, wenn die Aufzeichnungen nicht die individuelle Formprägung aufweisen, die für einen Urheberrechtsschutz erforderlich ist.

GrundG Artt 1, 2; BGB § 823 Abs. 1; LitUrhG § 1

I Zivilsenat. Urt. v. 25. Mai 1954 i.S. Dr. M. (Kl.) w. 'D. W.' Verlags GmbH. (Bekl.). I ZR 211/53.

I Landgericht Hamburg

II Oberlandesgericht Hamburg

Die Beklagte veröffentlichte am 29. Juni 1952 in ihrer Wochenzeitung ... einen Artikel mit der Überschrift: 'Dr. H.S. & Co.' und dem Untertitel 'Politische Betrachtung anläßlich der Gründung des neuen Bankhauses' von K.B. Der Artikel enthielt eine Stellungnahme zu der von Dr. S. in H. gegründeten neuen Außenhandelsbank und setzte sich in diesem Zusammenhang mit dem politischen Wirken des Dr. S. während des nationalsozialistischen Regimes und in den Jahren nach dem Krieg auseinander.

Im Auftrage von Dr. S. übersandte der Kläger, ein Rechtsanwalt, der Beklagten ein Schreiben vom 4. Juli 1952, in dem es auszugsweise heißt: 'Ich vertrete die Interessen des Dr. S. Gemäß § 11 des Pressegesetzes verlange ich hiermit in Ihrer am Sonntag, den 6. cr. erscheinenden Ausgabe zu obengenanntem Artikel die Aufnahme folgender Berichtigung:

1 Es ist unrichtig, daß ...

2 ...

Der vorstehende Berichtigungsanspruch stützt sich in rechtlicher Hinsicht auf das Pressegesetz in Verbindung mit dem BGB, ferner auf das Urheberrecht.

THE PUBLICATION OF A LETTER CASE

This was a case in which a letter was published in such a way as to give a misleading impression as to its nature. It was not clearly defamation or breach of copyright, but it was an infringement of the right of personality under Arts 1 and 2 of the Basic Law. It is therefore an example of the secondary effect of the Basic Rights.

BGHZ Volume 13 p 334

43 Letters or other private writings ought, as a rule, not to be published without the consent of the author while he is still alive; and only in the manner approved by the author. That follows from the protection of personality anchored in Arts 1 and 2 of the Basic Law and is therefore effective even if the writings do not exhibit the individual character form which is necessary for copyright protection.

GG, Arts 1 and 2 ; BGB, § 823 para 1; LitUrhG § 1

1st Civil Senate. Judgment of 25 May 1954 in the matter of Dr. M. (plaintiff) v 'DW' Publishers Ltd (defendant) – I ZR 211/53.

211/53

I State Court of Hamburg

II Upper State Court of Hamburg

The defendant published on 29 June 1952 in its weekly newspaper an article with the headline: 'Dr HS & Co' and the subheading 'Political consideration in respect of founding of new banking house' by KB The article contained an opinion on the new export trade bank founded by Dr S in H and considered fully in this connection the political activity of Dr S during the national socialist regime and in the years after the war.

On behalf of Dr S, the plaintiff, a lawyer, sent the defendant a letter dated 4 July 1952 from which the following are extracts: 'I represent the interests of Dr S In accordance with § 11 of the Press Act I hereby demand in your edition appearing on Sunday the 6th instant the inclusion of the following correction to the above-mentioned article:

1 It is incorrect that ...

2 ...

The above claim to a correction is based legally on the Press Act in combination with the BGB and, further, on copyright law.

Ich bitte Sie, mir Ihre Bestätigung über die uneingeschränkte Durchführung der verlangten Berichtigung bis morgen mittag, Sonnabend, den 5. Juli 1952, 12 Uhr, telefonisch oder schriftlich bekanntzugeben, bei Vermeidung sofort einzuleitender gerichtlicher Maßnahmen.'

Die Beklagte gab dem Kläger keine Antwort. Sie veröffentlichte in der Ausgabe vom 6. Juli 1952 unter der Rubrik 'Leserbriefe' in Zusammenstellung mit unterschiedlichen Meinungsäußerungen von Lesern zu dem Artikel von K. B. folgendes:

'Dr. H.S. & Co

An die ... (Anschrift der Zeitung)

Ich vertrete die Interessen des Dr. H.S.

1 Es ist unrichtig...

2 ...

Dr. M., Rechtsanwalt'

In den Ausführungen unter 1. fehlte die Wiedergabe von Auszügen aus dem Dr. S. betreffenden Nürnberger Urteil, die der Kläger in seinem Schreiben vom 4. Juli 1952 gebracht hatte.

Im übrigen waren die Ausführungen nicht verändert.

Der Kläger erblickt in dieser Art der Veröffentlichung seiner Aufforderung eine Verletzung seiner Persönlichkeitsrechte. Der Abdruck des durch die Streichung und die Wahl der Überschrift in seinem Inhalt verfälschten anwaltlichen Aufforderungsschreibens unter 'Leserbriefe' stelle eine vorsätzliche Irreführung des Publikums dar. Es werde dadurch der unrichtige Eindruck erweckt, es handle sich um bloße Meinungsäußerung eines Lesers zu dem vorangegangenen Artikel über Dr. S., wie dies bei den unter der gleichen Rubrik abgedruckten Leserzuschriften der Fall sei. Dem Kläger habe aber eine politische Stellungnahme völlig ferngelegen und er sei nur im Rahmen seines anwaltlichen Auftrags tätig geworden. Schon aus standesrechtlichen Erwägungen könne das Verhalten der Beklagten nicht geduldet werden. Ein Anwalt müsse sich darauf verlassen können, daß ein im Namen seines Mandanten gestelltes Berichtigungsverlangen nicht in irreführender Weise der Öffentlichkeit unterbreitet werde.

Der Kläger hat beantragt, die Beklagte zu verurteilen, in ihrer nächsten Ausgabe unter 'Leserbriefe' ihre Behauptung vom 6. Juli 1952 zu widerrufen, daß der Kläger einen Leserbrief in Sachen 'Dr. H. S. & Co.' an die Beklagte gesandt habe.

I ask you to notify me by telephone or in writing with your confirmation of the unrestricted implementation of the correction demanded by midday tomorrow, Saturday 5 July 1952, 12 o'clock, in order to avoid legal proceedings being immediately instituted'.

The defendant gave the plaintiff no answer. It published the following in the edition of 6 July 1952 under the heading 'Readers letters' together with various expressions of opinion by readers on the article by KB.

'Dr HS & Co

To the ... (address of the newspaper)

I represent the interests of Dr HS

1 It is incorrect ...

2 ...

Dr M, Lawyer'

In the statements under 1, the reproduction of extracts from the Nuremberg judgment concerning Dr S, which the plaintiff had included in his letter of 4 July 1952, was omitted.

In other respects the statements were not altered.

The plaintiff sees in this kind of publication of his demand a violation of his rights of personality. The reproduction of the lawyer's letter of demand, falsified in its contents by the omission and choice of heading, under 'Reader's letters', represents a deliberate misleading of the public. It would produce the incorrect impression that it concerned a mere expression of the opinion of a reader in relation to the preceding article about Dr S, as would be the case with the readers' letters printed under the same heading. A political opinion was however very far from the plaintiff's mind and he had only acted within the framework of his legal instructions. From professional considerations alone, the conduct of the defendant could not be tolerated. A lawyer must be able to rely on a demand for a correction made in the name of his client not being presented in a misleading manner to the public.

The plaintiff has proposed that the defendant should be ordered, in its next edition under 'Reader's letters', to recall its statement of 6 July 1952 that the plaintiff had sent a reader's letter in the matter of 'Dr HS & Co' to the defendant.

Die Beklagte ist der Auffassung, daß sie nicht verpflichtet gewesen sei, dem Berichtigungsverlangen des Klägers nachzukommen, weil das Schreiben des Klägers nicht den Anforderungen des § 11 PresseG entsprochen habe. Es habe deshalb in ihrem Belieben gestanden, ob und an welcher Stelle ihrer Zeitung sie diese Einsendung zum Abdruck bringen wollte.

Das Landgericht hat der Klage aus § 823 Abs. 2 BGB in Verb mit §§ 186, 187 StGB stattgegeben. Das Oberlandesgerichts hat die Klage abgewiesen. Nach Ansicht des Berufungsgerichts liegt in der Veröffentlichung des Schreibens des Klägers in abgekürzter Fassung unter der Rubrik 'Leserbriefe' keine widerrechtliche Beeinträchtigung des Klägers. Die Art dieser Veröffentlichung enthalte zwar die Behauptung einer unwahren Tatsache. Die unrichtige Behauptung, der Kläger habe an die Beklagte einen Leserbrief gesandt, sei aber weder geeignet, den Kredit des Klägers zu schädigen, noch ihn verächtlich zu machen oder in der öffentlichen Meinung herabzuwürdigen.

Die Revision führte zur Wiederherstellung des landgerichtlichen Urteils.

Aus den Gründen:

Das Berufungsgericht hat zu Unrecht ungeprüft gelassen, ob sich das Klagbegehren aus einer Beeinträchtigung eines Persönlichkeitsrechtes des Klägers rechtfertigt, und die Klage lediglich deshalb abgewiesen, weil es die objektiven Voraussetzungen einer unerlaubten Handlung im Sinn der §§ 823, 824 Abs 2 BGB in Verb mit §§ 186, 187 StGB nicht für gegeben erachtet. Dies wird von der Revision mit Recht beanstandet.

The defendant is of the opinion that it was not obliged to comply with the plaintiff's demand for a correction because the plaintiff's letter did not correspond with the requirements of § 11 of the Press Act. It was therefore a matter for its discretion whether and in what place in its newspaper it wished to print this contribution.

The State Court has allowed the claim on the basis of § 823 para 2 of the BGB in combination with §§ 186 and 187 of the StGB. The Upper State Court has rejected the action. According to the view of the appeal court there is no unlawful injury to the plaintiff in the publishing of the plaintiff's letter in shortened form under the heading 'Readers' letters'. The manner of this publication certainly contained the assertion of an untrue fact. The incorrect statement that the plaintiff had sent a reader's letter to the defendant was however apt neither to harm the credit of the plaintiff nor to make him contemptible or degrade him in the public opinion.

The appeal in law led to the restoration of the judgment of the State Court.

Reasons:

The appeal court incorrectly failed to examine the question of whether what was requested in the action is justified by an interference with the plaintiff's right of personality and merely rejected the action because it did not regard the objective requirements of a tort in the sense of §§ 823 and 824 para 2 of the BGB in combination with §§ 186 and 187 of the StGB as present. This is correctly objected to by the appeal in law.

Es kann dahingestellt bleiben, ob das Schreiben des Klägers vom 4. Juli 1952 als Schriftwerk im Sinn des § 1 LitUrhG anzusehen ist und damit unter Urheberrechtsschutz fällt. Das Reichsgericht hat zwar in ständiger Rechtsprechung den Veröffentlichungsschutz für Briefe davon abhängig gemacht, ob diese die für den Urheberschutz erforderliche individuelle Formprägung aufweisen (RGZ 41, 43 [48]; 69, 401 [403]). Demgegenüber ist mit Recht vom Schrifttum darauf hingewiesen worden, daß ein Bedürfnis nach der Anerkennung eines Persönlichkeitsschutzes hinsichtlich der Verwertung eigener Aufzeichnungen in gleicher Weise auch dann besteht, wenn dieser Schutz nicht aus dem Urheberpersönlichkeitsrecht abgeleitet werden kann, weil es an einer auf individueller geistiger Tätigkeit beruhenden Formgestaltung der fraglichen Aufzeichnungen fehlt (vgl. Ulmer, Urheber- und Verlagsrecht § 83 IV; Neumann-Duesberg, *Das gesprochene Wort im Urheber- und Persönlichkeitsrecht*, 1949 S. 158ff.; Georg Müller, Ufita 1929, 367 [383ff.]). Das Reichsgericht glaubte, einen solchen von dem Urheberrecht unabhängigen Persönlichkeitsschutz für Briefveröffentlichungen deshalb versagen zu müssen, weil die damals geltende deutsche Rechtsordnung keine positiven Gesetzesbestimmungen über ein allgemeines Persönlichkeitsrecht enthielt (RGZ 79, 397 [398]; 82, 333 [334]; 94, 1; 102, 134; 107, 277 [281]; 113, 414; 123, 312 [320]). Das Reichsgericht hat zwar in zahlreichen Entscheidungen über § 826 BGB Persönlichkeitsrechten Schutz zugebilligt (RGZ 72, 175; 85, 343; 115, 416; 162, 7), aber grundsätzlich Persönlichkeitsrechte mit der absoluten Wirkung der Ausschließlichkeitsbefugnis nur für bestimmte einzelne Persönlichkeitsgüter anerkannt. Im Schrifttum haben sich schon Gierke und Kohler für die Anerkennung eines umfassenden Persönlichkeitsrechts eingesetzt (*Otto v. Gierke, Deutsches Privatrecht*, Bd 1, 707; Bd 3, 887; Kohler, 'Das Recht an Briefen'in *Archiv für bürgerliches Recht*, Bd 7, 94ff. [101]; für das schweizerische Recht vgl. Schweizer ZivGB Art. 28).

Nachdem nunmehr das Grundgesetz das Recht des Menschen auf Achtung seiner Würde (Art. 1 GrundG) und das Recht auf freie Entfaltung seiner Persönlichkeit auch als privates, von jedermann zu achtendes Recht anerkennt, soweit dieses Recht nicht die Rechte anderer verletzt oder gegen die verfassungsmäßige Ordnung oder das Sittengesetz verstößt (Art. 2 GrundG), muß das allgemeine Persönlichkeitsrecht als ein verfassungsmäßig gewährleistetes Grundrecht angesehen werden (vgl. Enneccerus-Nipperdey, Allgemeiner Teil 14. Aufl., § 78 I 2; Enneccerus-Lehmann, *Schuldrecht*, 14. Aufl., § 233 2 c; Coing SJZ 1947, 642).

It can be left undecided whether the letter of the plaintiff of 4 July 1952 is to be regarded as a written work in the sense of § 1 of the LitUrhG and therefore comes under copyright protection. The Reich High Court has certainly in consistent case law made protection from publication for letters depend on whether these exhibit the necessary individual character form for copyright protection (RGZ 41, 43 [48]; 69, 401 [403]). Over against that, it has been correctly pointed out in the literature that a need for the recognition of protection of personality in relation to the utilisation of one's own writings exists in the same way, even if this protection cannot be derived from the author's right of personality because there is no formulation of the writings in question on the basis of individual intellectual activity (compare Ulmer, Copyright and Publication Law § 83 IV; Neuman-Duesberg, *The Spoken Word in Copyright and Personality Law* 1949, p 158 and onwards; George Müller, Ufita, 1929, 367 [383 and onwards]). The Reich High Court believed it had to deny such protection of personality for publication of letters on a basis independent of copyright law because the German legal order current at that time contained no positive statutory provisions about a general right to personality (RGZ 79, 397 [398]; 82, 333 [334]; 94, 1; 102, 134; 107, 277 [281]; 113, 414; 123, 312 [320]). The Reich High Court has certainly granted, in numerous decisions concerning § 826 of the BGB, the protection of rights of personality (RGZ 72, 175; 85, 343; 115, 416; 162, 7), but in principle rights of personality with the absolute effect of authority to exclude are only recognised for certain individual personality interests. In the literature, Gierke and Kohler have already come down in favour of the recognition of a comprehensive right of personality (*Otto v Gierke, German Private Law*, Vol 1, 707; Vol 3, 887; Kohler, 'Rights in Letters' in *Archives for Civil Law*, Vol 7, 94 and onwards [101]; for Swiss Law, compare Schweizer, Civil Code, Art 28).

Since the Basic Law now recognises the right of the human being to respect for his dignity (Art 1 of the GG) and the right to free development of his personality as being also a private right to be respected by all, insofar as this right does not violate the rights of others or offend against the constitutional order or the law as to good morals (Art 2 of the GG), the general right to personality must be seen as a constitutionally guaranteed basic right (compare Enneccerus-Nipperdey, General Part, 14th edn, § 78 I 2; Enneccerus-Lehmann, *Law of Obligations*, 14th edn, § 233 2 c; Coing SJZ 1947, 642).

Es bedarf hier keiner näheren Erörterung, ob und inwieweit der Schutz dieses allgemeinen Persönlichkeitsrechtes, dessen Abgrenzung in besonderem Maße einer Güterabwägung bedarf, im Einzelfall durch berechtigte private oder öffentliche Belange eingeschränkt ist, die gegenüber dem Interesse an der Unantastbarkeit der Eigensphäre der Persönlichkeit überwiegen; denn im Streitfall sind schutzwürdige Belange der Beklagten, aus denen sie eine Berechtigung zu ihrem von dem Kläger beanstandeten Vorgehen herleiten könnte, nicht ersichtlich. Dagegen sind durch die von der Beklagten gewählte Art der Veröffentlichung des Berichtigungsschreibens unter Weglassung wesentlicher Teile dieses Schreibens persönlichkeitsrechtliche Interessen des Klägers verletzt worden.

Jede sprachliche Festlegung eines bestimmten Gedankeninhalts ist, und zwar auch dann, wenn der Festlegungsform eine Urheberschutzfähigkeit nicht zugebilligt werden kann, Ausfluß der Persönlichkeit des Verfassers. Daraus folgt, daß grundsätzlich dem Verfasser allein die Befugnis zusteht, darüber zu entscheiden, ob und in welcher Form seine Aufzeichnungen der Öffentlichkeit zugänglich gemacht werden; denn jeder unter Namensnennung erfolgenden Veröffentlichung von Aufzeichnungen eines noch lebenden Menschen wird von der Allgemeinheit mit Recht eine entsprechende Willensrichtung des Verfassers entnommen. Die Fassung der Aufzeichnungen und die Art ihrer Bekanntgabe unterliegt der Kritik und Wertung der öffentlichen Meinung, die aus diesen Umständen Rückschlüsse auf die Persönlichkeit des Verfassers zieht. Während eine *ungenehmigte* Veröffentlichung privater Aufzeichnungen – in der Regel – einen unzulässigen Eingriff in die jedem Menschen geschützte Geheimsphäre darstellt, verletzt eine *veränderte* Wiedergabe der Aufzeichnungen die persönlichkeitsrechtliche Eigensphäre des Verfassers deshalb, weil solche vom Verfasser nicht gebilligten Änderungen ein falsches Persönlichkeitsbild vermitteln können. Unzulässig sind im allgemeinen nicht nur vom Verfasser nicht genehmigte Streichungen wesentlicher Teile seiner Aufzeichnungen, sondern auch Zusätze, durch die seine nur für bestimmte Zwecke zur Veröffentlichung freigegebenen Aufzeichnungen eine andere Färbung oder Tendenz erhalten, als er sie durch die von ihm gewählte Fassung und die Art der von ihm erlaubten Veröffentlichung zum Ausdruck gebracht hat.

Soweit es sich um urheberrechtlich geschützte Werke handelt, sind diese Rechtsgrundsätze bereits seit langem von der Rechtsprechung aus dem Urheberpersönlichkeitsrecht des Werkschöpfers, das nur eine besondere Erscheinungsform des allgemeinen Persönlichkeitsrechtes ist, abgeleitet worden (RGZ 69, 242 [244]; 79, 397 [399]; 151, 50). Vom Blickpunkt des Persönlichkeitsschutzes aus ist die Interessenlage des Autors für Aufzeichnungen, die nicht unter Urheberrechtsschutz stehen, im wesentlichen die gleiche.

There is no need here for more detailed discussion as to whether and how far the protection of this general right to personality, the boundaries of which need to a special extent the balancing of interests, is limited in the individual case by justified private or public interests which outweigh the interest in the inviolability of the proper sphere of personality; because, in the case in dispute, interests of the defendant which are worthy of protection, from which it could derive a justification for its action to which the plaintiff has objected, are not evident. On the contrary, legal personality interests of the plaintiff are violated by the manner of publication chosen by the defendant in respect of the correcting letter, by the omission of vital parts of this letter.

Every linguistic statement is of a certain thought content and, even if the form of the statement cannot be granted the capacity for copyright protection, is the expression of the personality of the author. It follows from this that in principle the authority to decide whether and in what form his writings are made accessible to the public belongs to the author alone; because every publication of the writings of a human being who is still alive which occurs under his name is correctly inferred by the general public to come from a corresponding direction of the will of the author. The form of the writings and the manner in which they are made public is subject to the criticism and evaluation of public opinion, which draw conclusions from these circumstances about the personality of the author. Whilst an *unapproved* publication of private writings, as a rule, represents an impermissible encroachment into the protected private sphere of any human being, an *altered* reproduction of the writings violates the proper sphere of the legal personality of the author, because such alterations, not approved by the author, can convey a false picture of personality. In general not only are omissions, not approved by the author, of vital parts of his writing not permissible, but also additions by which his writings, which are released to the public only for definite purposes, receive a different colouring or slant than he expressed in the form chosen by him and the type of publication allowed by him.

Insofar as it is a matter of works protected by copyright, these legal principles have been derived over a long period from the case law from the author's personality right of the creator of the work, which is only a special manifestation of the general right to personality (RGZ 69, 242 [244]; 79, 397 [399]; 151, 50). From the viewpoint of protection of personality, the position of the author as to his interest in writings which are not under copyright protection is substantially the same.

Im vorliegenden Fall hatte der Kläger eindeutig nur eine Berichtigungsaufforderung, und zwar in seiner Eigenschaft als Anwalt des Dr. S, an die Beklagte gerichtet. Damit wurde die Beklagte von dem Kläger nur ermächtigt, entweder das Schreiben in unverkürzter Gestalt oder unter Beschränkung auf die von ihm verlangte Tatsachenberichtigung unter Klarstellung, daß es sich um ein Berichtigungsverlangen handele, zu veröffentlichen. Da der Kläger im vorliegenden Rechtsstreit nicht die Durchsetzung seines ursprünglichen Berichtigungsbegehrens anstrebt, ist es für die Entscheidung bedeutungslos, ob sein Schreiben vom 4. Juli 1952 den Voraussetzungen des § 11 PresseG entsprochen hat. Wäre dies mit dem Berufungsgericht zu verneinen, so würde hieraus nur ein Recht der Beklagten folgen, von einer Veröffentlichung dieses Schreibens überhaupt abzusehen. Nicht aber war die Beklagte berechtigt, das Schreiben unter der Rubrik 'Leserbriefe' bekanntzugeben, und zwar unter Streichung derjenigen Sätze, aus denen klar ersichtlich war, daß der Kläger nicht etwa seiner persönlichen Meinung zugunsten des Dr. S. Ausdruck verleihen, sondern ein presserechtliches Berichtigungsverlangen durchsetzen wollte.

Es ist dem Landgericht beizupflichten, daß diese Art der Veröffentlichung – noch dazu unter Einreihung des Berichtigungsschreibens unter fünf weitere Zuschriften zu dem von der Beklagten veröffentlichen Artikel über Dr. S. – bei dem unbefangenen Leser den Eindruck hervorrufen mußte, das in Form eines Leserbriefes veröffentlichte Schreiben des Klägers gebe dessen persönliche Stellungnahme zu dem um Dr. S. entbrannten Meinungsstreit wieder. Diese Irreführung wurde auch nicht durch die wörtliche Wiedergabe des einleitenden Satzes des Klägers ausgeräumt; denn dieser Satz besagte in seiner allgemein gehaltenen Fassung für den Leser nur, daß es sich bei dem Einsender um den Anwalt des Dr. S. handle. Dieser Satz stellte aber nicht hinreichend klar, daß auch der Inhalt des fraglichen Schreibens auf einen anwaltlichen Auftrag zurückging und dieses Schreiben von dem Kläger nicht als Privatmann, sondern in Ausübung seines Berufes verfaßt worden war.

Dementsprechend hat das Berufungsgericht auch nicht verkannt, daß die Veröffentlichung des Berichtigungsschreibens in der gekürzten Fassung unter der Rubrik 'Leserbriefe' die Behauptung einer unwahren Tatsache enthält. Damit aber steht zugleich fest, daß durch diese Art der Veröffentlichung das Berichtigungsschreiben eine mit seiner ursprünglichen Fassung nicht übereinstimmende Tendenz erhalten hat, und daß diese Veröffentlichungsform nicht dem entspricht, wozu der Kläger allein seine Einwilligung erteilt hatte, nämlich die fraglichen Ausführungen unverändert in der von ihm gewählten Formgebung als ein Berichtigungsschreiben der Öffentlichkeit zu unterbreiten.

In the present case, the plaintiff had clearly only addressed to the defendant a demand for correction, and that in his capacity as lawyer for Dr S The defendant was only thereby empowered by the plaintiff either to publish the letter in unshortened form or, limiting it to the factual correction requested by him, with the explanation that it was a question of a request for a correction. As the plaintiff in the present action does not seek the implementation of his original desire for a correction, it is unimportant for the decision whether his letter of 4 July 1952 corresponded with the prerequisites of § 11 of the Press Act. Were this to be denied, as in the appeal court, there would only follow from this a right for the defendant to refrain altogether from a publication of this letter. But the defendant was not entitled to publish the letter under the heading 'Readers' letters' together with the omission of those sentences from which it was clearly evident that the plaintiff did not want to give expression to his personal opinion, in favour of Dr S, but to submit a demand for correction under media law.

The opinion of State Court is agreed that this kind of publication, and in addition putting the correction letter along with five other letters about the article published by the defendant about Dr S, had to give rise to the impression in the ingenuous reader that the published contribution of the plaintiff, in the form of a reader's letter, reproduced his personal opinion about the conflict of views which had broken out about Dr S. This misleading impression was not removed either by the literal reproduction of the introductory sentence of the plaintiff; because this sentence only said, in its generally understood version for the reader, that the contributor was the lawyer of Dr S. But this sentence did not explain sufficiently clearly that the content also of the letter in question originated in instructions to a lawyer and this letter had been composed by the plaintiff not as private individual, but in exercise of his profession.

Accordingly the appeal court also did not fail to recognise that the publication of the letter of correction in the abbreviated form under the heading of 'Readers' letters' contains the statement of an untrue fact. In connection with this, however, at the same time it is established that by this kind of publication the letter of correction acquired a propensity which did not agree with its original version and that this form of publication did not correspond with the only thing to which the plaintiff had given his consent, namely to submit to the public the statements in question in the formulation chosen by him as a letter of correction.

Das Landgericht hat mit Recht die beanstandete Veröffentlichung, die nach seinen Feststellungen einem außerordentlich großen Personenkreis bekannt geworden ist, als fortwirkende Beeinträchtigung angesehen und deshalb das auf Widerruf gerichtete Klagbegehren als berechtigt erachtet.

THE NEWSPAPER DELIVERY OBSTRUCTION CASE

BGHZ Band 59 S. 30

6 Zur Haftung der Teilnehmer einer auf die Verhinderung der Auslieferung einer Zeitung gerichteten Demonstration für Mehraufwendungen, die durch die erzwungene Verzögerung der Auslieferung entstanden sind.

BGB §§ 823, 830

VI Zivilsenat, Urt. vom 30. Mai 1972 i.S. A. (Bekl.) w. F. S. (Kl.). VI ZR 6/71.

I Landgericht Frankfurt/Main

II Oberlandesgericht Frankfurt/Main

Anläßlich des Attentats auf das SDS (= Sozialistische Deutscher Studentenbund) – Mitglied Rudi Dutschke am 11. April 1968 (Gründonnerstag) in Berlin fanden an den folgenden Tagen in verschiedenen Städten der Bundesrepublik Demonstration statt, bei denen versucht wurde, die Auslieferung der 'Bild-Zeitung' und anderer Zeitungen des Verlages Axel Springer zu verhindern. Auch das Verlags- und Druckereiunternehmen der Klägerin, die eigene Tageszeitungen herausgibt und die 'Frankfurter Allgemeine Zeitung' sowie eine Teilauflage der 'Bild-Zeitung' druckt, war am Karfreitag, dem 12. April 1968, und am Ostermontag, dem 15. April 1968, Ziel derartiger Demonstrationen.

Mit der Klage nimmt die Klägerin neben anderen den Beklagten, damals Sprecher des Bundesvorstandes des SDS und nach Ansicht der Klägerin einer der Initiatoren der Demonstration, auf Ersatz der ihr durch sie entstandenen Schäden (erhöhte Produktionskosten, Erlöseinbußen, Sachschäden) in Anspruch.

The State Court correctly regarded the publication objected to, which according to its findings became known to an unusually large group of persons, as a continuing violation and therefore considered the demand in the action for retraction as justified.

THE NEWSPAPER DELIVERY OBSTRUCTION CASE

This case concerns the liability of demonstrators for the harm they cause to a business against which they are demonstrating. Liability arose under § 823 I of the BGB, although other bases of liability are discussed. The significant content of the case, however, is concerned with the extent to which the plaintiff's right to demonstrate was protected by Art 8 of the Basic Law and the plaintiff's right to produce a newspaper was protected by Art 5 of the Basic Law. It was the interpretation of these basic rights which determined the actual outcome of the case.

BGHZ Volume 59 p 30

6 On the liability of the participants in a demonstration directed towards the obstruction of delivery of a newspaper for additional expenditure which arose through the enforced delay in delivery.

BGB §§ 823, 830

VIth Civil Senate. Judgment of 30 May 1972 in the matter of A (defendant) v FS (plaintiff) – VI ZR 6/71.

I State Court Frankfurt/Main

II Upper State Court Frankfurt/Main

As a result of the attack on the GSS (= German Socialist Student Union) member Rudi Dutschke on 11 April 1968 (Maundy Thursday) in Berlin, demonstrations took place in various cities in the Federal Republic on the following days. In these demonstrations, attempts were made to obstruct the delivery of the 'Bild Newspaper' and other newspapers of the publishing house of Axel Springer. The publishing and printing undertakings of the plaintiff which publish their own daily newspapers and print the 'Frankfurter Allgemeine Zeitung' (a newspaper) as well as the partial edition of the 'Bild Newspaper' were the target of demonstrations of the same kind on Good Friday 12 April 1968 and on Easter Monday 15 April 1968.

By the action, the plaintiff claims against, amongst others, the defendant, at that time spokesman of the board of the GSS and, in the view of the plaintiff, one of the initiators of the demonstration, for compensation for the harm thereby caused to it (increased cost of production, loss of proceeds, material harm).

Das Landgericht hat die aus der Demonstration in der Nacht vom 12. zum 13. April 1968 hergeleiteten Schadensersatzansprüche dem Grunde nach für gerechtfertigt erklärt. Auf die Berufung des Beklagten hat das Berufungsgericht die Klage hinsichtlich der auf die Schäden am Gebäude der Klägerin gestützten Schadensersatzansprüche abgewiesen. Im übrigen hat es die Berufung zurückgewiesen. Die Revision des Beklagten blieb ohne Erfolg.

Aus den Gründen:

I

Die von der Revision gegenüber dem Erlaß eines Teilurteils erhobenen verfahrensrechtlichen Bedenken sind nicht begründet (wird ausgeführt).

II

1 Das Berufungsgericht hat über den Verlauf der Demonstration am Karfreitag und über die Rolle, die der Beklagte bei ihrer Vorbereitung und ihrer Durchführung spielte, folgende Feststellungen getroffen:

Nachdem am 11. April 1968 Mitglieder einer kleineren Demonstrantengruppe, darunter auch der Beklagte, erfolglos versucht hatten, die bei der Klägerin beschäftigten Arbeiter durch Aufrufe und Diskussionen dazu zu bewegen, die Auslieferung der 'Bild-Zeitung' zu verhindern, wurde am 12. April 1968 (Karfreitag) in Frankfurt ein Flugblatt verteilt, in dem dazu aufgefordert wurde, um 17.00 Uhr in die Universität zu kommen, um von dort gemeinsam zum Geschäftsgebäude der Klägerin zu ziehen und die Auslieferung der 'Bild-Zeitung' zu verhindern. Im Lichthof der Universität fand dann eine als 'teach-in' bezeichnete Versammlung statt, in deren Verlauf neben anderen der Beklagte dazu aufforderte, durch Blockierung sämtlicher Ein- und Ausgänge des Geschäftsgebäudes der Klägerin die Auslieferung der 'Bild-Zeitung' zu verhindern. An Hand einer Tafel, auf welcher der Grundriß des Geschäftsgebäudes der Klägerin mit allen Ein- und Ausgängen sowie die angrenzenden Straßen aufgezeichnet waren, erläuterte er, in welcher Reihenfolge die Ein- und Ausgänge besetzt werden sollten.

The State Court has declared the claims to compensation for harm arising from the demonstrations in the night from 12 to 13 April 1968 to be justified in principle. On the appeal of the defendant, the appeal court dismissed the action insofar as it related to claims to compensation for damage to the plaintiff's building. In other respects it rejected the appeal. The appeal in law by the defendant was unsuccessful.

Reasons:

I

The procedural objections raised by the appeal in law against the issue of a partial judgment are unfounded (this is explained).

II

1 The appeal court made the following findings about the course of the demonstration on Good Friday and about the role which the defendant played in its preparation and execution:

After the members of a smaller group of demonstrators, which also included the defendant, had tried unsuccessfully on 11 April 1968 to induce the workers, employed by the plaintiff, by appeals and discussions to obstruct the delivery of the 'Bild Newspaper', on 12 April 1968 (Good Friday) a leaflet was distributed in Frankfurt which gave an invitation to come to the University at 17.00 hours, in order to proceed together from there to the business premises of the plaintiff and to prevent the delivery of the 'Bild Newspaper'. In the air well of the University a meeting described as a 'teach-in' then took place in the course of which the defendant, amongst others, proposed obstructing the delivery of the 'Bild Newspaper' by blockading all the entrances and exits of the business premises of the plaintiff. From a board, on which a plan of the premises of the plaintiff with all its entrances and exits as well as the streets adjoining it were drawn, he explained the order in which the entrances and exits should be occupied.

Gegen 18.00 Uhr zogen etwa 1500 Personen, darunter der Beklagte, von der Universität zum Geschäftsgebäude der Klägerin und versperrten dort sämtliche Ein- und Ausgänge. An die Demonstranten gerichtete Aufforderungen der Polizei, sich zu entfernen, blieben erfolglos. Lastwagen der Klägerin, die das Betriebsgrundstück verlassen wollten und dabei die Sperren zu durchbrechen suchten, wurden von den Demonstranten fahruntüchtig gemacht. Außerdem wurden einige Fensterscheiben zerstört, die Einfriedigung des Geschäftsgebäudes beschädigt und dessen Mauer mit Aufschriften in Ölfarben versehen. Die Auslieferungssperre zwang die Klägerin dazu, den Druck der Zeitungen – nicht nur der 'Bild-Zeitung' – zeitweise zu unterbrechen, da für die aus den Rotationsmaschinen kommenden normalerweise laufend abtransportierten Zeitungen nicht genügend Lagerraum zur Verfügung stand. Erst am 13. April 1968 gegen 2.00 Uhr konnten die ersten mit Zeitungen beladenen Lastwagen das Geschäftsgebäude verlassen, und von 2.30 Uhr an lief die Auslieferung wieder normal. Die verspätete Ausgabe hat nach der Behauptung der Klägerin Erlöseinbußen und Mehraufwendungen insbesondere für Überstunden verursacht.

Das Berufungsgericht hat aus diesen Vorgängen ferner die Überzeugung gewonnen, daß die Beteiligung des Beklagten an der Vorbereitung und der Durchführung der Demonstration von seiner Vorstellung und seinem Willen getragen war, zusammen mit anderen, gleichgesinnten Demonstranten durch eine Blockade des Betriebsgebäudes der Klägerin die Auslieferung der von ihr gedruckten, für den 13. April 1968 bestimmten Zeitungen zu verhindern.

2 Die gegen diese Feststellungen gerichteten Angriffe der Revision sind nicht begründet.

Die Feststellung des Berufungsgerichts, der Beklagte habe den Inhalt des Flugblattes, mit dem zu dem Treffen in der Universität eingeladen wurde, gekannt, findet entgegen der Auffassung der Revision eine hinreichende Stütze darin, daß dieses Flugblatt auch noch vor und während der Veranstaltung unmittelbar vor dem Versammlungsraum verteilt wurde und daß der Beklagte bei seiner Ansprache an die Versammelten sich die in dem Flugblatt enthaltene Aufforderung zur Blockade des Betriebsgebäudes der Klägerin zu eigen machte und sie durch Anleitungen zu ihrer Durchführung ergänzte.

At around 18.00 hours about 1,500 people, including the defendant, went from the University to the business premises of the plaintiff and blocked all the entrances and exits there. The requests of the police to the demonstrators to move away were unsuccessful. Lorries belonging to the plaintiff which wanted to leave the business site and sought in the process to break through the barriers, were rendered unfit to drive by the demonstrators. Besides this, several windows were broken, the boundary structures of the business premises were damaged and its wall was daubed with slogans in oil paint. The delivery blockade forced the plaintiff to suspend the printing of newspapers – and not only the 'Bild Newspaper' – for a time as there was insufficient storage space available for the newspapers which were coming off the rotary press and normally being continually transported. The first lorries loaded with newspapers were only able to leave the business premises at about 2.00 hours on 13 April 1968 and from 2.30 hours onwards the delivery ran normally again. The delayed distribution caused loss of proceeds and additional expenditure, especially for overtime, according to the assertion of the plaintiff.

The appeal court has further been convinced by these events that the participation of the defendant in the preparation and carrying out of the demonstration was supported by his idea and his intention, together with other like-minded demonstrators, to obstruct the delivery of the newspapers printed by the plaintiffs, which were intended for 13 April 1968, by a blockade of its business premises.

2 The arguments of the appeal in law directed against these findings are not well founded.

The finding of the appeal court that the defendant knew the contents of the leaflet by which invitations were given for the meeting at the University, finds, contrary to the view advanced in the appeal in law, sufficient support in the fact that this leaflet was also distributed before and during the event immediately in front of the place of meeting and that the defendant, in his speech to those assembled, adopted the invitation to the blockade of the business premises of the plaintiff contained in the leaflet and supplemented it by instructions for the implementing of it.

Bei seiner Feststellung, der Beklagte habe an der Demonstration mit dem Willen teilgenommen, gemeinsam mit anderen die Auslieferung der von der Klägerin gedruckten Zeitungen, insbesondere der 'Bild-Zeitung' zu verhindern, ist das Berufungsgericht nicht, wie die Revision meint, von einer Beweislast des Beklagten ausgegangen. Es hat vielmehr als bewiesen erachtet, daß der Beklagte sich bewußt und gewollt an der Auslieferungssperre beteiligt hat. Eine Verkennung der Beweislast läßt sich nicht daraus entnehmen, daß das Berufungsgericht bei der Auseinandersetzung mit der Behauptung des Beklagten, bei dem 'teach-in' sei von einer Blockade gar nicht die Rede gewesen, u. a. darauf hingewiesen hat, daß der Beklagte es unterlassen habe, für diese Gegendarstellung Beweis anzutreten, obwohl ihm das ohne weiteres möglich gewesen sei. Diese Überlegung besagt nicht, daß das Berufungsgericht der Auffassung gewesen sei, die Beweislast zu diesem Streitpunkt treffe den Beklagten, sondern stellt lediglich eine im Rahmen der Beweiswürdigung rechtlich zulässige Folgerung aus dem prozessualen Verhalten des Beklagten dar. Ebensowenig kommt eine Verkennung der Beweislast darin zum Ausdruck, daß das Berufungsgericht aus dem Umstand, daß der Beklagte trotz der bei Durchführung der Blockade geschehenen Gewalttätigkeiten, die von der Mehrheit der Demonstranten ausgingen, weiterhin an Ort und Stelle verblieben ist, unter Einbeziehung seines vorangegangenen Verhaltens Rückschlüsse auf seine innere Einstellung zu den Blockademaßnahmen gezogen hat.

Rechtlich nicht zu beanstanden ist schließlich, daß das Berufungsgericht auch aus dem Verhalten des Beklagten bei dem vorangegangenen 'teach-in' einen Rückschluß darauf gezogen hat, mit welcher inneren Einstellung er an der anschließenden Demonstration teilgenommen hat.

III

Die von den Demonstranten durchgeführte Blockade hat das Berufungsgericht als rechtswidrigen, schuldhaften Eingriff in das nach § 823 Abs. 1 BGB geschützte Recht der Klägerin am eingerichteten und ausgeübten Gewerbetrieb gewürdigt. Das läßt einen Rechtsfehler nicht erkennen.

1 Das Berufungsgericht erörtert nicht, ob das Verhalten des Beklagten als Nötigung (§§ 823 Abs. 2 BGB, 240 StGB) oder vorsätzliche sittenwidrige Schädigung (§ 826 BGB) gewertet werden kann. Es stellt insbesondere nicht ausdrücklich fest, daß der Beklagte mit dem Vorsatz der Vermögensschädigung gehandelt habe.

In finding that the defendant took part in the demonstration with the intention of, together with others, obstructing the delivery of the newspapers printed by the plaintiff, in particular the 'Bild Newspaper', the appeal court did not, as the appeal in law claims, proceed on the basis that the burden of proof lay on the defendant. Rather it regarded, as proved, that the defendant had consciously and willingly taken part in the delivery blockade. A failure to appreciate the burden of proof cannot be deduced from the fact that the appeal court, in its examination of the assertion of the defendant that there had certainly been no talk of a blockade at the 'teach-in', amongst other things pointed to the fact that the defendant had refrained from offering proof for this contrary assertion, although this would easily have been possible. This consideration does not mean that the appeal court was of the opinion that the burden of proof on this disputed issue fell on the defendant, but merely constitutes a conclusion from the procedural conduct of the defendant which is legally permissible within the framework of assessment of the evidence. Neither is a failure to appreciate the burden of proof indicated by the fact that the appeal court drew conclusions from his personal attitude to the blockade measures from the circumstance that he, in spite of the acts of violence which occurred in the carrying out of the blockade, which originated from the majority of the demonstrators, nevertheless remained on the scene, and also taking into account his previous conduct.

Finally, there is no legal objection to the fact that the appeal court also drew from the conduct of the defendant at the prior 'teach-in' a conclusion as to the personal attitude with which he took part in the ensuing demonstration.

III

The blockade carried out by the demonstrators was assessed by the appeal court as an illegal, culpable infringement of the right of the plaintiff protected by § 823 para 1 of the BGB, to established and exercised pursuit of business. That does not reveal any mistake in law.

1 The appeal court does not discuss whether the behaviour of the defendant can be assessed as coercion (§ 823 para 2 of the BGB, § 240 of the StGB) or intentional harm contrary to good morals (§ 826 of the BGB). In particular, it did not expressly find that the defendant had acted with the purpose of causing financial harm.

Diese Fragen bedürfen jedoch auch jetzt keiner Entscheidung. Zwar kann eine Schadensersatzpflicht unter dem Gesichtspunkt des Eingriffs in den Gewerbebetrieb nur begründet werden, wenn dies geboten ist, um eine sonst bleibende Lücke im Rechtsschutz zu schließen (BGHZ 36, 252, 257; 45, 296, 307; st. Rspr.). Es ist aber ebenfalls anerkannt, daß unmittelbare Eingriffe in fremden Gewerbebetrieb eine Ersatzpflicht auch dann auslösen können, wenn sie ohne das Bewußtsein der Schädigung vorgenommen oder nicht als sittenwidrig zu werten sind (BGHZ a.a.O. S. 256). Die notwendige Begrenzung dieser Haftung ergibt sich dadurch, daß die Frage nach der Rechtswidrigkeit des Handelns hier nicht schon wegen des Eingriffstatbestandes grundsätzlich zu bejahen, sondern in jedem Einzelfall unter Heranziehung aller Umstände zu prüfen ist (BGHZ 45, 296, 307 m. w. Nachw.; Urteil vom 14. Januar 1969 – VI ZR 196/67 = VersR 69, 352; Urteil vom 20. Juni 1969 – VI ZR 234/67 = VersR 69, 851). Steht, wie im Streitfall, politisch motiviertes Handeln in Frage, so muß diese Prüfung von den in Betracht kommenden, durch das Grundgesetz und die Landesverfassungen geschützten Freiheiten ausgehen. Das kann dazu führen, daß die Antwort auf die Frage der Rechtswidrigkeit auch durch die Willensrichtung des Handelnden mitbestimmt wird. Insbesondere bei Betriebsbehinderungen, die durch Demonstrationen verursacht werden, kann es für die Frage der Rechtswidrigkeit darauf ankommen, ob die Behinderung das Ziel oder nur eine unbeabsichtigte Nebenwirkung der Demonstration ist. Der Streitfall bietet hiernach angesichts der vom Berufungsgericht über die Willensrichtung des Beklagten getroffenen Feststellungen keinen Anlaß zur Prüfung der umstrittenen Frage, ob die Haftung für Vermögensschäden aus Eingriff in den Gewerbebetrieb durch Demonstrationen etwa auch bei nur fahrlässigem, insbesondere leicht fahrlässigem Handeln zu begründen wäre.

2 Daß die gegen den Betrieb der Klägerin gerichtete Blockade einen unmittelbaren, betriebsbezogenen Eingriff in das Recht der Klägerin an der ungestörten Ausübung ihres Gewerbebetriebes darstellt, ist nicht zweifelhaft (vgl. dazu BGHZ 29, 65, 74f.; BGH LM Nr. 36 zu § 823 [Ai] BGB).

Dieser Eingriff war auch rechtswidrig.

(a) Mit Recht hat das Berufungsgericht hierzu entscheidend auf die in der Auslieferungssperre liegende zielbewußte Anwendung unmittelbaren Zwanges gegen ein bestimmtes Unternehmen abgestellt. Die Einschließung des Gebäudes der Klägerin mit dem dann auch durchgeführten Zweck, die Ausfahrt ihrer Fahrzeuge zu verhindern, stellte die Anwendung von Gewalt dar (BGHSt 23, 46, 54).

The questions, however, need no decision even now. It is true that a duty to compensate for damage can only be established from the standpoint of an interference in the pursuit of a business if this is necessary in order to close a gap which would otherwise exist in legal protection (BGHZ 36, 252, 257; 45, 296, 307; established case law). But it is likewise recognised that direct interferences in the pursuit of business by others can produce a duty to compensate even if they are undertaken without the consciousness of causing harm or are not to be assessed as contrary to good morals (BGHZ, *loc cit*, 256). The necessary limits of this liability result from the fact that the question of the unlawfulness of the action is not here to be answered in principle positively simply because of the fact of interference, but in each individual case is to be examined by reference to all the circumstances (BGHZ 45, 296, 307 with further references; judgment of 14 January 1969 – VI ZR 196/67 = VersR 69, 352; judgment of 20 June 1969 – VI ZR 2 34/67 = VersR 69, 851). If, as in the case in dispute, politically motivated action is in question, this examination must start from the freedoms which come into consideration and which are protected in the Basic Law and the Constitutions of the States. That can lead to the answer to the question of unlawfulness being also partly determined by the intention of the person acting. Especially for obstructions to business which are caused by demonstrations, the issue of unlawfulness can depend upon whether the obstruction is the objective of the demonstration or only an unintended side effect. The case in dispute offers, in the light of the findings made by the appeal court about the intention of the defendant, no reason for examining the disputed question of whether liability for financial harm by interference by demonstrations in the carrying of the business could also be based on merely negligent, in particular slightly negligent, action.

2 It is not to be doubted that the blockade directed against the business of the plaintiff represents a direct business-related interference with the plaintiff's right to the undisturbed execution of its business (compare to this BGHZ; 29, 65, 74 and onwards; BGH LM no 36 at § 823 [Ai] of the BGB).

This interference was also unlawful.

(a) The appeal court has correctly taken into account the application of direct purposeful coercion against a certain undertaking in the delivery blockade which is decisive in this issue. The encirclement of the plaintiff's building with the purpose, which was then carried out, of obstructing the exit of their vehicles, represents the application of force (BGHSt 23, 46, 54).

Mit der Verhinderung der Auslieferung der 'Bild-Zeitung' sollte gegen die Pressekonzentration in den Händen des Verlegers Axel Springer und gegen die als tendenziös empfundene Berichterstattung der zu dessen Konzern gehörenden Zeitungen protestiert und es sollte die Öffentlichkeit auf die hieraus sich ergebenden Gefahren aufmerksam gemacht werden. Zu einem solchen Zweck gibt die Rechtsordnung u. a. das Mittel der Demonstration, gestattet jedoch nicht, diese zur Anwendung von Zwang der hier gegebenen Art zu benutzen.

In einem Teil des Schrifttums und der Rechtsprechung der Instanzgerichte ist zwar die Meinung vertreten worden, das durch Art. 5 und 8 GG gewährleistete Demonstrationsrecht rechtfertige unter gewissen Voraussetzungen auch die begrenzte Anwendung von Gewalt. Dem kann jedoch nicht beitreten werden. Art. 8 Abs. 1 GG gewährleistet das Recht zur friedlichen Versammlung, damit vor allem auch die gemeinsame Kundgabe einer übereinstimmenden Meinung durch einen öffentlichen Aufzug (Demonstration). Die Tragweite dieses Grundrechts ist aus dem Grundgesetz selbst zu entnehmen, insbesondere aus der Funktion, die der Versammlungsfreiheit im Rahmen der freiheitlich-demokratischen Grundordnung des Grundgesetzes zukommt, sowie aus ihrem systematischen Zusammenhang mit den anderen, von der Verfassung gewährleisteten Grundfreiheiten und -rechten, in erster Linie mit der in Art. 5 Abs. 1 Satz 1 GG verbürgten Meinungsfreiheit. Die Versammlungsfreiheit ergänzt die Meinungsfreiheit nach der kollektiven Seite hin; sie schützt den Vorgang der kollektiven Meinungskundgabe ebenso wie den des kollektiven Meinungsempfangs und dadurch die kollektive Meinungsbildung. Beide Grundrechte dienen dazu, die für das Funktionieren der freiheitlichen Demokratie unabdingbare öffentliche Diskussion über Gegenstände von allgemeinem Interesse und staatspolitischer Bedeutung zu gewährleisten. Das Demonstrationsrecht ist deshalb ebenso wie das Recht der freien Meinungsäußerung auf den geistigen Kampf der Meinungen angelegt, wenn auch nicht zu übersehen ist, daß in der Wirkungsweise zwischen einer Kollektivaussage durch eine Demonstration und einer individuellen Meinungsäußerung naturgemäß Unterschiede bestehen. Während letztere vor allem durch die Überzeugungskraft der verfochtenen Meinung wirken soll, zieht die in der Demonstration liegende Kollektivaussage zusätzliche Wirkung aus dem Kundgebungswillen derer, die sich durch ihre Beteiligung an der gemeinsamen Meinungskundgabe deren Inhalt zu eigen machen. Gerade wegen dieser zusätzlichen, überdies Belange der Allgemeinheit berührenden Wirkung solcher Kundgebungen ist das Demonstrationsrecht in Art. 8 GG neben dem Recht der freien Meinungsäußerung verankert. Durch dieses zusätzliche Element verliert sie jedoch nicht den Charakter eines Mittels der geistigen Auseinandersetzung. Sinn und Zweck der Demonstrationsfreiheit werden daher jedenfalls dann verfehlt, wenn die kollektive Meinungs- oder Willensäußerung ihr Ziel mit Hilfe eines auf Unterlassung fremder Meinungsäußerung gerichteten unmittelbaren Zwanges zu erreichen sucht. Eine Demonstration dieser Art ist nicht friedlich im Sinne des Art. 8 GG.

By obstruction of the delivery of the 'Bild Newspaper' a protest was to be made against the press concentration in the hands of the publisher Axel Springer and against news reporting, which was felt to be partisan, of the newspapers belonging to his concern, and the public were to made aware of the dangers arising from this. The legal order provides, amongst other things, the device of the demonstration for such a purpose but does not however allow this to be used for the application of coercion of the kind occurring here.

In a part of the literature and the case law of the trial courts the view has been taken that the right to demonstrate guaranteed by Arts 5 and 8 of the GG also justifies under certain conditions the limited application of force. This cannot, however, be acceded to. Art 8 para 1 of the GG guarantees the right to peaceful assembly and with that also, above all, the communal proclamation of an agreed opinion by a public procession (demonstration). The range of this basic right is to be deduced from the Basic Law itself, especially from the function which is appropriate to the freedom of assembly within the framework of the free democratic constitutional order of the Basic Law, as well as from its systematic correlation with the other basic freedoms and rights guaranteed by the Constitution, primarily the freedom of opinion guaranteed by Art 5 para 1, sentence 1 of the Basic Law. The freedom of assembly completes the freedom of opinion on the collective side; it protects the occurrence of collective proclamation of opinion as well as that of collective receiving of opinion and thereby collective formation of opinion. Both Basic Rights serve the purpose of guaranteeing public discussion about objects of general interest and political significance, which is indispensable for the functioning of a free democracy. The right of demonstration is therefore, like the right of free expression of opinion, designed for the intellectual conflict of opinions, even though it is not to be overlooked that differences naturally exist between the way a collective assertion of opinion through a demonstration and an individual expression of opinion work. While the latter should operate primarily through the persuasiveness of the opinion advocated, the collective assertion of opinion in a demonstration draws additional effect from the desire to give expression by those who, by participation in the general proclamation of opinion, make its content their own. It is precisely because of this additional effect of such declarations, affecting, moreover, the interests of the general public, that the right to demonstrate in Art 8 of the GG is anchored to the right of free expression of opinion. It does not however lose the character of a means of intellectual argument because of this additional element. The meaning and purpose of freedom to demonstrate are in any case missed if the collective expression of opinion or intention seeks to attain its objective with the help of direct coercion aimed at the discontinuance of a different expression of opinion. A demonstration of this kind is not peaceful in the sense of Art 8 of the GG.

Der verschiedentlich herangezogene Gedanke der Effektivität der Meinungsäußerung rechtfertigt kein anderes Ergebnis. Dieser Gesichtspunkt ist bei der Beurteilung verletzender Meinungsäußerungen von Bedeutung (BVerfGE 24, 278; 12, 113, 131; BGHZ 45, 296 'Höllenfeuer'). Dabei handelt es sich aber stets um die Beurteilung von Äußerungen auf der Ebene des geistigen Meinungskampfes. Die dabei entwickelten Grundsätze lassen sich, wie bereits der 2. Strafsenat des Bundesgerichtshofes (BGHSt 23, 46) ausgesprochen hat, nicht auf Verhaltensweisen übertragen, die sich zur Verhinderung fremder Meinungsäußerung des unmittelbaren Zwanges bedienen. Dem steht schon entgegen, daß das Grundgesetz nur den geistigen Meinungskampf schützt.

Auch der Gesichtspunkt der 'Chancengleichheit' vermag eine andere Beurteilung nicht zu rechtfertigen. Die Chance, mit einer Meinung zu Gehör zu kommen, gewährleistet das Grundgesetz gerade dadurch, daß Gewalt und Zwang als Mittel des Meinungskampfes ausgeschlossen werden zu Gunsten einer freien geistigen Auseinandersetzung einschließlich friedlicher Demonstrationen. Daß sich bei der Ausübung des Grundrechts der Meinungsfreiheit für den einzelnen Unterschiede hinsichtlich der Wirkungsmöglichkeiten deshalb ergeben, weil nicht jeder über die gleichen technischen und organisatorischen Möglichkeiten der Meinungsverbreitung verfügt, wird vom Grundgesetz als Ausfluß der Handlungsfreiheit grundsätzlich hingenommen. Sofern im Einzelfall eine übermäßige Pressekonzentration eine Gefahr für die Meinungs- und Pressefreiheit darstellt, die ein konstituierendes Prinzip der freiheitlichen Demokratie ist, mag das ein Eingreifen des Gesetzgebers oder des Bundesverfassungsgerichts zu ihrem Schutz erfordern (BVerfGE 20, 162, 176). Eine solche Sachlage gibt aber denjenigen, die auf eine derartige Gefahr hinweisen wollen, nicht die Befugnis, ihrer Warnung durch Anwendung von Zwang gegen bestimmte Personen oder Unternehmen vermehrte Aufmerksamkeit zu verschaffen.

Ob für Störungen und Beeinträchtigungen Dritter und der Allgemeinheit, die sich als bloße zwangsläufige Nebenwirkungen einer Demonstration darstellen, etwas anderes zu gelten hat, braucht hier nicht erörtert zu werden. Bei den gegen die Klägerin gerichteten Blockademaßnahmen handelte es sich eindeutig um die gegen ein bestimmtes Unternehmen gezielte Anwendung von Zwang und nicht lediglich um eine unvermeidbare Nebenwirkung einer kollektiven Meinungskundgabe.

The variously employed concept of the effectiveness of expression of opinion justifies no other outcome. This point of view is of importance in the assessment of hurtful expressions of opinion (BVerfGE 24, 278; 12, 113, 131; BGHZ 45, 296 'hellfire'). But at the same time it always concerns the assessment of statements on the level of intellectual conflict of opinion. The principles developed in this respect, as the second Criminal Senate of the Federal Supreme Court has already stated (BGHSt 23, 46) cannot be transferred to types of conduct which make use of direct coercion for the obstruction of the expression of a different opinion. The obstacle to that is that the Basic Law only protects the intellectual conflict of opinions.

The point of view of 'equality of chances' cannot justify a different assessment, either. The chance of getting a hearing for an opinion is guaranteed by the Basic Law simply by the fact that force and compulsion are excluded as a method in the conflict of opinions, in favour of a free intellectual debate, including peaceful demonstrations. The fact that, in the exercise of the basic right of freedom of opinion for the individual, differences arise in relation to the possibilities of effectiveness, because not everyone has at his disposal the same technical and organisational possibilities of dissemination of opinion, is accepted in principle by the Basic Law as the result of freedom of action. Insofar as a huge press concentration, in an individual case, represents a danger for freedom of opinion and of the press, which is a constituent principle of free democracy, that may require an intervention of the legislator or of the Federal Constitutional Court for protection of democracy (BVerfGE 20, 162, 176). But such a state of affairs does not give those who want to point out a danger of this kind the authority to provide increased attention for their warning by the application of coercion against certain persons or undertakings.

Whether different rules apply for disruptions to and interferences with third persons and the general public which show themselves to be mere unavoidable side effects of a demonstration does not need to be discussed here. With the blockade measures directed against the plaintiff, it is clearly a matter of the application of coercion directed against a certain undertaking and not merely an unavoidable side effect of a collective expression of opinion.

(b) Zutreffend hat das Berufungsgericht bei der zur Frage der Rechtswidrigkeit des Eingriffs in den Gewerbetrieb gebotenen Gesamtwürdigung ferner berücksichtigt, daß die Blockademaßnahmen gegen ein Presseunternehmen gerichtet waren und deshalb auch das Recht der Pressefreiheit verletzten. Selbstverständlich schützt die Pressefreiheit Presseorgane nicht vor wirtschaftlichen Nachteilen, die sich aus der Ausübung des Rechts der Meinungsfreiheit und des Demonstrationsrechts durch andere ergeben. Meinungs- und Pressefreiheit sollen aber die freie geistige Betätigung und den Prozeß der Meinungsbildung in der freiheitlichen Demokratie schützen; deshalb müssen zum Schutz des Instituts der freien Presse die Presseorgane –auch solche, die die Erzeugnisse der Presse zwar nicht gestalten, aber verbreiten – gegenüber Eingriffen gesichert werden, durch die ihre Handlungsfreiheit, wenn auch nur vorübergehend, unter Anwendung von Zwang aufgehoben wird (vgl. BVerfGE 25, 256 'Blinkfüer'). Die Auslieferungssperre verstieß gegen diese verfassungsmäßig gewährleistete Freiheit. Mit dieser Maßnahme überließen es die Demonstranten nicht mehr der freien Entscheidung der angesprochenen Leser, auf die Lektüre der 'Bild-Zeitung' zu verzichten; sie versuchten vielmehr, eine von ihnen wegen ihrer geistigen Haltung abgelehnte Zeitung – wenn auch nur vorübergehend – gewaltsam am Erscheinen zu hindern. Ein solches Verhalten läßt sich mit dem Grundsatz der Pressefreiheit nicht vereinbaren, weil es im Ergebnis auf eine unerlaubte Zensur durch Andersdenkende hinausläuft.

(c) Eine Rechtfertigung der Blockademaßnahmen durch Notwehr hat das Berufungsgericht zu Recht verneint. Es fehlte bereits an einem gegenwärtigen Angriff der Klägerin, da nicht festgestellt ist, daß die Zeitungen, deren Auslieferung die Demonstration verhindern wollte, irgendwelche Angriffe gegen Rechtsgüter Dritter enthielten. Notwehr liegt aber auch deshalb nicht vor, weil es bei dem Beklagten an dem dafür erforderlichen Verteidigungswillen fehlte. Das Berufungsgericht hat insoweit in tatrichterlicher Würdigung festgestellt, daß es darum gegangen sei, dem Springer-Konzern zur Warnung und um ihn wirtschaftlich zu schwächen, Schaden zuzufügen, sowie die Klägerin davon abzuhalten, in Zukunft die 'Bild-Zeitung' zu drucken. Der Beklagte versuche jetzt, Selbstjustiz als Notwehr hinzustellen. Damit ist der Verteidigungswille ausreichend verneint.

(d) Entsprechendes gilt für die Frage einer Rechtfertigung des Vorgehens der Demonstranten unter dem Gesichtspunkt des Notstandes (§ 904 BGB). Auch dieser Rechtfertigungsgrund setzt außer einer objektiven Notlage als subjektives Tatbestandselement einen durch die Notlage motivierten Willen des Handelnden voraus, woran es dem Beklagten fehlte.

(b) Pertinently, the appeal court has further considered in the total assessment necessary on the question of the unlawfulness of the interference in the pursuit of business, that the blockade measures were directed against a press undertaking and therefore violated the right of freedom of the press. Self-evidently, freedom of the press does not protect organs of the press from business disadvantages which arise from the exercise of the right of freedom of opinion and the right to demonstrate by others. Freedom of opinion and the press are however to protect free intellectual activity and the process of formation of opinion in a free democracy; therefore, for the protection of the institution of the free press, the organs of the press – even those which do not formulate the products of the press but disseminate them – must be protected against interferences by which their freedom of action is removed by application of coercion, even if only temporarily (compare BVerfGE 25, 256 'Blinkfüer'). The delivery blockade offends against this constitutionally guaranteed freedom. By this step, the demonstrators did not any longer leave it to the free decision of the readers who were addressed to give up reading the 'Bild Newspaper'; they attempted instead to obstruct by force, even if only temporarily, the appearance of a newspaper disapproved of by them because of its intellectual stance. Such conduct cannot be reconciled with the principle of press freedom, because it results in an unauthorised censorship by persons with other opinions.

(c) The appeal court correctly denied that there was any justification of the blockade measures resulting from self-defence. There was no current attack by the plaintiff, as it has not been established that the newspapers, the delivery of which the demonstrators wanted to obstruct, contained any attacks against the legal interests of others. Self-defence is however also not present because the defendant lacked the intention to defend necessary for it. The appeal court established in this respect, through the assessment by the judge of fact, that it was a case of inflicting harm on the Springer concern as a warning and to weaken it economically, as well as preventing the plaintiff from printing the 'Bild Newspaper' in the future. The defendant was now attempting to represent taking the law into his own hand as self-defence. In this respect an intention to act in defence is sufficiently contradicted.

(d) The same applies to the question of a justification of the demonstrators' action from the point of view of emergency (§ 904 of the BGB). This ground of justification also presupposes, besides an objective calamity, the subjective element of an intention of those acting which is motivated by the calamity and this was absent with the defendant.

(e) Ohne Rechtsverstoß hat das Berufungsgericht schließlich die Voraussetzungen eines Widerstandsrechts nach Art. 20 Abs. 4 GG verneint. Insoweit erhebt auch die Revision keine Bedenken.

3 Die gegen die Annahme eines Verschuldens des Beklagten gerichteten Revisionsangriffe sind nicht begründet.

(a) Ein zur Haftung ausreichendes Verschulden des Beklagten folgt schon daraus, daß der Eingriff in den Gewerbetrieb der Klägerin vom Vorsatz des Beklagten umfaßt war (RGZ 142, 116, 122; BGH LM Nr. 15 zu § 830 BGB). Nicht erforderlich war, daß der Beklagte die aus diesem Eingriff sich ergebenden Schäden vorhersah. Welche Vorstellungen der Beklagte sich über die wirtschaftlichen Auswirkungen der Auslieferungssperre bei der Klägerin machte, ist daher unerheblich. Den auf den Eingriff – die Verhinderung der Auslieferung der bei der Klägerin gedruckten Zeitungen – gerichteten Vorsatz des Beklagten hat das Berufungsgericht rechtsfehlerfrei bejaht.

(b) Dem Umstand, daß der Beklagte sein Tun möglicherweise für erlaubt hielt, hat das Berufungsgericht zu Recht keine Bedeutung beigemessen. Ein solcher Verbotsirrtum stellt nur ausnahmsweise einen Entschuldigungsgrund dar. Voraussetzung wäre, daß der Irrtum auch bei Anwendung der erforderlichen Sorgfalt unvermeidlich war. Daß das Berufungsgericht dies dem Beklagten nicht zuzugestehen vermochte, bedeutet entgegen der Auffassung der Revision keine Überspannung der an das Erkenntnisvermögen des Beklagten zu stellenden Anforderungen. Daß aus dem Recht zu friedlicher Versammlung kein Recht zur Auslieferungssperre gegen ein bestimmtes Druckereiunternehmen hergeleitet werden kann, ist für einen auf dem Boden des Grundgesetzes stehenden Staatsbürger erkennbar. Daran ändert auch nichts die Tatsache, daß die Auffassung des Beklagten, eine sogenannte 'begrenzte Gewaltanwendung' – was immer unter diesem Begriff zu verstehen sein und wo er seine Grenze finden mag – werde unter gewissen Voraussetzungen vom Demonstrationsrecht noch gedeckt, inzwischen auch von Juristen geäußert worden ist.

Der von der Revision in den Vordergrund gerückte Gesichtspunkt der vermeintlichen Notwehr vermag schon deshalb nicht Platz zu greifen, weil auch die vermeintliche Notwehr einen Verteidigungswillen erfordert.

IV

Das Berufungsgericht hat den Beklagten ferner für ersatzpflichtig erklärt, soweit drei Kraftfahrzeuge der Klägerin bei dem Versuch, die Blockade zu brechen, von den Demonstranten fahruntüchtig gemacht worden sind. Es stellt dazu fest, dies sei Teil der Handlung des Beklagten zur gewollten Verhinderung der Auslieferung der Zeitungen gewesen.

Für die Rechtswidrigkeit dieses Verhaltens des Beklagten und sein Verschulden hinsichtlich dieser Sachbeschädigung kann auf das zum Eingriff in den Gewerbebetrieb Ausgeführte verwiesen werden.

(e) Without any error in law, the appeal court finally denied the prerequisites of a right of resistance in accordance with Art 20 para 4 of the GG. In this respect the appeal in law also gives rise to no doubts.

3 The arguments of the appeal in law against the assumption of fault on the part of the defendant are not well founded.

(a) Fault of the defendant sufficient to give rise to liability follows merely from the fact that the interference in the carrying on of the plaintiff's business was included in the purpose of the defendant (RGZ 142, 116, 122; BGH LM no 15 on § 830 of the BGB). It was not necessary that the defendant should have foreseen the harm arising from this interference. What ideas the defendant had about the business consequences for the plaintiff of the delivery blockade is therefore unimportant. The defendant's purpose in relation to the interference, the obstruction of the delivery of newspapers printed by the plaintiff, has been confirmed by the appeal court, correctly in law.

(b) The appeal court correctly attached no importance to the fact that the defendant possibly considered his action to be permitted. Such a mistake of law only exceptionally represents a ground of excuse. It would be a pre-requisite that the mistake was unavoidable, even by the application of the necessary care. The fact that the appeal court was not able to concede this to the defendant does not, contrary to the view of the appeal in law, indicate an overstraining of the requirements to be placed on the defendant's capacity for discernment. The fact that no right to a delivery blockade of a certain printing undertaking can be derived from the right to peaceful assembly is recognisable for a citizen standing on the ground of the Basic Law. The fact that the opinion of the defendant, that a so-called 'limited application of force', whatever may be understood by the concept and whatever its limit may be, is, subject to certain conditions, covered by the right to demonstrate, has now also been expressed by jurists, does not change anything either.

The point of view, which has been brought into the foreground by the appeal in law, of supposed self-defence cannot take effect because the supposed self-defence also requires an intention to defend.

IV

The appeal court has further declared the defendant to be obliged to provide compensation insofar as three of the plaintiff's vehicles were, in the attempt to break the blockade, made unfit to drive by the demonstrators. It found that this had been part of the defendant's action for the intended obstruction of the delivery of the newspapers.

For the illegality of this conduct of the defendant, and his fault in relation to this material damage, reference can be made to the explanation in relation to the interference in the carrying on of the business.

V

1 Das Berufungsgericht hat den Beklagten als Mittäter hinsichtlich des gesamten durch die Demonstration vom 12./13. April 1968 angerichteten Vermögensschadens der Klägerin und ihres Sachschadens an Fahrzeugen dem Grunde nach für ersatzpflichtig erklärt. Lediglich die Gebäudeschaden hat es ausgenommen, da es sich trotz der Äußerung des Beklagten bei dem 'teach-in' in der Universität, er überlasse es der 'progressiven Phantasie' des einzelnen, welches Material er während der Demonstration mit sich führen wolle, nicht hat davon überzeugen können, daß auch die zu Sachschäden führenden Handlungen einzelner Demonstranten von seinem Willen gedeckt waren.

Die Revision verkennt nicht, daß die vom Berufungsgericht aus § 830 Abs. 2 Satz 1 BGB hergeleitete volle Haftung desjenigen Demonstranten, der sich wissend und willentlich an der Auslieferungssperre beteiligt hat, dem Inhalt der genannten Gesetzesvorschrift entspricht. Sie meint jedoch, die auf überholten Vorstellungen des 19. Jahrhunderts beruhende Vorschrift passe nicht mehr in die heutige Zeit. Wolle man die Ausübung des Demonstrationsrechts nicht mit unzumutbaren Risiken belasten, müsse die Haftung des einzelnen Demonstranten auf die Schäden beschränkt werden, die er selbst nachweislich verursacht habe.

Dieser Auffassung kann nicht beigetreten werden. Die in § 830 Abs. 1 Satz 1 BGB angeordnete volle Haftung eines jeden Mittäters beruht auf dem Gedanken, daß bei Beteiligung mehrerer es dem Geschädigten häufig nicht möglich ist nachzuweisen, inwieweit der Schaden von dem einen oder anderen Beteiligten verursacht worden ist. Eine Regelung, die jeden der mehreren Schädiger nur in dem Umfang haften ließe, in dem er durch eigene Handlungen zum Entstehen des Schadens beigetragen hat, hätte deshalb zur Folge, daß der Schaden häufig ganz oder teilweise von dem schuldlos Geschädigten getragen werden müßte, während die schuldigen Schädiger frei ausgingen. Das Gesetz legt daher das Risiko der Haftungsverteilung den Schädigern auf und überläßt es ihnen, sich untereinander nach Maßgabe ihres Schadensbeitrages auseinanderzusetzen (§§ 840, 426 BGB). Diese gesetzgeberische Wertung widerspricht keinem Verfassungsgrundsatz, insbesondere nicht dem der Verhältnismäßigkeit, und besitzt auch heute noch Gültigkeit. Sie trifft gerade auch auf die Fälle von Demonstrationsschäden zu, bei denen es dem Geschädigten in aller Regel nur möglich sein wird, einige der Teilnehmer an der Schädigungshandlung zu identifizieren und den Nachweis zu führen, daß sie zu denen gehören, die den rechtswidrigen Eingriff in seine Rechte auch gewollt haben.

V

1 The appeal court has declared the defendant, as a co-perpetrator in relation to the whole of the financial harm to the plaintiff caused by the demonstration of 12/13 April 1968 and the material damage to the vehicles, to be in principle liable to provide compensation. It has only excepted the damage to the buildings as, in spite of the statement of the defendant at the 'teach-in' in the University that he would leave it to the 'progressive imagination' of the individual what material he would want to take with him during the demonstration, it was not convinced that the actions of individual demonstrators leading to material damage were also covered by his intention.

The appeal in law does not fail to recognise that the full liability of those demonstrators who knowingly and willingly participated in the delivery blockade, which was derived by the appeal court from § 830 para 2 sentence 1 of the BGB, corresponds to the content of the said statutory provision. It considers, however, that the provision, based on out of date ideas of the 19th century, is not appropriate any more for the present day. If one does not want to burden the exercise of the right to demonstrate with unreasonable risks, the liability of the individual demonstrator must be limited to the harm which he himself demonstrably causes.

This view cannot be acceded to. The full liability of each accomplice provided for in § 830 para 1 sentence 1 of the BGB is based on the idea that where several people have participated, it is frequently not possible for the person harmed to prove how far the harm was caused by one or other of the participants. A regime which allows each of several tortfeasors to be liable only to the extent that he has contributed by his own actions to the production of the harm would have as its consequence that the harm would frequently have to be borne wholly or partly by the person, who was not at fault, who suffered the harm, while the tortfeasors, who were at fault, would escape. The law therefore puts the risk of allocation of liability on the tortfeasors and leaves it to them to come to terms amongst themselves according to the measure of their contribution to the harm (§§ 840, 426 of the BGB). This appraisal by the legislator does not contradict any constitutional principle, nor, in particular that of proportionality and still has validity today. It is also appropriate in cases of harm caused by demonstrations in which it will only be possible as a rule for the person suffering harm to identify some of the participants in the action causing the damage and to bring proof that they belong to those who wanted to interfere illegally with his rights.

Es kann der Revision auch nicht zugegeben werden, daß die in § 830 Abs. 1 Satz 1 BGB enthaltene Regelung die Ausübung des Demonstrationsrechts mit einem unzumutbaren Risiko belaste. Die Haftung nach dieser Vorschrift trifft nicht Demonstranten, ohne deren Willen andere Teilnehmer die Grenzen des Demonstrationsrechts überschreiten und in Rechte Dritter eingreifen. Sie kommt nur bei einem Demonstrationsteilnehmer in Betracht, der sich an schadenstiftenden Ausschreitungen beteiligt und Schäden dieser Art mit in seinen Willen aufgenommen hat, oder der sich an der Blockade eines bestimmten Unternehmens in Kenntnis dieses ihres Zieles beteiligt. Gegen eine Haftung unter diesem Gesichtspunkt bestehen jedenfalls dann keine Bedenken, wenn der so Beteiligte, wie hier, maßgeblich auch am Zustandekommen der unfriedlich geplanten Demonstration mitgewirkt hat.

2 Auch unter dem Gesichtspunkt des Mitverschuldens ist kein Raum für eine Minderung der Haftung des Beklagten. Daraus, daß die Klägerin die 'Bild-Zeitung' druckte, kann der Vorwurf des Verschuldens gegen sich selbst (§ 254 BGB) nicht hergeleitet werden.

It cannot be acknowledged, in favour of the appeal in law, that the rule contained in § 830 para 1 sentence 1 of the BGB burdens the exercise of the right to demonstrate with an unreasonable risk. Liability under this provision does not affect demonstrators if, without this being their intention, other participants overstep the limits of the right to demonstrate and intrude on the rights of third parties. Liability under this provision only has to be considered in relation to a participant in a demonstration who takes part in riots causing harm where damage of this kind was included in his intention, or who participates in the blockade of a certain undertaking in the knowledge that this is its objective. There are in any case no doubts about liability from this point of view if the participant, as here, contributed in a decisive way to the occurrence of the demonstration which was planned not to be peaceful.

2 Also, from the point of view of contributory fault, there is no room for a reduction in the liability of the defendant. An accusation of fault on the part of the plaintiff itself (§ 254 of the BGB) cannot be derived from the fact that it printed the 'Bild Newspaper'.

HARM TO FINANCIAL STATUS

§ 824 [Kreditgefährdung] (1) Wer der Wahrheit zuwider eine Tatsache behauptet oder verbreitet, die geeignet ist, den Kredit eines anderen zu gefährden oder sonstige Nachteile für dessen Erwerb oder Fortkommen herbeizuführen, hat dem anderen den daraus entstehenden Schaden auch dann zu ersetzen, wenn er die Unwahrheit zwar nicht kennt, aber kennen muß.

(2) Durch eine Mitteilung, deren Unwahrheit dem Mitteilenden unbekannt ist, wird dieser nicht zum Schadensersatze verpflichtet, wenn er oder der Empfänger der Mitteilung an ihr ein berechtiges Interesse hat.

HARM CONTRARY TO MORALITY

§ 825 [Bestimmung zur Beiwohnung] Wer eine Frauensperson durch Hinterlist, durch Drohung oder unter Mißbrauch eines Abhängigkeitsverhältnisses zur Gestattung der außerehelichen Beiwohnung bestimmt, ist ihr zum Ersatze des daraus entstehenden Schadens verpflichtet.

§ 826 [Sittenwidrige vorsätzliche Schädigung] Wer in einer gegen die guten Sitten verstoßenden Weise einem anderen vorsätzlich Schaden zufugt, ist dem anderen zum Ersatze des Schadens verpflichtet.

HARM TO FINANCIAL STATUS

§ 824 [Endangering of credit] (1) A person who, contrary to the truth, asserts or disseminates a fact which is apt to endanger the credit of another or to cause other disadvantages for his income or prospects must compensate that other for the harm arising from this, even if he did not know of the inaccuracy but ought to have known of it.

(2) A communication, the inaccuracy of which is unknown to the person making it, will not oblige that person to make compensation for harm if he or the recipient of the communication has a legitimate interest in it.

How does § 824 II compare and contrast with the defences of innocent dissemination and qualified privilege in the English tort of defamation?

HARM CONTRARY TO MORALITY

§ 825 [Inducement to cohabitation] A person who induces a female by fraud, by threat or through abuse of a relationship of dependency to consent to cohabitation outside marriage is obliged to compensate her for the harm arising from this.

§ 826 [Intentional harm contrary to morals] A person who intentionally inflicts harm on another in a manner which offends against good morals is obliged to make compensation to the other for the harm.

§ 826 covers a similar area to a number of English torts, eg, deceit, intimidation, procuring a breach of contract.

THE FILM DIRECTOR CASE

BVerfGE Band 7 S. 198

Nr. 28

1 Die Grundrechte sind in erster Linie Abwehrrechte des Bürgers gegen den Staat; in den Grundrechtsbestimmungen des Grundgesetzes verkörpert sich aber auch eine objektive Wertordnung, die als verfassungsrechtliche Grundentscheidung für alle Bereiche des Rechts gilt.

2 Im bürgerlichen Recht entfaltet sich der Rechtsgehalt der Grundrechte mittelbar durch die privatrechtlichen Vorschriften. Er ergreift vor allem Bestimmungen zwingenden Charakters und ist für den Richter besonders realisierbar durch die Generalklauseln.

3 Der Zivilrichter kann durch sein Urteil Grundrechte verletzen (§ 90 BVerfGG), wenn er die Einwirkung der Grundrechte auf das bürgerliche Recht verkennt. Das Bundesverfassungsgericht prüft zivilgerichtliche Urteile nur auf solche Verletzungen von Grundrechten, nicht allgemein auf Rechtsfehler nach.

4 Auch zivilrechtliche Vorschriften können 'allgemeine Gesetze' im Sinne des Art. 5 Abs. 2 GG sein und so das Grundrecht auf Freiheit der Meinungsäußerung beschränken.

5 Die 'allgemeinen Gesetze' müssen im Lichte der besonderen Bedeutung des Grundrechts der freien Meinungsäußerung für den freiheitlichen demokratischen Staat ausgelegt werden.

6 Das Grundrecht des Art. 5 GG schützt nicht nur das Äußern einer Meinung als solches, sondern auch das geistige Wirken durch die Meinungsäußerung.

7 Eine Meinungsäußerung, die eine Aufforderung zum Boykott enthält, verstößt nicht notwendig gegen die guten Sitten im Sinne des § 826 BGB; sie kann bei Abwägung aller Umstände des Falles durch die Freiheit der Meinungsäußerung verfassungsrechtlich gerechtfertigt sein.

Urteil des Ersten Senats vom 15. Januar 1958

– 1 BvR 400/51 –

in dem Verfahren über die Verfassungsbeschwerde des Senatsdirektors Erich L. in Hamburg gegen das Urteil des Landgerichts Hamburg vom 22. November 1951 - Az. 15. O. 87/51 -.

THE FILM DIRECTOR CASE

This is a case about public criticism of a film director who had associations with the Nazi regime. Consider therefore how the issues might have been dealt with in the context of the English tort of defamation (in particular, fair comment on a matter of public interest) and economic torts such as interference with contractual relations. The case was however chiefly concerned with the interaction between the basis of liability (§ 826 of the BGB) and the basic right under Art 5 of the GG of freedom of expression.

BVerfGE Volume 7 p 198

No 28

1 The Basic Rights are primarily protective rights of the citizen against the State; but in the provisions of the Basic Rights of the Basic Law there is also embodied an objective system of values, which, as a basic constitutional regime is valid for all areas of the law.

2 In civil law, the legal content of the Basic Rights develops indirectly through private law provisions. It uses above all provisions of a compulsory nature and, for the judge, it is, in particular, realisable through the general clauses.

3 The civil judge can, by his judgment, violate the Basic Rights (§ 90 of the BVerfGG) if he fails to recognise the effect of the Basic Rights on civil law. The Federal Constitutional Court examines civil court judgments only in respect of such violations of basic rights and not generally for mistakes in law.

4 Civil law provisions also can be 'general laws' in the sense of Art 5 para 2 of the GG and thus limit the basic right to freedom of expression of opinion.

5 The 'general laws' must be interpreted in the light of the special meaning of the basic right of free expression of opinion for the free democratic State.

6 The basic right in Art 5 of the GG not only protects the expression of an opinion as such but also the intellectual effect of the expression of opinion.

7 An expression of opinion which contains a call to boycott does not necessarily offend against good morals in the sense of § 826 of the BGB; it can, on weighing all the circumstances of the case, be justified in constitutional law by the freedom of expression of opinion.

Judgment of the First Senate of 15 January 1958

– 1 BvR 400/51 –

in the proceedings about the constitutional complaint of the Senate director Erich L. in Hamburg against the judgment of the State Court of Hamburg of 22 November 1951 -Az. 15. O. 87/15 -.

Entscheidungsformel:

Das Urteil des Landgerichts Hamburg vom 22. November 1951 – Az. 15. O. 87/51 – verletzt das Grundrecht des Beschwerdeführers aus Art. 5 Abs. 1 Satz 1 des Grundgesetzes und wird deshalb aufgehoben. Die Sache wird an das Landgericht Hamburg zurückverwiesen.

Gründe:

A

Der Beschwerdeführer – damals Senatsdirektor und Leiter der Staatlichen Pressestelle der Freien und Hansestadt Hamburg – hat am 20. September 1950 anläßlich der Eröffnung der 'Woche des deutschen Films' als Vorsitzender des Hamburger Presseklubs in einer Ansprache vor Filmverleihern und Filmproduzenten u. a. folgendes erklärt:

> Nachdem der deutsche Film im Dritten Reich seinen moralischen Ruf verwirkt hatte, ist allerdings ein Mann am wenigsten von allen geeignet, diesen Ruf wiederherzustellen: das ist der Drehbuchverfasser und Regisseur des Films 'Jud Süß'! Möge uns weiterer unabsehbarer Schaden vor der ganzen Welt erspart bleiben, der eintreten würde, indem man ausgerechnet ihn als Repräsentanten des deutschen Films herauszustellen sucht. Sein Freispruch in Hamburg war nur ein formeller. Die Urteilsbegründung war eine moralische Verdammung. Hier fordern wir von den Verleihern und Theaterbesitzern eine Haltung, die nicht ganz billig ist, die man sich aber etwas kosten lassen sollte: Charakter. Und diesen Charakter wünsche ich dem deutschen Film. Beweist er ihn und führt er den Nachweis durch Phantasie, optische Kühnheit und durch Sicherheit im Handwerk dann verdient er jede Hilfe und dann wird er eines erreichen, was er zum Leben braucht: Erfolg beim deutschen wie beim internationalen Publikum.

Die Firma Domnick-Film-Produktion GmbH, die zu dieser Zeit den Film 'Unsterbliche Geliebte' nach dem Drehbuch und unter der Regie des Filmregisseurs Veit Harlan herstellte, forderte daraufhin den Beschwerdeführer zu einer Äußerung darüber auf, mit welcher Berechtigung er die vorerwähnten Erklärungen gegen Harlan abgegeben habe. Der Beschwerdeführer erwiderte mit Schreiben vom 27. Oktober 1950, das er als 'Offenen Brief' der Presse übergab, u. a. folgendes:

> Das Schwurgericht hat ebensowenig widerlegt, daß Veit Harlan für einen großen Zeitabschnitt des Hitler-Reiches der 'Nazifilm-Regisseur Nr. 1' und durch seinen 'Jud Süß' - Film einer der wichtigsten Exponenten der mörderischen Judenhetze der Nazis war
> ...

Decision:

The judgment of the State Court of Hamburg of 22 November 1951 – Az. 15. O. 87/51 – violates the basic right of the constitutional complainant under Art 5 para 1 sentence 1 of the Basic Law and is therefore quashed. The matter is referred back to the State Court of Hamburg.

Reasons:

A

The complainant,who was, the at the time Senate director and manager of the State press office of the Free and Hanseatic City of Hamburg, on 20 September 1950 on the occasion of the opening of the 'Week of the German Film' as president of the Hamburg Press association in a speech to film distributors and producers stated, amongst other things, as follows:

> After the German film had forfeited its moral reputation, one man is certainly least suited of anyone to restore this reputation: he is the film script author and producer of the film 'Jew Süss'! May we be spared from the further incalculable harm in front of the whole world which would occur if anyone seeks to give him, of all people, prominence as the representative of German films. His acquittal in Hamburg was only a formal one. The basis of the judgment was a moral condemnation. We demand from film distributors and theatre proprietors a quality which is not cheap, but for which we ought to pay: character. And I want this character for the German film. And if it shows it, and brings proof by imagination, visual boldness and reliability in its trade, it deserves every assistance and it will then attain something which it needs for survival: success with the German as well as the international public.

The firm Domnick-Film-Production Ltd, which at this time was producing the film 'Immortal Beloved' according to the film script and under the management of the film producer Veit Harlan, thereupon demanded from the complainant a statement, as to what justification he had for making the said statements against Harlan. The complainant's reply in a letter of 27 October 1950, which he handed over to the press as an 'open letter', included the following:

> The jury court did not really refute that Veit Harlan was for a substantial period of the Hitler Reich the 'Nazi film producer no 1' and by his 'Jew Süss' film was one of the most important exponents of the murderous baiting of the Jews by the Nazis ...

Es mag im In- und Ausland Geschäftsleute geben, die sich an einer Wiederkehr Harlans nicht stoßen. Das moralische Ansehen Deutschlands in der Welt darf aber nicht von robusten Geldverdienern erneut ruiniert werden. Denn Harlans Wiederauftreten muß daum vernarbte Wunden wiederaufreißen und abklingendes Mißtrauen zum Schaden des deutschen Wiederaufbaus furchtbar erneuern. Es ist aus allen diesen Gründen nicht nur das Recht anständiger Deutscher, sondern sogar ihre Pflicht, sich im Kampf gegen diesen unwürdigen Repräsentanten des deutschen Films über den Protest hinaus auch zum Boycott bereitzuhalten.

Die Domnick-Film-Produktion GmbH und die Herzog-Film GmbH (diese als Verleiherin des Films 'Unsterbliche Geliebte' für das Bundesgebiet) erwirkten nun beim Landgericht Hamburg eine einstweilige Verfügung gegen den Beschwerdeführer, durch die ihm verboten wurde:

1 die deutschen Theaterbesitzer und Filmverleiher aufzufordern, den Film, 'Unsterbliche Geliebte' nicht in ihr Programm aufzunehmen,

2 das deutsche Publikum aufzufordern, diesen Film nicht zu besuchen.

Das Oberlandesgericht Hamburg wies die Berufung des Beschwerdeführers gegen das landgerichtliche Urteil zurück.

Auf Antrag des Beschwerdeführers wurde den beiden Film-gesellschaften eine Frist zur Klageerhebung gesetzt. Auf ihre Klage erließ das Landgericht Hamburg am 22. November 1951 folgendes Urteil:

Der Beklagte wird verurteilt, es bei Vermeidung einer gerichtsseitig festzusetzenden Geld- oder Haftstrafe zu unterlassen:

1 die deutschen Theaterbesitzer und Filmverleiher aufzufordern, den bei der Klägerin zu 1) produzierten und von der Klägerin zu 2) zum Verleih im Bundesgebiet übernommenen Film, 'Unsterbliche Geliebte' nicht in ihr Programm aufzunehmen,

2 das deutsche Publikum aufzufordern, diesen Film nicht zu besuchen.

Der Beklagte trägt die Kosten des Rechtsstreits.

Das Urteil ist gegen Sicherheitsleistung von 110 000 DM vorläufig vollstreckbar.

There may be business people at home and abroad who do not take offence at a return of Harlan. The moral reputation of Germany in the world ought not however to be ruined afresh by tough money-makers. Harlan's reappearance must tear open wounds which are scarcely healed, and formidably renew fading mistrust, to the harm of German reconstruction. For all these reasons it is not only the right of decent Germans but even their duty, in the struggle against this unworthy representative of the German film, to be ready not just to protest but also to boycott.

Domnick-Film-Production Ltd and Herzog-Film Ltd (as distributor of the film 'Immortal Beloved' for the area of the Federal Republic) secured from the State Court of Hamburg an interim injunction against the complainant by which he was forbidden:

1 to call upon German theatre proprietors and film distributors not to take the film 'Immortal Beloved' into their programmes; and

2 to call upon the German public not to see this film.

The Upper State Court of Hamburg rejected the appeal of the complainant against State Court judgment.

On the application of the complainant, the two film companies were set a period in which to institute proceedings. The State Court of Hamburg issued the following judgment in their action on 22 November 1951:

The defendant is ordered, upon pain of a monetary or custodial penalty to be set by the court, not:

1 to call on German theatre proprietors and film distributors not to include in their programmes the film 'Immortal Beloved' produced by the first plaintiff and taken up for distribution in the area of the Federal Republic from the second plaintiff; or

2 to call on the German public not to see this film.

The defendant is to bear the costs of the action.

The judgment is provisionally enforceable against a security of 110,000 DM.

Das Landgericht erblickt in den Äußerungen des Beschwerdeführers eine sittenwidrige Aufforderung zum Boykott. Ihr Ziel sei, ein Wiederauftreten Harlans 'als Schöpfer repräsentativer Filme' zu verhindern. Die Aufforderung des Beschwerdeführers laufe sogar 'praktisch darauf hinaus, Harlan von der Herstellung normaler Spielfilme überhaupt auszuschalten, denn jeder derartige Film könnte durch die Regieleistung zu einem repräsentativen Film werden'. Da Harlan aber in dem wegen seiner Beteiligung an dem Film 'Jud Süß' gegen ihn eingeleiteten Strafverfahren rechtskräftig freigesprochen worden sei und auf Grund der Entscheidung im Entnazifizierungsverfahren in der Ausübung seines Berufes keinen Beschränkungen mehr unterliege, verstoße dieses Vorgehen des Beschwerdeführers gegen 'die demokratische Rechts- und Sittenauffassung des deutschen Volkes'. Dem Beschwerdeführer werde nicht zum Vorwurf gemacht, daß er über das Wiederauftreten Harlans eine ablehnende Meinung geäußert habe, sondern daß er die Offentlichkeit aufgefordert habe, durch ein bestimmtes Verhalten die Aufführung von Harlan-Filmen und damit das Wiederauftreten Harlans als Filmregisseur unmöglich zu machen. Diese Boykottaufforderung richte sich auch gegen die klagenden Filmgesellschaften; denn wenn der in der Herstellung befindliche Film keinen Absatz finden könne, drohe ihnen ein empfindlicher Vermögensschaden. Der objektive Tatbestand einer unerlaubten Handlung nach § 826 BGB sei damit erfüllt, ein Unterlassungsanspruch also gegeben.

Der Beschwerdeführer legte gegen dieses Urteil Berufung zum Oberlandesgericht Hamburg ein. Gleichzeitig hat er Verfassungsbeschwerde erhoben, in der er die Verletzung seines Grundrechts auf freie Meinungsäußerung (Art. 5 Abs. 1 Satz 1 GG) rügt. Er habe am Verhalten Harlans und der Filmgesellschaften politische und moralische Kritik geübt. Dazu sei er berechtigt, denn Art. 5 GG verbürge nicht nur die Freiheit der Rede ohne Wirkungsabsicht, sondern gerade auch die Freiheit des Wirkens durch das Wort. Seine Äußerungen stellten Werturteile dar. Das Gericht habe irrigerweise geprüft, ob sie inhaltlich richtig seien und gebilligt werden könnten, während es nur darauf ankomme, ob sie rechtlich zulässig seien. Das aber seien sie, denn das Grundrecht der Meinungsfreiheit habe sozialen Charakter und gewähre ein subjektives öffentliches Recht darauf, durch geistiges Handeln die öffentliche Meinung mitzubestimmen und an der 'Gestaltung des Volkes zum Staat' mitzuwirken. Dieses Recht finde seine Grenze ausschließlich in den 'allgemeinen Gesetzen' (Art. 5 Abs. 2 GG). Soweit durch die Meinungsäußerung in das öffentliche, politische Leben hineingewirkt werden solle, könnten als 'allgemeine Gesetze' nur solche angesehen werden, die öffentliches Recht enthielten, nicht aber die Normen des Bürgerlichen Gesetzbuchs über unerlaubte Handlungen. Was dagegen in der Sphäre des bürgerlichen Rechts sonst unerlaubt sei, könne durch Verfassungsrecht in der Sphäre des öffentlichen Rechts gerechtfertigt sein; die Grundrechte als subjektive Rechte mit Verfassungsrang seien für das bürgerliche Recht 'Rechtfertigungsgründe mit Vorrang'.

The State Court sees in the statements of the complainant a boycott call which is contrary to good morals. Its objective would be to obstruct a reappearance of Harlan 'as creator of representative films'. The complainant's call 'amounted practically to eliminating Harlan altogether from the production of normal feature films, because every film of that kind could, by its quality of performance, become a representative film'. But as Harlan had been finally acquitted in the criminal proceedings taken against him because of his participation in the film 'Jew Süss' and on the basis of the verdict in the de-Nazification proceedings he was not subject to any more limitations in the exercise of his vocation, this action by the complainant contravened 'the democratic, legal and moral opinion of the German people'. The complainant is not accused of having expressed a disapproving opinion about the reappearance of Harlan, but on having called on the public to make, by certain conduct, the showing of Harlan films (and with that the reappearance of Harlan as a film producer) impossible. The call for a boycott is also directed against the plaintiff film companies; because if the film which is being produced can find no sales, a severe financial loss threatens them. The objective factual content of a tort in accordance with § 826 of the BGB has been satisfied and a claim for an injunction was therefore granted.

The complainant lodged an appeal against this judgment to the Upper State Court of Hamburg. At the same time he has made a constitutional complaint in which he claims the violation of his basic right to free expression of opinion (Art 5 para 1 sentence 1 of the GG). He exercised political and moral criticism in respect of the conduct of Harlan and of the film companies. He was entitled to do this because Art 5 of the GG not only guarantees the freedom of speech without intended effects but also the freedom to produce an effect by words. His statements represented value judgments. The court incorrectly examined whether they were correct in content and could be approved, whilst it was only a matter of whether they were legally permissible. This they were, however, because the basic right of freedom of opinion has a social character and grants a subjective public right to have an influence on public opinion by intellectual activity and to play a part in 'forming the people into a State'. This right finds its limit only in 'general laws' (Art 5 para 2 of the GG). Insofar as public political life is to be influenced by the expression of opinion, the only laws which could be regarded as general laws are those which contain public law, but not the norms of the Civil Code about torts. On the other hand, what is otherwise not permitted in the sphere of civil law could be justified by constitutional law in the sphere of public law; the Basic Rights as subjective rights with constitutional priority were in respect of civil law, 'grounds of justification having priority'.

Dem Bundesminister der Justiz, dem Senat der Freien und Hansestadt Hamburg und den beiden Filmgesellschaften wurde Gelegenheit zur Äußerung gegeben. Der Senat hat mitgeteilt, daß er sich den Ausführungen der Verfassungsbeschwerde anschließe. Die Filmgesellschaften halten das Urteil des Landgerichts für zutreffend.

In der mündlichen Verhandlung waren der Beschwerdeführer und die beiden Filmgesellschaften vertreten.

Die Akten des Landgerichts Hamburg 15 Q 35/50 und 15 O 87/51 sowie das Urteil des Schwurgerichts I in Hamburg vom 29. April 1950 – (50) 16/50/14 Ks 8/49 waren Gegenstand der mündlichen Verhandlung.

B–I.

Die Verfassungsbeschwerde ist zulässig; die Voraussetzungen für die Anwendung des § 90 Abs. 2 Satz 2 BVerfGG (Entscheidung vor Erschöpfung des Rechtsweges) liegen vor.

II

Der Beschwerdeführer behauptet, das Landgericht habe durch das Urteil sein Grundrecht auf freie Meinungsäußerung aus Art. 5 Abs. 1 Satz 1 des Grundgesetzes verletzt.

1 Das Urteil des Landgerichts, ein Akt der öffentlichen Gewalt in der besonderen Erscheinungsform der *rechtsprechenden* Gewalt, kann *durch seinen Inhalt* ein Grundrecht des Beschwerdeführers nur verletzen, wenn dieses Grundrecht bei der Urteilsfindung zu beachten war.

Das Urteil untersagt dem Beschwerdeführer Äußerungen, durch die er andere dahin beeinflussen könnte, sich seiner Auffassung über das Wiederauftreten Harlans anzuschließen und ihr Verhalten gegenüber den von ihm gestalteten Filmen entsprechend einzurichten. Das bedeutet objektiv eine Beschränkung des Beschwerdeführers in der freien Äußerung seiner Meinung. Das Landgericht begründet seinen Ausspruch damit, daß es die Äußerungen des Beschwerdeführers als eine unerlaubte Handlung nach § 826 BGB gegenüber den Klägerinnen betrachtet und diesen daher auf Grund der Vorschriften des bürgerlichen Rechts einen Anspruch auf Unterlassung der Äußerungen zuerkennt. So führt der vom Landgericht angenommene bürgerlich-rechtliche Anspruch der Klägerinnen durch das Urteil des Gerichts zu einem die Meinungsfreiheit des Beschwerdeführers beschränkenden Ausspruch der öffentlichen Gewalt. Dieser kann das Grundrecht des Beschwerdeführers aus Art. 5 Abs. 1 Satz 1 GG nur verletzen, wenn die angewendeten Vorschriften des bürgerlichen Rechts durch die Grundrechtsnorm inhaltlich so beeinflußt werden, daß sie das Urteil nicht mehr tragen.

Opportunity was given to make representations by the Federal Minister of Justice, the Senate of the Free and Hanseatic City of Hamburg and the two film companies. The Senate has announced that it supports the arguments in the constitutional complaint. The film companies consider the judgment of the State Court to be correct.

In the oral hearing the complainant and the two film companies were represented.

The records of the State Court of Hamburg 15 Q 35/50 and 15 O 87/51 as well as the judgment of Jury Court I in Hamburg of 29 April 1950 – (50) 16/50 / 14 Ks 8/49 were the subject of the oral proceedings.

B–I

The constitutional complaint is admissible; the pre-requisites for the application of § 90 para 2 sentence 2 of the BVerfGG (decision before exhaustion of legal action) are present.

II

The complainant asserts that the State Court has, by its judgment, violated his basic right to free expression of opinion in Art 5 para 1 sentence 1 of the Basic Law.

1 The judgment of the State Court, an act of public power in the particular manifestation of *judicial* power, can *by its content* only violate a basic right of the complainant if this basic right should have been taken into consideration in reaching a judgment.

The judgment prohibits the complainant from making statements through which he could influence others to support his view about the reappearance of Harlan and to arrange their conduct accordingly in relation to the films made by him. That means objectively a limiting of the complainant in the free expression of his opinion. The State Court bases its finding on the fact that it regards the statements of the complainant as a tort, under § 826 of the BGB, against the plaintiffs and therefore grants to them, on the basis of the provisions of civil law, a claim for cessation of the statements. Thus the plaintiffs' civil law claim accepted by the State Court leads through the judgment of the court to a decision by public power limiting the freedom of opinion of the complainant. This can only violate the basic right of the complainant under Art 5 para 1 sentence 1 of the GG if the provisions of civil law applied are so influenced in content by the basic right norm, that they cannot any longer support the judgment.

Die grundsätzliche Frage, ob Grundrechtsnormen auf das bürgerliche Recht einwirken und wie diese Wirkung im einzelnen gedacht werden müsse, ist umstritten (über den Stand der Meinungen siehe neustens Laufke in der Festschrift für Heinrich Lehmann, 1956 Band I S. 145ff., und Dürig in der Festschrift für Nawiasky, 1956, S. 157ff.). Die äußersten Positionen in diesem Streit liegen einerseits in der These, daß die Grundrechte ausschließlich gegen den Staat gerichtet seien, andererseits in der Auffassung, daß die Grundrechte oder doch einige und jedenfalls die wichtigsten von ihnen auch im Privatrechtsverkehr gegen jedermann gälten. Die bisherige Rechtsprechung des Bundesverfassungsgerichts kann weder für die eine noch für die andere dieser extremen Auffassungen in Anspruch genommen werden; die Folgerungen, die das Bundesarbeitsgericht in seinem Urteil vom 10. Mai 1957 – NJW 1957, S. 1688 – aus den Entscheidungen des Bundesverfassungsgerichts vom 17. und 23. Januar 1957 (BVerfGE 6, 55 und 6, 84) in dieser Hinsicht zieht, gehen zu weit. Auch jetzt besteht kein Anlaß, die Streitfrage der sogenannten 'Drittwirkung' der Grundrechte in vollem Umfang zu erörtern. Zur Gewinnung eines sachgerechten Ergebnisses genügt folgendes:

Ohne Zweifel sind die Grundrechte in erster Linie dazu bestimmt, die Freiheitssphäre des einzelnen vor Eingriffen der öffentlichen Gewalt zu sichern; sie sind Abwehrrechte des Bürgers gegen den Staat. Das ergibt sich aus der geistesgeschichtlichen Entwicklung der Grundrechtsidee wie aus den geschichtlichen Vorgängen, die zur Aufnahme von Grundrechten in die Verfassungen der einzelnen Staaten geführt haben. Diesen Sinn haben auch die Grundrechte des Grundgesetzes, das mit der Voranstellung des Grundrechtsabschnitts den Vorrang des Menschen und seiner Würde gegenüber der Macht des Staates betonen wollte. Dem entspricht es, daß der Gesetzgeber den besonderen Rechtsbehelf zur Wahrung dieser Rechte, die Verfassungsbeschwerde, nur gegen Akte der öffentlichen Gewalt gewährt hat.

Ebenso richtig ist aber, daß das Grundgesetz, das keine wertneutrale Ordnung sein will (BVerfGE 2, 1 [12]; 5, 85 [134ff., 197ff.]; 6, 32 [40 f.]), in seinem Grundrechtsabschnitt auch eine objektive Wertordnung aufgerichtet hat und daß gerade hierin eine prinzipielle Verstärkung der Geltungskraft der Grundrechte zum Ausdruck kommt (Klein-v. Mangoldt, Das Bonner Grundgesetz, Vorbem. B III 4 vor Art. 1 S. 93). Dieses Wertsystem, das seinen Mittelpunkt in der innerhalb der sozialen Gemeinschaft sich frei entfaltenden menschlichen Persönlichkeit und ihrer Würde findet, muß als verfassungsrechtliche Grundentscheidung für alle Bereiche des Rechts gelten; Gesetzgebung, Verwaltung und Rechtsprechung empfangen von ihm Richtlinien und Impulse. So beeinflußt es selbstverständlich auch das bürgerliche Recht; keine bürgerlich-rechtliche Vorschrift darf in Widerspruch zu ihm stehen, jede muß in seinem Geiste ausgelegt werden.

The question of principle of whether basic rights norms have an effect on civil law and what this effect should considered to be in detail is disputed (regarding the state of opinions see, recently, Laufke in the Festschrift for Heinrich Lehmann, 1956, Vol 1 p 145 and onwards and Dürig in the Commemorative Publication for Nawiasky, 1956, p 157 and onwards). The most extreme positions in this argument lie, on the one side, in the proposition that the Basic Rights are directed exclusively against the State and, on the other side, in the opinion that the Basic Rights or some, and in any case the most important, of them would be effective against everyone in private law. The case law so far of the Federal Constitutional Court cannot be claimed in support of either one or the other of these extreme views; the conclusions which the Federal Labour Court draws in this respect in its judgment of 10 May 1957 – NJW 1957, 1688 – from the decisions of the Federal Constitutional Court of 17 and 23 January 1957 (BVerfGE 6, 55 and 6, 84) go too far. There is even now no need to discuss the disputed question of the so-called 'secondary effect' of the Basic Rights in its full extent. To produce a proper conclusion, the following suffices:

Without doubt, the Basic Rights are primarily meant to secure the sphere of freedom of the individual from interferences from public power; they are defensive rights of the citizen against the State. That follows from the intellectual historical development of the basic rights idea as well as from the historical events which have led to the taking of basic rights into the constitutions of individual countries. The Basic Rights of the Basic Law also have this meaning; the Basic Law intended to emphasise the priority of the human being and his dignity as against the might of the State by giving first place to the Basic Rights section. The fact that the legislator has granted the special legal remedy of the constitutional complaint for the preservation of these rights only against acts of public power corresponds with this.

It is, however, just as correct that the Basic Law, which is not intended to be an order of neutral values (BVerfGE 2, 1 [12]; 5, 85 [134 and onwards; 197 and onwards]; 6, 32 [40 and onwards]), has set up in its Basic Rights section an objective order of values and that it is precisely in this that a strengthening in principle of the effective power of the Basic Rights is expressed (Klein-v Mangoldt, the Bonn Basic Law, preliminary note B III 4 preceding Art 1, p 93). This value system, which finds its focus in the freely developing human personality and its dignity within the social community must take effect as a basic provision of constitutional law for all areas of the law: legislation, administration and adjudication receive their guiding principles and impulses from it. Thus, it obviously influences the civil law as well; no civil law provision may stand in contradiction to it and each such provision must be interpreted in the spirit of it.

Der Rechtsgehalt der Grundrechte als objektiver Normen entfaltet sich im Privatrecht durch das Medium der dieses Rechtsgebiet unmittelbar beherrschenden Vorschriften. Wie neues Recht im Einklang mit dem grundrechtlichen Wertsystem stehen muß, so wird bestehendes älteres Recht inhaltlich auf dieses Wertsystem ausgerichtet; von ihm her fließt ihm ein spezifisch verfassungsrechtlicher Gehalt zu, der fortan seine Auslegung bestimmt. Ein Streit zwischen Privaten über Rechte und Pflichten aus solchen grundrechtlich beeinflußten Verhaltensnormen des bürgerlichen Rechts bleibt materiell und prozessual ein bürgerlicher Rechtsstreit. Ausgelegt und angewendet wird bürgerliches Recht, wenn auch seine Auslegung dem öffentlichen Recht, der Verfassung, zu folgen hat.

Der Einfluß grundrechtlicher Wertmaßstäbe wird sich vor allem bei denjenigen Vorschriften des Privatrechts geltend machen, die zwingendes Recht enthalten und so einen Teil des ordre public – im weiten Sinne – bilden, d. h. der Prinzipien, die aus Gründen des gemeinen Wohls auch für die Gestaltung der Rechtsbeziehungen zwischen den einzelnen verbindlich sein sollen und deshalb der Herrschaft des Privatwillens entzogen sind. Diese Bestimmungen haben nach ihrem Zweck eine nahe Verwandtschaft mit dem öffentlichen Recht, dem sie sich ergänzend anfügen. Das muß sie in besonderem Maße dem Einfluß des Verfassungsrechts aussetzen. Der Rechtsprechung bieten sich zur Realisierung dieses Einflusses vor allem die 'Generalklauseln', die, wie § 826 BGB, zur Beurteilung menschlichen Verhaltens auf außer-zivilrechtliche, ja zunächst überhaupt außerrechtliche Maßstäbe, wie die 'guten Sitten', verweisen. Denn bei der Entscheidung darüber, was diese sozialen Gebote jeweils im Einzelfall fordern, muß in erster Linie von der Gesamtheit der Wertvorstellungen ausgegangen werden, die das Volk in einem bestimmten Zeitpunkt seiner geistig-kulturellen Entwicklung erreicht und in seiner Verfassung fixiert hat. Deshalb sind mit Recht die Generalklauseln als die 'Einbruchstellen' der Grundrechte in das bürgerliche Recht bezeichnet worden (Dürig in Neumann-Nipperdey-Scheuner, *Die Grundrechte*, Band II S. 525).

The legal content of the Basic Rights as objective norms develops in private law through the medium of the provisions which directly control this area of law. In the same way as new law must be in harmony with the Basic Rights value system, so must existing older law adjust to this value system in its content; from this system, a specific constitutional law content flows into such law, which from then on determines its interpretation. A dispute between private parties about rights and duties arising from such norms about conduct in the civil law, which is influenced by the Basic Rights, remains substantively and procedurally a civil law legal dispute. Civil law is interpreted and applied, even if its interpretation has to follow public law, from the Constitution.

The influence of Basic Rights value yardsticks will arise primarily with those provisions of private law which contain compulsory law[1] and thus form a part of the public order – in the wide sense – ie, the principles which for reasons of the public benefit should also be binding for the formation of legal relationships between individuals and therefore are withdrawn from the control of the private will. These provisions have, in accordance with their purpose, a close relationship with public law, which they complement. That must expose them to a special extent to the influence of constitutional law. From case law, the 'general clauses' present themselves primarily for the realisation of this influence. They, like § 826 of the BGB, refer to the judging of human conduct by criteria which are outside civil law, in fact chiefly outside the law altogether, like 'good morals'. For in deciding what these social precepts require at any given time in the individual case, one must primarily proceed from the totality of value concepts which the people have reached at a certain point in time of their intellectual and cultural development and established in their Constitution. Therefore the general clauses have been correctly described as the 'break through points' of the Basic Rights into civil law (Dürig in Neumann-Nipperdey-Scheuner, *The Basic Rights*, Vol II p 525).

---

1   German law distinguishes between compulsory law (zwingendes Recht) and voluntary law (nachgiebiges Recht). The former applies regardless of the intention of the persons involved, but the latter can be excluded by them.

Der Richter hat kraft Verfassungsgebots zu prüfen, ob die von ihm anzuwendenden materiellen zivilrechtlichen Vorschriften in der beschriebenen Weise grundrechtlich beeinflußt sind; trifft das zu, dann hat er bei Auslegung und Anwendung dieser Vorschriften die sich hieraus ergebende Modifikation des Privatrechts zu beachten. Dies ist der Sinn der Bindung auch des Zivilrichters an die Grundrechte (Art. 1 Abs. 3 GG). Verfehlt er diese Maßstäbe und beruht sein Urteil auf der Außerachtlassung dieses verfassungsrechtlichen Einflusses auf die zivilrechtlichen Normen, so verstößt er nicht nur gegen objektives Verfassungsrecht, indem er den Gehalt der Grundrechtsnorm (als objektiver Norm) verkennt, er verletzt vielmehr als Träger öffentlicher Gewalt durch sein Urteil das Grundrecht, auf dessen Beachtung auch durch die rechtsprechende Gewalt der Bürger einen verfassungsrechtlichen Anspruch hat. Gegen ein solches Urteil kann – unbeschadet der Bekämpfung des Rechtsfehlers im bürgerlich-rechtlichen Instanzenzug – das Bundesverfassungsgericht im Wege der Verfassungsbeschwerde angerufen werden.

Das Verfassungsgericht hat zu prüfen, ob das ordentliche Gericht die Reichweite und Wirkkraft der Grundrechte im Gebiet des bürgerlichen Rechts zutreffend beurteilt hat. Daraus ergibt sich aber zugleich die Begrenzung der Nachprüfung: es ist nicht Sache des Verfassungsgerichts, Urteile des Zivilrichters in vollem Umfange auf Rechtsfehler zu prüfen; das Verfassungsgericht hat lediglich die bezeichnete 'Ausstrahlungswirkung' der Grundrechte auf das bürgerliche Recht zu beurteilen und den Wertgehalt des Verfassungsrechtssatzes auch hier zur Geltung zu bringen. Sinn des Instituts der Verfassungsbeschwerde ist es, daß *alle* Akte der gesetzgebenden, vollziehenden und richterlichen Gewalt auf ihre 'Grundrechtsmäßigkeit' nachprüfbar sein sollen (§ 90 BVerfGG). Sowenig das Bundesverfassungsgericht berufen ist, als Revisions- oder gar 'Superrevisions'-Instanz gegenüber den Zivilgerichten tätig zu werden, sowenig darf es von der Nachprüfung solcher Urteile allgemein absehen und an einer in ihnen etwa zutage tretenden Verkennung grundrechtlicher Normen und Maßstäbe vorübergehen.

2 Die Problematik des Verhältnisses der Grundrechte zum Privatrecht scheint im Falle des Grundrechts der freien Meinungsäußerung (Art. 5 GG) anders gelagert zu sein. Dieses Grundrecht ist – wie schon in der Weimarer Verfassung (Art. 118) – vom Grundgesetz nur in den Schranken der 'allgemeinen Gesetze' gewährleistet (Art. 5 Abs. 2). Ohne daß zunächst untersucht wird, welche Gesetze 'allgemeine' Gesetze in diesem Sinne sind, ließe sich die Auffassung vertreten, hier habe die Verfassung selbst durch die Verweisung auf die Schranke der allgemeinen Gesetze den Geltungsanspruch des Grundrechts von vornherein auf den Bereich beschränkt, den ihm die Gerichte durch ihre Auslegung dieser Gesetze noch belassen. Das Ergebnis dieser Auslegung müsse, soweit es eine Beschränkung des Grundrechts darstelle, hingenommen werden und könne deshalb niemals als eine 'Verletzung' des Grundrechts angesehen werden.

The judge must examine, by virtue of the requirement of the Constitution, whether the substantive civil law provisions to be applied by him are influenced by the Basic Rights in the manner described; if that is so, then in the interpretation and application of these provisions he must have regard to the modification of private law which arises from this. This is also the meaning of the civil judge being bound by the Basic Rights (Art 1 para 3 of the GG). If he fails to apply these criteria and his judgment is based on failure to take account of this constitutional law influence on the civil law norms, he not only violates objective constitutional law, in that he fails to recognise the content of the Basic Right norm as an objective norm; as the holder of public power he violates by his judgment the Basic Right, as to which the citizen has a claim in constitutional law that it shall be observed by the judicial power as well. The Federal Constitutional Court can be appealed to by way of a constitutional complaint against such a judgment – without prejudice to the contesting of the error in law by the stages of civil law appeal.

The Federal Constitutional Court must examine whether the ordinary court has appropriately assessed the scope and effect of the Basic Rights in the area of civil law. But the limit of the examination follows at the same time from this: it is not the affair of the constitutional court to examine judgments of the civil judge fully for mistakes in law; the constitutional court has merely to assess the 'radiation effect' of the Basic Rights on civil law as described above and also to bring into effect here the value content of the constitutional law requirement. The point of the institution of the constitutional complaint is that *all* acts of the legislative, executive and judicial powers should be examinable for their 'conformity to the Basic Rights' (§ 90 of the BVerfGG). The Federal Constitutional Court is no more called to be a court for appeals in law or even 'super appeals in law' for the civil courts than it may generally ignore the examination of such judgments and pass over a failure to recognise Basic Rights norms and criteria which comes to light in them.

2 The problem of the relationship of the Basic Rights to private law appears to be different in the case of the basic right of freedom of expression of opinion (Art 5 of the GG). This basic right is, as in the Weimar Constitution (Art 118), guaranteed by the Basic Law, only within the limits of 'general laws' (Art 5 para 2). Without first investigating which laws are 'general' laws in this sense, the opinion could be defended that here the Constitution itself had, by referring to the limitation of the general laws, limited this basic right's claim to effectiveness at the outset to the area which the courts, by their interpretation of these laws, still left to it. The outcome of this interpretation would have to be accepted insofar as it represents a limitation of the basic right and could therefore never be regarded as a violation of the basic right.

Dies ist indessen nicht der Sinn der Verweisung auf die 'allgemeinen Gesetze'. Das Grundrecht auf freie Meinungsäußerung ist als unmittelbarster Ausdruck der menschlichen Persönlichkeit in der Gesellschaft eines der vornehmsten Menschenrechte überhaupt (un des droits les plus précieux de l'homme nach Artikel 11 der Erklärung der Menschen- und Bürgerrechte von 1789). Für eine freiheitlich-demokratische Staatsordnung ist es schlechthin konstituierend, denn es ermöglicht erst die ständige geistige Auseinandersetzung, den Kampf der Meinungen, der ihr Lebenselement ist (BVerfGE 5, 85 [205]). Es ist in gewissem Sinn die Grundlage jeder Freiheit überhaupt, 'the matrix, the indispensable condition of nearly every other form of freedom' (Cardozo).

Aus dieser grundlegenden Bedeutung der Meinungsäußerungsfreiheit für den freiheitlich-demokratischen Staat ergibt sich, daß es vom Standpunkt dieses Verfassungssystems aus nicht folgerichtig wäre, die sachliche Reichweite gerade dieses Grundrechts jeder Relativierung durch einfaches Gesetz (und damit zwangsläufig durch die Rechtsprechung der die Gesetze auslegenden Gerichte) zu überlassen. Es gilt vielmehr im Prinzip auch hier, was oben allgemein über das Verhältnis der Grundrechte zur Privatrechtsordnung ausgeführt wurde: die allgemeinen Gesetze müssen in ihrer das Grundrecht beschränkenden Wirkung ihrerseits im Lichte der Bedeutung dieses Grundrechts gesehen und so interpretiert werden, daß der besondere Wertgehalt dieses Rechts, der in der freiheitlichen Demokratie zu einer grundsätzlichen Vermutung für die Freiheit der Rede in allen Bereichen, namentlich aber im öffentlichen Leben, führen muß, auf jeden Fall gewahrt bleibt. Die gegenseitige Beziehung zwischen Grundrecht und 'allgemeinem Gesetz' ist also nicht als einseitige Beschränkung der Geltungskraft des Grundrechts durch die 'allgemeinen Gesetze' aufzufassen; es findet vielmehr eine Wechselwirkung in dem Sinne statt, daß die 'allgemeinen Gesetze' zwar dem Wortlaut nach dem Grundrecht Schranken setzen, ihrerseits aber aus der Erkenntnis der Wertsetzenden Bedeutung dieses Grundrechts im freiheitlichen demokratischen Staat ausgelegt und so in ihrer das Grundrecht begrenzenden Wirkung selbst wieder eingeschränkt werden müssen.

This is however not the meaning of the reference to the 'general laws'. The basic right to free expression of opinion is, as the most direct expression of the human personality in society, really one of the most high ranking of human rights (one of the most precious rights of man according to Art 11 of the Declaration of the Rights of Men and Citizens of 1789). For a free democratic State order it is simply constitutive, because it enables continual intellectual debate, the conflict of opinions which is its vital element (BVerfGE 5, 85 [205]). It is, in a certain sense really the basis of every freedom, 'the matrix, the indispensable condition of nearly every other form of freedom' (Cardozo).

From this fundamental meaning of the freedom of expression of opinion for the free democratic State it follows that, from the standpoint of this constitutional system, it would not be logical to leave the essential scope of this basic right to every qualification by simple law (and at the same time inevitably by the case law of the courts interpreting the laws). Instead, what is stated above, generally, about the relationship of the Basic Rights to the private law order, is in principle valid here; the general laws must, in their effect which limits the basic right, for their part be looked at in the light of the meaning of the basic right and be interpreted so that the special value content of this right (which in a free democracy must lead to a presumption in principle in favour of freedom of speech in all areas, particularly however in public life) is in any case preserved. The mutual relationship between basic right and 'general law' is thus not to be understood as a one-sided limitation of the effective power of the basic right by 'general laws'; it is rather a case of reciprocal action in the sense that although the general laws, according to the wording, set limits to the basic right, they must on their side be interpreted in recognition of the value-prescribing meaning of this basic right in a free democratic State, and so themselves be limited in the effect which they have in limiting the basic right.

Das Bundesverfassungsgericht, das durch das Rechtsinstitut der Verfassungsbeschwerde zur Wahrung der Grundrechte letztlich berufen ist, muß demgemäß auch hier die rechtliche Möglichkeit besitzen, die Rechtsprechung der Gerichte dort zu kontrollieren, wo sie in Anwendung eines allgemeinen Gesetzes den grundrechtlich bestimmten Raum betreten und damit möglicherweise den Geltungsanspruch des Grundrechts im Einzelfall unzulässig beschränken. Es muß zu seiner Kompetenz gehören, den spezifischen Wert, der sich in diesem Grundrecht für die freiheitliche Demokratie verkörpert, *allen* Organen der öffentlichen Gewalt, also auch den Zivilgerichten, gegenüber zur Geltung zu bringen und den verfassungsrechtlich gewollten Ausgleich zwischen den sich gegenseitig widerstreitenden, hemmenden und beschränkenden Tendenzen des Grundrechts und der 'allgemeinen Gesetze' herzustellen.

3 Der Begriff des 'allgemeinen' Gesetzes war von Anfang an umstritten. Es mag dahinstehen, ob der Begriff nur infolge eines Redaktionsversehens in den Artikel 118 der Reichsverfassung von 1919 gelangt ist (siehe dazu Häntzschel im *Handbuch des deutschen Staatsrechts*, 1932 Band II S. 658). Jedenfalls ist er bereits während der Geltungsdauer dieser Verfassung dahin ausgelegt worden, daß darunter alle Gesetze zu verstehen sind, die 'nicht eine Meinung als solche verbieten, die sich nicht gegen die Äußerung der Meinung als solche richten', die vielmehr 'dem Schutze eines schlechthin, ohne Rücksicht auf eine bestimmte Meinung, zu schützenden Rechtsguts dienen', dem Schutze eines Gemeinschaftswerts, der gegenüber der Betätigung der Meinungsfreiheit den Vorrang hat (vgl. die Zusammenstellung der inhaltlich übereinstimmenden Formulierungen bei Klein-v Mangoldt, aaO, S. 250ff., sowie Veröffentl. der Vereinigung der Deutschen Staatsrechtslehrer, Heft 4, 1928, S. 6ff., bes. S. 18ff., 51ff.). Dem stimmen auch die Ausleger des Grundgesetzes zu (vgl. etwa Ridder in Neumann-Nipperdey-Scheuner, *Die Grundrechte*, Band II S. 282: 'Gesetze, die nicht die rein geistige Wirkung der reinen Meinungsäußerung inhibieren').

Wird der Begriff 'allgemeine Gesetze' so verstanden, dann ergibt sich zusammenfassend als Sinn des Grundrechtsschutzes:

Die Auffassung, daß nur das Äußern einer Meinung grundrechtlich geschützt sei, nicht die darin liegende oder damit bezweckte Wirkung auf andere, ist abzulehnen. Der Sinn einer Meinungsäußerung ist es gerade, 'geistige Wirkung auf die Umwelt' ausgehen zu lassen, 'meinungsbildend und überzeugend auf die Gesamtheit zu wirken' (Häntzschel, HdbDStR II, S. 655). Deshalb sind Werturteile, die immer eine geistige Wirkung erzielen, nämlich andere überzeugen wollen, vom Grundrecht des Art. 5 Abs. 1 Satz 1 GG geschützt; ja der Schutz des Grundrechts bezieht sich in erster Linie auf die im Werturteil zum Ausdruck kommende eigene Stellungnahme des Redenden, durch die er auf andere wirken will. Eine Trennung zwischen (geschützter) Äußerung und (nicht geschützter) Wirkung der Äußerung wäre sinnwidrig.

The Federal Constitutional Court, to which appeal is finally made for the protection of the Basic Rights through the legal institution of the constitutional complaint, must accordingly possess here also the legal power to control the adjudication of the courts at the point where they, in the application of a general law, enter the area governed by the basic right and therefore possibly limit the claim to effectiveness of the basic right in the individual case in a manner which is not permissible. It must be within the constitutional court's competence to bring into effect against *all* organs of public power, and therefore also the civil courts, the specific value which is embodied in this basic right for free democracy and to restore the balance intended by constitutional law between the mutually conflicting, inhibiting and limiting tendencies of the basic right and the 'general laws'.

3 The concept of the 'general' law was disputed at the start. It may be left undecided as to whether the concept was only admitted to Art 118 of the Reich Constitution of 1919 by an editorial error (see on this subject Häntzschel in the *Textbook of German Public Law*, 1932, Vol II p 658). In any case, it was interpreted, even during the period of validity of this Constitution, to the effect that all those laws were to be understood as included in it which 'did not forbid an opinion as such, which were not directed against the expression of opinion as such', but which rather 'ensured the protection of the subject matter of a legal right which was simply to be protected, without regard to any particular opinion', the protection of a community value which has priority over the expression of opinions (compare the compilation of formulations which agree as to content in Klein-v Mangoldt, *loc cit*, p 250 and onwards, as well as the Publication of the Association of German Teachers of Public Law, Book 4, 1928, p 6 and onwards, especially p 18 and onwards, and p 51 and onwards). The interpreters of the Basic Law also agree with this (compare, eg, Ridder in Neumann-Nipperdey-Scheuner, *The Basic Rights*, Vol II p 282: 'Laws which do not inhibit the purely intellectual effect of the pure expression of opinion').

If the concept of 'general laws' is understood in this way, the following is a summary of the meaning of basic right protection:

The opinion that only the expression of an opinion is protected by the basic right, and not the effect on others contained in it or intended by it, is to be rejected. The significance of an expression of opinion is to cause 'an intellectual influence' to go out 'into the world around', 'to have effect on the population in forming opinions and in convincing' (Häntzschel, *Textbook of German Public Law II*, p 655). Therefore value judgments, which always aim for an intellectual effect, that is, they are intended to convince others, are protected by the basic right in Art 5 para 1 sentence 1 of the GG; the protection of the basic right relates primarily to the individual point of view of the person speaking, by which he wants to have an effect on others and which comes into expression in the value judgment. Separating the (protected) utterance and the (not protected) effect of the utterance would be nonsensical.

Die – so verstandene – Meinungsäußerung ist als solche, d. h. in ihrer rein geistigen Wirkung, frei; wenn aber durch sie ein gesetzlich geschütztes Rechtsgut eines anderen beeinträchtigt wird, dessen Schutz gegenüber der Meinungsfreiheit den Vorrang verdient, so wird dieser Eingriff nicht dadurch erlaubt, daß er mittels einer Meinungsäußerung begangen wird. Es wird deshalb eine 'Güterabwägung' erforderlich: Das Recht zur Meinungsäußerung muß zurücktreten, wenn schutzwürdige Interessen eines anderen von höherem Rang durch die Betätigung der Meinungsfreiheit verletzt würden. Ob solche überwiegenden Interessen anderer vorliegen, ist auf Grund aller Umstände des Falles zu ermitteln.

4 Von dieser Auffassung aus bestehen keine Bedenken dagegen, auch Normen des bürgerlichen Rechts als 'allgemeine Gesetze' im Sinne des Art. 5 Abs. 2 GG anzuerkennen. Wenn das bisher in der Literatur im allgemeinen nicht geschehen ist (worauf auch Klein-v Mangoldt, aaO, S. 251, hinweist), so kommt darin nur zum Ausdruck, daß man die Grundrechte lediglich in ihrer Wirkung zwischen Bürger und Staat gesehen hat, so daß folgerichtig als einschränkende allgemeine Gesetze nur solche in Betracht kamen, die staatliches Handeln gegenüber dem einzelnen regeln, also Gesetze öffentlich-rechtlichen Charakters. Wenn aber das Grundrecht der freien Meinungsäußerung auch in den Privatrechtsverkehr hineinwirkt und sein Gewicht sich hier zugunsten der Zulässigkeit einer Meinungsäußerung auch dem einzelnen Mitbürger gegenüber geltend macht, so muß auf der andern Seite auch die das Grundrecht unter Umständen beschränkende Gegenwirkung einer privatrechtlichen Norm, soweit sie höhere Rechtsgüter zu schützen bestimmt ist, beachtet werden. Es wäre nicht einzusehen, warum zivilrechtliche Vorschriften, die die Ehre oder andere wesentliche Güter der menschlichen Persönlichkeit schützen, nicht ausreichen sollten, um der Ausübung des Grundrechts der freien Meinungsäußerung Schranken zu setzen, auch ohne daß zu dem gleichen Zweck Strafvorschriften erlassen werden.

The expression of opinion, understood in this sense, is as such, ie, in its pure intellectual effect, free; but if the subject matter of the right of another, which is protected by law, is encroached upon by it, and the protection of this right deserves priority over the freedom of opinion, this encroachment is not permitted just because it is committed by means of an expression of opinion. A 'balancing of interests' is therefore necessary: the right to expression of an opinion must recede if the interests of another, which are worthy of protection and are of higher rank, are violated by the expression of freedom of opinion. Whether such paramount interests of others are present is to be ascertained on the basis of all the circumstances of the case.

4 From this point of view there can be no doubts about recognising norms of civil law also as 'general laws' in the sense of Art 5 para 2 of the GG. If that has not happened so far in general in the literature (to which Klein-v Mangoldt, *loc cit*, p 251, also refers) that only expresses the fact that the Basic Rights have been seen merely in their effect between citizen and State, so that logically the only limiting general laws which came into consideration were those which regulate the dealings of the State as against the individual, ie, laws of a public law character. But if the basic right of freedom of expression of opinion also takes effect in private law matters, and its importance asserts itself here in favour of permitting an expression of opinion, and also as against the individual fellow citizen, so must on the other hand the contrary effect of a private law norm limiting the basic right in certain circumstances also be taken into consideration, insofar as the norm is intended to protect legal interests which are of higher rank. It could not be conceived why provisions of civil law which protect honour or other substantial interests of the human personality should not suffice to set limits on the exercise of the basic right of free expression of opinion, even without criminal provisions being enacted for the same purpose.

Der Beschwerdeführer befürchtet, daß durch Beschränkung der Redefreiheit einem einzelnen gegenüber die Gefahr heraufgeführt werden könnte, der Bürger werde in der Möglichkeit, durch seine Meinung in der Öffentlichkeit zu wirken, allzusehr beengt und die unerläßliche Freiheit der öffentlichen Erörterung gemeinschaftswichtiger Fragen sei nicht mehr gewährleistet. Diese Gefahr besteht in der Tat (vgl. dazu Ernst Helle, Der Schutz der persönlichen Ehre und des wirtschaftlichen Rufes im Privatrecht, 1957, S. 65, 83-85, 153). Um ihr zu begegnen, ist es aber nicht erforderlich, das bürgerliche Recht aus der Reihe der allgemeinen Gesetze schlechthin auszuscheiden. Es muß nur auch hier der freiheitliche Gehalt des Grundrechts entschieden festgehalten werden. Es wird vor allem dort in die Waagschale fallen müssen, wo von dem Grundrecht nicht zum Zwecke privater Auseinandersetzungen Gebrauch gemacht wird, der Redende vielmehr in erster Linie zur Bildung der öffentlichen Meinung beitragen will, so daß die etwaige Wirkung seiner Äußerung auf den privaten Rechtskreis eines anderen zwar eine unvermeidliche Folge, aber nicht das eigentliche Ziel der Äußerung darstellt. Gerade hier wird das Verhältnis von Zweck und Mittel bedeutsam. Der Schutz des privaten Rechtsguts kann und muß um so mehr zurücktreten, je mehr es sich nicht um eine unmittelbar gegen dieses Rechtsgut gerichtete Äußerung im privaten, namentlich im wirtschaftlichen Verkehr und in Verfolgung eigennütziger Ziele, sondern um einen Beitrag zum geistigen Meinungskampf in einer die Öffentlichkeit wesentlich berührenden Frage durch einen dazu Legitimierten handelt; hier spricht die Vermutung für die Zulässigkeit der freien Rede.

Es ergibt sich also: Auch Urteile des Zivilrichters, die auf Grund 'allgemeiner Gesetze' bürgerlich-rechtlicher Art im Ergebnis zu einer Beschränkung der Meinungsfreiheit gelangen, können das Grundrecht aus Art. 5 Abs. 1 Satz 1 GG verletzen. Auch der Zivilrichter hat jeweils die Bedeutung des Grundrechts gegenüber dem Wert des im 'allgemeinen Gesetz' geschützten Rechtsguts für den durch die Äußerung angeblich Verletzten abzuwägen. Die Entscheidung kann nur aus einer Gesamtanschauung des Einzelfalles unter Beachtung aller wesentlichen Umstände getroffen werden. Eine unrichtige Abwägung kann das Grundrecht verletzen und so die Verfassungsbeschwerde zum Bundesverfassungsgericht begründen.

The complainant fears that by limitation of the freedom of speech in respect of an individual, the danger could arise that the citizen would be too severely constrained in his chance of having an effect on the public through his opinion and the indispensable freedom of public discussion of questions important to the community would no longer be guaranteed. The danger exists in reality (compare on this Ernst Helle, The Protection of Personal Honour and Business Reputation in Private Law, 1957, pp 65, 83–85, 153). But in order to meet it, it is not necessary simply to take civil law out of the list of general laws. One must merely adhere decisively here to the freedom content of the basic right. It will in particular have to be put into the scales where use of the basic right is not made for the purpose of private arguments; the speaker primarily wishes instead to contribute to the formation of public opinion, so that the possible effect of his statement in the private law sphere of another is certainly an unavoidable consequence but not the real aim of the statement. It is just here that the relationship between purpose and means is important. The protection of the subject matter of a private right can and must recede to the extent that it does not concern a statement aimed directly against the subject matter of this right in private, especially business, communications and in pursuit of self-seeking goals, but a contribution to the intellectual conflict of opinions on a question substantially affecting the public, by a person legitimately making it; here the presumption is for the permissibility of free speech.

It therefore follows: even judgments of civil judges who, on the basis of general laws of the civil law kind, reach a result which limits the freedom of opinion can violate the basic right in Art 5 para 1 sentence 1 of the GG. The civil judge also must from time to time weigh up the importance of the basic right against the value of the subject matter of the right protected by the general law for the person allegedly injured by the statement. The decision can only be made by a complete survey of the individual case, taking into consideration all significant circumstances. An inaccurate balancing exercise can violate the basic right and thus form the ground for a constitutional complaint to the Federal Constitutional Court.

III

Die Beurteilung des Falles auf Grund der vorstehenden allgemeinen Darlegungen ergibt, daß die Rüge des Beschwerdeführers berechtigt ist. Gegenstand der verfassungsgerichtlichen Prüfung ist dabei der Inhalt des landgerichtlichen Urteils, wie er sich aus Tenor und Entscheidungsgründen ergibt. Ob die Entscheidung des Gerichts auch dann verfassungsrechtlichen Bedenken unterläge, wenn sie – im Anschluß an die Ausführungen im Urteil des Oberlandesgerichts Hamburg im Verfahren der einstweiligen Verfügung – auf die Bestimmung des § 823 Abs. 1 BGB gestützt worden wäre, kann das Bundesverfassungsgericht nicht abschließend entscheiden, weil nicht ohne weiteres unterstellt werden darf, daß das Landgericht sich die Begründung des Oberlandesgerichts in allen Einzelheiten zu eigen gemacht haben würde. Wegen der sich hier ergebenden Probleme mag auf die Ausführungen von Helle, aaO, S. 75ff. (bes. S. 83–85) verwiesen werden.

1 In der mündlichen Verhandlung ist erörtert worden, ob das Bundesverfassungsgericht an die tatsächlichen Feststellungen, die das Landgericht seinem Urteil zugrunde gelegt hat, gebunden ist. Das ist nicht lediglich mit dem Hinweis zu beantworten, daß nach § 26 BVerfGG im Verfahren vor dem Bundesverfassungsgericht der Grundsatz der materiellen Wahrheitsfindung gilt; denn der hier angegriffene Akt der öffentlichen Gewalt ist in einem Verfahren zustande gekommen, das seinerseits von der 'Dispositionsmaxime' beherrscht wird. Die Frage braucht jedoch hier nicht grundsätzlich entschieden zu werden. Die äußeren Tatsachen, namentlich der Wortlaut der Äußerungen des Beschwerdeführers, sind unbestritten; unbestritten ist auch, daß der Beschwerdeführer als Privatmann, nicht als Vertreter des hamburgischen Staates, gesprochen hat. In der Deutung der Äußerungen kann dem Landgericht jedenfalls soweit gefolgt werden, als es darin eine 'Aufforderung zum Boykott', auch in Richtung gegen die Filmgesellschaften, sieht. Der Beschwerdeführer selbst hat insoweit keine Bedenken erhoben. Was das Ziel der Äußerungen anlangt, so ist es unbedenklich, wenn das Landgericht feststellt, daß der Beschwerdeführer 'ein Wiederauftreten Harlans als Schöpfer repräsentativer Filme' habe verhindern wollen; ob die daran geknüpfte Folgerung, daß dies 'praktisch darauf hinauslaufe', Harlan von der Herstellung normaler Spielfilme überhaupt auszuschalten, angesichts des Wortlauts der Äußerungen nicht doch zu weit geht, muß freilich zweifelhaft erscheinen, kann aber dahingestellt bleiben, da es für die Entscheidung ohne Bedeutung ist.

III

The assessment of the case on the basis of the above general expositions results in the argument of the complainant being justified. The subject matter of the constitutional court examination is the content of the State court judgment, as it follows from the tenor and grounds of the decision. Whether the decision of the court would also succumb to doubts in constitutional law if it, following the explanations in the judgment of the Upper State Court of Hamburg in the proceedings for the interim injunction, had been based on the provisions of § 823 para 1 of the BGB cannot be decided finally by the Federal Constitutional Court, because it may not simply be assumed that the State Court would have adopted the reasoning of the Upper State Court in all its particulars. With regard to the problem which results here, the statements of Helle, *loc cit*, p 75 and onwards (especially pp 83–85) may be referred to.

1 In the oral hearing there was discussion as to whether the Federal Constitutional Court is bound by the factual findings on which the State Court based its judgment. That is not merely to be answered with the comment that according to § 26 of the BVerfGG the principle of the material finding of the truth takes effect in proceedings before the Federal Constitutional Court; because here the act of public power which is being attacked has come into existence in proceedings which for their part are governed by the 'disposition maxim'.[2] However, the question does not need to be decided in principle here. The external acts, particularly the wording of the statements of the complainant, are undisputed; it is also undisputed that the complainant spoke as a private person, not as a representative of the State of Hamburg. In the interpretation of the statements, the State Court can in any case be followed insofar as it sees in them a 'call for a boycott', which was also directed against the film companies. The complainant himself has raised no doubts in this respect. So far as the objective of the utterances is concerned, it is unobjectionable for the State Court to find that the complainant wanted to prevent 'a reappearance of Harlan as creator of representative films'; whether the conclusion linked with it that this 'practically amounts to' eliminating Harlan altogether from the production of normal feature films does not, however, go too far in the face of the wording of the statements must certainly appear doubtful, but can remain undecided as it is without significance for the decision.

---

2   This is the principle that the parties have control over court proceeeedings.

Für die rechtliche Beurteilung ist davon auszugehen, daß 'Boykott' kein eindeutiger Rechtsbegriff ist, der als solcher schon eine unerlaubte (sittenwidrige) Handlung bezeichnet. In der Rechtsprechung ist mit Recht darauf hingewiesen worden (so besonders RGZ 155, 257 [276ff.]), daß es keinen fest umgrenzten Tatbestand des sittenwidrigen Boykotts gibt, daß es vielmehr immer darauf ankommt, ob ein Verhalten in seinem konkreten Zusammenhang als 'sittenwidrig' anzusehen ist. Auch aus diesem Grunde ist es unbedenklich, die Deutung des Landgerichts zu übernehmen; denn sie sagt über die rechtlichen Folgen dieser Beurteilung noch nichts Entscheidendes aus. Man muß sich von der Suggestivkraft des Begriffs 'Boykott' freihalten und das Verhalten des Beschwerdeführers im Zusammenhang mit allen seinen Begleitumständen sehen.

2 Das Landgericht hat die Verurteilung des Beschwerdeführers auf § 826 BGB gestützt. Es nimmt an, daß das Verhalten des Beschwerdeführers im Sinne dieser Bestimmung gegen die guten Sitten, gegen die 'demokratische Rechts- und Sittenauffassung des deutschen Volkes', verstoßen habe und deshalb eine unerlaubte Handlung darstelle, da ein Rechtfertigungsgrund nicht erkennbar sei. Dabei brauche derjenige, dessen Recht sittenwidrig beeinträchtigt werde, nicht mit dem Geschädigten identisch zu sein.

Nach dem oben zu II 4 Ausgeführten muß § 826 BGB, der grundsätzlich *alle* Rechte und Güter gegen sittenwidrige Angriffe schützt, als ein 'allgemeines Gesetz' im Sinne des Art. 5 Abs. 2 GG angesehen werden. Die Prüfung des Bundesverfassungsgerichts beschränkt sich danach auf die Frage, ob das Landgericht bei der Anwendung dieser Generalklausel Bedeutung und Reichweite des Grundrechts der freien Meinungsäußerung richtig erkannt und gegen die Interessen Harlans und der Filmgesellschaften abgewogen hat.

§ 826 BGB verweist auf den Maßstab der 'guten Sitten'. Es handelt sich hier nicht um irgendwie vorgegebene und daher (grundsätzlich) unveränderliche Prinzipien reiner Sittlichkeit, sondern um die Anschauungen der 'anständigen Leute' davon, was im sozialen Verkehr zwischen den Rechtsgenossen 'sich gehört'. Diese Anschauungen sind geschichtlich wandelbar, können daher – in gewissen Grenzen – auch durch *rechtliche* Gebote und Verbote beeinflußt werden. Der Richter, der das hiernach sozial Geforderte oder Untersagte im Einzelfall ermitteln muß, hat sich, wie aus der Natur der Sache folgt, ihm aber auch in Art. 1 Abs. 3 GG ausdrücklich vorgeschrieben ist, dabei an jene grundsätzlichen Wertentscheidungen und sozialen Ordnungsprinzipien zu halten, die er im Grundrechtsabschnitt der Verfassung findet. Innerhalb dieser Wertordnung, die zugleich eine Wert*rang*ordnung ist, muß auch die hier erforderliche Abwägung zwischen dem Grundrecht aus Art. 5 Abs. 1 Satz 1 GG und den seine Ausübung beschränkenden Rechten und Rechtsgütern vorgenommen werden.

For the legal assessment one must proceed from the fact that 'boycott' is not an unambiguous legal concept which, as such, describes an impermissible action (a tort) which is contrary to morality. In case law it has been correctly pointed out (especially in RGZ 155, 257 [276 and onwards]) that there is no firmly defined factual content of a boycott which is contrary to morality, and that instead it is always a matter of whether conduct in its concrete context is to be regarded as 'contrary to morals'. For this reason also it is unobjectionable to accept the State Court's interpretation; for it does not yet say anything decisive about the legal consequences of this assessment. One must avoid the suggestive power of the concept 'boycott' and look at the conduct of the complainant in the context of all the accompanying circumstances.

2 The State Court has based judgment against the complainant on § 826 of the BGB. It accepts that the behaviour of the complainant has, in the sense of this provision contravened good morals and the 'democratic legal and moral view of the German people' and therefore constitutes a tort as no ground for justification is discernible. The person here whose right is encroached on, in a manner contrary to morals, does not need to be the same as the person who suffers harm.

According to what is explained at II 4 above, § 826 of the BGB which in principle protects *all* rights and property against attacks which are contrary to morals must be regarded as a 'general law' in the sense of Art 5 para 2 of the GG. Examination by the Federal Constitutional Court is accordingly confined to the question of whether the State Court, in the application of this general clause, understood correctly the meaning and scope of the basic right of free expression of opinion and weighed it against the interests of Harlan and the film companies.

§ 826 of the BGB refers to the standard of 'good morals'. It is not here a question of any professed, and therefore in principle unchangeable, rules of pure morality but of the ideas of 'decent people' about what 'is proper' in social contact between persons associating with one another on a legal plane. These ideas are historically changeable and can also therefore, within certain limits, be influenced by *legal* commands and prohibitions. The judge, who must determine what is accordingly socially required or forbidden in the individual case, must, as follows from the nature of the matter, but as is also laid down for him expressly in Art 1 para 3 of the GG, keep here to those fundamental value decisions and principles of social order which he finds in the Basic Rights section of the Constitution. Within this order of values, which is at the same time an order of *ranking* of values, there must also be undertaken the balancing exercise which is necessary here of the basic right in Art 5 para 1 sentence 1 of the GG and the rights and legal interests which limits its exercise.

Für die Entscheidung der Frage, ob eine Aufforderung zum Boykott nach diesen Maßstäben sittenwidrig ist, sind zunächst Motive, Ziel und Zweck der Äußerungen zu prüfen; ferner kommt es darauf an, ob der Beschwerdeführer bei der Verfolgung seiner Ziele das Maß der nach den Umständen notwendigen und angemessenen Beeinträchtigung der Interessen Harlans und der Filmgesellschaften nicht überschritten hat.

(a) Sicherlich haftet den Motiven, die den Beschwerdeführer zu seinen Äußerungen veranlaßt haben, nichts Sittenwidriges an. Der Beschwerdeführer hat keine eigenen Interessen wirtschaftlicher Art verfolgt; er stand namentlich weder mit den klagenden Filmgesellschaften noch mit Harlan in Konkurrenzbeziehungen. Das Landgericht hat selbst bereits in seinem Urteil im Verfahren der einstweiligen Verfügung festgestellt, die mündliche Verhandlung habe nicht die geringsten Anhaltspunkte dafür ergeben, daß der Beschwerdeführer etwa 'aus eigennützigen bzw. nicht achtenswerten Motiven' gehandelt habe. Dem ist von keiner Seite widersprochen worden.

(b) Das Ziel der Äußerungen des Beschwerdeführers war, wie er selbst angibt, Harlan als repräsentativen Vertreter des deutschen Films auszuschalten; er wollte verhindern, daß Harlan wieder als Schöpfer repräsentativer deutscher Filme herausgestellt werde und damit der Anschein entstehe, als sei ein neuer Aufstieg des deutschen Films notwendig mit der Person Harlans verbunden. Die Gerichte haben nicht zu beurteilen, ob diese Zielsetzung sachlich zu billigen ist, sondern nur, ob ihre Bekundung in der vom Beschwerdeführer gewählten Form rechtlich zulässig war.

Die Äußerungen des Beschwerdeführers müssen im Rahmen seiner allgemeinen politischen und kulturpolitischen Bestrebungen gesehen werden. Er war von der Sorge bewegt, das Wiederauftreten Harlans könne - vor allem im Ausland – so gedeutet werden, als habe sich im deutschen Kulturleben gegenüber der nationalsozialistischen Zeit nichts geändert; wie damals, so sei Harlan auch jetzt wieder der repräsentative deutsche Filmregisseur. Diese Befürchtungen betrafen eine für das deutsche Volk sehr wesentliche Frage, im Grunde die seiner sittlichen Haltung und seiner darauf beruhenden Geltung in der Welt. Dem deutschen Ansehen hat nichts so geschadet wie die grausame Verfolgung der Juden durch den Nationalsozialismus. Es besteht also ein entscheidendes Interesse daran, daß die Welt gewiß sein kann, das deutsche Volk habe sich von dieser Geisteshaltung abgewandt und verurteile sie nicht aus politischen Opportunitätsgründen, sondern aus der durch eigene innere Umkehr gewonnenen Einsicht in ihre Verwerflichkeit.

For a decision of the issue of whether a call to a boycott is contrary to good morals according to these standards, the motives, objective and purpose of the statements must first be examined; it is further a matter of whether the complainant has not overstepped, in the pursuit of his objectives, the extent of such encroachment on the interests of Harlan and the film companies as is necessary and appropriate according to the circumstances.

(a) Certainly nothing contrary to good morals attaches to the motives which caused the complainant to make his statements. The complainant did not pursue any interest of his own of a business kind; in particular he was not in any competitive relationship with the plaintiff film companies or with Harlan. The State Court has itself already established in its judgment in the proceedings regarding the interim injunction that the oral hearing did not reveal the least grounds for saying that the complainant had perhaps acted 'from selfish or unworthy motives'. Neither side has contradicted this.

(b) The objective of the statements of the complainant was, as he himself explains, to eliminate Harlan as the representative of the German film; he wanted to prevent Harlan again being given prominence as the creator of representative German films and the impression thereby arising that a new rise of the German film was necessarily connected with the person of Harlan. The courts do not have to decide whether this objective should be objectively approved, but only whether its expression in the form chosen by the complainant was legally permissible.

The statements of the complainant must be seen within the framework of his general political and politico-cultural endeavours. He was motivated by concern that the reappearance of Harlan could, especially in other countries, be interpreted as if nothing had changed in German cultural life in comparison with the national socialist period; as then, so again now, Harlan was the representative German film producer. These fears concerned a very important question for the German people which was basically that of its moral stance and its prestige in the world based on this. Nothing had harmed the German reputation as much as the cruel persecution of the Jews by National Socialism. There is, therefore, a crucial interest in the world being able to be certain that the German people had turned away from this attitude of mind and condemned it, not on grounds of political expediency, but on an insight into its reprehensibility obtained from its own inner change.

Die Befürchtungen des Beschwerdeführers sind von ihm nicht nachträglich konstruiert, sie entsprechen der Sachlage, wie sie sich damals für ihn darstellte. Das ist später unter anderem dadurch bestätigt worden, daß z. B. in der Schweiz der Versuch, den Film 'Unsterbliche Geliebte' zu zeigen, zu lebhaften Protesten, ja sogar zu einer Interpellation im Nationalrat und zu einer amtlichen Stellungnahme des Bundesrats geführt hat (vgl. Neue Zeitung Nr. 70 vom 22./23. März 1952 und Neue Zürcher Zeitung, Fernausgabe Nr. 327 vom 28. November 1951); der Film wurde einhellig nicht wegen seines Inhalts, sondern wegen der Mitwirkung Harlans abgelehnt und infolge dieser zahlreichen nachdrücklichen Interventionen auch nicht aufgeführt. Auch in mehreren deutschen Städten wurde aus den gleichen Gründen gegen die Aufführung des Films demonstriert. Der Beschwerdeführer konnte also in dem Wiederauftreten Harlans einen im Interesse der deutschen Entwicklung und des deutschen Ansehens in der Welt zu beklagenden Vorgang sehen. Die sich hiermit – nach seiner Auffassung – anbahnende Entwicklung wollte er verhindern.

Das Landgericht hält es für zulässig, daß der Beschwerdeführer über das Wiederauftreten Harlans eine Meinung geäußert hat, macht ihm aber zum Vorwurf, daß er die Öffentlichkeit aufgefordert habe, durch ein bestimmtes Verhalten das Wiederauftreten Harlans unmöglich zu machen. Bei dieser Unterscheidung wird übersehen, daß der Beschwerdeführer, wenn man ihm schon gestatten will, über das Wiederauftreten Harlans eine (ablehnende) Meinung zu äußern, kaum über das hinausging, was in diesem Werturteil bereits enthalten war. Denn die Aufforderung, Harlan-Filme nicht abzunehmen und nicht zu besuchen, ergab sich als Wirkung des negativen Werturteils über das Wiederauftreten Harlans geradezu von selbst. Das sachliche Anliegen des Beschwerdeführers war es, die Gefahr nationalsozialistischer Einflüsse auf das deutsche Filmwesen von vornherein abzuwehren; von da her hat er folgerichtig das Wiederauftreten Harlans bekämpft. Harlan erscheint hier als persönlicher Exponent einer bestimmten, vom Beschwerdeführer abgelehnten kulturpolitischen Entwicklung. Der zulässige Angriff gegen diese führte mit einer gewissen Notwendigkeit zu einem Eingriff in die persönliche Rechtssphäre Harlans.

The fears of the complainant have not been constructed by him with the benefit of hindsight; they correspond to the circumstances as they presented themselves to him at that time. That has been confirmed later by, amongst other things, the fact that, for instance in Switzerland, the attempt to show the film 'Immortal Beloved' has led to active protests and even to a parliamentary question in the National Assembly and to an official comment in the Federal Assembly (compare New Journal no 70 of 22/23 March 1952 and the *New Zürich Newspaper* Foreign Edition no 327 of 28 November 1951); the film was unanimously rejected not on account of its content but because of the participation of Harlan and it had also not been shown because of the numerous forcible interventions. There were also demonstrations in several German cities, for the same reasons, against the showing of the film. The complainant could thus see in the reappearance of Harlan an event to be deplored in the interest of German development and the reputation of Germany in the world. He wanted to prevent the development which would – in his view – follow on from this.

The State Court regards it as permissible that the complainant has expressed an opinion about the reappearance of Harlan, but blames him for having called upon the public to make the reappearance of Harlan impossible by a certain type of conduct. This distinction overlooks the fact that the complainant – if one intends to permit him to express a (negative) opinion about the appearance of Harlan – scarcely went beyond what was already contained in this value judgment. The call not to take up Harlan films and not to visit them follows of itself, directly, as the effect of the negative value judgment about the reappearance of Harlan. It was the actual wish of the complainant to prevent the danger of national socialist influences on the German film industry from the start; for this reason he, logically, resisted the reappearance of Harlan. Harlan appears here as the personal exponent of a certain politico-cultural development which the complainant is against. The permissible attack against this led with a certain necessity to an interference in the sphere of Harlan's personal rights.

Der Beschwerdeführer war durch seine besonders nahe persönliche Beziehung zu allem, was das deutsch-jüdische Verhältnis betraf, legitimiert, seine Auffassung in der Öffentlichkeit darzulegen. Er war damals bereits durch seine Bestrebungen um Wiederherstellung eines wahren inneren Friedens mit dem jüdischen Volke bekannt geworden. Er war führend in der Gesellschaft für christlich-jüdische Zusammenarbeit tätig; er hatte kurz vorher in Rundfunk und Presse die Aktion 'Friede mit Israel' eingeleitet, die in Deutschland und im Ausland lebhaft diskutiert worden war und ihm zahlreiche Zustimmungserklärungen eingebracht hatte. Es ist begreiflich, daß er befürchtete, alle diese Bestrebungen könnten durch das Wiederauftreten Harlans gestört und durchkreuzt werden. Er durfte aber auch davon ausgehen, daß man in der Öffentlichkeit gerade von ihm eine Äußerung dazu erwarte, zumal er aus Anlaß einer 'Woche des deutschen Films' ohnedies zu aktuellen Filmfragen zu sprechen hatte und die unmittelbar bevorstehende Aufführung des ersten neuen Harlan-Films in Fachkreisen sicherlich als ein wichtiges Ereignis gewertet wurde. Der Beschwerdeführer konnte die Empfindung haben, daß er hier einer Stellungnahme nicht ausweichen dürfe. Daraus ergab sich für ihn eine defensive Situation, die seine Äußerungen nicht als einen unmotivierten und jedenfalls unprovozierten Angriff, sondern als eine verständliche Reaktion der Abwehr erscheinen läßt.

The complainant was entitled, by his especially close personal relationship to everything that concerned the German-Jewish relationship, to state his opinion in public. He was at that time already known through his efforts for restoration of a true inward peace with the Jewish people. He played a leading role in the Association for Christian and Jewish Co-operation; shortly before he had introduced in broadcasting and the press the campaign 'Peace with Israel', which had been discussed vigorously in Germany and other countries and had brought him numerous declarations of agreement. It is conceivable that he feared that all these efforts could be disturbed and frustrated by the reappearance of Harlan. But he might also have proceeded on the basis that the public expected a statement from him on the subject especially as he had to speak anyway about topical film issues on the occasion of a 'Week of the German Film'; and the directly impending showing of the first new Harlan film would certainly be regarded in circles of experts as an important event. The complainant could have had the feeling that he ought not to avoid an expression of opinion here. This resulted in a defensive situation for him which causes his statements to appear not as an unmotivated and in any case unprovoked attack, but as an understandable reaction of defence.

Das Verlangen, der Beschwerdeführer hätte bei dieser Sachlage von der Kundgabe seiner Auffassung, daß Harlan von der Mitwirkung an repräsentativen Filmen ausgeschaltet werden solle, mit Rücksicht auf die beruflichen Interessen Harlans und die wirtschaftlichen Interessen der ihn beschäftigenden Filmgesellschaften trotzdem absehen müssen, ist unberechtigt. Die Filmgesellschaften mögen bei ihrem Entschluß, Harlan wieder zu beschäftigen, formal korrekt verfahren sein. Wenn sie dabei aber die darüber hinaus verbleibende moralische Problematik des Falles nicht berücksichtigt haben, dann kann das nicht dazu führen, das Vorgehen des Beschwerdeführers, der gerade diese Problematik aufgriff, als 'unsittlich' zu bezeichnen und ihm so die Freiheit der Meinungsäußerung zu beschneiden. Damit würde der Wert, den das Grundrecht der freien Meinungsäußerung für die freiheitliche Demokratie gerade dadurch besitzt, daß es die öffentliche Diskussion über Gegenstände von allgemeiner Bedeutung und ernstem Gehalt gewährleistet, empfindlich geschmälert. Wenn es darum geht, daß sich in einer für das Gemeinwohl wichtigen Frage eine öffentliche Meinung bildet, müssen private und namentlich wirtschaftliche Interessen einzelner grundsätzlich zurücktreten. Diese Interessen sind darum nicht schutzlos; denn der Wert des Grundrechts zeigt sich gerade auch darin, daß *jeder* von ihm Gebrauch machen kann. Wer sich durch die öffentliche Äußerung eines andern verletzt fühlt, kann ebenfalls vor der Öffentlichkeit erwidern. Erst im Widerstreit der in gleicher Freiheit vorgetragenen Auffassungen kommt die öffentliche Meinung zustande, bilden sich die einzelnen angesprochenen Mitglieder der Gesellschaft ihre persönliche Ansicht. Der Beschwerdeführer hat zu Recht darauf hingewiesen, daß es z. B. grundsätzlich zulässig ist, aus ernsthaften Motiven in der Öffentlichkeit den Absatz bestimmter Waren oder bestimmte Organisationsformen des Verkaufs zu bekämpfen, auch wenn bei Erfolg solcher Meinungsäußerungen wirtschaftliche Unternehmen zum Erliegen kämen, Arbeitsplätze verlorengingen u. dgl. Solche Äußerungen können nicht schon wegen dieser möglichen Folgen gerichtlich untersagt werden - den Angegriffenen steht es aber frei, sich durch Darlegung *ihrer* Auffassung zur Wehr zu setzen.

The claim that the complainant should, in these circumstances, out of consideration for the professional interests of Harlan and the business interests of the film companies employing him, have nevertheless abandoned the announcement of his opinion that Harlan should be excluded from participation in representative films is unjustified. The film companies may have acted in a formally correct manner in their decision to employ Harlan again. But if they did not at the same time consider the remaining moral problem of the case over and above this, that cannot lead to the action of the complainant, who took up precisely this problem, being described as 'contrary to good morals', and so to curtailing his freedom of expression of opinion. That would result in the value which the basic right of freedom of expression of opinion possesses for a free democracy, precisely due to the fact that it guarantees public discussion about subjects of general importance and serious content, being appreciably diminished. When it is a question of a public opinion being formed on an important question for the common good, private, and especially business, interests of individuals must in principle recede. These interests are not for this reason without protection; because the value of the basic right shows itself also in the fact that *everyone* can make use of it. A person who feels himself injured by the public statement of another can likewise reply in front of the public. It is only in the conflict of opinions expressed with equal freedom that public opinion can come into existence and the individual members of society addressed can form their personal view. The complainant has correctly referred to the fact that it is, eg, permissible in principle to oppose in public, from serious motives, the sale of certain wares or certain forms of marketing even when, if such expressions of opinion were successful, business undertakings would be brought to a standstill, jobs lost and the like. Such statements cannot be judicially forbidden simply on account of these possible consequences, but those attacked are at liberty to offer resistance by the explanation of *their* opinion.

In diesem Zusammenhang hat das Landgericht auf Art. 2 GG hingewiesen. Es geht davon aus, Harlan dürfe seinen Beruf als Filmregisseur wieder aufnehmen und ausüben, da er vom Schwurgericht, vor dem er wegen eines Verbrechens gegen die Menschlichkeit nach dem Kontrollratsgesetz Nr. 10 angeklagt war, freigesprochen, im Entnazifizierungsverfahren als 'Entlasteter' eingestuft worden sei und die Spitzenorganisation der Filmwirtschaft (Spio) alle Tätigkeitsbeschränkungen gegen ihn aufgehoben habe. Artikel 2 wirke allerdings nur gegen die öffentliche Gewalt; zugleich komme aber in der Bestimmung die sittliche Auffassung des deutschen Volkes zum Ausdruck, mit der Folge, daß die eigenmächtige Beschränkung dieses Grundrechts, 'von wem sie auch kommen mag', gegen die guten Sitten verstoße. Daran ist richtig, daß auch Art. 2 GG zu dem grundrechtlichen Wertsystem gehört und die Vorstellungen davon, was wider die 'guten Sitten' verstößt, maßgeblich beeinflussen kann. Trotzdem wird hier die Bedeutung des Artikels 2 nicht richtig gesehen. Daß der Staat, die öffentliche Gewalt, nur in den Schranken der Gesetze gegen Harlan vorgehen durfte und darf, ist selbstverständlich. Daraus folgt aber nichts dafür, was der einzelne Bürger gegenüber Harlan unternehmen und äußern darf. Denn hier ist entscheidend, daß jeder einzelne Träger derselben Grundrechte ist. Da im Zusammenleben in einer großen Gemeinschaft sich notwendig ständig Interessen- und Rechtskollisionen zwischen den einzelnen ergeben, hat im sozialen Bereich ständig ein Ausgleich und eine Abwägung der einander entgegenstehenden Rechte nach dem Grade ihrer Schutzwürdigkeit stattzufinden. Was als Ergebnis einer solchen Abwägung an Beschränkung der freien Entfaltungsmöglichkeit für den einzelnen verbleibt, muß hingenommen werden. Niemand kann sich hier auf die angeblich absolut geschützte Position des Art. 2 GG zurückziehen und jeden Angriff auf sie, 'von wem er auch kommen mag', als Unrecht oder Verstoß gegen die guten Sitten ansehen (vgl. auch H. Lehmann, MDR 1952, S. 298). Die Argumentation des Oberlandesgerichts Hamburg im Verfahren der einstweiligen Verfügung: 'weil der Staat das Recht (zu gewissen Maßnahmen) nicht hat, so kann dieses Recht erst recht nicht der einzelne Bürger haben', ist irrig, weil sie Nicht-Zusammengehöriges in ein einfaches Verhältnis von mehr und weniger bringen will.

In this connection, the State Court referred to Art 2 of the GG. It proceeds on the basis that Harlan might take up and exercise his profession as film producer again, as he was acquitted by the jury court before which he was accused of a crime against humanity according to the Control Council Act no 10, he was classified as 'exonerated' in the de-Nazification proceedings, and the Organisation of Heads in the Film Industry (Spio) had annulled all limitations on his activities. Article 2 would certainly only have effect against public power; but at the same time the moral opinion of the German people comes into expression in this provision with the consequence that the arbitrary limitation of this basic right 'from whomsoever it may come' contravenes good morals. In this connection it is correct that Art 2 of the GG also belongs to the basic right value system and can influence decisively the conceptions of what offends against good morals. Nevertheless, the significance of Art 2 is not seen rightly here. It is self-evident that the State, the public power, could and may only proceed against Harlan within the limits of the laws. But nothing follows from that as to what the individual citizen may undertake and state against Harlan. For here it is crucial that every individual is the beneficiary of the same basic rights. Since, in communal life in a large community, conflicts of interests and rights between individuals necessarily continually arise, in the social sphere a balancing and weighing up of the rights which are opposed to each other, according to the degree that they merit protection, must continually take place. What remains as the result of such a weighing up in the limitation of the possibility of free development for the individual must be accepted. No-one can fall back here on the allegedly absolutely protected position of Art 2 of the GG and regard every attack on it, 'from whomsoever it may come' as wrong or offending against good morals (compare also H Lehmann, MDR, 1952, p 298). The argument of the Upper State Court of Hamburg in the proceedings for the interim injunction: '... because the State does not have the right (to take certain measures), the individual citizen cannot have this right' is erroneous, because it seeks to bring unconnected things into a simple relationship of more and less.

Die Ausführungen des Landgerichts könnten auch so gedeutet werden, daß es in den Äußerungen des Beschwerdeführers einen Eingriff in den Kern der künstlerischen Persönlichkeit Harlans erblickt, den 'letzten unantastbaren Bereich menschlicher Freiheit' (BVerfGE 6, 32 [41]), einen Eingriff also, der durch keine noch so gewichtigen Interessen des Beschwerdeführers gerechtfertigt werden könne und deshalb, weil er die Menschenwürde Harlans verletze, unter allen Umständen sittenwidrig sei. Eine so weitreichende Folgerung läßt aber der festgestellte Sachverhalt nicht zu. Selbst wenn man – über den Wortlaut der Äußerungen hinaus – mit dem Landgericht annimmt, bei Erfolg der Aufforderung werde Harlan als Regisseur von Spielfilmen völlig ausgeschaltet, würden diesem doch noch andere künstlerische Betätigungsmöglichkeiten – auch im Filmwesen – verbleiben, so daß von einer gänzlichen Vernichtung seiner künstlerischen und menschlichen Existenz nicht gesprochen werden könnte. Eine solche Annahme würde aber überhaupt die Intensität des in den Äußerungen liegenden Eingriffs erheblich überschätzen. Die Äußerungen konnten als solche die künstlerische und menschliche Entfaltungsfreiheit Harlans unmittelbar und wirksam überhaupt nicht beschränken. Dem Beschwerdeführer standen keinerlei Zwangsmittel zu Gebote, um seiner Aufforderung Nachdruck zu verleihen; er konnte nur an das Verantwortungsbewußtsein und die sittliche Haltung der von ihm Angesprochenen appellieren und mußte es ihrer freien Willensentschließung überlassen, ob sie ihm folgen wollten. Daß er auf die Subventionierung von Filmen durch den hamburgischen Staat Einfluß gehabt hätte, also durch die Drohung mit dem Entzug oder der Versagung von Subventionen einen gewissen Druck wenigstens auf die Filmproduzenten hätte ausüben können, ist nicht dargetan.

(c) Die Gegner des Beschwerdeführers haben in der mündlichen Verhandlung vor dem Bundesverfassungsgericht besonderes Gewicht darauf gelegt, daß die vom Beschwerdeführer bei der Boykottaufforderung angewandten Mittel jedenfalls in einer Hinsicht in sich schon sittenwidrig gewesen seien. Der Beschwerdeführer habe nämlich die objektiv unwahre Behauptung aufgestellt, Harlan sei vom Schwurgericht nur formell freigesprochen worden, die Urteilsgründe seien eine moralische Verdammung gewesen.

Es mag dahinstehen, ob dieser Vorwurf, wenn er gerechtfertigt wäre, ein so umfassendes Verbot begründen könnte, wie es im Urteil des Landgerichts ausgesprochen ist. Das Landgericht selbst ist der Auffassung, 'daß die Verwendung sittenwidriger Mittel wohl ein Verbot der Boykottaufforderung mit diesen Mitteln, nicht aber ein Verbot der Boykottaufforderung schlechthin rechtfertigen würde'. Indessen kann nicht anerkannt werden, daß der Beschwerdeführer sich mit dieser Kennzeichnung des Schwurgerichtsurteils eines Sittenverstoßes schuldig gemacht habe.

The remarks of the State Court could also be interpreted to the effect that it sees in the statements of the complainant an intrusion into the kernel of the artistic personality of Harlan, 'the final inviolable realm of human freedom' (BVerfGE 6, 32 [41]), and therefore an intrusion which could not be justified by the most weighty of the complainant's interests and therefore, because it violated Harlan's human dignity, was under all the circumstances contrary to good morals. Such a far reaching conclusion is not however permitted by the established facts of the case. Even if one accepts with the State Court, going beyond the wording of the statements, that on the success of the call (for a boycott) Harlan would be completely eliminated as a producer of feature films, other possibilities of artistic activity would still remain open for him in the film industry as well, so that one could not speak of a total destruction of his artistic and human existence. Such an assumption would really considerably overvalue the intensity of the intrusion contained in the statements. The statements could as such not directly and effectively limit the free artistic and human development of Harlan at all. No kinds of means of coercion were at the complainant's disposal to lend emphasis to his call (for a boycott); he could only appeal to the sense of responsibility and the moral stance of those addressed by him and had to leave it to the free decision of their will as to whether they would follow him. It has not been demonstrated that he would have had influence on the subsidising of films by the State of Hamburg and therefore could have exercised a certain pressure, at least on film producers, by threatening the withdrawal or denial of subsidies.

(c) The complainant's opponents in the oral hearing before the Federal Constitutional Court laid particular weight on the fact that the means employed by the complainant in the call for a boycott were in any case in one respect in themselves contrary to good morals. That is, the complainant had made the objectively untrue assertion that Harlan had only been formally acquitted by the jury court and the grounds of the decision had been a moral condemnation.

It can be left undecided whether this accusation, if it were justified, could be the basis of such a comprehensive prohibition as has been pronounced in the judgment of the State Court. The State Court itself is of the opinion 'that the use of methods contrary to good morals would certainly justify a prohibition of a call to a boycott by these methods, but would not simply justify a prohibition of a call to a boycott'. Nevertheless it cannot be admitted that the complainant has committed a violation of good morals by characterising the judgment of the jury court in this way.

Aus dem Inhalt des Schwurgerichtsurteils ist festzustellen: Das Urteil schildert den Lebensgang Harlans, insbesondere seine Laufbahn als Filmregisseur, die nach 1933 begann und ihn alsbald zum 'Prestigeregisseur' (so kennzeichnet Harlan selbst seine Stellung in der Schrift 'Meine Beziehung zum Nationalsozialismus', S. 21) aufsteigen ließ. Das Urteil stellt dann die Entstehungsgeschichte des Films 'Jud Süß' und die Beteiligung Harlans an diesem Film als Regisseur und Drehbuchmitautor im einzelnen dar. Es schreibt dem Film 'klare antisemitische Tendenz' zu, würdigt ihn im Zusammenhang mit den allgemeinen Umständen zur Zeit seiner Entstehung und ersten Aufführung (1940) dahin, daß er durch die tendenziöse Beeinflussung der öffentlichen Meinung im judenfeindlichen Sinn mitursächlich für die Judenverfolgung gewesen sei, und kennzeichnet ihn deshalb in objektiver Hinsicht als ein 'Angriffsverhalten', wie es nach der Rechtsprechung für den Begriff des Verbrechens gegen die Menschlichkeit im Sinne des Kontrollratsgesetzes Nr. 10 erfordert werde. Da Harlan als Mitgestalter des Drehbuchs und Regisseur objektiv zum Kreis der Angriffstäter gehöre und da er auch die mit dem Film verfolgten Absichten erkannt sowie mit den voraussichtlichen Wirkungen des Films gerechnet habe, kommt das Urteil zur Feststellung, daß er durch seine maßgebende Mitwirkung bei der Schaffung dieses Film 'in objektiver und subjektiver Hinsicht den Tatbestand des Verbrechens gegen die Menschlichkeit erfüllt 'habe. Es spricht ihn trotzdem frei, weil es ihm den Schuldausschließungsgrund des sogenannten Nötigungsnotstands (§ 52 StGB) zubilligt. Dazu wird im einzelnen ausgeführt:

From the content of the judgment of the jury court it can be established: the judgment describes the course of Harlan's life, in particular his career as a film producer which began after 1933 and caused him to rise immediately to 'prestige producer' (Harlan himself describes his position in this way in the publication My Relationship with National Socialism, p 21). The judgment describes the history of the origin of the film 'Jew Süss' and the participation of Harlan in this film as producer and co-author of the film script in detail. It assigns the film to the category of 'clear anti-semitic tendency', evaluates it in the context of the general circumstances at the time of its origin and first showing (1940) to the effect that it was a contributory cause to the persecution of the Jews through its prejudicial influencing of public opinion towards an anti-Jewish frame of mind and characterises it therefore in an objective sense as 'aggressive conduct' of the kind required by case law for the concept of a crime against humanity in the sense of the Control Council Act no 10. Since Harlan, as co-creator of the film script and producer belonged objectively to the category of perpetrators of aggression and since he had also recognised the purposes pursued by the film and had reckoned with the probable effects of the film, the judgment arrives at the finding that he had, by his controlling participation in the creation of the film, 'fulfilled in an objective and subjective respect the factual content of a crime against humanity'. It acquitted him nevertheless because it allowed him the ground of exculpation of so-called coercion emergency (§ 52 of the StGB [in an earlier formulation of the StGB]). The details here are explained:

'Nach dem Ergebnis der Beweisaufnahme steht fest, daß Harlan sich nicht um die Mitwirkung an der Herstellung des Films 'Jud Süß' bemüht hat, sondern im Gegenteil erst auf Grund des ihm vom Propagandaminister Goebbels erteilten Befehls tätig geworden ist. Zur Beurteilung der Frage, wie Goebbels sich im Fall der offenen oder versteckten Ablehnung Harlans verhalten haben würde, war zunächst auf Grund allgemeiner gerichtsnotorischer Tatsachen festzustellen, daß im November 1939 bereits der Kriegszustand zwischen Deutschland und Polen und die Möglichkeit der weiteren Ausdehnung des Krieges auf andere Staaten bestand. Goebbels vertrat die These, daß im Kriege jeder Deutsche seine Aufgabe an dem Platz zu erfüllen habe, an den er gestellt sei, und daß jeder Deutsche 'Soldat des Führers' sei. Goebbels selbst betrachtete sich in seiner Eigenschaft als Propagandaminister als General des Führers und die unter ihm arbeitenden Beamten des Propagand-aministeriums und alle seinem Ministerium unterstellten Personen, auch Filmproduzenten, Regisseure, Schauspieler usw. als unter seinem Befehl stehende Soldaten. Die Nichtausführung eines von Goebbels gegebenen Befehles wurde seit Beginn des Krieges von ihm als Verweigerung eines kriegsdienstlichen Befehles angesehen und es bedarf keiner Erörterung darüber, daß eine solche von den damaligen Machthabern mit den schärfsten Strafen, auch mit der Todesstrafe, belegt worden wäre. In derartigen Fällen bewies Goebbels eine unmenschliche Härte und Skrupellosigkeit zur Durchführung seiner Absichten, so daß die Möglichkeit einer offenen Ablehnung von vornherein ausgeschlossen war. Darüber hinaus bewiesen die angeführten Einzelbeispiele, wie unberechenbar und gefährlich Goebbels in seinen Handlungen sein konnte. Weiter zeigt die Tatsache, daß Goebbels als Propagandaminister jahrelang zugesehen hat, wie deutsche Menschen, deutsche Städte durch einen sinnlosen Krieg zugrundegerichtet wurden und wie Millionen unschuldiger Menschen durch die Willkürmaßnahmen des nationalsozialistischen Regimes in einer jeder Menschlichkeit Hohn sprechenden Art und Weise gequält, gedemütigt, ja sogar gemordet wurden, und daß Goebbels alle diese Taten durch seine Propaganda zu rechtfertigen suchte, wie skrupellos und ohne moralische Hemmungen dieser Propagandadiktator war. Unter dem nationalsozialistischen Gewaltsystem sind ferner eine große Anzahl bedeutender und im Volke außerordentlich angesehener Männer aus den einflußreichsten Stellungen entfernt worden, in Konzentrationslager verbracht, zum Selbstmord getrieben oder hingerichtet worden, und zwar in vielen Fällen ohne daß auch nur der Schein des Rechtes gewahrt worden wäre. Alle diese Tatsachen erhellen, das Goebbels zur Durchsetzung seiner Absichten ebenso wie die andern nationalsozialistischen Machthaber vor keiner Gewalttat zurückschreckte.

'According to the outcome of the hearing of witnesses, it is established that Harlan did not himself take steps towards co-operation in the production of the film 'Jew Süss' but on the contrary only did so because of a command given to him by the Minister for Publicity, Goebbels. In deciding the question of how Goebbels would have behaved in the event of an open or covert refusal by Harlan, it was first established on the basis of general facts, of which the court can take notice, that in November 1939 a state of war existed between Germany and Poland and there was a possibility of further extension of the war to other States. Goebbels advocated the proposition that in the war every German had his duty to fulfil in the place in which he was put and every German was 'soldier of the Führer'. Goebbels regarded himself in his character as Minister for Publicity as General of the Führer and the officials of the Ministry of Publicity working under him, and all persons placed under his Ministry, including film manufacturers, producers, actors, etc. as soldiers under his command. The non-execution of a command given by Goebbels would from the start of the war be regarded by him as refusal of a military command and no discussion is needed about the fact that such a refusal would have been met with the severest penalties, even the death penalty, by the rulers at that time. In cases of this kind, Goebbels showed an inhuman hardness and unscrupulousness in the execution of his purposes, so that the possibility of an open refusal was excluded from the start. Besides this, the individual examples quoted proved how unpredictable and dangerous Goebbels could be in his actions. Further, the fact that Goebbels as Minister of Publicity had witnessed for years the destruction of German people and German cities by a senseless war and the torture, humiliation and even murder of millions of innocent human beings by the arbitrary measures of the National Socialist Regime in a manner which showed contempt for every kind of humanity, and that Goebbels sought to justify all these actions by his propaganda, showed how unscrupulous, and without moral restraints, this propaganda dictator was. Under the National Socialist power system a large number of persons who were important and especially respected by the people were removed from the most influential positions, brought to concentration camps, driven to suicide or executed and in many cases even without the appearance of justice having been maintained. All these facts reveal that Goebbels, just like the other National Socialist rulers, did not shrink from any act of violence for the accomplishment of his purposes.

Als Goebbels im Jahre 1938 die Auflage an die Filmgesellschaften erteilte, je einen antisemitischen Filmstoff herauszubringen, verfolgte er planmäßig die im nationalsozialistischen Programm festgelegten antisemitischen Thesen. Im Jahre 1939 mußte die antisemitische Propaganda nach der Auffassung der damaligen Machthaber eine noch weit größere Bedeutung erlangen, da sie das Weltjudentum als den Feind Europas und als ihren stärksten Gegner betrachteten, wie das auch in den Reden Adolf Hitlers ständig zum Ausdruck gekommen ist. Die Durchführung der von Goebbels erteilten Auflage gewann daher zunehmend größere Bedeutung. Sie mußte sogar von seinem Standpunkt aus von größtem staatspolitischen Wert sein. Goebbels war daher schon aus den hier aufgezeigten Gründen an der Durchführung seiner Befehle auf das heftigste interessiert. Bei dem Film 'Jud Süß' kam jedoch hinzu, daß Goebbels auch persönlich durch den von den Schauspielern geleisteten Widerstand gegen das Filmprojekt äußerst gereizt war. Es galt für ihn, seinen Willen in diktatorischer Weise gegenüber jedem Widerstand durchzusetzen. Unter Berücksichtigung aller dieser Umstände konnte zumindest die Möglichkeit nicht ausgeschlossen werden, daß für Harlan im Falle einer offenen oder versteckten Ablehnung, falls diese von Goebbels erkannt wurde, Gefahr für Leib und Leben bestand. Das Schwurgericht ist darüber hinaus sogar der Auffassung, daß diese Lebensbedrohung bei der 'Persönlichkeit Goebbels' durchaus ernsthaft gegeben war und zwar um so mehr, als das Verhältnis zwischen Goebbels und Harlan besonders im Jahre 1939/40 außerordentlich gespannt war. Von der großen Zahl der zu diesem Punkt vernommenen Zeugen hat nicht ein einziger mit Sicherheit sagen können, welche Folgewirkungen für Harlan hätten entstehen können. Sie stimmten jedoch weitgehend darin überein, daß Goebbels in irgendeiner Weise seine furchtbare Macht Harlan hätte spüren lassen. Für die rechtliche Entscheidung kann es jedoch nicht von Bedeutung sein, ob Goebbels gegen Harlan als Verweigerer eines kriegsdienstlichen Befehls etwa ein Verfahren vor dem Sondergericht in die Wege geleitet oder ihn der Wilkürbehandlung im Konzentrationslager überantwortet hätte, oder ob er schließlich irgendeinen anderen, nicht im Zusammenhang mit dem Filmprojekt stehenden Vorwand gesucht und gefunden hätte, Harlan als politischen Gegner, Saboteur oder wegen irgendeines anderen Deliktes den gleichen Maßnahmen auszusetzen. Daß die Harlan drohende Gefahr eine gegenwärtige war, bedarf keiner weiteren Ausführungen, da die Folgen der Nichtausführung des Goebbelsbefehles in jedem Augenblick eintreten konnten, in dem Goebbels Harlans wahre Absichten erkannte.'

When Goebbels in 1938 gave the order to the film companies to bring out anti-semitic film material he was pursuing methodically the anti-semitic propositions determined in the National Socialist programme. In 1939 anti-semitic propaganda, according to the opinion of the rulers of that time, had to attain far greater importance as they regarded world Jewry as the enemy of Europe and their strongest opponent, as was also continually expressed in the speeches of Adolf Hitler. The carrying out of the order given by Goebbels therefore obtained increasingly greater importance. From his point of view, it must have been of the greatest political value. Goebbels was therefore already interested to the greatest degree in the carrying out of his commands for the reasons shown here. There was however the added factor with the film 'Jew Süss' that Goebbels was personally extremely irritated by the opposition of the actors to the film project. His will had to be achieved in a dictatorial way, against all opposition. In consideration of all these circumstances, it cannot be excluded that there was at least a possibility of danger to life and limb for Harlan in the case of an open or covert refusal if this became known by Goebbels. In addition to this, the jury court is of the opinion that this threat to life from the 'personality of Goebbels' was submitted entirely seriously and so much more because the relationship between Goebbels and Harlan was unusually strained, especially in the years 1939/40. Out of the large number of witnesses examined on this issue, not one could say with certainty what consequences could have arisen for Harlan. They largely agreed, however, that Goebbels would in some way have let Harlan feel his formidable power. It cannot, however, be of importance for the legal decision whether Goebbels would perhaps have arranged for proceedings against Harlan before a special court for refusing a military command or would have consigned him to arbitrary treatment in a concentration camp or whether he would finally have sought and found some other pretext, not having a connection with the film project, to expose Harlan to the same measures as a political opponent, saboteur, or on account of some other offence. That the danger threatening Harlan was an actual one needs no further explanation, as the consequences of not carrying out a command by Goebbels could occur at any moment in which Goebbels realised Harlan's true intentions.'

Es wird dann geprüft, ob Harlan zu seiner Mitarbeit an dem Film etwa durch andere Beweggründe bestimmt worden sei. Solche Motive lassen sich nach Auffassung des Schwurgerichts nicht feststellen. Es heißt dann weiter:

> Es ist bereits ausgeführt worden, daß die offene Ablehnung der Mitarbeit an dem Filmprojekt 'Jud Süß' für Harlan eine schwere Bedrohung und Lebensgefahr bedeutet hätte. Es war aber weiter zu prüfen, welche Möglichkeiten für ihn bestanden haben, durch verstecktes Ausweichen dieser Gefahr zu entgehen und sich dennoch der Beteiligung an der Filmarbeit zu entziehen. Der Angeklagte hat nun behauptet, er habe alle Möglichkeiten, um den Goebbels'schen Befehl herumzukommen, voll ausgeschöpft, andere Möglichkeiten als die von ihm versuchten hätten ihm nicht zur Verfügung gestanden.
>
> Dem Angeklagten konnte nicht widerlegt werden, daß er verschiedene Ausweichmanöver versucht hat und zwar, daß er das Drehbuch bei Goebbels gründlich verrissen, sich zur Darstellung rein negativer Personen unfähig erklärt, auf seine dringenden Arbeiten an seinem Film 'Pedro soll hängen' und an dem neuen Projekt 'Agnes Bernauer' verwiesen hat und daß er sich schließlich freiwillig zum Kriegsdienst gemeldet hat. Soweit es sich bei den von dem Angeklagten behaupteten Ausweichmanövern um Einwendungen künstlerischer Art handelte, konnte seine Haltung ihre Erklärung auch in der Besorgnis eines Regisseurs finden, der auf Grund eines schlechten Drehbuchs einen schlechten Film zu drehen fürchtete. Trotzdem konnte das Gericht nicht mit Sicherheit ausschließen, daß alle diese Maßnahmen Harlans aus einer inneren Ablehnung gegen das Filmprojekt als solche ergriffen wurden. Es war daher die weitere Frage zu prüfen, ob sich Harlan über die von ihm behaupteten Ausweichversuche hinaus weitere Möglichkeiten zum Ausweichen geboten haben könnten. Das Gericht hat solche Möglichkeiten nicht feststellen können.

Das Urteil legt dann im einzelnen dar, daß zu der Zeit, als Harlan mit der Gestaltung des Films beauftragt wurde, für ihn kaum noch Möglichkeiten bestanden hätten, sich der Mitarbeit zu entziehen, den Film zu sabotieren oder seinen antisemitischen Inhalt wesentlich zu mildern; daß er das letztere wenigstens versucht habe, wird ihm ausdrücklich bescheinigt. In diesem Zusammenhang wird gesagt:

There is then an examination of whether Harlan's collaboration in the film had perhaps been induced by other motives. Such motives cannot be established, according to the opinion of the jury court. It states further:

It has already been explained that open refusal of collaboration in the film project 'Jew Süss' would have meant a severe threat to Harlan and danger to his life. But it had further to be examined what possibilities there were for him to escape this danger by hidden evasion and nevertheless to avoid participation in the film work. The accused has now claimed that he fully exhausted every possibility of avoiding Goebbels' command and possibilities other than those tried by him would not have been available to him.

It could not be refuted that the accused had tried various evasive manoeuvres and indeed that he thoroughly criticised the film script to Goebbels, had declared himself incapable of portraying purely negative persons, and referred to his pressing work on his film 'Pedro shall hang' and on the new project 'Agnes Bernauer', and that he had finally voluntarily reported for military service. So far as concerned the evasive manoeuvres regarding objections of an artistic nature which were asserted by the accused, his attitude could be explained by the apprehension of a producer who feared that on the basis of a bad film script a bad film would be produced. Nevertheless the court could not exclude with certainty that all these measures by Harlan were taken from an personal rejection of the film project as such. The further question therefore had to be examined of whether other possibilities for evasion could have presented themselves to Harlan besides the attempts at evasion asserted by him. The court has not been able to establish such possibilities.

The judgment then explains in detail that at the time Harlan was commissioned with the composition of the film, scarcely any possibilities would have existed for him to withdraw from participation, to sabotage the film or significantly to mitigate its anti-semitic content; that he had at least attempted this last course of action is expressly confirmed in his favour. In this connection it is said:

Dem Angeklagten konnte auch nicht zum strafrechtlichen Vorwurf gemacht werden, daß er den Film in einer seinen künstlerischen Fähigkeiten entsprechenden Form gestaltet hat. Es wird wohl zutreffen, daß der Film unter Zugrundelegung des Metzger-Möller'-schen Drehbuches oder unter der Regie Dr. Brauers einen weit geringeren Zulauf bei dem Filmpublikum erreicht hätte. Es ist logisch und zwingend, daß in diesem Falle die antisemitische Tendenz des Films keine so weite Verbreitung hätte finden können, wie dies bei dem von Harlan hergestellten Film der Fall war. Es war hierbei zu berücksichtigen, daß Harlan durch eine künstlerisch nicht so hoch zu wertende Gestaltung seinen Ruf als großer Regisseur auf das schwerste hätte gefährden können. Das Schwurgericht ist jedoch der Ansicht, daß ein Künstler – ob er nun freiwillig oder gezwungen an die Erfüllung eines Auftrages geht – gar nicht imstande ist, zu bestimmen, ob er einen guten, zukräftigen oder einen schlechten Film herstellt. In jedem Falle wird der Film so ausfallen, wie es seiner künstlerischen Begabung entspricht.

So gelangt das Urteil schließlich zu dem Ergebnis:

Zusammenfassend ist zu sagen, daß die Tätigkeit Harlans in objektiver und subjektiver Hinsicht zwar den Tatbestand des Verbrechens gegen die Menschlichkeit erfüllt hat, ihm jedoch der Entschuldigungsgrund des § 52 StGB zuzubilligen war.

Das Schwurgericht hat sonach nicht konkrete Tatsachen festgestellt, die für Harlan einen Notstand begründet hätten; es hat die von Harlan in dieser Richtung vorgetragenen Verteidigungsbehauptungen gewürdigt und ist zu dem Schluß gekommen, man müsse annehmen, daß bei Ablehnung einer Mitwirkung an dem Film für Harlan Gefahr für Leib und Leben bestanden habe; die aus allgemeinem geschichtlichen Wissen bekannten Charakterzüge von Goebbels machten eine solche Gefährdung sogar wahrscheinlich.

Diese Gedankenführung des schwurgerichtlichen Urteils hat der Beschwerdeführer zusammenfassend dahin gewertet, es handle sich hier um einen 'formellen Freispruch' und eine 'moralische Verdammung'. Was der Beschwerdeführer zum Ausdruck bringen wollte, war offenbar dies: Es liege hier nicht ein Freispruch wegen erwiesener Unschuld vor; Harlan sei durch die Urteilsgründe in Wahrheit schwer belastet, da er als maßgebender Mitgestalter eines Werkes erscheine, das als 'Verbrechen gegen die Menschlichkeit' zu charakterisieren sei und dessen mutmaßliche Wirkung auf die Behandlung der Juden er gekannt habe; das Gericht habe ihn nur freigesprochen, weil es ihm nicht habe widerlegen können, daß er unter Zwang an dem Film mitgewirkt habe.

It also cannot be turned into a criminal accusation against the accused that he shaped the film into a form corresponding with his artistic capabilities. It is certainly true that the film would have had a far smaller popularity with the film-going public taking a Metzger-Möller film script as a basis or under the management of Dr Brauer. It is logical and convincing that in this case the anti-semitic propensity of the film would not have been able to find so wide a circulation as was the case with a film produced by Harlan. It had to be considered in this connection that Harlan could have endangered his reputation as a great producer to the gravest extent by a production which was not to be so highly appraised from an artistic point of view. The jury court is however of the opinion that an artist, whether he fulfils a commission voluntarily or under compulsion, is certainly not able to decide whether he produces a good and attractive or a bad film. In each case the film will turn out in a way which corresponds to his artistic gift.

Thus the judgment finally reached the conclusion:

Summarising, it has to be said that Harlan's actions have certainly in an objective and subjective respect fulfilled the factual content of a crime against humanity but the ground of exculpation in § 52 of the StGB is to be allowed to him.

The jury court consequently did not establish concrete facts which would have substantiated an emergency for Harlan; it evaluated the defence assertions expressed by Harlan to this effect and came to the conclusion that one must accept that on refusal to participate in the film, danger to life and limb would have existed for Harlan; the features of the character of Goebbels known from general historical information made such danger even probable.

This train of thought in the judgment of the jury court was evaluated by the complainant in summary to the effect that it was here a question of a 'formal acquittal' and a 'moral condemnation'. What the complainant wanted to express was obviously this: This was not an acquittal on account of proved innocence; Harlan was, by the grounds of the judgment, in truth heavily incriminated, as he appeared as a controlling co-producer of a work which was to be characterised as a 'crime against humanity', the probable effect of which in the treatment of the Jews would have been known to him; the court only acquitted him because it had not been able to refute his claim that he collaborated in the film under coercion.

Wenn der Beschwerdeführer seinen Eindruck vom Inhalt des schwurgerichtlichen Urteils in die Worte 'formeller Freispruch' und 'moralische Verdammung' zusammengefaßt hat, so geht das nach Auffassung des Bundesverfassungsgerichts nicht über die Grenze des in der öffentlichen Diskussion eines Themas von ernstem Gehalt Zulässigen hinaus. Es bedeutet eine unannehmbare Einengung der Redefreiheit in einer freiheitlichen Demokratie, wenn das Landgericht hier von dem Beschwerdeführer, der nicht Jurist ist, die Sorgfalt sogar eines 'strafrechtlich geschulten Lesers' fordert, die ihn hätte veranlassen müssen, die Kennzeichnung 'formeller Freispruch' zu unterlassen, weil sie nur beim Fehlen objektiver Voraussetzungen der Strafbarkeit angängig sei. Die vom Beschwerdeführer gewählten Bezeichnungen sind keine Tatsachenbehauptungen, deren Wahrheit oder Unwahrheit bewiesen werden könnte; namentlich wird mit der Bezeichnung 'formeller Freispruch' kein eindeutiger rechtlicher Tatbestand bezeichnet. Es handelt sich um eine zusammenfassende, wertende Charakterisierung des gesamten Urteilsinhalts, die für zulässig gehalten werden muß, weil sie weder in der Form verletzend ist noch inhaltlich so sehr den gemeinten Sachverhalt verfehlt, daß sie bei Hörern und Lesern ganz irrige Vorstellungen über den Urteilsinhalt erwecken müßte, wie es etwa der Fall wäre, wenn von einem Freigesprochenen ohne nähere Erläuterung behauptet würde, er sei 'verurteilt' worden. Es ist hier auch von Bedeutung, daß der Freispruch Harlans in der breiteren Öffentlichkeit und erst recht in den Kreisen der Filmwirtschaft bereits bekannt war. Ebenso war bekannt, daß Harlan der Regisseur des Films 'Jud Süß' gewesen war. Damit stand fest, daß das Urteil nicht die völlige 'Unschuld' im Sinne einer Nichtbeteiligung Harlans an der Förderung der Judenverfolgung durch diesen Film festgestellt haben konnte, daß mithin der Freispruch auf einem anderen, vergleichsweise 'formalen' Gesichtspunkt beruhen mußte. Die Äußerung des Beschwerdeführers kann also nicht in Vergleich gesetzt werden mit den Fällen, in denen eine Boykottaufforderung durch Verbreitung einer summarischen Kennzeichnung eines Sachverhalts begründet wird, die von den Adressaten nicht ohne weiteres richtig verstanden werden kann.

If the complainant summarised his impression of the content of the judgment of the jury court in the words 'formal acquittal' and 'moral condemnation', that does not, in the view of the Federal Constitutional Court go beyond the boundary of what is permissible in the public discussion of a subject of serious content. It would signify an unacceptable narrowing of freedom of speech in a free democracy if the State Court demanded here from the complainant, who is not a jurist, the care even of a 'reader trained in criminal law', which would have had to make him omit the description 'formal acquittal', because it was permissible only in the absence of the objective prerequisites of liability to punishment. The descriptions chosen by the complainant are not assertions as to facts whose truth or falsehood could be proved; in particular, no unambiguous legal state of affairs is described by the designation 'formal acquittal'. It concerns a summarising, evaluating characterisation of the whole content of the judgment which must be held to be permissible because it is neither offensive in form nor does it fail in content to meet the facts of the case referred to so seriously that it would have induced quite false ideas in hearers and readers about the content of the judgment, as would perhaps be the case if it was asserted about a person who had been acquitted that he had been 'convicted', without more precise elucidation. It is also of importance here that the acquittal of Harlan was already known by the broader public and more especially in the circles of the film industry. It was just as well known that Harlan had been the producer of the film 'Jew Süss'. It was therefore established that the judgment could not have found complete 'innocence', in the sense of non-participation by Harlan in the furthering of persecution of the Jews by this film, and that therefore the acquittal must have been based on another, comparatively 'formal', point of view. The statement of the complainant can thus not be compared with the cases in which a call for a boycott is based on distribution of a summary description of the facts of a case which cannot, on its own, be properly understood by the addressee.

(d) Die vom Beschwerdeführer für seine Meinungsäußerung gewählten Formen der Ansprache vor dem Presseklub und des Offenen Briefes gingen nicht über das nach den Umständen Zulässige hinaus. Die Domnick-Film-Produktion GmbH hat in dem Schreiben, das sie nach der Ansprache des Beschwerdeführers an diesen richtete, hervorgehoben, daß ihr daran gelegen sei, die frühere künstlerische Höhe des deutschen Films wieder zu erreichen. In diesem 'Bestreben nach künstlerisch anspruchsvollen Filmen' habe sie Harlan zur Mitarbeit herangezogen. Daraus ergibt sich, daß die Gesellschaft sich gerade von der Mitwirkung Harlans an ihren Filmen viel versprach, und es war selbstverständlich, daß sie diese Mitwirkung in ihrer Werbung entsprechend hervorheben werde. Hiermit war ein starkes Hervortreten Harlans in der Öffentlichkeit auch ohne besonderes Zutun von seiner Seite verbunden. Das Massenunterhaltungsmittel des Films erreicht fast gleichzeitig Millionen von Zuschauern im In- und Ausland und läßt so die Mitwirkenden, namentlich die Darsteller und Regisseure, rasch in der breitesten Öffentlichkeit bekannt werden. Wer aber in dieser Weise vor die Öffentlichkeit tritt und dabei an den früheren Ruf eines Mitwirkenden anknüpft, muß sich gefallen lassen, daß auch die Kritik hieran vor der Öffentlichkeit erfolgt; und je intensiver mit einem Namen und unter Hinweis auf die früheren Leistungen eines Künstlers auf breite Bevölkerungskreise gewirkt wird, desto eindringlicher und schärfer darf auch die Form der vorsorglichen Abwehr solcher Wirkung sein. Deshalb ist es nicht zu beanstanden, daß der Beschwerdeführer für seine Kritik die Form einer Ansprache vor Filmproduzenten und Filmverleihern sowie die des Offenen Briefes gewählt hat, die letztere übrigens nur, weil die Domnick-Film-Produktion GmbH ihrerseits ihr Schreiben der Spio bekanntgegeben hatte.

Eine abschließende Gesamtbetrachtung des Falles kann schließlich an folgender Überlegung nicht vorübergehen: Der Beschwerdeführer hat aus lauteren Motiven an das sittliche Gefühl der von ihm angesprochenen Kreise appelliert und sie zu einer nicht zu beanstandenden moralischen Haltung aufgerufen. Das ist in der allgemeinen Volksanschauung nicht verkannt worden. Der Beschwerdeführer hat darauf hinweisen können, daß er sich bei seiner Bewertung des Wiederauftretens Harlans im Einklang mit der Haltung angesehener Persönlichkeiten des öffentlichen Lebens im Inland und Ausland befinde. Beweise dafür liegen vor; es mag nur auf die in Nr. 3 der Deutschen Universitätszeitung vom 8. Februar 1952 veröffentlichte Stellungnahme von 48 Göttinger Professoren verwiesen werden, ferner etwa auf die Beiträge in der erwähnten Ausgabe der Neuen Zürcher Zeitung. Vor allem aber hat in der 197. Sitzung des Deutschen Bundestags am 29. Februar 1952 der Abgeordnete Dr. Schmid-Tübingen folgendes erklärt (Prot. S. 8474):

(d) The forms chosen by the complainant for his expression of opinion – the speech before the press association and the open letter – do not go beyond what is permissible according to the circumstances. Domnick Film Production Ltd emphasised in the letter which, after the complainant's speech, it sent to him that it was concerned to reach the earlier artistic heights of the German film. In this 'striving for films laying claim to artistic merit' it had brought Harlan in to participate. It follows from this that the company promised itself much, simply from the participation of Harlan in its films, and it was self-evident that it would emphasise this participation in its publicity accordingly. This was linked with Harlan coming strongly into the public eye, even without any special help from his side. The mass entertainment method of the film reaches millions of viewers almost simultaneously in this country and others and so enables those who collaborate in it, especially the actors and producers, to become known very quickly to a very wide public. But whoever appears in this manner before the public and at the same time makes a link with the earlier reputation of a participant must put up with the fact that public criticism about this will also follow; and the more intensively use is made of a name, and reference is made to the earlier achievements of an artist, to wide circles of the population, the more forceful and sharp may the form of pre-emptive defence of such use be. Therefore, no objection can be made to the fact that the complainant chose for his criticism the form of a speech to film producers and film distributors as well as that of the open letter, the latter moreover only because Dominick Film Production Ltd on its side had made its letter known to Spio.

Finally, a concluding overall view of the case cannot pass over the following consideration: The complainant appealed from altruistic motives to the moral feeling of the circle addressed by him and called them to take a moral stance which cannot be objected to. The general perception of the people has not failed to recognise this. The complainant has been able to refer to the fact that in his assessment of the reappearance of Harlan he finds himself in agreement with the attitude of respected personalities in public life in this country and others. Proofs of this are present; reference may only be made to the opinion of 48 Göttingen professors, published in no 3 of the German University Journal of 8 February 1952 and further perhaps to the contributions in the said issue of the *New Zürich Newspaper*. Above all, however, in the 197th sitting of the German Parliament on 29 February 1952, the Deputy Dr. Schmid-Tübingen stated as follows (Protocol, p 8474):

In Bonn läuft zur Zeit der Film 'Immensee' aus der Produktion des Ihnen allen als Hersteller des Films 'Jud Süß' bekannten Regisseurs Veit Harlan. Es ist eine Schande, daß die Machwerke dieses Mannes in Deutschland überhaupt gezeigt und besucht werden können. Manche berufen sich darauf, daß es keine Gesetze gebe, die es ermöglichten, die Vorführung von Filmen dieses Mannes zu untersagen. Das ist richtig, und auch der Bundestag kann ihre Vorführung nicht verhindern. Ich glaube aber, daß man dem wahren Rechte dient, wenn in diesem Hause dagegen Protest erhoben wird, daß ausgerechnet am Sitze des deutschen Parlaments, das in diesem Lande in ganz besonderem Maße der Hüter und Herold echter Toleranz zu sein hat, Filme eines Mannes aufgeführt werden, der zumindest indirekt mit dazu beigetragen hat, die massenpsychologischen Voraussetzungen für die Vergasungen von Auschwitz zu schaffen.

Das Protokoll verzeichnet hierzu 'Beifall links und bei den Regierungsparteien'. Für die Beurteilung des Verhaltens des Beschwerdeführers kann die hier zum Ausdruck gekommene Auffassung des repräsentativen Vertretungsorgans des deutschen Volkes nicht gleichgültig sein. Sie macht es unmöglich, in den Äußerungen des Beschwerdeführers einen Vestoß gegen die 'Auffassungen der verständigen, billig und gerecht denkenden Bürger' zu sehen.

IV

Das Bundesverfassungsgericht ist auf Grund dieser Erwägungen zu der Überzeugung gelangt, daß das Landgericht bei seiner Beurteilung des Verhaltens des Beschwerdeführers die besondere Bedeutung verkannt hat, die dem Grundrecht auf freie Meinungsäußerung auch dort zukommt, wo es mit privaten Interessen anderer in Konflikt tritt. Das Urteil des Landgerichts beruht auf diesem Verfehlen grundrechtlicher Maßstäbe und verletzt so das Grundrecht des Beschwerdeführers aus Art. 5 Abs. 1 Satz 1 GG. Es ist deshalb aufzuheben.

LIMITATION OF LIABILITY

§ 827 [Ausschluß und Minderung der Verantwortlichkeit] Wer im Zustande der Bewußtlosigkeit oder in einem die freie Willensbestimmung ausschließenden Zustande krankhafter Störung der Geistestätigkeit einem anderen Schaden zufügt, ist für den Schaden nicht verantwortlich. Hat er sich durch geistige Getränke oder ähnliche Mittel in einen vorübergehenden Zustand dieser Art versetzt, so ist er für einen Schaden, den er in diesem Zustande widerrechtlich verursacht, in gleicher Weise verantwortlich, wie wenn ihm Fahrlässigkeit zur Last fiele; die Verantwortlichkeit tritt nicht ein, wenn er ohne Verschulden in den Zustand geraten ist.

In Bonn at the moment the film 'Immensee' is running which is produced by the film manager Veit Harlan, known to you all as the producer of the film 'Jew Süss'. It is a disgrace that the inferior works of this man can be shown and viewed in Germany. Many refer to the fact that there are no laws which made it possible to prohibit the presentation of films of this man. That is correct, and the Federal Parliament also cannot obstruct their presentation. But I believe that true justice is assisted if protest is raised against it in this House, that in this very seat of the German Parliament, which in this land has to be to a very special extent the guardian and herald of true tolerance, films of a man are shown who has at least indirectly contributed to create the mass psychological conditions for the gas chambers at Auschwitz.

The Protocol records here 'Applause from the left and by the Government parties'. In assessing the conduct of the complainant, the view expressed here by the representative organs of the German people cannot be a matter of indifference. It makes it impossible to see in the statements of the complainant a wrong contrary to the 'views of intelligent, fair and right thinking citizens'.

IV

The Federal Constitutional Court has, on the basis of these considerations, come to be convinced that the State Court, in its assessment of the conduct of the complainant, has failed to recognise the special meaning which the basic right to free expression of opinion receives where it comes into conflict with private interests of others. The judgment of the State Court is based on this failure to attain basic right standards and thus violates the basic right of the complainant in Art 5 para 1 sentence 1 of the GG. It is therefore to be quashed.

LIMITATION OF LIABILITY

§ 827 [Exclusion and reduction of responsibility] A person who, in a condition of unconsciousness or in a condition of pathological disturbance of the activity of the mind which excludes free determination of the will, inflicts harm on another is not responsible for the harm. If he has put himself in a temporary condition of this kind by alcoholic beverages or similar means, he is responsible for harm which he unlawfully causes in this condition in the same way as if he was to be charged with negligence; responsibility does not arise if he came into this condition without fault.

§ 828 [Minderjährige; Taubstumme] (1) Wer nicht das siebente Lebensjahr vollendet hat, ist für einen Schaden, den er einem anderen zufügt, nicht verantwortlich.

(2) Wer das siebente, aber nicht das achtzehnte Lebensjahr vollendet hat, ist für einen Schaden, den er einem anderen zufügt, nicht verantwortlich, wenn er bei der Begehung der schädigenden Handlung nicht die zur Erkenntnis der Verantwortlichkeit erforderliche Einsicht hat. Das gleiche gilt von einem Taubstummen.

§ 829 [Ersatzpflicht aus Billigkeitsgründen] Wer in einem der in den §§ 823 bis 826 bezeichneten Fälle für einen von ihm verursachten Schaden auf Grund der §§ 827, 828 nicht verantwortlich ist, hat gleichwohl, sofern der Ersatz des Schadens nicht von einem aufsichtspflichtigen Dritten erlangt werden kann, den Schaden insoweit zu ersetzen, als die Billigkeit nach den Umständen, insbesondere nach den Verhältnissen der Beteiligten, eine Schadloshaltung erfordert und ihm nicht die Mittel entzogen werden, deren er zum angemessenen Unterhalte sowie zur Erfüllung seiner gesetzlichen Unterhaltspflichten bedarf.

PLURALITY OF DEFENDANTS

§ 830 [Mittäter und Beteiligte] (1) Haben mehrere durch eine gemeinschaftlich begangene unerlaubte Handlung einen Schaden verursacht, so ist jeder für den Schaden verantwortlich. Das gleiche gilt, wenn sich nicht ermitteln läßt, wer von mehreren Beteiligten den Schaden durch seine Handlung verursacht hat.

(2) Anstifter und Gehilfen stehen Mittätern gleich.

§ 828 [Minors; deaf mutes] (1) A person who has not completed the 7th year of his life is not responsible for harm which he has inflicted on another.

(2) A person who has completed the 7th but not the 18th year of his life is not responsible for harm which he inflicts on another, if on committing the act causing harm he did not have the necessary understanding for realisation of responsibility. The same applies to a deaf mute.

Contrast this compromise position as to the liability of minors in tort with their liability under English law and their situation under French law.

§ 829 [Duty to compensate on grounds of fairness] A person who in one of the cases described in §§ 823–826 is not, on the basis of § 827 or 828, responsible for harm caused by him must nevertheless, insofar as compensation for harm cannot be obtained from a third party with a supervisory duty, compensate for the harm as far as an indemnification is required by fairness in accordance with the circumstances, in particular according to the relationships of the participants, and the means which he needs for appropriate maintenance as well as the fulfilment of his statutory duties of maintenance are not taken away from him.

PLURALITY OF DEFENDANTS

§ 830 [Joint perpetrators and participants] (1) If several people have caused harm by a tort committed jointly, each is responsible for the harm. The same applies when it cannot be ascertained which of the several participants has caused the harm by his action.

(2) Instigators and assistants are in the same position as joint perpetrators.

Consideration was given to § 830 I in the newspaper delivery obstruction case (see p 481). The defendant sought to argue in the context of harm caused by demonstrators that it was an outdated provision, and should not be used to determine liability. The court rejected this argument, and said there were good policy reasons for its applicability. Compare these concepts of civil liability with those relating to criminal liability contained in §§ 25, 26 and 27 of the StGB: see Chapter Seven, p 701.

VICARIOUS LIABILITY

Employers

§ 831 [Haftung für den Verrichtungsgehilfen] (1) Wer einen anderen zu einer Verrichtung bestellt, ist zum Ersatze des Schadens verpflichtet, den der andere in Ausführung der Verrichtung einem Dritten widerrechtlich zufügt. Die Ersatzpflicht tritt nicht ein, wenn der Geschäftsherr bei der Auswahl der bestellten Person und, sofern er Vorrichtungen oder Gerätschaften zu beschaffen oder die Ausführung der Verrichtung zu leiten hat, bei der Beschaffung oder der Leitung die im Verkehr erforderliche Sorgfalt beobachtet oder wenn der Schaden auch bei Anwendung dieser Sorgfalt entstanden sein würde.

(2) Die gleiche Verantwortlichkeit trifft denjenigen, welcher für den Geschäftsherrn die Besorgung eines der im Absatz 1 Satz 2 bezeichneten Geschäfte durch Vertrag übernimmt.

VICARIOUS LIABILITY

Employers

§ 831 [Liability for work assistants] (1) A person who employs another for work is obliged to make compensation for the harm which the other inflicts unlawfully on a third party in the carrying out of the work. The duty to compensate does not arise if the employer observes the care necessary in the affairs of life in the choice of the person employed and, insofar as he has to provide apparatus or implements or to supervise the carrying out of the work, in such provision or supervision; or if the harm would still have arisen despite application of this care.

(2) The same responsibility applies to a person who takes over for an employer by contract the control of one of the matters described in para 1 sentence 2.

§ 831 was considered in the fowl pest case: see p 439 and onwards and in the fallen telegraph pole case, p 565.

Compare the position here with vicarious liability in English law. The need for the tort to have been committed by an employee (who must be integrated into his employer's organisation) and in the scope of his duties (compare this with, for example, the English cases of *Limpus v London General Omnibus Co* (1862) I H & C 526; and *Rose v Plenty* [1976] 1 All ER 97) is similar to the position under English law; but there is a possibility, which does not exist in English law, of the employer escaping liability. (This may be harder in respect of certain categories of vicarious liability.) Liability for harm inflicted by an independent contractor is also possible. Does Germany appear to be satisfied with its vicarious liability rules?

THE FALLEN TELEGRAPH POLE CASE

BGH NJW 1954 Heft 24 S. 913

2 BGB §§ 839, 823, 831 (Haftung der Bundespost für Telegraphenanlagen)

(a) Die Pflicht der Bundespost zu einer verkehrssicheren Unterhaltung ihrer Telegraphenanlagen ergibt sich im Verhältnis zu unbeteiligten dritten Personen nicht aus § 839, sondern aus § 823 BGB.

(b) Zum Ausschluß der Haftung aus § 831 BGB bedarf es keines besonderen Entlastungsbeweises, wenn der Angestellte sich so verhalten hat, wie jede mit Sorgfalt ausgewählte Person sich verhalten hätte.

BGH, Urt. v. 14.1.1954 – III ZR 221/52 (Frankfurt/M.)

Der bei der Kl. versicherte M. fuhr mit seinem Motorrad nachts auf den ersten von vier quer über die Straße liegenden Telefonmasten auf und erlitt eine schwere Schädelverletzung. Das LG hat die Klage für dem Grunde nach gerechtfertigt erklärt. Das OLG hat sie abgewiesen. Die Rev. führte zur Aufhebung und Zurückverweisung.

Aus den Gründen:

I Eine Haftung der bekl. Post für die Unfallfolgen kann nur bejaht werden, wenn die Voraussetzungen einer bestimmten gesetzlichen Vorschrift als erfüllt anzusehen sind. Eine Haftung aus 'allgemeinen Grundsätzen' kennt das geltende Recht nicht, insbes. auch nicht eine Haftung dahin, daß jeder verpflichtet sei, einen durch seine Sachen verursachten Schaden zu ersetzen, wenn er nicht nachweisen kann, daß ihn an der für andere gefährlichen Lage dieser Sachen kein Verschulden trifft. Noch weniger kommt eine reine Gefährdungshaftung der Bekl. hinsichtlich der von ihr unterhaltenen Telefonleitungen in Betracht (vgl. RGZ 116, 287).

THE FALLEN TELEGRAPH POLE CASE

Although this case concerned the liability of a public authority, it was not based on § 839 of the Civil Code. It was instead based on § 823; § 836 was also considered. The chief interest in the case however is centred around the consideration of the availability of exculpatory proof to save an employer from liability under § 831, the application of the German equivalent of *res ipsa loquitur*, and the consideration of the issue of causation.

BGH NJW 1954 Volume 24 p 913

2 BGB §§ 839, 823, 831 (Liability of the Federal Post Office for telegraph installations)

(a) The duty of the Federal Post Office to maintain its telegraph installations so as to be safe for traffic arises, in relation to unconnected third parties, not from § 839 but from § 823 of the BGB.

(b) For the exclusion of liability under § 831 of the BGB no special exculpatory proof is necessary if the employee has behaved in a way in which any person chosen with care would have behaved.

BGH, judgment of 14 January 1954 – III ZR 221/52 (Frankfurt/M)

M, who was insured with the plaintiff, rode on his motorbike at night into the first of four telephone poles lying across the road and suffered a severe head injury. The State Court declared the action to be justified in principle. The Upper State Court dismissed it. The appeal in law led to quashing and reference back.

Reasons:

I Liability of the defendant Post Office for the consequences of an accident can only be accepted if the conditions of a certain statutory provision are to be regarded as fulfilled. Liability on 'general principles' is not known under current law, especially not a liability to the effect that everyone is under a duty to compensate in respect of harm caused by his things unless he can prove that no fault rests with him in respect of the dangerous condition to others of these things. It is even less appropriate to consider pure risk liability of the defendant in respect of the telephone lines maintained by it (compare RGZ 116, 287).

II Die Kl. wirft der Bekl. vor, daß sie ihre Anlagen nicht in einem verkehrssicheren Zustand gehalten und daß ihre Bediensteten nicht für die Beseitigung der eingetretenen Verkehrsbehinderung gesorgt hätten. -Unter keinem dieser Gesichtspunkte kann eine Haftung der Bekl. nach § 839 BGB, Art. 131 Weim Verf. in Betracht kommen; sowohl die Pflicht zu einer verkehrsgemäßen Unterhaltung einer Anlage als auch die zur Beseitigung eines eingetretenen Verkehrshindernisses ist eine Obliegenheit, die auch bei öffentlichen Körperschaften nicht erst aus einem besonderen Fürsorgeverhältnis der öffentlichen Hand zu den von ihrer Betätigung zufällig betroffenen Dritten entspringt, sondern schon darauf zurückzuführen ist, daß eine objektive Gefahrenlage geschaffen worden ist. Bei Sicherungspflichten, die auf dieser Gundlage beruhen, sind die öffentlichen Körperschaften nicht anders zu behandeln als jede Privatperson, mag auch die jeweils in Betracht kommende Betätigung einen hoheitlichen Charakter haben. Ihre Haftung bestimmt sich somit nach §§ 823, 831 BGB. Der Senat hat dies im Anschluß an die Rspr. des RG in seinem in BGHZ 9, 373 = NJW 53, 1297 veröffentlichten Urt. näher begründet; was dort zu der Verkehrssicherungspflicht hinsichtlich eines öffentlichen Weges ausgeführt worden ist, gilt auch für den vorl. Fall. Die RevErwiderung beruft sich deshalb in diesem Zusammenhang zu Unrecht darauf, daß der Tätigkeit der Post durch die Rspr. immer mehr ein hoheitlicher Charakter beigelegt worden sei. Verfehlt ist auch ihr Hinweis auf die in RGZ 127, 31ff. veröffentlichte Entsch; dort wird nämlich ausdrücklich der hier dargelegte Grundsatz auch für Beschädigungen, die beim Legen von Fernsprechkabeln verursacht werden, für anwendbar erklärt: im Verhältnis 'zu unbeteiligten dritten Personen' kommt keine Haftung nach § 839 BGB in Betracht, nur demjenigen gegenüber, der nach dem TelegraphenwegeG verpflichtet ist, Eingriffe in sein Eigentum zu dulden, besteht die Amtspflicht, ihn vor Schädigungen zu bewahren. Letzterer Sachverhalt liegt aber hier nicht vor.

III Das BerGer. hat ohne Rechtsirrtum eine Haftung der Bekl. verneint, soweit die Klage auf die nicht rechtzeitige Beseitigung der umgefallenen Masten von der Straße gestützt wird.

1 Die Angriffe der Rev. gegen die Annahme des BerRichters, daß auf Grund des § 831 BGB eine Haftung der Bekl. nicht bestehe, gehen fehl.

(a) Es entspricht einer feststehenden Rspr., daß eine Haftung nach § 831 BGB ausgeschlossen ist, ohne daß es noch eines besonderen Entlastungsbeweises bedürfte, wenn der Angestellte sich so verhalten hat, wie jede mit Sorgfalt ausgewählte Person sich verhalten hätte (vgl. Soergel-Lindenmaier. Anm. 7 zu § 831 mit Nachw. der Rspr.).

II The plaintiff alleges against the defendant that it did not keep its installations in a condition which was safe for traffic and its employees did not attend to the removal of the obstacle to traffic which had arisen. From no point of view can liability of the defendant under § 839 of the BGB, and Art 131 of the Weimar Constitution fall to be considered; the duty to maintain an installation in a manner suitable for traffic, as well as that of removal of an obstacle to traffic which has arisen, are obligations which even with public bodies does not just arise from a special relationship of care by the public enterprise to the third person coincidentally affected by its activities, but is to be traced back to the fact that an objective situation of danger has been created. As to duties to protect which rest on this basis, public bodies are not to be treated differently to any private person even though the activity coming under consideration at any given time may have a sovereign character. Its liability is accordingly determined by §§ 823 and 831 of the BGB. The Senate has given more detailed reasons, following the case law of the RG, in its judgment published in BGHZ 9, 373 = NJW 53, 1297; what was explained there about the duty to safeguard traffic in respect of a public highway is also valid for the present case. The reply in the appeal in law therefore refers incorrectly in this connection to the fact that sovereign character has been increasingly ascribed to the activities of the Post Office by case law. Its reference to the decision published in RGZ 127, 31 and onwards is also wrong; there, the principle laid down here is expressly declared also to be applicable to harm which is caused by the laying down of telephone cables: no liability under § 839 of the BGB falls to be considered in relation 'to unconnected third persons'. Only as against the person who is under a duty according to the Telegraph Lines Act to suffer encroachments to his property is there an official duty to protect him from harm. But the latter circumstances are not present here.

III The appeal court has denied liability on the part of the defendant without any error in law, insofar as the action is based on the delayed removal of the fallen poles from the road.

1 The arguments of the appeal in law against the assumption of the appeal judge that on the basis of § 831 of the BGB liability on the part of the defendant did not exist are unsuccessful.

(a) It corresponds with established case law that liability in accordance with § 831 of the BGB is excluded without there needing to be special exculpatory proof if the employee has conducted himself as any person selected with care would have behaved (compare Soergel-Lindenmaier, note 7 to § 831 with references to the case law).

(b) Das Verhalten des Betriebswartes war aber so, wie es auch ein anderer Angestellter, auch der mit der gebotenen Sorgfalt handelnde, gezeigt hätte. Es mag sein, daß in der fraglichen Nacht ein stärkerer Sturm geherrscht hat und daß dies auch vom Postamt L. aus wahrgenommen werden konnte. Dennoch läßt sich nicht sagen, daß unter solchen Umständen ein mit der erforderlichen Sorgfalt handelnder Postangestellter alsbald nach der Wahrnehmung einer teilweisen Störung der Telephonleitung mitten in der Nacht den Störtrupp auf den Weg gesandt hatte. Wenn von 30 Leitungen nur 7 ausgefallen waren, so lag es nicht nahe, anzunehmen, es könnten Masten umgeknickt und die Leitung eingestürzt sein. Die Bekl. hat ohne Widerspruch der Kl. ausgeführt, daß Störungen solcher Art auch schon früher vorgekommen seien, und zwar wegen Eindringens von Feuchtigkeit in das Kabel und wegen der 'Bleimüdigkeit' der Kabeladern. Auch in der Unfallnacht herrschte nach dem insoweit übereinstimmenden Parteivortrag feuchtes Wetter. Deshalb ist es verständlich, wenn der Betriebswart auch in diesem Falle die Störung im Leitungsnetz auf eine jener früher beobachteten Ursachen zurückführte. Daß es aber zur Beseitigung solcher Störungen wenig zweckmäßig war, in der Nacht den Störtrupp auf die Suche zu schicken, muß der Bekl. zugestanden werden. Auch das TelegraphenwegeG geht, wie sich aus § 12 Abs. 3 ergibt, davon aus, daß Störungen in der Regel nur während der Tagesstunden beseitigt werden.

2 Angesichts dieses Sachverhaltes kann auch die Meinung der Rev., daß die Bekl. die Beaufsichtigung des Telephonbetriebes unzulänglich organisiert habe und deshalb – unmittelbar nach § 823 BGB – für die aufgetretene Schädigung zu haften habe, ohne daß es notwendig wäre, ein schuldhaftes Handeln eines bestimmten Organs darzutun, nicht als richtig angesehen werden. Eine derartige Haftung ist in der Rspr. z. B. angenommen worden, wenn eine Körperschaft überhaupt nicht für eine der Verkehrssicherung dienende Aufsicht über ihre Anlagen Vorsorge getroffen hat (vgl. RGZ 157, 228). So liegen die Verhältnisse im vorl. Falle aber nicht. Auch in der Nacht v. 15./16.2 1948 war ein Angestellter der Post damit betraut, das Funktionieren der Telephonleitung zu überwachen. Ob der Betriebswart als 'Organ' der Bekl. i.S. der §§ 89, 30, 31 BGB angesehen werden könnte, kann dahingestellt bleiben; das BerGer. hat mit Recht verneint, daß er fahrlässig gehandelt hat. Daß kein schuldhaftes Handeln vorliegt, ergibt sich aus den obigen Ausführungen zu der Frage, ob sich ein sorgfältig ausgewählter Angestellter ebenso verhalten hätte. Daß sich ein anderer Angestellter der Bekl. oder eines ihrer Organe in der Unfallnacht in schuldhafter Weise nicht um die Telephonleitung gekümmert hätte, ist ebenfalls nicht ersichtlich. Irgendwelche Ansprüche wegen der nicht rechtzeitigen Entdeckung und Beseitigung des Verkehrshindernisses können somit nicht entstanden sein.

(b) The conduct of the duty foreman was such as another employee might also have shown, even one acting with the necessary care. It may be that in the night in question there was a violent storm and that this could also be perceived by the Post Office at L. However, it cannot be said that under such circumstances a postal employee, acting with the necessary care, would, immediately after the detection of a partial disturbance of the telephone circuit, have sent the breakdown team out in the middle of the night. If, out of 30 circuits, only seven had become defective, this does not suggest that one should assume that poles have snapped and the lines have collapsed. The defendant has explained, without contradiction from the plaintiff, that disturbances of such a kind had occurred previously because of the penetration of damp into the cable and because of 'lead fatigue' of the cable runs. On the night of the accident wet weather also prevailed, according to the report of the parties which is agreed in this respect. It is therefore understandable if the duty foreman in this case also attributed the breakdown in the circuit network to one of those causes observed earlier. It must be conceded in favour of the defendant that it was hardly appropriate to send the breakdown team out on search in the night in order to resolve such breakdowns. The Telegraph Lines Act proceeds on the basis that breakdowns will usually only be resolved during daytime, as follows from § 12 para 3.

2 In the light of the facts of this case, the view of the appeal in law that the defendant had not organised the surveillance of the telephone undertaking adequately and therefore, directly in accordance with § 823 of the BGB, must be liable for the harm which has arisen, without it being necessary to demonstrate a culpable action on the part of a specific organ, cannot be regarded as correct. A liability of this kind has been accepted in case law, eg, if a corporate body has not made any provision for a supervision of its installations which serves to protect others from risks (compare RGZ 157, 228). But the circumstances in the present case are not like that. In the night of 15/16 February 1948 an employee of the Post Office was entrusted with watching over the functioning of the telephone circuit. Whether the duty foreman could be regarded as an 'organ' of the defendant in the sense of §§ 89, 30 and 31 of the BGB can remain undecided; the appeal court has correctly denied that he acted negligently. It follows from the above statements on the question of whether a carefully chosen employee would have behaved in the same way, that no culpable conduct is present. It is likewise not evident that another employee of the defendant or of one of its organs failed to trouble about the telephone circuit in a culpable manner on the night of the accident. Any claims on account of the delayed discovery and removal of the obstruction to traffic can therefore not have arisen.

IV Die Kl. stützt ihren Anspruch aber auch darauf, daß die Bekl. die Telephonmasten nur mangelhaft unterhalten habe: Es sei deshalb zu dem Unfall gekommen, weil der Sturm den angefaulten Mast umgeworfen und dieser dann mittels des Telephonkabels die anderen unzureichend gesicherten Masten umgerissen habe. Diesem Vorbringen wird das angef. Urt. nicht ganz gerecht.

1 Der BerRichter geht auf diesen Vortrag als Anspruchsgrundlage nicht weiter ein, weil er in tatsächlicher Hinsicht es als nicht erwiesen und nicht beweisbar ansieht, daß der Unfall wirklich auf die von der Kl. behauptete Art und Weise verursacht worden sei; die Möglichkeit, daß ein amerikanischer Lkw. einen Mast angefahren habe und daß so der Bruch der Leitung herbeigeführt worden sei, könne nicht ausgeschlossen werden.

Soweit die Rev. dem BerRichter vorwirft, er habe die Beweislast verkannt, weil angesichts der tatsächlich eingetretenen verkehrswidrigen Situation die Bekl. den Beweis führen müßte, 'daß sie an diesem gefährlichen Zustand ihrer Anlage keine Schuld trifft', kann ihr nicht gefolgt werden. Die Behauptung, daß der Schaden durch eine mangelhafte Unterhaltung der Anlage herbeigeführt worden sei, muß die Kl. beweisen, nicht nur bei der Stützung ihres Anspruches auf § 823 BGB, sondern auch im Falle des § 836 BGB (vgl. Soergel-Lindenmaier, 9 zu § 836 mit weiteren Nachw.). Das ergibt sich aus der Regel, daß derjenige, der ein Recht beansprucht, das Vorliegen der tatsächlichen Voraussetzungen für die Entstehung seines Rechtes beweisen muß.

2 Das BerGer. übersieht aber, daß eine Haftung der Bekl. selbst dann möglich sein könnte, wenn ein Mast tatsächlich von dem amerik. Lkw. angefahren worden und es so zu dem Einsturz der Telephonleitung gekommen sein sollte. Die Möglichkeit, daß der Lkw. mit einer größeren Wucht auf einen der Masten aufgefahren wäre, scheidet nach der Überzeugung des BerRichters aus. Mangels einer Spur an einem der umgefallenen Masten spricht auch die Lebenserfahrung dafür, daß der Lkw. den Mast, wenn überhaupt, so nur ohne jede Stoßkraft angefahren haben könnte. Wenn aber schon ein leichteres Berühren eines Mastes zu einem völligen Niederbrechen eines Teiles der Anlage geführt hätte, so würde durchaus die Möglichkeit bestehen, daß tatsächlich eine mangelhafte Unterhaltung des Werkes für den Unfall mitursächlich war. Ob die von der Bekl. selbst zugestandene Beschädigung des einen Mastes durch Fäulnis so groß und im übrigen die Sicherung der Masten so gering war, daß von einem verkehrssicheren Zustand nicht mehr die Rede sein konnte, muß geprüft werden. Ob der Sturm oder der Lkw. den Mast geknickt hat, kann dann dahinstehen. Es besteht weder in jedem Falle eines Naturereignisses eine Haftung, noch schließt die Einwirkung eines Dritten die Haftung in jedem Falle aus. Dies ist auch im Rahmen des § 836 BGB anerkannten Rechtes. Entscheidend ist bei der Frage der Ursächlichkeit, ob das Bauwerk so mangelhaft unterhalten oder gesichert war, daß es schon durch Einwirkungen geringfügiger Art, mit denen man als etwas Üblichem rechnen muß, zum Einsturz gebracht werden konnte. Die 'letzte' Ursache kann möglicherweise überhaupt nicht feststellbar sein, und doch braucht deswegen eine Haftung nicht ausgeschlossen zu sein.

IV The plaintiff also bases its claim on the fact that the defendant maintained the telephone poles defectively: an accident therefore occurred because the storm overturned the rotten pole and this then tore down the other insufficiently secured poles by means of the telephone cable. The contested judgment does not entirely do justice to this allegation.

1 The appeal judge does not go further into this statement as a basis of claim because he did not regard it as proved or provable in a factual sense that the accident had really been caused in the manner asserted by the plaintiff; the possibility that an American lorry drove into a pole and that the break in the circuit was caused by this could not be excluded.

Insofar as the appeal in law reproaches the appeal court judge with having misunderstood the burden of proof, because in the light of the actual situation which had arisen and which was contrary to traffic regulations the defendant had to bring proof 'that no blame attached to it in connection with this dangerous condition of its installations', it cannot be followed. The assertion that the harm had been caused by defective maintenance of the installation must be proved by the plaintiff not only when its claim is based on § 823 of the BGB but also in the case of § 836 of the BGB (compare Soergel-Lindenmaier, 9 at § 836 with further references). That follows from the rule that the person who claims a right must prove the presence of the factual prerequisites for his right to come into existence.

2 The appeal court overlooks the fact, however, that liability of the defendant itself could be possible even if a pole really was driven into by the American lorry and this had resulted in the fall of the telephone line. The possibility that the lorry was driven against one of the poles with great force is, according to the belief of the appeal judge, ruled out. Experience of life indicates that in default of any trace on one of the fallen poles, the lorry, if it drove against the mast at all, could only have done so without any force. But if a light touching of a pole would have led to a complete breaking down of a part of the installation, the possibility would definitely exist that defective maintenance of the works was actually a contributing factor to the accident. Whether the damage to the one pole by rot, which was admitted by the defendant itself, was so great and the securing of the poles in other respects so inadequate that one could no longer speak of a condition which was safe for traffic, is a question which must be examined. Whether the storm or the lorry broke the pole can then be left undecided. Liability does not exist in every case of a natural event, nor does the action of a third party exclude liability in every case. This is also recognised law within the framework of § 836 of the BGB. The decisive issue in relation to the question of causality is whether the structure was so defectively maintained or secured that it could be made to collapse even by actions of a trifling kind, which one must reckon with as something usual. The 'last' cause can possibly not be ascertainable at all, and yet liability does not need to be excluded for this reason.

Sollte die weitere Aufklärung des Sachverhaltes zur Feststellung einer Mangelhaftigkeit der Telephonmasten in dem angegebenen Sinne führen, so würde sich eine Haftung der Bekl. schon aus § 823 BGB in Verb. mit §§ 89, 31, 30 ergeben, wenn sie nicht nachweist, daß keines ihrer Organe ein Verschulden trifft; denn das Bestehenlassen eines anderen gefährdenden Zustandes spricht schon als solches gegen die Beobachtung der Sorgfalt, die zwecks Sicherung des Verkehrs gefordert werden muß. Nach Lage der Sache kann auch nur die Bekl. selbst dartun, daß in ihrem Bereich alles Erforderliche getan worden ist. Die Kl., der die Bekl. eine Einsicht in ihre Akten verweigert hat, ist nicht in der Lage, den normalerweise dem Geschädigten obliegenden Verschuldensbeweis zu führen. Die Bekl. hat auch selbst Beweise für ein ordnungsmäßiges Verhalten ihrer Organe und Bediensteten angeboten, so daß eine weitere Aufklärung der tatsächlichen Verhältnisse möglich ist.

Nach der besonderen Gestaltung des vorl. Falles müßte somit, wenn eine mangelhafte Unterhaltung der Telephonleitung festgestellt wird, eine Haftung bereits nach § 823 BGB bejaht werden, wenn die Bekl. sich nicht zu entlasten vermag. Bei dieser Rechtslage bedarf es keines Eingehens auf die von der Rev. aufgeworfene Frage, ob eine Haftung nach § 836 BGB auch dann in Betracht kommen könnte, wenn die Schädigung nicht durch die 'bewegende Kraft' des einstürzenden Bauwerkes verursacht worden ist, sondern durch das Liegenbleiben des bereits eingestürzten Werkes auf einer dem öffentlichen Verkehr dienenden Straße. Bei § 836 handelt es sich 'nicht um einen anders gearteten Fall als in § 823, sondern nur um Umkehrung der Beweislast' (Palandt, I zu § 836 mit Rspr.). Deshalb kommt dem § 836 keine besondere Bedeutung zu, wenn erst im Rahmen des § 823 BGB ausnahmsweise der Schuldner seine Schuldlosigkeit beweisen muß.

Supervisors

§ 832 [Haftung des Aufsichtspflichtigen] (1) Wer kraft Gesetzes zur Führung der Aufsicht über eine Person verpflichtet ist, die wegen Minderjährigkeit oder wegen ihres geistigen oder körperlichen Zustandes der Beaufsichtigung bedarf, ist zum Ersatze des Schadens verpflichtet, den diese Person einem Dritten widerrechtlich zufügt. Die Ersatzpflicht tritt nicht ein, wenn er seiner Aufsichtspflicht genügt oder wenn der Schaden auch bei gehöriger Aufsichtsführung entstanden sein würde.

(2) Die gleiche Verantwortlichkeit trifft denjenigen, welcher die Führung der Aufsicht durch Vertrag übernimmt.

If further elucidation of the circumstances should lead to a finding of defectiveness of the telephone poles in the sense mentioned, liability of the defendant would arise under § 823 of the BGB in association with §§ 89, 31 and 30, if it does not prove that blame rests with none of its organs; for allowing the existence of a state of affairs endangering others is of itself sufficient to suggest failure to observe the care which must be demanded for the purpose of safety of traffic. According to the circumstances of the matter, only the defendant itself can demonstrate that everything necessary has been done in its sphere. The plaintiff, to whom the defendant has refused an inspection of its documents, is not in a position to bring the proof of blame which normally would be incumbent on the person suffering harm. The defendant has itself offered proofs of orderly conduct of its organs and employees, so that a further elucidation of the factual circumstances is possible.

According to the special circumstances of the present case therefore, if defective maintenance of the telephone circuit is established, liability under § 823 of the BGB must be affirmed, if the defendant cannot exculpate himself. In this legal situation, no investigation is needed of the question raised by the appeal in law as to whether liability under § 836 of the BGB could also come into consideration if the harm was not caused by the 'moving force' of the collapsing structure but by the leaving of the structure, which had already collapsed, lying on a road serving public traffic. With § 836 it is a matter 'not of a differently constituted case to that in § 823 but only of a reversal of the burden of proof' (Palandt, 1 at § 836 with case law). Therefore no special significance attaches to § 836 if exceptionally the obligor must prove his blamelessness within the framework of § 823.

Supervisors

§ 832 [Liability of persons with a supervisory duty] (1) A person who, by virtue of a statutory provision, is obliged to supervise a person who needs control on account of minority or on account of his mental or physical condition is obliged to compensate for the harm which this person inflicts unlawfully on a third party. The duty to compensate does not arise if he satisfies his supervisory duty or if the harm would still have arisen despite suitable supervision.

(2) The same responsibility applies to a person who takes over the supervision by contract.

German law follows French law in imposing vicarious liability on parents. Contrast the personal liability of a parent, which is the only kind that can apply to a parent in England, as in the case of *Bebee v Sales* **(1916) 32 TLR 413.**

STRICT LIABILITY AND ANIMALS

Animals

§ 833 [Haftung des Tierhalters] Wird durch ein Tier ein Mensch getötet oder der Körper oder die Gesundheit eines Menschen verletzt oder eine Sache beschädigt, so ist derjenige, welcher das Tier hält, verpflichtet, dem Verletzten den daraus entstehenden Schaden zu ersetzen. Die Ersatzpflicht tritt nicht ein, wenn der Schaden durch ein Haustier verursacht wird, das dem Berufe, der Erwerbstätigkeit oder dem Unterhalte des Tierhalters zu dienen bestimmt ist, und entweder der Tierhalter bei der Beaufsichtigung des Tieres die im Verkehr erforderliche Sorgfalt beobachtet oder der Schaden auch bei Anwendung dieser Sorgfalt entstanden sein würde.

§ 834 [Haftung des Tieraufsehers] Wer für denjenigen, welcher ein Tier hält, die Führung der Aufsicht über das Tier durch Vertrag übernimmt, ist für den Schaden verantwortlich, den das Tier einem Dritten in der im § 833 bezeichneten Weise zufügt. Die Verantwortlichkeit tritt nicht ein, wenn er bei der Führung der Aufsicht die im Verkehr erforderliche Sorgfalt beobachtet oder wenn der Schaden auch bei Anwendung dieser Sorgfalt entstanden sein würde.

Other cases

§ 835 (aufgehoben)

STRICT LIABILITY AND ANIMALS

Animals

§ 833 [Liability of the keeper of an animal] If a human being is killed or there is injury to the body or health of a human being, or a thing is damaged by an animal, the person who keeps the animal is obliged to compensate the person suffering the harm for the harm arising therefrom. The duty to compensate does not arise if the harm is caused by a domestic animal which is intended to serve the vocation, the work activity or the maintenance of the keeper of the animal and either the keeper of the animal observes the care necessary in affairs of life in the supervision of the animal or the harm would still have arisen despite application of this care.

How does the German categorisation of animals contrast with that contained in the English Animals Act 1971?

§ 834 [Liability of the supervisor of the animal] A person who by contract takes over the supervision of an animal on behalf of the person who keeps the animal is responsible for the harm which the animal inflicts on a third party in the manner described in § 833. The responsibility does not arise if he observes the care necessary in the affairs of life in the supervision or if the harm would still have arisen despite application of this care.

Other cases

Liability for what are known as luxury animals is the only example of strict liability under the Civil Code itself. There are a number of categories of statutory strict liability outside it, in particular in respect of motor vehicles under the Road Traffic Act; and product liability, under the Product Liability Act 1989 which was introduced to comply with the European Community Directive of 25 July 1985; railways; certain electricity, gas and other installations; aircraft; atomic energy; medicines; and pollution. See, for an instance of one of these categories, the kite case, p 605. The courts have not however been prepared to extend these categories by way of analogy. Some of them are subject to financial limits, but a claim based on general principles may still be possible.

§ 835 (repealed)

LIABILITY FOR BUILDINGS

§ 836 [Haftung bei Einsturz eines Bauwerkes] (1) Wird durch den Einsturz eines Gebäudes oder eines anderen mit einem Grundstücke verbundenen Werkes oder durch die Ablösung von Teilen des Gebäudes oder des Werkes ein Mensch getötet, der Körper oder die Gesundheit eines Menschen verletzt oder eine Sache beschädigt, so ist der Besitzer des Grundstücks, sofern der Einsturz oder die Ablösung die Folge fehlerhafter Errichtung oder mangelhafter Unterhaltung ist, verpflichtet, dem Verletzten den daraus entstehenden Schaden zu ersetzen. Die Ersatzpflicht tritt nicht ein, wenn der Besitzer zum Zwecke der Abwendung der Gefahr die im Verkehr erforderliche Sorgfalt beobachtet hat.

(2) Ein früherer Besitzer des Grundstücks ist für den Schaden verantwortlich, wenn der Einsturz oder die Ablösung innerhalb eines Jahres nach der Beendigung seines Besitzes eintritt, es sei denn, daß er während seines Besitzes die im Verkehr erforderliche Sorgfalt beobachtet hat oder ein späterer Besitzer durch Beobachtung dieser Sorgfalt die Gefahr hätte abwenden können.

(3) Besitzer im Sinne dieser Vorschriften ist der Eigenbesitzer.

§ 837 [Haftung des Gebäudebesitzers] Besitzt jemand auf einem fremden Grundstück in Ausübung eines Rechtes ein Gebäude oder ein anderes Werk, so trifft ihn an Stelle des Besitzers des Grundstücks die im § 836 bestimmte Verantwortlichkeit.

§ 838 [Haftung des Gebäudeunterhaltungspflichtigen] Wer die Unterhaltung eines Gebäudes oder eines mit einem Grundstücke verbundenen Werkes für den Besitzer übernimmt oder das Gebäude oder das Werk vermöge eines ihm zustehenden Nutzungsrechts zu unterhalten hat, ist für den durch den Einsturz oder die Ablösung von Teilen verursachten Schaden in gleicher Weise verantwortlich wie der Besitzer.

LIABILITY FOR BUILDINGS

§ 836 [Liability on the collapse of a building] (1) If a human being is killed, or there is injury to the body or health of a human being, or a thing is damaged by the collapse of a building or another structure connected to a piece of land or by the detachment of parts of the building or structure, the person in possession of the piece of land is obliged, insofar as the collapse or the detachment was the result of defective construction or deficient maintenance, to compensate the person suffering harm for the harm arising therefrom. The duty to compensate does not arise if the person in possession observed the care necessary in the affairs of life for the purpose of avoidance of danger.

(2) A person in possession of the piece of land at an earlier time is responsible for the harm if the collapse or detachment arises within a year of the end of his possession unless he, during his possession, observed the care necessary in the affairs of life or a person in possession at a later time could have avoided the danger by the observance of this care.

(3) The person in possession in the sense of these provisions is the person with personal possession.[3]

See, in this connection the fallen telegraph pole case, p 565. § 836 can cover such things as excavations and canals, but not natural things like trees.

§ 837 [Liability of the person in possession of the building] If a person possesses a building or another structure on another's land, in the exercise of a right, the responsibility provided for in § 836 applies to him in the place of the person in possession of the piece of land.

§ 838 [Liability of those responsible to maintain a building] A person who takes over the maintenance of a building or structure connected to a piece of land for the person in possession, or has to maintain the building or the structure by virtue of a right of use which belongs to him, is responsible for the harm caused by the collapse or the detachment of parts in the same manner as the person in possession.

---

3   The person with personal possession (Eigenbesitzer) is the person who possesses a thing as belonging to himself: § 872 of the BGB.

LIABILITY OF OFFICIALS

§ 839 [Haftung bei Amtspflichtverletzung] (1) Verletzt ein Beamter vorsätzlich oder fahrlässig die ihm einem Dritten gegenüber obliegende Amtspflicht, so hat er dem Dritten den daraus entstehenden Schaden zu ersetzen. Fällt dem Beamten nur Fahrlässigkeit zur Last, so kann er nur dann in Anspruch genommen werden, wenn der Verletzte nicht auf andere Weise Ersatz zu erlangen vermag.

(2) Verletzt ein Beamter bei dem Urteil in einer Rechtssache seine Amtspflicht, so ist er für den daraus entstehenden Schaden nur dann verantwortlich, wenn die Pflichtverletzung in einer Straftat besteht. Auf eine pflichtwidrige Verweigerung oder Verzögerung der Ausübung des Amtes findet diese Vorschrift keine Anwendung.

(3) Die Ersatzpflicht tritt nicht ein, wenn der Verletzte vorsätzlich oder fahrlässig unterlassen hat, den Schaden durch Gebrauch eines Rechtsmittels abzuwenden.

THE AIR TRAFFIC CONTROLLERS' STRIKE CASE

BGHZ Band 69 S. 128

18 (a) Die streikähnliche Aktion der Flugleiter (Fluglotsen) im Jahre 1973 stellte sich als (widerrechtlicher) Eingriff in Gewerbebetriebe dar, die sich auf das ungestörte Funktionieren der Flugsicherung in ihrer betrieblichen Planung eingerichtet hatten. Hierdurch verletzten die Flugleiter (Fluglotsen) Amtspflichten, die ihnen gegenüber solchen Betrieben als Dritten oblagen.

(b) Die Bundesrepublik Deutschland hat für den Schaden aufzukommen, den ein im Flugreisegeschäft tätiges Reiseunternehmen durch die streikähnliche Aktion der Flugleiter (Fluglotsen) im Jahre 1973 als Folge aufgetretener Verzögerungen im Flugverkehr erlitten hat.

GG Art. 34; BGB §§ 823, 839

III Zivilsenat, Urt. v. 16. Juni 1977 i.S. Bundesrep. Deutschland

(Bekl.) w. Fa. N. (Kl.) III ZR 179/75.

I Landgericht Bonn

LIABILITY OF OFFICIALS

§ 839 [Liability through violation of duty of office] (1) If an official intentionally or negligently violates the official duty which falls upon him as against a third party, he must compensate the third party for the harm arising therefrom. If the official can only be charged with negligence, a claim can only be made against him if the person suffering harm cannot obtain compensation in another manner.

(2) If an official violates his official duty through a decision on a legal issue, he is only responsible for the harm arising therefrom if the violation of duty consists in a criminal act. This provision has no application to a refusal or delay in the exercise of the office which is contrary to duty.

(3) The duty to compensate does not arise if the person suffering the harm has intentionally or negligently omitted to avert the harm by the use of a legal remedy.

Note also Art 34 of the GG (which relieves the official himself from liability where it applies) and the State Liability Act 1982.

THE AIR TRAFFIC CONTROLLERS' STRIKE CASE

This case concerns the liability of the State for a strike by officials. Compare the question of whether responsibility for the strike was to rest with the State with the issue of vicarious liability.

BGHZ Volume 69 p 128

18 (a) The action in the nature of a strike by the flight controllers (air traffic controllers) in 1973 represented an (illegal) interference with commercial enterprises, which had prepared for the undisturbed functioning of air traffic control in their business planning. The flight controllers (air traffic controllers) thereby violated official duties which were incumbent upon them as against such businesses as third parties.

(b) The Federal Republic of Germany has to accept responsibility for the harm which a travel undertaking, active in the air transport business, has suffered due to the action in the nature of a strike by flight controllers (air traffic controllers) in 1973 as a consequence of the delays in air traffic which occurred.

GG Art 34; BGB §§ 823, 839

IIIrd Civil Senate, Judgment of 16 June 1977 in the matter of Federal Republic of Germany (defendant) v Fa N (plaintiff) – III ZR 179/75.

I State Court of Bonn

II Oberlandesgericht Köln

Die Klägerin betreibt ein Reiseunternehmen. Sie veranstaltet u. a. Flugreisen, bei denen sie die Luftbeförderung, den Transfer der Reisenden vom und zum Zielflughafen und die Unterbringung in einem Hotel am Zielort als einheitliche Leistung zu einem Pauschalpreis anbietet. Zur Durchführung der Luftbeförderung bedient sie sich selbständiger Fluggesellschaften.

Die beklagte Bundesrepublik unterhält auf allen inländischen Verkehrsflughäfen Flugsicherungsdienste, die organisatorisch in der nicht rechtsfähigen Bundesanstalt für Flugsicherung zusammengefaßt sind. Die Bediensteten in den Flugsicherungsstellen (Flugleiter oder auch Fluglotsen genannt) stehen überwiegend im Beamtenverhältnis. Oberste Dienstbehörde ist der Bundesminister für Verkehr.

In den letzten Jahren herrschte unter den Flugleitern große Unruhe, weil sie mit ihren Arbeitsbedingungen und mit ihrer Besoldung nicht zufrieden waren. Da sie die von der Beklagten zugesagten technischen und finanziellen Verbesserungen für unzureichend hielten, entschlossen sie sich im Frühjahr 1973 zu Kampfmaßnahmen. Ihr Ziel war es, die Bundesregierung unter Druck zu setzen, um sie zu veranlassen, ihren standespolitischen Forderungen nachzugeben. In der Zeit vom 31. Mai bis 23. November 1973 meldeten sich auffallend viele Flugleiter zu bestimmten Stichtagen krank ('go sick'). Andere setzten über einen längeren Zeitraum ihre Arbeitsleistung herab ('go slow'). Durch diese Maßnahmen wurde der zivile Luftverkehr erheblich gestört. Viele Flüge konnten nur mit erheblicher Verspätung durchgeführt werden, andere fielen ganz aus. Ende Juni 1973 erreichten die Störungen ein derartiges Ausmaß, daß sich die Beklagte gezwungen sah, einzelne Flughäfen, darunter den Flugplatz Hannover, vorübergehend für den gesamten Flugverkehr zu sperren.

Von den Störungen des Flugverkehrs ist auch die Klägerin betroffen worden. Sie nimmt deshalb die Beklagte auf Schadensersatz in Anspruch. Im vorliegenden Verfahren macht sie einen Teil der Unkosten (45 000 DM) geltend, die ihr nach ihrem Vorbringen durch die Schließung des Flughafens Hannover in der Zeit vom 3. bis 5. Juli 1973 entstanden sind. Es handelt sich hierbei nach den Angaben der Klägerin um von ihr aufgewendete zusätzliche Transport-, Verpflegungs- und Übernachtungskosten für ihre Kunden sowie Personalkosten, die durch die Schließung des Flughafens Hannover zusätzlich entstanden sein sollen. Außerdem begehrt die Klägerin 5000 DM Schadensersatz wegen angeblichen Rückgangs ihrer Kurzfristbuchungen.

Das Landgericht hat die Klage abgewiesen, das Oberlandesgericht hat sie dem Grunde nach für gerechtfertigt erklärt. Die Revision der Beklagten blieb erfolglos.

II Upper State Court of Cologne

The plaintiff runs a travel agency. It arranges, amongst other things, air journeys in which it offers air transport, transfer of travellers to and from airport destinations and accommodation in an hotel at the destination as a single service at a lump sum price. For the carrying out of the air transport it makes use of independent airline companies.

The defendant Federal Republic maintains at all airports within the Federal Republic air traffic control services which, organisationally, are included in the legally non-competent Federal Institute for Air Traffic Control. The employees in air traffic control posts (called flight controllers or air traffic controllers) are predominantly officials. The chief administrative authority for the service is the Federal Minister for Transport.

In recent years, great unrest prevailed amongst flight controllers because they were not satisfied with their work conditions and their salary. As they regarded the technical and financial improvements promised by the defendant as insufficient, they decided early in the year 1973 in favour of combative measures. Their objective was to put the Federal Government under pressure to make it give way to their demands as to status policy. In the period from 31 May to 23 November 1973, a significantly large number of flight controllers reported themselves as sick on certain key dates ('go sick'). Others decreased their rate of work over a longer period ('go slow'). Civil air traffic was considerably disturbed by these measures. Many flights could only be made with considerable delay, and others were cancelled altogether. At the end of June 1973 the disturbances reached such an extent that the defendant was compelled temporarily to close individual airports, amongst them Hannover airport, to all air traffic.

The plaintiff also was affected by the disturbances in the air traffic. It therefore claims against the defendant for compensation for harm. In the present proceedings it claims a part of the expenses (45,000 DM) which, according to its allegations, have been incurred by it through the closing of Hannover airport during the period from 3 to 5 July 1973. It is here, according to the plaintiff's assertions, a question of the expenses of extra transport, board and lodging for the night expended by it for its customers as well as staff expenses which would have been additionally generated by the closing of Hannover airport. Besides this, the plaintiff demands 5,000 DM compensation for alleged decline in its short term bookings.

The State Court rejected the claim; the Upper State Court declared it to be justified in principle. The appeal in law of the defendant was unsuccessful.

Aus den Gründen:

Das Berufungsgericht hat den Klageanspruch aus dem Gesichtspunkt der Amtshaftung (Art. 34 GG i.V. m. § 839 BGB) im Ergebnis zutreffend dem Grunde nach für gerechtfertigt erklärt.

I

Das Berufungsgericht hat angenommen, die Flugleiter hätten in Ausübung eines ihnen anvertrauten öffentlichen Amtes (Art. 34 GG) gehandelt, als sie durch gehäufte Krankmeldungen ('go sick') und Herabsetzung ihrer Arbeitsleistung ('go slow') den Flugverkehr behinderten.

Die hiergegen gerichteten Angriffe der Revision haben keinen Erfolg.

1 Ob ein bestimmtes Verhalten einer Person als Ausübung eines öffentlichen Amtes anzusehen ist, bestimmt sich nach der ständigen Rechtsprechung des Senats danach, ob die eigentliche Zielsetzung, in deren Sinn die Person tätig wurde, hoheitlicher Tätigkeit zuzurechnen ist, und ob bejahendenfalls zwischen dieser Zielsetzung und der schädigenden Handlung ein so enger äußerer und innerer Zusammenhang besteht, daß die Handlung ebenfalls noch als dem Bereich hoheitlicher Betätigung angehörend angesehen werden muß (BGHZ 42, 176, 179; LM BGB § 839 Ca Nr. 23). Hiervon ist das Berufungsgericht zutreffend ausgegangen.

2 Nach § 1 Abs. 1 LuftVG ist die Benutzung des Luftraums durch Luftfahrzeuge frei, soweit sie nicht durch das Luftverkehrgesetz, das Gesetz über die Bundesanstalt für Flugsicherung und durch die zur Durchführung dieser Gesetze erlassenen Rechtsvorschriften beschränkt wird. Diese als 'magna carta' der Luftfahrt bezeichnete Regelung (vgl. Schleicher/Reymann/ Abraham, Das Recht der Luftfahrt, 3. Aufl. Bd. 2 S. 15) stellt eine Konkretisierung der in Art. 2 Abs. 1 GG verfassungsrechtlich als subjektives öffentliches Recht unter bestimmten Voraussetzungen gewährleisteten allgemeinen Handlungsfreiheit dar.

Nach den geltenden luftverkehrsrechtlichen Vorschriften ist Luftfahrt, jedenfalls soweit sie im hier interessierenden Umfang betrieben wird, nur unter Inanspruchnahme des Flugsicherungsdienstes, den die Beklagte in Form eines staatlichen Monopolbetriebs zur Verfügung stellt, zulässig und möglich. Diese Regelung findet ihre Rechtfertigung darin, daß Aufgaben der Flugsicherung aus Gründen der öffentlichen Sicherheit und Ordnung ihrer Natur nach *staatliche* Aufgaben sind und deshalb vom Staat wahrgenommen werden müssen. Nur so ist gewährleistet, daß Gefahren, die einerseits die Sicherheit des Luftverkehrs bedrohen und andererseits von der Luftfahrt ausgehen, wirksam abgewehrt werden.

Reasons:

The appeal court has, accurately in the outcome, declared the claim in the action to be justified in principle from the point of view of official liability (Art 34 of the GG in combination with § 839 of the BGB).

I

The appeal court has accepted that the flight controllers would have acted in exercise of a public office entrusted to them (Art 34 of the GG) when they impeded air traffic through the accumulated cases of reporting themselves as sick ('go sick') and decreasing their rate of work ('go slow').

The arguments of the appeal in law directed against this are unsuccessful.

1 Whether certain conduct of a person is to be regarded as exercise of a public office is to be determined, according to the established case law of the Senate, by whether the real object in the sense of which the person was acting is to be attributed to the exercise of sovereign authority, and whether, if this is the case, there exists between this object in view and the action causing the harm such a close external and internal connection that the action must be regarded as belonging to the realm of the exercise of sovereignty (BGHZ 42, 176, 179; LM BGB § 839 [Ca] no 23). The appeal court correctly proceeded from this position.

2 According to § 1 para 1 of the Air Traffic Act, use of the airspace by aeroplanes is free insofar as it is not limited by the Air Traffic Act, the Act regarding the Federal Institute for Air Traffic Control and by the statutory instruments issued for the implementation of these Acts. This regime, described as the 'magna carta' of air travel, (compare Schleicher/Reymann/Abraham, The Law of Air Travel, 3rd edn, vol 2 p 15) represents a concretization of the general freedom of action guaranteed under certain pre-requisites in Art 2 para 1 of the GG in constitutional law as subjective public law.

According to the current statutory instruments in respect of air traffic law, air travel, in any event so far as it is carried on to the extent concerned here, is permissible and possible only by taking advantage of the Air Traffic Control Service, which the defendant makes available in the form of a State monopoly business. This regime finds its justification in the fact that duties of air traffic control are *State* duties in accordance with their nature for reasons of public safety and order, and therefore must be attended to by the State. Only in this way can it be guaranteed that dangers, which on the one hand threaten the safety of air traffic and on the other hand proceed from air travel, are effectively prevented.

Die Flugleiter erfüllen als Bedienstete der Bundesanstalt für Flugsicherung, einer dem Bundesminister für Verkehr unterstellten nicht rechtsfähigen Anstalt (vgl. Gesetz über die Bundesanstalt für Flugsicherung vom 23. März 1953, BGBl I 70, BFSG) Aufgaben der Luftaufsicht (§§ 29, 31 Abs. 1 Satz 3, Abs. 2 Nr. 18 LuftVG). Diese besteht nach § 29 Abs. 1 Satz 1 LuftVG in der Abwehr von Gefahren für die Sicherheit des Luftverkehrs sowie für die öffentliche Sicherheit oder Ordnung durch die Luftfahrt. Sie ist damit ihrer Rechtsnatur nach *sonderpolizeilicher* Art. Der Bundesanstalt für Flugsicherung mit ihren Außenstellen (vgl. Reuss, Jahrbuch der Luft- und Raumfahrt 1975 S. 21ff.; Verwaltungsordnung für die Flugsicherung vom 24. Dezember 1953, VkBl 1954, 26) obliegt in diesem Rahmen u. a. die Durchführung des Flugsicherungsbetriebsdienstes, zu dem insbesondere die Luftverkehrskontrolle einschließlich der Bewegungslenkung im Luftraum und auf den Rollflächen der Flughäfen gehört (§§ 1, 2 BFSG, §§ 1, 3, 6ff. AVV vom. 8 April 1968, BAnz. Nr. 74). Der Flugverkehrskontrolldienst kann in Ausübung der Luftaufsicht Verwaltungsakte (Luftaufsichtsverfügungen) erlassen; er hat die von den Luftfahrzeugführern nach den Verkehrsvorschriften der Luftverkehrsordnung einzuholenden Flugverkehrsfreigaben zu erteilen (§ 29 Abs. 1 Satz 2 LuftVG, § 26 LuftVO, § 10 AVV). Dies alles ist Ausübung öffentlicher Gewalt (Schleicher/Reymann/Abraham, aaO Bd. 2 Vorb. 2 BFSG S. 692; Hofmann Luftverkehrs-Verordnungen, Vorb. 3 BFSG S. 515; Soergel/Glaser, BGB, 10. Aufl., § 839 Bem. 134; Bodenschatz, BFSG § 2 Anm. 1; ders., VersW 1960, 217, 220 Fn. 10; Wegerdt, ZLR 1953, 127, 134; Darsow, ZLR 1953, 295, 297ff.; Vierheilig, Die Polizei 1964, 363, 367).

3 Das Berufungsgericht hat darüber hinaus zu Recht angenommen, daß zwischen dieser Tätigkeit und den von der Klägerin beanstandeten Maßnahmen der Flugleiter nicht nur ein äußerer, sondern auch ein innerer Zusammenhang besteht.

The flight controllers, as employees of the Federal Institute for Air Traffic Control, an institute which is not legally competent and is placed under the Federal Minister for Transport, fulfil duties of air surveillance (compare Act regarding the Federal Institute for Air Traffic Control of 23 March 1953, BGBl I 70, BFSG) (§§ 29, 31 para 1 sentence 3, para 2 no 18 of the LuftVG). This consists, according to § 29 para 1 sentence 1 of the LuftVG, in the prevention of dangers to the safety of air traffic as well as to public safety or order through air travel. It is therefore, according to its legal nature, of a *special policing* kind. The Federal Institute for Air Traffic Control with its branch offices (compare Reuss, Yearbook of Air and Space Travel, 1975, p 21 and onwards; Administrative Order for Air Traffic Control of 24 December 1953 VkBI 1954, 26) is under a duty within this framework, amongst other things, to carry out the air traffic control operational service, to which in particular air traffic control, inclusive of direction of movement in the airspace and on the runways of the airports, belongs (§§ 1 and 2 BFSG, §§ 1, 3 and 6 and onwards AVV of 8 April 1968, BAnz no 74). The Air Traffic Control Service can issue administrative acts (Air Surveillance Decrees) in exercise of air surveillance; it has to dispense the air traffic releases which are to be obtained by aircraft pilots according to the traffic provisions of the Air Traffic Order (§ 29 para 1 sentence 2 of the LuftVG, § 26 of the LuftVO, § 10 of the GAO). All this is the exercise of public power (Schleicher/Reymann/Abraham *loc cit*, Vol 2, preliminary note 3 of the BFSG, p 692; Hofmann Air Traffic Regulations, preliminary note 3 of the BFSG, p 515; Soergel/Glaser, BGB, 10th edn, § 839, note 134; Bodenschatz BFSG § 2 note 1; the same, VersR 1960, 217, 220 footnote 10; Wegerdt ZLR 1953, 127, 134; Darsow, ZLR 1953, 295, 297 and onwards; Vierheilig, The Police, 1964, 363, 367).

3 Besides this, the appeal court has also correctly accepted that there is not only an external but also an internal connection between this activity and the measures taken by the flight controllers objected to by the plaintiff.

(a) Das Berufungsgericht hat insoweit, von der Revision nicht beanstandet, festgestellt, daß in dem hier fraglichen Zeitraum des Jahres 1973 ein Großteil der Flugleiter verabredungsgemäß entweder sich grundlos krank meldete ('go sick') oder seine Arbeitsleistung über einen längeren Zeitraum hinweg erheblich herabsetzte ('go slow'), so daß die vom Luftverkehrskontrolldienst zu treffenden Entscheidungen, insbesondere die Flugverkehrsfreigaben gem. § 26 LuftVO, erheblich verzögert wurden und zum Teil sogar ganz unterblieben sind. Diese Aktionen der Flugleiter sind entgegen der Annahme der Revision nicht nur 'bei Gelegenheit' ihrer dienstlichen Verrichtungen erfolgt, sondern sie waren derart eng mit der Dienstausübung verbunden, daß sie als ihr zugehörig angesehen werden müssen. Das eine ist von dem anderen schon rein tatsächlich nicht zu trennen Das beanstandete Vorgehen der Flugleiter (Krankmeldungen und Herabsetzung der Arbeitsleistung) steht zu der unmittelbaren Verwirklichung des hoheitlichen Ziels, der Sicherung des Flugverkehrs, in einer solchen Beziehung, daß es mit dieser als ein einheitlicher Lebensvorgang anzusehen ist (vgl. insoweit Senatsentscheidung LM GrundG Art. 34 Nr. 25). Erst recht ist der erforderliche Zusammenhang mit der aufgetragenen amtlichen Tätigkeit zu bejahen, soweit sich das beanstandete Verhalten der Flugleiter als amtspflichtwidrige *Unterlassung* gebotener Amtstätigkeit darstellt (Bender, Staatshaftungsrecht, 2. Aufl. Rdn. 432; Senatsurteil LM BGB § 839 Fg Nr. 5).

(b) Art. 34 GG findet grundsätzlich auch Anwendung, wenn mit der Ausübung hoheitlicher Gewalt betraute Bedienstete zum Zwecke der Verbesserung ihrer Arbeitsbedingungen in streikähnlicher Weise ihre Amtstätigkeit einstellen oder verzögern und hierdurch Dritte vorsätzlich schädigen, für die – was auf den Betrieb der Klägerin zutrifft, vgl. dazu nachst. unter II 4 d – nach ihrer betrieblichen Organisation und Planung die Amtstätigkeit eine rechtliche oder tatsächliche Voraussetzung der Unternehmensbetätigung bildet.

Es bedarf nicht der Erörterung, ob über diese Grenze hinaus der 'Beamtenstreik' dem Dienstherrn nach Art. 34 GG schlechthin zuzurechnen ist (so offenbar Nipperdey in Festschrift für Sitzler S. 82). Jedenfalls für den hier vorliegenden Sachverhalt ist der für eine Haftungsübernahme erforderliche innere Zusammenhang zwischen der Zielsetzung der streikähnlichen Aktion und dem öffentlichen Amt der Flugleiter zu bejahen.

(a) The appeal court has in this respect established (and this is not contested by the appeal in law) that in the period at issue here in the year 1973 a great part of the flight controllers, by agreement, either reported themselves groundlessly as sick ('go sick') or decreased their rate of work significantly over a longer period ('go slow') so that the decisions to be made by the air traffic control service, in particular the air traffic releases in accordance with § 26 of the LuftVO, were substantially delayed and in part did even not take place. These actions of the flight controllers did not, contrary to the argument of the appeal in law, occur merely 'on the occasion' of their official functions, but they were so closely connected with the exercise of their office that they must be seen as appertaining to it. The one is really not to be separated from the other. The action of the flight controllers which has been objected to (reporting as sick and decreasing rate of work) stands in such a relationship to the direct fulfilment of the sovereign objective of safety of air traffic that it is to be regarded as an undivided vital process with it (compare in this respect the decision of the Senate LM GG Art 34 no 25). The necessary connection with the official activity with which the flight controllers are charged is all the more to be affirmed insofar as their conduct which is the subject matter of the objection, shows itself as a failure, contrary to official duty, to carry out an official activity which has been ordered (Bender, State Liability Law, 2nd edn, marginal no 432; judgment of the Senate LM BGB § 839 Fg no 5).

(b) Article 34 of the GG is also applicable in principle when in the exercise of sovereign power, trusted employees stop or delay their work for the purpose of improving their conditions of work, in a manner similar to a strike, and as a result intentionally harm third parties, for whom – which applies to the business of the plaintiff, compare for this purpose what follows under II 4 d – according to their business organisation and planning, the official activity forms a legal and factual prerequisite for the activity of the undertaking.

There is no need for discussion as to whether beyond this limit the 'officials' strike' is simply to be attributed to the employer in accordance with Art 34 of the GG (as is stated plainly by Nipperdey in Festschrift for Sitzler, p 82). At all events, for the facts of the case present here, the internal connection between the objective of the action in the nature of a strike and the public office of the flight controllers, which is necessary for an assumption of responsibility, is to be confirmed.

(c) Die beabsichtigten Störungen im Ablauf der Flugsicherung betrafen im Kern die (polizeiliche) Aufgabe, die der Flugleiter als Amtsträger zu erfüllen hat. Soweit der Ausfall der Flugsicherung sich nachteilig auf Gewerbetriebe wie den der Klägerin ausgewirkt hat, drückt sich in diesen Folgen die funktionelle Abhängigkeit solcher Unternehmen von dem öffentlichen Amt aus. Die planmäßige Vernachlässigung eines öffentlichen Amtes der beschriebenen Art durch den Amtsträger stellt sich nicht so dar, als habe der Beamte lediglich eine durch die Amtsausübung geschaffene Lage zur Gewinnung persönlicher Vorteile ausgenutzt (was den Zusammenhang mit dem Amt aufheben würde, vgl. Maunz/Dürig/Herzog, GG Art. 34 Rdn. 18). Vielmehr hält sich eine solche Aktion nach Zielrichtung und verwendetem Mittel (noch) im Bereich des anvertrauten öffentlichen Amtes.

(d) Daß hier die Flugleiter sich letztlich gegen den eigenen Dientsherrn wandten, hebt den Zusammenhang zwischen ihrem 'Bummelstreik' und der Ausübung des anvertrauten öffentlichen Amtes nicht auf. Die Flugleiter haben ihre Aktion innerhalb des ihnen aufgetragenen Wirkungskreises und unter Ausnutzung ihrer amtlichen Stellung durchgeführt. Es lag ihnen fern, dem Staat allgemein und grundsätzlich den Gehorsam zu verweigern und sich aus der Bindung zum Dienstherrn schlechthin zu lösen. Nur bei einer solchen Sachlage, die sich durch die einseitige Aufkündigung der übertragenen Stellung als Organ des Staates kennzeichnet, könnte erwogen werden, die Haftung des Staats für seine Beamten einzuschränken oder auszuschließen (vgl. dazu RGZ 104, 257, 263).

(e) Dieses Verständnis des Art. 34 GG entspricht auch dem rechtsstaatlichen Anliegen der Vorschrift. Die Schadensersatzpflicht der öffentlichen Hand ist ein wichtiges Mittel zum Schutz des Bürgers vor Einwirkungen der öffentlichen Gewalt (vgl. BGHZ 11, 192, 198; 22, 383, 388). Besonders dann, wenn – wie hier – der (durch die Verwaltungsgerichte zu gewährende) unmittelbare Rechtsschutz gegen rechtswidrige Maßnahmen staatlicher Amtsträger wegen der Eigenart der Verwaltungstätigkeit im wesentlichen ausfällt, das Verhalten der Amtsträger jedoch zu erheblichen Einbußen des Einzelnen führt, gewinnt der durch Art. 34 GG vermittelte subsidiäre (mittelbare) Schutz in rechtsstaatlicher Sicht besondere Bedeutung (Bettermann in Bettermann/Nipperdey-Scheuner, Die Grundrechte III/2 S. 781, 852/3; Dagtoglou, Bonner Komm. GG Art. 34 – Zweitbearbeitung – Rdn. 3, 4). Unterstrichen wird dies durch die Erwägung, daß der Bürger im hoheitlichen Bereich auf den Staat in besonderer Weise angewiesen ist, ohne sich einzelne Beamte 'aussuchen' zu können. Hingegen stehen dem Dienstherrn die rechtlichen Mittel des öffentlichen Dienstrechts zu Gebote, die es ihm erlauben, die ordnungsgemäße Erfüllung der Amtspflichten – gegebenenfalls durch Abberufung einzelner Amtsträger und Einsatz von Ersatzkräften – sicherzustellen.

(c) The intended disturbances in the discharge of air traffic control related in essence to the (policing) duty which the flight controller has, as an official, to fulfil. Insofar as the results of air traffic control have operated disadvantageously on businesses like that of the plaintiff, the functional dependence of such undertakings on the public office expresses itself in these consequences. The methodical neglect by the office holder of a public office of the kind described does not present itself as if the official had merely utilised a situation created by the exercise of office to gain personal advantages (which would take away the connection with the office, compare Maunz/Dürig/Herzog GG Art 34 marginal no 18). Such action much rather remains, in accordance with its objective and the means employed (still) within the realm of the entrusted public office.

(d) The fact that the flight controllers finally turned against their own employer does not remove the connection between their 'go slow' and the exercise of the entrusted public office. The flight controllers have carried out their action within the field of activity with which they were charged, and by utilising their official position. It was far from their thoughts to refuse obedience to the State generally and in principle, and simply to free themselves from the obligation to their employer. Only in such a state of affairs, which is characterised by a unilateral notice of termination of the position assigned as organ of the State, could it be considered that the liability of the State for its officials should be limited or excluded (compare with this RGZ 104, 257, 263).

(e) This understanding of Art 34 of the GG also corresponds with the constitutional State context of the provision. The duty to compensate for harm out of the public purse is an important method for the protection of the citizen from the effect of public power (compare BGHZ 11, 192, 198; 22, 383, 388). Especially if – as here – the direct protection of the law (to be granted by the Administrative Courts) against unlawful measures by public officials substantially fails because of the peculiar nature of the administrative activity, but the conduct of the officials leads to significant losses to individuals, the subsidiary (indirect) protection procured by Art 34 of the GG gains special importance from the constitutional State viewpoint (Bettermann in Bettermann/Nipperdey-Scheuner, The Basic Rights III/2 p 781, 852/3; Dagtoglou, Bonn Commentary on the GG, Art 34 – Second Revision – marginal no 3, 4). This is underlined by the consideration that the citizen is, in the sovereign realm, in a special way cast upon the State without being able to 'seek out' individual officials. Over against this, the employer has at his command the legal methods of public service law which permit him to secure the orderly fulfilment of official duties – if necessary by recalling individual officials and the supply of reserve employees.

Schließlich entspricht die Anwendung des Art. 34 GG auf den vorliegenden Sachverhalt auch dem sozialstaatlichen Anliegen, den Bürger, der sich einem stetigen Anwachsen staatlicher Tätigkeit im hoheitlichen Bereich gegenübersieht, einen immer leistungsfähigen Schuldner zu gewährleisten (RGZ 96, 148; Bender aaO Rdn. 381).

II

1 Eine Haftung der Beklagten für die von der Klägerin geltend gemachten Schäden setzt weiter voraus, daß die Flugleiter eine ihnen gegenüber der Klägerin als 'Dritte' bestehende Amtspflicht schuldhaft verletzt haben (Art. 34 GG, § 839 Abs. 1 Satz 1 BGB). Das Berufungsgericht hat offen gelassen, ob die Flugleiter verpflichtet waren, die Klägerin – ggfs. in deren Eigenschaft als Luftfrachtführer – vor geschäftlichen Nachteilen zu bewahren, die sich aus einer gestörten, nicht zügigen Abwicklung des Flugreiseverkehrs ergeben konnten. Eine Amtspflichtverletzung zum Nachteil der Klägerin, so hat das Berufungsgericht weiter ausgeführt, sei schon deshalb zu bejahen, weil das Verhalten der Flugleiter gegen § 826 BGB verstoßen habe und daher als Amtsmißbrauch aufzufassen sei; dies verpflichte zum Ersatz aller bei den Betroffenen eingetretenen Nachteile einschließlich der Vermögensschäden.

Die Revision macht geltend, auch bei Annahme eines Amtsmißbrauchs könne die Klägerin nicht Ersatz ihres Vermögensschadens verlangen. Die Amtspflichten der Flugleiter beschränkten sich darauf, Leben, Gesundheit und Eigentum der unmittelbar Flugbeteiligten von bestimmten Gefahren des Luftverkehrs zu schützen. Das Interesse eines nicht überschaubaren Kreises von Personen an dem pünktlichen Starten, Landen oder Verkehren von Flugzeugen sei dagegen durch die Amtätigkeit nicht geschützt.

Im Ergebnis bleibt die Revision auch insoweit ohne Erfolg.

2 (a) Inhalt und Umfang der Amtspflichten eines Beamten bestimmen sich nach den seinen Aufgaben- und Pflichtenkreis regelnden Vorschriften, seien sie Gesetz oder Verordnung, Verwaltungsvorschrift oder dienstliche Einzelweisung, auch aus der Art der wahrzunehmenden Aufgaben selbst (vgl. BGB-RGRK, 11. Aufl., § 839 Anm. 32).

Finally, the application of Art 34 of the GG corresponds to the facts of the present case in the social State setting as well, in guaranteeing to the citizen who see himself faced with a continual growth of State activity in the sovereign realm an obligor who is always capable of performing his obligations (RGZ 96, 148; Bender, *loc cit*, marginal no 381).

II

1 Liability of the defendant for the harm claimed for by the plaintiff further presupposes that the flight controllers have culpably violated an official duty existing for them against the plaintiff as 'third party' (Art 34 of the GG, § 839 para 1 sentence 1 of the BGB). The appeal court has left open whether the flight controllers were under a duty to protect the plaintiff – if necessary in its capacity as air cargo manager – from business losses which could result from a disturbed and interrupted running of air traffic. A violation of official duty to the disadvantage of the plaintiff was, the appeal court further explained, to be affirmed because the conduct of the flight controllers had violated § 826 of the BGB and therefore was to be understood as a abuse of office; this created an obligation to provide compensation in respect of all the losses of those affected, inclusive of financial harm.

The appeal in law claims that even if abuse of office were accepted the plaintiff could not demand compensation for its financial harm. The official duties of the flight controllers were confined to protecting the life, health and property of the parties directly involved in flights from certain dangers of air traffic. The interest of a group of persons not readily comprehensible in extent in the punctual starting, landing or passage of aircraft was on the contrary not protected by official activity.

The appeal in law is also in this respect unsuccessful in its outcome.

2 (a) The content and scope of the official duties of an official are determined by the provisions regulating his area of tasks and duties, whether they are statutes, regulations, administrative provisions or official individual directions, or even from the kind of tasks to be attended to themselves (compare BGB-RGRK, 11th edn, § 839 note 32).

Ob der Geschädigte (hier: die Klägerin) im Sinne des § 839 BGB 'Dritter' ist, richtet sich danach, ob die Amtspflicht – wenn auch nicht notwendig allein, so doch auch – den Zweck hat, gerade sein Interesse wahrzunehmen. Nur wenn sich aus den die Amtspflicht begründenden und sie umreißenden Bestimmungen sowie aus der besonderen Natur des Amtsgeschäfts ergibt, daß der Geschädigte zu dem Personenkreis zählt, dessen Belange nach dem Zweck und der rechtlichen Bestimmung des Amtsgeschäfts geschützt und gefördert werden sollen, besteht ihm gegenüber bei schuldhafter Pflichtverletzung eine Schadensersatzpflicht. Hingegen ist anderen Personen gegenüber, selbst wenn die Amtspflichtverletzung sich für sie mehr oder weniger nachteilig ausgewirkt hat, eine Ersatzpflicht nicht begründet. Es muß mithin eine besondere Beziehung zwischen der verletzten Amtspflicht und dem geschädigten 'Dritten' bestehen (Senatsentscheidungen BGHZ 56, 40, 45; 63, 35, 39; 65, 196, 198; st. Rspr.).

Im übrigen muß eine Person, der gegenüber eine Amtspflicht zu erfüllen ist, nicht in allen ihren Belangen immer als 'Dritter' anzusehen sein. Vielmehr ist jeweils zu prüfen, ob gerade das im Einzelfall berührte Interesse nach dem Zweck und der rechtlichen Bestimmung des Amtsgeschäfts geschützt werden soll (Senatsentscheidungen BGHZ 63, 35, 41ff.; 65, 196, 198; BGH NJW 1976, 103f.). Es kommt demnach auf den Schutzzweck der verletzten Amtspflicht an.

(b) Die nach § 29 Abs. 1 LuftVG den Luftfahrtbehörden zugewiesene Abwehr von Gefahren für die Sicherheit des Luftverkehrs sowie für die öffentliche Sicherheit oder Ordnung durch die Luftfahrt ist auf dem Gebiet der Flugsicherung Aufgabe der Bundesanstalt für Flugsicherung (§§ 1, 2 BFSG). Diese führt – neben einer Reihe anderer Aufgaben – auf allen deutschen Verkehrsflughäfen den sog. Flugsicherungs-betriebsdienst durch (§ 2 Abs. 1 Nr. 9 BFSG). Zu diesem gehört (§ 2 Abs. 2 BFSG, § 1 AVV) insbesondere der Flugverkehrskontrolldienst, der die Bewegungslenkung im Luftraum und auf den Rollflächen der Flugplätze durchzuführen hat (§ 2 Abs. 2 Nr. 1 BFSG; § 6ff. AVV). Die im Flugverkehrskontrolldienst eingesetzten Flugleiter haben nach § 6 AVV namentlich eine dreifache Aufgabe: Einmal, Zusammenstöße zwischen Luftfahrzeugen in der Luft und auf dem Rollfeld der Flugplätze zu verhindern; zum anderen Zusammenstöße zwischen Luftfahrzeugen und anderen Fahrzeugen sowie sonstigen Hindernissen auf dem Rollfeld der Flugplätze zu verhindern; schließlich, den Luftverkehr möglichst schnell und flüssig abzuwickeln. § 26 Abs. 2 LuftVO bestimmt darüber hinaus, daß die von den Luftfahrzeugführern einzuholenden und nach § 10 Nr. 2 AVV vom Flugverke-hrskontrolldienst zu erteilenden sog. Flugverkehrsfreigaben *Schnelligkeit*, *Wirtschaftlichkeit* und *Regelmäßigkeit* des Luftverkehrs berücksichtigen sollen, soweit es die öffentliche Sicherheit oder Ordnung, insbesondere die Sicherheit des Luftverkehrs, zulassen.

Whether the person suffering harm (here: the plaintiff) is a 'third party' in the sense of § 839 of the BGB, is governed by whether the official duty has the purpose – not necessarily solely, but also additionally – of protecting his interest. Only if it follows from the provisions forming the basis of and outlining the official duty, as well as from the special nature of the official business, that the person suffering harm belongs to the group of persons whose interests should be protected and promoted according to the purpose and the legal regulation of the official business, does there exist a duty to compensate him for harm in the case of culpable violation of duty. On the other hand, a duty to compensate other persons is not established, even if the violation of official duty has had a more or less disadvantageous effect for them. There must therefore be a special relationship between the violated official duty and the 'third party' suffering harm (decisions of the Senate BGHZ 56, 40, 45; 63, 35, 39; 65, 196, 198; established case law).

Besides this, a person against whom an official duty has to be fulfilled does not always have to be regarded in all his interests as a 'third party'. It is rather a question of examining whether, at any given time, the interest affected in the individual case should be protected according to the purpose and legal regulation of the official business (decisions of the Senate BGHZ; 63, 35, 41 and onwards; 65, 196, 198; BGH NJW 1976, 103 and onwards). It is accordingly a matter of the protective purpose of the violated official duty.

(b) The prevention of dangers arising from air travel to the safety of air traffic, as well as to public safety or order, which is assigned to the air travel authorities according to § 29 para 1 of the LuftVG is, within the area of air traffic control, the task of the Federal Institute for Air Traffic Control (§§ 1 and 2 of the BFSG). This carries out, besides a range of other tasks, the so-called flight safety operational service at all German airports (§ 2 para 1 no 9 of the BFSG). Included in this (§ 2 para 2 of the BFSG, § 1 of the AVV) is in particular the flight traffic control service which has to carry out the direction of movement in the airspace and on the runways of the airfields (§ 2 para 2 no 1 of the BFSG; § 6 and onwards of the AVV). The flight controllers employed in the flight traffic control service have, according to § 6 of the AVV, in particular, a threefold task: first, to prevent accidents between aircraft in the air and on the runways of the airfields; next, to prevent accidents between aircraft and other vehicles as well as other obstacles on the runways of the airfields; and finally to deal with air traffic as quickly and smoothly as possible. § 26 para 2 of the LuftVO provides additionally that the so-called air traffic releases which are to be obtained by aircraft pilots and dispensed by the air traffic control service in accordance with § 10 no 2 of the AVV should have regard to the *speed, good management* and *regularity* of air traffic insofar as public safety or order, in particular the safety of air traffic, permit it.

Diese Regelung der Flugsicherung ist den einheitlichen internationalen Richtlinien nachgebildet, wie sie von der Internationalen Zivilluftfahrt-Organisation nach Art. 37 des in Chicago am 7. Dezember 1944 unterzeichneten Abkommens über die Internationale Zivilluftfahrt (BGBl II 1956, 411) herausgegeben werden (vgl. hierzu Schleicher/Reymann/Abraham aaO Bd. 1 S. 54f.; Bd. 2 S. 173; Hofmann, Luftverkehrs-Verordnungen BFSG § 1 Rdn. 1 S. 516; Darsow, ZLR 1953, 295, 296).

Daß die einzelnen Flugleiter, als sie durch grundlose Krankmeldungen oder erhebliche Herabsetzung ihrer Arbeitsleistung den Flugverkehr behinderten, gegen ihre vorbezeichneten Amtspflichten verstießen, insbesondere gegen die Pflicht zur zügigen Abwicklung des Luftverkehrs, wie sie in § 26 Abs. 2 LuftVO und § 6 Nr. 3 AVV (siehe auch §§ 13, 19 Nr. 1, 23 AVV für den Fluginformations-, Flugberatungs- und Flugfernmeldedienst) ausdrücklich niedergelegt ist, kann nicht zweifelhaft sein (vgl. insoweit BDiszG DVBl 1974, 820 = ZBR 1974, 369; NJW 1975, 1905).

3 Es spricht vieles dafür, daß die im vorliegenden Rechtsstreit von der Klägerin geltend gemachten Vermögensinteressen auch in den Schutzbereich der den Flugleitern insoweit obliegenden Amtspflichten fallen.

Wie sich aus § 1 Abs. 1 BFSG, § 29 Abs. 1 Satz 1 LuftVG, § 26 Abs. 2 LuftVO und § 3 AVV ergibt, dient allerdings die Flugsicherung in erster Linie der Gefahrenabwehr im polizeilichen Sinne. Diesem Ziel ist die Tätigkeit der Flugleiter grundsätzlich zugeordnet. Dies schließt es indessen nicht aus, daß sie *auch* vermögensrechtliche Belange solcher Personen zu schützen hat, die durch ihre Teilnahme an einem organisierten Flugreisedienst auf die regelmäßige und wirtschaftliche Abwicklung des Flugverkehrs angewiesen sind. Dafür könnte sprechen, daß eine zügig arbeitende Flugsicherung regelmäßig sowohl Gefahren abwehren als auch einen wirtschaftlichen Flugbetrieb gewährleisten wird und eine Aufspaltung dieses einheitlichen Ordnungsbereichs der Lebenswirklichkeit widersprechen würde. Diese Frage bedarf jedoch nicht der abschließenden Erörterung, weil das Begehren der Klägerin sich aus einer anderen - vom Berufungsgericht nicht angestellten -Überlegung rechtfertigt.

4 (a) Jeder Beamte darf die mit der Ausübung öffentlicher Gewalt verbundenen Mittel nur in den durch das Amt gezogenen Grenzen gebrauchen; ihm obliegt kraft seines Amtes die Fürsorgepflicht, bei der Amtsausübung in keiner Weise in den Bereich Unbeteiligter einzugreifen (RGZ 158, 83, 94). Hiernach ist der hoheitlich handelnde Beamte namentlich verpflichtet, sich bei der Amtsausübung aller Eingriffe in fremde Rechte zu enthalten, die eine unerlaubte Handlung im Sinne des bürgerlichen Rechts, so auch des § 823 Abs. 1 BGB darstellen. Ein Beamter, der in Ausübung seines öffentlichen Amtes in diesem Sinne eine unerlaubte Handlung begeht, verletzt dadurch zugleich eine ihm dem Träger des Rechts oder Rechtsguts gegenüber obliegende Amtspflicht (BGHZ 16, 111, 113; 23, 36, 47; RGZ 154, 117, 123; 158, 83, 94; BGB-RGRK aaO § 839 Anm. 36; Soergel/Siebert/Glaser, BGB aaO § 839 Bem. 33, 185).

This regime of flight safety is copied from uniform international guidelines as they are published by the International Civil Air Travel Organisation in accordance with Art 37 of the Agreement in respect of International Civil Air Travel signed in Chicago on 7 December 1944 (BGBl II 1956, 411) (compare on this Schleicher/Reymann/Abraham, *loc cit*, Vol 1 p 54 and onwards; Vol 2 p 173; Hofmann, Air Traffic Regulations BFSG, § 1 marginal no 1 p 516; Darsow, ZLR 1953, 295, 296).

It cannot be doubted that the individual flight controllers, when they impeded air traffic by reporting themselves, groundlessly, as sick or by significantly decreasing their rate of work, violated their official duties described above, especially the duty of uninterrupted running of air traffic as it is expressly laid down in § 26 para 2 of the LuftVO and § 6 no 3 of the AVV (see also §§ 13, 19 no 1 and 23 of the AVV for the Flight Information, Flight Advice and Flight Announcement Services) (compare in this respect BDiszG DVBI 1974, 820 = ZBR 1974, 369; NJW 1975, 1905).

3 There is much to indicate that the economic interests claimed by the plaintiff in the present dispute also fall within the area of protection of the official duties incumbent on the flight controllers in this respect.

As follows from § 1 para 1 of the BFSG, § 29 para 1 sentence 1 of the LuftVG, § 26 para 2 of the LuftVO and § 3 of the AVV, air traffic control certainly provides primarily for prevention of dangers in the policing sense. The activity of the flight controllers is in principle allied to this objective. This does not, however, exclude the fact that it *also* has to protect the legal economic interests of those persons who, by their participation in an organised air travel service, are reliant on the regular and well managed running of air traffic. It could be said in favour of this that an air traffic control service which operates without interruption will normally prevent dangers as well as guarantee a well managed flight operation, and a splitting up of this united sphere of order would contradict the realities of life. This question does not however need definitive discussion because the plaintiff's demand is justified by another consideration - not employed by the appeal court.

4 (a) Every official may use the means connected with the exercise of public power only within the boundaries drawn by the office; a duty of care is incumbent on him, by virtue of his office, not to interfere in any way in the exercise of his office in the sphere of persons who are not concerned (RGZ 158, 83, 94). According to this, the official acting in a sovereign manner is obliged in particular to refrain, in the exercise of his office, from all interferences with the rights of others which represent a tort in the sense of civil law and thus also of § 823 para 1 of the BGB. An official who commits a tort in the exercise of his public office in this sense thereby violates at the same time an official duty incumbent on him as against the holder of the right or the legal interest (BGHZ 16, 111, 113; 23, 36, 47; RGZ 154, 117, 123; 158, 83, 94; BGB-RGRK, *loc cit*, § 839 note 36; Soergel/Siebert/Glaser, BGB *loc cit*, § 839 note 33, 185).

(b) Zu den durch § 823 Abs. 1 BGB geschützten 'sonstigen Rechten' gehört nach der Rechtsprechung des Bundesgerichtshofs auch der eingerichtete und ausgeübte *Gewerbebetrieb* (BGHZ 29, 65; BGB-RGRK, 11. Aufl., § 823 Anm. 27). Der Schutz des eingerichteten und ausgeübten Gewerbetriebs bildet allerdings einen 'Auffangtatbestand', der nur zur Anwendung kommen soll, wenn andere Schutzvorschriften nicht durchgreifen (BGHZ 36, 252, 256f.; 38, 200, 204; 45, 296, 307; BGH NJW 1971, 886; MDR 1974, 921). Diese Auffassung steht hier einer Anwendung des § 823 Abs. 1 BGB nicht deshalb entgegen, weil möglicherweise die Voraussetzungen des § 826 BGB vorliegen. Der richterrechtlich entwickelte Schutz des Gewerbetriebs als 'sonstiges Recht' im Sinne von § 823 Abs. 1 BGB ist nicht zuletzt deshalb eingeführt worden, weil die Bestimmung des § 826 BGB insbesondere im Hinblick auf das Erfordernis eines vorsätzlichen Handelns den Bedürfnissen der Praxis nicht genügte (BGHZ 36, 252, 256). Diese Vorschrift ist – anders als wettbewerbsrechtliche Sondervorschriften – nicht speziell auf den Unternehmensschutz ausgerichtet. Sie gewährt namentlich gegenüber fahrlässigen Eingriffen in den Gewerbebetrieb keinen Schutz. Nicht zuletzt insoweit stellt die Anerkennung des Gewerbebetriebs als 'sonstiges Recht' im Sinne von § 823 Abs. 1 BGB einen erweiterten Vermögensschutz vor allem im Verhältnis zu § 824 BGB dar. Schon deshalb gilt der Rechtssatz, daß auf § 823 Abs. 1 BGB als Schutznorm erst zurückzugreifen ist, wenn keine andere Bestimmung zutrifft, bei vorsätzlichen Eingriffen in den fremden Gewerbebetrieb nicht. Auf eine Prüfung der strengeren Voraussetzungen des § 826 BGB kann bei einem solchen Sachverhalt verzichtet werden (Staudinger/Schäfer, BGB, 10./11. Aufl., § 823 Rdn. 9; im Ergebnis ebenso BGHZ 59, 30, 34).

Der Schutz des Gewerbetriebs durch § 823 Abs. 1 BGB beschränkt sich jedoch auf Eingriffe, die *betriebsbezogen* sind (BGHZ 29, 65, 74). Die Bezogenheit zum Gewerbebetrieb kann sich (u. a.) aus der Tendenz des Eingriffs ergeben, wenn es etwa in der *Willensrichtung* des Verletzers liegt, durch bestimmte Maßnahmen den Betrieb zu beeinträchtigen (BGHZ 59, 30, 35; BGH BGB § 823 Ai Nr. 36 = NJW 1969, 1207; Anm. Hauß bei LM BGB § 823 Nr. 16; H. Lehmann, NJW 1959, 670; Larenz Schuldrecht II, 11. Aufl., § 72 III 7 b; Staudinger/Schäfer aaO Rdn. 134).

(c) Die für den Flughafen Hannover zuständigen Flugleiter haben durch die Störung des Flugverkehrs, die zur vorübergehenden Schließung des Flughafens führte, unter Verletzung der ihnen gegenüber der Klägerin bestehenden Amtspflichten deren Recht am eingerichteten und ausgeübten Gewerbebetrieb in rechtswidriger Weise beeinträchtigt.

(b) In the 'other rights' protected by § 823 para 1 of the BGB, according to the case law of the Federal Supreme Court, there is also included the established and exercised *operation of a business* (BGHZ 29, 65; BGH-RGRK, 11th edn, § 823 note 27). It is true that the protection of the established and exercised operation of a business certainly forms a 'fallback situation' which should only come to be applied if other protective provisions do not operate effectively (BGHZ 36, 252, 256 and onwards; 38, 200, 204; 45, 296, 307; BGH NJW 1971, 886; MDR 1974, 921). This view is not opposed to an application of § 823 para 1 of the BGB just because the prerequisites of § 826 of the BGB are possibly present. The protection of the operation of a business developed in case law as an 'other right' in the sense of § 823 para 1 of the BGB has not ultimately been introduced merely because the provisions of § 826 of the BGB, especially with regard to the requirement of an intentional action, did not satisfy the needs of practice (BGHZ 36, 252, 256). This provision is – in contrast to the special provisions in relation to competition law – not specially adapted to the protection of undertakings. It grants in particular no protection as against negligent interferences in the operation of a business. Not least in this respect, the recognition of the operation of a business as an 'other right' in the sense of § 823 para 1 of the BGB represents an enlarged economic protection principally in relation to § 824 of the BGB. For this reason, the statement of law that § 823 para 1 of the BGB is only to be resorted to as a protective norm if no other provision is appropriate does not apply to intentional interferences in the operation of the business of another. In such circumstances an examination of the more stringent requirements of § 826 of the BGB can be waived (Staudinger/Schäfer, BGB, 10th/11th edn, § 823 marginal no 9; likewise, in its outcome, BGHZ 59, 30, 34).

The protection of the operation of a business by § 823 para 1 of the BGB limits itself, however, to interferences which are *business related* (BGHZ 29, 65, 74). The relationship to the operation of the business can result from (amongst other things) the tendency of the interference, if this is the *direction of the intention* of the person inflicting the harm, to prejudice the business by certain measures (BGHZ 59, 30, 35; BGH BGB § 823 Ai no 36 = NJW 1969, 1207; note by Hauß in LM BGB § 823 no 16; H Lehmann NJW 1959, 670; Larenz, Law of Obligations II, 11th edn, § 72 III 7 b; Staudinger/Schäfer, *loc cit*, marginal no 134).

(c) The flight controllers responsible for Hannover airport have, by disturbance of air traffic, which led to the temporary closure of the airport, prejudiced the right of the plaintiff to the established and exercised operation of a business through violation of their official duties as against the plaintiff.

Wie teils vom Oberlandesgericht bindend (§ 561 ZPO) festgestellt, teils unstreitig ist, stellten die gehäuften Krankmeldungen und der sog. Dienst nach Vorschrift eine verabredete Maßnahme kollektiver Verweigerung geordneter Amtstätigkeit der Flugleiter dar, die darauf abzielte, Druck auf die Bundesregierung auszuüben, um sie zu veranlassen, den standespolitischen Forderungen der Flugleiter nachzugeben. Die Besonderheit dieser Aktion bestand darin, daß sie grundsätzlich gegen Unbeteiligte geführt wurde, die ihrerseits nicht in der Lage waren, die standespolitischen Forderungen der Flugleiter zu erfüllen. Anders als bei einem Streik in der Wirtschaft richtete sich die streikähnliche Aktion der Flugleiter nicht gegen ein Betriebspotential ihres Dienstherrn, sondern unmittelbar gegen die wirtschaftliche Organisation von Dritten, deren unternehmerische Tätigkeit funktionell mit der Amtstätigkeit der Flugleiter eng verbunden und von ihr abhängig war. Es lag ganz wesentlich in der Willensrichtung der Flugleiter, diese (bestimmten) Unternehmen in ihrer betrieblichen Abhängigkeit von der Flugsicherung zu beeinträchtigen, um die Bundesregierung wegen der bei diesen Dritten eintretenden Schadensfolgen ihren Forderungen gefügig zu machen.

Eine solche vorsätzliche Störung der gewerblichen Betätigung eines Reiseunternehmens, das für die reibungslose Abwicklung seiner geplanten und organisierten Flugreisen auf die ordnungsmäßige Durchführung der Flugsicherung angewiesen ist, stellt einen betriebsbezogenen Eingriff in den geschützten Bereich dieses Gewerbebetriebes dar.

(d) Dieser Eingriff war auch rechtswidrig, weil das schädigende Vorgehen nach seinem Zweck und seiner Ausführung zu mißbilligen war (vgl. BGHZ 45, 296, 307).

Das streikähnliche Verhalten der Flugleiter verstieß gegen ihre besondere beamtenrechtliche Treuepflicht gegenüber dem Dienstherrn und war daher amtswidrig (BVerfGE 8, 1, 17; weitere Nachweise bei Isensee, Beamtenstreik S. 53 Fn. 1; ders. JZ 1971, 73 Fn. 2; gegen ein generelles Streikverbot u. a. Ramm, Koalitionsrecht und Streikrecht der Beamten, m. w. Nachw. S. 32 Fn. 36, 37). Diese Verletzung beamtenrechtlicher (Innen) Pflichten kennzeichnet indessen das Verhalten der Flugleiter nocht nicht als unzulässige Einwirkung auf einen fremden Gewerbebetrieb. Denn ein ersatzbewerter Eingriff in den Gewerbebetrieb liegt nur bei Verletzung einer Norm vor, die den (einzelnen) Betrieb schützen soll (v. Caemmerer, Wandlungen des Deliktsrechts in: Festschrift z. 100jährigen Bestehen des DJT Band 2 S. 49ff., 96; Nikisch, ArbRecht, 2. Aufl. Band 2 S. 133; Ramm aaO S. 156). Das Treueverhältnis des Beamten zum Staat bestimmt jedoch ausschließlich die dienstrechtlichen Beziehungen zwischen dem Dienstherrn und dem Beamten; es begründet als solches keinen Individualrechtsschutz bestimmer Betriebe. Abzustellen ist vielmehr auf die Eigenart der jeweiligen Amtstätigkeit und auf die Folgen, die ihr Fehlgebrauch für bestimmte, der Amtsausübung verbundene Betriebe haben kann.

As has in part been bindingly established by the Upper State Court (§ 561 of the ZPO) and is in part uncontroversial, the accumulated reportings of sickness and the so-called work to rule represented an agreed measure of collective refusal of prescribed official activity by the flight controllers which had as its objective the exercise of pressure on the Federal Government to cause them to give way to the demands of the flight controllers as to status policy. The particular characteristic of this action consisted in the fact that it was in principle conducted against persons not involved who for their part were not in a position to fulfil the status policy demands of the flight controllers. Unlike a strike in the business world, the action in the nature of a strike by the flight controllers was not directed against the business potential of their employer, but directly against the business organisation of third parties whose activity as undertakings was closely connected functionally with the official activity of the flight controllers and was dependent upon them. It lay quite substantially in the direction of the intention of the flight controllers to prejudice these (specific) undertakings in their business dependence on air traffic control, in order to make the Federal Government tractable to their demands, because of the harmful consequences arising in the case of these third parties.

Such an intentional disturbance of the business activity of a travel undertaking which is reliant on the orderly carrying out of air traffic control for the smooth running of its planned and organised air journeys represents a business related interference into the protected sphere of the operation of this business.

(d) This interference was also unlawful because the action causing the damage should, according to its purpose and implementation, be disapproved (compare BGHZ 45, 296, 307).

The conduct of the flight controllers in the nature of a strike violates their special duty of good faith in administrative law as against their employer and was therefore contrary to their office (BVerfGE 8, 1, 17; further references in Isensee, Strike by Officials, p 53 footnote 1; the same in JZ 1971, 73 footnote 2; against a general ban on strikes, *inter alia*, Ramm, The Right of Officials to Form Coalitions and to Strike, with further references, p 32 footnotes 36 and 37). This violation of (internal) duties in administrative law does not however characterise the conduct of the flight controllers as impermissible action against the operation of the business of another. This is because an interference, protected by compensation, into the operation of a business, is only present in the case of the violation of a norm which is to protect the (individual) business (v Caemmerer, Changes in the Law of Tort in: Festschrift on the 100th year of existence of the DJT Vol 2 p 49 and onwards, 96; Nikisch, ArbRecht, 2nd edn, Vol 2 p 133; Ramm, *loc cit*, p 156). The relationship of good faith of the official to the State determines exclusively however the employment law relationships between the employer and the official; it does not as such form the basis of any individual legal protection of specific businesses. It is to be assigned rather to the special character of actual official activity and to the consequences which its wrong use can have for certain businesses which are connected with the exercise of the office.

In diesem Zusammenhang ist es vor allem zu mißbilligen, daß die Flugleiter ihre polizeilichen Aufgaben planmäßig vernachlässigt und die ihnen für die Hoheitsverwaltung in die Hand gegebenen Mittel dazu gebraucht haben, unbeteiligte, auf ihre Amtstätigkeit angewiesene und gegen diese Aktion wehrlose Unternehmen zu schädigen, um hierdurch den Staat, den eigentlichen sozialen Gegenspieler, mittelbar unter Druck zu setzen.

Die Flugsicherung ist, wie bereits ausgeführt, eine notwendige Voraussetzung jedes geordneten und sicheren Luftverkehrs. Störungen der Flugsicherung bringen erhebliche Gefahren für Leben, Gesundheit und Eigentum mit sich. Gefährdet sind damit in erster Linie höchstpersönliche Rechtsgüter, die als solche nicht ersetzbar sind. Wegen dieser drohenden Schadensfolgen erscheint eine geordnete Flugsicherung unverzichtbar. Eine planmäßige Störung der Flugsicherung erschüttert aber auch das Vertrauen der Reisenden in die gefahrenfreie Teilnahme am Luftverkehr. Sie muß zum – zeitweisen – Zusammenbruch jedes geordneten Luftverkehrs führen.

Reiseunternehmen, die - wie die Klägerin - das Flugreisegeschäft im Wege vorausschauender Planung betreiben, richten sich auf das ungestörte Funktionieren der Flugsicherung ein. Dieses Vertrauen ist schutzwürdig, weil die Übernahme der Flugsicherung in die Hoheitsverwaltung ihnen eine entsprechende unternehmerische Betätigung, die das Risiko des Ausfalls dieser für den Luftreiseverkehr notwendigen Dienstleistung begrenzen oder ausschließen könnte, verwehrt. Die Beamten der Flugsicherung erfüllen bei einer solchen Sicht eine Aufgabe, deren Besorgung für Betriebe der beschriebenen Art Voraussetzung der gewerblichen Betätigung ist, eine Aufgabe also, die dem unternehmerischen Zweck besonders eng verbunden ist. Die vorsätzliche Störung der geordneten Flugsicherung bereitet solchen Betrieben ein unüberwindbares Hindernis, das sich als widerrechtlicher Eingriff in den geschützten Betriebsablauf darstellt.

Dieser den Flugleitern zuzurechnende Eingriff entfällt im übrigen nicht etwa deshalb, weil die Beklagte den Flugverkehrskontrolldienst Hannover vorübergehend eingestellt hat. Diese Maßnahme trug ersichtlich der durch den 'Bummelstreik' entstandenen Lage angemessen Rechnung. Sie ist also als durch die Aktion der Flugleiter adäquat mitverursachte Notmaßnahme anzusehen. Daß sie aus Gründen der Gefahrenabwehr im Interesse der zu schützenden Rechtsgüter geboten war, schließt die Rechtswidrigkeit der sie veranlassenden streikähnlichen Aktion nicht aus.

5 Durch diesen widerrechtlichen Eingriff in den Gewerbebetrieb der Klägerin haben die Flugleiter zugleich Amtspflichten verletzt, die ihnen gegenüber der Klägerin als einem 'Dritten' oblagen (§ 839 Abs. 1 Satz 1 BGB; vgl. dazu oben II 4 a).

In this connection one must above all disapprove of the fact that the flight controllers have neglected their policing duties in a systematic way and have used the means put in their hands for sovereign administration to harm unconnected organisations, which were reliant on their official activity and were defenceless against this action, in order thereby to put the State, the real social opponent, indirectly under pressure.

Air traffic control is, as already explained, a necessary prerequisite of all well ordered and safe air traffic. Disturbances of air traffic control bring substantial dangers for life, health and property with them. Highly personal legal interests are primarily endangered thereby which as such are not replaceable. Because of these threatening harmful consequences, well ordered air traffic control appears indispensable. A systematic disturbance of air traffic control, however, shakes the confidence of travellers in danger-free participation in air travel. It must lead – temporarily – to breakdown of any well ordered air traffic.

Travel undertakings which, like the plaintiff, manage air travel business by way of forward planning make preparations based on the undisturbed functioning of air traffic control. This confidence is worthy of protection because the acceptance of air traffic control into sovereign administration precludes them from corresponding entrepreneurial activity which could limit or exclude the risk of the deficiency of this service which is necessary for air travel traffic. The officials of air traffic control fulfil, under such a view, a duty the performance of which for businesses of the kind described is a prerequisite of business activity, a duty therefore which is especially closely connected with the entrepreneurial purpose. The intentional disturbance of well ordered air traffic control causes such businesses an insuperable obstacle which represents an unlawful interference in the protected discharge of the business.

This interference which is to be attributed to the flight controllers did not lapse simply because the defendant temporarily suspended the air traffic control service at Hannover. This measure evidently took appropriate account of the situation which had arisen through the 'go-slow'. It is therefore to be regarded as an emergency measure adequately caused by the action of the flight controllers. The fact that it was necessary for protection from danger in the interests of legal interests which should be protected does not exclude the unlawfulness of the action in the nature of a strike which caused it.

5 Through this illegal interference in the operation of the plaintiff's business, the flight controllers have at the same time violated official duties which were incumbent on them as against the plaintiff as a 'third party' (§ 839 para 1 sentence 1 of the BGB; compare to this II 4 a, above).

Entgegen der Auffassung der Revision hat das Berfungsgericht in revisionsrechtlich nicht zu beanstandender Weise auch festgestellt, daß die Flugleiter ihre Amtspflichten gegenüber der Klägerin *vorsätzlich* verletzt haben. Der Vorsatz wäre allerdings zu verneinen, wenn die Beamten ihre streikähnliche Maßnahme in der Auswirkung auf Gewerbebetrieb der beschriebenen Art *tatsächlich* für rechtmäßig gehalten hätten (Senatsurteile in BGHZ 34, 375, 381 und in VersR 1963, 339, 341; 1966, 875, 876; 1973, 443, 445). Das hat das Berufungsgericht aber nicht festgestellt.

Soweit das Berufungsgericht die Rechtslage für den Fall erörtert, daß ein möglicher Bewertungsirrtum der an der Aktion beteiligten Flugleiter etwa auf grober Fahrlässigkeit beruht habe, handelt es sich ersichtlich nur um eine Hilfsbegründung, mit der das Berufungsgericht seinen in erster Linie getroffenen Feststellungen zur inneren Tatseite nicht ihre tragende Bedeutung hat nehmen wollen. Diese Feststellungen gehen dahin, die Flugleiter hätten spätestens in dem hier kritischen Zeitpunkt (Ende Juni 1973) mit der Möglichkeit (positiv) gerechnet, daß ihre einen für die Volkswirtschaft wesentlichen Verkehrsbereich nachhaltig störende Aktion gegen ihre Amtspflichten verstoße. Dem Zusammenhang der Gründe des angefochtenen Urteils ist auch die weitere Festellung zu entnehmen, daß die Beamten die Möglichkeit, mit der Aktion ihre Amtspflichten zu verletzen, *gebilligt* haben. Das ergibt sich einmal aus dem vom Berufungsgericht ausgewerteten unstreitigen Umstand, daß die Flugleiter alle Erklärungen des zuständigen Bundesministers über die Rechtswidrigkeit ihres Verhaltens und die Kritik ihrer Aktion durch die Massenmedien unbeachtet gelassen haben, zum anderen daraus, daß sie ihren Arbeitskampf nicht offen, sondern in verschleierter Form geführt haben und damit dem Dienstherrn die Möglichkeit genommen haben, rechtzeitig die erforderlichen Gegenmaßnahmen zu ergreifen. Dem fügt sich die weitere Feststellung des Berufungsgerichts ein, der Plan der Flugleiter, die Bundesregierung politisch unter Druck zu setzen, habe geradezu darauf aufgebaut, alle diejenigen, die mit dem Luftverkehr wirtschaftlich verflochten seien, durch die Störungen zu beeinträchtigen.

Die Revision zeigt nicht auf, daß das Berufungsgericht tatsächliches Vorbringen der Beklagten, das den Schluß auf fehlendes Bewußtsein der Pflichtwidrigkeit rechtfertigen könnte, übergangen hat. Dies wirkt sich gegen die Beklagte aus, weil sie bei dem gegebenen Sachverhalt für das Vorliegen eines besonderen Umstandes, wie ihn der vorsatzausschließende Rechtsirrtum darstellt, darlegungs- und beweispflichtig ist (Staudinger/Schäfer aaO § 823 Rdn. 424 a.E.; Palandt/Heinrichs, BGB, 36. Aufl., § 276 Anm. 3 b; Leipold, Beweislastregeln und gesetzliche Vermutungen S. 155 m. w. Nachw. in Fn. 16; vgl. auch BGH NJW 1968, 1279, 1281 unter III; Musielak, Grundlagen der Beweislast im Zivilprozeß [1975] S. 159).

Contrary to the view of the appeal in law, the appeal court also established, in a manner to which there can be no legal objection by the appeal in law, that the flight controllers *intentionally* violated their official duties as against the plaintiff. Intention could certainly be denied if the officials had *really* regarded their action in the nature of a strike, in its effect on the operation of businesses of the kind described, as lawful (judgments of the Senate in BGHZ 34, 375, 381 and in VersR 1963, 339, 341; 1966, 875, 876; 1973, 443, 445). But that has not been established by the appeal court.

Insofar as the appeal court discussed the legal situation which would apply in the case of a possible error of assessment by the flight controllers participating in the action having been based on gross negligence, it is evidently only a question of a supplementary reason as to which the appeal court did not want to take the significance which it bears into its primary findings on the internal side of the act. These findings were to the effect that the flight controllers had at the latest at the point of time which is critical here (end of June 1973) reckoned (positively) with the possibility that their action, which caused sustained disruption to an area of traffic vital for the national economy, contravened their official duties. From the correlation of the reasons for the disputed judgment, it is also possible to infer the further finding that the officials *approved* of the possibility of violating their official duties by the action. That follows on the one hand from the indisputable circumstance, as interpreted by the appeal court, that the flight controllers left all the explanations by the relevant Federal minister about the illegality of their conduct and the criticism of their action by the mass media unheeded; and on the other hand from the fact that they did not conduct their industrial dispute openly, but in a veiled form, and thereby took away from their employer the possibility of making use of the necessary counter measures promptly. The further finding of the appeal court, that the plan of the flight controllers to put the Federal Republic under political pressure had built directly on prejudicing by the disruptions all those who were involved economically with air traffic, fits in with this.

The appeal in law does not show that the appeal court overlooked the actual allegation of the defendant that a conclusion of the lack of consciousness of the breach of duty could provide justification. This operates against the defendant because it is under an obligation in the given circumstances to produce explanation and proof for the presence of a special circumstance, as would be presented by an error of law which excludes intention (Staudinger/Schäfer, *loc cit*, § 823 marginal no 424 aE; Palandt/Heinrichs, BGB, 36th edn, § 276 note 3 b; Leipold, Rules as to the Burden of Proof and Statutory Presumptions, p 155 with further references in footnote 16; compare also BGH NJW 1968, 1279, 1281 under III; Musielak, Principles of the Burden of Proof in the Civil Process, 1975, p 159).

6 Bei dieser Rechtslage bedarf es nicht der Erörterung, ob die Klägerin als Luftfrachtführer anzusehen war und insoweit in einem öffentlich-rechtlichen Benutzungsverhältnis zur Bundesanstalt für Flugsicherung stand. Es kann auch dahinstehen, ob – wie das Berufungsgericht angenommen hat – in Richtung gegen die Klägerin ein Amtsmißbrauch wegen sittenwidriger vorsätzlicher Schädigung (§ 826 BGB) zu bejahen war.

III

Die geltend gemachten Schäden sind nach dem Vortrag der Klägerin solche, die auf der Grundlage eines widerrechtlichen und schuldhaften Eingriffs in den geschützten Gewerbebetrieb zu ersetzen sind (§§ 249, 252 BGB). Das schließt den behaupteten Ausfall von Kurzfristbuchungen ein. Diese Buchungen wären, wie die Klägerin vorträgt, nach dem gewöhnlichen Lauf der Dinge (§ 252 BGB) noch kurz vor Reisebeginn erflogt, wenn die Störungen der Flugsicherung die Reisenden nicht von der beabsichtigten Teilnahme abgehalten hätten.

Hiernach erweist sich das Grundurteil als gerechtfertigt.

THE KITE CASE

BGHZ Band 7 S. 338

49 Kommt ein elfjähriger Junge dadurch zu Schaden, daß sein in der Luft befindlicher Drachen eine Hochspannungsleitung berührt und durch die Verbindung zu dem Kind Strom geleitet wird, so liegt kein außergewöhnliches Ereignis im Sinne der höheren Gewalt vor.

RHaftPflG § 1 a

III Zivilsenat. Urt. v. 23. Oktober 1952 i.S. VEW (Bekl.) w. E. (Kl.). III ZR 364/51

I Landgericht Arnsberg

II Oberlandesgericht Hamm

6 In this legal situation it does not need to be discussed whether the plaintiff was to be regarded as an air cargo manager and stood in this respect in a public law use relationship to the Federal Institute for Flight Safety. It can also be left undecided whether - as the appeal court has accepted - an abuse of office directed against the plaintiff because of intentional harm contrary to good morals (§ 826 of the BGB) should be confirmed.

III

The harm claimed for is, according to the report of the plaintiff, such as should be compensated for on the principle of an unlawful and culpable interference in the protected operation of a business (§§ 249 and 252 of the BGB). That includes the claimed deficit in short term bookings. These bookings would, as the plaintiff alleges, according to the usual course of things (§ 252 of the BGB) have taken place shortly before the commencement of the journey, if the disturbances in air traffic control had not held back travellers from their intended involvement.

For these reasons the original judgment proves itself to be justified.

THE KITE CASE

The tortious liability provisions of the Code only include one (§ 833 sentence 1) which creates strict liability. There are however a number of separate statutes which create strict liability, and the case which follows is an example of one of them. The statutory provision in question creates liability for the escape of electricity, gas, steam or current. Although it is strict, force majeure is a possible defence.

BGHZ Volume 7 p 338

49 If a 12 year old boy is harmed by his kite when it is in the air touching a high tension cable, and as a result of the contact an electric current is passed through the child, this is not an extraordinary event in the sense of supervening force.

RHaftPflG § 1 a

III Civil Senate, judgment of 23rd October 1952 in the matter of VEW (defendant) v E (claimant) – III ZR 364/51

I State Court Arnsberg

II Upper State Court Hamm

Der elfjährige Kläger ließ auf einer Wiese einen Papierdrachen steigen, der nicht an einem Bindfaden, sondern an einem dünnen Bindedraht befestigt war. Dieser Draht berührte die in der Nähe befindliche Hochspannungsleitung der Beklagten. Der Kläger erlitt hierdurch erhebliche Verbrennungen. Er hat unter Berücksichtigung seines eigenen mitwirkenden Verschuldens von der Beklagten Ersatz der Hälfte seines Schadens verlangt.

Landgericht und Oberlandesgericht haben seiner Ersatzklage entsprochen. Die Revision blieb erfolglos.

Aus den Gründen:

Das Berufungsgericht sieht ohne Rechtsirrtum die Grundlage der erhobenen Klageansprüche in § 1 a des Reichshaftpflichtgesetzes.

1 ...

2 Eine Haftung der Beklagten würde dann ausgeschlossen sein, wenn der dem Kläger entstandene Schaden durch höhere Gewalt verursacht worden wäre. Das Berufungsgericht hat ausgeführt, höhere Gewalt liege nur vor, wenn das Verhalten des Klägers sich als ein betriebsfremdes ungewöhnliches Ereignis darstelle, das mit den der Beklagten zumutbaren Mitteln nicht abzuwenden wäre. Das Spielen mit Drachen sei zwar ein von außen kommender Vorgang; jedoch könne das Verhalten des Klägers nicht als ganz ungewöhnlich angesehen werden. Es sei vielmehr durch sein Alter bedingt, und es müsse unter diesen Umständen damit gerechnet werden, daß Drachen die Leitung berühren. Hierbei komme es nicht darauf an, ob der Unfall in seiner Eigenart nicht alltäglich sei.

Die Rüge der Revision, hierin liege eine Verkennung des Rechtsbegriffs 'höhere Gewalt', ist nicht begründet. Nach der ständigen Rechtsprechung des Reichsgerichts, die auch von der Revision nicht angegriffen wird, ist höhere Gewalt ein betriebsfremdes, von außen durch elementare Naturkräfte oder durch Handlungen dritter Personen herbeigeführtes Ereignis, das nach menschlicher Einsicht und Erfahrung unvorhersehbar ist, mit wirtschaftlich erträglichen Mitteln auch durch die äußerste nach der Sachlage vernünftigerweise zu erwartende Sorgfalt nicht verhütet werden oder unschädlich gemacht werden kann und auch nicht wegen seiner Häufigkeit vom Betriebsunternehmer in Kauf zu nehmen ist (RG JW 1931, 865). Das Reichsgericht hat unter Zugrundelegung dieser Begriffsbestimmung höhere Gewalt nur dann bejaht, wenn eine Einwirkung von außen, die außergewöhnlich und nicht abwendbar war, vorlag (vgl. Geigel 17. Kap; Wussow 1952 S 75; RG DR 1943, 993 mit Hinweis auf weitere Entscheidungen).

The 11 year old claimant let a paper kite rise up into the air on a meadow. It was not fastened to a string but to a thin wire. This wire touched a high tension cable of the defendants which was situated nearby. The claimant thereby suffered substantial burns. Taking into account his own contributory fault, he demanded from the defendants compensation for half of the harm.

The State Court and the Upper State Court met his claim to compensation. The appeal in law was unsuccessful.

Reasons:

The appeal court, without any mistake in law, sees the basis of the claims raised in the § 1 a of the Reich Liability Act.

1 ...

2 Liability on the part of the defendants would be excluded if the harm which has occurred to the claimant had been caused by supervening force. The appeal court has explained that supervening force is only present if the conduct of the claimant presents itself as an external unusual event which could not be averted by means which could reasonably be expected of the defendant. Playing with a kite is certainly an external event; yet the conduct of the claimant could not be regarded as entirely unusual. It was much rather conditioned by his age, and in these circumstances it had therefore to be taken into account that kites touch cables. In this connection, it was not a question of whether the accident in its peculiarity was not an everyday one.

The objection raised by the appeal in law that in this there is a misunderstanding of the legal concept of 'supervening force' is not well founded. According to the constant case law of the Reich High Court, which is not challenged by the appeal in law, supervening force is an external event, caused from outside by elemental powers of nature or by the actions of third persons which, according to human insight and experience, is unforeseeable, which cannot be prevented or rendered harmless by means which can be tolerated from a business point of view even by the utmost care sensibly to be expected according to the circumstances and which does not occur so frequently that it must be accepted by business undertakings (RG JW 1931, 865). The Reichsgericht has only confirmed the existence of supervening force on the basis of this concept if an external effect was present which was extraordinary and not preventable (see Geigel, 17th chapter; Wussow, 1952, p 75; RG DR 1943, 993 with reference to further decisions).

Zur Annahme des Haftungsausschlusses durch den Einwand der höheren Gewalt ist danach neben der Forderung, das Ereignis müsse von außen kommen und unabwendbar sein, noch das Merkmal der Außergewöhnlichkeit, des Elementaren zu verlangen. Es kann bei dem hier vorliegenden Unfall – mag er auch selten sein – jedenfalls nicht davon gesprochen werden, er sei in diesem Sinne außergewöhnlich, gewißermassen elementarer Art.

LIABILITY AS BETWEEN DEFENDANTS

§ 840 [Haftung mehrerer] (1) Sind für den aus einer unerlaubten Handlung entstehenden Schaden mehrere nebeneinander verantwortlich, so haften sie als Gesamtschuldner.

(2) Ist neben demjenigen, welcher nach den §§ 831, 832 zum Ersatze des von einem anderen verursachten Schadens verpflichtet ist, auch der andere für den Schaden verantwortlich, so ist in ihrem Verhältnisse zueinander der andere allein, im Falle des § 829 der Aufsichtspflichtige allein verpflichtet.

(3) Ist neben demjenigen, welcher nach den §§ 833 bis 838 zum Ersatze des Schadens verpflichtet ist, ein Dritter für den Schaden verantwortlich, so ist in ihrem Verhältnisse zueinander der Dritte allein verpflichtet.

COMPENSATION

Personal injury

§ 842 [Umfang der Ersatzpflicht bei Verletzung einer Person] Die Verpflichtung zum Schadensersatze wegen einer gegen die Person gerichteten unerlaubten Handlung erstreckt sich auf die Nachteile, welche die Handlung für den Erwerb oder das Fortkommen des Verletzten herbeiführt.

§ 843 [Geldrente oder Kapitalabfindung] (1) Wird infolge einer Verletzung des Körpers oder der Gesundheit die Erwerbsfähigkeit des Verletzten aufgehoben oder gemindert oder tritt eine Vermehrung seiner Bedürfnisse ein, so ist dem Verletzten durch Entrichtung einer Geldrente Schadensersatz zu leisten.

(2) Auf die Rente finden die Vorschriften des § 760 Anwendung. Ob, in welcher Art und für welchen Betrag der Ersatzpflichtige Sicherheit zu leisten hat, bestimmt sich nach den Umständen.

Accordingly, for acceptance of the exclusion of liability through the defence of supervening force, besides the requirement that the event must come from outside and not be capable of being averted, the feature of extraordinariness, of the elemental, is required. It cannot in any case be said in relation to the accident here – even if it is rare – that it is extraordinary in this sense, of a so to speak elemental kind.

LIABILITY AS BETWEEN DEFENDANTS

§ 840 [Liability of several persons] (1) If several people are responsible together for the harm arising from a tort, they are liable as joint obligors.

(2) If, besides the person who is obliged, according to §§ 831 and 832, to make compensation for the harm caused by another person, that other person is also responsible for the harm, in their relationship to each other only that other person, or in the case of § 829 only the person with the supervisory duty, is so obliged.

(3) If, besides the person who according to §§ 833 to 838 is obliged to make compensation for harm, a third party is responsible for the harm, the third party alone is so obliged in their relationship to each other.

§ 841 relates to the liability as between officials and others causing harm.

COMPENSATION

Personal injury

§ 842 [Scope of the duty to compensate on injury of a person] The obligation to compensate for harm on account of a tort directed against the person extends to disadvantages which the act brings about for the income or prospects of the person suffering harm.

§ 843 [Annuity or capital settlement] (1) If, in consequence of an injury to body or health, the capacity of the injured party to earn a living is ended or reduced or an increase in his needs arises, compensation for harm is to be made to the injured party by payment of an annuity.

(2) The provisions of § 760 apply to the annuity. Whether, in what way, and for what sum the person liable to pay compensation has to provide security is determined according to the circumstances.

(3) Statt der Rente kann der Verletzte eine Abfindung in Kapital verlangen, wenn ein wichtiger Grund vorliegt.

(4) Der Anspruch wird nicht dadurch ausgeschlossen, daß ein anderer dem Verletzten Unterhalt zu gewähren hat.

§ 844 [Ersatzansprüche Dritter bei Tötung] (1) Im Falle der Tötung hat der Ersatzpflichtige die Kosten der Beerdigung demjenigen zu ersetzen, welchem die Verpflichtung obliegt, diese Kosten zu tragen.

(2) Stand der Getötete zur Zeit der Verletzung zu einem Dritten in einem Verhältnisse, vermöge dessen er diesem gegenüber kraft Gesetzes unterhaltspflichtig war oder unterhaltspflichtig werden konnte, und ist dem Dritten infolge der Tötung das Recht auf den Unterhalt entzogen, so hat der Ersatzpflichtige dem Dritten durch Entrichtung einer Geldrente insoweit Schadensersatz zu leisten, als der Getötete während der mutmaßlichen Dauer seines Lebens zur Gewährung des Unterhalts verpflichtet gewesen sein würde; die Vorschriften des § 843 Abs. 2 bis 4 finden entsprechende Anwendung. Die Ersatzpflicht tritt auch dann ein, wenn der Dritte zur Zeit der Verletzung erzeugt, aber noch nicht geboren war.

§ 845 [Ersatzansprüche wegen entgangener Dienste] Im Falle der Tötung, der Verletzung des Körpers oder der Gesundheit sowie im Falle der Freiheitsentziehung hat der Ersatzpflichtige, wenn der Verletzte kraft Gesetzes einem Dritten zur Leistung von Diensten in dessen Hauswesen oder Gewerbe verpflichtet war, dem Dritten für die entgehenden Dienste durch Entrichtung einer Geldrente Ersatz zu leisten. Die Vorschriften des § 843 Abs. 2 bis 4 finden entsprechende Anwendung.

§ 846 [Mitverschulden des Verletzten] Hat in den Fällen der §§ 844, 845 bei der Entstehung des Schadens, den der Dritte erleidet, ein Verschulden des Verletzten mitgewirkt, so finden auf den Anspruch des Dritten die Vorschriften des § 254 Anwendung.

§ 847 [Schmerzensgeld] (1) Im Falle der Verletzung des Körpers oder der Gesundheit sowie im Falle der Freiheitsentziehung kann der Verletzte auch wegen des Schadens, der nicht Vermögensschaden ist, eine billige Entschädigung in Geld verlangen.

(2) Ein gleicher Anspruch steht einer Frauensperson zu, gegen die ein Verbrechen oder Vergehen wider die Sittlichkeit begangen oder die durch Hinterlist, durch Drohung oder unter Mißbrauch eines Abhängigkeitsverhältnisses zur Gestattung der außerehelichen Beiwohnung bestimmt wird.

(3) Instead of the annuity, the injured person can claim a capital settlement if a weighty reason exists.

(4) The claim is not excluded by the fact that another person has to provide maintenance for the injured party.

§ 844 [Claims of a third party to compensation in respect of a fatality] (1) In the case of a fatality the person liable to pay compensation has to compensate for the costs of the funeral the person who has the duty to bear those costs.

(2) If the person who was killed was, at the time of the injury, in a relationship to a third party by virtue of which he, by virtue of a statutory provision, was or could become under a duty of maintenance as against this person, and if as a consequence of the fatality the right to maintenance has been removed from the third party, the person liable to pay compensation must make compensation to the third party for harm by payment of an annuity insofar as the person killed would, during the probable length of his life, have been obliged to provide maintenance; the provisions of § 843 paras 2–4 have corresponding application. The duty to compensate also arises if the third party was conceived at the time of the injury but was not yet born.

§ 845 [Claims to compensation because of lost services] In the case of a fatality or injury to body or health as well as the case of a deprivation of freedom, the person liable to pay compensation must, if the person suffering harm was obliged by virtue of a statutory provision to perform services for a third party in that person's household or business, make compensation to that third party for the lost services by payment of an annuity. The provisions of § 843 paras 2–4 have corresponding application.

§ 846 [Joint fault of the person suffering harm] If in the cases of §§ 844 or 845 fault on the part of the person suffering harm has contributed to the generation of the harm which the third party suffers, the provisions of § 254 have application to the claim of the third party.

§ 847 [Compensation for pain and suffering] (1) In the case of an injury to body or health as well as in the case of a deprivation of freedom, the person suffering harm can also claim fair compensation in money for harm which is not financial harm.

(2) A similar claim is available to a female against whom a crime or an offence against morality has been committed or who by fraud, by threat or through abuse of a relationship of dependency has been induced to consent to cohabitation outside marriage.

See note to § 253, Chapter Five, p 375.

Other cases

§ 848 [Haftung für Zufall bei Entziehung einer Sache] Wer zur Rückgabe einer Sache verpflichtet ist, die er einem anderen durch eine unerlaubte Handlung entzogen hat, ist auch für den zufälligen Untergang, eine aus einem anderen Grunde eintretende zufällige Unmöglichkeit der Herausgabe oder eine zufällige Verschlechterung der Sache verantwortlich, es sei denn, daß der Untergang, die anderweitige Unmöglichkeit der Herausgabe oder die Verschlechterung auch ohne die Entziehung eingetreten sein würde.

§ 849 [Verzinsung der Ersatzsumme] Ist wegen der Entziehung einer Sache der Wert oder wegen der Beschädigung einer Sache die Wertminderung zu ersetzen, so kann der Verletzte Zinsen des zu ersetzenden Betrags von dem Zeitpunkt an verlangen, welcher der Bestimmung des Wertes zugrunde gelegt wird.

§ 850 [Ersatz von Verwendungen] Macht der zur Herausgabe einer entzogenen Sache Verpflichtete Verwendungen auf die Sache, so stehen ihm dem Verletzten gegenüber die Rechte zu, die der Besitzer dem Eigentümer gegenüber wegen Verwendungen hat.

§ 851 [Ersatzleistung an Nichtberechtigten] Leistet der wegen der Entziehung oder Beschädigung einer beweglichen Sache zum Schadensersatze Verpflichtete den Ersatz an denjenigen, in dessen Besitze sich die Sache zur Zeit der Entziehung oder der Beschädigung befunden hat, so wird er durch die Leistung auch dann befreit, wenn ein Dritter Eigentümer der Sache war oder ein sonstiges Recht an der Sache hatte, es sei denn, daß ihm das Recht des Dritten bekannt oder infolge grober Fahrlässigkeit unbekannt ist.

Other cases

§ 848 [Liability for accident on the taking away of a thing] A person who is obliged to return a thing which he took away from another by a tort is also responsible for accidental destruction, accidental impossibility of surrender due to some other reason or accidental deterioration in the thing, unless the destruction, the other kind of impossibility of surrender or the deterioration would also have occurred without the thing being taken away.

§ 849 [Payment of interest on the compensation sum] If because of the taking away of a thing the value is to be the subject of compensation or because of the damaging of a thing the reduction in value is to be the subject of compensation, the person suffering the harm can claim interest on the compensation sum from the point in time at which the assessment of the value is established.

§ 850 [Compensation for expenditure] If a person who is obliged to surrender a thing which has been taken away expends money on the thing, he is entitled to the rights, as against the person suffering harm, which a possessor has as against an owner because of expenditure.

§ 851 [Payment of compensation to those not entitled] If the person obliged to make compensation for harm because of the taking away of, or damage to, a moveable thing pays the compensation to the person in whose possession the thing was at the time it was taken away or damaged, his liability is discharged by the payment, even though a third party was the owner of the thing or had another right in the thing, unless the right of the third party is known to him or is unknown in consequence of gross negligence.

LIMITATION

§ 852 [Herausgabeanspruch nach Eintritt der Verjährung] Hat der Ersatzpflichtige durch eine unerlaubte Handlung auf Kosten des Verletzten etwas erlangt, so ist er auch nach Eintritt der Verjährung des Anspruchs auf Ersatz des aus einer unerlaubten Handlung entstandenen Schadens zur Herausgabe nach den Vorschriften über die Herausgabe einer ungerechtfertigten Bereicherung verpflichtet. Dieser Anspruch verjährt in zehn Jahren von seiner Entstehung an, ohne Rücksicht auf die Entstehung in 30 Jahren von der Begehung der Verletzungshandlung oder dem sonstigen, den Schaden auslösenden Ereignis an.

LIMITATION

§ 852 [Restitution after expiry of limitation period] If the person obliged to make compensation as a result of a tort has acquired something at the cost of the victim, he is obliged even after expiry of the limitation period for the claim to compensation in respect of the harm which has arisen from a tort to make restitution in accordance with the provisions about restitution of unjustified enrichment. This claim is time barred after 10 years from the time it arose or without regard to the time it arose after 30 years from the commission of the act causing the injury or the other event triggering the harm.

There are special rules as to limitation in respect of liability for defective construction of buildings.

(§ 853 makes special provision for certain cases where someone obtains a claim against another by means of a tort.)

CHAPTER SEVEN

CRIMINAL LAW

HISTORY AND EFFECTIVE SCOPE

The original Criminal Code for the German Reich dates from 1871. The words 'for the German Reich' were dropped in 1953 and the StGB was issued in its new form in 1987, although further amendments have, of course, since been made. The Unification Treaty provided for its application to the new States, subject to certain reservations, but also for certain provisions of the StGB of the DDR to remain in force.

The StGB is divided into a General Part which deals with general principles of the criminal law, and a Special Part which deals with specific crimes and offences.

Non-retroactivity

Strafgesetzbuch

Allgemeiner Teil

Erster Abschnitt. Das Strafgesetz

Erster Titel. Geltungsbereich

§ 1 [Keine Strafe ohne Gesetz] Eine Tat kann nur bestraft werden, wenn die Strafbarkeit gesetzlich bestimmt war, bevor die Tat begangen wurde.

Temporal scope

§ 2 [Zeitliche Geltung] (1) Die Strafe und ihre Nebenfolgen bestimmen sich nach dem Gesetz, das zur Zeit der Tat gilt.

(2) Wird die Strafdrohung während der Begehung der Tat geändert, so ist das Gesetz anzuwenden, das bei Beendigung der Tat gilt.

(3) Wird das Gesetz, das bei Beendigung der Tat gilt, vor der Entscheidung geändert, so ist das mildeste Gesetz anzuwenden.

(4) Ein Gesetz, das nur für eine bestimmte Zeit gelten soll, ist auf Taten, die während seiner Geltung begangen sind, auch dann anzuwenden, wenn es außer Kraft getreten ist. Dies gilt nicht, soweit ein Gesetz etwas anderes bestimmt.

...

Non-retroactivity

Criminal Code

General Part

First section. The Criminal Law

First title. Scope of application

§ 1 [No punishment without statutory provision] An act can only be punished if the criminality was provided for by statute before the act was committed.

This reflects Art 103 II of the Basic Law: see Chapter Two.

Temporal scope

§ 2 [Temporal effect] (1) The punishment and its additional incidents[1] are to be determined in accordance with statute law which applies at the time of the act.

(2) If the punishment provided for is changed during the commission of the act, the statute law to be applied is that which was effective at the end of the act.

(3) If statute law, which applies at the end of the act, is changed before the court's decision, the least severe statute law is to applied.

(4) A statutory provision which is only to be effective for a determined period is also to be applied to acts which are committed during its validity when it has ceased to be effective. This does not apply insofar as a statutory provision provides otherwise.

(5) and (6) contain supplementary provisions about other consequences of criminal acts.

---

1 These additonal incidents are the legal consequences of a crime which do not have a specifically criminal character. They may concern the loss of rights like the right to hold office or to vote.

THE SHOOTINGS AT THE BERLIN WALL CASE

BGHSt Band 39 S. 1

1 Zur Beurteilung vorsätzlicher Tötungshandlungen von Grenzsoldaten der DDR an der Berliner Mauer.

StGB §§ 2, 7; GG Art. 103 Abs. 2;

Internationaler Pakt über bürgerliche und politische Rechte vom 19. Dezember 1966;

WStG § 5; Grenzgesetz-DDR.

5. Strafsenat. Urt. vom 3. November 1992 g. W.u.H.

5 StR 370/92

Landgericht Berlin

THE SHOOTINGS AT THE BERLIN WALL CASE

The theme which runs through this case is the issue of whether the criminal law applicable in the German Democratic Republic (DDR) at the time these shootings took place was, in its application to the crime which those shootings constituted, more or less severe than the equivalent law in the Federal Republic. The Federal Supreme Court came to the conclusion that it was more severe in every respect; this therefore justified the conviction of the defendants under the Criminal Code of the Federal Republic, in the light of the wording of § 2 III of that Code. The difficulty about reaching this conclusion was that if the instructions which the border guards were obeying when they fired constituted any sort of legal justification for what they did, the Federal Supreme Court would have had to come to the conclusion that the law of the DDR was less severe. However, the Federal Supreme Court considered that the defence of act of State did not apply; and although they disagreed with the opinion of the court of first instance that the defendants were not acting in accordance with the internal law of the DDR, they considered that such law (insofar as it justified the shooting) was so wrong as to be invalid law. International law, as it should have been applied in the DDR, was cited to support this conclusion. This same search for the system of law which had more lenient consequences for the defendants was then applied to other aspects of the case.

More recently, East German political leaders have been prosecuted in connection with killings at the border.

BGHSt Volume 39 p 1

1 On the conviction of border soldiers of the DDR for intentional homicide at the Berlin wall.

StGB §§ 2 and 7; GG Art 103 para 2;

International agreement regarding civil and political rights of 19 December 1966;

WStG § 5; Border Act-DDR

5th Criminal Senate. Judgment of 3 November 1992 v W and H

5 StR 370/92

State Court of Berlin

Gründe:

A Die Jugendkammer hat die Angeklagten W. (geboren am 11. April 1964) und H. (geboren am 16. Juli 1961) wegen Totschlags verurteilt, und zwar den Angeklagten W. zu einer Jugendstrafe von einem Jahr und sechs Monaten und den Angeklagten H. zu einer Freiheitsstrafe von einem Jahr und neun Monaten; sie hat die Vollstreckung beider Strafen zur Bewährung ausgesetzt.

Die Angeklagten waren als Angehörige der Grenztruppen der DDR – W. als Unteroffizier und Führer eines aus zwei Personen bestehenden Postens, H. als Soldat – an der Berliner Mauer eingesetzt. Dort haben sie am 1. Dezember 1984 um 3.15 Uhr auf den 20 Jahre alten, aus der DDR stammenden S. geschossen, der sich anschickte, die Mauer vom Stadbezirk Pankow aus in Richtung auf den Bezirk Wedding zu übersteigen. S. wurde, während er auf einer an die Mauer gelehnten Leiter hochstieg, von Geschossen aus den automatischen Infanteriegewehren der Angeklagten getroffen. Ein Geschoß aus der Waffe des Angeklagten W. drang in seinen Rücken ein, als er bereits eine Hand auf die Mauerkrone gelegt hatte; diese Verletzung führte zum Tode. S. wurde auch von einem Geschoß aus der Waffe des Angeklagten H. getroffen, und zwar am Knie; diese Verletzung war für den Tod ohne Bedeutung. Die zeitliche Abfolge der beiden Schußverletzungen ist nicht geklärt. S. wurde erst kurz vor 5.30 Uhr in das Krankenhaus der Volkspolizei eingeliefert, wo er um 6.20 Uhr starb. Er wäre bei unverzüglicher ärztlicher Hilfe gerettet worden. Die Verzögerung war die Folge von Geheimhaltungs- und Zuständigkeitsregeln, die den Angeklagten nicht bekannt waren. Die Angeklagten sind nicht bei der Bergung und dem Abtransport des Opfers eingesetzt worden.

Bei den Schüssen, die S. getroffen haben, waren die Gewehre der beiden Angeklagten auf 'Dauerfeuer' eingestellt. Der Angeklagte H. hat in den fünf Sekunden, während derer S. auf der Leiter nach oben stieg, insgesamt 25 Patronen verschossen; aus dem Gewehr des Angeklagten W. wurden 27 Patronen verschossen. Der Angeklagte W., der zuvor durch Zuruf zum Stehenbleiben aufgefordert und Warnschüsse abgegeben hatte, schoß aus einer Entfernung von 150 m aus dem Postenturm auf S. Der Angeklagte H., der beim Auftauchen des Flüchtlings auf Anweisung des Angeklagten W. den Turm verlassen hatte, schoß, an die Mauer gelehnt, aus einer Entfernung von ca. 110 m. Beide Angeklagte wollten S., den sie nicht für einen Spion, Saboteur oder 'Kriminellen' hielten, nicht töten. Sie erkannten aber die Möglichkeit eines tödlichen Treffers. 'Auch um diesen Preis wollten sie aber gemäß dem Befehl, den sie für bindend hielten, das Gelingen der Flucht verhindern. Um die Ausführung des Befehls auf jeden Fall sicherzustellen, der zur Vereitelung der Flucht auch die bewußte Tötung des Flüchtenden einschloß, schossen sie – das als Vorstufe vorgeschriebene gezielte Einzelfeuer auslassend – in kurzen Feuerstößen Dauerfeuer. Sie wußten, daß dieses zwar die Trefferwahrscheinlichkeit, wenn auch nicht in dem anvisierten Bereich, erhöhte, damit aber auch das Risiko eines tödlichen Schusses.'

Reasons:

A The Young Persons Chamber convicted the accused W (born on 11 April 1964) and H (born on 16 July 1961) of homicide and sentenced the accused W to a borstal sentence of one year and six months and the accused H to a prison sentence of one year and nine months; it suspended the execution of both sentences.

The defendants, as members of the border troops of the DDR – W as non-commissioned officer and as leader of a post consisting of two persons, and H as a soldier – were stationed at the Berlin wall. There, on 1 December 1984, at 3.15 hours, they fired at S who was 20 years old and came from the DDR. He was preparing to climb over the wall, from the city district of Pankow in the direction of the district of Wedding. S while he was climbing up a ladder leaning against the wall, was hit by bullets from the automatic infantry rifles of the defendants. A bullet from the weapon of the defendant W penetrated his back, when he had already laid one hand on the top of the wall; this injury was fatal. S was also hit in the knee by a bullet from the weapon of the defendant H; this injury had no connection with his death. The time sequence of the two gunshot wounds has not been established. S was not brought into the People's Police Hospital until shortly before 5.30 hours, where he died at 6.20 hours. He would have been saved by immediate assistance from a doctor. The delay was the consequence of rules as to secrecy and competence, which were not known to the defendants. The defendants were not employed in the recovery and removal of the victim.

For the shots which hit S, the rifles of both defendants were adjusted to 'continuous firing'. The defendant H fired 25 rounds altogether in the five seconds during which S climbed up the ladder; from the rifle of the defendant W 27 rounds were fired. The defendant W who had previously shouted to S to stay still, and had given warning shots, fired at S from a distance of 150 m, from the watch tower. The defendant H who, on the appearance of the fugitive, had left the tower at the direction of the defendant W fired, leaning against the wall, from a distance of about 110 m. Neither of the defendants intended to kill S whom they did not consider to be a spy, saboteur or 'criminal'. But they recognised the possibility of a fatal hit. 'Even at this price, however, they intended to prevent the success of the flight, in accordance with the command, which they considered to be binding. In order to secure in any event the carrying out of the command, which even included the conscious killing of the fugitive so as to frustrate the flight, they fired – omitting as a first stage the prescribed aimed individual shots – in short bursts of continuous fire. They knew that this increased the probability of a hit, even if not in the area aimed at, and with that also the risk of a fatal shot.'

Die Angeklagten waren vor dem Antritt ihres Dienstes an der Grenze gefragt worden, ob sie bereit seien, gegen 'Grenzbrecher' die Waffe einzusetzen; sie hatten die Frage ohne innere Vorbehalte bejaht. Die §§ 26, 27 des Grenzgesetzes vom 25. März 1982 (GB1 DDR I 197) waren bei ihrer Ausbildung erörtert worden. Nach § 27 Abs. 2 Satz 1 dieses Gesetzes war die Anwendung der Schußwaffe 'gerechtfertigt, um die unmittelbar bevorstehende Ausführung oder die Fortsetzung einer Straftat zu verhindern, die sich den Umständen nach als ein Verbrechen darstellt'. Die Jugendkammer hat als wahr unterstellt, daß Verstöße gegen § 213 StGB-DDR ('Ungesetzlicher Grenzübertritt') mit unmittelbarem Kontakt zur Berliner Mauer zur Tatzeit in den meisten Fällen nach § 213 Abs. 3 StGB-DDR als Verbrechen gewertet und mit mehr als zwei Jahren Freiheitsstrafe bestraft wurden; der Tatrichter hält es für möglich, daß bei der Schulung der Angeklagten die Vorschrift des § 213 StGB-DDR, deren Grundtatbestand ein Vergehen war, ohne Differenzierung nach der Tatschwere besprochen, also der Fluchtversuch an der Mauer generell als Verbrechen dargestellt worden ist.

Zur Befehlslage heißt es in den Urteilsgründen: 'Die auch für die Angeklagten maßgebliche, von ihnen so verstandene und akzeptierte Befehlslage ging dahin, auf jeden Fall und letztlich mit allen Mitteln zu verhindern, daß der Flüchtende "feindliches Territorium" (hier: Berlin-West) erreichte. Dementsprechend lautete eine der bei der 'Vergatterung' auch gegenüber den Angeklagten verwendeten Formulierungen in ihrem Kernsatz: "Grenzdurchbrüche sind auf keinen Fall zuzulassen. Grenzverletzer sind zu stellen oder zu vernichten" ... Vor jedem Ausrücken zum Grenzdienst erfolgte die Vergatterung; durch sie wurde den Grenzposten noch einmal der konkrete Einsatz und in allgemeiner Form die gestellte Aufgabe bewußt gemach.' Die in der Shulung behandelte Befehlslage sah folgendes Handlungsschema vor, wobei jeweils zur nächsten Handlungsstufe überzugehen war, wenn die vorherige keinen Erfolg zeigte oder sich von vornherein als nicht erfolgversprechend darstellte: Anrufen des Flüchtenden – Versuch des Postens, den Flüchtenden zu Fuß zu erreichen - Warnschuß – gezieltes Einzelfeuer, falls erforderlich mehrmals, auf die Beine – 'Weiterschießen, egal wie, notfalls auch erschießen, bis die Flucht verhindert ist'. Als Faustregel galt: 'Besser der Flüchtling ist tot, als daß die Flucht gelingt.'

The defendants were asked before the start of their service at the border whether they were prepared to use weapons against 'border violators'; they answered the question in the affirmative without inward reservations. §§ 26 and 27 of the Border Act of 25 March 1982 (GBl DDR I 197) had been discussed during their training. According to § 27 para 2 sentence 1 of this Act, the use of the gun was 'justified in order to prevent the immediately impending execution or continuation of a punishable act, which in the circumstances presents itself as a crime'. The Young Persons Chamber accepted as true that contraventions of § 213 of the StGB-DDR ('unlawful crossing of the border') in direct contact with the Berlin wall at the time of the act were in most cases assessed to be a crime in accordance with § 213 para 3 of the StGB-DDR and were punished with more than two years imprisonment; the judge of fact considers it to be possible that in the training of the defendants the provisions of § 213 of the StGB-DDR, whose basic elements constituted an offence, were discussed without differentiating according to the seriousness of the act and therefore the attempted flight at the wall was generally described as a crime.

As to the total context of the command, it says in the reasons for the judgment: 'The total context of the command which was authoritative for the defendants as well and was so understood and accepted by them, was to the effect that the reaching of "enemy territory" (here: West Berlin) by the fugitive was to be prevented in every case and, in the end, by all methods. Accordingly one of the formulations used, to the defendants as well, at the "gatherings",[2] stated in its key sentence: 'Border escapes are not to be permitted in any case. "Border violators are to be arrested or destroyed"... Before every move out to border service, the "gathering" took place; by it, once again, the specific action and, in general form, the duty imposed were made known to the border guards.' The total context of the command, as dealt with in training, provided for the following scheme of action, under which at any time the next action stage was to be proceeded to if the previous one showed no result or showed itself from the outset not to promise results: calling to the fugitive – attempt by the guard to reach the fugitive on foot – warning shot – aimed single shots, several times if necessary, at the legs– 'further shooting, no matter how, if necessary also shooting to kill, until the flight has been prevented'. The rule of thumb was: 'Better that the fugitive should be dead than that the flight should succeed.'

---

2 This expression implies a 'pep-talk' or indoctrination session.

Die Jugendkammer nimmt an, daß die Angeklagten mit bedingtem Vorsatz einen gemeinschaftlichen Totschlag begangen haben. Sie wendet die §§ 212, 213 StGB als das gegenüber dem Strafrecht der DDR mildere Recht an (Art. 315 Abs. 1 EGStGB i.V.m. § 2 Abs. 3 StGB). Nach ihrer Ansicht war zwar das durch § 27 des Grenzgesetzes i.V.m. § 213 Abs. 3 StGB-DDR bestimmte Grenzregime an der Demarkationslinie mit den völkerrechtlichen Verpflichtungen der DDR und mit dem ordre public der Bundesrepublik Deutschland unvereinbar. Daraus folgt aber nach Auffassung der Jugendkammer nicht, daß zum Nachteil der Angeklagten der im Recht der DDR vorgesehene Rechtfertigungsgrund außer Betracht bleiben kann. Die Jugendkammer beruft sich insoweit auf Artikel 103 Abs. 2 GG sowie auf den Gesichtspunkt der Rechtssicherheit; die Rechtssicherheit habe hier Vorrang, weil ein Extremfall, wie er etwa in BGHSt 2, 234 zur Entscheidung stand, nicht vorgelegen habe.

Die Jugendkammer führt jedoch weiter aus: Auch wenn hiernach ein Rechtfertigungsgrund nach dem Recht der DDR in Betracht komme, so sei er gleichwohl wegen der besonderen Umstände der Tat auf die Schüsse der Angeklagten nicht anwendbar. Wie sich aus der Systematik der §§ 26, 27 des Grenzgesetzes ergebe, seien diese Vorschriften, ebenso wie die Bestimmungen des UZwG über den Schußwaffengebrauch, am Prinzip der Verhältnismäßigkeit orientiert; § 27 Abs. 1 Satz 1 bezeichne die Anwendung der Schußwaffe als 'die äußerste Maßnahme der Gewaltanwendung'. Eine den Gesichtspunkt der Verhältnismäßigkeit beachtende Auslegung des Rechtfertigungsgrundes ergebe hier, daß das von den Angeklagten abgegebene Dauerfeuer nicht durch § 27 des Grenzgesetzes gedeckt, sondern nur Einzelfeuer gestattet gewesen sei; dafür spreche auch die Regelung des § 27 Abs. 5 des Grenzgesetzes, nach der Menschenleben nach Möglichkeit zu schonen sei. Zwar hätten die Angeklagten auf die Beine gezielt. Ihnen sei aber bewußt gewesen, daß bei einem Dauerfeuer mit kurzen Feuerstößen die Waffe nach dem ersten Schuß 'auswandere'.

Das Verhalten der Angeklagten ist nach Ansicht des Landgerichts nicht durch dienstlichen Befehl (§ 5 WStG; § 258 StGB-DDR) entschuldigt gewesen. Befohlen sei in der Tatsituation Einzelfeuer auf die Beine gewesen; die Angeklagten seien in vorauseilendem Gehorsam über diesen Befehl hinausgegangen, um durch Dauerfeuer die Chance, den Flüchtling zu treffen und damit an der Überschreitung der Grenze zu hindern, zu erhöhen. 'Daß die Angeklagten dabei geglaubt haben, dieses Vorgehen sei durch den Befehl, den Grenzverletzer in jedem Fall zu stellen, ihn als letztes Mittel sogar zu vernichten (=töten), gedeckt, vermag sie nicht zu entlasten, denn die Ausführung des Befehls, einen Flüchtling notfalls zu erschießen ... verstieß offensichtlich gegen das Strafgesetz, nämlich das Tötungsverbot der §§ 112, 113 StGB-DDR'. Das Mißverhältnis des wirtschaftlichen und politischen Interesses der DDR an der Verhinderung einer unkontrollierten Ausreise ihrer Bürger zu dem Rechtsgut des Lebens sei offensichtlich gewesen; Rechtsblindheit werde auch durch § 258 StGB-DDR nicht privilegiert. Deswegen sei ein Verbotsirrtum (§ 17 StGB) vermeidbar gewesen.

The Young Persons Chamber accepts that the defendants committed joint homicide with a conditional intention. It applies §§ 212 and 213 of the StGB as the more lenient law as against the criminal law of the DDR (Art 315 para 1 of the EGStGB in association with § 2 para 3 of the StGB). According to their view, the border regime determined by § 27 of the Border Act in association with § 213 para 3 of the StGB-DDR on the demarcation line was not reconcilable with the international law duties of the DDR and with the public order of the Federal Republic of Germany. It does not however follow from this according to the view of the Young Persons Chamber that the ground of justification provided for in the law of the DDR can remain out of consideration to the disadvantage of the defendants. The Young Persons Chamber refers in this respect to Art 103 para 2 of the GG as well as to the viewpoint of legal certainty; legal certainty would have priority here, because an extreme case, such as perhaps arose for decision in BGHSt 2, 234, would not have been present.

The Young Persons Chamber however further states: even if a ground of justification under the law of the DDR comes into consideration in accordance with the above, it would nevertheless not be applicable to the shots of the defendants because of the special circumstances of the act. As follows from the layout of §§ 26 and 27 of the Border Act, these provisions, like the provisions of the UZwG about the use of firearms, are orientated by the principle of proportionality; § 27 para 1 sentence 1 describes the use of firearms as 'the most extreme measure of the application of force'. An interpretation of the ground of justification which has regard to the viewpoint of proportionality would result here in the continuous fire given by the defendants not being covered by § 27 of the Border Act and only the single shots having been permitted; the requirement of § 27 para 5 of the Border Act that human life is to be spared if possible also argues in favour of this. Admittedly the defendants aimed at the legs. They were however aware that with continuous fire in short bursts, the weapon 'wanders' after the first shot.

The conduct of the defendants was not, according to the view of the State Court, excused by official command (§ 5 WStG; § 258 StGB-DDR). Single shots at the legs were prescribed in this factual situation; the defendants in their haste for obedience, went beyond this command, so as to increase the chance, by continuous fire, of hitting the fugitive and therefore preventing the crossing of the border. 'The fact that the defendants at the same time believed that this procedure was covered by the command to arrest the border violator in every case and even, as a final method, to destroy (ie, kill) him cannot exonerate them, because the carrying out of the command to shoot a fugitive dead if necessary ... obviously violates the criminal law, namely the prohibition on homicide in § 112 and 113 of the StGB-DDR.' The disproportionate relationship of the economic and politic interest of the DDR in the prevention of the uncontrolled emigration of its citizens as compared with the legal value of life was obvious; ignorance of the law was also, by § 258 of the StGB-DDR, not privileged. Therefore an error of law (§ 17 of the StGB) was avoidable.

Die Jugendkammer hat bei der Strafbemessung, auch hinsichtlich des Angeklagten W., angenommen, daß die Voraussetzungen des § 213 StGB (minder schwerer Fall des Totschlages) vorlägen.

B Die Revision des Angeklagten W. beanstandet, das Landgericht habe gegen ein 'Bestrafungsverbot' verstoßen, das aus der 'act of State doctrine' herzuleiten sei; der Angeklagte habe nämlich als Funktionsträger, im Auftrag und im Interesse eines anderen Staates, der DDR, gehandelt und dürfe deswegen nicht zur Verantwortung gezogen werden. Damit soll ersichtlich ein Verfahrenshindernis geltend gemacht werden. Es besteht nicht.

I Die in Staaten des angelsächsischen Rechtskreises in unterschiedlicher Weise formulierte 'act of State doctrine' ist keine allgemeine Regel des Völkerrechts im Sinne des Art. 25 GG. Sie betrifft vielmehr die Auslegung innerstaatlichen Rechts, nämlich die Frage, ob und in welchem Maße von der Wirksamkeit der Akte fremder Staaten auszugehen ist (Ipsen, Völkerrecht, 3. Aufl., S. 335, 619; Verdross/Simma, Universelles Völlkerrecht, 3. Aufl., S. 775; Dahm/Delbrück/Wolfrum, Völkerrecht, 2. Aufl., S. 487; Kimminich, Völkerrecht, 4. Aufl., S. 316). Die kontinentaleuropäische, auch die deutsche, Rechtspraxis greift auf diese Doktrin nicht zurück (Dahm/Delbruck/Wolfrum aaO S. 490f.). Hier gibt es keine verbindliche Regel, daß die Wirksamkeit ausländischer Hoheitsakte bei der Anwendung innerstaatlichen Rechtes der gerichtlichen Nachprüfung entzogen sei (vgl. für den Bereich des Strafrechts insbesondere M. Herdegen ZaöRV 47 (1987), 221ff.). Im Einigungsvertrag ist nicht vereinbart worden, daß Akte, die der Staatstätigkeit der DDR zuzuordnen sind, der Nachprüfung durch Gerichte der Bundesrepublik Deutschland entzogen sein sollen. Das Gegenteil trifft zu: In den Artikeln 18 und 19 des Einigungsvertrags ist bestimmt, daß Entscheidungen der Gerichte und der Verwaltung der DDR zwar grundsätzlich wirksam bleiben, jedoch aufgehoben werden können, wenn sie mit rechtsstaatlichen Grundsätzen nicht zu vereinbaren sind (vgl. auch die Anlage I zum Einigungsvertrag Kapitel III Sachgebiet A Abschnitt III Nr. 14 d).

II Möglicherweise meint die Revision mit ihrem Einwand, Gerichte der Bundesrepublik Deutschland dürften mit Rücksicht auf die Immunität fremder Staaten und ihrer Repräsentanten keine Gerichtsbarkeit ausüben; die Revision beruft sich auf eine zu Immunitätsfragen ergangene Entscheidung des VI. Zivilsenats des Bundesgerichtshofs (NJW 1979, 1101) sowie auf die Entscheidung BGHSt 33, 97, mit der dem Staatsratsvorsitzenden der DDR im Jahre 1984 Immunität zuerkannt worden ist, wie sie einem Staatsoberhaupt zukommt. Die Angeklagten sind schon deswegen nicht als Repräsentanten eines fremden Staates zu behandeln, weil die Deutsche Demokratische Republik nicht mehr besteht.

C Die sachlichrechtliche Nachprüfung ergibt, daß die Revisionen der Angeklagten im Ergebnis unbegründet sind.

The Young Persons Chamber accepted in the assessment of punishment, in relation to the defendant W as well, that the prerequisites of § 213 of the StGB (less serious case of manslaughter) were present.

B The appeal in law of the defendant W raises the objection that the State Court violated a 'prohibition on punishment' which is to be derived from the 'act of State doctrine'; the defendant had namely acted as an office holder on behalf of and in the interest of another State, the DDR, and therefore could not be held responsible. An obstacle to the proceedings was obviously thereby being claimed. It fails.

I The 'act of State doctrine',[3] formulated in different ways in States in the Anglo-Saxon legal circle is not a general rule of international law in the sense of Art 25 of the GG. Rather does it affect the interpretation of internal national law, that is to say the question of whether and in what degree one should proceed on the basis of the effectiveness of acts of foreign States (Ipsen, International Law, 3rd edn, pp 335, 619; Verdross/Simma, Universal International Law, 3rd edn, p 775; Dahm/ Delbrück/ Wolfrum, International Law, 2nd edn, p 487; Kimminich, International Law, 4th edn, p 316). The continental European and also the German legal practice does not refer to this doctrine (Dahm/Delbrück/Wolfrum, *loc cit*, p 490 and onwards). Here there is no binding rule that the effectiveness of foreign sovereign acts is withdrawn from judicial examination by the application of internal national law (compare, for the area of criminal law, in particular M. Herdegen ZaöRV 47 (1987), 221 and onwards). In the Unification Treaty it was not agreed that acts which are to be associated with the State activity of the DDR should be withdrawn from examination by the courts of the Federal Republic of Germany. The opposite is true: in Arts 18 and 19 of the Unification Treaty it is provided that decisions of the courts and of the administration of the DDR remain effective in principle but can be annulled if they are not reconcilable with the principles of a constitutional State (compare also Appendix I to the Unification Treaty, Chapter III, Subject Area A, Section III no 14 d).

II Possibly the appeal in law means by its objection that courts of the Federal Republic of Germany should not be permitted to exercise jurisdiction having regard to the immunity of foreign States and their representatives; the appeal in law refers to a decision of the VIth Civil Senate of the Federal Supreme Court (NJW 1979, 1101) made on questions of immunity, as well as to the decision BGHSt 33, 97 by which the President of the Council of State of the DDR was granted the immunity due to a head of State in the year 1984. The defendants are not on that account to be treated as representatives of a foreign State, because the DDR no longer exists.

C The factual and legal examination shows that the appeals in law of the defendants are, in their outcome, unfounded.

---

3 Examples of Act of State in English law are the cases of *Musgrave v Pulido* (1879) 5 App Cas 102; and *Buron v Denman* (1848) 2 Exch 167. Would the defence have been available in England in these circumstances?

I Die Angeklagten und das Tatopfer hatten zur Tatzeit ihre Lebensgrundlage in der DDR; dort ist das Opfer von den Schüssen der Angeklagten getroffen worden und gestorben. Das Landgericht hat Artikel 315 Abs. 1 EGStGB (idF des Einigungsvertrags Anl. I Kap III Sachgebiet C Abschn. II Nr. 1 b) angewandt und ermittelt, ob das Recht der Bundesrepublik Deutschland oder das Recht der DDR milder im Sinne des § 2 Abs. 3 StGB sei. Dieser Ausgangspunkt entspricht der ständigen Rechtsprechung des Bundesgerichtshofs (vgl. BGHSt 37, 320; 38, 1, 3; 38, 18; 38, 88; BGHR StGB § 2 Abs. 3 DDR-StGB 5).

Etwas anderes würde gelten, wenn die Tat schon vor dem 3. Oktober 1990 nach dem Recht der Bundesrepublik Deutschland zu beurteilen gewesen wäre (Art. 315 Abs. 4 EGStGB idF des Einigungsvertrags).

1 Der Senat hat die Frage geprüft, ob die in BGHSt 32, 293 im Jahre 1984 entwickelten Grundsätze mit dem Ergebnis anzuwenden sind, daß schon vor der Vereinigung Deutschlands Taten der hier in Rede stehenden Art nach dem Strafrecht der Bundesrepublik Deutschland zu beurteilen waren (vgl. Laufhütte in LK, 11. Aufl. vor § 80 Rdn. 35). Er hat die Frage verneint.

Der 3. Strafsenat hatte in der Entscheidung BGHSt 32, 293 im Anschluß an seine Entscheidung BGHSt 30, 1 ausgeführt, das Strafrecht der Bundesrepublik Deutschland gelte für eine in der damaligen DDR unter Einheimischen durch politische Verdächtigung bewirkte Freiheitsberaubung, und zwar aus folgenden Gründen: Zwar schütze das Strafrecht der Bundesrepublik Deutschland spätestens seit dem Grundlagenvertrag vom 21. Dezember 1972 (BGBl 1973 II, 421) nicht mehr alle in der DDR lebenden Deutschen in dem Sinne, daß die gegen sie auf dem Gebiet der DDR begangenen Taten ohne weiteres nach § 7 Abs. 1 StGB, mithin nach dem Strafrecht der Bundesrepublik Deutschland zu beurteilen seien. Etwas anderes gelte aber jedenfalls für Taten, in denen die mit politischer Verdächtigung oder Verschleppung verbundene Gefahr rechtsstaatswidriger Verfolgung in eine Verletzung, insbesondere in eine Freiheitsberaubung, übergehe; der in § 5 Nr. 6 StGB gewährte umfassende Schutz (BGHSt 30, 1) könne nach dem Zweck dieser Vorschrift nicht auf die Ahndung des Gefährdungstatbestands beschränkt bleiben (BGHSt 32, 293, 298).

Im vorliegenden Fall sind die Regeln des § 5 StGB nicht betroffen; eine Anknüpfung an die Vorschrift des § 5 Nr. 6 StGB ist, anders als in den Fällen BGHSt 30, 1; 32, 293, nicht möglich. Den Schüssen an der Mauer war kein Gefährdungsdelikt vorausgegangen. S. ist zwar, ebenso wie die Opfer der in den §§ 234 a, 241 a StGB bezeichneten Straftaten, das Opfer eines Freiheitsrechte mißachtenden politischen Systems geworden. Dieser Gesichtspunkt ist für sich allein aber nicht bestimmt genug, um die gegen ihn begangene Tat im Hinblick auf das Rechtsanwendungsrecht (§§ 3 bis 7 StGB) hinreichend deutlich zu beschreiben und von anderen in der DDR begangenen Taten abzugrenzen, für die die Vorschrift des § 7 Abs. 1 StGB nicht galt.

I The lives of defendants and the victim were based in the DDR at the time of the deed; there the victim was hit by the defendants shots and died. The State Court applied Art 315 para 1 of the EGStGB (in the version contained in the Unification Treaty, App I Chapter III, Subject Area C, Section II no 1 b) and determined whether the law of the Federal Republic of Germany or the law of the DDR was more lenient in the sense of § 2 para 3 of the StGB. This starting point corresponds with the consistent case law of the Federal Supreme Court (compare BGHSt 37, 320; 38, 1, 3; 38, 18; 38, 88; BGHR StGB § 2 para 3 of the DDR-StGB 5).

The position would be different if the deed were to be judged before 3 October 1990 according to the law of the Federal Republic of Germany (Art 315 para 4 of the EGStGB in the version contained in the Unification Treaty).

1 The Senate examined the question of whether the principles developed in BGHSt 32, 293 in the year 1984 are to be applied with the result that even before the unification of Germany, deeds of the kind being spoken of here were to be judged in accordance with the criminal law of the Federal Republic of Germany (compare Laufhütte in LK, 11th edn, before § 80 marginal no 35). It answered the question in the negative.

The third Criminal Senate had explained in the decision BGHSt 32, 293 in connection with its decision BGHSt 30, 1 that the criminal law of the Federal Republic of Germany would apply to a deprivation of freedom in respect of natives in the former DDR brought about through political suspicion, and this was for the following reasons: the criminal law of the Federal Republic of Germany since the Fundamental Principles Treaty of 21 December 1972 (BGBl 1973 II, 421) at the latest no longer protects all Germans living in the DDR in the sense that the acts committed against them on the territory of the DDR are, simply for this reason, to be judged in accordance with § 7 para 1 of the StGB and therefore in accordance with the criminal law of the Federal Republic of Germany. The position would however be different for acts in which the danger of persecution contrary to the principle of a constitutional State and connected with political suspicion or deportation turns into a violation, especially a deprivation of freedom; the comprehensive protection granted in § 5 no 6 of the StGB (BGHSt 30, 1) could, in accordance with the purpose of this provision, not remain limited to punishment for the elements of the criminal offence of endangering.[4]

In the present case, the rules in § 5 of the StGB are not involved; a connection with the provisions of § 5 no 6 of the StGB is, in contrast to the cases BGHSt 30, 1; 32, 293, not possible. No criminal offence of endangering preceded the shots at the wall. S. became, just like the victims of the criminal acts described in §§ 234 a and 241 a of the StGB, the victim of a political system disregarding rights of freedom. This point of view is, however, not by itself definite enough in order to describe the act committed against him sufficiently clearly with regard to the law as to application of the law (§§ 3 to 7 of the StGB) and to differentiate it from other acts committed in the DDR for which the provisions of § 7 para 1 of the StGB did not apply.

---

4 Endangering can in some circumstances come within a certain category of criminal offences.

Hinzu kommt folgende Überlegung: Der Gesetzgeber hat ersichtlich den Meinungsstand hinsichtlich der Anwendung der §§ 3 bis 7 StGB auf DDR-Fälle, insbesondere die Rechtsprechung des Bundesgerichtshofs (BGHSt 30, 1; 32, 293), gekannt, als er mit der Neufassung des Artikels 315 EGStGB durch den Einigungsvertrag in das System des Rechtsanwendungsrechts eingriff. Würde die Rechtsprechung, die sich nur noch auf Taten bezieht, die vor dem Inkrafttreten des Einigungsvertrags begangen worden sind, im jetzigen Zeitpunkt wesentlich geändert, so erhielte die Neufassung des Art. 315 EGStGB einen Inhalt, mit dem der Gesetzgeber nicht gerechnet hat. Unter diesen Umständen ist der Anwendungsbereich des Artikels 315 Abs. 4 EGStGB nicht anders zu beurteilen, als es dem gesicherten Stand der bisherigen Rechtsprechung entspricht.

2 Aus den gleichen Gründen folgt der Senat nicht dem weitergehenden, in jüngster Zeit wieder aufgegriffenen Vorschlag, Deutsche, die ihren Lebensmittelpunkt in der DDR hatten, ausnahmslos als Deutsche im Sinne des § 7 Abs. 1 StGB aufzufassen (Küpper/Wilms ZRP 1992, 91; Bath Deutschland-Archiv 1990, 1733; im Ergebnis ähnlich Hruschka JZ 1992, 665; aus der Zeit vor 1989 vgl. Oehler JZ 1984, 948; Woesner ZRP 1976, 248 sowie OLG Düsseldorf NJW 1979, 59; 1983, 1277). Daß dem Einigungsvertrag diese Auslegung nicht zugrunde gelegen hat, ergibt sich schon aus der Beobachtung, daß für die Vorschrift des Artikel 315 Abs. 1 EGStGB nur ein sehr geringer Anwendungsbereich (Taten ohne individuelle Opfer sowie Taten gegen Ausländer) übrig bliebe, wenn alle Taten, die sich gegen DDR-Bürger richteten, unter Artikel 315 Abs. 4 EGStGB fielen; wie die Gesamtheit der in den Artikeln 315 bis 315 c EGStGB idF des Einigungsvertrags enthaltenen Regelungen zeigt, ist der Gesetzgeber aber ersichtlich davon ausgegangen, daß der Anwendungsbereich des – allerdings an § 2 Abs. 3 StGB zu messenden – DDR-Rechts breit sein werde.

II Das Recht der ehemaligen DDR wäre im Sinne des § 2 Abs. 3 StGB (i.V.m. Art. 315 Abs. 1 EGStGB idF des Einigungsvertrags) im Vergleich mit dem Recht der Bundesrepublik Deutschland das mildere Recht, wenn der abgeurteilte tödliche Schußwaffengebrauch nach dem Recht der DDR (§ 27 Abs. 2 des Grenzgesetzes i.V.m. § 213 Abs. 3 StGB-DDR) gerechtfertigt gewesen wäre und dieser Rechtfertigungsgrund auch heute zugunsten der Angeklagten beachtet werden müßte. Die Nachprüfung ergibt, daß die Angeklagten zwar – nach der zur Tatzeit in der DDR praktizierten Auslegung – den in § 27 Abs. 2 des Grenzgesetzes bezeichneten Anforderungen entsprochen haben, daß sich daraus jedoch kein wirksamer Rechtfertigungsgrund ergibt.

1 Die Grenztruppen der DDR hatten nach § 18 Abs. 2 des Grenzgesetzes vom 25. März 1982 (GBl DDR I 197) die 'Unverletzlichkeit' der Grenze zu 'gewährleisten'; als Verletzung galt u. a. das widerrechtliche Passieren der Grenze (§ 17 Satz 2 Buchst. b des Grenzgesetzes).

Besides this there is the following consideration: the legislator evidently knew the state of opinion in relation to the application of §§ 3 to 7 of the StGB to DDR cases, especially the case law of the Federal Supreme Court (BGHSt 30, 1; 32, 293) when he intervened by the Unification Treaty in the system of law as to the application of the law with the new form of Art 315 of the EGStGB. If the case law which only relates to acts which were committed before the coming into effect of the Unification Treaty were to be substantially changed at the present point in time, the new form of Art 315 of the EGStGB would be given a content with which the legislator did not reckon. Under these circumstances, the area of application of Art 315 para 4 of the EGStGB is not to be judged otherwise than as would correspond with the established position of the case law hitherto.

2 On the same grounds, the Senate does not follow the far-reaching proposition propounded again recently that Germans whose lives were centred in the DDR are to be understood without exception as being Germans in the sense § 7 para 1 of the StGB (Küpper/Wilms ZRP 1992, 91; Bath, Archives of Germany, 1990, 1773; JZ 1992, 665 – similar in its outcome; from the period before 1989, compare Oehler JZ 1984, 948; Woesner ZRP 1976, 248 as well as OLG Düsseldorf NJW 1979, 59; 1983, 1277). The fact that the Unification Treaty was not based on this interpretation follows from the observation that only a very small area of application (acts without individual victims, as well as acts against foreigners) is left for the provisions of Art 315 para 1 of the EGStGB if all acts which were directed against DDR citizens fell within Art 315 para 4 of the EGStGB; however, as the totality of the rules contained in Arts 315–315 c of the EGStGB in the form contained in the Unification Treaty shows, the legislator has evidently proceeded on the basis that the area of application of DDR law would be broad - certainly as measured by § 2 para 3 of the StGB.

II The law of the former DDR would, in the sense of § 2 para 3 of the StGB (in association with Art 315 para 1 of the EGStGB in the form contained in the Unification Treaty), be, in comparison with the law of the Federal Republic of Germany, the more lenient law if the fatal use of firearms which was the subject of the judgment had been justified in accordance with the law of the DDR (§ 27 para 2 of the Border Act in association with § 213 para 3 of the StGB-DDR), and this ground of justification had to be taken into consideration even today in favour of the defendants. The examination shows that the defendants – according to the interpretation employed in the DDR at the time of the act – complied with the requirements described in § 27 para 2 of the Border Act, but that no effective ground of justification follows from this.

1 The border troops of the DDR had, in accordance with § 18 para 2 of the Border Act of 25 March 1982 (GBl DDR I 197) to 'guarantee' the 'inviolability' of the border; the unlawful crossing of the border, amongst other things, counted as a violation (§ 17 sentence 2 letter b of the Border Act).

Nach § 27 Abs. 2 Satz 1 des Grenzgesetzes war die Anwendung der Schußwaffe 'gerechtfertigt, um die unmittelbar bevorstehende Ausführung oder die Fortsetzung einer Straftat zu verhindern, die sich den Umständen nach als ein Verbrechen darstellt'. In § 27 Abs. 5 Satz 1 des Gesetzes hieß es, das Leben von Personen sei bei der Anwedung der Schußwaffe 'nach Möglichkeit zu schonen'. Als Verbrechen wurden nach § 1 Abs. 3 Satz 2 StGB-DDR u. a. 'gesellschaftsgefährliche' Straftaten gegen 'Rechte und Interessen der Gesellschaft' verstanden, die eine 'schwerwiegende Mißachtung der sozialistischen Gesetzlichkeit darstellen und ... für die innerhalb des vorgesehenen Strafrahmens im Einzelfall eine Freiheitsstrafe von über zwei Jahren ausgesprochen wird'. Mit einer solchen Strafe, nämlich mit Freiheitsstrafe von einem Jahr bis zu acht Jahren, war der ungesetzliche Grenzübertritt in schweren Fällen bedroht (§ 213 Abs. 3 StGB-DDR idF des 3. StrÄndG vom 28. Juni 1979, GBl DDR I 139). Ein schwerer Fall lag nach § 213 Abs. 3 Satz 2 Nr. 2 StGB-DDR 'insbesondere' vor, wenn die Tat mit 'gefährlichen Mitteln oder Methoden' durchgeführt wurde. Daß die Praxis der DDR zur Tatzeit die 'Republikflucht' mit unmittelbarem Grenzkontakt in den meisten Fällen als Verbrechen wertete und mit Freiheitsstrafen von mehr als zwei Jahren ahndete, hat der Tatrichter unterstellt. Dem entspricht es, daß das Oberste Gericht der DDR und der Generalstaatsanwalt der DDR am 15. Januar 1988 in ihrem 'Gemeinsamen Standpunkt zur Anwendung des § 213 StGB' ausgeführt haben, eine gefährliche Methode im Sinne des § 213 Abs. 3 Satz 2 Nr. 2 StGB sei u. a. das Benutzen von 'Steighilfen zur Überwindung von Grenzsicherungsanlagen' (OG-Informationen 2/1988 S. 9, 14); bereits am 17. Oktober 1980 war ein 'Gemeinsamer Standpunkt' des Obersten Gerichtes und des Generalstaatsanwalts mit entsprechendem Inhalt formuliert worden (OG-Informationen -Sonderdruck 1980 S. 3).

Nach dem vom Ministerium der Justiz und der Akademie für Staats- und Rechtswissenschaft der DDR herausgegebenen Kommentar zum Strafgesetzbuch (Strafrecht der Deutschen Demokratischen Republik, 5. Aufl. 1987 – fortan als 'DDR-Kommentar' zitiert, § 213 Anm. 16) fiel das Verhalten des Tatopfers auch unter § 213 Abs. 3 Satz 2 Nr. 5 StGB-DDR: S. hatte bis zum Übersteigen der Hinterlandmauer gemeinschaftlich mit einem anderen gehandelt; dessen Rücktritt vom Versuch des unerlaubten Grenzübertritts bewirkte nicht, daß für S. die Voraussetzungen des § 213 Abs. 3 Satz 2 Nr. 5 StGB-DDR (Begehung der Tat 'zusammen mit anderen') wegfielen (DDR-Kommentar aaO).

2 Entgegen der Auffassung der Judendkammer kommt eine Auslegung dieser Vorschriften in dem Sinne in Betracht, daß das Verhalten der Angeklagten von ihnen gedeckt war.

According to § 27 para 2 sentence 1 of the Border Act the use of firearms was 'justified, in order to prevent the immediately impending carrying out or continuation of a criminal act, which according to the circumstances presents itself as a crime'. In § 27 para 5 sentence 1 of the Act, it says that on the use of firearms lives of persons are 'to be spared as far as possible'. According to § 1 para 3 sentence 2 of the StGB DDR, amongst other things, criminal acts 'dangerous to society' against 'rights and interests of society' which 'represent a grave disregard of socialist legality and ... for which, within the penal framework provided for, a sentence of imprisonment of over two years is imposed in the individual case' were to be understood as crimes. The unlawful crossing of the border was, in serious cases, threatened with such a penalty, namely a sentence of imprisonment of from one year to eight years (§ 213 para 3 of the StGB-DDR in the form contained in the third StrÄndG of 28 June 1979, GBl DDR I 139). A serious case in accordance with § 213 para 3 sentence 2 no 2 of the StGB-DDR existed 'in particular' if the act was carried out by 'dangerous means or methods'. The judge of fact assumed that the practice of the DDR at the time of the act regarded 'flight to the Republic' in direct contact with the border in most cases as a crime and punished it with sentences of imprisonment of more than two years. It corresponds with this that the Upper Court of the DDR and the general public prosecutor of the DDR on 15 January 1988 stated in their 'Common Standpoint on the Application of § 213 of the StGB' that a dangerous method in the sense of § 213 para 3 sentence 2 no 2 of the StGB included, amongst other things, the use of 'climbing aids for surmounting the border security installations' (OG Information 2/1988 pp 9 and 14); a 'Common Standpoint' of the Upper Court and the general public prosecutor with corresponding content had been formulated as early as 17 October 1980 (OG Information – Separate Impression, 1980, p 3).

According to the commentary on the Criminal Code published by the Ministry of Justice and the Academy for Political and Legal Science of the DDR (*Criminal Law of the German Democratic Republic*, 5th edn, 1987 – from now on referred to as the 'DDR Commentary' – § 213 note 16), the conduct of the victim also fell within § 213 para 3 sentence 2 no 5 of the StGB-DDR: S. had acted jointly with another up to the climbing of the first border wall; his retreat from the attempted unlawful crossing of the border did not have the effect for S. of causing the prerequisites of § 213 para 3 sentence 2 no 5 of the StGB DDR (commission of the act 'together with others') to cease to apply (DDR Commentary, *loc cit*).

2 Contrary to the view of the Young Persons Chamber, consideration should be given to interpreting these provisions as meaning that the conduct of the defendants was covered by them.

(a) Der Wortsinn des § 27 des Grenzgesetzes läßt eine solche Auslegung zu: Der Grenzübertritt, der in Anwendung des § 213 Abs. 3 StGB-DDR als Verbrechen angesehen wurde, sollte, sofern er unmittelbar bevorstand, durch Anwendung der Schußwaffe 'verhindert' werden (§ 27 Abs. 2 Satz 1 des Grenzgesetzes). Zwar bezeichnete das Gesetz die Anwendung der Schußwaffe als 'äußerste Maßnahme' (§ 27 Abs. 1 Satz 1 des Grenzgesetzes); andere Mittel, den Grenzübertritt zu verhindern, standen den Angeklagten aber nicht zur Verfügung. Nach § 27 Abs. 5 des Grenzgesetzes war das Leben anderer 'nach Möglichkeit', also nicht in jedem Falle zu schonen. Hiernach läßt der Wortlaut des Gesetzes die Auslegung zu, daß auch mit (jedenfalls bedingtem) Tötungsvorsatz geschossen werden durfte, wenn das Ziel, Grenzverletzungen zu verhindern, nicht auf andere Weise erreicht werden konnte.

Voraussetzung für diese Auslegung des § 27 des Grenzgesetzes ist allerdings, daß das Ziel, Grenzverletzungen zu verhindern, im Konfliktfalle Vorrang vor der Schonung menschlichen Lebens hatte. Wie die Abwägung zwischen dem Leben des Flüchtlings und der 'Unverletzlichkeit der Staatsgrenze' auszufallen hatte, war aus dem Gesetz nicht abzulesen. Rechtsprechung von Gerichten der DDR ist zu dieser Frage nicht veröffentlicht worden. Äußerungen im Schrifttum der DDR zum Schußwaffengebrauch an der Grenze beschränken sich auf die Darlegung, daß die Bestimmungen über den Schußwaffengebrauch den westdeutschen Vorschriften entsprächen (Kaul/Graefrath NJ 1964, 272, 273) und im Einklang mit dem Völkerrecht dem Schutz der nationalen Sicherheit und öffentlichen Ordnung dienten (Buchholz/Wieland NJ 1977, 22, 26); diese Äußerungen stammen aus der Zeit vor dem Inkrafttreten des Grenzgesetzes. Unter diesen Umständen sind die vom Tatrichter festgestellte Befehlslage und die – ebenfalls auf vorgegebenen Befehlen beruhenden – Begleitumstände des Tatgeschehens heranzuziehen, um zu ermitteln, wie die Vorschrift des § 27 des Grenzgesetzes zur Tatzeit von den für ihre Anwendung und Auslegung Verantwortlichen verstanden worden ist.

(a) The literal meaning of § 27 of the Border Act permits such an interpretation: the crossing of the border which, by application of § 213 para 3 of the StGB-DDR was regarded as a crime, should, so far as it was directly imminent, be 'prevented' by the use of firearms (§ 27 para 2 sentence 1 of the Border Act). The Act certainly described the use of firearms as the 'ultimate measure' (§ 27, para 1 sentence 1 of the Border Act); other means of preventing the crossing of the border were however not available for the defendants. According to § 27 para 5 of the Border Act, the lives of others were to be spared 'as far as possible', and therefore not in every case. According to this, the literal meaning of the Act permits the interpretation that it was permissible to fire, even with the intention (conditional,[5] however) of killing if the objective of preventing border violations could not be attained in another way.

The prerequisite for this interpretation of § 27 of the Border Act is, of course, that the objective of preventing border violations had priority over the sparing of human life in case of conflict. How the balancing of the life of the fugitive with the 'inviolability of the State border' was to turn out could not be gathered from the Act. Case law of courts of the DDR on this question has not been published. Remarks in the literature of the DDR on the use of firearms at the border limit themselves to the statement that rules on the use of firearms corresponded to the West German provisions (Kaul/Graefrath NJ 1964, 272, 273) and, in harmony with international law, served the protection of national security and public order (Buchholz/Wieland NJ 1977, 22, 26); these remarks originate from the time before the Border Act came into effect. Under these circumstances, the total context of the command established by the judge of fact and the circumstances – likewise based on alleged commands – surrounding the occurrence of the act are to be referred to in order to ascertain how the provisions of § 27 of the Border Act was understood by those responsible for its application and interpretation at the time of the act.

---

5 Conditional intention means the perpetrator foresaw that his action might fit the elements of a crime, and approved of this; or foresaw it as a serious possibility and accepted it.

Compare this, and the shootings at the Berlin Wall case itself, with *R v Desmond, Barrett and Others, The Times,* 28 April 1868. This concerned an attempt by the defendant to free two Irish Fenians who were in prison. He blew up the wall near where he (incorrectly) thought they would be exercising. Several people living nearby were killed. Since he was considered to have foreseen the death or serious injury of these persons, he was convicted of their murder.

In some cases, conditional intention will not suffice for a crime: for instance, the use of the words 'contrary to his better knowledge' as in the offence of Calumny: § 187 of the StGB.

(aa) Die Befehlslage schloß – so das angefochtene Urteil - 'zur Vereitelung der Flucht auch die bewußte Tötung des Flüchtenden' ein, falls mildere Mittel zur Fluchtverhinderung nicht ausreichten. Daß der Flüchtende den Westteil von Berlin erreichte, war danach 'auf jeden Fall und letztlich mit allen Mitteln zu verhindern'. In der regelmäßig wiederkehrenden Vergatterung war nach den Feststellungen der 'Kernsatz' enthalten: 'Grenzdurchbrüche sind auf keinen Fall zuzulassen. Grenzverletzer sind zu stellen oder zu vernichten'. Bei der Schulung der Grenzsoldaten galt als Faustregel: 'Besser der Flüchtling ist tot, als daß die Flucht gelingt.' Das Interesse, die Flucht zu verhindern, hatte hiernach Vorrang vor dem Leben des Flüchtlings. Eine gelungene Flucht war 'das Schlimmste, was der Kompanie passieren konnte, da sie der ihr gestellten Aufgabe nicht gerecht geworden wäre'. Die Erschießung eines Flüchtlings an der Mauer hatte dagegen 'keine negativen Konsequenzen'; sie hat nie zu einem Verfahren gegen den Schützen geführt. Vielmehr wurde der Posten, der eine Flucht, wie auch immer, verhindert hatte, ausgezeichnet und belohnt. Der Tatrichter hat keinerlei Anhaltspunkte dafür gefunden, daß Gerichte, Staatsanwaltschaften oder andere staatliche Instanzen der DDR jemals beanstandet hätten, der durch die Befehlslage bezeichnete Schußwaffengebrauch überschreite die in § 27 des Grenzgesetzes gesteckten Grenzen.

(bb) Daß der Schutz des Lebens von 'Grenzverletzern' hinter andere Ziele, auch das Ziel der Geheimhaltung schwerer Verletzungen, zurücktrat, zeigen auch die folgenden Feststellungen des Tatrichters:

(aa) The total context of the command included – according to the contested judgment – 'even the deliberate killing of the fugitive in order to frustrate the flight' if less severe means did not suffice for the prevention of the flight. The reaching by the fugitive of the western sector of Berlin was accordingly 'to be prevented in every case and in the end by all means'. In the regularly recurring 'gathering' the 'key sentence' was, according to the findings, included: 'Border escapes are not to be permitted in any case. Border violators are to be arrested or destroyed.' In the training of border soldiers, the following counted as a rule of thumb: 'Better that the fugitive should be dead than that the flight should succeed.' The interest in prevention of the flight accordingly had priority over the life of fugitive. A successful flight was 'the worst thing that could happen for the company as it would not be consistent with the duty placed upon it'. On the other hand, the fatal shooting of a fugitive at the wall had 'no negative consequences'; it never led to proceedings against the marksman. Instead, the guard who had, in whatever way, prevented a flight would be treated with distinction and rewarded. The judge of fact found no basis for saying that courts, public prosecutors' offices or other State authorities of the DDR had ever objected that the use of firearms described in the total context of the command exceeded the boundaries laid down in § 27 of the Border Act.

(bb) The fact that the protection of the life of 'border violators' receded behind other objectives, even the objective of keeping serious injuries secret, is also shown by the following findings of the judge of fact:

Obwohl § 27 Abs. 5 des Grenzgesetzes vorschrieb, das Leben von Personen nach Möglichkeit zu schonen und unter Beachtung der notwendigen Sicherheitsmaßnahmen Erste Hilfe zu gewähren, hat keiner der nach den Schüssen der Angeklagten hinzugekommenen Angehörigen der Grenztruppen und anderer Einheiten S. geholfen, obwohl dieser mehrfach darum bat. Der Verletzte wurde zu einem Turm 'geschleift' und dort an einer vom Westen nicht einsehbaren Stelle 'abgelegt'. S. ist nicht mit dem gewöhnlichen Krankenwagen der 'Schnellen medizinischen Hilfe', sondern mit einem Sanitätswagen des Regiments, der zunächst 45 Minuten für die Anfahrt benötigt hatte, abtransportiert worden, und zwar nicht zum nächstgelegenen Krankenhaus, sondern zu dem entfernteren Krankenhaus der Volkspolizei, wo er mehr als zwei Stunden nach den Verletzungen eingeliefert wurde. In dem Sanitätswagen war kein Arzt, weil bei der Anforderung des Wagens nicht mitgeteilt werden durfte, daß jemand schwer verletzt worden war. Bei schneller ärztlicher Hilfeleistung hätte S. gerettet werden können. Die genannten Maßnahmen, die eine erhebliche Verzögerung bewirkten, entsprachen der Befehlslage, die vorrangig nicht an der Lebensrettung, sondern an dem Interesse orientiert war, daß der Vorfall auf beiden Seiten der Grenze unerkannt blieb; möglicherweise galt diese Geheimhaltung als 'notwendige Sicherheitsmaßnahme' im Sinne des § 27 Abs. 5 Satz 2 des Grenzgesetzes. Dem Vorrang der Geheimhaltung vor der Lebensrettung entsprach es, daß die Sanitäter die Fahrt nicht ihrem Regimentsarzt melden durften, daß der Zugführer unterschreiben mußte, der Nachtdienst sei ohne besondere Vorkommnisse verlaufen, und daß der Name des Opfers im Eingangsbuch des Krankenhauses sowie auf dem Totenschein nicht genannt wurde; auch wurde der Vater der Opfers erst am 4. Dezember 1984 vom Tod seines Sohnes unterrichtet.

Ein Hinweis auf die Bedeutung politischer Interessen ergibt sich auch daraus, daß der Befehl, an der Grenze zu schießen, anläßlich von Staatsbesuchen, Parteitagen und FDJ-Treffen auf Fälle der Notwehr, der Verwendung 'schwerer Technik' und der Fahnenflucht beschränkt wurde. Gleichzeitig wurde die Postendichte verstärkt.

Although § 27 para 5 of the Border Act directed that the lives of persons were to be spared as far as possible and they were to be given first aid subject to consideration of the necessary security measures, none of the members of the border troops and other units coming up after the shots of the defendants helped S although he asked for this several times. He was 'dragged' to a tower and 'put down' there in a place which was not visible from the West. S was not taken away by the usual ambulance of the 'Rapid Medical Aid', but by a regiment ambulance which first took 45 minutes to arrive, and not to the nearest hospital but to the more distant hospital of the Peoples Police, where he was delivered more than two hours after the injuries. There was no doctor in the ambulance, because on the requesting of the ambulance no communication was permitted to the effect that someone had been seriously injured. With rapid medical assistance, S could have been saved. The measures mentioned, which produced a substantial delay, corresponded to the total context of the command which was primarily orientated, not towards the saving of life, but towards the interest in ensuring that the incident remained unknown on both sides of the border; possibly this secrecy counted as a 'necessary security measure' in the sense of § 27 para 5 sentence 2 of the Border Act. It corresponded with the priority of secrecy over the saving of life that the medical orderlies were not permitted to notify their regimental doctor of the journey, that the section commander had to sign to say that the night duty had passed without any special occurrences and that the name of the victim was not mentioned in the admittance book for the hospital or on the death certificate; and also the father of the victim was only informed of the death of his son for the first time on 4 December 1984.

An indication of the importance of political interests also follows from the fact that the command to shoot at the border was, on the occasion of State visits, party conferences and meetings of the Free German Youth, restricted to cases of self-defence, the use of 'major equipment' and desertion. At the same time, the number of guards was increased.

(cc) Die genannten tatsächlichen Umstände ergeben in ihrer Gesamtheit, daß die Verhinderung des Grenzübertritts als überragendes Interesse aufgefaßt wurde, hinter das persönliche Rechtsgüter einschließlich des Lebens zurücktraten. Der Senat gelangt deswegen zu dem Ergebnis, daß nach der zur Tatzeit in der DDR geübten Staatspraxis die Anwendung von Dauerfeuer ohne vorgeschaltetes, auf die Beine gerichtetes Einzelfeuer nicht als rechtswidrig angesehen worden wäre. Denn die Angeklagten haben mit dem Dauerfeuer die Chance, die Flucht zu verhindern, freilich auch das Risiko eines tödlichen Treffers, erhöht und damit dem entsprochen, was ihnen im Einklang mit der herrschenden Auslegung des Grenzgesetzes als das wichtigste Ziel vermittelt wurde, nämlich die Verhinderung von Grenzübertritten. Sie hatten sich nach den genannten Beurteilungsmaßstäben allenfalls dann einer auf § 27 Abs. 5 Satz 1 des Grenzgesetzes gestützten Kritik ausgesetzt, wenn eine hohe Wahrscheinlichkeit dafür gesprochen hätte, daß das Einzelfeuer auf die Beine die Flucht zuverlässig verhindert hätte. Das liegt hier angesichts der zeitlichen Verhältnisse fern: S. befand sich, als die Angeklagten schossen, im zügigen Aufstieg auf der Leiter. Er hat fünf Sekunden bis zum Erreichen einer Höhe benötigt, aus der er an die Mauerkrone greifen konnte. Es muß angenommen werden, daß er zu diesem Zeitpunkt in der Lage war, innerhalb weniger Sekunden die Mauerkrone zu übersteigen und sich dadurch in Sicherheit zu bringen. Bei der Abgabe von Einzelfeuer betrug nach den Feststellungen der Mindestabstand zwischen zwei Schüssen 1,5 Sekunden; angesichts der Kürze der für die Fluchtverhinderung verbliebenen Zeit war hiernach die Chance, dieses Ziel zu erreichen, bei Dauerfeuer (mit einer Frequenz von 10 Schüssen je Sekunde) wesentlich höher. Im übrigen ist auch zu berücksichtigen, daß die Entfernung der Schützen von S. nicht unbeträchtlich war und daß sich die Ereignisse zur Nachtzeit zutrugen.

(dd) Hiernach entsprach das Verhalten der Angeklagten der rechtfertigenden Vorschrift des § 27 Abs. 2 des Grenzgesetzes so wie sie in der Staatspraxis angewandt wurde. Diese Staatspraxis ist durch den Vorrang der Fluchtverhinderung von dem Lebensschutz gekennzeichnet; die zur Rechtskontrolle berufenen Gerichte und Behörden der DDR haben dieser Staatspraxis nicht widersprochen. Sofern man das darin zum Ausdruck gekommene Verständnis des § 27 Abs. 2 des Grenzgesetzes zugrunde legt, waren die mit bedingtem Vorsatz und Dauerfeuer abgegebenen Schüsse der Angeklagten gerechtfertigt.

(cc) All the factual circumstances mentioned show that the prevention of a crossing of the border was understood as an overriding interest, behind which personal legal interests, inclusive of that of life, receded. The Senate therefore reached the conclusion that, according to State practice in the DDR at the time of the act, the use of continuous fire without preliminary single shots directed at the legs had not been regarded as unlawful. This is because the defendants, by continuous fire, increased the chance of preventing the flight (although admittedly also the risk of a fatal shot) and thereby complied with what was, in harmony with the prevailing interpretation of the Border Act, conveyed to them as the most important objective, namely the prevention of crossings of the border. They would, according to the stated criteria for assessment, possibly have laid themselves open to criticism, supported by § 27 para 5 sentence 1 of the Border Act, if there was a high probability that single shots at the legs would have reliably prevented flight. That is certainly not the position here in view of the timing: S was, when the defendants fired, rapidly climbing the ladder. He needed five seconds to reach a height from which he could grasp the top of the wall. It must be accepted that he was at this point in time in a position to climb over the top of the wall within a few seconds and thereby to bring himself into safety. On the firing of single shots, according to the findings, the least interval between two shots amounted to 1.5 seconds; in view of the shortness of the time remaining for prevention of the flight, the chance of attaining this objective was accordingly substantially higher with continuous fire (with a frequency of 10 shots per second). Incidentally, it must also be borne in mind that the distance of the marksmen from S was not inconsiderable and that the events took place at night.

(dd) Accordingly, the conduct of the defendants complied with the justification provisions of § 27 para 2 of the Border Act as they were applied in State practice. This State practice is characterised by the priority of prevention of flight over protection of life; the courts and authorities of the DDR which are competent to exercise legal control have not contradicted this State practice. Insofar as one takes as a basis the understanding of § 27 para 2 of the Border Act expressed in it, the shots of the defendants given with conditional intent and by continuous fire were justified.

In dieser Betrachtungsweise weicht der Senat von Vorgehen der Jugendkammer ab. Diese hat das Grenzgesetz wegen des von ihm erweckten 'Anscheins von Rechtsstaatlichkeit' nach rechtsstaatlichen Maßstäben, insbesondere im Lichte des Verhältnismäßigkeitsgrundsatzes ausgelegt; sie ist der Auffassung, daß staatliche Präventionszwecke niemals die vorsätzliche, auch nicht die bedingt vorsätzliche Tötung eines Menschen, der das Leben anderer nicht gefährdet, rechtfertigten, weil das Leben das höchste Rechtsgut sei. Nach Ansicht der Jugendkammer rechtfertigt § 27 Abs. 2 des Grenzgesetzes die (unbedingt oder bedingt) vorsätzliche Tötung auch dann nicht, wenn die in § 27 des Grenzgesetzes umschriebenen staatlichen Zwecke anders nicht zu erreichen wären. Diese Rechtsauffassung der Jugendkammer ist dem Grundgesetz und der Europäischen Menschenrechtskonvention verpflichtet. Sie wäre deshalb ein geeigneter Ausgangspunkt für die Auslegung des § 11 UZwG sowie des § 16 UZwGBw. Hier geht es indessen nicht um die Auslegung dieser Vorschriften, sondern im Hinblick auf § 2 Abs. 3 StGB um die Prüfung, ob als milderes Gesetz ein Rechtfertigungsgrund nach dem zur Tatzeit geltenden fremden Recht in Betracht kommt.

(b) Von der Frage, ob das Verhalten der Angeklagten nach dem Recht der DDR, wie es in der Staatpraxis angewandt wurde, gerechtfertigt war, ist die andere Frage zu unterscheiden, ob ein so verstandener Rechtfertigungsgrund (§ 27 Abs. 2 des Grenzgesetzes) wegen Verletzung vorgeordneter, auch von der DDR zu beachtender allgemeiner Rechtsprinzipien und wegen eines extremen Verstoßes gegen das Verhältnismäßigkeitsprinzip bei der Rechtsfindung außer Betracht bleiben muß, und zwar auch dann, wenn die Prüfung des fremden Rechtfertigungsgrundes im Rahmen des § 2 Abs. 3 StGB stattfindet. Der Senat bejaht diese Frage.

Der in § 27 Abs. 2 des Grenzgesetzes genannte Rechtfertigungsgrund, wie ihn die damalige Staatspraxis, vermittelt durch die Befehlslage, handhabe, hat, sofern der Grenzübertritt auf andere Weise nicht verhindert werden konnte, das (bedingt oder unbedingt) vorsätzliche Töten von Personen gedeckt, die nichts weiter wollten, als unbewaffnet und ohne Gefährdung allgemein anerkannter Rechtsgüter die Grenze zu überschreiten. Die Durchsetzung des Verbots, die Grenze ohne besondere Erlaubnis zu überschreiten, hatte hiernach Vorrang vor dem Lebensrecht von Menschen. Unter diesen besonderen Umständen ist der Rechtfertigungsgrund, wie er sich in der Staatspraxis darstellte, bei der Rechtsanwendung nicht zu beachten.

(aa) Allerdings müssen Fälle, in denen ein zur Tatzeit angenommener Rechtfertigungsgrund als unbeachtlich angesehen wird, auf extreme Ausnahmen beschränkt bleiben.

Daß ein Rechtfertigungsgrund gegen den ordre public der Bundesrepublik Deutschland (vgl. Art. 6 EGBGB) verstoßen hat, ist -entgegen Küpper/Wilms ZRP 1992, 91, 93 – für sich allein kein ausreichender Grund, ihm bei der Aburteilung einer unter dem früheren Recht begangenen Tat die Berücksichtigung zu versagen. Das Landgericht hat mit Recht auf die hohe Bedeutung der Rechtssicherheit hingewiesen. Sie spricht dafür, in den Fällen des § 2 Abs. 3 StGB bei der Ermittlung des milderen Rechtes grundsätzlich die Rechtfertigungsgründe des früheren Rechtes mit zu berücksichtigen.

In looking at the matter in this way, the Senate diverges from the proceedings of the Young Persons Chamber. The latter interpreted the Border Act, because of the 'appearance of constitutionality' suggested by it, in accordance with constitutional criteria, in particular in the light of the principle of proportionality; it was of the view that preventative objectives of the State never justified the intentional or even the conditionally intentional killing of a human being who does not endanger the life of others, because life is the highest legal interest. According to the view of the Young Persons Chamber § 27 para 2 of the Border Act does not even justify (unconditional or conditional) intentional killing if the State objectives described in § 27 of the Border Act could not otherwise be attained. The Young Persons Chamber is indebted to the Basic Law and the European Human Rights Convention for this view of the law. It was therefore an appropriate starting point for the interpretation of § 11 of the UZwG as well as of § 16 of the UZwGBw. Here, however, it is not a question of the interpretation of these provisions, but, having regard to § 2 para 3 of the StGB, of examining whether a ground of justification under the foreign law applicable at the time of the act is to be considered as a less severe statutory provision.

(b) One must distinguish from the question of whether the conduct of the defendants was justified by the law of the DDR as it was applied in State practice the other question of whether a ground of justification understood in this way (§ 27 para 2 of the Border Act) must be left out of consideration in the determining legal situation because it infringes pre-ordained general legal principles which should be observed in the DDR as well, and because of an extreme violation of the principle of proportionality, especially if the examination of the foreign ground of justification takes place within the framework of § 2 para 3 of the StGB. The Senate answers this question in the affirmative.

The ground of justification mentioned in § 27 para 2 of the Border Act as operated by the State practice of that time, communicated by the total context of the command, covered, insofar as the crossing of the border could not be prevented in another manner, the (conditionally or unconditionally) intentional killing of persons who did not want to do anything more than cross the border unarmed, and without endangering generally recognised legal interests. According to this, the enforcement of the prohibition against crossing the border without special permission had priority over the right of human beings to life. In these special circumstances, the ground of justification, as presented in State practice, is not to be taken into consideration in the application of the law.

(aa) Cases in which a ground of justification accepted at the time of the act is regarded as not appropriate for consideration must certainly remain limited to extreme exceptions.

The fact that a ground of justification offends against the public order of the Federal Republic of Germany (compare Art 6 of the EGBGB) is – contrary to the view of Küpper/Wilms ZRP 1992, 91, 93 – not on its own a sufficient ground to deny it consideration in passing judgment on an act committed under the earlier law. The State Court has correctly referred to the great importance of legal certainty. This argues in favour of in principle taking into account the grounds of justification in earlier law in determining which is the less severe law for cases under § 2 para 3 of the StGB.

(bb) Ein zur Tatzeit angenommener Rechtfertigungsgrund kann vielmehr nur dann wegen Verstoßes gegen höherrangiges Recht unbeachtet bleiben, wenn in ihm ein offensichtlich grober Verstoß gegen Grundgedanken der Gerechtigkeit und Menschlichkeit zum Ausdruck kommt; der Verstoß muß so schwer wiegen, daß er die allen Völkern gemeinsamen, auf Wert und Würde des Menschen bezogenen Rechtsüberzeugungen verletzt (BGHSt 2, 234, 239). Der Widerspruch des positiven Gesetzes zur Gerechtigkeit muß so unerträglich sein, daß das Gesetz als unrichtiges Recht der Gerechtigkeit zu weichen hat (Radbruch SJZ 1946, 105, 107). Mit diesen Formulierungen (vgl. auch BVerfGE 3, 225, 232; 6, 132, 198f.) ist nach dem Ende der nationalsozialistischen Gewaltherrschaft versucht worden, schwerste Rechtsverletzungen zu kennzeichnen. Die Übertragung dieser Gesichtspunkte auf den vorliegenden Fall ist nicht einfach, weil die Tötung von Menschen an der innerdeutschen Grenze nicht mit dem nationalsozialistischen Massenmord gleichgesetzt werden kann. Gleichwohl bleibt die damals gewonnene Einsicht gültig, daß bei der Beurteilung von Taten, die in staatlichem Auftrag begangen worden sind, darauf zu achten ist, ob der Staat die äußerste Grenze überschritten hat, die ihm nach allgemeiner Überzeugung in jedem Land gesetzt ist.

(bb) A ground of justification accepted at the time of the act can only remain out of consideration because of a violation of law with a higher priority if an obviously gross violation of basic concepts of justice and humanity is expressed in it; the violation must be so serious that it offends against convictions about law, which are common to all people, referring to the worth and dignity of the human being (BGHSt 2, 234, 239). The conflict of positive law with justice must be so intolerable that the statutory provision has, as false law, to give way to justice (Radbruch SJZ 1946, 105, 107). An attempt was made (compare also BVerfGE 3, 225, 232; 6, 132, 198 and onwards) after the end of the National Socialist despotism to characterise the most serious violations of law in this way. The transfer of these points of view to the present case is not simple, because the killing of human beings at the internal German frontier cannot be equated with national socialist mass murder. Nevertheless, the insight obtained at that time remains valid, that in assessing acts which have been committed at the order of the State, regard has to be had to whether the State has overstepped the uttermost limit which is set for it according to the general conviction in every country.

(cc) Heute sind konkretere Prüfungsmaßstäbe hinzugekommen: Die internationalen Menschenrechtspakte bieten Anhaltspunkte dafür, wann der Staat nach der Überzeugung der weltweiten Rechtsgemeinschaft Menschenrechte verletzt. Hierbei ist der Internationale Pakt über bürgerliche und politische Rechte vom 19. Dezember 1966 (BGBl 1973 II, 1534 – IPbürgR –) von besonderer Bedeutung. Die DDR ist ihm im Jahre 1974 beigetreten (GBl DDR II 57); sie hat die Ratifizierungsurkunde am 8. November 1974 hinterlegt (GBl. aaO). Der Internationale Pakt (im Sprachgebrauch der DDR 'Konvention über zivile und politische Rechte' genannt) ist für beide deutsche Staaten am 23. März 1976 in Kraft getreten (BGBl II, 1068; GBl DDR II 108). Allerdings hat die DDR es unterlassen, den Pakt gemäß Art. 51 der DDR-Verfassung zum Anlaß für innerstaatliche Gesetzesänderungen zu nehmen und bei dieser Gelegenheit nach der genannten Verfassungsvorschrift von der Volkskammer 'bestätigen' zu lassen. An der völkerrechtlichen Bindung der DDR ändert dieser Sachverhalt nichts. Ein Staat kann sich 'nicht durch eine Berufung auf seine innerstaatliche Rechtsordnung der Erfüllung von ihm eingegangener Verpflichtungen entziehen' (Völkerrecht, Lehrbuch Berlin-Ost 1981 I S. 59); er ist 'kraft Völkerrechts verpflichtet, im Bereich seiner innerstaatlichen Gesetzgebung entsprechend diesen Verpflichtungen zu handeln und sie zu erfüllen' (aaO). Ergeben sich bei der Bewertung des Rechts der DDR Widersprüche zwischen den von ihr völkerrechtlich anerkannten Menschenrechten und der tatsächlichen Anwendung der Grenz- und Waffengebrauchsvorschriften, so kann dieser Widerspruch auch bei der Beurteilung der Frage berücksichtigt werden, ob derjenige rechtswidrig handelt, der auf staatlichen Befehl Menschenrechte verletzt, die durch den völkerrechtlichen Vertrag geschützt sind. Deswegen kann die Frage offenbleiben, ob entgegen der in der DDR vertretenen Auffassung (Buchholz/Wieland NJ 1977, 22, 26; vgl. auch Graefrath, Menschenrechte und internationale Kooperation Berlin-Ost 1988 S. 55ff. sowie R. Hofmann, Die Ausreisefreiheit nach Völkerrecht und staatlichem Recht Berlin-West 1988 S. 243ff.) aus dem besonderen Inhalt des IPbürgR abzuleiten ist, daß schon die Ratifikation den Menschen in den Vertragsstaaten eine Rechtsposition gegenüber ihrem Staat verschafft hat (vgl. Tomuschat, Vereinte Nationen 1976 H. 6 S. 166ff.; Buergenthal in: Henkin [Hrsg.], The International Bill of Rights 1981 S. 72ff.).

(1) Art. 12 Abs. 2 IPbürgR lautet: 'Jedermann steht es frei, jedes Land, einschließlich seines eigenen, zu verlassen' (Übersetzung im DDR-Gesetzblatt: 'Es steht jedem frei, jedes Land, auch sein eigenes, zu verlassen'). Nach Art. 12 Abs. 3 IPbürgR darf dieses Recht nur durch Gesetz und nur zu bestimmten Zwecken, darunter zum Schutz der nationalen Sicherheit und der öffentlichen Ordnung, eingeschränkt werden.

(cc) Today, more concrete standards for investigation have been added: the international human rights agreements offer criteria for saying when the State violates human rights according to the belief of the world wide legal community. In this connection, the International Convention on Civil and Political Rights of 19 December 1966 (BGBl 1973 II, 1534 – IPburgR) is of special significance. The DDR acceded to it in 1974 (GBl DDR II 57); it deposited the ratification document on 8 November 1974 (GBl, *loc cit*). The International Agreement (called 'Convention regarding Civil and Political Rights' in the parlance of the DDR) came into effect for both German States on 23 March 1976 (BGBl II, 1068; GBl DDR II 108). The DDR however neglected to use the agreement in accordance with Art 51 of the DDR Constitution as an opportunity for internal statutory amendments and to have it 'confirmed' on this occasion by the People's Chamber in accordance with the said constitutional provision. These circumstances do not change anything so far as the international law obligation of the DDR is concerned. A State can 'not evade the fulfilment of obligations entered into by it by an appeal to its internal legal order' (International Law, Textbook, East Berlin 1981, I p 59); it is 'obliged by virtue of international law to act in the sphere of its internal legislation in accordance with these obligations and to fulfil them' (*loc cit*). If contradictions result between the human rights recognised by the DDR in international law and the actual application of provisions as to the border and the use of weapons when the law of the DDR is assessed, this contradiction can also be taken into account when considering the question of whether a person is acting unlawfully if he violates human rights which are protected by the international law agreement, at the command of the State. For that reason, the question can remain open of whether, contrary to the view held in the DDR (Buchholz/Wieland NJ 1977, 22, 26; compare also Graefrath, Human Rights and International Co-operation, East Berlin, 1988, p 55 and onwards, as well as R Hoffmann, The Freedom to Travel Abroad in international Law and National Law, West Berlin, 1988, p 243 and onwards), it can be derived from the special content of the IPburgR that ratification alone has created for persons in the contracting States a legal standing as against their State (compare Tomuschat, United Nations 1976 H 6, p 166 and onwards; Buergenthal in: Henkin [Ed.], The International Bill of Rights, 1981, p 72 and onwards).

(1) Article 12 para 2 of the IPburgR states 'Every person is free to leave any country including his own' (Translation in the *DDR Law Gazette*: 'Everyone is free to leave any country and also his own'). According to Art 12 para 3 of the IPburgR, this right may only be limited by statute and only for certain purposes, amongst which are the protection of national security and the public order.

Das Erfordernis, daß die Einschränkung durch Gesetz erfolgen muß, hat das Paßgesetz der DDR vom 28. Juni 1979 (GBl DDR I 148) erfüllt. Darauf, daß die im Paßgesetz und in den zugehörigen Anordnungen enthaltenen Beschränkungen dem Schutz der öffentlichen Ordnung dienten, hat sich die DDR stets berufen. Doch ergibt sich aus dem verbindlichen englischen Wortlaut des Art. 12 Abs. 3 IPbürgR ('The ... rights shall not be subject to any restrictions except ...') und der Entstehungsgeschichte sowie der internationalen Auslegung der Vorschrift, daß mit dem Gesichtspunkt der öffentlichen Ordnung (ordre public) nicht etwa ein umfassender Gesetzesvorbehalt gemeint war; vielmehr sollten die Einschränkungen auf Ausnahmefälle beschränkt bleiben und keinesfalls die Substanz der Freizügigkeit und des Ausreiserechts zerstören (Nowak, UNO-Pakt über bürgerliche und politische Rechte, Art. 12 Rdn. 23, 32f.; Jagerskiold in: Henkin [Hrsg.], The International Bill of Rights S. 166, 172, 179; R. Hofmann, Die Ausreisefreiheit nach Völkerrecht und staatlichem Recht S. 123, 251; Polakiewicz EuGRZ 1992, 177, 186; Hannum, The Right to leave and return in International Law and Practice S. 52f.; Empfehlungen der internationalen Konferenzen von Uppsala [1972] und Syrakus [1984], mitgeteilt bei Hannum aaO S. 150f., 22; Reinke, Columbia Journal of Transnational Law 24 S. 647, 665). Gesichtspunkte des wirtschaftlichen oder sozialen Wohls sollten, wie die Materialien ergeben, kein zulässiges Motiv für die Einschränkung der Freizügigkeit sein (R. Hofmann aaO S. 43; Nowak aaO Rdn. 37 Fn. 86; Bossuyt, Guide to the Travaux Préparatoires of the IPburgR S. 255).

Die DDR ist in den Jahren 1977 und 1984 vom Menschenrechtsausschuß der Vereinten Nationen zu den Verhältnissen an der innerdeutschen Grenze gehört worden. Sie hat 1977 erklärt, die Einschränkung der Freizügigkeit entspreche dem IPbürgR (vgl. Bruns Deutschland-Archiv 1978, 848, 851; UNO-Dokument A 33/Suppl. 40 [1978] S. 26ff., 29). In ihrem Bericht für die Vereinten Nationen von 1984 hat sich die DDR auf die große Zahl erlaubter Ausreisen berufen und betont, die Beschränkungen dienten dem Schutz der nationalen Sicherheit und öffentlichen Ordnung (vgl. Bruns Deutschland-Archiv 1984, 1183, 1185; R. Hofmann aaO S. 117ff., 251). In der mündlichen Befragung hat damals der Vertreter der DDR behauptet, das Grenzgesetz von 1982 sei mit dem IPbürgR, auch mit dessen Art. 6 (Recht auf Leben), vereinbar; Grenzsoldaten schössen nur im äußersten Notfall, wenn andere Mittel nicht ausreichten, um ein Verbrechen – erwähnt wurde der Fall der Gewalttat (violence) – zu verhindern (R. Hofmann aaO S. 121; vgl. Bruns aaO 1984, 1186).

The requirement that the limitation must take place by statute has been fulfilled by the Passport Act of the DDR of 28 June 1979 (GBl DDR I 148). The DDR has continually referred to the fact that the limitations contained in the Passport Act and the directives appertaining to it served the protection of the public order. However, it follows from the binding English wording of Art 12 para 3 of the IPburgR ('The ... rights shall not be subject to any restrictions except ... ') and the history of origin as well as the international interpretation of the provision that a comprehensive statutory reservation was not intended from the viewpoint of public order (ordre public); the limitations should much rather remain limited to exceptional cases and not in any way destroy the substance of the freedom to move around and the right to travel abroad (Novak, UNO Agreement regarding Civil and Political Rights, Art 12 marginal no 23, 32 and onwards; Jagerskiold in: Herkin [Ed], The International Bill of Rights, pp 166, 172, 179; R Hofmann, The Right to Travel Abroad in International and National Law, pp 123, 251; Polakiewicz EuGRZ, 1992, 177, 186; Hannum, The right to leave and return in International Law and Practice, p 52 and onwards; Recommendations of the International Conference of Uppsala [1972] and Syrakus [1984], reported by Hannum, *loc cit*, p 150 and onwards, 22; Reinke, Columbia Journal of Transnational Law 24, pp 647, 665). Economic or social welfare points of view, as the materials show, should not be a permissible motive for the limitation of the freedom to move around (R Hofmann, *loc cit*, p 43; Nowak, *loc cit*, marginal no 37 footnote 86; Bossuyt, Guide to the Preparatory works to the IPburgR, p 255).

The DDR was heard in the years 1977 and 1984 before the Human Rights Committee of the United Nations on the circumstances at the inner German border. It explained in 1977 that the limitation on the freedom to move around complied with the IPburgR (compare Bruns German Archives 1978, 848, 851; UNO Document A 33/Suppl 40 [1978] p 26 and onwards, 29). In their report for the United Nations of 1984, the DDR referred to the large number of permitted journeys abroad and emphasised that the limitations served the protection of national security and public order (compare Bruns German Archives 1984, 1183, 1185; R. Hoffmann, *loc cit*, p 117 and onwards, 251). In the oral interrogation, the representative of the DDR asserted at that time that the Border Act of 1982 was reconcilable with the IPburgR, and with Art 6 of it (right to life); border soldiers only fired in the most extreme case of emergency, if other means did not suffice to prevent a crime - the case of violence was mentioned (R Hofmann, *loc cit*, p 121; compare Bruns, *loc cit*, 1984, 1186).

Es ist zwar nicht anzunehmen, daß der Inhalt des Art. 12 IPbürgR zu den 'allgemein anerkannten, dem friedlichen Zusammenleben und der Zusammenarbeit der Völker dienenden Regeln des Völkerrechts' im Sinne des Art. 8 der DDR-Verfassung gezählt wurde; Art. 8 dieser Verfassung bezog sich ersichtlich auf einen engeren Ausschnitt aus dem Völkerrecht, der die Zusammenarbeit und Koexistenz verschiedener Staaten betraf (vgl. Sorgenicht u. a., Verfassung der DDR Art. 8 Anm.1; siehe auch Mampel, Die sozialistische Verfassung der DDR, 2. Aufl., Art. 8 Rdn. 2). Die dem Art. 12 IPbürgR entsprechenden Regeln gehören aber zu den Werten, die das Verhältnis des Staates zu seinen Bürgern bestimmen und deswegen bei der Auslegung von Gesetzen berücksichtigt werden müssen.

(2) Das in Art. 12 IPbürgR bezeichnete Menschenrecht auf Ausreisefreiheit wurde durch das Grenzregime der DDR verletzt, weil den Bewohnern der DDR das Recht auf freie Ausreise nicht nur in Ausnahmefällen, sondern in aller Regel vorenthalten wurde.

Nach den Vorschriften des DDR-Rechts über die Ausgabe von Pässen als Voraussetzung für das legale Überschreiten der deutsch-deutschen Grenze (Paßgesetz und Paß- und Visaanordnung vom 28. Juni 1979 - GBl DDR I 148, 151 -, ergänzt durch die Anordnung vom 15. Februar 1982 - GBl DDR I 187 -) gab es, jedenfalls bis zum 1. Januar 1989 (Inkrafttreten der VO vom 30. November 1988, GBl DDR I 271), für nicht politisch privilegierte Bürger unterhalb des Rentenalters, abgesehen von einzelnen dringenden Familienangelegenheiten, keine Möglichkeit der legalen Ausreise; Entscheidungen über Anträge auf Ausreise bedurften bis zum 1. Januar 1989 nach § 17 der Anordnung vom 28. Juni 1979 (GBl DDR I 151) keiner Begründung und konnten bis zu diesem Zeitpunkt (§ 23 der VO vom 30. November 1988) nicht mit der Beschwerde angefochten werden.

Diese Regelung verstieß gegen die Einschränkungskriterien des Art. 12 Abs. 3 IPbürgR, gegen den Grundsatz, daß Einschränkungen die Ausnahme bleiben sollten, und gegen das allenthalben aufgestellte Prinzip, daß die Versagung der Ausreise mit Rechtsbehelfen anfechtbar sein müsse (Hannum aaO S. 148). Der Senat übersieht nicht, daß auch andere Länder die Ausreise ihrer eigenen Bürger beschränken, daß die Ausreisefreiheit bei der Schaffung des Grundgesetzes nicht zu einem selbständigen Grundrecht gemacht worden ist (vgl. Pieroth JuS 1985, 81, 84; Rittstieg in AK-GG, 2. Aufl., Art. 11 Rdn. 1ff., 37) und daß dies damals auch mit der Besorgnis begründet wurde, die arbeitsfähigen Jahrgänge würden in unerwünschtem Maße auswandern (Jahrbuch des Öffentlichen Rechtes der Gegewart Neue Folge Bd. 1 (1951), 44). Ihm ist auch bewußt, daß es in den Vereinten Nationen Meinungsunterschiede zwischen Entwicklungsländern, die das Abwandern der Intelligenz verhüten wollen, und den westeuropäischen Mitgliedsstaaten gibt, die auf eine möglichst unbeschränkte Ausreisefreiheit dringen (Hannum aaO S. 31, 52, 55, 109ff.), und daß zur Tatzeit in den unter sowjetischem Einfluß stehenden Staaten durchweg Ausreisebeschränkungen bestanden (vgl. R. Hofmann aaO S. 239ff.; Hannum aaO S. 96ff.; G. Brunner in: Menschenrechte in den Staaten des Warschauer Pakts, Bericht der Unabhängigen Wissenschaftlerkommission 1988 S. 165ff.; Kuss EuGRZ 1987, 305).

It cannot be accepted that the content of Art 12 of the IPburgR was included in the 'generally recognised rules of international law serving the peaceful co-existence and co-operation of peoples' in the sense of Art 8 of the DDR Constitution; Art 8 of this Constitution evidently referred to a narrower section of international law which related to the co-operation and co-existence of different States (compare Soergenicht, *inter alia*, Constitution of the DDR Art 8, note 1; see also Mampel, The Socialist Constitution of the DDR, 2nd edn, Art 8 marginal no 2). The rules corresponding to Art 12 of the IPburgR belong however to the values which determine the relationship of the State to its citizens and for that reason must be considered in the interpretation of statutes.

(2) The human right to freedom to travel abroad described in Art 12 of the IPburgR was violated by the border regime of the DDR because the right to free travel abroad was withheld from inhabitants of the DDR not only in exceptional cases but as a rule.

According to the provisions of DDR law regarding the issuing of passports as a prerequisite for the legal crossing of the German border (Passport Act and Passport and Visa Order of 28 June 1979 - GBl DDR I 148, 151 -, supplemented by the Directive of 15 February 1982 - GBl DDR I 187 -) there was, in any case, for citizens who were not politically privileged and were below pensionable age, no possibility of legal travel abroad until 1 January 1989 (coming into force of the Regulation of 30 November 1988, GBl DDR I 271) apart from individual cases of pressing family matters; decisions regarding proposals to travel abroad needed no reasons until 1 January 1989 according to § 17 of the Directive of 28 June 1979 (GBl DDR I 151) and could until this point in time (§ 23 of the VO of 30 November 1988) not be challenged by way of complaint.

This rule contravened the limitation criteria of Art 12 para 3 of the IPburgR, the principle that limitations should remain the exception and the principle established everywhere that denial of travel abroad must be capable of being challenged by legal remedies (Hannum, *loc cit*, p 148). The Senate does not overlook the fact that other countries also limit the travel abroad of their own citizens, that the freedom to travel abroad was not made an independent basic right on the creation of the Basic Law (compare Pieroth JuS 1985, 81, 84; Rittstieg in AK-GG, 2nd edn, Art 11 marginal no 1 and onwards, 37) and that this was at that time based on the fear that age groups capable of work would emigrate to an undesired extent (Yearbook of Current Public Law, New Series, Vol 1, 1951, 44). It is also aware that in the United Nations there are divisions of opinion between developing countries, who want to prevent emigration of the intelligentsia, and Western European Member States who insist on as unlimited a freedom to travel abroad as possible (Hannum, *loc cit*, p 31, 52, 55, 109 and onwards) and that at the time of the Act, in the States which were under Soviet influence, limitations on travel abroad always existed (compare R Hoffmann, *loc cit*, p 239 and onwards; Hannum, *loc cit*, p 96 and onwards; G. Brunner in: Human Rights in the States of the Warsaw Pact, Report of the Independent Commission of Academics, 1988, p 165 and onwards; Kuss EuGRZ 1987, 305).

Das Grenzregime der DDR empfing jedoch seine besondere Härte dadurch, daß Deutsche aus der DDR ein besonderes Motiv für den Wunsch, die Grenze nach West-Berlin und West-Deutschland zu überqueren, hatten: Sie gehörten mit den Menschen auf der anderen Seite der Grenze zu einer Nation und waren mit ihnen durch vielfältige verwandtschaftliche und sonstige persönliche Beziehungen verbunden.

(3) Insbesondere kann die durch die restriktiven Paß- und Ausreisevorschriften begründete Lage unter dem Gesichtspunkt der Menschenrechte nicht ohne Beachtung der tatsächlichen Verhältnisse an der Grenze gewürdigt werden, die durch 'Mauer, Stacheldraht, Todesstreifen und Schießbefehl' (BVerfGE 36, 1, 35) gekennzeichnet waren und damit gegen Art. 6 IPbürgR verstießen. Nach dieser Vorschrift hat 'jeder Mensch ein angeborenes Recht auf Leben'; 'niemand darf willkürlich seines Lebens beraubt werden' (Art. 6 Abs. 1 Satz 1 und 3). Auch wenn die Auslegung des Merkmals 'willkürlich' insgesamt bisher nicht sehr ergiebig gewesen ist (vgl. Nowak aaO Art. 6 Rdn. 12ff.; Nowak EuGRZ 1983, 11, 12; Polakiewicz EuGRZ 1992, 177, 182; Ramcharan, Netherlands Internat. Law Review 30 (1983), 297, 316ff.; Boyle in: Ramcharan [Hrsg.], The Right to Life in International Law S. 221ff.), so zeichnet sich doch, auch in der Rechtsprechung anderer Staaten (vgl. insbesondere US Supreme Court 471 US 1 in der Sache *Tennessee v Garner*, 1985), die Tendenz ab, den mit der Möglichkeit tödlicher Wirkung verbundenen Schußwaffengebrauch von Staatsorganen unter starker Betonung des Verhältnismäßigkeitsgrundsatzes auf Fälle einzugrenzen, in denen eine Gefährdung von Leib und Leben anderer zu befürchten ist (Boyle aaO S. 241f.; Desch, Österr. Zeitschr. f. öff. Recht u. Völkerrecht 36 (1985) 77, 102; Ramcharan aaO S. 318). In der 'Allgemeinen Bemerkung' des Menschenrechtsausschusses der Vereinten Nationen zum Recht auf Leben aus dem Jahre 1982 (General Comment 6/16 - A/37/40 S. 93ff. -, abgedruckt bei Nowak, UNO-Pakt über bürgerliche und politische Rechte S. 879 sowie bei Graefrath, Menschenrechte und internationale Kooperation S. 263) heißt es, der Schutz des Lebens vor willkürlicher Tötung sei von überragender Bedeutung; das Gesetz müsse die Umstände, unter denen staatliche Organe jemanden seines Lebens berauben dürfen, 'strikt kontrollieren und begrenzen' (aaO Abschnitt 3).

Die Grenze zur Willkür ist nach der Auffassung des Senats insbesondere überschritten, wenn der Schußwaffengebrauch an der Grenze dem Zweck dient, Dritte vom unerlaubten Grenzübertritt abzuschrecken. Daß die 'Befehlslage', die die vorsätzliche Tötung von 'Grenzverletzern' einschloß, auch dieses Ziel hatte, liegt auf der Hand.

The border regime of the DDR however took its particular harshness from the fact that Germans from the DDR had a special motive for the wish to cross the border to West Berlin and West Germany: they belonged, with people on the other side of the border, to one nation and were bound to them by various relationships of kindred and of other personal kinds.

(3) In particular, the position based on the restrictive provisions as to passports and travel abroad cannot be appreciated from the point of view of human rights without having regard to the actual circumstances at the border, which were characterised by 'wall, barbed wire, no man's land and command to shoot' (BVerfGE 36, 1, 35) and therefore violated Art 6 of the IPburgR. According to this provision 'every human being has an inherent right to life'; 'no-one may be deprived of his life arbitrarily' (Art 6 para 1 sentences 1 and 3). Even if the interpretation of the characteristic 'arbitrarily' has up till now, on the whole, not been very productive (compare Nowak, *loc cit*, Art 6 marginal no 12 and onwards; Nowak EuGRZ 1983, 11, 12; Polakiewicz EuGRZ 1992, 177, 182; Ramcharan, Netherlands Internat. Law Review 30 (1983), 297, 316 and onwards; Boyle in: Ramcharan (Ed), The Right to Life in International Law, p 221 and onwards) the tendency becomes apparent, in the case law of other States as well (compare in particular US Supreme Court 471 US 1 in the case *Tennessee v Garner*, 1985) to limit the use by the organs of State of firearms which have possible fatal effect, by strong emphasis on the principle of proportionality, to cases in which an endangering of life and limb of others is to be feared (Boyle, *loc cit*, p 241 and onwards; Desch, Austrian Journal of Public Law and International Law 36 (1985) 77, 102; Ramcharan, *loc cit*, p 318). In the 'General Comment' of the Human Rights Committee of the United Nations on the Right to Life from the year 1982 (General Comment 6/16 - A/37/40, p 93 and onwards -, printed by Nowak, UNO – Convention on Civil and Political Rights, p 879 as well as by Graefrath, Human Rights and International Co-operation, p 263) it says that the protection of life from arbitrary killing is of transcending importance; statute must 'strictly control and limit' the circumstances in which State organs may deprive a person of his life (*loc cit*, § 3).

The limit of arbitrary action is, according to the view of the Senate, in particular overstepped if the use of firearms at the border serves the purpose of frightening third persons away from the unauthorised crossing of the border. It is obvious that the 'total context of the command' which included the intentional killing of 'border violators' also had this objective.

Im vorliegenden Fall ergibt sich bei gleichzeitiger Verletzung der Artikel 6 und 12 IPbürgR eine Menschenrechtsverletzung ferner daraus, daß das Grenzregime in seiner beispiellosen Perfektion und dem durch § 27 des Grenzgesetzes i.V.m. § 213 Abs. 3 StGB-DDR bestimmten, in der Praxis rücksichtslos angewandten Schußwaffengebrauch Menschen betraf, denen aufgrund einer die Ausreise regelmäßig und ohne Begründung versagenden Verwaltungspraxis verwehrt wurde, aus der DDR in den westlichen Teil Deutschlands und insbesondere Berlins zu reisen.

(4) Der Senat nimmt, was das Recht auf Leben angeht, die von der Revision des Angeklagten W. gemachten kritischen Hinweise auf die Auslegung des § 11 UZwG sowie der §§ 15, 16 UZwGBw (ebenso Polakiewicz EuGRZ 1992, 177, 185) ernst. Er findet es befremdlich, daß im Schrifttum bei der Auslegung des § 16 UZwGBw ein bedingter Tötungsvorsatz als von der Vorschrift gedeckt bezeichnet worden ist (Jess/Mann, UZwGBw, 2. Aufl., § 16 Rdn. 4), und pflichtet Frowein (in: Kritik und Vertrauen, FS für Peter Schneider S. 112ff.) darin bei, daß in der Bundesrepublik Deutschland der Schußwaffengebrauch gegen Menschen angesichts seiner unkontrollierbaren Gefährlichkeit (vgl. dazu BGHSt 35, 379, 386) auch im Grenzgebiet (§ 11 UZwG) auf die Verteidigung von Menschen beschränkt werden sollte (aaO S. 117), also auf Fälle, in denen von demjenigen, auf den geschossen wird, eine Gefährdung von Leib oder Leben anderer zu befürchten ist. Der Umstand, daß die derzeitige Auslegung der Schußwaffenvorschriften des geltenden Rechts im Lichte des Verhältnismäßigkeitsprinzips nicht in jeder Weise befriedigend ist (vgl. auch BGHSt 26, 99), rechtfertigt indessen kein Verständnis für den Schußwaffengebrauch durch die Grenztruppen der DDR; dieser war durch eine Konstellation gekennzeichnet, die in der Bundesrepublik Deutschland angesichts ihrer offenen Grenzen keine Parallele hat.

(dd) Die Verletzung der in den Artikeln 6 und 12 des Internationalen Pakts garantierten Menschenrechte in ihrem spezifischen, durch die Verhältnisse an der innerdeutschen Grenze gekennzeichneten Zusammenhang macht es dem Senat unmöglich, bei der Rechtsanwendung die Vorschriften des § 27 des Grenzgesetzes sowie des § 213 Abs. 3 StGB-DDR in dem Umfang, wie sie in der Staatspraxis der DDR verstanden worden sind, als Rechtfertigungsgrund zugrundezulegen. Die Verhältnisse an der Grenze waren auch unter Berücksichtigung der wirtschaftlichen und sozialen Nachteile, die für den betroffenen Staat mit einer starken Abwanderung arbeitsfähiger Menschen verbunden sein können, Ausdruck einer Einstellung, die das Lebensrecht der Menschen niedriger einschätzt als das Interesse, sie am Verlassen des Staates zu hindern. Der im DDR-Recht vorgesehene, in § 27 des Grenzgesetzes bezeichnete Rechtfertigungsgrund hat deswegen von Angang an in der Auslegung, die durch die tatsächlichen Verhältnisse an der Grenze gekennzeichnet war, keine Wirksamkeit gehabt. Er hat bei der Suche nach dem milderen Recht (§ 2 Abs. 3 StGB i.V.m. Art. 315 Abs.1 EGStGB) außer Betracht zu bleiben, weil bereits die DDR bei Zugrundelegung der von ihr anerkannten Prinzipien den Rechtfertigungsgrund hätte einschränkend auslegen müssen.

In the present case, a violation of human rights also follows from the simultaneous violation of Arts 6 and 12 of the IPburgR, in that the border regime in its unprecedented perfection and the use of firearms, defined by § 27 of the Border Act in association with § 213 para 3 of the StGB-DDR but in practice applied ruthlessly, affected persons to whom it was forbidden, on the basis of an administrative practice denying travel abroad regularly and without reasons, to travel from the DDR into the western part of Germany and in particular of Berlin.

(4) As to the right to life, the Senate takes seriously the critical references made by the appeal in law of the defendant W to the interpretation of § 11 of the UZwG as well as to §§ 15 and 16 of the UZwGBw (likewise Polakiewicz EuGRZ 1992, 177, 185). It finds it strange that in the literature in the interpretation of § 16 of the UZwGBw a conditional intention to kill has been described as covered by the provision (Jess/Mann, UZwGBw, 2nd edn, § 16 marginal no 4) and Frowein (in: Criticism and Trust, FS for Peter Schneider, p 112 and onwards) agrees that in the Federal Republic of Germany the use of firearms against human beings in view of its uncontrollable danger (compare to this BGHSt 35, 379, 386) should, even in the border area (§ 11 of the UZwG), be limited to the defence of human beings (*loc cit*, p 117) and therefore to cases in which a danger to the life or limb of others is to be feared from the person fired at. The fact that the current interpretation of the firearms provisions of the applicable law in the light of the principle of proportionality is not in every respect satisfactory (compare also BGHSt 26, 99) does not however justify sympathy for the use of firearms by the border troops of the DDR; this was characterised by a combination of criteria which has no parallels in the Federal Republic of Germany in the light of its open borders.

(dd) The violation of the human rights guaranteed in Arts 6 and 12 of the International Convention in their specific context, characterised by the relationships at the inner German border, makes it impossible for the Senate, in application of the law, to base a ground of justification on the provisions of § 27 of the Border Act as well as those of § 213 para 3 of the StGB-DDR to the extent to which they were understood in the State practice of the DDR. The circumstances at the border were, even considering the economic and social disadvantages for the State affected which could be connected with a substantial emigration of persons who were capable of work, an expression of an attitude which valued the right of human beings to life at a lower level than its interest in preventing them from leaving the State. The ground of justification provided for in DDR law and described in § 27 of the Border Act was for this reason, in the interpretation which was indicated by the actual circumstances at the border, ineffective from the start. It must be left out of consideration in the search for a less severe law (§ 2 para 3 of the StGB in association with Art 315 para 1 of the EGStGB), because the DDR would have had to interpret the ground of justification restrictively on the basis of principles recognised by it.

3 Der Senat hatte sodann der Frage nachzugehen, ob § 27 des Grenzgesetzes mit Auslegungsmethoden, die dem Recht der DDR eigentümlich waren, so hätte ausgelegt werden können, daß die genannten Menschenrechtsverletzungen vermieden wurden; ein so eingegrenzter Rechtfertigungsgrund wäre mit Rücksicht auf Art. 103 Abs. 2 GG zu beachten. Die Prüfung ergibt, daß eine solche Auslegung möglich gewesen wäre, daß der so bestimmte Rechtfertigungsgrund jedoch das Verhalten der Angeklagten (Dauerfeuer mit bedingtem Tötungsvorsatz) nicht gedeckt hätte.

(a) Der Senat legt bei dieser Auslegung nicht die Wertordnung des Grundgesetzes oder der Menschenrechtskonvention zugrunde; er beschränkt sich darauf, die Vorgaben zu berücksichtigen, die im Recht der DDR für eine menschenrechtsfreundliche Gesetzesauslegung angelegt waren. Ausgangspunkt ist Art. 89 Abs.2 der Verfassung der DDR; danach durften Rechtsvorschriften der Verfassung nicht widersprechen. Nach Art. 30 der Verfassung waren Persönlichkeit und Freiheit eines jeden Bürgers der DDR unantastbar und Einschränkungen nur dann zulässig, wenn sie im Zusammenhang mit strafbaren Handlungen oder einer Heilbehandlung gesetzlich begründet waren; Rechte durften 'nur insoweit eingeschränkt werden, als dies gesetzlich zulässig und unumgänglich ist' (Art. 30 Abs. 2). Das Recht auf Leben und körperliche Unversehrtheit war in der Verfassung der DDR nicht ausdrücklich genannt; auch ist dieses Recht in dem Sinne, wie es Gegenstand westlicher Verfassungen ist, in der Literatur der DDR nicht ausdrücklich behandelt worden (vgl. z.B. E. Poppe [Hrsg.] Grundrechte des Bürgers in der sozialistischen Gesellschaft S. 163, 265). Schon im Blick auf Art. 6 IPbürgR kann es aber keinem Zweifel unterliegen, daß die Verfassungsvorschrift des Art. 30 Abs.1 VerfDDR, indem sie die Persönlichkeit für unantastbar erklärte, den Schutz des Lebens einschloß; demnach ist Art. 30 Abs. 2 VerfDDR zu entnehmen, daß Eingriffe in das Leben gesetzlich begründet sein mußten (vgl. K. Sorgenicht u. a., Verfassung der DDR Art. 30 Anm. 1; G. Brunner, Menschenrechte in der DDR S. 111, 113). Mit der Abschaffung der Todesstrafe durch das 4. StRÄndG vom 18. Dezember 1987 (GBl DDR I 301) wollte die DDR ersichtlich dem Menschenrecht auf Leben Rechnung tragen. Die Vorschrift des Art. 30 Abs. 2 Satz 2 der Verfassung der DDR brachte einen Gesichtspunkt zum Ausdruck, der im Verfassungsrecht der Bundesrepublik Deutschland als Grundsatz der Verhältnismäßigkeit bezeichnet wird.

3 The Senate then had to investigate the question of whether § 27 of the Border Act could, by the interpretation methods which were peculiar to the law of the DDR, have been interpreted in such a way as to avoid the violations of human rights mentioned; a ground of justification limited in this manner should then be considered, having regard to Art 103 para 2 of the GG. The examination shows that an interpretation that the ground of justification determined in this way would not however have covered the conduct of the defendants (continuous fire with conditional intention to kill) would have been possible.

(a) In this interpretation the Senate does not take the order of values in the Basic Law or in the Human Rights Convention as a basis; it limits itself to considering the provisions which were made in the law of the DDR for statutory interpretation which is sympathetic to human rights. The starting point is Art 89 para 2 of the Constitution of the DDR; according to this, legal provisions were not permitted to contradict the Constitution. According to Art 30 of the Constitution, the personality and freedom of each citizen of the DDR were inviolable and restrictions were only permissible if they were based on statute and in relation to criminal acts or treatment for illness; laws could 'only be limited insofar as this is permissible by statute and unavoidable' (Art 30 para 2). The right to life and physical integrity was not expressly mentioned in the Constitution of the DDR; this right is also not expressly dealt with in the literature of the DDR in the sense in which it is a subject in western constitutions (compare, eg, E Poppe [Ed], Basic Rights of Citizens in Socialist Society, pp 163, 265). There can, however, be no doubt in the light of Art 6 of the IPburgR that the constitutional provisions of Art 30 para 1 of the Constitution of the DDR, in that it declared personality to be inviolable, included the protection of life; consequently it is to be inferred from Art 30 para 2 of the Constitution of the DDR that invasions into the sphere of life had to be statutorily based (compare K Sorgenicht, *inter alia*, Constitution of the DDR, Art 30 note 1; G.Brunner, Human Rights in the DDR, pp 111, 113). By the abolition of the death penalty by the 4th Penal Law Amendment Act of 18 December 1987 (GBl DDR I 301) the DDR evidently wanted to take account of the human right to life. The provisions of Art 30 para 2 sentence 2 of the Constitution of the DDR expressed a point of view which in the constitutional law of the Federal Republic of Germany is called the principle of proportionality.

Anders als im nationalsozialistischen Führerstaat gab es in der DDR keine Doktrin, nach der der bloße Wille der Inhaber tatsächlicher Macht Recht zu schaffen vermochte. Gesetze waren verbindlich (vgl. Art. 49 Abs.1 der Verfassung); sie konnten allein von der Volkskammer erlassen werden (Art. 48 Abs. 2 der Verfassung). Zur 'Durchführung der sozialistischen Gesetzlichkeit' war die Rechtspflege berufen, die die Freiheit, das friedliche Leben, die Rechte und die Würde der Menschen zu schützen hatte (Art. 90 Abs. 1 der Verfassung). Die Richter sollten nach Art. 96 Abs. 1 der Verfasung in ihrer Rechtsprechung unabhängig sein. Hiernach beanspruchten die Gesetze eine Geltung, die nicht durch Weisungen oder die tatsächliche Staatspraxis bestimmt war. Wer heute den Inhalt der Gesetze der DDR unter Berücksichtigung der DDR-Verfassung und der Bindung der DDR an die internationalen Menschenrechtspakte zu ermitteln sucht, unterschiebt demnach nicht dem Recht der DDR Inhalte, die mit dem eigenen Anspruch dieses Rechtes unvereinbar wären. Der Erste Stellvertreter des Vorsitzenden des Ministerrates der DDR hat am 25.März 1982 in der Volkskammer bei der Einbringung des Grenzgesetzes u. a. ausgeführt, die Regelung über den Schußwaffengebrauch (§ 27) enthalte 'nicht mehr und nicht weniger, als auch andere Staaten für ihre Schutzorgane festgelegt haben'; die Anwendung der Schußwaffe sei 'die äußerste Maßnahme' gegen Personen, die 'Verbrechen gegen die Rechtsordnung der DDR begangen haben oder sich der Verantwortung für die begangene Rechtsverletzung zu entziehen suchen' (Volkskammer 8. Wahlper. 4. Tagung, S. 88 f. der Sten. Niederschrift).

In contrast to the National Socialist dictator State, there was no doctrine in the DDR according to which the mere will of the possessor of factual power was able to make law. Statutes were binding (compare Art 49 para 1 of the Constitution); they could only be issued by the People's Chamber (Art 48 para 2 of the Constitution). The administration of justice, which had to protect freedom, peaceful life and the rights and dignity of humans was called to 'realise socialist legality' (Art 90 para 1 of the Constitution). The judges were to be independent, according to Art 96 para 1 of the Constitution, in their application of the law. Accordingly statutes laid claim to a validity which was not determined by directions or actual State practice. A person who seeks today to ascertain the content of the statutes of the DDR by having regard to the Constitution of the DDR and the fact that the DDR was bound by international human rights agreements does not thereby impute to the law of the DDR contents which would be irreconcilable with this law's own pretensions. The First Deputy for the President of the Council of Ministers of the DDR on 25 March 1982 in the Peoples Chamber explained on the introduction of the Border Act, *inter alia*, that the regime regarding the use of firearms (§ 27) contained 'no more and no less than other States have laid down for their protective organs'; the use of firearms was 'the most extreme measure' against persons who 'have committed crimes against the legal order of the DDR or seek to evade responsibility for the violation of the law they have committed' (People's Chamber, 8th electoral period, 4th session, p 88 and onwards of the shorthand copy).

(b) Eine an den Artikeln 6, 12 IPbürgR orientierte Auslegung des § 27 des Grenzgesetzes kann sich auf den genannten, in Art. 30 Abs. 2 Satz 2 der DDR-Verfassung enthaltenen Verhältnismäßigkeitsgrundsatz stützen; dieser Grundsatz hat in anderem Zusammenhang auch in § 26 Abs. 2 Satz 2, 3 des Grenzgesetzes sowie in seiner Formulierung, daß die Anwendung der Schußwaffe 'die äußerste Maßnahme der Gewaltanwendung gegenüber Personen' sei (§ 27 Abs. 1 Satz 1 des Grenzgesetzes), Ausdruck gefunden. Es liegt deshalb nahe anzunehmen, daß der Verhältnismäßigkeitsgrundsatz, so wie er in der DDR galt, verletzt wurde, wenn derjenige als Täter eines Verbrechens nach § 213 Abs. 3 Satz 2 Nr. 2 StGB-DDR verstanden wurde, der die Mauer mit einer Leiter überstieg. Verhält es sich so, dann war der Gebrauch der Schußwaffe nach § 27 Abs. 2 des Grenzgesetzes unzulässig, weil sich die Flucht nicht als ein Verbrechen nach § 213 Abs. 3 Satz 2 Nr. 2 StGB-DDR darstellte. Aber selbst wenn die vom Obersten Gericht und vom Generalstaatsanwalt vorgegebene Auslegung, im übrigen auch die Anwendbarkeit des § 213 Abs. 3 Satz 2 Nr. 5 StGB-DDR zugrunde gelegt wird, so gestattete doch der Wortlaut des § 27 Abs. 2 des Grenzgesetzes eine Auslegung, die dem auch im Recht der DDR (eingeschränkt) vorhandenen Verhältnismäßigkeitsgrundsatz Rechnung trug. § 27 Abs. 2 Satz 1 des Grenzgesetzes ist dann so zu verstehen: Der Grenzsoldat durfte zwar in den dort bezeichneten Fällen die Schußwaffe zur Verhinderung der Flucht einsetzen; der Rechtfertigungsgrund fand aber eine Grenze, wenn auf einen nach den Umständen unbewaffneten und auch sonst nicht für Leib oder Leben anderer gefährlichen Flüchtling mit dem - bedingten oder unbedingten – Vorsatz, ihn zu töten, geschossen wurde. Hiernach war die bedingt vorsätzliche Tötung, wie sie unter den gegebenen Umständen in der Anwendung von Dauerfeuer zum Ausdruck kam, vom dem in menschenrechtsfreundlicher Weise ausgelegten § 27 Abs. 2 des Grenzgesetzes nicht gedeckt; das würde auch dann gelten, wenn der Sachverhalt unter § 27 Abs. 2 Satz 2 des Grenzgesetzes (Ergreifung von Personen, die eines Verbrechens nach § 213 Abs. 3 StGB-DDR dringend verdächtig sind) subsumiert würde. In diesen Fällen hat der Schutz des Lebens Vorrang; dies kann auch auf den Rechtsgedanken des § 27 Abs. 5 Satz 1 des Grenzgesetzes – bei menschenrechtsfreundlicher Auslegung – gestützt werden.

(c) Bei dieser Auslegung ist das Verhalten der Angeklagten nicht von dem Rechtfertigungsgrund des § 27 Abs. 2 des Grenzgesetzes gedeckt gewesen; sie haben danach auch nach dem Recht der DDR einen rechtswidrigen Totschlag begangen.

4 Nach Art. 103 Abs. 2 GG kann eine Tat nur bestraft werden, wenn die Strafbarkeit zur Tatzeit gesetzlich bestimmt war (Rückwirkungsverbot). Diese Verfassungsbestimmung verbietet die Bestrafung der Beschwerdeführer nicht.

(b) An interpretation of § 27 of the Border Act which is orientated to Arts 6 and 12 of the IPburgR can be based on the principle of proportionality which has been mentioned and which was contained in Art 30 para 2 sentence 2 of the DDR Constitution; this principle has found expression in another context in § 26 para 2 sentences 2 and 3 of the Border Act, as well as in its formulation that the use of firearms was 'the most extreme measure of the application of force against persons' (§ 27 para 1 sentence 1 of the Border Act). It is therefore natural to accept that the principle of proportionality, as it applied in the DDR, was violated if a person who climbed over the wall with a ladder was understood to be the perpetrator of a crime in accordance with § 213 para 3 sentence 2 no 2 of the StGB-DDR. If that is the case, then the use of firearms in accordance with § 27 para 2 of the Border Act was not permissible, because the flight did not present itself as a crime in accordance with § 213 para 3 sentence 2 no 2 of the StGB-DDR. But even if the interpretation asserted by the Supreme Court and the General State Attorney, and further even the applicability of § 213 para 3 sentence 2 no 5 of the StGB-DDR is taken as a basis, the wording of § 27 para 2 of the Border Act permitted an interpretation which took into account the principle of proportionality which is also present (in a limited form) in the law of the DDR. § 27 para 2 sentence 1 of the Border Act is then to be understood in this way: the border soldier might certainly use firearms for prevention of flight in the cases described there. But the ground of justification reached its limit when shots were fired at a fugitive, who, according to the circumstances, was unarmed and not otherwise a danger to the life and limb of others, with the – conditional or unconditional – intention to kill him. Accordingly, the conditionally intentional killing, as expressed in the given circumstances in the use of continuous fire, was not covered by § 27 para 2 of the Border Act as interpreted in a manner sympathetic to human rights; that would also apply if the facts of the case were comprised within § 27 para 2 sentence 2 of the Border Act (capture of persons who are seriously suspected of a crime in accordance with § 213 para 3 of the StGB-DDR). In these cases, the protection of life has priority; this can also be supported by the legal concept of § 27 para 5 sentence 1 of the Border Act – interpreted in a manner sympathetic to human rights.

(c) On this interpretation, the conduct of the defendants was not covered by the ground of justification in § 27 para 2 of the Border Act; and accordingly they have also committed an unlawful homicide according to the law of the DDR.

4 According to Art 103 para 2 of the GG, an act can only be punished if the criminality was determined by statute at the time of the act (prohibition on retroactivity). This constitutional provision does not forbid the punishment of the complainants.

(a) Unter den vorstehend (zu 2, 3) dargelegten Umständen gibt es Gründe für die Auffassung, daß Art. 103 Abs. 2 GG die Bestrafung der Angeklagten von vornherein nicht hindert, weil die Tat nach dem richtig ausgelegten Recht der DDR zur Tatzeit strafbar war. Ob die Angeklagten dies erkannt haben, ist eine Frage, die lediglich Entschuldigungsgründe betrifft.

(b) Der Senat hat jedoch nicht übersehen, daß im Hinblick auf Art. 103 Abs. 2 GG die Frage aufgeworfen werden kann, welches Verständnis vom Recht der Tatzeit zugrunde zu legen ist. Wird an das Tatzeitrecht ein Beurteilungsmaßstab angelegt, der die Handlung, obwohl sie vom Staat befohlen worden war, als rechtswidrig erscheinen läßt (vorstehend zu 2, 3), so ergibt sich, daß das Rückwirkungsverbot der Bestrafung nicht entgegensteht. Wird dagegen bei der Würdigung der Rechtslage, die zur Tatzeit bestanden hat, hauptsächlich auf die tatsächlichen Machtverhältnisse im Staat abgestellt, so kann die Anwendung des Art. 103 Abs.2 GG zu einem anderen Ergebnis führen. Das gilt vor allem, wenn dem Angeklagten von einer staatlichen Stelle befohlen worden ist, ein allgemein anerkanntes Recht, zumal das Recht auf Leben, zu verletzen. Hier kann sich die Frage stellen, ob und unter welchen Umständen aus einem solchen Befehl zugunsten des Angeklagten die Annahme hergeleitet werden muß, die Strafbarkeit sei zur Tatzeit nicht gesetzlich bestimmt gewesen.

(aa) Die Frage, welche Bedeutung Art. 103 Abs. 2 GG für die Beurteilung von Handlungen hat, die unter einem früheren Regime im staatlichen Auftrag vorgenommen worden sind und Menschenrechte wie das Recht auf Leben verletzen, ist noch nicht vollständig geklärt (vgl. Schünemann in FS für Hans-Jürgen Bruns S. 223ff.; Dencker, Krit V 73 (1990), 299, 304 und Polakiewicz EuGRZ 1992, 177, 188). Die in diesem Zusammenhang genannten Entscheidungen des Bundesverfassungsgerichts (BVerfGE 3, 225ff.; 6, 195ff.) betreffen nicht das Strafrecht; auch die Frage, ob eine laufende strafrechtliche Verjährungsfrist verlängert werden kann (BVerfGE 25, 269ff.), ist nicht einschlägig. Das Problem des Rückswirkungsverbots bei Rechtfertigungsgründen ist in der deutschen Rechtsprechung vom Obersten Gerichtshof für die Britische Zone aufgeworfen worden (OGHSt 2, 231ff.).

(a) In the circumstances explained above (at 2 and 3) there are grounds for the view that Art 103 para 2 of the GG does not prevent, from the outset, the punishment of the defendants because the act was punishable according to the law of the DDR at the time of the act as correctly interpreted. Whether the defendants knew this is a question which merely concerns grounds of excuse.

(b) The Senate has not however overlooked the fact that with regard to Art 103 para 2 of the GG the question can be raised as to which understanding of the law at the time of the act is to be taken as a basis. If a standard of assessment is applied to the law at the time of the act which causes the action, although it was commanded by the State, to appear as contrary to law (above, at 2 and 3), it follows that the prohibition on retroactivity does not oppose punishment. If on the other hand on assessment of the legal position which existed at the time of the act the actual conditions of power in the State are taken cheifly into consideration, the application of Art 103 para 2 of the GG can lead to another result. That applies primarily if the defendant has been commanded by a State department to violate a generally recognised law, especially the right to life. Here the question can present itself as to whether and in what circumstances the hypothesis in the defendant's favour that the criminality was not statutorily determined at the time of the act must be derived from such a command.

(aa) The question of what meaning Art 103 para 2 of the GG has for the assessment of actions which have been undertaken by order of the State under a former regime, and which violate human rights like the right to life, has not yet been made completely clear (compare Schüneman in FS for Hans-Jürgen Bruns, p 223 and onwards; Dencker, KritV 73 (1990), 299, 304 and Polakiewicz EuGRZ 1992, 177, 188). The decisions of the Federal Constitutional Court mentioned in this connection (BVerfGE 3, 225 and onwards; 6, 195 and onwards) do not concern criminal law; even the question of whether a current criminal law limitation period can be lengthened (BVerfGE 25, 269 and onwards) is not relevant. The problem of the prohibition on retroactivity in relation to grounds of justification has been raised in German case law by the Supreme Court for the British Zone (OHGSt 2, 231 and onwards).

Die in der Rechtsprechung des Internationalen Militärtribunals von Nürnberg sowie insbesondere in der Entscheidung im sogenannten Juristenprozeß (III. US-Militärgerichtshof, Urteil vom 4.12.1947 S. 29ff. des offiziellen Textes) unter wesentlichem Einfluß angelsächsischer Rechtsüberzeugungen entwickelten Gesichtspunkte sind von der späteren deutschen Rechtsprechung nicht übernommen worden. Das Verbot der Verurteilung von Taten, die zur Zeit ihrer Begehung nicht strafbar waren, findet sich auch in Art. 15 des Internationalen Pakts sowie in Art. 7 MRK. Doch ist beiden Vorschriften ein zweiter Absatz angefügt, in dem es heißt, das grundsätzliche Rückwirkungsverbot schließe nicht die Verurteilung von Personen aus, deren Tat zur Zeit ihrer Begehung nach den von der Völkergemeinschaft anerkannten allgemeinen Rechtsgrundsätzen strafbar war. Die Bundesrepublik Deutschland hat jedoch gegenüber Art. 7 Abs. 2 MRK den Vorbehalt (Art. 64 MRK) gemacht, daß die Vorschrift nur in den Grenzen des Art. 103 Abs. 2 GG angewandt werden würde (BGBl 1954 II, 14). Gegen Art. 15 Abs. 2 des Internationalen Pakts hat die Bundesrepublik Deutschland keinen Vorbehalt erklärt; das ändert nichts daran, daß auch insoweit Art. 103 Abs. 2 GG als Verfassungsrecht vorgeht.

Rechtfertigungsgründe sind nicht generell von dem Schutzbereich des Art. 103 Abs. 2 GG ausgeschlossen (vgl. Rüping, Bonner Kommentar – Zweitbearbeitung – Art. 103 Abs. 2 Rdn. 50; Kratzsch GA 1971, 65ff.; Engels GA 1982, 109, 114ff.). Das gilt auch für das in Art. 103 Abs. 2 GG enthaltene Rückwirkungsverbot. Der Senat folgt nicht dem Vorschlag (vgl. neuestens F.C. Schroeder JZ 1992, 990, 991), das Rückwirkungsverbot generell nur auf die Tatbestandsstufe und nicht auf die Rechtswidrigkeitsstufe zu beziehen. Nicht immer spiegelt das Verhältnis von Tatbestand und Rechtfertigungsgrund einen Sachverhalt wider, bei dem die Rechtsgutverletzung auch in den gerechtfertigten Fällen ein soziales Unwerturteil erlaubt; die Entscheidung des Gesetzgebers, den Tatbestand einzuschränken oder aber bei uneingeschränktem Tatbestand einen Rechtfertigungsgrund vorzusehen, ist unter Umständen nur technischer Natur. War eine tatbestandsmäßige Handlung zur Tatzeit nicht rechtswidrig, so kann sie demnach grundsätzlich nicht bestraft werden, wenn der Rechtfertigungsgrund nachträglich beseitigt worden ist (Eser in Schönke/Schröder, StGB, 24. Aufl., § 2 Rdn. 3). Bleibt nämlich ein früher vorgesehener Rechtfertigungsgrund außer Bertracht, so wird das frühere Recht zum Nachteil des Angeklagten verändert (vgl. Jakobs, Strafrecht AT, 2. Aufl., S. 121). Insoweit ist mithin auch im Rahmen der Prüfung nach § 2 Abs. 3 StGB grundsätzlich das Rückwirkungsverbot zu beachten.

The points of view developed under substantial influence of Anglo-Saxon legal opinions in the case law of the International Military Tribunal of Nuremberg as well as in particular in the decision in the so-called lawyers' proceedings (IIIrd US Military Court, judgment of the 4.12.1947, p 29 and onwards of the official text) were not taken over by later German case law. The prohibition against conviction in respect of acts which were not punishable at the time they were committed also occurs in Art 15 of the International Agreement as well as in Art 7 MRK. But a second paragraph is added to both provisions in which it says that the prohibition in principle on retroactivity does not exclude the conviction of persons whose act was punishable at the time it was committed according to the general principles of law recognised by the international community. The Federal Republic of Germany has however made the reservation (Art 64 MRK) in respect of Art 7 para 2 MRK that the provision would only be applied within the limits of Art 103 para 2 of the GG (BGBl 1954 II, 14). The Federal Republic of Germany has declared no reservation in respect of Art 15 para 2 of the International Agreement; that does not alter the fact that in this respect Art 103 para 2 of the GG takes precedence, as constitutional law.

Grounds of justification are not generally excluded from the area of protection of Art 103 para 2 of the GG (compare Rüping, Bonn Commentary – Second Revision – Art 103 para 2 marginal no 50; Kratzsch GA 1971, 65 and onwards; Engels GA 1982, 109, 114 and onwards). That also applies to the prohibition on retroactivity contained in Art 103 para 2 of the GG. The Senate does not follow the proposition (compare, very recently, FC Schroeder JZ 1992, 990, 991) that the prohibition on retroactivity should generally be referred to only at the stage of the constituent elements and not the stage of unlawfulness. The relationship of constituent elements and ground of justification does not always reflect a situation in which the violation of a legal interest permits an adverse social judgment even in the justified cases; the decision of the legislator to limit the constituent elements or to provide instead for a ground of justification for unlimited constituent elements is in certain circumstances only of a technical nature. If an action which corresponds to the constituent elements of the crime was not unlawful at the time of the act, it can consequently not in principle be punished, if the ground of justification is subsequently removed (Eser in Schönke/Schröder, StGB, 24th edn, § 2 marginal no 3). That is to say that if a ground of justification which was provided for earlier is left out of consideration, the earlier law is changed to the disadvantage of the accused (compare Jakobs, Criminal Law AT, 2nd edn, p 121). In this respect, the prohibition on retroactivity should therefore also be considered within the framework of the examination in accordance with § 2 para 3 of the StGB.

Aus dieser Erwägung ist in der neuesten Diskussion im Hinblick auf Fälle der vorliegende Art die Folgerung abgeleitet worden, daß ein zur Tatzeit praktizierter Rechtfertigungsgrund, mag er auch übergeordneten Normen widersprechen, nicht zum Nachteil des Angeklagten außer Betracht bleiben darf, weil dann unter Verstoß gegen Art. 103 Abs. 2 GG eine Strafbarkeit begründet würde, die zur Tatzeit nicht bestanden hat (Jakobs in J. Isensee [Hrsg.], Vergangenheitsbewältigung durch Recht S.36ff., dort auch Isensee S. 91, 105ff.; Grünwald StV 1991, 31, 33; Rittstieg, Demokratie und Recht 1991, 404; Pieroth VVDStRL 51 (1992) 92ff., 102ff., 144ff., 168ff.; dort auch Isensee S. 134ff.; Dencker KritV 73 (1990), 299, 306; differenzierend Polakiewicz EuGRZ 1992, 177, 188ff.; vgl. auch Dreier, VVDStRL 51 (1992), 137).

(bb) Der Senat folgt dieser Auffassung im Ergebnis nicht.

(1) Dabei sind allerdings nicht die Vorschriften der DDR über die Bestrafung von Verbrechen gegen den Frieden, die Menschlichkeit und von Kriegsverbrechen (insbesondere Art. 91 Satz 1 der Verfassung der DDR) oder die Bestimmung des § 95 StGB-DDR heranzuziehen. Die letztgenannte Bestimmung schließt zwar anscheinend ohne Einschränkung die Berufung auf grund- und menschenrechtswidrige Gesetze aus. Wie ihre Stellung im Gesetz zeigt, betrifft die Vorschrift aber nur die in den §§ 85 bis 94 StGB-DDR bezeichneten Verbrechen; eine Nachprüfung von Gesetzen am Maßstab der Grund- und Menschenrechte sollte sie nicht generell begründen. Dem entspricht es, daß § 95 StGB-DDR nach der damaligen offiziellen Auslegung (DDR-Kommentar § 95 Anm. 1) den Inhalt von Art. 8 des Statuts des Internationalen Militärtribunals von Nürnberg übernehmen sollte.

From this consideration, the inference has been derived in the most recent discussion with regard to cases of the present kind that a ground of justification employed at the time of the act, even if it also contradicts superior norms, should not be permitted to be left out of consideration to the disadvantage of the accused, because then a criminality, which did not exist at the time of the act, would be established in a manner which violates Art 103 para 2 of the GG (Jakobs in J Isensee [Ed], Overcoming the Past by Law, p 36 and onwards; also, in the same volume, Isensee, pp 91, 105 and onwards; Grünwald StV 1991, 31, 33; Rittstieg, Democracy and Law, 1991, 404; Pieroth VVDStRL 51 (1992) 92 and onwards, 102 and onwards, 144 and onwards, 168 and onwards; also, in the same volume, Isensee, p 134 and onwards; Dencker KritV 73 (1990), 299, 306; differentiating, Polakiewicz EuGRZ 1992, 177, 188 and onwards; compare also Dreier VVDStRL 51 (1992), 137).

(bb) The Senate does not follow this view in its outcome.

(1) In this connection, the provisions of the DDR concerning the punishment of crimes against peace and humanity and of war crimes (especially Art 91 sentence 1 of the Constitution of the DDR) or the provisions of § 95 of the StGB-DDR are certainly not to be called upon. It is true that the last named provision excludes, apparently without limitation, reference to statutory provisions which are contrary to basic rights and human rights. As its position in the statute shows, however, the provisions only concern the crimes designated in §§ 85–94 of the StGB-DDR; it was not to establish generally a testing of statutory provisions against the standard of basic rights and human rights. The fact that § 95 of the StGB-DDR in accordance with the official interpretation at that time (DDR Commentary § 95 note 1) was to take over the content of Art 8 of the Statute of the International Military Tribunal of Nuremberg corresponds with this.

(2) Der Senat ist aus folgendem Grunde der Ansicht, daß Art. 103 Abs. 2 GG hier nicht der Annahme entgegensteht, die Tat sei rechtswidrig: Entscheidend ist, wie dargestellt, ob die Strafbarkeit 'geseztlich bestimmt war', bevor die Tat begangen wurde. Bei der Prüfung, ob es sich so verhalten hat, ist der Richter nicht im Sinne reiner Faktizität an diejenige Interpretation gebunden, die zur Tatzeit in der Staatspraxis Ausdruck gefunden hat. Konnte das Tatzeitrecht bei Beachtung der vom Wortsinn des Gesetzes gegebenen Grenzen im Lichte der Verfassung der DDR so auslegelegt werden, daß den völkerrechtlichen Bindungen der DDR im Hinblick auf Menschenrechte entsprochen wurde, so ist das Tatzeitrecht in dieser menschenrechtsfreundlichen Auslegung als das Recht zu verstehen, das die Strafbarkeit zur Zeit der Tat im Sinne des Art. 103 Abs. 2 GG 'gesetzlich bestimmt' hat (im Ergebnis ähnlich Alexy VVDStRL 51 (1992), 132ff.; Schünemann aaO; Lüderssen ZStW 104 [1992], 735, 779ff.; vgl. ferner Starck und Maurer VVDStRL 51 (1992), 141ff., 147f.). Ein Rechtfertigungsgrund, der das Verhalten der Angeklagten gerechtfertigt hätte, wurde zwar in der Staatspraxis, wie sie sich in der Befehlslage ausdrückte, angenommen; er durfte aber dem richtig interpretierten Gesetz schon damals nicht entnommen werden. Das Rückwirkungsverbot soll den Angeklagten vor Willkür schützen und die Strafgewalt auf den Vollzug der allgemeinen Gesetze beschränken (Schreiber, Gesetz und Richter S. 217); es schützt das Vertrauen, das der Angeklagte zur Tatzeit in den Fortbestand des damals geltenden Rechts gesetzt hat (Rüping, Bonner Kommentar – Zweitbearbeitung – Art. 103 Abs.2 GG Rdn. 16 m. w.Nachw.). Diese verfassungsrechtlichen Schutzrichtungen werden hier nicht verfehlt: Die Erwartung, das Recht werde, wie in der Staatspraxis zur Tatzeit, auch in Zukunft so angewandt werden, daß ein menschenrechtswidriger Rechtfertigungsgrund anerkannt wird, ist nicht schutzwürdig. Es ist keine Willkür, wenn der Angeklagte, was die Rechtswidrigkeit seines Tuns angeht, so beurteilt wird, wie er bei richtiger Auslegung des DDR-Rechts schon zur Tatzeit hätte behandelt werden müssen. Nichts anderes könnte im übrigen im Ergebnis gelten, wenn ein gesetzlicher Rechtfertigungsgrund, der gleich gewichtigen Einwendungen ausgesetzt ist, überhaupt keiner Auslegung zugänglich wäre, die sich an den Menschenrechten orientiert.

(c) Steht hiernach den Angeklagten kein Rechtfertigungsgrund zur Seite, so haben sie rechtswidrig den Tatbestand des § 212 StGB erfüllt. Deswegen trifft im Ergebnis die Auffassung der Judendkammer zu, daß das Recht der Bundesrepublik Deutschland anwendbar ist, weil es im Sinne des § 2 Abs. 3 StGB milder ist als die entsprechenden Tatbestände (§§ 112, 113) des Strafgesetzbuchs der DDR; dies ergibt sich daraus, daß in § 213 StGB für minder schwere Fälle ein niedrigerer Strafrahmen vorgesehen ist.

(2) The Senate is, for the following reason, of the view that Art 103 para 2 of the GG is not opposed to the proposition that the act is unlawful; the decisive issue is, as stated, whether the criminality 'was determined by statute' before the act was committed. In examining whether this was the case, the judge is not bound in the sense of pure factuality to that interpretation which found expression in State practice at the time of the act. If the law at the time of the act could, taking into account the limits provided by the literal meaning of the statute and in the light of the constitution of the DDR be so interpreted that the international law obligations of the DDR with regard to human rights were complied with, the law at the time of the act is to be understood according to this interpretation sympathetic to human rights as the law which 'statutorily determined' the criminality at the time of the act in the sense of Art 103 para 2 of the GG (similar in outcome to Alexy VVDStRL 51 (1992), 132 and onwards; Schünemann *loc cit*; Lüderssen ZStW 104 [1992], 735, 779 and onwards; compare further Starck and Maurer VVDStRL 51 (1992), 141 and onwards, 147 and onwards). A ground of justification which would have justified the conduct of the defendants was certainly accepted in State practice as was expressed in the total context of the command; but it ought not to be inferred at that time from the statute as correctly interpreted. The prohibition on retroactivity should protect the accused from arbitrary action and limit penal authority to the enforcement of general laws (Schreiber, Statute and Judges, p 217); it protects the trust which the defendant has put, at the time of the act, in the continuing existence of the law applicable at that time (Rüping, Bonn Commentary – Second Revision – GG, Art 103 para 2 marginal no 16 with further references). These protective principles of constitutional law are not being ignored here: the expectation that the law would also be applied in the future as it was in State practice at the time of the act, in such a way that a ground of justification which was contrary to human rights was acknowledged, is not worthy of protection. It is not arbitrary treatment if the accused, so far as the unlawfulness of his action is concerned, is judged in the way in which he ought to have been treated on the correct interpretation of DDR law at the time of the act. Besides this, no other outcome could apply if a statutory ground of justification which is open to equally weighty objections would be susceptible to no interpretation at all which is orientated to human rights.

(c) If no ground of justification is accordingly available to the defendants, they have fulfilled the constituent elements of § 212 of the StGB in an unlawful manner. Therefore, the view of the Young Peoples Chamber that the law of the Federal Republic of Germany is applicable proves correct in its outcome, because it is less severe, in the sense of § 2 para 3 of the StGB, than the corresponding constituent elements (§§ 112 and 113) of the Criminal Code of the DDR; this follows from the fact that in § 213 of the StGB a lower punishment structure is provided for in respect of less serious cases.

III

1 Auf dieser Grundlage ergibt die sachlichrechtliche Nachprüfung, daß die Jugendkammer das Verhalten der Angeklagten zutreffend als gemeinschaftlichen Totschlag (§§ 212, 25 Abs. 2 StGB) gewertet hat.

(a) Die mit der Abgabe von Dauerfeuer verbundene, den Angeklagten bewußte besondere Gefährdung des Tatopfers ist von der Jugendkammer im Zusammenhang mit der Befehlslage, der die Angeklagten entsprechen wollten, ohne Rechtsverstoß zur Grundlage ihrer Annahme gemacht worden, die Angeklagten hätten mit bedingtem Tötungsvorsatz gehandelt. Durch diesen Vorsatz unterscheidet sich die abgeurteilte Tat von dem in der Entscheidung BGHSt 35, 379 behandelten Fall; dort hatte der Beamte nach der vom Revisionsgericht hingenommenen Feststellung des Tatrichter eine tödliche Verletzung des Fliehenden nicht billigend in Kauf genommen (aaO S. 386).

(b) Auch der Angeklagte H. war Täter. Zwar hat er das Tatopfer nur am Knie getroffen, wie er es beabsichtigt hatte. Indessen haben beide Angeklagte übereinstimmend mit Dauerfeuer geschossen, um S. am Übersteigen der Mauer zu hindern, selbst wenn es ihn das Leben kosten sollte. Zwar hat, seitdem der Angeklagte H. den Turm verließ, kein Kontakt zwischen den beiden Angeklagten bestanden. Beide handelten jedoch unter dem Einfluß des gleichen Befehls mit gleicher Zielsetzung. Allerdings sind bei nur bedingtem Vorsatz an die Gemeinschaftlichkeit der Tatbegehung (§ 25 Abs. 2 StGB) hohe Anforderungen zu stellen. Ihnen wird das Urteil der Jugendkammer indessen noch gerecht. Beiden Angeklagten war befohlen, selbst unter Inkaufnahme einer Tötung auf den Flüchtling zu schießen, wenn dessen Flucht nicht anders sicher zu verhindern war. Beide gingen, wie der Tatrichter festgestellt hat, davon aus, daß jeweils der andere dem Befehl entsprechen werde. Mit ihrem jeweiligen Verhalten gaben sie dem anderen zu erkennen, daß sie das Ziel verfolgten, das ihnen beiden durch den Befehl vorgegeben war. Es entsprach der Befehlslage, daß jeder der beiden Soldaten durch sein Schießen zur Fluchtverhinderung beitrug. Unter diesen Umständen muß sich der Angeklagte H. das Verhalten des Mitangeklagten, das zur tödlichen Verletzung führte, im Sinne arbeitsteiliger Mittäterschaft zurechnen lassen.

Die Vorschrift des StGB-DDR über die Mittäterschaft (§ 22 Abs. 2 Nr. 2) begründete keine mildere Beurteilung im Sinne des § 2 Abs. 3 StGB. Die Angeklagten haben die Tat auch im Sinne des § 22 Abs. 2 Nr. 2 StGB-DDR gemeinschaftlich ausgeführt, indem beide mit bedingtem Tötungsvorsatz schossen. Für S. wurde ungeachtet der – nicht geklärten – Reihenfolge der Schüsse jedenfalls die Chance, sich den Schüssen des Angeklagten W. durch Übersteigen der Mauer zu entziehen, dadurch vermindert, daß auch der Angeklagte H. auf ihn schoß. Insofern hat auch dieser Angeklagte Haundlungen vorgenommen, die geeignet waren, den Tod des Opfers herbeizuführen (vgl. DDR-Kommentar § 22 StGB Anm. 5 unter Hinweis auf OGNJ 1973, 87 und 177).

III

1 On this basis the relevant factual and legal examination shows that the Young Peoples Chamber correctly assessed the conduct of the defendants as joint manslaughter (§§ 212 and 25 para 2 of the StGB).

(a) The Young Peoples Chamber, without any mistake in law, based their proposition that the defendants had acted with a conditional intention to kill on the particular endangering of the victim, of which the defendants were aware, and which was associated with the discharge of continuous fire, connected with the total context of the command with which the defendants wished to comply. This intention distinguishes the act which was the subject of the judgment from the case dealt with in the decision BGHSt 35, 379; there, the official had, according to the finding of the judge of fact which was accepted by the court hearing the appeal in law, accepted the possibility of a fatal injury of the fugitive without approving of it (*loc cit*, p 386).

(b) The defendant H was also a perpetrator. It is true that he only hit the victim on the knee, as he had intended. However, both the defendants used continuous fire by agreement to prevent S climbing over the wall, even if it was to cost him his life. It is true that there was no contact between the two defendants after the defendant H left the tower. Both acted however under the influence of the same command, with the same object in view. Certainly when the intention is only conditional higher standards are to be set as to whether the act has been committed jointly (§ 25 para 2 of the StGB). The judgment of the Young Peoples Chamber is however correct in relation to these standards. Both defendants were commanded to shoot at the fugitive, even if this resulted in killing him, if his flight could not otherwise be prevented. Both proceeded on the basis, as the judge of fact has established, that, at any given time, the other would comply with the command. By their actual conduct, they each gave the other to understand that they were pursuing the objective which was given to them both by the command. It corresponded with the total context of the command that each of the two soldiers contributed by shooting to prevent the flight. Under these circumstances, the conduct of the co-defendant, which led to fatal injury must be attributed to the accused H in the sense of complicity based on their joint task.

The provisions of the StGB-DDR regarding complicity (§ 22 para 2 no 2) did not form the basis of a less severe assessment in the sense of § 2 para 3 of the StGB. The defendants also carried out the act jointly in the sense of § 22 para 2 no 2 of the StGB-DDR, in that both fired with conditional intention to kill. For S, regardless of the sequence – which was not made clear – of the shots, the chance of escaping from the shots of the defendant W. by climbing over the wall would in any case be diminished by the fact that the defendant H also fired at him. In this respect this defendant also took steps which were appropriate for bringing about the death of the victim (compare DDR Commentary § 22 StGB note 5 with reference to OGNJ 1973, 87 and 177).

(c) Beide Beschwerdeführer waren nicht etwa nur Gehilfen derer, auf die die Befehle zurückgingen. Der Senat braucht nicht auf die Frage einzugehen, ob und in welcher Weise die Neufassung der Vorschrift des § 25 Abs.1 StGB durch das 2. StrRG eine Beurteilung ausschließt, wie sie der Bundesgerichtshof in BGHSt 18, 87 zugunsten bloßer Teilnahme vorgenommen hatte (vgl. auch BGH NStZ 1987, 224ff.). Hier haben die Angeklagten nicht nur alle Tatbestandsmerkmale, auch durch wechselseitige Zurechnung arbeitsteiligen Verhaltens, erfüllt. Sie haben auch, anders etwa als diejenigen, die unmittelbar vor dem Schießen einen Befehl entgegennehmen, einen gewissen Handlungsspielraum gehabt, weil sie beim plötzlichen Erscheinen des Flüchtlings auf sich allein gestellt waren. Schon dieser Umstand kennzeichnet ihr Verhalten als Täterschaft.

2 Die Angeklagten haben den – mangels eines beachtlichen Rechtfertigungsgrundes rechtswidrigen – Totschlag auf Befehl begangen. Die Feststellungen ergeben, daß sie bei ihrer Tat nicht erkannt haben, daß die Ausführung des Befehls gegen Strafgesetze verstieß. Dies steht indessen ihrer Schuld nicht entgegen.

(a) Der Senat hatte in diesem Zusammenhang zunächst zu prüfen, ob bei einem Handeln auf Befehl § 258 Abs.1 StGB-DDR im Hinblick auf § 2 Abs. 3 StGB milder ist als die entsprechende Vorschrift des Bundesrechts (§ 5 Abs. 1 WStG). Das wäre der Fall, sofern der Soldat nach § 258 Abs. 1 StGB-DDR immer schon dann von Verantwortung frei wäre, wenn er nicht positiv erkannt hat, daß die Ausführung des Befehls gegen Strafgesetze verstieß. In diesem Sinne können Ausführungen in dem DDR-Kommentar verstanden werden (§ 258 StGB Anm. 2, 3 d). Indessen ist diese Kommentierung mit dem Wortsinn des Gesetzes nicht vereinbar. Nach § 258 Abs. 1 StGB-DDR wird der Soldat nicht von seiner Verantwortung befreit, wenn die Ausführung des Befehls offensichtlich gegen die anerkannten Normen des Völkerrechts oder gegen Strafgesetze verstößt. Die Vorschrift kann nur so verstanden werden, daß in diesem Falle auch derjenige, der den Verstoß gegen das Strafrecht nicht erkannt hat, für seine Handlung bestraft werden kann; nur für diese Personengruppe ist der Bezug auf die Offensichtlichkeit des Strafrechtsverstoßes sinnvoll, während es bei demjenigen, der die Strafrechtswidrigkeit eingesehen hat, nicht darauf ankommen kann, ob diese offensichtlich war oder nicht.

Hiernach war im Rahmen des sonst milderen Bundesrechts § 5 Abs. 1 WStG anzuwenden. Allerdings gilt das Wehrstrafgesetz unmittelbar nur für Soldaten der Bundeswehr (§ 1 Abs. 1 WStG). Da es aber unbillig wäre, das Untergebenenverhältnis der beiden Angeklagten gegenüber ihren Befehlsgebern weder nach dem Recht der DDR noch nach Bundesrecht zu berücksichtigen, ist die Vorschrift des § 5 WStG zugunsten der Angeklagten entsprechend anzuwenden.

(c) Both complainants were not only assistants of those from whom the commands originated. The Senate does not need to go into the question of whether and in what manner the new form of the provisions of § 25 para 1 of the StGB introduced by the 2nd StrRG excludes a judgment like that taken by the Federal Supreme Court in BGHSt 18, 87 in favour of mere participation (compare also BGH NStZ 1987, 224 and onwards). Here the defendants have not only fulfilled all the constituent elements, by reciprocal assignment of the carrying out of the shared joint task. They also had, in contrast to those who receive a command immediately before the shooting, a certain latitude in respect of their actions, because on the sudden appearance of the fugitive they were dependent on themselves alone. This circumstance characterises their behaviour as perpetration.

2 The defendants committed the – in default of any ground of justification which could be taken into account, unlawful – killing on command. The findings show that they did not recognise as they committed their act that the carrying out of the command violated criminal statutory provisions. This is not, however, inconsistent with their guilt.

(a) The Senate had to examine first in this connection whether for an action carried out by command § 258 para 1 of the StGB-DDR is, with regard to § 2 para 3 of the StGB, less severe than the corresponding provisions of the Federal law (§ 5 para 1 of the WStG). That would be the case insofar as the soldier would always be free from responsibility according to § 258 para 1 of the StGB-DDR if he did not positively recognise that the execution of the command violated criminal statutory provisions. Statements in the DDR Commentary can be understood in this sense (§ 258 of the StGB, note 2, 3 d). However, this comment is not reconcilable with the literal sense of the statute. According to § 258 para 1 of the StGB-DDR, the soldier is not freed from his responsibility if the carrying out of the command obviously violates the recognised norms of international law or criminal statutes. The provision can only be understood in such a way that in this case even the person who did not recognise the violation of the criminal law can be punished for his act; only for this group of persons is the reference to the obviousness of the violation of the criminal law meaningful, whilst for the person who perceived the criminal unlawfulness, it cannot matter whether this was obvious or not.

According to this, § 5 para 1 of the WStG was to be applied in the framework of the – in other respects less severe – Federal law. It is true that the Military Crimes Act only applies directly for soldiers of the Federal Army (§ 1, para 1 of the WStG). But as it would be unfair to consider the relationship of subordination of the two defendants as against those issuing commands to them neither in accordance with the law of the DDR nor in accordance with Federal law, the provisions of § 5 of the WStG are to be applied correspondingly in favour of the defendants.

(b) Nach § 5 Abs. 1 WStG trifft den Untergebenen eine Schuld nur, wenn er erkennt, daß es sich um eine rechtswidrige Tat handelt oder dies nach den ihm bekannten Umständen offensichtlich ist. Die erste der genannten Voraussetzungen liegt, wie dargelegt, nicht vor. Ob die Angeklagten nach § 5 Abs. 1 WStG entchuldigt sind, hängt demnach davon ab, ob es nach den ihnen bekannten Umständen offensichtlich war, daß ihnen eine rechtswidrige Tat im Sinne des Strafgesetzbuchs (§ 11 Abs.1 Nr. 5 StGB) befohlen worden war.

Die Jugendkammer nimmt an, es sei für die Angeklagten nach den ihnen bekannten Umständen offensichtlich gewesen, daß sie mit dem ihnen befohlenen Schießen ein Tötungsdelikt im Sinne des Strafgesetzbuches begingen. Diese Bewertung hält im Ergebnis der sachlichrechtlichen Nachprüfung stand.

Die Jugendkammer hat nicht übersehen, daß die Angeklagten als Grenzsoldaten der DDR einer besonders intensiven politischen Indoktrination ausgesetzt waren und daß sie zuvor 'im Geiste des Sozialismus mit entsprechenden Feindbildern von der Bundesrepublik Deutschland und von Personen, die unter Überwindung der Sperranlagen die DDR verlassen wollen, aufgewachsen' sind. Sie hat auch unter diesen Umständen nicht die hohen Anforderungen verfehlt, die an die Offensichtlichkeit im Sinne des § 5 Abs. 1 WStG zu stellen sind. Der Soldat hat keine Prüfungspflicht (Scherer/Alff, Soldatengesetz, 6. Aufl., § 11 Rdn. 29). Wo er Zweifel hegt, die er nicht beheben kann, darf er dem Befehl folgen; offensichtlich ist der Strafrechtsverstoß nur dann, wenn er jenseits aller Zweifel liegt (Amtliche Begründung zum Entwurf des Soldatengesetzes BTDrucks. 2/1700 S. 21; vgl. auch Schölz/Lingens WStG, 3. Aufl., § 5 Rdn. 12).

(b) According to § 5 para 1 of the WStG, the subordinate is only guilty if he recognises that it is a question of an unlawful act or this is obvious according to the circumstances known to him. The first of the stated prerequisites is, as has been explained, not present. Whether the defendants are excused in accordance with § 5 para 1 of the WStG is consequently dependent on whether it was obvious according to the circumstances known to them that a command had been given to them to commit an unlawful act in the sense of the Criminal Code (§ 11 para 1 no 5 of the StGB).

The Young Peoples Chamber accepts that it was obvious for the defendants according to the circumstances known to them that they were committing a delict of homicide in the sense of the Criminal Code by the shooting which was the subject of the command to them. This assessment stands firm as a result of the factual and legal examination.

The Young Peoples Chamber did not overlook the fact that the defendants as border soldiers of the DDR were exposed to an especially intensive political indoctrination and that they had previously 'grown up in the spirit of socialism with corresponding hostile images of the Federal Republic of Germany and of persons who wanted to leave the DDR by surmounting the barrier installations'. Even in these circumstances the Chamber did not ignore the high requirements which are to be placed on obviousness in the sense of § 5 para 1 of the WStG. The soldier has no duty of examination (Scherer/Alff, Military Law, 6th edn, § 11 marginal no 29). If he harbours doubts which he cannot get rid of, he may follow the command; the violation of the criminal law is only obvious when it is beyond all doubt (Official Basis of the Scheme of Military Law BTDrucks 2/1700, p 21; compare also Schölz Lingens WStG, 3rd edn, § 5 marginal no 12).

Es ist aus Rechtsgründen nicht zu beanstanden, wenn die Jugendkammer gleichwohl angenommen hat, es sei nach den Umständen offensichtlich gewesen, daß das Schießen hier gegen das Strafrecht verstieß. Die Jugendkammer hebt zutreffend auf das 'Gebot der Menschlichkeit' ab, zu dem u. a. gehöre, daß auch der Straftäter ein Recht auf Leben hat. Damit will sie sagen, es sei ohne weiteres ersichtlich gewesen, daß der Staat nicht das Recht habe, einen Menschen, der, ohne andere zu bedrohen, unter Überwindung der Mauer von einem Teil Berlins in einen anderen hinüberwechseln wollte, zur Verhinderung dieses unerlaubten Grenzübertritts töten zu lassen. Den Revisionen ist zuzugeben, daß die Anwendung des Merkmals 'offensichtlich' hier sehr schwierig ist. Immerhin ist während der langen Jahre, in denen an der Mauer und an den sonstigen innerdeutschen Grenzen geschossen wurde, nicht bekannt geworden, daß Menschen, die in der DDR in Politik, Truppenführung, Justiz und Wissenschaft Verantwortung trugen, gegen das Töten an der Grenze öffentlich Stellung genommen haben. Verfahren gegen Schützen waren nicht durchgeführt worden. Angesichts des Lebensweges und der Umwelt der Angeklagten erscheint es auch nicht angemessen, ihnen 'Bequemlichkeit', 'Rechtsblindheit' und Verzicht auf eigenes Denken zum Vorwurf zu machen. Schließlich sollte es den Angeklagten H. nicht belasten, daß er 'nach seiner eigenen Einlassung unmittelbar nach der Tat erkannt hat, daß sein Vorgehen gegenüber S. unmenschlich war'; dieser Umstand kann auch so gedeutet werden, daß die Konfrontation mit den Folgen der Schüsse das Gewissen des Angeklagten erstmals geweckt hat.

Gleichwohl ist der Jugendkammer letztlich darin zuzustimmen, daß die Tötung eines unbewaffneten Flüchtlings durch Dauerfeuer unter den gegebenen Umständen ein derart schreckliches und jeder vernünftigen Rechtfertigung entzogenes Tun war, daß der Verstoß gegen das elementare Tötungsverbot auch für einen indoktrinierten Menschen ohne weiteres einsichtig, also offensichtlich war. Dem entspricht es, daß die große Mehrheit der Bevölkerung in der DDR die Anwendung von Schußwaffen an der Grenze mißbilligte. Daß es sich so verhielt, ist allgemeinkundig. Auch der Umstand, daß die Befehlslage der Geheimhaltung des Vorganges Vorrang vor einer schnellen Lebensrettung des Opfers gab, zeigt, in welchem Maße die Verantwortlichen eine Mißbilligung der Todesschüsse durch die Bevölkerung voraussetzten. Das Tatopfer S., ein Zimmermann, hatte es strikt abgelehnt, zu den Grenztruppen zu gehen.

There can be no objection on legal grounds to the Young Peoples Chamber nevertheless accepting that it was obvious in the circumstances that the shooting here violated criminal law. The Young Peoples Chamber emphasises pertinently the 'requirement of humanity' which includes, amongst other things, the principle that the criminal also has a right to life. By this it meant that it was plainly self-evident that the State does not have the right, in order to prevent this impermissible crossing of the border, to cause the killing of a person who, without threatening others, intended to go from one part of Berlin into another by surmounting the wall. It is conceded in favour of the appeals in law that the application of the characteristic 'obvious' is very difficult here. After all, during the long years in which there were shootings at the wall and at the other inner German borders, the people in the DDR who bore responsibility in politics, military leadership, justice and knowledge were not known to have expressed a view publicly about killing on the border. Proceedings against marksmen had not been taken. In the light of the life history and environment of the defendants it also does not seem appropriate to reproach them with 'complacency', 'blindness to the law' and renunciation of their own thought processes. Finally, it should not be held against the accused H that 'according to his own admission he recognised immediately after the act that his action against S was inhuman'; this circumstance can also have as its explanation that confrontation with the consequences of the shots awoke the conscience of the accused for the first time.

Nevertheless, the view of the Young Peoples Chamber that the killing of an unarmed fugitive by continuous fire in the given circumstances was an act so dreadful and so beyond any rational justification that the violation of the elementary prohibition of killing was easily comprehensible, and therefore obvious, even for an indoctrinated person, should, in the end, be agreed. The fact that the great majority of the population of the DDR disapproved of the use of firearms at the border corresponds with this. It is generally known that this was the case. Even the circumstance that whole context of the command gave secrecy of the event priority over taking rapid steps to save the life of the victim shows to what degree those responsible assumed disapproval by the population of fatal shots. The victim S, a carpenter, had strictly refused to join the border troops.

3 Der Tatrichter hat nicht ausgeschlossen, daß die Angeklagten geglaubt haben, sie müßten einen Grenzbrecher zur Verhinderung der Flucht auch dann, dem Befehl entsprechend, töten, wenn der Befehl rechtswidrig war. Es ist aus Rechtsgründen nicht zu beanstanden, daß der Tatrichter angenommen hat, dieser Irrtum stelle als Annahme eines nicht anerkannten Rechtfertigungsgrundes einen Verbotsirrtum dar, der im Sinne des § 17 Satz 2 StGB von den Angeklagten vermieden werden konnte. Der Tatrichter hat zur Begründung der letztgenannten Wertung wiederum darauf hingewiesen, daß das Leben das höchste aller Rechtsgüter sei. Dem kann aus Rechtsgründen nicht entgegengetreten werden. Der Tatrichter hätte in diesem Zusammenhang auch darauf hinweisen können, daß den Angeklagten bei ihrer Schulung gesagt worden ist, Befehle, die gegen die Menschlichkeit verstießen, brauchten nicht befolgt zu werden.

Auch im Zusammenhang mit der Frage des Verbotsirrtums würde die Anwendung des DDR-Rechts zu keiner milderen Beurteilung führen (§ 2 Abs. 3 StGB). Zwar ist im Schrifttum der DDR ausgeführt worden, der Täter handele (nur dann) vorsätzlich, wenn er sich bewußt sei, gegen die sozialen Grundnormen zu verstoßen (DDR-Kommentar § 6 Anm.1). Nach Lekschas u. a. schließt der Vorsatz die 'Selbsterkenntnis ein, sich entgegen den Grundregeln menschlichen Zusammenlebens zu einem sozial negativen Verhalten entschieden zu haben' (Strafrecht der DDR, Lehrbuch 1988 S. 237). Doch gab es hierzu keine einheitliche Auffassung (Lekschas u. a. aaO). Aus der veröffentlichten Rechtsprechung der Gerichte der DDR ergibt sich zu dieser Frage nichts. Aus alldem kann der Senat nicht entnehmen, daß die irrige Annahme, ein offensichtlich gegen das Strafrecht verstoßender Befehl müsse befolgt werden, bei der Anwendung des DDR-Rechts Anlaß gegeben hätte, den Vorsatz zu verneinen.

4 Die Strafzumessung hält der sachlichrechtlichen Nachprüfung stand. Der Tatrichter hat, wie der Zusammenhang der Urteilsgründe zeigt, nicht übersehen, daß die Angeklagten erst nach dem Bau der Berliner Mauer aufgewachsen sind und nach Herkunft und Lebensweg keine Möglichkeit hatten, der Indoktrination eine kritische Einschätzung entgegenzustellen. Ihre handwerkliche Berufsausbildung hat dazu ersichtlich ebenso wie die Schulausbildung nicht beitragen können. Die Angeklagten standen in der militärischen Hierarchie ganz unten. Sie sind in gewisser Weise auch Opfer der mit dieser Grenze verbundenen Verhältnisse. Wie die Verteidigung zutreffend ausgeführt hat, haben Umstände, die die Angeklagten nicht zu vertreten haben, dazu geführt, daß sie vor Funktionsträgern, die über einen größeren Überblick und eine differenziertere Ausbildung verfügten, strafrechtlich zur Verantwortung gezogen worden sind. Dies alles drängte zu milden Strafen. Dem hat die Jugendkammer Rechnung getragen.

3 The judge of fact did not exclude the possibility that the defendants believed, in accordance with the command, they had to kill a violator of the border in order to prevent his flight even if the command was unlawful. There can be no objection on legal grounds to the fact that the judge of fact accepted that this mistake represented, as an assumption of a ground of justification which was not recognised, a mistake of law which, in the sense of § 17 sentence 2 of the StGB, could have been avoided by the defendants. The judge of fact, as a basis for the last mentioned assessment, again referred to the fact that life was the highest of all legal interests. That cannot be opposed on legal grounds. The judge of fact would also have been able to refer in this connection to the fact that the defendants were told in their training that commands which offended against humanity did not need to be followed.

In connection also with the question of a mistake of law, the application of the law of the DDR would not lead to a more lenient judgment (§ 2 para 3 of the StGB). It is true that it has been stated in the literature of the DDR that the perpetrator would (only) be acting intentionally if he was aware that he was violating the basic social norms (DDR Commentary § 6 note 1). According to Lekschas, amongst others, intention includes the 'self-knowledge that one has decided in favour of socially negative conduct contrary to the basic rules of human communal life' (Criminal Law of the DDR, Textbook, 1988, p 237). There was, however, on this issue, no uniform view (Leckschas, amongst others, *loc cit*). Nothing emerges from the published case law of the courts of the DDR on this question. The Senate cannot infer from all this that the mistaken supposition that a command which obviously violated the criminal law had to be followed would have given rise, on the application of DDR law, to a denial of intention.

4 The assessment of the punishment withstands the factual and legal examination. The judge of fact, as the correlation of the grounds of the judgment shows, did not overlook the fact that the defendants had only grown up after the building of the Berlin wall and according to their origin and life history had no opportunity to subject their indoctrination to a critical assessment. Their vocational training as manual workers and likewise their school education obviously could not have contributed to this. The defendants were quite far down in the military hierarchy. They are in a certain way also victims of the relationships connected with this border. As the defence pertinently explained, circumstances which the defendants do not have to defend have led to them having been called to account under the criminal law before officials who have at their disposal a larger overview and a more discriminating education. All this urged towards lenient punishments. The Young Peoples Chamber took account of this.

Spatial scope

§ 3 [Geltung für Inlandstaten] Das deutsche Strafrecht gilt für Taten, die im Inland begangen werden.

§ 5 [Auslandstaten gegen inländische Rechtsgüter] Das deutsche Strafrecht gilt, unabhängig vom Recht des Tatorts, für folgende Taten, die im Ausland begangen werden:

1 Vorbereitung eines Angriffskrieges (§ 80);

2 Hochverrat (§§ 81 bis 83);

3 Gefährdung des demokratischen Rechtsstaates;

...

4 Landesverrat und Gefährdung der äußeren Sicherheit (§§ 94 bis 100 a);

5 Straftaten gegen die Landesverteidigung;

...

6 Verschleppung und politische Verdächtigung (§§ 234 a, 241 a), wenn die Tat sich gegen einen Deutschen richtet, der im Inland seinen Wohnsitz oder gewöhnlichen Aufenthalt hat;

(6 a–15 ...)

§ 6 [Auslandstaten gegen international geschützter Rechtsgüter] Das deutsche Strafrecht gilt weiter, unabhängig vom Recht des Tatorts, für folgende Taten, die im Ausland begangen werden:

1 Völkermord (§ 220 a);

(2–8 ...)

9 Taten, die auf Grund eines für die Bundesrepublik Deutschland verbindlichen zwischenstaatlichen Abkommens auch dann zu verfolgen sind, wenn sie im Ausland begangen werden.

Time and place of act

§ 8 [Zeit der Tat] Eine Tat ist zu der Zeit begangen, zu welcher der Täter oder der Teilnehmer gehandelt hat oder im Falle des Unterlassens hätte handeln müssen. Wann der Erfolg eintritt, ist nicht maßgebend.

Spatial scope

§ 3 [Effect for acts within the country] German criminal law applies for acts which are committed within the country.

§ 4 applies to acts on German ships and aircraft.

§ 5 [Acts in other countries against domestic legal interests] German criminal law applies, independently of the law of the place of the act, for the following acts which are committed in other countries:

1 Preparation for a war of aggression (§ 80);

2 High treason (§§ 81 to 83);

3 Endangering of the democratic constitutional State;

...

4 Betrayal of the country and endangering of external security (§§ 94 to 100 a);

5 Criminal acts against the country's defence;

...

6 Abduction and political inculpation (§§ 234 a, 241 a), if the act is directed against a German person who has his domicile or normal residence within the country;

(6a–15: other criminal acts)

§ 6 [Acts in other countries against internationally protected legal interests] German criminal law also applies, independently of the law of the place of the act, for the following acts which are committed in other countries:

1 Genocide (§ 220 a);

(2–8: other criminal acts)

9 Acts which are to be prosecuted, even if they are committed in another country, on the basis of an international treaty which is binding on the Federal Republic.

§ 7 relates to acts in other countries in other cases.

Time and place of act

§ 8 [Time of the act] An act is committed at the time at which the perpetrator or participant has acted or, in the case of an omission, ought to have acted. When the result occurs is not decisive.

§ 9 relates to the place of the act.

Young people

§ 10 [Sondervorschriften für Jugendliche und Heranwachsende] Für Taten von Jugendlichen und Heranwachsenden gilt dieses Gesetz nur, soweit im Jugendgerichtsgesetz nichts anderes bestimmt ist.

DEFINITIONS

Zweiter Titel. Sprachgebrauch

§ 11 [Personen- und Sachbegriffe] (1) Im Sinne dieses Gesetzes ist

1 Angehöriger:

wer zu den folgenden Personen gehört:

(a) Verwandte und Verschwägerte gerader Linie, der Ehegatte, der Lebenspartner, der Verlobte, Geschwister, Ehegatten der Geschwister, Geschwister der Ehegatten, und zwar auch dann, wenn die Ehe oder die Lebenspartnerschaft, welche die Beziehung begründet hat, nicht mehr besteht oder wenn die Verwandtschaft oder Schwägerschaft erloschen ist.

(b) Pflegeeltern und Pflegekinder;

...

5 rechtswidrige Tat:

nur eine solche, die den Tatbestand eines Strafgesetzes verwirklicht;

6 Unternehmen einer Tat:

deren Versuch und deren Vollendung;

7 Behörde:

auch ein Gericht;

...

§ 12 [Verbrechen und Vergehen] (1) Verbrechen sind rechtswidrige Taten, die im Mindestmaß mit Freiheitsstrafe von einem Jahr oder darüber bedroht sind.

(2) Vergehen sind rechtswidrige Taten, die im Mindestmaß mit einer geringeren Freiheitsstrafe oder die mit Geldstrafe bedroht sind.

(3) Schärfungen oder Milderungen, die nach den Vorschriften des Allgemeinen Teils oder für besonders schwere oder minder schwere Fälle vorgesehen sind, bleiben für die Einteilung außer Betracht.

Young people

§ 10 [Special provisions for the young and adolescent] For acts of young people and adolescents, this Code only applies insofar as the Juvenile Court Act does not provide otherwise.

DEFINITIONS

Second Title. Use of language

§ 11 [Concepts as to persons and things] (1) For the purpose of this Code,

1 relative:

means anyone included amongst the following persons:

(a) relatives and in-laws in the direct line, spouse, life partner, fiancé, siblings, spouses of siblings, siblings of spouses, including when the marriage or the life partnership which has founded the relationship does not exist any more or when the relationship or relationship by marriage has lapsed;

(b) foster parents and foster children;

(2–4: certain official positions)

5 Unlawful act:

only one which embodies the elements of a criminal statutory provision;

6 undertaking of an act:

its attempt and its completion;

7 authority:

includes a court;

(8 and 9: 'measures' and 'recompense')

((2) and (3): extended meanings of 'intentional' and 'writings')

§ 12 [Crimes and offences] (1) Crimes are unlawful acts for which a sentence of imprisonment of at least one year or more may be imposed.

(2) Offences are unlawful acts for which at least a lesser sentence of imprisonment or a monetary penalty may be imposed.

(3) For the purpose of the division, increases or reductions, which are provided for according to the provisions of the General Part or for especially severe or less severe cases, are left out of consideration.

PRINCIPLES

Omissions, acting for another, intention and negligence

Zweiter Abschnitt. Die Tat

Erster Titel. Grundlagen der Strafbarkeit

§ 13 [Begehen durch Unterlassen] (1) Wer es unterläßt, einen Erfolg abzuwenden, der zum Tatbestand eines Strafgesetzes gehört, ist nach diesem Gesetz nur dann strafbar, wenn er rechtlich dafür einzustehen hat, daß der Erfolg nicht eintritt, und wenn das Unterlassen der Verwirklichung des gesetzlichen Tatbestandes durch ein Tun entspricht.

(2) Die Strafe kann nach § 49 Abs. 1 gemildert werden.

§ 15 [Vorsätzliches und fahrlässiges Handeln] Strafbar ist nur vorsätzliches Handeln, wenn nicht das Gesetz fahrlässiges Handeln ausdrücklich mit Strafe bedroht.

Mistakes

§ 16 [Irrtum über Tatumstände] (1) Wer bei Begehung der Tat einen Umstand nicht kennt, der zum gesetzlichen Tatbestand gehört, handelt nicht vorsätzlich. Die Strafbarkeit wegen fahrlässiger Begehung bleibt unberührt.

(2) Wer bei Begehung der Tat irrig Umstände annimmt, welche den Tatbestand eines milderen Gesetzes verwirklichen würden, kann wegen vorsätzlicher Begehung nur nach dem milderen Gesetz bestraft werden.

§ 17 [Verbotsirrtum] Fehlt dem Täter bei Begehung der Tat die Einsicht, Unrecht zu tun, so handelt er ohne Schuld, wenn er diesen Irrtum nicht vermeiden konnte. Konnte der Täter den Irrtum vermeiden, so kann die Strafe nach § 49 Abs. 1 gemildert werden.

PRINCIPLES

Omissions, acting for another, intention and negligence

Second section. The act

First title. Principles of criminal liability

§ 13 [Commission by omission] (1) A person who omits to prevent a consequence which belongs to the elements of a criminal statutory provision is only punishable according to this Code if he is legally responsible for the fact that the consequence does not occur and if the omission corresponds to the realisation of the statutory elements of an act.

(2) The punishment can be reduced in accordance with § 49 para 1.

§ 14 relates to action on behalf of another.

§ 15 [Intentional and negligent action] Only intentional action is punishable, unless statute expressly provides for punishment of negligent action.

Mistakes

§ 16 [Mistake regarding circumstances in connection with the act] (1) A person who on commission of an act does not know a circumstance which belongs to the statutory elements of the crime involved does not act intentionally. Criminal liability for negligent commission remains unaffected.

(2) A person who, on commission of an act, erroneously assumes circumstances which would fulfil the elements of a less serious statutory provision can be punished on account of intentional commission only in accordance with the less serious statutory provision.

§ 17 [Error of law] If the perpetrator on commission of the act lacks the understanding that he is doing wrong, he is acting without guilt if he could not avoid this mistake. If the perpetrator could avoid the mistake, the punishment can be reduced in accordance with § 49 para 1.

THE REFERENDUM MISTAKE CASE

BGHSt 4, 1

1 Die im Beschluss des Großen Senats für Strafsachen vom 18. März 1952
– GSSt 2/51, BGHSt 2, 194ff. – aufgestellten Grundsätze gelten auch für
Strafbestimmungen, die dem Schutze der öffentlichen Ordnung dienen.

2 Mit der 'Gewissensanspannung' im Sinne des Entscheidungssatzes
dieses Beschlusses ist gemeint, daß der Täter verpflichtet sei, alle seine
Erkenntniskräfte und alle seine sittlichen Wertvorstellungen
einzusetzen, wenn es gilt, sich über die Rechtmäßigkeit oder die
Rechtswidrigkeit eines bestimmten Verhaltens ein Urteil zu bilden.

StGB § 59

2 Strafsenat. Beschluss vom 23. Dezember 1952 g. Z. u. B.

2 StR 612/52

1 Oberlandesgericht Hamburg

Aus den Gründen:

Das Amtsgericht hat die Angeklagten wegen Verstoßes gegen die
Hamburgische Polizeiverordnung vom 11. Mai 1951 (Hamb Ges und
VOBl S 45) über das Verbot der Förderung der Volksbefragung gegen
die Remilitarisierung Deutschlands verurteilt, weil sie für das
sogenannte 'Friedenskomitee' in Hamburg am 21. Juni 1951 die von der
SED betriebene Volksbefragung 'durchgeführt' hätten. Auf die
Revisionen der Angeklagten hat das Oberlandesgericht die Sache gemäß
§ 121 Abs. 2 GVG dem Bundesgerichtshof vorgelegt, weil es in der Frage
des Bewußtseins der Rechtswidrigkeit von der Entscheidung des
Großen Senats für Strafsachen vom 18. März 1952 – GSSt 2/51 –
abzuweichen beabsichtige.

THE REFERENDUM MISTAKE CASE

The particular interest in this case for the English reader is its consideration of mistake of law as a defence to a crime. In fact, § 17 was only introduced into the Criminal Code in 1975, but it enacted a principle which had already been established in a case in 1952 (BGHSt 2, 194). The court in the present case makes it clear that if the defendants knew what they were doing was forbidden by the law of the community in which they lived, even if they rejected its legal order on political or philosophical grounds, they could not use the defence; but it would be otherwise if their rejection of the legal order and its prohibitions was associated with a belief that it contradicted a higher norm (here the Basic Law). See 'Mistake of law in Germany: opening up Pandora's Box' (2000) 64 Journal of Criminal Law 339.

BGHSt 4, 1

1 The principles laid down in the judgment of the Great Senate for Criminal Cases of the 18 March 1952 – GSSt 2/51, BGHSt 2, 194ff and onwards – also apply for criminal provisions which serve the protection of the public order.

2 'Exertion of the conscience' in the sense of the principle in the decision in this judgment means that the perpetrator is obliged to employ all his powers of understanding and all his moral conceptions of value when it is a question of forming a judgement about the legality or the illegality of certain conduct.

StGB § 59

2nd Criminal Senate judgment of the 23 December 1952 against Z and B.

2 StR 612/52

1 Upper State Court of Hamburg

Reasons:

The local court has convicted the defendants for violation of the Hamburg Police Regulation of the 11 May 1951 (*Hamburg Statutes and Regulations Gazette*, p 45) about the prohibition of the promotion of a referendum against the remilitarisation of Germany, because they had 'implemented' the referendum run by the Socialist Unity Party of Germany for the so-called 'Peace Committee' in Hamburg on the 21 June 1951. On the defendants' appeal in law, the Upper State Court referred the matter to the Bundesgerichtshof in accordance with § 121 para 2 of the GVG because, in relation to the question of the consciousness of illegality, it intended to deviate from the decision of the Great Senate for Criminal Cases of the 18 March 1952 – GSSt 2/51.

Zur Begründung führt das Oberlandesgericht aus:

Das angefochtene Urteil unterliegt jedoch Bedenken insoweit, als das Bewußtsein der Rechtswidrigkeit nicht geprüft ist, wie es gemäß dem Beschluß des Großen Senats für Strafsachen des Bundesgerichtshofs vom 18. März 1952 Voraussetzung für die Schuldfeststellung wäre. Der Senat ist demgegenüber der Auffassung, daß es auf die Feststellung der 'Gewissensanspannung' bei Strafbestimmungen, die zum Schutz der öffentlichen Ordnung dienen, nicht ankommen kann, vielmehr hier die Kenntnis von dem Vorliegen einer positiven Rechtsbestimmung, die als solche wegen ihrer formalen Ordnungsmäßigkeit die Vermutung der Rechtmäßigkeit für sich hat, als ausreichend für die Feststellung des Unrechtsbewußtseins anzusehen ist. Weder eine fehlende Gewissensanspannung noch eine mangelhafte Erkundigung liegt in derartigen Fällen vor, in denen der Betroffene zB aus grundsätzlichen politischen Erwägungen sich einer Verordnung nicht unterwerfen zu müssen glaubt. Ein Maßstab für die richtige Einstellung des Rechtsbrechers ist hier nach Auffassung des Senats aus ethischen Wertungen nicht zu gewinnen, während das allgemeine Ordnungsbedürfnis der Gemeinschaft dazu zwingt, auf eine Nachprüfung der psychologischen Vorgänge zu verzichten, wenn die innere Einstellung zu der Rechtmäßigkeit des Handelns überwiegend zB von der politischen Grundhaltung und Einstellung des betreffenden Täters beeinflußt sein kann. Der Senat ist danach der Auffassung, daß die Kenntnis von dem Verbotensein des Handelns, wie es von dem Amtsgericht zwar nicht ausdrücklich ausgesprochen ist, aber aus dem Urteilszusammenhang hervorgeht, zu einer Verurteilung ausreicht (vgl. auch HansOLG Ss 7/52). Da hierin eine Abweichung von dem Beschluß des Bundesgerichtshofs liegt, soweit er ausdrückliche Erwägungen in dieser Richtung auf Grund der besonderen Persönlichkeit der Täter voraussetzt, beabsichtigt der Senat, davon abzuweichen.

Hierzu ist folgendes zu sagen:

I Wenn die Angeklagten das Verbotensein ihres Handelns kannten, was das Oberlandesgericht dem Urteilszusammenhang entnehmen zu können glaubt, dann haben sie sich nicht in einem Verbotsirrtum befunden, sondern sie sind sich des Unrechts ihres Handelns bewußt gewesen. Für diesen Fall kann das Oberlandesgericht von dem Beschluß des Großen Senats nicht abweichen wollen; denn das Bewußtsein der Rechtswidrigkeit bedeutet auch für ihn: Der Täter weiß, daß das, was er tut, rechtlich nicht erlaubt, sondern verboten ist, BGHSt 2, 196. Auf eine 'Gewissensanspannung' kommt es nach dem Beschluß erst dann an, wenn der Täter das Unrecht seines Verhaltens *nicht* eingesehen hat. Die Ausführungen des Oberlandesgerichts sind deshalb offenbar anders zu verstehen.

On the reasoning, the Upper State Court states:

The judgment under challenge is however subject to doubts insofar as consciousness of illegality is not examined, as this would be a prerequisite in accordance with the decision of the Great Senate for Criminal Cases of the Bundesgerichtshof of the 18 March 1952 for the finding of guilt. The Senate is on the other hand of the view that in relation to criminal provisions which serve protection of the public order, it cannot be a question of finding an 'exertion of the conscience'. Here, instead, the knowledge of the presence of a positive legal provision, which as such has the presumption of legality for itself because of its formal conformity with the legal order, is to be regarded as sufficient for the finding of consciousness of illegality. Neither a lack of exertion of the conscience nor a deficient enquiry is present in those kinds of cases in which the person affected, eg, out of fundamental political considerations believes he does not have to subject himself to a regulation. A standard for the correct attitude of the lawbreaker is not to be derived here, according to the view of the Senate, from ethical values, while the general need for order in the community compels the abandoning of an examination of psychological processes when the inward attitude to the legality of the action can be overwhelmingly influenced, eg, by the basic political position and attitude of the perpetrator concerned. The Senate is accordingly of the opinion that the knowledge that the action is prohibited, which is admittedly not expressly stated by the local court, but proceeds from the context of the judgment, suffices for a conviction (see also HansOLG pp 7/52). As there is in this a deviation from the decision of the Bundesgerichtshof, insofar as it requires express considerations in this direction on the basis of the special personality of the perpetrator, the Senate intends to deviate from it.

The following has to be said on this subject:
I If the defendants knew that their action was forbidden, which the Upper State Court thinks it can derive from the context of the judgment, then they are not to be found to be in error of law, but were conscious of the illegality of their action. For this case, the Upper State Court cannot intend to deviate from the decision of the Great Senate. This is because consciousness of illegality means for it as well: the perpetrator knows that what he is doing is not legally allowed, but is forbidden, BGHSt 2, 196. It is only a question of an 'exertion of the conscience', according to the decision, if the perpetrator has *not* realised the illegality of his conduct. The statements of the Upper State Court are therefore obviously to be understood in a different way.

II Das Oberlandesgericht verweist auf die Fälle, in denen der Betroffene sich zB aus grundsätzlichen politischen Erwägungen einer Verordnung nicht unterwerfen zu müssen glaube. Es meint, hier liege weder eine fehlende Gewissensanspannung noch eine mangelhafte Erkundigung vor. Das Bewußtsein der Rechtswidrigkeit fehle dem Täter wegen seiner politischen Grundhaltung. Deshalb sei ein auf sittlichen Wertungen beruhender Maßstab fragwürdig. Das Ordnungsbedürfnis der Gemeinschaft zwinge, auf eine Nachprüfung psychologischer Vorgänge zu verzichten.

Diese Ausführungen lassen nicht klar erkennen, welcher Art der Irrtum der Angeklagten nach der Auffassung des Oberlandesgerichts gewesen sein könne. Zwei Möglichkeiten kommen in Betracht:

1 Der Täter weiß, daß das, was er tut, nach dem Recht der Gemeinschaft, in der er sich befindet, verboten ist. In diesem Falle kennt er das Verbotensein seines Handelns. Ein Verbotsirrtum scheidet deshalb aus. Daß er die Rechtsordnung der Gemeinschaft, der er angehört, aus politischen oder weltanschaulichen Gründen ablehnt und deshalb die Verbindlichkeit ihrer Normen bestreitet, ist rechtlich bedeutungslos. Wer in einer Gemeinschaft lebt, muß das Recht, das in ihr gilt, auch gegen sich gelten lassen.

2 Der Täter kennt die Verbotsnorm (hier: Verbot der Volksbefragung), nimmt jedoch an, daß sie einer höheren Norm (hier: Grundgesetz) widerspreche und deshalb unwirksam sei. In diesem Falle liegt ein echter Verbotsirrtum im Sinne des Beschlusses vom 18. März 1952 vor. Im Gegensatz zum Oberlandesgericht ist der Senat der Ansicht, daß auch auf ihn die dort entwickelten Grundsätze zutreffen.

(a) Eine begrifflich einwandfreie und befriedigende Abgrenzung der Strafvorschriften, 'die zum Schutze der öffentlichen Ordnung dienen', von anderen ist kaum möglich. Ihr gelten im Endergebnis alle Strafbestimmungen. Sogar die Verfolgung von Beleidigungen, die dem ersten Anschein nach rein persönliche Interessen zu berühren scheinen, kann im öffentlichen Interesse erforderlich sein (§ 376 StPO). Eine Beschränkung der Grundsätze des Beschlusses vom 18. März 1952 auf Strafbestimmungen, die nicht zum Schutze der öffentlichen Ordnung dienen, hätte daher unaufhörlichen Streit über die Abgrenzung dieser Bestimmungen von andern und damit allgemeine Rechtsunsicherheit zur Folge.

II The Upper State Court refers to the cases in which the person concerned thinks he does not have to submit to a regulation, eg, on fundamental political considerations. It thinks that here there is neither the lack of exertion of the conscience nor deficient enquiry. The perpetrator lacks consciousness of illegality because of his basic political position. Therefore a standard based on moral values is questionable. The need for order in the community compels abandonment of an examination of psychological processes.

These statements do not allow clear identification of the kind of mistake, according to the view of the Upper State Court, the defendants could have made. Two possibilities come into consideration:

1 The perpetrator knows that what he is doing is forbidden according to the law of the community in which he finds himself. In this case he knows that his action is forbidden. A mistake of law is therefore ruled out. The fact that he rejects the legal order of the community to which he belongs, out of political or philosophical grounds and therefore contests the binding nature of its norms, is not of legal significance. A person who lives in a community must permit the law which applies in it to be applied against himself as well.

2 The perpetrator knows the prohibition norm (here: the prohibition of the referendum) but assumes that it contradicts a higher norm (here: the Basic Law) and therefore is ineffective. In this case, a true mistake of law is present in the sense of the decision of the 18 March 1952. In contrast to the Upper State Court, the Senate is of the view that the principles developed there also apply to it.

(a) A differentiation of the criminal provisions 'which serve the protection of the public order' from others which is conceptually free from objections and satisfactory is hardly possible. In the end result all criminal provisions have this purpose in view. Even prosecution for insults, which appear at first sight to affect purely personal interests, can be necessary in the public interest (§ 376 of the StPO). Limitation of the principles of the decision of the 18 March 1952 to criminal provisions which do not serve the protection of public order would therefore have as its consequence continuous dispute about the differentiation of these provisions from others and therefore general legal uncertainty.

(b) Auch sachlich ist es geboten, die Grundsätze des Beschlusses auf alle Strafbestimmungen zu beziehen. Denn nur dann ist gewährleistet, daß jeder nach dem Maße seiner Schuld bestraft wird. Dabei macht es keinen Unterschied, ob es sich um sogenannte sittlich fundierte Strafrechtsnormen oder um Bestimmungen handelt, die aus Erwägungen sozialer oder rein staatlicher Zweckmäßigkeit formale Ordnungsvorschriften aufstellen. Gerade Bestimmungen der letzten Art bieten der Möglichkeit eines Verbotsirrtums ein weites Feld, BGHSt 2, 203.

Im übrigen zeigt der vorliegende Fall, daß auch gegenüber Verboten, die eine Polizei Verordnung enthält, ein Irrtum möglich ist, der die Grundlagen der Rechtsordnung betrifft, zB wenn der Täter glaubt, das Verbot der Volksbefragung schränke das verfassungsmäßige Recht der freien Meinungsäußerung ein. Daß eine 'positive Bestimmung' wegen ihrer 'formalen Ordnungsmäßigkeit' die 'Vermutung der Rechtmäßigkeit' für sich habe, wie das Oberlandesgericht meint, mag im allgemeinen zutreffen. Das schließt aber nicht aus, daß sie im Einzelfalle sich als rechtsunwirksam erweist. Solange aber diese Möglichkeit besteht, muß der unvermeidbare Irrtum des Täters beachtlich sein. Allerdings wird in solchen Fällen der Täter im allgemeinen damit rechnen, sein Verhalten könne verboten sein und diese Möglichkeit in seinen Willen aufnehmen, wenn er der Bestimmung zuwiderhandelt. Damit wäre auch das Unrechtsbewußtsein gegeben, BGH Urt vom 20. Mai 1952 – 1 StR 490/51 – Lindenmaier-Möhring, Das Nachschlagewerk des BGH Nr. 6 zu § 59 StGB.

(b) It is also objectively necessary to apply the principles of the decision to all criminal provisions. This is because it will only then be guaranteed that everyone will be punished according to the measure of his guilt. In this connection it makes no difference whether it is a question of so-called morally based criminal law norms or of provisions which establish formal rules relating to order out of considerations of social or purely State expediency. It is in fact provisions of the latter kind which offer the possibility of mistake of law a wide field, BGHSt 2, 203.

Besides this, the present case shows that, even in respect of prohibitions which a police regulation contains, a mistake is possible which concerns the foundations of the legal order, eg, if the perpetrator believes that the ban on the referendum limits the constitutional right to free expression of opinion. The idea that a 'positive provision' because of its 'formal conformity to the legal order' has in its favour the 'presumption of legality', as the Upper State Court thinks, may in general be correct. But that does not exclude the possibility that in the individual case it may prove to be legally ineffective. As long as this possibility exists, however, the unavoidable mistake of the perpetrator must be important. It is true that in such cases the perpetrator will in general take into account that his conduct could be forbidden and include this possibility in his intention if he acts in a manner contrary to the provision. His consciousness of the illegality would therefore be present, BGH judgment of 20 May 1952 – 1 StR 490/51 – Lindenmaier-Möhring, Reference work of the BGH no 6 on § 59 of the StGB.

(c) Richtig ist allerdings der Gedanke des Oberlandsgerichts, daß demjenigen, der aus politischen Gründen glaube, sich einem Verbot nicht unterwerfen zu sollen, auch eine 'Anspannung des Gewissens' nicht zu der richtigen Einsicht verhelfen werde. In den unter 1 aufgeführten Fällen ist dies aber auch nicht erforderlich. Im übrigen ist der Entscheidungssatz des Beschlusses vom 18. März 1952 nicht so aufzufassen, als ob der Täter nur dann in einem vermeidbaren Verbotsirrtum handele, wenn er bei Anspannung seines Gewissens im engeren Sinne das Unrecht seines Verhaltens einsehen könne. Denn dann würden die meisten Fälle der Ordnungswidrigkeit ohne Sühne bleiben, weil hier dem Täter die Gewissensanspannung kaum zu der richtigen Einsicht verhelfen wird. Hier liegt aber gerade nach der Auffassung des Großen Senats ein 'weites Feld' für die Möglichkeit eines Verbotsirrtums. An anderer Stelle des Beschlusses heißt es, der Täter habe sich 'bei allem, was er zu tun im Begriff stehe, bewußt zu machen, ob es mit den Sätzen des rechtlichen Sollens in Einklang stehe; Zweifel habe er durch *Nachdenken oder Erkundigen* zu beseitigen', BGHSt 2, 201. Mit den Worten 'Anspannung des Gewissens' ist deshalb offenbar gemeint, daß der Täter verpflichtet sei, alle seine geistigen Erkenntniskräfte und alle seine sittlichen Wertvorstellungen einzusetzen, wenn es gilt, sich über die Rechtmäßigkeit oder die Rechtswidrigkeit eines bestimmten Verhaltens ein Urteil zu bilden. Nur so ist die abschließende Folgerung des Beschlusses (BGHSt 2, 209) verständlich, 'daß der Verbotsirrtum, wenn er unüberwindlich ist, die Schuld ausschließt, wenn er überwindlich ist, sie mindert, aber den Tatvorsatz nicht beseitigt'.

Naturgemäß darf der Täter nicht solche Wertvorstellungen von Recht und Unrecht zugrunde legen, die einem fremden Kulturkreis angehören (etwa die des kommunistischen Rußlands), sondern nur diejenigen, die seine Rechtsgemeinschaft anerkennt d.h. die Gemeinschaft, in der er lebt (so BGH vom 10. Juli 1952 – 4 StR 73/52). Wenn die Gerichte dies beachten, so besteht keine Gefahr, daß bei der Prüfung der Vorstellungen des Täters politische Überzeugungen Beachtung finden, die zu den sittlichen und rechtlichen Grundanschauungen des westeuropäischen Kulturkreises in Widerspruch stehen.

Punishment linked to consequence

§ 18 [Schwerere Strafe bei besonderen Tatfolgen] Knüpft das Gesetz an eine besondere Folge der Tat eine schwerere Strafe, so trifft sie den Täter oder den Teilnehmer nur, wenn ihm hinsichtlich dieser Folge wenigstens Fahrlässigkeit zur Last fällt.

(c) The idea of the Upper State Court that a person who on political grounds believes himself not be subject to a prohibition will not be helped to the right view by an 'exertion of conscience' is admittedly correct. This is also not necessary however in the cases listed under 1. Besides this, the principle of the decision of the 18 March 1952 is not to be regarded as if the perpetrator only acts under an avoidable mistake of law if he could, on exertion of his conscience in the narrower sense, perceive the wrongness of his conduct. This is because most cases of administrative offences would then remain without expiation, because here exertion of the conscience would hardly assist the perpetrator to obtain a correct insight. But it is precisely here, according to the opinion of the Great Senate, that there is a 'wide field' for the possibility of a mistake of law. In another place in the judgment it says that the perpetrator must 'make himself aware in everything that he is about to do whether he is in harmony with the principles of legal norms; he must eliminate doubts by reflection or enquiry': BGHSt 2, 201. The words 'exertion of the conscience' obviously therefore mean that the perpetrator is under an obligation to use all his mental powers of perception and all his ideas of moral values when it is a question of forming a judgement about the lawfulness or the unlawfulness of certain behaviour. Only in this way is the final conclusion of the judgment (BGHSt 2, 209) comprehensible 'that a mistake of law, if it is insurmountable, excludes guilt, and if it is surmountable reduces it, but does not eliminate intention to commit the act'.

Naturally the perpetrator ought not to take as a basis values of right and wrong which belong to a circle of foreign culture (for instance, those of communist Russia), but only those which are recognised by his legal community, ie, the community in which he lives (as in BGH 10 July 1952 – 4 StR 73/52). If the courts pay attention to this, there is no danger that, in examination of the perpetrator's ideas, political convictions will receive attention which are in contradiction to the basic moral and legal opinions of the circle of western European culture.

Punishment linked to consequence

§ 18 [Severer punishment in case of special consequences of the act] If statute links a more severe punishment with a specific consequence of an act, this only affects the perpetrator or the participant if at least negligence in relation to this consequence can be laid to his charge.

Criminal incapacity

§ 19 [Schuldunfähigkeit des Kindes] Schuldunfähig ist, wer bei Begehung der Tat noch nicht vierzehn Jahre alt ist.

§ 20 [Schuldunfähigkeit wegen seelischer Störungen] Ohne Schuld handelt, wer bei Begehung der Tat wegen einer krankhaften seelischen Störung, wegen einer tiefgreifenden Bewußtseinsstörung oder wegen Schwachsinns oder einer schweren anderen seelischen Abartigkeit unfähig ist, das Unrecht der Tat einzusehen oder nach dieser Einsicht zu handeln.

§ 21 [Verminderte Schuldfähigkeit] Ist die Fähigkeit des Täters, das Unrecht der Tat einzusehen oder nach dieser Einsicht zu handeln, aus einem der in § 20 bezeichneten Gründe bei Begehung der Tat erheblich vermindert, so kann die Strafe nach § 49 Abs. 1 gemildert werden.

ATTEMPT

Zweiter Titel. Versuch

§ 22 [Begriffsbestimmung] Eine Straftat versucht, wer nach seiner Vorstellung von der Tat zur Verwirklichung des Tatbestandes unmittelbar ansetzt.

§ 23 [Strafbarkeit des Versuchs] (1) Der Versuch eines Verbrechens ist stets strafbar, der Versuch eines Vergehens nur dann, wenn das Gesetz es ausdrücklich bestimmt.

(2) Der Versuch kann milder bestraft werden als sie vollendete Tat (§ 49 Abs. 1).

(3) Hat der Täter aus grobem Unverstand verkannt, daß der Versuch nach der Art des Gegenstandes, an dem, oder des Mittels, mit dem die Tat begangen werden sollte, überhaupt nicht zur Vollendung führen konnte, so kann das Gericht von Strafe absehen oder die Strafe nach seinem Ermessen mildern (§ 49 Abs. 2).

Criminal incapacity

§ 19 [Child's incapacity for criminal guilt] A person who is not yet 14-years old on commission of an act is incapable of criminal guilt.

§ 20 [Incapacity for criminal guilt on account of mental disturbances] A person who, on commission of an act, is, because of a pathological mental disturbance, a fundamental disturbance of consciousness or imbecility or another severe mental abnormality, incapable of understanding the wrongfulness of an act, or acting according to this understanding, acts without criminal guilt.

§ 21 [Reduced capacity for criminal guilt] If the capacity of the perpetrator to understand the wrongness of an act or to act according to this understanding has been substantially reduced on commission of the act due to one of the reasons described in § 20, the punishment can be reduced in accordance with § 49 para 1.

German criminal law permits diminished responsibility to be pleaded in the case of any crimes or offences. In English criminal law it is only available for murder.

ATTEMPT

Second Title. Attempt

§ 22 [Definition] A person attempts a criminal act if he starts directly to bring about the elements of the act, according to his conception of the act.

§ 23 [Liability to punishment for attempt] (1) An attempt to commit a crime is always punishable; an attempt to commit an offence only if statute expressly so provides.

(2) The attempt can be punished more leniently than the completed deed (§ 49 para 1).

(3) If the perpetrator has, through gross misunderstanding, failed to recognise that the attempt, considering the type of object by which or the means by which the act should be committed, could not really lead to completion, the court can refrain from punishing or can reduce the punishment in accordance with its discretion (§ 49 para 1).

§ 24 [Rücktritt] (1) Wegen Versuchs wird nicht bestraft, wer freiwillig die weitere Ausführung der Tat aufgibt oder deren Vollendung verhindert. Wird die Tat ohne Zutun des Zurücktretenden nicht vollendet, so wird er straflos, wenn er sich freiwillig und ernsthaft bemüht, die Vollendung zu verhindern.

(2) Sind an der Tat mehrere beteiligt, so wird wegen Versuchs nicht bestraft, wer freiwillig die Vollendung verhindert. Jedoch genügt zu seiner Straflosigkeit sein freiwilliges und ernsthaftes Bemühen, die Vollendung der Tat zu verhindern, wenn sie ohne sein Zutun nicht vollendet oder unabhängig von seinem früheren Tatbeitrag begangen wird.

PERPETRATORS AND PARTICIPANTS

Perpertrators

Dritter Titel. Täterschaft und Teilnahme

§ 25 [Täterschaft] (1) Als Täter wird bestraft, wer die Straftat selbst oder durch einen anderen begeht.

(2) Begehen mehrere die Straftat gemeinschaftlich, so wird jeder als Täter bestraft (Mittäter).

§ 26 [Anstiftung] Als Anstifter wird gleich einem Täter bestraft, wer vorsätzlich einen anderen zu dessen vorsätzlich begangener rechtswidriger Tat bestimmt hat.

Participants

§ 27 [Beihilfe] (1) Als Gehilfe wird bestraft, wer vorsätzlich einem anderen zu dessen vorsätzlich begangener rechtswidriger Tat Hilfe geleistet hat.

(2) Die Strafe für den Gehilfen richtet sich nach der Strafdrohung für den Täter. Sie ist nach § 49 Abs. 1 zu mildern.

§ 28 [Besondere persönliche Merkmale] (1) Fehlen besondere persönliche Merkmale (§ 14 Abs. 1), welche die Strafbarkeit des Täters begründen, beim Teilnehmer (Anstifter oder Gehilfe), so ist dessen Strafe nach § 49 Abs. 1 zu mildern.

(2) Bestimmt das Gesetz, daß besondere persönliche Merkmale die Strafe schärfen, mildern oder ausschließen, so gilt das nur für den Beteiligten (Täter oder Teilnehmer), bei dem sie vorliegen.

§ 24 [Withdrawal] (1) A person will not be punished because of an attempt if he willingly gives up the further carrying out of the deed or prevents its completion. If the act will not be completed without the assistance of the person withdrawing, he will be exempt from punishment if he willingly and seriously endeavours to prevent completion.

(2) If several people have participated in the act, any person who willingly prevents completion will not be punished because of the attempt. However, his willing and earnest endeavour to prevent completion of the act suffices to exempt him from punishment if it will not be completed without his assistance or it will be committed independently of his earlier contribution to the act.

PERPETRATORS AND PARTICIPANTS

Perpetrators

Third Title. Perpetration and Participation

§ 25 [Perpetration] (1) A person who commits the criminal act himself or through another will be punished as the perpetrator.

(2) If several people commit the criminal act jointly, each one will be punished as the perpetrator (co-perpetrator).

§ 26 [Inciting] A person will be punished as an inciter in the same way as a perpetrator if he intentionally induced another to do an unlawful act and that other has committed it intentionally.

Participants

§ 27 [Assistance] (1) A person will be punished as an assistant if he has intentionally given assistance to another for an unlawful act which that other has committed intentionally.

(2) The punishment for the assistant depends upon the punishment threatened for the perpetrator. It is to be reduced in accordance with § 49 para 1.

§ 28 [Special personal characteristics] (1) If special personal characteristics (§ 14 para 1), which are the basis of the perpetrator's liability to punishment, are not present with the accessory (inciter or assistant), his punishment is to be reduced in accordance with § 49 para 1.

(2) If statute provides that special personal characteristics increase, reduce or exclude punishment, that is only effective in relation to the participant (perpetrator or accessory) with whom they are present.

§ 29 [Selbständige Strafbarkeit des Beteiligten] Jeder Beteiligte wird ohne Rücksicht auf die Schuld des anderen nach seiner Schuld bestraft.

§ 30 [Versuch der Beteiligung] (1) Wer einen anderen zu bestimmen versucht, ein Verbrechen zu begehen oder zu ihm anzustiften, wird nach den Vorschriften über den Versuch des Verbrechens bestraft. Jedoch ist die Strafe nach § 49 Abs. 1 zu mildern. § 23 Abs. 3 gilt entsprechend.

(2) Ebenso wird bestraft, wer sich bereit erklärt, wer das Erbieten eines anderen annimmt oder wer mit einem anderen verabredet, ein Verbrechen zu begehen oder zu ihm anzustiften.

§ 31 [Rücktritt vom Versuch der Beteiligung] (1) Nach § 30 wird nicht bestraft, wer freiwillig:

1 den Versuch aufgibt, einen anderen zu einem Verbrechen zu bestimmen, und eine etwa bestehende Gefahr, daß der andere die Tat begeht, abwendet;

2 nachdem er sich zu einem Verbrechen bereit erklärt hatte, sein Vorhaben aufgibt oder;

3 nachdem er ein Verbrechen verabredet oder das Erbieten eines anderen zu einem Verbrechen angenommen hatte, die Tat verhindert.

(2) Unterbleibt die Tat ohne Zutun des Zurücktretenden oder wird sie unabhängig von seinem früheren Verhalten begangen, so genügt zu seiner Straflosigkeit sein freiwilliges und ernsthaftes Bemühen, die Tat zu verhindern.

SELF-DEFENCE AND EMERGENCIES

Self-defence

Vierter Titel. Notwehr und Notstand

§ 32 [Notwehr] (1) Wer eine Tat begeht, die durch Notwehr geboten ist, handelt nicht rechtswidrig.

(2) Notwehr ist die Verteidigung, die erforderlich ist, um einen gegenwärtigen rechtswidrigen Angriff von sich oder einem anderen abzuwenden.

§ 33 [Überschreitung der Notwehr] Überschreitet der Täter die Grenzen der Notwehr aus Verwirrung, Furcht oder Schrecken, so wird er nicht bestraft.

§ 29 [Independent liability of the participant to punishment] Every participant will be punished according to his guilt, without regard to the guilt of the others.

§ 30 [Attempt to participate] (1) A person who seeks to induce another to commit a crime or to incite him to do so will be punished in accordance with the provisions regarding the attempt to commit the crime. The punishment is however to be reduced in accordance with § 49 para 1. § 23 para 3 applies correspondingly.

(2) Anyone who declares willingness, accepts the offer of another or agrees with another to commit a crime or to incite another to commit it will be punished in the same way.

§ 31 [Withdrawal from attempt to participate] (1) A person will not be punished in accordance with § 30 if he willingly:

1 gives up the attempt to induce another to commit a crime and averts a possibly existing danger that the other will commit the act;

2 gives up his purpose after he had declared his willingness to commit a crime; or

3 prevents the act after he had agreed to a crime or had accepted the offer of another to commit a crime.

(2) If the act will not take place without the assistance of the person withdrawing or if it will be committed independently of his earlier conduct, his willing and serious endeavour to prevent the act will suffice to exempt him from punishment.

SELF-DEFENCE AND EMERGENCIES

Self-defence

Fourth Title. Self-defence and emergency

§ 32 [Self-defence] (1) A person who commits an act which is required by self-defence does not act contrary to the law.

(2) Self-defence is the defence which is necessary in order to avert a present unlawful attack against oneself or another.

§ 33 [Excessive self-defence] If the perpetrator exceeds the limits of self-defence due to confusion, fear or terror, he will not be punished.

Emergency

§ 34 [Rechtfertigender Notstand] Wer in einer gegenwärtigen, nicht anders abwendbaren Gefahr für Leben, Leib, Freiheit, Ehre, Eigentum oder ein anderes Rechtsgut eine Tat begeht, um die Gefahr von sich oder einem anderen abzuwenden, handelt nicht rechtswidrig, wenn bei Abwägung der widerstreitenden Interessen, namentlich der betroffenen Rechtsgüter und des Grades der ihnen drohenden Gefahren, das geschützte Interesse das beeinträchtigte wesentlich überwiegt. Dies gilt jedoch nur, soweit die Tat ein angemessenes Mittel ist, die Gefahr abzuwenden.

§ 35 [Entschuldigender Notstand] (1) Wer in einer gegenwärtigen, nicht anders abwendbaren Gefahr für Leben, Leib oder Freiheit eine rechtswidrige Tat begeht, um die Gefahr von sich, einem Angehörigen oder einer anderen ihm nahestehenden Person abzuwenden, handelt ohne Schuld. Dies gilt nicht, soweit dem Täter nach den Umständen, namentlich weil er die Gefahr selbst verursacht hat oder weil er in einem besonderen Rechtsverhältnis stand, zugemutet werden konnte, die Gefahr hinzunehmen; jedoch kann die Strafe nach § 49 Abs. 1 gemildert werden, wenn der Täter nicht mit Rücksicht auf ein besonderes Rechtsverhältnis die Gefahr hinzunehmen hatte.

(2) Nimmt der Täter bei Begehung der Tat irrig Umstände an, welche ihn nach Absatz 1 entschuldigen würden, so wird er nur dann bestraft, wenn er den Irrtum vermeiden konnte. Die Strafe ist nach § 49 Abs. 1 zu mildern.

Emergency

§ 34 [Justifying emergency] A person who commits an act in present danger, not to be otherwise averted, to life, body, freedom, honour, property or another legal interest, in order to avert the danger to himself or another, does not act contrary to law if, on balancing the conflicting interests, particularly the legal interests affected and the degree of the dangers threatening them, the protected interest significantly outweighs the one which has been encroached upon. This only applies insofar as the act is an appropriate means of averting the danger.

§ 35 [Excusing emergency] (1) A person who commits an unlawful act in present danger, not otherwise to be averted, to life, body or freedom in order to avert the danger to himself, a relative, or another person close to him, acts without guilt. This does not apply insofar as it could, in accordance with the circumstances, be expected of the perpetrator that he accept the danger, particularly because he has caused the danger himself or because he was in a special legal relationship; however, the punishment can be reduced in accordance with § 49 para 1, if the perpetrator did not have to accept the danger, having regard to a special legal relationship.

(2) If the perpetrator on commission of the act erroneously assumes circumstances which would excuse him according to para 1, he will only be punished if he could have avoided the error. The punishment is to be reduced in accordance with § 49 para 1.

ASSESSMENT OF PUNISHMENT

One crime or offence

Dritter Abschnitt. Rechtsfolgen der Tat

Zweiter Titel. Strafbemessung

§ 46 [Grundsätze der Strafzumessung] (1) Die Schuld des Täters ist Grundlage für die Zumessung der Strafe. Die Wirkungen, die von der Strafe für das künftige Leben des Täters in der Gesellschaft zu erwarten sind, sind zu berücksichtigen.

(2) Bei der Zumessung wägt das Gericht die Umstände, die für und gegen den Täter sprechen, gegeneinander ab. Dabei kommen namentlich in Betracht:

die Beweggründe und die Ziele des Täters;

die Gesinnung, die aus der Tat spricht, und der bei der Tat aufgewendete Wille;

das Maß der Pflichtwidrigkeit;

die Art der Ausführung und die verschuldeten Auswirkungen der Tat;

das Vorleben des Täters, seine persönlichen und wirtschaftlichen Verhältnisse sowie;

sein Verhalten nach der Tat, besonders sein Bemühen, den Schaden wiedergutzumachen, sowie das Bemühen des Täters, einen Ausgleich mit dem Verletzten zu erreichen.

(3) Umstände, die schon Merkmale des gesetzlichen Tatbestandes sind, dürfen nicht berücksichtigt werden.

§ 46 a [Täter-Opfer-Ausgleich, Schadenswiedergutmachung] Hat der Täter:

1 in dem Bemühen, einen Ausgleich mit dem Verletzten zu erreichen (Täter-Opfer-Ausgleich), seine Tat ganz oder zum überwiegenden Teil wiedergutgemacht oder deren Wiedergutmachung ernsthaft erstrebt oder;

2 in einem Fall, in welchem die Schadenswiedergutmachung von ihm erhebliche persönliche Leistungen oder persönlichen Verzicht erfordert hat, das Opfer ganz oder zum überwiegenden Teil entschädigt,

so kann das Gericht die Strafe nach § 49 Abs. 1 mildern oder, wenn keine höhere Strafe als Freiheitsstrafe bis zu einem Jahr oder Geldstrafe bis zu dreihundertsechzig Tagessätzen verwirkt ist, von Strafe absehen.

ASSESSMENT OF PUNISHMENT

The preciseness of the rules here are in contrast to the comparatively wide discretion of the English judge.

One crime or offence

Third section. Legal consequences of the act

Second Title. Ascertainment of punishment

§ 46 [Principles for assessment of punishment] (1) The guilt of the perpetrator is the basis for assessment of punishment. The effects which are to be expected from the punishment for the future life of the perpetrator in society are to be considered.

(2) In the assessment, the court weighs the circumstances which speak for and against the perpetrator against each other. In this connection, the following matters should in particular be considered:

the motives and the aims of the perpetrator;

the attitude which the act indicates and the intention which was operative in the act;

the extent of any breach of duty;

the manner of perpetration and the blameworthy consequences of the act;

the previous life of the perpetrator, his personal and business interests; and

his attitude after the act, in particular his efforts to make good the damage, as well as the efforts of the perpetrator to reach a settlement with the injured party.

(3) Circumstances which are already characteristics of statutory ingredients of the crime should not be taken into consideration.

§ 46 a [Perpetrator-victim settlement, reparation for harm] If the perpetrator:

1 in the effort to make a settlement with the injured party (perpetrator-victim settlement) makes reparation wholly or predominantly for his act or seriously seeks its reparation; or

2 in a case in which reparation for the harm has required from him substantial personal action or personal sacrifice, has compensated the victim completely or predominantly,

the court can mitigate the punishment in accordance with § 49 para 1 or refrain from punishment if no higher punishment than a prison sentence of up to one year or a fine of up to 360 daily income amounts has been incurred.

§ 47 [Kurze Freiheitsstrafe nur in Ausnahmefällen] (1) Eine Freiheitsstrafe unter sechs Monaten verhängt das Gericht nur, wenn besondere Umstände, die in der Tat oder der Persönlichkeit des Täters liegen, die Verhängung einer Freiheitsstrafe zur Einwirkung auf den Täter oder zur Verteidigung der Rechtsordnung unerläßlich machen.

(2) Droht das Gesetz keine Geldstrafe an und kommt eine Freiheitsstrafe von sechs Monaten oder darüber nicht in Betracht, so verhängt das Gericht eine Geldstrafe, wenn nicht die Verhängung einer Freiheitsstrafe nach Absatz 1 unerläßlich ist. Droht das Gesetz ein erhöhtes Mindestmaß der Freiheitsstrafe an, so bestimmt sich das Mindestmaß der Geldstrafe in den Fällen des Satzes 1 nach dem Mindestmaß der angedrohten Freiheitsstrafe; dabei entsprechen dreißig Tagessätze einem Monat Freiheitsstrafe.

§ 48 (weggefallen)

§ 49 [Besondere gesetzliche Milderungsgründe] (1) Ist eine Milderung nach dieser Vorschrift vorgeschrieben oder zugelassen, so gilt für die Milderung folgendes:

1 An die Stelle von lebenslanger Freiheitsstrafe tritt Freiheitsstrafe nicht unter drei Jahren.

2 Bei zeitiger Freiheitsstrafe darf höchstens auf drei Viertel des angedrohten Höchstmaßes erkannt werden. Bei Geldstrafe gilt dasselbe für die Höchstzahl der Tagessätze.

3 Das erhöhte Mindestmaß einer Freiheitsstrafe ermäßigt sich:

im Falle eines Mindesmaßes von zehn oder fünf Jahren auf zwei Jahre;

im Falle eines Mindestmaßes von drei oder zwei Jahren auf sechs Monate;

im Falle eines Mindestmaßes von einem Jahr auf drei Monate;

im übrigen auf das gesetzliche Mindestmaß.

(2) Darf das Gericht nach einem Gesetz, das auf diese Vorschrift verweist, die Strafe nach seinem Ermessen mildern, so kann es bis zum gesetzlichen Mindestmaß der angedrohten Strafe herabgehen oder statt auf Freiheitsstrafe auf Geldstrafe erkennen.

§ 50 [Zusammentreffen von Milderungsgründen] Ein Umstand, der allein oder mit anderen Umständen die Annahme eines minder schweren Falles begründet und der zugleich ein besonderer gesetzlicher Milderungsgrund nach § 49 ist, darf nur einmal berücksichtigt werden.

§ 47 [Short sentence of imprisonment only in exceptional cases] (1) The court will only impose a sentence of imprisonment of less than six months if special circumstances, present in the act or the personality of the perpetrator make the imposition of a sentence of imprisonment essential for its effect on the perpetrator or for defence of the legal order.

(2) If statute does not provide for a monetary penalty, and a sentence of imprisonment of six months or more does not come into consideration, the court will impose a monetary penalty if the imposition of a sentence of imprisonment is not essential according to para 1. If statute provides for an increased lower limit of the sentence of imprisonment, the lower limit of the monetary penalty is to be determined in cases under sentence 1 according to the lower limit of the sentence of imprisonment provided for; and in this connection 30 daily income amounts[6] correspond to a month's imprisonment.

§ 48 (repealed)

§ 49 [Special statutory grounds for mitigation] (1) If mitigation is prescribed or permitted in accordance with this provision, the following applies to the mitigation:

1 In place of life imprisonment, imprisonment will not be for less than three years.

2 For terms of imprisonment only up to three quarters of the highest amount provided for may be imposed. For monetary penalties, the same applies for the highest number of daily income amounts.

3 The increased lower limit of a sentence of imprisonment is reduced:

in the case of a lower limit of 10 or five years, to two years;

in the case of a lower limit of three or two years, to six months;

in the case of a lower limit of one year, to three months;

otherwise to the statutory lower limit.

(2) If the court may, according to a statute which refers to this provision, mitigate the punishment in accordance with its discretion, it can reduce the sentence provided to the statutory minimum or impose a monetary penalty instead of a sentence of imprisonment.

§ 50 [Coinciding of grounds for mitigation] A circumstance which alone or with other circumstances forms the basis of acceptance of a less serious case, and which at the same time is a special statutory ground for mitigation according to § 49, may only be considered once.

---

6   Daily income amounts are the building blocks for financial penalties. It is the average net income which the perpetrator receives or could receive per day (within stated limits). A court will, however, also take the personal and economic circumstances into account.

§ 51 [Anrechnung] (1) Hat der Verurteilte aus Anlaß einer Tat, die Gegenstand des Verfahrens ist oder gewesen ist, Untersuchungshaft oder eine andere Freiheitsentziehung erlitten, so wird sie auf zeitige Freiheitsstrafe und auf Geldstrafe angerechnet. Das Gericht kann jedoch anordnen, daß die Anrechnung ganz oder zum Teil unterbleibt, wenn sie im Hinblick auf das Verhalten des Verurteilten nach der Tat nicht gerechtfertigt ist.

(2) Wird eine rechtskräftig verhängte Strafe in einem späteren Verfahren durch eine andere Strafe ersetzt, so wird auf diese die frühere Strafe angerechnet, soweit sie vollstreckt oder durch Anrechnung erledigt ist.

(3) Ist der Verurteilte wegen derselben Tat im Ausland bestraft worden, so wird auf die neue Strafe die ausländische angerechnet, soweit sie vollstreckt ist. Für eine andere im Ausland erlittene Freiheitsentziehung gilt Absatz 1 entsprechend.

(4) Bei der Anrechnung von Geldstrafe oder auf Geldstrafe entspricht ein Tag Freiheitsentziehung einem Tagessatz. Wird eine ausländische Strafe oder Freiheitsentziehung angerechnet, so bestimmt das Gericht den Maßstab nach seinem Ermessen.

(5) Für die Anrechnung der Dauer einer vorläufigen Entziehung der Fahrerlaubnis (§ 11 a der Strafprozeßordnung) auf das Fahrverbot nach § 44 gilt Absatz 1 entsprechend. In diesem Sinne steht der vorläufigen Entziehung der Fahrerlaubnis die Verwahrung, Sicherstellung oder Beschlagnahme des Führerscheins (§ 94 der Strafprozeßordnung) gleich.

Several crimes or offences

Dritter Titel. Strafbemessung bei mehreren Gesetzesverletzungen

§ 52 [Tateinheit] (1) Verletzt dieselbe Handlung mehrere Strafgesetze oder dasselbe Strafgesetz mehrmals, so wird nur auf eine Strafe erkannt.

(2) Sind mehrere Strafgesetze verletzt, so wird die Strafe nach dem Gesetz bestimmt, das die schwerste Strafe androht. Sie darf nicht milder sein, als sie anderen anwendbaren Gesetze es zulassen.

(3) Geldstrafe kann das Gericht unter den Voraussetzungen des § 41 neben Freiheitsstrafe gesondert verhängen.

§ 51 [Setting off] (1) If a convicted person has, by reason of an act which is or has been the subject of proceedings, suffered arrest for investigation or some other deprivation of freedom, this will be set against a sentence of imprisonment or a monetary penalty. The court can, however, arrange for the setting off not to take place in whole or in part, if it is not justified having regard to the conduct of the convicted person after the act.

(2) If a lawfully imposed punishment is replaced by another punishment in later proceedings, the earlier punishment will be set against this, insofar as it has been served or discharged by set off.

(3) If the convicted person has been punished for the same act in another country, the foreign punishment will be set off against the new punishment insofar as it has been served. Paragraph 1 applies correspondingly for any other deprivation of freedom suffered in another country.

(4) In setting off of or against a monetary penalty, one day's deprivation of freedom corresponds to a daily income amount. If a foreign punishment or deprivation of freedom is set off, the court will determine the extent in accordance with its discretion.

(5) For setting off the length of a temporary deprivation of permission to drive (§ 11 a of the Criminal Procedure Code) against a ban on driving in accordance with § 44 para 1 applies correspondingly. In this sense temporary deprivation of permission to drive is like the taking into custody, securing or confiscation of a driving licence (§ 94 of the Criminal Procedure Code).

Several crimes or offences

Third Title. Assessment of punishment in respect of several statutory violations

§ 52 [Unity of act] (1) If the same action violates several criminal statutory provisions, or the same statutory provision several times, only one punishment will be imposed.

(2) If several criminal statutory provisions are violated, punishment will be determined according to the statutory provision which provides for the severest punishment. It cannot be milder than the other applicable statutory provisions permit.

(3) A money penalty can be imposed by the court under the prerequisites of § 41 separately, in addition to a sentence of imprisonment.

(4) Lässt eines der anwendbaren Gesetze die Vermögensstrafe zu, so kann das Gericht auf sie neben einer lebenslangen oder einer zeitigen Freiheitstrafe von mehr als zwei Jahren gesondert erkennen. Im übrigen muß oder kann auf Nebenstrafen, Nebenfolgen und Maßnahmen (§ 11 Abs. 1 Nr. 8) erkannt werden, wenn eines der anwendbaren Gesetze sie vorschreibt oder zuläßt.

§ 53 [Tatmehrheit] (1) Hat jemand mehrere Straftaten begangen, die gleichzeitig abgeurteilt werden, und dadurch mehrere Freiheitsstrafen oder mehrere Geldstrafen verwirkt, so wird auf eine Gesamtstrafe erkannt.

(2) Trifft Freiheitsstrafe mit Geldstrafe zusammen, so wird auf eine Gesamtstrafe erkannt. Jedoch kann das Gericht auf Geldstrafe auch gesondert erkennen; soll in diesen Fällen wegen mehrerer Straftaten Geldstrafe verhängt werden, so wird insoweit auf eine Gesamtgeldstrafe erkannt.

(3) Hat der Täter nach dem Gesetz, nach welchem § 43 a Anwendung findet, oder im Fall des § 52 Abs. 4 als Einzelstrafe eine lebenslange oder eine zeitige Freiheitstrafe von mehr als zwei Jahren verwirkt, so kann das Gericht neben der nach Absatz 1 oder 2 zu bildenden Gesamtstrafe gesondert eine Vermögensstrafe verhängen; soll in diesen Fällen wegen mehrerer Straftaten Vermögensstrafe verhängt werden, so wird insoweit auf eine Gesamtvermögensstrafe erkannt. § 43 a Abs. 3 gilt entsprechend.

(4) § 52 Abs. 3 und 4 Satz 2 gilt sinngemäß.

(4) If one of the applicable statutory provisions permits a wealth-related monetary penalty, the court can impose it separately in addition to sentences of life imprisonment or imprisonment for a term of more than two years. Apart form this, additional punishments, additional incidents and measures (§ 11 para 1 no 8) must or can be imposed if one of the applicable statutory provisions prescribes or permits them.

§ 53 [Plurality of acts] (1) If someone has committed several criminal acts on which judgment is passed simultaneously and he thereby incurs several sentences of imprisonment or several monetary penalties, a combined punishment will be imposed.

(2) If a sentence of imprisonment and a monetary penalty coincide, a combined punishment will be imposed. The court can also however impose a monetary penalty separately; if in these cases a monetary penalty is imposed because of several criminal acts, in this respect a combined monetary penalty is imposed.

(3) If the perpetrator has, in accordance with a statutory provision under which § 43 a is to be applied, or in the case of § 52 para 4 as a single punishment, incurred a sentence of life imprisonment or imprisonment for a term of more than two years, the court can, in addition to the combined punishment to be formed in accordance with paras 1 or 2 impose a wealth-related monetary penalty separately; if in these cases a wealth-related monetary penalty is imposed because of several criminal acts, in this respect a combined wealth related penalty is imposed. § 43 a para 3 applies correspondingly.

(4) § 52 paras 3 and 4 sentence 2 apply by analogy.

§§ 54 and 55 contain further provisions about combined punishments.

CRIMES OF INSULT

Vierzehnter Abschnitt. Beleidigung

§ 185 [Beleidigung] Die Beleidigung wird mit Freiheitstrafe bis zu einem Jahr oder mit Geldstrafe und, wenn die Beleidigung mittels einer Tätlichkeit begangen wird, mit Freiheitsstrafe bis zu zwei Jahren oder mit Geldstrafe bestraft.

THE INSULT OF SOLDIERS CASE

BGHSt Band 36 S. 83

14.1 Die aktiven Soldaten der Bundeswehr können kollektiv beleidigt werden.

2 Beleidigungen von Soldaten als Angriffe auf die Menschenwürde?

StGB §§ 185, 130

1 Strafsenat. Urt. vom 19. Januar 1989 g.P.

1 StR 641/88.

Landgericht Traunstein

CRIMES OF INSULT

These criminal offences cover an area for which English law makes little provision. They are also torts, by virtue of § 823 II of the BGB. Only §§ 186 and 187 strictly correspond to defamation, and the distinction between them is not based on whether the communication is in permanent or transient form; it is based on whether the untruth is contrary to the better knowledge of the person making the communication. For consideration of the relevance of §§ 186 and 187 in a tort case, see the publication of a letter case, Chapter Six, p 469.

In contrast to §§ 186 and 187, § 185 may relate to statements of opinion as well as of fact, which may be made to the person concerned as well as to a third person.

Fourteenth section. Insult

§ 185 [Insult] Insult will be punished with a sentence of imprisonment of up to one year or with a monetary penalty and, if the insult is committed by means of an act of violence, with a sentence of imprisonment of up to two years or with a monetary penalty.

THE INSULT OF SOLDIERS CASE

Although this case approximates to defamation in English law, it was brought as a prosecution under German law. There is some logic in this, as the only available civil law remedy, damages, would not seem appropriate. However, two particular comparisons worth making here with English law are how it compares with the rules about defamation of a class and whether an analogy can be drawn with *Derbyshire County Council v Times Newspapers* [1992] 3 All ER 65 in which Art 10 of the European Convention on Human Rights was considered and it was held that a local authority, despite its corporate status, had no right to sue in defamation where the allegations went to its governing or administrative functions. The issue of whether soldiers may be called murderers has since been considered by the Federal Constitutional Court.

BGHSt Volume 36 p 83

14.1 The active soldiers of the Federal Army can be collectively insulted.

2 Insulting of soldiers as attacks on human dignity?

StGB §§ 185, 130

1st Criminal Senate. Judgment of 9 January 1989 v P.

1 StR 641/88.

State Court of Traunstein

Gründe:

Nach den Feststellungen des angefochtenen Urteils hat der Angeklagte als Mitglied des Redaktionskollektivs einen in der Ausgabe Nr. 35 der 'br.er fliegenden blätter' am 18. Dezember 1987 veröffentlichen Artikel verfaßt, der sich mit den öffentlichen Gelöbnisfeiern der Bundeswehr kritisch auseinandersetzt. In dem knapp zwei DIN A4-Seiten umfassenden Beitrag finden sich folgende Wendungen:

> In dieser Richtung war von der SPD-Fraktion nichts zu hören, als das Militärspektakel im Gemeinderat erörtert wurde. Sie hielt sich in ihrer Ablehnung zur Verärgerung vieler friedliebender Menschen sehr zurück. Der Soldatenberuf sei ein Beruf wie jeder andere und die Angehörigen anderer Berufsgruppen würden auch nicht öffentlich vereidigt, war als fadenscheinige Begründung zu hören.

> Damit befindet sich die SPD-Fraktion aber sauber auf dem Holzweg. Es ist im Gegenteil sogar so, daß es kaum einen Beruf gibt, der mit dem Soldatenberuf vergleichbar wäre. Höchstens noch der des Folterknechts, des KZ-Aufsehers oder des Henkers. Denn wo sonst wird man schon dazu ausgebildet, möglichst perfekt Menschen umzubringen? ...

> Aber: Ob notwendig oder nicht, daß man zum Killen abgerichtet wird, das läßt sich nicht wegdiskutieren. Und ein Beruf, dessen eigentlicher Zweck das Morden und Aufrechterhalten einer gigantischen Mordmaschinerie ist, ist eben ein moralisch verwerflicher Beruf.

> Um so mehr sind normale Wehrdienstpflichtige und alte Weltkriegsteilnehmer zu bedauern weil sie vom hochheiligen Vaterland (d.h. das Vaterland kann ja auch nichts dafür, nur dessen schäbige Politiker) zu diesem blutigen Handwerk gepreßt wurden und immer noch werden. Sie können – sofern sie nicht auch Militär-Enthusiasten sind – Entschuldigungen für sich in Anspruch nehmen, die für den echten Berufssoldaten nicht gelten ...

Das Landgericht hat den Angeklagten deshalb wegen Beleidigung aller aktiven und ehemaligen Soldaten der Bundeswehr zu einer Geldstrafe verurteilt.

Die gegen dieses Urteil eingelegte Revision der Staatsanwaltschaft erhebt die Sachrüge und beanstandet, daß der Angeklagte aufgrund des festgestellten Sachverhalts nicht auch wegen Beleidigung der Bundeswehr sowie wegen Verleumdung und Volksverhetzung verurteilt worden ist. Das Rechtsmittel führt zur Aufhebung der angefochtenen Entscheidung und zur Zurückverweisung der Sache an das Landgericht.

Reasons:

According to the findings of the judgment under challenge, the accused as a member of an editorial collective wrote an article published in issue no 35 of the 'Br Flying Leaves' on 18 December 1987, which took a critical look at the public swearing-in ceremony in the Federal Army. In the contribution, comprising barely two A4 (German Industrial Standard) sides, the following comments are found:

> Nothing like this was to be heard from the SPD Party when the military spectacle was discussed in the local council. It showed excessive restraint in its refusal (to address this subject) to the exasperation of many peace-loving people. The soldiers profession was a job like any other, and the members of other professional groups were not publicly sworn in; this was the threadbare basis of the argument.

> But the SPD Party finds itself in this respect completely on the wrong track. On the contrary, it is a case of there being scarcely any vocation comparable with that of a soldier. At best, that of torturer, concentration camp supervisor or hangman. For where else are people trained to kill people as perfectly as possible? ...

> But: whether or not it is necessary to train people to kill, cannot be argued away. And a job, where the real purpose is murder and the maintenance of a gigantic murder machine is simply a morally reprehensible one.

> Normal conscripts and World War veterans are so much the more to be pitied because they were pressed into this bloody trade, and still are, by the sacred Fatherland (that is, it's not the fault of the Fatherland, but of its shabby politicians). They can – insofar as they are not military enthusiasts – claim excuses for themselves which would not apply to the genuine professional soldier ...

The State Court imposed a fine on the defendant for insult of all active and former soldiers of the Federal Army.

The appeal in law lodged against this judgment by the State Prosecutor raises a criticism of the case and objects to the fact that, on the basis of the established factual content, the defendant was not convicted for insult of the Federal Army nor for slander or incitement of the people. The legal proceedings lead to annulment of the contested decision and to reference of the case back to the State Court.

1 Die Verurteilung wegen Beleidigung weist Rechtsfehler zu Gunsten und zu Lasten des Angeklagten auf.

(a) Das Landgericht hat die Äußerungen des Angeklagten ohne Rechtsfehler dahin ausgelegt (vgl. BGHSt 21, 371, 372; 32, 310, 311), daß sich die Angriffe des Angeklagten vordergründig zwar gegen den Beruf des Soldaten richten, daß damit aber auch die Menschen getroffen werden sollen, die die Aufgabe des Soldaten wahrnehmen; dieser Schluß rechtfertigt sich daraus, daß sich der Beitrag in vielfacher Hinsicht mit der Lage und den Problemen der Soldaten befaßt.

Die vom Angeklagten gebrauchten Vergleiche und Wertungen sind auch grundsätzlich geeignet, Soldaten der Bundeswehr in ihrer Ehre zu kränken. Das Landgericht hat zutreffend dargelegt, daß die angeführten undifferenzierten Vergleiche Mißachtung gegen Soldaten ausdrücken und daß diese Wirkung dadurch verstärkt wird, daß mit drastischen Formulierungen auf die mit der Tätigkeit der Soldaten verbundene Ausbildung zu töten – z.B. mit der Wendung 'gigantische Mordmaschinerie' – hingewiesen wird.

Der Angeklagte kann sich zur Rechtfertigung seiner Äußerungen nicht auf das Grundrecht der Meinungsfreiheit (Art. 5 Abs. 1 Satz 1 GG) berufen. Zwar stand es ihm frei, sich mit den öffentlichen Gelöbnisfeiern der Bundeswehr kritisch auseinanderzusetzen und dabei auch scharfe und polemische Formulierungen, überspitzte und plakative Wertungen zu gebrauchen (vgl. BVerfGE 24, 278, 286: 42, 163, 169; BGH(Z) NJW 1981, 2117, 2119; BayObLG NStZ 1983, 265); das rechtfertigt jedoch nicht Beschimpfungen, Schmähungen und Diffamierungen [vgl. BGH(Z) NJW 1974, 1762, 1763; 1977, 626, 627; BayObLG NStZ 1983, 126 und 265; OLG Düsseldorf(Z) NJW 1986, 1262], wie sie hier verwendet wurden.

(b) Zu weit gefaßt ist jedoch der Schuldumfang insoweit, als das Landgericht auch alle ehemalige Soldaten als beleidigt angesehen hat.

In der Rechtsprechung ist zwar seit jeher anerkannt, daß die Beleidigung einer Mehrheit einzelner Personen unter einer Kollektivbezeichnung in der Weise möglich ist, daß mit der Bezeichnung einer bestimmten Personengruppe alle ihre Angehörigen getroffen werden sollen, wobei der Täter selbst diese Personen nicht zu kennen und sich vorzustellen braucht. Demgemäß wurde eine kollektive Beleidigung u. a. anerkannt für den preußischen Richterstand (RGRspr. 1, 292), die Großgrundbesitzer mit Ausnahme etwa sozialdemokratisch gesinnter (RGSt 33, 46, 47), die deutschen Offiziere (RG LZ 1915, 60), die deutschen Ärzte (RG JW 1932, 31, 13), die in Deutschland lebenden Juden, die Opfer der nationalsozialistischen Verfolgungsmaßnahmen waren (BGHSt 11, 207, 208); verneint wurde die Beleidigungsfähigkeit für 'alle an der Entnazifizierung Beteiligten', die Katholiken, die Protestanten, die Akademiker (BGHSt 11, 207, 209), 'die Robenknechte von Moabit' (KG JR 1978, 422), die Polizei in ihrer Gesamtheit (OLG Düsseldorf NJW 1981, 1522).

1 The conviction for insult shows errors of law in favour of and against the defendant.

(a) The State Court has, without error of law, interpreted the statements of the defendant to the effect that (compare BGHSt 21, 371, 372; 32, 310, 311) the attacks of the defendant were primarily directed against the vocation of the soldier, but that persons were also to be affected by it who carry out the tasks of a soldier; this conclusion was justified by the fact that the article in many respects addresses the situation and problems of soldiers.

The comparisons and assessments used by the defendant are also in principle appropriate to insult the honour of soldiers in the Federal Army. The State Court has pertinently stated that the undifferentiated comparisons quoted express disdain of soldiers and that this effect is strengthened by the fact that reference is made with drastic formulations to the training to kill connected with the activity of soldiers – eg, with the expression 'gigantic murder machinery'.

The defendant cannot rely on the basic right of freedom of opinion (Art 5 para 1 sentence 1 of the GG) for justification of his statements. He was certainly at liberty to take a critical look at the public swearing-in ceremony of the Federal Army and also at the same time to use sharp and polemic formulations and exaggerated and bold assessments (compare BVerfGE 24, 278, 286; 42, 163, 169; BGH(Z) NJW 1981, 2117, 2119; BayObLG NStZ 1983, 265); that, however, did not justify insult, invective and defamation [compare BGH(Z) NJW 1974, 1762, 1763; 1977, 626, 627; BayObLG NStZ 1983, 126 and 265; OLG Düsseldorf (Z) NJW 1986, 1262], as they were used here.

(b) The scope of guilt is however too widely conceived insofar as the State Court also regarded all former soldiers as insulted.

In the case law it has certainly always been recognised that the insulting of a number of individual persons under a collective description is possible in such a way that by the description of a certain group of persons all its members are to be affected, in which connection the perpetrator himself does not need to know these persons or to picture them. Accordingly, a collective insult was acknowledged, amongst other cases, in relation to the Prussian judicial bench, (RG case law 1, 292), the landed proprietors with the exception perhaps of the social democratically minded (RGSt 33, 46, 47) German officers (RG LZ 1915, 60) German doctors (RG JW 1932, 31, 13) Jews living in Germany who were victims of the National Socialist persecution measures (BGHSt 11, 207, 208); the capacity to be insulted was denied to 'all participants in de-Nazification', Catholics, Protestants, academics (BGHSt 11, 207, 209), 'the robed servants of Moabit' (KG JR 1978, 422) and the police in their totality (OLG Düsseldorf NJW 1981, 1522).

Als wesentliches Kriterium für die Möglichkeit der Kollektivbeleidigung wurde in der bisherigen Rechtsprechung – weil feststehen müsse, welche einzelnen Personen beleidigt sind – angesehen, daß sich die bezeichnete Personengruppe auf Grund bestimmter Merkmale so deutlich aus der Allgemeinheit heraushebe, daß der Kreis der Betroffenen klar abgegrenzt sei (vgl. z.B. BGHSt 2, 38, 39; 11, 207, 208; RGSt 33, 46, 47). Jedoch hatte bereits das Reichsgericht (RGSt 31, 185) für Unsicherheiten der Abgrenzung anerkannt, daß diese nicht geeignet seien, die Kränkung derjenigen Personen in Frage zu stellen, deren Zugehörigkeit zur Gruppe außer Zweifel stehe. Tatsächlich reicht das Kriterium der klaren Abgrenzung nicht aus, eine Ausuferung der Kollektivbeleidigung zu verhindern, weil derjenige, der der angesprochenen Personengruppe unzweifelhaft angehört, jedenfalls Strafverfolgung verlangen könnte (Androulakis, Die Sammelbeleidigung 1970 S. 46); es ist aber jederzeit feststellbar, wer etwa Katholik oder Mitglied des Deutschen Gewerkschaftsbundes ist und wer nicht.

Demgemäß kann der eigentliche Grund, warum große Gruppen wie Katholiken und Protestanten, aber auch die Frauen, die Gewerkschafter, die Arbeitgeber nicht kolletiv beleidigungsfähig sind, nicht allein die mangelnde Abgrenzbarkeit des Kreises der Betroffenen sein. Infolgedessen wird in der Literatur als weiteres Kriterium für die Annahme der Kollektivbeleidigung gefordert, daß der fragliche Personenkreis zahlenmäßig überschaubar ist (Lenckner in Schönke/Schröder, StGB, 23. Aufl. Vorbem. §§ 185ff. Rdn. 7; Arzt JuS 1982, 717, 719; kritisch auch Androulakis aaO S. 63ff. 79ff.; Wagner JuS 1978, 674, 677). Andere Überlegungen zielen darauf ab, daß Kollektivbeleidigungen übertreiben und stereotypisieren; es handele sich um Verallgemeinerungen, bei welchen die individuelle Ausnahme stets miterklärt sei, wenn die Kollektivbezeichnung eine nicht überschaubare Personenmenge umfasse und infolgedessen eine konkrete Beziehung der Nachrede oder des Werturteils des Täters auf bestimmte Personen nicht erkennbar sei. Da offen bleibe, wer überhaupt beleidigt sei, sei niemand beleidigt (Herdegen in LK, 10. Aufl. vor § 185 Rdn. 22 unter Hinweis auf BayObLGSt 1958, 34, 35; vgl. Androulakis aaO S. 79ff.; Liepmann, Die Beleidigung, VDB Bd. IV 1906 S. 217; Wagner JuS 1978, 674, 678).

Der Senat ist der Meinung, daß allein die Größe der beleidigten Gruppe kein ausreichendes Kriterium ist, um zusammen mit der Abgrenzbarkeit zu der an sich aus rechtsstaatlichen Gründen gebotenen Einschränkung der Kollektivbeleidigung zu gelangen; es ist nicht zuverlässig abzugrenzen, wo die nicht mehr überschaubare Menge beginnen würde. Dagegen ist richtig, daß Kollektivbeleidigungen vielfach allgemeine Werturteile enthalten, die nicht geeignet sind, einzelne Menschen in ihre Ehre zu kränken. Bei Äußerungen wie 'alle deutschen Ärzte sind Kurpfuscher' oder 'alle deutschen Richter beugen das Recht' liegt auf der Hand, daß solche Behauptungen – und zwar auch in den Augen des sich so Äußernden – nicht zutreffen; mangels Bezug auf individualisierbare Personen kann sich auch niemand betroffen sehen.

It was regarded in the case law so far as an essential criterion for the possibility of collective insult – because it has to be established which individual persons are insulted – that the group of persons described stand out so clearly from the general public on the basis of certain characteristics that the circle of those affected is clearly delineated (compare, eg, BGHSt 2, 38, 39; 11, 207, 208; RGSt 33, 46, 47). However, the Reich High Court (RGSt 31, 185) had already recognised, in relation to uncertainties as to the limits, that these were not appropriate for questioning the insult to those persons whose membership of the group was beyond doubt. In fact the criterion of clear limits does not suffice to prevent an expansion of collective insult, because the person who undoubtedly belongs to the group of persons addressed could in any case demand criminal prosecution (Androulakis, Collective Insult 1970, p 46); it is however always ascertainable who is a Catholic, or a member of the German Federation of Trade Unions, and who is not.

Accordingly the real reason why large groups like Catholics and Protestants, and also women, trade unionists and employers are not capable of being collectively insulted, cannot only be the fact that the circle of those affected cannot be delimited. In consequence, a further criterion is required in the literature for the acceptance of collective insult, which is that the group of persons in question be comprehensible from a numerical point of view (Lenckner in Schönke/Schröder StGB, 23rd edn, preliminary note §§ 185 and onwards marginal no 7; Arzt JuS 1982, 717, 719; also, critically, Androulakis, *loc cit,* p 63 and onwards, p 79 and onwards; Wagner JuS 1978, 674, 677). Other considerations lead to the view that collective insults exaggerate and stereotype; it is a question of generalizations as to which the individual exception is always implied along with them if the collective insult comprises a multitude of people which cannot be comprehended; and as a consequence a concrete relationship of the calumny or value judgment of the perpetrator to certain persons is not discernible. Since it remains open as to who is insulted, no-one is insulted (Herdegen in LK, 10th edn, before § 185 marginal no 22 with reference to BayObLG Cr 1958, 34, 35; compare Androulakis, *loc cit,* p 79 and onwards; Liepmann, Insult VDB Vol IV, 1906, p 217; Wagner JuS 1978, 674, 678).

The Senate is of the opinion that the size alone of the insulted group is not a sufficient criterion in order, together with the concept of delimitation, to attain on its own the restriction on collective insult required on constitutional grounds; it is not reliable to delimit where a multitude, which could no longer be comprehended, would begin. Over against this it is true that collective insults on many occasions contain general value judgments which are not appropriate for offending the honour of individual persons. With statements like 'all German doctors are quacks' or 'all German judges bend the law', it is obvious that such assertions – and in the eyes of the person making them, too – are not true; in the absence of reference to persons who can be individualised, no-one can see themselves as affected.

Jedoch gibt es abwertendende Äußerungen über Kollektive, für die dieser Einwand nicht greift. So liegt es hier. Der Angeklagte hat sein Unwerturteil mit einem Kriterium verbunden, das eindeutig allen Soldaten zuzuordnen ist, weil es ein äußeres Verhalten und ein objektives Eingebundensein in das angefochtene Kollektiv beschreibt. Wer, wie er, den Soldatenberuf mit der Tätigkeit von KZ-Aufsehern, Henkern und Folterknechten vergleicht, greift deshalb ohne Einschränkung alle Soldaten an; die Frage, wem die abwertenden Äußerungen zuzuordnen sein könnten, stellt sich nicht.

Der Senat ist daher der Auffassung, daß der Angeklagte entsprechend dem Strafantrag des Bundesministers der Verteidigung alle Soldaten beleidigt hat, die im Zeitpunkt der Veröffentlichung des Artikels im aktiven Dienst standen; für Reservisten gilt das nur insoweit, als sie sich in einem Wehrdienstverhältnis befanden (§ 1 Abs. 2 SoldatenG, § 4 Abs. 1, 3, 4 WPflG). Der damit gezogene Kreis der Betroffenen ist zwar groß, aber klar abgrenzbar und insoweit auch überschaubar. Nicht auszuschließen ist freilich, daß auch aktive Soldaten der Bundeswehr – etwa Wehrpflichtige - die Wertungen des Angeklagten teilen. Insoweit läge ein tatbestandsausschließendes Einverständnis vor (vgl. Herdegen aaO § 185 Rdn. 41). Dieser Personenkreis wäre jedoch so gering, daß er für den Schuldumfang nicht ins Gewicht fallen würde.

Anders liegt es hinsichtlich der ehemaligen Soldaten der Bundeswehr. Insoweit ist zunächst der Schuldumfang schon deshalb zu weit gefaßt, weil es an den erforderlichen Strafanträgen (§ 194 Abs. 1 StGB) fehlt. Der Strafantrag des Bundesministers der Verteidigung konnte und sollte nur die zur Tatzeit aktiven Soldaten erfassen; Strafanträge ehemaliger Soldaten sind nur in zwei Fällen gestellt worden.

Darüber hinaus ist der Kreis ehemaliger Soldaten derart groß und unüberschaubar, daß er insgesamt keine beleidigungsfähige Personenmehrheit mehr bildet. Abgesehen davon, daß auch unter den ehemaligen Soldaten einzelne die Beurteilung des Angeklagten teilen mögen, werden sich, etwa weil sie – manchmal seit Jahrzehnten – keine Verbindung mehr zur Bundeswehr haben, nicht wenige von seinen Äußerungen nicht getroffen fühlen. Als Betroffene können daher nur ehemalige Soldaten in Frage kommen die sich weiterhin der Bundeswehr verbunden fühlen und diese Einstellung durch ihr Verhalten manifestieren, etwa durch regelmäßige Teilnahme an Wehrübungen oder Mitarbeit in soldatischen Interessenverbänden. Ob diese Voraussetzungen bei den beiden Antragstellern vorliegen, wird das Landgericht in der neuen Hauptverhandlung zu prüfen haben.

(c) Gleichfalls rechtlichen Bedenken unterliegen jedoch die Erwägungen, mit denen das Landgericht eine Beleidigung der Bundeswehr als Institution verneint hat.

There are however disparaging statements about groups to which this exception does not apply. That is the case here. The defendant has connected his disparaging judgment with a criterion which is to be associated unequivocally with all soldiers because it describes external behaviour and an objective integration in the group under attack. A person who, like him, compares the vocation of a soldier with the activity of concentration camp supervisors, hangmen and torturers attacks all soldiers without limitation; the question of whom the disparaging statement could be associated with does not arise.

The Senate is therefore of the view that the defendant in accordance with the criminal complaint[7] by the Federal Minister of Defence has insulted all soldiers who were in active service at the time of the publication of the article; for reservists it only took effect insofar as they were in a military service relationship (§ 1 para 2 Soldiers Act, § 4 paras 1, 3 and 4 WPflG). The circle of persons affected thereby drawn is certainly large, but capable of clear delimitation and, to that extent, also comprehensible. It is true that it cannot be excluded that active soldiers of the Federal Army – perhaps conscripts – share the assessments of the defendant. To that extent a consent excluding the necessary elements of the offence would be present (compare Herdegen, *loc cit*, § 185 marginal no 41). This circle of persons would however be so small that it would be immaterial to the extent of the guilt.

It is otherwise in relation to former soldiers of the Federal Army. In this respect the extent of the guilt is first of all too widely conceived because the necessary criminal complaints are lacking (§ 194 para 1 StGB). The criminal complaint by the Federal Minister of Defence could and should only relate to the soldiers active at the time of the act; criminal complaints by former soldiers have only been made in two cases.

Besides this, the circle of former soldiers is so large and incapable of being comprehended that it does not together form a group of persons capable of being insulted. Apart from the fact that even amongst former soldiers individuals may share the judgment of the defendant, not a few will feel themselves not to be affected by his statements, perhaps because they no longer have any connection with the Federal Army – sometimes over several decades. Therefore, former soldiers only fall to be considered as being affected if they feel themselves to be still connected to the Federal Army and they manifest this attitude by their conduct, perhaps by regular participation in reserve duty training exercises or collaboration with soldiers' interest groups. Whether these prerequisites are present with the two complainants will have to be examined by the State Court in the new main proceedings.

(c) In the same way, the considerations on which the State Court has denied an insult of the Federal Army as an institution are subject to legal doubts.

---

7 This complaint must be made in the case of certain criminal offences, by an appropriate person other than the State prosecution service before proceedings can be taken in respect of the criminal offence. This person will be the person harmed by the offence or someone else sufficiently connected to that person.

Neben Einzelpersonen sind auch Personengemeinschaften unter gewissen Voraussetzungen beleidigungsfähig (vgl. z.B. BGHSt 6, 186ff. m. w. Nachw.). Für Behörden, politische Körperschaften und sonstige Stellen, die Aufgaben der öffentlichen Verwaltung wahrnehmen, folgt das schon aus § 194 Abs. 3, 4 StGB. Demgemäß ist auch die Bundeswehr als Institution passiv beleidigungsfähig (OLG Hamm NZWehrr 1977, 70 mit zustimmender Anmerkung Hennings).

Das Landgericht hat das nicht verkannt, eine Beleidigung der Bundeswehr jedoch wegen fehlenden Vorsatzes verneint. Die Erwägungen dazu geben zu rechtlichen Bedenken Anlaß. Zwar ist die Auslegung der Publikation des Angeklagten und damit auch die Feststellung des Zieles seiner Angriffe Sache des Tatrichters (BGHSt 21, 371, 372; 32, 310, 311). Der Schluß, der Artikel befasse sich in erster Linie mit den Soldaten, nicht mit deren Dienstherrn, berücksichtigt jedoch entgegenstehende Textstellen nur unzureichend und ist damit nicht in Einklang zu bringen. Schon der Anlaß des Artikels, die geplante öffentliche Gelöbnisfeier der Bundeswehr in Br., zeigt, daß die Stoßrichtung der Angriffe eher auf die Institution Bundeswehr als auf den einzelnen Soldaten zielt. Demgemäß stehen im Vordergrund nicht beleidigende Äußerungen über einzelne oder eine Vielzahl von Soldaten oder konkret von ihnen durchgeführte Tätigkeiten, sondern abstrakte Betrachtungen über den Beruf des Soldaten, dessen eigentlicher Zweck das Morden und Aufrechterhalten einer 'gigantischen Mordmaschinerie' sei. Bei diesen Äußerungen ist der Schluß, der Angeklagte habe nicht erwogen, seine Äußerungen seien geeignet, die Bundeswehr als Institution zu beleidigen, durch den Text der Publikation nicht belegt.

Anzumerken ist insoweit jedoch, daß besonderer Prüfung bedarf, ob bei Bejahung der Voraussetzungen des § 185 StGB hinsichtlich der Bundeswehr als Institution angesichts des Gewichts des Interesses der Öffentlichkeit an freier Kritik und ungebundener Diskussion gerade im hier fraglichen Bereich sowie unter Berücksichtigung der Zielsetzung des Angeklagten bei Verbreitung seiner Schrift der Bereich dessen überschritten ist, was einer Institution wie der Bundeswehr, die sich auch unsachlicher und massiver Kritik eher stellen muß als eine Einzelperson, noch hinzunehmen zumutbar ist (vgl. OLG Hamm NZWehrr 1977, 70, 71; zur Anwendung des § 193 StGB in Fällen der Beleidigung BGH NStZ 1987, 554; BGH, Urt. vom 27. Januar 1984 – 5 StR 866/83; verneinend noch BGH, Urt. vom 31. März 1953 – 1 StR 584/52 bei Dallinger MDR 1953, 401).

Demgemäß kann das Urteil schon aus den angeführten Gründen keinen Bestand haben.

Besides individual persons, associations of persons are also, under certain conditions, capable of being insulted (compare, eg, BGHSt 6, 186 and onwards with further references). For administrative authorities, political bodies, and other authorities which look after the tasks of the public administration, this follows from § 194 paras 3 and 4 of the StGB. Accordingly the Federal Army also is passively capable of being insulted (OLG Hamm NZWehrr 1977, 70 with concurring note by Henning).

The State Court did not fail to recognise that but denied an insult of the Federal Army because of lack of intention. The considerations for this give cause for legal doubts. The interpretation of the defendant's publication and with this also the establishment of the objective of his attacks is, of course, a matter for the judge of fact (BGHSt 21, 371, 372; 32, 310, 311). The conclusion however that the article was primarily concerned with soldiers, not with their superiors, takes insufficient account of the parts of the text which are opposed to this, and cannot therefore be reconciled with them. The cause of the article, the planned public swearing-in ceremony of the Federal Army in Br, shows that the thrust of the attacks was rather directed towards the institution of the Federal Army than towards individual soldiers. Accordingly, what stands in the foreground is not insulting statements about individual soldiers or a number of soldiers or actual activities carried out by them, but abstract opinions about the vocation of soldiers the real purpose of which was murder and the maintenance of a 'gigantic murder machine'. From these statements, the conclusion that the defendant did not consider that his statements were appropriate to insult the Federal Army as an institution is not verified by the text of the publication.

It is however to be observed in this respect that special examination is needed as to whether on confirmation of the presence of the prerequisites of § 185 of the StGB with regard to the Federal Army as an institution, there has in the light of the weight of public interest in free criticism and unrestrained discussion in the sphere in question here as well as in consideration of the objective of the defendant in disseminating his publication, been an overstepping of the area of what it is reasonable for an institution like the Federal Army, which must expose itself to subjective and massive criticism to a greater degree than an individual person, to accept (compare OLG Hamm NZWehrr 1977, 70, 71; on application of § 193 of the StGB in cases of insult, BGH NStZ 1987, 554; BGH judgment of 27 January 1984 – 5 StR 866/83; disagreeing, BGH, judgment of 31 March 1953 – 1 StR 584/52 in Dallinger MDR 1953, 401).

Accordingly, the judgment cannot stand for the reasons cited.

2 Der Tatbestand der Verleumdung nach § 187 StGB ist entgegen der Meinung der beschwerdeführenden Staatsanwaltschaft nicht erfüllt.

Bei seiner Auseinandersetzung mit dem Soldatenberuf geht der Angeklagte nicht davon aus, daß die von ihm kritisierte Tötung anderer Menschen anders als im offenen Kampf erfolgen würde. Er behauptet nicht, Soldaten der Bundeswehr würden tatsächlich wie Folterknechte, KZ-Aufseher oder Henker Menschen zu Tode bringen; daß diese Vergleiche nur seine Bewertung darstellen, liegt auf der Hand.

Der Angeklagte läßt freilich bei seinen Betrachtungen außer acht, daß die Streitkräfte der Bundesrepublik Deutschland grundsätzlich nur zur Verteidigung eingesetzt werden dürfen (Art. 87 a Abs. 2 GG). Jede Tötungshandlung durch Soldaten der Bundeswehr erhält dadurch den Charakter einer kollektiven Notwehr; dadurch, daß der Angeklagte in seinem Pamphlet diesen Gesichtspunkt übersieht, stellt er jedoch keine unwahren Tatsachenbehauptungen auf und will dies ersichtlich auch nicht, zumal der Verteidigungsauftrag der Bundeswehr allgemein bekannt ist.

3 Auch den Tatbestand der Volksverhetzung nach § 130 StGB hat das Landgericht im Ergebnis zu Recht als nicht erfüllt angesehen.

Dabei kann dahinstehen, ob der Wertung, die Äußerungen des Angeklagten seien nicht als Beschimpfungen oder böswillige Verächtlichmachung anzusehen, beigetreten werden kann. Jedenfalls enthält der Artikel des Angeklagten, im Zusammenhang gelesen, keine Angriffe gegen die Menschenwürde der Soldaten der Bundeswehr.

2 The necessary elements of calumny in accordance with § 187 of the StGB are, contrary to the opinion of the complainant State prosecutor, not fulfilled.

In his argument against the vocation of the soldier, the defendant does not proceed on the basis that the killing of other humans which he criticises would ensue otherwise than in open battle. He does not assert that soldiers of the Federal Army would actually kill people like torturers, concentration camp supervisors or hangmen; it is obvious that these comparisons only represent his assessment.

The defendant, of course, in his observations leaves out of account the fact that the forces of the Federal Republic of Germany may only in principle be used for defence (Art 87 a para 2 of the GG). Every act of killing by soldiers of the Federal Army thereby obtains the character of collective self-defence; but the defendant did not put forward any untrue factual assertions by virtue of the fact that he overlooks this point of view in his pamphlet and he evidently did not intend to put any such assertions forward, especially as the defence mission of the Federal Army is generally known.

3 The necessary elements of incitement of the people in accordance with § 130 of the StGB have also, in the result, been correctly seen by the State Court as not fulfilled.

In this connection it can be left undecided whether the assessment that the statements of the defendant were not to be regarded as affronts or malicious exposure to contempt can be agreed. In any case, the defendant's article, read in context, includes no attacks against the human dignity of the soldiers of the Federal Army.

Dieses Merkmal ist verwirklicht, wenn den angegriffenen Personen 'ihr Lebensrecht als gleichwertige Persönlichkeit in der staatlichen Gemeinschaft' bestritten wird und sie als 'unterwertige Wesen' behandelt werden. Das 'Menschentum' der Angegriffenen muß bestritten oder relativiert, der Betroffene im Kernbereich seiner Persönlichkeit getroffen werden; die Beeinträchtigung einzelner Persönlichkeitsrechte genügt nicht (Bericht des Rechtsausschusses BTDrucks. III/1746 S. 3; vgl. Schafheutle JZ 1960, 470, 473; Streng in Festschrift für Lackner 1987 S. 501, 504f.; Giering StV 1985, 30, 34). Angriffe, die sich ausschließlich mit den beruflichen Funktionen der angegriffenen Gruppenmitglieder befassen, sind daher regelmäßig nur geeignet, diese im Kernbereich ihrer Persönlichkeit zu treffen, wenn sich daraus zugleich der Schluß ergibt, diese Tätigkeit charakterisiere den, der sie ausübe, als 'unterwertiges Wesen' und nehme ihm sein Lebensrecht als gleichwertige Persönlichkeit. So können aber die Darlegungen des Angeklagten insgesamt nicht verstanden werden. Er hat zwar verletzende Kritik an den beruflichen Funktionen der Soldaten der Bundeswehr und damit auch an ihnen selbst geübt, andererseits aber auch für die mißliche Lage, in der sich nach seiner Sicht 'die armen Teufel, die sich zum Bund verpflichtet' haben, befinden, Verständnis gezeigt und gemeint, da 'dämmere es dem einen oder anderen doch einmal, daß er eine äußerst fragwürdige Existenz' führe. Diese Ausführungen machen hinreichend deutlich, daß der Angeklagte den Soldaten der Bundeswehr ein Lebensrecht in der Gemeinschaft nicht absprechen will. Dieser Eindruck wird dadurch verstärkt, daß sich der Angriff des Angeklagten in erster Linie gegen den Beruf des Soldaten richtete. Er nähert sich damit in seiner Tendenz einem Angriff auf die Institution Bundeswehr. Es ist jedoch anerkannt, daß zu den in § 130 StGB geschützten Teilen der Bevölkerung nicht institutionalisierte Personenmehrheiten zählen, soweit es um die Institution als solche geht und nicht um die hinter ihr stehenden Menschen (Lenckner aaO § 130 Rdn. 4; v. Bubnoff in LK, 10. Aufl., § 130 Rdn. 4; Giehring aaO S. 32). So liegt es zwar hier nicht, doch mindert der vorrangige Angriff gegen die Einrichtung das Gewicht der mittelbaren Kränkung der hinter ihr stehenden Menschen und zeigt, daß es dem Angeklagten nicht darum ging, die Menschenwürde der Soldaten anzutasten.

This characteristic is realised when the persons attacked have 'their right to life as an equal personality in the State community' disputed and they are treated as 'inferior beings'. The 'humanity' of those attacked must be disputed or qualified and the person concerned affected in the core area of his personality; the infringement of individual rights of personality does not suffice (Report of the Legal Committee BTDrucks III/1746, p 3; compare Schafheutle JZ 1960, 470, 473; Streng in Festschrift for Lackner, 1987, pp 501, 504 and onwards; Giering StV 1985, 30, 34). Attacks which concern themselves exclusively with the vocational functions of the group members attacked are therefore ordinarily only appropriate to affect them in the core area of their personality if at the same time the conclusion follows that this activity would characterise the person who carries it out as an 'inferior being' and would take away his right to life as an equal personality. The statements of the defendant cannot however, taken as a whole, be understood in this way. He has certainly used insulting criticism in relation to the vocational functions of the soldiers of the Federal Army and thereby also in relation to themselves, but on the other hand also shown understanding for the awkward situation in which, according to his view, 'the poor fellows who' have 'pledged themselves to the Federation' find themselves and considered 'it would' then 'dawn on one or other of them one day that he' was leading 'an extremely questionable existence'. These statements make it sufficiently clear that the defendant does not intend to deny soldiers of the Federal Army a right to life in the community. This impression is strengthened by the fact that the defendant's attack was directed primarily against the vocation of the soldier. He thereby comes close in his intention to an attack on the institution of the Federal Army. It is however recognised that institutionalised groups of persons are not included in the sections of the population protected by § 130 of the StGB insofar as the issue concerns the institution as such and not the people who stand behind it (Lenckner, *loc cit*, § 130 marginal no 4; v Bubnoff in LK, 10th edn, § 130 marginal no 4; Giehring, *loc cit*, p 32). That is certainly not the case here, but the primary attack on the institution lessens the importance of the indirect insult to the persons standing behind it and shows that it was not the defendant's aim to offend the human dignity of soldiers.

§ 186 [Üble Nachrede] Wer in Beziehung auf einen anderen eine Tatsache behauptet oder verbreitet, welche denselben verächtlich zu machen oder in der öffentlichen Meinung herabzuwürdigen geeignet ist, wird, wenn nicht diese Tatsache erweislich wahr ist, mit Freiheitsstrafe bis zu einem Jahr oder mit Geldstrafe und, wenn die Tat öffentlich oder durch Verbreiten von Schriften (§ 11 Abs. 3) begangen ist, mit Freiheitsstrafe bis zu zwei Jahren oder mit Geldstrafe bestraft.

§ 187 [Verleumdung] Wer wider besseres Wissen in Beziehung auf einen anderen eine unwahre Tatsache behauptet oder verbreitet, welche denselben verächtlich zu machen oder in der öffentlichen Meinung herabzuwürdigen oder dessen Kredit zu gefährden geeignet ist, wird mit Freiheitsstrafe bis zu zwei Jahren oder mit Geldstrafe und, wenn die Tat öffentlich, in einer Versammlung oder durch Verbreiten von Schriften (§ 11 Abs. 3) begangen ist, mit Freiheitsstrafe bis zu fünf Jahren oder mit Geldstrafe bestraft.

§ 188 [Üble Nachrede und Verleumdung gegen Personen des politischen Lebens] (1) Wird gegen eine im politischen Leben des Volkes stehende Person öffentlich, in einer Versammlung oder durch Verbreiten von Schriften (§ 11 Abs. 3) eine üble Nachrede (§ 186) aus Beweggründen begangen, die mit der Stellung des Beleidigten im öffentlichen Leben zusammenhängen, und ist die Tat geeignet, sein öffentliches Wirken erheblich zu erschweren, so ist die Strafe Freiheitsstrafe von drei Monaten bis zu fünf Jahren.

(2) Eine Verleumdung (§ 187) wird unter den gleichen Voraussetzungen mit Freiheitsstrafe von sechs Monaten bis zu fünf Jahren bestraft.

§ 189 [Verunglimpfung des Andenkens Verstorbener] Wer das Andenken eines Verstorbenen verunglimpft, wird mit Freiheitstrafe bis zu zwei Jahren oder mit Geldstrafe bestraft.

CRIMES AGAINST LIFE

Sechzehnter Abschnitt. Straftaten gegen das Leben

§ 211 [Mord] (1) Der Mörder wird mit lebenslanger Freiheitsstrafe bestraft.

§ 186 [Defamation] A person who, in relation to another, asserts or disseminates a fact which is apt to make him contemptible or to degrade him in public opinion will, if this fact is not demonstrably true, be punished with a sentence of imprisonment of up to one year or with a monetary penalty, and if the act is committed publicly or by the dissemination of written material (§ 11 para 3), with a sentence of imprisonment of up to two years or with a monetary penalty.

§ 187 [Calumny] A person who, contrary to his better knowledge, in relation to another, asserts or disseminates an untrue fact, which is apt to make him contemptible or to degrade him in public opinion or to endanger his credit, will be punished with a sentence of imprisonment of up to two years or with a monetary penalty, and if the act is committed publicly, in a meeting, or by dissemination of written material (§ 11 para 3) with a sentence of imprisonment of up to five years or with a monetary penalty.

§ 188 [Defamation and calumny against persons in political life] (1) If defamation (§ 186) is committed against a person with a status in the political life of the people publicly, in a meeting or by dissemination of written material (§ 11 para 3) from motives which are connected with the position of the person insulted in public life and if the act is apt for making his public work substantially more difficult, the punishment is a sentence of imprisonment of three months to five years.

(2) Calumny (§ 187) will be punished under the same conditions with a sentence of imprisonment of six months to five years.

§ 189 [Disparagement of the memory of a deceased person] A person who disparages the memory of a deceased person will be punished with a sentence of imprisonment of up to two years or with a monetary penalty.

§§ 190, 192–194, and 199 and 200 contain supplementary provisions about insult. §§ 195–198 have been repealed.

CRIMES AGAINST LIFE

The simple division of these acts in English law into murder, manslaughter and infanticide contrasts with more complex categorisation in German law, which again generally reduces the discretion of the judge. Abortion has been the subject of Federal Constitutional Court decisions, and finally an amendment of the law following reunification.

Sixteenth section. Criminal acts against life

§ 211 [Murder] (1) A murderer will be punished with life imprisonment.

(2) Mörder ist, wer aus Mordlust, zur Befriedigung des Geschlechtstriebs, aus Habgier oder sonst aus niedrigen Beweggründen, heimtückisch oder grausam oder mit gemeingefährlichen Mitteln oder um eine andere Straftat zu ermöglichen oder zu verdecken, einen Mensch tötet.

THE BASE MOTIVE CASE

BGHSt Band 3 S. 132

30 Niedrig ist ein Tötungsbeweggrund, der nach allgemeiner sittlicher Wertung auf tiefster Stufe steht, durch hemmungslose, triebhafte Eigensucht bestimmt und deshalb besonders verwerflich, ja verächtlich ist (hier: Tötung der Ehefrau als Hindernis eines Liebesverhältnisses).

StGB § 211

1 Ferienstrafsenat. Urt vom 25. Juli 1952 g. Sch. 1 StR 272/52

I Schwurgericht Nürnberg-Fürth

Aus den Gründen:

Die Angeklagten haben die Ehefrau Sch. gemeinsam getötet, weil sie ihnen bei ihrem Liebesverhältnis im Wege war. Die Verurteilung wegen Mordes (§ 211 StGB) ist nicht zu beanstanden.

(2) A person is a murderer if he, from a lust to kill, to satisfy a sexual urge, from greed or from other base motives insidiously or cruelly or by methods constituting a public danger or in order to facilitate a criminal act or to conceal such an act kills a human being.

'Greed' means something more than a mere intention to benefit financially. It means unrestrained and ruthless pursuit of gain. A contract killer would satisfy this requirement. 'Other base motive' means something particularly reprehensible, eg, revenge, racial hatred.

THE BASE MOTIVE CASE

The particular features of interest in this brief case are the application of a moral assessment to distinguish between murder and manslaughter; and the evidence it provides that not all German criminal cases are as lengthy and complicated as the shootings at the Berlin wall case!

BGHSt Volume 3 p 132

30 A motive for killing is base if, according to general moral assessment, it stands at the lowest level, dictated by unrestrained unbridled selfishness and therefore especially reprehensible - in fact contemptible (here: the killing of a wife who is a hindrance to a love affair).

StGB § 211

1st Vacational Criminal Senate. Judgment of 25 July 1952 v Sch 1 StR 272/52

I Jury Court of Nuremberg-Fürth

Reasons:

The defendants killed Mrs Sch. together because she stood in the way of their love affair. Objection cannot be raised to the conviction for murder (§ 211 of the StGB).

Daß die Angeklagten aus niedrigem Beweggrunde getötet haben, unterliegt keinem Zweifel. Die gesetzlichen Beispiele niedriger Beweggründe im § 211 StGB (Mordlust, Habgier, zur Befriedigung des Geschlechtstriebs) zeigen, daß dieser unbestimmte Begriff solche Beweggründe der vorsätzlichen Tötung umfaßt, die nach allgemeiner sittlicher Wertung auf tiefster Stufe stehen, durch ungehemmte, triebhafte Eigensucht bestimmt und deshalb besonders verwerflich, ja verächtlich sind. Dabei kommt es nicht, wie die Revision meint, auf die sittliche Bewertung etwa des Strebens nach Gewinn oder nach geschlechtlicher Vereinigung an sich an, sondern auf dessen antreibende Verknüpfung mit einer vorsätzlichen Tötung, von der oder deren Folgen der Täter die Befriedigung dieser Begierde erwartet. Daß der Täter seiner Begierde so stark unterliegt, daß er um ihretwillen alle natürlichen, menschlichen Hemmungen überwindet und sogar vorsätzlich tötet, zeigt, daß er in seinen Vorstellungen, Wünschen und Antrieben unter das Mindestmaß der Anforderungen herabgesunken ist, die die Gemeinschaft allgemein stellen muß. Auf dieser Stufe verleugnet er die sittliche Verantwortung, vor die jedermann gestellt ist, bewußt so stark, daß der Antrieb seines Tuns keinerlei Rechtfertigung oder selbst Verständnis mehr verdient, sondern nur noch Verachtung. Einen solchen niedrigen Beweggrund hat das Schwurgericht hier mit Recht angenommen. Den Angeklagten war die Ehefrau Sch. lästig. Sie hatte zwar ihre Geschlechtsbeziehungen nicht wesentlich hindern können; ihre Unterhaltsansprüche gefährdeten nach Meinung der Angeklagten aber die ungestörte Fortsetzung dieser Beziehungen und auch die angestrebte Ehe. In der Ehefrau sahen sie das einzige Hindernis, das ihren Wünschen im Wege stand; deshalb haben sie sie nach der Überzeugung des Schwurgerichts getötet. Dieser Beweggrund war in dem geschilderten Sinne niedrig.

§ 212 [Totschlag] (1) Wer einen Menschen tötet, ohne Mörder zu sein, wird als Totschläger mit Freiheitsstrafe nicht unter fünf Jahren bestraft.

(2) In besonders schweren Fällen ist auf lebenslange Freiheitsstrafe zu erkennen.

§ 213 [Minder schwerer Fall des Totschlags] War der Totschläger ohne eigene Schuld durch eine ihm oder einem Angehörigen zugefügte Mißhandlung oder schwere Beleidigung von dem getöteten Menschen zum Zorn gereizt und hierdurch auf der Stelle zur Tat hingerissen worden oder liegt sonst ein minder schwerer Fall vor, so ist die Strafe Freiheitsstrafe von einem Jahr bis zu zehn Jahren.

§§ 214, 215 (weggefallen)

There can be no doubt that the defendants killed from a base motive. The statutory examples of base motives in § 211 of the StGB (desire to kill, greed, satisfaction of sexual urge) show that this indefinite concept includes motives for intentional killing which, according to general moral assessment, stand at the lowest level, dictated by unrestrained unbridled selfishness and therefore especially reprehensible – in fact contemptible. It is not a question, as is argued in the appeal in law, of the moral assessment of striving for gain or for sexual union in themselves, but of the linking of this, as a driving force, with an intentional killing, from which, or from the consequences of which, the perpetrator expects the gratification of his desire. That the perpetrator succumbs so violently to this desire, that he overcomes all natural human restraints for its sake and even kills intentionally, shows that he has in his ideas, wishes and urges, sunk beneath the lowest measure of requirements which society must generally make. At this level, he consciously denies so strongly the moral responsibility before which everyone is placed that the motive of his action no longer deserves any kind of justification or even understanding but only contempt. Such a base motive has correctly been assumed here by the Jury Court. Mrs Sch was an inconvenience to the defendants. She could certainly not have substantially hindered their sexual relations; but her claims to maintenance, according to the opinion of the defendants, endangered the undisturbed continuation of these relations and also the marriage to which they aspired. In the wife, they saw the only hindrance which stood in the way of their wishes; for this reason, according to the belief of the Jury Court, they killed her. This motive was base in the sense described.

§ 212 [Manslaughter] (1) A person who kills a human being, otherwise than by murder, will be punished for manslaughter with a sentence of imprisonment of not less than five years.

(2) In especially serious cases a sentence of life imprisonment is to be imposed.

§ 213 [Less serious case of manslaughter] If a person who commits manslaughter was provoked to anger, without blame on his part, by ill-treatment or serious insult to him or a relative by the person killed and as a result had been impelled to commit the act on the spot, or the case is otherwise less serious, the punishment is a sentence of imprisonment of one year to 10 years.

§§ 214, 215 (repealed)

§ 216 [Tötung auf Verlangen] (1) Ist jemand durch das ausdrückliche und ernstliche Verlangen des Getöteten zur Tötung bestimmt worden, so ist auf Freiheitsstrafe von sechs Monaten bis zu fünf Jahren zu erkennen.

(2) Der Versuch ist strafbar.

§ 220 a [Völkermord] (1) Wer in der Absicht, eine nationale, rassische, religiöse oder durch ihr Volkstum bestimmte Gruppe als solche ganz oder teilweise zu zerstören:

1 Mitglieder der Gruppe tötet,

2 Mitgliedern der Gruppe schwere körperliche oder seelische Schäden, insbesondere der in § 226 bezeichneten Art, zufügt,

3 die Gruppe unter Lebensbedingungen stellt, die geeignet sind, deren körperliche Zerstörung ganz oder teilweise herbeizuführen,

4 Maßregeln verhängt, die Geburten innerhalb der Gruppe verhindern sollen,

5 Kinder der Gruppe in eine andere Gruppe gewaltsam überführt,

wird mit lebenslanger Freiheitsstrafe bestraft.

(2) In minder schweren Fällen des Absatzes 1 Nr. 2 bis 5 ist die Strafe Freiheitsstrafe nicht unter fünf Jahren.

§ 221 [Aussetzung] (1) Wer einen Menschen:

1 in eine hilflose Lage versetzt oder,

2 in einer hilflosen Lage im Stich läßt, obwohl er ihn in seiner Obhut hat oder ihm sonst beizustehen verpflichtet ist,

und ihn dadurch der Gefahr des Todes oder einer schweren Gesundheitsschädigung aussetzt, wird mit Freiheitsstrafe von drei Monaten bis zu fünf Jahren bestraft.

(2) Auf Freiheitsstrafe von einem Jahr bis zu zehn Jahren ist zu erkennen, wenn der Täter:

1 die Tat gegen sein Kind oder eine Person begeht, die ihm zur Erziehung oder zur Betreuung in der Lebensführung anvertraut ist, oder

2 durch die Tat eine schwere Gesundheitsschädigung des Opfers verursacht.

(3) Verursacht der Täter durch die Tat den Tod des Opfers, so ist die Strafe Freiheitsstrafe nicht unter drei Jahren.

(4) In minder schweren Fällen des Absatzes 2 ist auf Freiheitsstrafe von sechs Monaten bis zu fünf Jahren, in minder schweren Fällen des Absatzes 3 auf Freiheitsstrafe von einem Jahr bis zu zehn Jahren zu erkennen.

§ 216 [Killing on request] (1) If someone had decided to kill as a result of the express and earnest request of the person killed, a sentence of imprisonment is to be imposed of six months to five years.

(2) The attempt is punishable.

§ 217 has been repealed, §§ 218–219 b relate to abortion. § 220 has been repealed.

§ 220 a [Genocide] (1) A person who, with the intention of wholly or partially destroying as such a national, racial or religious group or a group which is determined by its national traditions:

1 kills members of the group,

2 causes to members of the group severe physical or mental harm, especially of the kind described in § 226,

3 puts the group under conditions of life which are apt to bring about its physical destruction, wholly or partly,

4 imposes rules which are to prevent births within the group,

5 forcefully transfers children of the group into another group,

will be punished by life imprisonment.

(2) In less serious cases of para 1 nos 2–5 the punishment is a sentence of imprisonment of not less than five years.

§ 221 [Abandonment] (1) A person who:

1 places another person in a helpless situation, or

2 deserts another person in a helpless situation, even though he has him in his care or is otherwise obliged to assist him,

and thereby exposes him to the risk of death or of serious harm to his health will be punished with a sentence of imprisonment of three months to five years.

(2) A sentence of imprisonment of from one to 10 years is to be imposed if the perpetrator:

1 commits the act against his child or a person who is entrusted to him for his upbringing or care in the conduct of his life, or

2 causes serious harm to the health of the victim by the act.

(3) If the perpetrator causes the death of the victim by the act, the penalty is imprisonment for not less than three years.

(4) In less serious cases of para 2 a sentence of imprisonment of six months to five years and in less serious cases of para 3 a sentence of imprisonment of one year to 10 years is to be imposed.

§ 222 [Fahrlässige Tötung] Wer durch Fahrlässigkeit den Tod eines Menschen verursacht, wird mit Freiheitsstrafe bis zu fünf Jahren oder mit Geldstrafe bestraft.

BODILY INJURY

Siebzehnter Abschnitt. Körperverletzung

§ 223 [Körperverletzung] (1) Wer eine andere Person körperlich mißhandelt oder an der Gesundheit schädigt, wird mit Freiheitsstrafe bis zu funf Jahren oder mit Geldstrafe bestraft.

(2) Der Versuch ist strafbar.

§ 224 [Gefährliche Körperverletzung] (1) Wer die Körperverletzung:

1 durch Beibringung von Gift oder anderen gesundheitsschädlichen Stoffen,

2 mittels einer Waffe oder eines anderen gefährlichen Werkzeugs,

3 mittels eines hinterlistigen Überfalls,

4 mit einem anderen Beteiligten gemeinschaftlich oder,

5 mittels einer das Leben gefährdenden Behandlung

begeht, wird mit Freiheitstrafe von sechs Monaten bis zu zehn Jahren, in minder schweren Fällen mit Freiheitstrafe von drei Monaten bis zu fünf Jahren bestraft.

(2) Der Versuch ist strafbar:

§ 225 [Mißhandlung von Schutzbefohlenen] (1) Wer eine Person unter achtzehn Jahren oder eine wegen Gebrechlichkeit oder Krankheit wehrlose Person, die:

1 seiner Fürsorge oder Obhut untersteht,

2 seinem Hausstand angehört,

3 von dem Fürsorgepflichtigen seiner Gewalt überlassen worden oder

4 ihm im Rahmen eines Dienst- oder Arbeitsverhältnisses untergeordnet ist,

quält oder roh mißhandelt, oder wer durch böswillige Vernachlässigung seiner Pflicht, für sie zu sorgen, sie an der Gesundheit schädigt, wird mit Freiheitsstrafe von sechs Monaten bis zu zehn Jahren bestraft.

(2) Der Versuch ist strafbar.

(3) Auf Freiheitsstrafe nicht unter einem Jahr ist zu erkennen, wenn der Täter die schutzbefohlene Person durch die Tat in die Gefahr:

1 des Todes oder einer schweren Gesundheitsschädigung oder

§ 222 [Negligent killing] A person who causes the death of a human being by negligence will be punished by a sentence of imprisonment of up to five years or with a monetary penalty.

BODILY INJURY

Seventeenth section. Physical injury

§ 223 [Physical injury] (1) A person who ill-treats another person physically or harms his health will be punished with a sentence of imprisonment of up to five years or with a monetary penalty.

(2) The attempt is punishable.

§ 224 [Dangerous physical injury] (1) A person who commits a physical injury:

1 by administering poison or other material harmful to health;

2 by means of a weapon or another dangerous tool;

3 by means of a deceitful attack;

4 jointly with another participant; or

5 by means of treatment endangering life,

will be punished by a sentence of imprisonment of six months to 10 years, and in less serious cases with a sentence of imprisonment of three months to five years.

(2) The attempt is punishable.

§ 225 [Ill treatment of persons under one's protection] (1) A person who torments or roughly ill-treats a person under the age of 18 years, or a person who is defenceless because of infirmity or illness, who:

1 is under his care or keeping,

2 belongs to his household,

3 has been left in his power by the person responsible for him, or

4 is subordinated to him within the framework of a service or work relationship,

or who harms him in his health by wilful neglect of his duty to care for him, will be punished by a sentence of imprisonment of six months to 10 years.

(2) The attempt is punishable.

(3) A sentence of imprisonment of not less than one year is to be imposed if by the act the perpetrator puts the person under his protection in danger:

1 of death or serious harm to health or

2 einer erheblichen Schädigung der körperlichen oder seelischen Entwicklung bringt.

(4) In minder schweren Fällen des Absatzes 1 ist auf Freiheitsstrafe von drei Monaten bis zu fünf Jahren, in minder schweren Fällen des Absatzes 3 auf Freiheitsstrafe von sechs Monaten bis zu fünf Jahren zu erkennen.

THE ROUGH ILL-TREATMENT CASE

BGHSt Band 25 S. 277

73 Eine rohe Mißhandlung im Sinne des § 223 b StGB liegt vor, wenn der Täter einem anderen eine Körperverletzung aus gefühlloser Gesinnung zufügt, die sich in erheblichen Handlungsfolgen äußert. Solches Vorgehen wird zwar regelmäßig seinen Niederschlag in beträchtlichen Schmerzen oder Leiden finden, jedoch braucht dies – z.B. bei infolge geistiger Erkrankung vermindert schmerzempfindlichen oder schmerzunempfindlichen Personen – nicht notwendig der Fall zu sein. Entscheidend ist die Schwere des körperlichen Eingriffs, in dem sich die gefühllose Gesinnung widerspiegelt und der so beschaffen sein muß, daß ein normaler Mensch ihn als erheblich schmerzhaft empfinden würde.

StGB § 223 b

3 Strafsenat. Urt. vom. 23 Januar 1974 g. W. 3 StR 324/73

Landgericht Kleve

Aus den Gründen:

Das Landgericht hat den Angeklagten wegen Mißhandlung Abhängiger in vier Fällen zu einer Gesamtfreiheitsstrafe von zwei Jahren verurteilt. Seine Revision bleibt erfolglos.

2 of substantial harm to physical or mental development.

(4) In less serious cases of para 1 a sentence of imprisonment of three months to five years and in less serious cases of para 3 a sentence of imprisonment of six months to five years is to be imposed.

THE ROUGH ILL-TREATMENT CASE

The issue in this case is one of interpretation: whether the offence of rough ill-treatment could be committed against persons who through mental illness were not (or not very) sensitive to pain. For this purpose there is a historical investigation of the case law. The case was based on § 223 b of the Criminal Code, which was the predecessor to § 225.

BGHSt Volume 25 p 277

73 Rough ill-treatment in the sense of § 223 b of the StGB occurs if the perpetrator inflicts on another a physical injury out of an unfeeling attitude, which expresses itself in substantial practical consequences. Such action will certainly ordinarily result in considerable pain or suffering, but this does not – eg, with persons who, in consequence of mental illness, are less sensitive or not sensitive to pain – need necessarily to be the case. The decisive issue is the seriousness of the physical interference in which the unfeeling attitude reflects itself and which must be of such a nature that a normal human being would feel it to be considerably painful.

StGB § 223 b

3rd Criminal Senate judgment of 23 January 1974 v.W. 3 StR 324/73

State Court of Kleve

Reasons:

The State Court sentenced the accused to a total prison sentence of imprisonment of two years for ill-treatment of defendants in four cases. His appeal in law is unsuccessful.

1 Keinen Bedenken begegnet zunächst die Annahme der Strafkammer, das Verhalten des Angeklagten gegenüber den vier Patienten sei eine üble, unangemessene Behandlung, durch die diese mehr als nur unerheblich in ihrem körperlichen Wohlbefinden beeinträchtigt worden sind, so daß der Tatbestand der Körperverletzung vorliegt. Das gilt auch für das Herbeiführen einer schweren Erregung des Patienten F. (vgl. Hirsch in LK, 9. Aufl. Rdn. 8 zu § 223 unter Hinweis auf RGSt 32, 113). Unerheblich ist insoweit, ob die Patienten, wie die Revision geltend macht, wegen ihres Geisteszustandes möglicherweise erheblich vermindert schmerzempfindlich gewesen sind. Schmerzerregung ist kein notwendiges Erfordernis der Körperverletzung (RGSt 19, 136, 139 und HRR 1931 Nr. 376).

2 Entgegen der Ansicht der Revision hat die Strafkammer auch zu Recht angenommen, daß die Mißhandlungen roh waren und somit nicht nur der Tatbestand des § 223 StGB, sondern der des § 223 b StGB gegeben ist. Eine Mißhandlung ist roh, wenn der Täter aus gefühlloser, fremde Leiden mißachtender Gesinnung handelt und diese sich in erheblichen Handlungsfolgen für das Wohlbefinden des Opfers offenbart (vgl. Schaefer in LK, 8. Aufl., Anm III b zu § 223 b StGB und Mezger/Blei, Strafrecht Besonderer Teil 8. Aufl., § 13 III b). Daß nur solche Folgen beachtlich seien, die ihren Niederschlag in erheblichen Schmerzen finden, trifft - entgegen der Ansicht der Revision - nicht zu.

Die Frage, ob zur Verwirklichung des Merkmals der Mißhandlung die gefühllose, fremde Leiden mißachtende Gesinnung des Täters in der Zufügung erheblicher Schmerzen hervortreten muß, wird im Schrifttum nicht einheitlich beantwortet. Teils wird die Zufügung besonderer Schmerzen überhaupt nicht verlangt oder nicht erwähnt (Lackner/Maassen, StGB, 8. Aufl. Anm. 6 zu § 223 b; Petters/Preisendanz, StGB, 28. Aufl. Anm. 3 b zu § 223 b; Mezger/Blei aaO); teils wird ohne ausdrückliche Stellungnahme hierzu auf die Rechtsprechung des Reichsgerichts verwiesen (Dreher, StGB, 34. Aufl. Anm. 3 A zu § 223 b und Kohlrausch/Lange, StGB, 43. Aufl. Anm. V zu § 223 b), und schließlich wird unter Bezugnahme auf diese Rechtsprechung die Erregung erheblicher Schmerzen ausdrücklich für erforderlich gehalten (Olshausen, StGB, 12. Aufl. Anm. 3 zu § 223 b; Niethammer, Lehrbuch des Besonderen Teils des Strafrechts, 1950 S. 150; Hirsch in LK, 9. Aufl. Rdn. 14 zu § 223 b; ferner Schönke/Schröder, StGB, 17. Aufl. Rdn. 13 zu § 223 b und Schaefer, aaO – beide nur für den Regelfall). Indes kommt diesem Erfordernis sowohl nach Ansicht von Schönke/Schröder als auch von Hirsch, Schaefer und Maurach (Deutsches Strafrecht, Besonderer Teil 5. Aufl., § 10 II A 2) nur die Funktion einer Objektivierung der gefühllosen Gesinnung zu. Als solche kann sie in der Tat Bedeutung erlangen, hat aber nicht die allein ausschlaggebende Bedeutung, die ihr die Revision beilegen will.

1 There is first of all no doubt as to the criminal court's assumption that the conduct of the accused towards the four patients was improper and evil treatment by which they were impaired in their physical well being to an extent that was more than insignificant, so that the elements of physical injury are present. That also applies to the causing of severe agitation in patient F (compare Hirsch in LK, 9th edn, marginal no 8 at § 223 with reference to the RGSt 32, 113). It is unimportant in this respect whether the patients, as the appeal in law claims, were possibly significantly less sensitive to pain on account of their mental condition. The arousing of pain is not a necessary requirement of physical injury (RGSt 19, 136, 139 and HRR 1931 no 376).

2 Contrary to the view of the appeal in law, the criminal court also correctly accepted that the ill-treatment was rough and therefore not only the elements of § 223 of the StGB but also those of § 223 b of the StGB are satisfied. Ill-treatment is rough if the perpetrator acts out of a unfeeling attitude which disregards the suffering of others and this reveals itself in substantial practical consequences for the well being of the victim (compare Schaefer in LK, 8th edn, note III b at § 223 b of the StGB and Mezger/Blei, Criminal Law – Special Part, 8th edn, § 13 III b). Contrary to the view of the appeal in law, it is not correct that only those consequences are noteworthy which result in substantial pain.

The question whether, for the realisation of the characteristics of ill-treatment, the unfeeling attitude of the perpetrator, disregarding the suffering of others, must be evidential in the infliction of substantial pain is not answered uniformly in the literature. In some places the infliction of particular pain is not asked for at all or not mentioned (Lackner/Maasson, StGB, 8th edn, note 6 at § 223 b; Petters/Preisendanz, StGB, 28th edn, note 3 b at § 223 b; Mezger/Blei, *loc cit*); in other places the case law of the Reich High Court is referred to without an express opinion on this subject (Dreher, StGB, 34th edn, note 3 A at § 223 b and Kohlrausch/Lange, StGB, 43rd edn, note V at § 223 b); and finally the arousing of substantial pain is expressly held to be necessary with reference to the case law (Olshausen, StGB, 12th edn, note 3 at § 223 b; Niethammer, Textbook on the Special Part of the Criminal Law, 1950, p 150; Hirsch in LK, 9th edn, § 223 b marginal no 14; further Schönke/Schröder, StGB, 17th edn, § 223 b marginal no 13 and Schäefer, *loc cit* – both only for the ordinary case). However, according to the view of Schönke/Schröder as well as that of Hirsch, Schaefer and Maurach (German Criminal Law, Special Part, 5th edn, § 10 II A 2) this requirement only serves the function of an objectivisation of the unfeeling attitude. As such it can indeed acquire significance, but it does not have the sole decisive significance which the appeal in law wants to ascribe to it.

Aus der Rechtsprechung des Reichgerichts, auf die sich die Revision und ein Teil des Schrifttums berufen, ergibt sich nicht, daß eine rohe Mißhandlung stets nur dann anzunehmen wäre, wenn dem Opfer erhebliche Schmerzen zugefügt worden waren. Das hat das Reichsgericht zwar in seinen – soweit ersichtlich – zuletzt veröffentlichen Entscheidungen RG DR 1944, 330 und 1941, 492 ausgesprochen. Es bezieht sich aber zur Begründung dieser Ansicht in der Entscheidung aus dem Jahre 1944 nur auf ein vorangegangenes, in DR 1940, 26 veröffentliches Urteil, in der Entscheidung aus dem Jahre 1941 – nur Leitsatz – darüber hinaus auch auf ein früheres Urteil aus dem Jahre 1938 (RG JW 1938, 1879). In RG DR 1940, 26 heißt es allerdings, daß die Rechtsprechung unter einer rohen Mißhandlung die Erregung erheblicher Schmerzen oder Leiden aus gefühlloser Gesinnung verstehe, jedoch verweist auch diese Entscheidung wiederum nur auf die früheren Urteile RG JW 1938, 2808 und 1879. In dem letztgenannten Urteil und schon im Urteil HRR 1935 Nr. 1276 verstand das Reichsgericht unter einer rohen Mißhandlung jede körperliche Mißhandlung, die einer gefühllosen Gesinnung des Täters entspringt; von der (notwendig erforderlichen) Zufügung erheblicher Schmerzen war hier (noch) nicht die Rede. Nur in der in JW 1938, 2808 veröffentlichten Entscheidung hat es – offensichtlich aus Gründen der Rechtssicherheit – noch eine Objektivierung der gefühllosen Gesinnung verlangt, die es in der Zufügung erheblicher Schmerzen sah. Dieses Kriterium bot sich in jenem Falle an: Wer einem in normaler Geistesverfassung Befindlichen ohne Rechtfertigungs- oder Entschuldigungsgrund erhebliche Schmerzen beibringt oder Leiden verursacht, handelt in der Regel aus gefühlloser Gesinnung. Das Reichsgericht wollte ersichtlich aber damit nicht aussprechen, daß *nur* die Zufügung erheblicher Schmerzen oder Leiden den Tatbestand des § 223 b StGB erfülle. Diese ist zwar die regelmäßige, aber nicht die einzige Form, in der gefühllose Gesinnung in Erscheinung treten kann. Fälle herabgesetzter Schmerzempfindlichkeit oder gar völliger Schmerzunempfindlichkeit lagen den genannten Entscheidungen, soweit erkennbar, nicht zugrunde. In einem solchen Falle hat nämlich das Reichsgericht selbst auf einen anderen Gesichtspunkt abgehoben und – noch zu § 223 a StGB in der vor dem 1. Juni 1933 geltenden Fassung – entschieden, der Umstand, daß ein Opfer in seinem Gefühlsleben stark abgestumpft sei, schließe es nicht aus, die Behandlung als eine grausame anzusehen. Sie könne dies auch dann sein, wenn sie zwar nicht von der betroffenen Person selbst wegen deren besonderen körperlichen oder seelischen Beschaffenheit als grausam empfunden wird, wohl aber von anderen Personen, die die Behandlung wahrnehmen und deren Gefühlsleben natürlich und gesund ist (RGSt 62, 160, 161).

From the case law of the Reich High Court, to which the appeal in law and a part of the literature refer, it does not always follow that rough ill-treatment would only be assumed if substantial pain had been inflicted on the victim. The Reich High Court has certainly stated that in its – so far as is evident – last published decisions RG DR 1944, 330 and 1941, 492. But in the decision in the year 1944, it refers for the reason for this view only to a previous judgment, published in DR 1940, 26, and in the decision in the year 1941 – only the summarising sentence[8] – besides this also to an earlier judgment from the year 1938 (RG JW 1938, 1879). In RG DR 1940, 26 it does say that the case law sees rough ill-treatment as including the arousing of substantial pain or suffering through an unfeeling attitude, but this decision also refers again only to the earlier judgments RG JW 1938, 2808 and 1879. In the last named judgment and in the judgment HRR 1935 No 1276 the Reich High Court understood, as included in the category of rough ill-treatment, any physical ill-treatment which originates in a unfeeling attitude by the perpetrator; there was (still) no mention here of the (indispensably necessary) infliction of substantial pain. Only in the decision published in JW 1938, 2808 did it – obviously on the grounds of legal certainty – still require an objectivisation of the unfeeling attitude, which it saw in the infliction of substantial pain. This criterion was presented in that case: a person who inflicts substantial pain or causes suffering to someone in a normal state of mind without grounds of justification or excuse acts as a rule from a unfeeling attitude. The Reich High Court evidently did not however thereby wish to state that *only* the infliction of substantial pain or suffering would fulfil the elements of § 223 b of the StGB. This is certainly the usual, but not the only, form in which an unfeeling attitude can become apparent. Cases of reduced sensitivity to pain or even complete insensitivity to pain were not the basis of the decisions referred to, so far as can be discerned. In such a case the Reich High Court itself emphasised another point of view and decided – in relation to § 223 a of the StGB in the form applying before 1 June 1933 – that the circumstance of a victim's capacity to feel was considerably truncated did not exclude regarding the treatment as cruel. It could also be so if it was not felt by the person affected himself to be cruel because of his special bodily or mental condition, but would be by other persons who observe the treatment and whose capacity to feel is natural and healthy (RGSt 62, 160, 161).

---

8 This is a brief statement of the essential content of a court decision. Such a statement will usually appear at the beginning of a case report.

Diese Rechtsansicht trifft auch auf die rohe Mißhandlung zu, die gegenüber der grausamen ein Weniger ist. Entscheidend ist die Schwere des körperlichen Eingriffs, in dem sich die gefühllose Gesinnung widerspiegelt, und der so beschaffen sein muß, daß ein normaler Mensch ihn als erheblich schmerzhaft empfindet. Anderenfalls würden des besonderen Schutzes des § 223 b StGB – je nach dem Grade ihrer Empfindlichkeit – gerade die Personen entbehren müssen, die seiner in vermehrtem Maße bedürfen, wie z.B. bestimmte Gruppen von Geisteskranken in vorgerücktem Stadium, die nicht in der Lage sind, ihr Schmerzempfinden mitzuteilen.

3 Die gegenüber den Patienten begangenen Handlungen des Angeklagten waren, so wie sie das Landgericht festgestellt hat, von erheblichem Gewicht und geeignet, bei Personen mit normalen Empfinden erhebliche Schmerzen oder Leiden hervorzurufen.

(Wird ausgeführt).

§ 226 [Schwere Körperverletzung] (1) Hat die Körperverletzung zur Folge, daß die verletzte Person:

1 das Sehvermögen auf einem Auge oder beiden Augen, das Gehör, das Sprechvermögen oder die Fortpflanzungsfähigkeit verliert,

2 ein wichtiges Glied des Körpers verliert oder dauernd nicht mehr gebrauchen kann oder

3 in erheblicher Weise dauernd entstellt wird oder in Siechtum, Lähmung oder geistige Krankheit oder Behinderung verfällt,

so ist die Strafe Freiheitsstrafe von einem Jahr bis zu zehn Jahren.

(2) Verursacht der Täter eine der in Absatz 1 bezeichneten Folgen absichtlich oder wissentlich, so ist die Strafe Freiheitsstrafe nicht unter drei Jahren.

(3) In minder schweren Fällen des Absatzes 1 ist auf Freiheitstrafe von sechs Monaten bis zu fünf Jahren, in minder schweren Fällen des Absatzes 2 auf Freiheitstrafe von einem Jahr bis zu zehn Jahren zu erkennen.

§ 227 [Körperverletzung mit Todesfolge] (1) Verursacht der Täter durch die Körperverletzung (§§ 223 bis 226) denTod der verletzten Person, so ist die Strafe Freiheitsstrafe nicht unter drei Jahren.

(2) In minder schweren Fällen ist auf Freiheitstrafe von einem Jahr bis zu zehn Jahren zu erkennen.

This view of the law is also correct in relation to rough ill-treatment which is less than cruel. The decisive issue is the severity of the physical interference in which the unfeeling attitude is reflected and which must be so constituted that a normal human being would feel it to be substantially painful. Otherwise it would be the very persons who need the special protection of § 223 b of the StGB to an increased extent – according to the level of their sensitivity – who would have to do without it, like, eg, certain groups of persons in an advanced phase of mental sickness who are not in a position to communicate their sensitivity to pain.

3 The treatment of the patients by the accused was, as the State Court has established, of substantial gravity and apt to cause substantial pain or suffering in persons with normal sensitivity.

(Details are given).

§ 226 [Serious physical injury] (1) If the physical injury has as its consequence that the injured person:

1 loses his sight in one or both eyes, hearing, power of speech or power of reproduction,

2 loses or can permanently no longer use an important member of his body, or

3 is permanently disfigured in a substantial way or becomes infirm, paralysed, mentally ill or disabled,

the penalty is a sentence of imprisonment of one year to 10 years.

(2) If the perpetrator causes one of the consequences described in para 1 intentionally or knowingly, the penalty is a sentence of imprisonment of not less than three years.

(3) In less serious cases of para 1 a sentence of imprisonment of six months to five years, and in less serious cases of para 2 a sentence of imprisonment of one year to 10 years is to be imposed.

§ 227 [Physical injury resulting in death] (1) If the perpetrator causes the death of the injured person by the physical injury (§§ 223 to 226), the penalty is a sentence of imprisonment of not under three years.

(2) In less serious cases a sentence of imprisonment of one year to 10 years is to be imposed.

§ 228 [Einwilligung] Wer eine Körperverletzung mit Einwilligung der verletzten Person vornimmt, handelt nur dann rechtswidrig, wenn die Tat trotz der Einwilligung gegen die guten Sitten verstößt.

§ 229 [Fahrlässige Körperverletzung] Wer durch Fahrlässigkeit die Körperverletzung einer anderen Person verursacht, wird mit Freiheitsstrafe bis zu drei Jahren oder mit Geldstrafe bestraft.

§ 231 [Beteiligung an einer Schlägerei] (1) Wer sich an einer Schlägerei oder an einem von mehreren verübten Angriff beteiligt, wird schon wegen dieser Beteiligung mit Freiheitsstrafe bis zu drei Jahren oder mit Geldstrafe bestraft, wenn durch die Schlägerei oder den Angriff den Tod eines Menschen oder eine schwere Körperverletzung (§ 226) verursacht worden ist.

(2) Nach Absatz 1 ist nicht strafbar, wer an der Schlägerei oder dem Angriff beteiligt war, ohne daß ihm dies vorzuwerfen ist.

§ 228 [Consent] A person who carries out a physical injury with the consent of the injured person only acts unlawfully if the act, in spite of the consent, violates good morals.

§ 229 [Negligent physical injury] A person who causes physical injury to another person through negligence will be punished by a sentence of imprisonment of up to three years or by a fine.

§ 230 deals with procedure.

§ 231 [Participation in a brawl] (1) A person who takes part in a brawl or in an attack perpetrated by several people will be punished because of this participation by a sentence of imprisonment of up to three years or by a fine if the death of a human being or a serious physical injury (§ 226) has been caused by the brawl or the attack.

(2) A person whose participation in the brawl or the attack is not something for which he can be held responsible is not punishable under para 1.

BIBLIOGRAPHY

Currie, D, *The Constitution of the Federal Republic of Germany*, 1994, London and Chicago: University of Chicago Press

Dannemann, G, *An Introduction to German Civil and Commercial Law*, 1993, London: British Institute of International and Comparative Law

Ebke, WF and Finkin, MW (eds), *Introduction to German Law*, 1996, London: Kluwer

Fisher, HD, *The German Legal System and Legal Language*, 3rd edn, 2002, London: Cavendish Publishing

Foster, NG, *German Legal System and Laws*, 2nd edn, 1996 (see 3rd edn, 2002 forthcoming, Oxford: OUP), London: Blackstone

Horn, N, Kötz, H and Leser, HG, *German Private and Commercial Law, An Introduction*, Weir, JA (trans), 1982, Oxford: Clarendon

Kommers, DP, *The Case Law of the Federal Constitutional Court of Germany*, 2nd edn, 1997, Chicago: Duke Press

Kötz, H and Flessner, A, *European Contract Law,* Weir, JA (trans), 1997, Oxford: Clarendon

Markesinis, BS, Lorenz, W and Dannemann, G, *The German Law of Obligations, The Law of Contracts and Restitution: A Comparative Introduction*, 1997, Oxford: Clarendon, Vol I

Markesinis, BS, *The German Law of Obligations, The Law of Torts: A Comparative Introduction*, 3rd edn with corrections and additions, 1994, Oxford: Clarendon, Vol II

Marsh, PDV, *Comparative Contract Law, England, France, Germany*, 1994, Aldershot: Gower

Michalowski, S and Woods, L, *German Constitutional Law*, 1999, Aldershot: Dartmouth

Van Gerven, W, *Cases, Materials and Text on National, Supranational and International Tort Law*, 2000, Oxford: Hart

von Bar, C, *The Common European Law of Torts*, 1998, Beck: München, Vols I and II

Vranken, M, *Fundamentals of European Civil Law*, 1996, London: Blackstone

Youngs, R, *English, French and German Comparative Law*, 1998, London: Cavendish Publishing

Zimmermann, R, *The Law of Obligations*, 1989, London: Clarendon

Zweigert, K and Kötz, H, *An Introduction to Comparative Law*, Weir, JA (trans), 3rd edn, 1995, Oxford: Clarendon

INDEX

Note: page references in *italics* refer to case studies

A

Abandonment 737

Abortion 731

Academic writings
on law 1, 5
declaration of will 249, 265–271
self-defence 325

Act of State
(as defence) 629, 659–671

Action, freedom of 207

AGBG (General
Conditions of
Business Act) 333, 371
on offer/acceptance 341–349

Agriculture/forestry 213

Air traffic controllers
strike case 51, 373,
435, *579–605*
facts of case 579–581
legality of strike 583–591
determination of
responsibility 591–605

Alcohol (and
responsibility) 559

Alienation 313

All Germany
election case *53–81*
Barrier Clause 57–63, 75–81
combination of
party lists 67–73
special circumstances
of election 63–67

Allergy to hair tonic case *399–411*
facts of case 401
judgment and reasons 403–411

Amsterdam, Treaty of 133

Animals,
owners' liabilities 575
rights of *129–139*

Appeals, types of 2

Army, Federal
See also Military service
collective insult to *715–729*
international role *19–39*

Arrest,
grounds for 111–113,
121–127
rights/duties relating to 99

Arrested admiral
case 109, *111–127*
background 111–113
facts of case 113–115
judgment and
reasons 115–127

Assembly,
freedom of 183, 491, 497

Assistance
(in criminal acts) 701

Association,
freedom of 183–185, 221

Asylum, rights of 223–225

Attempted acts
(criminal) 699–701, 703
withdrawal from 701, 703

Auctions 363
See also Internet auction case

Avoidance 259, *261–279*,
315–317
declarations of 247, 257–259
grounds for 281, *283–295*,
355–357
time constraints 279, 295

B

Bailiffs, role/duties of 311

Balancing,
Basic Law 7, 19
Basic Rights 7, 105, 527,
531, 541
proportionality
principle 109

Barrier (5%) clause 53, 55–81
lowering of
requirements
(proposed) 55, 75–77
regionalisation of 55–57, 77–81

Base motive case *733–735*

Basic Law (*Grundgesetz*) 1, 9–103
See also Basic Rights
animal rights 129, 135–137
balancing 7, 19
business law 193, *201–211*,
221–223

criminal law........ 97–99, *663–669*
and EU law 13–15
Federal institutions....... 53, 89–97
Federal
 organisation......... 9–11, 83, 99
general laws.............. 519–527
history................... 7, 9, 15
international
 relations 17, 41, 49
interpretation............... 7, 481
judicial process 87–99
legal status 4, 101
legislation............... 53, 83–87
modifications............ 81, 83–85
officials/authorities 51–53
publication................... 101
sexual equality 145–149, 149
social/economic
 order 193, 209
States 43–49,
 43–53, 83,
 89–91
termination 103
as transitional 101
Unity of (as legal
 principle) 7
vs international law *19–39*

Basic Rights (*Grundrechte*).... 105–227
See also Expression (of opinion),
 freedom of
balancing............... 105, 527,
 531, 541
and civil law............ 106–107,
 515–527
conflicts between..... 105, *481–501*,
 541
constitutional
 freedoms 106, 157, 173,
 183–187
constitutional status 105
definition 105
equality before the law 141
and EU law 13
extent of application .. 106–108, 505,
 515–519
forfeiture.................... 227
human dignity 107, 129, 475
interpretation............. 481, 505
limitations.............. 107–108,
 227, 317
military service
 (refusal of) 157, 187
misuse...................... 227
of personality 139, 233,
 469–481

political................. 223–225
primary purpose............. 515
property 189–191
pursuit of business *487–501*,
 597–601
and State law 43
statutory reservation 107–108
violations of 91, 106–107,
 469–481, 505

Berlin Wall, shootings at
 See Shootings at the Berlin
 Wall case

Bodily injury,
 offences causing.......... 739–741,
 741–747,
 747–749
 consent to................... 749

Bosnia flight exclusion
 zone case *19–39*
 facts of case 19–21
 role of FCC................. 29–31
 role of NATO 25–29, 33–39
 role of UN 21–23

Boycott (and
 good morals) *505–511*,
 529–559

Brawls........................ 749

Buildings, collapse/
 maintenance of 577

Burden of proof *399–411*,
 435, 439,
 457–467

Bürgerliches Gesetzbuch
 (BGB)
 See Civil Code (BGB)

Bye-laws.................... 4, 107

C

Cannabis application
 rejection case *159–173*

Cases, selection of................. 1

Cattle slaughter case 15, *129–139*
 facts of case 131
 judgment and
 reasons 133–139

Chemist's case................. 185

Children
 See Minors; Parental duties/rights

Citizenship, German 223

Civil Code (BGB) 1, 7
See also AGBG
contract law 331–333, 359–367
declarations
of will 243, 259,
279–281, 295–301,
311–313, 311–315
history 229
legal competence 235–239
legal transactions 313–317
mistake 259
obligations 369–377, 397–399,
411–431
persons, definitions/
rights of 229–233
special defences 319–321
tort 435–437, 503,
559–563, 573–579,
609–615

Coercion,
as defence 545–553
Federal (of States) 53

Communist Party
of Germany 11

Company law
and Basic Rights 106
definitions 2

Compensation 281, 373–375
See also Liability
by annuity 609–611
breakdown of
negotiations 393–395
contractual liability 363–365
contributory fault 375, 501
for criminal acts 707
expenditure 411, 613
for fatalities 611
on grounds of
fairness 561
for harm to livestock 439–467
joint liability 609
in lieu of
performance 397–399, 411
limitation 379
nationalisation 223
for personal
injury 321–329,
377–391, 565–573,
605–609, 609–611
time limits 615
transfer of claims 375
and withdrawal 427

Competence, legal
(Rechtsfähigkeit) 229, 235–239
and declarations
of will 311
disqualifications
from 235
limited 235, 311
of minors 235

Computer
non-disclosure case 283–295
judgment and
reasons 287–295

Consent (to legal
transactions) 367

Constitution
See Basic Law; Weimar
Constitution

Constitutional complaints 91
admissibility 199–201
grounds for 527
industrial finance 197–223
lodgement of 193
wrongful arrest 111–127

Consumers,
compensation 449–467
definition 233
rights/obligations 369, 413

Contracts 331–431
See also Avoidance; Deception,
fraudulent; Mistake;
Obligations
acceptance 331, 359–361
agreement 361
alteration 371
basis,
disturbance of 421
conditions 363–365, 415–419
consent 367
content 415–425
culpa in contrahendo 383–385
definition 239
interpretation 313, 363, 417
long term 421
and minors 235–237
mutual 425–429
negotiations
(pre-contractual) 393–395
offer 331–333,
333–357, 359
prohibited/
ineffective content 417–419
ratification 235–237

revocation. 237
of service *301–311*
third parties,
  liability towards *385–391*
time limits. 359, 365,
                                    425–427
withdrawal
  from *301–311*, 425–429
Copyright. 475–477
Corporations
  (and Basic Rights). 106
Courts,
  establishment of 97
Creditors/debtors,
  definition 2–3
Criminal law
  See also Criminal Code;
    Penalties
  definitions/translation
    of terms. 3
  provisions in
    Basic Law. 97–99, *663–669*
Criminal Code
  (*Strafgesetzbuch*) 1, 7, 437,
                                    617–749
  assistance 701
  attempts 699–701, 703
  basic principles 619, 687
  bodily injury. 739–741,
                                    747–749
  definitions 685–687
  emergency 705
  guilt,
    (in)capacity for 699
  history. 617
  insult. 715
  intent. 687
  life, crimes against 731–739
  omission. 683, 687
  penalties. 707–713
  perpetration/
    participation 701–703
  retroactivity,
    prohibition of 619, *663–669*
  self-defence 703
  spatial scope 683
  temporal scope. 619, *621–681*,
                                    683
  withdrawal 703
  young offenders 685
Culpa in contrahendo 383–385

Currency reform
  (1951). 195
Custom,
  legal status of. 4

D

Damages
  See Compensation; Liability
DDR (German
  Democratic Republic)
  See also Unification (1990)
  Civil Code 229
  Constitution. 659–661, 669
  human rights law 649–657,
                                    659–661,
                                    669, 679
  policy on attempted
    border crossings. 625–629,
                                    633–643,
                                    653–657, 677
  relationship with
    Federal law 109, 621, 629,
                                    631–635, 665
  relationship with
    international law. 649–657
Deaf mutes. 561
Death penalty 97
Deception,
  fraudulent. 261, 263,
                                    275–277, 281,
                                    283–295, 295
  by silence 281, 287, 291–295
Declarations
  of will. 241–243, *243–259*,
                                    261–279
  See also Avoidance; Contracts;
    Deception, fraudulent; Mistake;
    Wills
  authentication 299
  definition 239
  effectiveness 299,
                                    301–311, 311
  form. 297–299
  interpretation. 313
  invalidity. 243, 279,
                                    281, 295–297
Defamation. 437, 505,
                                    715, *715–729*
  collective
    (possibility of) 719–725

Defences,
 coercion *545–553*
 in criminal law 703–705
 emergency 319, 705
 force majeure *605–609*
 mistake *689–697*
 self-defence 319, *321–329*, 703
 self-help 319

Defendants,
 multiple 561, 609
 rights of 97

Delivery (of goods) 377, 413

Demonstrations, liability
 arising out of *481–501*

Dignity (human),
 protection of 129, 219, 475
 applied to animals *129–139*
 balanced against other
  considerations 515, 543
 and insult 715, 727–729

Diminished
 responsibility 559–561, 699

Disclosure, duty of 281, *283–295*

Drugs (illicit), cultivation/
 consumption of *159–173*

E

East Germany
 See DDR

Education 181–183

Elections 53
 See also All Germany
  election case

Electrical damage *605–609*

Electronic text,
 validity of 297

Emergency
 as defence 319,
  545–553, 705
 states of 51, 187

Employers,
 liability of *439–467*, 563,
  565–573

Equality (before the
 law), right of 141, 541
 access to public
  office 49
 business law 209–211, 215–221
 between sexes *141–157*

European Charter of
 Fundamental Rights 131, 135

European Convention
 on Human Rights 715
 status in national law 105

European Court
 of Justice 15, 97, 135,
  137–139

European Union/
 Community Directives 369, 371,
  413, 419,
  427, 429, 575
 extradition/
  political asylum 223, 225
 and human/
  animal rights *129–139*
 laws, status of
  (vs national law) 4, 13–15
 proportionality
  principle 108
 Treaties 15, 133, 225

Euthanasia 139

Expression (of
 opinion), freedom of 173,
  173–181,
  505–559
 scope of, analysed 519–527

Extradition 223

F

Fall in the
 supermarket case *377–391*, 429
 facts of case 377–379
 issue of liability 379–383
 role of third party 385–391

Fallen telegraph
 pole case 433, 435, 563,
  565–573, 577

Fatalities,
 compensation for 611

Fault,
 contributory 375, 381,
  501, 607, 611
 of obligor 377, *377–391*

Federal Border
 Protection Force 51, 187

Federal Constitutional
 Court 1, 89–91
 arbitration on
  State issues 89–91, 95–97

banning of
  unconstitutional
  organisations 11
and Basic Rights. 99, 515,
                              519, 523,
                          527, 529–559
composition 91
electoral rulings 53, 57–81
on EU jurisdiction. 15
interim injunctions 175, 179
international
  jurisdiction 29–31
interpretation of
  Basic Law 7, 89, 108
jurisdiction 89–91, 99,
                          201, 211, 215,
                              519, 529
rulings 107, 109, 185,
                          515, 529–559

Federal Council
  (*Bundesrat*) 83, 85
role in composition
  of FCC. 91
role in EU 13–15

Federal Courts. 93, 97
See also Federal Constitutional
  Court; Federal Supreme Court

Federal Parliament
  (*Bundestag*) 4, 91
elections to 53, 53–81
proceedings 557–559
role in EU 13

Federal Supreme Court 1, 93
rulings 251, 265,
                                  597

Federation (*Bund*)
  administration. 83, 87
constitutional
  status. 4, 9, 83
defence. 51, 99,
                              187, 683
See also Army, Federal
economy. 99, 193–223, 229
electoral system. 53
flag. 11
international
  relations 17, 19, 41, 49
political
  organisation. 11
relationship with EU 13–15
relationship
  with States 43, 53, 83

responsibility
  (for acts of officials) 579–605
territory,
  reorganisation of. 43–45

Film director
  case. 105, 107, 139,
                              173, 505–559
facts of case 505–511
general findings
  (on Basic Rights) 511–527
case assessment. 529–559
coercion, defence of 545–553
public opinion. 557–559

Firearms,
  possession/use of. 321–329
in DDR law 627, 633–635,
                              661–663

5% Clause
  See Barrier (5%) clause

Food labelling 109

Foreign countries,
  crimes committed in. 683

Foreign nationals
  (and Basic Rights) 106

Fowl pest case 371, 373, 435,
                          437, 439–467, 563
facts of case 439–441
judgment and
  reasons 441–467

Freedom, rights of 49, 99, 139,
                              157, 183–185
of belief. 159–173
of expression 173–181, 505–559
limitations on 117–121, 127,
                          173, 207, 527
physical liberty 111–127

French law (compared
  with German)
Civil Code. 259, 331,
                              433–435
minors. 561, 573
vicarious liability 573

French Revolution 521

G

'Gazumping' 393

Genocide 683, 737

Goebbels, Joseph. 545–553

Good faith, role in
  business law 299, 365, 369–371

Good morals
    and boycott *505–511, 529–559*
    offences against. 313, 503, 749
'Grace and favour' 241
Gravel extraction case 191
Guardianship Court. 237–239
Gysi, Gregor 173–181

H
Harlan, Veit. *505–511, 529–559*
Health, protection of
    See also Public safety
    as constitutional
      right. 165
    and drug offences. 165–171
Herzog, Roman, Dr 89
Hierarchy
    (of legal norms) 4
Housework day case *141–157*
    facts of case 143, 147
    historical/legal
      background 145
    rejection of claim. 143, 147
    result of appeal 143, 149–157
Human rights
    See also Basic Rights
    in DDR law 649–657,
                      659–661, 669, 679
    European
      statements of. 105, 131,
                         135, 715
    in international law 649–657
    UN Declarations on 119, 659

I
IHG
    See Investment Aid Act case
Imprisonment
    See also Penalties
    and human dignity. 129
Industrial action *579–605*
Industry,
    investment in. *193–223*
Inheritance 191
Insult of soldiers
    case 139, 173, *715–729*

Interest,
    payment of. 371–373, 613
    base rates 371
    on debts 413
Interim injunctions. *173–181*
International law
    See also European Union/
      Community; NATO
    on human rights 649–657
    relationship with
      Federal law 17, *19–39*,
                         41, 97
    States' role in 49
Internet auction case. . . . 259, 279, 317,
                      333–357, 411,
                         415, 423
    facts of case 333–339
    judgement and
      reasons 339–357
Investment Aid
    Act case 139, *193–223*
    admissibility of
      complaints 197–201
    and Basic Rights 205–223
    challenges to
      complete statute 201–211
    challenges to individual
      parts of statute. 211–223
    and Federal
      competence 201–205
    historical/legislative
      background 195–197
Inviolability of the home,
    right of 189–191

J
Judges,
    appointment 89, 93
    dismissal/retirement 95
    function 5, 87, 99
    legal position 93–95
    politics. 89
    status of decisions. 5, 7, 527

K
Kite case 575, *605–609*
Krenz, Egon 173

L

Land purchase
  mistake case. *261–279*, 281

Legal persons 229, 233
  rights. 199, 209

Legal transactions
  See also Contracts
  avoidance. 315–317
  conditions. 363
  consent 367
  definition 239
  invalidity 239, 313–315, 371
  one-/many-sided 237, 239,
                                     317, 367

Legislation, institutions/
  processes of 53, 83–87

Liability
  See also Compensation; Negligence;
    Third parties
  accident (following
    deprivation). 613
  buildings 577, 615
  criminal 687, 701–703
  damage to property *497–501*
  financial harm 373, *487–489*,
                                     503, 511
  general principles. 433, 435–437
  joint 609
  limitation 559–561, 615
  manufacturers *399–411*,
                                     439–467, 575
  moral harm 503
  officials. 579, *579–605*
  strict 575, 605, *605–609*
  vicarious 563, *565–573*,
                                     573–575

Loans,
  forced 205
  repayment 371–373

Local government. 9, 43

Locus standi (in
  constitutional complaints). 91

M

Maastricht Treaty 15

Manslaughter 735–737

Manufacturers
  (liability of) *399–411*,
                                     439–467

Markesinis, BS, Prof 2

Maternity law 153

Mentally incapacitated
  persons 235, 573, 699
  ill-treatment of . . . 739–741, *741–747*

Mephisto case 173

Military service. 187, 227
  conscientious objection 157, 187

Minors 235–239
  and criminal law. 685, 699
  definition 231
  education 181–183
  ill-treatment of 739–741
  injuries to *605–609*
  legal competence 235, 239
  legal representation 235–239
  responsibility. 561, 573, 699
  rights. 106, 181
  supervision 573

Misdirected withdrawal
  declaration case. *301–311*
  facts of case 303
  judgment and
    reasons 305–311

Mistake 247, 259,
                                     261–279
  in criminal law 687, *689–697*

Mitigation. 709

Morality
  See also Good morals
  of military life 717
  offences against. 503, 611

Movement, freedom of 185

Murder. 731–733
  motives. 733, *733–735*

N

Name, right to. 233

Nationalisation 223

NATO,
  role in Bosnia. 23, 25–29, 33–39

Natural disasters. 51

Natural persons 229–233
  legal competence 231

Nazi regime 139, *505–511*,
                                     529–559, 647, 661
  film industry/
    coercive methods 545–553

Negligence 321–329,
                    377–391, 397
  criminal 687, 749
  definition 377
  during delay 377
  fatal 739
Newspaper delivery
  obstruction case 9, 173, 183,
                    435, 437,
                    481–501, 561

O

Obligations 369–431
  on behalf of
      third parties 397
  liability 377, 377–395
  performance 369–375
      See also Performance (of
      obligations)
  relationships (defined) 419
  termination 421
  towards third
      parties 385–391, 419–431
Officials,
  determination/
      performance of
      duties 591–605
  Federal/State 51–53
  freedom to strike 583–591
  liability 51, 579,
                    591–605

P

Parental duties/
  rights 106, 181, 435, 573
Parties, political
  See also Barrier (5%) clause
  banning of 11
  combination of lists 55, 67–73
  conflicts over
      international issues 19–39
  effect of unification 53, 65–67
  and judiciary 89
Partnerships, rights of 201
Penalties,
  attempted acts 699, 703
  bodily injury 739–741, 747–749
  combined 711–713
  determination of 619, 697,
                    707–713

linked to consequence 697
murder/
    manslaughter 731, 735–739
reduction 687, 701,
                    705, 707–709
Performance
  (of obligations) 369–375
  delay 411–413
  determination 423–425
  failure to provide 425–429
  frustration/
      impossibility 375–377, 397
  hindrance 419–421
  mutual 425
  for third parties 429–431
Personality,
  rights of 139, 469–481, 729
  See also Dignity
Persons,
  natural vs legal 229
  See also Legal persons; Natural
      persons
Petition, right of 225
Police
  border control 51
  rights of detention 99
Precedent, role of 5
Press, freedom of 173, 173–181
Privacy, right to 139, 185
Product liability 399–411,
                    439–467, 575
Property,
  definitions 191
  expropriation 191
  inheritance 191
  inviolability 189–191
  owners' liability 577
  ownership/sale 261–279
  rights of 189–191, 207–209
Proportionality,
  principle of 108–109
  arrest 119–121, 125–127
  in DDR law 627, 659
  drug offences 168–169
Public safety,
  air travel 593–595, 599–601
  emergency
      provisions 51
  vs property rights 189–191

Public sector industries 213

Public transport,
  contracts 415
  taxation 213

Publication of a
  letter case 139, 233,
                    469–481, 715
  facts of case 469–473
  judgment and
    reasons 473–481

Punishment
  See Penalties

R

Referenda 43–45
  legality of *689–697*

Referendum mistake
  case 689–697

Refugees 223–225

Regulations,
  and Basic Rights 107
  business law 217
  legal status 4
  passing of 85

Religion,
  in education 181–183
  freedom of 49, 157, *159–173*

Retirement ages 141

Retroactivity
  (of Criminal Law
  Code), prohibition of 619,
                      663–669

Right to give the
  opposite view cases *173–181*
  facts 175, 179
  judgment and
    reasons 175–179, 181

Rights
  See also Basic Rights; Human
    Rights
  of accused/defendants 97, 99
  catalogue of 435
  civic 49
  translation of terms 3

Rome, Treaty of 141

Rough ill-treatment case *741–747*

S

Schäuble, Dr 67

Schmid-Tübingen, Dr 557–559

Self-defence 319, *321–329*,
                        495–497
  in criminal law 703

Self-help (as defence) 319

Service(s)
  contracts of *301–311*
  of process 311
  unsolicited 369

Shooting at the
  disco case 319, *321–329*, 435

Shootings at the
  Berlin Wall case 97, 109,
                    621–681, 733
  DDR law/
    policy 625–629, 631–643
  facts of case 623–625
  international law 649–657
  justification,
    grounds for 629, 643–647,
                      659–671
  ultimate findings 673–681

Silence,
  as consent 241
  deception by 281, 287,
                    291–295

Socialist Reich Party 11

Somalia, sending of
  troops to 19

Springer, Axel 491

State(s) (*Länder*),
  assistance, mutual 51
  Constitutional
    Courts 91, 95–97
  constitutional status 4, 9, 83
  definition of term 3
  internal government 43, 83
  international
    relations 49
  law, vs Federal law 47, 83, 89
  names, listed 9
  relations with EU 13–15
  relations with
    Federation 43, 53
  reorganisation 43–47
  representation on
    Federal bodies 101

treaties with other
States/foreign
powers 47, 49

Statutes,
and Basic Rights 107–108
business law 193, 201
extradition 223
general 173
legal status 4, 97
nationalisation............... 223
passing of.............. 83, 85–87
political asylum.............. 225
strict liability *605–609*
violation 437

Supervisors/carers,
ill-treatment by *741–747*
liability 573

T

Taxation,
public sector
industries 213
scope of definition 203–205

Telecommunications 417

Termination of
negotiations case.......... *393–395*

Territory,
reorganisation of........... 43–45

Third parties,
claims to
compensation 611
consent of.................. 367
determination by 423–425
liability towards......... 385–391,
419–431, 429–431,
441–447, 613
responsibility for............. 397

Threats 281, 295

Tort(s).................... 433–615
contrasted with
contract law 443, 457
joint perpetrators 561, 609
limitations 559–561
minors...................... 561
overlap with
contract law 377, 381, 439
overlap with
criminal law............... 715
third party liability........ 441–447
time limits 615

Translation,
principles of................ 2–3

Treason...................... 683

Treaties,
conclusion of 47, 49, 225

U

UK law (compared to
German)
contracts 259, 281, 331,
333, 361, 393
criminal law.......... 699, 707, 731
declarations of will....... 241, 259
defamation.................. 707
duress/threats............... 281
human rights................ 105
legal transactions 315
local government 9
minors...................... 561
precedent, role of 5
proportionality
principle.............. 108, 111
sexual equality 141
torts 433, 435, 503,
505, 561, 563
vicarious liability 563, 575

Unification (1990)
See also All Germany election case
applicability of former
DDR law.............. 631–635
effect on Basic Law........ 15, 101
effect on Civil Code 229
effect on criminal law 617, 621,
631–633
effect on electoral
system.................. 53, 81

Unintended declaration
of will case *243–259*, 279
facts of case 243–247
judgment and reasons..... 247–255
results of appeal 255–259

United Nations,
Human Rights
Committee/
Declarations........ 119, 651, 659
role in Bosnia.............. 21–23

V

Vocation, freedom of.... 107–108, 185

W

Weimar Constitution.... 519, 523, 567

Weimar Republic,
  conditions in 371

Wills 241
  See also Declarations of will
    interpretation............... 313

Withdrawal
  from contracts 425–429
  from criminal acts......... 701, 703